New
Perspectives

Microsoft® 365®
Excel®

First Edition

Comprehensive

Patrick Carey

Australia • Brazil • Canada • Mexico • Singapore • United Kingdom • United States

New Perspectives Microsoft® 365® Excel®
Comprehensive, **First Edition**
Patrick Carey

SVP, Product: Cheryl Costantini

VP, Product: Thais Alencar

Senior Product Director: Mark Santee

Portfolio Product Director: Rita Lombard

Senior Portfolio Product Manager: Amy Savino

Senior Product Assistant: Ciara Boynton

Learning Designer: Zenya Molnar

Content Manager: Christina Nyren

Digital Project Manager: Jim Vaughey

Developmental Editor: Robin Romer

VP, Product Marketing: Jason Sakos

Senior Director, Product Marketing: Danae April

Senior Product Marketing Manager:
Mackenzie Paine

Product Specialist: Matt Schiesl

Content Acquisition Analyst: Callum Panno

Production Service: Lumina Datamatics Ltd.

Designer: Erin Griffin

Cover Image Source: Marco Bottigelli/Moment/
Getty Images, Mr. Simon Paul/shutterstock.com

Previous editions: © 2023, © 2020, © 2017

For product information and technology assistance, contact us at
**Cengage Customer & Sales Support, 1-800-354-9706
or support.cengage.com.**

For permission to use material from this text or product, submit all requests online at **www.copyright.com.**

Library of Congress Control Number: 2024931360

Student Edition ISBN: 978-0-357-88222-1

Loose-leaf Edition ISBN: 978-0-357-88223-8

Cengage
5191 Natorp Boulevard
Mason, OH 45040
USA

Cengage is a leading provider of customized learning solutions with employees residing in nearly 40 different countries and sales in more than 125 countries around the world. Find your local representative at **www.cengage.com.**

To learn more about Cengage platforms and services, register or access your online learning solution, or purchase materials for your course, visit **www.cengage.com.**

Notice to the Reader

Printed in the United States of America
Print Number: 01   Print Year: 2024

Brief Contents

Preface .... NPP-i

Getting to Know Microsoft Office Versions... OFF-1

Using SAM Projects and Textbook Projects SAM-1

Excel

Module 1: Getting Started with Excel.. EX 1-1
Developing a Purchase Order Report

Module 2: Formatting a Workbook... EX 2-1
Creating a Sales Report

Module 3: Calculating with Formulas and Functions .... EX 3-1
Staffing a Call Center

Module 4: Analyzing and Charting Financial Data .... EX 4-1
Preparing an Investment Report

Module 5: Generating Reports from Multiple Worksheets and Workbooks .... EX 5-1
Summarizing Profit and Loss Statements

Module 6: Managing Data with the Excel Data Tools .... EX 6-1
Analyzing Employee Data

Module 7: Summarizing Data with PivotTables... EX 7-1
Creating a Customer Relationship Management Report

Module 8: Performing What-If Analyses .... EX 8-1
Maximizing Profits with the Best Product Mix

Module 9: Exploring Financial Tools and Functions... EX 9-1
Analyzing a Business Plan

Module 10: Analyzing Data with Business Intelligence Tools .... EX 10-1
Presenting Sales and Revenue Data

Module 11: Exploring PivotTable Design and Data .... EX 11-1
Tracking Daily Revenue Estimates

Module 12: Developing an Excel Application .... EX 12-1
Tracking Donations to a Nonprofit

Index... Index-1

Contents

Preface...NPP-i
Getting to Know Microsoft Office Versions..OFF-1
Using SAM Projects and Textbook Projects SAM-1

Excel

Module 1: Getting Started with Excel
Developing a Purchase Order Report

Developing a Purchase Order Report...EX 1-1

Part 1.1 Visual Overview: The Excel Workbook............EX 1-2
Using the Excel Interface.......................................EX 1-4
Navigating Between Sheets ....EX 1-7
Selecting Worksheet Cells and Cell Ranges..................EX 1-9
Closing a Workbook...EX 1-13
Starting a New Workbook.....................................EX 1-14
Inserting, Naming, and Moving Worksheets...............EX 1-16
Entering Text into a Worksheet.............................EX 1-18
Editing Cells and Using AutoComplete.....................EX 1-18
Entering Dates and Numeric Values ....EX 1-22
Resizing Worksheet Columns and Rows....................EX 1-26
   Resizing Worksheet Columns ....EX 1-26
   Wrapping Text Within a Cell.............................EX 1-28
   Resizing Worksheet Rows...............................EX 1-30
Part 1.2 Visual Overview: Excel Formulas
and Functions..EX 1-32
Calculating with Formulas...................................EX 1-34
Copying and Pasting a Formula.............................EX 1-37
Calculating with Functions..................................EX 1-38

Inserting Functions with AutoSum ....EX 1-39
Moving Worksheet Cells...EX 1-42
Counting Numeric Values with the
COUNT Function ....EX 1-44
Inserting and Deleting Rows and Columns...............EX 1-45
Inserting and Deleting a Range..................................EX 1-47
Generating Text with Flash Fill ....EX 1-50
Formatting a Worksheet ....EX 1-51
   Adding Cell Borders ....EX 1-51
   Changing the Font Size ....EX 1-52
Printing a Workbook..EX 1-53
   Changing Worksheet Views.....................................EX 1-53
   Changing the Page Orientation.................................EX 1-55
   Scaling a Printed Page..EX 1-56
   Setting the Print Options.......................................EX 1-57
Viewing Worksheet Formulas.....................................EX 1-58
Practice: Review Assignments ....EX 1-61
Apply: Case Problem 1...EX 1-62
Challenge: Case Problem 2 ....EX 1-63

Module 2: Formatting a Workbook
Creating a Sales Report

Creating a Sales Report...EX 2-1

Part 2.1 Visual Overview: Formatting a Worksheet ....EX 2-2
Formatting Text..EX 2-4
   Applying a Font Color ....EX 2-7
   Formatting Text Selections Within a Cell ....EX 2-9
Working with Fill Colors and Backgrounds..................EX 2-9
   Changing a Fill Color ....EX 2-9
   Adding a Background Image...............................EX 2-11
   Changing the Sheet Tab Color............................EX 2-12
Formatting Numbers...EX 2-13
   Applying the Accounting and Currency Formats......EX 2-13
   Formatting Percentages ....EX 2-15
   Formatting Dates and Times ....EX 2-16

Copying and Pasting Formats.....................................EX 2-17
   Copying Formats with the Format Painter ....EX 2-17
   Copying Formats with the Paste Options
   Button ....EX 2-19
   Copying Formats with Paste Special..........................EX 2-19
   Transposing Data...EX 2-20
Working with Border Styles..EX 2-21
Aligning Cell Contents ....EX 2-24
   Indenting Cell Text...EX 2-25
   Merging Cells ....EX 2-26
   Rotating Text...EX 2-27
Exploring the Format Cells Dialog Box ....EX 2-28

Part 2.2 Visual Overview: Designing a Printed Worksheet .... EX 2-32

Applying Cell Styles .... EX 2-34

Creating a Custom Cell Style .... EX 2-36

Merging Custom Cell Styles .... EX 2-38

Working with Themes .... EX 2-38

Applying a Theme .... EX 2-38

Setting Theme Colors and Fonts .... EX 2-40

Saving a Theme .... EX 2-40

Finding and Replacing Text and Formats .... EX 2-40

Calculating Averages .... EX 2-43

Highlighting Data with Conditional Formats .... EX 2-45

Highlighting Cells with a Top/Bottom Rule .... EX 2-48

Editing a Conditional Format .... EX 2-49

Documenting Conditional Formats .... EX 2-51

Clearing Conditional Formatting Rules .... EX 2-53

Formatting a Workbook for Printing .... EX 2-53

Using Page Break Preview .... EX 2-53

Defining the Print Area .... EX 2-54

Setting the Print Titles .... EX 2-56

Moving, Adding, and Removing Page Breaks .... EX 2-57

Adding Headers and Footers .... EX 2-60

Setting the Page Margins .... EX 2-62

Practice: Review Assignments .... EX 2-66

Apply: Case Problem 1 .... EX 2-67

Challenge: Case Problem 2 .... EX 2-69

Module 3: Calculating with Formulas and Functions
Staffing a Call Center .... EX 3-1

Part 3.1 Visual Overview: References and Ranges ...... EX 3-2

Designing a Workbook for Calculations .... EX 3-4

Documenting Calculations .... EX 3-5

Constants and Units .... EX 3-5

Calculating with Dates and Times .... EX 3-6

AutoFilling Formulas and Data Patterns .... EX 3-6

AutoFilling a Formula .... EX 3-6

Exploring Auto Fill Options .... EX 3-7

Filling a Series .... EX 3-8

Exploring Cell References .... EX 3-11

Relative Cell References .... EX 3-11

Absolute Cell References .... EX 3-11

Mixed Cell References .... EX 3-12

Calculating with Dynamic Arrays .... EX 3-14

Spill Ranges .... EX 3-15

Referencing a Spill Range .... EX 3-16

Performing Calculations with the Quick Analysis Tool .... EX 3-18

Interpreting Error Values .... EX 3-20

Part 3.2 Visual Overview: Formulas and Functions .... EX 3-22

Analyzing Data with Excel Functions .... EX 3-24

Calculating Minimums and Maximums .... EX 3-24

Measures of Central Tendency .... EX 3-26

Rounding Data Values .... EX 3-29

Nesting Functions .... EX 3-33

The Role of Blanks and Zeroes .... EX 3-34

Date and Time Functions .... EX 3-35

Working with the Logical IF Function .... EX 3-37

Looking Up Data .... EX 3-41

Finding an Exact Match with the XLOOKUP Function .... EX 3-42

Finding an Exact Match with VLOOKUP and HLOOKUP .... EX 3-45

Performing What-If Analysis with Formulas and Functions .... EX 3-47

Using Trial and Error .... EX 3-47

Using Goal Seek .... EX 3-48

Practice: Review Assignments .... EX 3-51

Apply: Case Problem 1 .... EX 3-52

Challenge: Case Problem 2 .... EX 3-53

Module 4: Analyzing and Charting Financial Data
Preparing an Investment Report .... EX 4-1

Part 4.1 Visual Overview: Charts and Chart Elements .... EX 4-2

Getting Started with Excel Charts .... EX 4-4

Creating a Pie Chart .... EX 4-6

Selecting the Data Source .... EX 4-6

Charting with the Quick Analysis Tool .... EX 4-7

Moving and Resizing a Chart .... EX 4-8

Working with Chart Elements .... EX 4-10

Formatting a Chart Element .... EX 4-11

Choosing a Chart Style .... EX 4-14

Changing the Color Scheme .... EX 4-15

Filtering a Chart .... EX 4-16

Performing What-If Analyses with Charts .... EX 4-17

Creating a Column Chart .... EX 4-18

Comparing Column Chart Subtypes...........................EX 4-18

Creating a Clustered Column Chart............................EX 4-19

Editing a Chart Title...EX 4-21

Setting the Gap Width..EX 4-21

Adding Gridlines to a Chart.....................................EX 4-22

Creating a Line Chart...EX 4-23

Editing the Category Axis..EX 4-24

Formatting Data Markers ....EX 4-25

Creating a Combination Chart ....EX 4-27

Adding an Axis Title...EX 4-29

Editing a Value Axis Scale ....EX 4-30

Part 4.2 Visual Overview: Scatter Charts,
Data Bars, and Sparklines...EX 4-32

Creating a Scatter Chart...EX 4-34

Editing the Chart Data Source ....EX 4-38

Adding Graphic Objects to a Workbook......................EX 4-40

Adding a Data Callout to a Chart..............................EX 4-40

Inserting a Graphic Shape..EX 4-41

Exploring Other Chart Types ....EX 4-42

Hierarchy Charts...EX 4-43

Pareto Charts..EX 4-43

Histogram Charts..EX 4-44

Waterfall Charts..EX 4-45

Creating Data Bars..EX 4-45

Modifying a Data Bar Rule.......................................EX 4-46

Creating Sparklines...EX 4-48

Formatting a Sparkline...EX 4-50

Sparkline Groups and Sparkline Axes ....EX 4-51

Practice: Review Assignments ....EX 4-54

Apply: Case Problem 1..EX 4-55

Challenge: Case Problem 2 ....EX 4-57

Module 5: Generating Reports from Multiple Worksheets and Workbooks
Summarizing Profit and Loss Statements...EX 5-1

Part 5.1 Visual Overview: Worksheet Groups
and 3-D References ....EX 5-2

Working with Multiple Worksheets.............................EX 5-4

Copying Worksheets ....EX 5-4

Viewing a Workbook in Multiple Windows ....EX 5-6

Arranging Multiple Workbook Windows ....EX 5-7

Using Synchronized Scrolling Between Windows.......EX 5-9

Working with Worksheet Groups ....EX 5-10

Editing a Worksheet Group......................................EX 5-12

Ungrouping a Worksheet Group ....EX 5-13

Writing 3-D References...EX 5-14

Referencing Cells in Other Worksheets.....................EX 5-14

Applying 3-D References to Formulas
and Functions..EX 5-14

Part 5.2 Visual Overview: External References
and Links ....EX 5-20

Linking to External Workbooks...................................EX 5-22

Creating an External Reference ....EX 5-22

External References and Security Concerns ....EX 5-25

Reviewing Links Within a Workbook ....EX 5-26

Managing Workbook Links ....EX 5-27

Creating Hyperlinks ....EX 5-28

Linking to a Location Within a Workbook...................EX 5-29

Linking to an Email Address......................................EX 5-31

Part 5.3 Visual Overview: Named Ranges
and Templates..EX 5-34

Simplifying Formulas with Named Ranges ....EX 5-36

Defining a Named Range..EX 5-36

Using Range Names in Formulas ....EX 5-38

Determining the Scope of Range Names ....EX 5-41

Using Defined Names in Existing Formulas..............EX 5-44

Exploring Workbook Templates..................................EX 5-46

Setting Up a Workbook Template..............................EX 5-47

Creating a Workbook Based on a Template ....EX 5-49

Practice: Review Assignments ....EX 5-53

Apply: Case Problem 1..EX 5-54

Challenge: Case Problem 2 ....EX 5-55

Module 6: Managing Data with the Excel Data Tools
Analyzing Employee Data...EX 6-1

Part 6.1 Visual Overview: Data Ranges
and Subtotals...EX 6-2

Managing Data in Excel...EX 6-4

Using Panes to Navigate Data...................................EX 6-6

Dividing the Workbook Window into Panes................EX 6-6

Freezing Panes..EX 6-8

Locating Duplicate Records.......................................EX 6-10

Highlighting Duplicate Values...................................EX 6-10

Removing Duplicate Records....................................EX 6-12

Sorting Records in a Data Range ....EX 6-13

Sorting by a Single Field..EX 6-13

Sorting by Multiple Fields...EX 6-14

Sorting with a Custom List ....EX 6-16

Calculating Subtotals...EX 6-18

Using the Subtotal Outline View...................EX 6-21

Part 6.2 Visual Overview: Filters and
Excel Tables .... EX 6-24

Locating Cells Within a Worksheet .... EX 6-26

Finding and Selecting Multiple Cells ....EX 6-26

Finding Cells by Type ....EX 6-27

Filtering Data .... EX 6-27

Filtering Based on One Field..........................EX 6-27

Filtering Based on Multiple Fields ....EX 6-29

Using Criteria Filters ....EX 6-30

Creating an Excel Table.. EX 6-33

Converting a Range to a Table.......................EX 6-33

Using Table Styles...EX 6-35

Adding a Total Row..EX 6-36

Adding and Deleting Records.........................EX 6-37

Creating a Calculated Field............................EX 6-38

Part 6.3 Visual Overview: Slicers and Dashboards ..... EX 6-44

Filtering Data with Slicers .... EX 6-46

Creating a Dashboard.. EX 6-48

Formatting a Slicer ....EX 6-49

Using the SUBTOTAL Function.. EX 6-51

Creating Dynamic Charts .... EX 6-54

Looking Up Data with Tables .... EX 6-57

Creating Tables with Excel Filter Tools .... EX 6-58

Applying an Advanced Filter ....EX 6-58

Filtering Data with the FILTER Function ....EX 6-62

Filtering with Multiple Criteria ....EX 6-63

Sorting Data with the SORT Function.........................EX 6-65

Sorting Data with the SORTBY Function ....EX 6-66

Combining Sorting and Filtering...................EX 6-67

Exploring Other Dynamic Array Functions.................EX 6-68

Practice: Review Assignments .... EX 6-72

Apply: Case Problem 1...................................... EX 6-73

Challenge: Case Problem 2 .... EX 6-75

Module 7: Summarizing Data with PivotTables
Creating a Customer Relationship Management Report..EX 7-1

Part 7.1 Visual Overview: XLOOKUP and Summary
IF Functions ....EX 7-2

Retrieving Data with Lookup Functions ....EX 7-4

Creating Approximate Match Lookups .... EX 7-6

Approximate Match Lookups with VLOOKUP
and HLOOKUP...EX 7-10

Using XLOOKUP with Multiple Lookup Values ....EX 7-10

Two-Way Lookups with XLOOKUP................................EX 7-12

Retrieving Data with Index Match Lookups ....EX 7-13

Exploring Logical Functions .... EX 7-15

Generating Multiple Outcomes from
a Logical Function...EX 7-20

Using the AND, OR, and NOT Functions ....EX 7-20

Applying Summary IF functions.................................... EX 7-21

Conditional Counting with COUNTIF
and COUNTIFS..EX 7-21

Calculating Conditional Sums ....EX 7-24

Calculating Other Conditional Statistics ....EX 7-26

Summary Calculations Using the
FILTER Function..EX 7-27

Part 7.2 Visual Overview: PivotTables .... EX 7-30

Creating a PivotTable.. EX 7-32

Inserting a PivotTable ....EX 7-33

Defining a PivotTable Layout ....EX 7-35

Adding Multiple Fields to a Row or Column..............EX 7-37

Filtering a PivotTable...EX 7-38

Formatting a PivotTable .... EX 7-40

Changing PivotTable Labels ....EX 7-42

Changing a PivotTable Summary Function.................EX 7-43

Choosing a PivotTable Style ....EX 7-44

Setting PivotTable Options ....EX 7-45

Part 7.3 Visual Overview: PivotCharts and Slicers.... EX 7-50

Introducing PivotCharts .... EX 7-52

Creating a PivotChart.....................................EX 7-53

Moving a PivotChart to Another Worksheet..............EX 7-55

Sorting PivotTable Categories .... EX 7-58

Adding Date Fields to PivotTables............................. EX 7-60

Using Slicers with PivotTables .... EX 7-64

Applying a Slicer to Multiple PivotTables ....EX 7-65

Creating a Timeline Slicer .... EX 7-67

Drilling Down a PivotTable.. EX 7-70

Practice: Review Assignments .... EX 7-74

Apply: Case Problem 1...................................... EX 7-75

Challenge: Case Problem 2 .... EX 7-77

Module 8: Performing What-If Analyses
Maximizing Profits with the Best Product Mix........................ EX 8-1

Part 8.1 Visual Overview: Data Tables and What-If Analysis.................... EX 8-2
Understanding Cost–Volume Relationships .... EX 8-4
  Comparing Expenses and Revenue............................ EX 8-4
  Exploring the Break-Even Point .... EX 8-6
  Finding the Break-Even Point with What-If Analysis.................... EX 8-7
Working with Data Tables .... EX 8-9
  Creating a One-Variable Data Table.............................. EX 8-9
  Charting a One-Variable Data Table.......................... EX 8-12
  Modifying a Data Table.. EX 8-13
Creating a Two-Variable Data Table............................ EX 8-14
  Formatting the Result Cell.. EX 8-16
  Charting a Two-Variable Data Table....................... EX 8-17
Part 8.2 Visual Overview: What-If Scenarios .... EX 8-22
Exploring Financial Scenarios with Scenario Manager.................... EX 8-24

Defining a Scenario .... EX 8-25
Viewing Scenarios .... EX 8-28
Editing a Scenario.. EX 8-30
Creating Scenario Summary Reports........................ EX 8-31
Part 8.3 Visual Overview: Optimal Solutions with Solver.................... EX 8-38
Optimizing a Product Mix .... EX 8-40
Finding the Optimal Solution with Solver.................. EX 8-42
  Activating Solver.. EX 8-43
  Setting the Objective Cell and Variable Cells............ EX 8-44
  Adding Constraints to Solver .... EX 8-46
Exploring the Iterative Process .... EX 8-52
Creating a Solver Answer Report .... EX 8-53
Saving and Loading Solver Models............................. EX 8-56
Practice: Review Assignments .... EX 8-60
Apply: Case Problem 1 .... EX 8-61
Challenge: Case Problem 2 .... EX 8-63

Module 9: Exploring Financial Tools and Functions
Analyzing a Business Plan........................ EX 9-1

Part 9.1 Visual Overview: Loan and Investment Functions........................ EX 9-2
Introducing Financial Functions....................................... EX 9-4
Calculating the Cost of Borrowing .... EX 9-4
  Calculating Payments with the PMT Function .... EX 9-5
  Calculating a Future Value with the FV Function .... EX 9-7
  Calculating the Payment Period with the NPER Function.................... EX 9-9
  Calculating the Present Value with the PV Function .... EX 9-10
Creating an Amortization Schedule........................... EX 9-12
  Calculating Interest and Principal Payments............. EX 9-13
  Calculating Cumulative Interest and Principal Payments................ EX 9-16
  Loan and Investment Schedules with Variable Interest Rates.................... EX 9-18
Part 9.2 Visual Overview: Income Statements and Depreciations.................... EX 9-20
Projecting Future Income and Expenses .... EX 9-22
  Exploring Linear and Growth Trends........................ EX 9-22
  Interpolating from a Starting Value to an Ending Value .... EX 9-23
  Calculating the Cost of Goods Sold .... EX 9-26
  Extrapolating from a Series of Values .... EX 9-27
Calculating Depreciation of Assets .... EX 9-30
  Straight-Line Depreciation .... EX 9-30

Declining Balance Depreciation................................... EX 9-30
Adding Depreciation to an Income Statement .... EX 9-35
Adding Taxes and Interest Expenses to an Income Statement........................ EX 9-35
Part 9.3 Visual Overview: NPV and IRR and Auditing........................ EX 9-38
Calculating Interest Rates with the RATE Function ..... EX 9-40
Viewing the Payback Period of an Investment.......... EX 9-42
Calculating Net Present Value .... EX 9-44
  The Time Value of Money .... EX 9-44
  Using the NPV Function .... EX 9-44
  Choosing a Rate of Return .... EX 9-45
Calculating the Internal Rate of Return..................... EX 9-47
  Using the IRR Function .... EX 9-48
  Exploring the XNPV and XIRR Functions................... EX 9-50
  Viewing the Modified Internal Rate of Return .... EX 9-52
Auditing a Workbook.. EX 9-52
  Tracing an Error .... EX 9-53
  Evaluating a Formula .... EX 9-56
Using the Watch Window.. EX 9-58
Practice: Review Assignments .... EX 9-61
Apply: Case Problem 1 .... EX 9-63
Challenge: Case Problem 2 .... EX 9-65

Module 10: Analyzing Data with Business Intelligence Tools
Presenting Sales and Revenue Data .... EX 10-1

Part 10.1 Visual Overview: Queries
and Trendlines .... EX 10-2

Introducing Business Intelligence .... EX 10-4

Writing a Data Query .... EX 10-4

   Using Power Query .... EX 10-4

   Retrieving Data into an Excel Table .... EX 10-8

   Editing a Query .... EX 10-9

   Refreshing Query Data .... EX 10-10

Transforming Data with Queries .... EX 10-10

   Adding a New Column .... EX 10-12

   Grouping Values in a Query .... EX 10-12

Charting Trends .... EX 10-15

Creating a Forecast Sheet .... EX 10-18

Part 10.2 Visual Overview: Power Pivot and
the Data Model .... EX 10-24

Introducing Databases .... EX 10-26

   Relational Databases .... EX 10-26

   Querying an Access Database .... EX 10-27

Exploring the Data Model .... EX 10-28

   Transforming Data with Power Pivot .... EX 10-31

   Exploring the Data Model in Diagram View .... EX 10-32

   Managing Table Relationships .... EX 10-33

Creating a PivotTable from the Data Model .... EX 10-35

   Tabulating Across Fields from Multiple Tables .... EX 10-37

   Applying Slicers and Timelines
   from the Data Model .... EX 10-38

Part 10.3 Visual Overview:
Hierarchies and Maps .... EX 10-42

Working with Outlines and Hierarchies .... EX 10-44

   Outlining a PivotTable by Nested Fields .... EX 10-44

   Drilling Down a Field Hierarchy .... EX 10-46

   Viewing Data with the Quick Explore Tool .... EX 10-50

Viewing Data with Map Charts .... EX 10-53

   Creating a Value Map Chart .... EX 10-54

   Formatting a Map Chart .... EX 10-59

Visualizing Data with 3D Maps .... EX 10-60

   Choosing a Map Style .... EX 10-62

   Creating New Scenes .... EX 10-64

   Setting Scene Options .... EX 10-65

   Playing a Tour .... EX 10-66

Practice: Review Assignments .... EX 10-68

Apply: Case Problem 1 .... EX 10-70

Challenge: Case Problem 2 .... EX 10-72

Module 11: Exploring PivotTable Design and Data
Tracking Daily Revenue Estimates .... EX 11-1

Part 11.1 Visual Overview: Layouts,
Sorting, Filtering, and Grouping .... EX 11-2

Laying Out a PivotTable .... EX 11-4

   Working with Grand Totals and Subtotals .... EX 11-4

   Changing the PivotTable Layout .... EX 11-6

Sorting a PivotTable .... EX 11-9

   Manually Sorting a Field .... EX 11-9

   Sorting by Value .... EX 11-9

Filtering a PivotTable .... EX 11-12

Grouping PivotTable Fields .... EX 11-15

   Manual Grouping .... EX 11-16

   Grouping by Dates .... EX 11-19

   Grouping by Numeric Fields .... EX 11-22

Part 11.2 Visual Overview: Conditional
Formats and Calculations .... EX 11-26

Calculations with PivotTables .... EX 11-28

   Calculating Ranks .... EX 11-30

   Calculating Percent Differences .... EX 11-31

Displaying PivotTables with
Conditional Formats .... EX 11-33

   Creating an Icon Set .... EX 11-34

   Working with Color Scales .... EX 11-36

Exploring the PivotTable Cache .... EX 11-37

   Sharing a Cache Between PivotTables .... EX 11-38

   Creating a New Cache .... EX 11-39

Working with Calculated Items and
Calculated Fields .... EX 11-41

   Creating a Calculated Item .... EX 11-41

   Creating a Calculated Field .... EX 11-44

   Behind the Math of Calculated Items and Fields ... EX 11-47

Part 11.3 Visual Overview: PivotTable Measures .... EX 11-50

Introducing PivotTable Design under
the Data Model .... EX 11-52

Calculating Distinct Counts .... EX 11-53

Creating a Measure .... EX 11-55

   Introducing DAX .... EX 11-55

   Adding a Measure to a Table .... EX 11-56

Calculating Measures Across Tables and Rows .... EX 11-59

   The RELATED Function .... EX 11-60

   The SUMX Function .... EX 11-61

Retrieving PivotTable Data with GETPIVOTDATA ...... EX 11-63

Exploring Database Functions .... EX 11-67

Analyzing Data with Linked Data Types .... EX 11-69

Getting Insights into Data... EX 11-71

Practice: Review Assignments .... EX 11-73

Apply: Case Problem 1 .... EX 11-74

Challenge: Case Problem 2 .... EX 11-76

Module 12: Developing an Excel Application
Tracking Donations to a Nonprofit...EX 12-1

Part 12.1 Visual Overview:
Error Control and Data Validation.............................. EX 12-2

Planning an Excel Application .... EX 12-4

Managing Error Values .... EX 12-6

   Using the IFERROR Function.................................... EX 12-7

   Handling Errors in Dynamic Array Functions............ EX 12-8

Validating Data Entry.. EX 12-11

   Validating Numbers .... EX 12-12

   Creating a Validation Message .... EX 12-15

   Creating an Input Message .... EX 12-17

   Validating Against a List .... EX 12-18

   Creating a Custom Validation Rule.......................... EX 12-20

   Validating Existing Data... EX 12-21

Protecting a Worksheet.. EX 12-23

   Enabling Protection.. EX 12-23

   Locking and Unlocking Cells .... EX 12-25

   Highlighting Unlocked Cells .... EX 12-27

Part 12.2 Visual Overview: LET and
LAMBDA Functions .... EX 12-30

Writing Formulas with the LET Function .... EX 12-32

   Examining the Syntax of LET..................................... EX 12-32

   Writing a LET Function .... EX 12-34

Writing Formulas with LAMBDA .... EX 12-35

Combining LET and LAMBDA...................................... EX 12-37

Creating Custom Functions with LAMBDA .... EX 12-40

   Creating a Custom Function for the 80|20 Rule ... EX 12-43

Creating an Optional Argument................................ EX 12-46

Using LAMBDA Helper Functions .... EX 12-50

Part 12.3 Visual Overview: Macros and
Visual Basic for Applications .... EX 12-56

Getting Started with Macros .... EX 12-58

   Loading the Excel Developer Tab .... EX 12-58

   Saving a Macro-Enabled Workbook .... EX 12-59

Creating an Excel Macro... EX 12-60

   Recording a Macro .... EX 12-60

   Running a Macro .... EX 12-62

   Assigning a Macro to a Graphic Object................... EX 12-63

Creating a Data Entry Worksheet............................... EX 12-65

   Recording a Macro to Enter Donor Information.... EX 12-65

   Assigning a Macro to a Form Button .... EX 12-67

Working with the VBA Editor....................................... EX 12-71

   Opening the VBA Editor.. EX 12-71

   Understanding Sub Procedures .... EX 12-72

   Editing a Macro with the VBA Editor .... EX 12-72

   Displaying a Message Box .... EX 12-73

Finishing an Excel Application .... EX 12-76

   Hiding Workbook Content... EX 12-76

   Setting Macro Security .... EX 12-78

   Protecting a Workbook .... EX 12-79

Practice: Review Assignments .... EX 12-81

Apply: Case Problem 1 .... EX 12-83

Challenge: Case Problem 2 .... EX 12-85

Index..Index-1

Preface for New Perspectives Series Microsoft 365 and Office

About the Authors

Access: Dr. Mark Shellman is an instructor and chair of the Information Technology Department at Gaston College in Dallas, North Carolina. Dr. Mark, as his students call him, prides himself on being student-centered and loves learning himself. His favorite subjects in the information technology realm include databases and programming languages. Dr. Mark has been teaching for more than 30 years and has co-authored several texts in the New Perspective series on Microsoft® Office 365 & Access® along with a textbook on Structured Query Language.

Excel: A leading textbook author, lecturer, and instructor, Patrick Carey has authored or co-authored more than 40 popular educational and trade texts for the academic market. He has taught and written about a wide range of topics, including website design, JavaScript programming, Microsoft Office and Excel, statistics, data analysis, and mathematics. Mr. Carey received his M.S. in biostatistics from the University of Wisconsin, where he worked as a researcher designing and analyzing clinical studies. Today, he splits his time between Wisconsin and Colorado, and when he is not writing, he can be found hiking and cycling.

PowerPoint: Jennifer T. Campbell has written and co-authored several leading technology texts, including *New Perspectives on Microsoft® PowerPoint 365*, *Technology for Success*; *Discovering Computers: Digital Technology, Data, and Devices*; *Discovering the Internet; Web Design: Introductory*; and many others. For over 25 years, she has served integral roles in computer educational publishing as an editor, author, and marketing manager. She holds a B.A. in English from The College of William and Mary.

Word: Ann Shaffer is the author of *New Perspectives on Microsoft® Word 365* and has contributed to many other Cengage publications. She has more than 30 years of experience as a developmental editor and co-author of books, journal articles, and multimedia in a variety of fields, including computer science, mathematics, history, engineering, and social sciences. She holds a master's degree in English from the University of Wisconsin-Madison.

Preface for the Instructor

The New Perspectives series' unique in-depth, case-based approach helps students apply Microsoft Office skills to real-world business scenarios based on market insights while reinforcing critical thinking and problem solving abilities. Professional tips and insights are incorporated throughout, and ProSkills boxes help students strengthen their employability. Module learning objectives are mapped to Microsoft Office Specialist (MOS) certification objectives, preparing students to take the MOS exam, which they can leverage in their career. MindTap and updated SAM (Skills Assessment Manager) online resources are also available to guide additional study and ensure successful results.

New Perspectives is designed primarily for students at four-year schools. It can also be used at two-year schools and in continuing education programs. The New Perspectives series is comprised of three parts: introductory, intermediate, and advanced. The series offers a comprehensive title that includes the four main Microsoft applications (Word, Excel, PowerPoint, and Access) at the introductory level. The MindTap Collection includes additional module coverage, including Outlook, Operating Systems, and Teams.

Market research is conducted semi-annually with both current Cengage users and those who use other learning materials. The focus of our market research is to gain insights into the user experience and overall learner needs so we can continuously evolve our content to exceed user expectations. We survey hundreds of instructors to ensure we gather insights from a large and varied demographic.

New to This Edition

Access: New features in the Access Collection include updated, real-world scenarios from a variety of industries that illustrate the relevance of Access databases in today's businesses. Completely updated projects use gapped Start and Solution files to ensure students use new, authentic files for each project from one module to the next.

Excel: With the thoroughly updated coverage in the Excel Collection, students learn both long-standing Excel functions and tools as well as the most recent innovations. New Microsoft® Excel 365® features include dynamic arrays and dynamic array functions such as the FILTER, SORT, SORTBY, and UNIQUE functions. This edition also introduces LAMBDA and LET for generating custom functions and function variables, Excel data types, and the Analyze Data tool for spotting trends and gaining insight into data.

PowerPoint: The PowerPoint Collection introduces the new commenting experience, which lets users display comments in contextual view or in the Comments pane. The comment anchor helps reviewers identify specific slide elements with comments and place the comment bubble anywhere on the slide. With the revised search feature, users can enter a word or phrase in the Search box to find the definition. Microsoft Search also provides support articles to help perform tasks.

Word: New features in the Word Collection include the enhanced Accessibility Checker, which identifies potential accessibility issues and presents suggestions to make documents more inclusive. The Word Collection also introduces Focus mode, the updated collaboration experience, Microsoft's expanded search tool, and voice options. The Immersive Reader is covered, as is the ability to create a private document copy and use Word's screen reader.

Organization of the Text

New Perspectives Microsoft 365 & Office, First Edition is a comprehensive introduction to Microsoft applications—Word, Excel, PowerPoint, and Access—and is well-suited for business programs. Each application is divided into modules within the three levels—introductory, intermediate, and advanced. Each module introduces a topic through an engaging real-world case scenario and presents content that aligns directly with the learning objectives listed at the beginning of the module. Skills are taught progressively to encourage student learning and advancement to proficiency. After completing each part in the module, students verify their understanding by answering Quick Check questions. End-of-module activities range from applying skills to working independently as they explore new features and solutions. All the activities are based on real-life scenarios from the top industries for each application and provide students with opportunities to engage in higher-level thinking and increase their confidence in their abilities.

Features of the Text

The features of the text, which are found consistently throughout all modules, are designed to aid the student in a specific way.

The projects present authentic case scenarios, which are focused on employability and based on research and data.

The Visual Overview is a screenshot of the application and spans a two-page spread at the start of each part in the module. It serves as a preview of the part content and a study tool for later reference. Callouts in the image align to the learning objectives for the module.

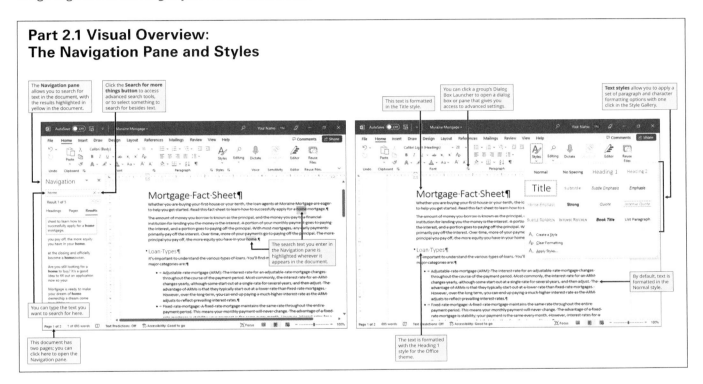

Heading levels organize topics within a module. Step-by-step task sequences provide numbered steps that guide students to complete the case project.

Step-by-step sequences include the following features:

Key Steps draw attention to a particular step that students must complete accurately to avoid real difficulty later on. The Key Step text reminds students how to perform the step correctly.

> ### To center-align the text:
>
> 1. Make sure the Home tab is still selected, and press **CTRL+A** to select the entire document.
>
>   **Key Step** Use CTRL+A to select the entire document, instead of dragging the pointer. It's easy to miss part of the document when you drag the pointer.

Course Solutions
Online Learning Platform: MindTap with SAM

The New Perspectives Series MindTap Collection, powered by SAM (Skills Assessment Manager), enables proficiency in Microsoft Office and computing concepts for your Introductory Computing courses. With a library of renowned course materials, including ready-to-assign, auto-graded learning modules, you can easily adapt your course to best prepare students for the evolving job market. In addition to an eReader that includes the full content of the printed book, the New Perspectives Collection, First Edition MindTap course includes the following:

- SAM Textbook Projects: Follow the steps and scenarios outlined in the textbook readings; enable students to complete projects based on a real-world scenario live in Microsoft Office applications and submit them in SAM for automatic grading and feedback.
- SAM Training and Exam: Trainings teach students to complete specific skills in a simulated Microsoft application environment while exams allow students to demonstrate their proficiency (also in a simulated environment).
- SAM Projects: Students complete projects based on real-world scenarios live in Microsoft applications and submit the projects in SAM for automatic grading and feedback. SAM offers several types of projects, each with a unique purpose: 1A and 1B, critical thinking, end of module, capstone, and integration.
- Microsoft Office Specialist (MOS) resources: Training and exams are based on the Microsoft Office 365 Objective Domains for the MOS Exam and exam simulation that replicates the test-taking environment of the MOS exam for Word, Excel, Access, PowerPoint, and Outlook.

To learn more, go to: https://www.cengage.com/mindtap-collections/

Ancillary Package

Additional instructor and student resources for this product are available online. Instructor assets include an Instructor Manual, an Educator Guide, PowerPoint® slides, a Guide to Teaching Online, Solution Files, a test bank powered by Cognero®, and a Transition Guide. Student assets include data files and a glossary. Sign up or sign in at **www.cengage.com** to search for and access this product and its online resources. The instructor and student companion sites contain ancillary material for the full New Perspectives Series Collection, along with instructions on how to find specific content within the companion site.

- Instructor Manual: This guide provides additional instructional material to assist in class preparation, including module objectives, module outlines, discussion questions, and additional activities and assignments. Each outline corresponds directly with the content in the module, and additional discussion questions and activities are aligned to headings in the book.
- Educator Guide: The MindTap Educator Guide contains a detailed outline of the corresponding MindTap course, including activity types and time on task. The SAM Educator Guide explains how to use SAM functionality to maximize your course.
- PowerPoint slides: The slides may be used to guide classroom presentations, to provide to students for module review, or to print as classroom handouts. The slides align closely with the book while activities and the self-assessment align with module learning objectives and supplement the content in the book.
- Guide to Teaching Online: This guide presents technological and pedagogical considerations and suggestions for teaching the Introductory Computing course when you can't be in the same room with students.

- Solution files: These files provide solutions to all textbook projects for instructors to use to grade student work.
    - Instructors using SAM do not need solution files since projects are auto-graded within SAM.
    - Solution files are provided on the instructor companion site for instructors *not* using SAM.
- Data files: These files are provided for students to complete the projects in each module.
    - Students using SAM to complete the projects download the required data files directly from SAM.
    - Students who are *not* using SAM to complete the projects can find data files on the student companion site and within MindTap.
- Test banks: A comprehensive test bank, offered in Cognero, Word, Blackboard, Moodle, Desire2Learn, Canvas, and SAM formats, contains questions aligned with each module's learning objectives and are written by subject matter experts. Powered by Cognero, Cengage Testing is a flexible, online system that allows you to author, edit, and manage test bank content from multiple Cengage solutions and to create multiple test versions that you can deliver from your LMS, your classroom, or wherever you want.
- Transition Guide: This guide highlights all the changes in the text and in the digital offerings from the previous edition to the current one so that instructors know what to expect.

Acknowledgments

Mark Shellman: I would first like to dedicate this text to the memory of my parents, Mickey and Shelba Shellman. No child has ever been more loved and supported in their life than I. I would also like to thank my wonderful wife Donna Sue, and my children, Taylor and Kimberly, for their support and patience during this project. All of you girls are my world! Last, but certainly not least, I would like to thank the entire development team of Amy Savino, Christina Nyren, and Lisa Ruffolo. Thank you all from the bottom of my heart for all of your support, caring, and patience during this project. It means more that you will ever know. You are truly the best!

Patrick Carey: I would like to thank the people who worked so hard to make this book possible. Special thanks to my developmental editor, Robin Romer, for her hard work, attention to detail, and valuable insights, and to Content Manager Christina Nyren, who has worked tirelessly in overseeing this project and made my task so much easier with enthusiasm and good humor. Other people at Cengage who deserve credit are Amy Savino, senior portfolio product manager; Amberlea Cogan, technical content program manager; Zenya Molnar, learning designer; Ciara Boynton, product assistant; Erin Griffin, senior designer; Seth Cohn, senior planner buyer; and Lumina Datamatics Ltd., compositor. This book is dedicated to my wife Joan who is my inspiration and role model for her good humor, dedication, and tireless support.

Jennifer T. Campbell: Many thanks to my editor, Mike Sanford, for his wisdom and hard work, as well as the team at Cengage, including Christina Nyren, Amy Savino, Zenya Molnar, and Ciara Boynton. As always, Mike, Emma, and Lucy were my biggest cheerleaders and inspiration.

Ann Shaffer: Thanks to the publishing professionals at Cengage Learning who are smart, fun to work with, and great at their jobs: Amy Savino, senior product manager; Zenya Molnar, learning designer; Christina Nyren, content manager; Ciara Boynton, senior product assistant. They made this revision a total pleasure. Many thanks to Neha Bhargava, project manager, and the team at Lumina Datamatics, who magically turned a pile of text and art manuscript files into the finished product. I will never understand how they can manage the 10 million details involved in publishing books like this, but somehow, they do it. I am grateful to Amit Tomar and the team at Qualitest for checking every step and exercise for errors. Their thoroughness made every module better. My biggest thank you goes to Mary Pat Shaffer, development editor extraordinaire, who pulled me along through the long process of this revision with endless patience, stunning attention to detail, an ability to remember everything that needed to be remembered, and a warm-hearted sense of humor that made me look forward to every morning's conversation as the highlight of my day. This book is dedicated to Mary Pat, whose fortitude and kindness always amazes me.

Getting to Know Microsoft Office Versions

Cengage is proud to bring you the next edition of Microsoft Office. This edition was designed to provide a robust learning experience that is not dependent upon a specific version of Office.

Microsoft supports several versions and editions of Office: (Refer to Table 1 below for more information)

- **Microsoft 365 (formerly known as Office 365):** A service that delivers the most up-to-date, feature-rich, modern Microsoft productivity applications direct to your device. There are several combinations of Microsoft 365 programs for business, educational, and personal use. Microsoft 365 is cloud-based, meaning it is stored, managed, and processed on a network of remote servers hosted on the Internet, rather than on local servers or personal computers. Microsoft 365 offers extra online storage and cloud-connected features, as well as updates with the latest features, fixes, and security updates. Microsoft 365 is purchased for a monthly subscription fee that keeps your software up to date with the latest features.

- **Office 2021:** The Microsoft "on-premises" version of the Office apps, available for both PCs and Macintosh computers, offered as a static, one-time purchase and outside of the subscription model. Unlike Microsoft 365, Office 2021 does not include online product updates with new features.

- **Microsoft 365 Online (formerly known as Office Online):** A free, simplified version of Microsoft web applications (Teams, Access, Word, Excel, PowerPoint, and OneNote) that lets users create and edit files collaboratively.

- **Office 365 Education:** A free subscription including Word, Excel, PowerPoint, OneNote, and now Microsoft Teams, plus additional classroom tools. Only available for students and educators at select institutions.

Table 1 Microsoft Office applications — uses and availability

Application	Use	Availability/Editions
Word	Create documents and improve your writing with intelligent assistance features.	Microsoft 365 Family, Home, Business, Office 2021, Office 365 Education
Excel	Simplify complex data into easy-to-read spreadsheets.	Microsoft 365 Personal, Home, Business, Office 2021, Office 365 Education
PowerPoint	Create presentations that stand out.	Home, Business, Office 2021, Office 365 Education
OneNote	A digital notebook for all your note-taking needs.	Home, Office 365 Education
OneDrive	Save and share your files and photos wherever you are.	Home, Business
Outlook	Manage your email, calendar, tasks, and contacts all in one place.	Home, Business
SharePoint	Create team sites to share information, files, and resources.	Business
Publisher	Create polished, professional layouts without the hassle.	Home, Business, Office 2021 (PC only)
Access	Create your own database apps easily in formats that serve your business best.	Home, Business, Office 2021 (PC only)
Teams	Bring everyone together in one place to meet, chat, call, and collaborate.	Business, Office 365 Education
Exchange	Business-class email and calendaring.	Business

Over time, the Microsoft 365 cloud interface will continuously update using its web connection, offering new application features and functions, while Office 2021 will remain static.

Because Microsoft 365 releases updates continuously, your onscreen experience may differ from what you see in this product. For example, the more advanced features and functionalities covered in this product may not be available in Microsoft 365 Online, may have updated from what you see in Office 2021, or may be from a post-publication update of Microsoft 365.

For up-to-date information on the differences between Microsoft 365, Office 2021, and Microsoft 365 Online, please visit the Microsoft Support website.

Cengage is committed to providing high-quality learning solutions for you to gain the knowledge and skills that will empower you throughout your educational and professional careers.

Thank you for using our product, and we look forward to exploring the future of Microsoft Office with you!

Using SAM Projects and Textbook Projects

SAM (Skills Assessment Manager) **Projects** allow you to actively apply the skills you learned in Microsoft Word, Excel, PowerPoint, or Access. You can also submit your work to SAM for online grading. You can use SAM Projects to become a more productive student and use these skills throughout your career.

To complete SAM Textbook Projects, please follow these steps:

SAM Textbook Projects allow you to complete a project as you follow along with the steps in the textbook. As you read the module, look for icons that indicate when you should download **sam**⬇ your SAM Start file(s) and when to upload **sam**⬆ your solution file to SAM for grading.

Everything you need to complete this project is provided within SAM. You can launch the eBook directly from SAM, which will allow you to take notes, highlight, and create a custom study guide, or you can use a print textbook or your mobile app. Download IOS or Download Android.

To get started, launch your SAM Project assignment from SAM, MindTap, or a link within your learning management system.

1. Step 1:
   Download Files
   - Click the "Download All" button or the individual links to download your **Start File** and **Support File(s)** (when available). You must use the SAM Start file.
   - Click the Instructions link to launch the eBook (or use the print textbook or mobile app).
   - Disregard any steps in the textbook that ask you to create a new file or to use a file from a location outside of SAM.
   - Look for the SAM Download icon **sam**⬇ to begin working with your start file.
   - Follow the module's step-by-step instructions until you reach the SAM Upload icon **sam**⬆.
   - Save and close the file.

2. Step 2:
   Save Work to SAM
   - Ensure you rename your project file to match the Expected File Name.
   - Upload your in-progress or completed file to SAM. You can download the file to continue working or submit it for grading in the next step.

3. Step 3:
   Submit for Grading
   - Upload your completed solution file to SAM for immediate feedback and to view the available Reports.
     - The **Graded Summary Report** provides a detailed list of project steps, your score, and feedback to aid you in revising and resubmitting the project.
     - The **Study Guide** provides your score for each project step and links to the associated training and textbook pages.
   - If additional attempts are allowed, use your reports to assist with revising and resubmitting your project.
   - To re-submit your project, download the file you saved in step 2.
   - Edit, save, and close the file, then re-upload and submit it again.

For all other SAM Projects, please follow these steps:

To get started, launch your SAM Project assignment from SAM, MindTap, or a link within your learning management system.

1. Step 1:
   Download Files
   - Click the "Download All" button or the individual links to download your **Instruction File**, **Start File**, and **Support File(s)** (when available). You must use the SAM Start file.
   - Open the Instruction file and follow the step-by-step instructions. Ensure you rename your project file to match the Expected File Name (change _1 to _2 at the end of the file name).

2. Step 2:
   Save Work to SAM

   o Upload your in-progress or completed file to SAM. You can download the file to continue working or submit it for grading in the next step.

3. Step 3:
   Submit for Grading

   o Upload the completed file to SAM for immediate feedback and to view available Reports.

   ▪ The **Graded Summary Report** provides a detailed list of project steps, your score, and feedback to aid you in revising and resubmitting the project.

   ▪ The **Study Guide** provides your score for each project step and links to the associated training and textbook pages.

   o If additional attempts are allowed, use your reports to assist with revising and resubmitting your project.

   o To re-submit the project, download the file saved in step 2.

   o Edit, save, and close the file, then re-upload and submit it again.

For additional tips to successfully complete your SAM Projects, please view our SAM Video Tutorials.

Getting Started with Excel

Developing a Purchase Order Report

Case: Insight Video Solutions

Sofi Feng is an account assistant for Insight Video Solutions, a startup company that designs and installs high-end video equipment for video conferencing and online seminars. One of Sofi's responsibilities is to maintain documentation on customer accounts, relating that information to the general financial health of the company. Sofi wants to use Excel to create purchase order reports for Insight Video Solution customers. You'll help her to develop those reports.

Starting Data Files

Excel1	Case1
Module	NP_EX_1-3.xlsx
NP_EX_1-1.xlsx	**Case2**
Review	NP_EX_1-4.xlsx
NP_EX_1-2.xlsx	

Objectives

Part 1.1

- Open and close a workbook
- Navigate through a workbook and worksheet
- Select cells and ranges
- Plan and create a workbook
- Insert, rename, and move worksheets
- Enter text, dates, and numbers
- Undo and redo actions
- Resize columns and rows

Part 1.2

- Enter formulas and the SUM and COUNT functions
- Copy and paste formulas
- Move or copy cells and ranges
- Insert and delete rows, columns, and ranges
- Create patterned text with Flash Fill
- Add cell borders and change font size
- Change worksheet views
- Prepare a workbook for printing

Part 1.1 Visual Overview: The Excel Workbook

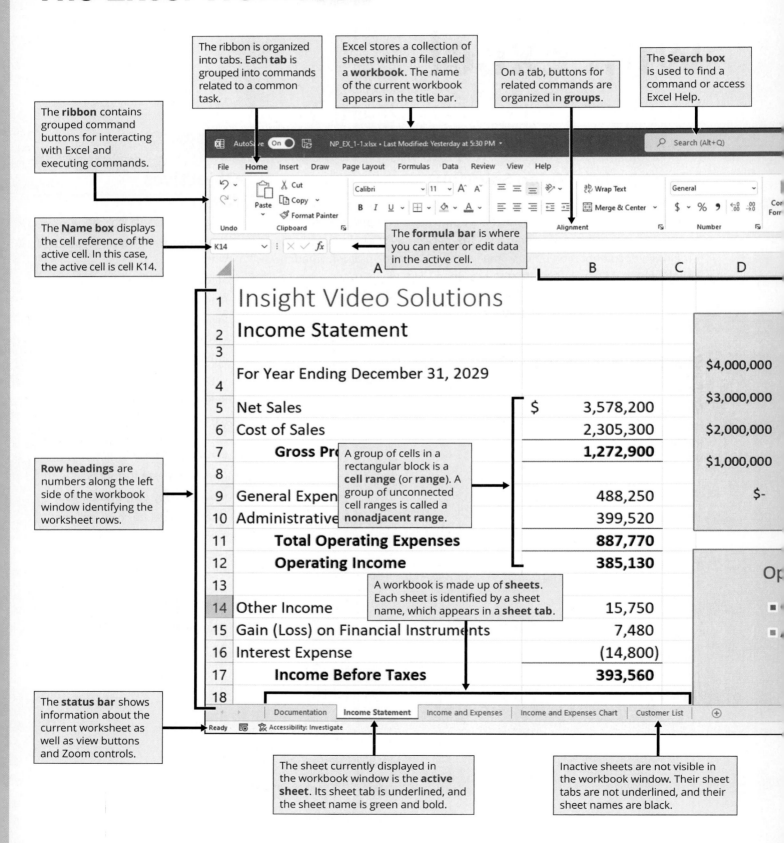

The ribbon is organized into tabs. Each **tab** is grouped into commands related to a common task.

Excel stores a collection of sheets within a file called a **workbook**. The name of the current workbook appears in the title bar.

On a tab, buttons for related commands are organized in **groups**.

The **Search box** is used to find a command or access Excel Help.

The **ribbon** contains grouped command buttons for interacting with Excel and executing commands.

The **Name box** displays the cell reference of the active cell. In this case, the active cell is cell K14.

The **formula bar** is where you can enter or edit data in the active cell.

Row headings are numbers along the left side of the workbook window identifying the worksheet rows.

A group of cells in a rectangular block is a **cell range** (or **range**). A group of unconnected cell ranges is called a **nonadjacent range**.

A workbook is made up of **sheets**. Each sheet is identified by a sheet name, which appears in a **sheet tab**.

The **status bar** shows information about the current worksheet as well as view buttons and Zoom controls.

The sheet currently displayed in the workbook window is the **active sheet**. Its sheet tab is underlined, and the sheet name is green and bold.

Inactive sheets are not visible in the workbook window. Their sheet tabs are not underlined, and their sheet names are black.

The **Minimize button** reduces a window so that only its program icon is visible on the taskbar.

The **Restore Down button** returns a window to its previous size. If the **Maximize button** appears, it expands the window to fill the entire screen.

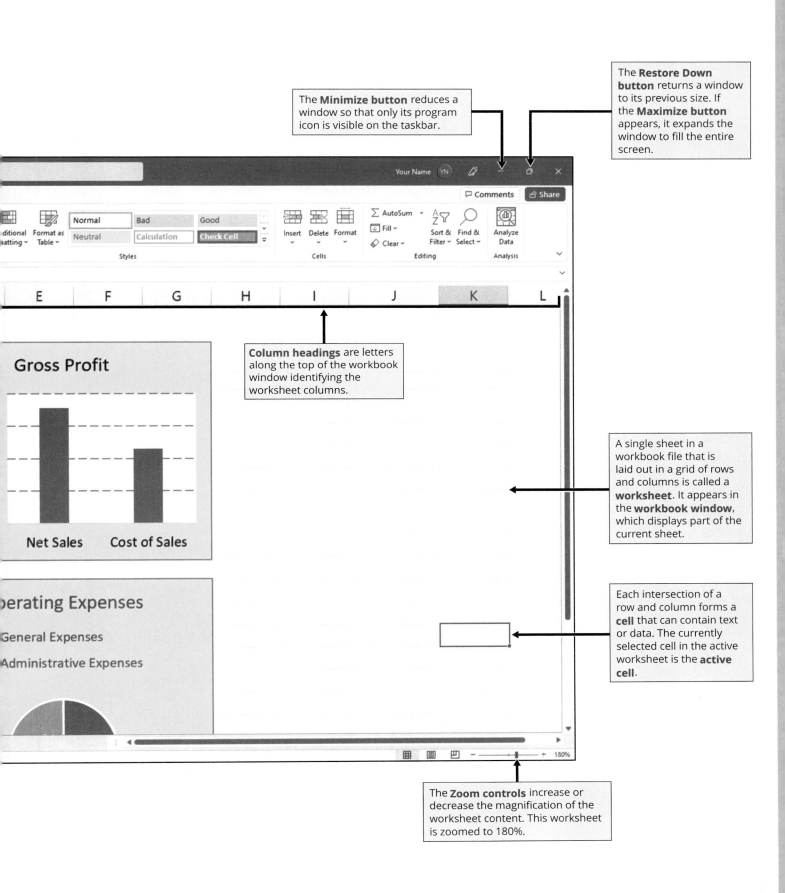

Column headings are letters along the top of the workbook window identifying the worksheet columns.

A single sheet in a workbook file that is laid out in a grid of rows and columns is called a **worksheet**. It appears in the **workbook window**, which displays part of the current sheet.

Each intersection of a row and column forms a **cell** that can contain text or data. The currently selected cell in the active worksheet is the **active cell**.

The **Zoom controls** increase or decrease the magnification of the worksheet content. This worksheet is zoomed to 180%.

Gross Profit

Net Sales   Cost of Sales

perating Expenses

General Expenses

Administrative Expenses

Using the Excel Interface

Microsoft Excel (or just **Excel**) is a program to store, analyze, and report data arranged in the form of a spreadsheet. A **spreadsheet** is a grouping of text and numbers in a rectangular grid or table. Spreadsheets are often used in business for budgeting, inventory management, and financial reporting because they unite text, numbers, and graphics within a single document. Spreadsheets can also be used for personal needs such as planning a family budget, tracking expenses, or listing personal items. The advantage of an electronic spreadsheet is that the content can be easily edited and updated to reflect changing financial conditions.

To start Excel:

1. On the Windows taskbar, click the **Start** button ⊞ . The Start menu opens.

2. On the Start menu, scroll the list, and then click **Excel.** Excel starts and displays the Home screen in Backstage view. Refer to Figure 1–1.

Figure 1–1   Backstage view

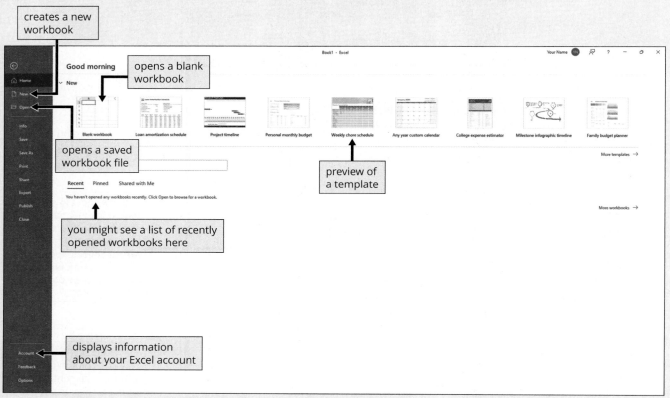

> **Trouble?** If Excel is not in the Start menu, click the Type here to search box, type Excel, and then press Enter. Excel starts with the Home screen in Backstage view.

Backstage view displays commands and screens for managing your interface with the Excel app and your account on Microsoft Office. From this view, you can also open recently viewed files, create and save new documents, and share your work with your colleagues.

Excel documents are called workbooks. You can open a blank workbook or an existing workbook, or you can create a new workbook based on a template. A **template** is a preformatted workbook containing designs and content already created for the users. Templates can speed up your work because much of the effort in designing the workbook and entering its initial content has already been done.

Sofi created an Excel workbook with financial income statements drawn from the current accounts of Insight Video Solutions customers. You will open that workbook and review its contents.

To open the Income Statement workbook:

1. In Backstage view, click **Open**. The Open screen is displayed, providing access to locations where workbooks might be saved.

2. Click **Browse**. The Open dialog box appears.

3. Navigate to the **Excel1 > Module** folder included with your Data Files.

   > **Trouble?** If you don't have the starting Data Files, you need to get them before you can proceed. Your instructor will either give you the Data Files or indicate how to access them. If you have any questions about the Data Files, ask your instructor or technical support person for assistance.

4. Click **NP_EX_1-1.xlsx** in the file list to select it.

   If your instructor wants you to submit your work as a SAM Project for automatic grading, you must download the Data File in Step 4 from the assignment launch page.

5. Click the **Open** button. The workbook opens in Excel.

   > **Trouble?** If only the tab names appear at the top of the Excel window instead of the full ribbon as it appears in the Part 1.1 Visual Overview, right-click any tab name to display a shortcut menu, and then click Collapse the Ribbon to display the full ribbon.

6. If the Excel window doesn't fill the screen, click the **Maximize** button ◻ in the upper-right corner of the title bar. Refer to Figure 1–2.

Figure 1–2　　　Financial workbook

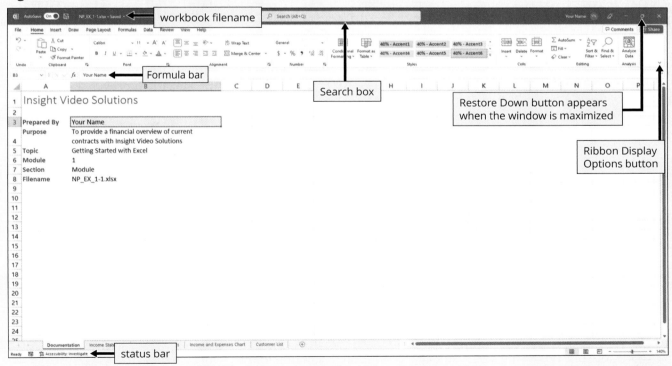

Nearly everything you do in Excel uses a command. You can access Excel commands on the ribbon using a mouse or pointing device. Or, you can use keyboard shortcuts.

> **Tip** If you want help with a task, you can use Excel Help. To access Help, press F1. You can also enter a descriptive phrase or keyword in the Search box on the title bar to view help on that topic.

A **keyboard shortcut** is a key or combination of keys that you press together to perform a command or access a feature. For example, the keyboard shortcut to save a document is CTRL+S, which means you press the CTRL and S keys at the same time. When available, a keyboard shortcut is listed next to the command's name in a ScreenTip. A **ScreenTip** is a label that appears next to an object, providing information about that object or giving a link to additional information in Excel Help. Figure 1–3 lists some of the keyboard shortcuts commonly used in Excel.

Figure 1–3   Excel keyboard shortcuts

Press	To	Press	To
ALT	Display the Key Tips for the commands and tools on the ribbon	CTRL+V	Paste content that was cut or copied
CTRL+A	Select all objects in a range	CTRL+W	Close the current workbook
CTRL+C	Copy the selected object(s)	CTRL+X	Cut the selected object(s)
CTRL+G	Go to a location in the workbook	CTRL+Y	Repeat the last command
CTRL+N	Open a new blank workbook	CTRL+Z	Undo the last command
CTRL+O	Open a saved workbook file	F1	Open the Excel Help window
CTRL+P	Print the current workbook	F5	Go to a location in the workbook
CTRL+S	Save the current workbook	F12	Save the current workbook with a new name or to a new location

You can also use the keyboard to access commands on the ribbon. Press ALT to display **Key Tips**, which are labels with keys that appear on the ribbon. Then press the key or key combination listed to access the corresponding tab, command, or button. For example, pressing ALT followed by Y accesses the commands on the Help tab, and then pressing W accesses the What's New command in the Help group.

With touchscreen devices, you access commands using your finger(s) or a stylus. You can switch Excel to **Touch Mode**, which adds space around the icons on the ribbon to make them more convenient to tap. The figures in these modules show Excel in **Mouse Mode**, which is the standard spacing for the ribbon for use with a mouse or pointing device. If you switch between a touchscreen device and a non-touchscreen monitor, you might want to switch between Touch and Mouse modes. You'll try that now.

To switch between Mouse Mode and Touch Mode:

1. Click the **Ribbon Display Options** button in the lower-right corner of the ribbon.

2. Click **Show Quick Access Toolbar** if it is not checked to display the Quick Access Toolbar.

3. Below the ribbon on the left edge of the Excel window, click the **Quick Access Toolbar** button. A list of options appears.

   Trouble? If the Quick Access Toolbar button appears above the ribbon, you can change its position. Click the Quick Access Toolbar button, and then click Show Below the Ribbon. The toolbar moves below the ribbon.

4. Click **Touch/Mouse Mode** if it is not checked to add this button to the Quick Access Toolbar.

5. On the Quick Access Toolbar, click the **Touch/Mouse Mode** button, and then click **Touch**. The display is in Touch Mode with more space between the commands and buttons on the ribbon. Refer to Figure 1–4.

Figure 1–4   Excel displayed in Touch Mode

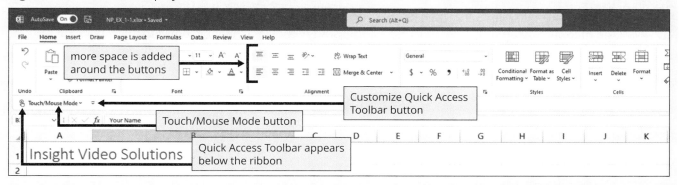

> **Trouble?** If the screen display doesn't change, you were already in Touch mode. Continue with the next step.

Next, you will switch back to Mouse Mode. If you are working with a touchscreen and want to continue using Touch Mode, skip Step 6.

6. On the Quick Access Toolbar, click the **Touch/Mouse Mode** button, and then click **Mouse**. The display returns to Mouse Mode (refer to Figure 1–2). The figures in these modules show the ribbon in Mouse Mode.

7. To remove the Touch/Mouse Mode button from the Quick Access Toolbar, click the **Customize Quick Access Toolbar** button ⯆ , and then click **Touch/Mouse Mode** to deselect it. The Touch/Mouse Mode button is removed from the Quick Access Toolbar.

8. To hide the Quick Access Toolbar, click the **Ribbon Display Options** button, and then click **Hide Quick Access Toolbar**.

The Quick Access Toolbar is useful for accessing commands that might take several clicks to access on the ribbon. However, these modules do not use the Quick Access Toolbar.

Navigating Between Sheets

The contents of a workbook are displayed in the workbook window located below the ribbon. Workbooks are organized into separate pages called sheets. Excel supports two types of sheets: worksheets and chart sheets. A worksheet contains a grid of rows and columns organized into cells in which you can enter text, numbers, dates, and formulas. Worksheets can also contain graphical elements such as charts, maps, and clip art. A **chart sheet** contains a single chart linked to data within a workbook. A chart sheet can also contain other graphical elements like clip art, but it doesn't contain a grid for entering data values.

Worksheets and chart sheets are identified by the sheet tabs at the bottom of the workbook window. Sofi's workbook contains five sheets labeled Documentation, Income Statement, Income and Expenses, Income and Expenses Chart, and Customer List. If a workbook contains more sheet tabs than can fit in the workbook window, the list of tabs will end with an ellipsis (…), indicating there are additional sheets. You can use the sheet tab scrolling buttons, located to the left of the sheet tabs, to scroll through the complete sheet tab list. Scrolling through the tab list does not change the active sheet; it changes only which sheet tabs are visible within the workbook window.

The sheet currently displayed in the workbook window is the active sheet, which in this case is the Documentation sheet. The sheet tab of the active sheet has a green underline, and the sheet name appears in bold. To change the active sheet, you click its sheet tab.

> **Tip** Some workbooks have hidden sheets; even though these sheets aren't displayed, they are still part of the workbook.

You will view the different sheets in Sofi's workbook.

To view the sheets in Sofi's workbook:

1. Click the **Income Statement** sheet tab. The Income Statement worksheet becomes the active sheet, and its name is now bold green. Refer to Figure 1–5.

Figure 1–5   Income Statement worksheet

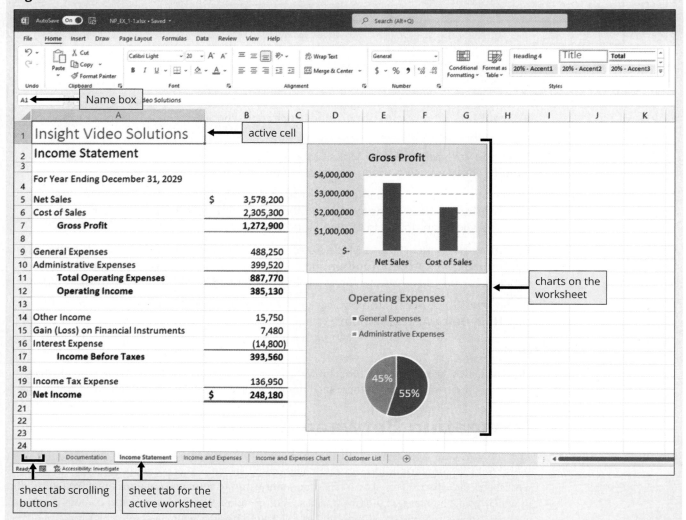

sheet tab scrolling buttons

sheet tab for the active worksheet

The Income Statement worksheet sheet contains financial data on the company's sales, profit, expenses, and net income. The sheet also contains a chart comparing the company's net sales to its cost of sales and a chart that breaks down the company's operating expense into general and administrative expenses. The charts provide a visual interpretation of the data contained in the income statement.

2. Click the **Income and Expenses** sheet tab. The active sheet displays sales and expense data for each month of the fiscal year. From viewing the final data in this worksheet, you can learn that the company showed a negative operating income for the first three months of the year but a positive income for the remaining months as sales increased.

3. Click the **Income and Expenses Chart** sheet tab. The active chart sheet shows the monthly profit and expenses for the company and the operating income. The chart provides a visual summary of the data in the Income and Expenses worksheet. Refer to Figure 1–6.

Figure 1-6   Income and Expenses Chart sheet

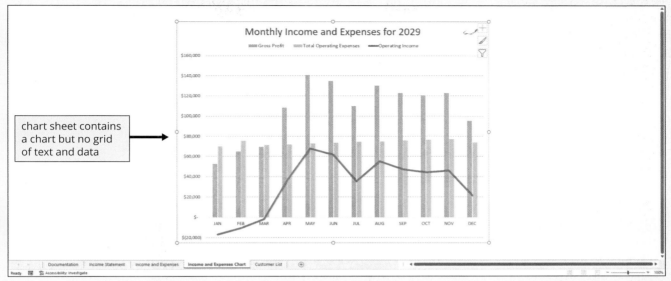

chart sheet contains a chart but no grid of text and data

4. Click the **Customer List** sheet tab. The active sheet shows a list of Insight Video Solutions customers from the current fiscal year. The worksheet provides contact information for each customer as well as the order total from each customer's account with the company.

Selecting Worksheet Cells and Cell Ranges

Rows within a worksheet are identified by numbers; the columns are identified by letters. Row headings range from 1 to 1,048,576. Column headings start with letters from A to Z. After Z, the next columns are labeled AA, AB, AC, and so forth. The last possible column heading is XFD, which means there are 16,384 available columns in a worksheet. The total number of possible cells in a single Excel worksheet is more than 17 billion, providing an extremely large working space for reports.

Each cell is identified by a **cell reference** that indicates the column and row of that cell. The company's net income of $248,180 (refer to Figure 1–5) is in cell B20, which is the intersection of row B and column 20. In every cell reference, the column letter always appears first.

The cell currently selected in the worksheet is the active cell, indicated by a thick green border. The corresponding column and row headings for the active cell are shaded. The cell reference of the active cell appears in the Name box, which is on the left edge of the window just below the ribbon. The active cell in Figure 1–5 is cell A1, containing the company name, Insight Video Solutions.

To move different parts of the worksheet into view, use the horizontal and vertical scroll bars located at the bottom and right edges of the workbook window. Each scroll bar has clickable arrow buttons to move the worksheet one column or row and a scroll box that can be dragged to shift the worksheet larger amounts in the direction you choose.

You will use these tools to scroll through the contents of the Customer List worksheet.

To scroll through the Customer List worksheet:

1. On the Customer List worksheet, click the **down arrow** button ▼ on the vertical scroll bar three times to scroll down the worksheet three rows.

2. Drag the vertical scroll box down until you reach row 140 containing information on the last customer in the list (Zohne & Haus Group).

3. On the horizontal scroll bar, click the **right arrow** button ▶ three times. The worksheet scrolls three columns to the right, moving columns A through C out of view.

4. On the horizontal scroll bar, drag the scroll box to the left until you reach column A.

5. On the vertical scroll bar, drag the scroll box up until you reach the top of the worksheet and cell A1.

Scrolling through the worksheet does not change the location of the active cell. Although the active cell might shift out of view, its cell reference is in the Name box. To choose a different active cell, either click a new cell or use keyboard shortcuts describe in Figure 1–7 to navigate to a new cell.

Figure 1–7   Navigation keyboard shortcuts

Press	To move the active cell
↑↓←→	Up, down, left, or right one cell
HOME	To column A of the current row
CTRL+HOME	To cell A1
CTRL+END	To the last cell in the worksheet that contains data
ENTER	Down one row or to the start of the next row of data
SHIFT+ENTER	Up one row
TAB	One column to the right
SHIFT+TAB	One column to the left
PGUP, PGDN	Up or down one screen
CTRL+PGUP, CTRL+PGDN	To the previous or next sheet in the workbook

Keyboard shortcuts are especially useful in large scientific and financial worksheets in which data is spread across hundreds or thousands of rows and columns. You will use keyboard shortcuts to change the active cell in the Customer List worksheet.

To change the active cell using keyboard shortcuts:

1. On the Customer List worksheet, move the pointer over cell D10 containing the text "Detroit," and then click the mouse button. The active cell moves from cell A1 to cell D10. A green border appears around cell D10 indicating that it's now the active cell. The labels for row 10 and column D are shaded, and the cell reference in the Name box changes to D10.

2. Press **TAB**. The active cell moves one column to the right to cell E10 containing the text "MI".

3. Press **PGDN**. The active cell moves down one full screen.

4. Press **PGUP**. The active cell moves up one full screen, returning to cell E10.

5. Press **CTRL+END**. The active cell is cell L140, the last worksheet cell containing data.

6. Press **CTRL+HOME**. The active cell returns to the first cell in the worksheet, cell A1.

To change the active cell to a specific cell location, you can enter the cell's address in either the Go To dialog box or the Name box. You'll try both methods.

To change the active cell using the Go To dialog box and Name box:

1. On the Home tab, in the Editing group, click the **Find & Select** button, and then click **Go To** on the menu that opens (or press **CTRL+G** or **F5**). The Go To dialog box opens.

2. Type **A104** in the Reference box. Refer to Figure 1–8.

Figure 1–8   Go To dialog box

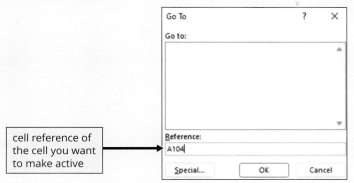

cell reference of the cell you want to make active

3. Click **OK**. Cell A104 becomes the active cell, showing account information for customer CD7586, New Tech Construction.

4. Click the **Name** box, type **A42**, and then press **ENTER**. Cell A42 becomes the active cell of the row showing account information for customer CD2939, Reed & Stribling Financial.

Many tasks in Excel involve working with groups of cells, called a cell range or simply a range. Cell ranges are identified with a **range reference** that specify which cells are included in the range. Cells in an adjacent range are in a rectangular block. The reference for an adjacent range includes the reference for the top-left and bottom-right cells separated by a colon. For example, A1:G5 references a rectangular block including all cells from cell A1 through cell G5.

As with individual cells, you can select cell ranges using your mouse or pointing device, the keyboard, or commands. You will select a cell range in the Income Statement worksheet.

To select a cell range in the Income Statement worksheet:

1. Click the **Income Statement** sheet tab. The Income Statement worksheet is the active sheet.

2. Click cell **A5** to select it and, without releasing the mouse button, drag down and right to cell **B7**.

3. Release the mouse button. All cells from cell A5 down to cell B7 are selected, and the block of cells is surrounded by a green border. The first cell selected, A5, is the active cell in the worksheet. The Quick Analysis button appears next to the selected range, providing options for analyzing the data in the selected range. Refer to Figure 1–9.

Figure 1-9   Range A5:B7 selected in the worksheet

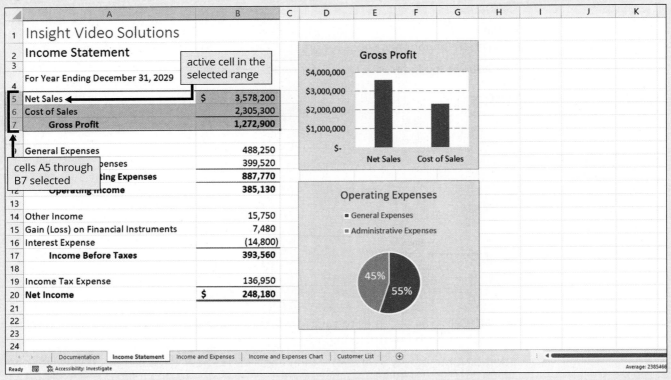

Tip You can also select a range by clicking the top-left cell in the range, holding down SHIFT, clicking the bottom-right cell in the range, and then releasing SHIFT.

4. Click cell **A1** to deselect the range.

You can select separate adjacent ranges, known as a nonadjacent range. References for nonadjacent ranges includes the reference to each adjacent range separated by commas. For example, the reference A1:G5,A10:G15 includes two ranges—the first is the rectangular block of cells from cell A1 to cell G5, and the second is the rectangular block of cells from cell A10 to cell G15.

To reference entire rows or columns, you include only the row or column headings. For example, the reference A:B includes all cells in columns A and B, and the reference 10:12,15:18 includes all cells in rows 10 through 12 and 15 through 18. To reference all cells in a single row or column, repeat the row or column heading. For example, the reference A:A selects all cells in column A, and the reference 20:20 selects all cells in row 20.

You will use select cells in a nonadjacent range in the Income Statement worksheet.

To select a nonadjacent range in the Income Statement worksheet:

1. Click cell **A5**, hold down **SHIFT** as you click cell **B7**, and then release **SHIFT** to select the range A5:B7.

2. Hold down **CTRL** as you drag to select the range **A9:B12**, and then release **CTRL**. The two separate blocks of cells in the nonadjacent range A5:B7, A9:B12 are selected. Refer to Figure 1–10.

Figure 1–10   Nonadjacent range A5:B7, A9:B12 selected

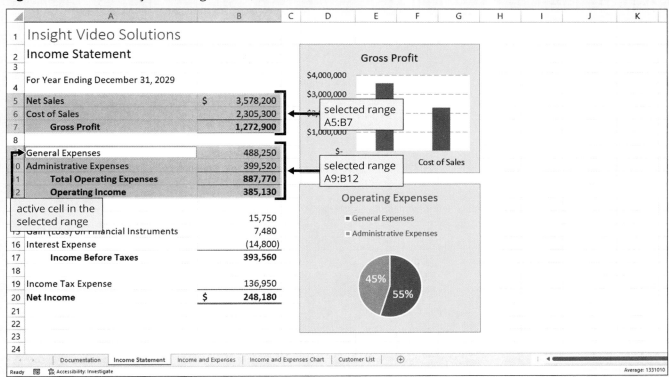

> **Tip** You can select a range by typing its reference, such as A5:B7, A9:B12, in the Go To dialog box or the Name box and pressing ENTER.

Closing a Workbook

When you are finished with a workbook, you should close it. A dialog box might appear, asking whether you want to save any changes made to the workbook. If you have made changes that you want to keep, save the workbook with the changes. Because you have finished reviewing Sofi's workbook for the company, you will close the workbook without saving any changes you may have inadvertently made to its contents.

To close Sofi's workbook:

1. On the ribbon, click the **File** tab to display Backstage view, and then click **Close** in the navigation bar (or press **CTRL+W**).

2. If a dialog box opens, asking whether you want to save your changes to the workbook, click **Don't Save**. The workbook closes without saving any changes. Excel remains opens, ready for you to create or open another workbook.

Now that you've reviewed Sofi's workbook of the company's incomes and expenses, you are ready to create your own workbook. Sofi wants you to create a workbook providing details on a purchase order made by an Insight Video Solutions customer.

Starting a New Workbook

Before starting a new workbook, it is often useful to plan out its contents and structure. You can do this with a planning analysis sheet, which includes the following questions to help you think about the workbook's purpose and how to achieve your intended results:

1. **What problems do I want to solve?** The answer identifies the goal or purpose of the workbook. For this module, you need to create a workbook that will document purchase order information from an Insight Video Solutions customer.

2. **What data do I need?** The answer identifies the type of data that you need to collect for the workbook. A purchase order needs to describe the items purchased, the per-unit cost of each item, and the total number of items ordered. It should also contain contact information for the customer so that you can do follow up if necessary.

3. **What calculations do I need?** The answer identifies the formulas you need to apply to your data. The purchase order needs to calculate to the total cost of each item ordered, the tax levied on the order, and the final overall cost of all items ordered plus tax.

4. **What form should my solution take?** The answer impacts the appearance of the workbook content and how it should be presented to others. Sofi wants the estimates stored in a single worksheet that is easy to read and prints clearly.

You will create a workbook based on this plan. Sofi will then use your solution in other workbooks that track customer purchase orders and income for the company.

Proskills

Written Communication: Creating Effective Workbooks

Workbooks convey information in written form. As with any type of writing, the final product creates an impression and provides an indicator of your interest, knowledge, and attention to detail. To create the best impression, all workbooks—especially those you intend to share with others such as coworkers and clients—should be well planned, well organized, and well written.

A well-designed workbook should clearly identify its overall goal and present information in an organized format. The data it includes—both the entered values and the calculated values—should be accurate. The process of developing an effective workbook includes the following steps:

1. Determine the workbook's purpose, content, and organization before you start.

2. Create a list of the sheets used in the workbook, noting each sheet's purpose.

3. Insert a documentation sheet that describes the workbook's purpose and organization. Include the name of the workbook's author, the date the workbook was created, and any additional information that will help others to track the workbook to its source.

4. Enter all the data in the workbook. Add labels to indicate what the values represent and, if possible, where they originated so others can view the source of your data.

5. Enter formulas for calculated items rather than entering the calculated values into the workbook. For more complicated calculations, provide documentation explaining them.

6. Test the workbook with a variety of values; edit the data and formulas to correct errors.

7. Save the workbook and create a backup copy when the project is completed. Print the workbook's contents if you need to provide a hard-copy version to others or for your files.

8. Maintain a history of your workbook as it goes through different versions, so that you and others can quickly review how the workbook has changed during revisions.

By including clearly written documentation, explanatory text, a logical organization, and accurate data and formulas, you will create effective workbooks that others can easily use.

You create new workbooks from the New screen in Backstage view. The New screen includes template icons that preview different types of workbooks with preplaced content and formatting. You will create a workbook from the Blank workbook template and then add all the content Sofi wants.

To start a new, blank workbook for a customer purchase order:

1. **sam↓** On the ribbon, click the **File** tab to display Backstage view.

2. Click **New** in the navigation bar to display the New screen, which includes access to templates for a variety of workbooks.

3. Click **Blank workbook**. A blank workbook opens.

   ▌ **Tip** You can also create a new blank workbook by pressing CTRL+N.

   In these modules, the workbook window is zoomed to 140% for better readability. If you want to zoom your workbook window to match the figures, complete Step 4. If you prefer to work in the default zoom of 100% or at another zoom level, read but do not complete Step 4; more or less of the worksheet might display on your screen, but this will not affect your work in the modules.

4. If you want your workbook window zoomed to 140% to match the figures, on the Zoom slider at the lower-right of the Excel window, click the **Zoom In** button ➕ four times to increase the percentage to **140%**. The 140% magnification increases the size of each cell but reduces the number of worksheet cells visible in the workbook window. Refer to Figure 1–11.

Figure 1–11   Blank workbook

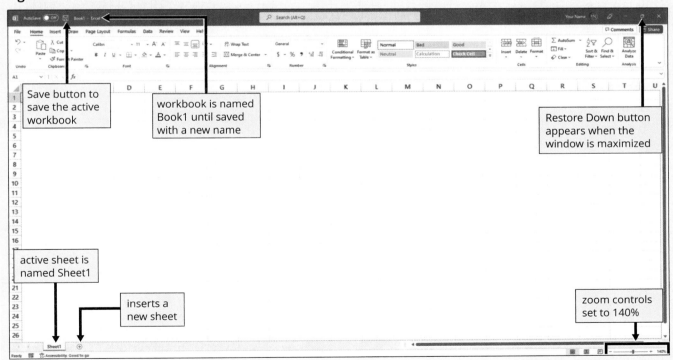

The name of the active workbook, Book1, appears in the title bar. If you open multiple blank workbooks, they are named Book1, Book2, Book3, and so forth until you save them with more descriptive names.

Inserting, Naming, and Moving Worksheets

Blank workbooks open with a single blank worksheet named Sheet1. It's a good practice to give sheets more descriptive names that indicate the purpose and content of each sheet. Sheet names cannot exceed 31 characters, but they can contain blank spaces and include uppercase and lowercase letters.

Because Sheet1 is not a descriptive name, Sofi asks you to rename the worksheet as Purchase Order.

To rename the Sheet1 worksheet:

1. Double-click the **Sheet1** tab to select the text of the sheet name.

2. Type **Purchase Order** as the new name, and then press **ENTER**. The width of the sheet tab expands to fit the longer sheet name

Many workbooks include multiple sheets to organize the report into logical sections. A common practice is to include a documentation worksheet containing a description of the workbook, the name of the person who prepared the workbook, and the date it was created.

Sofi wants you to create two new worksheets and name them Documentation and Customer Information. The Customer Information worksheet will store information about the customer making the purchase.

To insert and name the Documentation and Customer Information worksheets:

1. To the right of the Purchase Order sheet tab, click the **New sheet** button ⊕. A new sheet named Sheet2 is inserted to the right of the Purchase Order sheet.

2. Double-click the **Sheet2** sheet tab, type **Documentation** as the new name, and press **ENTER**. The worksheet is renamed.

3. To the right of the Documentation sheet, click the **New sheet** button ⊕ to insert a new worksheet, and name the Sheet3 worksheet with **Customer Information** as the descriptive name.

4. If you want these worksheets zoomed to 140% to match the figures, go to each worksheet, and then on the Zoom slider, click the **Zoom In** button ➕ four times to increase the percentage to 140%.

Often the first worksheet in a workbook provides an overview of the book's contents. Sheets that provide more specific or detailed information are placed later in the workbook. To change the placement of a sheet, click and drag its sheet tab to a new location in the workbook.

Sofi wants the Documentation worksheet to be of the first sheet in the workbook.

To move the Documentation worksheet:

1. Point to the **Documentation** sheet tab. The sheet tab name changes to bold.

2. Press and hold the mouse button. The pointer changes to the move sheet pointer ⬚, and a small arrow appears in the upper-left corner of the sheet tab.

3. Drag to the left until the small arrow appears in the upper-left corner of the Purchase Order sheet tab, and then release the mouse button. The Documentation worksheet is now the first sheet in the workbook.

> **Tip** You can make a copy of a worksheet by holding down CTRL as you drag and drop the sheet tab.

You might find a workbook has sheets that can be deleted. The easiest way to delete a sheet is by using a **shortcut menu**, which is a list of commands related to an object that opens when you right-click the object. Sofi asks you to include customer information on the Purchase Order worksheet. The Customer Information worksheet is no longer needed and can be removed.

To delete the Customer Information worksheet:

1. Right-click the **Customer Information** sheet tab. A shortcut menu opens.
2. Click **Delete**. The Customer Information worksheet is removed from the workbook.

When you delete a sheet, you also delete any text and data it contains. So be careful that you do not remove important and irretrievable information.

Save changes to your workbook frequently so that you don't lose any work. The first time you save a workbook, the Save As dialog box opens so you can name the file and choose where to save it. You can save the workbook on your computer or network or to your account on OneDrive.

If you save a file to your OneDrive account, you can turn on AutoSave. The workbook is then saved to your OneDrive account every few seconds. You can also access a previously saved version of the file using the version history in OneDrive. If you do not turn on AutoSave, remember to save your workbook periodically so you do not lose any work.

You'll save the workbook you just created.

To save the workbook you created for the first time:

1. On the title bar, click the **Save** button (or press **CTRL+S**). The Save this file dialog box opens.
2. Click **More options**. The Save As screen in Backstage view appears.
3. Click the **Browse** button. The Save As dialog box opens.
4. Navigate to the location specified by your instructor for your saved files.
5. In the File name box, select **Book1.xlsx** (the default file name assigned to your workbook) if it is not already selected, and then type **NP_EX_1_Order** as the new name.
6. Verify that **Excel Workbook** appears in the Save as type box.
7. Click **Save**. The workbook is saved, the dialog box closes, and the workbook window reappears with the new file name in the title bar.

As you modify a workbook, you will need to resave the file. Because you already saved the workbook with a file name, the next time you click the Save button, the changes you made to the workbook are saved without opening the Save As dialog box.

> **Tip** You can save a workbook to your OneDrive account by clicking its file name in the title bar and then clicking Upload.

Sometimes you will want to save a workbook with a new file name. This is useful when you want to modify a workbook but keep a copy with the original content and structure or when you want to save a copy of the workbook to a new location. To save a workbook with a new name, click the File tab to return to Backstage view, click Save As on the navigation bar, specify the new file name and location, and then click Save.

Entering Text into a Worksheet

Worksheet cells can contain text, numbers, dates, and times. **Text data** is any combination of letters, numbers, and symbols. A **text string** is a series of text data characters. **Numeric data** is any number that can be used in a mathematical operation. **Date data** and **time data** are values displayed in commonly recognized date and time formats. For example, Excel interprets the cell entry April 15, 2029, as a date and not as text. By default, text is left-aligned within worksheet cells, and numbers, dates, and times are right-aligned.

Text is often used in worksheets as labels for the numeric values and calculations displayed in the workbook. Sofi wants you to enter text content into the Documentation sheet.

To enter text into the Documentation sheet:

1. Go to the **Documentation** sheet, and then press **CTRL+HOME** to make sure cell A1 is the active cell.

2. Type **Insight Video Solutions** in cell A1. As you type, the text appears in the cell and in the formula bar.

3. Press **ENTER** twice. The text is entered into cell A1, and the active cell moves down two rows to cell A3.

4. Type **Author** in cell A3, and then press **TAB**. The text is entered, and the active cell moves one column to the right to cell B3.

5. Type your name in cell B3, and then press **ENTER**. The text is entered, and the active cell moves one cell down and to the left to cell A4.

6. Type **Date** in cell A4, and then press **TAB**. The text is entered, and the active cell moves one column to the right to cell B4, where you would enter the date on which the workbook is created. For now, you will leave the cell for the date blank.

7. Press **ENTER** to make cell A5 the active cell, type **Purpose** in the cell, and then press **TAB**. The active cell moves one column to the right to cell B5.

8. Type **To display a purchase order** in cell B5, and then press **ENTER**.

The text entered in cells A1, B3, and B5 is displayed over their adjacent cells. Though the company name in cell A1 appears to occupy three cells, it is still only entered in cell A1. If the adjacent cells also contain content, only the text that fits into the cell is displayed while the remaining text is hidden. You will learn how to increase the width of cell to accommodate its extended content in the next session.

Editing Cells and Using AutoComplete

Excel keeps a list of the actions you took during your current session. If you need to undo an action, you can use the Undo button ↶ on the Home tab of the ribbon or press CTRL+Z to reverse your most recent action. To reverse addition actions, continue to click the Undo button (or press CTRL+Z), and each action stored in the list will be reversed one at a time.

You will undo the most recent change you made to the Documentation sheet—the text you entered in cell B5. Then you will enter a different description of the workbook's purpose in that cell.

To undo the text entry in cell B5:

1. On the Home tab in the Undo group, click the **Undo** button ↺ (or press **CTRL+Z**). The last action is reversed, removing the text you entered in cell B5.

2. In cell B5, type **To document a purchase order for the company** and then press **ENTER**. The new purpose statement is entered in cell B5. Figure 1–12 shows the text entered in the Documentation sheet.

Figure 1–12   Text entered in the Documentation sheet

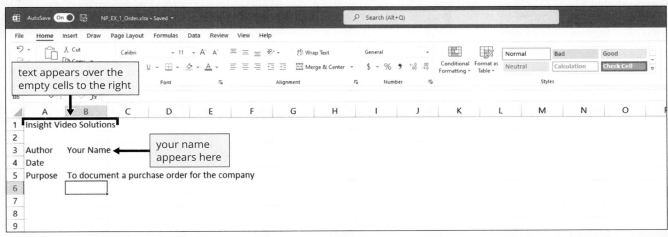

If you need to restore actions you have undone, you can redo them. To redo one action at a time, click the Redo button ↻ in the Undo group on the Home tab or press CTRL+Y. To redo additional actions, continue click the Redo button or press CTRL+Y. After you undo or redo an action, Excel continues the action list, starting with the new changes you make to the workbook.

To replace an entire cell entry, you can overwrite the previous entry. Select the cell and then type the new entry. If you want to replace only part of the entry, you can switch to Edit mode to make the changes directly in the cell. To switch to Edit mode, double-click the cell. A blinking insertion point indicates where the new content will be inserted. In the cell or formula bar, the pointer changes to an I-beam, which you can use to select sections of text with the cell. Anything you type replaces the selected content.

Sofi wants you rewrite the purpose statement to clarify that the workbook documents a customer's purchase order with the company.

To edit the text in cell B5:

1. Double-click cell **B5** to select the cell and switch to Edit mode. A blinking insertion point appears within the text of cell B5. The status bar displays Edit instead of Ready to indicate that the cell is in Edit mode.

2. Press **LEFT ARROW** or **RIGHT ARROW** as needed to move the insertion point directly to the left of the word "purchase" in the cell text.

3. Type **customer's** following by a space to change the text to "To document a customer's purchase order for the company" in the cell.

4. Select the word **for** and then type **with** to change the text to "To document a customer's purchase order with the company" in cell B5. Refer to Figure 1–13.

Figure 1–13   Edited text in the Documentation sheet

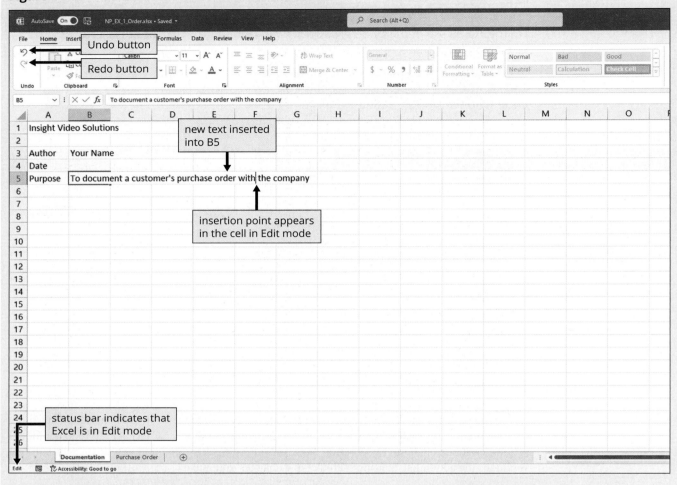

5. Press **ENTER** to accept the edits.

As you type text into the active cell, Excel anticipates the remaining characters by displaying text that begins with the same letters as a previous entry of the same column. This feature, known as **AutoComplete**, makes entering repetitive text easier and reduces data entry errors. To accept the suggested text, press TAB or ENTER. To override the suggested text, continue to type the text you want to enter in the cell. AutoComplete does not work with dates or numbers or when a blank cell is positioned between the previous entry and the text you are typing.

AutoComplete entries might appear as you enter descriptive text about the customer's order in the Purchase Order worksheet.

To enter information about the purchase order:

1. Click the **Purchase Order** sheet tab to make it the active sheet.

2. In cell **A1**, type **Insight Video Solutions** as the worksheet title, and then press **ENTER**.

3. In cell **A2**, type **Purchase Order** and then press **ENTER** twice to move the insertion point to cell A4.

    First, enter the labels for the customer information in column A.

4. In the range **A4:A8**, enter the following text labels, pressing **ENTER** after each entry: **Customer**, **Street**, **City**, **State**, and **Postal Code**.

5. In the range **A10:A12**, enter the following text labels: **Contact**, **Phone**, and **Email**.

   Next, enter the customer data in column B alongside each category label.

6. In the range **B4:B8**, enter the customer's name and address using the following text values: **Davis Financial Services**, **45 West Lancet Drive**, **Boston**, **MA**, and **02109**.

7. In the range **B10:B12**, enter information about the customer's contact person using the following text values: **Lishan Zola, 800-555-1048**, and **l.zola@example.com**. Figure 1–14 shows the completed customer information for the purchase order.

Figure 1–14   Customer information in the Purchase Order worksheet

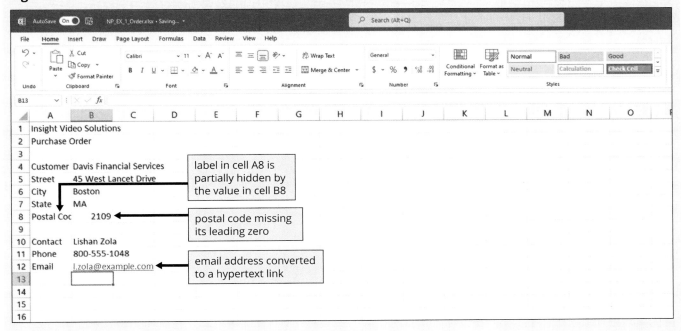

Excel converts any email or website address into a hypertext link, which opens in an email app or web browser when clicked. An email link, like the one in cell B12, is displayed in blue and underlined.

When you enter a number in a cell, Excel removes leading zeroes from integer values. So, the postal code value 02109 you entered in cell B7 appears as 2109. Excel removed the zero because it treated the postal code as number rather than text. To correct this problem, you can instruct Excel to treat a number as text so its leading zero is not dropped. You'll make this change for the postal code in cell B8.

To display the postal code as text:

1. Click cell **B8** to select the cell. The value is right-aligned, indicating that Excel considers it a number.

2. On the Home tab, in the Number group, click the **Number Format arrow**. A list of number format options appears.

3. Scroll down the list, and then click **Text**. Anything entered in the cell will be treated by Excel as text. The value in B8 is left-aligned, indicating that Excel considers it text.

   Tip You can also display a number as text by typing an apostrophe (') before the number.

4. Type **02109** and press **ENTER**. The cell retains the leading zero. Refer to Figure 1–15.

Figure 1–15   Postal code displayed as text

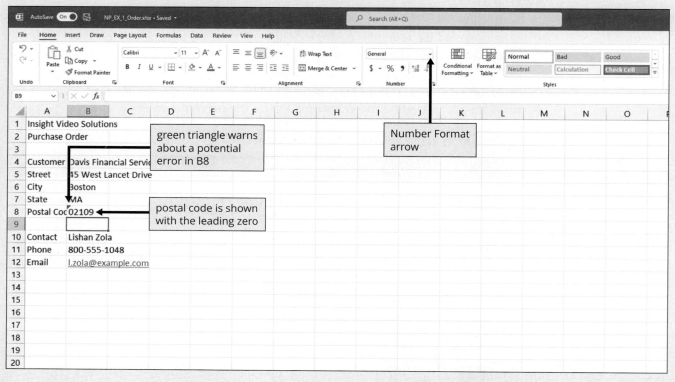

Notice that a green triangle appears in the upper-left corner of cell B8. Excel uses green triangles to flag potential errors. In this case, Excel is warning that a number is displayed as text. Because this is intentional, you do not have to edit the cell to fix the "error." To remove a green triangle, click the cell, click the icon that appears, and then click Ignore Error.

Entering Dates and Numeric Values

Excel recognizes dates in any of the following standard date formats:

- 4/6/2029
- 4/6/29
- 4-6-2029
- April 6, 2029
- 6-Apr-29

Even though dates appear as text, they are stored as numbers equal to the number of days between the specified date and January 0, 1900. Times also appear as text but are stored as numbers equal to fractions of a 24-hour day. For example, a date and time of April 15, 2029, 6:00 PM is stored as the number 47,223.75, which is 47,223 days after January 0, 1900, plus three-quarters of one day. Excel stores dates and times as numbers so they can be used for date and time calculations, such as determining the elapsed time between two dates.

Based on how your computer displays dates, Excel might change the appearance of a date after you type it. For example, if you enter the date 4/15/29 into the active cell, Excel might display the date with the four-digit year value, 4/15/2029. If you enter the text April 15, 2029, Excel might change the date format to 15-Apr-29. Changing the date format does not affect the underlying date or time value.

Insight

International Date Formats

For international business transactions, you may need to adopt international standards for expressing dates, times, and currency values in your workbooks. For example, a worksheet cell might contain the date 06/05/29, which could be interpreted as either the 5th of June 2029, or the 6th of May 2029.

The interpretation depends on which country the workbook has been designed for. You can avoid this problem by entering the full date, as in June 5, 2029. However, this might not work with documents written in foreign languages, such as Japanese, that use different character symbols.

To solve this problem, many international businesses adopt ISO (International Organization for Standardization) dates in the format *yyyy-mm-dd*, where *yyyy* is the four-digit year value, *mm* is the two-digit month value, and *dd* is the two-digit day value. A date such as June 5, 2029, is entered as 2029/06/05. If you choose to use this international date format, make sure that everyone else using your workbook understands this format so they interpret dates correctly. You can include information about the date format in the Documentation sheet.

The purchase order report needs the date of the customer order. For your work, you will enter dates in the format *mm/dd/yyyy*, where *mm* is the two-digit month number, *dd* is the two-digit day number, and *yyyy* is the four-digit year number. You also need to enter the order ID.

To enter the order date and order ID:

1. In cell A14, type **Order Date** and then press **TAB** to make B14 the active cell.

2. Type **1/6/2029** in cell B14, and then press **ENTER** to make A15 the active cell.

   Trouble? Depending on your system configuration, Excel might change the date to the date format *dd-mmm-yy*. This difference will not affect your work.

3. Type **Order ID** in cell A15. AutoComplete feature will suggest inserting Order Date into the cell. Ignore the suggestion and press **TAB** to make B15 the active cell.

4. Type **OR2055-1506** in cell B15 and press **ENTER**. Figure 1–16 shows the completed customer information.

Figure 1–16   Customer order date and ID

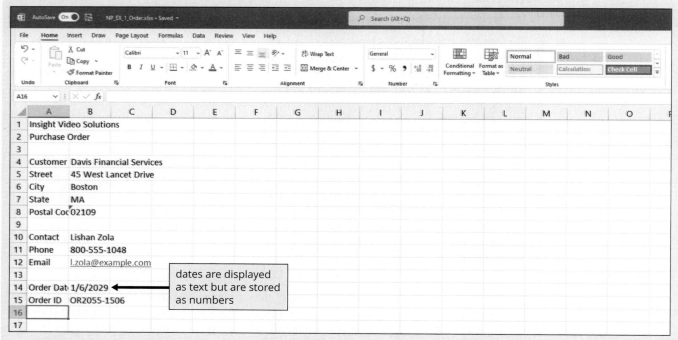

5. Click the **Documentation** sheet tab, and then enter the current date in cell B4.

The next part of the Purchase Order worksheet will document what products and services the customer ordered from Insight Video Solutions. Figure 1–17 lists the data you will add to the worksheet.

Figure 1–17   Customer order data

Category	Subcategory	Description	QTY	Cost
AUD	9010	TruSound AT100T wireless audio transmitter	12	$24.50
AUD	9020	TruSound AT100R wireless audio receiver	12	$28.00
VID	7050	TruVideo SCX5G green screen backdrop and storage case	1	$45.50
AUD	5100	TruSound TS100 wireless headset	20	$65.50
VID	4020	Eagleview EV45W conference camera	5	$325.50
TEL	7010	SureTalk V9200 VOIP conference phone with wiring harness and control board	5	$475.50
SER	4020	Installation and wiring	1	$650.00

You'll enter the first three columns of this list into the worksheet.

To enter the first of the list of purchased items:

1. Click the **Purchase Order** sheet tab to return to the Purchase Order worksheet.

2. Click **A17** to make it the active cell, type **Category** as the column label, and then press **TAB** to move to cell B17.

3. Type **Subcategory** in B17, press **TAB** to move to C17, type **Description** and then press **ENTER**. Note that the Subcategory label in cell B17 is only partially visible because of the text in cell C17.

4. In the range **A18:C24**, enter the Category, Subcategory, and Description text for the seven products and services listed in Figure 1–17, pressing **TAB** to move from one column to next and pressing **ENTER** to move to the start of the next row. Refer to Figure 1–18.

Figure 1–18   Products and services on the purchase order

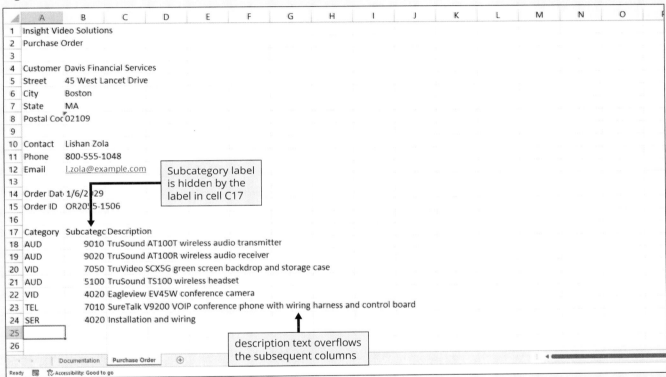

Numbers are entered in a worksheet in a variety of formats, including integers (378), decimals (3.14), negative numbers (−4.27), and scientific notation (1.25E3 for 1.25×10^3). Currency values like $125.50 or percentages like 95% are special number formats. As with dates, currency and percentages entered in a cell are displayed with their symbols but stored as numbers. For example, a currency value such as $87.25 is stored as the number 87.25, and a percentage such as 95% is stored as 0.95.

An integer that is too long to fit in a cell is displayed in scientific notation. A decimal value with too many decimal places is rounded (but its full value is stored). Hashtag symbols (#####) in a cell indicate the cell is too narrow to display its stored number.

You'll complete the purchase order by entering the quantity and cost of each product or service ordered by the customer.

To enter the quantity and cost of each product or service:

1. Click cell **D17**, type **QTY** as the label, and then press **TAB**. Cell E17 becomes the active cell.

2. Type **Cost** in cell E17, and then press **ENTER**. Cell D18 becomes the active cell.

3. In the range **D18:E24**, enter the quantity and cost of the products and services ordered by the customer (refer to Figure 1–17). Note that as you enter this information, the description values in column C will be hidden. Refer to Figure 1–19.

Figure 1–19　　Quantities and costs on the purchase order

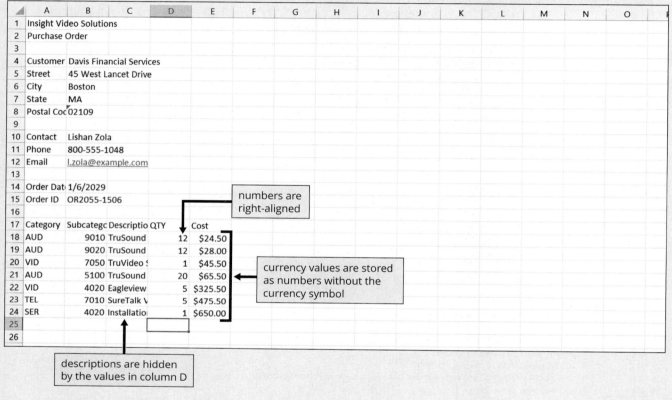

4. Press **CTRL+S** to save the workbook.

Some of the labels and all the descriptions are hidden by the text and values entered in adjacent cells, making the worksheet unreadable. You can display the hidden cell content by increasing the column widths.

Resizing Worksheet Columns and Rows

Resizing columns and rows in worksheet let you modify the worksheet layout to create the best fit for your data.

Resizing Worksheet Columns

Column widths are expressed as the number of characters a column can fit. The default column width is 8.43 standard-sized characters. In general, this means that you can type eight characters in a cell. Any additional text will overlap the adjacent cell or be hidden by it. Column widths are also expressed in terms of pixels. A **pixel** is an individual point on a computer monitor or printout. A column width of 8.43 characters is equivalent to 64 pixels.

Insight

Column Widths and Pixels

On a computer monitor, pixel size is based on screen resolution. As a result, cell content that looks fine on one screen might appear differently when viewed on a screen with a different resolution. If you work on multiple computers or share workbooks with others, you should set column widths based on the maximum number of characters you want displayed in the cells rather than pixel size. This ensures that everyone sees the cell contents the way you intended.

You will increase the width of column A so that all the text labels in that column are completely displayed.

To increase the width of column A:

1. Point to the **right border** of the column A heading until the pointer changes to the column resize pointer ✛ .

2. Click and drag to the right until the width of the column heading reaches **12** characters, but do not release the mouse button. The ScreenTip that appears as you resize the column shows the new column width in characters and in pixels. Refer to Figure 1–20.

Figure 1–20   Width of column A increased to 12 characters

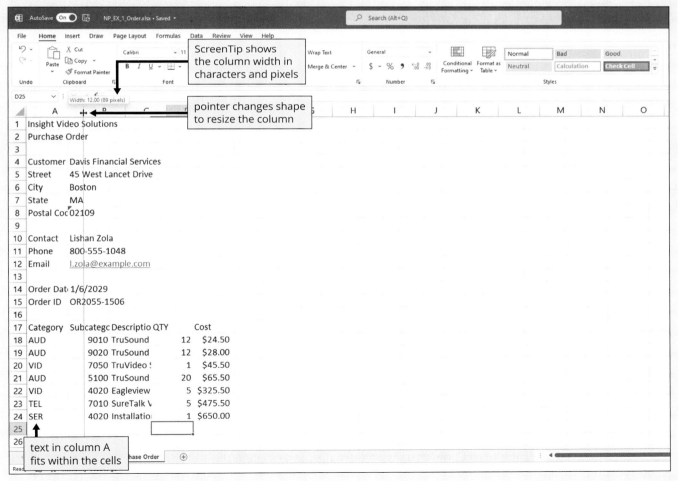

3. Release the mouse button. The width of column A expands to 12 characters, and all the text in that column is visible.

You can change the widths of multiple columns at once. When you change the width of one column in a group of selected columns, the widths of all the columns in that group are similarly resized.

To select a group of adjacent columns, click the first column heading in the group, hold down SHIFT, and then click the last column heading in the group. Another way to select a group of adjacent columns is to hold down the mouse button as you drag the pointer over the headings of the columns you want to include in the group. To select nonadjacent columns, hold down CTRL and click the heading of each column in the group.

Using the click-and-drag method to resize columns can be imprecise. Instead, you can use the Format command in the Cells group on the Home tab to set an exact column width and row height. You'll use the Format command to set the width of column B to 14 characters so all the text in column B is visible.

To set the width of column B using the Format command:

1. Click the **column B** heading. The entire column is selected.

2. On the Home tab, in the Cells group, click the **Format** button, and then click **Column Width**. The Column Width dialog box opens.

3. Type **14** in the Column width box to set the width to 14 characters.

4. Click **OK**. The width of column B is increased to 14 characters.

5. Click **A2** to deselect column B.

You can also use the **AutoFit** feature to automatically adjust a column width or row height to its widest or tallest entry. To AutoFit a column to the width of its contents, double-click the right border of the column heading or click the Format button in the Cells group the Home tab and click AutoFit Column Width. You'll use AutoFit to resize column C so that the descriptions are fully displayed.

To use AutoFit to resize the width of column C:

1. Point to the **right border** of column C until the pointer changes to the resize column width pointer ✛.

2. Double-click the **right border** of the column C heading. The width of column C increases to about 70.86 characters so that the longest item description is completely visible.

Sometimes AutoFit creates a column that is too wide for the worksheet layout. Another way to display long text entries is to wrap the text within the cell.

Wrapping Text Within a Cell

When text is wrapped within a cell, any content that doesn't fit along a single line is moved to the next line within the cell. As more lines are added to the cell, the row height increases to display them. You can wrap only text within a cell; numbers, dates, and times do not wrap.

> **Tip** To force a new line within a cell, press ALT+ENTER where you want the new line created.

You'll reduce the width of column C, and then wrap the descriptions so all the text is still visible within the narrower columns.

To wrap text in column C:

1. Resize the width of column C to **30** characters.

2. Select the range **C18:C24**. These cells contain descriptions of the products and services.

3. On the Home tab, in the Alignment group, click the **Wrap Text** button. The Wrap Text button is highlighted, indicating that it is applied to the selected range. Any text in the selected cells that exceeds the column width wraps to a new line in those cells.

4. Click **C17** to make it the active cell. Refer to Figure 1–21.

Figure 1–21   Text wrapped within cells

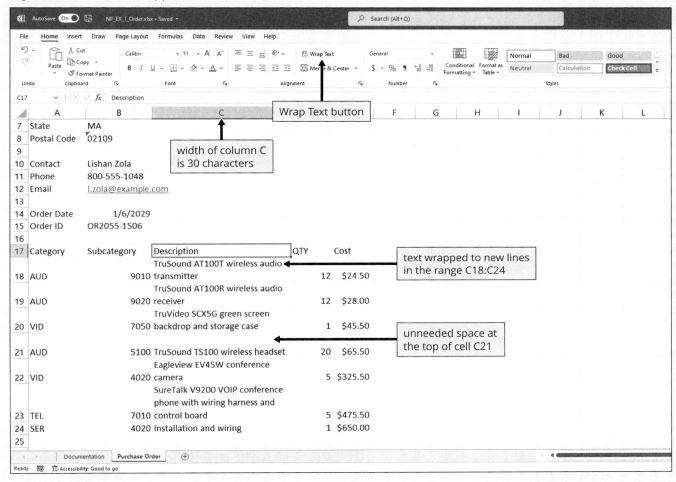

Resizing Worksheet Rows

Row heights are measured in points or pixels. A **point** is approximately 1/72 of an inch. The default row height is 15 points or 20 pixels. There are several ways to change row height. You can drag the bottom border of the row heading to a new height. You can click the Format button in the Cells group on the Home tab, click Row Height, and then set an exact row height. Also, you can double-click the bottom border of the row to AutoFit the row to its contents.

After you wrapped the text in the range C18:C24, row 21 has unneeded space above the description. You'll decrease the height of row 21 to remove the extra space at the top of cell C21.

To change a row height of cell C21:

1. Point to the **bottom border** of the row 21 heading until the pointer changes to the resize row height pointer ╪ .

2. Drag the bottom border up until the height of the row is equal to **18** points (or **24** pixels), and then release the mouse button. The empty space at the top of cell C21 is removed.

3. Save the workbook.

You have entered the products and services in the customer's purchase order. In the next session, you will use formulas and functions to calculate the total cost of that order.

Part 1.1 Quick Check

1. How do worksheets and chart sheets differ?

2. What is the cell reference for the cell located in the fourth column and fifth row of a worksheet?

3. What is the range reference for the block of cells A10 through D15?

4. What is the range reference for cells A10 through C20 and cells A22 through C32?

5. Text entered in cell A3 exceeds the cell's width. If the cell to the right is empty, how is the text displayed? If the cell to the right contains content, how is that text displayed?

6. Cell B10 contains the percentage 75%. What numeric value is stored in the cell?

7. Cell C10 contains the date May 3, 2029. Is this content stored as a text string or a number?

8. What does a series of hashtag symbols (#####) in a cell indicate?

Part 1.2 Visual Overview: Excel Formulas and Functions

The Page Layout tab specifies how the worksheet will be arranged and printed.

Font size specifies the size of text characters measured in points.

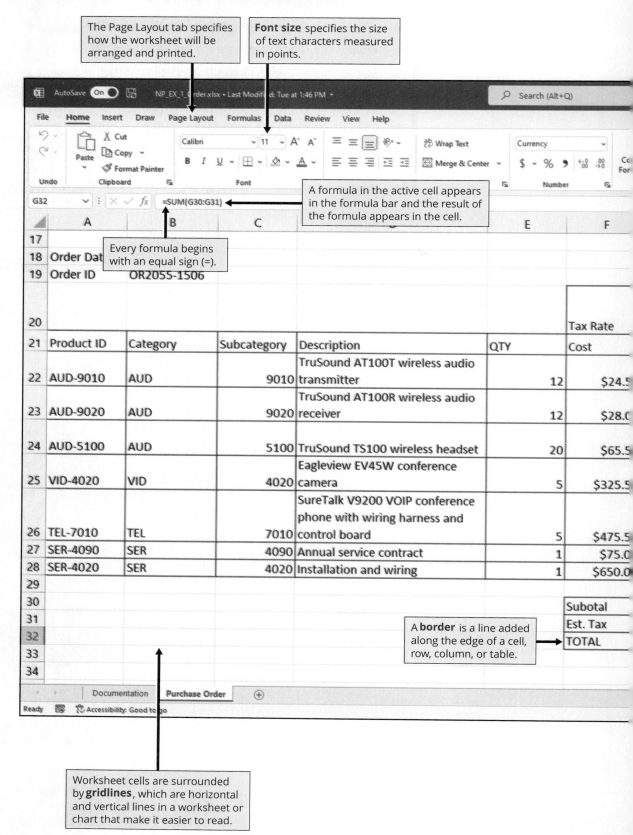

A formula in the active cell appears in the formula bar and the result of the formula appears in the cell.

Every formula begins with an equal sign (=).

A border is a line added along the edge of a cell, row, column, or table.

Worksheet cells are surrounded by gridlines, which are horizontal and vertical lines in a worksheet or chart that make it easier to read.

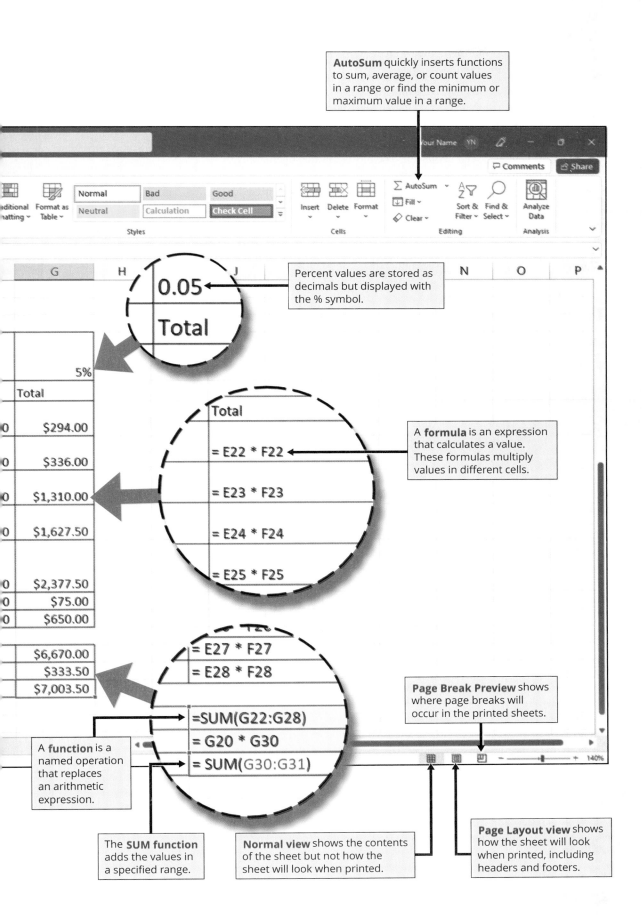

AutoSum quickly inserts functions to sum, average, or count values in a range or find the minimum or maximum value in a range.

Percent values are stored as decimals but displayed with the % symbol.

A **formula** is an expression that calculates a value. These formulas multiply values in different cells.

Page Break Preview shows where page breaks will occur in the printed sheets.

A **function** is a named operation that replaces an arithmetic expression.

The **SUM function** adds the values in a specified range.

Normal view shows the contents of the sheet but not how the sheet will look when printed.

Page Layout view shows how the sheet will look when printed, including headers and footers.

Calculating with Formulas

So far you have entered text, numbers, and dates in the worksheet. However, the main reason for using Excel is to perform calculations and analysis on data. Sofi wants the workbook to report on the number of items in the purchase order and the total cost of those items including tax. Such calculations are added to a worksheet using formulas and functions.

A formula is an expression returning a value. In most cases, that value is a number—though it could also be text or a date. In Excel, every formula begins with an equal sign (=) followed by an expression containing the operations used to calculate a value.

A formula is written using **operators**, or mathematical symbols, that combine different values, resulting in a single value that is then displayed in the cell. The most common operators are **arithmetic operators** that perform mathematical calculations such as addition (+), subtraction (−), multiplication (*), division (/), and exponentiation (^). For example, the following formula adds 3 and 8, returning a value of 11:

    =3+8

Most Excel formulas contain references to cells rather than specific values. For example, the following formula returns the result of adding the values stored in cells C3 and D10:

    =C3+D10

If a value changes, you can update that value in its cell without having to modify the formula. Continuing the example, if the value 3 is stored in cell C3 and the value 8 is stored in cell D10, this formula would also return a value of 11. If the value in cell C3 is later changed to 10, the formula would return a value of 18. Figure 1–22 describes the different arithmetic operators and provides examples of formulas.

Figure 1–22   Arithmetic operators and example formulas

Operation	Arithmetic Operator	Example	Description
Addition	+	=B1+B2+B3	Adds the values in cells B1, B2, and B3
Subtraction	−	=C9-B2	Subtracts the value in cell B2 from the value in cell C9
Multiplication	*	=C9*B9	Multiplies the values in cells C9 and B9
Division	/	=C9/B9	Divides the value in cell C9 by the value in cell B9
Exponentiation	^	=B5^3	Raises the value of cell B5 to the third power

If a formula contains more than one arithmetic operator, Excel performs the calculation based on the following order of operations:

1. Operations within parentheses
2. Exponentiation (^)
3. Multiplication (*) or division (/)
4. Addition (+) or subtraction (−)

Based on the order of operations, the following formula returns the value 23 because multiplying 4 by 5 is done before adding 3:

    =3+4*5

If a formula contains two or more operators at the same level, the calculations are done from left to right. In the following formula, Excel first multiplies 4 by 10 and then divides that result by 8 to return the value 5:

    =4*10/8

When parentheses are used, the expression inside them is calculated first. In the following formula, Excel calculates (3+4) first, and then multiplies that result by 5 to return the value 35:

$$= (3+4) * 5$$

Figure 1–23 shows how changes in a formula affect the order of operations and the result of the formula.

Figure 1–23   Order of operations applied to formulas

Formula	Order of Operations	Result
=50+10*5	10 * 5 calculated first and then 50 is added	100
=(50+10)*5	(50 + 10) calculated first and then 60 is multiplied by 5	300
=50/10−5	50/10 calculated first and then 5 is subtracted	0
=50/(10−5)	(10 − 5) calculated first and then 50 is divided by that value	10
=50/10*5	Two operators at same precedence level, so the calculation is done left to right with 50/10 calculated first and that value is then multiplied by 5	25
=50/(10*5)	(10 * 5) is calculated first and then 50 is divided by that value	1

The purchase order report should calculate the total cost of each product or service ordered by the customer. The total cost is equal to the number of units ordered multiplied by the cost per unit. You already entered this information in columns D and E. Now you will enter a formula in cell F11 to calculate the total cost of each product or service.

To enter a formula calculating the total for wireless audio transmitters:

1. If you took a break after the previous session, make sure the NP_EX_1_Order.xlsx workbook is open and the Purchase Order worksheet is active.

2. Click cell **F17**, type **Total** as the label, and then press **ENTER**. The label is entered in the cell, and cell F18 becomes the active cell.

3. In cell F18, type **=D18 * E18** (the quantity multiplied by the cost of each item). As you type the formula, a list of Excel function names appears in a ScreenTip, which provides a quick method for entering functions. The list will close when you complete the formula. You will learn more about Excel functions shortly. Also, Excel color codes each cell reference and its corresponding cell with the same color. Refer to Figure 1–24.

Figure 1–24   Formula with cell references

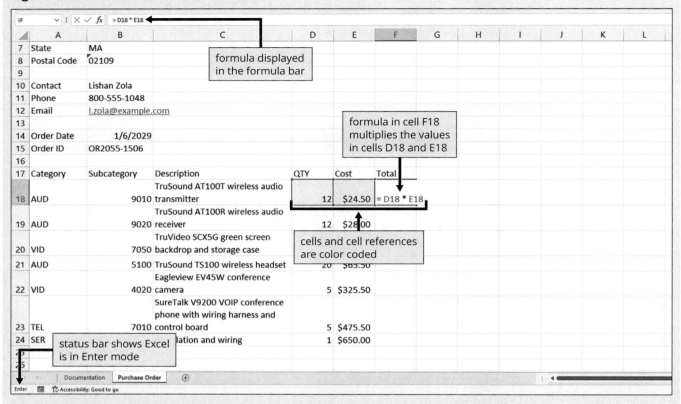

4. Press **ENTER**. The formula result $294.00 appears in cell F18, which is the total cost of purchasing 12 wireless audio transmitters at a cost of $24.50 each. The result is displayed as currency because cell E18, which is referenced in the formula, contains a currency value.

5. Click cell **F18** to make it the active cell. The cell displays the result of the formula, but the formula bar displays the formula you entered so that you can review both the formula and its value.

For the first item, you entered the formula by typing each cell reference in the expression. You can also insert a cell reference by clicking the cell as you type the formula. This technique reduces the possibility of error caused by typing an incorrect cell reference. You will use this method to enter the formula to calculate the cost of ordering 12 wireless audio receivers.

To enter a formula for purchasing wireless audio receivers using a mouse:

1. Click cell **F19** to make it active cell.

2. Type **=** to indicate the beginning of a formula. Excel will insert the cell reference to any cell you click.

> **Key Step** Be sure to type = first; otherwise, Excel will not recognize the entry as a formula.

3. Click cell **D19**. The cell reference is inserted into the formula in the formula bar. At this point, any cell you click changes the cell reference used in the formula. The cell reference isn't locked until you type an operator.

4. Type ***** to enter the multiplication operator. The cell reference for cell D19 is locked in the formula, and the next cell you click will be inserted after the operator.

5. Click cell **E19** to enter its cell reference in the formula. The formula, =D19*E19, is complete.

6. Press **ENTER**. A total cost of $336.00 for the 12 wireless audio receivers appears in F19.

Next, you will enter formulas to complete the calculations of the remaining items in the purchase order.

Copying and Pasting a Formula

Many worksheets have the same formula repeated across several rows or columns. Rather than retyping the formula, you can copy a formula from one cell and paste it into another cell or an entire range of cells. When you copy a formula, Excel places the formula onto the **Clipboard**, which is a temporary storage area for selections you copy or cut. When you **paste**, Excel retrieves the formula from the Clipboard and places it into its new location in the workbook.

The cell references in the copied formula change to reflect the formula's new location. A formula from a cell in column C that add values from other cells in column C will change its reference to column E when copied to a cell in that column. In this way, Excel makes it easier to reuse the same general formula in different locations in your workbook.

You will calculate the cost of the remaining items on the purchase order by copying the formula in cell F19 and pasting it into the range F20:F24.

To copy and paste the formula in F19:

1. Click cell **F19** to make it the active cell. This is the cell with the formula you want to copy.

2. On the Home tab, in the Clipboard group, click the **Copy** button (or press **CTRL+C**). Excel copies the formula to the Clipboard. A blinking green box surrounds the cell being copied.

3. Select the range **F20:F24**. These are the cells where you will paste the formula.

4. In the Clipboard group, click the **Paste** button (or press **CTRL+V**). Excel pastes the formula into the selected cells, adjusting each formula so that the total cost of each item is based on the quantity and cost values in that row. Hashtag symbols appear in the range F21:F23 because those cells are not wide enough to display the currency values. The Paste Options button, containing additional options for pasting the contents of the Clipboard, appears in the lower-right corner of the selected range.

5. Increase the width of column F to **15** characters. All the values in column F are visible. Refer to Figure 1–25.

Figure 1–25   Copied and pasted formula

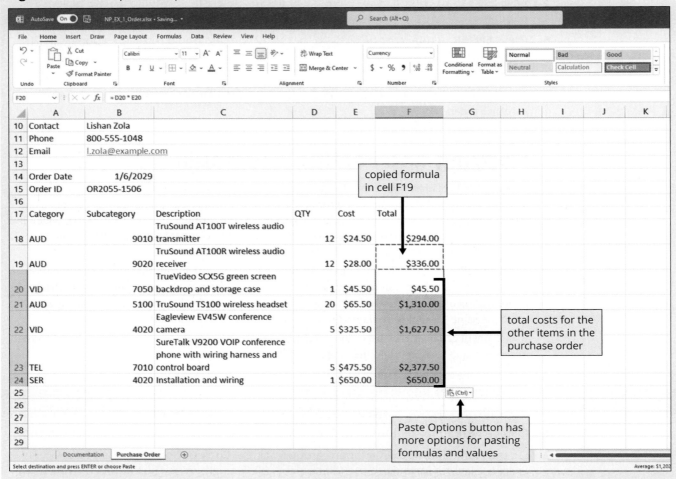

6. Click **F20** to make it the active cell. The formula =D20*E20 appears in the formula bar. Notice that the cell references from the copied formula are updated to reflect its new location in the worksheet.

7. Examine the remaining formulas from cells in the range F21:F24 to verify that the copied formula in each cell has been updated to reflect that cell's location in the worksheet.

As more cell references are included, the formula becomes more and more complicated. One way of simplifying a formula is with a function.

Calculating with Functions

A function is a named operation that returns a value. Every function follows a set of rules, or **syntax**, specifying how the function should be written. The general syntax of all Excel functions is

FUNCTION(arg1,arg2,[arg3],[arg4],…)

where FUNCTION is the function name, and arg1, arg2, and so forth are arguments. An **argument** is information the function uses to return a value. Arguments required by the function are listed first. Optional arguments, indicated by the brackets in the function syntax, are listed last. If an optional argument is not included, Excel might assign it a default value (depending on the function). For example, the syntax of the SUM function used to calculate totals is

SUM(number1,[number2],[number3],…)

where *number1* is a required argument containing a number or range of values to sum and *number2*, *number3*, and so on are optional arguments for other numbers or ranges to add to that sum. To calculate the sum of values from nine worksheet cells, you could enter the following long formula:

$$=A1+A2+A3+C11+C12+C13+E21+E22+E23$$

Or you can do the same calculation with a SUM function that references those cells as arguments of the function.

$$=SUM(A1:A3, \; C11:C13, \; E21:E23)$$

Both expressions return the same value, but the formula with the SUM function is more compact and less prone to a typing error. Excel supports more than 300 functions from the fields of finance, business, science, and engineering, including functions that work with numbers, text, and dates.

> **Tip** If a function does not have any arguments, enter the function name followed by an empty parentheses, such as = NOW() for the NOW function to display the current time.

The syntax of every Excel function is described in Excel Help, including examples and a summary of the required and optional arguments.

Inserting Functions with AutoSum

A fast and convenient way to enter some commonly used functions is with AutoSum. The AutoSum button, located in the Editing group on the Home tab of the ribbon, can insert the following functions into a selected cell or range:

- SUM—Adds the values in a specified range
- AVERAGE—Averages the values in a specified range
- COUNT—Counts the total numeric values in a specified range
- MAX—Returns the maximum value in a specified range
- MIN—Returns the minimum value in a specified range

After you select one of the AutoSum options, Excel includes the most likely range from the adjacent data and enters it as the argument. You should always verify that the range included in the AutoSum function matches the range that you want to use.

You'll use AutoSum to calculate the total cost of all items on the purchase order.

To calculate the total cost of all items on the purchase order:

1. Click cell **E25** to make it the active cell, type **Subtotal** as the label, and then press **TAB**. Cell F25 is the active cell.

2. On the Home tab, in the Editing group, click the **AutoSum arrow**. The button's menu opens and displays five common functions: Sum, Average, Count Numbers, Max, and Min.

3. On the AutoSum menu, point to Sum.

4. Click **Sum** to enter the SUM function. The formula =SUM(F18:F24) is entered in cell F25. The cells being summed are selected and highlighted in the worksheet so you can quickly confirm that Excel selected the appropriate range from the available data. A ScreenTip appears below the formula describing the function's syntax. Refer to Figure 1–26.

> **Tip** You can quickly insert the SUM function by clicking the worksheet cell where the sum should be calculated and pressing ALT+=.

Figure 1-26   SUM function entered using the AutoSum button

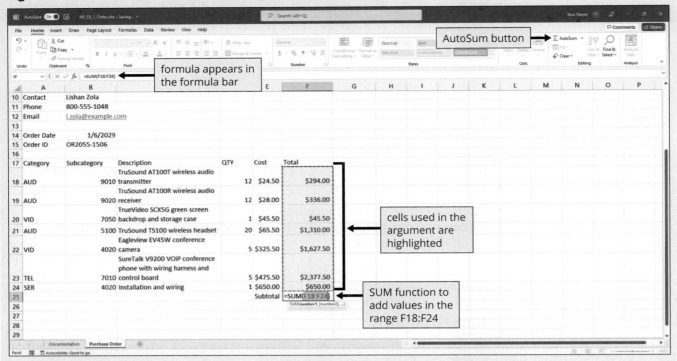

5. Press **ENTER** to accept the formula. Cell F25 shows the total cost of the seven items on the purchase order, which is $6,640.50.

Every order from Insight Video Solutions is subject to a 5% sales tax. You'll add formulas to calculate the amount of tax due on this order and then add the subtotal value to the tax.

To calculate the sales tax and total expenses:

1. Click cell **E16**, type **Tax Rate** as the label, and then press **TAB**. Cell F16 is the active cell.

2. Type **5%** in cell F16, and then press **ENTER**. The 5% value is displayed in the cell, but the stored value is 0.05.

3. Click cell **E26** to make it the active cell, type **Est**. **Tax** as the label, and then press **TAB**. Cell F26 is the active cell.

4. Type the formula **=F16*F25** in cell F26 to calculate the tax on all items bought in the purchase order, and then press **ENTER**. The formula multiplies the tax rate in cell F16 (0.05) by the subtotal in cell F25 ($6,640.56). The estimated tax is $332.03.

5. Click cell **E27**, type **TOTAL** as the label, and then press **TAB**. Cell F27 is the active cell.

6. Type the formula = **SUM(F25:F26)** in cell F27 to calculate the total cost of the purchase order, adding the subtotal to the estimate text, and then press **ENTER**. The total for the purchase order of $6,972.53.

7. Click cell **F27**. Refer to Figure 1-27.

Figure 1-27   Total cost of the purchase order

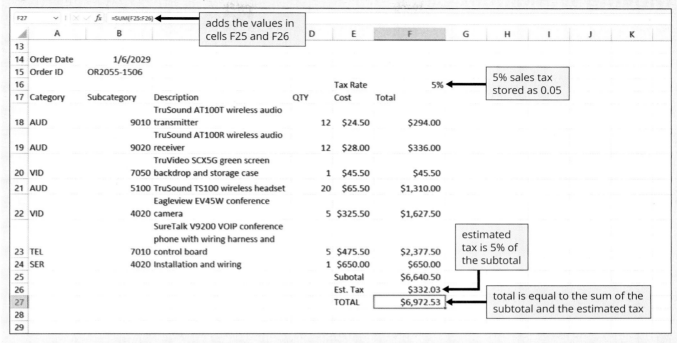

If you want to add all the numbers in a column or row, you need to reference the entire column or row in the SUM function. For example, SUM(E:E) will return the sum of all numeric values in column E and SUM(5:5) will return the sum of all numeric values in row 5. Any cells with text in those columns or rows will be ignored.

Proskills

Problem Solving: Writing Effective Formulas

You can use formulas to quickly perform calculations and solve problems. First, identify the problem you need to solve. Then, gather the data needed to solve the problem. Finally, create accurate and effective formulas that use the data to answer or resolve the problem. To write effective and useful formulas, consider these guidelines:

- **Keep your formulas simple.** Use functions in place of long, complex formulas whenever possible. For example, use the SUM function instead of entering a formula that adds individual cells, making it easier to confirm that the formula is providing accurate information.
- **Do not hide data values within formulas.** The worksheet displays formula results, not the actual formula. For example, to calculate a 5% interest rate on a currency value in cell A5, you could enter the formula =0.05*A5. However, this approach doesn't reveal how the value is calculated. A better practice places the 5% value in a cell accompanied by a descriptive label and uses the cell reference in the formula, making it clear to others what calculation is being performed.
- **Break up long formulas to display intermediate results.** Long formulas can be difficult to interpret and are prone to error. For example, the formula =SUM(A1:A10)/SUM(B1:B10) calculates the ratio of two sums but hides the two sum values. Consider calculating each sum in separate cells, such as A11 and B11, and use the formula =A11/B11 to calculate the ratio. The worksheet will then include both the sums and the calculation of their ratio.
- **Test complicated formulas with simple values.** Use values you can calculate in your head to confirm that your formula works as intended. For example, using 1s or 10s as the input values makes it easier to verify that your formula is working as intended.

Finding a solution to a problem requires accurate data and analysis. In a workbook, this means using formulas for calculations, showing all the values used in the formulas clearly in the worksheet, and testing to verify their accuracy.

Moving Worksheet Cells

As you develop a worksheet, you will often need to modify its content and structure to create a cleaner and more readable document. You can move cells and ranges without affecting the data or the formulas they contain.

One way to move a cell or range is to select it, point to the bottom border of the selection, drag the selection to a new location, and then release the mouse button. This technique is called **drag and drop** because you are dragging the range and dropping it in a new location.

> **Tip** If the drop location is not visible, drag the selection to the edge of the workbook window to scroll the worksheet, and then drop the selection.

You can also use the drag-and-drop technique to copy cells by pressing CTRL as you drag the selected range to its new location. A copy of the original range is placed in the new location without removing the original range from the worksheet.

Reference

Moving or Copying a Cell Range

- Select the cell range to move or copy.
- Move the pointer over the border of the selection until the pointer changes shape.
- To move the range, click the border and drag the selection to a new location. To copy the range, hold down CTRL and drag the selection to a new location.

or

- Select the cell range to move or copy.
- On the Home tab, in the Clipboard group, click the Cut or Copy button; or right-click the selection, and then click Cut or Copy on the shortcut menu; or press CTRL+X or CTRL+C.
- Select the cell or the upper-left cell of the range where you want to paste the copied content.
- In the Clipboard group, click the Paste button; or right-click the selection and then click Paste on the shortcut menu; or press CTRL+V.

Sofi wants the labels and values in the range E25:F27 moved down one row to the range E26:F28 to set those calculations off from the list of purchase order items. You will use the drag-and-drop method to move the range.

To drag and drop the range E25:F27:

1. Select the range **E25:F27**. This is the range you want to move.

2. Point to the **bottom border** of the selected range so that the pointer changes to the move pointer ⊹.

3. Press and hold the mouse button to change the pointer to the arrow pointer ⊳, and then drag the selection down one row. Do not release the mouse button. A ScreenTip appears, indicating that the new range of the selected cells will be E26:F28. A dark green border also appears around the new range. Refer to Figure 1–28.

Figure 1–28   Range being moved with drag and drop

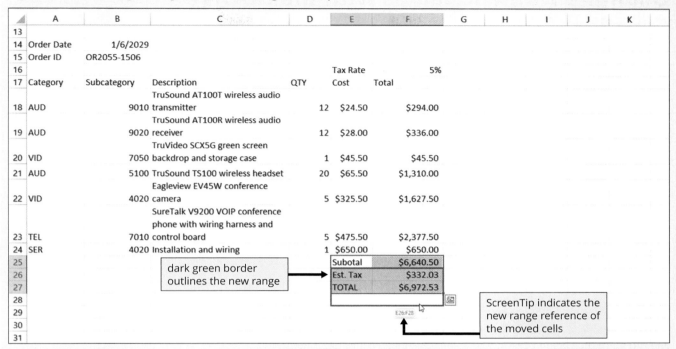

4. Verify that the ScreenTip displays the range E26:F28, and then release the mouse button. The selected cells move to their new location.

The drag-and-drop technique can be slow and awkward in larger worksheets. In that situation, it is often more efficient to cut or copy a selected range and then paste it into the new location. Cutting moves the selected content. Copying duplicates the selected content in the new location.

Sofi wants to include a summary of the purchase order totals at the top of the worksheet. To free up space for this summary, you'll cut the contents of the range A4:F28 and paste it into the range A8:F32.

To move the range A4:F28 using cut and copy:

1. Click the **Name** box to the left of the formula bar, type **A4:F28** as the range to select, and then press **ENTER**. The range A4:F28 is selected.

2. On the Home tab, in the Clipboard group, click the **Cut** button (or press **CTRL+X**). The range is surrounded by a moving border, indicating that it has been cut.

3. Click cell **A8** to select it. This is the upper-left corner of the range where you want to paste the selection that you cut.

4. In the Clipboard group, click the **Paste** button (or press **CTRL+V**). The range A4:F28 is pasted into the range A8:F32. Note that the cell references in the formulas were automatically updated to reflect the new location of those cells in the worksheet.

Next you will add a summary of the purchase order to top of the worksheet, starting with a count of the total items ordered by the customer.

Counting Numeric Values with the COUNT Function

Many financial workbooks need to report the number of entries, such as the number of products in an order or the number of items in an expense or revenue category. To calculate the total number of items, you can use the COUNT function. The COUNT function has the syntax

COUNT(*value1*, [*value2*], [*value3*],…)

where *value1* is the range of numeric values to count and *value2*, *value3*, and so forth are optional arguments to specify other numbers and ranges.

The COUNT function counts only numeric values. Any cells containing text are not included in the tally. To also count cells containing nonnumeric data such as text strings, you use the COUNTA function. The COUNTA function has the syntax

COUNTA(*value1*, [*value2*], [*value3*],…)

where *value1* is the range containing numeric or text values, and *value2*, *value3*, and so forth specify other ranges to be included in the tally.

Tip Numeric functions like SUM and COUNT ignore text values and use only the numeric values within their function arguments.

You'll use the COUNT function to display the number of distinct items ordered by the customer and reference the value in cell F32 to display the total cost of those items.

To apply the COUNT function:

1. Scroll up the worksheet, click cell **A4** to make it the active cell, type **Summary** as the label, and then press **ENTER** to make cell A5 the active cell.

2. In cell A5, type **Products** as the label, and press **TAB** to make cell B5 the active cell.

3. In cell B5, type **= COUNT(** to begin the COUNT function.

4. Select the range **F22:F28**. The range reference F22:F28 is entered as the first (and only argument) of the COUNT function.

5. Type **)** to complete the function, and then press **ENTER** to make cell A6 the active cell. Cell B5 displays 7, indicating that the purchase order contains seven distinct items.

6. In cell A6, type **Total Charge** as the label, and then press **TAB** to make cell B6 the active cell.

7. In cell B6, type **= F32** as the formula, and then press **ENTER**. This formula displays $6,972.53, which is the total cost of the order calculated in cell F32. Refer to Figure 1–29.

Figure 1–29   Purchase Order summary

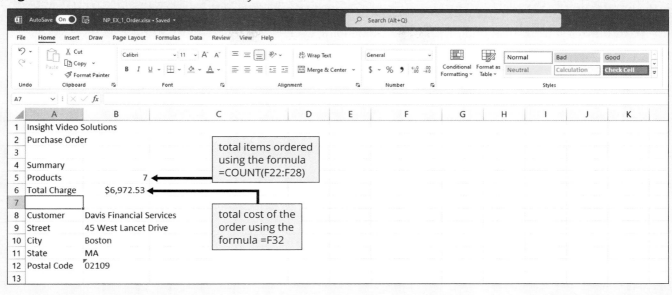

The formula in cell B6 displaying the total cost of the order as calculated in cell F32 illustrates an important practice: Don't repeat the same formula multiple times. Instead, reference the cell containing the formula. If the formula is changed later, the new results will appear throughout the workbook.

Inserting and Deleting Rows and Columns

Another way to modify the structure of a workbook is to insert or remove whole rows and columns from a worksheet. When you insert a new column, the existing columns are shifted to the right, and the new column has the same width as the column directly to its left. When you insert a new row, the existing rows are shifted down, and the new row has the same height as the row above it. Because inserting a new row or column moves the location of the other cells in the worksheet, any cell references in a formula or function are updated to reflect the new layout.

Reference

Inserting and Deleting Rows and Columns

- Select the row or column headings where you want to insert or delete content.
- To insert rows and columns, on the Home tab, in the Cells group, click the Insert button; or right-click the selected headings and click Insert on the shortcut menu; or press CTRL+SHIFT+ =.
- To delete rows or columns, on the Home tab, in the Cells group, click the Delete button; or right-click the selecting headings, and then click Delete on the shortcut menu; or press CTRL+ -.

Davis Financial Services has decided to purchase an annual service contract for technical support and maintenance. Sofi wants you to add the new item to the purchase order. You'll insert a new row in the worksheet and enter the new item in the list.

To enter a new purchased item in the list:

1. Scroll down the worksheet and click the **row 28** heading to select the entire row.

2. On the Home tab, in the Cells group, click the **Insert** button (or press **CTRL+SHIFT+=**). A new row 28 is inserted in the worksheet, and all the rows below the new row are shifted down.

   | **Tip** To insert multiple rows or columns, select multiple row or column headings from the worksheet and then click the Insert button (or press CTRL+SHIFT+=).

3. In the range A28:E28, enter the following data pressing TAB after each entry: **SER**, **4090**, **Annual service contract**, **1**, and **$75.00**.

   Cell F28 is the active cell and $75.00 appears in the cell because AutoFill entered the formula =D28*E28 into the cell following the pattern of formulas in column F. Also, the Subtotal, Est. Tax, and TOTAL formulas adjust to include the inserted row. The total cost of the purchase order in cell F33 is increased to $7,051.28, reflecting the added item. Refer to Figure 1–30.

Figure 1–30   New row inserted into the purchase order

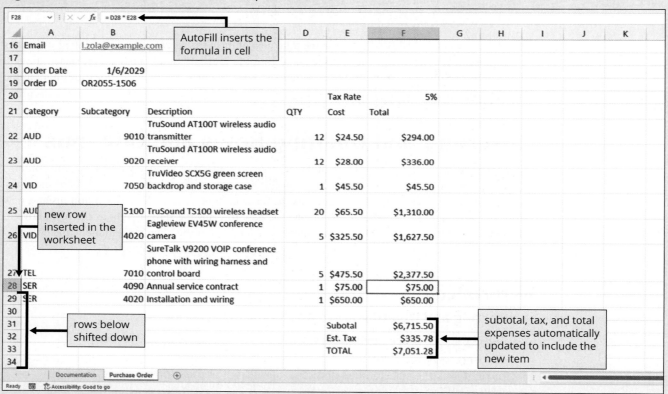

4. Scroll to the top of the worksheet and verify that the number of items in the purchase order in cell B5 is now eight.

There are two ways to remove content from a worksheet: deleting and clearing. **Deleting** removes both the data and rows or columns from the worksheet. The rows below the deleted row shift up to fill the vacated space. Likewise, the columns to the right of the deleted column shift left to fill the vacated space. Also, all cell references in worksheet formulas are adjusted to reflect the change that removing the row or column makes to the worksheet structure. To delete a selected row or column, click the Delete button in the Cells group on the Home tab.

Clearing removes the data from the selected cells, leaving those cells blank but preserving the worksheet structure. No formulas in the worksheet are modified when data is cleared. To clear data from a selected cell or range, press DELETE.

Sofi tells you that the customer did not order the green screen backdrop. You'll correct the purchase order by deleting row 24 from worksheet.

To delete the green screen row from the worksheet:

1. Click the **row 24** heading to select the entire row containing the order of the green screen backdrop.

2. On the Home tab, in the Cells group, click the **Delete** button (or press **CTRL+ -**). Row 24 is deleted, and the rows below it shift up to fill the space.

> **Tip** To delete multiple rows or columns, select multiple row or column headings from the worksheet and click the Delete button (or press CTRL+ -).

All cell references in the formulas are updated to reflect the deleted row. The subtotal value in cell F30 changes to $6,670.00, which is the sum of the range F22:F28. The estimated tax in cell F31 decreases to $333.50. The total cost of the purchase order drops to $7,003.50. Also, the result of the COUNT function in cell B7 shows that seven items were purchased by the customer.

Inserting and Deleting a Range

You can also insert or delete cell ranges within a worksheet. By default, inserting a range shifts cells to right when the selected range is longer than it is wide and shift cells down when the selected range is wider than it is long. You can specify the direction shifted cells move using the Insert command in the Cells group on the Home tab. All cell references in formulas are automatically changed to reflect the new structure of the worksheet. Refer to Figure 1–31.

Figure 1–31   Cell range inserted into a worksheet

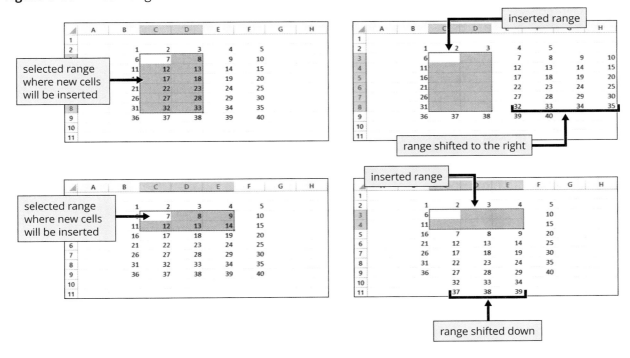

The process works in reverse when you delete a range. Cells adjacent to the deleted range either move up or left to fill in the space vacated by the deleted cells. You can specify the direction shifted cells move using the Delete command in the Cells group on the Home tab. Whether you insert or delete a range, cells shifting to a new location adopt the widths of the columns and heights of the rows that they shift into. As a result, you may need to resize column widths and row heights after inserting or deleting cells.

Reference

Inserting or Deleting a Range

- Select a range that matches the area you want to insert or delete.
- On the Home tab, in the Cells group, click the Insert button or the Delete button.

or

- Select the range that matches the range you want to insert or delete.
- On the Home tab, in the Cells group, click the Insert arrow and then click Insert Cells or click the Delete arrow and then click Delete Cells; or right-click the selected range, and then click Insert or Delete on the shortcut menu.
- Click the option button for the direction to shift the cells, columns, or rows.
- Click OK.

Insight Video Solutions assigns a product ID for each item appearing in a purchase order. Sofi asks you to insert a new range of cells into the purchase order list for this data.

To insert a new range to enter the product IDs:

1. Select the range **A20:A32**.

2. On the Home tab, in the Cells group, click the **Insert arrow**. A menu of insert options appears.

3. Click **Insert Cells**. The Insert dialog box opens.

4. Verify that the **Shift cells right** option button is selected, and then click **OK**. New cells are inserted into the selected range, and the adjacent cells move to the right. The shifted content does not fit well in the adjacent columns. You'll resize the columns and rows to fit their data.

5. Change the width of column C to **12** characters, the width of column D to **30** characters, and the widths of columns E through G to **12** characters.

   You will autofit the row heights to the row contents.

6. Select rows **22** through **28**. These rows are too high.

7. In the Cells group, click the **Format** button, and then click **AutoFit Row Height**. The row heights now better fit the data.

   > **Tip** You can also autofit rows by double-clicking the bottom border of the selected rows.

8. Resize the height of row 20 to **42** points, creating additional space between the summary information and the purchase order list.

9. Click **A21** to deselect row 20. Refer to Figure 1–32 for the appearance of the purchase order list after the rows and columns have been resized.

Figure 1–32   New range inserted in the purchase order

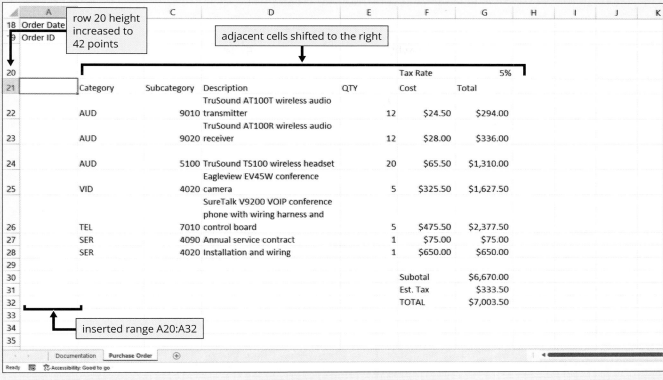

Notice that even though the product IDs will be entered in the range A21:A28, you inserted new cells in the range A20:A32 to retain the layout of the worksheet contents. Selecting the additional rows ensures that the tax rate and summary values still line up with the Cost and Total columns. Whenever you insert a new range, be sure to consider its impact on the entire layout of the worksheet.

Insight

Hiding and Unhiding Rows, Columns, and Worksheets

Workbooks can become long and complicated, filled with formulas and data that are important for performing calculations but are of little interest to readers. In those situations, you can simplify your workbooks by hiding rows, columns, and even worksheets. Although the contents of hidden cells cannot be seen, the data in those cells is still available for use in formulas and functions throughout the workbook.

Hiding removes a row or column from view while keeping it part of the worksheet. To hide a row or column, select the row or column heading, click the Format button in the Cells group on the Home tab, point to Hide & Unhide on the menu that appears, and then click Hide Rows or Hide Columns. The border of the row or column heading is doubled to mark the location of hidden rows or columns.

A worksheet is hidden when the entire worksheet contains data that is not of interest to the reader and is better summarized elsewhere in the workbook. To hide a worksheet, make that worksheet active, click the Format button in the Cells group, point to Hide & Unhide, and then click Hide Sheet.

Unhiding redisplays the hidden content in the workbook. To unhide a row or column, click in a cell below the hidden row or to the right of the hidden column, click the Format button, point to Hide & Unhide, and then click Unhide Rows or Unhide Columns. To unhide a worksheet, click the Format button, point to Hide & Unhide, and then click Unhide Sheet. The Unhide dialog box opens. Click the sheets you want to unhide, and then click OK. The hidden content is redisplayed in the workbook.

Although hiding data can make a worksheet and workbook easier to read, be sure never to hide information that is important to the reader.

You will complete the content of the purchase order list by adding the product IDs for each item purchased. You can use Flash Fill to automatically create the account IDs.

Generating Text with Flash Fill

Flash Fill enters text based on patterns it finds from preceding rows in the same columns of data. For example, Flash Fill can use the first names, middle initials, and last names stored in separate columns to display complete names in another column (refer to Figure 1–33). To accept the suggested full names, press ENTER. To reject the suggested text, continue typing the text you want to enter.

Figure 1–33   Text automatically entered with Flash Fill

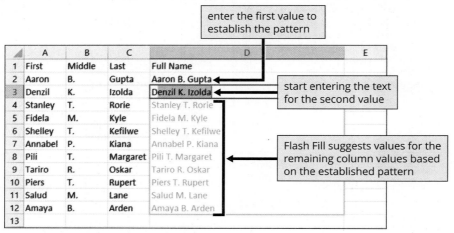

Flash Fill works best when the pattern is clearly recognized from the values in the data. Be sure to enter the data pattern in the column or row next to the related data. The data used to generate the pattern must be in a rectangular grid and cannot have blank columns or rows.

Insight Video Solution generates product IDs by combining the text of the Category and Subcategory columns. For example, installation and wiring, in the SER category and 4020 subcategory, has a product ID of SER-4020. You'll use Flash Fill to generate the product ID values for all items on the purchase order.

To generate product IDs using Flash Fill:

1. In cell A21, type **Product ID** and then press **ENTER**. Cell A22 becomes the active cell.

2. Type **AUD-9010** in cell A22, and then press **ENTER** to establish the pattern for the product IDs. Cell A23 is the active cell.

3. Type **AUD-9020** in cell A23. After you type 2, Flash Fill generates the remaining entries in column based on the established pattern. Refer to Figure 1–34.

Figure 1-34   Product IDs generated by Flash Fill

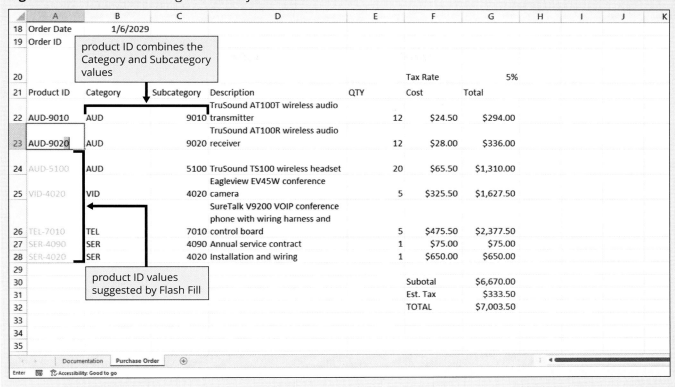

4. Press **ENTER** to accept the suggested text values.

> **Trouble?** If you pause for an extended time between entering text to establish the pattern, Flash Fill might not extend the pattern for you. Delete the text you entered in the cell, and then repeat Steps 3 and 4.

Flash Fill generates text, not formulas. If you edit or replace the entry originally used to create the Flash Fill pattern, the other entries generated by Flash Fill in the column will not be updated.

Formatting a Worksheet

Formatting enhances the appearance of the worksheet data by changing its font, size, color, or alignment or adding cell borders. Two common formatting changes are adding cell borders and changing the font size of text.

Adding Cell Borders

You can make worksheet content easier to read by adding borders around the worksheet cells. Borders can be added to the left, top, right, or bottom edge of any cell or range. You can set the color, thickness of and the number of lines in each border. Borders are especially useful when you print a worksheet because the gridlines that surround the cells in the workbook window are not printed by default. They appear only in the worksheet window as a guide.

Sofi wants borders around the cells listing the items in the purchase order to make the content easier to read.

To add borders around cells in the purchase order:

1. Select the range **F20:G20**. You will add borders to these cells.

2. On the Home tab, in the Font group, click the **Borders arrow** ⊞ ⌄ , and then click **All Borders**. Borders are added around each cell in the selected range. The Borders button changes to reflect the last selected border option, which in this case is All Borders. The name of the selected border option appears in the button's ScreenTip.

3. Select the nonadjacent range **A21:G28,F30:F32**.

4. On the Home tab, in the Font group, click the **All Borders** button ⊞ . Borders appear around all the cells in this range as well.

5. Click cell **A32** to deselect the range. Refer to Figure 1–35.

Figure 1–35   Borders added to the purchase order

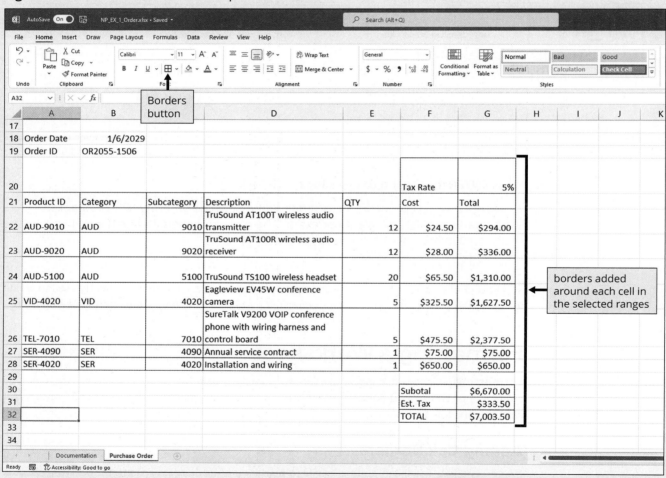

Changing the Font Size

Changing the size of text in a sheet provides a way to identify different parts of a worksheet, such as distinguishing a title or section heading from data. The size of the text is referred to as the font size and is measured in points. The default font size for worksheets is 11 points, but it can be made larger or smaller as needed. You can resize text in selected cells using the Font Size button in the Font group on the Home tab. You can also use the Increase Font Size and Decrease Font Size buttons to resize cell content to the next higher or lower standard font size.

Sofi wants you to increase the size of the worksheet title to 36 points and the subtitle to 22 points to make them more visible and stand out from the rest of the worksheet content.

To change font sizes of worksheet title and subtitle:

1. Scroll up the worksheet and click cell **A1** to select the worksheet title.

2. On the Home tab, in the Font group, click the **Font Size arrow** `11 ▼` to display a list of font sizes, and then click **36**. The worksheet title changes to 36 points.

3. Click cell **A2**, and then in the Font group, click the **Increase Font Size** button `A^` six times until the font size is **22** points. Refer to Figure 1–36.

Figure 1–36   Font sizes increased for worksheet text

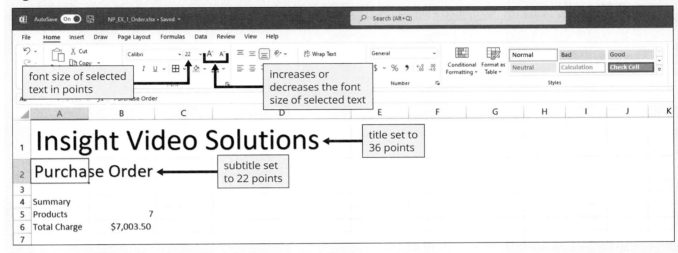

4. Press **CTRL+S** to save the workbook.

Now that the workbook content and formatting are final, you can print the report on the customer's purchase order.

Printing a Workbook

Excel has many tools to control the print layout and appearance of a workbook. Before printing a worksheet, you will want to preview the printout to make sure that it will print correctly.

Changing Worksheet Views

You can view a workbook in three ways. Normal view, which you have been using throughout this module, shows the contents of the worksheet. Page Layout view shows how the worksheet will appear when printed. Page Break Preview displays the location of the different page breaks within the worksheet. This view is useful when a worksheet spans several printed pages, and you need to control what content appears on each page.

Sofi wants you to preview the print version of the Purchase Order worksheet. You will do this by switching between views.

To switch worksheet views:

1. Click the **Page Layout** button 📃 on the status bar. The page layout of the worksheet appears in the workbook window.

2. On the Zoom slider at the lower-right corner of the workbook window, click the **Zoom Out** button until the percentage is **70%**. The reduced magnification makes it clear that the worksheet will spread over two pages when printed. Refer to Figure 1–37.

Figure 1–37   Worksheet in Page Layout view

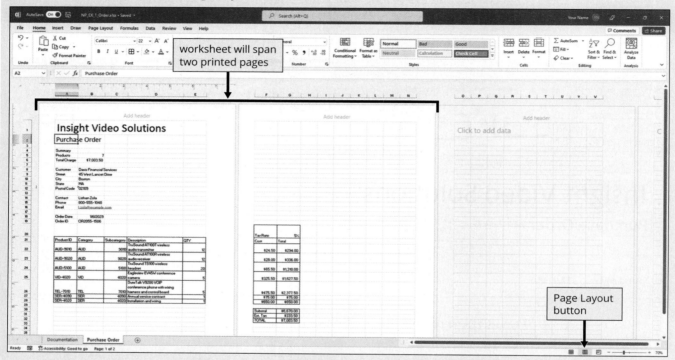

3. Click the **Page Break Preview** button 凹 on the status bar. The view switches to Page Break Preview, which shows only those parts of the current worksheet that will print. A dotted blue border separates one page from another.

    Tip You can relocate a page break by dragging the dotted blue border in the Page Break Preview window.

4. On the Zoom slider, drag the slider button to the right until the percentage is **90%**. You can now more easily read the contents of the worksheet. Refer to Figure 1–38.

Figure 1–38   Worksheet in Page Break Preview view

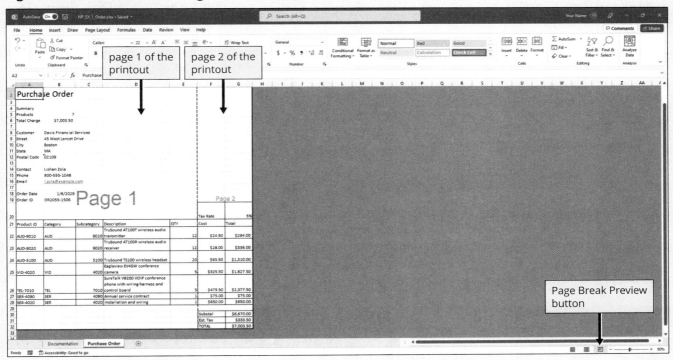

5. Click the **Normal** button ⊞ on the status bar. The worksheet returns to Normal view. After viewing the worksheet in Page Layout or Page Break Preview, a dotted black line appears between columns D and E in Normal view to indicate where the page breaks occur.

Changing the Page Orientation

Page orientation specifies in which direction content is printed on the page. In **portrait orientation**, the page is taller than it is wide. In **landscape orientation**, the page is wider than it is tall. By default, Excel displays pages in portrait orientation. Changing the page orientation affects only the active sheet in the workbook and not the other, unselected, sheets.

As you saw in Page Layout view and Page Break Preview, the Purchase Order worksheet will print on two pages—columns A through E will print on the first page, while columns F and G will print on the second page. Keep in mind that the columns that print on each page may differ slightly depending on the printer. Sofi wants the entire worksheet to print on a single page, so you'll change the page orientation from portrait to landscape.

To change the page orientation of the Purchase Order worksheet:

1. On the ribbon, click the **Page Layout** tab. The tab includes options for changing how the worksheet is arranged.

2. In the Page Setup group, click the **Orientation** button, and then click **Landscape**. The worksheet switches to landscape orientation, though you cannot tell this change occurred in Normal view.

3. Click the **Page Layout** button 🗐 on the status bar to switch to Page Layout view.

The worksheet will still print on two pages with rows 1 through 25 on the first page and rows 26 through 32 on the second. You can fit the entire worksheet on a single page by rescaling the page.

Scaling a Printed Page

Scaling resizes the worksheet to fit within a single page or set of pages. You can scale a worksheet so the printout:

1. Fits all columns or all rows on a single page.

2. Fits all columns and all rows on a single page.

3. Fits on a specified number of pages.

4. Adjusts to a specified percentage of its default size, such as 50% of its normal size.

When scaling a printout, make sure that the worksheet is still readable after it is resized. Scaling affects only the active worksheet, so you can scale each worksheet to best fit its contents. That scaling will be retained even if you add more rows and columns of data to the worksheet.

Sofi asks you to scale the printout so that all rows and columns of the Purchase Order worksheet fit on one page in landscape orientation.

To scale the printout of the worksheet:

1. On the Page Layout tab, in the Scale to Fit group, click the **Width arrow**, and then click **1 page**. All the columns in the worksheet fit on one page.

2. In the Scale to Fit group, click the **Height arrow**, and then click **1 page**. All the rows in the worksheet fit on one page. Refer to Figure 1–39.

Figure 1–39   Printout scaled to fit on one page

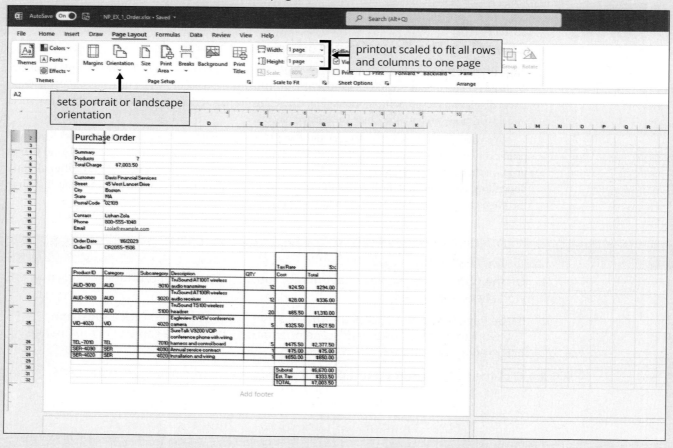

Setting the Print Options

You can print the contents of a workbook by using the Print screen in Backstage view. The Print screen provides options for choosing where to print, how many copies to print, and what to print. You can choose to print only a selected range of cells, only the currently active sheet, or all the worksheets in the workbook.

By default, a printout includes only the worksheet content. The other elements of the Excel window, such as the row and column headings and the gridlines, will not be printed. The print preview shows you exactly how the printed pages will look with the current settings. You should always preview before printing to ensure that the printout looks exactly as you intend.

> **Tip** To print the gridlines or the column and row headings, click the corresponding Print check box in the Sheet Options group on the Page Layout tab.

Sofi asks you to preview and print the workbook containing the purchase order for the customer.

To preview and print the workbook:

1. On the ribbon, click the **File** tab to display Backstage view.

2. Click **Print** in the navigation bar. The Print screen appears with the print options and a preview of the printout of the Purchase Order worksheet. Refer to Figure 1–40.

Figure 1–40   Print screen in Backstage view

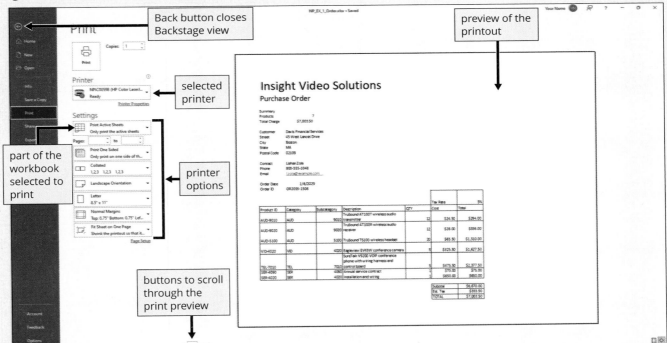

3. Click the **Printer** button, and then click the printer you want to print to, if it is not already selected. By default, Excel will print only the active sheet.

4. In the Settings options, click the top button, and then click **Print Entire Workbook** to print all sheets in the workbook—in this case, both the Documentation and the Purchase Order worksheets. The preview shows the first sheet in the workbook—the Documentation worksheet. Note that this sheet is still in portrait orientation.

5. Below the preview, click the **Next Page** button ▶ to view the print preview for the Purchase Order worksheet, which will print on a single page in landscape orientation.

6. If you are instructed to print, click the **Print** button to send the contents of the workbook to the specified printer. If you are not instructed to print, click the **Back** button ⬅ in the navigation bar to exit Backstage view.

Viewing Worksheet Formulas

Most of the time, you will be interested viewing and printing the data and formula results, not the formulas used to calculate those results. However, in some cases, you might want to view the formulas contained within a worksheet. Displaying that information is useful when you encounter unexpected results and need to examine the underlying formulas, or when you want to discuss the formulas with a colleague. You can view a worksheet in **formula view**, which displays the formulas in place of the results.

In formula view, any printout will include the formulas instead of the values. To make the printout easier to interpret, you should also print the worksheet gridlines, row headings, and column headings, so that cell references from the formulas are easy locate.

You'll look at the formulas in the Purchase Order worksheet.

To view the formulas in the Purchase Order worksheet:

1. Make sure the Purchase Order worksheet is displayed in Page Layout view.

2. On the ribbon, click the **Formulas** tab.

3. In the Formula Auditing group, click the **Show Formulas** button. The worksheet changes to display formulas instead of the values. Notice that the columns widen to display the complete formula text within each cell. Refer to Figure 1–41.

Figure 1–41   Worksheet with formulas displayed

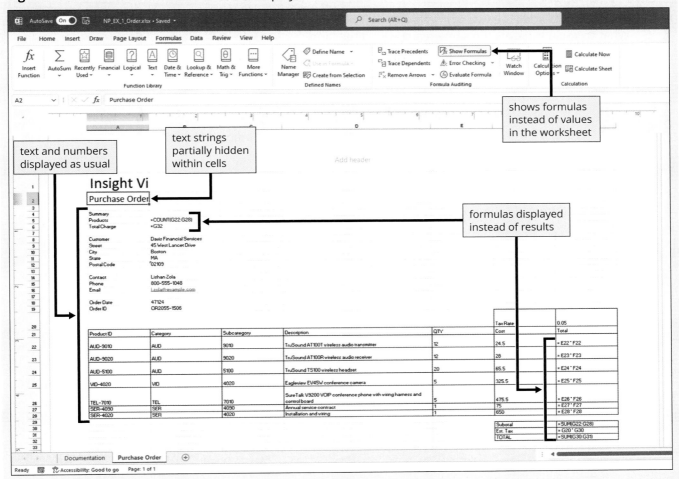

4. When you are done reviewing the formulas, click the **Show Formulas** button again to hide the formulas and display the resulting values.

   | **Tip** You can also toggle between formula view and Normal view by pressing CTRL+` (the grave accent symbol ` is usually located above TAB).

5. Click the **Normal** button ⊞ on the status bar to return the workbook to Normal view.

6. On the Zoom slider, drag the slider button to the right until the percentage is **140%** (or the magnification you want to use).

7. **sam**⬆ Save the workbook, and then close it.

Sofi is pleased with the workbook you created and will use it to create purchase orders for other customer of Insight Video Solutions.

Part 1.2 Quick Check

1. What formula adds the values in cells A1, B1, and C1 without using a function? What formula achieves the same result with a function?

2. What formula counts the number of numeric values in the range A1:A30. What formula counts the number of numeric values and text values in that range?

3. If you insert cells into the range C1:D10, shifting cells to the right, what is the new location of the data that was previously in cell F4?

4. Cell E11 contains the formula =SUM(E1:E10). How is the formula adjusted when a new row is inserted above row 5?

5. In the following AVERAGE function, which arguments are required and which are optional?

    AVERAGE(*number1*, [*number2*], [*number3*], ...)

6. What formula sums all numeric values in column E?

7. What is the difference between deleting a range and clearing a range?

8. Describe the four ways of viewing worksheet content in Excel.

Practice: Review Assignments

Data File needed for the Review Assignments: NP_EX_1-2.xlsx

Sofi wants you to create a workbook to provide quarterly summaries of the Insight Video Solutions income and expenses. The report should also provide the total income and expenses from the entire fiscal year and the percent change in operating income from one quarter to the next. Complete the following:

1. Open the **NP_EX_1-2.xlsx** workbook located in the Excel1 > Review folder included with your Data Files, and then save the workbook as **NP_EX_2_Quarterly** in the location specified by your instructor.
2. Move the Documentation sheet to from the last to the first sheet in the workbook, and then enter your name in cell B3 and the current date in cell B4.
3. Edit the purpose statement in cell B5 by adding the phrase **in the current fiscal year** to the end of the text.
4. Wrap the text in cell B5, set the width of column B to **30** characters and the height of row 5 to **60** points.
5. Set the font size of the title in cell A1 to **26** points.
6. Add all borders around the range A3:B5.
7. Remove the Notes about the Company worksheet from the workbook.
8. Change the name of the Income worksheet to **Quarterly Report**.
9. In the ranges B5:E6 and B9:E10, enter the data from Figure 1–42.

Figure 1–42   Quarterly income and expenses

	QTR 1	QTR 2	QTR 3	QTR 4
Net Sales	$648,150	$988,750	$982,750	$1,018,550
Cost of Sales	$401,200	$604,950	$619,650	$679,500
General Expenses	$99,400	$120,000	$123,650	$125,200
Administrative Expenses	$77,350	$98,300	$101,620	$102,250

10. In the range B7:E7, enter a formula to calculate the gross profit per quarter by subtracting the cost of sales from the net sales.
11. In the range B11:E11, enter a formula to calculate the total operating expenses per quarter by adding the general and administrative expenses.
12. In the range B13:E13, enter a formula to calculate the operating income per quarter by subtracting total operating expenses from gross profit.
13. In the range C14:E14, enter the following formula to calculate the percent change in operating income from one quarter to the next:

$$\% \text{ change} = \frac{\text{current operating income} - \text{previous operating income}}{\text{previous operating income}} \times 100$$

14. Move the range A4:E14 to the range A17:E27.
15. Copy the labels from the range A18:A26 into the range A5:A13. Enter **End-of-Year Total** in cell B4 and **Average per Quarter** in cell C4. Wrap the text in cells B4 and C4.
16. In cell B5, use the SUM function to calculate the sum of all net sales in the range B18:E18.
17. In cell C5, enter a formula that divides the value in cell B5 by 4.
18. Copy the formulas in the range B5:C5 into the nonadjacent range B6:C7,B9:C11,B13:C13 to calculate the end-of-year totals and quarterly averages for each income and expense category.
19. Change the page orientation of the Quarterly Report worksheet to landscape.
20. Scale the Quarterly Report worksheet so that all the columns and rows print on one page.
21. Save the workbook. If you are instructed to print the workbook, print both sheets in the document.
22. Display the formula used in the Quarterly Report worksheet. If you are instructed to print the formulas, print the entire sheet. Hide the formulas.
23. Save the workbook, and then close it.

Apply: Case Problem 1

Data File needed for this Case Problem: NP_EX_1-3.xlsx

Boxes Express Kiran Avanti manages delivery drivers in the southwest region for Boxes Express, a shipping company specializing in overnight and two-day deliveries. One of Kiran's monthly responsibilities is to monitor the distances and hours traveled by Boxes Express drivers to ensure that they follow safety regulations for distance and travel times. Kiran also monitors the driving costs incurred by each driver. Kiran asks you to work on an Excel report detailing the trips and costs of a typical Boxes Express driver. Complete the following:

1. Open the **NP_EX_1-3.xlsx** workbook located in the Excel1 > Case1 folder included with your Data Files, and then save the workbook as **NP_EX_1_Boxes** in the location specified by your instructor.
2. On the Documentation sheet, enter your name in cell B3 and the current date in cell B4.
3. Change the name of the Log worksheet to **Driving Log**.
4. In the Driving Log worksheet, move the data in the range D1:O23 to the range D4:O26.
5. Increase the font size of cell A1 to **24** points. Increase the font size of cells A2, A4, D4, and L4 to **16** points. Increase the font size of row 5 to **12** points.
6. Use AutoFit to increase the width of columns E and F to match their contents.
7. In the range J6:J26, determine the miles driven by entering formulas to calculate the difference between the ending and beginning mileage for each day.
8. In the range N6:N26, determine the cost of fuel each day by entering formulas to multiply the number of gallons used by the cost per gallon.
9. Summarize the driving time during the month by entering the following calculations:
   a. In cell B5, use the COUNT function to count the number of numeric values in column D.
   b. In cell B6, use the SUM function to determine the total driving hours from column G.
   c. In cell B7, determine the average hours of driving per day by entering a formula to divide the value in cell B6 by the value in cell B5.
10. Summarize the expenses incurred during the month by entering the following calculations:
    a. In cell B9, use the SUM function to calculate the total expenses in column range N:0.
    b. In cell B10, use the SUM function to calculate the total spent on fuel in column N.
    c. In cell B11, use the SUM function to calculate the total miscellaneous expenses from column O.
11. Summarize the data on fuel consumption by entering the following calculations:
    a. In cell B13, use the SUM function to add up the gallons consumed in column L.
    b. In cell B14, use the SUM function to add up the total mileage from column J.
    c. In cell B15, calculate the miles per gallon by dividing the total mileage by the total gallons consumed.
    d. In cell B16, calculate the cost of delivery by dividing the total expenses incurred during the month by the total mileage driven.
12. The company wants to keep the cost per mile of delivery packages to the hubs and distribution centers to $1 or less per mile. In cell B18, enter **over budget** if the cost per mile is over this goal or **under budget** if it meets this goal.
13. Add all borders around the cells in the nonadjacent ranges D5:J26,L5:O26.
14. Change the page orientation of the Driving Log worksheet to landscape.
15. Scale the Driving Log worksheet so that all rows and columns fit on one page. If you are instructed to print your solution, print the contents of the entire workbook.
16. Save the workbook, and then close it.

Challenge: Case Problem 2

Data File needed for this Case Problem: NP_EX_1-4.xlsx

Eat Well, Inc. Marta Arlet works in the Human Resources Department of the national grocery store chain Eat Well, Inc. Marta is finalizing a workbook that summarizes data from almost 500 employees from all stores in the chain. The report will include information on the employee's average salaries, years of employment with the company, personal days, sicks days, and performance evaluation.

To complete Marta's workbook, you will use the AVERAGE function to calculate averages from ranges of numeric values. The syntax of the AVERAGE function is:

    AVERAGE(number1, [number2], [number3],…)

You will also combine employee first and last names into a single text string using the & operator. To apply the & operator to create a full name from a first and last name, you use the formula

    = first &""& last

where *first* is the cell reference to the employee's first name and *last* is the cell reference to the employee's last name. Complete the following:

1. Open the **NP_EX_1-4.xlsx** workbook located in the Excel1 > Case2 folder included with your Data Files, and then save the workbook as **NP_EX_1_EatWell** in the location specified by your instructor.
2. In the Documentation sheet, enter your name and the current date in cells B3 and B4.
3. Wrap the text in cell B5 and set the width of column B to **25** characters and the height of row 5 to **80** points.
4. In the Employees worksheet, AutoFit the width of column A. Set the width of column B to **16** characters.
5. In cell J4, enter a formula to determine the first employee's number of days employed by subtracting the date hired from the current date value.
6. In cell K4, enter a formula to determine the years hired for the first employee by dividing the value in cell J4 by 365.25.
7. Copy the formulas from the range J4:K4 into the range J5:K495 to estimate the days and years hired for the rest of the employees.
8. **Explore:** In cell F4, enter the formula **= D4 &" "& E4** to display the full name for the first employee.
9. Copy the formula in cell F4 into the range F5:F495 to display the other employee full names.
10. Summarize the employee data for the company by entering the following calculations into the worksheet:
    a. In cell B4, use the COUNT function to count the number of values in column I.
    b. In cell B5, use the SUM function with the values in column L to calculate the total of employee salaries to the company.
    c. In cell B6, use the SUM function with the values in column M to calculate the total number of personal days taken by company employees.
    d. In cell B7, use the SUM function with the values in column N to calculate the total number of sick days taken by company employees.
11. **Explore:** Calculate employee averages by inserting the following calculations into the worksheet:
    a. In cell B10, use the AVERAGE function to calculate the average salary using the values from column L.
    b. In cell B11, use the AVERAGE function to calculate the average years employed using values from column K.
    c. In cell B12, use the AVERAGE function to calculate the average number of personal days using the values from column M.
    d. In cell B13, use the AVERAGE function to calculate the average number of sicks days using the values from column N.
    e. In cell B14, use the AVERAGE function to calculate the average performance rating using the values from column O.

12. A new employee was hired at Eat Well. Insert cells into the range D10:O10, shifting the current cells down the worksheet.

13. Enter the following information about the new employee: **Andrew** in cell D10, **Alito** in cell E10, **IT** in cell G10, **3/31/2029** in cell H10, **3/23/2029** in cell I10, **$81,000** in cell L10, **0** in cell M10, **0** in cell N10, and **75** in cell O10. (Note that the formulas will automatically be inserted into cells F10, J10, and K10.)

14. In the range D3:O496, add all borders around the cells.

15. Change the page orientation of the worksheet to landscape.

16. Change the page scaling of the worksheet so that all the columns fit on one page.

17. **Explore:** Select the range A1:B14, and then using the Print Settings options on the Print page in Backstage View, print only the selected cells (not the entire worksheet or workbook).

18. Save the workbook, and then close it.

Formatting a Workbook

Creating a Sales Report

Case: Hook and Line Seafood

Robert Coby is a sales manager for Hook and Line Seafood, a chain of seafood restaurants in Florida, Georgia, and Alabama. Robert creates an annual sales report using data from 12 restaurants in the Hook and Line chain. The report includes monthly summaries of each restaurant's total revenue, total expenses, net profit, and profit margin. That is a lot of data on a single worksheet. You will format the worksheet for Robert to improve its readability and to highlight important results such as months when a restaurant had a net loss instead of a profit. The workbook will also be released in a print version, so you will need to format the workbook for print as well as for the screen.

Starting Data Files

Excel2

Module

NP_EX_2-1.xlsx
Support_EX_2_Background.jpg

Review

NP_EX_2-2.xlsx
Support_EX_2_Texture.jpg

Case1

NP_EX_2-3.xlsx

Case2

NP_EX_2-4.xlsx
Support_EX_2_Home.thmx

Objectives

Part 2.1

- Change fonts, font style, and font color
- Add fill colors and a background image
- Format numbers as currency and percentages
- Format dates and times
- Copy and paste formats with the Format Painter
- Align, indent, and rotate cell contents
- Merge a group of cells

Part 2.2

- Use the AVERAGE function
- Apply cell styles
- Find and replace text and formatting
- Change workbook themes
- Highlight cells with conditional formats
- Format a worksheet for printing

Part 2.1 Visual Overview: Formatting a Worksheet

The Font group has buttons for setting the font, font size, font color, and **font style**, which indicates how characters are emphasized, such as **bold**, *italic*, or underline.

The Alignment group has buttons for setting horizontal and vertical alignment, orientation, and indents; wrapping text in cells; and merging cells.

A **font** defines the appearance and shape of letters, numbers, and special characters.

You can format text strings within a cell in Edit mode.

The Number group has buttons for applying the Accounting format, Percent style, and Comma style, as well as changing how many decimal places are displayed.

The number of digits to the right of the decimal point can be increased or decreased without affecting the cell's value.

You can rotate content within a cell.

You can **merge**, or combine, adjacent cells into one cell. The range A12:A31 is merged into cell A12.

You can change the fill colors of sheet tabs to help organize a workbook.

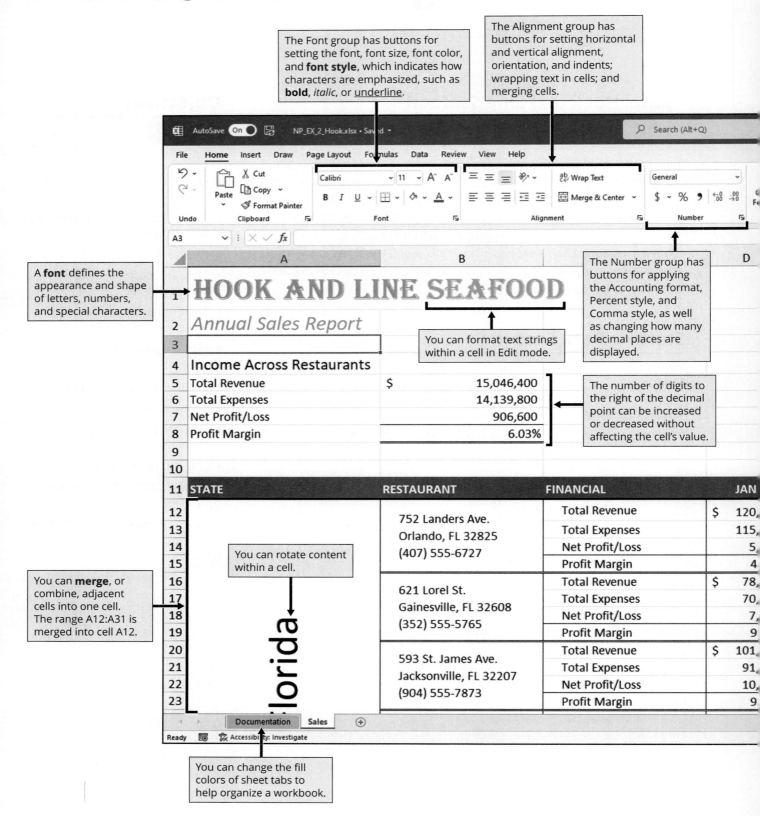

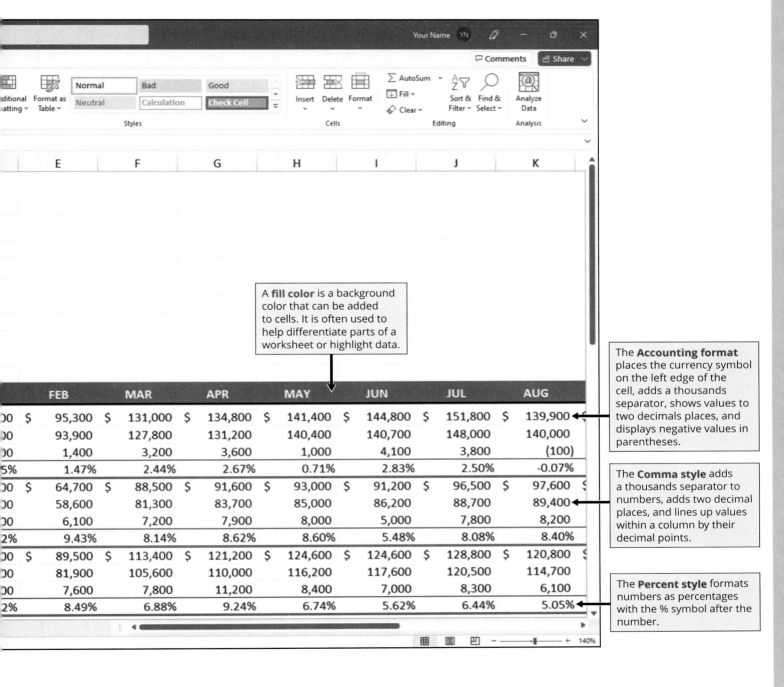

A **fill color** is a background color that can be added to cells. It is often used to help differentiate parts of a worksheet or highlight data.

The **Accounting format** places the currency symbol on the left edge of the cell, adds a thousands separator, shows values to two decimals places, and displays negative values in parentheses.

The **Comma style** adds a thousands separator to numbers, adds two decimal places, and lines up values within a column by their decimal points.

The **Percent style** formats numbers as percentages with the % symbol after the number.

	FEB	MAR	APR	MAY	JUN	JUL	AUG
)0 $	95,300 $	131,000 $	134,800 $	141,400 $	144,800 $	151,800 $	139,900
)0	93,900	127,800	131,200	140,400	140,700	148,000	140,000
)0	1,400	3,200	3,600	1,000	4,100	3,800	(100)
5%	1.47%	2.44%	2.67%	0.71%	2.83%	2.50%	-0.07%
)0 $	64,700 $	88,500 $	91,600 $	93,000 $	91,200 $	96,500 $	97,600
)0	58,600	81,300	83,700	85,000	86,200	88,700	89,400
)0	6,100	7,200	7,900	8,000	5,000	7,800	8,200
2%	9.43%	8.14%	8.62%	8.60%	5.48%	8.08%	8.40%
)0 $	89,500 $	113,400 $	121,200 $	124,600 $	124,600 $	128,800 $	120,800
)0	81,900	105,600	110,000	116,200	117,600	120,500	114,700
)0	7,600	7,800	11,200	8,400	7,000	8,300	6,100
2%	8.49%	6.88%	9.24%	6.74%	5.62%	6.44%	5.05%

Formatting Text

The appearance of a workbook is often as important as the calculations it contains. A poorly organized and formatted workbook can obscure useful information and insights. A well-formatted workbook helps make data accessible for users to analyze and review. Note that formatting changes only the appearance of data. It does not alter the content of the data.

Robert has sales information for the restaurant chain stored in a workbook. He wants you to turn the data into a document that will be both insightful and impactful. You'll start by reviewing the data in Robert's workbook.

To open and review Robert's workbook:

1. **sam ↓** Open the **NP_EX_2-1.xlsx** workbook located in the **Excel2 > Module** folder included with your Data Files, and then save the workbook as **NP_EX_2_Hook** in the location specified by your instructor.

2. In the Documentation sheet, enter your name in cell B4 and the current date in cell B5.

3. Go to the **Sales** worksheet, which summarizes sales from all 12 restaurants in the Hook and Line Seafood chain. Refer to Figure 2-1.

Figure 2-1   Unformatted Sales worksheet

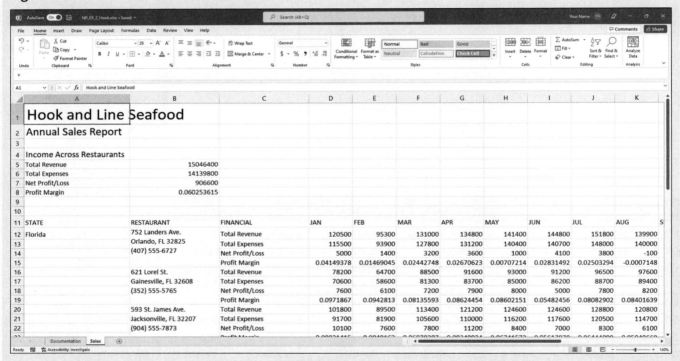

The Sales worksheet contains a lot of useful information about sales. However, in its current form, the worksheet is difficult to read and users cannot make any important insights about monthly or annual sales. To fix that problem, you will change the workbook's appearance.

A workbook's appearance is based on a theme. A **theme** is a predefined set of formats for text, colors, and graphic effects that provide a workbook with a consistent, professional look that is informative for the user. All new workbooks use the Office theme, but you can choose a different theme from the Excel library or create your own. Themes are saved as files, so that the same theme can be shared by multiple workbooks.

The theme impacts the appearance of text used in the workbook. Text design is based on fonts, which are sets of characters that share a common appearance and shape. **Serif fonts**, such as Times New Roman, have extra strokes at the end of each character. **Sans serif fonts**, such as Arial, do not include these flourishes. Other fonts are purely decorative, such as a font associated with a company's logo.

Excel organizes fonts into theme fonts and standard fonts. A **theme font** is associated with a particular theme and is used to format headings and body text within the workbook. If you change a workbook's theme, text formatted with a theme font will also change. A **standard font** is not associated with any theme and retains its appearance no matter what theme the workbook uses.

Every font can be formatted with a font style that can add special emphasis to the characters, such as *italic*, **bold**, ***bold italic***, underline, and color. You can also increase or decrease the font size to change its impact.

Reference

Formatting Text

- To choose the font, select the cell or range. On the Home tab, in the Font group, click the Font arrow, and then select a font name.
- To set the font size, select the cell or range. On the Home tab, in the Font group, click the Font Size arrow, and then select a size.
- To set the font style, select the cell or range. On the Home tab, in the Font group, click the Bold, Italic, or Underline button; or press CTRL+B, CTRL+I, or CTRL+U.
- To set the font color, select the cell or range. On the Home tab, in the Font group, click the Font Color arrow, and then select a color.
- To format a text selection, double-click the cell to enter Edit mode, select the text to format, change the font, size, style, or color, and then press ENTER.

As you design a workbook, you can test different formatting options using **Live Preview**, which shows the results of a format change before it is selected. Robert wants the company name to use the same font as the corporate logo. He also wants other text in the Documentation sheet to stand out more.

To format text in the Documentation sheet:

1. Go to the **Documentation** sheet, and then click cell **A1** if necessary to select it.

2. On the Home tab, in the Font group, click the **Font arrow** to display a gallery of available fonts. Each name is previewed in its font typeface. The first two fonts listed are the Office theme fonts for headings and body text—Calibri Light and Calibri. The remaining fonts are standard fonts not associated with any theme.

3. In the Font gallery, scroll down as needed and point to **Algerian**. Live Preview shows the effect of the font on the text in cell A1. Refer to Figure 2-2.

Figure 2–2   Font gallery

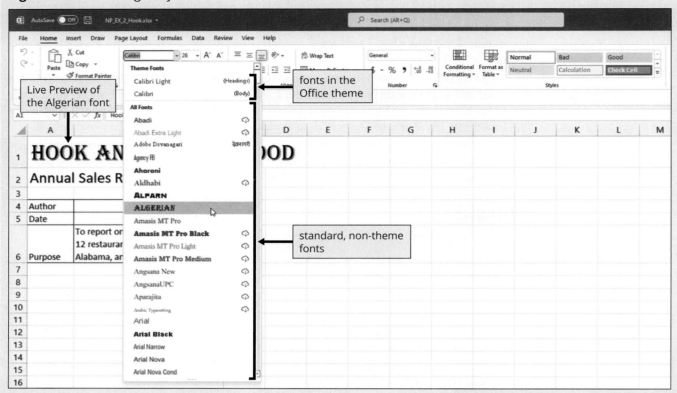

> **Trouble?** If Algerian is not in your list of standard fonts, use a font suggested by your instructor or choose a different decorative font.

4. Click **Algerian** in the list of standard fonts. The text in cell A1 changes to the selected font.

5. In the Font group, click the **Bold** button B (or press **CTRL+B**). The text changes to a bold font.

6. Click cell **A2** containing the subtitle for the worksheet.

7. In the Font group, click the **Italic** button I (or press **CTRL+I**). The Annual Sales Report subtitle is italicized.

8. Select the range **A4:A6** containing the labels, and then press **CTRL+B**. The text in the selected range changes to bold.

9. Click cell **A8** to deselect the range. Refer to Figure 2–3.

Figure 2-3   Font styles applied to text

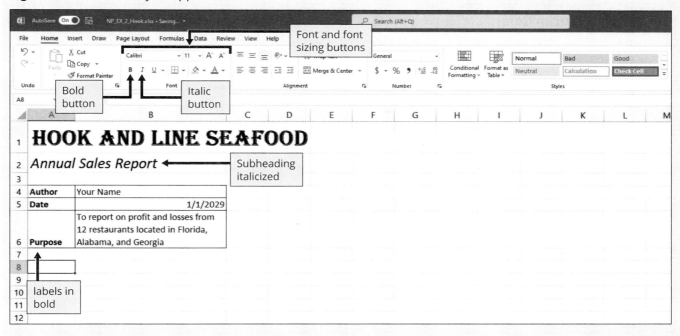

Applying a Font Color

Color can transform a plain workbook filled with numbers and text into a powerful presentation that captures the user's attention. Color can also emphasize important points in a data analysis.

Like fonts, colors are organized into theme and standard colors. **Theme colors** are a set of 12 coordinated colors that belong to the workbook's theme. Four colors are designated for text and backgrounds, six colors are used for accents and highlights, and two colors are used for hyperlinks (followed and not followed links). These 12 colors are designed to complement each other while remaining readable when used in combination. Each theme color has five variations, or accents, with a different tint of shading of the color.

Ten **standard colors**—dark red, red, orange, yellow, light green, green, light blue, blue, dark blue, and purple—are always available regardless of the workbook's theme. Beyond these easily accessible standard colors is an extended palette of 134 colors. You can also create a custom color by specifying a mixture of red, blue, and green color values, making available 16.7 million custom color combinations, which are more colors than the human eye can distinguish. Some dialog boxes have an automatic color option that uses your Windows default text and background colors, usually black text on a white background.

Insight

Creating Custom Colors

Custom colors let you add subtle and striking colors to a formatted workbook. To create custom colors, you use the **RGB Color model** in which each color is expressed with varying intensities of red, green, and blue. RGB color values are often represented as a set of numbers in the format

        (red, green, blue)

where `red` is an intensity value assigned to red light, `green` is an intensity value assigned to green light, and `blue` is an intensity value assigned to blue light. The intensities are measured on a scale of 0 to 255—0 indicates no intensity (or the absence of the color) and 255 indicates the highest intensity. So, the RGB color value (255, 255, 0) represents a mixture of high-intensity red (255) and high-intensity green (255) with the absence of blue (0), creating yellow.

To create colors in Excel using the RGB model, click the More Colors option located in a color menu or dialog box to open the Colors dialog box. In the Colors dialog box, click the Custom tab, and then enter the red, green, and blue intensity values. A preview box displays the resulting RGB color.

Robert wants the title and subtitle in the Documentation sheet to stand out. You'll change the font color in cells A1 and A2 to light blue.

To change the text color of the title and subtitle:

1. In the Documentation sheet, select the range **A1:A2** containing the title and subtitle.

2. On the Home tab, in the Font group, click the **Font Color arrow** A ▾. The gallery of theme and standard colors opens.

3. In the Standard Colors section, point to the **Light Blue** color (the seventh color). The color name appears in a ScreenTip, and Live Preview shows the text with the light blue font color. Refer to Figure 2–4.

Figure 2–4   Font color gallery

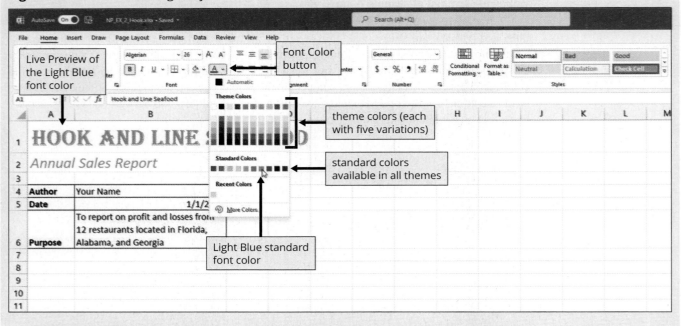

4. Click the **Light Blue** standard color. The title and subtitle text change that font color.

Formatting Text Selections Within a Cell

Not all text in a cell must be the same color. In Edit mode, you can select and format selections of text within a cell. You can make these changes to selected text from the ribbon or from the Mini toolbar. The **Mini toolbar** is a small toolbar that appears next to selected content, containing the most frequently used formatting commands for that content.

Robert asks you to format the company name in cell A1 so that "Seafood" is light green.

To change the color of "Seafood" in cell A1 to light green:

1. Double-click cell **A1** to select the cell and enter Edit mode. The status bar reads "Edit" and the insertion point changes to the I-beam pointer to indicate that you are working with the cell in Edit mode.

   Tip You can also enter Edit mode by clicking a cell and pressing F2.

2. Drag the pointer over the word **Seafood** to select it. The Mini toolbar appears next to the selected text with button to change the font, size, style, and color of the selected text.

3. On the Mini toolbar, click the **Font Color arrow** ▣▾ , and then in the Standard Colors section, point to the **Light Green** color (the fifth color). Live Preview changes the color of the selected text to light green. Refer to Figure 2–5.

Figure 2–5   Mini toolbar in Edit mode

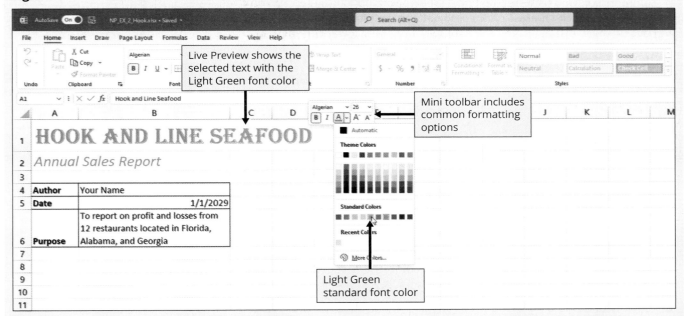

4. Click the **Light Green** standard color. The Mini toolbar closes and the selected text changes to light green.

Working with Fill Colors and Backgrounds

Another way to distinguish sections of a worksheet is by formatting the cell backgrounds. You can fill the cell background with color or with an image.

Changing a Fill Color

In the Office theme, worksheet cells do not include any background color. But filling a cell's background with color, also known as a fill color, can be helpful for highlighting data, differentiating parts of a worksheet, or adding visual interest to a report. The colors available for fonts are also available for cell backgrounds.

Insight

Using Color to Enhance a Workbook

When used wisely, color can enhance any workbook. However, when used improperly, color can distract the user, making the workbook difficult to read. As you add color to a workbook, keep in mind the following tips:

- Use colors from the same theme to maintain a consistent look and feel across the worksheets. If the built-in themes do not fit your needs, you can create a custom theme.
- Use colors to differentiate types of cell content and to direct users where to enter data. For example, format a worksheet so that formula results appear in cells without a fill color and users enter data in cells with a light gray fill color.
- Avoid color combinations that are difficult to read.
- Print the workbook in both color and black-and-white to ensure the printed copy is readable in both versions.
- Understand your printer's limitations and features. Colors that look good on your monitor might not look as good when printed.
- Don't overdo it. Too many color choices will distract rather than enhance your document.

  Be sensitive to your audience. About 8% of all men and 0.5% of all women have some type of color vision impairment and might not be able to distinguish the text when certain color combinations are used. Red–green color vision impairment is the most common, so avoid using red text on a green background or green text on a red background. High contrast color combinations are often better choices for users who have difficulty distinguishing color combinations with lower contrasts.

Robert wants you to change the background color of the range A4:A6 in the Documentation sheet to white text on a blue background. He also wants you to change the content in the range B4:B6 to blue text on a white background.

To change the font and fill colors on the Documentation sheet:

1. Select the range **A4:A6**.

2. On the Home tab, in the Font group, click the **Fill Color arrow** [🖉 ▾], and then in the Theme Colors section, click the **Blue, Accent 1** color (the fifth color in the first row).

3. In the Font group, click the **Font Color arrow** [A ▾], and then in the Theme Colors section, click the **White, Background 1** color (the first color in the first row). The labels are formatted as white text on a blue background.

4. Select the range **B4:B6**, and then format the cells with the **Blue, Accent 1** theme font color and the **White, Background 1** theme fill color.

5. Click cell **A8** to deselect the range. Refer to Figure 2–6.

Figure 2-6   Font and fill colors applied to ranges

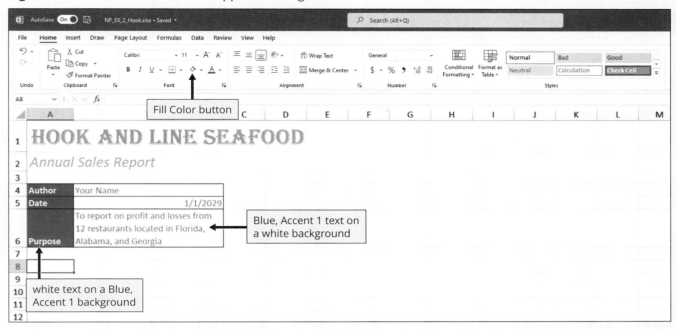

You can change the background color of an entire worksheet by first selecting all the cells in the sheet and then changing the fill color. To select all cells in a worksheet, click the Select All button above the row headers or press CTRL+A.

Adding a Background Image

Another way to format the worksheet background is with a background image. Background images are usually based on image files of textures such as granite, wood, or fibered paper. The image does not need to match the size of the worksheet. A small image repeats, or tiles, until it fills the entire sheet. Background images do not affect any cell's format or content. Any fill colors will appear on top of the background image.

> **Tip** A background image appears only in the workbook window. It is not printed. To print a graphic image, add it to the worksheet as a graphic object.

Robert has an image file he wants to use as the background for the Documentation sheet. You'll add that background image now.

To add a background image to the Documentation sheet:

1. On the ribbon, click the **Page Layout** tab to display the page layout options.

2. In the Page Setup group, click the **Background** button. The Insert Pictures dialog box opens with options to search for an image from a file on your computer, from the Bing Image server, or on your OneDrive account.

3. Click the **From a file** option. The Sheet Background dialog box opens.

4. Navigate to the **Excel2 > Module** folder included with your Data Files, click the **Support_ EX_2_Background.jpg** image file, and then click **Insert**. The image is added to the background of the Documentation sheet. The worksheet gridlines remain visible on the background image.

5. In the Sheet Options group, in the Gridlines list, click the **View** checkbox to deselect it. The gridlines for the Documentation sheet are hidden, creating a cleaner background. Hiding the gridlines in this worksheet does not affect the gridlines in other worksheets. Refer to Figure 2-7.

Figure 2-7   Background image added to the worksheet

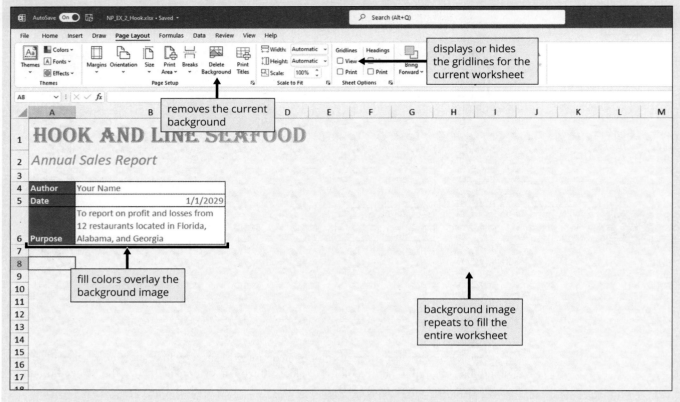

To remove a background image from a worksheet, click the Delete Background button in the Page Setup group on the Page Layout tab.

Changing the Sheet Tab Color

You can add colors to sheet tabs to visually group worksheets sharing a common topic. Although you can change the sheet tab fill color, you cannot change its text color or text style. Robert wants you to change the fill color of the Documentation sheet tab to gold.

To change the tab color of the Documentation sheet:

1. Right-click the **Documentation** sheet tab. A shortcut menu appears with options related to the sheet tab.

2. On the shortcut menu, point to **Tab Color** to display the palette of theme and standard colors.

3. In the Theme Colors section, click **Gold, Accent 4** (the eighth color in the first row). The Documentation sheet tab has a gold highlight.

4. Click the **Sales** sheet tab to make that the active sheet. The Documentation sheet tab has a solid gold fill color.

Formatting Numbers

Formatting the numerical values in a worksheet makes them easier to read. All cells start out in the **General format**, which displays the value stored in the cell without any extra characters (such as currency symbols or commas) or specialized formatting. The General format is fine for some values, but other numbers are easier to interpret with additional formatting, such as:

- Adding commas to separate thousands within larger numbers
- Changing the number of digits displayed to the right of the decimal point
- Including currency symbols to identify the monetary unit of exchange
- Identifying percentages with the % symbol

All the numbers in the Sales worksheet are in the General format. It is not immediately apparent whether the values represent currency or quantities. Also, values without commas, such as the total revenue 15046400 in cell B5, may be misread.

Applying the Accounting and Currency Formats

Excel supports two monetary formats—Accounting and Currency. Both formats add thousands separators to the values and display two digits to the right of the decimal point. The **Accounting format** places the currency symbol at the left edge of the cell and displays negative numbers within parentheses and zero values with a dash. It also slightly indents the values from the right edge of the cell to allow room for parentheses around negative values. The **Currency format** places the currency symbol directly to the left of the first digit of the monetary value and displays negative numbers with a negative sign. Figure 2–8 compares the two formats for the same set of numbers.

Figure 2–8   Accounting and Currency format

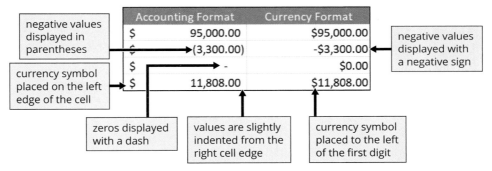

When choosing between the Accounting format and the Currency format, consider accounting principles that govern how financial data should be formatted and displayed. Note that changing the number format does not alter the value stored in the cell.

Proskills

Written Communication: Formatting Monetary Values

Spreadsheets commonly include monetary values. To make these values more readable and comprehensible, keep in mind the following guidelines when formatting the currency data in a worksheet:

- **Format for your audience.** General financial reports often round values to the nearest hundred, thousand, or million. Investors are more interested in the big picture than in exact values. However, for accounting reports, accuracy is important and often legally required. For those reports, be sure to display the exact monetary value.

- **Use thousands separators.** A long string of numbers can be challenging to read. Use the thousands separator to make the number easier to comprehend.

- **Apply the Accounting format to columns of monetary values.** The Accounting format makes columns of numbers easier to read than the Currency format. Use the Currency format for individual cells that are not part of long columns of numbers.

- **Use only two currency symbols in a column of monetary values.** Standard accounting format displays one currency symbol with the first monetary value in the column and optionally displays a second currency symbol with the last value in that column. Use the Accounting format to fix the currency symbols, aligning them in the column.

Following these standard accounting principles will make financial data easier to read both on the screen and in printouts.

Robert wants you to format the total revenue value in cell B5 with the Accounting format.

To display the total revenue in the Accounting format:

1. Click cell **B5** containing the total revenue from the 12 restaurants for the year.

2. On the ribbon, click the **Home** tab.

3. In the Number group, click the **Accounting Number Format** button ⬚$⬚ . The number is formatted with the Accounting format.

   > **Tip** To apply the Currency format to a selected range, click the Number Format arrow and then click Currency (or press CTRL+SHIFT+$).

The value $15,046,400.00 in cell B5 indicates that the total revenue for all the restaurants is more than $15 million. The Accounting format displays both dollars and cents, but that level of precision is not needed in this sales report. You can decrease or increase the number of decimal places displayed without affecting the underlying cell value. To choose a different currency symbol, click the Accounting Number Format arrow and then click the currency symbol you want.

Robert wants you to hide the digits to the right of the decimal point.

To change the number of decimal places displayed in cell B5:

1. Make sure cell **B5** is still selected. You'll change remove the decimal places from this cell.

2. Click the **Decrease Decimal** button ⬚ twice. The cents value for the total revenue are hidden, and cell B5 displays $15,046,400.

The Comma style is identical to the Accounting format except that it does not place a currency symbol on the left edge of the cell. A general approach with financial reports is to apply the Accounting format only to the top and bottom values of a long column and then format the other values with the Comma style to add comma separators and cents values. The advantage of using the Comma style and the Accounting format together is that the numbers and the commas will be aligned within the column. Also, this approach streamlines the worksheet, since the same currency symbols are not repeated down an entire column of financial data.

The next two values in column B are the total expenses from the 12 restaurants and those restaurants' total net profit or loss (equal to the total revenue minus the total expenses). You'll format the total expenses and net profit/loss values with the Comma style, which adds a thousands separator and cents values to numbers. Then you'll decrease the number of decimal places to hide the cents values.

To apply the Comma style to financial data:

1. Select the range **B6:B7** containing the total expenses and net profit/loss values.

2. On the Home tab, in the Number group, click the **Comma Style** button. A comma separator and cent values are added to the numbers.

3. Click the **Decrease Decimal** button twice to hide the two digits to the right of the decimal point.

4. Click cell **B8** to deselect the range. Refer to Figure 2–9.

Figure 2–9   Accounting format and Comma style added to financial data

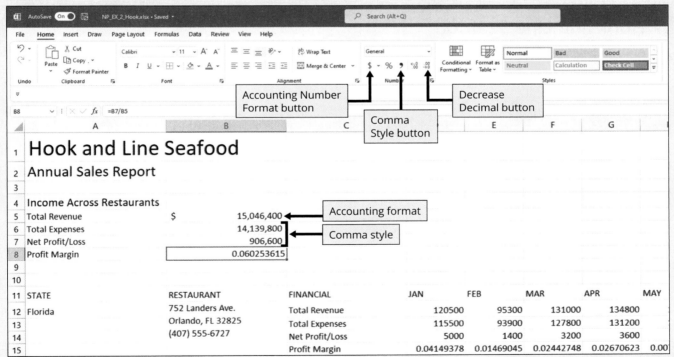

Formatting Percentages

To format a percentage with no decimal places, you use the Percent Style button. For example, the number 0.124 would be formatted as 12%. You can change how many decimal places are displayed in the cell by increasing the number of decimal places displayed in the cell.

The final entry in the Income Across Restaurants section of the worksheet is the company's profit margin. A company's profit margin is equal to the net profit or loss divided by the total revenue. Profit margins are displayed as percentages (the percentage of total revenue that is profit). Restaurants often achieve profit margins of 4% to 7% on their sales. The financial statement already includes a formula to calculate profit margin for the entire franchise and for each restaurant's monthly sales. You'll format this value as a percentage.

To format the overall profit margin as a percentage:

1. If it is not already selected, click cell **B8** to select it.

2. On the Home tab in the Number group, click the **Percent Style** button %. The profit margin is displayed as 6%.

3. In the Number group, click the **Increase Decimal** button twice. The percentage now includes two decimal places—6.03%. Refer to Figure 2–10.

Figure 2–10   Percent style applied

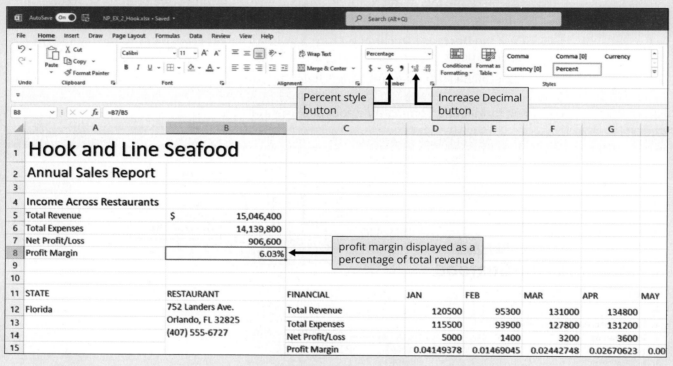

The financial report more clearly reveals that the 12 restaurants have a bit more than a 6% profit margin, which is typical for businesses of this type.

Formatting Dates and Times

Dates and times are stored as numbers. You can format a date or time like any other number without affecting its underlying value in the cell. The **Short Date format** displays dates in the form *mm/dd/yyyy* and the **Long Date format** displays dates with day of the week and the full month name as a text and the day and the year in numbers.

Robert wants you to display the date in the Documentation sheet in the Long Date format.

To format the date in the Documentation sheet with the Long Date format:

1. Go to the **Documentation** sheet, and then select cell **B5**.

2. On the Home tab, in the Number group, click the **Number Format arrow** to display a list of number formats, and then click **Long Date**. The weekday, month name, day, and year appear in cell B5.

    ▌ **Tip** To view the numeric value of a date and time, apply the General format to the cell.

Other built-in numeric formats in Excel include:

- **Time** for displaying time values in a 12-hour time format
- **Fraction** for displaying decimals as fractions to a specified number of digits
- **Scientific** for displaying numeric values in scientific notation
- **Text** for displaying numeric values as text

Excel also has customizable formats that you can modify to fit a wide variety of situations. In the Number group, click the Number Format arrow, and then click More Number Formats to create a custom format.

Copying and Pasting Formats

You formatted the overall sales values in the range B5:B8, but the monthly sales figures for each restaurant in the range D12:P59 are still in the General format. Rather than repeat the same steps to format the monthly sales results, you can copy and paste the formats you just applied.

Copying Formats with the Format Painter

The **Format Painter** copies and pastes formatting from one cell or range to another. The cells with the formatting you want to copy are called the **source range**. The cells where you want to paste the formatting are called the **destination range**. The Format Painter does not copy formulas or values. If the destination range is larger than the source range, the copied format will be repeated across and down the destination range until all cells in the range are formatted.

You will use the Format Painter to copy the formats from the range B5:B8 into the table of monthly sales for the restaurants in the chain.

To copy and paste monthly sales formats with the Format Painter:

1. Go to the **Sales** worksheet, and then select the range **B5:B8**. This is the source range with formats you want to copy.

2. On the Home tab, in the Clipboard group, click the **Format Painter** button ✎ . The pointer changes to the Format Painter pointer ⊕⬛.

3. Select the range **D12:P59** containing the monthly sales data for each restaurant. This the destination range where the copied formats will be pasted. The copied format is repeated until it fills the entire range. Refer to Figure 2–11.

Figure 2–11   Formats copied and pasted

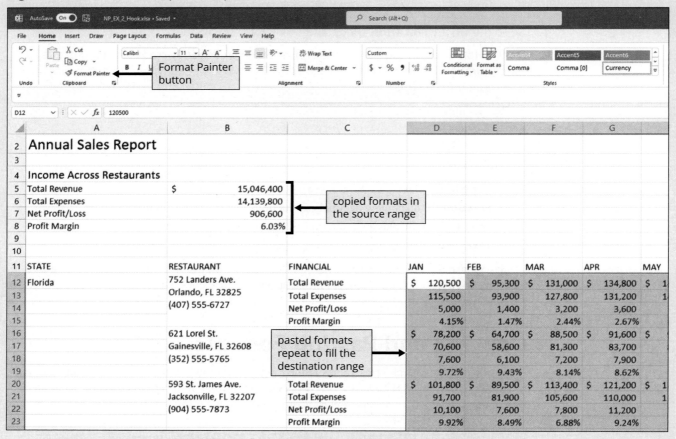

> **Tip** To copy and paste the formats into several nonadjacent ranges, select the source range, double-click the Format Painter button, select destination ranges, and then press ESC to turn off the Format Painter.

You can also use the Format Painter to copy and paste formats between worksheets. You'll use the Format Painter to copy the title and subheading formats in the Documentation sheet to the same title and subheading in the Sales worksheet.

To copy and paste formats between worksheets:

1. Go to the **Documentation** sheet.

2. Select the range **A1:A2** containing the formatted title and subheading.

3. On the Home tab, in the Clipboard group, click the **Format Painter** button. The selected formats are copied.

4. Go to the **Sales** worksheet, and then select the range **A1:A2** to paste the formats. The title and subheading formats match the Documentation sheet.

   The green font color from the word "Seafood" was not included in the pasted formats because the Format Painter does not copy and paste formats of text within a cell. You'll add that formatting to the cell A1.

5. Double-click cell **A1** to enter Edit mode, select **Seafood**, and then change the font color to the **Light Green** standard color.

6. Press **ENTER** to exit Edit mode and select cell A2.

The format of the company title and the subheading on the Sales worksheet now matches the title and subheading in the Documentation sheet.

Copying Formats with the Paste Options Button

Another way to copy and paste formats is with the Paste Options button ⌧ (Ctrl) ▾, which provides options for pasting only values, only formats, or a combination of values and formats. Each time a copied range is pasted, the Paste Options button appears in the lower-right corner of the destination range. Clicking the Paste Options buttons opens a list of options; refer to Figure 2–12. When you point to an icon in the Paste Options list, a ScreenTip will appear explaining the meaning of the icon and its impact on pasting the copied cell range.

Figure 2–12   Paste Options list

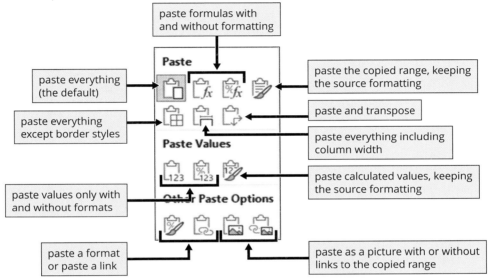

Copying Formats with Paste Special

Paste Special give you more control over what is pasted. To use Paste Special, copy a range of cells, select the range to paste the copied content, click the Paste arrow in the Clipboard group on the Home tab or right-click the selected range, and then click Paste Special. The Paste Special dialog box opens; refer to Figure 2–13.

Figure 2–13   Paste Special options

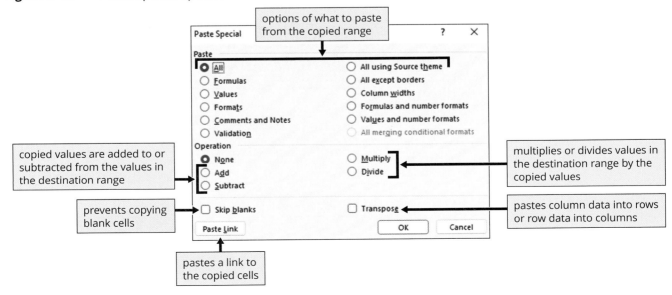

By default, Excel pastes everything except column widths.

Insight

Performing Special Tasks with Paste Special

Paste Special gives you a large amount of control over what is pasted into a range. You can also use Paste Special to modify cell values and formulas. The following are a few special tasks you can perform using Paste Special:

- **Paste values only.** Rather than pasting cell formulas and formatting, paste only the calculated values from the source range by selecting the Values option in the Paste Special dialog box. Any formatting already applied to the destination range is unaffected.
- **Paste column widths.** Copy the source range containing the column widths to duplicate and then select the destination range. In the Paste Special dialog box, select the Column widths option to paste only columns widths and no content.
- **Paste with no borders.** Copy all formats from a range except border styles by selecting the All except borders option in the Paste Special dialog box.
- **Skip blanks.** If the source range contains cells that are empty or blank, use the Skip Blanks option in the Paste Special dialog box to copy only those cells with content.
- **Perform a mathematical operation.** Add, subtract, multiply, or divide the values in the destination range by the copied values. For example, copying the value 2 from a cell and choosing the Multiply option from the Paste Special dialog box will double the values in the destination range.
- **Paste a link.** Rather than pasting a value, paste a cell reference to the range using the Paste Link button in the Paste Special dialog box. For example, copying cell B10 and pasting a link, places the formula =B10 into every cell of the destination range.

These Paste Special features help you work more efficiently as you worksheets.

Transposing Data

Data values are often arranged in a rectangular grid. However, you might want to change the orientation of that grid, switching rows for columns and columns for row. You can do this with the Transpose option. In Figure 2–14, a range of sales data that was copied and then pasted so that the rows and columns are transposed with the store data switched from the rows to the columns and the month data switched from columns to rows. Cell formulas and formats are automatically adjusted for the data's new orientation.

Figure 2–14 Pasted range transposed

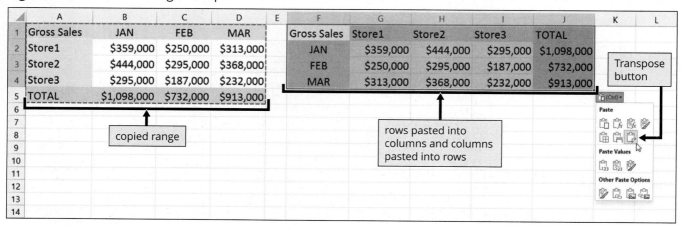

The Paste Transpose option is useful when you want to quickly modify a worksheet's layout without redoing the formulas and formats to reflect the new layout.

Working with Border Styles

Accountants follow specific style rules to distinguish financial figures representing raw data from those figures representing calculated values. Subtotals calculated from a column of values are underlined. A grand total calculated from several subtotals has a double underline. The financial term "the bottom line" refers to this accounting practice of using underlines to indicate the final and most important calculation from a column of figures. You can use borders to apply these accounting practices to workbooks.

To add borders to cells, you use the Borders button in the Font group on the Home tab. You can also use your mouse or stylus to draw borders around a cell or range by clicking the Borders arrow, and then clicking Draw Border or Draw Border Grid.

You will use border styles to format Robert's financial report, adding a single bottom border to the net profit and loss value calculated from all restaurants in the Hook and Line Seafood chain and a double bottom border to the profit margin from all the chain restaurants. The profit margin represents "the bottom line" for Robert's financial analysis.

To add border styles to the restaurants' financial summaries:

1. Click cell **B7** containing the net profit and loss for the company across all restaurants.
2. On the Home tab, in the Font group, click the **Border arrow** to display a list of border style options.
3. Click **Bottom Border**. A single black line is added at the bottom of the cell.
4. Click cell **B8** containing the profit margin for the company.
5. In the Font group, click the **Border arrow**, and then click **Bottom Double Border**. A double black line is added to the bottom of the cell.
6. Select the range **B5:B8** containing the cells you just formatted. You'll copy these border styles to the table of monthly sales for each restaurant.
7. On the Home tab, in the Clipboard group, click the **Format Painter** button.
8. Select the range **D12:P59** to paste the copied formats into the table.
9. Click cell **A10** to deselect the range. Refer to Figure 2–15.

Figure 2–15   Border styles copied and pasted

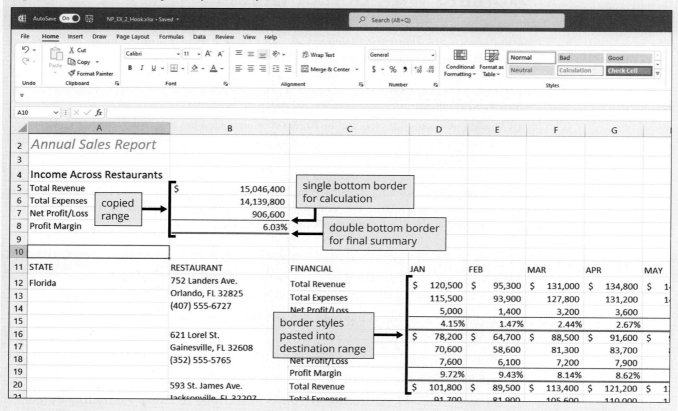

Border styles can be customized by changing their color, thickness, and placement within a range of cells. You can also add different border styles to a range of cells using the More Borders option from the Border button.

Robert wants to add borders around the financial labels, the address of each restaurant and state name. You will use the More Borders option to set a border style for those cells.

To add borders to the financial labels and restaurant names and addresses:

1. Click cell **C14** containing the Net Profit/Loss label.

2. On the Home tab, in the Font group, click the **Border arrow** ⊞ ▾ to display the list of border options, and then click **Bottom Border**. A bottom border is added to that cell.

3. Select the range **A12:C15** containing the labels of the state name, restaurant address, and financial category.

4. In the Font group, click the **Border arrow** ⊞ ▾ to display the list of border options, and then click **More Borders**. The Format Cells dialog box opens to the Border tab, displaying a preview of the border appearance.

5. In the Line Style section, click the **single border line** at the bottom of the first column of border styles to select it, if necessary.

6. In the Border section, click the outside left line, vertical middle line, and outside right line of the border preview to apply the border style to those edges.

7. In the Line Style section, click the **double border line** at the bottom of the second column of border styles to select it.

8. In the Border section, click the bottom edge of the border preview to add a double bottom to the cells. Refer to Figure 2–16.

Figure 2–16   Border tab in the Format Cells dialog box

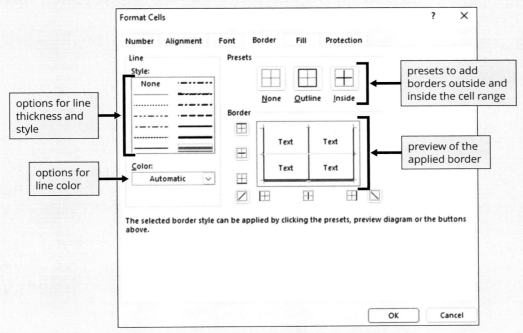

9. Click **OK**. The border styles are applied to the range A12:C15.

> **Trouble?** If you make a mistake, you can erase borders from the worksheet. On the Home tab, in the Font group, click the Border button, and then click Erase Border. The pointer changes to an eraser. Drag the eraser over any border you want to remove.

10. Make sure the range A12:C15 is still selected, and then use the Format Painter to copy the format from the selected range to the range **A16:C59**. The border styles are applied to all the labels in the financial table.

11. Click cell **A1** to deselect the range. Refer to Figure 2–17.

Figure 2–17   Borders applied to the table labels

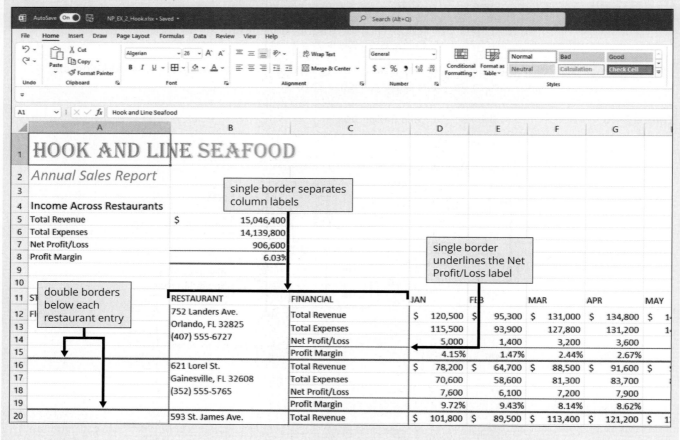

Aligning Cell Contents

By default, text aligns with the left edge of the cell and numbers align with the right edge. Both text and numbers are aligned vertically at the bottom edge of the cell. You might want to change the alignment to make the text and numbers more readable or visually appealing. In general, you should center column titles, left-align other text, and right-align numbers to keep their decimal places lined up within a column. Figure 2–18 describes the buttons located in the Alignment group on the Home tab that you use to set these alignment options.

Figure 2–18   Cell alignment options

Button	Name	Description
	Top Align	Aligns the cell content with the cell's top edge
	Middle Align	Vertically centers the cell content within the cell
	Bottom Align	Aligns the cell content with the cell's bottom edge
	Align Left	Aligns the cell content with the cell's left edge
	Align Center	Horizontally centers the cell content within the cell
	Align Right	Aligns the cell content with the cell's right edge
	Decrease Indent	Decreases the size of the indentation used in the cell
	Increase Indent	Increases the size of the indentation used in the cell
	Orientation	Rotates the cell content to any angle within the cell
	Wrap Text	Forces the cell text to wrap within the cell borders
	Merge & Center	Merges the selected cells into a single cell

The date in the Documentation sheet is right aligned in cell B5 because Excel treats dates and times as numbers. Robert wants you to left-align the date in the Documentation sheet and center some of the column titles in the Sales worksheet.

To left-align the date and center labels:

1. Go to the **Documentation** sheet, and then click cell **B5**.

2. On the Home tab, in the Alignment group, click the **Align Left** button ☰. The date shifts to the left edge of the cell, matching the other entries.

3. Go to the **Sales** worksheet, and then select the range **D11:P11** containing some of the column labels in the financial table.

4. In the Alignment group, click the **Center** button ☰. The column labels are centered horizontally within their cells.

Indenting Cell Text

Text at the left edge of a cell or numbers at the right edge of a cell can appear crowded at the cell's border. You can add more space between a cell's content and border by indenting. Increasing the indent moves cell content away from the border. Decreasing the indent moves cell content closer to the border.

Robert wants the restaurant addresses in column B and the financial categories in column C to be indented two spaces from the left borders of their cells. He also wants that text to be vertically aligned in the middle of their cells.

To indent the content of the addresses and financial categories:

1. In the Sales worksheet, select the range **B12:C59** containing the restaurant addresses and the financial categories.

2. On the Home tab, in the Alignment group, click the **Increase Indent** button ☷ twice. The selected text moves two spaces to the right within their cells.

   Tip To shift cell contents closer to the border, click the Decrease Indent button ☷ in the Alignment group on the Home tab.

3. In the Alignment group, click the **Middle Align** button ☰. The text is vertically centered in the middle of the cells.

4. Click cell **A10** to deselect the range. Refer to Figure 2–19.

Figure 2-19   Cell content aligned in the worksheet

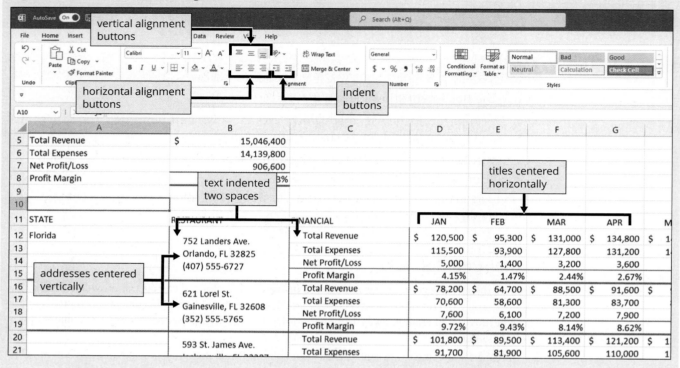

Merging Cells

So far, every cell is in a single row and column. You can also merge, or combine, a range of cells into a single cell. The merged cell can span multiple rows and/or columns. When a range is merged, only the content from the upper-left cell of the range is retained. The upper-left cell also becomes the cell reference for the merged range. For example, if you merge the range A10:C15 into a single cell, its merged cell reference is A10. References to cells below and to the right of the merged cell do not change. Below the merged cell A10, the cell references for the next three cells remain A16, B16, and C16, and the references to the five cells to the right remain D10 through D15. But no cells that have the reference B11 or C12 because those cells are merged into cell A10.

You can align the content of a merged cell by clicking the Merge & Center arrow in the Alignment group on the Home tab, and then using one of the following options:

- **Merge & Center**—merges the range into one cell and horizontally centers the content
- **Merge Across**—merges each row in the selected range across the columns in the range
- **Merge Cells**—merges the range into a single cell but does not horizontally center the cell merged
- **Unmerge Cells**—reverses a merge, returning the merged cell to a range of individual cells

The Sales worksheet already has some merged cells. For example, the address for the first restaurant spans the range B12:B15 but is merged into the single cell B12. Similarly, the address for second restaurant is in the merged cell B16, which includes range B16:B19. The merged cells allow the restaurant addresses to line up with the rows containing their financial information. This makes the connection between the data clearer.

Column A in the table of monthly restaurant financials contains the names of the three states in the report. Robert wants you to merge those cells so that the state name is in a single cell.

To merge each state into a single cell:

1. In the Sales worksheet, select the range **A12:A31** containing the cells for the five Florida restaurants.

2. On the Home tab, in the Alignment group, click the **Merge & Center** button. The five cells are merged into a single cell with the reference A12. "Florida" is centered horizontally in the cell and aligned with the bottom border.

3. Select the range **A32:A43** containing the Georgia restaurants, and then click the **Merge & Center** button. The cells associated with the three Georgia restaurants merge into cell A32. "Georgia" is centered at the bottom of the merged cell.

4. Select the range **A44:A59** containing the Alabama restaurants, and then click the **Merge & Center** button. The cells associated with the four Alabama restaurants are merged and centered into cell A44. Refer to Figure 2–20.

Figure 2–20   Ranges merged into single cells

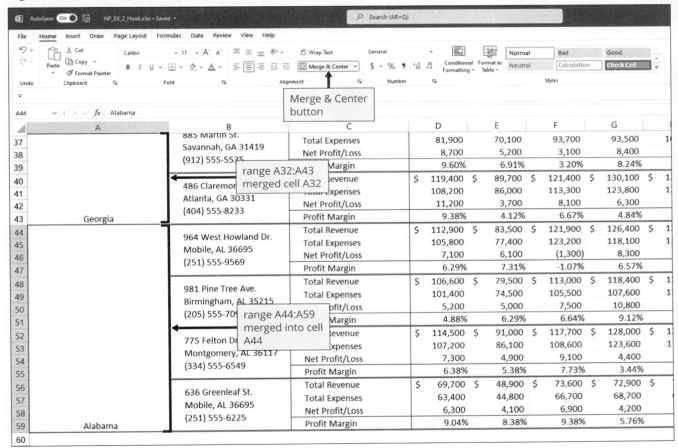

Rotating Text

Text and numbers are displayed horizontally within cells. However, you can rotate cell text to any angle to save space, better connect data, or to visual interest to a worksheet. Merging the state cells better connected the state name with its restaurants. However, the merged cells take up a lot of room. You will remove the extra space by rotating the state names vertically within their cells. You will also increase the font size of the state names.

To rotate and resize the state names in the merged cells:

1. Select the range **A12:A59** containing the three merged cells for the state names of Florida, Georgia, and Alabama.

2. On the Home tab, in the Alignment group, click the **Orientation** button ⬀ ⌄ to display a list of rotation options.

3. Click **Rotate Text Up**. The state names rotate 90 degrees counterclockwise.

4. In the Alignment group, click the **Middle Align** button ≡ to vertically center the rotated state name.

5. Change the font size to **36** points.

6. Click cell **A1** to select it.

7. Zoom the worksheet to **60%** so the entire formatted table is visible. Refer to Figure 2–21.

Figure 2–21   Rotated cell contents

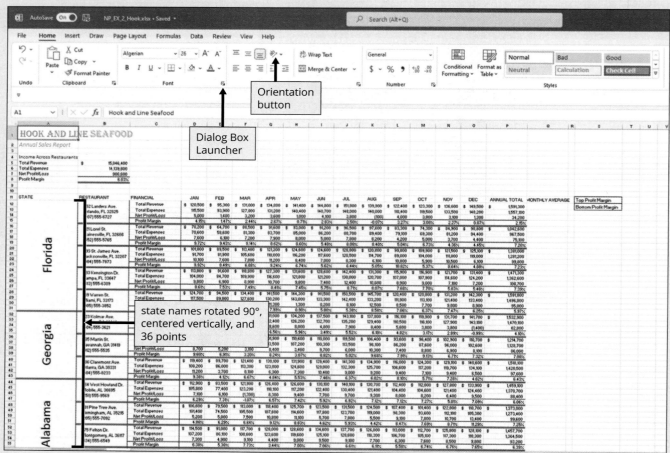

8. Zoom the worksheet back to **140%**.

Exploring the Format Cells Dialog Box

Although many formatting options appear on the ribbon, all these options and more are available in the Format Cells dialog box. The dialog box contains the following six tabs, each focusing on different formatting options:

- **Number**—options for formatting the appearance of numbers, including dates and numbers treated as text such as telephone or Social Security numbers
- **Alignment**—options for how data is aligned within a cell

- **Font**—options for selecting font types, sizes, styles, and other formatting attributes such as underlining and font colors
- **Border**—options for adding and removing cell borders as well as selecting a line style and color
- **Fill**—options for creating and applying background colors and patterns to cells
- **Protection**—options for locking or hiding cells to prevent other users from modifying their contents

You can open the Format Cells dialog box in a variety of ways. You can access it from options on the ribbon, such as when you used the Border tab earlier. You can right-click a selected range and then click Format Cells on the shortcut menu. Or you can click the Dialog Box launcher in the lower-right corner of the Font, Alignment, or Number group on the Home tab.

The final part of the table of monthly restaurants revenue and expenses to be formatted are the column labels in row 11. You will use the Format Cells dialog box to format the labels in white font on a light blue background with a thick bottom border.

To format the revenue and expenses labels with the Format Cells dialog box:

1. Select the range **A11:P11** containing the labels for the table of monthly revenue and expenses for the restaurants.

2. On the Home tab, in the Font group, click the **Dialog Box Launcher** located to the right of the group name (refer to Figure 2–21). The Format Cells dialog box opens with the Font tab displayed.

3. Click the **Color** box to display the available colors, and then click the **White, Background 1** theme color (the first color in the first row).

4. In the Font style list, click **Bold**. Refer to Figure 2–22.

Figure 2–22   Font tab in the Format Cells dialog box

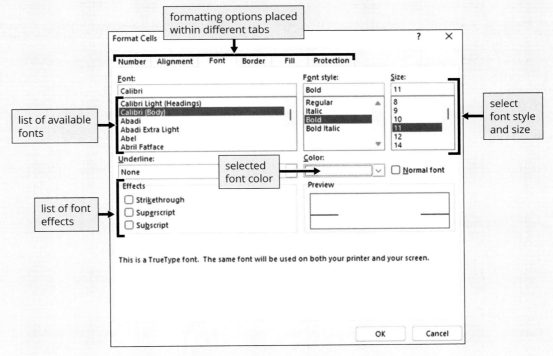

5. Click the **Fill** tab to display background color options.

6. In the Background Color section, click the **Blue, Accent 1** theme color (the fifth color in the first row). The background is set to blue, as previewed in the Sample box.

7. Click the **Border** tab, and then in the Style box, click the **Thick** line (the sixth line in the second column).

8. In the Border section, click the bottom border of the border preview. The thick line style is set for the bottom border.

9. Click **OK** to apply the formatting choices you made in the dialog box to the range A11:P11.

10. Click cell **A1**. Refer to Figure 2–23.

Figure 2–23   Column labels formatted in the worksheet

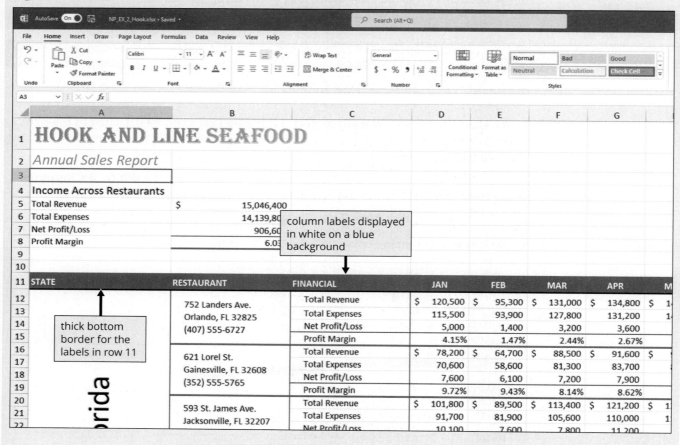

The contents of the formatted Sales worksheet are clearer to read and interpret.

Proskills

Written Communication: Formatting Workbooks for Readability and Appeal

Designing a workbook requires the same care as designing any written document or report. A well-formatted workbook provides a structure and establishes a sense of professionalism with readers. You can improve the readability of your worksheets with the following guidelines:

- **Clearly identify each worksheet's purpose.** Include column or row titles and a descriptive sheet name.
- **Include only one or two topics on each worksheet.** Do not crowd individual worksheets with too much information. Place extra topics on separate sheets. Readers should be able to interpret each worksheet with minimal horizontal and vertical scrolling.
- **Organize worksheets in order of importance.** Place worksheets summarizing findings near the front of the workbook. Place worksheets with detailed and involved analysis near the end as an appendix.
- **Use consistent formatting throughout the workbook.** If negative values appear in red in one worksheet, format them in the same way in all sheets. Also, be consistent in the use of thousands separators, decimal places, and percentages.
- **Pay attention to the format of the printed workbook.** Make sure printouts are legible with informative headers and footers. Check that the printed content is scaled correctly to the page size and that page breaks divide the information into logical sections.

Be aware that much formatting can be intrusive, overwhelming data and making the document less readable. Remember that the goal of formatting is not to make a "pretty workbook" but to accentuate important trends and relationships in the data. A well-formatted workbook should seamlessly convey information to the reader. If the reader is thinking about how the workbook looks, the reader is not thinking about the data.

You have made great progress in formatting Robert's sales report. You will continue this process in the next part of this module. You will apply cell styles and workbook themes to the workbook. You will also use conditional formatting to highlight important results from Robert's financial analysis. Finally, you will explore formatting print versions of workbooks.

Part 2.1 Quick Check

1. What is the difference between a serif font and a sans serif font?

2. What is the difference between a theme color and a standard color?

3. If you need to display a graphic image with your printed workbook, explain why you should not insert the graphic as a background image on the worksheet.

4. What is the General format?

5. How does the Accounting format differ from the Currency format?

6. How do the Short Date format and the Long Date format display dates?

7. Describe three ways of copying a format from one range to another.

8. The range C5:E7 is merged into a single cell. What is the cell reference of the merged cell? What are the cell references to the cells directly below and directly to the right of the merged cell?

Part 2.2 Visual Overview:
Designing a Printed Worksheet

The Page Layout tab has options for setting how the worksheet will print.

Print titles are rows and/or columns printed on every page. In this page columns A through C are print titles.

Ranges that are not printed are marked in gray.

The **print area** is the cell range marked for printing.

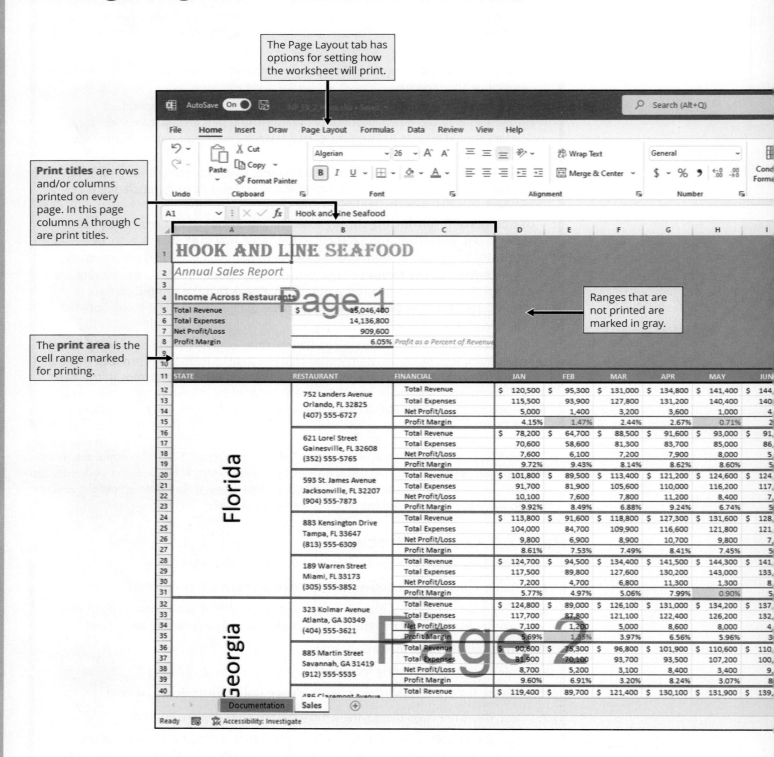

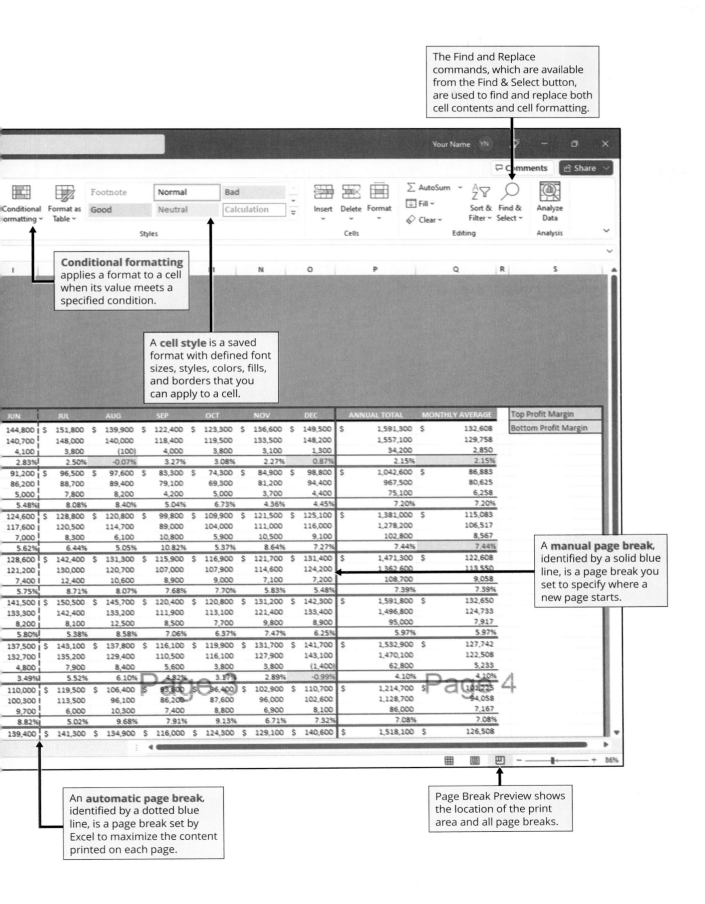

The Find and Replace commands, which are available from the Find & Select button, are used to find and replace both cell contents and cell formatting.

Conditional formatting applies a format to a cell when its value meets a specified condition.

A **cell style** is a saved format with defined font sizes, styles, colors, fills, and borders that you can apply to a cell.

A **manual page break**, identified by a solid blue line, is a page break you set to specify where a new page starts.

An **automatic page break**, identified by a dotted blue line, is a page break set by Excel to maximize the content printed on each page.

Page Break Preview shows the location of the print area and all page breaks.

Applying Cell Styles

Cells throughout a workbook often store the same type of data. For example, cells in each worksheet might contain the same heading and subheading, or several worksheets might contain related tables of financial figures. A good design practice is to apply a common format to cells that contain the same type of data.

One way to ensure that similar data is displayed with a consistent format is with cell styles. A cell style is a collection of formatting options—such as a specified font, font size, font styles, font color, fill color, and borders—that you can apply to a cell or cell range. Excel has a library of built-in cell styles that you can use to format workbooks. You can also create custom styles for each workbook. When you apply a cell style, any formatting that is part of the cell style override any formatting previously applied to that range.

All cell styles are listed in the Cell Styles gallery, located in the Styles group on the Home tab. The Cell Styles gallery also includes the Accounting, Comma, and Percent number format styles that you applied to the Sales worksheet using buttons in the Number group on the Home tab.

Reference

Applying a Cell Style

- Select the cell or range you want to apply a cell style to.
- On the Home tab, in the Styles group, click the Cell Styles button.
- Point to each cell style in the Cell Styles gallery for a Live Preview of that cell style on the selected cell or range.
- Click the cell style you want to apply to the selected cell or range.

Robert asks you to add more color and interest to the Sales worksheet. You will use cell styles to format the labels at the top of the worksheet.

To apply cell styles to the labels:

1. If you took a break after the previous part, make sure the NP_EX_2_Hook.xlsx workbook is open and the Sales worksheet is active.
2. Select the range **A4:B4** containing the title at the top of the worksheet.
3. On the Home tab, in the Styles group, click the **Cell Styles** button to expand the gallery of available cell styles.
4. In the Titles and Headings section, point to the **Heading 1** style. Live Preview shows a preview of the style applied to the selected cells. Refer to Figure 2–24.

Figure 2–24   Cell Styles gallery

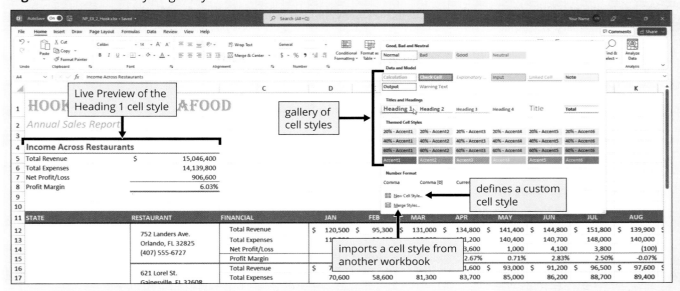

5. Click the **Heading 1** style to apply the style to the range A4:B4.

6. Select the range **A5:A8** containing the financial category labels.

7. In the Styles group, click the **Cell Styles** button, and then click the **20% - Accent 3** style in the Cell Styles gallery.

8. In cell **C8**, enter **Profit as a Percent of Revenue** to add an explanatory note about the meaning of profit margin.

9. Click cell **C8** to select it, click the **Cell Styles** button to open the Cell Styles gallery, and then in the Data and Model section, click the **Explanatory** style. The new note is formatted.

10. Click cell **A1**. Refer to Figure 2–25.

Figure 2–25   Worksheet formatted with cell styles

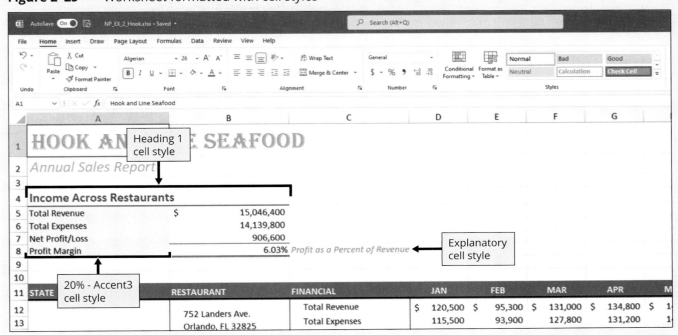

All cells start out formatted with the Normal cell style. To restore cells with other added formatting to the Normal style, select the cell or range, and then apply the Normal cell style from the Cell Styles gallery.

> **Tip** The Cell Style gallery includes Comma, Currency, and Percent styles. Be aware that this Currency style matches the Accounting format in the Number format box in the Numbers group on the Home tab!

Creating a Custom Cell Style

When you create a custom cell style, you define the font, font size, font styles, alignment, number format, borders, and fill you want to include in that style. You can base a new cell style on an existing style or on formatting already applied to a cell or range. Custom cell styles appear in the Cell Styles gallery so you can apply them to any range in the workbook.

Robert wants you to create a custom style for footnotes. The Footnote style will display cell text in a 10-point gray Georgia font.

To create a custom cell style for footnotes:

1. In cell **A61**, enter **Financial figures rounded to nearest hundred dollars.** as the footnote text.

2. Right-click cell **A61**, and then click **Format Cells** on the shortcut menu. The Format Cells dialog box opens.

3. Click the **Font** tab, click **Georgia** in the Font box, and then click **10** in the Size box.

4. Click the **Color** box, and then click the **White, Background 1, Darker 50%** theme color (the last color in the first column).

5. Click **OK** to close the Format Cells dialog box. Cell A61 is still selected.

6. On the Home tab, in the Styles group, click the **Cell Styles** button, and then click **New Cell Style**. The Style dialog box opens. From this dialog box, you name the custom style and select which formatting of the selected cell to include in the custom style.

7. In the Style name box, type **Footnote** as the name for the custom style.

8. In the Style includes section, deselect all of the checkboxes except the Font checkbox. Refer to Figure 2–26.

Figure 2–26   Style dialog box

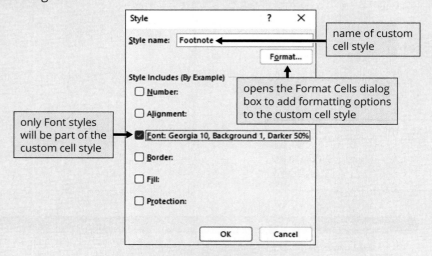

9. Click **OK**. The new style is created and added to the Cell Style gallery.

10. In the Styles group, click the **Cell Styles** button to display the Cell Style gallery, and verify that the Footnote cell style appears in the Custom section at the top of the gallery.

11. With cell A61 still selected, click **Footnote** to apply the custom style to the cell.

You can apply custom cell styles to any cell in the workbook. Robert wants you to add a footnote for the Documentation sheet and format it with the new Footnote style.

To apply the Footnote cell style in the Documentation sheet:

1. Go to the **Documentation** sheet.

2. In cell **A10**, enter **Report presented at the sales conference in Orlando, FL.** as the new footnote text.

3. Click cell **A10**, and then on the Home tab, in the Styles group, click the **Cell Styles** button. The Cell Styles gallery opens and includes the custom Footnote cell style.

4. In the Custom section, click **Footnote**. The text you just entered is formatted in the Footnote cell style. Refer to Figure 2-27.

Figure 2-27   Custom cell style applied to the worksheet

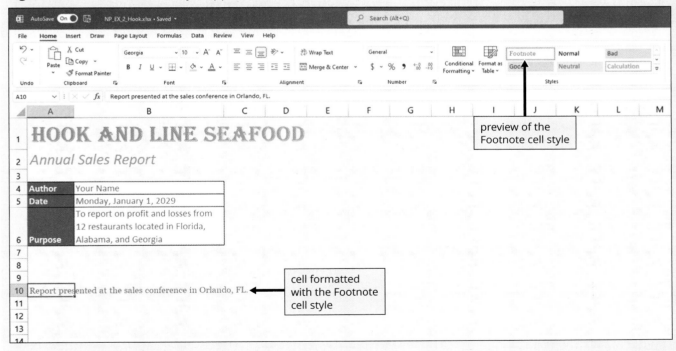

To change the formatting included in a custom cell style, right-click the style's name in the Cell Styles gallery and then click Modify on the shortcut menu. In the Style dialog box, enter the new formatting options. Any cells in the workbook formatted with that style automatically update to reflect the latest style.

Merging Custom Cell Styles

Custom cell styles are part of the workbook in which they are created. To use a custom cell style in another workbook, it must be copied from one workbook to another. Copying cells styles is useful for companies and organizations that need a consistent format in their workbooks and reports. To copy custom cell styles from one workbook to another, do the following:

1. Open the workbook containing the custom cell styles (the source workbook) and the workbook that will receive the custom cell style (the destination workbook).

2. In the destination workbook, open the Cell Styles gallery, and then click Merge Styles at the bottom of the gallery.

3. In the Merge Styles dialog box, select the source workbook containing the custom cell styles, and then click OK.

The custom cell styles from the source workbook are then copied into the destination workbook. Note that if the custom cell style in the source workbook is changed, that change will not appear in the destination workbook until the merge process is repeated.

Working with Themes

Another way to make multiple changes to the formats used in a workbook is with themes. Recall that a theme is a predefined set of formats that are applied throughout a workbook to give it a consistent, professional look.

Applying a Theme

When you change a workbook's theme, all the formats and cell styles based on that theme change to reflect the new theme's formats. Formats based on standard fonts and colors remain unchanged.

Many of the formatted choices applied to Robert's workbook use theme fonts and colors. Robert wants you to change to workbook's theme.

To change the workbook's theme:

1. Go to the **Sales** worksheet, and then click cell **A1**.

2. On the ribbon, click the **Page Layout** tab, and then in the Themes group, click the **Themes** button. The Themes gallery opens.

3. Point to the **Retrospect** theme. Live Preview shows the impact of that theme on the workbook's appearance. Refer to Figure 2–28.

Figure 2–28   Live Preview of the Retrospect theme

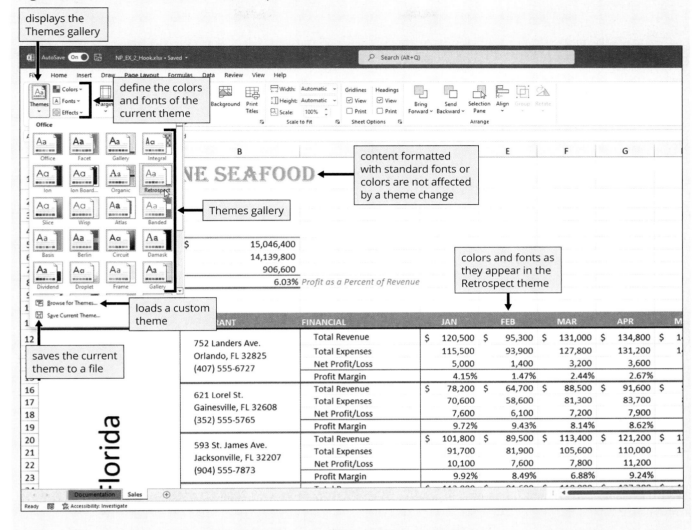

4. Click **Retrospect** to apply that theme to the workbook.

   Trouble? If Retrospect does not appear in the gallery, choose a different theme to apply to the workbook. Note that the colors and fonts in your workbook might differ from those in the figures.

Changing the theme made a significant difference in the worksheet's appearance. The most obvious changes to the worksheet are the fill colors and the fonts. The font and text colors for the company name in cell A1 did not change because they use standard fonts and colors. You can view the fonts and colors used by the Retrospect theme in the Format Cells dialog box.

To view the theme font and colors for the current theme:

1. Right-click cell **A11**, and then click **Format Cells** on the shortcut menu. The Format Cells dialog box opens.

2. Click the **Font** tab, if necessary. The first two fonts in the font list are always the theme fonts. In this case, the fonts used by the Retrospect theme are Calibri Light for headings and Calibri for body—the same fonts that the Office theme uses.

3. Click the **Fill** tab. The theme colors at the top of the color gallery range from ice blue to orange to green. A fill color that was blue in the Office theme is orange in the Retrospect theme.

   Trouble? If you applied a theme other than Retrospect for your workbook, the theme fonts and colors might be different than described.

4. Click **Cancel** to close the Format Cells dialog box without making any changes.

If you do not like the color or fonts associated with a particular theme you can change them using the tools in the Themes group on the Page Layout tab.

Setting Theme Colors and Fonts

Businesses often design custom themes for their workbooks that reflect the color and fonts used in the company's logo and business mailings. To change theme colors, click the Colors button in the Themes group on the Page Layout tab, and then select one of the color palettes. To create a color palette not in the predefined list, click Customize Colors to open the Create New Theme Colors dialog box. In this dialog box, you can select colors for the text and background and the six accent colors used by that theme and then save the custom colors with a name you choose.

To change the theme fonts, click the Fonts button in the Themes group on the Page Layout tab, and then select one of the font themes for heading and body text. To create your own theme fonts, click Customize Fonts to open the Create New Theme Fonts dialog box. In this dialog box, select fonts for heading and body text, and then save the custom fonts with a new name.

Saving a Theme

Once you have changed a theme's colors or fonts, you can save your custom theme as its own theme file. To do this, click the Themes button in the Themes group on the Page Layout tab, and then click Save Current Theme. Theme files are stored in the Office Theme folder on your computer and are available to all Office applications, including Excel, Word, and PowerPoint. You can choose a different location for a theme file, such as a network folder that is accessible to your colleagues.

Finding and Replacing Text and Formats

You can use Find and Replace to make global changes to formats that do not involve cell styles or themes. Find and Replace searches through the current cell selection, worksheet, or workbook, looking for content that matches a set of search criteria. The criteria can be based on text, numbers, formats, or some combination of all three. When cells are found matching the search criteria, their contents or formats can be replaced with new content or formats. You can review each match found one at a time, deciding whether to replace its content or formats. You can also highlight all matches found in the workbook. Or you can replace all matches at once without reviewing them.

Robert wants you to replace all street title abbreviations (such as St. or Ave.) in the restaurant addresses with the full street titles (such as Street or Avenue). You'll use Find and Replace to make these changes.

To find and replace the street title abbreviations:

1. On the ribbon, click the **Home** tab. In the Editing group, click the **Find & Select** button, and then click **Replace** (or press **CTRL+H**). The Find and Replace dialog box opens.

2. In the Find what box, type **St.** as the text to locate.

3. Press **TAB** to move the insertion point to the Replace with box, and then type **Street** as the new text.

4. Click the **Options** button, if necessary, to expand the list of find and replace options. Refer to Figure 2–29.

Figure 2–29   Find and Replace dialog box

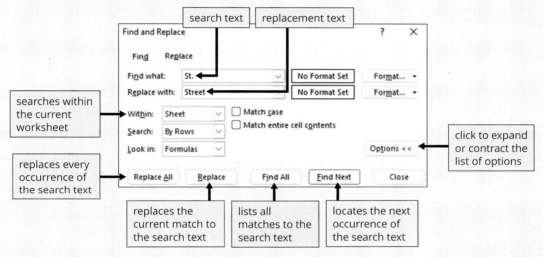

5. Click **Find Next** to locate the next occurrence of "St." in the Sales worksheet. Cell B16 containing the address "621 Lorel St." is selected.

> **Key Step** Always check the matched text so that you do not inadvertently replace text that should not be replaced.

6. Click **Replace** to replace "St." with "Street" in cell B16. Cell B20, containing the address "593 St. James Ave." is selected as the next matching cell. You do not want to replace "St." in this address because it is not an abbreviation for Street.

7. Click **Find Next**. Cell B28 containing the address "189 Warren St." is selected.

8. Click **Replace** to change the address to 189 Warren Street.

9. Click **Replace** twice to change the remaining two occurrences of "St." with "Street" in the range B36:B56. When you have finished, the Find and Replace dialog box remains open.

Rather than reviewing each possible replacement, you can use the Replace All button in the Find and Replace dialog box to make all the replacements at once. You should do this only if you are sure there is no chance for a replacement error. You will use the Replace All button to change all instances of "Ave." in the store addresses with "Avenue" and all instances of "Dr." with "Drive."

To replace all matches of "Ave." and "Dr.":

1. In the Find and Replace dialog box, type **Ave.** in the Find what box, and then type **Avenue** in the Replace with box.

2. Click **Replace All**. A dialog box appears, indicating that five matches were replaced.

3. Click **OK** to return to the Find and Replace dialog box.

   > **Tip** By default, searches do not differentiate between uppercase and lowercase letters. To search using uppercase and lowercase letters, select the Match Case check box.

4. Type **Dr.** in the Find what box, and then type **Drive** in the Replace with box.

5. Click **Replace All**. A dialog box appears, indicating that three replacements were made.

6. Click **OK** to return to the Find and Replace dialog box.

You can also use Find and Replace to replace formatting. Robert want you to change the Orange Accent 1 theme fill color to a standard light blue color to match the font color of the company title and subheading. You will use Find and Replace to ensure to change all instances of the formatting.

To find and replace the fill color throughout the workbook:

1. In the Find and Replace dialog box, delete the search text from the Find what and Replace with box, leaving those two boxes empty. By not specifying a text string, Find and Replace will check every cell regardless of its content.

2. Click **Format** in the Find what row. The Find Format dialog box, similar to the Format Cells dialog box, opens.

3. Click the **Fill** tab, and then click the **Orange, Accent 1** theme color (the fifth color in the first row).

4. Click **OK** to return to the Find and Replace dialog box.

5. Click **Format** in the Replace with row. The Find Format dialog box opens.

6. On the Fill tab, click the **Light Blue** standard color (the seventh color in the non-theme colors) and then click **OK**.

7. Click the Within box, and then click **Workbook** to search throughout the entire workbook. Refer to Figure 2–30.

Figure 2–30   Format replacement

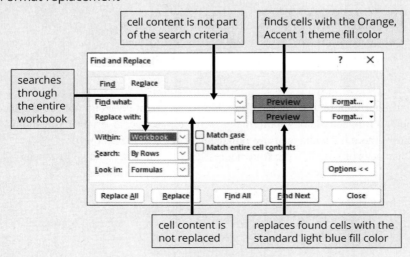

8. Click **Replace All**. A dialog box indicates that 19 cells were reformatted. The column labels in the Sales worksheet are displayed with the light blue fill color.

9. Click **OK** to return to the Find and Replace dialog box, and then **Close** to return to the worksheet.

10. Go the **Documentation** sheet and verify that the labels in A4:A6 are also displayed with a light blue fill.

A good practice is to clear find-and-replace formats from the Find and Replace dialog box after you are done so they won't affect any future searches and replacements. You will do this now.

To clear the find and replace options:

1. On the Home tab, in the Editing group, click the **Find & Select** button, and then click **Replace**. The Find and Replace dialog box opens.

2. In the Find what row, click the **Format arrow**, and then click **Clear Find Format**. The search format is removed.

3. In the Replace with row, click the **Format arrow**, and then click **Clear Replace Format**. The replacement format is also removed.

4. Click **Close**. The Find and Replace dialog box closes.

When finding and replacing a format, any formatting options you choose in the Find Format dialog box will be part of the search criteria, but formatting within a selected cell that is not part of that search criteria (such a font size of border style) will not be affected.

Proskills

Using Wildcards with Find and Replace

You can create flexible searches by adding wildcards to your search criteria. A **wildcard** is a symbol that represents any character or combination of characters. Two useful wildcards are the question mark (?) character representing any single character and the asterisk character (*) representing any string of characters.

For example, the search string St?ck would match Stack, Stick, Stock, Stuck, or any text string with a single character between the "St" and "ck" characters. The text string St*k would match Stock, Streak, Stack, or any text string that begins with "St" and ends with "k."

Calculating Averages

The monthly sales table includes the annual overall total for each restaurant in the Hook and Line Seafood chain. Robert is aware that monthly sales vary throughout the year, but he wants to know what a typical month looks like for each restaurant. You'll calculate each restaurant's monthly average revenue, expenses, and net profit or loss.

The AVERAGE function calculates the average value from a collection of numbers. Its syntax is

```
AVERAGE(number1, [number2], [number3],...)
```

where *number1*, *number2*, *number3*, and so forth are either numbers or references to ranges containing numbers. For example, the following formula calculates the average of the numbers in the ranges B2:B10 and D2:D10:

```
=AVERAGE(B2:B10, D2:D10)
```

Only numeric values in the ranges are included in the calculations. Nonnumeric content is ignored.

You will use the AVERAGE function to calculate the monthly average revenue, expenses, and net profit/loss for each restaurant and then calculate the profit margin for a typical month.

To calculate the monthly financial averages for the restaurants:

1. Go to the **Sales** worksheet.

2. In cell **Q11**, enter **MONTHLY AVERAGE** as the column title. The cell is automatically formatted to match the adjacent cell P11.

3. In cell **Q12**, type **= AVERAGE(** to begin the function, select the range **D12:O12** as the range to average, type **)** to close the function arguments, and then press **ENTER**. The average monthly revenue for the first restaurant is $132,608.

   > **Trouble?** If cell Q12 returns $244,815, you included cell P12 in the range reference. You do not want to include the annual total in the average calculation. Edit the function in cell Q11 so that the range reference is D12:O12.

4. In cell **Q13**, enter the formula **= AVERAGE(D13:O13)** to calculate the average monthly expenses for the first restaurant, and then press **ENTER**. The restaurant's average monthly expenses are 129,758 (dollars).

5. In cell **Q14**, enter the formula **= Q12 – Q13** to subtract the first restaurant's average monthly expenses from its average monthly revenue, and then press **ENTER**. The first restaurant's expected monthly profit is $2,850.

6. In cell **Q15**, enter the formula **= Q14/Q12** to divide the restaurant's monthly profits by its monthly revenue, and press **ENTER**. The first restaurant's typical monthly profit margin is 2.15%.

   Excel formatted the calculations but didn't include the border styles and didn't format the net profit/loss value in cell Q13 in the Accounting format.

7. Use the Format Painter to copy the formats from the range **P11:P15** to the range **Q11:Q15**. The formats in the two columns should now match.

8. Copy the range **Q12:Q15** containing the monthly averages for the first restaurant and paste them to the range **Q16:Q59**. The monthly averages for the remaining restaurants appear in column Q.

   > **Trouble?** If the column label was duplicated, you copied the range Q11:Q15. Press CTRL+Z to under the paste. Then redo Step 8, being sure to copy the range Q12:Q15 without the column label.

9. Click cell **Q12** to deselect the pasted range. Refer to Figure 2–31.

Figure 2–31   Monthly averages across restaurants

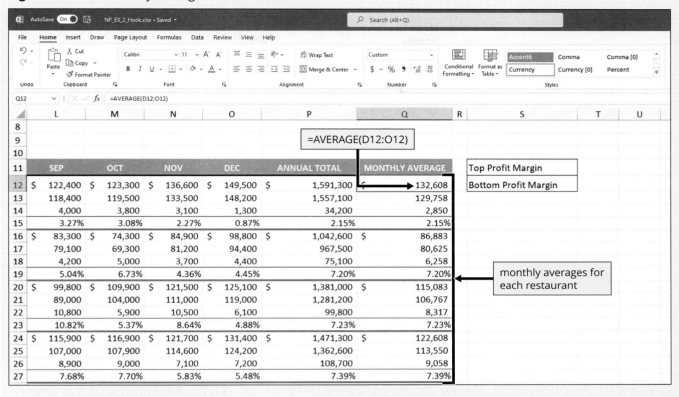

The monthly averages indicate that a typical restaurant in the Hook and Line Seafood chain can expect monthly profit margins in the range of 2% to 7% and higher. Sometimes restaurants in smaller markets can outperform restaurants in larger markets in terms of their profit margins. However, large revenues are no guarantee of financial success if they are accompanied by large expenses.

Highlighting Data with Conditional Formats

A conditional format is applied to a cell based on the cell's content. As the cell's content changes, the format of the cell might change in response. Conditional formats draw attention to important or unusual results, such as a sales total that exceeds a specified goal or an unusually large expense from a company's balance sheet.

The four types of conditional formats in Excel are data bars, highlighting, color scales, and icon sets. In this module, you will use conditional formats to highlight cells based on their content.

Reference

Highlighting Cells with Conditional Formats

- Select the range in which you want to highlight cells.
- On the Home tab, in the Styles group, click the Conditional Formatting button, point to Highlight Cells Rules or Top/Bottom Rules, and then click the appropriate rule.
- Select the appropriate options in the dialog box.
- Click OK.

Figure 2–32 describes the seven ways a conditional format can highlight a cell based on content.

Figure 2–32   Conditional Format highlighting rules

Rule	Highlights Cell Values
Greater Than	Greater than a specified number
Less Than	Less than a specified number
Between	Between two specified numbers
Equal To	Equal to a specified number
Text that Contains	That contain specified text
A Date Occurring	That contain a specified date
Duplicate Values	That contain duplicate or unique values

Robert wants to highlight months in which a restaurant's profit margin dropped below 2%. You will create a conditional format that displays profit margins below 2% in dark red text on a light red background.

To create a conditional format to highlight profit margins below 2%:

1. In the Sales worksheet, select the range **D15:O15** containing the monthly profit margins from January to December for the Orlando location.

2. On the Home tab, in the Styles group, click the **Conditional Formatting** button, and then point to **Highlight Cells Rules**. A list of highlighting options opens.

3. Click **Less Than**. The Less Than dialog box opens.

4. Type **2%** in the left box, and then press **TAB**. The right box lists the formatting options you can apply to cells whose value is less than 2%.

5. Verify that **Light Red Fill with Dark Red Text**, the first formatting option in the list, is selected. Refer to Figure 2–33.

Figure 2–33   Less than dialog box

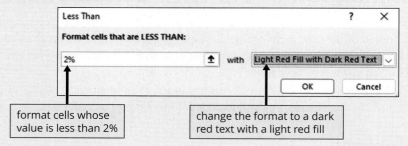

format cells whose value is less than 2%

change the format to a dark red text with a light red fill

Tip To create your own format for highlighting cells, select Custom Format in the formats list and then choose formatting options in the Format Cells dialog box.

6. Click **OK** to apply the conditional format.

7. Click cell **O9** to deselect the range. Refer to Figure 2–34.

Figure 2–34   Conditional format highlighting cells less than 2%

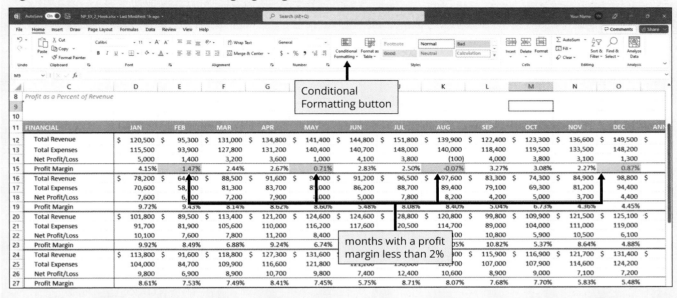

With the conditional format, Robert can quickly locate the months when the Orlando restaurant reported a profit margin of less than 2%: cell E15 (February), cell H15 (May), cell K15 (August), and cell O15 (December).

Like other formats, a conditional format can be copied and pasted from one cell range to another. You'll copy the conditional format you just defined and paste it into the range containing the monthly profit margins of the other 11 restaurants.

To copy and paste the Less than conditional format:

1. Select the range **D12:O15** containing the formats applied to the financial figures for the Orlando restaurant (including the conditional formats in row 15).

2. On the Home tab, in the Clipboard group, click the **Format Painter** button.

3. Select the range **D16:O59** containing the monthly financial data for the other restaurants.

4. Click cell **A1** to deselect the range, and then scroll down the worksheet to view the other months that have profit margins of below 2%. Refer to Figure 2–35.

Figure 2-35   Low monthly profit margins for other restaurants highlighted

	B	C	D	E	F	G	H	I	J
28	189 Warren Street Miami, FL 33173 (305) 555-3852	Total Revenue	$ 124,700	$ 94,500	$ 134,400	$ 141,500	$ 144,300	$ 141,500	$ 150,50
29		Total Expenses	117,500	89,800	127,600	130,200	143,000	133,300	142,40
30		Net Profit/Loss	7,200	4,700	6,800	11,300	1,300	8,200	8,10
31		Profit Margin	5.77%	4.97%	5.06%	7.99%	0.90%	5.80%	5.38
32	323 Kolmar Avenue Atlanta, GA 30349 (404) 555-3621	Total Revenue	$ 124,800	$ 89,000	$ 126,100	$ 131,000	$ 134,200	$ 137,500	$ 143,10
33		Total Expenses	117,700	87,800	121,100	122,400	126,200	132,700	135,20
34		Net Profit/Loss	7,100	1,200	5,000	8,600	8,000	4,800	7,90
35		Profit Margin	5.69%	1.35%	3.97%	6.56%	5.96%	3.49%	5.52
36	885 Martin Street Savannah, GA 31419 (912) 555-5535	Total Revenue	$ 90,600	$ 75,300	$ 96,800	$ 101,900	$ 110,600	$ 110,000	$ 119,50
37		Total Expenses	81,900	70,100	93,700	93,500	107,200	100,300	113,50
38			8,700	5,200	3,100	8,400	3,400	9,700	6,00
39			9.60%	6.91%	3.20%	8.24%	3.07%	8.82%	5.02
40	486 Claremont Avenue Atlanta, GA 30331 (404) 555-8233		$ 119,400	$ 89,700	$ 121,400	$ 130,100	$ 131,900	$ 139,400	$ 141,30
41		Total Expenses	108,200	86,000	113,300	123,800	124,600	129,000	132,30
42		Net Profit/Loss	11,200	3,700	8,100	6,300	7,300	10,400	9,00
43		Profit Margin	9.38%	4.12%	6.67%	4.84%	5.53%	7.46%	6.37
44	964 West Howland Drive Mobile, AL 36695 (251) 555-9569	Total Revenue	$ 112,900	$ 83,500	$ 121,900	$ 126,400	$ 126,600	$ 130,100	$ 140,10
45		Total Expenses	105,800	77,400	123,200	118,100	117,200	122,400	130,40
46		Net Profit/Loss	7,100	6,100	(1,300)	8,300	9,400	7,700	9,70
47		Profit Margin	6.29%	7.31%	-1.07%	6.57%	7.42%	5.92%	6.92
48	981 Pine Tree Avenue Birmingham, AL 35215 (205) 555-7092	Total Revenue	$ 106,600	$ 79,500	$ 113,000	$ 118,400	$ 125,700	$ 123,500	$ 131,50
49		Total Expenses	101,400	74,500	105,500	107,600	114,600	117,800	123,70
50		Net Profit/Loss	5,200	5,000	7,500	10,800	11,100	5,700	7,80
51		Profit Margin	4.88%	6.29%	6.64%	9.12%	8.83%	4.62%	5.93

> **Trouble?** If you make a mistake applying the formats with the Format Painter button, click the Undo button in the Undo group on the Home tab (or press CTRL+Z) to undo your actions and repeat Steps 1 through 4.

The conditional format reveals to Robert that the only months in which profit margins dropped below 2% occurred with the May sales of the Miami restaurant (cell H31), the February and December sales of the Atlanta restaurant (cells E35 and O35), the March sales of the first Mobile restaurant (cell F47), and the August sales of the second Mobile restaurant cell (K59).

Conditional formats highlight that four of the nine monthly profit margins that dropped below 2% occurred in the Orlando restaurant. This result could indicate problems with management or the economic challenges of the Orlando location.

Highlighting Cells with a Top/Bottom Rule

A top/bottom rule formats cells with the highest or lowest numbers in the selected range. Robert wants you to use this rule to highlight the restaurants with the best three average profit margins. You will create this conditional format.

To highlight the restaurants the best average profit margins by a top/bottom rule:

1. Select the nonadjacent range **Q15,Q19,Q23,Q27,Q31,Q35,Q39,Q43,Q47,Q51,Q55,Q59** containing the average monthly profit margins for the restaurants.

2. On the Home tab, in the Styles group, click the **Conditional Formatting** button, click **Top/Bottom Rules**, and then click **Top 10 Items**. the Top 10 Items dialog box opens.

3. In the left box from 10 to **3**, and then press **TAB**.

4. In the right box, select **Green Fill with Dark Green Text**. Refer to Figure 2–36.

Figure 2–36   Top 10 Items dialog box

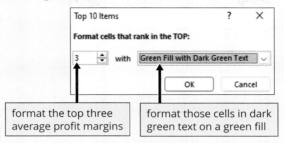

5. Click **OK**. The profit margins for the top three restaurants are displayed in a dark green text on a green file.

The restaurants with the top three average profit margins are Jacksonville with a profit margin of 7.23% (cell Q23), Tampa with a profit margin of 7.39% (cell Q27), and Birmingham with a profit margin of 7.25% (cell Q51).

Editing a Conditional Format

You can modify a conditional format by changing what is being highlighted or the format applied to those cells. With only 12 restaurants, Robert wants to highlight only the top restaurant in the chain. You'll use the Manage Rules command to edit the conditional format.

To edit the top conditional format rule:

1. Make sure the nonadjacent range **Q15,Q19,Q23,Q27,Q31,Q35,Q39,Q43,Q47,Q51,Q55,Q59** containing the profit margins for each restaurant is still selected.

2. On the Home tab, in the Styles group, click the **Conditional Formatting** button, and then click **Manage Rules**. The Conditional Formatting Rules Manager dialog box opens, listing all the conditional formats applied to the current selection. Refer to Figure 2–37.

Figure 2–37   Conditional Formatting Rule Manager dialog box

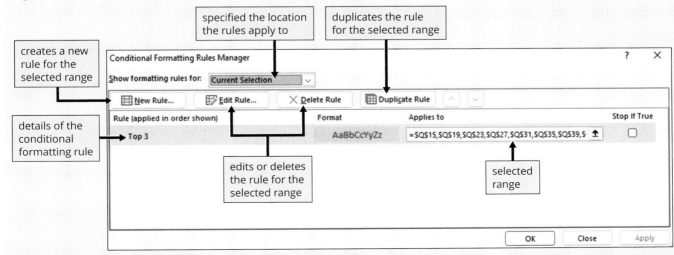

3. Click **Edit Rule** to edit the rule selected in the dialog box. The Edit Formatting Rule dialog box opens.

4. In the Edit the Rule Description section, change the value in the middle box from 3 to **1** so that only the top profit margin is highlighted. Refer to Figure 2–38.

Figure 2–38   Edit Formatting Rule dialog box

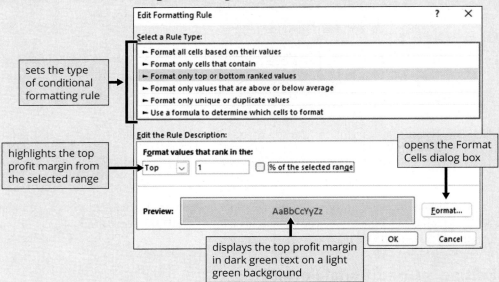

5. Click **OK** in each dialog box to return to the worksheet.

The only cell highlighted in green is cell Q27, containing the 7.39% monthly average profit margin for the Tampa location, which is the restaurant with the best in the chain.

A cell range can contain multiple conditional formats. You'll add another rule to the selected cells to highlight the restaurant with the lowest average profit margin in the chain.

To highlight the restaurant with the lowest profit margin:

1. Make sure the nonadjacent range **Q15,O19,Q23,Q27,Q31,Q35,Q39,Q43,Q47,Q51,Q55,Q59** is still selected.

2. On the Home tab, in the Styles group, click the **Conditional Formatting** button, click **Top/Bottom Rules**, and then click **Bottom 10 Items**. The Bottom 10 Items dialog box opens.

3. In the left box, change the value from 10 to **1**.

4. In the right box, verify that **Light Red Fill with Dark Red Text** is selected as the format.

5. Click **OK**.

Cell Q15 is highlighted with red, indicating that the Orlando restaurant has the lowest average profit margin of 2.15%. This result is not surprising given the low monthly profit margins highlighted by the conditional format you added earlier.

Insight

Conditional Formatting with Cell References

Conditional formats can be based on cell references. For example, you can use a conditional format to highlight all cells whose value is greater than the value stored in cell B10 by doing the following:

1. Select the range to be formatted.
2. On the Home tab, in the Styles group, click the Conditional Formatting button, click Highlight Cells Rules, and then click Greater Than.
3. In the Greater Than dialog box, enter = $B$10 in the Format cells that are GREATER THAN box.
4. Click OK.

All cells in the selected range that are greater than the value in cell B10 are highlighted. If the value in cell B10 changes, the cells highlighted with the conditional format will also change. The $ symbol in the cell reference locks the reference so that the formula always points to cell B10 for every cell in the selected range. If the formula was entered as = B10, the cell reference would change for every cell.

A conditional format is based on the current cell values. If any cell value changes, the highlighted cells can also change. Robert notices an incorrect data entry for the Jacksonville restaurant. December expenses were $116,000 and not $119,000. You'll edit the value in cell O21 and check how this change impacts the results of the conditional format.

To correct the value in cell O21 and check the impact on the conditional format:

1. Click cell **O21** containing the incorrect expense value.
2. Type **116,000** as the corrected December expense value.
3. Press **ENTER**. The average monthly profit margin for the Jacksonville location in cell Q23 increases to 7.44%, making it the top restaurant in the chain instead of Tampa.

Because a cell can have several conditional formats, the rule listed last in the Conditional Formatting Rules Manager take precedence over any other rule. To allow an earlier conditional formatting rule to take precedence over later rules, click the Stop if True checkbox next to the rule you want to have precedence.

Documenting Conditional Formats

You should document all the conditional formats used in a workbook to ensure that users understand why some cells are formatted differently than others. A legend is an effective way to document the conditional format rules in a workbook.

In cells S11 and S12 of the Sales worksheet, Robert created the legend text for the top and bottom profit margins. You will format those cells to match the conditional formats you applied to the restaurant profit margins.

To document the top and bottom conditional formats:

1. In the Sales worksheet, click cell **S11** to select it.

2. On the Home tab, in the Styles group, click the **Conditional Formatting** button, click **Highlight Cell Rules**, and then click **Text that Contains**. The Text That Contains Dialog box opens.

3. Verify that **Top Profit Margin** (the text in cell S11) appears in the left box, select **Green Fill with Dark Green Text** as the format in the right box, and then click **OK**. The format of cell S11 matches the top profit margin conditional format.

4. Click cell **S12** to select it.

5. Click the **Conditional Formatting** button, click **Highlight Cell Rules**, and then click **Text that Contains**. The Text That Contains Dialog box opens.

6. Verify that **Bottom Profit Margin** (the text entered in cell S12) appears in the left box, select **Light Red Fill with Dark Red Text** format is selected in the right box, and then click **OK**. The format of cell S12 matches the bottom profit margin conditional format.

7. Click cell **S9** to deselect the legend text. Refer to Figure 2–39.

Figure 2–39   Highlighting the top and bottom profit margins

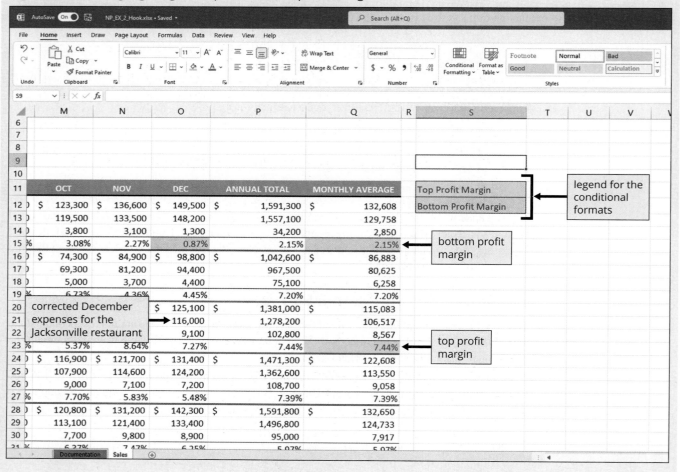

Clearing Conditional Formatting Rules

You can remove a conditional format at any time without affecting the underlying data. Select the range containing the conditional format, click the Conditional Formatting button in the Styles group on the Home tab, and then click Clear Rules. A menu opens, providing options to clear the conditional formatting rules from the selected cells or the entire worksheet.

Proskills

Written Communication: Using Conditional Formats Effectively

Conditional formats are an excellent way to highlight important trends and data values to clients and colleagues. However, be sure to use them judiciously. Overusing conditional formats might obscure the very data you want to emphasize. Keep in mind the following tips as you make decisions about what to highlight and how it should be highlighted:

- **Document the conditional formats you use.** If a bold, green font means that a sales number is in the top 10% of all sales, document that information in the worksheet.
- **Do not clutter data with too much highlighting.** Limit highlighting rules to one or two per data set. Highlights are designed to draw attention to points of interest. If you use too many, you will end up highlighting everything—and, therefore, nothing.
- **Consider alternatives to conditional formats.** If you want to highlight the top 10 sales regions, it might be more effective to simply sort the data with the best-selling regions at the top of the list.

Remember that the goal of highlighting is to showcase important data or results. Careful use of conditional formats helps readers to focus on the important points you want to make rather than distracting them with secondary issues and facts.

Formatting a Workbook for Printing

Many workbooks are distributed in print versions. In addition to formatting workbooks for the computer screen, you also need to consider how they appear when printed. The requirements for a printed worksheet are different than the requirements for the same worksheet viewed on a monitor. For printed page, consider how the data appears on each page. If the content spans several pages, you do not want column and row labels printed on one page while financial figures end up on a different page without any context or explanation.

The Page Layout tab includes many tools to format and lay out the print version of workbooks. You can change the page orientation, set the print area, add page breaks, and create headers and footers. The print settings can be applied to the entire workbook or to individual sheets within the workbook.

Using Page Break Preview

As you begin formatting the printed version of a workbook, you want to check how the sheets will print. Page Break Preview shows how many total pages will be printed and what will be printed on each page. In Page Break Preview, a solid or dotted blue order indicates that the page boundaries and page numbers appear in the workbook window. As you develop the print version of a workbook, you can refer to Page Break Preview to ensure that each page contains the appropriate content in a clear and informative design.

Robert wants you to check how the Sales worksheet would print in portrait orientation. You'll use Page Break Preview to review the page layout.

To preview the print layout in Page Break Preview:

1. Click cell **A1** to select it.

2. On the ribbon, click the **Page Layout** tab.

3. In the Page Setup group, verify that page orientation is set to **Portrait**.

4. On the status bar, click the **Page Break Preview** button ⊞. The worksheet switches to Page Break Preview.

5. Change the zoom level so all pages of the printed report are displayed the workbook window. Refer to Figure 2–40.

Figure 2–40   Sales worksheet in Page Break Preview

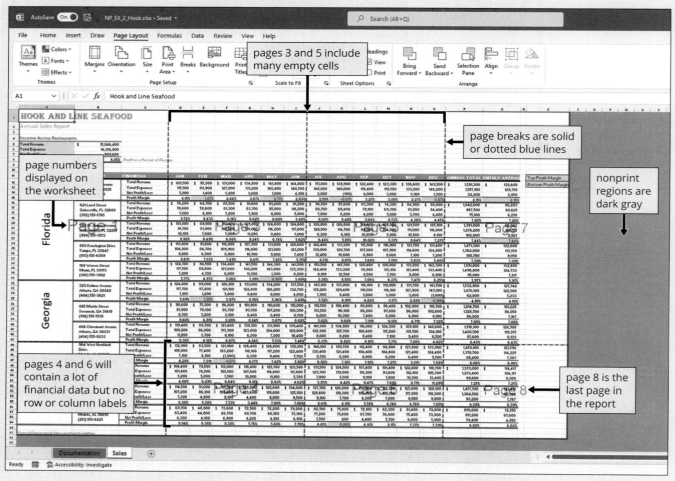

Trouble? If your layout is different than Figure 2–40, don't worry. The layout depends on your printer and monitor.

Page Break Preview reveals that the printed Sales worksheet would require eight pages. Some of the pages would be very confusing to a reader. For example, pages 4 and 6 are filled with financial data without any labels identifying the month or the restaurant. Half of pages 3 and 5 contain empty cells, wasting space. The report needs reformatting before it is suitable for printing.

Defining the Print Area

The print area specifies which range or ranges in a worksheet will be printed. The default print area is the range that extends from cell A1 to the rightmost column and lowest row containing printable content. In many worksheets, this includes a lot of empty cells. For example, in the Sales worksheet, the range D1:S10 has no content, and the printed report would be more effective without those cells. To remove cells from a printed worksheet, you can set a more different print area that includes nonadjacent ranges. Each worksheet has its own print area.

Robert wants you to define a print area for the Sales worksheet that eliminates the blank cells. You'll do that in Page Break Preview, which clearly indicates what areas will print.

To define the print area for the Sales worksheet:

1. Increase the zoom level of the workbook window to **90%** to make it easier to select cells and cell ranges.

2. Select the nonadjacent range **A1:C10,A11:S61** covering the summary information at the top of the worksheet and the complete financial table including the conditional formatting legends and the footnote.

3. On the Page Layout tab, in the Page Setup group, click the **Print Area** button, and then click **Set Print Area**. The print area covers an L-shaped region for the nonadjacent range A1:C10,A11:S61. The rest of the worksheet is shaded dark gray, indicating that those cells are not part of the printout.

4. Click **A1** to deselect the range.

5. Reduce the zoom level until the complete preview of the printed report is displayed in the workbook window. Refer to Figure 2–41.

Figure 2–41   Print area set for the Sales worksheet

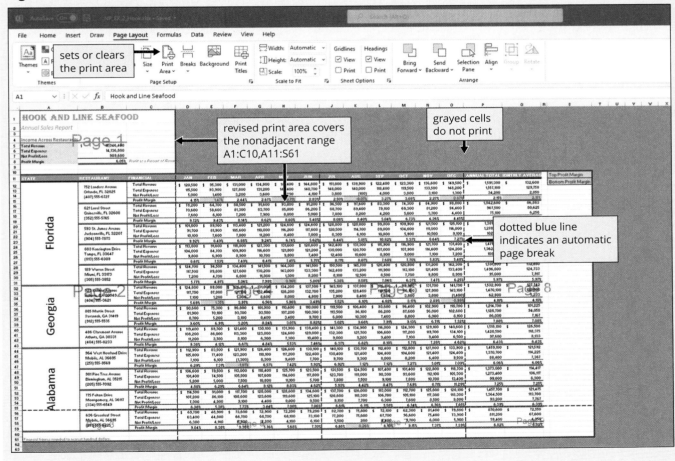

To reset the print area, click the Print Area button in the Page Setup group on the Page Layout tab, and then click Clear Print Area. The print area returns to its original setting, a rectangle extending from cell A1 to the right and bottom edges of the sheet content.

Setting the Print Titles

A good practice is for every page of a printed report to include descriptive text such as the company's name, titles and subheadings, and row and column labels for any content. You can repeat important information like this on every page by specifying which rows and columns in the worksheet should print on all pages. Those rows and columns act as print titles, adding context to every printed page.

In the Sales worksheet, as currently set, the company name and report subheading will be printed only on the first page and many pages will have financial data with no labels. Robert wants the company name and report subheading in rows 1 and 2 and the labels containing the state name, restaurant location, and financial category in columns A through C repeated on every page. You will mark them as print titles.

To define the print titles for the Sales worksheet:

1. On the Page Layout tab, in the Page Setup group, click the **Print Titles** button. The Page Setup dialog box opens with the Sheet tab displayed.

   Tip You can also open the Page Setup dialog box by clicking the Dialog Box Launcher in the Page Setup group on the Page Layout tab.

2. In the Print titles section, click the **Rows to repeat at top** box, and then in the Sales worksheet, select rows **1:3**. The row reference $1:$3 appears in the Rows to repeat at top box. A flashing border appears around the three rows of the worksheet to indicate that the contents of these rows will be repeated on each page of the printout.

3. Click the **Columns to repeat at left** box, and then in the Sales worksheet, select columns **A:C**. The column reference **$A:$C** appears in the Columns to repeat at left box. Refer to Figure 2–42.

Figure 2–42   Sheet tab in the Page Setup dialog box

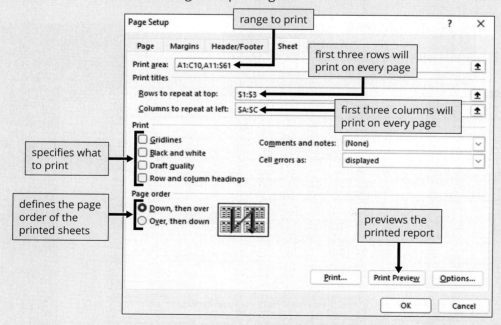

4. Click **Print Preview** to preview the current format of the printed report. The printed report will be 35 pages.

5. Click the **Next Page** button ▶ to go through the printout page by page. The content of rows 1 through 3 and columns A through C appear on every page.

6. In the page number box, enter **4** to return to the preview of that page. Refer to Figure 2–43.

Figure 2–43   Page 4 printout with page titles

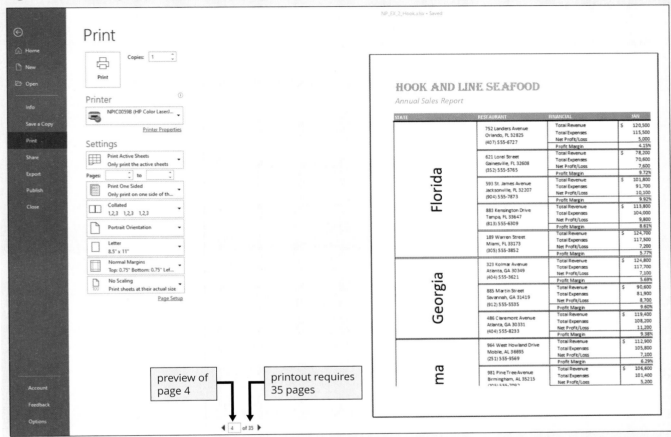

Trouble? Depending on your printer, the content of your printed pages might be slightly different.

7. Click the **Back** button ⊖ to exit Backstage view and return to the Sales worksheet.

Moving, Adding, and Removing Page Breaks

When a worksheet will not fit on to a single printed page, Excel adds page breaks throughout the worksheet. These automatic page breaks are placed to fit the most content possible on each printed page. However, automatic page breaks can split pages at awkward locations, such as within the middle of a table. They can also create long and unwieldy printouts.

To better split a printout into logical segments, you can manually set page breaks. In Page Break Preview, automatic page breaks are dotted blue lines and manual page breaks are solid blue lines. You encountered these page breaks when you set the print area for the Sales worksheet. To move a page break, you click and drag the break to a new row or new column. Each time you move, add, or remove a page break, the printout rescales to adjust to the new page layout.

Reference

Moving, Adding, and Removing Page Breaks

To move a page break:
- Drag a page break line to a new location within the print area.

To add a page break:
- Click the worksheet where you want to insert a page break.
- On the Page Layout tab, in the Page Setup group, click the Breaks button, and then click Insert Page Break. Page breaks are inserted to the left and above the selected cell, column, or row.

To remove a page break:
- Select any cell below or to the right of the page break you want to remove.
- On the Page Layout tab, in the Page Setup group, click the Breaks button, and then click Remove Page Break.

or

- In Page Break Preview, drag the page break line out of the print area.

As currently formatted, the printout will require 35 pages. That is too many pages. Robert wants you to reduce the report to a more manageable size. You do this by adjusting the page breaks. You'll start by removing the automatic page breaks.

To remove the automatic page breaks from the Sales report:

1. In Page Break Preview, point to the vertical dotted blue line between columns R and S. The pointer changes to a double-headed horizontal pointer ↔.

2. Drag the dotted blue line out of the print area. The automatic page break is removed, and the printout rescales, reducing the number of pages from 35 to 10.

   Tip To restore all automatic page breaks, click the Breaks button in the Page Setup group and then click Reset All Page Breaks.

3. Drag the dotted blue line between columns P and Q out of the print area. The printout rescales again, and the number of pages reduces to 4. A manual page break is placed between columns O and P. An automatic page break is placed between columns I and J. Refer to Figure 2–44.

Figure 2–44   Rescaled printout of the Sales report after removing automatic breaks

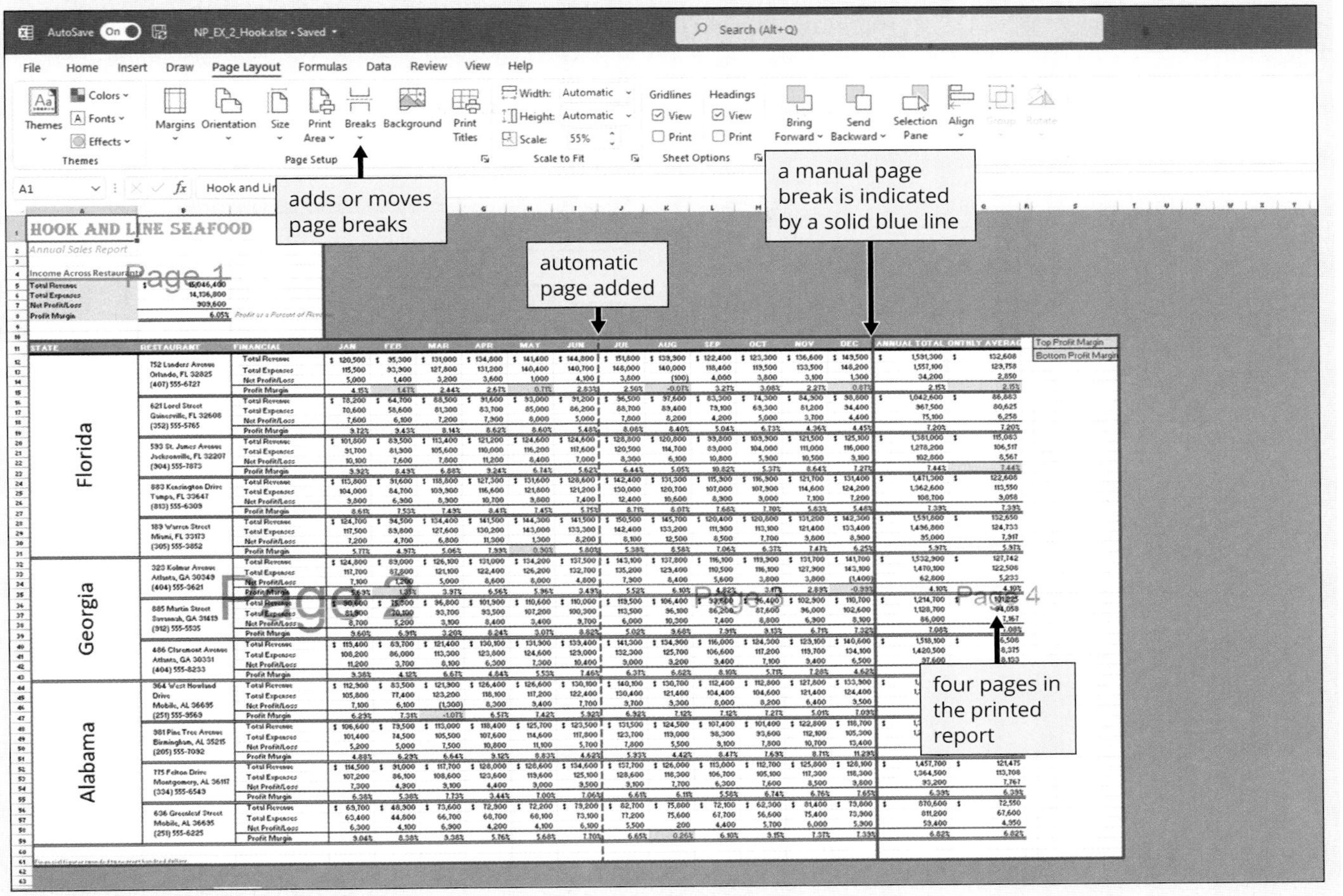

The printout of the Sales worksheet now has four pages. Robert wants the summary data from the 12 restaurants on page 1, the financial figures of all the restaurants from January to June on page 2, the July to December figures on page 3, and the final totals and monthly averages on page 4. The automatic page breaks match Robert's the report layout. To ensure that the page breaks stay in place, you will change the automatic page break between column I and J to a manual break.

To move and insert page breaks:

1. In Page Break Preview, click the column **J** column header containing the July figures.

2. On the Page Layout tab, in the Page Setup group, click the **Breaks** button, and then click **Insert Page Break**. The page break between column I and column J changes to a solid blue line, indicating a manual page break.

3. Click cell **A1** to deselect column J and then verify that manual page break appears between columns I and J.

4. In the lower-right corner of the Page Setup group, click the **Dialog Box Launcher**. The Page Setup dialog box opens.

5. Click **Print Preview** to preview the printed report, and then verify that the report is four pages and the last three pages display the company name, subheading, state name, restaurant address, and financial labels. Refer to Figure 2–45.

Figure 2–45   Preview of page 2 of the Sales report printout

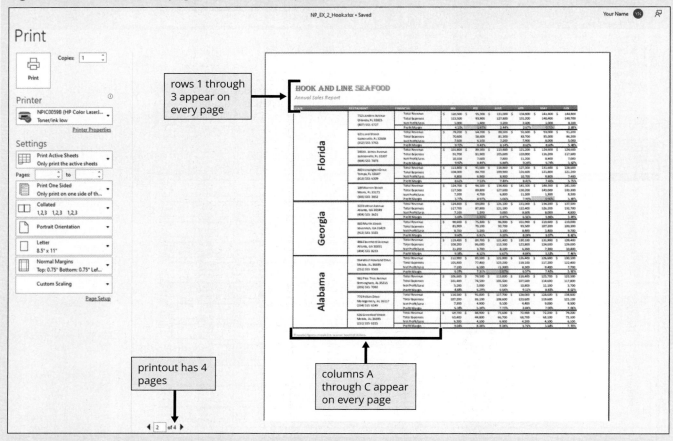

Trouble? If your report is not four pages, return to Page Break Preview and insert, move, or remove page breaks as needed until the printout is four pages with titles on each page.

Adding Headers and Footers

Headers and footers appear only on printed pages. A **header** is text placed at the top of a printed page, and a **footer** is text placed at the page bottom of a printed page. Headers and footers are divided into three sections—left, center, and right—into which you can enter information.

Headers and footers often contain information that does not appear in the workbook itself. The information can be dynamic, such as the workbook or worksheet name, page numbers, the total number of pages, or the date the pages printed. If you later change the workbook name or the number of pages in the report, the header and footer will reflect that change. You can also enter text into the header and footer that doesn't change, such as your name as the report's author.

A printout can contain different sets of headers and footers. You can design one set for the first page of the report. Then, you can create another set for the remaining pages or for odd- and even-numbered pages.

Robert wants you to add headers and footers to the report. For the header, you'll display workbook's file name in left section and the current date in the right section. For the footer, you'll display the current page number and the total number of pages in the center section and your name in the right section.

To set up the page header for the Sales report:

1. In Print Preview, at the bottom of the Settings section, click the **Page Setup** link. The Page Setup dialog box opens.

2. Click the **Header/Footer** tab to display options for the header and footer.

> **Tip** You can create or edit headers and footers in Page Layout view by clicking in the Header & Footer section and using the tools on the Design tab.

3. Click the **Different first page** check box to select it, creating one set of headers and footers for the first page and another set for subsequent pages.

4. Click the **Customer Header** button. The Header dialog box opens. Because you selected the Different first page option, the dialog box contains a Header tab and a First Page Header tab.

5. Click the **First Page Header** tab.

6. Click in the Left section box, type **File name:** and press **SPACEBAR**, and then click the **Insert File Name** button. The code &[File], representing the file name of the current workbook, is added to the header text.

7. Press **TAB** twice to move to the Right section box, and then click the **Insert Date** button. The code &[Date] is added to the right section. Refer to Figure 2-46.

Figure 2-46   Header dialog box

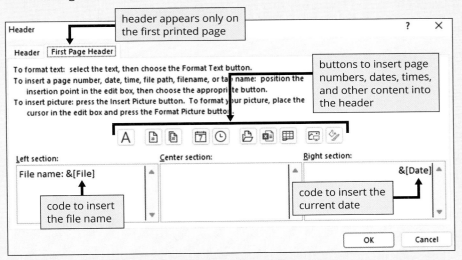

8. Click **OK** to return to the Page Setup dialog box.

The header text you just created will print only on the first page of the report. Robert wants a footer to print on all pages. Because you selected different headers and footers for the first page, you will create one footer for the first page and another footer for subsequent pages.

To create footers for the printed report:

1. In the Page Setup dialog box, on the Header/Footer tab, click the **Custom Footer** button. The Footer dialog box opens.

2. On the Footer tab, click the **Center section** box, type **Page** and press **SPACEBAR**, and then click the **Insert Page Number** button. The code &[Page] is added to the center footer.

3. Press **SPACEBAR**, type **of** and press **SPACEBAR**, and then click the **Insert Number of Pages** button ⬚ . The code &[Pages] is added to the center footer. Refer to Figure 2–47.

Figure 2–47   Footer dialog box

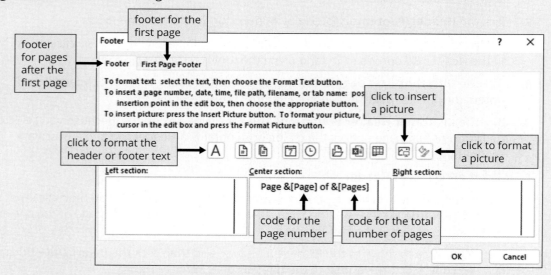

4. Click the **First Page Footer** tab to design the footer of the first page.

5. Click the **Center section** box, and then type **Page &[Page] of &[Pages]** as the center footer of the first page.

6. Click the **Right section** box, type **Prepared by:** and press **SPACEBAR**, and then type your name.

7. Click **OK** to return to the Page Setup dialog box.

Header and footer text are plain unformatted text. You can set the font style, size, and color by clicking the Format Text button in the Header or Footer dialog box.

Setting the Page Margins

A **margin** is the space between the page content and the edges of the page. By default, Excel sets the page margins to 0.7 inch on the left and right sides and 0.75 inch on the top and bottom and allows for 0.3-inch margins around the header and footer. You can reduce or increase these margins as needed by selecting predefined margin sizes or setting your own.

Hook and Line Seafood requires all company reports to use larger top margins to accommodate the company letterhead. You will increase the top margin to 1.5 inches.

To set the top margin for the printed report:

1. In the Page Setup dialog box, click the **Margins** tab to display options for changing the page margins.

   Tip To apply preset margins, click the Margins button in the Page Setup group on the Page Layout tab.

2. Double-click the **Top** box to select the current setting, and then type **1.5** to increase the size of the top margin to 1.5 inches. Refer to Figure 2–48.

Figure 2–48   Margin tab of the Page Setup dialog box

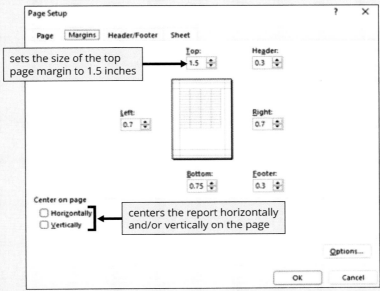

3. Click **OK**. The Page Setup dialog box closes. The new margin appears in the preview.

Page content can be centered both horizontally and vertically on the page. You can do this in the Page Setup dialog box on the Margins tab by selecting the Horizontally and Vertically check boxes.

Robert wants you to print the final version of the Sales report. Before you print, you'll preview the formatted pages.

To preview and print the Sales report:

1. On the Print screen in Backstage view, click the **Zoom to Page** button located in the lower-right corner of the preview window. The display changes to include the entire first page. Refer to Figure 2–49.

Figure 2–49   Preview of the first page

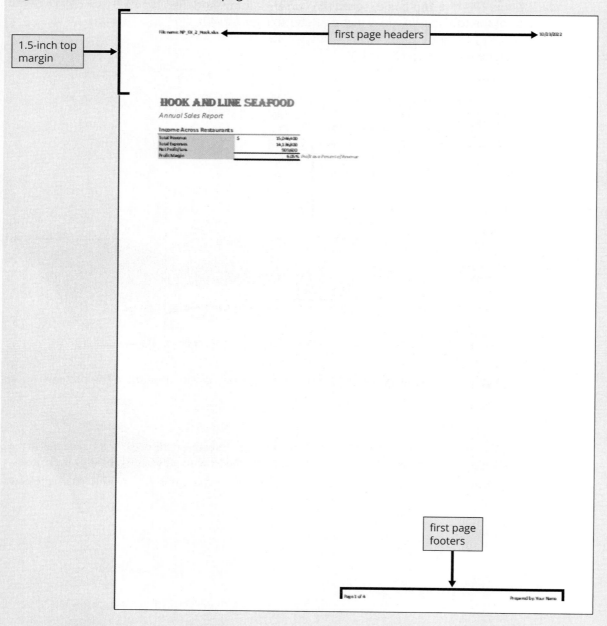

2. Navigate through the rest of the four pages in the Print Preview window.

3. On the Print screen, in the Settings section, click the first box, and then click **Print Entire Workbook**. The printout will include five pages—one page for the Documentation sheet and four pages for the Sales worksheet.

4. If you are instructed to print, click the **Print** button to print the entire workbook. If you are not instructed to print, click the **Back** button ⬅ on the Backstage view navigation bar to return to the workbook window.

5. Click the **Normal** button ⊞ on the status bar to return the view of the workbook to normal.

6. **sam**⬆ Save the workbook, and then close it.

Robert is pleased that your work formatting the workbook has made the sales report more readable and the data more accessible.

Part 2.2 Quick Check

1. If you change the definition of a custom cell style, what impact does that have on cells formatted with that style in the workbook?

2. If you change the definition of a custom cell style, what impact does that have on cells formatted with that style in other workbooks?

3. If you change a workbook's theme, what impact does that have on a cell whose background is filled with a standard color?

4. What is the formula to calculate the average of the values in columns F through H?

5. Why would you use a conditional format to highlight cells rather than formatting those cells directly?

6. What are print titles?

7. In Page Break Preview, how can you tell the difference between automatic page breaks and manual page breaks?

8. What is the code to display the text "Page *number* of *total*" in a page header or footer where *number* is the page number and *total* is the total number of pages?

Practice: Review Assignments

Data Files needed for the Review Assignments: NP_EX_2-2.xlsx, Support_EX_2_Texture.jpg

The Hook and Line Seafood chain wants to expand its market and increase its visibility. It has started a fleet of mobile food trucks to cater to parks, beaches, and festivals in southern Florida. Robert is working on a report analyzing August revenue from Food Truck 3. His analysis has four sections: a summary section, a table of revenue by weekday, a table of revenue by location, and a calendar of daily revenue by location during August. Robert wants each section to print on a separate page. He also wants the report to highlight the days and the locations with the highest and lowest revenue. The worksheet has almost no formatting. You'll format the report for both the computer screen and the printed page. Complete the following:

1. Open the **NP_EX_2-2.xlsx** workbook located in the Excel2 > Review folder included with your Data Files, and then save the workbook as **NP_EX_2_Truck** in the location specified by your instructor.
2. In the Documentation sheet, enter your name in cell B4 and the date in cell B5.
3. Set the background of the Documentation sheet to the **Support_EX_2_Texture.jpg** image file located in the Excel2 > Review folder included with your Data Files.
4. In the August worksheet, format the calendar as follows:
   a. Format cell A39 with the Title cell style.
   b. Merge and center the range B40:H40 containing the month and year, and then format the merged cell with the 60% – Accent4 cell style.
   c. In the range B41:H41, format the day abbreviations with the Accent6 cell style, and then center the text in each cell.
   d. In cell B42, format containing the day number with the 20% – Accent3 cell style.
   e. Format cell B44 containing the day's revenue with Currency format and decrease the decimal to remove the cents value.
   f. Add an outside border around the range B42:B44.
   g. Use the Format Painter to copy the format from the range B42:B44 to the rest of the calendar days in the range B42:H56.
   h. In the range A42:A44, merge and center the title, middle-align the text vertically, increase the font size to 14 points, orient the text Angle Counterclockwise, and then add a border around the merged cell.
   i. Copy the format from the merged cell A42 to the range A45:A56.
5. Format the Revenue by Location summary as follows:
   a. Format cell A22 using the Title cell style and format the range A23:C23 using the Accent6 cell style.
   b. In the range A24:A37 containing the addresses, decrease the font to 9 points and increase the indent twice.
6. Copy and paste the format in the range A22:C23 into the range A12:C13. Copy and paste the format in the range A24:C24 into the range A14:C20.
7. Apply the following formatting to the Revenue by Day summary:
   a. Apply the Title cell style to cell A4.
   b. In cell B5, apply the Accounting format and reduce the number of decimals to hide the cents values.
   c. In the range B6:B7, apply the Comma format and hide the cents values.
   d. In cell B8, apply the Percent and display two decimal places.
   e. In cell B8, add a single border line above the cell and a double border line below the cell.
8. Create a custom style for the August summary by doing the following:
   a. In cell C6, format the note in 9 points, italic, Gray, Accent3 font and increase the indent one space.
   b. Save the format you applied to cell C6 as custom cell style named **sidenote** and include only the Alignment and Font settings in the style.
   c. Apply the sidenote custom cell style to the range C5:C8.

9. Highlight the top and bottom days in August by selecting the range B44:H44,B47:H47,B50:H50,B53:H53,B56:H56 containing the daily revenue totals. Create a conditional format to display the top day in green fill with dark green text. Create another conditional format to display the bottom day in light red fill with dark red text.

10. Use conditional formats to highlight the best and worst locations by selecting the range C24:C37 and changing the top location to a green fill with dark green text and the worst location to a light red fill with dark red text.

11. Repeat Step 10 for the weekday averages in the range C14:C20.

12. Format the print version of the August worksheet as follows:
   a. Verify that sheet will print in portrait orientation.
   b. Set the print area of the report to A1:C38,A39:H56.
   c. Repeat rows 1 through 3 as print titles on every page of the report.
   d. Insert a manual page break directly above rows 12, 22, and 39. Remove all automatic page breaks from the document so that it prints on four pages.
   e. Add a different first page for headers and footers. On the first page header, enter your name in the left section, the file name in center, and the date in the right section.
   f. For the first page footer and subsequent page footers, enter the code **Page &[Page] of &[Pages]** in the center section.

13. Preview the printed version of the August worksheet. Verify that the report has four pages, the first rows of the worksheet will print on each page, the overall summary is on page 1, the revenue by day of the week is on page 2, the revenue by location is on page 3, and the revenue for day in the calendar is on page 4. Make sure your name, the file name, and the date appear on the first page header and that the page number and total number of pages appear on every footer.

14. If you are instructed to print, print the entire workbook.

15. Save the workbook, and then close it.

Apply: Case Problem 1

Data File needed for this Case Problem: NP_EX_2-3.xlsx

Thrill Managers Alya Jannat is an analyst for Thrill Managers, a web company that analyzes usage data for theme parks and thrill rides. One of the services provided by Thrill Managers is an hourly analysis of wait times at different parks. Using their reports, park visitors can arrange their visits to minimize wait times and park owners can distribute their resources to improve the customer experience. Alya wants you to finish formatting a worksheet displaying hourly wait times for a popular theme park over the past month. You will use conditional formats to create a "heat map" that shows the times during each day and across each week where wait times increase in response to customer demand. Complete the following:

1. Open the **NP_EX_2-3.xlsx** workbook located in the Excel2 > Case1 folder included with your Data Files, and then save the workbook as **NP_EX_2_Thrill** in the location specified by your instructor.

2. In the Documentation sheet, enter your name in cell B4 and the current date in cell B5. Format the date in cell B5 using the Long Date format and left-align it in the cell.

3. Copy the format from the range A1:A2 of the Documentation sheet into the range A1:A2 of the Wait Times worksheet.

4. In the Wait Times worksheet, in the range J21:K21, merge and center the title and apply the Accent1 cell style. In the range J22:J28, indent the wait times one space to the right. In the range J21:K28, add a thick outside border.

5. Define the color scale for the range of wait times with the following fill colors:
   a. In cell K22, set the fill color to Olive Green, Accent 3.
   b. In cell K23, set the fill color to Olive Green, Accent 3, Lighter 40%.
   c. In cell K24, set the fill color to Olive Green, Accent 3, Lighter 60%.
   d. In cell K25, set the fill color to Orange, Accent 6, Lighter 60%.
   e. In cell K26, set the fill color to Red, Accent 2, Lighter 60%.
   f. In cell K27, set the fill color to Red, Accent 2, Lighter 40%.
   g. In cell K28, set the fill color to Red, Accent 2.

6. In the range B22:H34, create the following conditional formats in the order specified:
   a. Highlight values greater than 60 with the Red, Accent 2 fill color. (Note: Use the Custom Format option in the Greater Than dialog box and then set the fill color in the Fill tab.)
   b. Highlight values less than 10 with an Olive Green, Accent 3 fill (seventh color in the first row).
   c. Highlight values between 10 and 20 with an Olive Green, Accent 3, Lighter 40% fill (seventh color in the fourth row).
   d. Highlight values between 20 and 30 with an Olive Green, Accent 3, Lighter 60% fill (seventh color in the third row).
   e. Highlight values between 30 and 40 with an Orange, Accent 6, Lighter 60% fill (last color in the third row).
   f. Highlight values between 40 and 50 with Red, Accent 2, Lighter 60% fill (sixth color in the third row).
   g. Highlight values between 50 and 60 with Red, Accent 2, Lighter 40% fill (sixth color in the fourth row).

7. In the range B21:H21, apply the Accent1 cell style to the day abbreviations and center the text horizontally.

8. In the range B20:H20, merge and center the date range and increase the font size to 14 points.

9. In the range A22:A34, right-align the hour values and increase the indent one space (to move the values the left).

10. In the range B21:H34, add thick outside borders.

11. Use the Format Painter to copy the formats in the range A20:K34 and paste the formats to the ranges A36:K50, A52:K66, and A68:K82.

12. Enter the following calculations to determine the average wait times during each of the four weeks in June:
    a. In cell B5, use the AVERAGE function to calculate the average ride wait time for values in the range B22:H34.
    b. In cell B6, calculate the average wait time for values in the range B38:H50.
    c. In cell B7, calculate the average wait time for values in the range B54:H66.
    d. In cell B8, calculate the average wait time for values in the range B70:H82.
    e. In the range A5:A8, decrease the font size to 10 points and indent the text one space to the right.
    f. Merge and center the range A4:C4, apply the Accent1 cell style to the merged cell, and then add thick outside borders to the range A4:C8.

13. Enter the following calculations to determine average wait times from Sunday to Saturday:
    a. In cell B11, calculate the average of value in the nonadjacent range B22:B34, B38:B50, B54:B66, B70:B82.
    b. In cell B12 calculate the average of values in the range C22:C34, C38:C50, C54:C66, C70:C82.
    c. In cell B13, calculate the average of values in the range D22:D34, D38:D50, D54:D66, D70:D82.
    d. In cells B14 through B17, calculate the averages of the wait times for Wednesday through Saturday, revising the cell references to point to in columns E through H.
    e. In the range A11:A17, decrease the font size to 10 points and indent the text one space to the right.
    f. Merge and center the range A10:C10, apply the Accent1 cell style to the merged cell, and then add thick outside borders to the range A10:C17.

14. Format the print version of the report as follows:
    a. Repeat rows 1 through 3 on every page.
    b. Remove all automatic page breaks from the printout and add manual page breaks above rows 20, 36, 52, and 68.
    c. Verify that the orientation is portrait and scale the printout to 75%.
    d. Display your name and the date in the right section of the first page header.
    e. On every page after the first page, display the text Page *page* of *number* in the center footer, where *page* is the page number and *total* is the number of pages.

15. Preview the printout to verify that the report is printed on five pages, your name and the date are on the right side in the header of the first page, and that the page number and total number of pages are centered in the footer on the remaining pages.

16. If you are instructed to print, print the entire workbook.

17. Save the workbook, and then close it.

Challenge: Case Problem 2

Data Files needed for this Case Problem: NP_EX_2-4.xlsx, Support_EX_2_Home.thmx

Home Tracker Samuel Javier is an analyst for Home Tracker, a property listing service. Part of Samuel's job is to maintain a current listing of homes in different markets. Each listing includes the home address, market price, square footage, number of bedrooms, and the number of bathrooms. Samuel stores this information in a workbook and wants to add search tools he can use to highlight the entire row of each property that matches specified criteria.

To highlight those properties, you will use a conditional format based on a formula. These formulas need locked cell references so that the format can be copied across a range of cells without the cell references changing. To lock a cell reference, include the $ symbol before the row and/or column addresses. The following formula highlights cells when the values in column E (starting with cell E2) are less than or equal to the value in cell K2 and the values in column G (starting with cell G2) are equal to the value in cell K3.

        = AND($E2 <= $K$2, $G2 = $K$3)

As the values stored in cells K2 and K3 change, the cells matched by this formula also change. You will use a similar formula for Samuel's workbook to highlight properties with a specified price, number of bedrooms, and number of bathrooms. Complete the following:

1. Open the **NP_EX_2-4.xlsx** workbook located in the Excel2 > Case2 folder included with your Data Files, and then save the workbook as **NP_EX_2_Tracker** in the location specified by your instructor.
2. In the Documentation sheet, in the range B3:B4, enter your name and the date.
3. **Explore:** On the Page Layout tab, in the Themes group, click the Themes button, and click Browse for Themes. Open the **Support_EX_2_Home.thmx** theme file located in the Excel2 > Case2 folder included with your Data Files. Verify that the colors and fonts in the Documentation sheet change.
4. In the Home Listings worksheet, apply the following formatting to the range containing criteria for the conditional format:
   a. In the range A4:B4, merge and center the contents of the cells, and then apply the Accent2 cell style.
   b. Format cell B5 in Currency format (*not* the Currency cell style) with no digits to the right of the decimal point.
   c. In the range A5:A7, change the fill color of to the theme color Gold, Accent3, Lighter 80%.
   d. In the range A4:B7, add thick outside borders with the Orange, Accent2 color and a dotted inside border in black.
5. Insert the following formulas and formats to summarize the home listing data:
   a. In cell B10, use the COUNT function to count the number of values in column H.
   b. In cell B11, use the AVERAGE function to display the average listing price from column H.
   c. In cell B12, use the AVERAGE function to calculate the average square footage in column I.
   d. Copy the formats from the range A4:B7 and paste them into the range A9:B12.
   e. In cell B10, change the format to General. In cell B11, change the format to Currency with no digits to the right of the decimal point. In cell B12, change the format to Comma with no digits to the right of the decimal point.
6. Apply the following formatting to the property listings:
   a. In the range D1:K1, apply the Accent6 cell style to the column labels.
   b. In the range G1:G226, apply the Text format to the postal code values. In the range H1:H226, apply the Currency format with no decimal places to the listed prices. In the range I1:I226, apply the Comma Style format with no decimal places to the square footage.
   c. Add a dotted border around all cells in the range D2:K226.
7. **Explore:** Select the range D2:K226 containing information on each property, and then apply the following conditional format:
   a. On the Home tab, in the Styles group, click the Conditional Formatting button, click Highlight Cell Rules, and then click More Rules.
   b. In the New Formatting Rule dialog box, click Use a formula to determine which cells to format.

   c. In the Format values where this formula is true box, enter the following formula (exactly as written):

      `= AND($H2 <= $B$5, $J2 = $B$6, $K2 = $B$7)`

   d. Click the Format button, and then in the Format Cells dialog box, format the font as bold, standard red, and format the fill to the Light Yellow, Background 2 theme color (the third color in the first row).

   e. Close the dialog box, and then verify that only one property (524 East Lakewood Street, Coraopolis, PA) matches the search criteria and that the entire row of data for that property is highlighted.

8. Change the values in the range B5:B7 to highlight properties listed for $300,000 or less with three bedrooms and two baths. Verify that nine properties are highlighted in the table.

9. Apply the following print formats to the worksheet:
   a. Set the orientation of the printout to landscape.
   b. Set the print area to the nonadjacent range A1:B12,D1:K226.
   c. Set the print titles to display row 1 on every page.
   d. Remove any automatic page breaks from printout. Add manual page breaks above rows 50, 100, 150, and 200.
   e. Add a header to the first page displaying your name, the date, and the name of the workbook on separate lines in the right section of the header.
   f. **Explore:** In the Header dialog box, select the code for the header and click the Format Text button to open the Font dialog box. Set the font size of the header text to 20 points.
   g. On each page, display a center footer displaying the word **Page** followed by the page number and the number of pages in the printed report.

10. Preview the printout to verify that the report is printed on six pages and that your name, the date, and the workbook file name are in right header of the first page. Verify that the page number and total number of pages are centered in the footer on every page.

11. If you are instructed to print, print the entire workbook.

12. Save the workbook, and then close it.

Calculating with Formulas and Functions

Staffing a Call Center

Case: MediCOH

Chryssa Fontini manages the national call center for MediCOH, a nationwide health care insurer based in central Ohio. The call center is open Monday through Friday from 8 AM to 6 PM, Central Time. It is Chryssa's responsibility to ensure that the center is adequately staffed to handle customer queries and requests. To accomplish that task, Chryssa analyzes the volume of calls made to the center, paying particular attention to the amount of time customers wait on hold. If the hold times are too long or if too many customers hang up before reaching an operator, MediCOH will lose business and the trust of its customers. Chryssa has created an Excel workbook of call data. You will analyze this data to help Chryssa meet the staffing needs of the call center.

Starting Data Files

Excel3	Case1
Module	NP_EX_3-4.xlsx
NP_EX_3-1.xlsx	**Case2**
NP_EX_3-2.xlsx	NP_EX_3-5.xlsx
Review	
NP_EX_3-3.xlsx	

Objectives

Part 3.1

- Perform calculations on dates and times
- Extend a formula or data series with AutoFill
- Use relative, absolute, and mixed cell references
- Write formulas using dynamic arrays
- Analyze data with the Quick Analysis tool
- Interpret an error value

Part 3.2

- Calculate minimums, maximums, averages, medians, and modes
- Round a value to a specified number of digits
- Write a logical formula with the IF function
- Retrieve data with XLOOKUP, VLOOKUP, and HLOOKUP
- Use Goal Seek to do a What-If Analysis

Part 3.1 Visual Overview: References and Ranges

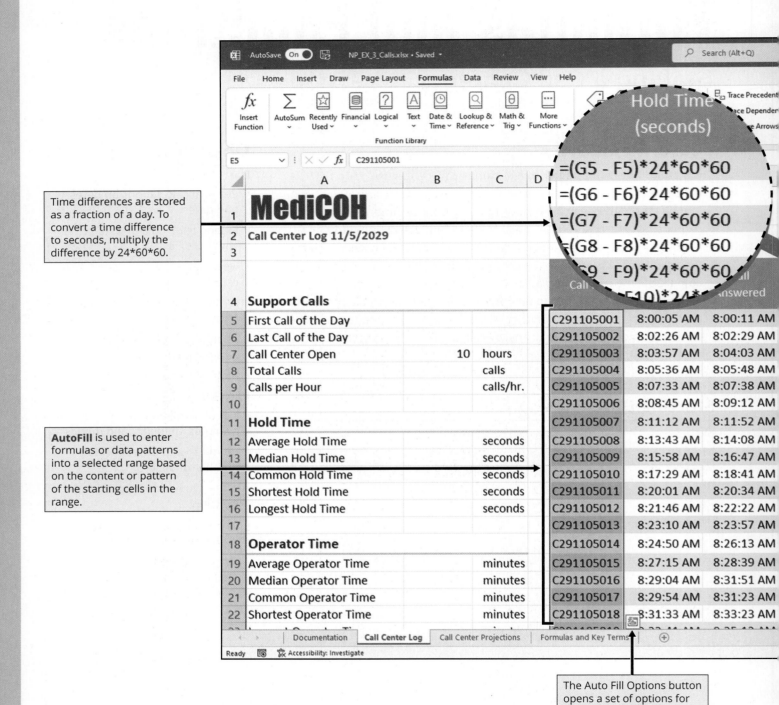

Time differences are stored as a fraction of a day. To convert a time difference to seconds, multiply the difference by 24*60*60.

$$=(G5 - F5)*24*60*60$$
$$=(G6 - F6)*24*60*60$$
$$=(G7 - F7)*24*60*60$$
$$=(G8 - F8)*24*60*60$$
$$=(G9 - F9)*24*60*60$$

Hold Time (seconds)

AutoFill is used to enter formulas or data patterns into a selected range based on the content or pattern of the starting cells in the range.

The Auto Fill Options button opens a set of options for the AutoFill selection.

E5   C291105001

	A	B	C	D
1	**MediCOH**			
2	Call Center Log 11/5/2029			
3				
4	**Support Calls**			
5	First Call of the Day			C291105001
6	Last Call of the Day			C291105002
7	Call Center Open	10	hours	C291105003
8	Total Calls		calls	C291105004
9	Calls per Hour		calls/hr.	C291105005
10				C291105006
11	**Hold Time**			C291105007
12	Average Hold Time		seconds	C291105008
13	Median Hold Time		seconds	C291105009
14	Common Hold Time		seconds	C291105010
15	Shortest Hold Time		seconds	C291105011
16	Longest Hold Time		seconds	C291105012
17				C291105013
18	**Operator Time**			C291105014
19	Average Operator Time		minutes	C291105015
20	Median Operator Time		minutes	C291105016
21	Common Operator Time		minutes	C291105017
22	Shortest Operator Time		minutes	C291105018

Call times:
8:00:05 AM — 8:00:11 AM
8:02:26 AM — 8:02:29 AM
8:03:57 AM — 8:04:03 AM
8:05:36 AM — 8:05:48 AM
8:07:33 AM — 8:07:38 AM
8:08:45 AM — 8:09:12 AM
8:11:12 AM — 8:11:52 AM
8:13:43 AM — 8:14:08 AM
8:15:58 AM — 8:16:47 AM
8:17:29 AM — 8:18:41 AM
8:20:01 AM — 8:20:34 AM
8:21:46 AM — 8:22:22 AM
8:23:10 AM — 8:23:57 AM
8:24:50 AM — 8:26:13 AM
8:27:15 AM — 8:28:39 AM
8:29:04 AM — 8:31:51 AM
8:29:54 AM — 8:31:23 AM
8:31:33 AM — 8:33:23 AM

Documentation   **Call Center Log**   Call Center Projections   Formulas and Key Terms

Ready   Accessibility: Investigate

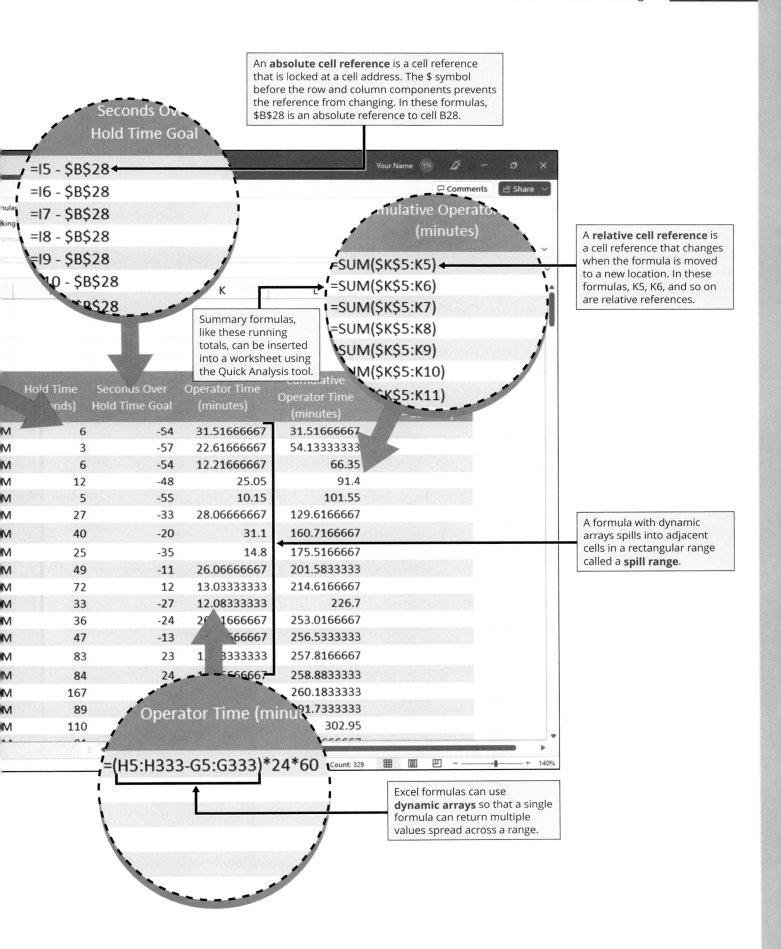

An **absolute cell reference** is a cell reference that is locked at a cell address. The $ symbol before the row and column components prevents the reference from changing. In these formulas, $B$28 is an absolute reference to cell B28.

Seconds Over Hold Time Goal

=I5 - $B$28
=I6 - $B$28
=I7 - $B$28
=I8 - $B$28
=I9 - $B$28
=I10 - $B$28
$B$28

A **relative cell reference** is a cell reference that changes when the formula is moved to a new location. In these formulas, K5, K6, and so on are relative references.

Cumulative Operator Time (minutes)

=SUM($K$5:K5)
=SUM($K$5:K6)
=SUM($K$5:K7)
=SUM($K$5:K8)
=SUM($K$5:K9)
=SUM($K$5:K10)
=SUM($K$5:K11)

Summary formulas, like these running totals, can be inserted into a worksheet using the Quick Analysis tool.

A formula with dynamic arrays spills into adjacent cells in a rectangular range called a **spill range**.

Hold Time (seconds)	Seconds Over Hold Time Goal	Operator Time (minutes)	Cumulative Operator Time (minutes)
6	-54	31.51666667	31.51666667
3	-57	22.61666667	54.13333333
6	-54	12.21666667	66.35
12	-48	25.05	91.4
5	-55	10.15	101.55
27	-33	28.06666667	129.6166667
40	-20	31.1	160.7166667
25	-35	14.8	175.5166667
49	-11	26.06666667	201.5833333
72	12	13.03333333	214.6166667
33	-27	12.08333333	226.7
36	-24	26.1666667	253.0166667
47	-13	.66667	256.5333333
83	23	1.8333333	257.8166667
84	24	1.66667	258.8833333
167			260.1833333
89			91.7333333
110			302.95

Operator Time (minutes)

=(H5:H333-G5:G333)*24*60   Count: 329   140%

Excel formulas can use **dynamic arrays** so that a single formula can return multiple values spread across a range.

Your Name   YN
Comments   Share

Designing a Workbook for Calculations

Excel is a powerful application for interpreting a wide range of data from finance to marketing to scientific research. In this module, you will use Excel to analyze data from a call center. Call center science is a rich field of research using mathematical tools to answer questions such as, "How many operators are necessary to handle the call center traffic?" and "What are the expected wait times with a given number of operators?"

The call center manager, Chryssa Fontini, created a workbook containing the call log from a typical day at the MediCOH call center. You will use this data to determine how long a customer typically waits on hold before reaching an operator and how long conversations with those operators last. Based on your calculations and analysis, Chryssa will project how many operators are needed to handle the call traffic with the goal of providing good customer service without exceeding the department's budget.

To open the call center workbook:

1. **sam** ⬇ Open the **NP_EX_3-1.xlsx** workbook located in th**e Excel3 > Module** folder included with your Data Files, and then save the workbook as **NP_EX_3_Calls** in the location specified by your instructor.

2. In the Documentation worksheet, enter your name in cell B4 and the date in cell B5.

3. Go to the **Call Center Log** worksheet. This worksheet contains the raw call center data. Refer to Figure 3–1.

Figure 3–1   Call center log

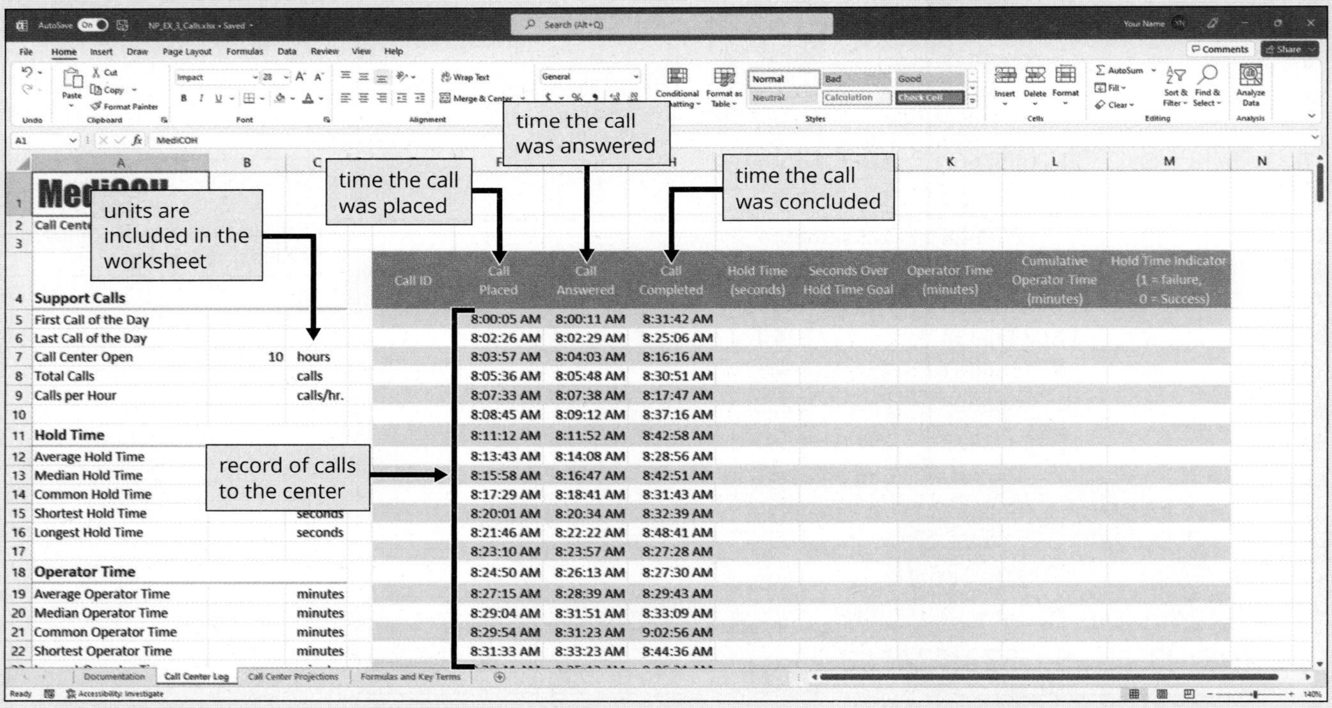

The Call Center Log worksheet displays the time each call was placed, the time an operator answered the call, and the time the conversation with the operator ended. Other information, such as how long the customer was on hold and the length of each conversation with the operator, is not included in the call log and needs to be calculated.

Documenting Calculations

A workbook with many calculations and formulas can be challenging to interpret. It is helpful to list the formulas used in the workbook and explain the assumptions and key terms behind those formulas. These can be placed in a separate worksheet.

Chryssa included a worksheet containing explanations of the equations and key terms that are used in this workbook. You will review the formulas and key terms used in the workbook.

To review the workbook's formulas and key terms:

1. Go to the **Formulas and Key Terms** worksheet.

2. Review the worksheet contents, paying attention to the equations and key terms that you will be using in this workbook.

3. Go to the **Call Center Log** worksheet.

Constants and Units

An important Excel skill is the ability to translate a mathematical equation into an Excel formula. Some equations use **constants**, which are terms in an equation whose values don't change. For example, the following equation converts a time interval measured in days to an interval measured in seconds by multiplying the *day* value by three constants—24, 60, and 60, because there are 24 hours in a day, 60 minutes in each hour, and 60 seconds in each minute:

$$\texttt{seconds = day} \times \texttt{24} \times \texttt{60} \times \texttt{60}$$

A good practice is to include the units in any calculation next to the calculated value. In some situations, the unit is obvious, such as when a currency value is formatted with the appropriate currency symbol. In other situations, such as reporting time intervals, the unit is unknown unless you include it (hours, minutes, or seconds) as text in the worksheet.

Insight

Deciding Where to Place a Constant

Constants can be placed in an Excel formula or in a worksheet cell referenced by the formula. Which approach is better?

The answer depends on the constant being used, the purpose of the workbook, and the intended audience. Placing constants in separate cells referenced by the formulas can help users better understand the worksheet because all the values are visible. You can also add explanatory text next to each constant, documenting its meaning and use within the calculations. On the other hand, you don't want anyone to inadvertently change the value of a constant, which then alters a calculation.

You will need to evaluate how important it is for other people to immediately locate the constant and whether the constant requires any explanation for other people to understand the formula. In general, if the constant is commonly known, such as the constant 60 used to multiply hour values into minutes, you can place the constant directly in a formula. However, if the constant is less well-known, such as a tax rate, it is better to place the constant in its own cell, making it more visible. If you decide to place a constant in a cell, you can lock that cell value to ensure that the constant remains unchanged and unchangeable.

You will use constants to calculate each customer's hold time during their call to the center.

Calculating with Dates and Times

Excel stores dates and times as the number of days since January 0, 1900. Full days are a whole number. Partial days are a fraction, such as 0.5 for a half day or 12 hours. Storing dates and times as numbers makes it easier to calculate time and date intervals.

Chryssa wants you to calculate the length of time the first customer in the call log spent on hold.

To calculate the first customer's hold time:

1. In cell **I5**, enter the formula **= G5 − F5** to calculate the hold time of the first call, equal to the difference between the time when the call was placed and the time when the call was answered by an operator. The time 12:00:06 AM appears in this cell.

2. Click cell **I5** to select it. When Excel performs calculations with dates and times, it retains the date/time format. In this instance, you want to display the numerical difference between the time values and not the time.

3. On the Home tab, in the Number group, click the **Number Format arrow**, and then click **General**. The General number format changes the value displayed in the cell to 6.9444E-05.

The value 6.9444E-05 is a decimal value in scientific notation, equal to 6.9444×10^{-5} or 0.000069444. Because Excel measures times in days, this value represents the fractional part of one day. You will convert this value to seconds by multiplying it by 24 times 60 times 60 (the total number of seconds in a single day).

To convert the first customer's hold time to seconds:

1. In cell **I5**, change the formula to **= (G5 − F5)*24*60*60** to convert the value to seconds.

2. Click cell **I5** to select it, and then change the number format to **General**. The value 6 appears in the cell, indicating that the first customer was on hold for 6 seconds.

Now that you have calculated the hold time for the first customer, you will apply this formula and number format to the rest of calls in the log. Although you could copy and paste the formula for the remaining entries in the log, you will use a more efficient method to enter the formulas and formats.

AutoFilling Formulas and Data Patterns

One way to efficiently enter long columns or rows of formulas and data values is with AutoFill. AutoFill extends a formula or a pattern of data values into a selected range. This method is often faster than copying and pasting, which requires two distinct actions.

AutoFilling a Formula

To extend a formula into a range with AutoFill, you select the cell containing the formula. When the cell is selected, a **fill handle** appears as a green square in the lower-right corner of the cell. Double-clicking or dragging the fill handle over a range extends the formula and format of the selected cell into the range.

Tip You can also click the Fill button in the Editing group on the Home tab, and then select the direction to fill.

You will use AutoFill to extend the formula in cell I5 down the remaining cells in the Hold Time column.

To extend the formula and format in cell I5 with AutoFill:

1. Verify that cell **I5** is still selected. The fill handle, the small green square, appears in the lower-right corner of the cell.

2. Point to the **fill handle** in the lower-right corner of the cell. The pointer changes to a plus pointer **+**.

3. Double-click the **fill handle**. The formula and format in cell I5 extend through the rest of the hold time cells in the range I5:I333. Refer to Figure 3–2.

Figure 3–2   Formula and format extended with AutoFill

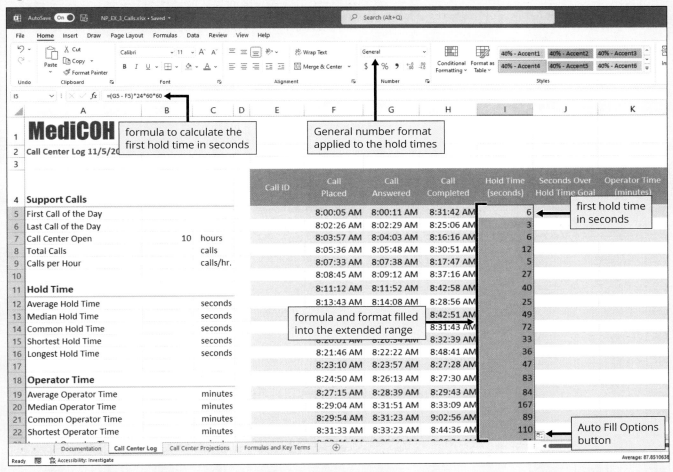

AutoFill also extends formulas and formats from a range. You select the range with the formulas and formats you want to extend, and then either drag the fill handle over the range you want to fill or double-click the fill handle.

Exploring Auto Fill Options

AutoFill extends both the formulas and the formatting of the initial cell or range. However, you might want to extend only the formulas or only the formatting from the initial cells. You use the Auto Fill Options button that appears after AutoFill is complete to do that. The Auto Fill Options button lets you specify what to extend. Refer to Figure 3–3.

Figure 3–3   Auto Fill Options menu

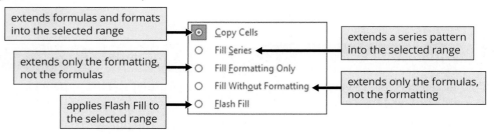

Chryssa used banded rows to make the call log easier to read. By extending cell I5 into the rest column I, you copied cell I5's formatting as well as its formula, removing the banded row effect for column I. You will use the Auto Fill Options button to restore the banded row effect to column I.

To use the Auto Fill Options button to copy only formulas:

1. Click the **Auto Fill Options** button 🔲. A menu of AutoFill options appears.

2. Click the **Fill Without Formatting** option button. The original formatting of the range is restored without affecting the copied formulas.

3. Click cell **I5** to select it, and then verify that the banded rows effect still appears with the calculated hold times from column I.

4. Verify that hold times are calculated for every call in the column. Refer to Figure 3–4.

Figure 3–4   Hold times for the last calls of the day

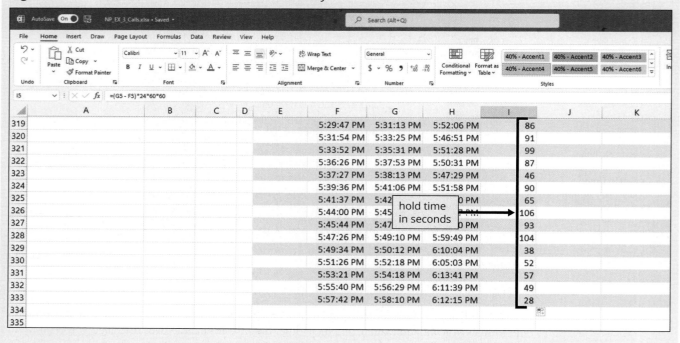

Filling a Series

AutoFill can extend any data pattern involving dates, times, numbers, and text. To extend a series of data values based on a pattern, enter enough values to establish the pattern, select the cells containing the pattern, and then drag the fill handle into a larger range. Figure 3–5 shows how AutoFill can be used to extend an initial series of odd numbers established in cells A2 and A3 into the range A2:A9.

Figure 3–5   AutoFill used to extend a series

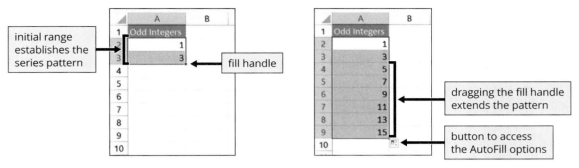

initial range establishes the series pattern

fill handle

dragging the fill handle extends the pattern

button to access the AutoFill options

Figure 3–6 describes other extended patterns created with AutoFill. In each case, you must provide enough information to identify the pattern. AutoFill recognizes some patterns from only a single entry—such as Jan or January to create a series of month abbreviations or names, and Mon or Monday to create a series of the days of the week. A text pattern that includes text and a number such as Region 1, Region 2, and so on can also be automatically extended using AutoFill. You can start the series at any point, such as Weds, June, or Region 10, and AutoFill will continue with the next days, months, or text.

Figure 3–6   Series patterns extended with AutoFill

Type	Initial Value(s)	Extended Values
Numbers	1, 2, 3	4, 5, 6, …
	2, 4, 6	8, 10, 12, …
Dates and Times	Jan	Feb, Mar, Apr, …
	January	February, March, April, …
	15-Jan, 15-Feb	15-Mar, 15-Apr, 15-May, …
	12/30/2029	12/31/2029, 1/1/2029, 1/2/2029, …
	1/31/2029, 2/28/2029	3/31/2029, 4/30/2029, 5/31/2029, …
	Mon	Tue, Wed, Thu, …
	Monday	Tuesday, Wednesday, Thursday, …
	11:00 AM	12:00 PM, 1:00 PM, 2:00 PM, …
	11:58 AM, 11:59 AM	12:00 PM, 12:01 PM, 12:02 PM, …
Patterned Text	1st period	2nd period, 3rd period, 4th period, …
	Region 1	Region 2, Region 3, Region 4, …
	Quarter 3	Quarter 4, Quarter 1, Quarter 2, …
	Qtr3	Qtr4, Qtr1, Qtr2, …

AutoFill can extend patterns either horizontally across columns within a single row or vertically across rows within a single column.

Reference

Extending a Series with AutoFill

- Enter the first few values of the series into a range.
- Select the range, and then drag the fill handle over the cells you want to fill; or double-click to fill handle to extend the series alongside the adjacent data.
- To copy only the formats or only the formulas, click the Auto Fill Options button and select the appropriate option.

or

- Enter the first few values of the series into a range.
- Select the entire range into which you want to extend the series.
- On the Home tab, in the Editing group, click the Fill button, and then click Down, Right, Up, Left, Series, or Justify.

At the MediCOH call center, calls are automatically assigned a sequential call ID number with the pattern C*YearMonthDateNumber*, where *Year* is the two-digit year value, *Month* is the two-digit month value, *Date* is the two-digit day value, and *Number* is three-digit number indicating the placement of the call on that day. For example, the 12th call on 11/9/2029 would have a call ID of C291109012. You will use AutoFill to insert the call IDs in column E of the Call Center Log worksheet.

To insert the call ID number series in the call log:

1. In cell **E5**, enter **C291105001** as the call ID number for the first call received on November 5, 2029.

2. Click cell **E5** to select it, and then double-click the **fill handle** in the lower-right corner of the cell. The text series extends through remaining cells in the Call ID column.

3. At the bottom of the Call ID column, click the **Auto Fill Options** button ⊞ , and then click **Fill Without Formatting**. The original formatting is retained.

    > **Tip** Another way to retain banded rows in a table is to select the two cells in the column and then autofill the series.

4. Go to cell **E333** and verify that the last call ID is C291105329.

5. Click cell **E5** to select it. Refer to Figure 3–7.

Figure 3–7   Text pattern extended with AutoFill

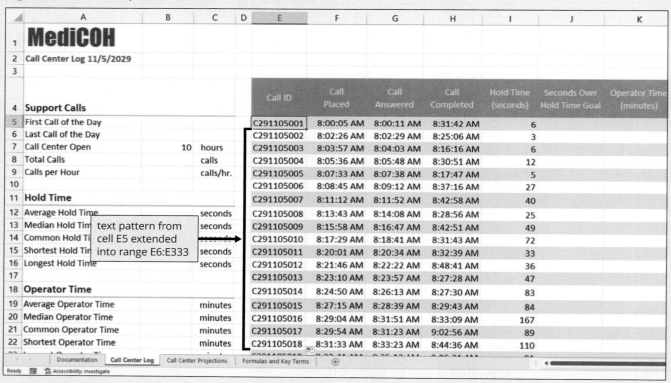

6. Save the workbook.

Another way to define a series is with the Series dialog box; refer to Figure 3–8. To access the Series dialog box, select the range in which you want to place a series of values, click the Fill button in the Editing group on the Home tab, and then select Series. You can specify a linear or growth series for numbers; a date series for dates that increase by day, weekday, month, or year; or an AutoFill series for patterned text. With numbers, you can also specify the step value (how much each number increases over the previous entry) and a stop value (the endpoint for the entire series).

Figure 3–8   Series dialog box

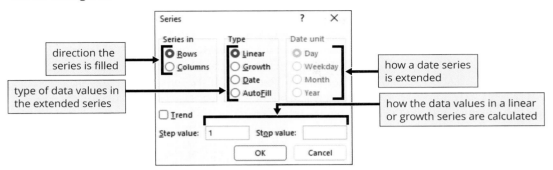

Exploring Cell References

You entered the formula = (G5 − F5)*24*60*60 in cell E5. When you extended the formula, AutoFill not only copied the formula but also adjusted the cell references in the formula to reflect the formula's new location in the worksheet. For example, AutoFill entered the formula = (G6 − F6)*24*60*60 in cell E6. If you do not want Excel to adjust cell references, you need to modify the type of cell reference used.

Excel has four types of cell references: relative, absolute, mixed, and spill. Each type of cell reference reacts differently when a formula or function is copied and pasted to a new location.

Relative Cell References

A relative cell reference changes based on its position to the cell containing the formula. For example, if cell A1 contains the formula = B1 + A2, Excel interprets that formula as, "Add the value of the cell one column to the right of cell A1 (cell B1) to the value of the cell one row down from cell A1 (cell A2)." This relative interpretation of the references is retained when the formula is copied to a new location. If the formula in cell A1 is copied to cell D3, the cell that is one column to the right is cell E3 and the cell that is one row down is cell D4. The formula copied from cell A1 = B1 + A2 into cell D3 becomes = E3 + D4.

Similarly, the hold time formula = (G5 − F5)*24*60*60 in cell E5 instructed Excel to calculate the difference of the cell one column to the left (cell F5) and the cell two columns to the left (cell G5). Because the formula uses relative references, the other hold time calculations used the same pattern. For example, the formula in cell E6 is = (G6 − F6)*24*60*60 and so on. But with some formulas, you don't want the cell references to change. This is when an absolute cell reference is useful.

Absolute Cell References

An absolute cell reference remains locked to a cell even when the formula it's used in is copied to a new location. Absolute references use the dollar sign symbol, $, before each column and row designation. For example, B8 is a relative reference to cell B8, while $B$8 is an absolute reference to that cell. If cell A1 contains the formula = $B$8 + $A$2, Excel interprets that formula as, "Add the value of cell B8 to the value of cell A2." That interpretation is always the same no matter where the formula is copied.

Mixed Cell References

A **mixed cell reference** contains both relative and absolute components, locking either the column reference or the row reference, but not both. For example, a mixed cell reference to cell A2 can be either $A2 where the column is locked and the row is relative, or it can be A$2 where the column is relative and the row is locked. When copied to a new location, the absolute portion of the cell reference remains locked, but the relative portion shifts. If the formula = $B2 + A$2 in cell A1 is copied to cell D3, the formula changes to =$B4 + E$2 because the locked parts of the row and column references don't change, but the relative parts adjust based on the location of the new cell (one row down for the first cell reference and one column to the right for the second cell reference).

You can cycle between relative, absolute, and mixed references using the F4 key. After you type a cell reference, such as A1, in a formula, pressing F4 once changes it to the absolute reference $A$1, pressing F4 again changes it to the mixed reference A$1, and pressing F4 a third time changes it to the mixed reference $A1. Pressing F4 a fourth time repeats the cycle with the relative reference A1.

Proskills

Problem Solving: When to Use Relative, Absolute, and Mixed Cell References

Part of effective workbook design is knowing when to use relative, absolute, and mixed cell references. Use relative references when you want to apply the same formula with input cells that share a common layout or pattern. Relative references are commonly used when copying a formula that calculates summary statistics across columns or rows of data values. Use absolute references when you want copied formulas to always refer to the same cell. This usually occurs when a cell contains a constant value, such as a tax rate, that will be referenced in formulas throughout the worksheet. Mixed references are seldom used other than when creating tables of calculated values such as a multiplication table in which the values of the formula or function can be found at the intersection of the rows and columns of the table.

Mixed references are useful in tables where the first row and column contain data applied to every cell within table. You will use mixed cell reference to create a multiplication table.

To use mixed references to formulas in a table:

1. Open the **NP_EX_3-2.xlsx** workbook located in the **Excel3 > Module** folder included with your Data Files, and then save the workbook as **NP_EX_3_Explore** in the location specified by your instructor.

2. In the Documentation worksheet, enter your name in cell B3 and the date in cell B4.

3. Go to the **Mixed References** worksheet, and then click cell **B5**. This cell will contain the first entry in the multiplication table.

4. Type the equal sign **=** to begin the formula.

5. Click cell **A5**, and then press the **F4** key three times. The cell reference changes to the mixed reference $A5.

6. Type ***** as the operator.

7. Click cell **B4**, and then press the **F4** key twice. The cell reference changes to B$4.

8. Press **ENTER**. The formula =$A5*B$4 is entered in the cell, returning the value 1.

9. Use AutoFill to extend the formula in cell B5 down to cell **B14** and then across the range B5:F14. The multiplication table is complete.

10. Click cell **B5**, and then click the **Formulas** tab on the ribbon.

11. In the Formula Auditing group, click the **Show Formulas** button. The formulas with the mixed references copied across the multiplication table appear in the worksheet. Refer to Figure 3–9.

Figure 3–9   Multiplication table formulas with mixed references

▲	A	B	C	D	E	F	G	H	I
1	Mixed Ref								
2	Multiplication T								
3									
4		1	2	3	4	5			
5	1	=$A5*B$4	=$A5*C$4	=$A5*D$4	=$A5*E$4	=$A5*F$4			
6	2	=$A6*B$4	=$A6*C$4	=$A6*D$4	=$A6*E$4	=$A6*F$4			
7	3	=$A7*B$4	=$A7*C$4	=$A7*D$4	=$A7*E$4	=$A7*F$4			
8	4	=$A8*B$4	=$A8*C$4	=$A8*D$4	=$A8*E$4	=$A8*F$4			
9	5	=$A9*B$4	=$A9*C$4	=$A9*D$4	=$A9*E$4	=$A9*F$4			
10	6	=$A10*B$4	=$A10*C$4	=$A10*D$4	=$A10*E$4	=$A10*F$4			
11	7	=$A11*B$4	=$A11*C$4	=$A11*D$4	=$A11*E$4	=$A11*F$4			
12	8	=$A12*B$4	=$A12*C$4	=$A12*D$4	=$A12*E$4	=$A12*F$4			
13	9	=$A13*B$4	=$A13*C$4	=$A13*D$4	=$A13*E$4	=$A13*F$4			
14	10	=$A14*B$4	=$A14*C$4	=$A14*D$4	=$A14*E$4	=$A14*F$4			
15									

12. Click the **Show Formulas** button again. The calculated values are displayed.

13. Save the workbook.

Now that you've worked with relative, absolute, and mixed cell references, you will return to the call center log.

Chryssa's goal for the call center is to have every call answered within one minute. To document how well the call center is meeting that goal, you will determine by how much each call meets or exceeds that 60-second challenge.

To calculate the difference between each hold time and the 60-second goal:

1. Return to the **NP_EX_Calls** workbook, and make sure the Call Center Log worksheet is active.

2. In cell **B28**, enter **60** as the hold-time goal.

3. In cell **J5**, enter the formula **= I5 − $B$28** to subtract the 60-second goal from the first call of the day. The calculated value is −54, indicating that the first call had a hold time that was 54 seconds below the call center goal.

   > **Key Step** Be sure to enter the absolute cell reference $B$28 rather than the relative reference so the reference is locked when you extend the formula down the column.

4. Click cell **J5** to select it, and then double-click the **fill handle** to autofill the Seconds Over Hold Time Goal column.

5. Click the **Auto Fill Options** button, and then click the **Fill Without Formatting** option to retain the banded rows.

6. Click cell **J5** to deselect the range. Refer to Figure 3–10.

Figure 3-10   Formulas with absolute cell references

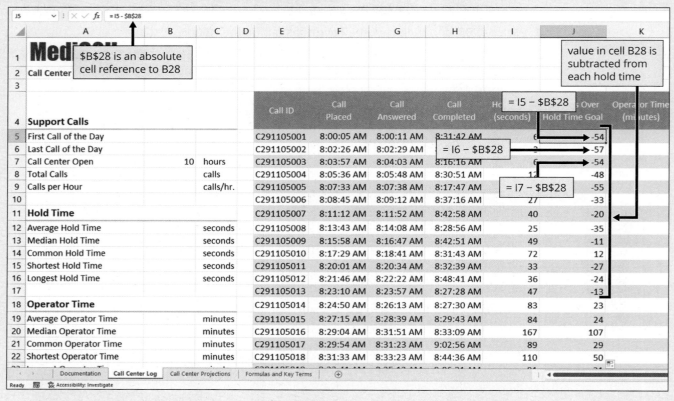

7.   Save the workbook.

Because the formula uses an absolute reference to cell B28, it will always point to cell B28 even when extended through the range J5:J333. For example, the formula in cell J6 is = I6 − $B$28, the formula in J7 is = I7 − $B$28, and so forth.

Calculating with Dynamic Arrays

So far you have entered formulas that return a single value in a single cell. You can also enter formulas that use dynamic arrays to return multiple values across multiple cells. An **array** is a collection of elements or data values. A **dynamic array** is an array that automatically increases in size as more values are added to it.

An Excel formula with dynamic arrays populates multiple cells in a rectangular range of cells. You enter the formula only once in the upper-left cell of the range, and then Excel automatically applies the formula across and down the rectangular range. You don't have to copy or paste the formula. Excel determines where to place the calculated values based on the arrays specified in that single formula.

You will return to the Explore workbook and use a dynamic array to create another multiplication table.

To create a multiplication table with dynamic arrays:

1.   Go to the **NP_EX_3_Explore** workbook, and then go to the **Dynamic Arrays** worksheet.

2.   In cell **B5**, type the equal sign **=** to begin a formula.

3.   Select the range **A5:A14** containing the first array of values for the multiplication table.

4.   Type ***** as the multiplication operator, and then select the range **B4:F4** containing the second array of values for the multiplication table. The formula =A5:A14*B4:F4 is displayed in the formula bar.

5. Press **ENTER**. The dynamic array formula is applied to the rest of table, showing the multiplication of each combination of row and column values.

6. Click cell **B5** to select it. Refer to Figure 3–11.

Figure 3–11   Multiplication table with a dynamic array

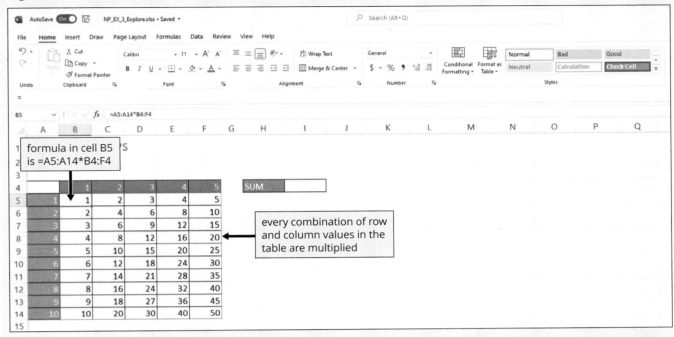

7. Click cell **E10** displaying the value 24 (the product of 6 and 4). This cell displays the same formula you entered in cell B5, =A5:A14*B4:F4, but grayed out. This is because the formula only exists in cell B5 but is applied everywhere in the table.

   As with other formulas, when you change a cell value, the calculated values update to reflect that change.

8. In cell **F4**, enter **6** as the new value. Column F now displays multiples of 6 instead of 5.

9. In cell **F4**, return cell value to **5**.

Every formula or function that uses a single value can be turned into a dynamic array. You just replace the single values with arrays to return multiple values. For example, the formula = A1 + B1 returns a single value containing the sum of cells A1 and B1. But the formula = A1:A10 + B1:B10 returns a column of 10 values: the first cell contains the sum of cells A1 and B1, the second cell contains the sum of cells A2 and B2, and so on.

Spill Ranges

The range of values returned by a dynamic array formula is called a spill range because the formula in the upper-left corner of the rectangular range "spills" into the other cells. All the cells in the spill range use the same formula, but only the formula in the upper-left cell can be edited.

Dynamic array formulas can only spill into empty cells, ensuring that any content in the path of the spill range is not overwritten. If a dynamic array formula cannot be spilled because one of the cells in the dynamic array already contains content, #SPILL! appears in upper-left cell. You'll try this now.

To change the spill range for the multiplication table:

1. In cell **E10**, enter **Excel**. The values are removed from the original spill range. Cell B5 displays #SPILL! indicating that the spill range could not be generated because the range contains other content. Refer to Figure 3–12.

Figure 3–12   Spill range obstructed

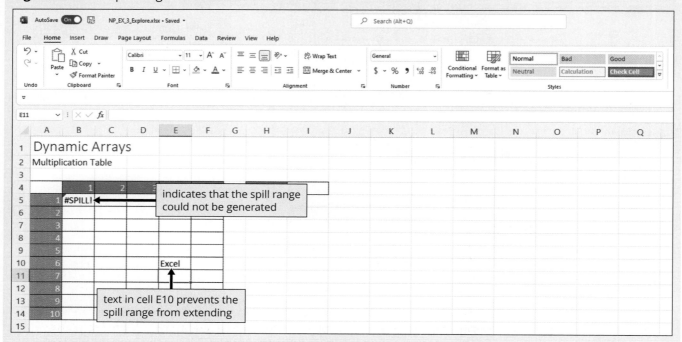

2. Click cell **E10**, and then press **DELETE** to remove the text in the cell. The dynamic array formula once again fills the multiplication table with values.

Referencing a Spill Range

A spill range reference includes the reference of the upper-left cell of the spill range followed by the pound sign (#). For example, A10# references a spill range that starts from cell A10. Because the size of the spill range is determined by the dynamic array formula, you do not need to specify the exact rows and columns in the range. Excel will automatically include all cells that contain the formula spilled from cell A10.

You'll use the SUM function with a spill range reference to calculate the sum of the values in the multiplication table.

To calculate the sum of the values in the multiplication table with a spill range:

1. In the Dynamic Arrays worksheet, click cell **I4** to select it.

2. Type **= SUM(B5#)** as the formula, and then press **ENTER**. Excel returns a value of 825, the total sum of the values in the spill range of the multiplication table.

3. Click cell **I4** to select it. Refer to Figure 3–13.

Figure 3–13   Function with a spill range reference

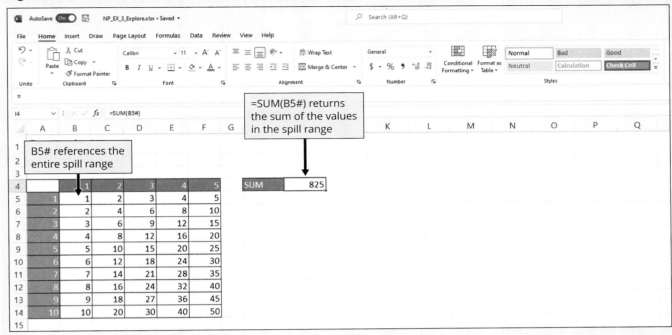

4. Save the workbook, and then close it

The next column in the call log calculates the number of minutes operators spend on the phone with customers. You will use dynamic arrays to calculate the difference between the time each call was completed and the time the call was answered. Because this difference is expressed in days, you will multiply the difference by 24 times 60 to convert it to minutes.

To calculate the operator time in minutes:

1. Go to the **NP_EX_3_Calls** workbook, and make sure the **Call Center Log** worksheet is active.

2. In cell **K5**, enter **= (H5:H333 − G5:G333)*24*60** as the dynamic array formula. The difference in minutes for each call is displayed in the spill range K5:K333. A thin blue border surrounds the cells in the spill as a reminder that the dynamic array formula in cell K5 is spilled into these cells.

3. Click cell **K5** to select it. The duration of the first call in this cell is displayed as a time value.

4. On the Home tab, in the Number group, click the **Number Format arrow**, and then click **General** to apply the General number format to cell K5. Refer to Figure 3–14.

Figure 3-14   Duration of each call with an operator

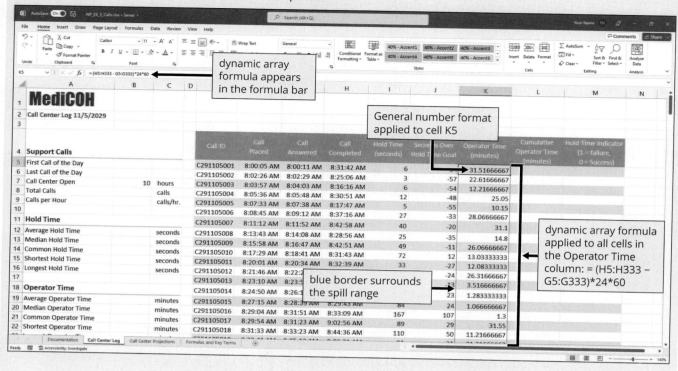

Performing Calculations with the Quick Analysis Tool

When you select a range of cells, the Quick Analysis tool appears to provide quick access to tools for data analysis, chart creation, and conditional formatting. The tool is organized into the following five categories:

- **Formatting** to apply conditional formats to the selected range
- **Charts** to create charts from the data in the range
- **Totals** to calculate sums, counts, and averages of the selected data
- **Tables** to convert the selected range into an Excel table
- **Sparklines** to create sparkline charts from the selected data

Many of the Quick Analysis tools are also accessible in other ways. For example, the conditional formatting commands are also available in the Styles group on the Home tab, and the SUM function is also available in the Editing group on the Home tab or in the Function Library group on the Formulas tab as well as by typing it in the cell.

Chryssa wants a running total of the time that operators spend on the phone as the day progresses. Although you can calculate the total from this column of data by directly entering the SUM function into a cell, you will use the Quick Analysis tool to apply that calculation to the values in column K.

To calculate a running total with the Quick Analysis tool:

1. Select the range **K5:K333** containing the operator time in minutes for each call.

2. In the lower-right corner of the selected range, click the **Quick Analysis** button 📖 (or press **CTRL+Q**). A menu of Quick Analysis categories and buttons appears.

3. In the Quick Analysis tool categories, click **Totals**. The tools for calculating summary statistics in the selected range appear. Refer to Figure 3-15.

Figure 3–15   Totals category on the Quick Analysis tool

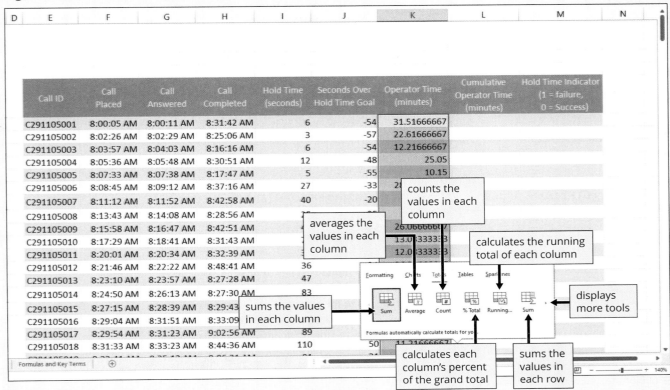

4. Click the **right arrow** to access additional Quick Analysis tools.

5. Click the **Running** tool (the last icon in the list). The running total of call durations is added to the adjacent range L5:L333.

6. Scroll up and click cell **L5**. Refer to Figure 3–16.

Figure 3–16   Running total of operator time

| | D | E | F | G | H | I | J | K | L | M | N |

Call ID	Call Placed	Call Answered	Call Completed	Hold Time (seconds)	Seconds Over Hold Time Goal	Operator Time (minutes)	Cumulative Operator Time (minutes)	Hold Time Indicator (1 = failure, 0 = Success)
C291105001	8:00:05 AM	8:00:11 AM	8:31:42 AM	6	-54	31.51666667	31.51666667	
C291105002	8:02:26 AM	8:02:29 AM	8:25:06 AM	3			54.13333333	
C291105003	8:03:57 AM	8:04:03 AM	8:16:16 AM	6	-54	12.216	66.35	
C291105004	8:05:36 AM	8:05:48 AM	8:30:51 AM	12	-48	25.05	91.4	
C291105005	8:07:33 AM	8:07:38 AM	8:17:47 AM	5			101.55	
C291105006	8:08:45 AM	8:09:12 AM	8:37:16 AM	27	-33	28.06666667	129.6166667	
C291105007	8:11:12 AM	8:11:52 AM	8:42:58 AM	40	-20	31.1	160.7166667	
C291105008	8:13:43 AM	8:14:08 AM	8:28:56 AM	25	-35	14.8	175.5166667	
C291105009	8:15:58 AM	8:16:47 AM	8:42:51 AM	49	-11	26.06666667	201.5833333	
C291105010	8:17:29 AM	8:18:41 AM	8:31:43 AM	72	12	13.03333333	214.6166667	
C291105011	8:20:01 AM	8:20:34 AM	8:32:39 AM	33	-27	12.08333333	226.7	
C291105012	8:21:46 AM	8:22:22 AM	8:48:41 AM	36	-24	26.31666667	253.0166667	
C291105013	8:23:10 AM	8:23:57 AM	8:27:28 AM	47	-13	3.516666667	256.5333333	
C291105014	8:24:50 AM	8:26:13 AM	8:27:30 AM	83	23	1.283333333	257.8166667	
C291105015	8:27:15 AM	8:28:39 AM	8:29:43 AM	84	24	1.066666667	258.8833333	
C291105016	8:29:04 AM	8:31:51 AM	8:33:09 AM	167	107	1.3	260.1833333	
C291105017	8:29:54 AM	8:31:23 AM	9:02:56 AM	89	29	31.55	291.7333333	
C291105018	8:31:33 AM	8:33:23 AM	8:44:36 AM	110	50	11.21666667	302.95	

= SUM($K$5:K5)

= SUM($K$5:K6)

= SUM($K$5:K7)

running totals calculated using the Quick Analysis tool

Formulas and Key Terms

Column L shows the running totals of operator time in minutes. For each cell in column L, the Quick Analysis tool inserts a formula that calculates the sum of all values from the first cell through the cell in the current row. The initial cell reference is locked at cell K5 ($K$5), but the second cell reference is relative and changes for each row (K5, K6, K7, and so on). So, the function in cell L5 is SUM($K$5:K5), the function in cell L6 is SUM(KK:K6), and so on.

The Quick Analysis calculations are in bold. You'll remove the bold formatting so that the values in column L have same formatting as column K.

To remove bold formatting from the running totals:

1. Select the range **L5:L333** containing the running totals.

2. On the ribbon, click **Home** tab, and then in the Font group, click the **Bold** button ⬚ᴮ (or press **CTRL+B**) to remove bold formatting from the selected range.

3. Click cell **L5** to deselect the range.

Column L now shows the running total of the time in minutes spent by operators answering calls. The first two calls required more than 54 minutes of operator time. The first three calls required more than 66 minutes. With the duration of each call added to the previous total, Chryssa can track the increase of total operator time throughout the day. For example, by 9 AM (cell L24), MediCOH operators have logged about 359 minutes, or almost 6 hours, dealing with customers. By the end of the day (cell L333), more than 7,590 operator minutes, or 126.5 operator hours, were spent answering customer inquiries. Hiring and training enough operators to answer that volume of calls each day is one of the call center's greatest challenges.

Interpreting Error Values

When Excel encounters a formula that it cannot resolve, it returns an **error value** indicating that no results can be returned from the formula. For example, when Excel could not complete the dynamic array earlier because of the obstructing text in cell E10, it returned the error value #SPILL! to indicate that the formula in cell B5 could not be spilled (refer back to Figure 3–12). Common error values you might encounter are listed in Figure 3–17.

Figure 3–17   Error values

Error Value	Description
#DIV/0!	The formula or function contains a number divided by 0.
#NAME?	Excel doesn't recognize text in the formula or function, such as when the function name is misspelled.
#N/A	A value is not available to a function or formula, which can occur when a workbook is initially set up prior to entering actual data values.
#NULL!	A formula or function requires two cell ranges to intersect, but they don't.
#NUM!	Invalid numbers are used in a formula or function, such as text entered for a function argument requiring a number.
#REF!	A cell reference used in a formula or function is no longer valid, which can occur when the cell used by the function was deleted from the worksheet.
#SPILL!	A spill range could not be completed, often because of text already present in one of the spill range cells
#VALUE!	The wrong type of argument is used in a function or formula. This can occur when you reference a text value for an argument that should be strictly numeric.

When a formula returns an error, an error indicator appears in the upper-left corner of that cell. You can point to the error indicator to display a ScreenTip with more information about the error. Although the ScreenTips provide hints as to the reason for the error, you usually need to examine the formula to determine exactly what went wrong and how to fix it.

You have completed your initial work on the call center log by calculating the hold time experienced by each customer and the total time operators spent helping customers during a typical day. In the next part, you will use functions to summarize this data. Your analysis will help Chryssa develop a plan for the center's staffing needs.

Part 3.1 Quick Check

1. Write a formula to convert the number of days entered in cell B10 to seconds.

2. If 4/30/2029 and 5/31/2029 are the initial values in a range, what are the next two values that AutoFill will insert?

3. You need to reference cell Q57 in a formula. What is its relative reference? What is its absolute reference? What are its two mixed references?

4. If cell R10 contains the formula =R1+R2 that is then copied to cell S20, what formula is entered in cell S20?

5. If cell R10 contains the formula =$R1+R$2 that is then copied to cell S20, what formula is entered in cell S20?

6. The range A1:A10 contains the integers from 1 to 10. If you enter the dynamic array formula =2*A1:A10 in cell B1, what will be the result?

7. The range A2:A11 contains the integers from 1 to 10. The range B1:D1 contains the values 10, 20, and 30. If the dynamic array formula =A2:A11+B1:D1 is entered in cell B2, what will be the result?

8. Cell A10 displays the #SPILL! error value. What might have caused that error?

9. Cell B2 contains the formula =SUME(A1:A100) with the name of the SUM function misspelled as SUME. What error value will appear in cell B2?

Part 3.2 Visual Overview:
Formulas and Functions

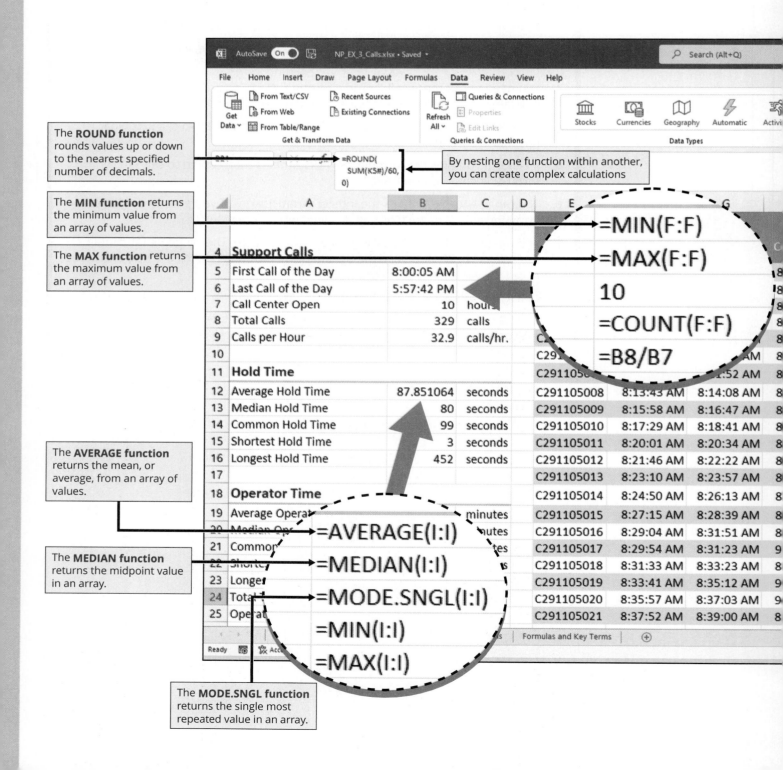

The **ROUND function** rounds values up or down to the nearest specified number of decimals.

By nesting one function within another, you can create complex calculations

```
=ROUND(
    SUM(K5#)/60,
    0)
```

The **MIN function** returns the minimum value from an array of values.

The **MAX function** returns the maximum value from an array of values.

The **AVERAGE function** returns the mean, or average, from an array of values.

The **MEDIAN function** returns the midpoint value in an array.

The **MODE.SNGL function** returns the single most repeated value in an array.

=MIN(F:F)

=MAX(F:F)

10

=COUNT(F:F)

=B8/B7

=AVERAGE(I:I)

=MEDIAN(I:I)

=MODE.SNGL(I:I)

=MIN(I:I)

=MAX(I:I)

	A	B	C	D	E	F	G
4	**Support Calls**						
5	First Call of the Day	8:00:05 AM					
6	Last Call of the Day	5:57:42 PM					
7	Call Center Open	10	hours				
8	Total Calls	329	calls				
9	Calls per Hour	32.9	calls/hr.				
10					C29...		
11	**Hold Time**				C291105...		:52 AM
12	Average Hold Time	87.851064	seconds		C291105008	8:13:43 AM	8:14:08 AM
13	Median Hold Time	80	seconds		C291105009	8:15:58 AM	8:16:47 AM
14	Common Hold Time	99	seconds		C291105010	8:17:29 AM	8:18:41 AM
15	Shortest Hold Time	3	seconds		C291105011	8:20:01 AM	8:20:34 AM
16	Longest Hold Time	452	seconds		C291105012	8:21:46 AM	8:22:22 AM
17					C291105013	8:23:10 AM	8:23:57 AM
18	**Operator Time**				C291105014	8:24:50 AM	8:26:13 AM
19	Average Opera...		minutes		C291105015	8:27:15 AM	8:28:39 AM
20	Median Op...		...utes		C291105016	8:29:04 AM	8:31:51 AM
21	Common...		...tes		C291105017	8:29:54 AM	9...
22	Shorte...		s		C291105018	8:31:33 AM	8:33:23 AM
23	Longe...				C291105019	8:33:41 AM	8:35:12 AM
24	Total...				C291105020	8:35:57 AM	8:37:03 AM
25	Opera...				C291105021	8:37:52 AM	8:39:00 AM

The What-If Analysis button lets you perform what-if analyses and goal seeks to explore different scenarios for data calculations.

The expand and contract arrows on the formula bar lets you display and then hide several lines of a formula.

The **IF function** returns one value if a specified condition is met and a different value if the condition is not met.

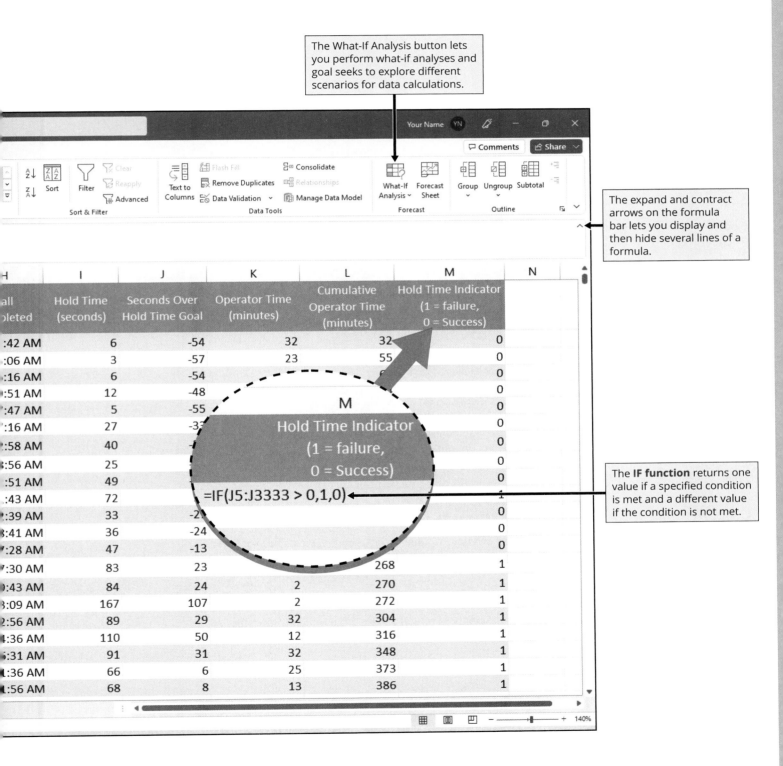

H all pleted	Hold Time (seconds)	Seconds Over Hold Time Goal	Operator Time (minutes)	Cumulative Operator Time (minutes)	Hold Time Indicator (1 = failure, 0 = Success)
:42 AM	6	-54	32	32	0
:06 AM	3	-57	23	55	0
:16 AM	6	-54			0
:51 AM	12	-48			0
:47 AM	5	-55			0
:16 AM	27	-33			0
:58 AM	40				0
:56 AM	25				0
:51 AM	49				0
:43 AM	72				1
:39 AM	33	-2			0
:41 AM	36	-24			0
:28 AM	47	-13			0
:30 AM	83	23		268	1
:43 AM	84	24	2	270	1
:09 AM	167	107	2	272	1
:56 AM	89	29	32	304	1
:36 AM	110	50	12	316	1
:31 AM	91	31	32	348	1
:36 AM	66	6	25	373	1
:56 AM	68	8	13	386	1

M

Hold Time Indicator
(1 = failure,
0 = Success)

=IF(J5:J3333 > 0,1,0)

Analyzing Data with Excel Functions

Excel supports several hundred functions covering a wide range of topics, including finance, statistics, and engineering. With so many functions, it can be challenging to find the function you need. To help you locate functions, Excel organizes the functions into a function library with the 13 categories described in Figure 3–18.

Figure 3–18   Function library categories

Category	Description
Compatibility	Functions from Excel 2010 or earlier, still supported to provide backward compatibility
Cube	Retrieve data from multidimensional databases involving online analytical processing (OLAP)
Database	Retrieve and analyze data stored in databases
Date & Time	Analyze or create date and time values and time intervals
Engineering	Analyze engineering problems
Financial	Analyze information for business and finance
Information	Return information about the format, location, or contents of worksheet cells
Logical	Return logical (true-false) values
Lookup & Reference	Look up and return data matching a set of specified conditions from a range
Math & Trig	Perform math and trigonometry calculations
Statistical	Provide statistical analyses of data sets
Text	Return text values or evaluate text
Web	Provide information on web-based connections

You can access the function library from the Function Library group on the Formulas tab or from the Insert Function dialog box. The Insert Function dialog box includes a search tool to find a function based on a general description. It also displays the function syntax, helping you to enter a function without syntax errors.

Calculating Minimums and Maximums

The MIN and MAX functions return the smallest and largest values from a set of values. The syntax of the two functions is:

```
MIN(number1, [number2], …)
MAX(number1, [number2], …)
```

where *number1*, *number2*, and so on are the numbers or cell ranges from which to find the smallest or largest value.

Reference

Using Functions to Find Minimums and Maximums

- To return the smallest value from a data series, use

```
MIN(number1, [number2], …)
```

where *number1*, *number2* … are the cell ranges or numbers in the data series.

- To return the largest value from a data series, use

```
MAX(number1, [number2], …)
```

Chryssa wants the call center report to note the times of the first and last calls of the day. You will do that calculation with the MIN and MAX functions.

To calculate the first and last calls of the day:

1. If you took a break after the previous part, make sure the NP_EX_3_Calls.xlsx workbook is open and the Call Center Log worksheet is active.

2. Click cell **B5** to select it.

3. On the ribbon, click the **Formulas** tab. In the Function Library group, click the **More Functions** button, and then point to **Statistical** to display a list of all the statistical functions.

4. Scroll down the list, and then click **MIN**. The Function Arguments dialog box for the MIN function opens.

5. In the Number1 box, type **F:F** to return the smallest value from all of the time values in column F. You won't enter anything in the Number2 box because you want to search only this range of cells.

6. Click **OK**. The function returns 0.3333912, which is the numeric value of the minimum time value in column F.

7. On the ribbon, click the **Home** tab. In the Number group, click the **Number Format arrow**, and then click **Time**. The value displayed in cell B5 changes to 8:00:05 AM (the time of the first call).

8. Click cell **B6**, and then repeat Steps 2 through 7, clicking the **MAX** function in Step 4 to return the time of the last call of the day. Cell B6 displays 5:57:42 PM, indicating that the last call was placed just before the call center closed.

The Call Center Log worksheet should also display the number of calls received and the number of calls per hour. You'll add these calculations to the worksheet.

To count the number of calls during the day and per hour:

1. In cell **B8**, enter the formula **= COUNT(F:F)** to count all the cells containing numbers in column F. A total of 329 calls were made that day.

2. In cell **B9**, enter the formula **= B8/B7** to calculate the number of calls per hour. Cell B9 displays 32.9, indicating that the national call center received almost 33 calls per hour. Refer to Figure 3–19.

Figure 3–19   Completed support calls calculations

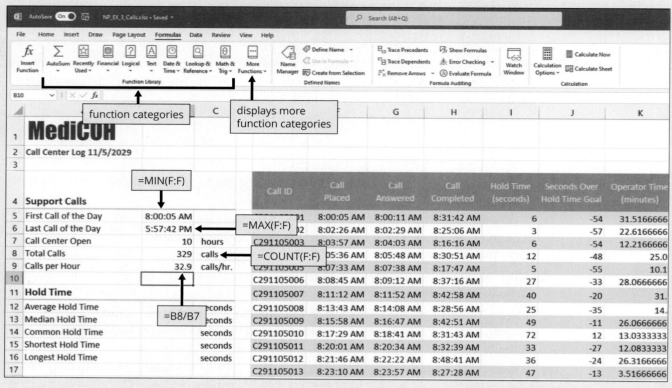

Chryssa now has a better picture of the level of traffic at the call center. Next, you will calculate how long a typical caller will wait on hold before reaching an operator.

Measures of Central Tendency

Central tendency is a single measurement from a data series that returns the most typical or "central" data value. There are several measures of central tendency. This module focuses on the three most used measures—average, median, and mode. The **average**, also known as the **mean**, is equal to the sum of the data values divided by their count. The **median** is the center data value so that half the values are less than the median and half are greater. Finally, the **mode** is the value repeated most often in the data series. A data series can have several modes if different values are repeated the same number of times. These three measures are calculated using the following functions

```
AVERAGE(number1, [number2], …)
MEDIAN(number1, [number2], …)
MODE.SNGL(number1, [number2], …)
MODE.MULT(number1, [number2], …)
MODE(number1, [number2], …)
```

where number1, number2, and so on reference the data values. Notice that Excel includes three different mode functions. The MODE.SNGL function returns a single value representing the mode of the data. The **MODE.MULT function** returns either a single value or a list of values if more than one value is repeated the same number of times. The MODE function is the older version of the function for calculating modes and is equivalent to the MODE.SNGL function.

> **Tip** If there are several possible modes, both the MODE.SNGL and MODE functions return the first mode value listed in the data series.

The average, while the most used measure of central tendency, can be adversely affected by extreme values. Consider an exam in which every student receives a 90 except one student who receives a zero. That single zero value will cause the class average to drop, making it appear that class did poorly on the exam. On the other hand, the median and the mode will both be 90, providing a more accurate assessment of a typical student's performance on the exam. However, the median and the mode are also limited because they obscure information that might be useful. The instructor might want to know that one student did extremely poorly on the exam, which only the average indicates. For these reasons, it is often best to compare the results of all three measures.

Reference

Calculating Measures of Central Tendency

- To calculate the average from a data series, use

    AVERAGE(*number1*, [*number2*], …)

- To calculate the median or midpoint from a data series, use

    MEDIAN(*number1*, [*number2*], …)

- To return a single value that is repeated most often in a data series, use

    MODE.SNGL(*number1*, [*number2*], …)

- To return the value or list of values that is repeated most often in a data series, use

    MODE.MULT(*number1*, [*number2*], …)

Chryssa wants to know the typical hold time that customers will experience at the call center based on the average, median, and mode measures of the hold-time data. Chryssa also wants to know the shortest and longest hold times that customers experienced during the day. You'll calculate these measures using the AVERAGE, MEDIAN, MODE.SNGL, MIN, and MAX functions.

To calculate the average, median, and mode hold times:

1. Click cell **B12**, and then click the **Formulas** tab on the ribbon.

2. In the Function Library group, click the **More Functions** button, and then point to **Statistical** in the list of function categories. A list of statistical functions appears.

3. Click **AVERAGE**. The Function Arguments dialog box opens.

4. In the Number1 box, type **I:I** to reference the column containing the calculated hold times, and then click **OK**. The average hold time of was about 87.85 seconds, or almost a minute and a half.

5. Click cell **B13**, and the repeat Steps 2 through 4, selecting **MEDIAN** as the statistical function in Step 3. The medium hold time was 80 seconds.

6. Click cell **B14**, and then repeat Steps 2 through 4, selecting **MODE.SNGL** as the function in Step 3. the most common hold time was 99 seconds.

7. In cell **B15**, enter the formula **=MIN(I:I)** to calculate the minimum hold-time value in column I. The shortest hold time was 3 seconds.

8. In cell **B16**, enter the formula **= MAX(I:I)** to calculate the longest hold time. The longest hold time of the day was 452 seconds, or about seven and a half minutes. Refer to Figure 3–20.

Figure 3–20   Hold-time summary statistics

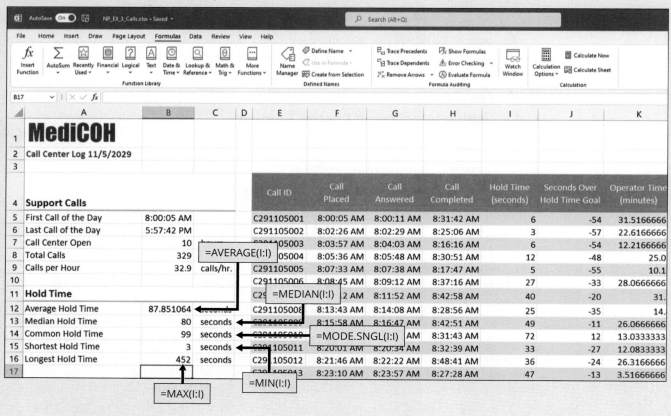

The average, median, and mode values all indicate that a typical customer will wait on hold for about a minute and a half, though it can be much longer. Chryssa wants you to do a similar analysis for the length of time an operator spends on a call. Recall that the operator time calculations in column K were done using a dynamic array formula, so you will reference the data values in that column using the spill range reference K5#.

To calculate the typical length of an operator conversation:

1. In cell **B19**, enter the formula **= AVERAGE(K5#)** to calculate the average length of the conversations. The average conversation lasted 25.471125 minutes.

2. In cell **B20**, enter the formula **= MEDIAN(K5#)** to return the midpoint value. The median conversation lasted 22.75 minutes.

3. In cell **B21**, enter the formula **= MODE.SNGL(K5#)** to return the most common conversation length. Conversations most commonly lasted 13.25 minutes.

4. In cell **B22**, enter the formula **= MIN(K5#)** to return the shortest operator conversation. The shortest conversation lasted 1.0666 minutes.

5. In cell **B23**, enter the formula **= MAX(K5#)** to determine the duration of the longest conversation. of the longest conversation lasted 109.46667 minutes, or about1 hour and 50 minutes. Refer to Figure 3–21.

Figure 3-21   Operator time summary statistics

	A	B	C	D	E	F	G	H	I	J	K
					Call ID	Call Placed	Call Answered	Call Completed	Hold Time (seconds)	Seconds Over Hold Time Goal	Operator Time (minutes)
4	**Support Calls**										
5	First Call of the Day	8:00:05 AM			C291105001	8:00:05 AM	8:00:11 AM	8:31:42 AM	[first cell of the spill range K5#]		31.51666667
6	Last Call of the Day	5:57:42 PM			C291105002	8:02:26 AM	8:02:29 AM	8:25:06 AM		-57	22.61666667
7	Call Center Open	10	hours		C291105003	8:03:57 AM	8:04:03 AM	8:16:16 AM	6	-54	12.21666667
8	Total Calls	329	calls		C291105004	8:05:36 AM	8:05:48 AM	8:30:51 AM	12	-48	25.05
9	Calls per Hour	32.9	calls/hr.		C291105005	8:07:33 AM	8:07:38 AM	8:17:47 AM	5	-55	10.15
10					C291105006	8:08:45 AM	8:09:12 AM	8:37:16 AM	27	-33	28.06666667
11	**Hold Time**				C291105007	8:11:12 AM	8:11:52 AM	8:42:58 AM	40	-20	31.1
12	Average Hold Time	87.851064	seconds		C291105008	8:13:43 AM	8:14:08 AM	8:28:56 AM	25	-35	14.8
13	Median Hold Time	80	seconds		C291105009	8:15:58 AM	8:16:47 AM	8:42:51 AM	49	-11	26.06666667
14	Common Hold Time	99	seconds		C291105010	8:17:29 AM	8:18:41 AM	8:31:43 AM	72	12	13.03333333
15	Shortest Hold Time	3	[=AVERAGE(K5#)]		011	8:20:01 AM	8:20:34 AM	8:32:39 AM	33	-27	12.08333333
16	Longest Hold Time	452			012	8:21:46 AM	8:22:22 AM	8:48:41 AM	36	-24	26.31666667
17					C291105013	8:23:10 AM	8:23:57 AM	8:27:28 AM	47	-13	3.516666667
18	**Operator Time**			[=MEDIAN(K5#)]	50 AM	8:26:13 AM	8:27:30 AM	83	23	1.283333333
19	Average Operator Time	25.471125	minutes		C2911050 5	8:27:15 AM	8:28:39 AM	8:29:43 AM	84	24	1.066666667
20	Median Operator Time	22.75	minutes			8:29:04 AM	8:31:51 AM	8:33:09 AM	167	107	1.3
21	Common Operator Time	13.25	[=MODE.SNGL(K5#)]	AM	9:02:56 AM	89	29	31.55
22	Shortest Operator Time	1.0666667		05018	8:31:33 AM	8:33:23 AM	8:44:36 AM	110	50	11.21666667
23	Longest Operator Time	109.46667	minutes		C291105019	8:33:41 AM	8:35:12 AM	9:06:31 AM	91	31	31.31666667
24	Total Time with Operators		hours		C291105020	8:35:57 AM	8:37:03 AM	9:01:36 AM	66	6	24.55
25	Operator Workload per Hour		[=MAX(K5#)]	[=MIN(K5#)]	8:37:52 AM	8:39:00 AM	8:51:56 AM	68	8	12.93333333
26						8:39:43 AM	8:40:18 AM	8:46:53 AM	35	-25	6.583333333
27	**Key Performance Indicator (KPI)**				C291105023	8:42:26 AM	8:44:13 AM	9:41:37 AM	107	47	57.4

Documentation | **Call Center Log** | Call Center Projections | Formulas and Key Terms   ⊕

Ready   Accessibility: Investigate

The three measures of central tendency for the length of the conversations show distinctly different values. The average conversation with an operator lasts about 25 and half minutes, but the most common conversation length, as indicated by the mode, is 13.25 minutes with a median of 22.75 minutes. One interpretation is that many calls could be dealt with in a short time, although some longer calls (up to almost 110 minutes) require more operator time, bringing up the average. This information tells Chryssa that the call center might handle calls more efficiently by routing more difficult, time-consuming calls to the most experienced operators.

Rounding Data Values

Three rounding functions supported by Excel are ROUND, ROUNDDOWN, and ROUNDUP. The ROUND function rounds a value to the nearest digit, the **ROUNDDOWN function** rounds the value to the next lowest digit, and the **ROUNDUP function** rounds the value up to the next highest digit. These syntax of these three functions are

```
ROUND(number, Num_digits)
ROUNDDOWN(number, Num_digits)
ROUNDUP(number, Num_digits)
```

where *number* is the number to be rounded and *Num_digits* is the digit to round the number to. A positive *Num_digits* rounds values to the right of the decimal point and a negative *Num_digits* rounds digits to the left of decimal point. A *Num_digits* value of zero rounds the number to the nearest integer. Refer to Figure 3-22 for examples of rounding a value to different digits.

Figure 3-22   ROUND function examples

Formula	Interpretation	Result
= ROUND(137.438, 2)	Round to the nearest hundredth	137.44
= ROUND(137.438, 1)	Round to the nearest tenth	137.4
= ROUND(137.438, 0)	Round to the nearest integer	137
= ROUND(137.438, −1)	Round to nearest multiple of ten	140
= ROUND(137.438, −2)	Round to the nearest multiple of one hundred	100

Values returned from the ROUNDDOWN and ROUNDUP functions are similar except that they round the value down or up. The function ROUNDUP(137.438, −2) rounds the value up to the next multiple of 100, returning a value of 200. The function ROUNDDOWN(132.438, −1) rounds the value down to the previous multiple of 10, returning a value of 130.

Unlike number formats, which change how many digits are displayed in a cell, the rounding functions change the value stored in a cell.

Reference

Using Functions to Round Values

- To round a number to the nearest digit, use

    ROUND(*number*, *Num_digits*)

    where *number* is the numeric value and *Num_digits* is the number of digits the numeric value is rounded to.

- To round a number down to the next lowest digit, use

    ROUNDDOWN(*number*, *Num_digits*)

- To round a number to the next highest digit, use

    ROUNDUP(*number*, *Num_digits*)

- To round a number to the nearest integer, use

    INT(*number*)

- To round a number to the nearest multiple of a value, use

    MROUND(*number*, *multiple*)

    where *multiple* is a multiple to be rounded to.

The operator time values in column K show time values to fractions of a minute. Chryssa doesn't need that kind of accuracy in the analysis. Instead, she wants the call durations to be rounded to whole minutes. For example, a call lasting 12.2 minutes would round up to 13 minutes. You will use rounding functions to round up the operator times.

To roundup the operator times:

1. Click cell **K5**, and then press **DELETE** to remove the dynamic array formula. The multiple values in column K disappear and the running totals in column L change to zero.

2. On the Formulas tab, in the Function Library group, click the **Insert Function** button. The Insert Function dialog box opens.

3. In the Search for a function box, type **round** to describe the function you want to use, and then click **Go**. Functions related to rounding appear in the search results. Refer to Figure 3–23.

Figure 3–23   Insert Function dialog box

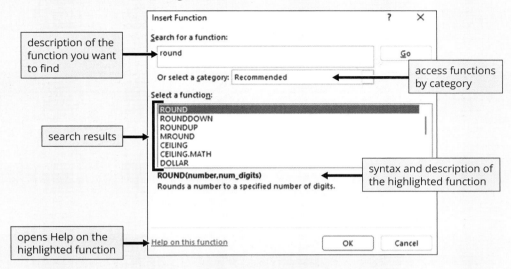

4. In the Select a function box, click **ROUNDUP**, and then click **OK**. The Function Arguments dialog box opens, describing the arguments used by the function.

5. In the Number box, type the formula **(H5:H333 – G5:G333)*24*60** to calculate the duration of the operator times in minutes.

6. Press **TAB**, and then type **0** in the Num_digits box to round up the calculated value to the next highest integer. For cell K5, the formula result 31.51666667 will be rounded up to 32. Refer to Figure 3–24.

Figure 3–24   Function Arguments dialog box

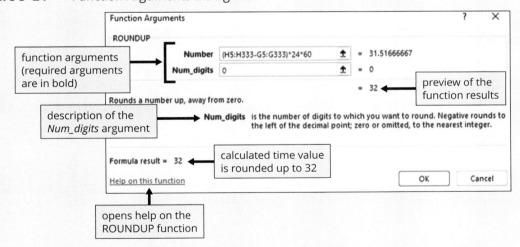

7. Click **OK** to close the dialog box. The formula =ROUNDUP((H5:H333 − G5:G333)*24*60, 0) is entered in cell K5. The rounded values appear in column K starting with the first call lasting 32 minutes (cell K5) through the last call lasting 15 minutes (cell K333). Refer to Figure 3–25.

Figure 3–25   Rounded operator times

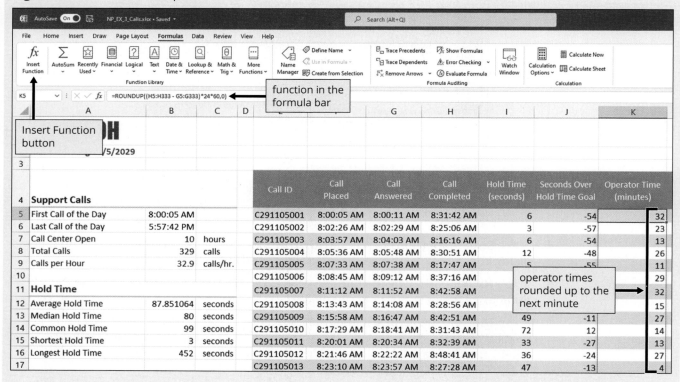

The ROUND, ROUNDDOWN, and ROUNDUP functions all round values to the nearest power of 10 such as 1/100, 1/10, 1, 10, 100, and so forth. To round values to powers other than 10, you can use the **MROUND function**, which has the syntax

    MROUND(*number*, *multiple*)

where *number* is the number to be rounded and *multiple* is a multiple of a value to be rounded to. For example, MROUND(17, 5) returns a value 5 since 5 is the closest multiple of 5 to 17 and MROUND(60, 9) returns a value of 63 since 63 is the closest multiple of 9 to 60.

To always rounds a value down to the next lowest integer, use the **INT function**, which has the syntax

    INT(*number*)

For example, the function INT(52.817) returns a value of 52. You can learn more about the rounding functions in Excel Help.

Proskills

Written Communication: Displaying Significant Digits

Excel stores numbers with a precision up to 15 digits and displays as many digits as will fit into the cell. So even the result of a simple formula such as =10/3 will display 3.33333333333333 if the cell is wide enough.

A number with 15-digit accuracy is difficult to read, and calculations rarely need that level of precision. Many scientific disciplines, such as chemistry or physics, have rules specifying exactly how many digits should be displayed with any calculation. These digits are called **significant digits** because they indicate the accuracy of the measured and calculated values. For example, the value 19.32 has four significant digits.

The rules for determining the number of significant digits reported in a calculation vary between disciplines. Generally, a calculated value should display no more digits than are found in any of the values used in the calculation. For example, any calculations based on the value 19.32 should have no more than four significant digits even if other numbers are measured with greater precision. Showing more digits would be misleading because it implies a level of accuracy beyond what was measured.

Because Excel displays calculated values with as many digits as can fit into a cell, you need to know the standards of your profession to report the number of digits correctly.

Nesting Functions

Functions can be **nested**, or placed inside within, other functions. When functions are nested, Excel evaluates the innermost function first and then moves outward, evaluating the remaining functions with the inner function acting as an argument for the next outer function. For example, the following expression nests the AVERAGE function within the ROUND function. In this expression, the average of the values in the range A1:A100 is calculated first, and then that average is rounded to the nearest integer:

```
ROUND(AVERAGE(A1:A100),0)
```

Formulas that involve several layers of nested functions can be challenging to read. The more nested functions there are, the more difficult it becomes to associate each set of arguments with its corresponding function. To help interpret nested functions, Excel displays the opening and closing parentheses of each function level in a different color. You can also expand the formula bar and then enter different levels of nested functions on separate lines, making each function clearer.

The last part of the Operator Time section in the Call Center Log worksheet calculates the total time operators spend on the phone during the day. Knowing how long operators are actively engaged with customers is important to determining the call center's staffing needs. Chryssa wants the total support time rounded to the nearest hour. To do that, you will use both the SUM function and the ROUND function nested in a single formula. Chyrssa also wants to know the total operator time per hour. You will calculate this value by dividing the total operator time by the total number of hours the call center is open.

To calculate and round the total operator time and the operator time per hour:

1. Click cell **B24** to make it the active cell.

2. Click the **down arrow** in the bottom-right corner of the formula bar. The formula bar expands in height.

3. Type **=ROUND(** to begin the formula. As you type the formula, the syntax of the ROUND function appears in a ScreenTip. The number argument is in bold to indicate that you are entering this part of the function.

4. Press **ALT+ENTER** to create a new line on the formula bar.

5. Press the **SPACEBAR** three times to indent the line three spaces.

6. Type **SUM(K5#)/60,** to calculate the total operator, divided by 60 to convert that sum to hours.

7. Press **ALT+ENTER** to create a new line on the formula bar.

8. Type **0)** to end the ROUND function, rounding the sum to the nearest hour, and then press **ENTER**.

> **Key Step** To round a value to the nearest integer, specify 0 as the last argument in the function to indicate that the value is rounded to zero digits.

9. Click cell **B24** to make it the active cell. The value 142 appears in cell B24, indicating that center operators have logged about 142 hours during the day dealing with customer inquiries. Refer to Figure 3–26.

Figure 3–26   Rounded sum of total operator hours

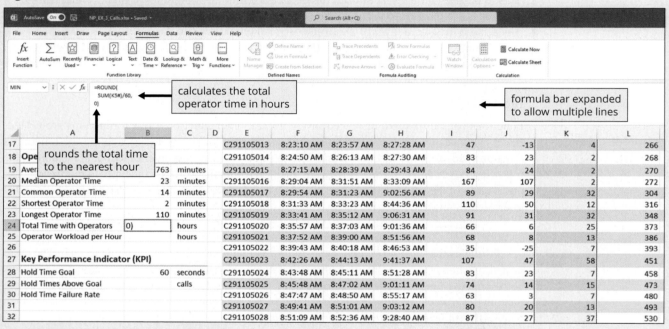

10. Click the **up arrow** in the upper-right corner of the expanded formula bar. The formula bar collapses to one line.

11. In cell **B25**, enter the formula **=B24/B7** to divide the total operator time by the number of hours the call center is open. The total operator time per hour is 14.2.

Chryssa learns that on average, the call center staff spends 14.2 hours with customers every hour. In other words, the call center needs at least 15 operators available every hour to keep up with call volume. Fewer than 15 operators will result in a backlog that would increase throughout the day as more calls pile up in the queue.

The Role of Blanks and Zeroes

The functions you've entered were applied to whole columns of data even though those columns contained empty cells and cells with text strings. Mathematical and statistical functions such as SUM, COUNT, AVERAGE, and MEDIAN include only numeric data in their calculations, ignoring empty cells and text entries. A blank cell is considered a text entry and is not treated as the number zero. Refer to Figure 3–27 for how the results differ when a blank replaces a zero in a data series.

Figure 3–27   Calculations with blanks and zeroes

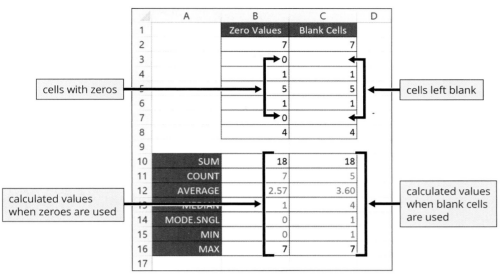

cells with zeros

cells left blank

calculated values when zeroes are used

calculated values when blank cells are used

Whether you use a blank cell or a zero in a data series depends on what you are trying to measure. For example, to calculate the average number of hours per day that the call center is open, Chryssa could enter 0 or a blank for days that the call center is closed. Using a zero returns the average hours worked across all calendar days and gives a good overall summary of the company's annual staffing needs. Using a blank cell would summarize staffing needs only for the days that the call center is open. Both approaches have their uses. Consider the purpose of your calculations and choose the approach that best achieves your goal.

Date and Time Functions

Excel supports a large collection of date and time functions. Figure 3–28 summarizes some of the most useful ones.

Figure 3–28   Date and time functions

Function	Description
DATE(*year,month,day*)	Creates a date value for the date represented by the *year*, *month*, and *day* arguments
DAY(*serial_number*)	Extracts the day of the month from a date value stored as *serial_number*
MONTH(*serial_number*)	Extracts the month number from a date value stored as serial_number, where 1=January, 2=February, and so on
YEAR(*serial_number*)	Extracts the 4-digit year value from a date value stored as *serial_number*
NETWORKDAYS(*start_date, end_date,[holidays]*)	Calculates the number of whole working days between *start_date* and *end_date*; to exclude holidays, add the optional holidays argument containing a list of holiday dates to skip
WEEKDAY(*serial_number, [return_type]*)	Calculates the weekday from a date value stored as *serial_number*, where 1=Sunday, 2=Monday, and so forth; to choose a different numbering scheme, set *return_type* to 1 (1=Sunday, 2=Monday, ...), 2 (1=Monday, 2=Tuesday, ...), or 3 (0=Monday, 1=Tuesday, ...)
WORKDAY(*start_date, days,[holidays]*)	Returns the workday after *days* workdays have passed since the *start_date*; to exclude holidays, add the optional holidays argument containing a list of holiday dates to skip
NOW( )	Returns the current date and time
TODAY( )	Returns the current date

Many workbooks include the current date so that any reports generated by the workbook are identified by date. To display the current date, you can use the following **TODAY function**:

```
TODAY()
```

The date displayed by the TODAY function is updated automatically whenever you enter a new formula or reopen the workbook. You'll use the TODAY function to display the current date on the Documentation sheet.

To display the current date:

1. Go to the **Documentation** sheet.

2. Click cell **B5**, and then type **=TODAY()** as the formula

3. Press **ENTER**. The current date appears in the cell. The date will be updated every time the workbook is reopened.

To display the current date and the current time, use the NOW function. The NOW function, like the TODAY function, is automatically updated whenever you add a new calculation to the workbook or reopen it.

Insight

Date Calculations with Working Days

Businesses are often more interested in workdays rather than calendar days. For example, to estimate a delivery date in which packages are not shipped or delivered on weekends, it is more useful to know the date of the next weekday rather than the date of the next day.

To display the date of a working day that is a specified number of workdays past a start date, use the **WORKDAY function** with the syntax

```
WORKDAY(start_date, days, [holidays])
```

where `start_date` is the starting date, `days` is the number of workdays after that starting date, and `holidays` is an optional list of holiday dates to skip. For example, if cell A1 contains the date 12/20/2029, a Thursday, the following formula displays the date 1/2/2029, a Wednesday that is nine working days later:

```
WORKDAY(A1,9)
```

The optional `holidays` argument references a series of dates that the WORKDAY function will skip in performing its calculations. So, if 12/24/2029, 12/25/2029, and 1/1/2030 are entered in the range B1:B2 as holidays, the following function will return the date 1/4/2030, a Friday, that is nine working days (excluding the holidays) after 12/20/2029:

```
WORKDAY(A1,9,B1:B3)
```

To reverse the process and calculate the number of working days between two dates, use the **NETWORKDAYS function**, which has the syntax

```
NETWORKDAYS(start_date, end_date, [holidays])
```

where `start_date` is the starting date, `end_date` is the ending date, and `holidays` is an optional list of holiday dates to skip. So, if cell A1 contains the date 12/20/2029 and cell A2 contains the date 1/7/2030, the following function returns the value 11, indicating that there are 11 working days between the start and ending date, excluding the holidays specified in the range B1:B3:

```
NETWORKDAYS(A1,A2,B1:B3)
```

For international applications, which might have a different definition of working day, Excel supports the WORKDAY.INTL function. Refer to Excel Help for more information.

Chryssa wants to keep hold times down to a minute or less. She wants to know how many calls in the call log meet this goal. You can use logical functions to find the answer.

Working with the Logical IF Function

A **logical function** is a function that returns one of two possible values depending on whether a given condition is true or false. The condition is entered as an expression, such as A5 = 3. If cell A5 is equal to 3, the condition is true; if cell A5 is not equal to 3, the condition is false. A common logical function is the following IF function:

```
IF(logical_test, value_if_true, [value_if_false])
```

where `logical_test` is a condition that is either true or false, `value_if_true` is the value returned by the function if the condition is true, and `value_if_false` is an optional argument containing the value if the condition is false.

> **Tip** If no `value_if_false` argument is provided, the IF function returns the value FALSE when the condition is false.

For example, the following function returns a value of 100 if A1 = B1. Otherwise, it returns a value of 50:

```
IF(A1 = B1, 100, 50)
```

The `value_if_true` and the `value_if_false` arguments in the IF function can also be cell references. For example, the following function returns the value of cell C1 if the condition is true, otherwise it returns the value of cell D1:

```
IF(A1 = B1, C1, D1)
```

The = symbol in IF function is a **comparison operator**, which is an operator expressing the relationship between two values. Figure 3–29 describes other comparison operators that can be used with logical functions.

Figure 3–29   Logical comparison operators

Operator	Expression	Tests
=	A1 = B1	If value in cell A1 is equal to the value in cell B1
>	A1 > B1	If the value in cell A1 is greater than the value in cell B1
<	A1 < B1	If the value in cell A1 is less than the value in cell B1
>=	A1 >= B1	If the value in cell A1 is greater than or equal to the value in cell B1
<=	A1 <= B1	If the value in cell A1 is less than or equal to the value in cell B1
<>	A1 <> B1	If the value in cell A1 is not equal to the value in cell B1

The following function returns the text string "goal met" if the value in cell A1 is less than or equal to the value of cell B1. Otherwise, it returns the text string "goal failed":

```
IF(A1 <= B1, "goal met", "goal failed")
```

> **Tip** To apply multiple logical conditions, you can nest one IF function within another.

To determine whether a customer was on hold longer than a minute, you will use the IF function to test the values in column J, containing the difference between each customer's hold time and the hold time goal of 60 seconds. If the difference is positive (indicating a hold time longer than 60 seconds), the IF function will return a value of 1. Otherwise, it will return a value of zero.

To use the IF function to indicate that a call has exceed the hold-time goal:

1. Go to the **Call Center Log** worksheet.
2. Click cell **M5** to select that cell.
3. On the Formulas tab, in the Function Library group, click the **Logical** button to display a list of all the logical functions.
4. Click **IF** to open the Function Arguments dialog box for the IF function.
5. In the Logical_test box, type the **J5:J333 > 0** to test whether the array of values in column J are greater than zero.
6. In the Value_if_true box, type **1** as the value to display if the hold time is over 60 seconds.
7. In the Value_if_false box, type **0** as the value to display if the hold time is 60 seconds or less.
8. Click **OK** to enter the formula = IF(J5:J333 > 0, 1, 0) in cell M5. An array of 0s and 1s appear in column M. The tenth call, in cell M14, is the first call that exceeds the 1-minute hold-time goal. Refer to Figure 3–30.

Figure 3–30 Hold times exceeding 1 minute

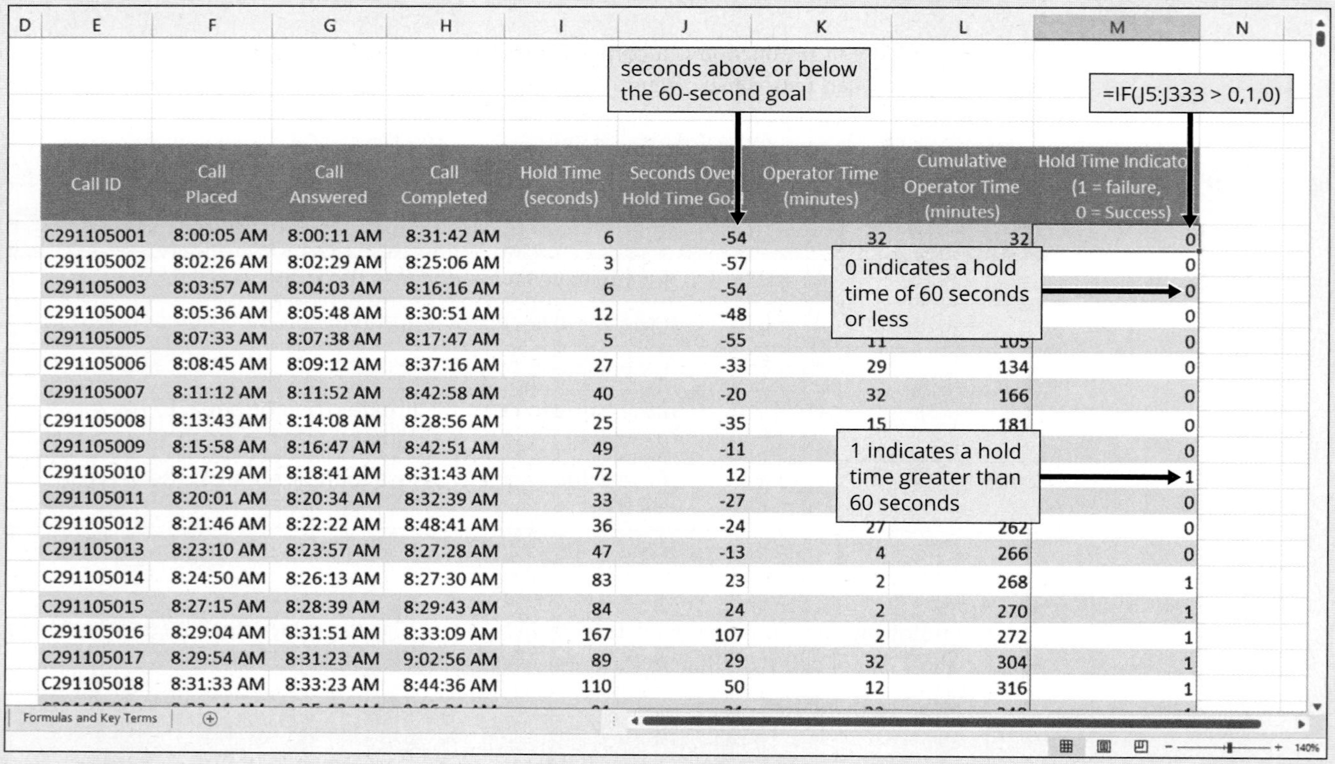

Call ID	Call Placed	Call Answered	Call Completed	Hold Time (seconds)	Seconds Over Hold Time Goal	Operator Time (minutes)	Cumulative Operator Time (minutes)	Hold Time Indicator (1 = failure, 0 = Success)
C291105001	8:00:05 AM	8:00:11 AM	8:31:42 AM	6	-54	32	32	0
C291105002	8:02:26 AM	8:02:29 AM	8:25:06 AM	3	-57			0
C291105003	8:03:57 AM	8:04:03 AM	8:16:16 AM	6	-54			0
C291105004	8:05:36 AM	8:05:48 AM	8:30:51 AM	12	-48			0
C291105005	8:07:33 AM	8:07:38 AM	8:17:47 AM	5	-55	11	105	0
C291105006	8:08:45 AM	8:09:12 AM	8:37:16 AM	27	-33	29	134	0
C291105007	8:11:12 AM	8:11:52 AM	8:42:58 AM	40	-20	32	166	0
C291105008	8:13:43 AM	8:14:08 AM	8:28:56 AM	25	-35	15	181	0
C291105009	8:15:58 AM	8:16:47 AM	8:42:51 AM	49	-11			0
C291105010	8:17:29 AM	8:18:41 AM	8:31:43 AM	72	12			1
C291105011	8:20:01 AM	8:20:34 AM	8:32:39 AM	33	-27			0
C291105012	8:21:46 AM	8:22:22 AM	8:48:41 AM	36	-24	27	262	0
C291105013	8:23:10 AM	8:23:57 AM	8:27:28 AM	47	-13	4	266	0
C291105014	8:24:50 AM	8:26:13 AM	8:27:30 AM	83	23	2	268	1
C291105015	8:27:15 AM	8:28:39 AM	8:29:43 AM	84	24	2	270	1
C291105016	8:29:04 AM	8:31:51 AM	8:33:09 AM	167	107	2	272	1
C291105017	8:29:54 AM	8:31:23 AM	9:02:56 AM	89	29	32	304	1
C291105018	8:31:33 AM	8:33:23 AM	8:44:36 AM	110	50	12	316	1

Businesses often track success with a **key performance indicator (KPI)**, which compares a measured outcome to an established norm or baseline. The percentage of customers experiencing long hold times is one KPI that Chryssa uses to measure the success of the call center. A high percentage of long hold times indicates that the call center needs to improve its service.

Since every call is graded as either a failure (1) or a success (0), you can calculate the percent of calls with long hold times by summing the values in column M and dividing that sum by the total number of calls.

To calculate the number and percent of long hold times:

1. In cell **B29**, enter the formula **= SUM(M5#)** to add the values in column M. Cell B29 displays 265, indicating that 265 callers experienced hold times of longer than a minute.

2. In cell **B30**, enter the formula **= B29/B8** to calculate the percentage of calls with long hold times.

3. Click cell **B30**. You'll format cell B30 to display the value as a percentage to two decimal places.

4. On the ribbon, click the **Home** tab. In the Number group, click the **Number Format** box, and then click **Percentage**. The result of 80.55% indicates that more than 80% of callers experienced a long hold time based on the 60-second standard that Chryssa is trying to maintain for the center. Refer to Figure 3–31.

Figure 3–31   Percentage of failed calls with long hold times

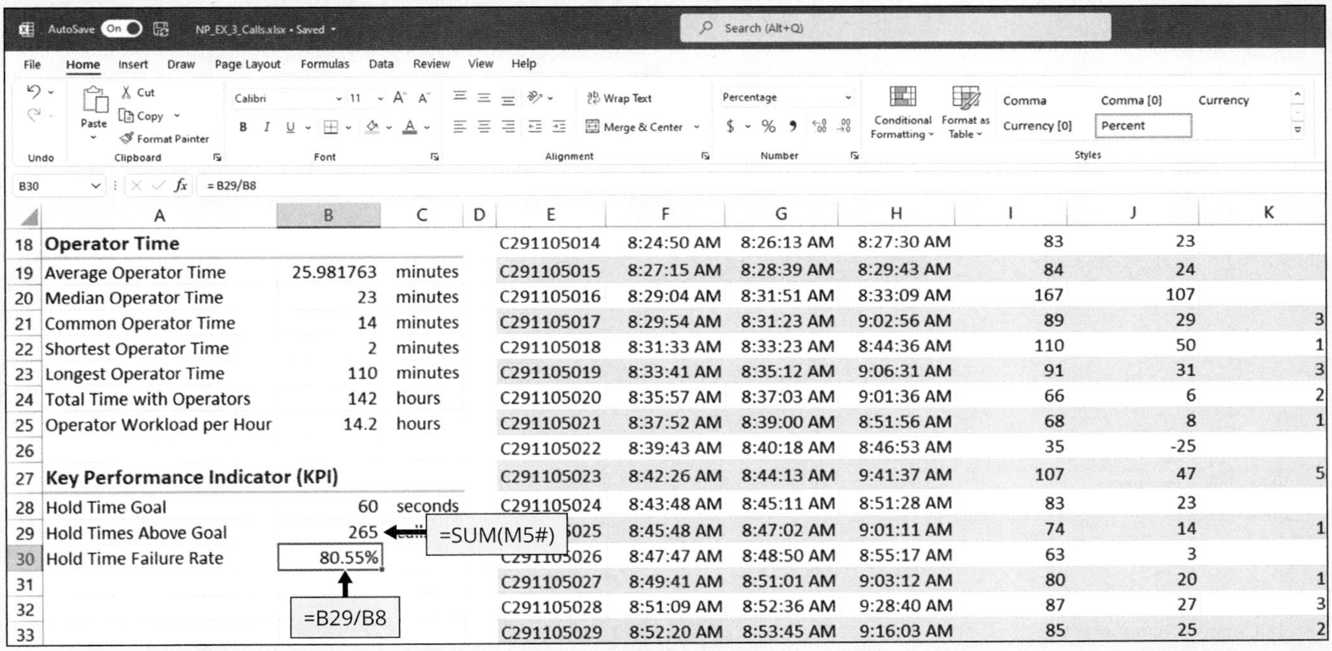

You have compiled a lot of useful information about the call center. Based on your analysis, you know the following:

- The national call center receives about 33 calls per hour.
- Callers wait on hold for an average of about 88 seconds with more than 80% of the callers waiting longer than a minute to reach an operator.
- Operators spend an average of about 26 minutes on each call with some calls lasting up to an hour and a half.
- At least 15 operators must be available every hour to handle the call volume.

More operators will reduce the hold times, but Chryssa wants to know how many more operators are needed to make a significant difference. To answer this question, you will enter what you have learned about the call center.

To enter the call center metrics:

1. Go to the **Call Center Projections** worksheet.

2. In cell **B6**, enter **33** as the anticipated calls per hour to the center.

3. In cell **B7**, enter **15** as the number of operators available to answer calls.

4. In cell **B8**, enter **60** as the hold time goal in seconds.

5. In cell **B9**, enter **26** as the average call duration in minutes.

6. In cell **B12**, enter the formula **= B9/60** to calculate the average call duration in hours. The average call duration is 0.43 hours.

   > **Tip** A green triangle appears next to some calculated values in this worksheet. You can ignore them. They do not affect the calculated values and just indicate some calculations in the workbook use custom functions created specifically for this report.

7. In cell **B13**, enter the formula **= B6*B12** to calculate the number of operators required each hour to handle the call volume. The number of operators hours per workload is 14.30. The Hold Time Lookup Table entries are generated based on the value in cell B13. You will use this table shortly.

8. In cell **B14**, enter the formula **= B13/B7** to calculate the anticipated percentage of operators occupied with callers. At the current call volume and 15 operators, 95.33% of the operators will be occupied with a call at any one time.

9. In cell **B15**, enter the formula **= 1 − B14** to calculate the percent of operators who are free to answer calls. The percentage of available operators is 4.67%. Refer to Figure 3–32.

Figure 3–32   Metrics of the call center

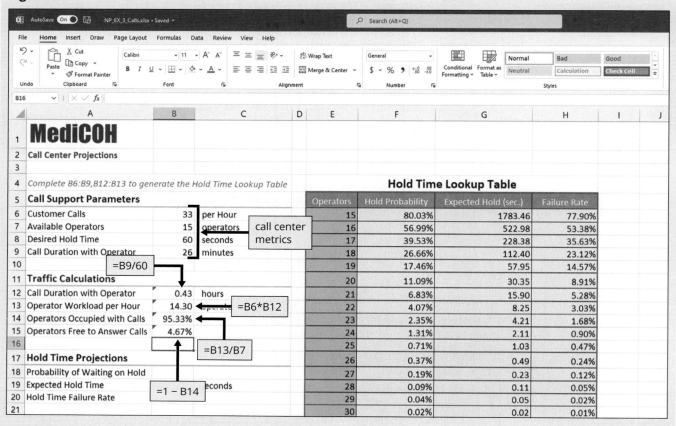

As you entered the call center data, a table of hold time probabilities and projections was populated in the range E5:H32. The table was generated by MediCOH statisticians using a branch of mathematics called "queuing theory" to predict call center performance based on call volume, the number of available operators, and the average length of each call. A study of queueing theory is beyond the scope of this module, but you can extract information from the table using lookup functions, answering questions about the optimal number of operators required at the center.

Insight

Using the IFERROR Function to Catch Error Values

An error value does not mean that your formula is wrong. Some errors appear simply because you have not yet entered any data into the workbook. For example, if you apply the AVERAGE function to a range that does not yet contain any data values, the #DIV/0! error value appears because Excel cannot calculate averages without data. However, as soon as you enter your data, the #DIV/0! error value disappears, replaced with the calculated average.

Error values of this type can make your workbook confusing and difficult to read. One way to hide them is with the following **IFERROR function**

```
IFERROR (Value, Value_if_error)
```

where `Value` is the value to be calculated and `Value_if_error` is the value returned by Excel if any error is encountered in the function. For example, the following IFERROR function returns the average of the values in column F, but if no values have yet been entered in that column, it returns a blank text string (" "):

```
IFERROR(AVERAGE(F:F), "")
```

Using this logical function results in a cleaner workbook that is more usable without distracting error values.

Looking Up Data

A **lookup function** retrieves a value matching a specified condition from a table of data. For example, a lookup function can be used to retrieve a shipping rate given a package's size and destination or a tax rate for a specified income.

The table storing the data to be retrieved is called a **lookup table**. The row or column with values to be matched is called the **lookup array**. If the values in the lookup array are organized in a row, the table is a **horizontal lookup table**; if the values are arranged in a column, the table is a **vertical lookup table**. The remaining rows or columns contain the **return array**, which are values retrieved from the lookup table when a match is found.

Figure 3–33 displays a vertical lookup table for retrieving data about MediCOH employees. The first column contains the lookup array (Employee ID), and the other columns contain return arrays (First Name, Last Name, Department). In this example, a lookup value for the employee ID "E86-2-2044" is supplied to the lookup table. A matching ID is found in cell A6—the fifth entry in the lookup array. The fifth entry from the return array for employee last names is returned, which in this case is "Aziz" located in cell C6.

Figure 3–33   Exact match returned from a lookup table

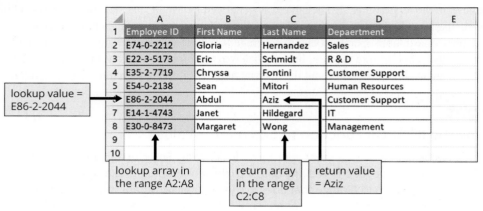

Lookup tables can be constructed for exact matches or approximate matches. In an **exact match lookup**, like the one in Figure 3–33, the lookup value must exactly match one of the values in the lookup array. If the lookup value falls within a range of values in the lookup arrow, you use an **approximate match lookup**. For example, in an approximate match lookup, you might match each employee's salary not to a specific amount but to a range of values, such as salaries between $70,000 and $80,000. Any salary falling within that range would constitute a match. In this module you will work with only exact match lookups.

Finding an Exact Match with the XLOOKUP Function

To retrieve a value from a lookup table, you use the following **XLOOKUP function**, which matches a supplied value to the lookup array and retrieves a corresponding value in the return array

```
XLOOKUP(lookup_value, lookup_array, return_array,
[if_not_found], [match_mode], [search_mode])
```

where *lookup_value* is the value to match, *lookup_array* is the column or row containing the lookup values, *return_array* is the column or row containing the return values, *if_not_found* is an optional value returned if no match is found, *match_mode* is the type of match, and *search_mode* specifies how the lookup array will be searched for matches.

The optional *match_mode* argument supports the following values defining what constitutes a match:

- match = 0   (default) Exact match. If none is found, returns the error value #N/A or the value specified by the *if_not_found* argument.
- match = −1   Exact match. If none is found, returns the next smaller value in the lookup array.
- match = 1   Exact match. If none is found, returns the next larger value in the lookup array.
- match = 2   Wildcard match using the *, ? and ~ symbols to locate a match within the lookup array.

The optional *search_mode* argument supports the following values defining how Excel will search through the lookup array:

- search = 1   (default) Perform a search starting down from the first value in the lookup array.
- search = −1   Perform a reverse search, starting up from the last value in the lookup array.
- search = 2   Perform a binary search that relies on lookup values being sorted in ascending order. If not sorted, invalid results will be returned.
- search = −2   Perform a binary search that relies on lookup values being sorted in descending order. If not sorted, invalid results will be returned.

If you do not include values for the *match_mode* and *search_mode* arguments, the XLOOKUP function performs an exact match lookup starting down from the first value in the lookup array.

The following XLOOKUP function performs the exact match lookup presented in Figure 3–33 with "E86-2-2044"as the lookup value, the range A2:A8 as the lookup array, and the range C2:C8 as the return array. If no employee with that ID is found in the lookup array, the text string "No employee found" is returned by the function.

```
XLOOKUP("E86-2-2044", A2:A8, C2:C8, "No employee found")
```

The Call Center Projection worksheet contains the following lookup and return arrays:

- **Operators.** The number of operators available to answer calls.
- **Hold Probability.** The probability that a customer will be placed on hold.
- **Expected Hold (sec).** The expected hold time in seconds for a customer calling the support center.
- **Failure Rate.** The probability that the customer's hold time will exceed the hold-time goal.

The number of operators in the lookup table starts with 15 operators. This is due to the mathematics of queueing theory. If the number of operators answering calls is less than the workload, the call center is understaffed and cannot keep up with demand. The workload of the call center was estimated in cell B13 as 14.30 operator hours every hour so the center must have at least 15 operators available to always answer calls.

You will use the XLOOKUP function to return the probability that a customer will have to wait on hold if 15 operators are staffing the call center.

To determine customers' hold probability with exact match lookup with XLOOKUP:

1. Click cell **B18** to select it.
2. On the ribbon, click the **Formulas** tab. In the Function Library group, click the **Lookup & Reference** button, and then click **XLOOKUP**. The Function Arguments dialog box opens.
3. In the Lookup_value box, enter **B7** as the cell containing the number of available operators.
4. In the Lookup_array box, enter **E6:E32** as the range containing the array of possible lookup matches.
5. In the Return_array box, enter **F6:F32** as the range containing the array of possible return values. You will not enter any other arguments for the XLOOKUP function, but instead will use their default values. Refer to Figure 3–34.

value. The `col_index_num` refers to the column number of the lookup table, not the worksheet column. So, a `col_index_num` of 2 refers to the lookup table's second column no matter where the lookup table is located within the worksheet. For the HLOOKUP function, you enter the lookup table's row number, not the worksheet row number. Finally, `range_lookup` is an optional argument that specifies whether the lookup should be done as an exact match or an approximate match. Its default value is TRUE, creating an approximate match. To create an exact match, enter FALSE for the `range_lookup` argument.

The following VLOOKUP function uses the lookup table presented in Figure 3–33 to perform an exact match look of the employee ID E86-2-2044, returning a matching value from the third column of the lookup table located in the A2:D8 range:

```
VLOOKUP("E86-2-2044", A2:D8, 3, FALSE)
```

The VLOOKUP and HLOOKUP functions have several important differences from the XLOOKUP function:

1. The lookup array must be the first column of the lookup table for VLOOKUP or the first row for HLOOKUP, but it can be in any column or row for XLOOKUP.

2. For exact matches, the first column or first row must be sorted in ascending order for VLOOKUP and HLOOKUP, but the lookup array (wherever it is located) does not need to be sorted for XLOOKUP.

3. Specify the index number of the column or row containing the return values for VLOOKUP and HLOOKUP, but provide the reference to the range containing the return array for XLOOKUP.

4. If no match is found, VLOOKUP and HLOOKUP always return the #N/A error value, but XLOOKUP can return a specified value.

5. Both VLOOKUP and HLOOKUP use approximate match lookups by default; XLOOKUP uses an exact match lookup by default.

The XLOOKUP function is much more flexible and powerful than VLOOKUP or HLOOKUP, allowing for a wide variety of matching conditions. Because XLOOKUP works with lookup tables that are arranged by column or by row, it can replace both VLOOKUP and HLOOKUP. However, VLOOKUP and HLOOKUP have been the established standard. So, you should be comfortable with both approaches.

Insight

Generating Random Data

For some projects, you will want to simulate scenarios using randomly generated data. The following RAND function can generate a random decimal number between 0 and 1:

```
RAND()
```

To convert this random number to any decimal within a given range, include the function within the formula

```
(top - bottom)*RAND() + bottom
```

where `bottom` is the bottom of the range and `top` is the top of the range. For example, the following expression generates a random decimal number between 10 and 50:

```
(50-10)*RAND()+10
```

To limit the random numbers to integers, use the following RANDBETWEEN function:

```
RANDBETWEEN(bottom, top)
```

For example, the following formula generates a random integer between 10 and 50:

```
RANDBETWEEN(10, 50)
```

Random number functions are **volatile functions** in that they will automatically recalculate their values every time Excel does any calculation in the workbook. This means a different set of random numbers will appear with every new calculation in the workbook.

Performing What-If Analysis with Formulas and Functions

A **what-if analysis** explores the impact that changing input values has on calculated values and output values. By exploring a wide range of different input values, you will achieve a better understanding of data and its implications.

Using Trial and Error

One way to perform a what-if analysis is by **trial and error** where you change one or more of the input values to explore how they impact the calculated values in the workbook. Trial and error requires some guesswork and patience as you estimate which values to change and by how much. You'll use trial and error to investigate how changing the number of available operators impacts the hold-time projections.

To use trial and error to evaluate the impact changing the number of operators:

1. In cell **B7**, enter **16**. With one additional operator on call, the probability of waiting on hold drops to about 57% (cell B18), the expected hold time decreases to about 523 seconds (cell B19), and the hold time failure rate falls to 53.38% (cell B20).

2. In cell **B7**, enter **17**. With 17 operators available to answer calls, the probability of waiting on hold drops to about 40%, the expected hold time decreases to about 228 seconds, and the hold time failure rate falls to 35.63%.

3. In cell **B7**, enter **19**. With 19 available operators, the expected hold time drops just below one minute to about 58 seconds. Refer to Figure 3–36.

Figure 3–36   Using trial and error to determine the number of operators

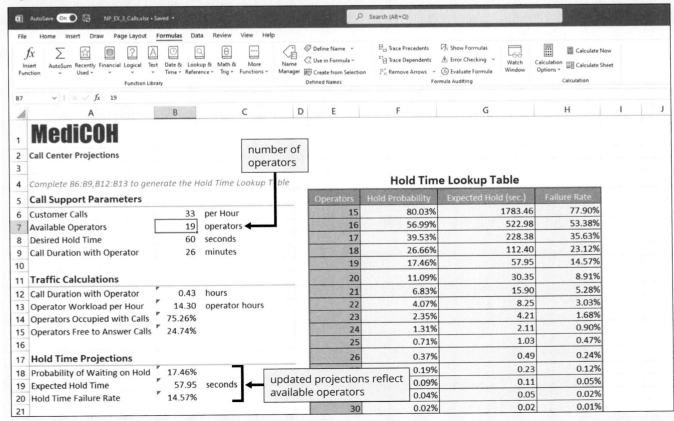

Based on the trial-and-error analysis, Chryssa recommended to management that the call center staff be expanded to 19 operators. However, the company does not have the budget to staff the call center to that level. Chryssa must come up with another solution. Other than hiring more staff, the only other factor in the company's control is how long operators spend on calls. If operators could handle calls more efficiently without sacrificing quality, the same number of operators could handle more callers. Chryssa needs to know by how much time each call would have to be trimmed to accommodate the daily call volume. That calculation can be done using Goal Seek.

Using Goal Seek

Goal Seek reverses the trial-and-error process by specifying an output value and working backward to find the input value needed to reach that goal. The output is always a calculated value, and the input is always a constant that can be changed using the Goal Seek tool. Goal Seek can be used only with calculated numbers, not with text.

Reference

Performing What-If Analysis and Goal Seek

To perform a what-if analysis by trial and error:
- Change the value of a worksheet cell (the input cell).
- Observe its impact on one or more calculated cells (the result cells).
- Repeat until the desired results are achieved.

To perform a what-if analysis using Goal Seek:
- On the Data tab, in the Forecast group, click the What-If Analysis button, and then click Goal Seek.
- Select the result cell in the Set cell box, and then specify its value (goal) in the To value box.
- In the By changing cell box, specify the input cell.
- Click OK. The value of the input cell changes to set the value of the result cell.

Management wants Chryssa to get the expected hold time down to 45 seconds with only 17 operators. The only parameter that Chryssa can change to meet that goal is the length of time operators spend with customers. Currently that value is set to 26 minutes. You will use Goal Seek to find out how much that value must be reduced to achieve the target hold time of 45 seconds.

To use Goal Seek to set the expected hold time to 45 seconds:

1. In cell **B7**, enter **17** as the number of operators on-call to answer customer queries.
2. In cell **B8**, enter **45** seconds as the desired hold time.
3. On the ribbon, click the **Data** tab. In the Forecast group, click the **What-If Analysis** button, and then click **Goal Seek**. The Goal Seek dialog box opens.
4. In the Set cell box, type **B19** as the output cell whose value you want to set using Goal Seek.
5. In the To value box, type **45** to set the value of cell B19 to 45.
6. In the By changing cell box, type **B9** as the cell whose value you want changed to meet the desired goal. Refer to Figure 3–37.

Figure 3–37   Goal Seek dialog box

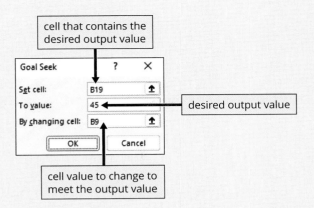

cell that contains the desired output value

Goal Seek

Set cell: B19

To value: 45 ← desired output value

By changing cell: B9

OK   Cancel

cell value to change to meet the output value

7. Click **OK**. The Goal Seek dialog box closes and the Goal Seek Status dialog box opens, indicating that Goal Seek has found a solution.

8. Click **OK**. The value in cell B9 changes from 26 to 22.4611 minutes and the value in cell B19 changes to the goal value of 45 seconds. Refer to Figure 3–38.

Figure 3–38   Goal Seek solution

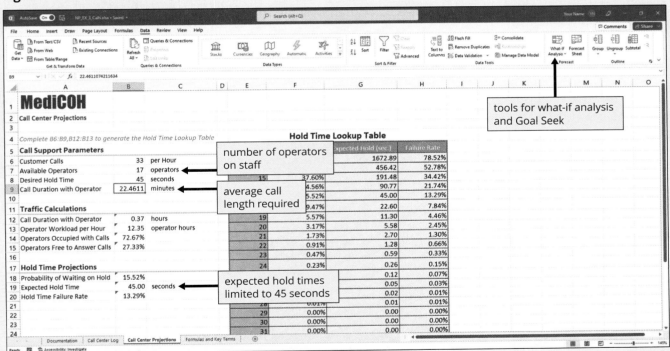

number of operators on staff

average call length required

expected hold times limited to 45 seconds

tools for what-if analysis and Goal Seek

9. **sam** ⬆ Save the workbook, and then close it.

The Goal Seek results tell Chryssa that if the average length of calls can be reduced to about 22.46 minutes (rough 22 and half minutes), 17 operators can handle the call volume with an expected hold time of 45 seconds.

Your analysis of the call center log has provided Chryssa a better understanding of the challenges facing the call center and how to meet those challenges. If the call center could route the most difficult calls to the most experienced operators, the average call length could be reduced, resulting in shorter hold times for MediCOH customers. With increased efficiency in handling calls, operators could be given more breaks so that they remain fresh and alert when helping customers.

Part 3.2 Quick Check

1. Write the formula that rounds the value in cell A5 down to the nearest multiple of 1000.

2. The range is defined as the maximum value from a set of numbers minus the minimum value from that set. Write the nested formula that calculates the range of the values in stored in the range Y1:Y100 and then rounds that value to the nearest integer.

3. Write the formula that calculates the number of working days between a starting date stored in cell H2 and an ending date stored in cell H3, using a list of holiday dates stored in the range G2:G10.

4. Stephen is entering thousands of temperature values into a worksheet for a climate research project and wants to speed up data entry by entering blanks rather than typing zeroes. Why will this cause complications in the calculation of the average temperature.

5. If the value in cell Q3 is greater than the value in cell Q4, you want to display the text "OK"; otherwise, display the text "RETRY". Write the formula that accomplishes this.

6. A vertical lookup table is placed in the range D1:H50. If the lookup value is in cell B2, the lookup array is in the range D2:D50, and the return array is in the range G2:G50, what is the XLOOKUP function that returns an exact match for the lookup value?

7. For the previous question, what is the VLOOKUP function that returns the exact match to the lookup value? (Note that the return values are in fourth column of the lookup table.)

8. If the XLOOKUP function cannot find a match, what value is returned by default from the function?

9. What is the difference between a what-if analysis done by trial and error and one that is done by Goal Seek?

Practice: Review Assignments

Data File needed for the Review Assignments: NP_EX_3-3.xlsx

Chryssa needs you to perform another analysis of the call center log. Callers who wait on hold often hang up before reaching an operator. Chryssa wants to examine the relationship between abandoned calls and the length of the hold time. To explore that relationship, you will analyze a call center log that lists all calls made on a typical day with information on whether the caller hung up before reaching an operator. Complete the following:

1. Open the **NP_EX_3-3.xlsx** workbook located in the Excel3 > Review folder included with your Data Files, and then save the workbook as **NP_EX_3_Abandon** in the location specified by your instructor.
2. In the Documentation sheet, enter your name in cell B4 and use the TODAY function to enter the current date in cell B5.
3. In the Caller Log worksheet, in cell E5, enter **C291208001**. Calls that were answered by an operator have the ID format C*YearMonthDateNumber*, where *Year* is the two-digit year value, *Month* is the two-digit month value, *Date* is the two-digit day value, and *Number* is three-digit number indicating the placement of the call on that day.
4. Drag the fill handle from cell E5 to cell E306 to enter the IDs of the rest of the answered calls. Fill the IDs without formatting.
5. Calls that were abandoned before reaching an operator have the ID format X*yearMonthDateNumber*. Use AutoFill to fill in the abandoned call IDs in the range E307:E344, starting with X291208001 in cell E307. Again, fill without formatting.
6. In cell I5, calculate the time in seconds that clients were on hold before reaching an operator or hanging up by entering the following dynamic array formula:

   `=(G5:G344 – F5:F344)*24*60*60`

7. The hold time goal is 45 seconds. In cell J5, enter the following dynamic array formula and absolute cell reference to calculate the number seconds above or below the hold time goal for every call made that day to the center:

   `=I5:I344 – $B$8`

8. Create indicator values that determine whether a hold time is greater or less than 1 minute and whether a call was abandoned by entering the following formulas and functions:
   a. In cell K5, enter an IF function with dynamic arrays to return a value of 1 if the corresponding values in the range I5:I344 are less than or equal to 60, and return 0 if otherwise.
   b. In cell L5, enter an IF function with dynamic arrays to return a value of 1 if the corresponding values in the range I5:I344 are greater than 60, and return a value of 0 if otherwise.
   c. In cell M5, enter an IF function with dynamic arrays to return a value of 1 if the corresponding values in the range H5:H344 are equal to "hung up" and 0 if otherwise.
   d. In cell N5, enter a dynamic array formula that multiplies the values in the range K5:K344 by the values in the range M5:M344. In the results, the value 1 indicates the caller hung up within 1 minute and 0 otherwise.
   e. In cell O5, enter a dynamic array formula that multiplies the values in the range L5:L344 by the values in the range M5:M344. In the results, the value 1 indicates the caller hung up after 1 minute and 0 otherwise.
9. Summarize the calls made that day to the center by entering the following formulas and functions:
   a. In cell B5, enter the COUNT function to count the values in column F.
   b. In cell B6, enter the SUM function to sum up the values in the spill range starting with the cell M5#.
   c. In cell B7, calculate the difference between the value in cell B5 and the value in cell B6.
   d. In cell C6, calculate the percent of calls abandoned by dividing the value in cell B6 by the value in cell B5.
   e. In cell C7, calculate the percent of calls answered by dividing the value in cell B7 by the value in cell B5.

10. Summarize information on the call that were answered or abandoned within the first minute by entering the following formulas and functions:

   a. In cell B11, use the SUM function to sum up the values in the spill range starting with the cell K5#.

   b. In cell B12, use the SUM function to sum up the values in the spill range starting with the cell N5#.

   c. In cell B13, calculate the difference between the values of cell B11 and cell B12.

   d. In cell C12, calculate the percent of calls abandoned in the first minute by dividing the value in cell B12 by the value in cell B11.

   e. In cell C13, calculate the percent of calls answered by dividing the value in cell B13 by the value in cell B11.

11. In the range B16:B18, repeat Step 10 to perform the same calculations for calls with hold times longer than 1 minute. The total number of calls with hold times longer than 1 minute are in the spill range starting with cell L5#. The total number of calls abandoned after 1 minute are in the spill range starting with cell O5#.

12. Provide summary statistics on the abandoned calls by entering the following functions:

   a. In cell B21, use the AVERAGE function with the range I307:I344 to calculate the average time at which calls were abandoned. Nest the AVERAGE function within the ROUND function and round the calculated average to the nearest second.

   b. In cell B22, use the MEDIAN function with the range I307:I344 to calculate the midpoint time of the abandoned calls.

   c. In cell B23, use the MIN function with the range I307:I344 to calculate the quickest a client abandoned a call.

   d. In cell B24, use the MAX function with the range I307:I344 to calculate the longest a client waited before abandoning a call.

13. Perform the following steps to retrieve information on a specified call by the call ID:

   a. In cell B27, enter **X291208027** as the call ID.

   b. In cell B28, use the XLOOKUP function with cell B27 as the lookup value, column E as the lookup array, and column F as the return array. If no match is found, return the value "No call with that ID".

   c. In cell B29, enter the same function as in cell B28, except use column G as the return array.

   d. In cell B30, enter the same function as in cell B28 except use column H as the return array.

   e. Verify that the return values match the values for call X291208027 located in row 333.

14. Statisticians employed by MediCOH have derived an equation to predict the probability that a client will abandon a call after a specified number of seconds. Chryssa wants you to determine the length of time at which the probability of a client hanging up is 50%.

   a. Do a what-if analysis by entering **60** in cell B33 as an initial guess for probability of waiting on hold. Confirm that cell B34 shows a probability that 10% of customers will hang up if put on hold for one minute.

   b. Use Goal Seek to set cell B34 to the value 50% by changing cell B33.

15. Save the workbook, and then close it.

Apply: Case Problem 1

Data File needed for this Case Problem: NP_EX_3-4.xlsx

Curbside Thai Sajja Adulet is the owner and master chef of Curbside Thai, a popular food truck that operates in Charlotte, North Carolina. Sajja has compiled daily sales figures from the most recent fiscal year. You will analyze the data to calculate both the annual total and daily average of the restaurant's sales and expenses. You also will calculate the daily net income. You will also compare weekend and weekday sales. Finally, you will use Goal Seek to determine how to increase the restaurant's profit margin by reducing costs on space rental in downtown Charlotte. Complete the following:

1. Open the **NP_EX_3-4.xlsx** workbook located in the Excel3 > Case1 folder included with your Data Files, and then save the workbook as **NP_EX_3_Thai** in the location specified by your instructor.

2. In the Documentation sheet, enter your name and the date.

3. In the Daily Sales worksheet, in cell G5, calculate the net income for the first day using the sales in cell E5 minus the sum of cell F5 and the daily rental fee in cell B13. Use an absolute cell reference to cell B13 in your formula.

4. AutoFill the formula in cell G5 to the range G5:G368 and fill without formatting.

5. In cell H5, enter a number representing the day of the week using the formula = WEEKDAY(D5, 2) so that Mondays have the value 1, Tuesdays have the value 2, and so on. AutoFill the formula in cell H5 to the range H5:H368 and fill without formatting.

6. Sajja also wants to display the name of the day of the week. In cell I5, use the XLOOKUP function to retrieve the weekday name with cell H5 as the lookup value, the range M5:M11 as the lookup array, and the range N5:N11 as the return array. Use absolute cell references to the range M5:M11 and the range N5:N11. AutoFill the formula to range I5:I368 and fill without formatting.

7. In cell J5, enter the dynamic array formula = IF(H5:H368 < 6, E5:E368, "") to return the sales values from column E when the weekday numbers in column H are less than 6 (Monday through Friday) and a blank text string if otherwise.

8. In cell K5, enter the dynamic array formula = IF(H5:H368 >= 6, E5:E368, "") to return the sales values from column E when the weekday numbers in column H are greater than 6 (Saturday and Sunday) and a blank text string if otherwise.

9. Summarize the total sales figures by entering the following formulas:
   a. In cell B5, calculate the sum of the values in column E to estimate the total sales for the year.
   b. In cell B6, calculate the sum of the values in column F to estimate the total cost of goods sold for the year.
   c. In cell B7, multiply the value in cell B13 by the count of values in column D to estimate the annual cost of renting public space for the year.
   d. In cell B8, calculate the value of cell B5 minus the sum of cells B6 and B7 to determine the net income for the year.
   e. In cell B9, divide cell B8 by cell B5 to display the company's profit margin for the year.

10. Estimate daily averages for food truck sales by entering the following formulas:
    a. In cell B12, calculate the average of the values in column E to estimate the average daily sales.
    b. In cell B14, calculate the average of the values in column F to estimate the average daily cost of goods sold.
    c. In cell B15, enter cell B12 minus the sum of cell B13 and B14 to estimate the daily net income.

11. Compare average daily sales between the weekday and weekend by entering the following calculations:
    a. In cell B18, use the AVERAGE function to calculate the average sales values in column J.
    b. In cell B19, use the AVERAGE function to calculate the average sales value in column K.
    c. In cell B20, calculate the difference in weekend and weekday sales by subtracting the value in cell B18 from the value in cell B19.

12. Sajja wants to increase the company's profit margin. One way of doing this might be to find ways of renting public space at a reduced cost. Use Goal Seek to determine how low the space rental fee would have been to achieve a profit margin of 8.5%. Set the value in cell B9 to 8.5% by changing the value of cell B13.

13. Save the workbook, and then close it.

Challenge: Case Problem 2

Data File needed for this Case Problem: NP_EX_3-5.xlsx

Up Range Construction Owen Meuric is a production manager for Up Range Construction, a builder of homes and office spaces in Missouri. Building projects need to follow carefully designed construction schedules involving several different phases often occurring at the same time. Each construction phase requires a set number of days to complete and cannot be started until a specified prior phase is done. For example, painting cannot be started until the drywall work is completed, and drywall work can't be started until the insulation is in. Some construction phases also must be delayed several days before they can be started to allow materials to dry and settle.

Owen has created a workbook within information on a proposed building project, listing the construction phases, the number of days allotted for each phase, and the delay required before each phase can be begin. You will use this raw data to calculate the ending date for the entire building project. To create the production schedule, you will use the WORKDAY and NETWORKDAYS functions described in Figure 3–28 and in the Insight box, "Date Calculations with Working Days." Complete the following:

1. Open the **NP_EX_3-5.xlsx** workbook located in the Excel3 > Review folder included with your Data Files, and then save the workbook as **NP_EX_3_Schedule1** in the location specified by your instructor.

2. In the Documentation sheet, enter your name and the current date.

3. Go to the Production Schedule worksheet. Owen has set a starting date for the project of 2/5/2029. The client wants the building completed by 12/7/2029. Owen has listed all the phases of the project, the number of days to complete each phase, the prior phase that must be completed first, and the delay before each phase can begin.

4. **Explore:** In cell C13, use the WORKDAY function to calculate the ending date for the Site Work phase. Use cell B13 as the starting date, cell D13 as the number days, and the dates in the range I13:I28 as the holiday dates. Enter the holiday dates using an absolute cell reference.

5. AutoFill the formula in cell C13 across the range C13:C34 without formatting. The dates won't make sense because not all the information for the production schedule has been calculated yet.

6. Retrieve the ending date for the prior phase of each construction phase. In cell F14, use an XLOOKUP function with cell E14 as the lookup value, the range A13:A34 as the lookup array, and the range C13:C34 as the return array. Use absolute cell references to the ranges A13:A34 and C13:C34.

7. AutoFill the formula in cell F14 to the range F14:F34 without formatting.

8. **Explore:** Calculate the starting date of each construction phase. In cell B14, use the WORKDAY function with cell F14 (the ending date of the prior phase) as the starting date, cell G14 as the number of days delayed from the prior phase, and the range I13:I28 as the list of holiday dates. Enter the range I13:I28 as absolute cell references.

9. AutoFill the formula in cell B14 to the range B14:B34 without formatting. The worksheet now displays the starting and ending dates for each phase of the project as well as the completion date for the entire building.

10. In cell B5, enter a reference to cell C34 to display the ending date of the project.

11. Indicate if the building will be completed at or before the client's deadline. In cell B7, use the IF function to display the text "Acceptable" if cell B5 is less than or equal to cell B6 and "Unacceptable" otherwise.

12. Create two conditional formatting rules for cell B7. If the cell value is equal to "Acceptable" display the contents in a dark green font on a green background. If the value is "Unacceptable" display the cell in a dark red font on a light red background.

13. **Explore:** In cell B9, use the NETWORKDAYS function to calculate the number of working days spent on the project, using cell B4 as the starting date, cell B5 as the ending date, and the range I13:I28 as the holiday dates.

14. In cell B10, calculate the difference between cell B5 and cell B4 to display number of calendars days between the start of the project and the ending.

15. Save the workbook. The completion date on the project will not satisfy the client, and so you will draw up a new schedule.

16. Save the workbook as **NP_EX_3_Schedule2** in the same folder.

17. The company should be able to meet the client's deadline by starting the project earlier. Use Goal Seek to determine the starting date that will meet the client's deadline, setting the value of cell B5 (completion date) to 12/7/2029 by changing the value in cell B4 (start date).

18. Save the workbook, and then close it.

Analyzing and Charting Financial Data

Preparing an Investment Report

Case: Proxis Financial

Lydia Adessa is an analyst for Proxis Financial, an investment firm located in Grand Rapids, Michigan. Lydia needs to prepare financial reports that the company's clients will receive at meetings with a Proxis Financial advisor. One of the products handled by the company is the Hamilton Fund, a large-growth/large-risk investment fund. Lydia needs to summarize the fund's financial holdings as well as document its recent and long-term performance. Lydia has already entered the financial data into a workbook but wants you to finish the report. Because many clients are overwhelmed by tables of numbers, you will summarize the data using Excel financial charts and graphics.

Starting Data Files

Excel4

Module

NP_EX_4-1.xlsx

Review

NP_EX_4-2.xlsx

Case1

NP_EX_4-3.xlsx

Case2

NP_EX_4-4.xlsx

Objectives

Part 4.1

- Create a pie chart
- Format chart elements
- Create a line chart
- Work with chart legends
- Create a combination chart

Part 4.2

- Create a scatter chart
- Edit a chart data source
- Create a data callout
- Insert a text box into a chart
- Create and edit a data bar
- Create and edit a group of sparklines

Part 4.1 Visual Overview:
Charts and Chart Elements

Each chart has a **data source**, which is the range containing the data to display in the chart. The data source in the range A5:B9 is used in the pie chart.

Chart **gridlines** extend the values of the major or minor tick marks across the plot area.

The **chart title** is a descriptive label or name for the chart.

A **data marker** displays an individual value from a data series. These data markers are columns in a column chart.

A **chart legend** identifies the data markers associated with each data series.

A **line chart** displays data values using a connected line rather than columns or bars.

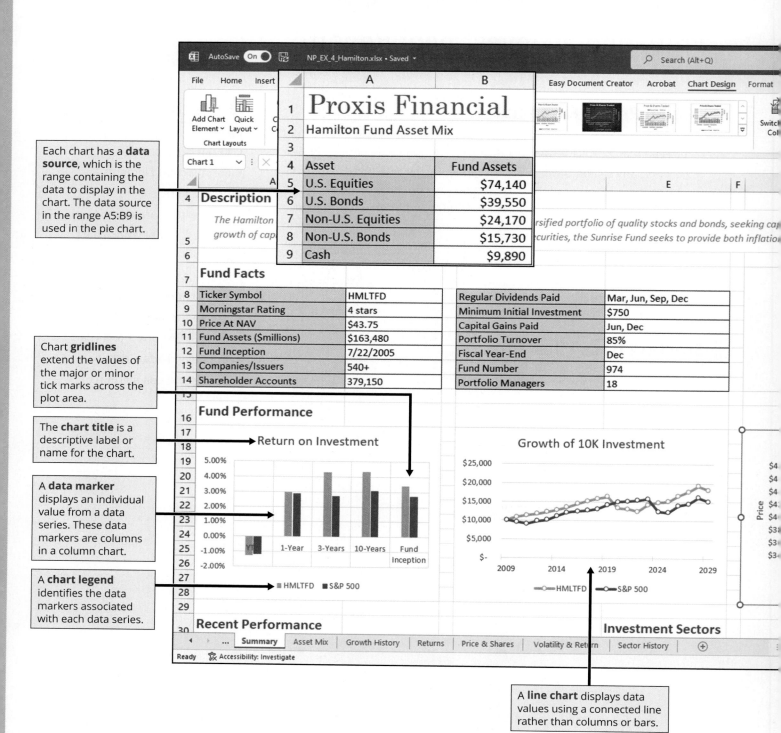

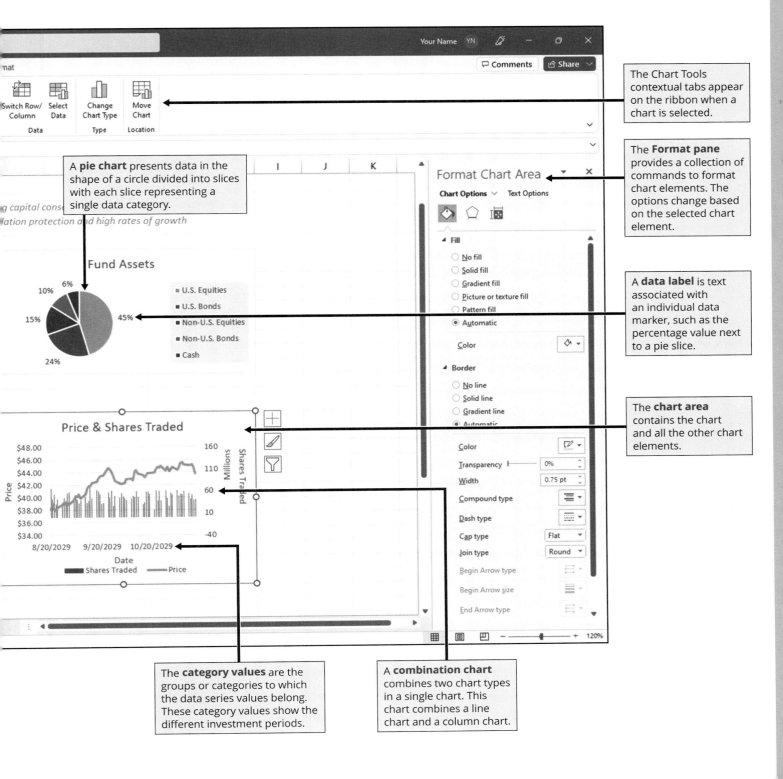

A **pie chart** presents data in the shape of a circle divided into slices with each slice representing a single data category.

The Chart Tools contextual tabs appear on the ribbon when a chart is selected.

The **Format pane** provides a collection of commands to format chart elements. The options change based on the selected chart element.

A **data label** is text associated with an individual data marker, such as the percentage value next to a pie slice.

The **chart area** contains the chart and all the other chart elements.

The **category values** are the groups or categories to which the data series values belong. These category values show the different investment periods.

A **combination chart** combines two chart types in a single chart. This chart combines a line chart and a column chart.

Getting Started with Excel Charts

In this module, you will learn how to analyze financial data using Excel charts and graphics. Lydia Adessa from Proxis Financial has already entered the financial data you need into an Excel workbook. You'll open and review that workbook now.

To open Lydia's financial workbook:

1. **sam** ⬇ Open the **NP_EX_4-1.xlsx** workbook located in the **Excel4 > Module** folder included with your Data Files, and then save the workbook as **NP_EX_4_Hamilton** in the location specified by your instructor.

2. In the Documentation sheet, enter your name in cell B3 and the date in cell B4.

3. Review the financial data stored in the workbook, and then return to the **Summary** worksheet. You'll summarize data stored in the other sheets of the workbook in this worksheet.

A properly constructed chart can be as valuable for a data analyst as a thousand lines of financial facts and figures. Excel has more than 60 types of charts organized into the 10 categories described in Figure 4–1. Within each chart category are chart variations called chart subtypes. You can also design custom chart types to meet your specific needs.

Figure 4–1   Excel chart types and subtypes

Chart Category	Description	Chart Subtypes
Column or Bar	Compares values from different categories. Values are indicated by the height of the columns or the length of a bar.	2D Column, 3D Column, 2D Bar, 3D Bar
Hierarchy	Displays data that is organized into a hierarchy of categories where the size of the groups is based on a number.	Treemap, Sunburst
Waterfall or Stock	Displays financial cash flow values or stock market data.	Waterfall, Funnel, Stock
Line or Area	Compares values from different categories. Values are indicated by the height of the lines. Often used to show trends and changes over time.	2D Line, 3D Line, 2D Area, 3D Area
Statistic	Displays a chart summarizing the distribution of values from a sample population.	Histogram, Pareto, Box and Whisker
Pie	Compares relative values of different categories to the whole. Values are indicated by the areas of the pie slices.	2D Pie, 3D Pie, Doughnut
X Y (Scatter) or Bubble	Shows the patterns or relationship between two or more sets of values. Often used in scientific studies and statistical analyses.	Scatter, Bubble
Surface or Radar	Compares three sets of values in a three-dimensional chart.	Surface, Radar
Combo	Combines two or more chart types so the data can be compared.	Clustered Column-Line, Clustered Column-Line on Secondary Axis, Stacked Area-Clustered Column

Each chart type provides a different insight into data. Figure 4–2 presents the same financial data displayed in different Excel charts—a pie chart, a column chart, a treemap chart, and a map chart. The chart you choose depends on what aspect of the data you are trying to highlight.

Figure 4–2   Data displayed in different Excel chart types

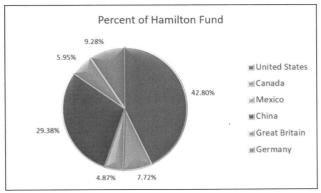

Pie chart

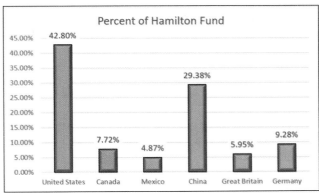

Column chart

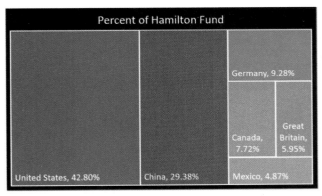

Treemap chart

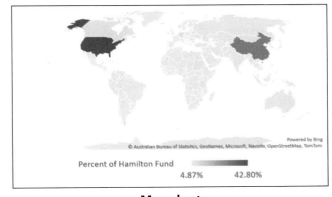

Map chart

Creating a chart is a multistep process. First, you select the data to display. Then, you choose the chart type best suited to that data. Finally, you format the chart's appearance to make it clearer to read and interpret. The first chart you will create for the Hamilton Fund report is a pie chart depicting the different assets of the fund.

Reference

Creating a Chart

- Select the range containing the data you want to chart.
- On the Insert tab, in the Charts group, click the Recommended Charts button or a button representing the general chart type, and then click the chart you want to create; or click the Quick Analysis button, click the Charts category, and then click the chart you want to create.
- On the Chart Design tab, in the Location group, click the Move Chart button, select whether to embed the chart in a worksheet or place it in a chart sheet, and then click OK.
- Use the chart tools to format the appearance of individual chart elements.

Creating a Pie Chart

A pie chart presents data in a circle graph divided into slices with each slice representing a single data category. Categories whose data values take up larger percentages of the whole are represented with larger slices; categories that take up a smaller percentage of the whole are presented as smaller slices. Pie charts are most effective when the data can be divided into six or fewer categories. With more categories, each slice becomes a smaller part of the whole, making comparisons between categories more difficult.

Selecting the Data Source

The data displayed in a chart come from a data source, which includes one or more data series and a set of category values. A **data series** contains the data values plotted within the chart. The category values groups those values into descriptive categories. Categories are usually listed in the first column or row of the data source, and the data series values are placed in subsequent columns or rows.

> **Tip** Do not include row or column totals in the pie chart data because Excel will treat those totals as another category.

The Asset Mix worksheet in Lydia's workbook breaks down the assets in the Hamilton Fund. The assets are organized into equities, bonds, and cash from sources within and outside of the United States. You will display this data in a pie chart. You will start creating the pie chart by selecting the chart's data source.

To select the data source for the pie chart:

1. Go to the **Asset Mix** worksheet.

2. Select the range **A4:B9**. This range contains the names of the assets and the amount invested within each asset category. Refer to Figure 4–3.

Figure 4–3　　Selected chart data source

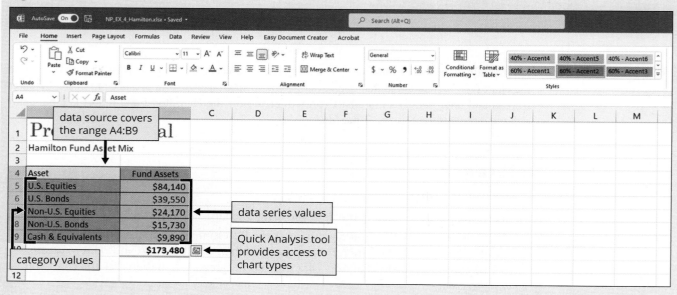

The selected data source covers two columns. The categories in the first column (Asset) identify each pie slice. The data series in the second column (Fund Assets) sets the size of each slice.

Charting with the Quick Analysis Tool

After you select a data source, the Quick Analysis tool appears in the lower-right corner of the selection. The Charts category in the Quick Analysis tool displays chart types that are appropriate for the selected data source. For this data source, a pie chart provides a good way to compare the relative amount that the Hamilton Fund invests in five asset categories. You'll use the Quick Analysis tool to generate the pie chart for Lydia.

To create a pie chart with the Quick Analysis tool:

1. With the range A4:B9 still selected, click the **Quick Analysis** button in the lower-right corner of the selected range (or press **CTRL+Q**) to open the Quick Analysis tool.

2. Click the **Charts** category. The chart types you will most likely want to use with the selected data source are listed.

3. Point to each chart type to preview that type of chart and a description of the data rendered as that chart. Refer to Figure 4–4.

Figure 4–4   Charts category of the Quick Analysis tool

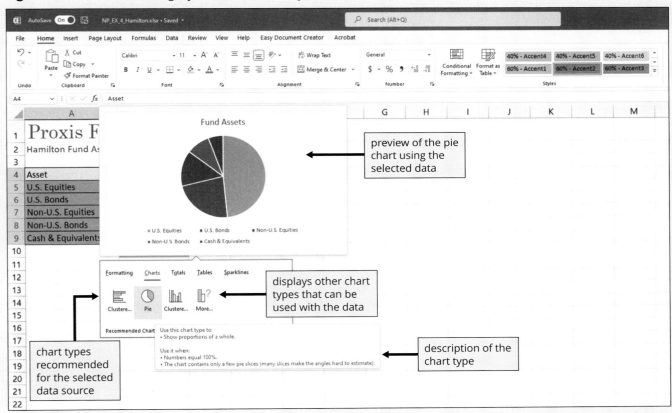

4. Click **Pie**. A pie chart appears in the Asset Mix worksheet.

> **Tip** You can also insert a chart by selecting a chart type in the Charts group on the Insert tab.

Excel identifies the slice categories and the slice values from the data source. When the selected range is taller than it is wide, Excel assumes that the category values and data series are laid out in columns. Conversely, a data source that is wider than it is tall is assumed to have the category values and data series laid out in rows. The biggest slice in this pie chart represents the amount of the fund invested in U.S. equities, and the smallest slice represents the amount invested in cash and equivalents. Slices start at the top of the pie and are added to the right around the pie.

Each new chart is given a reference name, which appears in the Reference box at the upper-left corner of the worksheet. The initial chart names are Chart 1, Chart 2, and so forth, but you can click the Reference box and enter a different, more descriptive name. When a chart is selected, two chart contextual tabs appear on the ribbon. The Chart Design tab contains tools to modify the chart's overall design and its data source, and the Format tab contains tools to format the individual parts of the chart, such as the chart's title, border, or background. When the chart is not selected, the contextual tabs disappear.

Moving and Resizing a Chart

A chart is placed in its own chart sheet or embedded in a worksheet. The advantage of an embedded chart is that it can be displayed alongside relevant text and tables in the worksheet. Chart sheets are best used for charts that occupy a single page in a report or printout. In this report, you will embed all the charts in the Summary worksheet.

> **Tip** You can print an embedded chart with its worksheet, or you can print the selected embedded chart without its worksheet.

You will move the fund assets pie chart to the Summary worksheet.

To move the embedded chart to the Summary worksheet:

1. Verify that the pie chart is selected.

2. On the ribbon, click the **Chart Design** tab, if necessary, to display it.

3. In the Location group, click the **Move Chart** button. The Move Chart dialog box opens.

4. Click the **Object in** arrow to open a list of worksheets in the workbook, and then click **Summary** to indicate that the pie chart should be placed in the Summary worksheet. Refer to Figure 4–5.

Figure 4–5   Move Chart dialog box

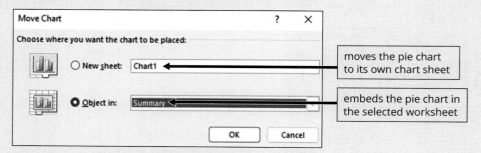

5. Click **OK** to close the Move Chart dialog box and move the chart to the Summary worksheet.

You can also use cut and paste to move an embedded chart to a different worksheet. Select the chart, click the Cut button in the Clipboard group on the Home tab, and then select the worksheet cell where you want to place the chart. Click the Paste button to place the upper-left corner of the chart at the selected cell.

Because an embedded chart covers the worksheet grid, it can obscure some of the content. You can fix that problem by moving the chart to an empty location and resizing it. To move and resize a chart, the chart must be selected, which adds a selection box around the chart. The selection box has sizing handles to change the chart's width and height. As you move and resize a chart, holding down ALT snaps the chart to the worksheet grid. If you do not hold down ALT, you can move and resize the chart to any location on the grid.

Lydia wants the pie chart to cover the range G7:H14 in the Summary worksheet. You'll move and resize the chart to fit this space.

To move and resize the pie chart:

1. Move the pointer over an empty part of the chart so that the pointer changes to the Move pointer and the ScreenTip displays "Chart Area."

   > **Key Step** Make sure the ScreenTip shows "Chart Area" so that the entire chart moves when you drag.

2. Hold down **ALT**, drag the chart to cell **G7** until its upper-left corner snaps to the upper-left corner of the cell, and then release the mouse button and **ALT**. The upper-left corner of the chart now aligns with the upper-left corner of cell G7.

   > **Trouble?** If the pie chart resizes or does not move to the new location, you probably didn't drag the chart from an empty part of the chart area. Press CTRL+Z to undo your last action, and then repeat Steps 1 and 2, being sure to drag the pie chart from the chart area.

3. Point to the sizing handle in the lower-right corner of the selection box until the pointer changes to the Resizing pointer.

4. Hold down **ALT**, drag the sizing handle up to the lower-right corner of cell **H14**, and then release the mouse button and **ALT**. The chart resizes to cover the range G7:H14 and remains selected. Refer to Figure 4–6.

Figure 4–6   Moved and resized pie chart

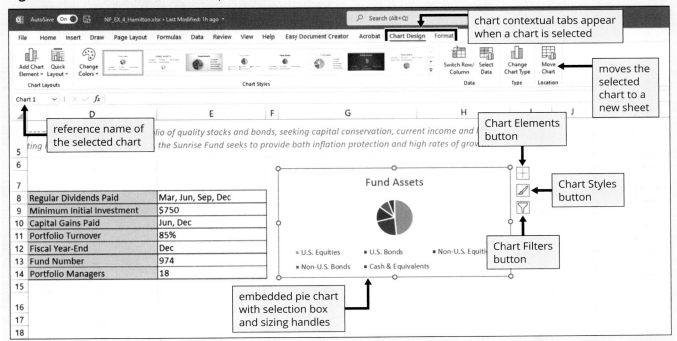

Even though a chart is not part of the worksheet grid, it resizes with the grid. If the size of a column or row is changed, the chart's width and height will also change, ensuring that an embedded chart will stay in the same location relative to other worksheet content.

Insight

Exploding a Pie Chart

Pie slices do not need to be fixed within the pie. An **exploded pie chart** moves one slice away from the others as if someone were taking the piece away from the pie. Exploded pie charts are useful for emphasizing one category above the others. For example, to emphasize the fact that Hamilton Fund invests heavily in U.S. equities, you could explode that single slice, moving it away from the other slices.

To explode a pie slice, first click the pie to select it, and then click the single slice you want to move. Make sure that a selection box appears around only that slice. Drag the slice away from the other slices in the pie. You can explode multiple slices by selecting each slice in turn and dragging them away. To explode all the slices, select the entire pie and drag the pointer away from the pie's center. Although you can explode more than one slice, the resulting pie chart is rarely effective at conveying information to the reader.

Working with Chart Elements

The individual parts of the chart are called **chart elements**. Figure 4–7 shows elements that are common to many charts. You can access the properties of these chart elements by clicking the Chart Elements button  that appears to the right of the chart.

Figure 4–7   Common chart elements

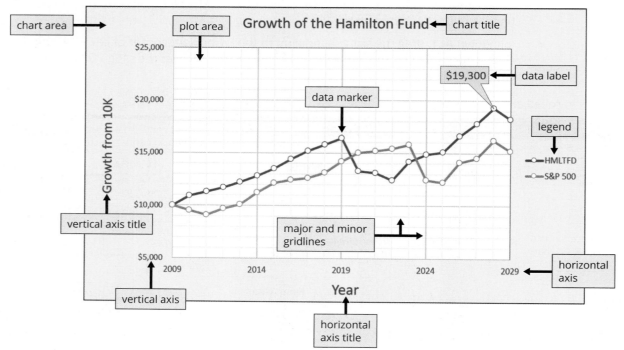

The pie chart you created does not contain any data labels. Lydia thinks adding the data values associated with each pie slice would make the chart more informative. You will use the Chart Elements button  to add that element to the pie chart.

To add the data labels chart element to the pie chart:

1. With the pie chart still selected, click the **Chart Elements** button ⊞. A menu of chart elements associated with the pie chart opens. As the checkmarks indicate, only the chart title and the chart legend are displayed in the pie chart.

   > **Tip** You can also add and remove chart elements with the Add Chart Element button in the Chart Layouts group on the Chart Design tab.

2. Point to the **Data Labels** check box. Live Preview displays the chart with data labels of the dollar amount (in millions) invested within each category.

3. Click the **Data Labels** check box to select it. The data labels are added to the chart. Refer to Figure 4–8.

Figure 4–8   Data labels added to the pie chart

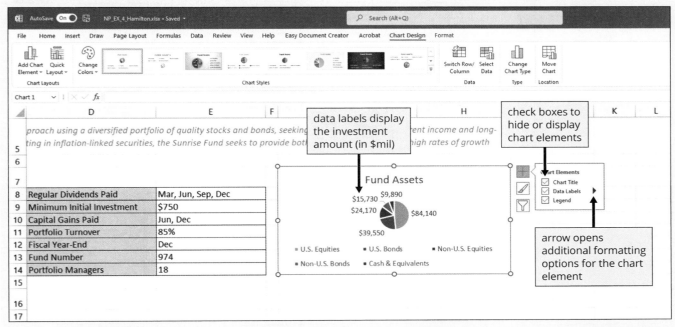

Lydia does not want the data labels to show the amount invested in each asset, but rather the percentage of the total invested in each asset. You can make that change by editing the Data Labels element.

Formatting a Chart Element

Each element listed in the Chart Elements button contains a submenu of common formatting choices. Explore the formatting choices available with data labels now to move the placement of the data labels.

To format a data label:

1. With the pie chart still selected, click the **Chart Elements** button ⊞ if necessary to display the menu, point to **Data Labels**, and then click the **right arrow** icon ▶ to display the list of common formatting choices for data labels.

2. Point to each of the following options for a Live Preview of data labels positioned at different locations around the pie chart: **Center, Inside End, Outside End, Best Fit**, and **Data Callout**.

3. Click **More Options** to view the extensive menu of formatting options for data labels in the Format Data Labels pane. The Format Data Labels pane is divided into different sections indicated by the icons near the top of the pane. The formatting options for the data labels is selected by default.

4. Click the **Percentage** check box to add percentages to the data labels for each pie slice.

5. Click the **Value** check box to deselect it, removing the data values from the data labels.

6. In the Label Position section, click the **Outside End** option button in the Label Position section to always place the data labels outside and at the end of each pie slice. Refer to Figure 4–9.

Figure 4–9   Format Data Labels pane

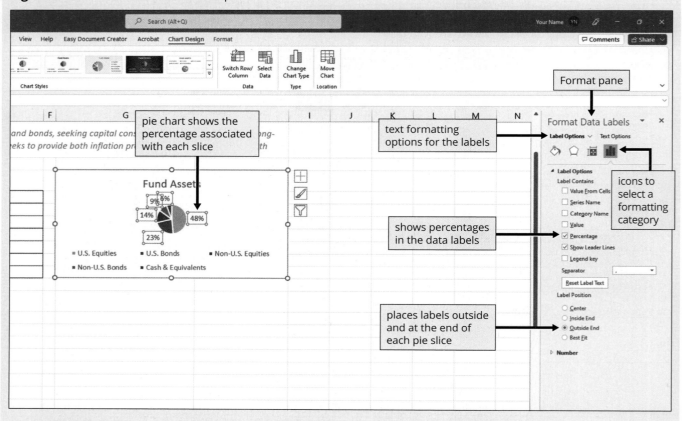

The Format pane is attached, or docked, to the right side of the workbook window. You can undock the pane so that it floats free above the worksheet grid by pointing to a blank area of the pane until the pointer changes to the Move pointer ⁺k̟ and then clicking and dragging the pane over the worksheet grid. To redock the pane, point to the floating pane until the pointer changes to the Move pointer ⁺k̟ and then drag to the right until the pane reattaches to the workbook window.

From the Format pane, you can format other chart elements. Lydia thinks the pie chart would be more effective if the legend were aligned with the right edge of the chart area rather than its current position at the bottom. Lydia also wants the background of the legend to be a light tan color. You'll use the Format pane to make those changes now.

To move and format the pie chart legend:

1. In the Format Data Labels pane, click the **Label Options arrow** directly below the Format Data Labels title, and then click **Legend** in the list of chart elements. The name of the Format pane changes to Format Legend and options for formatting the pie chart legend appear in the pane.

   ▌ **Tip** You can also double-click any chart element to open its Format pane.

2. In the Legend Options section, click the **Right** option button to place the pie chart legend on the right side of the chart area. Refer to Figure 4–10.

Figure 4–10   Chart legend in chart area

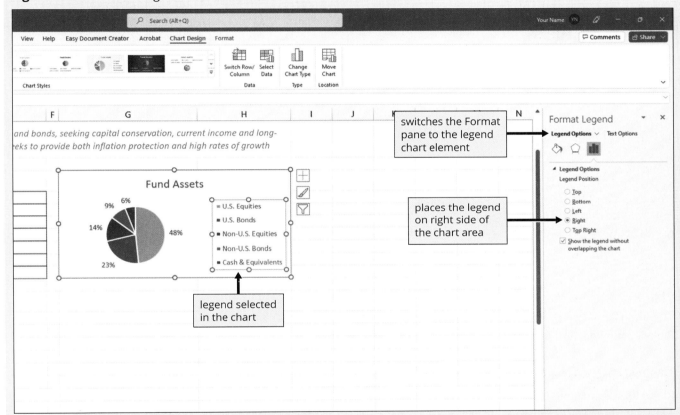

3. Click the **Fill & Line** icon ◈ , and then click the **Fill** heading to expand the fill options for the legend.

4. Click the **Solid fill** option button, click the **Color** button ◢▾ , and then click **Tan, Accent 6, Lighter 80%** (the last theme color in the second row) in the color palette. Refer to Figure 4–11.

Figure 4–11   Fill color for the chart legend

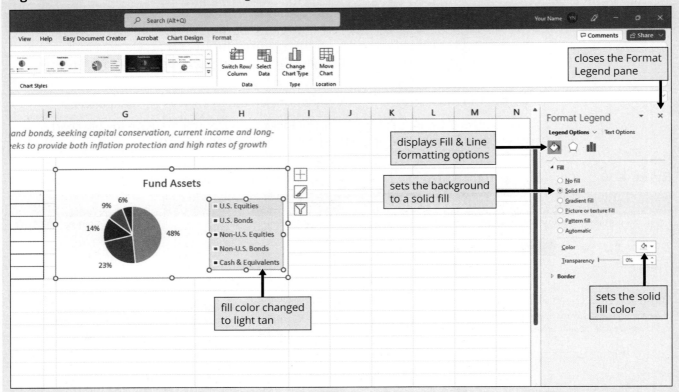

5. Click the **Close** button ☒ in the upper-right corner of the Format Legend pane to close the pane.

Another way of modifying the chart layout is to choose a predefined layout from the Quick Layout button on the Chart Design tab.

Choosing a Chart Style

Rather than formatting individual chart elements, you can apply one of the built-in chart styles to apply a professional design to all elements of the chart. You can access chart styles either from the Chart Styles button ✎ next to a selected chart or in the Chart Styles gallery on the Chart Tools tab. You'll use Live Preview to test different chart styles you can apply to pie charts.

To use the built-in pie chart styles:

1. With the pie chart still selected, click the **Chart Styles** button ✎ next to the chart.

2. Scroll through the gallery of chart styles, pointing to each entry in the gallery to see a preview of the chart with that style. Figure 4–12 shows a preview of design of the Style 6 chart style applied to the Asset Mix pie chart.

Figure 4–12   Preview of a chart style

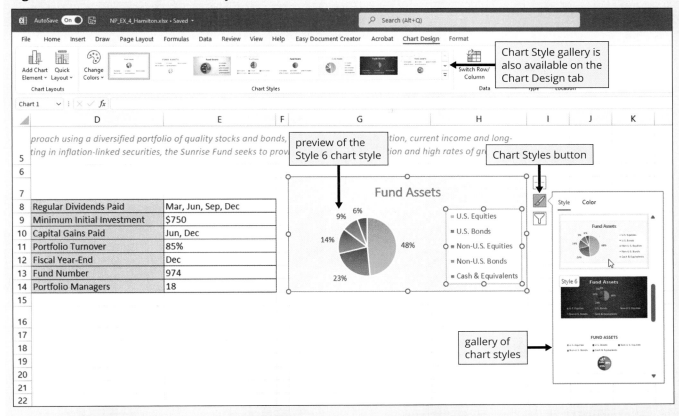

3. Press **ESC** to close the chart style gallery without changing the style of the Asset Mix pie chart.

    Trouble? If you accidentally apply a chart style, click the Undo button ↩ on the Quick Access Toolbar to restore the chart to its previous style.

Although Lydia does not want you to change the chart style of the Asset Mix pie chart, she is concerned that the pie chart is challenging to interpret with its mix of colors. You can eliminate this issue by choosing a different color scheme.

Changing the Color Scheme

By default, Excel applies a color scheme to a chart using theme colors. You can select a different color scheme from the Chart Styles button in the Colors submenu. Lydia wants you to use colors in the same orange hue but with different levels of saturation so that the largest slice is displayed in dark orange and the smallest slice displayed in a light orange. You will apply this color scheme to the Asset Mix pie chart.

To change the pie slice colors:

1. Click the **Chart Styles** button 🖌 to reopen the gallery of chart styles.

    Tip You can also use the Change Colors button in the Chart Styles group on the Chart Design tab.

2. Click the **Color** tab to display a gallery of possible color schemes.

3. In the Monochromatic section, click the orange monochromatic color scheme labeled **Monochromatic Palette 1**. Refer to Figure 4–13.

Figure 4–13   Pie chart with updated color scheme

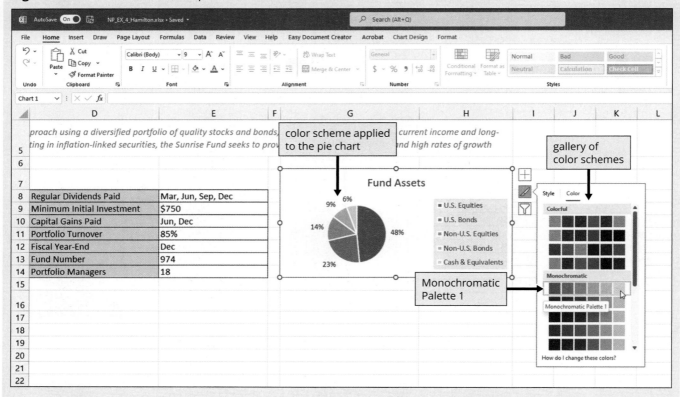

4. Press **ESC** to close the chart styles gallery.

Because the color schemes are based on the theme colors, you can change the color schemes by selecting new theme colors from the Colors box in the Themes group on the Page Layout tab. If you don't want to change the workbook's color theme, you can change the color of individual pie slices. To change a pie slice to another color, double-click the slice to select only that slice (and no other elements on the chart), and then choose a color from the Fill Color button [⬥ ▾] in the Font group on the Home tab.

Filtering a Chart

If you want a chart to focus on fewer categories, you can filter the chart by removing one or more categories. To remove a category, click the Filter button [▽] next to the chart, opening a list of data categories. Check the data categories you want to appear in chart, and then click the Apply button. Removing a data category has no effect on the data source. It affects only the categories that Excel will display in the chart.

The pie chart in Figure 4–14 is filtered and does not display all its possible categories. The size of the slices is modified to match the number of categories that appear in the chart, not the total number of possible categories and their values.

Figure 4–14   Filtered pie chart

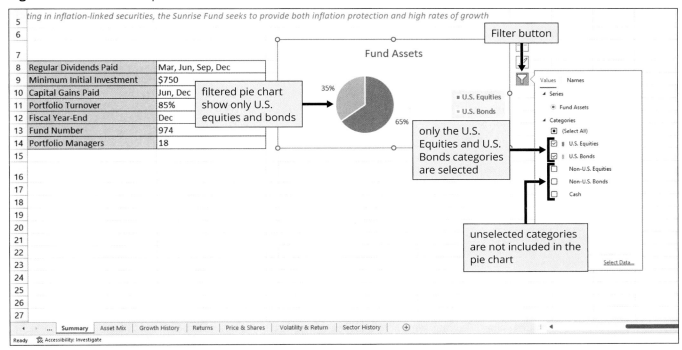

To redisplay a data category, click its check box to select it, and then click the Apply button. You can also use Live Preview to review the effects of filtering without applying the filter to the pie chart.

Insight

Overlaying Chart Elements

An embedded chart takes up less space than a chart sheet. However, it can be challenging to fit all the chart elements into that smaller space. One solution is to overlay one element on top of another. The most commonly overlaid elements are the chart title and the chart legend. To overlay the chart title, click the Chart Title arrow in the Chart Elements list and select Centered Overlay as the position option. Excel will place the chart title on top of the plot area, freeing up more space for other chart elements. Chart legends can also be overlaid by opening the Format pane for the legend and deselecting the Show the legend without overlapping the chart check box in the Legend Options section. Other chart elements can be overlaid by dragging them to new locations in the chart area and then resizing the plot area to recover the empty space.

Do not overuse the technique of overlaying chart elements. Too much overlaying of chart elements can make a chart difficult to understand.

Performing What-If Analyses with Charts

Because a chart is linked to its data source, any changes in the data source values will be reflected in the chart. This link between a chart and its data source provides a powerful tool for data exploration. For the Asset Mix pie chart, the chart title is linked to the text in cell B4 of the Asset Mix worksheet, the size of the pie slices is based on values in the range B5:B9, and the category names are linked to the category values in the range A4:A9.

Lydia notes that the value in cell B5 for the amount invested in U.S. equities should be $74,140 instead of $84,140. You will change the value in the cell and change the category name in cell B9 from "Cash & Equivalents" to simply "Cash."

To modify the pie chart's data:

1. Go to the **Asset Mix** worksheet, and then in cell **B5**, change the value to **$74,140** to reflect the correct amount invested in U.S. equities.

2. In cell **A9**, change the text to **Cash** to update the label.

3. Return to the **Summary** worksheet and confirm that the percentage of assets invested in U.S. equities has decreased to 45% and that the last legend entry changed to "Cash."

The pie chart revealed some important information about the assets of the Hamilton Fund. Next, you will use a column chart to explore the level of returns that the fund has provided for investors over the past 10 years.

Creating a Column Chart

A **column chart** displays data values as columns with the height of each column based on the data value. A column chart turned on its side is called a **bar chart**, with the length of the bar determined by the data value. It is better to use column and bar charts than pie charts when the number of categories is large or when the data categories are close in value. Figure 4–15 displays the same data as a pie chart and a column chart. As you can see, it is difficult to determine which pie slice is biggest and by how much. It is much simpler to make those comparisons in a column or bar chart.

Figure 4–15   Pie and column charts with the same data

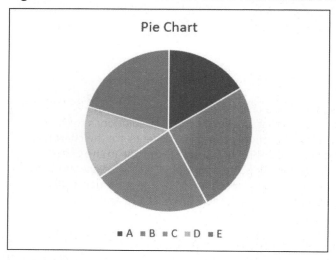
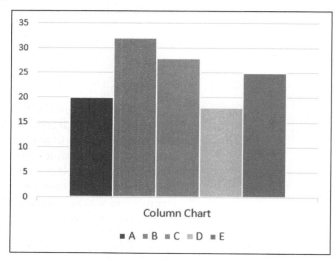

Comparing Column Chart Subtypes

Unlike pie charts, which have only one data series, column and bar charts can include multiple data series. Figure 4–16 presents three examples of column charts in which five data series (U.S. Equities, U.S. Bonds, Non-U.S. Equities, Non-U.S. Bonds, and Cash) are plotted against one category series (Years). Column charts are plotted against a **value axis** along the vertical side of the chart displaying the values from the data series and a **category axis** along the horizontal side of the chart displaying the category values associated with each data series.

Figure 4–16   Column chart subtypes

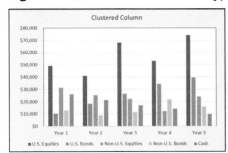 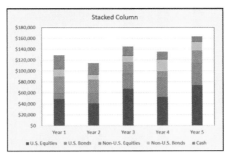 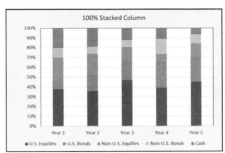

A **clustered column chart** displays the data series values in separate columns side by side so that you can compare the relative heights of values across categories. The clustered column chart in Figure 4–16 compares the amount invested in each category in Year 1 through Year 5. Note that the amount invested in U.S. bonds steadily increases as the amount invested in cash decreases over the same period.

A **stacked column chart** combines the data series values within a single column to show how much of the total is contributed by each item. The stacked column chart in Figure 4–16 gives information on the total amount invested each year in the fund and how each year's investment is split among five investment categories. This chart makes it clear that the total investment in the fund dropped from Year 3 to Year 4 before rising again in Year 5.

Finally, a **100% stacked column chart** makes the same comparison as the stacked column chart except that the stacked sections are expressed as percentages of the whole. As you can see from the 100% stacked column chart in Figure 4–16, the investment in U.S. equities and bonds starts out at about 45% in the first year and steadily increases to about 70% by Year 5. Each chart, while working with the same data source, reveals something different about the activity of the investment fund over the five-year period.

Creating a Clustered Column Chart

The process for creating a column chart is the same as for creating a pie chart: Select the data source and then choose a chart type and subtype. After the chart is embedded in the worksheet, you can move and resize the chart and change the chart's design, layout, and format.

Lydia wants a column chart presenting the returns of the Hamilton Fund adjusted over 1-year, 3-year, and 10-year periods, as well as year-to-date (YTD) and since the fund's inception. The column chart will include the returns from the Standard & Poor's 500 index (S&P 500) to indicate how the fund compares to an industry standard. You will create that chart now.

To create a clustered column chart:

1. Go to the **Returns** worksheet containing the returns based on month-end values.

2. Select the range **A4:C9** containing the categories and values to chart.

3. On the ribbon, click the **Insert** tab, and then in the Charts group, click the **Recommended Charts** button. The Insert Chart dialog box opens to the Recommended Charts tab. From this tab, you can preview and select a chart best suited to the data source. Refer to Figure 4–17.

Figure 4–17   Recommended Charts tab in the Insert Chart dialog box

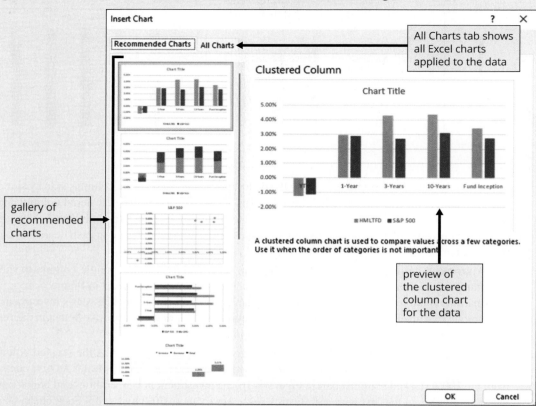

4. Confirm that the **Clustered Column** chart is selected, and then click **OK**.

5. On the Chart Design tab, in the Location group, click the **Move Chart** button.

6. From the Object in box, click **Summary**.

7. Click **OK** to move the column chart to the Summary worksheet.

> **Tip** To set an exact chart size, enter the height and width values in the Size group on the Format tab.

8. In the Summary worksheet, move and resize the chart to cover the range **A17:B28**, using **ALT** to snap the chart to the grid. Refer to Figure 4–18.

Figure 4–18   Clustered column chart

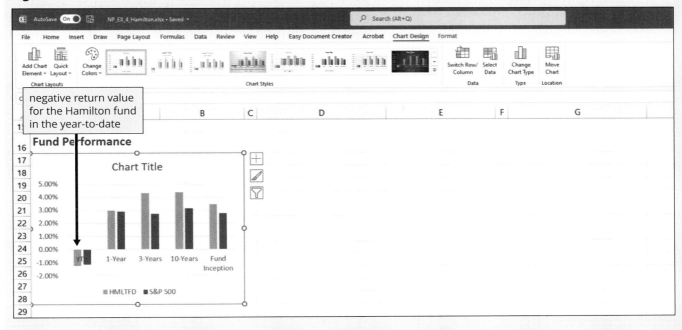

The column chart shows that the Hamilton Fund has generally outperformed the S&P 500 index for most of its life and especially during the previous 3-year and 10-year periods. However, in the current year-to-date, the fund is performing worse than the S&P 500 and, in fact, is showing a negative return in value.

Editing a Chart Title

When a chart has a single data series, the name of the data series is used for the chart title. When a chart has more than one data series, "Chart Title" is used as the temporary title of the chart. Lydia wants you to change the chart title to "Return on Investment." You will edit the chart title now.

To change the title of the column chart:

1. At the top of the column chart, click **Chart Title** to select it.

   Tip You can change the font size and style of the chart title by clicking the formatting buttons in the Font group on the Home tab.

2. Type **Return on Investment** as the new title, and then press **ENTER**. The new title is inserted into the chart.

Because the chart title is not linked to any worksheet cell, the title will not be updated if changes are made to the data source.

Setting the Gap Width

Excel automatically sets the space between the data series in a column chart as well as the gap width between one category value and the next. If a column chart contains several data series, there might be too little room between the categories, making it difficult to know when one category ends and the next begins. You can modify the space between the data series and gap width using the Format pane.

Lydia wants you to reduce the space between the two data series and increase the interval width between the Year categories.

To set the column chart gap and interval widths:

1. Double-click any column in the column chart to display the Format Data Series pane with the Series Options section 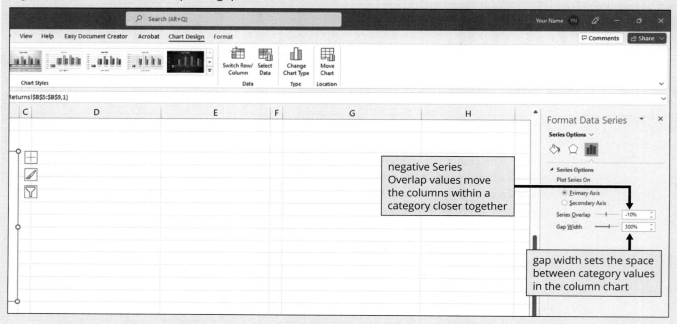 already selected.

2. Select the **Series Overlap** box, and then change the space between the data series to **−10%**.

> **Tip** Use the up and down spin arrows in the Series Overlap and Gap Width boxes to change the values in 1% increments.

3. Select the **Gap Width** box, and then increase the value of the gap between the category values to **300%**. Refer to Figure 4–19.

Figure 4–19   Series overlap and gap width values

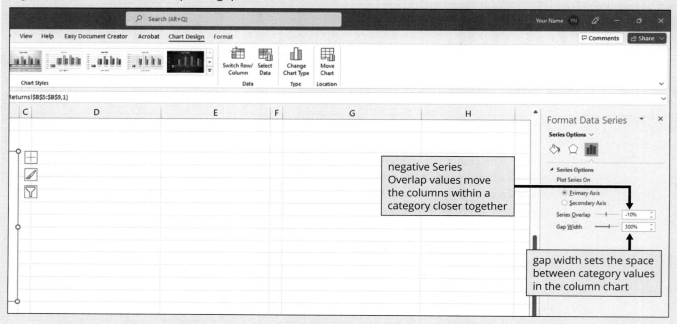

4. Close the Format Data Series pane.

Adding Gridlines to a Chart

Another way of distinguishing columns in separate categories is with gridlines. A gridline is a line that extends from the chart's horizontal and vertical axis into the plot area, making it easier to identify the values or categories associated with the chart's data markers. For example, the horizontal gridlines in the Return on Investment chart make it clearer that the return from the Hamilton Fund exceeds 4% growth for the 3-year and 10-year time periods.

Lydia wants you to add vertical gridlines to provide an additional visual aid for separating the time intervals from each other.

Creating a Line Chart

To add vertical gridlines to the chart:

1. With the column chart still selected, click the **Chart Elements** button ⊞ to the right of chart to display the list of chart elements associated with column charts.

2. To the right of Gridlines, click the **arrow** ▶ to display the gridline options, and then click **Primary Major Vertical** to add vertical gridlines to the chart. Refer to Figure 4–20.

Figure 4–20 Gridlines added to the column chart

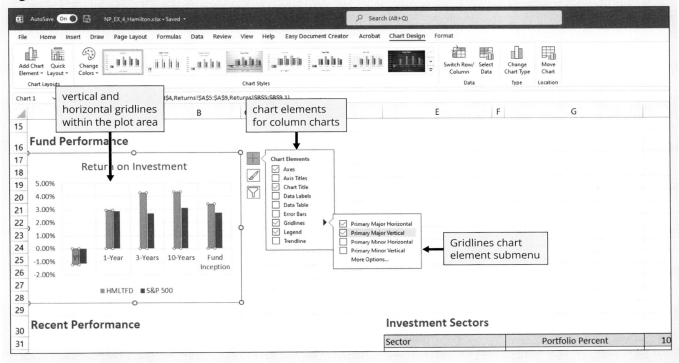

The column chart is complete. The next chart that Lydia wants added to the Summary worksheet analyzes how the value of the fund has changed over the past 20 years.

Insight

Adding Data Tables to Charts

You can use data labels to add data directly to a chart. Another way of viewing the data values associated with a chart is by adding a data table. The data table will be inserted within the chart area directly below the plot area. Each data series will appear as a separate row within the data table with category values placed in the first column of the table.

Creating a Line Chart

A line chart uses lines to plot one or more data series against a set of categories. The categories should follow a sequential order that is evenly spaced. For example, if the categories represent calendar months, the space between one month and the next must be constant. Otherwise, the line chart will give an inaccurate depiction of change over time.

Lydia wants a line chart comparing the growth of an investment in the Hamilton Fund over the past 20 years to the same investment in the Standard & Poor's 500 index. You will create this line chart using the data in the Growth History worksheet.

To create the growth history line chart:

1. Go to the **Growth History** worksheet, and then select the range **A4:C25** containing the growth of the Hamilton Fund and the S&P 500 index from a hypothetical $10,000 initial investment.

2. On the ribbon, click the **Insert** tab, and then in the Charts group, click the **Recommended Charts** button. The Insert Chart dialog box opens to the Recommended Charts tab.

3. Confirm that the **Line** chart type is selected, and then click **OK** to insert the line chart into the Growth History worksheet.

4. Move the chart to the **Summary** worksheet.

5. Move and resize the line chart so that it covers the range **D17:E28**, holding down **ALT** to snap the chart to the worksheet grid.

6. In the chart, click **Chart Title** to select it, type **Growth of 10K Investment** as the title, and then press **ENTER**. Refer to Figure 4–21.

Figure 4–21   Line chart of two data series

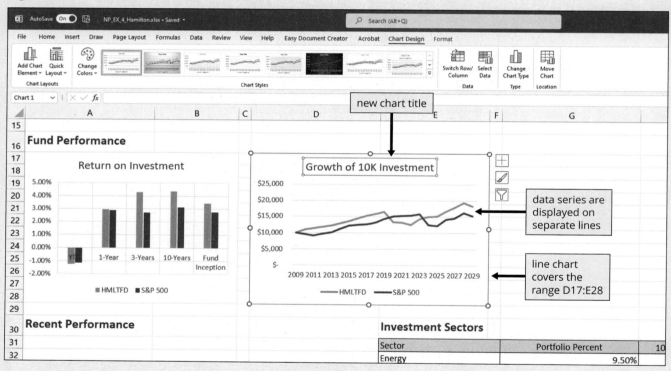

The line chart shows that the value of the Hamilton Fund exceeds the S&P 500 index for most of the past 20 years except between 2019 and 2023 when the index performed better. Lydia also notes that in the last year both the Hamilton Fund and the index have lost value.

Editing the Category Axis

You can modify the axis labels and tick marks to change which category values are displayed in the chart. The year values in the horizontal axis of the line chart are crowded, making the dates unclear. Lydia wants you to revise the axis so that it lists years in 5-year increments.

To format the horizontal axis:

1. Double-click one of the years on the horizontal axis to open the Format Axis pane.
2. If necessary, at the top of the Format pane, click the **Axis Options** button 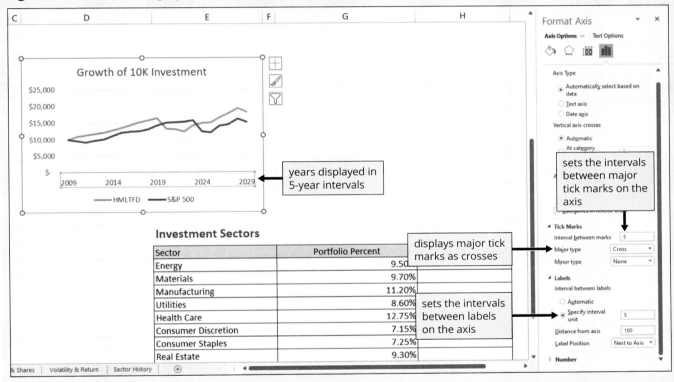 to select it.
3. Click **Tick Marks** to view options for modifying the tick marks on the category axis.
4. In the Interval between marks box, change the value to **5** so that the tick marks are laid out in 5-year intervals.
5. Click the **Major type** arrow, and then click **Cross** so that the tick marks are displayed as crosses.
6. Click **Labels** to expand that section, click the **Specify interval unit** option button, enter **5** in the Specify interval unit box, and then press **ENTER**. The year labels appear at 5-year intervals. Refer to Figure 4–22.

Figure 4–22   New category intervals for the horizontal axis

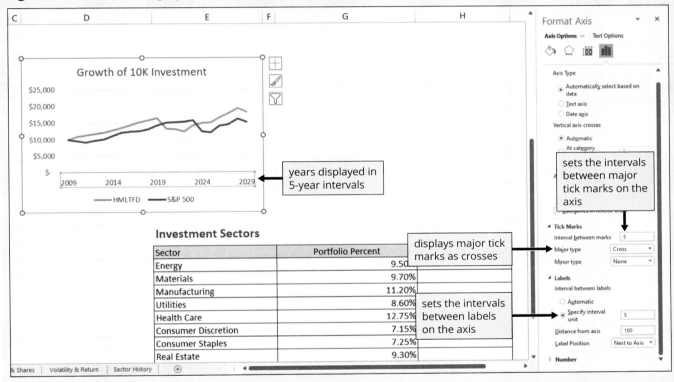

You can modify date categories by clicking the Date axis option button in the Axis Type section of the Format Axis pane. The pane will then show an input box from which you specify the number of days, weeks, months, and so forth between date values.

Formatting Data Markers

Each value from a data series is represented by a data marker. In pie charts, the data markers are the individual pie slices. In column charts, the columns are the data markers. In a line chart, the data markers are the points connected by the line. Depending on the line chart style, these data marker points can be displayed or hidden.

In the line chart you created, the data marker points are hidden, and only the line connecting those markers is visible. Lydia wants you to display those data markers and change their fill color to white so that they stand out, making the data values obvious.

To display and format the line chart data markers:

1. In the line chart, double-click the orange line for the Hamilton Fund (HMLTFD) to display the Format Data Series pane.

2. At the top of the Format pane, click the **Fill & Line** button ⟨🖌⟩.

3. At the top of the pane, click **Marker**, and then click **Marker Options** to display options specific to data markers.

4. Click the **Automatic** option button to automatically display the markers along with the line for the Hamilton Fund data series. The data markers are now visible in the line chart, but they have an orange fill color. You will change this fill color to white.

5. In the Fill section, click the **Solid fill** option button, click the **Color** button, and then select the **White, Background 1** theme color. The fill color for the data markers for the Hamilton Fund line changes to white.

6. Repeat Steps 1 through 5 for the maroon line representing the S&P 500 index. Refer to Figure 4–23.

Figure 4–23   Formatted data markers in a line chart

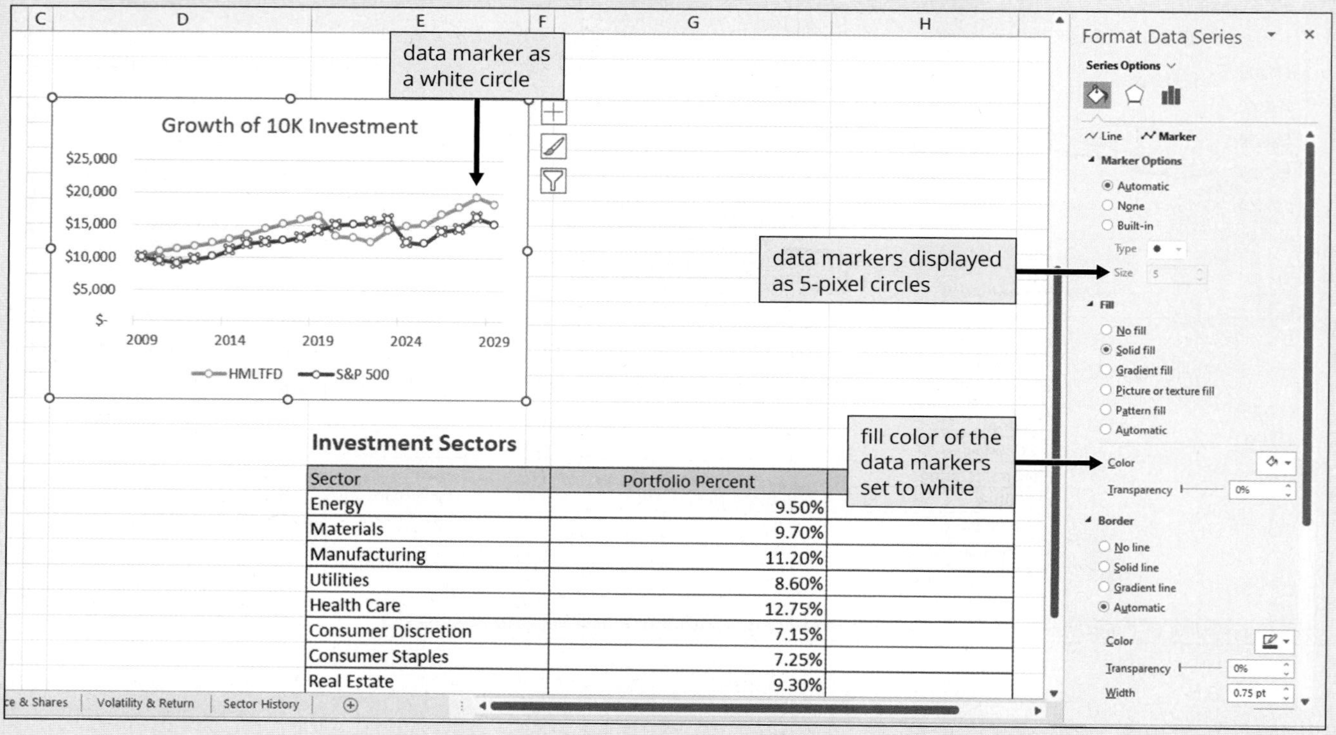

7. Close the Format Data Series pane.

By adding the data markers, you now have a better view of individual values in plotted in the line chart.

Proskills

Written Communication: Communicating Effectively with Charts

Studies show that people better interpret information when it is presented as a graphic rather than in a table. As a result, charts can help communicate the real story underlying the facts and figures you present to colleagues and clients. A well-designed chart can illuminate the bigger picture that might be hidden by viewing only the numbers. However, poorly designed charts can mislead readers and make it more difficult to interpret data.

To create effective and useful charts, keep in mind the following tips as you design your charts:

- **Keep it simple.** Do not clutter a chart with too many graphical elements. Focus attention on the data rather than on decorative elements that do not inform.
- **Focus on the message.** Design the chart to highlight the points you want to convey to readers.
- **Limit the number of data series.** Most charts should display no more than four or five data series. Pie charts should have no more than six slices.
- **Choose colors carefully.** Display different data series in contrasting colors to make it easier to distinguish one series from another. Modify the default colors as needed to make them distinct on the screen and in the printed copy.
- **Limit text styles.** Use a maximum of two or three different text styles in the same chart. Too many text styles in one chart can distract attention from the data.

The goal of written communication is always to inform the reader in the simplest, most accurate, and most direct way possible. Everything in your workbook should be directed toward that aim.

Creating a Combination Chart

So far, the charts you created are based on one chart type. A combination chart combines two chart types, enabling you to display each data series using the chart type best suited for it.

When the data series values cover vastly different ranges, you can plot one data series against the **primary axis**, the vertical axis appearing along the left edge of the chart, and the other data series against the **secondary axis**, the vertical axis on the chart's right edge.

The next chart that Lydia wants added to the Summary worksheet will display the recent performance of the Hamilton Fund, showing its daily selling price and the number of shares traded over the past three months. You'll display the daily selling price in a line chart plotted against the primary axis and the number of shares traded in a column chart plotted against the secondary axis.

To create a combination chart:

1. Go to the **Price & Shares** worksheet, and then select the range **A4:C69**.

2. On the ribbon, click the **Insert** tab, and then in the Charts group, click the **Recommended Charts** button. The Insert Chart dialog box opens showing the recommended Line chart.

3. Click the **All Charts** tab for a list of all Excel chart types.

4. In the list of chart types, click **Combo**.

5. Click the **Custom Combination** chart subtype (the last subtype listed for the Combo chart). At the bottom of the dialog box, the "Choose the chart type and axis for your data series" box lists two data series in the selected data.

6. In the "Choose the chart type and axis for your data series" box, click the **Price** Chart Type arrow, and then in the Line section, click **Line**. The Price data series will be displayed as a line chart.

Creating a Scatter Chart

The charts you created so far all involve plotting numeric data against categorical data. Another important type of chart is the scatter chart, which plots two data series of numeric values against each other. Scatter charts are widely used in science and engineering applications when investigators want to discover how two numeric variables are related. For example, an economist might want to investigate the effect of high tax rates on tax revenue or the effect of increasing the minimum wage on the unemployment rate.

Lydia wants you to create a scatter chart exploring the relationship between the Hamilton Fund's rate of return and its volatility. The rate of return indicates how much an investment can earn for the investor while volatility measures the degree by which that return estimate can vary. In general, investments that have high rates of return are often volatile so that the investor faces the prospect of either making or losing a lot of money. On the other hand, safe investments, while usually not very volatile, also do not often offer high return rates. Figure 4–28 presents a typical scatter chart showing the relationship between return rate and volatility in which the return rates are plotted on the vertical axis and the volatility values are plotted on the horizontal axis.

Figure 4–28   Scatter chart of return rate vs. volatility

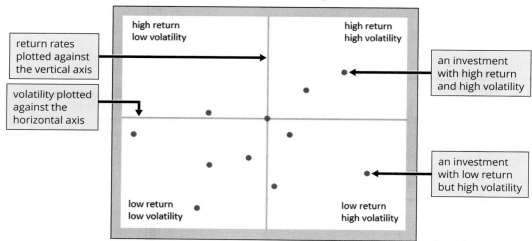

Lydia's clients want to know where the Hamilton Fund falls in its rate of return versus its volatility. Is the fund a high-risk/high-reward venture, or does it offer low risk but also low reward? You will create a scatter chart of those two data series to provide this information.

To create a scatter chart for the Hamilton Fund:

1. If you took a break at the end of the previous part, make sure the NP_EX_4_Hamilton workbook is open.

2. Go to the **Volatility & Return** worksheet, and then select the range **B5:C7** containing the volatility and return rates for the S&P 500 index and the Hamilton Fund calculated over a 10-year interval.

3. On the ribbon, click the **Insert** tab, and then in the Charts group, click the **Recommended Charts** button. The Insert Chart dialog box opens to the Recommended Charts tab.

4. In the recommended chart types, click **Scatter**. Refer to Figure 4–29.

Figure 4–29   Scatter chart preview

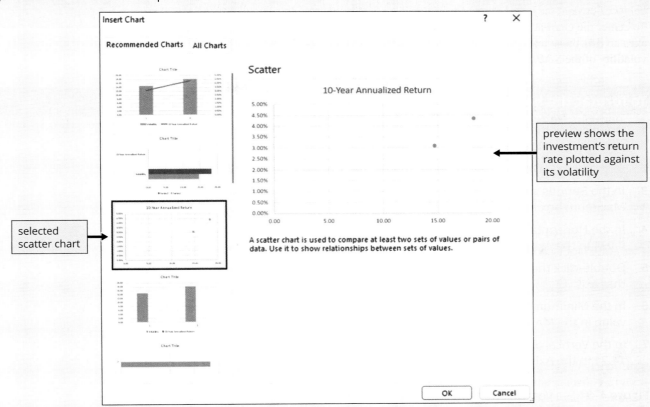

5. Click **OK** to insert the scatter chart.

6. Move the scatter chart to the Summary worksheet.

7. Move and resize the scatter chart to cover the range **G17:H28**, holding down the **ALT** key to snap the chart to the worksheet grid. Refer to Figure 4–30.

Figure 4–30   Scatter chart

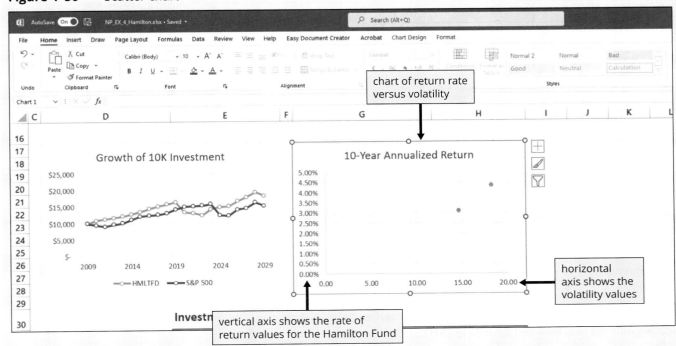

Insight

Copying and Pasting Chart Formats

You will often want to repeat the same design for the charts in your worksheet. Rather than repeat the same steps, you can copy the formatting from one chart to another. To copy a chart format, first select the chart with the existing design that you want to replicate, and then click the Copy button in the Clipboard group on the Home tab (or press CTRL+C). Next, select the chart that you want to format, click the Paste arrow in the Clipboard group, and then click Paste Special to open the Paste Special dialog box. In the Paste Special dialog box, select the Formats option button, and then click OK. All the copied formats from the original chart—including fill colors, font styles, axis scales, and chart types—are then pasted into the new chart. Be aware that the pasted formats will overwrite any formats previously used in the new chart.

The scatter chart now contains only the two data points and the two axis lines. But with only two data markers in the chart, there is not a lot of basis for comparison with other investments. Lydia asks you to add data markers representing other funds to the scatter chart.

Editing the Chart Data Source

Excel automates most of the process of assigning a data source to the chart. However, sometimes the completed chart is not what you want, and you need to edit the chart's data source. At any time, you can modify the chart's data source to add more data series or change the current data series in the chart.

Reference

Modifying a Chart's Data Source

- Select the chart to make it active.
- On the Chart Design tab, in the Data group, click the Select Data button.
- In the Legend Entries (Series) section of the Select Data Source dialog box, click the Add button to add another data series to the chart or click the Remove button to remove a data series from the chart.
- Click the Edit button in the Horizontal (Category) Axis Labels section to select the category values for the chart.
- Click OK.

Lydia wants you to add a data series containing information from other funds to the scatter chart of returns versus volatility. You will edit the chart's data source definition to make that change.

To edit the chart's data source:

1. With the scatter chart still selected, on the Chart Design tab, in the Data group, click the **Select Data** button. The Select Data Source dialog box opens. Refer to Figure 4–33.

Figure 4–33   Select Data Source dialog box

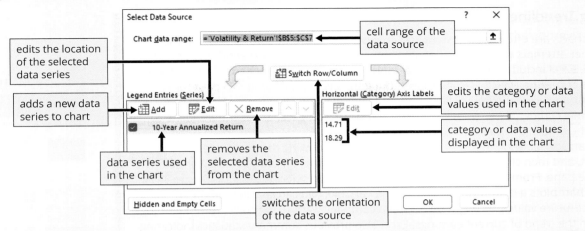

2. Click **Add** to open the Edit Series dialog box. You can add another data series to the chart from here.

   > **Tip** To organize a chart's data source by rows rather than columns (or vice versa), click the Switch Row/Column button in the Select Data Source dialog box.

3. With the insertion point in the Series name box, click the **Volatility & Return** sheet tab, and then click cell **G5** in that worksheet. The expression =`'Volatility & Return'!$G$5` is entered into the Series name box.

4. Click the **Series X values** box, and then in the Volatility & Return worksheet, select the range **F6:F14** to enter the expression =`'Volatility & Return'!$F$6:$F$14`.

5. Click the **Series Y values** box, delete the expression in that box, and then in the Volatility & Return worksheet, select the range **G6:G14** to enter the expression =`'Volatility & Return!'$G$6:$G$14`. Refer to Figure 4–34.

Figure 4–34   Edit Series dialog box

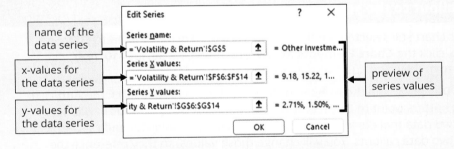

> **Key Step** Values or expressions might already be entered into the Edit Series dialog box, so you must delete any expressions before inserting a new reference.

6. Click **OK** to return to Select Data Source dialog box. Note that the data series "Other Investment Fund Returns" has been added to the list of data series.

7. Click **OK** to return to the Summary worksheet. Data markers for the second data series are added to the scatter chart.

You have simplified the scatter chart by removing elements that Lydia thinks will not be of interest to the company's investors (such as the exact values of the stock's volatility). However, the chart still needs some descriptive information to aid in its interpretation. You will add this additional text and graphics to the chart and worksheet next.

4. Click near the upper-left corner of the scatter chart. A text box is added. You will enter text here.

5. Type **high return** as the first line of text in the text box, press **ENTER**, and then type **low volatility** as the second line of text in the text box.

6. Click and drag the **sizing handles** around the selected text box as needed to reduce the text box to fit the text.

7. Point to the text box border so the pointer changes to the Move pointer, and then drag the text box so that it aligns with the upper-left corner of the scatter chart.

> **Trouble?** If the chart or another chart element moves, you didn't select the text box. Undo that move, and then make sure you click the text in the text box and verify that the selection handles appear around the box before attempting to move it.

8. Repeat Steps 2 through 7 to insert a text box containing **high return** and **high volatility** on separate lines in the upper-right corner of the chart.

9. Repeat Steps 2 through 7 to insert a text box containing **low return** and **low volatility** on separate lines in the lower-left corner of the chart.

10. Repeat Steps 2 through 7 to insert a text box containing **low return** and **high volatility** on separate lines in the lower-right corner of the chart. Refer to Figure 4–36.

Figure 4–36   Text boxes added to an Excel chart

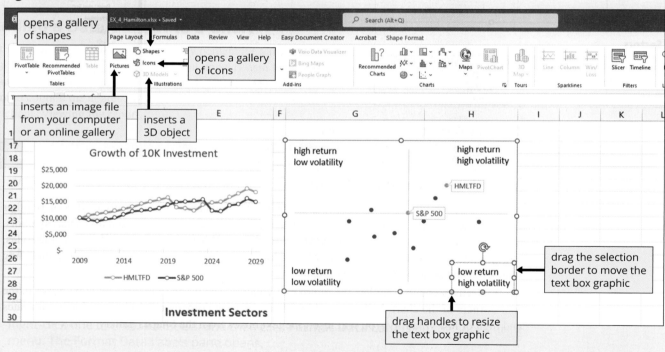

With the final version of the scatter chart, Lydia's clients can quickly identify the Hamilton Fund as a high return, high volatility investment, particularly when compared to the S&P 500 index and other sample investments.

Exploring Other Chart Types

At this point, you have used only a few of the many Excel chart types. Excel has other chart types that are useful for financial and scientific research, which you can access from the Charts group on the Insert tab. If you want to change the chart type of an existing chart, click the Change Chart Type button in the Type group on the Chart Design tab and then select the new chart type from the dialog box.

Hierarchy Charts

Hierarchy charts are like pie charts in that they show the relative contribution of groups to a whole. Unlike pie charts, a hierarchy chart also shows the organizational structure of the data with subcategories displayed within main categories. Excel supports two types of hierarchy charts: treemap charts and sunburst charts.

In a **treemap chart**, each category is placed within a rectangle, and subcategories are nested as rectangles within those rectangles. The rectangles are sized to show the relative proportions of the two groups based on values from a data series. The treemap chart in Figure 4–37 shows the investor sectors of the Hamilton Fund broken down by group and category. You can create a treemap chart by clicking the Recommended Charts button and then selecting Treemap from the list of chart types on the All Charts tab.

Figure 4–37   Treemap and Sunburst charts

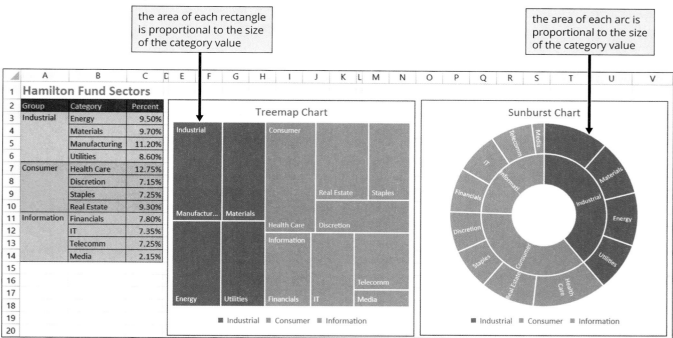

A **sunburst chart** organizes hierarchical data through a series of concentric rings with the innermost rings showing the highest category levels and the outer rings showing categories from lower levels. The size of the rings indicates the relative proportions of the different groups and categories within groups. Refer back to Figure 4–37. Sunburst charts are better than treemap charts at conveying information from multiple levels of nested groups. But treemaps are better at displaying the relative sizes of the categories within each group level. You can create a sunburst chart by clicking the Recommended Charts button and then selecting Sunburst from the list of chart types on the All Charts tab.

Pareto Charts

A special kind of combination chart is the **Pareto chart**, which combines a column chart and a line chart to indicate which factors are the largest contributors to the whole. Figure 4–38 shows a Pareto chart of investment categories. The categories are sorted in descending order of importance so that the largest investment category, Health Care, is listed first followed by Manufacturing, Materials, Energy, and so forth. The line chart provides a running total of the percentage that each category adds to the overall total. Roughly 50% of the Hamilton Fund is invested in the first five categories listed in the chart.

Pareto charts are often used in quality control studies to isolate the most significant factors in the failure of a manufacturer process. They are also used in market research to indicate which factors and combination of factors are the most crucial in consumer choices. You can create a Pareto chart by clicking the Recommended Charts button, clicking Histogram on the All Charts tab, and then clicking the Pareto chart type.

Figure 4–38   Pareto chart

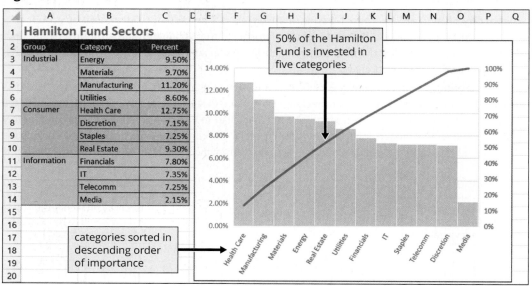

Histogram Charts

A **histogram** is a column chart displaying the distribution of values from a single data series. For example, a professor might create a histogram to display the distribution of scores from a midterm exam. There is no category series for a histogram. Instead, the categories are determined based on the data series values with the data values allocated to **bins** and the size of the columns determined by the number of items within each bin. The number of bins is arbitrary and can be chosen to best represent the shape of the distribution.

Figure 4–39 shows a histogram of the distribution of the weekly price of the Hamilton Fund over a 15-month period. From the histogram the midpoint price of the Hamilton Fund falls between about $41 and $42, but there were a few values as low as $35 to $36 and as high as $48 to $49. You can create a Histogram by clicking the Recommended Charts button, clicking Histogram on the All Charts tab, and then selecting the Histogram chart type. To modify the bins used in the histogram, double-click the horizontal axis to open the Format Axis pane and then set the bin size or the number of bins in the Bins section of the Axis Options section.

Figure 4–39   Histogram chart

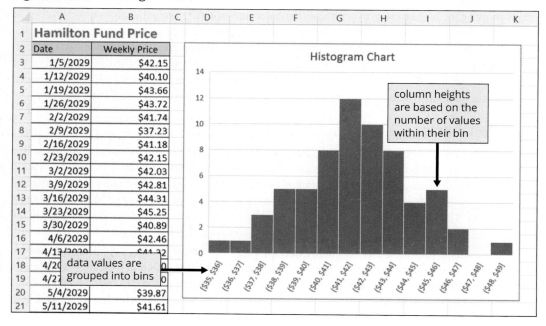

Waterfall Charts

A **waterfall chart** tracks the addition and subtraction of values within a sum. Figure 4–40 shows a waterfall chart of the value of an investment in the Hamilton Fund over 10 years. The initial and final value of the fund are shown in dark gray. Positive changes in the fund's value are shown in green. Years in which the fund decreased in value are shown in red. The waterfall chart is so named because the increasing and decreasing steps in the graph resemble a waterfall. Waterfall charts are often used with Profit and Loss statements to track the impact of revenue and expenses on a company's net profit.

Figure 4–40   Waterfall chart

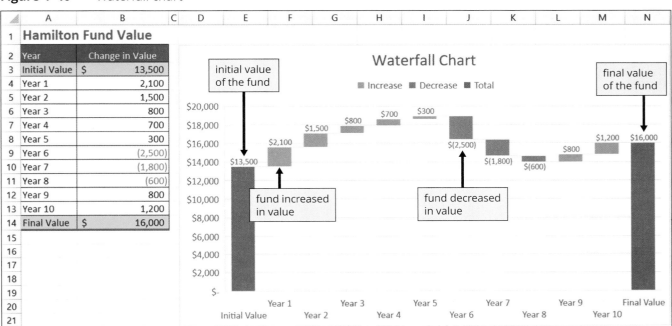

Creating Data Bars

So far, the charts you created have been embedded as objects on a worksheet. You can also create charts that appear in worksheet cells. Data bars are one of these types of charts.

A data bar is a conditional format that adds a horizontal bar to a cell background. The length of the bar is based on the value stored in the cell. Cells storing larger values display longer data bars; cells with smaller values have shorter bars. When applied to a range of cells, the data bars have the same appearance as a bar chart, with each cell displaying a single bar. Like all conditional formats, data bars are dynamic, changing their lengths as the cell's value changes.

Reference

Creating Data Bars

- Select the range containing the data to be charted.
- On the Home tab, in the Styles group, click the Conditional Formatting button, point to Data Bars, and then click the data bar style you want to use.
- To modify the data bar rules, click the Conditional Formatting button, and then click Manage Rules.

The Hamilton Fund invests in different sectors of the economy. The percentage invested in each sector is displayed in the range E31:G43 of the Summary worksheet. You'll enhance the percentage values in column G using data bars with the length of each bar matching the percentage invested.

To add data bars to the portfolio percentages in the worksheet:

1. On the Summary worksheet, select the range **G32:G43**.

2. On the ribbon, click the **Home** tab. In the Styles group, click the **Conditional Formatting** button, and then click **Data Bars**. A gallery of data bar styles opens.

3. In the Gradient Fill section, click the **Orange Data Bar** style (the first style in the second row). Orange data bars are added to the selected cells.

4. Click cell **E30** to deselect the range. Refer to Figure 4–41.

Figure 4–41   Portfolio percentages displayed with data bars

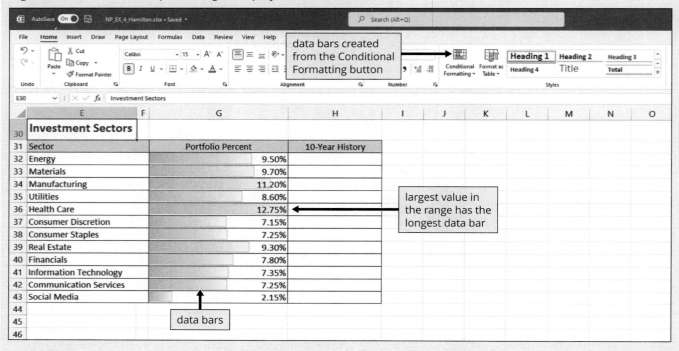

The data bars allow comparison of the relative size of the investment sectors for the Hamilton Fund. However, some of the data bars cover their cell value. Lydia wants you to shorten the length of the bars so that there is no overlap.

Modifying a Data Bar Rule

By default, the cell with the largest value in the range will have a data bar that stretches across the entire width of the cell. You can modify the length of the data bars by altering the rules of the conditional format.

> **Tip** When the range contains negative values, the data bars originate from the center of the cell—negative bars extend to the left, and positive bars extend to the right.

The longest data bar is in cell G36, representing the amount of the fund invested in health care (12.75%). You'll modify the conditional format rule for the data bar, setting the maximum length to 0.25 so that the longest bar doesn't overlap the value in its cell.

To modify the data bar conditional formatting rule:

1. On the Home tab, in the Styles group, click the **Conditional Formatting** button, and then click **Manage Rules**. The Conditional Formatting Rules Manager dialog box opens, displaying all the rules applied to any conditional format in the workbook.

2. In the Show formatting rules for box, select **This Worksheet** to show all the conditional formatting rules for the current sheet.

3. With the Data Bar rule selected, click the **Edit Rule** button. The Edit Formatting Rule dialog box opens.

4. In the Type row, click the **Maximum arrow**, and then click **Number**.

5. Press **TAB** to move the insertion point to the Maximum box in the Value row, and then type **0.25**. All data bar lengths will then be defined relative to this value. Refer to Figure 4–42.

Figure 4–42   Edit Formatting Rule dialog box

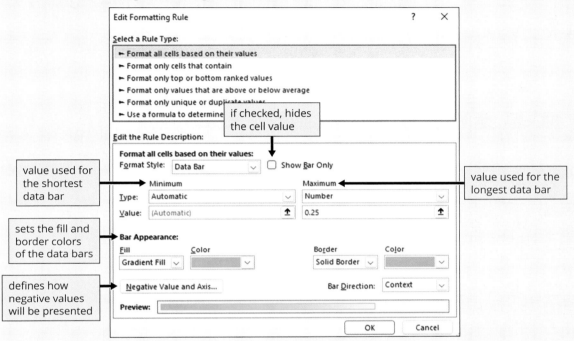

6. Click **OK** in each dialog box to return to the worksheet, and then verify that the data bars no longer span the width of the selected cells. Refer to Figure 4–43.

Figure 4–43   Resized data bars

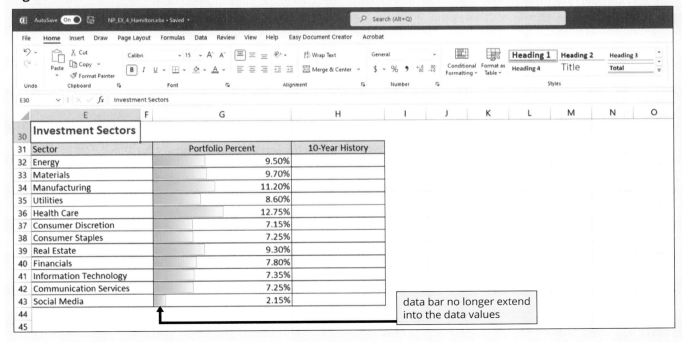

Creating Sparklines

Another way of adding a chart to a cell is with a sparkline, which is a small chart completely confined to the borders of a single cell. Because of their small size, sparklines do not include chart elements such as legends, titles, or gridlines. The goal of a sparkline is to display the maximum amount of information in the smallest space. As a result, sparklines are useful when you only need to convey a general impression of the data without specific details.

Excel supports three types of sparklines: line sparklines, column sparklines, and win/loss sparklines. Figure 4–44 includes an example of each type of sparkline in which the price history, shares traded, and increases and declines of 10 investments are displayed within a worksheet.

Figure 4–44   Sparklines types

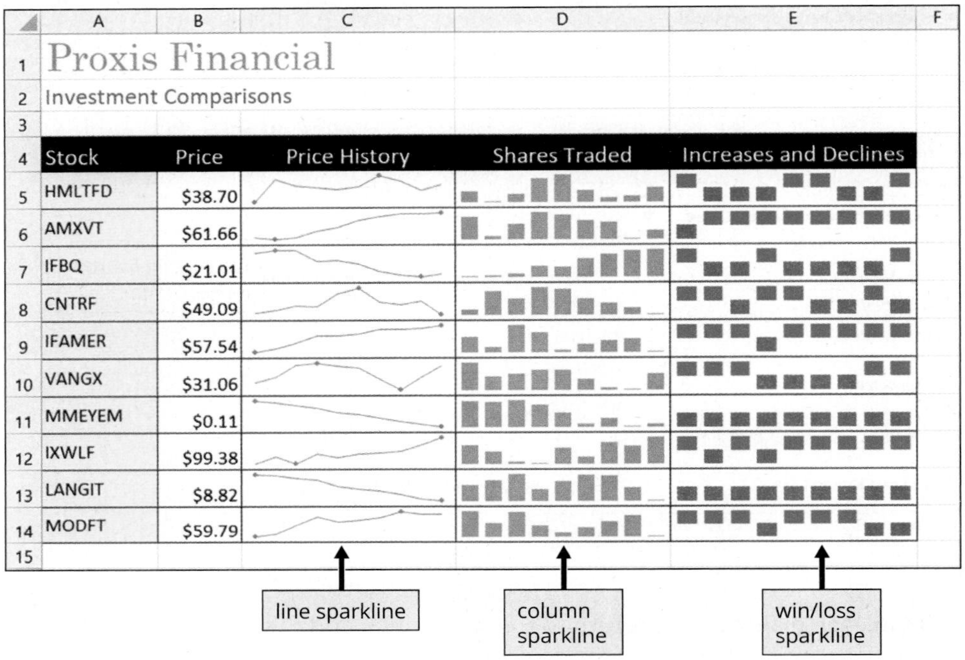

The line sparkline indicates the daily fluctuation in the selling price of each investment. While the sparkline does not provide specific prices, it clearly demonstrates that the selling price of the Hamilton Fund (HMTLTFD) has seen increases followed by declines over its history, with prices rebounding in the last few days. Other investments such as the IFBQ stock (cell C7) have shown a steady decline in price while the IFAMER stock (cell C9) has shown a steady increase.

The column sparkline indicates the volume of shares traded. Once again, specific details are not provided, but an investor can see that the trading volume for the Hamilton Fund has gone up and down over the last few days.

Finally, the win/loss sparkline displays a green block for positive values on those days in which the investment's selling price increased and a red block for days in which the selling price declined. The selling price of an investment like MMEYEM (cell E11) is quickly seen to have declined every day, while the IFAMER investment (cell E9) showed an increase in its selling price every day except the first.

The range C5:E14 in Figure 4–44 displays 30 different charts. Although these charts show only general trends, they give the investor a quick and easily interpreted snapshot of the 10 investments and their recent performance. More details can always be provided elsewhere with more informative Excel charts.

Insight

Edward Tufte and Chart Design Theory

Any study of chart design will include the works of Edward Tufte, who pioneered the field of information design. One of Tufte's most important works is *The Visual Display of Quantitative Information*, in which he laid out several principles for the design of charts and graphics.

Tufte was concerned with what he termed as "chart junk," in which a proliferation of chart elements—chosen because they look "nice"—confuse and distract the reader. One measure of chart junk is Tufte's data–ink ratio, which is the amount of "ink" used to display quantitative information compared to the total ink required by the chart. Tufte advocated limiting nondata ink, which is any part of the chart that does not convey information about the data. One way of measuring the data–ink ratio is to determine how much of the chart you can erase without affecting the user's ability to interpret your data. Tufte argued for high data–ink ratios with a minimum of extraneous elements and graphics.

To this end, Tufte helped develop sparklines, which convey information with a high data–ink ratio within a compact space. Tufte believed that charts that can be viewed and comprehended briefly have a greater impact on the reader than large and cluttered graphs, no matter how attractive they might be.

Note that the cells containing sparklines do not need to be blank because the sparklines are part of the cell background and do not replace any content.

Reference

Creating and Editing Sparklines

- On the Insert tab, in the Sparklines group, click the Line, Column, or Win/Loss button to open the Create Sparklines dialog box.
- In the Data Range box, enter the range for the data source of the sparkline.
- In the Location Range box, enter the range into which to place the sparkline.
- Click OK.
- On the Sparkline tab, in the Show group, click the appropriate check boxes to specify which markers to display on the sparkline.
- In the Group group, click the Axis button, and then click Show Axis to add an axis to the sparkline.

Lydia wants you to use line sparklines in the range H32:H43 of the Summary worksheet to display the general trend of the growth of the Hamilton Fund's investment into 12 economic sectors.

To create the line sparklines showing the sector history growth trends:

1. Select the range **H32:H43** in the Summary worksheet.

2. On the ribbon, click the **Insert** tab, and then in the Sparklines group, click the **Line** button. The Create Sparklines dialog box opens.

3. Make sure the insertion point is in the Data Range box, click the **Sector History** sheet tab, and then select the range **B6:M45** in the Sector History worksheet. This range contains the growth of investments in 12 economic sectors given a hypothetical $10,000 initial investment.

4. Verify that the range **$H$32:$H$43** is entered in the Location Range box. Refer to
    Figure 4–45.

Figure 4–45   Create Sparklines dialog box

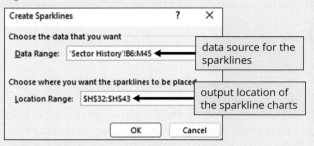

5. Click **OK** to insert the sparklines into the range H32:H43 of the Summary worksheet.
    Refer to Figure 4–46.

Figure 4–46   Line sparklines in the Summary worksheet

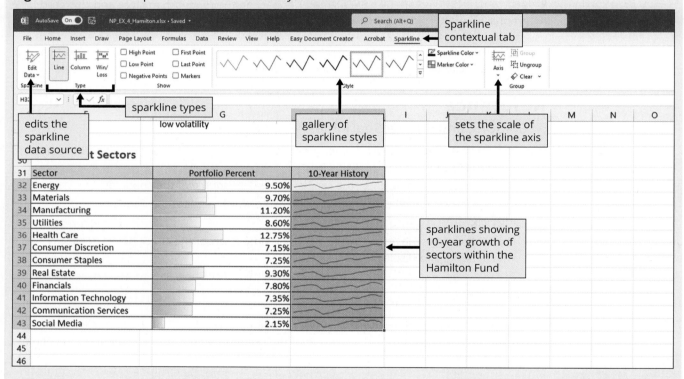

The Sparkline contextual tab appears on the ribbon when a sparkline is selected. From this
tab, you can change the sparkline type, edit the sparkline's data source, and format the sparkline's
appearance.

Formatting a Sparkline

Because of their compact size, sparklines have fewer formatting options than other Excel charts.
You can add data markers to highlight low and high values, initial and ending values, and negative
values. From the Style gallery on the Sparkline tab, you can apply built-in styles to the sparklines.
From the Sparkline Color and Marker Color buttons in the Style group, you can set the color of the
sparklines and their data markers.

Lydia wants you to add data markers identifying the low and high points within the time interval
to each sparkline and to change the sparkline color to dark orange.

To format the sparklines:

1. In the Summary worksheet, make sure the sparklines in the range H32:H43 are still selected.

2. On the Sparkline tab, in the Show group, click the **High Point** and **Low Point** check boxes. Two data markers appear on each sparkline identifying the high and low points.

3. In the Style group, click the **Sparkline Color** button, and then click the **Orange, Accent 1, Darker 25%** theme color (the fifth theme color in the fifth row) in the color palette. The sparkline colors change to orange.

4. In the Style group, click the **Marker Color** button, point to **High Point**, and then click the **Green** standard color. The high point data marker color changes to green.

5. Click the **Marker Color** button, click **Low Point**, and then click the **Red** standard color. The low point data marker color changes to red.

6. Click cell **I30** to deselect the sparklines. Refer to Figure 4–47.

Figure 4–47   Formatted sparklines

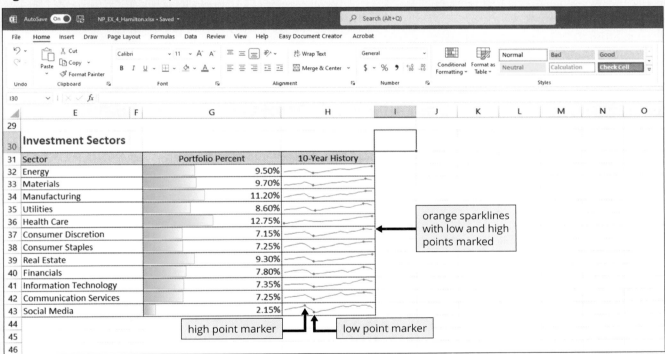

7. **sam**⬆ Save the workbook, and then close it.

The sparklines show that the 12 economic sectors experienced the same general growth trend over the previous 10 years with negative growth occurring around years 3 and 4 followed by steady growth thereafter. The lowest for all sectors seem to come around the fourth year.

Sparkline Groups and Sparkline Axes

Sparklines are grouped together by default so that the format choices are applied to every sparkline chart in the group. Grouping ensures that sparklines for related data series are formatted consistently. To format a single sparkline, click the cell containing the sparkline and then click the Ungroup button in the Group group on the Sparkline tab. The selected sparkline is split from the rest of the sparkline group. You can then apply a unique format to it. To regroup the sparklines, select all the cells containing the sparklines, and then click the Group button in the Group group.

Excel displays each sparkline on its own vertical axis ranging from the data series' low point and high point. That means comparing one sparkline to another can be misleading if they are all plotted on a different scale. You can modify the vertical axes by clicking the Axis button in the Group group on the Sparkline tab. To ensure that the vertical scale is the same for all charts in the sparkline group, click the Same for All Sparklines option for both the minimum and maximum scale values. To explicitly define the scale of the vertical axis, click the Custom Value option and specify the minimum and maximum values.

Proskills

Written Communication: Honesty in Charting

One of the great challenges in chart design is to not mislead your audience by misrepresenting the data. Here are a few of the ways in which a chart, created even with the best of intentions, can mislead the viewer:

- **Improper scaling.** This is a very common mistake in which the range of the data scale is set so narrow that even small changes seem large or so wide that all values appear to be the same. For example, a 1% change in a data value will appear large if the scale goes from 0% to 2%, and it will appear insignificant if the scale goes from 0% to 100%.

- **Scaling data values differently.** If improper scaling can exaggerate or minimize differences, the problem can be compounded with combination charts in which two data series that should be plotted on the same scale are instead plotted against vastly different scales. For example, one data series might appear to show a significant trend while the other shows none, and yet the only difference is the scale on which the values have been plotted.

- **Truncating the vertical axis.** You can make trends appear more significant than they are if you cut off what might appear to be irrelevant information. Is an increase in the interest rate from 4% to 4.05% a significant jump? If you set the scale of the vertical axis to cover the range from 0% to 4.1%, it will not appear to be. However, if your chart only covers the range from 4% to 4.1%, it will appear to be significant jump.

- **3D distortions.** Displaying charts in 3D can be eye-catching, but the effect of perspective in which objects appear to recede into the distance can exaggerate or minimize important differences that would be more apparent with a 2D chart.

To be fair, one should not assume that a misleading chart was designed with malicious intent. Because Excel and other software packages include charting, they can lead to the kinds of mistakes discussed here. To avoid misleading the audience, check your assumptions and verify that you are not altering your chart to make it appear more dramatic or interesting. View your charts under different formatting options to confirm that it is truly the data that is telling the story.

You have finished creating charts and graphics to summarize the history and performance of the Hamilton Fund. Lydia is pleased that so much information fits on a single worksheet. Figure 4–48 shows a preview of the printed Summary sheet containing all the charts created for the report.

Figure 4–48   Final Summary report

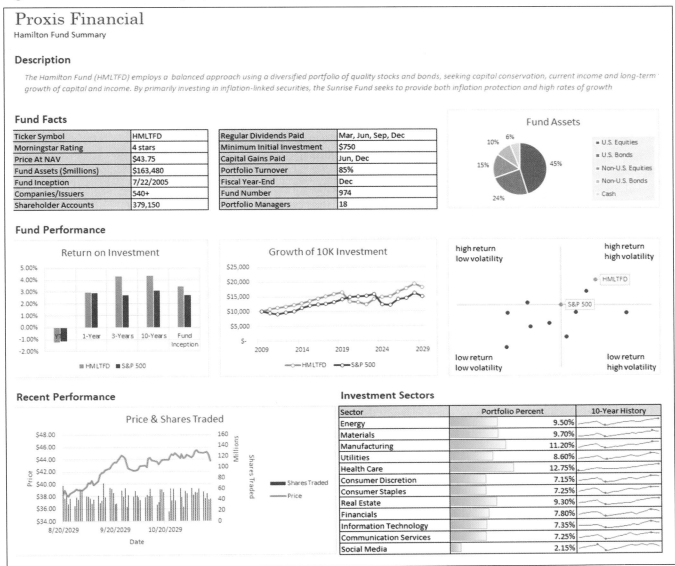

Lydia appreciates your help in creating the summary report. Later you will help her apply this type of formatting to workbooks containing investment data from other funds.

Part 4.2 Quick Check

1. You want to create a chart of temperature versus time, but the time points are not evenly spaced. Should you create a scatter chart or a line chart? Why?

2. When would you use a treemap or sunburst chart?

3. Which chart should you use to display categories arranged in descending order of value along with a line chart that tracks the cumulative percentage from the categories?

4. When would you use a Waterfall chart?

5. Which chart should you use to display the distribution of values from a data series?

6. When would you use a sparkline in place of a line chart in a report?

7. Describe the three types of sparklines.

8. When would you use data bars in place of a column or bar chart in a report?

Practice: Review Assignments

Data File needed for the Review Assignments: NP_EX_4-2.xlsx

Lydia wants you to develop another investment report for the Adams Fund. As with the report you generated for the Hamilton Fund, this workbook will include a worksheet that uses Excel charts and graphics to summarize financial data about the fund. Complete the following:

1. Open the **NP_EX_4-2.xlsx** workbook located in the Excel4 > Review folder included with your Data Files, and then save the workbook as **NP_EX_4_Adams** in the location specified by your instructor.
2. In the Documentation sheet, enter your name and the date in the range B3:B4.
3. Lydia wants a pie chart that breaks down the allocation of the assets in the Adams Fund. Do the following:
   a. In the Allocation worksheet, create a pie chart from the data in the range A4:B8.
   b. Move the pie chart to the Prospectus worksheet, and then resize the chart to cover the range D7:E14.
   c. Place the legend on the right side of the chart area.
   d. Change the color scheme to the Monochromatic Palette 6.
   e. Add data labels showing the percentage allocated to each category, positioning the label on the outside end of each pie slice.
4. Lydia wants the report to display a column chart of the month-end returns for the Adams Fund and the S&P 500 over different time intervals. Do the following:
   a. In the Returns worksheet, create a clustered column chart from the data in the range A4:C9.
   b. Move the chart to the Prospectus worksheet, and then resize the chart to cover the range F7:H14.
   c. Change the chart title to **Investment Comparison**.
   d. Place the legend on the right side of the chart area.
5. Lydia wants a line chart comparing the growth of a theoretical investment of $10,000 in the Adams Fund and the S&P 500 over the past 10 years. Do the following:
   a. In the Growth worksheet, create a line chart of the data in the range A4:C25, using the line chart from the list of recommended charts. (The Year value appears on the horizontal axis.)
   b. Move the chart to the Prospectus worksheet, and then resize the chart to cover the range D15:E24.
   c. Change the chart title to **Growth of 10K Investment**.
   d. Add primary major vertical gridlines to the chart.
   e. Place the legend on the right side of the chart area.
   f. Change the interval between the major tick marks and between labels on the category axis to 5 units so that the years 2009, 2014, 2019, 2024, and 2029 appear on the horizontal axis.
6. Lydia wants the report to show the recent selling price and shares traded of the Adams Fund in a combination chart. Do the following:
   a. In the Recent History worksheet, create a combination chart of the data in the range A4:C58. Display the price data as a line chart plotted on the primary axis and the shares traded data as a clustered column chart plotted on the secondary axis.
   b. Move the chart to the Prospectus worksheet, and then resize the chart to cover the range A26:D39.
   c. Change the chart title to **Recent History**.
   d. Display axis titles on the chart. Change the primary vertical axis title to **Price**, the secondary vertical axis title to **Shares Traded**, and the category axis title to **Date**. Change the angle of rotation of the Shares Traded axis title to Rotate Text Down.
   e. Place the legend on the right side of the chart area.
   f. Change the scale of the secondary axis to go from 0 to 1.6E08 and display the scale in units of 1 million and display the unit label on the chart.

7. Lydia needs to compare the return rate and volatility of the Adams Fund to other investment vehicles. Do the following:
   a. In the Performance worksheet, create a scatter chart from the data in the range B5:C7 using the scatter chart from the list of recommended charts.
   b. Move the chart to the Prospectus worksheet, and then resize the chart to cover the range F15:H24.
   c. Remove the chart title and the gridlines from the chart.
   d. Rescale the vertical axis to go from 0.0 to 0.06 with the horizontal axis crossing at 0.031. Rescale the horizontal axis to go from 4 to 24 with the vertical axis crossing at 14.71.
   e. Set the label position to none for both the vertical and horizontal axis labels.
   f. Add data labels to the data markers in the data series. Format the data labels to show data callout bubbles and show only the text from the range A6:A7 in the Performance worksheet. Do not show X or Y values in the callout.

8. Complete the scatter chart by adding a new data series to the chart with cell G5 in the Performance worksheet as the series name, the range F6:F15 in the Performance worksheet as the Series X values, and the range G6:G15 in the Performance worksheet as the Series Y values. If necessary, remove any callouts for the new data values by selecting them and pressing DELETE.

9. Add the four text boxes shown earlier in Figure 4–28 to the scatter chart, placing the return and volatility descriptions on separate lines. Resize and move the text boxes so that they align with the chart corners.

10. Add solid blue data bars to the values in the range G28:G39. Keep the data bars from overlapping the values in those cells by modifying the conditional formatting rule so that the maximum length of the data bar corresponds to a value of 0.30.

11. Add line sparklines to the range H28:H39 using the data values from the range B6:M45 of the Sectors worksheet. Add data markers for the high and low points of each sparkline using the Red standard color.

12. Save the workbook, and then close it.

Apply: Case Problem 1

Data File needed for this Case Problem: NP_EX_4-3.xlsx

Proko Car Rental Miguel Rubens is an account manager for Proko Car Rental, an industry-leading car rental firm that serves customers across the United States and overseas. Miguel is developing a market report for an upcoming sales conference and needs your assistance in summarizing market information into a collection of Excel charts and graphics. Complete the following:

1. Open the **NP_EX_4-3.xlsx** workbook located in the Excel4 > Case1 folder included with your Data Files. Save the workbook as **NP_EX_4_Proko** in the location specified by your instructor.
2. In the Documentation sheet, enter your name and the date in the range B3:B4.
3. Miguel wants the report to include pie charts breaking down the current year's revenue in terms of market (Airport vs. Off-Airport), car type (Leisure vs. Commercial), and location (Americas vs. International). Do the following:
   a. In the Rentals by Type worksheet, create a pie chart of the data in the range A6:B7. Move the chart to the Analysis worksheet and resize it to cover the range D5:F9.
   b. Remove the chart title from the pie chart.
   c. Add data labels to the outside end of the two slices showing the percentage of the Airport versus Off-Airport sales.
   d. Change the color of the chart to Colorful Palette 3.
4. Repeat Step 3 for the data in the range A11:B12 of the Rentals by Type worksheet, placing the pie chart comparing Leisure and Commercial sales in the range H5:H9 of the Analysis worksheet.
5. Repeat Step 3 for the data in the range A16:B17 of the Rentals by Type worksheet, placing the pie chart comparing revenue between the Americas and International sales in the range J5:J9 of the Analysis worksheet.

6. Miguel wants to present the company revenue broken down by car type. Do the following:

   a. In the Car Models worksheet, create a clustered column chart of the data in the range A4:B9. Move the chart to the range B11:F22 in the Analysis worksheet.

   b. Remove the chart legend if it exists.

   c. Add data labels to the outside end of the data markers showing the revenue for each car model.

   d. Format the data series so that the gap width between the chart columns is 25%.

   e. Change the color palette of the chart to Colorful Palette 3.

7. Miguel also wants to track revenue for each car model over the years to determine whether certain car models have increased or decreased in popularity. Do the following:

   a. In the Revenue by Year worksheet, create a line chart of the data in the range A4:F15. Move the chart to the range H11:J22 in the Analysis worksheet.

   b. Remove the chart title.

   c. Add gridlines for the primary major vertical and horizontal axes.

   d. Move the chart legend to the right side of the plot area.

   e. Add axis titles to the chart. Set the vertical axis title to the text **Revenue ($bil)** and the horizontal axis title to **Year**.

   f. Set the interval between tick marks and between the labels on the category (horizontal) axis to 2 units so that the category labels are Y2019, Y2021, Y2023, Y2025, Y2027, and Y2029.

   g. Change the color of the chart to Colorful Palette 3.

8. Miguel wants to compare the Proko brand to competing car rental companies. Do the following:

   a. In the range F25:F29 of the Analysis worksheet, insert line sparklines showing the trend in market share percentages using the data in the range B19:F29 in the Market Share worksheet.

   b. Add a marker to each sparkline showing the high point.

   c. Change the sparkline color to the Lime, Accent 3 theme color.

9. Repeat Step 9 in the range F32:F36 using the data in the range B5:F15 in the Market Share worksheet.

10. In the range E25:E29, add green data bars with a gradient fill to the data values. Set the size of the largest data bar to the maximum value of 0.75.

11. Repeat Step 10, adding green data bars with a gradient fill to the data values in the range E32:E36. Set the size of the largest data bar to the maximum value of 32.

12. Miguel wants to present a more detailed chart of the revenue values from the five competing rental car agencies over the past several years.

   a. In the Market Share worksheet, create a stacked column chart from the data in the range A4:F15. Move the chart to cover the range H24:J36 in the Analysis worksheet.

   b. Remove the chart title.

   c. Add axis titles to the chart. Change the vertical axis title to **Revenue ($bil)** and the horizontal axis title to **Year**.

   d. Move the legend to the right side of the chart area.

   e. Set the interval between tick marks and between the labels on the category (horizontal) axis to 2 units to display the category values Y2019, Y2021, Y2023, Y2025, Y2027, and Y2029.

   f. Change the color of the chart to Colorful Palette 3.

   g. Set the gap width between the bars in the chart to 25%.

   h. In the lower right corner of the chart, insert a text box with the text **Car Rental Revenues in Decline** on one line.

13. Save the workbook, and then close it.

Challenge: Case Problem 2 ———————————————————————

Data File needed for this Case Problem: NP_EX_4-4.xlsx

Crystal Creek Hospital & Clinic Inola Cochise is a facilities administrator at Crystal Creek Hospital Clinic in southwest Utah. As part of an annual report for the clinic's trustees, Inola documents patient care at the clinic, including inpatient and outpatient admissions, length of stay, average waiting time, and nurse/patient ratios. Inola has asked your help in supplementing the report with informative charts and graphics. Complete the following.

1. Open the **NP_EX_4-4.xlsx** workbook located in the Excel4 > Case2 folder included with your Data Files. Save the workbook as **NP_EX_4_Crystal** in the location specified by your instructor.

2. In the Documentation sheet, enter your name in cell B3 and the current date in cell B4.

3. In the Summary worksheet, in the range D5:D11, Inola has broken down the number of inpatient admissions by department. Add gradient blue data bars to the range and set the maximum length of the data bars to 8000.

4. Repeat Step 3 for the outpatient admissions in the range E5:E11, using gradient green data bars.

5. **Explore:** Inola wants to report on the number of inpatient and outpatient admissions at the clinic. Do the following:
   a. In the Patients by Month worksheet, create a Sunburst chart of the data in the nonadjacent range A4:C4,A17:C17. Move the chart to the Summary worksheet covering the range G4:J11.
   b. Remove the chart title.
   c. Display the chart legend at the top of the chart.
   d. Change the data labels to show the values and not the category names.

6. **Explore:** Inola also wants to view the admission data by month. Do the following:
   a. In the Patients by Month worksheet, create a stacked area chart of the data in the range A4:C16. Move the chart to the Summary worksheet covering the range L4:P11.
   b. Remove the chart title.
   c. Add primary major vertical gridlines to the chart.

7. **Explore:** The report will also include an analysis of the length of inpatient stays. Inola has retrieved length of stay data for 300 randomly selected patients and wants you to display the distribution of those stays in a histogram chart. Do the following:
   a. In the Length of Stay worksheet, create a histogram of the data in the range A4:A304. Move the chart to the range C13:E25 in the Summary worksheet. (Note: If necessary, you can quickly move the chart to the top of the worksheet by cutting and pasting the chart.)
   b. Change the chart title to **Length of Stay (Days)**.
   c. Double-click the histogram categories along the horizontal axis to open the Format Axis pane. Change the Bin Width value to **1**. Change the Overflow Bin value to 10 so that length of stay values larger than 10 are pooled together in a single category.

8. When patients are admitted to the hospital and then discharged, they might be readmitted within 30 days. Inola wants the report to include the inpatient admission totals and the 30-day readmission rates for each quarter of the past year. Do the following:
   a. In the Readmission worksheet, create a combination chart of the data in the range A4:C8. Display the Inpatient Admissions data series as a clustered column chart. Display the Readmission Rate data series as a line chart on the secondary axis. Move the chart to the range G13:J25 of the Summary worksheet.
   b. Change the chart title to **Admissions and 30-Day Readmission Rate**.
   c. Add axis titles to the chart. Change the primary vertical axis to **Inpatient Admissions**. Change the secondary vertical axis to **Readmission Rate** and rotate the text down. Change the category axis to **Quarter**.
   d. Change the bounds of the secondary axis to go from 0.1 to 0.3.

9. **Explore:** Inola's report needs to break down admissions by payer (Medicare, Medicaid, Private Insurance, or Other). Inola thinks this data would be best presented in a Pareto chart. In the Payer worksheet, create a Pareto chart of the data in the range A4:B8. Move the chart to range L13:P25 in the Summary worksheet and change the chart title to **Admissions by Payer**. (Note: You can find the Pareto chart by selecting the data range, clicking the Recommended Charts button, clicking Histogram on the All Charts tab, and then clicking the Pareto chart type.)

10. Monitoring the length of time that patients must wait before being treated is an important task for Inola. On the Summary worksheet, add gradient red data bars to range D29:D35 containing the wait times for different departments. Set the maximum length of the data bars to 40.

11. Inola wants to track how wait times within each department have changed over the past year. Add line sparklines to the range E29:E35 using the data in the range B5:H16 of the Waiting Times worksheet. Mark the high and low point within each sparkline.

12. **Explore:** Trustees want to examine the nurse-to-patient ratio from different units at the hospital and clinic. Do the following:

    a. In the Nurse Ratio worksheet, create a treemap chart from the data in the range A5:C14. Move the chart to the range G29:P45 of the Summary worksheet.

    b. Remove the chart title.

    c. Select the data legend and increase the font size to 14 points.

    d. Add data labels to the chart showing both the category name and the data value.

    e. With the data labels selected, increase their font size to 14 points.

13. Save the workbook, and then close it.

Generating Reports from Multiple Worksheets and Workbooks

Summarizing Profit and Loss Statements

Case: Rusty's Subs

Kendis Coleman is a financial officer for Rusty's Subs, a national restaurant chain specializing in sub sandwiches and soups. As a financial officer, Kendis needs to retrieve and combine financial statements from each Rusty's Subs location into a single summary report that will be analyzed by upper management. Kendis is currently working on an annual report of financial statements from eight stores in Ohio and Indiana. You'll help Kendis summarize the data from these restaurants into a single worksheet.

Starting Data Files

Excel5
Module
NP_EX_5-1.xlsx
NP_EX_5-2.xlsx
Support_EX_5_Store008.xlsx
Support_EX_5_2025.xlsx
Support_EX_5_2026.xlsx
Support_EX_5_2027.xlsx
Support_EX_5_2028.xlsx
Review
NP_EX_5-3.xlsx
Support_EX_5_Akron.xlsx
Support_EX_5_Region1.xlsx
Support_EX_5_Region2.xlsx

Support_EX_5_Region3.xlsx
Support_EX_5_Region4.xlsx
Case1
NP_EX_5-4.xlsx
Support_EX_5_Dec.xlsx
Support_EX_5_MVPL2028.xlsx
Case2
NP_EX_5-5.xlsx
Support_EX_5_Fund01.xlsx
Support_EX_5_Fund02.xlsx
Support_EX_5_Fund03.xlsx
Support_EX_5_Fund04.xlsx
Support_EX_5_Fund05.xlsx

Objectives

Part 5.1
- Copy worksheets between workbooks
- View a workbook in multiple windows
- Organize worksheets in worksheet group
- Write a 3-D cell reference

Part 5.2
- Write an external reference
- Manage the security features of linked documents
- Create a hyperlink to a document source
- Link to an email address

Part 5.3
- Create and apply a named range
- Determine the scope of a range name
- Create a workbook template

Part 5.1 Visual Overview:
Worksheet Groups and 3-D References

When sheets are grouped, the workbook is in group-editing mode and the word "Group" appears in the title bar.

The New Window button creates multiple windows of the same workbook.

The Arrange All button defines how multiple windows are arranged on the screen.

In a worksheet group, any edit made to one sheet is applied to all sheets in the group.

A **worksheet group** is the collection of two or more selected worksheets. All sheet tabs in the group are highlighted.

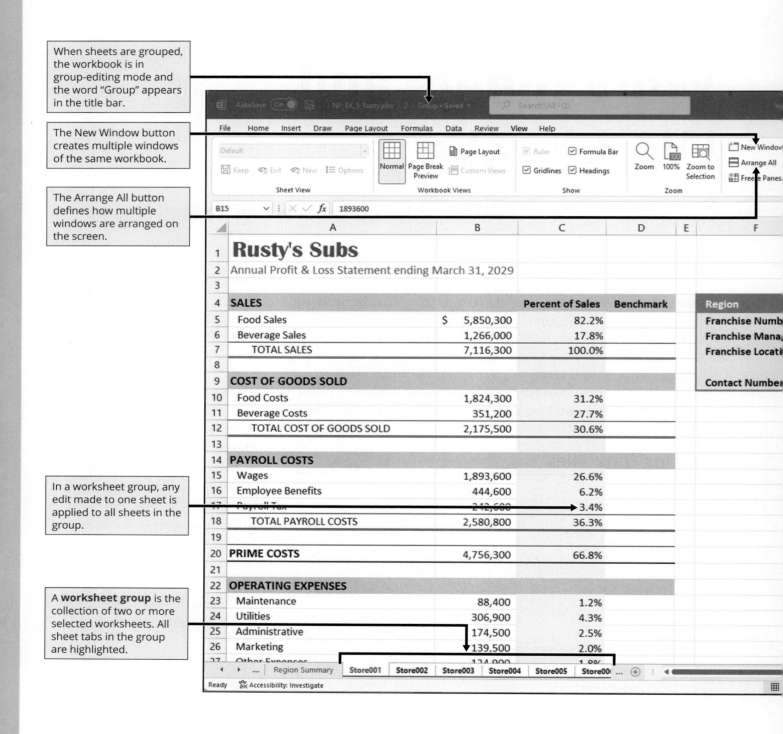

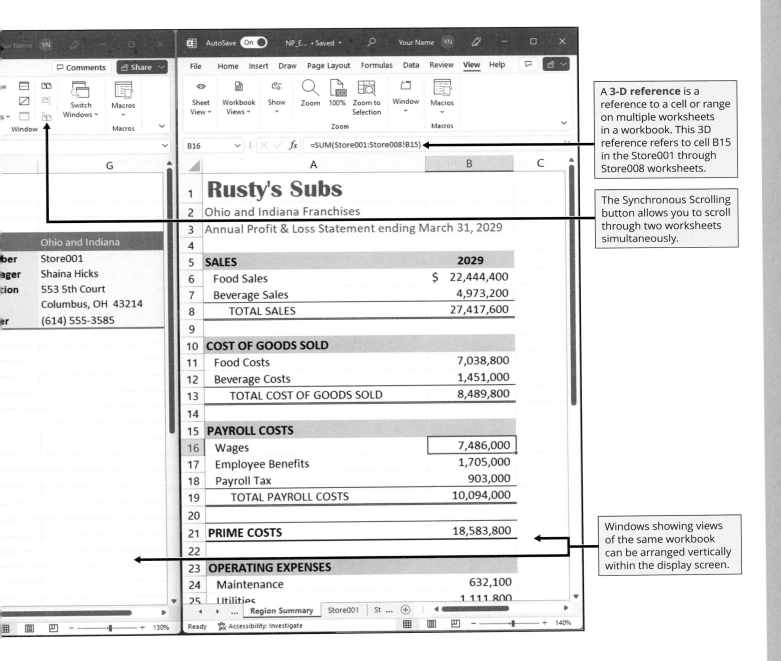

A **3-D reference** is a reference to a cell or range on multiple worksheets in a workbook. This 3D reference refers to cell B15 in the Store001 through Store008 worksheets.

The Synchronous Scrolling button allows you to scroll through two worksheets simultaneously.

Windows showing views of the same workbook can be arranged vertically within the display screen.

B16   =SUM(Store001:Store008!B15)

Rusty's Subs

Ohio and Indiana Franchises

Annual Profit & Loss Statement ending March 31, 2029

	A	B
5	**SALES**	**2029**
6	Food Sales	$ 22,444,400
7	Beverage Sales	4,973,200
8	TOTAL SALES	27,417,600
9		
10	**COST OF GOODS SOLD**	
11	Food Costs	7,038,800
12	Beverage Costs	1,451,000
13	TOTAL COST OF GOODS SOLD	8,489,800
14		
15	**PAYROLL COSTS**	
16	Wages	7,486,000
17	Employee Benefits	1,705,000
18	Payroll Tax	903,000
19	TOTAL PAYROLL COSTS	10,094,000
20		
21	**PRIME COSTS**	18,583,800
22		
23	**OPERATING EXPENSES**	
24	Maintenance	632,100
25	Utilities	1,111,800

Ohio and Indiana

ber	Store001
ager	Shaina Hicks
tion	553 5th Court
	Columbus, OH 43214
er	(614) 555-3585

Region Summary   Store001   St ...

Working with Multiple Worksheets

So far, you have worked with formulas and functions that referenced cells in a single worksheet within a single workbook. However, data is often stored across several worksheets and workbooks. In this module, you will learn to effectively manage data across multiple worksheets and workbooks.

Kendis Coleman has been developing a workbook to summarize profit and loss statements from Rusty's Subs stores operating in Indiana and Ohio. A **profit and loss (P&L) statement**, also called an **income statement**, is a financial statement summarizing income and expenses incurred during a specified interval. Profit and loss statements are usually released monthly, quarterly, and annually. Such statements are useful in tracking expenditures and locating ways in which a business might be able to operate more efficiently and profitably. Kendis wants to use Excel to analyze the annual profit and loss figures for the Indiana/Ohio region.

To open the workbook containing profit and loss statements:

1. **sam** ↓ Open the **NP_EX_5-1.xlsx** workbook located in the **Excel5 > Module** folder included with your Data Files, and then save the workbook as **NP_EX_5_Rusty** in the location specified by your instructor.

2. In the **Documentation** sheet, enter your name in cell B3 and the date in cell B4.

3. Review each of the worksheets in the workbook. P&L statements are stored in the Store001 through Store007 worksheets. Financial definitions are entered in the Terms and Definitions worksheet. The Region Summary worksheet is where you will summarize the data from all stores in the Indiana/Ohio region.

4. Go to the **Store001** worksheet.

The workbook contains profit and loss statements from seven restaurants. Kendis has just received a workbook containing a P&L statement from an eighth store in the region and wants you to copy it into the NP_EX_5_Rusty workbook.

Copying Worksheets

One way to use data from another workbook is to copy and paste worksheets from one workbook into another. The copied worksheets can be placed anywhere within the new workbook. Once copied, any changes made to the worksheets in the new workbook will not affect the original sheets from the original workbook.

Reference

Moving and Copying a Worksheet

- Right-click the sheet tab of the worksheet you want to move or copy, and then click Move or Copy on the shortcut menu.
- Click the To book arrow, and then click the name of an existing workbook or click (new book) to create a new workbook for the sheet.
- In the Before sheet box, click the worksheet before which you want to insert the sheet.
- Click the Create a copy check box to copy the sheet rather than moving it.
- Click OK.

or

- Drag the sheet tab of the worksheet you want to move and drop it in a new location within the current workbook or within another open workbook. Hold down CTRL as you drag and drop the sheet tab to copy rather than move the sheet.

Kendis has a workbook showing the profit and loss statement from the Rusty's Subs restaurant in Akron, Ohio. You will copy the worksheet from that workbook into the NP_EX_5_Rusty workbook.

To open the Akron workbook:

1. Open the **Support_EX_5_Store008.xlsx** workbook located in the **Excel5 > Module** folder included with your Data Files.

2. Go to the **Store008** worksheet.

3. Right-click the **Store008** sheet tab, and then click **Move or Copy** on the shortcut menu. The Move or Copy dialog box opens.

4. Click the **To book** arrow, and then click **NP_EX_5_Rusty.xlsx** in the list.

   Tip You can create a new workbook and move or copy a sheet into that workbook by clicking (new book) in the To book list.

5. In the Before sheet box, scroll down and click **Terms and Definitions** to place the copied Store008 worksheet before the Terms and Definitions worksheet.

6. Click the **Create a copy** check box to place a copy of the Store008 worksheet in the NP_EX_5_Rusty workbook rather than move it. Refer to Figure 5–1.

   Key Step Be sure to click the Create a copy check box to copy, not move, the worksheet.

Figure 5–1   Move or Copy dialog box

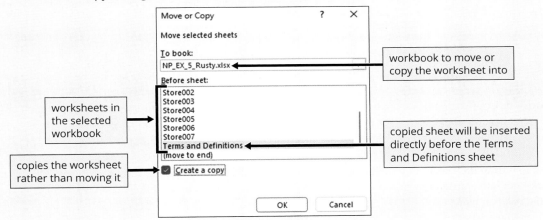

7. Click **OK**. The Store008 worksheet is copied into the Rusty workbook.

8. Close the **Support_EX_5_Store008** workbook without saving changes.

9. Return to the **NP_EX_5_Rusty** workbook and scroll through the sheets and verify that the Store008 worksheet appears directly after the Store007 sheet. Refer to Figure 5–2.

Figure 5–2   Copied worksheet

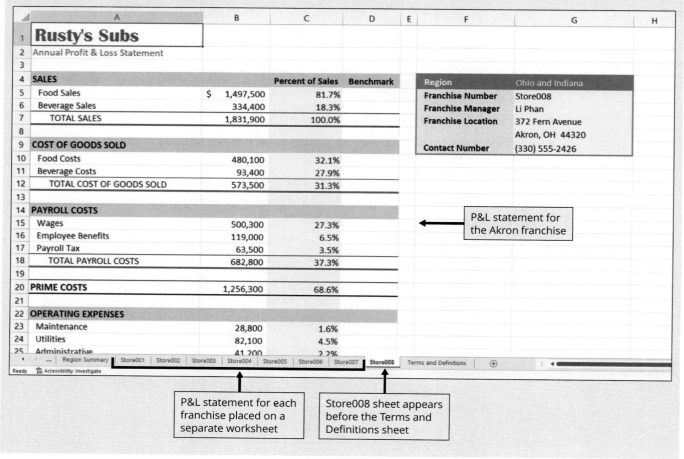

P&L statement for the Akron franchise

P&L statement for each franchise placed on a separate worksheet

Store008 sheet appears before the Terms and Definitions sheet

The Move or Copy dialog box can also be used to move or copy worksheets within the current workbook. This is particularly useful for large workbooks that contain dozens of worksheets. You can also move or copy a worksheet by dragging its sheet tab to a new location within the current workbook or to another open workbook displayed in a visible workbook window. Hold down CTRL as you drag and drop the sheet tab to create a copy of the sheet rather than moving it. Once you copy a worksheet into a different workbook, any changes you make to the copied worksheet do not appear in the original worksheet.

Viewing a Workbook in Multiple Windows

When a workbook has several worksheets, you might find yourself constantly switching worksheets to compare data from different sheets. Instead, you can work on different parts of the workbook at the same time by displaying worksheets in separate windows. You do this with the New Window button in the Window group on the View tab.

Kendis wants to compare the income and expenses from the eight stores to determine whether any stores are underperforming or exceeding expectations. Because the franchise profit and loss statements are on separate worksheets, Kendis would have to switch between eight sheets to complete this analysis. Instead, you can view information from different sheets simultaneously by displaying the sheets in separate windows.

To create a new viewing window for the workbook:

1. On the ribbon, click the **View** tab to display the commands for viewing the workbook's contents.

2. In the Window group, click the **New Window** button. A second window displaying the same workbook opens.

Two windows now display the same workbook. Excel distinguishes the different windows by adding a number after the file name in the title bar. In this case, the two windows for the NP_EX_5_Rusty.xlsx workbook are appended with numbers 1 and 2. If you opened a third workbook window, the number 3 would appear after the file name, and so forth.

Arranging Multiple Workbook Windows

When you have multiple windows, you can change how they are sized and arranged so you can access all windows at one time. When you use the Arrange All button in the Window group on the View tab, you can choose from the following four layout options (refer to Figure 5–3).

- **Tiled.** Resizes the height and width of windows to fill the screen in both horizontal and vertical directions.
- **Horizontal.** Expands the width of the windows to fill the screen and places them in a single column.
- **Vertical.** Expands the height of the windows to fill the screen and places them in a single row.
- **Cascade.** Layers the windows in an overlapping stack.

Figure 5–3   Workbook window layouts

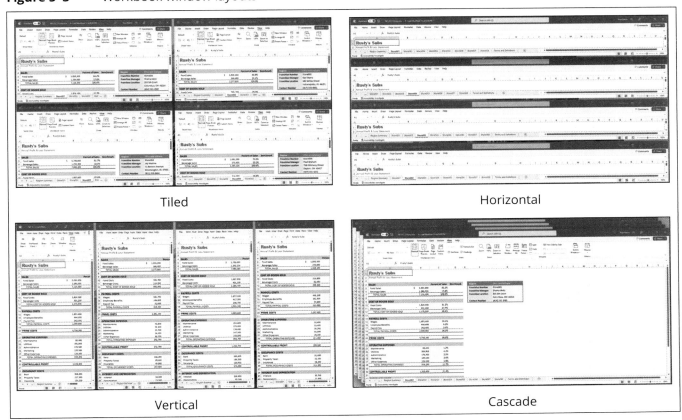

Tiled

Horizontal

Vertical

Cascade

The window arrangement is not part of the saved workbook. If you have multiple workbook windows open and arranged in a specific layout, that layout will not be present the next time you open the workbook, and you will have to arrange the windows again.

Generally, you do not want to tile more than four windows at a time. With more windows, the contents become small and difficult to view. You will use the Arrange All command to display the two windows of the NP_EX_5_Rusty workbook in a vertical layout.

To view the Rusty workbook windows in a vertical layout:

1. On the ribbon, click the **View** tab, and then in the Window group, click the **Arrange All** button. The Arrange Windows dialog box opens.

2. Click the **Vertical** option button to select a vertical layout for the workbook windows.

3. Click the **Windows of active workbook** check box to select it. Now, only windows for the active workbook, and not any other open workbooks, will be arranged. Refer to Figure 5–4.

Figure 5–4   Arrange Windows dialog box

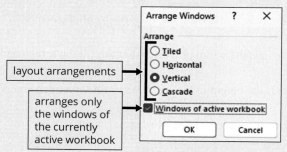

4. Click **OK**. The windows of the current workbook change to a vertical layout with one window on the left and another on the right.

5. Click the **title bar** of left workbook window to select it, and then click the **Store001** sheet tab to display the profit and loss statement for the Columbus location.

6. Increase the zoom level of the worksheet to **140%**.

7. Click the title bar of the right workbook window to select it, and then click the **Store002** sheet tab to display the profit and loss statement for the Indianapolis location.

8. If necessary, increase the zoom level of the worksheet to **140%**. Refer to Figure 5–5.

Figure 5–5   Workbook windows in a vertical layout

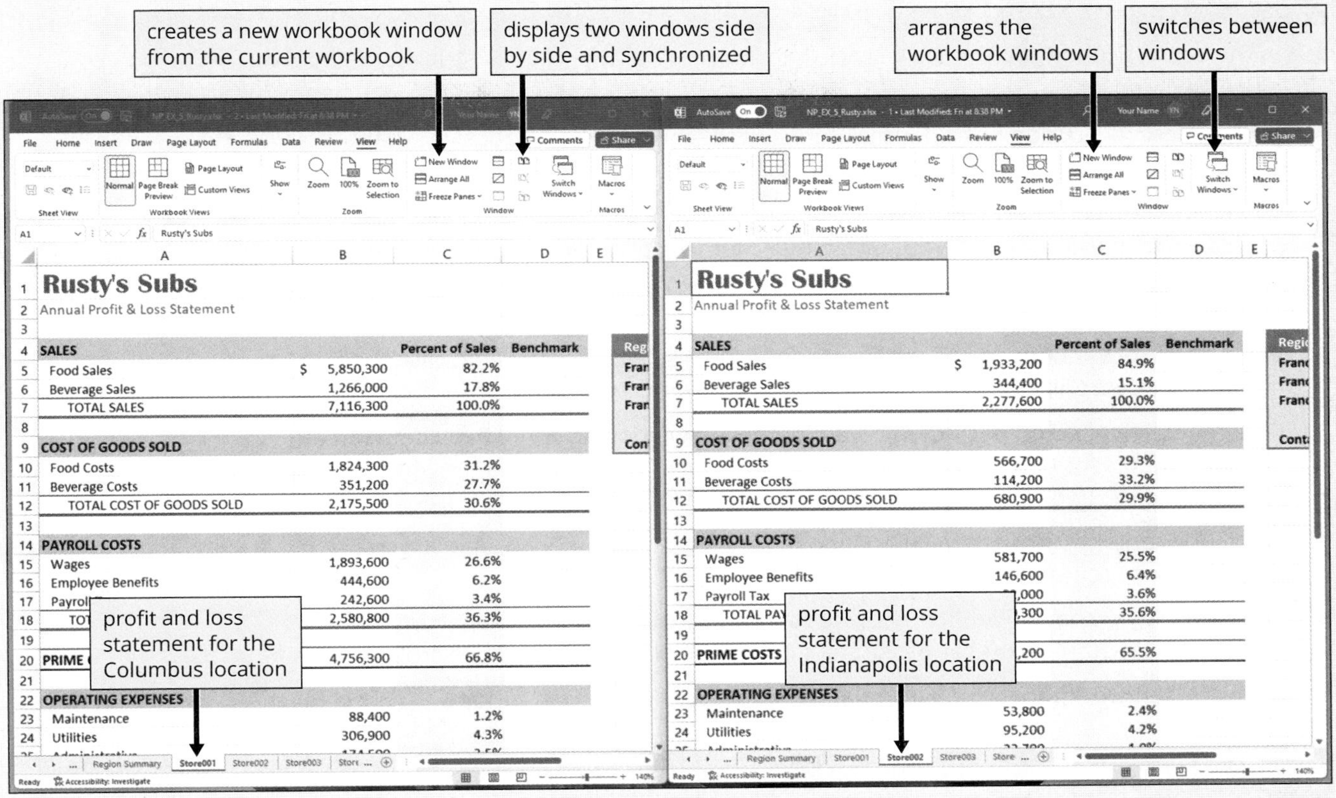

creates a new workbook window from the current workbook

displays two windows side by side and synchronized

arranges the workbook windows

switches between windows

profit and loss statement for the Columbus location

profit and loss statement for the Indianapolis location

The two workbook windows allow you to compare the contents of one sheet with another. Because the windows are not maximized, more of the sheet contents area are hidden. You can deal with that problem with synchronized scrolling.

Reference

Arranging Multiple Workbook Windows

- To create a new window for the current workbook, on the View tab, in the Window group, click the New Window button.
- To arrange multiple workbook windows, on the View tab, in the Window group, click the Arrange All button, click an arrangement option button, click the Windows of active workbook check box to arrange only windows for the current workbook, and then click OK.
- To view two workbook windows side by side, on the View tab, in the Window group, click the View Side by Side button and select the workbook window to view along with the current window. If necessary, select the Synchronous Scrolling button to scroll both windows simultaneously.

Using Synchronized Scrolling Between Windows

With synchronized scrolling, you scroll both windows at the same time, keeping their rows and column aligned. Synchronized scrolling lets you more easily compare two workbooks whose contents extend beyond the workbook window. You will use synchronized scrolling to compare the contents of the Store001 and Store002 worksheets.

To view the workbook windows side-by-side:

1. In the active window, on the View tab, in the Windows group, click the **View Side by Side** button ⊞.

   > **Trouble?** If a dialog box opens so you can select which workbooks you want to view side by side, you have multiple workbooks open. Select the window for NP_EX_5_Rusty.xlsx - 2 workbook as the other window.

   > **Trouble?** If the vertical layout of the two windows disappears, you need to restore the vertical layout. Click the Arrange All button in the Window group on the View tab.

2. Verify that the **Synchronous Scrolling** button ⊞ is selected. If it is not, click the button to enable synchronized scrolling between the two windows.

3. Click the **vertical scroll bar down arrow** of the left window to verify that the profit and loss statements for both franchises scroll up and down together. There might be a slight lag between the two windows as the second window tries to mirror the actions of the first.

4. Scroll horizontally through the left window, verifying the right window also scrolls horizontally to match it.

5. View other worksheets with the two windows and confirm that you can compare the profit and loss statements for other pairs of stores using synchronized scrolling.

6. Close the left workbook window so that only the right workbook window is visible for the workbook.

7. If necessary, click the **Maximize** button ☐ on the title bar so that the workbook window fills the entire screen.

After comparing the profit and loss statements from the different locations, Kendis notices several errors. Each statement needs a subtitle specifying the end date on which the profit and loss numbers are calculated as well as a calculation of pretax profit for the year. Rather than fixing each worksheet individually, you can edit all the sheets simultaneously by grouping them.

Working with Worksheet Groups

You can edit several worksheets simultaneously by grouping the worksheets. In a worksheet group, any changes made to one worksheet are automatically applied to all sheets in the group, including entering formulas and data, changing row heights and widths, applying conditional formats, inserting or deleting rows and columns, defining page layouts, and setting view options. Worksheet groups save time and improve consistency because identical actions are performed within several sheets at the same time.

Reference

Grouping and Ungrouping Worksheets

- To select an adjacent group, click the sheet tab of the first worksheet in the group, press and hold SHIFT, click the sheet tab of the last worksheet in the group, and then release SHIFT.

- To select a nonadjacent group, click the sheet tab of one worksheet in the group, press and hold CTRL, click the sheet tabs of the remaining worksheets in the group, and then release CTRL.

- To ungroup the worksheets, click the sheet tab of a worksheet that is not in the group; or right-click the sheet tab of one worksheet in the group, and then click Ungroup Sheets on the shortcut menu.

You will group the profit and loss statements for the eight Rusty's Subs restaurants in the region.

To group the Store001 through Store008 worksheets:

1. Click the **Store001** sheet tab to select that worksheet.

2. Scroll the sheet tabs to the right to display the sheet tab for the Store008 worksheet.

3. Hold down **SHIFT**, click the **Store008** sheet tab, and then release **SHIFT**. All the worksheets from the Store001 worksheet to the Store008 worksheet are selected. The sheet tab names are in bold, and the word "Group" is added to the title bar as a reminder that you selected a worksheet group.

4. Scroll the sheet tabs back to the front of the workbook, displaying the contents of the Store001 worksheet. Refer to Figure 5–6.

Figure 5–6   Grouped worksheets

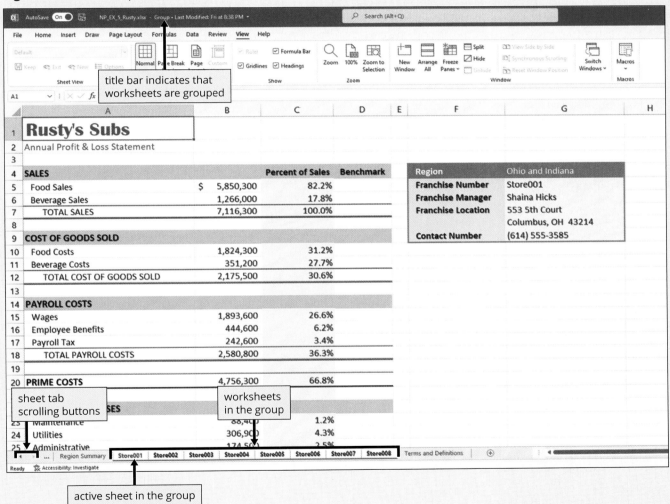

Trouble? If the sheets ungrouped, you probably clicked a sheet tab outside of the group. Repeat Steps 1 through 4 to regroup the sheets.

Editing a Worksheet Group

With the worksheets selected as a single group, you can now edit all of them at the same time. Remember, any changes you make to one worksheet will be made to all sheets in the group. Add a new subheading to each sheet in the selected group and calculate the pretax profit for each franchise.

To edit the worksheet group:

1. Make sure the **Store001** worksheet is still the active sheet in the group, and then click cell **A2**. Cell A2 is selected in all the worksheets in the group.

2. In cell A2, change the subheading to **Annual Profit & Loss Statement ending March 31, 2029** to add the ending date, and then press **ENTER**. The subheading is updated for all worksheets in the group.

3. Scroll down and click cell **A43**, type **PRETAX PROFIT** as the label, and then press **TAB**. The label is added to all sheets in the group.

4. In cell **B43**, enter the formula **= B30 – B36 – B41** to subtract the total occupancy costs, interest, and depreciation from the franchise's controllable profit, and then press **TAB**. The pretax profit for Store001 is $417,300.

5. In cell **C43**, enter the formula **= B43/B7** to calculate pretax profit divided by total sales, and then press **ENTER**. Store001's pretax profit, expressed as a percentage of total sales, is 0.058640024.

6. Select the range **A29:D30**, click the **Home** tab on the ribbon, and then in the Clipboard group, click the **Format Painter** button to copy the format from the selected range.

7. Click cell **A42** to paste the copied format to the pretax figures you just calculated.

8. Click cell **A45** to deselect the range. Refer to Figure 5–7.

Figure 5–7   Pretax profit calculations

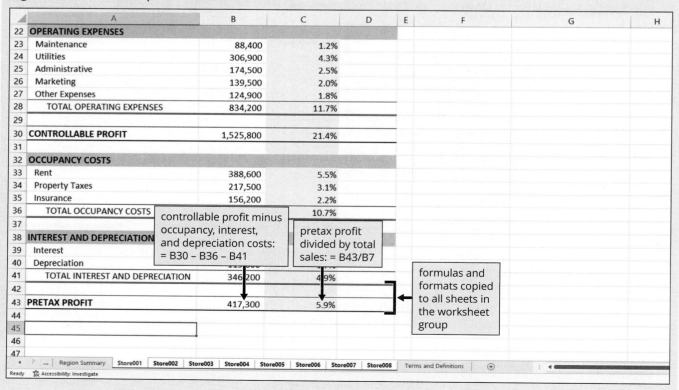

The Columbus store's pretax profit as a percent of total sales is 5.9%, which is a good profit margin in the restaurant industry. Because you made these edits in a worksheet group, the text, data, and formulas you entered in the Store001 worksheet also appear in the other sheets of the worksheet group. You will review those other sheets to check the pretax profits and percentages at the other locations.

To verify the pretax profits and percentages in the other sheets in the group:

1. Click the **Store002** sheet tab to view the profit and loss statement for the Indianapolis location.

2. Scroll up the worksheet and verify that the subheading in cell A2 includes the date for the profit and loss statement.

3. Scroll down to row **43** and verify that the pretax profit for Indianapolis is $204,800 with a percent of total sales value of 9.0%.

4. Click each of the other sheet tabs in the worksheet group to verify that the subheading in cell A2 was updated and the pretax profit and percentage appear in row 43.

After reviewing the other sheets in the worksheet group, only Store004 in Dayton, Ohio, showed a net loss for the last fiscal year of $53,300 with a pretax profit of –3.9%. The other stores showed pretax profits ranging from 0.2% (Store005 in Cincinnati, Ohio) to 7.7% (Store006 in Cleveland, Ohio).

Ungrouping a Worksheet Group

Once you are finished with a worksheet group, you should ungroup the selected sheets so that all sheets start acting independently again. To ungroup worksheets, click the sheet tab of any sheet that is not part of the group. If the group includes all sheets in the workbook, clicking any sheet tab will ungroup the worksheets. You can also right-click any sheet tab in the selected group and click Ungroup Sheets on the shortcut menu.

You will ungroup the selected sheets in the worksheet group.

To ungroup the sheets in the worksheet group:

1. Right-click any **sheet tab** in the worksheet group to display the shortcut menu.

2. Click **Ungroup Sheets** on the shortcut menu.

3. Verify that the sheets are ungrouped, and the word "Group" no longer appears in the title bar.

Be cautious when editing a worksheet group. If the layout and structure of the sheets are not the same, you might inadvertently overwrite important data in one of the worksheets. Also, remember to ungroup the worksheet group after you finish editing it. Otherwise, changes you intend to make to only one worksheet will be made to all the sheets in the group, potentially producing incorrect results.

Insight

Printing a Worksheet Group

Page layouts can be duplicated across multiple sheets. By grouping the worksheets, any of your choices for page orientation, margins, headers, footers, and other layout options will be applied to every other sheet in the group.

You can also print a worksheet group. To print a worksheet group, first group the sheets to be printed. Next, on the ribbon, click File to open Backstage view, and then click Print in the navigation bar. Then, on the Print screen, in the Settings section, verify that the Print Active Sheets option is selected. Finally, click the Print button to send the contents of all the worksheets in the group to the printer.

Kendis reviewed the financial information from the eight Rusty's Subs stores in Indiana and Ohio, and now Kendis wants you to summarize the data from all stores in the region in a single worksheet.

Writing 3-D References

So far, all the formulas you have written have been based on data stored in the same sheet as the formula. But as workbooks get larger and more complex, data can be spread across many sheets within the workbook. To analyze data across a workbook, you need that data using a 3-D cell reference.

Referencing Cells in Other Worksheets

Formulas with references to cells on the same sheet can be thought of as 2-D (or two-dimensional) references because they involve only a row address and a column address. A 3-D reference includes the row address, the column address, and the worksheet address, expressed within a single reference as:

```
Sheet!Range
```

where *Sheet* is the worksheet name and *Range* is the 2-D cell reference within that worksheet. The following expression references cell B10 on the Summary worksheet:

```
Summary!B10
```

If the worksheet title contains spaces, enclose the sheet name within a set of single quotation marks. The following expression uses this form to reference cell B10 on the Summary Report worksheet.

```
'Summary Report'!B10
```

The reference to a cell within a worksheet can be relative, absolute, or mixed so that the expression 'Summary Report'!$B$10 provides an absolute reference to cell B10 in the Summary Report worksheet.

Applying 3-D References to Formulas and Functions

3-D cell references can be used within any Excel formula and function. For example, the following formula calculates the combined total of cell B10 from the Jan, Feb, Mar, Apr, and May worksheets.

```
=Jan!B10+Feb!B10+Mar!B10+Apr!B10+May!B10
```

Another way to reference several worksheets is to treat them as worksheet group starting from the group's first sheet and ending at the last sheet. The syntax of the worksheet group reference is

```
FirstSheet:LastSheet!Range
```

where *FirstSheet* is the first sheet in the group, *LastSheet* is the last sheet in the group, and *Range* is a cell range common to all grouped sheets. The following expression references cell B10 from all sheets in a group starting with the Jan worksheet and ending with the May worksheet:

```
Jan:May!B10
```

Any worksheet between the Jan and May sheets is part of the group reference. The following formula calculates the total of the B10 cells within that group:

```
=SUM(Jan:May!B10)
```

If the Feb, Mar, and Apr sheets are placed between the Jan and May worksheets in the workbook, they will be included in the calculation.

Proskills

Problem Solving: Managing 3-D Group References

Worksheet group references are based on the *current order* of worksheets in the workbook. Rearranging the worksheets will affect what values are included in the calculation. Here are some tips to keep in mind when you revised the structure of a workbook containing a reference to a worksheet group:

- If you insert a new sheet between the first and last sheets of the group, it automatically becomes part of the worksheet group reference.
- If you move a worksheet out from between the first and last sheets, it is no longer part of the worksheet group reference.
- If you move the positions of the first or last sheets, the worksheet group will automatically refer to the new position of the group within the workbook.
- If the first sheet in the group is deleted, the sheet to the right of the first sheet becomes the new first sheet in the worksheet group reference.
- If the last sheet in the group is deleted, the sheet to the left of the last sheet becomes the new last sheet in the worksheet group reference.

  Relative references within the worksheets will not update if you change the structure of the sheets. For example, if you insert a new column B in the Jan through May worksheets, which moves cell B10 to cell C10 in those sheets, the formula remains =SUM(Jan:May!B10).
  A good practice is to use formulas that include a worksheet group reference only when you are confident that the sheet order and the row/column structure of the worksheets within the group will not change.

A 3-D reference can be used with most statistical functions, including the MIN, MAX, COUNT, AVERAGE, and MEDIAN functions. You can insert a 3-D reference into a formula by using your mouse to select the worksheet and then the cell range within the worksheet group.

Reference

Entering a 3-D Reference

- To create a 3-D reference to a range within a worksheet, enter *Sheet!Range* where *Sheet* is the worksheet name and *Range* is the cell address within that worksheet (enclose worksheet names that include spaces within a set of single quotes).
- To insert a 3-D reference in a formula, click the sheet tab of the worksheet, click the cell range in that worksheet, and then press ENTER.
- To copy the range from the worksheet, on the Home tab, in the Clipboard group, click the Paste arrow, and then click the Paste Link button.
- To create a 3-D reference to a range within a worksheet group, enter *FirstSheet:LastSheet!Range* where *FirstSheet* is the first sheet in the group, *LastSheet* is the last sheet in the group, and *Range* is a cell range common to all sheets in the group.
- To insert a 3-D reference to a range in a worksheet group, click the sheet tab of the first worksheet in the worksheet group, hold down SHIFT, click the tab for the last sheet in the group, release SHIFT, select the cell range in the selected worksheet group, and then press ENTER.

Kendis wants you to determine the total food sales for all eight Rusty's Subs stores in the Indiana/Ohio region. You will calculate that value using the SUM function with a 3-D cell reference.

To calculate total food sales using a 3-D cell reference:

1. Go to the **Region Summary** worksheet, and then click cell **B6** to select it.

2. Type **=SUM(** to begin the SUM function.

3. Click the **Store001** sheet tab. The formula displayed in the formula bar is =SUM('Store001'! showing the first worksheet used in the 3-D reference.

4. Scroll the sheet tabs until the Store008 sheet tab is visible.

5. Press and hold **SHIFT**, click the **Store008** sheet tab, and then release **SHIFT**. The formula changes to =SUM('Store001:Store008'! showing the entire worksheet group used in the reference.

6. Click cell **B5** to complete the 3-D reference. The formula changes to =SUM('Store001:Store008'!B5 in the formula bar.

7. Type **)** to complete the formula, and then press **ENTER**. The formula returns the value $22,426,900, which is the sum of food sales from the eight stores in the Indiana/Ohio region. Refer to Figure 5–8.

Figure 5–8   3-D reference in the SUM function

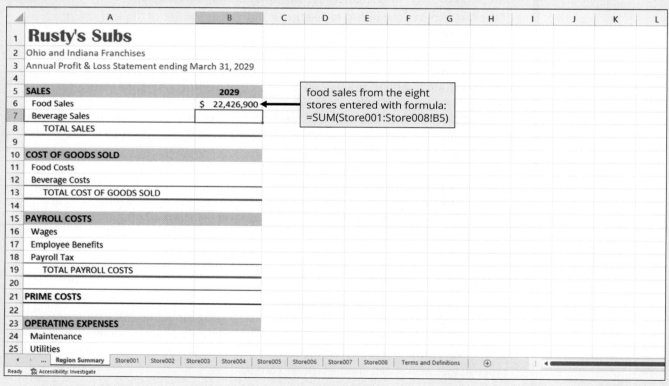

Rather than typing the SUM formula for the rest of the cells in the Region Summary worksheet, you can use AutoFill to copy the formula you created in cell B6.

To calculate the totals for the rest of the worksheet:

1. Select cell **B6**, and then drag the fill handle down to cell **B44**. The 3-D formula is copied down through the range B7:B44.

2. Click the **Auto Fill Options** button, and then click the **Fill Without Formatting** option button. The cells return to their original formatting. Some cells that were blank now display the value 0.

3. In the range B6:B44, select all cells displaying 0 or -, and then press **DELETE** to clear the formulas from those cells.

4. Click cell **B44** to select it. The total pretax profit from all eight stores is $1,317,500. Refer to Figure 5–9.

Figure 5–9   3-D cell reference copied through Region Summary worksheet

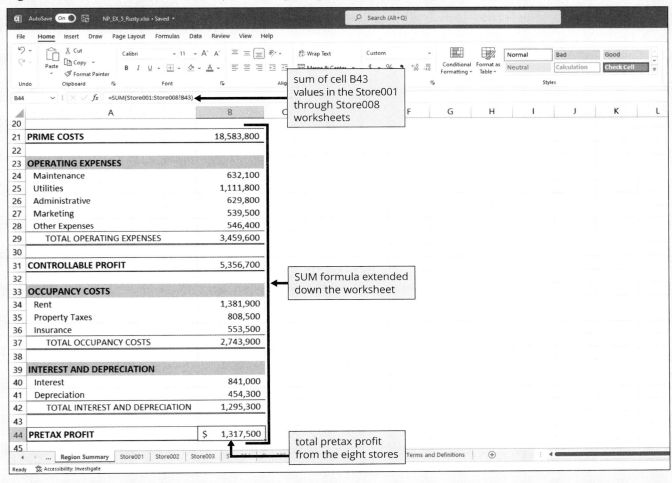

As with 2-D cell references, formulas with 3-D cell references update automatically when any of the values in a referenced worksheet cell change, making 3-D cell references a dynamic tool for analyzing data scattered across a workbook.

Insight

Wildcards and 3-D References

You can create flexible 3-D references using wildcards. Two useful wildcards are the question mark (?) wildcard representing any single character and the asterisk (*) wildcard representing any string of characters. For example, to sum the value of cell B5 from all worksheets beginning with the text string 'Store', you could use the formula

```
=SUM('Store*'!B5)
```

which would include worksheets named Store001, Store002, and so on in the calculation. If that wildcard expression matches worksheets you don't want to include, use the ? wildcard to narrow down the list of matching worksheets. In the following formula, only sheets that have names starting with Store00' and followed by a single character would be included in the sum:

```
=SUM(Store00?'!B5)
```

You can also omit any text string and use only wildcards. The following formula calculates the sum of cell B5 from any worksheet with three letters in its name, such as sheet names like Jan, Feb, Mar, and so forth:

```
=SUM('???'!B5)
```

When Excel encounters a wildcard in a worksheet reference, it automatically converts the reference to one in which the sheet name is explicitly entered.

Kendis discovered that the food sales values entered in the Store008 worksheet are incorrect. You will update the data in that sheet and then confirm that the values in the Region Summary worksheet updated automatically.

To change the food sales value in the Store008 worksheet:

1. Click the **Store008** sheet tab to make Store008 worksheet the active sheet.

2. Click cell **B5**, and then enter **1,515,000** as the correct value for food sales.

3. Go to the **Region Summary** worksheet and verify that the value in cell B6 increased from $22,426,900 to $22,444,400 and that the total pretax profit in cell B44 has increased from $1,317,500 to $1,335,000.

4. Save the workbook.

Kendis now has a summary of the profit and losses for the restaurants in the Indiana/Ohio region over the past year. But how do those values compare to previous years? You will answer that question when you compare the profit and loss statements in this workbook to profit and loss statements from workbooks created over the past several years.

Part 5.1 Quick Check

1. Why would you display the same workbook in multiple windows?

2. What are the four ways of arranging multiple workbook windows?

3. Why would you want to group worksheets?

4. How do you create a worksheet group of sheets that are not adjacent in the workbook?

5. How do you ungroup a worksheet group consisting of all sheets in the workbook?

6. What is the 3-D cell reference to cell C20 in the Monday worksheet?

7. What is the absolute 3-D cell reference to cell C20 in the Monday worksheet?

8. What is the 3-D cell reference to cell C20 in the Monday through Friday worksheet group?

9. What is the formula that uses the MAX function to return the maximum value of cell C20 of the Monday through Friday worksheet group?

Part 5.2 Visual Overview: External References and Links

To view a list of links created with external references, click the Edit Links button from the Queries & Connections group on the Data tab.

An **external reference** is a reference to a cell or range in a worksheet in a different workbook. This external reference refers to cell B7 in the Profit and Loss worksheet in the Support_EX_5_2026 workbook.

An external reference establishes a **link** between the data in the external document, known as the **source workbook**, and the current document, known as the **destination workbook**.

AutoSave On   NP_EX_5_Rusty.xlsx • Saved ▾

Search (Alt+Q)

File   Home   Insert   Draw   Page Layout   Formulas   Data   Review   View   Help

From Text/CSV   Recent Sources   Queries & Connections
From Web   Existing Connections   Properties
Get   From Table/Range   Refresh All   Edit Links
Data   Organization   Stocks   Currencies   Geography   Automatic

Get & Transform Data   Queries & Connections   Data Types

E7 fx ='https://data/Excel5/Module/[Support_EX_5_2026.xlsx]Profit and Loss'!B7

	A	B	C	D	E
1	**Rusty's Subs**				
2	Ohio and Indiana Franchises				
3	Annual Profit & Loss Statement ending March 31, 2029				
4					
5	**SALES**	**2029**	**2028**	**2027**	**2026**
6	Food Sales	$ 22,444,400	$ 22,172,000	$ 21,580,000	$ 21,463,0
7	Beverage Sales	4,973,200	4,920,000	4,850,000	4,836,0
8	TOTAL SALES	27,417,600	27,092,000	26,430,000	26,299,0
9					
10	**COST OF GOODS SOLD**				
11	Food Costs	7,038,800	6,886,000	6,795,000	6,749,0
12	Beverage Costs	1,451,000	1,455,000	1,427,000	1,440,0
13	TOTAL COST OF GOODS SOLD	8,489,800	8,341,000	8,222,000	8,189,0
14					
15	**PAYROLL COSTS**				
16	Wages	7,486,000	7,278,000	7,068,000	6,988,0
17	Employee Benefits	1,705,000	1,643,000	1,616,000	1,632,0
18	Payroll Tax	903,000	883,000	894,000	894,0
19	TOTAL PAYROLL COSTS	10,094,000	9,804,000	9,578,000	9,514,0
20					
21	**PRIME COSTS**	18,583,800	18,145,000	17,800,000	17,703,0
22					
23	**OPERATING EXPENSES**				
24	Maintenance	632,100	566,000	549,000	547,0
25	Utilities	1,111,800	1,065,000	1,039,000	1,034,0

Documentation   Region Summary   Store001   Store002   Store003   Store004   Store005   Store006   Store007   Store008

Ready   Accessibility: Investigate

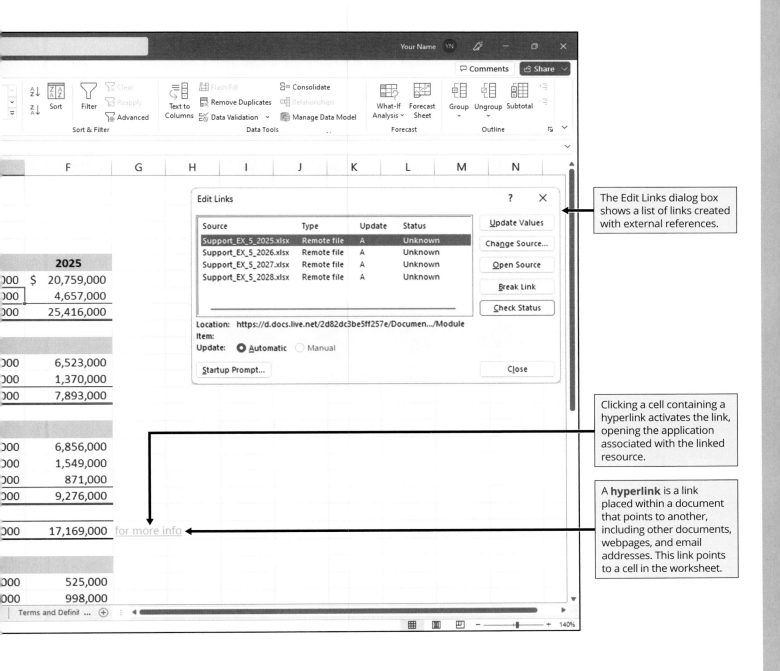

The Edit Links dialog box shows a list of links created with external references.

Clicking a cell containing a hyperlink activates the link, opening the application associated with the linked resource.

A **hyperlink** is a link placed within a document that points to another, including other documents, webpages, and email addresses. This link points to a cell in the worksheet.

Linking to External Workbooks

Just as you can reference cells across worksheets, you can reference cells stored in worksheets of other workbooks. References to cells in other workbooks, also known as external references, establish a **link**, or a connection, between a **source workbook** containing the data and the **destination workbook** receiving the data. Links to cells within a source workbook and a worksheet within that workbook are expressed with the external reference

> `[Workbook]Sheet!Range`

where `Workbook` is the file name of the source workbook, `Sheet` is a worksheet within the workbook, and `Range` is a cell range within that worksheet. The following expression references cell B10 of the Summary worksheet within the Report.xlsx workbook.

> `[Report.xlsx]Summary!B10`

If either the source workbook file name or the worksheet name includes blank spaces, you must enclose the entire `[Workbook]Sheet` portion of the reference within single quotes. For example, the following expression references cell B10 in the Summary worksheet of the Annual Report.xlsx file.

> `'[Annual Report.xlsx]Summary'!B10`

To reference cells within a worksheet group of the source workbook, place the workbook file name in brackets, and then list the worksheet group and cell reference as you would in a 3-D reference. The following expression references cell B10 within the Jan through May worksheet group of the Annual Report.xlsx workbook:

> `'[Annual Report.xlsx]Jan:May'!B10`

> **Tip** Unlike with worksheets, there is no such thing as a workbook group. You can specify only one workbook at a time.

If the source workbook is saved in the same folder as the destination workbook, you need to include only the workbook name in the reference. If the source workbook is stored in a different location, you need to include the **path**, or the exact location of the workbook file using the expression

> `Path\[Workbook]Sheet!Range`

where `Path` is an expression that points to the location of the workbook file. The following expression references cell B10 of the Summary worksheet in the Annual Report.xlsx workbook located in the C:\Documents\Reports folder:

> `'C:\Documents\Reports\[Annual Report.xlsx]Summary'!B10`

You must enclose the entire path, workbook name, and worksheet name portion of the reference in single quotes if any one of those names contains spaces.

Creating an External Reference

External references can be long and complicated. To speed up the process of entering an external reference as well as to avoid a mistake, you can begin entering the formula by typing the equal sign, and then use your mouse to select the cell or range from an already opened workbook. Excel will insert the external reference for you. Another approach is to copy the cell range from the external workbook, and then use the Paste Link command to paste the external reference to that range into the destination workbook.

Reference

Entering an External Reference

- To create an external reference to a range from another workbook, enter

  `[Workbook] Sheet!Range`

  where `Workbook` is the file name of an Excel workbook, `Sheet` is a worksheet within that workbook, and `Range` is a cell range within that worksheet (enclose workbook or worksheet names that include spaces within a set of single quotes).
- To insert the external reference into a formula as you type, click the cell range from the source workbook and press ENTER.
- To enter the external reference into a formula, copy the range from the source workbook, in the destination workbook, on the Home tab, in the Clipboard group, click the Paste arrow, and then click the Paste Link button.
- To create an external reference to a source workbook stored at a different location than the destination workbook, enter

  `Path\ [Workbook] Sheet!Range`

  where `Path` is the location of the folder containing the source workbook (enclose the path, workbook, or worksheet names that include spaces within a set of single quotes).

Kendis wants you to create a link to the profit and loss statement in the previous year's report. You will use the Paste Link feature to insert this external reference.

To insert an external reference to the previous year's data:

1. If you took a break after the previous part, make sure that the NP_EX_5_Rusty workbook is open and the Region Summary worksheet is active.

2. Open the **Support_EX_5_2028.xlsx** workbook located in the **Excel5 > Module** folder included with your Data Files.

3. In the Profit and Loss worksheet, select the range **B5:B44** containing the previous year's profit and loss values.

4. On the Home tab, in the Clipboard group, click the **Copy** button to copy the data.

5. Return to the **NP_EX_5_Rusty** workbook, and then click cell **C5** in the Region Summary worksheet to select it.

6. On the Home tab, in the Clipboard group, click the **Paste arrow** to open the Paste gallery, and then in the Other Paste Options section, click the **Paste Link** button 📋. Excel inserts links to the cells in the Support_EX_5_2028 workbook, starting with the formula ='[Support_EX_5_2028.xlsx]Profit and Loss'!B5 in cell C5 and extending down through cell C44 showing the pretax profit from 2028.

   | **Key Step** Make sure to use the Paste Link option so you paste the reference to the copied cells rather than pasting the cell values.

7. Click the **column B** header to select the entire column, and then in the Clipboard group, click the **Format Painter** button to copy the format from that column.

8. Click the **column C** header to paste the copied formats.

9. Click cell **C5** to select it. Refer to Figure 5–10.

Figure 5–10   Formula with an external reference

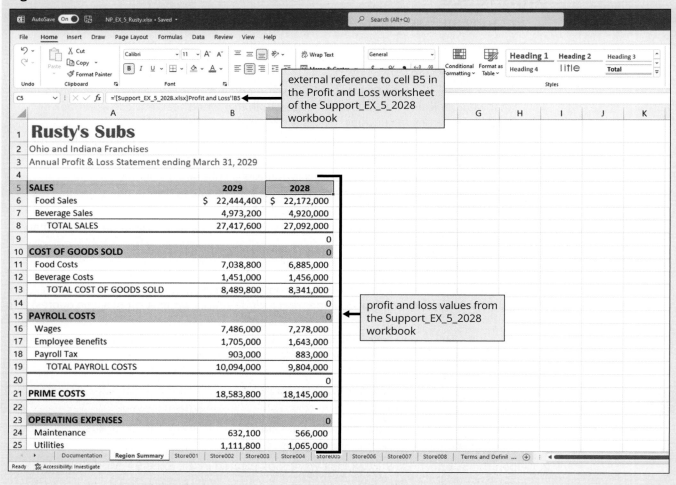

Kendis tells you that total sales increased from the previous year, but the total cost of goods sold has also increased. Kendis wants to know if this part of a trend. To find out, you will retrieve profit and loss data from other years.

To insert internal references to more years of data:

1. Repeat the previous set of steps, using the Paste Link command to create external references to the profit and loss values in the **Support_EX_5_2027.xlsx**, **Support_EX_5_2026.xlsx**, and **Support_EX_5_2025.xlsx** workbooks, placing the linked data in columns D through F. Several rows display zero or - because they contain formulas that reference empty cells in the source documents. You will remove those formulas.

2. Use **DELETE** on your keyboard to clear the zeros or - from rows 9, 10, 14, 15, 20, 22, 23, 30, 32, 33, 38, 39, and 43 in columns C through F of the Region Summary worksheet.

3. Scroll up the worksheet and click cell **F5** to select it. Refer to Figure 5–11.

Figure 5–11　Profit and loss values from 2025 through 2029

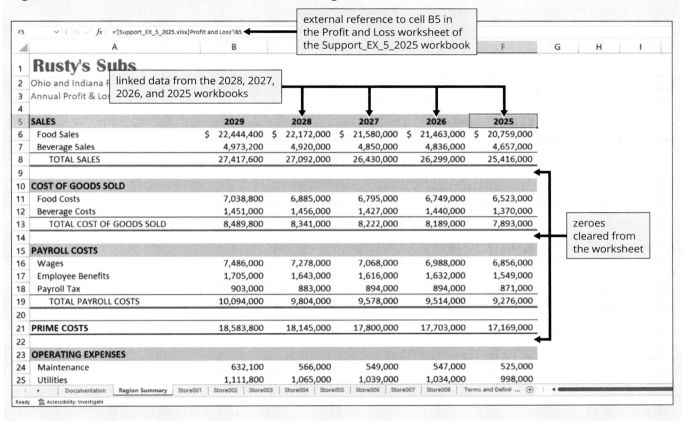

The annual profit and loss values indicate an interesting trend. Food sales have increased every year from the eight restaurants, rising from $20,759,000 in 2025 to $22,444,400 in 2029 (the range B8:F8). But pretax profits have decreased in the last year, dropping from $1,418,000 in 2028 (cell C44) to $1,335,000 in 2029 (cell B44). The decreased profit margin in the face of increasing sales indicates that rising costs are eating into profits. Kendis also notices that total payroll costs have increased by almost $300,000 from $9,804,000 in 2028 (cell C19) to $10,094,000 in 2029 (cell B19), which might be the important factor in the decline in profits. These are the types of insights that a workbook combining data from multiple worksheets and workbooks can provide.

When both the destination and source workbooks are open, any changes made to data in the source workbook immediately appear in the destination workbook. If the source workbook is open but the destination workbook is not, then the impact of the changes to the source workbook won't be apparent until you open the destination workbook. At that point, you can update the destination workbook to reflect the latest changes.

External References and Security Concerns

Linking to external source documents involves security issues. You might open a workbook that contains links to malicious software. For that reason, Excel disables links to source workbooks unless you explicitly indicate that you trust the data source. Once you indicate that you trust the source, Excel will add the source document to its list of trusted documents, and you will not be prompted again.

> **Tip** To view and edit the Excel security settings, click the File on the ribbon, click Options in Backstage view, and then click Trust Center in the Excel Options dialog box.

You will explore the Excel security measures as you work with the NP_EX_5_Rusty workbook.

To open the linked workbooks for the restaurants:

1. Save the **NP_EX_5_Rusty** and **Support_EX_5_2028** workbooks, and then close them.

2. Close the **Support_EX_5_2027**, **Support_EX_5_2026**, and **Support_EX_5_2025** workbooks, but do *not* save any changes that you inadvertently made during this session.

3. Reopen the **NP_EX_5_Rusty** workbook. A security warning appears below the ribbon requesting confirmation that the links in this workbook are from known and trusted data sources.

4. Click the **Enable Content** button.

5. If Excel displays a dialog box asking if you want to treat this file as a trusted document, click **Yes**.

6. Close the **NP_EX_5_Rusty** workbook without saving any changes you inadvertently made to the workbook.

7. Reopen the **NP_EX_5_Rusty** workbook. Because you already indicated that this workbook is a trusted data source, you are not prompted to enable the external content. Instead, a message dialog box opens. Refer to Figure 5–12.

Figure 5–12　　Dialog box prompting for action on links to external files

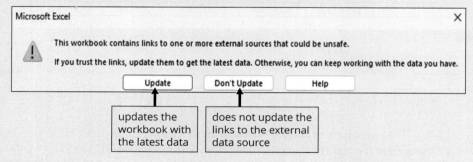

8. Click **Update** to update the links to the source documents.

Excel prompts you to update the links every time you open the workbook to ensure that you are working with the most current data. When a workbook contains links to other workbooks, it can be confusing to know which data are current. If you are working in a team, several individuals could be editing the same workbook at the same time. In that case, you will want to review a summary of the links in your workbook.

Reviewing Links Within a Workbook

A list of all links in your workbook is available in the Edit Links dialog box. For each link, the Edit Links dialog box displays the following information:

- **Source.** Indicates the source file for a given link.
- **Type.** Identifies the type of source file, such as an Excel worksheet, a Word document, or a PowerPoint slideshow.
- **Update.** Specifies how values are updated from the linked data source, where the letter *A* indicates the link is updated automatically upon opening the workbook, and *M* indicates that the link is updated manually in response to your request.
- **Status.** Reveals whether the data source has been accessed during the current session and, if so, whether the link has been updated.

In the Edit Links dialog box, you can manually update each link, change a link's data source, open a link's data source, break the connection to the link's data source, or check the status of the link. You will review the links in the NP_EX_5_Rusty workbook.

To review the links in the NP_EX_5_Rusty workbook:

1. On the ribbon, click the **Data** tab to access commands for working with data.

2. In the Queries and Connections group, click the **Edit Links** button. The Edit Links dialog box opens, showing the four links in the workbook, their source file, the type of data source, how the data source is updated, and whether the link has been accessed during this session.

3. Click **Support_EX_5_2028.xlsx** (the last link) in the list.

4. Click **Update Values** to connect to the data source and update the values displayed in the workbook. The status for the Support_EX_5_2028.xlsx workbook changes from Unknown to OK, indicating that Excel has successfully accessed and updated it. Refer to Figure 5–13.

Figure 5–13   Edit Links dialog box

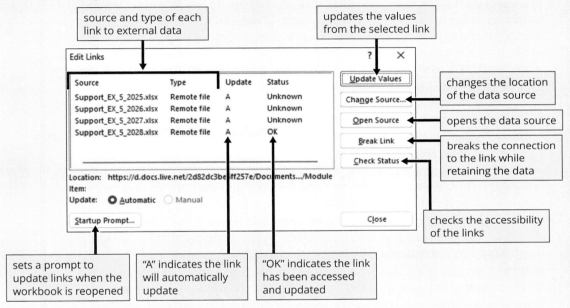

5. Click **Check Status** to check the accessibility of all listed links. That status of the other links changes from Unknown to OK, indicating that they have also been accessed and updated.

6. Click **Close** to close the dialog box and return to the workbook.

Managing Workbook Links

In some cases, you want to display only a "snapshot" of the data source at a single moment in time, as with financial statements that show final sales and expense figures at the end of the current month or year. To prevent a workbook from updating its content with data you do not want, you can break its link to the data source by clicking the Break Link button in the Edit Links dialog box. Breaking the link will remove the external references from your workbook, replacing them with the data values themselves.

> **Tip** You cannot undo the break link action. To restore the link, you must reenter the external reference formulas.

Sometimes the source workbook that a workbook is linked to is renamed or moved. Such a situation can occur for organizations that are restructuring their file system or switching to a new file server. To keep workbook links active and updateable, click the Change Source button in the Edit Links dialog box, and then replace the link to the old location with a link to the data in its new location or with its new name. You do not need to use the Change Source button if the destination and source workbooks both move to a new location and their relative positions within the folder structure are unchanged. Using the Change Source button is necessary only if the location of the source workbook alone is changed.

Proskills

Decision Making: Deciding When to Link Workbooks

At most businesses, a team works together to assemble data used in formulating policy and making decisions. Linked workbooks provide one way to make information compiled by different people or departments accessible to the decision-makers. When choosing whether to create a structure of linked workbooks, consider the following questions:

- **Is a large workbook too difficult to use?** While it may appear simpler to just keep everything within a single file, such workbooks can quickly become large and unwieldy. It is often better to divide information among several workbooks, allowing teams to focus on their own areas of expertise. However, keep in mind that a workbook with many links can also take a long time to open and update.

- **Can separate workbooks share a common design and structure?** Workbooks from different stores, branches, or departments need to have a uniform structure to avoid errors in data entry and analysis. Someone needs to be responsible for ensuring that all related documents adhere to a shared layout and structure.

- **Can information from different workbooks be summarized?** Is there an obvious way to summarize data from several source files within a single workbook, leaving the source files available for more in-depth analysis? Would important information be lost in such a summary?

- **Can source workbooks continually be updated?** Users of the summary workbook will often assume that the information is current and accurate. Are mechanisms in place for the timely update of key data?

- **Will the source workbooks be available to the destination workbook?** Data sources need to be accessible to relevant users so that links can be updated as needed and so the data itself can be reviewed for accuracy and completeness.

If you can answer yes to these questions, then linked workbooks might be the solution to your data needs. Creating a system of linked files can lead to more reliable data management and ultimately better and more informed decisions. A system of linked workbooks can also provide the company with flexibility as data sources become more expansive and complex.

An external reference is only one type of link supported by Excel. You can create links to a wide variety of data sources.

Creating Hyperlinks

Another type of link supported by Excel is a hyperlink, which is a text string or graphic image connected to a wide variety of resources, including:

- Websites
- Files on your computer, such as Word documents, PowerPoint presentations, text files, and PDF documents

- Cells and cell ranges within the current workbook
- Email addresses
- New documents created specifically as the source of the hyperlink

Clicking a hyperlink opens its linked resource using the application associated with that resource. Clicking a cell with a hyperlink to a website opens the website in your default browser, a hyperlink to a Word document opens the document file in Microsoft Word, and so forth. Hyperlinks are helpful in providing users with additional information not found in your workbook. For example, Kendis can use hyperlinks to connect the workbook to the company's website or to an operation manual for store managers.

> **Tip** You can create a hyperlink using the HYPERLINK function in which you specify the text of the link and the link's source.

Excel recognizes website addresses and email addresses as links. If you enter a website or email address into a cell, Excel will automatically convert that text into a hyperlink. You must manually define other types of links based on the location of their resource.

Linking to a Location Within a Workbook

You can manually create a link within a worksheet cell. Select the cell where you want to place the link. On the ribbon, click the Insert tab, and then in the Links group, click the Link button. The Insert Hyperlink dialog box opens. From the Insert Hyperlink dialog box, specify the type of resource to link to and the hyperlink text associated with that link. You can provide additional information about the hyperlink by adding a ScreenTip.

Reference

Working with Hyperlinks

- To create a hyperlink, select the text, graphic, or cell in which you want to insert the hyperlink. On the Insert tab, in the Links group, click the Hyperlink button. In the Insert Hyperlink dialog box, specify the link's location and the text as needed. Click the ScreenTip button to add a ScreenTip. Click OK.
- To create a hyperlink to a website or email address, type the address in a cell, and then press ENTER or TAB to convert the text into a hyperlink.
- To use a hyperlink, click the text, graphic, or cell containing the hyperlink; or right-click the hyperlink, and then click Open Hyperlink on the shortcut menu.
- To remove a hyperlink, right-click the hyperlink, and then click Remove Hyperlink on the shortcut menu.
- To edit a hyperlink, right-click the hyperlink, and then click Edit Hyperlink on the shortcut menu.

Kendis thinks that some of the terms in the profit and loss statement might not be familiar to users and asks you to create a hyperlink between those terms and their definitions on the Terms and Definitions worksheet. You will create some of these hyperlinks now.

To create hyperlinks within a workbook:

1. On the Region Summary worksheet, click cell **G21**, which is next to the data on prime costs.

2. On the ribbon, click the **Insert** tab, and then in the Links group, click the **Link** button. The Insert Hyperlink dialog box opens.

3. In the Text to display box, type **for more info** as the text of the hyperlink.

   > **Tip** To link to a location in different workbook, click Existing File or Web Page, select the workbook file, click the Bookmark button, enter the cell reference, and then click OK.

4. In the Link to section, click **Place in This Document** to display a list of places in the workbook you can link to.

5. In the Type the cell reference box, type **C16** as the cell reference, and then in the Or select a place in this document list, click **Terms and Definitions** to specify that the link be created to cell C16 in the Terms and Definitions worksheet. Refer to Figure 5–14.

Figure 5–14   Insert Hyperlink dialog box

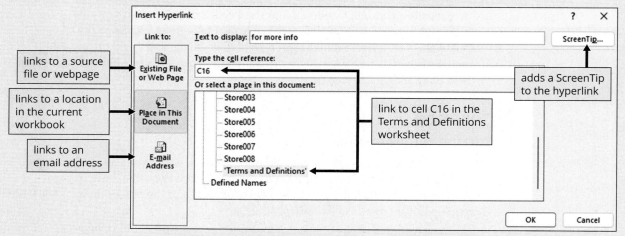

6. Click **ScreenTip** to open the Set Hyperlink ScreenTip dialog box.

7. In the ScreenTip text box, type **Click to learn more about Prime Costs** as the ScreenTip text, and then click **OK** to return to the Insert Hyperlink dialog box.

8. Click **OK** to insert the hyperlink into cell G21. The text "for more info" appears underlined in cell G21.

9. Repeat Steps 2 through 8 to link cell **G31** in the Region Summary worksheet to cell **C18** in the **Terms and Definitions worksheet** using **Click to learn more about Controllable Profit** as the ScreenTip text.

To use a link, click the cell containing the hyperlink. Excel will then jump to the linked location in the workbook. You will test the hyperlinks you created in cells G21 and G31 now.

To use the hyperlinks you created:

1. Point to cell **G21** to view the ScreenTip for that hyperlink. Refer to Figure 5–15.

Figure 5–15   Hyperlink text within a worksheet

	A	B	C	D	E	F	G	H	I
15	**PAYROLL COSTS**								
16	Wages	7,486,000	7,278,000	7,068,000	6,988,000	6,856,000			
17	Employee Benefits	1,705,000	1,643,000	1,616,000	1,632,000	1,549,000			
18	Payroll Tax	903,000	883,000	894,000	894,000	871,000			
19	TOTAL PAYROLL COSTS	10,094,000	9,804,000	9,578,000	9,514,000	9,276,000			
20									
21	**PRIME COSTS**	18,583,800	18,145,000	17,800,000	17,703,000	17,169,000	for more info		
22									
23	**OPERATING EXPENSES**								
24	Maintenance	632,100	566,000	549,000	547,000	525,000			
25	Utilities	1,111,800	1,065,000	1,039,000	1,034,000	998,000			
26	Administrative	629,800	635,000	621,000	624,000	594,000			
27	Marketing	539,500	602,000	586,000	589,000	563,000			
28	Other Expenses	546,400	547,000	541,000	542,000	518,000			
29	TOTAL OPERATING EXPENSES	3,459,600	3,415,000	3,336,000	3,336,000	3,198,000			
30									
31	**CONTROLLABLE PROFIT**	5,374,200	5,532,000	5,294,000	5,260,000	5,049,000	for more info		
32									
33	**OCCUPANCY COSTS**								
34	Rent	1,381,900	1,449,000	1,427,000	1,438,000	1,381,000			
35	Property Taxes	808,500	779,000	770,000	773,000	739,000			
36	Insurance	553,500	577,000	564,000	561,000	541,000			
37	TOTAL OCCUPANCY COSTS	2,743,900	2,805,000	2,761,000	2,772,000	2,661,000			
38									
39	**INTEREST AND DEPRECIATION**								
40	Interest	841,000	844,000	825,000	818,000	788,000			

Callouts in figure: "hyperlink to more information about prime costs"; "ScreenTip gives more information about the hyperlink" (Click to learn more about Prime Costs); "hyperlink to more information about controllable profit".

Sheet tabs: Documentation | Region Summary | Store001 | Store002 | Store003 | Store004 | Store005 | Store006 | Store007 | Store008 | Terms and Defini ...

Ready   Accessibility: Investigate

2. Click cell **G21** to make cell C16 in the Terms and Definitions worksheet the active cell.

   > **Tip** Only linked text within a cell is treated as a hyperlink; text extending beyond the cell's borders is not.

3. Read the definition of the Prime Costs definition entered in cell C16.

4. Return to the **Region Summary** worksheet and click cell **G31** to make cell C18 in the Terms and Definitions worksheet the active cell.

5. Read the definition of Controllable Profit and return to the **Region Summary** worksheet.

If you need to edit an existing hyperlink, right-click the cell, text, or graphic containing the link, and then click Edit Hyperlink on the shortcut menu to open the Edit Hyperlink dialog box. To remove a hyperlink, right-click the link, and then click Remove Hyperlink on the shortcut menu. To change the style of hyperlink text, click the Cell Styles button in the Styles group on the Home tab, right-click the Hyperlink cell style, and then click Modify.

Linking to an Email Address

You can make it easier for users to send you messages about your workbook by adding a hyperlink to your email address. Clicking a linked email address automatically opens the user's email program to a new message with your email address and a preset subject line already inserted. Kendis wants you to add an email address to the Documentation sheet of the NP_EX_5_Rusty workbook so users can easily submit questions and queries about the workbook's contents. You will create this email link now.

To link to an email address:

1. Go to the **Documentation** sheet, and then click cell **B3** containing your name.

2. On the Insert tab, in the Links group, click the **Link** button. The Insert Hyperlink dialog box opens.

3. In the Link to section, click **E-mail Address** to display the options for creating a link to an email address.

4. In the E-mail address box, type your email address (or the email address specified by your instructor). The text *mailto:*, which is an Internet communication protocol used for linking to email addresses, appears before the email address.

5. In the Subject box, type **Regarding the Profit and Loss Statement** as the subject line of any email created using this link. Refer to Figure 5–16.

Figure 5–16   Insert Hyperlink dialog box for an email address

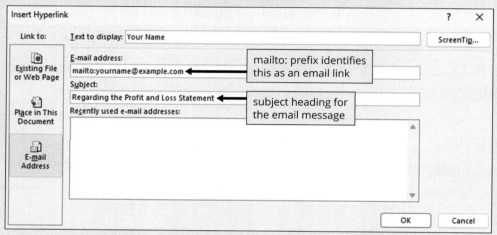

6. Click the **ScreenTip** button, type **Email me for questions about the workbook** in the Set Hyperlink ScreenTip dialog box, and then click **OK**.

7. In the Insert Hyperlink dialog box, click **OK** to insert the hyperlink in cell B3 of the Documentation sheet.

8. Click cell **B3** and verify that your email program opens to a new message with your email address and the subject line already filled in.

   Tip To select a cell containing a hyperlink without activating the link, right-click the cell.

9. Close the email message without sending it.

10. Save the workbook.

Note that the hyperlinks you added are part of the workbook, but they won't appear in the Edit Links dialog box. That dialog box is used only for data values retrieved from external sources.

You have completed your work on external reference and links. In the next session, you will learn how to assign names to references to make it easier to write and understand formulas.

Part 5.2 Quick Check

1. What is the external reference to cell C20 of the Final Report worksheet located in the Annual Statement.xlsx workbook?

2. What is the external reference to cell D10 of the Sunday worksheet located in the Weekly Report.xlsx workbook that is stored in the C:\Documents\Reports folder?

3. When would you paste a copied cell using the Paste Link option?

4. How do you check the status of a link within the current workbook to determine whether the link's source file is accessible and up to date?

5. How does Excel indicate that a cell contains linked text?

6. What does Excel do when a hyperlink is clicked by the user?

Part 5.3 Visual Overview: Named Ranges and Templates

The title bar shows the name of the template the workbook is based on. This workbook is based on the NP_EX_5_PLStatement.xltx template.

The list of named ranges in the workbook is displayed in the Name Manager dialog box.

A **named range**, or **defined name**, is a user-defined name that replaces a cell or range reference. Here, the defined range named TOTAL_SALES replaces the reference to cell B7.

A template is a predefined workbook in which all formulas and design elements are already built in, leaving the user to enter the data of interest.

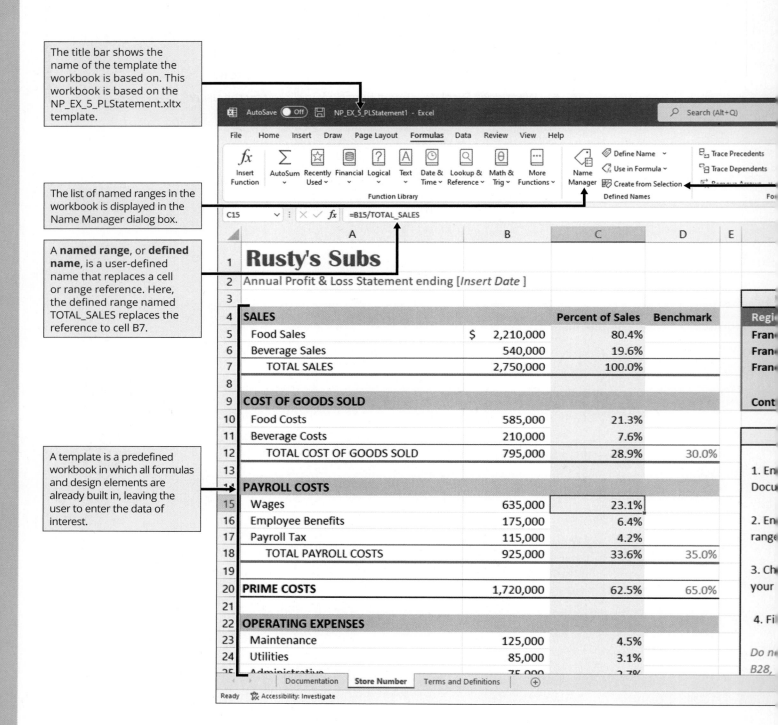

	A	B	C	D	E
1	**Rusty's Subs**				
2	Annual Profit & Loss Statement ending [*Insert Date*]				
3					
4	**SALES**		**Percent of Sales**	**Benchmark**	
5	Food Sales	$ 2,210,000	80.4%		
6	Beverage Sales	540,000	19.6%		
7	TOTAL SALES	2,750,000	100.0%		
8					
9	**COST OF GOODS SOLD**				
10	Food Costs	585,000	21.3%		
11	Beverage Costs	210,000	7.6%		
12	TOTAL COST OF GOODS SOLD	795,000	28.9%	30.0%	
13					
14	**PAYROLL COSTS**				
15	Wages	635,000	23.1%		
16	Employee Benefits	175,000	6.4%		
17	Payroll Tax	115,000	4.2%		
18	TOTAL PAYROLL COSTS	925,000	33.6%	35.0%	
19					
20	**PRIME COSTS**	1,720,000	62.5%	65.0%	
21					
22	**OPERATING EXPENSES**				
23	Maintenance	125,000	4.5%		
24	Utilities	85,000	3.1%		
25	Administrative	75,000	2.7%		

Cell reference box: C15   =B15/TOTAL_SALES

Sheet tabs: Documentation | Store Number | Terms and Definitions

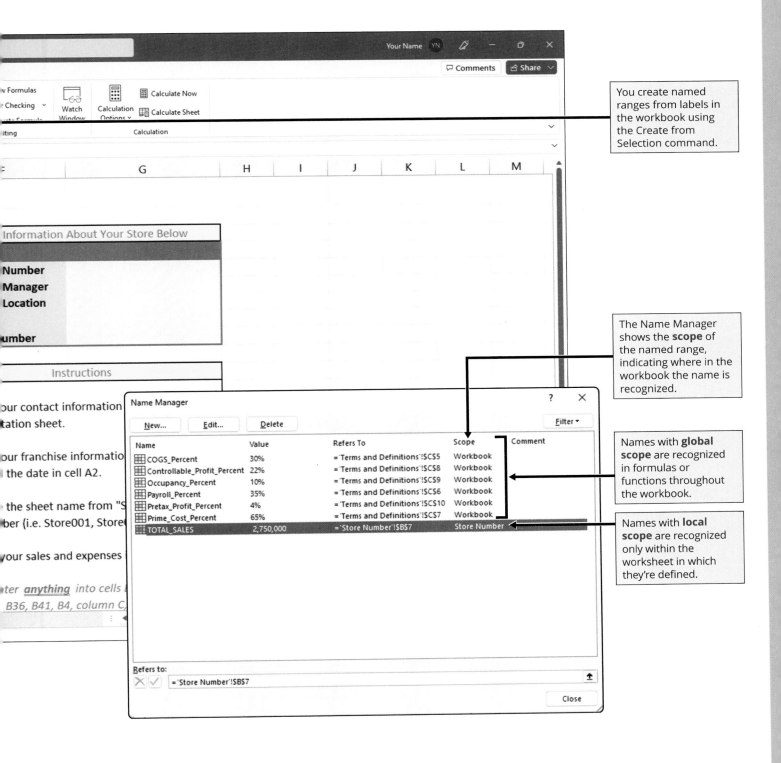

You create named ranges from labels in the workbook using the Create from Selection command.

The Name Manager shows the **scope** of the named range, indicating where in the workbook the name is recognized.

Names with **global scope** are recognized in formulas or functions throughout the workbook.

Names with **local scope** are recognized only within the worksheet in which they're defined.

Simplifying Formulas with Named Ranges

Formulas that use cell references do not describe what is being calculated. For example, compare the following formulas:

```
=B7 - B28
=Income - Expenses
```

In the first formula, the terms are cell references, which don't specify what is being calculated. In the second formula, the terms describe what is being calculated. That is the idea behind range names, which replace range references with descriptive names. A range name can refer to any cell or range within the workbook, so you can replace a reference such as `Sheet1!B7:B43` with the more descriptive name `SalesData2029`.

Defining a Named Range

A quick way to define a range name is to select a range and enter the name in the Name box located above the upper-left corner of the worksheet window. You can also go to the Formulas tab, click the Define Name button in the Defined Names group, and then enter the name in the New Names dialog box. Once a name is defined, it can be used in place of range references in any Excel formula or function.

Names should be short, meaningful, and descriptive of the range being defined. Keep in mind that any name you choose must follow these rules:

- The name must begin with a letter or _ (an underscore).
- The name can include letters and numbers as well as periods and underscores, but not other symbols or spaces. To distinguish multiword names, use an underscore between the words or capitalize the first letter of each word. For example, the names Net_Income and NetIncome are valid, but Net Income and Net-Income are not.
- The name cannot be a valid cell address (such as A20), a function name (such as Average), or any word that Excel reserves for other purposes (such as Print_Area).
- The name can include as many as 255 characters, although short, meaningful names of 5 to 15 characters are more practical.

Names are not case sensitive; Sales and SALES are treated by Excel as the same name.

Reference

Defining a Named Range

- Select the range, type the name in the Name box, and then press ENTER.

or

- Select the range, and then on the Formulas tab, in the Defined Names group, click the Define Name button.
- Type a name in the Name box, and then click OK.

or

- Select the data values and labels you want used as named ranges.
- On the Formulas tab, in the Defined Names group, click the Create from Selection button.
- Click the check box to indicate where the labels appear in the selection.
- Click OK.

You will use range names as you analyze the profit and loss statements in the Rusty's Subs workbook. In the restaurant industry, incomes and expenses are often expressed in terms of their percent of total sales. For example, instead of only noting that the Cleveland restaurant has total payroll costs of $2,553,000, a profit and loss statement would also include the fact that Cleveland's payroll costs were 35.4% of its total sales. This is done to compare restaurants operating in differently sized markets. The Rusty's Subs operating in Cleveland should show a larger income, expense, and hopefully, profit than a restaurant operating in a smaller market like Akron. But that does not mean the Cleveland franchise is better managed. Expressing the profit and loss figures as a percent of total sales provides a way of determining whether the franchise is adequately managing its expenses regardless of the size of its market.

Kendis entered industry benchmarks for different parts of the profit and loss statement in the Terms and Definitions worksheet. The worksheet shows a benchmark percentage for payroll costs of 35%, meaning that, regardless of the size of the market, a restaurant should spend no more than about 35% of its total sales income on payroll. You will create range names for these benchmark values so that you can display their values in the profit and loss statements for the eight locations.

To define a named range using the Name box:

1. If you took a break at the end of the previous part, make sure the NP_EX_5_Rusty workbook is open.

2. Go to the **Terms and Definitions** worksheet, and then click cell **C5** containing 30% as the benchmark for cost of goods as a percentage of total sales.

3. Click the **Name box** to select the cell reference.

4. Type **COGS_Percent** as the name of the defined range, and then press **ENTER**. The COGS_Percent named range now points to cell C5 of the Terms and Definitions worksheet. Refer to Figure 5-17.

Figure 5-17   Named range defined in the Name box

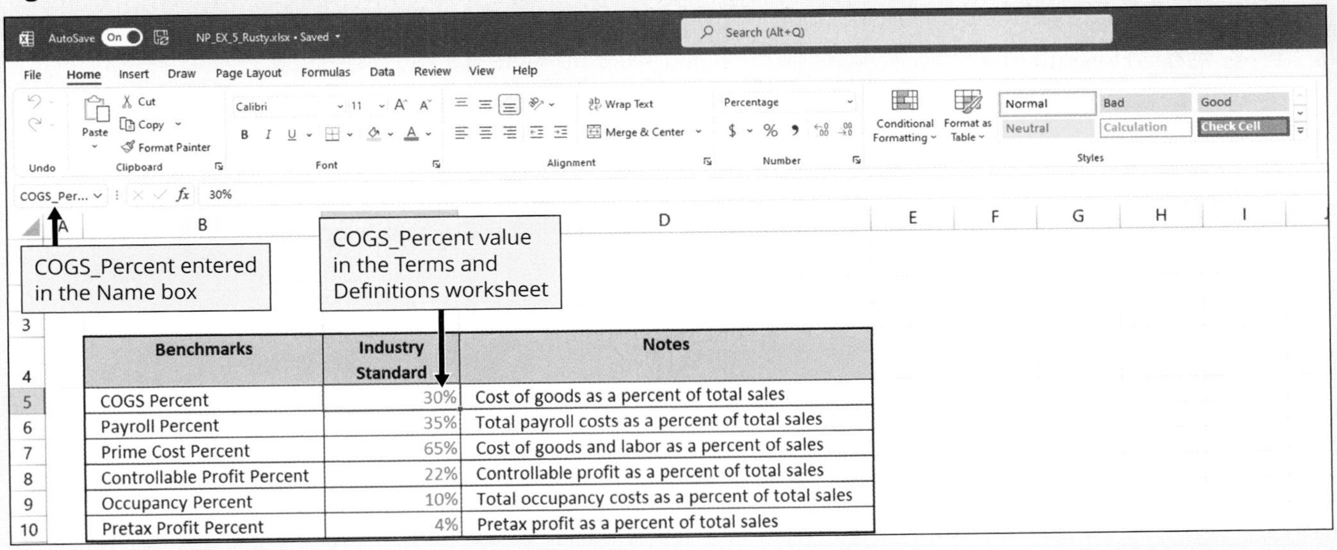

If you have many names to define, a more efficient approach is to create names drawn from the labels in the cells adjacent to the data cells. The Create from Selection button in the Defined Names group on the Formulas tab generates the named ranges based on the label text. In the Terms and Definitions worksheet, the range B6:B10 contains labels for other industry benchmarks, and the range C6:C10 contains the benchmark percentages. You will use those labels to define named ranges for the values in the range C6:C10.

To define named ranges using labels in adjacent cells:

1. In the Terms and Definitions worksheet, select the range **B6:C10** containing the industry benchmark labels and their associated values.

2. On the ribbon, click the **Formulas** tab, and then in the Defined Names group, click the **Create from Selection** button. The Create Names from Selection dialog box opens.

    > **Tip** You can also press CTRL+SHIFT+F3 to open the Create Names from Selection dialog box.

3. If necessary, click the **Left column** check box to insert a checkmark, leaving the other check boxes unselected. Refer to Figure 5–18.

Figure 5–18   Create Names from Selection dialog box

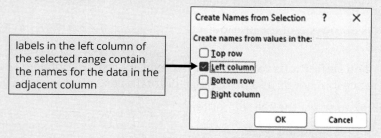

labels in the left column of the selected range contain the names for the data in the adjacent column

4. Click **OK** to define the named ranges.

5. Click the **Name box arrow** to display all six named ranges. These names match the labels in the range B5:B10. Because the names cannot contain spaces, an underscore (_) replaced the spaces in the benchmark labels.

6. Press **ESC** to close the Name box.

By default, Excel treats range names as absolute cell references. However, the reference is dynamic. If you add new cells within the range, the reference for the range name will expand to include the new cells. Likewise, the reference will contract if cells within the range are deleted. If you remove all the cells, the range name will no longer point to existing cells, and any formulas using that range name will return the #REF error value. Finally, if you move the referenced cells to a new location, the reference for the range name is updated automatically so that the name will always point to your data.

Using Range Names in Formulas

A range name can be used in place of a cell reference in any Excel formula or function. The 3-D reference in the formula

```
=SUM('Sales Data'!E4:E20)
```

can be replaced with

```
=SUM(salesFigures)
```

where `salesFigures` refers to the `'Sales Data'!E4:E20` location.

You can insert names into a formula by typing them directly in the formula or by clicking the Use in Formula button in the Defined Names group on the Formulas tab.

> **Tip** You can select a range name in the Name box to jump to its location wherever it is in the workbook and select it.

Kendis wants you to display the benchmark values within each location's profit and loss statement. To enter the formulas at the same time across all eight worksheets, you will group the eight worksheets and then create formulas using the named ranges you defined.

To create formulas for the benchmark values:

1. Click the **Store001** sheet tab, hold down **SHIFT**, click the **Store008** sheet tab, and then release **SHIFT** to group the Store001 through Store008 worksheets.

2. Click cell **D12**, and then type **=** to begin the formula.

3. Type **cog** as the first letters of the COGS_Percent named range. As you type, a list of functions and named ranges that start with those letters appear. Refer to Figure 5–19.

Figure 5–19   Named range being added to a formula

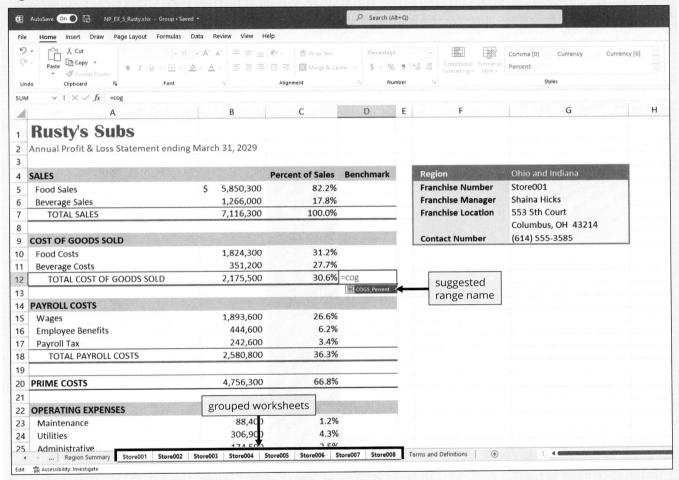

4. Press **TAB** to complete the formula =COGS_Percent, and then press **ENTER**. The value 30.0% is displayed in cell D12, which is also the value of C5 in the Terms and Definitions worksheet.

   Tip You can also click the Use in Formula button in the Defined Names group on the Formulas tab and select the name from a list of available named ranges.

5. In cell **D18**, enter **=Payroll_Percent** as the formula. The value 35.0% is displayed in the cell.

6. In cell **D20**, enter **=Prime_Cost_Percent** as the formula. The value 65.0% is displayed in the cell.

7. In cell **D30**, enter **=Controllable_Profit_Percent** as the formula. The value 22.0% is displayed in the cell.

8. In cell **D36**, enter **=Occupancy_Percent** as the formula. The value 10.0% appears in the cell.

9. In cell **D43**, enter **=Pretax_Profit_Percent** as the formula. The value 4.0% appears in the cell. Refer to Figure 5–20.

Figure 5–20   Named ranges used in formulas

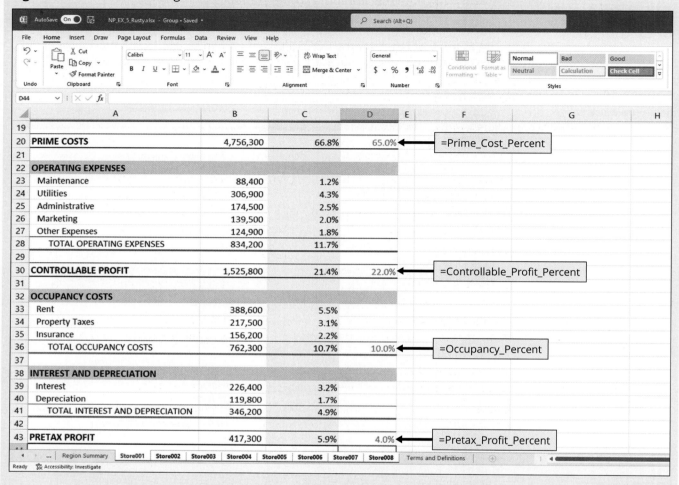

10. Click each sheet tab in the worksheet group, verifying that the formulas containing named ranges are duplicated on every sheet in the group.

Comparing the franchise figures with the industry benchmarks helps Kendis locate possible sources of trouble. For example, the Dayton location (Store004), which showed a net loss of 3.9% during the past year, also spent 44.6% of its total sales on payroll, far exceeding the recommended 35% goal (cell D18).

Because total sales are involved in so many calculations in the profit and loss statements, Kendis wants you to create a range name for total sales in each of the eight profit and loss worksheets.

To define a named range for total sales:

1. In the worksheet group, click the **Store001** sheet tab to make it the active sheet within the group.

2. Select the range **A7:B7**. Because the worksheets are still grouped, you are also selecting this range in each worksheet in the group.

3. On the Formulas tab, in the Defined Names group, click the **Create from Selection** button. The Create Names from Selection dialog box opens.

4. Make sure only the **Left column** check box is selected, and then click **OK**. The named range TOTAL_SALES associated with cell B7 is created for each worksheet in the group.

5. On the formula bar, click the **Name box arrow** to display a list of defined names and verify that the new defined name TOTAL_SALES appears in the list of names.

Because the worksheets were grouped when you used the Create from Selection commands, the action of creating the named range TOTAL_SALES was duplicated on each of the grouped worksheets. So how does Excel manage eight TOTAL_SALES named ranges? That question brings up the issue of scope.

Proskills

Written Communication: Saving Time with Defined Names

Words can be more descriptive than numbers. This is especially true with cell references. Compared to the letter and number references for cells, a named range provides a more intuitive reference, which is increasingly important as the workbook becomes longer and more complex. Other advantages of named ranges are:

- Names such as TaxRate and TotalSales are more descriptive than cell references and are easier to remember and apply.
- Names in formulas clearly show users exactly what is being calculated. For example, a formula like = GrossPay−Deductions is more easily interpreted than = C15−C16.
- Names remain associated with their range. If a range is moved within the workbook, its name moves with it. Any formulas that contain the name automatically reference the new location.
- Named ranges operate like absolute cell references. If a formula containing a named range is moved or copied, the reference remains pointed to the correct range.

Using defined names saves time and gives everyone reviewing the worksheet a clearer understanding of what that worksheet is doing and what the results mean.

Determining the Scope of Range Names

Scope indicates where in the workbook the range name is recognized. Names with global scope are recognized in formulas or functions throughout the workbook. Names with local scope are recognized only within the worksheet in which they are defined. So, if TOTAL_SALES is defined with local scope for cell B7 in the Store002 worksheet, you can apply the TOTAL_SALES range name only within that sheet. To reference a name with a local scope outside of its worksheet, you must include the sheet along with the range name, such as Store002!TOTAL_SALES. Names with global scope do not require the sheet name because they are recognized throughout the workbook.

Local scope avoids name conflicts that would occur when the same name is duplicated across multiple worksheets, as is the case with the TOTAL_SALES name. All range names are given global scope when they are created unless that name is already being used. If the name is already in use, the new name is given local scope. The Name Manager lets you view and manage all the named ranges defined for a workbook. From the Name Manager, you can learn the current value stored with each named range, the cell range they reference, and the name's scope.

Kendis wants to avoid confusion between the total sales stored in one worksheet versus another sheet, so all TOTAL_SALES range names should be limited to local scope. You can determine the scope of each range name using the Name Manager. Open the Name Manager to review the named ranges you have created.

To open the Name Manager:

1. If necessary, click the **Formulas** tab on the ribbon.

2. In the Defined Names group, click the **Name Manager** button (or press **CTRL+F3**). The Name Manager dialog box opens. Refer to Figure 5–21.

Figure 5–21   Name Manager dialog box

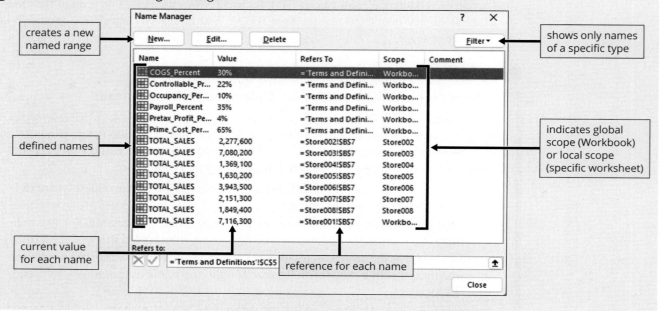

The Name Manager lists the 14 names defined for the workbook. The first six have global scope and point to ranges in the Terms and Definitions worksheet. The next eight are all named TOTAL_SALES and have local scope associating them with a specific worksheet. Only the TOTAL_SALES name from the Store001 worksheet has global scope and can be referenced anywhere within the workbook.

The TOTAL_SALES name for the Store001 worksheet has global scope because it was the first TOTAL_SALES name created when you were defining names in the worksheet group (Store001 was the active sheet in that group). Once that named range had global scope, the other TOTAL_SALES names were forced to have local scope because the same name cannot be used more than once if it has global scope. If it did, Excel would have no way of resolving the conflict.

Kendis wants the TOTAL_SALES name for the Store001 worksheet to also have local scope to avoid confusion. Once created, you cannot change the scope of a range name. Instead, you must delete and recreate the name using the Name Manager. You will use the Name Manager to delete and recreate the TOTAL_SALES name as a name with local scope for the Store001 worksheet.

To delete and recreate the TOTAL_SALES range name:

1. In the Name Manager dialog box, click the **TOTAL_SALES** named range that references cell B7 in the Store001 worksheet and has a current value of 7,116,300.

2. Click **Delete** to delete the TOTAL_SALES name, and then click **OK** in the dialog box that appears to confirm the deletion. The TOTAL_SALES name for the Store001 worksheet no longer appears in the Name list.

3. Click **New** to open the New Name dialog box.

4. In the Name box, type **TOTAL_SALES** as the name for the new defined name, and then press **TAB**.

5. Click the **Scope** box, and then select **Store001** as the worksheet, specifying that the scope of the TOTAL_SALES named range you are creating will be restricted to the Store001 worksheet.

> **Key Step** Make sure you select the worksheet from the Scope list to create a named range of local scope.

6. Press **TAB** twice to move to the Refers to box.

7. Click cell **B7** in the Store001 worksheet. The reference ='Store001'$B$7 appears in the Refers to box. Refer to Figure 5-22.

Figure 5-22　　New Name dialog box

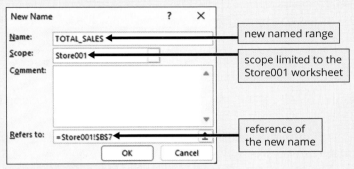

8. Click **OK** to close the New Name dialog box and return to the Name Manager dialog box.

9. Verify that the TOTAL_SALES name with the Scope value set to Store001 appears in the list of named ranges.

10. Click **Close** to close the Name Manager dialog box.

Next you will use the TOTAL_SALES range names in the calculations from the eight profit and loss statements.

Insight

Naming Constants

In addition to referencing ranges in a workbook, names can also store specific values. If you commonly use constants in your formulas, you can name the constant by completing the following steps:

1. In the Name Manager dialog box, click the New button. The New Name dialog box opens.

2. In the New name box, enter a name for the defined name.

3. In the Refers to box, enter the expression =value where value is the constant value stored in the defined name.

4. Click OK.

Once the constant is named, it can be used in any formula or function. For example, you can create a constant named salesTax that stores the value 0.05. Then the formula =B10*salesTax would multiply the value in cell B10 by 0.05. By storing named constants rather than using a worksheet cell, you can simplify your workbook and make it easier to write meaningful formulas and functions.

Using Defined Names in Existing Formulas

Once you have defined a named range, you can have Excel replace all cell references in formulas and functions with the equivalent name. To apply names to an existing set of formulas, click the Define Name arrow in the Defined Names group on the Formulas tab, and then click Apply Names. The Apply Names command cannot be used with a worksheet group. It can be used only with ranges in individual sheets. You will apply the TOTAL_SALES range names to formulas in the eight profit and loss statements.

To apply defined names to existing formulas in the profit and loss worksheets:

1. Right-click the **Store001** sheet tab, and then click **Ungroup Sheets** on the shortcut menu.

2. Save the workbook. You want to save before using the Apply Names command in case you make a mistake in the substitution.

3. Select the range **C5:C43** containing the formulas that calculate the percent of total sales values.

4. On the Formulas tab, in the Defined Names group, click the **Define Name arrow**, and then click **Apply Names**. The Apply Names dialog box opens.

5. In the Apply names list, make sure **TOTAL_SALES** is selected. You want to replace every reference to cell B7 in the current worksheet with the TOTAL_SALES name.

6. Verify that the **Ignore Relative/Absolute** check box is selected so that the name is applied whether cell B7 is referenced using an absolute or relative reference. Refer to Figure 5–23.

Figure 5–23   Apply Names dialog box

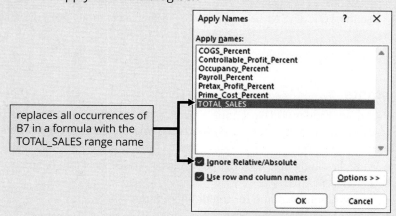

replaces all occurrences of B7 in a formula with the TOTAL_SALES range name

7. Click **OK** to apply the named range to formulas in the selected cells.

8. Click each cell in the range C5:C43 of the Store001 worksheet, verifying that references to cell B7 have been replaced with TOTAL_SALES.

> **Trouble?** If the replacement was not made, you may have made a mistake when using the Apply Names command. Close the workbook without saving changes, reopen the workbook, and then repeat Steps 3 through 7.

You cannot use the Apply Names command for worksheet groups, but you can use the Find and Replace command to replace every occurrence of a cell reference with its equivalent range name within a worksheet group. You will use this technique to replace every reference to cell B7 with TOTAL_SALES in the remaining franchise profit and loss statements.

To replace cell references with the TOTAL_SALES defined name:

1. Save the workbook so that if you make a mistake, you can close the workbook without saving changes and then reopen the workbook and repeat this set of steps.

2. Click the **Store002** sheet tab, hold down **SHIFT**, click the **Store008** sheet tab, and then release **SHIFT**. The Store002 through Store008 sheets are selected in a worksheet group.

3. In the worksheet group, select the range **C5:C43**.

4. On the ribbon, click the **Home** tab. In the Editing group, click the **Find & Select** button, and then click **Replace** (or press **CTRL+H**). The Find and Replace dialog box opens.

5. Type **B7** in the Find what box, press **TAB**, and then type **TOTAL_SALES** in the Replace with box. Refer to Figure 5–24.

Figure 5–24   Find and Replace dialog box

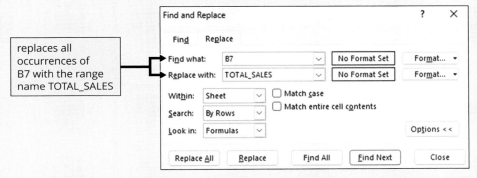

6. Click **Replace All**. In the worksheet group, 161 occurrences of B7 in the selected formulas are replaced with the TOTAL_SALES defined name.

7. Click **OK** in the message dialog box, and then click **Close** in the Find and Replace dialog box to return to the workbook.

8. Examine the formulas in the range C5:C43 and verify that the references to cell B7 in the worksheet group have been replaced with the TOTAL_SALES name.

   Trouble? If the cell references are not changed to the defined name, you made a mistake in the steps. Close the workbook without saving changes, reopen the workbook, and then repeat Steps 2 through 7.

9. **sam↑** Ungroup the selected worksheets, and then save and close the workbook.

If a workbook has many defined names, you might want a way to record all the defined names. In addition to viewing the list of names in the Name Manager, you can paste a list of the defined names into a worksheet table. To create a list of defined names, click the Use in Formula arrow in the Defined Names group on the Formulas tab, and then click Paste Names. In the Paste Names dialog box that opens, click Paste List to paste a list of all the names and the ranges they reference. The pasted list will not be updated as you add, modify, or delete the names. So, be sure to paste the list of defined names only when your workbook is complete.

Insight

Indirect Referencing

A cell reference tells a formula or function exactly where to find the data it needs. However, some formulas need to retrieve data from several possible locations. An application might need the same SUM function to calculate the sum of values from the range C1:C10 in one case and from the range D1:D10 in another. Being able to change a cell reference without having to rewrite a formula is the purpose of **indirect referencing** in which the range reference itself is a calculated value. Indirect references are created with the INDIRECT function

```
INDIRECT(ref_text, [a1])
```

where ref_text is a text string that specifies the reference address and $a1$ is an optional argument specifying how that reference is written. If cell A1 contains the text string 'C1:C10', then the expression

```
INDIRECT(A1)
```

is equivalent to the range reference C1:C10. Nesting the INDIRECT function in the formula

```
=SUM(INDIRECT(A1))
```

is the equivalent to the formula =SUM(C1:C10). If the text within cell A1 is changed to 'D1:D10', Excel evaluates the expression as =SUM(D1:D10), and so forth. You can also use a named range so that if the text of cell A1 is changed to 'TotalExpenses', Excel evaluates the formula as =SUM(TotalExpenses).

Indirect referencing gives Excel authors the ability to create dynamic formulas that change in response to user input. The INDIRECT function can also be used to reference data in separate worksheets or even separate workbooks. However, an indirectly referenced workbook must be open for Excel to access its contents.

Exploring Workbook Templates

In this module, you collected data from several workbooks. It was efficient because those source workbooks had an identical structure and design. Templates, or predesigned workbooks in which all the formulas and design elements are already built in, ensure a consistent design among workbooks. An additional advantage is that users can focus on data entry because all the structure, formatting, and formulas are already in place.

Proskills

Teamwork: Using Excel Templates

A team working together will often need to create the same types of workbooks. Rather than each person or group designing a different workbook, each team member should create a workbook from the same template. The completed workbooks will then all have the same structure with identical formatting and formulas. Not only does this ensure consistency and accuracy, it also makes it easier to compile and summarize the results. Templates help teams work better together and avoid misunderstandings.

For example, a large organization may need to collect the same information from several regions. By creating and distributing a workbook template, each region knows what data to track and where to enter it. The template already includes the formulas, so the results are calculated consistently.

The following are just some of the advantages of using a template to create multiple workbooks with the same features:

- Templates save time and ensure consistency in the design and content of workbooks because all labels, formatting, and formulas are entered once.
- Templates ensure accuracy because formulas can be entered and verified once, and then used with confidence in all workbooks.
- Templates standardize the appearance and content of workbooks.
- Templates prevent data from being overwritten when an existing workbook is inadvertently saved with new data rather than saved as a new workbook.

If you are part of a team that needs to create the same type of workbook repeatedly, it is a good idea to use templates to save time and ensure consistency in the design and content of your workbooks.

Setting Up a Workbook Template

Any workbook can be turned into a template by just deleting all its current data, leaving only the formulas and design elements. The data is left blank for end users to fill in later when they start creating their own documents.

Kendis is concerned that the restaurant managers may not complete their profit and loss reports in the same way, which makes it more difficult to combine their results in a summary workbook. Kendis has already created a workbook to use as a model for future reports and wants you to convert that workbook into a template. You'll open that workbook now.

To open Kendis's workbook:

1. Open the **NP_EX_5-2.xlsx** workbook located in the **Excel5 > Module** folder included with your Data Files.

2. Review the **Documentation**, **Store Number**, and **Terms and Definitions** worksheets. Do not make any changes to the contents of those sheets. Figure 5–25 shows the contents of the Store Number worksheet.

Figure 5-25   Template for profit and loss statements

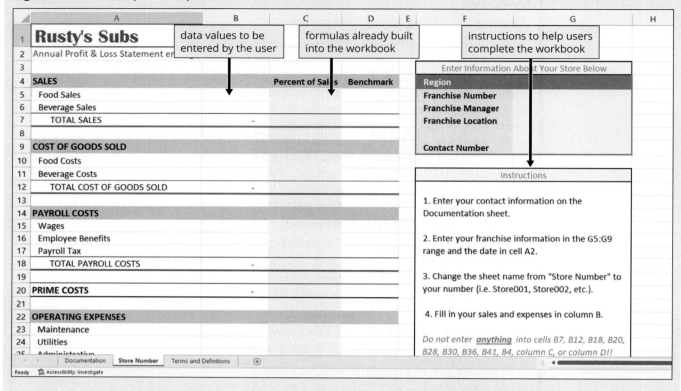

3. In each worksheet, scroll up to the top of the worksheet and click cell **A1**.

4. Click the **Documentation** sheet tab to make it the active sheet.

The Store Number worksheet contains the framework Kendis wants all stores to use for their profit and loss reports. It does not include data values because those will be entered by the franchise managers. However, the worksheet does include all the formulas required to calculate sales and expense totals as well as percentages. The formulas in the worksheet use the TOTAL_SALES defined name to make the formulas easier to understand. Kendis added detailed instructions about how the workbook should be filled out. Kendis's email address is included as a hyperlink in case users want help completing the workbook.

> **Tip** Good template designs assume users are not Excel experts and make it easy to fill out the workbook correctly.

Kendis wants you to convert this workbook into a template. When you save the workbook as a template, Excel will save the file to the user's Custom Office Templates folder. An icon for the template will appear in the New screen in Background view so users can easily create workbooks based on the template design. However, you can save a template to any folder you choose. You will save Kendis's workbook as a template to a different folder.

To save Kendis's workbook as a template:

1. On the ribbon, click the **File** tab to open Backstage view, and then in the navigation bar, click **Save As**. The Save As screen appears.

2. Click the **More options** link. The Save As dialog box opens.

3. In the File name box, type **NP_EX_5_PLStatement** as the file name for the template.

4. Click the **Save as type arrow**, and then click **Excel Template (*.xltx)** to save the file as a template. The default location for Excel templates, the Custom Office Templates folder, is displayed.

> **Tip** Excel template files have the .xltx file extension.

5. Navigate to the **Excel5 > Module** folder included with your Data Files.

6. Click **Save** to save the template, and then close the file.

Now that you have created the template file, your next step is to create a new workbook based on this template design.

Insight

Creating a Chart Template

Templates can also be created for Excel charts. These chart templates store customized chart designs that can be added as a new type in the chart gallery. Complete the following steps to save a chart template on your computer:

1. Create a chart, choosing the chart type and design of the chart elements.
2. Right-click the completed chart and click Save as Template on the shortcut menu.
3. Enter a name for the chart template file. All chart template files have the *.crtx file extension.
4. Save the chart template file. All chart templates are saved in the Microsoft > Templates > Charts folder within your user account on your computer.

Once you've saved the chart template file, it will appear as an option in the Recommended Charts dialog box, under the All Charts tab in the Templates folder. Select the chart template to apply it to the next chart you create.

Creating a Workbook Based on a Template

The great advantage of templates is that new workbooks are created based on the template design without altering the template file itself. As shown in Figure 5–26, each new workbook is a copy of the template design. Just as a blank workbook is named Book1, Book2, and so on based on the default "Book" template for new workbooks, files based on customized template are named *template*1, *template*2, and so on, where *template* is the file name of the original template file.

Figure 5–26   Workbooks created from a template

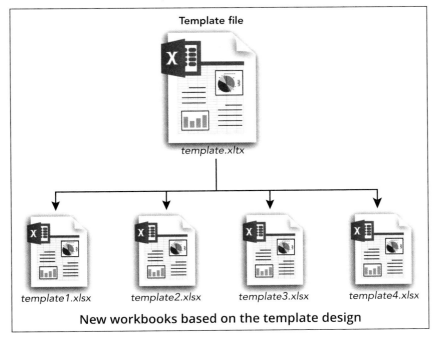

Template file

template.xltx

template1.xlsx   template2.xlsx   template3.xlsx   template4.xlsx

New workbooks based on the template design

There are two ways to create a workbook based on a template. If you save the template file to the Custom Office Templates folder, the template is always available on the New screen in Backstage view in the Personal section of the gallery of new file designs. Figure 5–27 shows how the NP_EX_5_PLStatement would appear in Backstage view.

Figure 5–27   New screen with templates

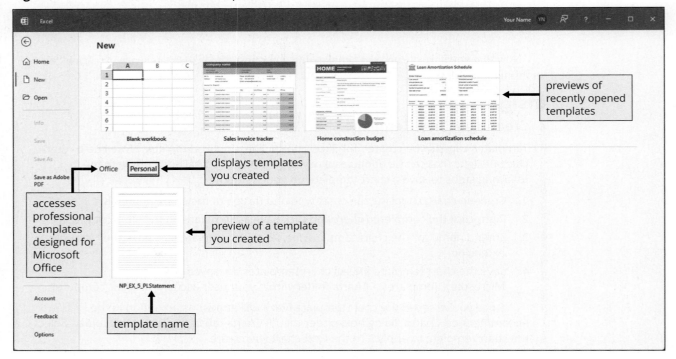

Clicking the template's icon in the gallery creates a new workbook based on the template design. You can also use one of the built-in templates displayed in the Featured gallery or use the Search box to search online for other templates created by professional designers.

When the template file is not stored in the Custom Office Templates folder, you can create a new workbook based on the template design by opening the template file from the File Explorer. You cannot use the Open screen in Backstage view of Excel because that would reopen the actual template file. Remember, you do not want users editing the template file. You only want to create new workbooks based on the template design.

Insight

Copying Styles Between Templates

Consistency is a hallmark of professional documents. If you want to reuse the styles that you created for the workbook but do not want to recreate the entire workbook, you can copy only the styles from that template. To copy styles from one template to another:

1. Open the template with the styles you want to copy.
2. Open the workbook or template in which you want to place the copied styles.
3. On the Home tab, in the Styles group, click the Cell Styles button, and then click Merge Styles. The Merge Styles dialog box opens, listing the currently open workbooks and templates.
4. Select the workbook or template with the styles you want to copy, and then click OK to copy those styles into the current workbook or template.
5. If a dialog box opens, asking if you want to "Merge Styles that have the same names?", click YES.
6. Save the workbook with the new styles as the Excel Template file type.

Copying template styles is much faster and more accurate than trying to recreate all those styles in a new workbook. However, the styles are not linked, so if you modify the design, you will have to recopy all the styles again.

You will create a new workbook from the NP_EX_5_PLStatement template, and then enter some test data.

To create a new workbook based on a PLStatement template:

1. Open **File Explorer** and navigate to the **Excel5 > Module** folder included with your Data Files.

2. Double-click the **NP_EX_5_PLStatement** template file. A workbook named NP_EX_5_PLStatement1 opens in the workbook window.

3. In the Documentation worksheet, enter your name and the date.

4. Go to the **Store Number** worksheet.

5. In cell **B5**, enter **2,210,000** for the food sales, and then in cell **B6**, enter **540,000** for the beverage sales.

6. In cell **B10**, enter **585,000** for the food costs, and then in cell **B11**, enter **210,000** for the beverage costs.

7. In cell **B15**, enter **635,000** for wages, in cell **B16**, enter **175,000** for employee benefits, and then in cell **B17**, enter **115,000** for payroll tax. The worksheet automatically calculates the total sales, the total cost of goods sold, the total payroll costs, and the percent of total sales for each number. Refer to Figure 5–28.

Figure 5–28   New workbook based on a template

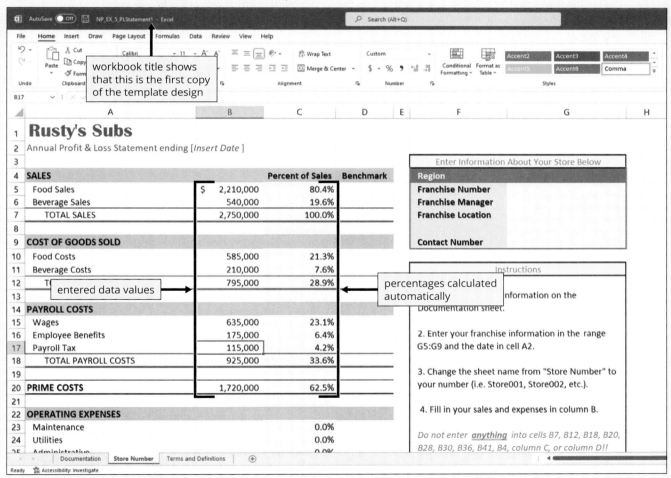

8. Save the workbook as **NP_EX_5_Sample** in the location specified by your instructor, and then close the workbook.

If you want to edit the template file, you can reopen the file from the Open screen in Backstage view. Any changes you make to the template file will not be reflected in workbooks already created based on earlier versions of the template.

Kendis appreciates your work on the template and will forward the template to the store managers so that they can base their next profit and loss statements on its design.

Part 5.3 Quick Check

1. Why is Report-Date not a valid named range?

2. What is the difference between a defined name with global scope and one with local scope?

3. If the range name SalesData references the range C2:C20 of the Sales worksheet with global scope, rewrite the following formula to use that range name:
   = SUM(Sales!C2:C20)

4. If the range name SalesData references the range C2:C20 of the Sales worksheet with local scope, rewrite the following formula to use that range name:
   = SUM(Sales!C2:C20)

5. Explain why you cannot have global scoped range names with the names TotalSales and TOTALSALES.

6. When would you create a template rather than just providing a coworker with the copy of your workbook?

7. What is displayed in the title bar for a workbook created from the EmployeeList.xltx template file?

8. By default, where does Excel store workbook templates?

Practice: Review Assignments

Data Files needed for the Review Assignments: NP_EX_5-3.xlsx, Support_EX_5_Akron.xlsx, Support_EX_5_Region1.xlsx, Support_EX_5_Region2.xlsx, Support_EX_5_Region3.xlsx, Support_EX_5_Region4.xlsx

Kendis wants to get a monthly sales and expense report from each location so that the company can catch issues early and offer suggestions to restaurants that are underperforming. Kendis started a summary workbook that will contain the collected data and needs you to finalize the workbook. Complete the following:

1. Open the **NP_EX_5-3.xlsx** workbook located in the Excel5 > Review folder included with your Data Files. Save the workbook as **NP_EX_5_Month** in the location specified by your instructor.

2. In the Documentation sheet, in the range B3:B4, enter your name and the date.

3. Change your name to a hyperlink pointing to your email address using the subject heading **Monthly Sales and Expenses Report** for the message and **Email me for more info** as the ScreenTip text.

4. Open the **Support_EX_5_Akron.xlsx** workbook located in the Excel5 > Review folder. Copy the Store008 worksheet into the NP_EX_5_Month workbook, placing the worksheet at the end of the workbook.

5. Create a worksheet group from the Store001 through Store008 worksheets. In the worksheet group, select the nonadjacent range A7:B7,A11:B11,A16:B16, and then create named ranges from the selection using the labels in the left column.

6. Use the Name Manager to change the TOTAL_COST_OF_GOODS_SOLD, TOTAL_PAYROLL_COSTS, and TOTAL_SALES named ranges for the Store001 worksheet from global scope to local scope by deleting those names and recreating them, limiting them to the scope of the Store001 worksheet. Verify in the Name Manager that all the defined names in the workbook have local scope.

7. In the range B5:C17 of the Store001 through Store008 worksheets, replace the cell references to cells B7, B11, and B16 with the TOTAL_SALES, TOTAL_COST_OF_GOODS_SOLD, and TOTAL_PAYROLL_COSTS defined names. You can either use the Apply Names command or find and replace the cell reference with the range name.

8. In the Region Report worksheet, in cell F5, use the SUM function to calculate the sum of cell B5 in the Store001 through Store008 worksheet group, displaying the total income from food sales.

9. Use AutoFill to extend the formula in cell F5 through the range F5:F17. Fill without formatting in the range. Delete the zeros in cells F8 and F12.

10. Open the **Support_EX_5_Region1.xlsx** file located in the Excel5 > Review folder. Copy the range B5:B17 of the Region 1 worksheet, and then use the Paste Link command to paste the external reference to the copied cells in the range B5:B17 of the Region Report worksheet. Delete the zeroes in cells B8 and B12.

11. Repeat Step 10 for the Region 2 through Region 4 data located in the **Support_EX_5_Region2.xlsx** through **Support_EX_5_Region4.xlsx** workbooks, pasting their external references in the ranges C5:C17, D5:D17, and E5:E17, respectively. Delete the zeroes in rows 8 and 12.

12. Copy the Store001 worksheet to a new workbook so you can create a template of the Sales and Expenses worksheet with all the data removed, but the formulas and formatting retained. Make the following changes to the workbook:
    a. Change the worksheet name to **Store Number**.
    b. Change the text of cell A2 to **[Region] Monthly Sales and Expenses**.
    c. Delete the data in the nonadjacent range **B5:B6, B9:B10, B13:B15, F4:F9**.
    d. From the Page Layout tab, go to the Themes group, click the Colors button, and change the design color to Red Orange.

13. Save the workbook as a template with the file name **NP_EX_5_SalesForm.xltx** in the location specified by your instructor.

14. Save and close all the workbooks.

Apply: Case Problem 1

Data Files needed for this Case Problem: NP_EX_5-4.xlsx, Support_EX_5_Dec.xlsx, Support_EX_5_MVPL2028.xlsx

Maple View Public Library Joan Wells is the executive director of the Maple View Public Library in Bowling Green, Kentucky. Each year the executive director presents a report to the trustees summarizing the year's total income and receipts and comparing the fiscal status of the library to budget projections. Joan wants your help in finalizing the Excel workbook, drawing data from multiple worksheets as well as the workbook used for the previous year's budget report. Complete the following:

1. Open the **NP_EX_5-4.xlsx** workbook located in the Excel5 > Review folder included with your Data Files, and then save the workbook as **NP_EX_5_MVPL2029.xlsx** in the location specified by your instructor.

2. In the Documentation sheet, in the range B3:B4, enter your name and the date.

3. Open the **Support_EX_5_Dec.xlsx** workbook and copy (not move) the Dec worksheet to the end of the NP_EX_5_MVPL2029 workbook.

4. Save the Support_EX_5_Dec.xlsx workbook as the template file **NP_EX_5_MVPLBudget.xltx** to a location specified by your instructor.

5. In the Dec worksheet, make the following changes in the template:
   a. In cell A2, change the text to **Monthly Receipts and Expenses**.
   b. Delete the data in the nonadjacent range C6:C9, C12:C17, C23:C30, C33:C38, C41:C45, C48:C50.
   c. Change the name of the worksheet to **Mon**.

6. Save the template workbook, and then close it.

7. Return the NP_EX_5_MVPL2029 workbook and go to the Annual worksheet. In cell C6, use the SUM function to calculate the total fines collected by the library in the current year by summing up the values of cell C6 in the Jan through Dec worksheets.

8. Copy the formula in cell C6 to the nonadjacent range C7:C9, C12:C17, C23:C30, C33:C38, C41:C45, C48:C50 using Paste Special to paste only the copied formulas and not the formats into the selected range to calculate the annual total for the other budget line items.

9. In cells C10, C18, C31, C39, C46, and C51, calculate the subtotals of each receipt and expense category.

10. In cell C19, calculate the total receipts by adding cell C10 and cell C18. In cell C52, calculate the total costs by adding cells C31, C39, C46, and C51. In cell C55, display the library's net income by calculating the difference of the total receipts in cell C19 and the total costs in cell C52.

11. In column E, calculate the difference between the 2029 Actuals in column C and the budgeted values in column D for every line item of the budget summary.

12. Joan wants to compare the 2029 Actuals with the 2028 Actuals to explore how receipts and expenses changed from the previous year. Open the **NP_EX_5_MVPL2028.xlsx** workbook, and then in the Annual worksheet, copy cell C6.

13. In the NP_EX_5_MVPL2029 workbook, use the Paste Link option to paste the copied content into cell F6 of the Annual worksheet. Edit the formula, changing the absolute cell reference $C$6 to a relative reference.

14. Use Paste Special to copy the formula only with no formatting in cell C6 to the nonadjacent range C7:C10, C12:C19, C23:C31, C33:C39, C41:C46, C48:C52, C55.

15. In cell G6, display the percent change from the 2028 Actuals to the 2029 Actuals by calculating the difference of cell C6 and F6 and dividing that difference by cell F6. Copy the formula in cell G6 to remaining budget items in column G, using Paste Special to paste only the formula and not the format.

16. In the Annual worksheet, assign the following range names:
   a. Assign the name **Actual_Total_Receipts** to cell C19.
   b. Assign the name **Budgeted_Total_Receipts** to cell D19.
   c. Assign the name **Actual_Total_Costs** to cell C52.
   d. Assign the name **Budgeted_Total_Costs** to cell D52.
   e. Assign the name **Actual_Net_Income** cell C55.
   f. Assign the name **Budgeted_Net_Income** to cell D55.

17. In the Summary worksheet, in the range B5:C7, use the range names you created in the previous step to the display the actual and budgeted figures for total receipts, total costs, and net income.

18. In the Annual worksheet, select the nonadjacent range B6:C9, B12:C17, B23:C30, B33:C38, B41:C45, B48:C50 and then use the Create from Selection button in the Defined Names group of the Formulas tab to create global range names from the account numbers in the left column.

19. Group the Jan through Dec worksheets, select the nonadjacent range B6:C9, B12:C17, B23:C30, B33:C38, B41:C45, B48:C50, and then use the Create from Selection button to create local range names from the account numbers in the left column of each monthly worksheet.

20. Return to the Summary worksheet. In cells H5 through H7, use the account numbers and the global range names for Fundraising, Utilities, and Wages to display the value of those 2,029 line items.

21. Save the NP_EX_5_MVPL2029.xlsx file, and then close it.

Challenge: Case Problem 2

Data Files needed for this Case Problem: NP_EX_5-5.xlsx, Support_EX_5_Fund01.xlsx, Support_EX_5_Fund02.xlsx, Support_EX_5_Fund03.xlsx, Support_EX_5_Fund04.xlsx, Support_EX_5_Fund05.xlsx

Granita Financial Jose Lupjic is an accounts manager at Granita Financial. Jose wants your help in developing a workbook to report on investments funds. In Jose's workbook, information on five funds has been entered into five worksheets. Eventually, Jose wants this workbook to contain dozens of worksheets with detailed information on funds handled by the company. As the number of worksheets increases, it will be cumbersome to scroll through the entire workbook to locate and view this data.

Instead, Jose wants to use range names and the INDIRECT function to retrieve and display information on specific investments based on their stock symbol so that the user only would need to type the symbol text into a single cell of a worksheet to view all the relevant statistics on the investment. The syntax of the INDIRECT function is:

```
INDIRECT(ref_text, [a1])
```

where ref_text is a text string providing the range reference and $a1$ is an optional argument specifying how that reference is written. You can learn more about the INDIRECT function in the Insight Box "Indirect Referencing" in this module or using Excel online help. Complete the following:

1. Open the **NP_EX_5-5.xlsx** workbook located in the Excel5 > Case2 folder included with your Data Files, and then save the workbook as **NP_EX_5_Granita** in the location specified by your instructor.

2. In the Documentation sheet, enter your name and the date in cells B3 and B4.

3. In the Reporter worksheet, select the range C4:D15, and then create global scope range names from the selection using the text in the left column.

4. Group the AIF through SNRFD worksheets, and then define the following range names:
   a. For the range A4:B15, create local scope range names from the selection using the text in the left column.
   b. For the range D4:F34, create local scope range names from the selection using the text in the top row.

5. Change Date, Closing, and Shares range names defined the AIF worksheet from global scope to local as follows:
   a. Ungroup the worksheets, and then go to the AIF worksheet.
   b. Using the Name Manager, delete the Date, Closing, and Shares range names, which have global (workbook) scope.
   c. Use the Name Manager to create new range names for Date, Closing, and Shares that have local scope limited to the AIF worksheet for the ranges D5:D34, E5:E34, and F5:F34, respectively.

6. **Explore:** In the Reporter worksheet, in cell D5, enter the following INDIRECT formula to return the name of the investment fund based on the current value of the Symbol range name:

```
=INDIRECT(Symbol&"!"&C5)
```

Confirm that the formula returns the text string "American Investment Fund". Note that the Symbol range name used in the formula references the AIF worksheet and C5 references the Morning_Star_Rating range name within that sheet.

7. Copy the formula from cell D5 into the range D6:D15, pasting the formula without formatting.

8. Change the value of cell D4 to IHGF, LTDX, ORTFD, and SNRFD, confirming that the descriptions in the range D5:D15 change with each investment fund. (Note: For your protection, cell D4 will only allow the fund symbols listed in the range A5:A9. Validation tests, often used for an app like this, are beyond the scope of this module.)

9. **Explore:** Range names can reference other range names using the INDIRECT function. You will create range names for Date, Closing, and Shares that will have global (workbook) scope, always pointing to the date, closing, and shares values from the worksheet matching the current value of the Symbol range name. Open the Name Manager and do the following:

    a. Create a **Date** range name with workbook scope, and then in the Refers to box, enter the following formula:

    ```
    = INDIRECT(Symbol&"!Date")
    ```

    b. Create a **Closing** range name with workbook scope, and then in the Refers to box, enter the following formula:

    ```
    = INDIRECT(Symbol&"!Closing")
    ```

    c. Create a **Shares** range name with workbook scope, and then in the Refers to box, enter the following formula:

    ```
    = INDIRECT(Symbol&"!Shares")
    ```

10. In the Reporter worksheet, in the 30-Day Summary table, enter the following formulas to summarize the performance of the investment over the previous month:

    a. In cell D18, enter the formula **=MIN(Date)** and in cell D19, enter the formula **=MAX(Date)** to show starting and ending dates of the 30-day window.

    b. In cells D20 through D22, enter the formulas **=MAX(Closing)**, **=MIN(Closing)**, and **=AVERAGE(Closing)** respectively to describe the closing values of the investment on each day.

    c. In cell D23, enter the formula **=AVERAGE(Shares)** to display average number of shares traded each day.

11. Change the value of cell D4 to one of the five symbols listed in the range A5:A9. Verify that the data in the 30-Day summary table changes to match the new symbol value. Note that the starting and ending dates will not change because those are the same for each of the five funds.

12. **Explore:** A data series within an Excel chart can reference a range name, but that range name must include the name of the workbook. The final part of the fund reporting app will modify the contents of the combination chart embedded in the Reporter worksheet. To make this chart a dynamic chart, do the following:

    a. Select the chart, and then on the Chart Design tab, click the Select Data button.

    b. In the Select Data Source dialog box, select Closing from the Series list, click Edit, and then change the entry in the Series value box to:

    ```
    = NP_EX_5_Granita.xlsx!Closing
    ```

    c. Select Shares from the Series list, click Edit, and then change the entry in the Series value box to:

    ```
    = NP_EX_5_Granita.xlsx!Shares
    ```

    d. Click the Edit button beneath the Horizontal (Category) Axis Labels box, and then change the Axis label range value to:

    ```
    = NP_EX_5_Granita.xlsx!Date
    ```

13. In the Reporter worksheet, change the symbol value in cell D4 to one of the five listed in the range A5:A9. Verify that the combo chart changes with each change in symbol. Enter **SNRFD** in cell D4 as the final symbol value.

14. **Explore:** In the Documentation worksheet, do the following:

    a. Click cell A8.

    b. On the Formulas tab, in the Defined Names group, click the Use in Formula button, and then click Paste Names.

    c. In the Paste Name dialog box, click Paste List to paste the names and references of all global scoped range names in the workbook.

15. Save the NP_EX_5_Granita.xlsx file, and then close it.

Managing Data with the Excel Data Tools

Analyzing Employee Data

Case: RevoluTEC

Amit Hadassah is a Human Resources (HR) analyst for RevoluTEC, a tech company specializing in the manufacture of integrated circuits and computer processors with offices in Atlanta, Houston, Phoenix, Pittsburgh, and Syracuse. As an HR analyst, Amit prepares employee reports involving a large amount of employee data, including information on salary, health benefits, and employee evaluations. You will help Amit finalize a workbook that provides an overview of the employee situation at RevoluTEC.

Starting Data Files

Excel6	Case1
Module	NP_EX_6-3.xlsx
NP_EX_6-1.xlsx	**Case2**
Review	NP_EX_6-4.xlsx
NP_EX_6-2.xlsx	

Objectives

Part 6.1

- Split a workbook window into panes
- Highlight and remove duplicate data
- Sort a data range by one or more fields
- Add subtotals to a data range
- Find and select workbook data

Part 6.2

- Filter data based on one or more fields
- Convert a data range to an Excel table
- Design an Excel table

Part 6.3

- Create and apply a slicer
- Calculate summary statistics from a table
- Design and create an interactive dashboard
- Create an advanced filter
- Apply the dynamic array functions

Part 6.1 Visual Overview: Data Ranges and Subtotals

The Split command in the Window group on the View tab divides the workbook window into separate areas. Each area is called a **pane**. This worksheet is divided into four panes.

A **split bar** separates one pane from another.

A **data range** is a data set that is organized into columns and rows representing fields and records, such as employee information.

Excel organizes subtotals using an outline that can be expanded or contracted to view or hide details about the data.

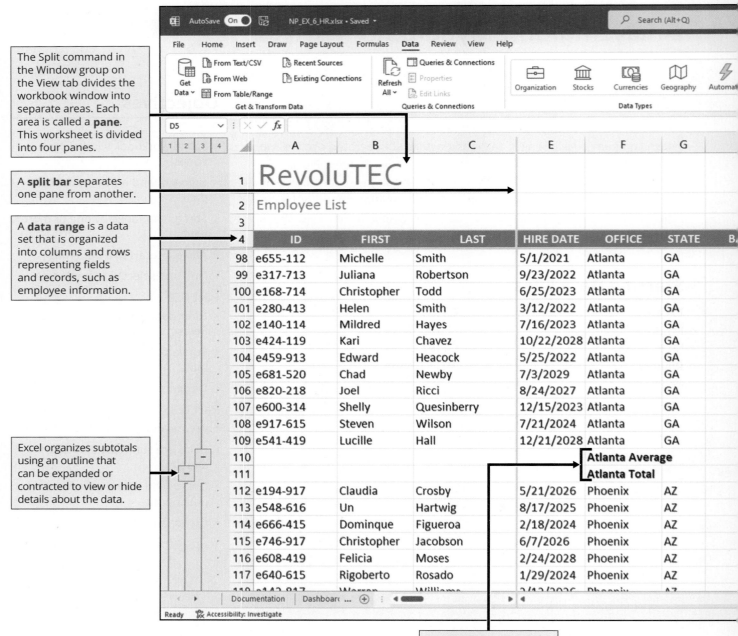

The Subtotal tool includes summary statistics for each group of records. These subtotals show the average and total by office location.

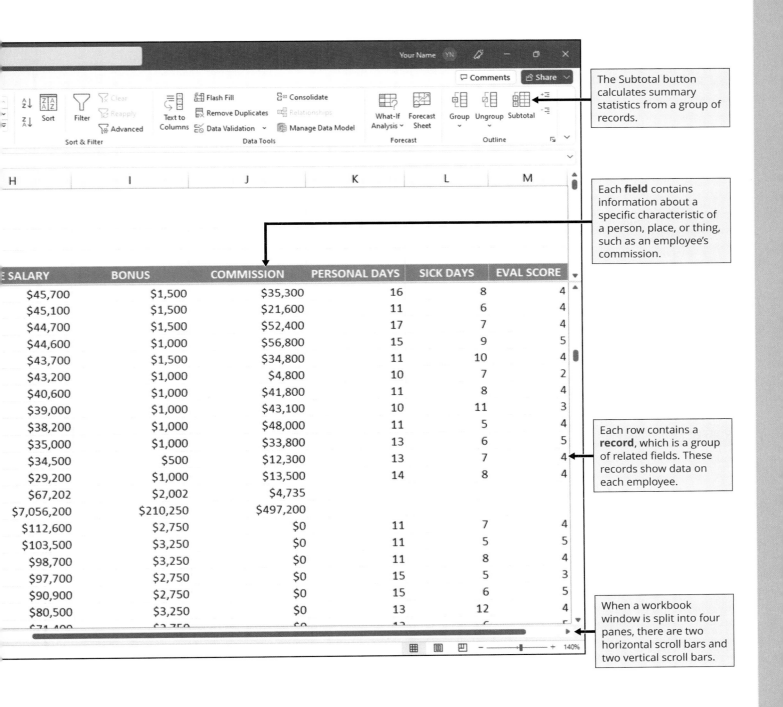

The Subtotal button calculates summary statistics from a group of records.

Each **field** contains information about a specific characteristic of a person, place, or thing, such as an employee's commission.

Each row contains a **record**, which is a group of related fields. These records show data on each employee.

When a workbook window is split into four panes, there are two horizontal scroll bars and two vertical scroll bars.

SALARY	BONUS	COMMISSION	PERSONAL DAYS	SICK DAYS	EVAL SCORE
$45,700	$1,500	$35,300	16	8	4
$45,100	$1,500	$21,600	11	6	4
$44,700	$1,500	$52,400	17	7	4
$44,600	$1,000	$56,800	15	9	5
$43,700	$1,500	$34,800	11	10	4
$43,200	$1,000	$4,800	10	7	2
$40,600	$1,000	$41,800	11	8	4
$39,000	$1,000	$43,100	10	11	3
$38,200	$1,000	$48,000	11	5	4
$35,000	$1,000	$33,800	13	6	5
$34,500	$500	$12,300	13	7	4
$29,200	$1,000	$13,500	14	8	4
$67,202	$2,002	$4,735			
$7,056,200	$210,250	$497,200			
$112,600	$2,750	$0	11	7	4
$103,500	$3,250	$0	11	5	5
$98,700	$3,250	$0	11	8	4
$97,700	$2,750	$0	15	5	3
$90,900	$2,750	$0	15	6	5
$80,500	$3,250	$0	13	12	4
$71,400	$3,750	$0	13	6	5

Managing Data in Excel

Excel has many data tools that companies use to manage data sets containing information about employees, sales, customer contacts, and financial transactions. Amit Hadassah relies on Excel to analyze data on the hundreds of employees who work full time for RevoluTEC across its various offices. You will open and review the data in Amit's workbook.

To open Amit's workbook of employee data:

1. **sam'** ⬇ Open the **NP_EX_6-1.xlsx** workbook located in the **Excel6 > Module** folder included with your Data Files, and then save the workbook as **NP_EX_6_HR** in the location specified by your instructor.

2. In the Documentation sheet, enter your name in cell B3 and the date in cell B4.

3. Review the contents of the worksheets in the NP_EX_6_HR workbook.

Amit's workbook contains worksheets that provide an overview of the employee situation at RevoluTEC. Amit has organized employee data into the following worksheets:

- **Evaluation**—Current and previous employee evaluations
- **Benefits**—Data on health care benefits, personal days, and sick days
- **Directory**—Contact information for each employee
- **Wages**—Data on salary, bonuses, and commissions
- **Demographics**—Data on each employee's age and date hired
- **Confidential**—Confidential salary data and the name of each employee
- **Wages**—A summary of each employee's total wages

Other worksheets are empty, and you will complete them throughout the module as you create an analysis for RevoluTEC. The data in each worksheet is organized into a rectangular range of cells, or data range. Figure 6–1 shows the current content of the Directory worksheet.

Figure 6–1   Directory worksheet

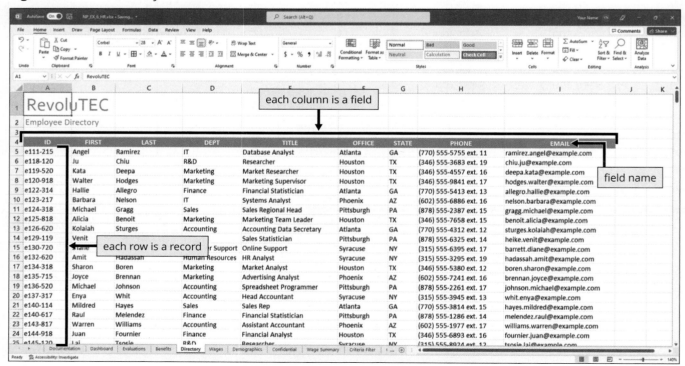

Each column of the data range stores information, known as a field, describing a characteristic of a person, place, or thing. Each row stores a data record containing a collection of field values. The first row of a data range, known as the **header row**, typically contains the names or labels associated with each field. Excel automatically recognizes data organized in this format and uses the labels from the header row to identify the fields in the data range. To avoid confusion with other worksheet content, a data range should be separated from other content by at least one blank row and one blank column.

The field names for the employee directory are stored in row 4 of columns A through I of the Directory worksheet. Amit included fields for employee ID, first name, last name, department, job title, office location, state, phone number, and email address. Each subsequent row contains the record of an individual employee.

A good practice is to include a **data definition table** describing each data range, including a list of the fields in the data range, the type of data stored in each field (such as numbers, text, or dates), a short description of the field, and any notes that would assist others in data entry. A properly constructed data definition table helps others to interpret the data stored in the workbook.

Amit entered data definition tables for all data ranges in the workbook. You will review that table to learn more about the data Amit has compiled.

To review the data definition tables for the employee data:

1. Go to the **Terms and Definitions** worksheet containing the data definition tables. Refer to Figure 6-2.

Figure 6-2   Terms and Definitions worksheet

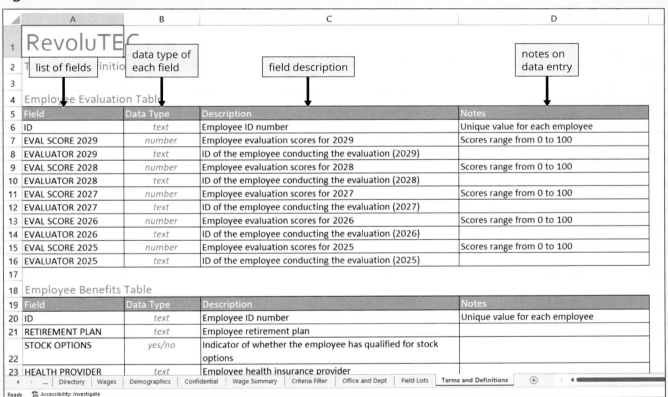

2. Review the information in the different fields.

Amit wants you to start by examining employee evaluations data, which is stored in the Evaluations worksheet.

Proskills

Written Communication: Planning for Data Entry

Before entering data, you should plan how that data should be structured to best achieve your goals. Those goals help to determine the fields needed for each record. Consider each of the following:

- **Who can access the data?** Some fields might contain confidential information accessible to a select few.
- **What questions do you want answered?** You collect data for a reason. Think about the types of questions you need to explore and how data helps you reach your conclusions.
- **What reports do you need to create?** Your answers will often be presented to others. Think about the reports that your audience (supervisors, colleagues, customers, and so forth) will need.
- **How is the data maintained?** Is the data generated daily, monthly, or in response to an event? Who is responsible for ensuring the data is updated and accurate?

After you have identified what data you need, you can set up the worksheet. Keep in mind the following guidelines:

- Use short field names that accurately describe the data, rather than long and cumbersome labels. If you need descriptive text, put it in a data definition table.
- Distinguish field names from data values using distinct colors and font styles.
- Break fields into single units of information, such as one field for the city name and another field for the state name.
- Separate the data from other workbook content. It is often best if you keep your data in one worksheet and your calculations and analysis in a separate worksheet.

Finally, whenever possible, avoid duplicate data entry. If the same data is entered multiple times, it increases the possibility that a data entry error will occur. Consider using 3D cell address to reference the same data multiple times rather than entering the same data multiple times.

With careful planning, you can avoid data entry errors and the expensive and time-consuming task of redesigning a workbook after others have begun data entry.

Using Panes to Navigate Data

The data in the Evaluation worksheet spans 11 columns and 534 rows. When data spans that large of a range, it will extend well beyond the workbook window. But even that is not a large worksheet in the business world where a typical worksheet might cover several dozen columns and thousands of rows. One way to efficiently navigate a large worksheet is with panes.

Dividing the Workbook Window into Panes

Panes divide the workbook into separate sections, each of which can display a different part of a large and extended data range. Worksheets can be split into as many as four panes. Once the worksheet is in panes, split bars appear in the workbook window to divide the workbook window along the top and left border of the selected cell or range. By scrolling through the contents of individual panes, you can compare cells from different sections of a large worksheet within the same workbook window.

Reference

Splitting the Workbook Window into Panes

- To split the workbook window into four panes, click any cell or range, and then click the Split button in the Window group on the View tab.
- To split the window into two vertical panes, select a cell in the first row, and then click the Split button.
- To split the window into two horizontal panes, select a cell in the first column, and then click the Split button.
- To close the panes and return to one window, click the Split button again.

The Evaluations worksheet contains data on current employee evaluations as well as evaluations going back four years. Each evaluation is recorded as a score on the 0 to 100 scale alongside the ID of the supervisor who made the evaluation. Amit wants to compare the 2029 evaluation scores to scores from three and four years prior. To make that comparison, you will split the worksheet into four panes.

To split the Evaluations worksheet into panes:

1. Go to the **Evaluations** worksheet, and then click cell **D5** to select it.

2. On the ribbon, click the **View** tab, and then in the Window group, click the **Split** button (or press **ALT,W,S**). Two split bars divide the workbook window into four panes with two sets of scroll bars along the horizontal and vertical edges of the workbook window.

3. Drag the **lower vertical scroll bar** down until row 70 is aligned with the horizontal split bar. Notice that scrolling is synchronized between the lower-left and lower-right panes so that both panes show the same rows.

   Tip To resize the panes, point to a pane split bar, and then use the double-headed split arrow to drag the split bar to a new location.

4. Drag the **right horizontal scroll bar** until column H is aligned with the vertical split bar. Scrolling between the upper-right and lower-right panes is also synchronized so that both panes show the same columns. Note that there are blank cells for employees who do not have evaluations from 2026 or 2025. Refer to Figure 6–3.

Figure 6–3   Workbook window split into four panes

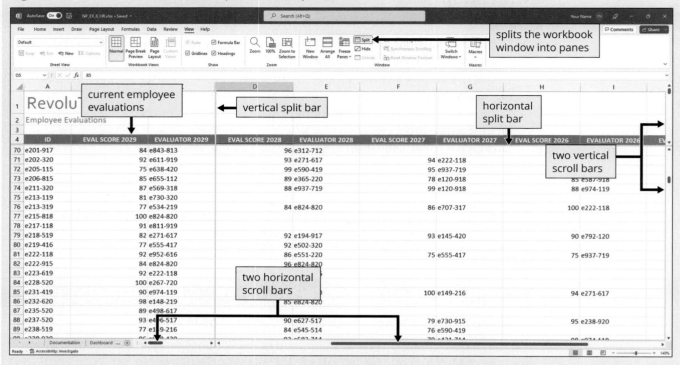

5. Continue to drag the **lower vertical scroll bar** down until row 534 appears in the workbook window.

With the workbook window split into four panes, you can compare different field values within a record. For example, note that in Figure 6–3, the latest evaluation for employee e202-320 (row 71) is 92, much higher than the 81 and 77 scores given previously. On the other hand, the evaluation for employee e213-319 (row 76) has dropped to 77 from a previous score of 100, which might indicate issues that the supervisor will want to investigate. Identifying this information without panes would be much more difficult because scrolling through the workbook window would hide the employee IDs and the current evaluation scores.

Splitting the workbook window affects only the active sheet or worksheet group. Other sheets will still be displayed in a workbook window containing one pane. To return the workbook window to a single pane, click the Split button again in the Window group on the View tab.

Freezing Panes

Another way of displaying different sections of a worksheet is by freezing panes. When you **freeze** a pane, its contents are locked on the screen though you can scroll within it. You can freeze the panes located above and to the left of a selected cell, allowing scrolling within the lower-right pane. This is commonly used with large data ranges to keep the field names and select fields always in view while the other data fields and records are free for scrolling. You can also freeze only the top row of the worksheet, allowing scrolling for subsequent rows. Or, you can freeze the first column of the worksheet, allowing scrolling across subsequent columns.

Reference

Freezing Window Panes

- To split the workbook window into four panes with the top and left panes frozen, click the cell where you want to freeze panes to the top and left, and then on the View tab, in the Window group, click the Freeze Panes button and click Freeze Panes.
- To freeze the top row of the worksheet, click the Freeze Panes button, and then click Freeze Top Row.
- To freeze the first column of the worksheet, click the Freeze Panes button, and then click Freeze First Column.
- To remove the frozen panes, click the Freeze Panes button, and then click Unfreeze Panes.

The Benefits worksheet contains extensive data on each employee's benefits package as well as the number of personal and sick days used and remaining in the current year. Amit wants to review only the data on personal days and sick days. To keep the field names and the employee ID always in view, you will freeze the first four rows of the worksheet and the first column.

To freeze rows and columns in the Benefits worksheet:

1. Go to the **Benefits** worksheet and click cell **B5** to select it.

2. On the View tab, in the Window group, click the **Freeze Panes** button, and then click **Freeze Panes** on the menu that appears below the button. Narrow dividing lines appear between columns A and B and rows 4 and 5. The worksheet has only one set of scroll bars.

   > **Tip** To unfreeze the panes, click the Freeze Pane button in the Window group on the View tab, and then click Unfreeze Panes on the menu.

3. Scroll down to row 210 and scroll to the right so that column G is displayed next to column A. As you scroll through the worksheet, the contents of the first four rows and first column remain locked in place. Refer to Figure 6–4.

Figure 6–4   Benefits worksheet with frozen panes

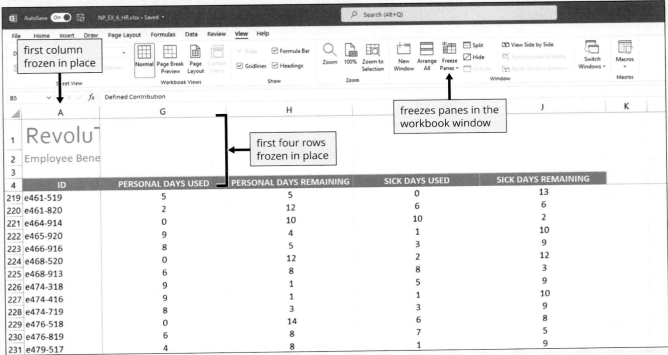

Using freeze panes, you can quickly associate each employee ID with personal and sick days used and unused. note that in Figure 6–4, the employee with ID e464-914 (row 221) has all 10 personal days remaining but has used 10 sick days with 2 remaining.

Locating Duplicate Records

Data entry errors are an almost unavoidable problem when dealing with large data sets. One common error is creating a duplicate record so that the same data appears multiple times in a data range. Duplicate records can occur when several people enter data into a worksheet or when data is combined from multiple sources. To resolve this issue, Excel provides tools to find and remove duplicates. One approach is to use conditional formatting.

Highlighting Duplicate Values

Conditional formatting can help locate duplicates by highlighting duplicated values within a selected range. Once you have located a duplicate, you can decide whether that entire record needs to be edited or deleted.

Reference

Highlighting Duplicate Values Within a Range

- Select the range you want to locate duplicate values within.
- On the Home tab, in the Styles group, click the Conditional Formatting button.
- On the conditional formatting menu, point to Highlight Cells Rules, and then click Duplicate Values.
- In the Duplicate Values dialog box, specify the highlighting style for duplicate values.
- Click OK.

Amit received the contents of the Directory worksheet from a colleague, but suspects that it contains some data entry errors and duplicate records. You will use conditional formatting to locate any records containing duplicate employee IDs.

To highlight duplicate employee IDs in the Directory worksheet:

1. Go to the **Directory** worksheet.

2. Click the **Name** box, type **A5:A538** as the range to select, and then press **ENTER**. All the ID values in column A are selected.

3. On the ribbon, click the **Home** tab. In the Styles group, click the **Conditional Formatting** button, point to **Highlight Cell Rules**, and then click **Duplicate Values**. The Duplicate Values dialog box opens.

4. Click **OK**. Cells that contain duplicate values are formatted with a light red fill with dark red text.

5. Scroll down the worksheet until rows 38 and 39 appear in the workbook window. The red formatting in cells A38 and A39 highlight that these two employees have duplicate ID numbers. Refer to Figure 6–5.

Figure 6-5   Conditional formatting highlights cells with duplicate values

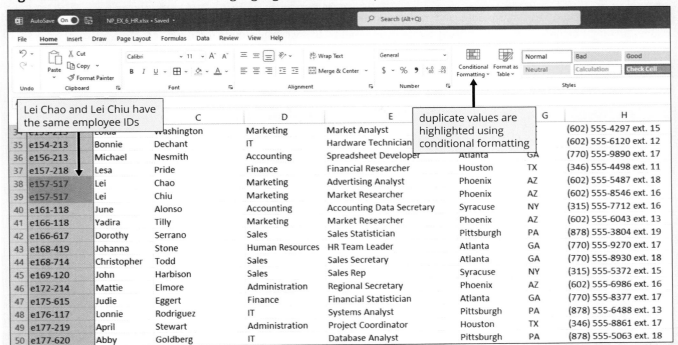

Lei Chiu's ID should have been entered as e157-617 and not e157-517. You will correct this mistake.

6. Click cell **A39**, and then enter **e157-617** as the ID value. Highlighting disappears from cells A38 and A39 because those IDs are no longer duplicates.

> **Tip** The conditional formatting rule will highlight duplicate values even if they are not adjacent to each other.

7. Scroll down the worksheet until the next set of highlighted duplicate IDs appear in the workbook window. In rows 86 through 88, the employee record for Marissa Schock is repeated three times. The directory should have only one record per employee.

8. Drag the pointer over the **row 87** and **row 88** row headers to select both rows.

9. Right-click the selected rows, and then click **Delete** on the shortcut menu. These rows are removed from the worksheet and highlighting disappears from row 86.

10. Scroll down the worksheet to rows 295 and 296. The employee record for James Orozco is duplicated.

11. Right-click the **row 296** row header, and then click **Delete** on the shortcut menu. Row 296 is removed from the worksheet and highlighting disappears from row 295.

12. Scroll down the worksheet to verify that no other IDs are duplicated.

13. Scroll back up to row 296, and then click cell **A295** to select it.

James Orozco is listed in both row 295 and row 296, but the row 295 record has an employee ID of e575-716 and the row 296 record has an ID of e575-761. Although it is not uncommon in a large company to have employees with the same name, these two records are completely identical except for the IDs. It would be extremely unlikely that two James Orozcos were hired to the same position in the same city with the same phone number and email address. These are duplicate records in which the wrong ID was entered for one of the records, resulting in two records for the same employee. The second record has the incorrect employee ID and should be deleted. However, Amit is concerned that the worksheet may contain other duplicates like this.

Removing Duplicate Records

Conditional formatting can locate duplicate records when the duplicates occur in a single field. It cannot highlight records that are duplicated across several fields. In a worksheet with thousands of records, it would be extremely time-consuming to compare every field from every record. Instead, you can use the Remove Duplicates tool to locate and delete records that are duplicated across multiple fields. Excel keeps the first instance of any duplicate records it finds and automatically deletes subsequent duplicates.

Reference

Removing Duplicate Records from a Data Range

- Click any cell in the data range.
- On the Data tab, in the Data Tools group, click the Remove Duplicates button.
- Select the check boxes for the fields that you want to check for duplicates.
- Click OK to remove records containing duplicates of all the selected fields.

Amit asks you to remove records in which *all* field values are duplicated except for the employee ID because it is extremely unlikely that two employees share every other possible employee characteristic. You will use the Remove Duplicates tool to remove those duplicate records.

To find and delete duplicate records:

1. On the ribbon, click the **Data** tab, and then in the Data Tools group, click the **Remove Duplicates** button ▣. The Remove Duplicates dialog box opens. All the employee data in the Directory worksheet is selected, and the dialog box lists the column labels from the header row to identify the field names (ID through EMAIL).

   Trouble? If the Remove Duplicates Warning dialog box appears, verify that the Expand the selection option is selected, and then click Remove Duplicates.

2. Click the **ID** check box to deselect it, and then verify that every other field check box is selected. You deselected the ID field because you want to delete duplicate records in which only the ID value is different while all other field values are identical. Refer to Figure 6–6.

Figure 6–6   Remove Duplicates dialog box

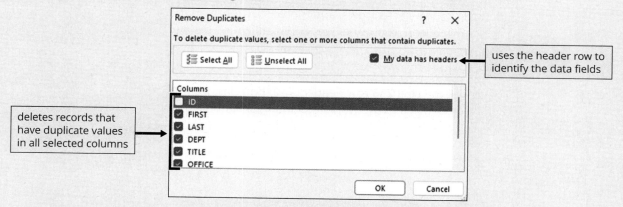

3. Click **OK** to remove the duplicate records. A dialog box opens, indicating that 1 duplicate record was found and deleted, leaving 530 unique records in the data range.

4. Click **OK** to close the dialog box and return to the worksheet.

5. Scroll to row **295** and verify that only one record exists for James Orozco.

   Tip If you delete records by mistake, click the Undo button on the Quick Access Toolbar (or press CTRL+Z).

Be *extremely cautious* when using the Remove Duplicates tool! You are *not* prompted to confirm deletion of duplicate records. Make sure that you are deleting records based only on fields that should *never* be completely duplicated. For example, you would not want to delete records with the same first and last names because two people can share the same name. But, if all other field values are identical, then a duplicate record almost certainly exists.

Sorting Records in a Data Range

Data records appear in the order in which they are entered. You can gain valuable insights into data by arranging the records by one or more chosen fields. Fields can be sorted in **ascending order** so that text entries are arranged alphabetically from A to Z, numeric values from smallest to largest, and date and time values from oldest to most recent. You can also sort the data in **descending order** so that text entries are sorted from Z to A, numeric values from largest to smallest, and dates and times from most recent to oldest.

In all the worksheets, the data records are entered in ascending order of employee ID number. Amit often finds it useful to have employee records organized by offices and departments. You can make that change by sorting the data values.

Sorting by a Single Field

To sort a data range by a field, select any cell within a column, and then on the Data tab in the Sort & Filter group, click the Sort A to Z ↕️ to sort the data in ascending order of the field. To sort the data in descending order of that field, click the Sort Z to A button ↕️. Sorting does not change the data; it merely reorders the records. Excel recognizes the data types in the selected field, so that text values are always sorted alphabetically, numbers are sorted numerically, and date and time values are always sorted by date and time.

Reference

Sorting Records in a Data Range

To sort by a single field:

- Click any cell in the field you want to sort by.
- On the Data tab, in the Sort & Filter group, click the Sort A to Z button or click the Sort Z to A button.

To sort records by multiple fields:

- Click any cell in the data range you want to sort.
- On the Data tab, in the Sort & Filter group, click the Sort button to open the Sort dialog box.
- Click the Sort by arrow and select a field to sort by. Click the Order arrow and select how the field should be sorted.
- For each additional field you want to sort by, click the Then by arrow to add a new row, click the Sort arrow and select a field, and then click the Order arrow and select how the field should be sorted.
- Click OK.

Amit wants to analyze employee wages. You will start by sorting the data in the Wages worksheet to determine which employees have the lowest and the highest base salaries.

To sort the wage data in descending order of the base salary:

1. Go to the **Wages** worksheet.

2. Click cell **E5** to select a cell within the Base Salary column.

    > **Tip** You can also click the Sort & Filter button in the Editing group on the Home tab to sort records by values in a single column.

3. On the Data tab, in the Sort & Filter group, click the **Sort Z to A** button ⫬. The records are rearranged in descending order of the Base Salary field with the highest paid employees listed first. Refer to Figure 6–7.

Figure 6–7   Data sorted based on a single column

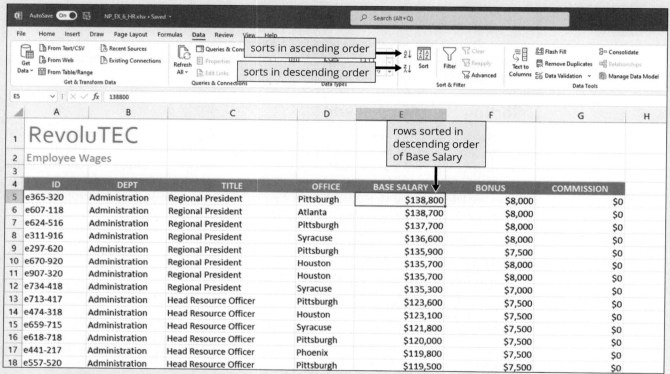

4. Scroll down the worksheet to verify that the values in the Base Salary column appear in descending order, ending with the employees with the lowest annual base salaries.

The sorted records show that the highest paid employees are the regional presidents followed by head resource officers and administrators. The highest paid employee has a base salary of $138,800 (row 5) while the lowest paid employee—an online support person in the Houston office—is paid $27,000 per year (row 534).

Sorting by Multiple Fields

The Sort A to Z and Sort Z to A buttons provide a fast way to sort data, but they are limited to sorting the data one field at a time. To sort by multiple fields, you need to use the Sort dialog box. With sorts involving multiple fields or columns, identify one field as the **primary sort field** for initially sorting the data and then a second field as the **secondary sort field** for sorting data within the primary sort field. You can continue this process by identifying a third sort field for values within values of the first two fields and so forth. Excel supports 64 levels of sort fields, so you can continue to add more sorting levels as needed. However, you probably will not use more than three for most reports.

Amit wants to organize the employee records in the Wages worksheet first by office, then by department, and finally by descending order of base salary within department. Once the data is sorted, Amit can compare salaries within departments and offices. You will use sort by multiple fields to reorder the records in the Wages worksheet.

To sort the employee data by the Office, Dept, and Base Salary fields:

1. On the Data tab, in the Sort & Filter group, click the **Sort** button. The Sort dialog box opens. The selected data range is currently set to sort in descending order of the Base Salary field. You will change that that first sort field to the Office field.

   > **Tip** You must have at least one cell selected in the data range before you click the Sort button.

2. Click the **Sort by arrow** to display a list of fields in the data range, and then click **OFFICE** in the list. The first sort is now set the Office field.

3. Click the **Order arrow** to display the sort order options, and then click **A to Z** to sort the data in ascending order of office name. The first sort level is complete.

4. Click the **Add Level** button. A second sort level is added to the sort.

5. Click the **Then by arrow**, and then click **DEPT** to sort the values by department within office location. The sort order is already ascending, so you do not need to change it.

6. Click the **Add Level** button to add a third sort level, click its **Then by arrow** and click **BASE SALARY** to add the Base Salary as the third sort field, and then click its **Order arrow** and click **Largest to Smallest** to change the sort order to descending. Refer to Figure 6–8.

Figure 6–8   Sort dialog box with three sorted fields

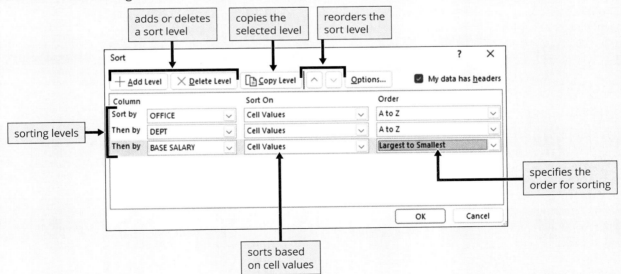

7. Click **OK** to sort the data in the Wages worksheet.

8. Scroll down the worksheet and verify that the data is sorted in ascending order by Office, then ascending order by department name within each office, and finally in descending order by base salary within each department. Refer to Figure 6–9.

Figure 6-9   Records sorted by the Office, Dept, and Base Salary fields

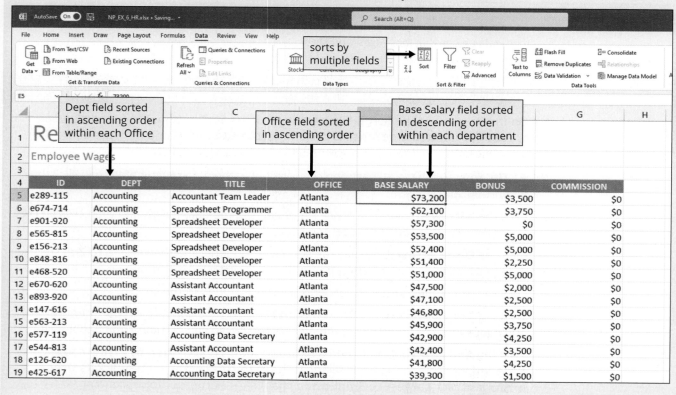

Using the sort data, Amit knows the range of base salaries within each department and within each office. For example, the highest paid employee in the Atlanta Accounting department is the accountant team leader (row 5) and the lowest paid employee in that department is the accountant data secretary (row 19).

Insight

Choosing Sort Options

Typically, you sort data based on field values. You can also sort data based on formatting, such as sorting the cells by the fill color, font color, or conditional formatting. To choose a different way of sorting, click the Sort On arrow in the Sort dialog box and select how you want the cells sorted.

All sorts assume that records are in rows and sort the data from top to bottom. If the records are in columns, you can change the sort orientation to sort the records from left to right. To do this, click the Options button in the Sort dialog box and change the orientation.

The default option for sorting text fields is to ignore capitalization so that values like "Chicago" and "CHICAGO" are treated the same. To identify different capitalizations as unique entries, click the Options button in the Sort dialog box, and then click the Case Sensitive check box. If the records are sorted in ascending order, lowercase letters will be displayed first. For example, Chicago will come before CHICAGO.

Sorting with a Custom List

So far, you have sorted data in ascending or descending order. However, some types of text data have their own special sort order. For example, Excel sorts the months of January February, March, and so forth in time order, not alphabetically. Excel applies this same sorting order to the abbreviated month names, Jan, Feb, Mar, and so forth. The days of the week (Sunday, Monday, Tuesday,…)

also have a sort order that is neither alphabetical nor numeric. The Sort dialog box already includes sort order options for month and day names. For other data types you can create a **custom list** that arranges the field values in the order you specify.

Amit wants you to sort the RevoluTEC offices in the order they opened rather than alphabetically. Each office opened in a different year: Phoenix in 2022, Syracuse in 2023, Pittsburgh in 2025, and Houston in 2027. You will create a custom list of those city names in the order the offices were established and use it to sort the employee data.

To create and apply a custom list of city names for sorting:

1. On the Data tab, in the Sort & Filter group, click the **Sort** button. The Sort dialog box opens.

2. In the Office field row, click the **A to Z** box, and then click **Custom List**. The Custom Lists dialog box opens.

3. Click **Add** to begin a new custom list.

4. In the List Entries box, type **Atlanta** and press **ENTER**. Atlanta is added to the List Entries box.

   ▌ **Tip** Any custom list can be sorted in either ascending or descending order.

5. Type the following city names, pressing **ENTER** after each name: **Phoenix**, **Syracuse**, **Pittsburgh**, and **Houston**. Refer to Figure 6–10.

Figure 6–10   Custom Lists dialog box

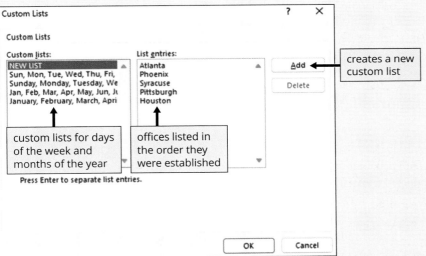

6. Click **OK** to create the list and return to the Sort dialog box. The Order box for the Office field shows the custom sort order: Atlanta, Phoenix, Syracuse, Pittsburgh, and Houston.

7. Click **OK** to apply this sort order to the employee data.

8. Scroll down the Wages worksheet and verify that employees are sorted in the new order with Atlanta employees listed first and Houston employees listed last.

Custom lists become part of your Excel settings, making them available to all your workbooks. A custom list can be used for tasks other than sorting. For example, the AutoFill tool will automatically fill in data based on a custom list. When you no longer need a custom list, you can remove it from the workbook. You will remove the city names custom list.

To delete the city names custom list:

1. On the Data tab, in the Sort & Filter group, click the **Sort** button. The Sort dialog box opens.

2. In the Office field row, click the **Atlanta**, **Phoenix**, **Syracuse**, **Pittsburgh**, **Houston** box, and then click **Custom List**. The Custom Lists dialog box opens.

3. In the Custom lists box, click **Atlanta**, **Phoenix**, **Syracuse**, **Pittsburgh**, **Houston**. The offices appear in the List entries box. You could edit the list entries if needed. Instead, you want to delete the entire list.

4. Click **Delete** to delete the custom list, and then click **OK** in the dialog box that opens to confirm that you want to permanently delete this custom list.

5. Click **OK** in each dialog box to return to the Wages worksheet.

Even though you removed this custom list, the employee data is still sorted in the order that the RevoluTEC offices opened. The sort order will remain unchanged until you sort the data in a different way.

Calculating Subtotals

With a large set of data, it is often helpful to add **subtotals**, which are summary functions applied to a part of a data range. You can use subtotals to calculate the total salaries or the average salary within each office or department. To calculate a subtotal, the data must first be sorted, which you have already done. The Subtotal tool will then insert a new row of subtotal calculations wherever the sort field changes value.

Reference

Adding a Subtotal to a Data Range

- Sort the data range by the field where you want to place the subtotal values.
- On the Data tab, in the Outline group, click the Subtotal button.
- Click the At each change in arrow and select the field where the subtotals will be added to the data range.
- Click the Use function arrow and select the summary function to use in the subtotal calculation.
- In the Add subtotal to box, select the fields for which the subtotal will be calculated.
- Click OK to generate the subtotals.
- Use the outline buttons on the worksheet to expand and collapse groups within the data range.

Amit wants you to provide summary statistics for the sorted base salary data. You will use the Subtotal button to calculate the total of the Base Salary, Bonus, and Commission fields within each office.

To calculate the salary subtotal for each office:

1. On the Data tab, in the Outline group, click the **Subtotal** button. The Subtotal dialog box opens.

2. Click the **At each change in arrow**, and then click **OFFICE** in the list of fields to specify adding a subtotal for each Office field value.

3. If necessary, click the **Use function arrow**, and then click **Sum** to calculate the sum at each change in the Office field.

4. In the Add subtotal to box, if necessary, click the **BASE SALARY**, **BONUS**, and **COMMISSION** check boxes to select them.

5. Verify that the **Replace current subtotals** and **Summary below data** check boxes are selected. Refer to Figure 6–11.

Figure 6–11   Subtotal dialog box

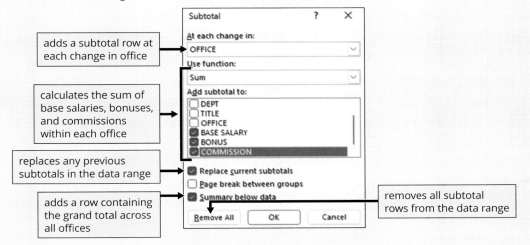

adds a subtotal row at each change in office

calculates the sum of base salaries, bonuses, and commissions within each office

replaces any previous subtotals in the data range

adds a row containing the grand total across all offices

removes all subtotal rows from the data range

6. Click **OK** to generate the subtotal rows.

7. Scroll down the worksheet to review the total spent on base salaries, bonuses, and commissions at the Atlanta office. Refer to Figure 6–12.

Figure 6–12   Subtotal row added to a data range

	A	B	C	D	E	F	G
97	e681-520	Sales	Sales Supervisor	Atlanta	$69,700	$5,000	$43,100
98	e502-320	Sales	Sales Supervisor	Atlanta	$57,200	$2,500	$47,800
99	e459-913	Sales	Sales Rep	Atlanta	$47,800	$3,250	$41,800
100	e541-419	Sales	Sales Rep	Atlanta	$47,200	$5,000	$13,500
101	e385-413	Sales	Sales Rep	Atlanta	$46,700	$5,000	$21,200
102	e507-915	Sales	Sales Rep	Atlanta	$45,300	$5,000	$30,000
103	e140-114	Sales	Sales Rep	Atlanta	$44,600	$3,750	$34,800
104	e317-713	Sales	Sales Rep	Atlanta	$44,600	$2,500	$21,600
105	e280-413	Sales	Sales Rep	Atlanta	$44,100	$5,000	$56,800
106	e424-119	Sales	Sales Statistician	Atlanta	$38,700	$1,500	$0
107	e600-314	Sales	Sales Secretary	Atlanta	$37,000	$1,500	$0
108	e917-615	Sales	Sales Statistician	Atlanta	$34,600	$1,000	$0
109	e820-218	Sales	Sales Secretary	Atlanta	$33,800	$1,000	$0
110	e168-714	Sales	Sales Secretary	Atlanta	$33,000	$1,000	$0
111				**Atlanta Total**	$5,361,300	$364,450	$345,900
112	e194-917	Accounting	Accountant Supervisor	Phoenix	$82,200	$7,000	$0
113	e545-514	Accounting	Accountant Team Leader	Phoenix	$78,200	$6,000	$0
114	e232-620	Accounting	Accountant Team Leader	Phoenix	$76,500	$6,000	$0

Subtotal row inserted at the change in Office value

totals spent on base salaries, bonuses, and commissions in the Atlanta office

8. Continue to scroll down the worksheet to review the subtotals for offices in Phoenix, Syracuse, Pittsburgh, and Houston. Row 540 at the bottom of data range shows the grand total spent on commissions across all five offices.

The subtotal rows show that the Atlanta office spent $5,361,300 on base salaries, $364,450 on bonuses, and $345,900 on commissions. Other offices have similar totals. The grand total in row 540 shows that the entire company spent $28,551,700 on base salaries, $1,965,450 on bonuses, and $1,708,200 on commissions.

You can include several summary statistics in the subtotals row. Amit wants this report to also include the average employee compensation in each office and across all offices. You will add the AVERAGE function to the subtotal report.

To add a second summary statistic to the employees subtotals:

1. On the Data tab, in the Outline group, click the **Subtotal** button. The Subtotal dialog box opens.

2. Click the **Use function arrow**, and then click **Average** in the list of summary statics.

3. Click the **Replace current subtotals** check box to deselect it, ensuring that the averages are added to the current subtotal values instead of replacing them.

> **Key Step** Be sure to uncheck the Replace current subtotals check box so new statistics do not overwrite the current ones.

4. Click **OK** to add an average calculation to the subtotals.

5. Scroll down the worksheet and verify that each office shows the average and the total amount RevoluTEC spends on employee compensation.

6. Increase the width of column D to **20 characters** so that the column displays the complete text of the subtotal labels. Refer to Figure 6–13.

Figure 6–13   Sums and averages for the subtotal rows

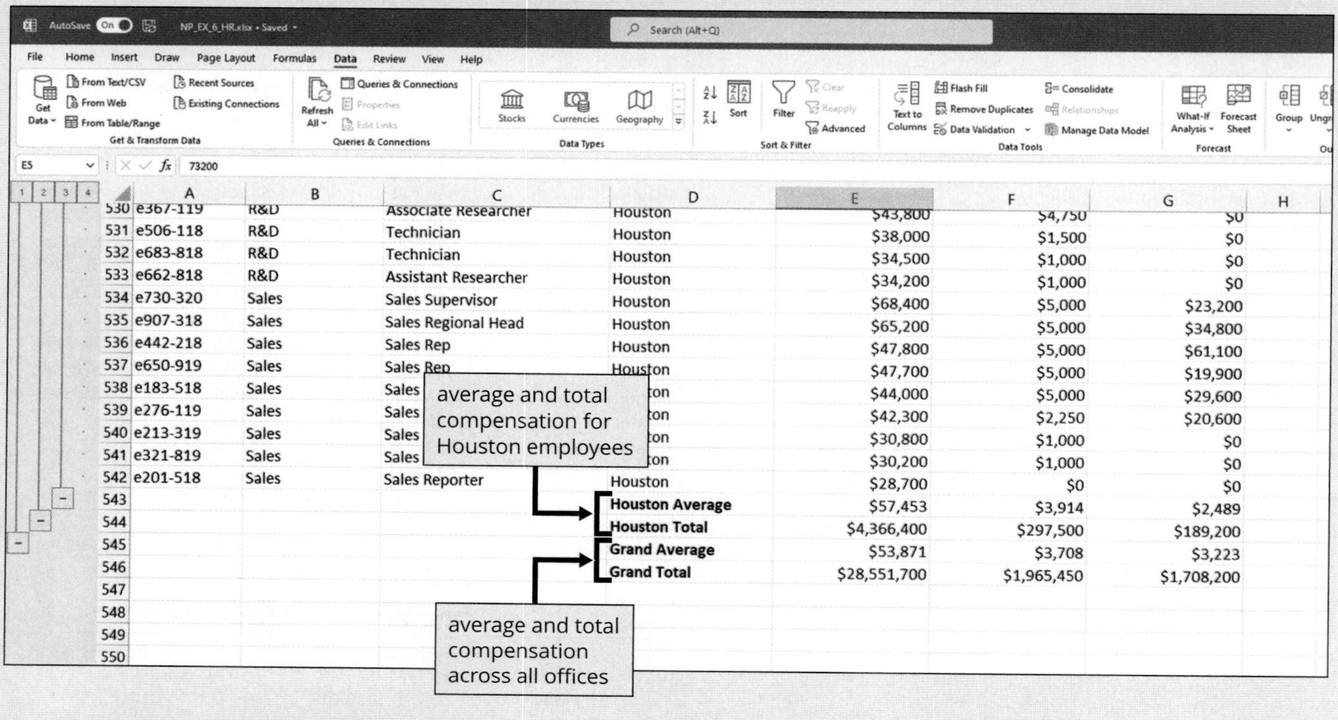

7. Scroll to the top of the Wages worksheet.

The subtotals let Amit know that across all offices, RevoluTEC pays its employees an average of $53,871 in base salary, $3,708 in bonuses, and $3,223 in commissions.

Using the Subtotal Outline View

Rather than display detailed information for every employee record, you might want to view only summary statistics. The outline tool lets you control the level of detail displayed in the worksheet. The Wages worksheet has four levels in the outline of its data range. The topmost level, or Level 1, displays the grand totals. Level 2 displays the total spent at each office. Level 3 displays both the total and average spent at each office. Finally, the bottommost level, Level 4, displays individual records. Clicking the outline buttons located to the left of the row numbers lets you choose how much detail to display in the worksheet. You will use the outline buttons to expand and collapse different sections of the data range.

To expand and collapse the employee data outline:

1. Click the **Level 1 Outline** button `1` to collapse the outline. All the rows between row 4 and row 545 are hidden. Only the grand average and grand total values for all offices are visible.

2. Click the **Level 2 Outline** button `2` to expand the outline to the second level. The totals for all offices as well as grand average and grand total are visible.

3. Click the **Level 3 Outline** button `3` to show the averages and totals for each office and for all offices. Refer to Figure 6–14.

Figure 6–14   Collapsed outline of a data range

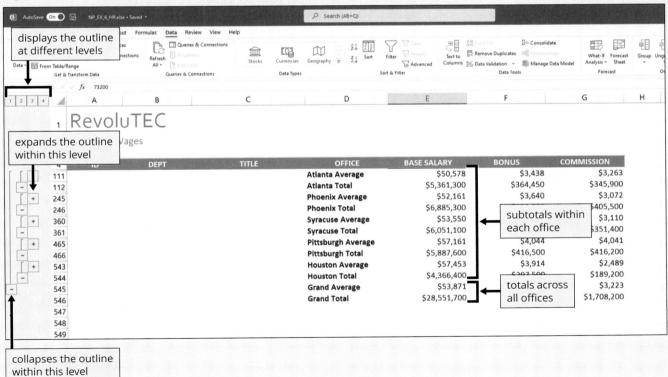

4. Click the **Show Detail** button ⊞ by row 465 to display employee records for only the Pittsburgh office. The outline expands to show rows 362 through 464. This lets you display select sections of the outline.

5. Click the **Hide Detail** ⊟ by row 465 to hide the rows 362 through 464 in the worksheet. The employee records from the Pittsburgh office are again hidden.

6. Click the **Level 4 Outline** button ④ to display all employee records.

7. Save the workbook.

To remove subtotals and outlines from a data range, click the Subtotal button in the Outline group on the Data tab to open the Subtotal dialog box, click the Remove All button, and then click OK. Subtotals and outlines will then be removed from the data range. You can add them back at any time using the Subtotal button.

Insight

Creating Manual Outlines

You can create outlines with any data range. Outlines can be applied to the range's rows or columns. To outline data, select the rows or columns you want to group and then click the Group button in the Outline group on the Data tab. Outline buttons appear in the worksheet. You can use these buttons to expand or collapse the outline. To remove the outlining, click the Ungroup button in the Outline group on the Data tab, and then click Clear Outline.

Many financial statements, such as profit and loss statements, already have subtotals. If you want to add outlining to a long and complicated financial statement, select anywhere within the statement and click the Group button and then click Auto Outline. The financial statement will automatically be grouped and outlined at each location of a subtotal.

You have completed your initial work with the employee records. In the next session, you will learn how to show subsets of the data range and how to convert a data range into an Excel table.

Part 6.1 Quick Check

1. What is a field? What is a record?

2. If you split a worksheet into panes at cell E3, how many panes are created?

3. What are the three freeze pane options?

4. When highlighting duplicate values with a conditional format, do the duplicate values have to be adjacent to each other?

5. Why is it *not* a good idea for a company to treat employee records with duplicate first and last names as duplicate records?

6. When an ascending sort order is used, how is a date-time field sorted?

7. If you want to sort employees by the value of the Hire Date field within each value of the Dept field, which field is the primary sort field? Which is the secondary sort field?

8. Before you can add subtotals to a data range, what must you first do with the data?

Part 6.2 Visual Overview: Filters and Excel Tables

An Excel table can be referenced by its assigned name.

Excel table fields are referenced using the bracket notation. Here, the BASE SALARY and COMMISSION fields are referenced by [BASE SALARY] and [COMMISSION].

Excel tables are organized into different structural elements, such as Header Row, Total Row, First Column, and Last Column.

Filtered rows, or records, are displayed in the worksheet. Records that do not match the filter criteria are hidden.

An **Excel table** is a structured range of data that is managed independently from other data in the workbook.

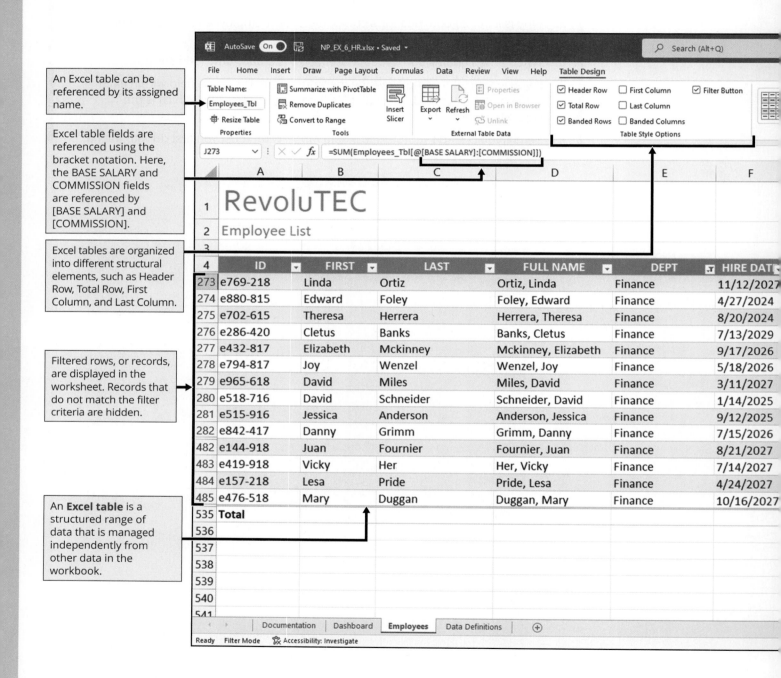

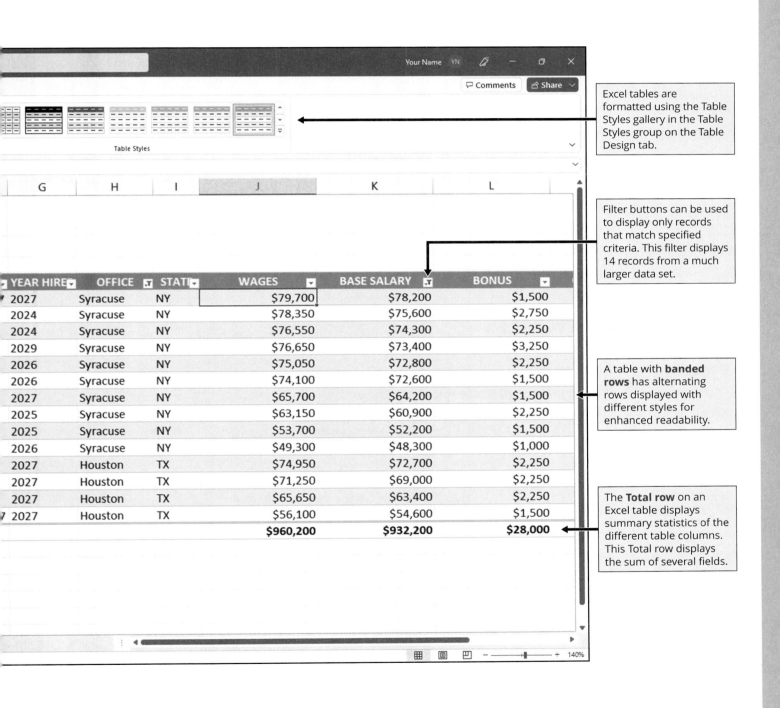

Excel tables are formatted using the Table Styles gallery in the Table Styles group on the Table Design tab.

Filter buttons can be used to display only records that match specified criteria. This filter displays 14 records from a much larger data set.

A table with **banded rows** has alternating rows displayed with different styles for enhanced readability.

The **Total row** on an Excel table displays summary statistics of the different table columns. This Total row displays the sum of several fields.

YEAR HIRED	OFFICE	STATE	WAGES	BASE SALARY	BONUS
2027	Syracuse	NY	$79,700	$78,200	$1,500
2024	Syracuse	NY	$78,350	$75,600	$2,750
2024	Syracuse	NY	$76,550	$74,300	$2,250
2029	Syracuse	NY	$76,650	$73,400	$3,250
2026	Syracuse	NY	$75,050	$72,800	$2,250
2026	Syracuse	NY	$74,100	$72,600	$1,500
2027	Syracuse	NY	$65,700	$64,200	$1,500
2025	Syracuse	NY	$63,150	$60,900	$2,250
2025	Syracuse	NY	$53,700	$52,200	$1,500
2026	Syracuse	NY	$49,300	$48,300	$1,000
2027	Houston	TX	$74,950	$72,700	$2,250
2027	Houston	TX	$71,250	$69,000	$2,250
2027	Houston	TX	$65,650	$63,400	$2,250
2027	Houston	TX	$56,100	$54,600	$1,500
			$960,200	$932,200	$28,000

Locating Cells Within a Worksheet

As the amount of data stored within a workbook increases, it becomes more difficult to finding specific pieces of information. One way of locating key data is with the Find & Select tool.

Finding and Selecting Multiple Cells

Find & Select locates cells that match specified criteria. You can use Find & Select to locate employees by their last name, base salary, or date of hire. Find & Select can list all cells within a selected range, worksheet, or workbook that satisfy the specified criterion.

Amit has been asked to review data for Mary Moreno, a recent hire working in the Finance office of the Pittsburgh office. Because Mary's data is spread out across several worksheets, you will search for the employee ID, e485-320 to examine all records pertaining to Mary's employment.

To find all cells in the workbook containing the employee ID e485-320:

1. If you took a break at the end of the previous part, make sure the NP_EX_6_HR workbook is open.

2. Go to the **Documentation** worksheet. You will start your search from the first sheet in the workbook.

3. On the ribbon, click the **Home** tab. In the Editing group, click the **Find & Select** button, and then click **Find** (or press **CTRL+F**). The Find and Replace dialog box opens.

4. In the Find what box, type **e485-320** as the value to locate.

5. Click **Options** if necessary to display an expanded list of find and replace options.

6. Click the **Within** box, and then click **Workbook** to search across the entire workbook.

7. Click the **Look in** box, and then click **Values** to search based on the values displayed in the cells rather than the formulas used in those cells.

8. Click the **Match entire cell contents** check box to limit the search only to those cells whose displayed value is exactly e485-320.

9. Click **Find All**. Seven cells in the workbook match the specified criterion. Refer to Figure 6–15.

Figure 6–15   Find and Replace dialog box

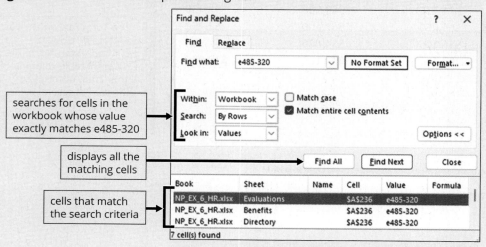

Excel jumps to the first match in the workbook—cell A236 in the Evaluations worksheet. The data in row 236 shows Mary's evaluation score of 90.

10. Click **Find Next** to go to the next match—cell A236 in the Benefits worksheet. This record shows that Mary has signed up for a Traditional IRA retirement plan, does not have any stock options, and is enrolled in a Family Plus health plan offered by Regency Health.

> **Tip** You can scroll through a worksheet's contents without closing the Find and Replace dialog box.

11. Click **Find Next** four times to review other worksheets containing Mary's contact information, salary data, age, and date of hire.

12. Click **Close** to close the Find and Replace dialog box.

Searches are not case sensitive. In this case, the search will match either e485-320 or E485-320. To make a search case sensitive, click the Match case check box to select it in the Find and Replace dialog box.

Finding Cells by Type

Find & Select can also locate cells based on criteria other than cell value, such as whether the cell contains a formula, constant, blank, or conditional formatting rule. To locate cells of a specific type, click the Find & Select button in the Editing group on the Home tab, and then click Go To Special. The Go To dialog box shown in Figure 6–16 opens.

Figure 6–16   Go To Special dialog box

The dialog box includes many ways to locate cells by types. For example, to select all of the records in a data range, click any cell in the data range, open the Go To Special dialog box, click the Current region option button, and then click OK. This approach is a big time-saver if you are working with a data range composed of thousands of records and dozens of fields.

Filtering Data

Find & Select is a quick way of locating cells of a specific type within a worksheet and across worksheets, but it does not search based on multiple criteria and it does not distinguish between fields. For example, searching for an accounting value of $8,000 might match an employee bonus or a commission or the employer contribution to a health plan. To find records based on search criteria involving multiple fields, you can filter the data.

Filtering Based on One Field

Filtering is a process that hides records that do not match specified criteria. You add filters to a data range by clicking the filter button displayed next to a field name. Records matching the filter criteria are displayed. Records that do not match the criteria are hidden but not removed from the worksheet. Hidden records can be redisplayed at any time either by removing filter or by replacing the filter with new criteria.

Reference

Filtering Data

- To add filter buttons to a data range or table, on the Data tab, in the Sort & Filter group, click the Filter button.
- To filter by a single field, click its filter button, click the check boxes for the values to include in the filter, and then click OK.
- To filter by a numeric field, click the filter button, click Number Filters, click the filter to apply, and then click OK.
- To filter by a date field, click the filter button, click Date Filters, click the filter to apply, and then click OK.
- To filter by a text field, click the filter button, click Text Filters, click the filter to apply, and then click OK.

Amit wants to examine the ages of the employees and the dates they were hired. This information is stored in the Demographics worksheet. You will start by limiting the data to the Phoenix employees.

To filter the list to display only the Phoenix records:

1. Go to the **Demographics** worksheet and click cell **A4** to select a cell in the data range.

2. On the ribbon, click the **Data** tab, and then in the Sort & Filter group, click the **Filter** button. Filter buttons appear next to each field name in the range A4:F4.

3. In cell D4, click the **filter** button next to the Office field name. The filter menu opens, listing the five unique office values within the Office field. Currently all offices are displayed in the data range. Refer to Figure 6–17.

Figure 6–17   Filter criteria

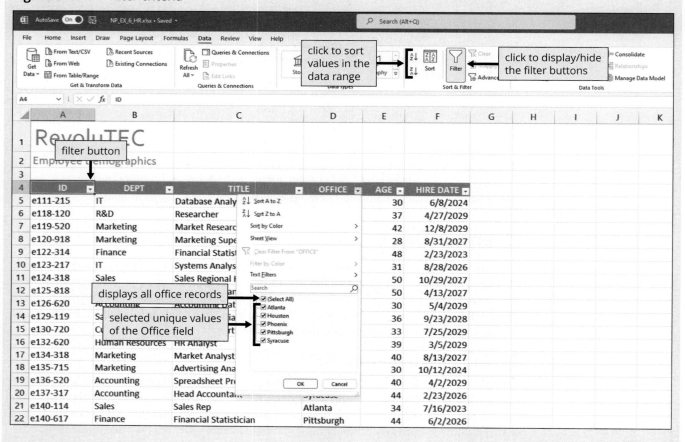

4. Click the **Select All** check box to deselect all the check boxes, and then click the **Phoenix** check box so that only the Phoenix office is selected.

5. Click **OK** to apply the filter. The status bar indicates that 132 of 530 records match the filter criteria. The records for other employees are hidden. Refer to Figure 6–18.

Figure 6–18   Employee records for the Phoenix office

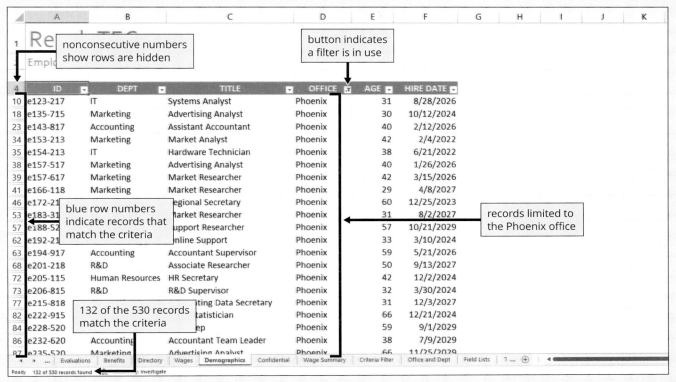

6. Scroll down the worksheet to verify that only employees from the Phoenix office are listed.

When a field or column is filtered, the filter button changes from ▾ to ⊤ as a visual reminder that some data records are hidden because of the filter. Row numbers for records matching the criteria are displayed in blue.

Filtering Based on Multiple Fields

You can filter a data range based on criteria from multiple fields. Each additional filter reduces the number of records displayed because a record must fulfill all criteria to be selected. To use filters from multiple fields, select the filter button from other column headers in the data range.

Amit wants you to add a filter to display only those Phoenix employees working in the IT or R&D departments. You will add that filter to the employees list.

To add a second filter to the employee lists:

1. In cell B4, click the **filter** button next to the Dept field name. The filter menu opens.

2. Click the **Select All** check box to deselect all the department check boxes.

3. Click the **IT** and **R&D** check boxes to select only those two departments from the list.

4. Click **OK** to add this filter to the data range. The number of records found reduces to 35, which is the number of people employed in the Phoenix IT or R&D departments. Refer to Figure 6–19.

Figure 6–19   IT and R&D employees from the Phoenix office

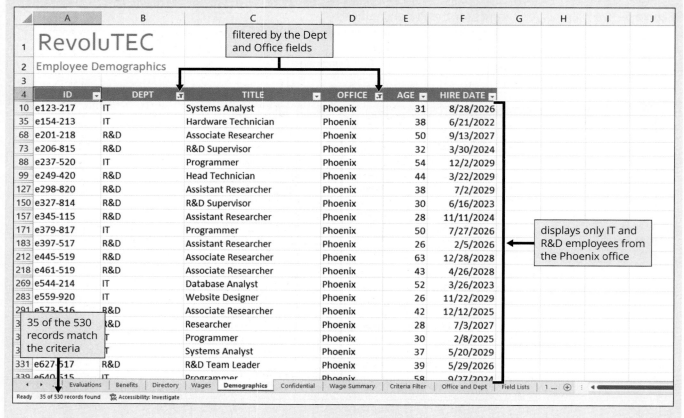

The two filters you have applied have selected records based on field categories. You can also filter data based on date and time, numbers, and text.

Using Criteria Filters

The filters created are limited to selecting records for fields matching a specific value or set of values. For more general criteria, you can create **criteria filters**, which are expressions involving dates and times, numeric values, and text strings. For example, you can filter the employee data to show only those employees hired within a specific date range or who receive a base salary above a certain amount. Figure 6–20 describes some of the criteria filters that you can apply to your data.

Figure 6–20   Text, number, and date criteria filters

Filter	Criteria	Records Displayed
Text	Equals	Exactly match the specified text
	Does Not Equal	Do not exactly match the specified text
	Begins With	Begin with the specified text
	Ends With	End with the specified text
	Contains	Have the specified text anywhere
	Does Not Contain	Do not have the specified text anywhere
Number	Equals	Exactly match the specified number
	Greater Than or Equal to	Are greater than or equal to the specified number
	Less Than	Are less than the specified number
	Between	Are greater than or equal to and less than or equal to the specified numbers
	Top 10	Are the top or bottom 10 (or the specified number)
	Above Average	Are greater than the average
Date	Today	Have the current date
	Last Week	Are in the prior week
	Next Month	Are in the month following the current month
	Last Quarter	Are in the previous quarter of the year (quarters defined as Jan, Feb, Mar; Apr, May, June; and so on)
	Year to Date	Are since January 1 of the current year to the current date
	Last Year	Are in the previous year (based on the current date)

Amit wants to further limit the employees list to include only those Phoenix IT and R&D employees hired between 2008 and 2009 and who are younger than 30 years old. You will use criteria filters for the Age and Hire Date fields to filter the data range.

To filter the employee list for dates and values:

1. In cell E4, click the **filter** button next to the Age field name.
2. On the filter menu, point to **Number Filters**, and then click **Less Than Or Equal To**. The Custom Autofilter dialog box opens.
3. Click text box to the right of the **is less than or equal to** arrow and enter **30** as the numeric value.

   Tip You can select a number from the list of field values by clicking the arrow button in the text box and choosing a number from the list.

4. Click **OK** to add the criteria to the filter. Eight employees in the Phoenix IT or R&D office are 30 years old or less.
5. Click the **filter** button next to the Hire Date field name.
6. On the filter menu, point to **Date Filters** and click **Between**. The Custom Autofilter dialog box opens.
7. Click the text box to the right of the **is after or equal to** arrow and enter **1/1/2028** as the starting date.

8. Click the text box to the right of **is before or equal to** arrow and enter **12/31/2029**. Refer to Figure 6–21.

Figure 6–21   Custom AutoFilter dialog box

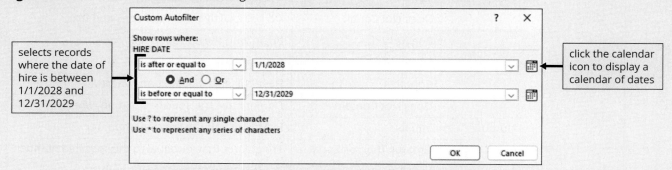

9. Click **OK** to add the criteria to the filter. The number of records reduces to two. Refer to Figure 6–22.

Figure 6–22   Age and Hire Date added to the filter

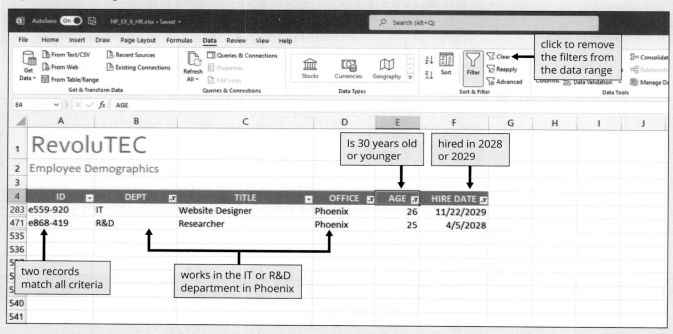

You report to Amit there are two employees in the Phoenix IT or R&D departments that are 30 years old or younger and were hired in 2028 or 2029. After you have narrowed down a data range to a select few records, you can copy the data in the data range by selecting the filtered rows and columns and pasting only the visible data to a new worksheet or workbook. Hidden cells are not copied or pasted. If you want to link the pasted records to the original data range, use the Paste Link option when pasting the selection.

If you need to remove the filters, click the Clear button in the Sort & Filter group on the Data tab. You can also turn off the filters by clicking the Filter button again. You can add, revise, or change the filters as often as you wish without affecting the data.

Insight

Exploring Text Filters

Text filters are useful for locating records based on all or part of a specified text string. If you want to match a certain pattern of characters within a text string, use the text filter options Begins With, Ends With, or Contains operators to filter a text field based on the characters the string starts with, ends with, or includes. The following are some text fields that can be applied to names and addresses:

- Use the Begins With text filter with the text string "Sm" to match names such as Smith, Smithe, or Smythe.
- Use the Ends With filter with the text string "son" to match names like Roberston, Anderson, Gibson, or Dawson.
- Use the Contains text with the text string "Main" to match street addresses like 101 East Main Street, 45B West Main Street, or 778 West Main Street.

For more advanced text filters, you can use wildcard characters to match a character pattern. The ? character represents any single character and the * character represents any series of characters. For example, a text filter based on the criteria "Will?" will match any name starting with "Wil" followed by 0 or 1 character, like Will, Wills, or Wille, but not Williams. A text file based on the criteria "Wil*son" will match any name that starts with "Wil" and ends with "son" separated by 0 or more characters, such as Wilson, Wilkerson, and Williamson.

Creating an Excel Table

So far, you have relied on Excel to recognize that a range of cells with labels in the first row and data values in subsequent rows contained fields and records to be analyzed. To explicitly indicate that a range contains fields and records, you can create a structured range of data called an Excel table.

Converting a Range to a Table

An Excel table is a data range treated by Excel as a single object incorporating the properties of a table. The advantage of converting a data range into a table is that a table includes features not available to data ranges, including:

- Sorting and filtering tools built into the table structure
- Table styles to format different features of the table, including banded rows and columns
- Automatic insertion of a totals row containing summary statistics for each field, which update automatically as records are inserted or deleted from the table
- Calculated values that use field names rather than cell references to make formulas easier to write and understand
- Named references to different parts of the table structure, including table columns, total rows, and header rows

Almost anything you can do with a data range, such as filtering and sorting, you can do with an Excel table. The main exception is that you *cannot* add subtotals to an Excel table because the table structure of field and records must be preserved, which does not allow for the insertion of subtotal rows.

Reference

Converting a Data Range to an Excel Table

- Click any cell in a data range.
- On the Insert tab, in the Tables group, click Tables.
- Confirm the data range and whether your data range contains headers.
- Click OK to create the Excel table.

Amit has created a data range containing employee salaries as well as the names of the employees. Because this information is confidential, Amit has placed the data in its own worksheet. You will convert this data range to an Excel table.

To convert the confidential employee data to an Excel table:

1. Go to the **Confidential** worksheet and click cell **A4** to select a cell within the data range.

2. On the ribbon, click the **Insert** tab, and then in the Tables group, click the **Table** button (or press **CTRL+T**). The Create Table dialog box opens.

3. Verify that **=$A$4:$J$534** is specified as the data range. This range contains all the employee data and the header row.

4. Verify that the **My tables has headers** check box is selected. This generates field names based on the labels entered in the header row.

5. Click **OK** to convert the data range to a table. Filter buttons are added to each field name and banded rows distinguish one row from the next. The Table Design tab appears on the ribbon, which includes commands for formatting the Excel table.

6. Click cell **A4** to remove highlighting from the entire table. Refer to Figure 6–23.

Figure 6–23   Employees data converted to an Excel table

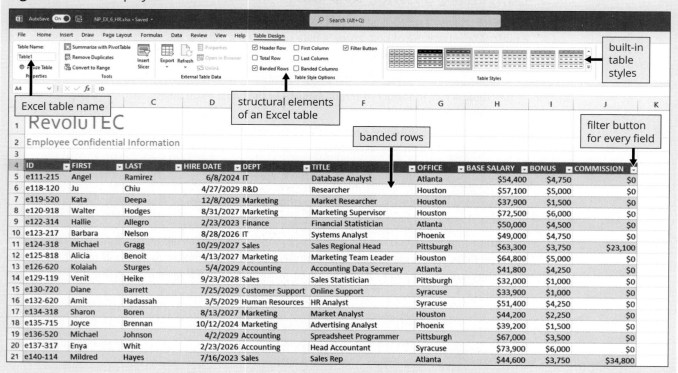

7. Scroll down the Confidential worksheet. As you scroll down the list, the field names replace the column letters, eliminating the need for freeze panes to keep field names in view.

An Excel table has the following structural elements:

- **Header row**—The first row of the table containing the field names
- **Total row**—A row at the bottom of the table containing summary statistics for selected fields
- **First column**—The leftmost column of the table
- **Last column**—The rightmost column of the table
- **Banded rows**—The odd- and even-numbered rows of the table formatted differently to make records easier to distinguish
- **Banded columns**—The odd- and even-numbered columns of the table formatted differently to make fields easier to distinguish
- **Filter buttons**—Buttons next to each field name for filtering and sorting the table data

Tables are automatically assigned names that can be referenced in any formula. The first table is named Table1, the next is named Table2, and so forth, but you can change this to a more meaningful and descriptive name. Table names must start with a letter or an underscore but can use any combination of letters, numbers, and underscores for the rest of the name. Table names cannot include spaces.

Amit wants you to use a more descriptive name for this table. You will rename Table1 as Employees.

To rename the Table1 Excel table:

1. With the table still selected, on the ribbon, click the **Table Design** tab, if necessary.

2. In the Properties group, click the **Table Name** box.

3. Type **Employees** as the new name, and then press **ENTER**. The Excel table is renamed.

An Excel table name is added to the Name box with global scope, so you can reference an Excel table anywhere within the workbook or from an external workbook. To convert an Excel table back to a data range, click the Convert to Range button in the Tools group on the Table Design tab.

Using Table Styles

Because an Excel table is composed of structural elements, you can apply styles to different parts of the table. For example, you can create a special style for the table's first or last columns or the header row. Excel also includes a gallery of built-in table styles that apply a professional look to the table. Amit wants you to change the Excel table style to make the Employees table easier to read.

To apply styles to the Employees table:

1. On the Table Design tab, in the Table Style Options group, click the **First Column** and **Last Column** check boxes to select those table elements.

2. Scroll through the worksheet and verify that values for the ID field in column A and the Commission field in column J are displayed in bold.

3. In the Table Style Options group, click the **Banded Rows**, **First Column** and **Last Column** check boxes to deselect them, leaving only the Header Row and Filter Buttons selected as part of the table design.

4. In the Table Styles group, click the **More** button to display different styles that can be applied to the table.

> **Tip** To remove table styles, click Clear in the Table Styles gallery. To create your own table style, click New Table Style in the gallery.

5. In the Table Styles gallery, click **Green, Table Style Medium 5** (the fifth style in the first row of the Medium table styles). Refer to Figure 6–24.

Figure 6–24   Table style applied to an Excel table

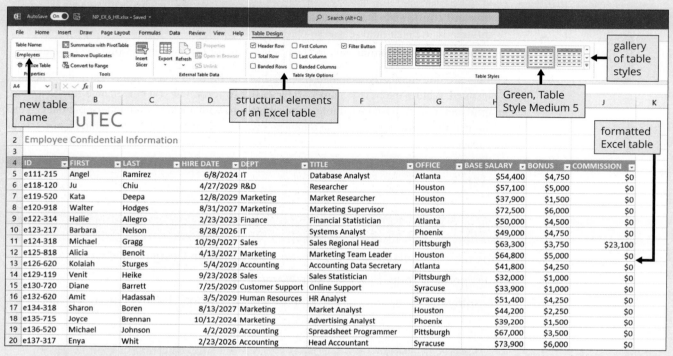

Table styles do not, by default, override the formatting applied to individual cells. Any format applied directly to a cell or range will be unaffected by your choice of table styles. To override a cell format with the table style, right-click the table style in the gallery, and then click Apply and Clear Formatting on the shortcut menu.

Adding a Total Row

A useful table element for data analysis is the Total row, which is added to the end of the table after the last data record. The Total row calculates summary statistics, including the average, sum, minimum, and maximum of select fields within the table. Summary statistics are displayed in bold with a double border line separating the data records from the Total row.

Amit wants you to add summary statistics to the Employees table. You will calculate those statistics by adding a Total row.

To add a Total Row to the Employees table:

1. On the Table Design tab, in the Table Style Options group, click the **Total Row** check box to select it (or press **CTRL+SHIFT+T**). The Total row is added at the bottom of the table. Excel has already calculated the sum of the values in the Commission field.

2. Click the cell in the Total row for the BASE SALARY column. An arrow button appears. You use this button to select a summary statistic.

3. Click the **arrow** button, and then click **Sum** in the list of summary statistics. The cell displays $28,543,100, which is the amount that company spent on base salaries.

4. Press **TAB** to move to the Bonus column in the Total row, click the **arrow** button, and then click **Sum** in the list of summary statistics. The cell displays $1,970,450, which is the amount that the company spent on bonuses.

5. Press **TAB** to move to the Commission column in the Total row, and then click the **arrow** button to display the list of summary functions, confirming that the SUM function is selected. Refer Figure 6–25.

Figure 6–25   Total row added to an Excel table

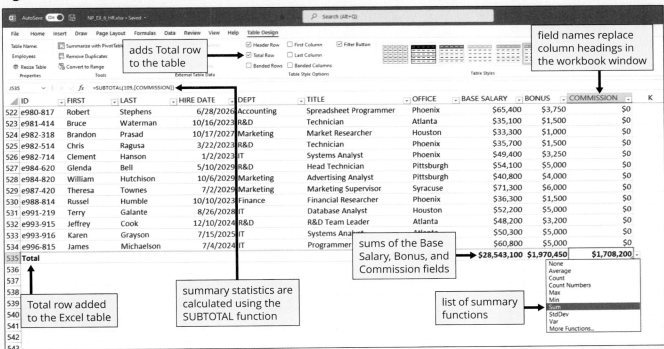

6. Press **ESC** to close the menu without changing this summary statistic.

The values in the Total row automatically update to reflect any filters applied to the table. If the Employees table is filtered to show only records from the Houston office, the Total row shows the sums and averages of those Houston employees. As the number of records in the filtered table increase and decrease, the Total row will always appear below the last visible row.

Adding and Deleting Records

When you edit, add, or delete records within an Excel table, the table adjusts to the new contents. Formats are updated to accommodate the new table size. Calculations in the Total row are updated to include the new and revised data.

Diane Soo of the Accounting department in Atlanta is no longer with the company. Karl Ruiz has been hired for that position. Amit wants you to update the data in the Employees table by removing Diana Soo's record and replacing it with the employee data for Karl Ruiz.

To modify the Employees table by adding and deleting records:

1. Scroll up the worksheet, click the **row 169** header containing the record for Diane Soo.

2. On the ribbon, click the **Home** tab, and then in the Cells group, click the **Delete** button. The record for Diane Soo is deleted from the table.

3. With row 169 still selected, in the Cells group, click the **Insert** button. A new row is added to the worksheet.

4. In row 169, enter the following information to create the record for Karl Ruiz: **e901-920** in the ID field, **Karl** in the First field, **Ruiz** in the Last field, **12/4/2029** in the Hire Date field, **Accounting** in the Dept field, **Spreadsheet Developer** in the Title field, **Atlanta** in the Office field, **$57,300** in the Base Salary field, **$0** in Bonus field, and **$0** in the Commission field.

In addition to adding or deleting table records, you can also insert or delete table fields. You will modify the Employees table by adding new fields containing formulas.

Creating a Calculated Field

So far, all the fields in the Employees table contain values. A field can also contain a formula that references other fields in the table. Such a field is called a **calculated field**, and it updates automatically as other field values in the table change. Instead of cell references, formulas in a calculated field use field names enclosed in brackets

> `[field]`

where `field` is a field or a group of fields. Field names are not case sensitive so that the field name "BASE SALARY" is identical to the "Base Salary" or "base salary" field name. To include the name of the table in a reference, preface the field name with the table name

> `table[field]`

where `table` is the name of an Excel table. Field names can be included in any formula in place of cell references. The following formula returns the sum of all values of the Base Salary field within the Employees table:

> `=SUM(Employees[Base Salary])`

To reference a group of fields, insert the first and last fields in the group, separated by a colon. The following formula returns the sum of all values of the Base Salary through Commission fields in the Employees table:

> `=SUM(Employees[BASE SALARY]:Employees[COMMISSION])`

To avoid repeating the table name, you can place the field group within its own set of square brackets as in the following formula:

> `=SUM(Employees[[BASE SALARY]:[COMMISSION]])`

An important symbol in calculated fields is the @ symbol, which references the current record or row within the table. The @ symbol is used in formulas that calculate values within each table record. For example, the following formula multiplies the value of the SalesPrice field by the UnitSold field within the table's current row:

    =[@SalesPrice]*[@UnitsSold]

If the field name contains a space, you must enclose the field name within another set of square brackets. The formula to multiply the values of the Sales Price and Units Sold fields within the current record is:

    =[@[Sales Price]]*[@[Units Sold]]

Amit wants to add a Name field to the Employees table, displaying each employee's last name followed by a comma and then the employee's first name. To combine the three text strings, you will use the CONCAT function, which concatenates (or combines) multiple text strings. The formula is:

    =CONCAT([@LAST], ", ", [@FIRST])

A formula entered in one record of an Excel table is automatically applied to all records. It is often easier to use the mouse to select and enter field references. You will use that technique to create a calculated value for the NAME field.

To add the Name calculated field to the Employees table:

1. Scroll to the top of the worksheet, and then click the **Column D** header.

2. On the Home tab, in the Cells group, click the **Insert** button. A new field named "Column1" is added to the table between the Last and Hire Date fields.

3. Click cell **D4**, type **NAME** as the field label, and then press **ENTER**.

4. In cell **D5**, type **=CONCAT(** to begin the CONCAT function.

5. Click cell **C5**. Excel enters the reference to the LAST field for the current row, insert the reference [@LAST] to the formula.

   | **Key Step** Be sure to enclose references to field or column names of an Excel table in square brackets.

6. Type **, ", ",** to add a comma followed by a blank space to the text string.

7. Click cell **B5** to reference the FIRST field. Excel inserts the field reference [@FIRST] in the formula.

8. Type **)** to complete the formula =CONCAT([@LAST], ", ", [@FIRST]) and press **ENTER**. The formula is added to add all records in the NAME column.

9. Increase the width of the Name column to **20 characters**. Refer to Figure 6–26.

Figure 6-26   Calculated field

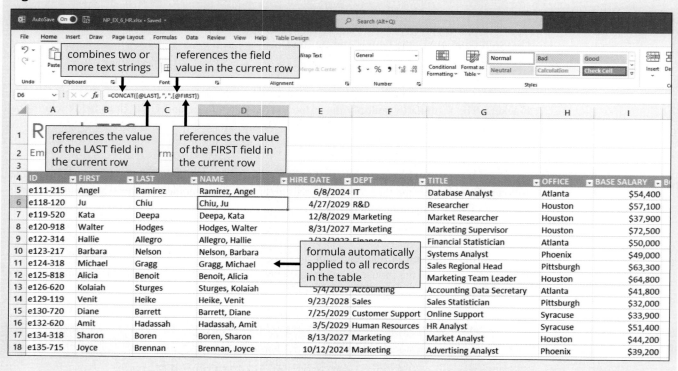

Amit wants you to create a calculated field to display the year the employee was hired. You can extract the year value from a date using the YEAR function.

To add the Year Hired field to the Employees table:

1. Click the **Column F** header, and then on the Home tab, in the Cells group, click the **Insert** button.

2. Click cell **F4**, type **YEAR HIRED** as the field name, and then press **ENTER**.

3. In cell **F5**, type **= YEAR(** to begin the formula.

4. Click cell **E5** so that [@[HIRE DATE]] is added to the formula.

5. Type **)** and then press **ENTER** to close the field name and insert the formula = YEAR([@[HIRE DATE]]).

   Excel displays the year values in date format, so they erroneously appear as 1905 dates. You will reformat the values using the General format.

6. Press **CTRL+SPACEBAR** to select all the data records in the HIRE YEAR column.

   ▮ **Tip** You can select all the fields in a record by pressing SHIFT+SPACEBAR.

7. On the Home tab, in the Number group, click the **Number Format arrow**, and then click **General**. The year value appears for each record. Refer to Figure 6-27.

Figure 6-27 Year hired for each employee

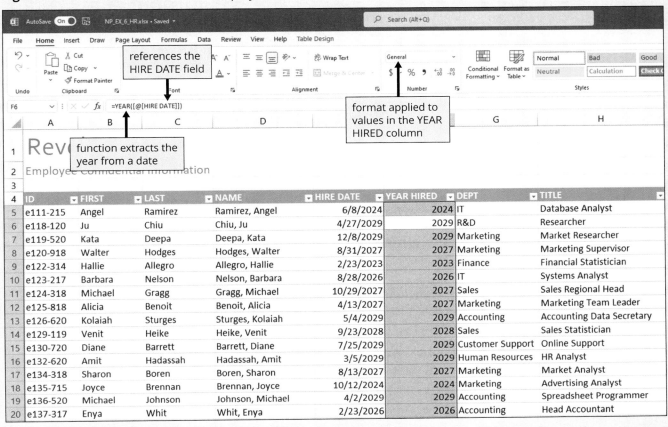

References to fields and elements in an Excel table are called **structural references** and are always enclosed within square brackets. Other parts of the Excel table, such as the header row and the Total row can be referenced with [#Headers] and [#Totals], respectively.

Amit wants you to complete the Excel table with a calculated field named Wages calculating the sum of the Base Salary, Bonus, and Commission field for each employee.

To add the Wages field to the Employees table:

1. Click cell **M4**, type **WAGES** as the new field name, and then press **ENTER**. Excel automatically recognizes this entry as a new field in the Employees table.

2. In cell **M5**, type **= SUM(** to begin the formula.

3. Use your mouse to select the range **J5:L5**. The structural reference Employees[@[BASE SALARY]:[COMMISSION]] is added to reference the Base Salary through Commission fields for the current employee record.

4. Type **)** to end the formula, and then press **ENTER**. The formula =SUM(Employees[@[BASE SALARY]:[COMMISSION]]) is entered for every record, calculating every employees total wages.

5. Press **CTRL+SPACEBAR** to select the entire column of wages.

6. On the Home tab, in the Number group, click the **Number Format arrow**, and then click **Currency** to display the values in currency format.

7. Remove the decimals from the currency values. Refer to Figure 6-28.

Figure 6–28   Total wages paid to each employee

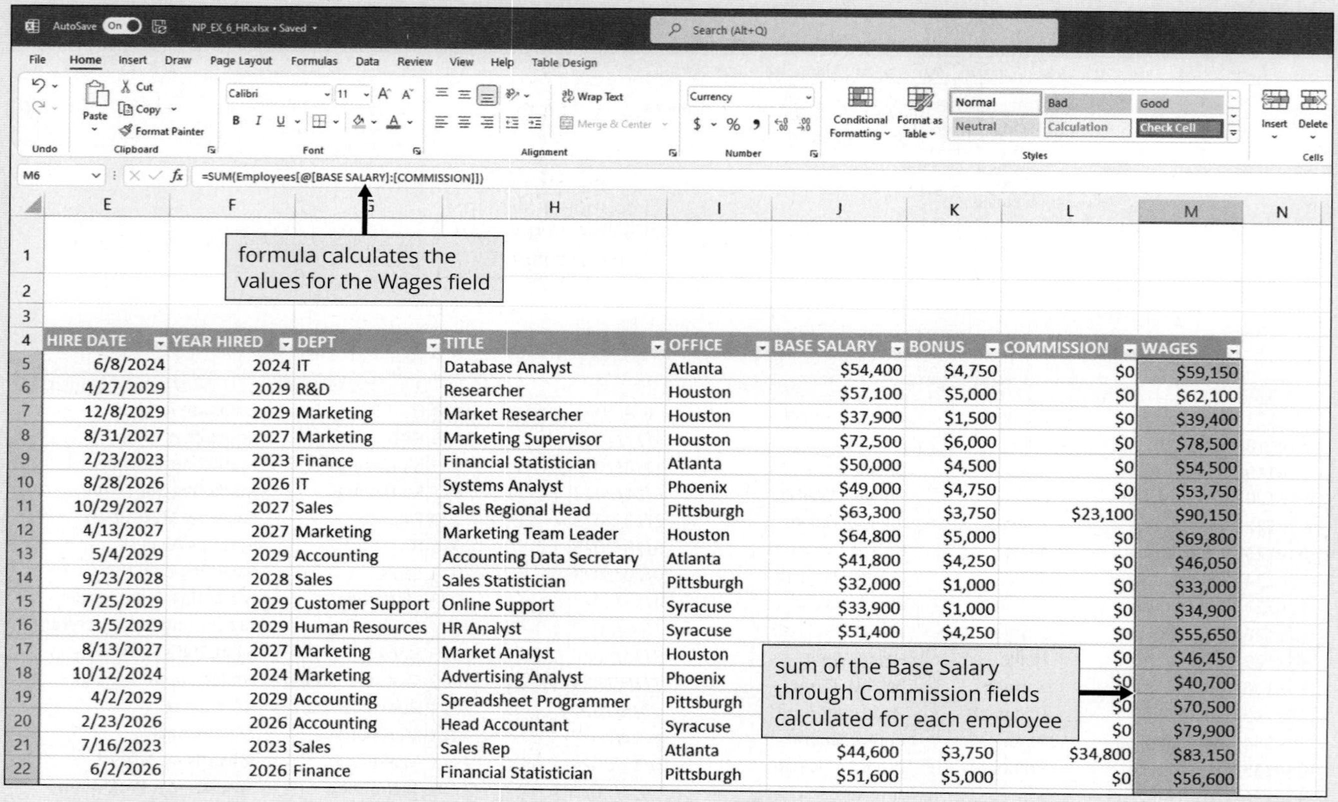

Cell M6 formula bar: =SUM(Employees[@[BASE SALARY]:[COMMISSION]])

formula calculates the values for the Wages field

	HIRE DATE	YEAR HIRED	DEPT	TITLE	OFFICE	BASE SALARY	BONUS	COMMISSION	WAGES
5	6/8/2024	2024	IT	Database Analyst	Atlanta	$54,400	$4,750	$0	$59,150
6	4/27/2029	2029	R&D	Researcher	Houston	$57,100	$5,000	$0	$62,100
7	12/8/2029	2029	Marketing	Market Researcher	Houston	$37,900	$1,500	$0	$39,400
8	8/31/2027	2027	Marketing	Marketing Supervisor	Houston	$72,500	$6,000	$0	$78,500
9	2/23/2023	2023	Finance	Financial Statistician	Atlanta	$50,000	$4,500	$0	$54,500
10	8/28/2026	2026	IT	Systems Analyst	Phoenix	$49,000	$4,750	$0	$53,750
11	10/29/2027	2027	Sales	Sales Regional Head	Pittsburgh	$63,300	$3,750	$23,100	$90,150
12	4/13/2027	2027	Marketing	Marketing Team Leader	Houston	$64,800	$5,000	$0	$69,800
13	5/4/2029	2029	Accounting	Accounting Data Secretary	Atlanta	$41,800	$4,250	$0	$46,050
14	9/23/2028	2028	Sales	Sales Statistician	Pittsburgh	$32,000	$1,000	$0	$33,000
15	7/25/2029	2029	Customer Support	Online Support	Syracuse	$33,900	$1,000	$0	$34,900
16	3/5/2029	2029	Human Resources	HR Analyst	Syracuse	$51,400	$4,250	$0	$55,650
17	8/13/2027	2027	Marketing	Market Analyst	Houston			$0	$46,450
18	10/12/2024	2024	Marketing	Advertising Analyst	Phoenix			$0	$40,700
19	4/2/2029	2029	Accounting	Spreadsheet Programmer	Pittsburgh			$0	$70,500
20	2/23/2026	2026	Accounting	Head Accountant	Syracuse			$0	$79,900
21	7/16/2023	2023	Sales	Sales Rep	Atlanta	$44,600	$3,750	$34,800	$83,150
22	6/2/2026	2026	Finance	Financial Statistician	Pittsburgh	$51,600	$5,000	$0	$56,600

sum of the Base Salary through Commission fields calculated for each employee

8. Save the workbook.

All formulas that involve structural references are updated to reflect any changes made to the workbook. For example, if you change a field name any formula referencing that field will update automatically to use the new name.

Proskills

Written Communication: Making Tables and Data Ranges More Accessible

Excel tables are excellent for storing structured data within a workbook. However, you should try to make them accessible to all users. The following guidelines will help ensure your Excel tables are more accessible.

- **Use descriptive table names and field labels.** Screen readers use the table name and column names to identify the key features of a table. To make an Excel table more accessible, provide a descriptive table name and descriptive field labels for all the table columns. Also, if possible, start table rows with a meaningful piece of data, such as an employee name or company title.
- **Avoid blank cells, columns, or rows within a table.** Blank or empty content can confuse a screen reader into believing that the end of the table has been reached. As an alternative, you can replace blanks with error values such as #N/A or a single dot.
- **Create a consistent table structure.** Screen readers keep track of their location by counting table rows and columns. Merged cells can cause a screen reader to lose count of its location. For the same reason, avoid nesting one table or data range within another. The best table layout has a set number of rows and columns across the entire structure.
- **Do not use only visual elements to differentiate parts of the table.** Avoid using visual elements such as color, shading, and borders as the only way to distinguish the different parts of the table structure. Your table should be easily interpreted with and without those elements to be truly accessible.
- **Add the table name and description above the table.** While not part of an Excel table structure, placing the table name and a description in the row immediately above the table can make it more accessible. For example, include a title cell containing the text "Table 1: Employee Ages and Date Hired" directly above the table. The screen reader can then provide the user with that detailed information about the table's content and purpose.
- **Perform a final accessibility check.** Excel includes an Accessibility Checker tool that will flag accessibility issues in your workbook. Run the Accessibility Checker before releasing your workbook to your colleagues as a final check of its accessibility to all your coworkers.

In this part, you worked with Excel tables to analyze employee data for Amit. Next, you will use slicers to create an interactive dashboard that Amit can use to quickly generate reports on the employee data.

Part 6.2 Quick Check

1. True or false and why: Records that do not match a filter criterion are deleted from the workbook.
2. When multiple filter buttons are used with a data range, how are criteria in different fields combined?
3. When would you use an advanced filter in place of the filter buttons?
4. What is the reference to the Price field in the Sales table?
5. What does the @ symbol represent in an Excel table formula?
6. Write the formula calculate the total of the Sales field from the Accounts table.
7. Write the formula to return the sum of the Sales field and the Tax field of the current row in the current Excel table.
8. True or false and why: If a field name contains a space, it should be enclosed within quotation marks in any Excel formula.

Part 6.3 Visual Overview: Slicers and Dashboards

The Clear Filter button removes all the criteria from the slicer.

The Slicer tab appears on the ribbon when a slicer is selected.

The Multi-Select button lets you select multiple categories in a slicer.

A **dashboard** is a page or screen providing informative visuals of data, key performance indicators, and statistics.

A **slicer** is an object used to filter data in an Excel table. It has a button for each unique value in a field.

The **SUBTOTAL function** calculates summary statistics from filtered data. The formula =SUBTOTAL(3,Employees[ID]) counts the number of employees in the Pittsburgh Finance office.

Selected criteria are highlighted in the slicer. In these two slicers, the Pittsburgh office and Finance department are highlighted.

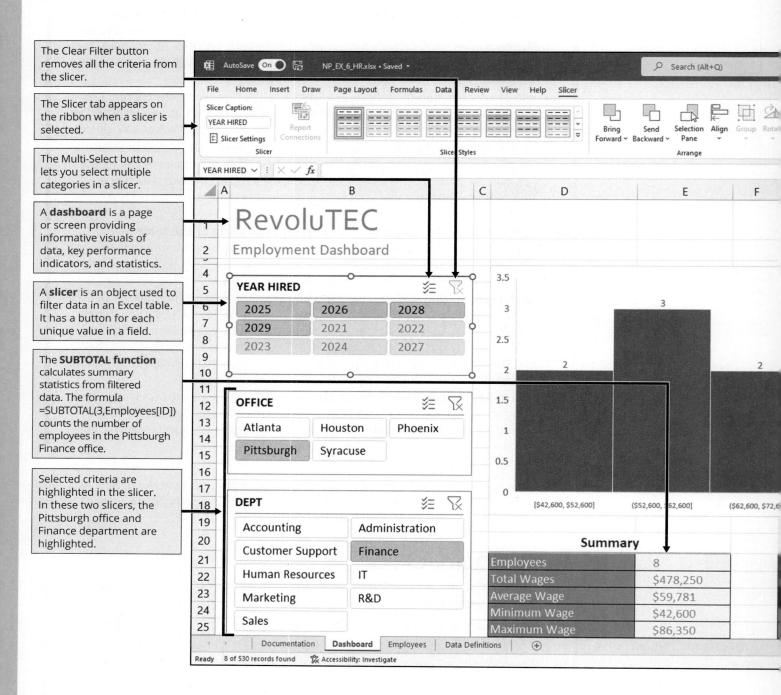

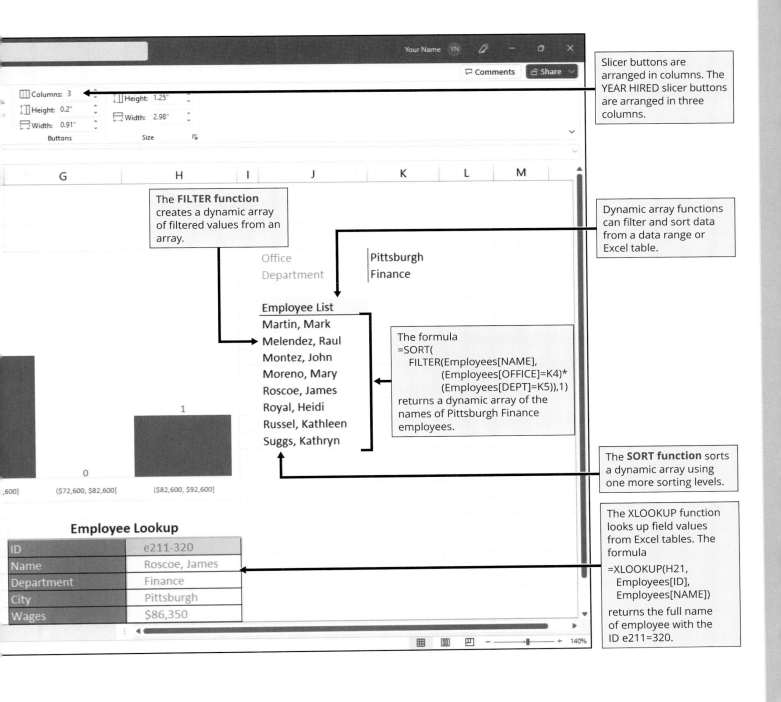

Slicer buttons are arranged in columns. The YEAR HIRED slicer buttons are arranged in three columns.

	Columns: 3		Height: 1.25"
Height: 0.2"		Width: 2.98"	
Width: 0.91"			
Buttons		Size	

The **FILTER function** creates a dynamic array of filtered values from an array.

Dynamic array functions can filter and sort data from a data range or Excel table.

| | G | H | I | J | K | L | M |

Office   Pittsburgh
Department   Finance

Employee List
Martin, Mark
Melendez, Raul
Montez, John
Moreno, Mary
Roscoe, James
Royal, Heidi
Russel, Kathleen
Suggs, Kathryn

The formula
=SORT(
    FILTER(Employees[NAME],
        (Employees[OFFICE]=K4)*
        (Employees[DEPT]=K5)),1)
returns a dynamic array of the names of Pittsburgh Finance employees.

1

0

[,600]   [$72,600, $82,600]   [$82,600, $92,600]

The **SORT function** sorts a dynamic array using one more sorting levels.

Employee Lookup

ID	e211-320
Name	Roscoe, James
Department	Finance
City	Pittsburgh
Wages	$86,350

The XLOOKUP function looks up field values from Excel tables. The formula
=XLOOKUP(H21,
    Employees[ID],
    Employees[NAME])
returns the full name of employee with the ID e211=320.

Filtering Data with Slicers

In the previous part, you used filter buttons to filter data. Another way to filter an Excel table is with slicers. A slicer is an object containing buttons for each value from a field. For example, a slicer for the Office field would have buttons for the Atlanta, Houston, Phoenix, Pittsburgh, and Syracuse offices. When slicer buttons are clicked or selected, the data is filtered to show those records only from the selected buttons. Slicers make it clear what filters are being applied to the data at any moment.

> ▌ **Tip** Slicers cannot be used with data ranges.

A table can have multiple slicers, each linked to a different field. Multiple slicers are connected with the AND logical operator so that filtered records must meet all of the criteria indicated in the slicers.

Reference

Creating a Slicer

- Select any cell in the Excel table to make the table active.
- On the Insert tab, in the Filters group, click the Slicer button.
- In the Insert Slicers dialog box, select the field or column names of the slicers you want to create.
- Click OK to add the slicers to the current worksheet.

Amit wants you to create three slicers for the Employees table linked to the Dept, Year Hired, and Office fields.

To add slicers to the Employees table:

1. If you took a break at the end of the previous part, make sure the NP_EX_6_HR workbook is open and the Confidential worksheet is active.
2. Click cell **A4** to make the Employees table active.
3. On the ribbon, click the **Insert** tab, and then in the Filters group, click the **Slicer** button. The Insert Slicers dialog box opens.
4. Click the **YEAR HIRED, DEPT,** and **OFFICE** check boxes in the list of fields.
5. Click **OK** to create the slicers. Three slicers float over the worksheet with values from the Year Hired, Dept, and Office fields.
6. Point to a blank part of the YEAR HIRED slicer to change the pointer to the Move pointer ⁺⇖.
7. Click and drag the YEAR HIRED slicer cell over cell **A1**.
8. Drag the DEPT slicer to the right of the YEAR HIRED slicer over cell **C1**.
9. Drag the OFFICE slicer to the right of the DEPT slicer. Refer to Figure 6–29.

Figure 6–29   Slicers for the Year Hired, Dept, and Office fields

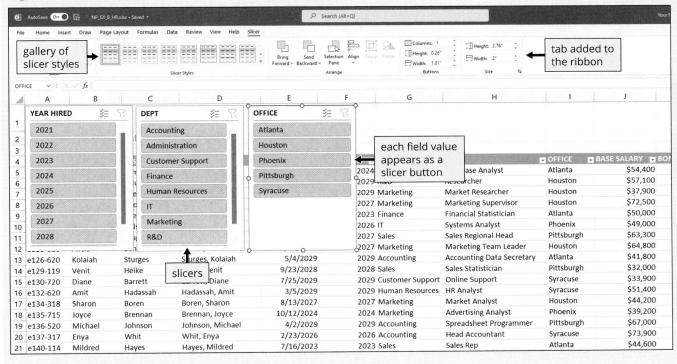

Each slicer shows the unique values for the selected field. The field name appears in the slicer title bar along with two buttons. The Multi-Select button 🗮 lets you select multiple slicer buttons. The Clear Filter button 🗷 clears the slicer filters from the table. When a slicer is selected, the Slicer tab appears on the ribbon. You use this tab to format slicers.

Amit wants to filter the records in the Employees table to display only those employees hired in the Houston Customer Support department from 2026 through 2029. You will use the three slicers to filter the data.

To filter the Employees table using slicers:

1. In the YEAR HIRED slicer, click the **Multi-Select** button 🗮 (or press **ALT+S**) so you can select multiple field categories.

2. Click the **2021** through **2025** buttons to deselect them, leaving the 2026 through 2029 buttons selected. Of the 530 records in the table, 348 records are for employees hired from 2026 to 2029.

3. In the DEPT slicer, click **Customer Support** to show only those employee records from the Customer Support department. Only 21 of the 530 records match this criterion.

4. In the Office slicer, click the **Houston** button. Five employees match the filter criteria. Notice that the 2021 through 2026 buttons in the YEAR HIRED slicer are greyed out because they have no matching records in the table. The Houston office opened in 2020, so no employee records exist before that year. Refer to Figure 6–30.

Figure 6–30   Slicers applied to an Excel table

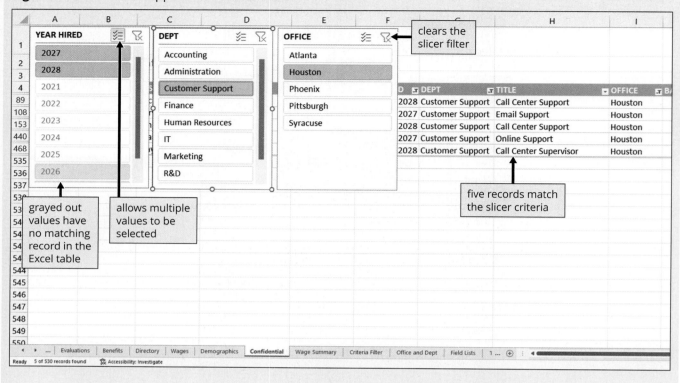

The slicers obscure much of the table data, making it difficult to read the records. Slicers can be moved to anywhere within the workbook and they will still filter the data records from their linked table. Amit wants you to move these slicers to another sheet to create a dashboard.

Insight

Choosing Between Slicers and Filter Buttons

Slicers and filter buttons are two ways to filter data in an Excel table. Use slicers when data has a few distinct values that can be easily listed within the slicer. Also, use slicers when you want to perform data from a table on another worksheet.

Use filter buttons when you need to use criteria filters involving text, date, or numeric values. For example, use filter buttons to filter for records that fall within a specified time interval or for a specific range of incomes or expenses.

Creating a Dashboard

A dashboard is a page or screen providing informative visuals of data, key performance indicators, and statistics. Most dashboards contain interactive tools to help users explore data under different conditions and assumptions. The term *dashboard* evokes the idea of an automobile dashboard that presents important information to the driver that can be quickly interpreted. Slicers are often used in dashboards because they provide a quick way to filter data.

Amit included a Dashboard worksheet in the workbook and wants you to place the three slicers you created for the Employees table on this sheet.

To move the slicers for the Employees table to the Dashboard worksheet:

1. In the Confidential worksheet, click the **YEAR HIRED** slicer to select it. Sizing handles are displayed in the corners and along the sides of the selected object.

2. On the ribbon, click the **Home** tab, and then in the Clipboard group, click the **Cut** button (or press **CTRL+X**).

3. Go to the **Dashboard** worksheet, click cell **B4** as the location for pasting the slicer, and then in the Clipboard group, click the **Paste** button (or press **CTRL+V**). The HIRE YEAR slicer is pasted into the worksheet.

   Tip You can cut and paste slicers between worksheets; you cannot cut and paste slicers between workbooks.

4. Hold down **ALT** as you drag the lower-right sizing handle of the slicer to the lower-right corner of cell **B9**. The slicer resizes to cover the range B4:B9.

5. Repeat Steps 1 through 4 to cut and paste the **OFFICE** slicer to cover the range **B11:B15** on the Dashboard worksheet.

6. Repeat Steps 1 through 4 to cut and paste the **DEPT** slicer to cover the range **B17:B25** on the Dashboard worksheet. Refer to Figure 6–31.

Figure 6–31   Slicers moved to the Dashboard worksheet

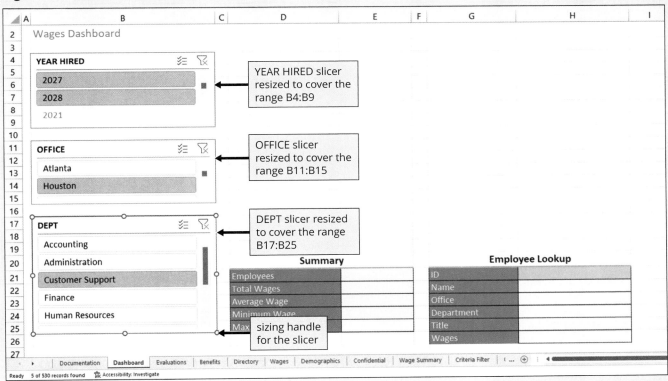

Even though the slicers are on a different worksheet, they still filter the data in the Employees table.

Formatting a Slicer

By default, slicer buttons are arranged in a single column. Amit wants you increase the number of columns for the Hire Year, Office, and Dept slicers so that all the buttons can be viewed together without needing to use the scroll bar.

To change the number of columns in the slicers:

1. Click the title bar of the YEAR HIRED slicer to select it.

2. On the ribbon, click the **Slicer** tab, and then in the Buttons group, click the **Columns** box.

3. In the Columns box, type **3** and then press **ENTER**. The buttons in the HIRE YEAR slicer are laid out in three columns and three rows.

4. Click the title bar of the OFFICE slicer to select it, and then enter **3** in the Columns box in the Buttons group.

5. Click the title bar of the DEPT slicer, and then enter **2** in the Columns box. The three slicers now have all buttons visible without scrolling. Refer to Figure 6–32.

Figure 6–32   Formatted slicers

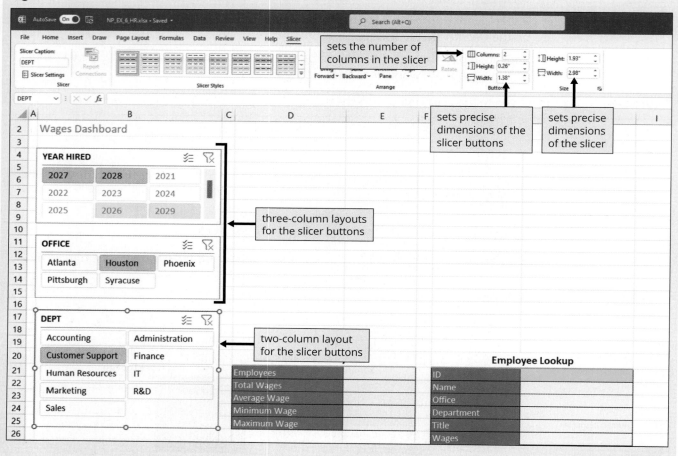

There are other ways to format a slicer's appearance using tools on the Slicer tab. You can set the exact size of the slicer and its buttons using the Height and Width boxes in the Buttons and Size groups. You can change the color scheme by selecting a slicer style from the Slicer Styles gallery. You can change the button order by clicking the Slicer Settings button in the Slicer group and then choosing the button sorting order (or create a custom sorting list) in the Slicer Settings dialog box. You can also change the slicer's title bar text from the field name to one of your own choosing by entering text in the Slicer Caption box in the Slicer group of the Slicer tab.

Proskills

Written Communication: Designing a Dashboard

A dashboard is designed to tell a story. It can be a springboard to reports providing more in-depth analysis, but fundamentally a dashboard needs to present useful information at a glance. As you create dashboards, keep in mind the following design tips:

- **Go Big. Go Bold.** Do not be afraid to use extremely large fonts and bright colors for important results. You want viewers to be attracted to those results first, and you want those results to be remembered.
- **Start from the Upper-Left Corner.** Excel menus are located at the top of the screen and read from left to right, so put your most important information in the upper-left corner where it will be noticed first.
- **Keep It Simple.** Focus on a few key points, and keep the clutter of charts, graphics, and text to a minimum. You can always create additional dashboards.
- **Do Not Let Color Overwhelm.** Keep the design of charts and graphics to a few complementary colors and use them consistently. Adding too many colors is distracting and reduces the dashboard's impact.
- **Make It User Friendly.** The use and purpose of interactive tools like slicers and menus should be clear. You may not have room to explain how to use the dashboard.
- **Be Focused.** Settle on a few key points. If a chart or graphic does not relate to that idea, remove it or place it in a different dashboard.

When you design a dashboard, always keep your audience in mind. What are they looking for? The dashboard you present to a sales director might be very different from one you present to a marketing manager or an HR executive. A dashboard is most useful and has the greatest impact when it is tailored to the needs of your audience.

Using the SUBTOTAL Function

Amit wants the dashboard to display summary statistics on the employee data filtered by the slicers. The first summary statistic will count the number of employees listed in the filtered table. You will use the COUNTA function to count the number of entries in the ID field of the Employees table.

To use the COUNTA function in the dashboard:

1. In each slicer's title bar, click the **Clear Filter** button to clear the filters. No filters are applied to the Employees table.

2. Click cell **E21**, and type the formula **= COUNTA(Employees[ID])** to count the number of entries in the ID field. As you type the formula, the name of the Excel table and a list of fields within that table appear.

   Tip Use the TAB key to select the highlighted names provided by Excel and insert them into your formula.

3. Press **ENTER**. The formula returns 530, which is the number of records in the Employees table.

4. In the OFFICE slicer, click **Atlanta**. The status bar indicates 106 of 530 records in the Employees table match the slicer criteria. However, the value in cell E21 is unchanged and still shows 530 as the number of employees.

Why does the dashboard show the same number of employees after limiting the employee list to the Atlanta office? The reason is that statistical functions like the COUNTA, AVERAGE, SUM, MAX, and MIN functions are applied to the *entire table*, regardless of any filter criteria. To count only records that match the filter criteria, use the SUBTOTAL function

SUBTOTAL(*Function_Num*, *ref1*, [*ref2*], [*ref3*], …)

where *Function_Num* is a number corresponding to a statistical function, *ref1* is a reference to the data to be analyzed, and *ref2*, *ref3*, and so forth are optional arguments for additional data references. Figure 6–33 lists some of the function numbers recognized by the SUBTOTAL function.

Figure 6-33   Function numbers of the SUBTOTAL function

Function Number	Function	Function Number	Function
1	AVERAGE	6	PRODUCT
2	COUNT	7	STDEV
3	COUNTA	8	STDEVP
4	MAX	9	SUM
5	MIN	10	VAR

The following formula uses the SUBTOTAL function with function number 3 to apply the COUNTA function to the ID field of the Employees table, but only for those records selected by any filters applied to the table:

= SUBTOTAL(3, Employees[ID])

> **Tip** To apply the SUBTOTAL function to data with manually hidden rows, add 100 to the function number.

You have already worked with the SUBTOTAL function without realizing it when you had Excel calculate subtotals in the Employees table (refer back to Figure 6–25).

Reference

Applying the SUBTOTAL Function

- To apply summary statistics records that match a filter criteria, apply the function

  SUBTOTAL(*Function_Num*, *ref1*, [*ref2*], [*ref3*], …)

  where *Function_Num* is an integer representing a statistical function to use in the subtotal calculation, *ref1* is a reference to the data to be analyzed, and *ref2*, *ref3*, and so on are optional arguments for additional data references.
- To calculate SUM from the filtered records of a table, set *Function_Num* to 9.
- To calculate AVERAGE from the filtered records, set *Function_Num* to 1.
- To calculate COUNT from the filtered records, set *Function_Num* to 2.
- To calculate COUNTA from the filtered records, set *Function_Num* to 3.

You will use the SUBTOTAL function to calculate summary statistics from the Employees table based on whatever records are selected the slicers on the dashboard.

To apply the SUBTOTAL function to the Employees table:

1. Click cell **E21**, and then type **= SUBTOTAL(** to begin the formula. A list of function numbers for statistical functions appears.

2. Press **DOWN ARROW** twice to select 3. - COUNTA from the list, and then press **TAB** to insert 3 into the formula.

   > **Key Step** Use the arrow keys or mouse to select the function number to ensure that you use the correct summary statistic.

3. Type **, Employees[ID])** to complete the formula, and then press **ENTER**. The formula returns 106, which is the number of records that match the filter criteria in the slicers.

4. In cell **E22**, enter the formula **= SUBTOTAL(9, Employees[WAGES])** to calculate the sum that RevoluTEC spends on wages for the 106 employees. The formula returns $6,071,650 as the total wages paid to the 106 employees.

5. In cell **E23**, enter the formula **= SUBTOTAL(1, Employees[WAGES])** to calculate the average of those wages. The formula returns $57,280 as the average wage for Atlanta employees.

6. In cell **E24**, enter the formula **= SUBTOTAL(5, Employees[WAGES])** to calculate the minimum wage paid to Atlanta employees. The formula returns $31,200 as the minimum wage.

7. In cell **E25**, enter the formula **= SUBTOTAL(4, Employees[WAGES])** to calculate the maximum wage paid to Atlanta employees. The formula returns a maximum wage of $146,700. Refer to Figure 6–34.

Figure 6–34   SUBTOTAL function applied to the Employees table

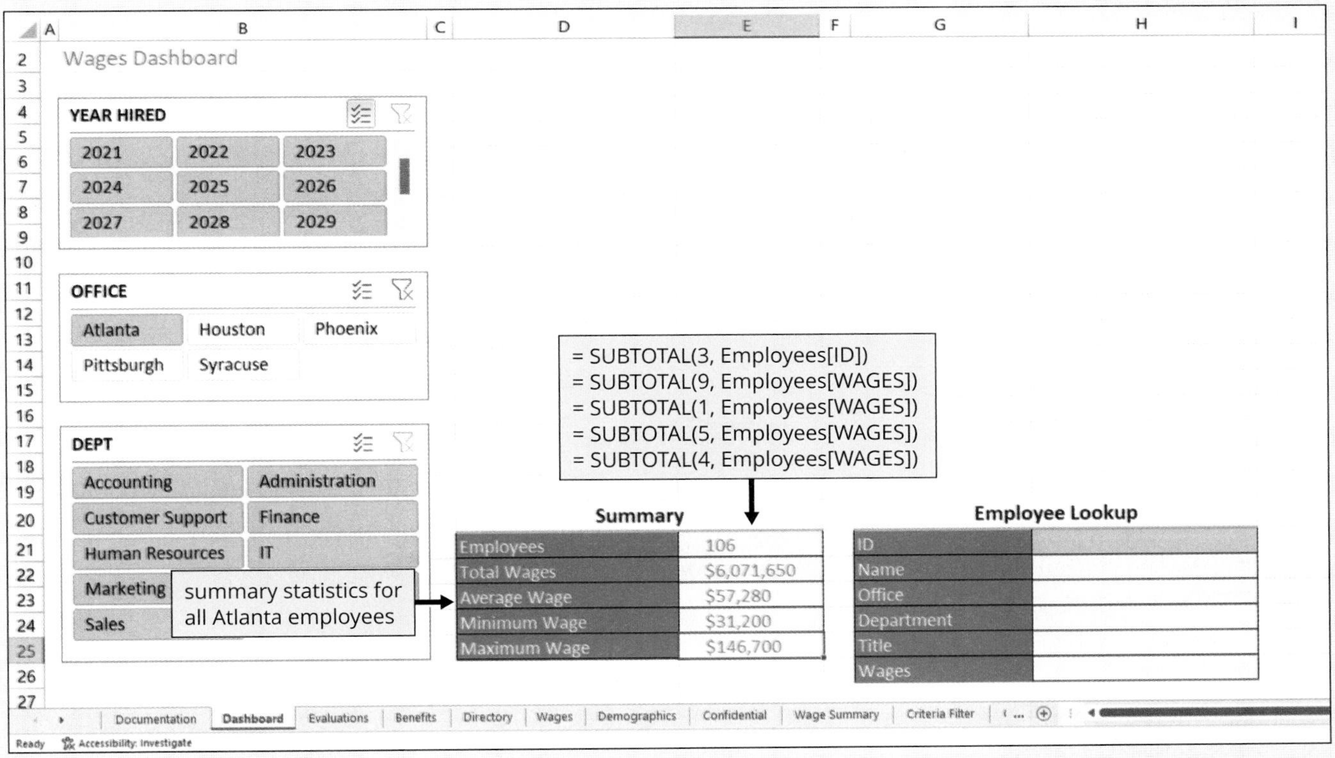

8. In the YEAR HIRED slicer, deselect all values except **2029** to limit the report to employees hired in 2029.

9. In the DEPT slicer, click **Accounting** to limit the report to employees of the Accounting department. The dashboard shows the results for five employees with total wages of $258,450, average wages of $51,690, ranging from $46,050 up to $57,300.

10. In each slicer, click the **Clear Filter** button to show the wages summary for all 530 employee records.

In addition to the summary statistics, dashboards often contain informative charts. You will add a chart describing the distribution of employee wages to the dashboard.

Creating Dynamic Charts

Charts based on Excel tables are dynamic so that they update automatically as the source data is filtered. Hidden records are not included in the chart, making charts ideal for dashboards because they present visual representations of the data under varying criteria.

Amit wants to be able to review the distribution of wages for different groups of employees. You will add a histogram to the Dashboard worksheet to show this information.

To add a histogram to the dashboard:

1. Go to the **Confidential** worksheet, and then click cell **M5** containing the wages in the first employee record.

2. Press **CTRL+SPACEBAR** to select all the data in the Wages column.

3. On the ribbon, click the **Insert** tab, and then in the Charts group, click the **Recommended Charts** button. The Insert Chart dialog box opens.

4. Click the **Histogram** chart, the third recommended chart, and then click **OK**. The histogram chart is created on the Confidential worksheet.

5. On the ribbon, click the **Home** tab, and then in the Clipboard group, click the **Cut** button (or press **CTRL+X**).

6. Go to the **Dashboard** worksheet, click cell **D4**, and then in the Clipboard group, click the **Paste** button (or press **CTRL+V**) to paste the chart.

7. In the Dashboard worksheet, hold down **ALT** as you move and resize the histogram chart so it covers the range D4:H18. Refer to Figure 6–35.

Figure 6–35   Histogram chart of the distribution of employee wages

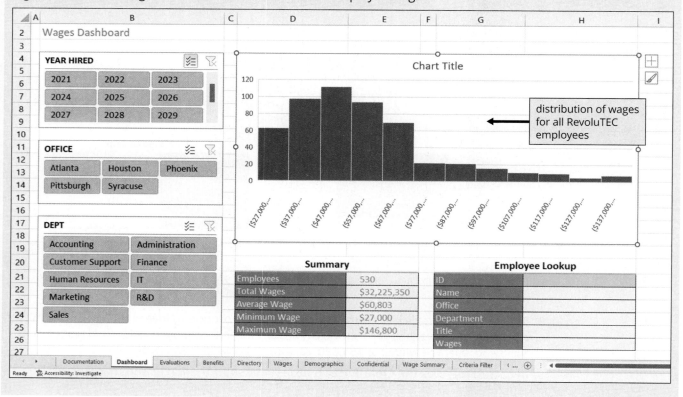

Amit asks you to remove the chart title and gridlines and to change the bin intervals for the histogram chart. You will change the axis scale to group the wages in intervals of $20,000 from $40,000 up to $120,000. Wages below or above that interval will be grouped together in the histogram.

To format the histogram chart:

1. With the chart still selected, click the **Chart Elements** button ⊞, and then click the **Chart Title** and **Gridlines** check boxes to deselect them. The chart title and horizontal gridlines disappear from the chart.

2. Click the **Data Labels** check box to show the number of employees in each wage group on the chart.

3. Double-click the labels in the horizontal axis. The Format Axis pane opens.

4. In the Axis Options section, click the **Bin width** option button to set a bin width for the histogram intervals and type **20000** in the Bin width box.

5. Click the **Overflow bin** check box, and then type **120000** in the Overflow bin box.

6. Click the **Underflow bin** check box, and then type **40000** in the Underflow bin box. Refer to Figure 6–36.

Figure 6–36   Formatted histogram chart

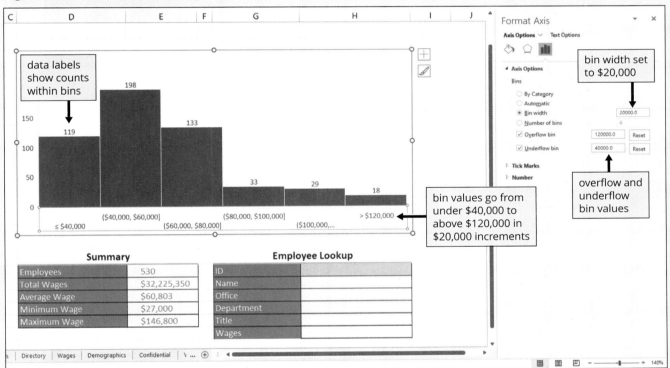

7. In the Format Axis pane, click the **Close** button ✖ to close the pane, and then click cell **A2** to deselect the chart.

The histogram chart you created is dynamic and will show the distribution for employees based on the selected criteria. Amit wants to review the distribution of wages for employees hired in the Houston IT department in 2028 and 2029.

To display the distribution of wages for Houston IT employees hired in 2028 and 2029:

1. In the YEAR HIRED slicer, deselect all slicer buttons except **2028** and **2029**.

   > **Trouble?** If you cannot select 2028 and 2029, make sure that the Multi-Select button is active in the slicer.

2. In the OFFICE slicer, click the **Houston** button.

3. In the DEPT slicer, click the **IT** button to select only that department. Refer to Figure 6–37.

Figure 6–37   Distribution of wages for Houston IT employees hired in 2028 and 2029

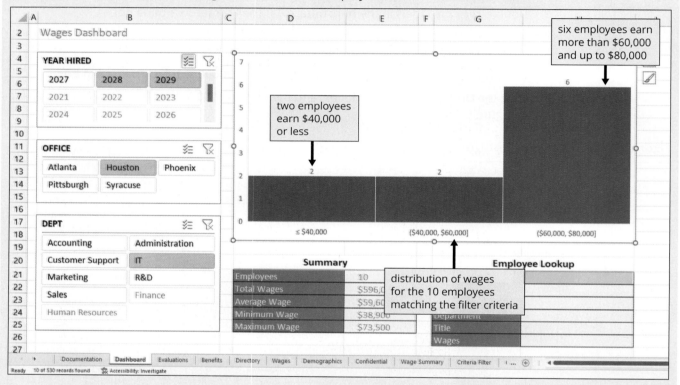

In 2028 and 2029, 10 employees were hired in Houston's IT department. The summary statistics show that the average wage for these 10 employees is $59,600. The histogram chart shows that two employees received less than $40,000 in wages and that six employees have annual wages from $60,000 to $80,000.

The slicers provide information on which field categories are missing. Notice that in Figure 6–37, the years 2021 through 2026 are grayed out in the YEAR HIRED slicer indicating that no Houston IT employees were hired in those years. Also, the Finance and Human Resources buttons are grayed out for the DEPT slicer, indicating that in Houston during 2028 and 2029, no employees were hired in those departments.

Insight

Exploring Boxplots

Another way of showing the distribution of data values is with a boxplot. A boxplot is a schematic diagram of the distribution in which the location of the central 50% of the data is displayed as a box with edges at the 25th and 75th percentiles. Extending beyond the 25th and 75th percentiles are straight lines, or whiskers, that indicate the range of the data values. The median of the data set is displayed as a central line within the box. Extremely small or large values are displayed as open circles beyond the whiskers. A typical boxplot would appear as follows:

Boxplots are extremely useful charts for statisticians who want a quick overview of the data and as a way of identifying unusually small or large data values. You can create a boxplot from the Insert Chart dialog box by selecting the Box and Whisker chart type.

Looking Up Data with Tables

Excel tables work well with the XLOOKUP function to retrieve data from lookup tables. As you add more records to the lookup table, the XLOOKUP function will automatically include the additional rows. If you filter the data, the lookup table will be restricted only to those rows that match filter criteria. Also, you can use the table names and field names to reference lookup and return columns rather than entering cell addresses.

Amit wants to be able to retrieve information about specific employees using their employee ID number right from the dashboard. You will add XLOOKUP functions to the Dashboard worksheet to retrieve this information.

To look up data from the Employees table from the dashboard:

1. Click cell **H21**, type the employee ID **e405-517** as the lookup entry, and then press **ENTER**.

2. In cell **H22**, type **= XLOOKUP(H21, Employees[ID], Employees[NAME])** to locate the record with the ID e405-517 from ID field in the Employees table and return the corresponding value in the Name field.

3. Press **ENTER**. The full name of the employee with the ID e405-517, Bentz, Manuel, appears in cell H22.

4. In cell **H23**, enter the formula **= XLOOKUP(H21,Employees[ID],Employees[OFFICE])** to retrieve the office from the table. Pittsburgh is displayed in cell H23.

5. In cell **H24**, enter the formula **= XLOOKUP(H21,Employees[ID],Employees[DEPT])** to retrieve data from the Dept field in the Employees table. Human Resources is displayed in cell H24.

6. In cell **H25**, enter the formula **= XLOOKUP(H21,Employees[ID],Employees[TITLE])** to retrieve data from the Title field. HR Programmer is displayed in cell H25.

7. In cell **H26**, enter the formula **= XLOOKUP(H21,Employees[ID],Employees[WAGES])** to retrieve the wages of Manuel Bentz. The value $60,300 is displayed in cell H26. Refer to Figure 6–38.

Figure 6–38   Employee data retrieved using the XLOOKUP function

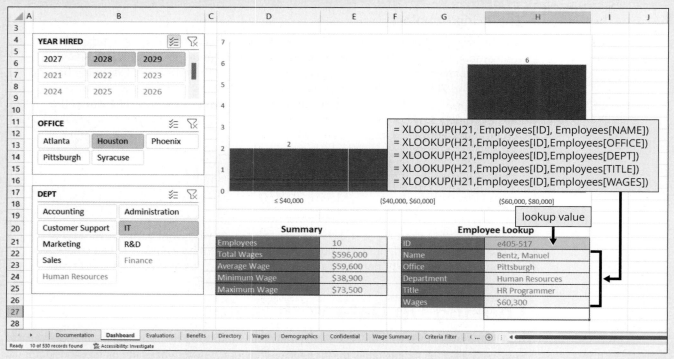

8. In cell **H21**, enter the employee ID **e119-520** to retrieve information on Kata Deepa.

> **Trouble?** If the lookup fails to retrieve the employee record, you might have mistyped the employee ID. Reenter the value in cell H21, making sure you enter the ID correctly.

You have completed your work on the Employee dashboard. With this dashboard, Amit can quickly retrieve payroll information for different groups of employees. By inserting even more slicers, Amit can add more factors and depth to that analysis.

Creating Tables with Excel Filter Tools

Data tables can be large and cumbersome, involving hundreds of fields and thousands of records. You will often find it more convenient to work with smaller versions of those tables, limited to a few select fields and records. You can create such tables using advanced filters and the FILTER function.

Applying an Advanced Filter

Filter and slicer buttons combine field values using the AND logical operator. In filtering the dashboard earlier, you retrieved only records of employees who were hired from 2028 to 2029 AND who worked in the IT department AND were based in the Houston office. Each criterion had to be met for a record to be chosen. However, you cannot use filter and slicer buttons for more complicated criteria involving both AND and OR logical operators. You cannot use the filter buttons for a search that returns employees who work in the Phoenix office (regardless of salary) OR make at least $90,000 a year (regardless of location).

Advanced filtering provides a way of writing more complicated filter criteria that involve expressions that combine fields using the AND and OR logical operators. To write an advanced filter, first define a **criteria range** laying out the specifications of the filter in a table using the following structure:

1. Field names are listed in the first row of the table and must exactly match the field names from the data range. The same field name can be repeated in the table to apply multiple criterion to same field.

2. Criteria for each field are listed in subsequent rows of the table.

3. Criteria within the same row are combined using the AND logical operator.

4. Criteria in different rows are combined using the OR logical operator.

Advanced filters can filter the data records in place as was done with the filter buttons applied to a data range or an Excel table, or they can be used to copy records matching the filter criteria to a new location, creating a new and smaller table.

Reference

Applying an Advanced Filter

- Create a criteria range in which the field names are in the first row, criteria for each field are listed in subsequent rows, criteria within the same row are combined with the AND operator, and criteria in different rows are combined with the OR operator.
- On the Data tab, in the Sort & Filter group, click the Advanced button.
- Specify whether to filter the data in place or copy to another location.
- In the List range box, specify the range containing the data values. In the Criteria range box, specify the range containing the criteria.
- Click OK to apply the advanced filter.

Amit's colleague wants a listing either of employees in the Syracuse Accounting department with total wages between $50,000 and $60,000 or employees in the Phoenix Finance department with total wages between $60,000 and $70,000. You will first create an advanced filter containing the criteria set by Amit's colleague.

To enter the criteria range for an advanced filter:

1. Go to the **Criteria Filter** worksheet. Amit has already entered the field names for this advanced filter in this sheet.

2. In cell **A6**, type **Syracuse** as the office to include in the filter, and then press **TAB**.

3. In cell B6, type **Accounting** as the department to include, and then press **TAB.**

4. In cell C6, type **>=50000** as the minimum base salary to include, and then press **TAB.**

5. In cell D6, type **<=60000** as the maximum base salary to include, and then press **ENTER**. The first row of the criteria range will filter the employee records to display only employees in the Syracuse office who work in the Accounting department and have a base salary between $50,000 and $60,000.

6. In the second row of the criteria range, type **Phoenix** in cell A7, press **TAB**, type **Finance** in cell B7, press **TAB**, type **>=60000** in cell C7, press **TAB**, type **<=70000** in cell D7, and then press **ENTER**. Refer to Figure 6–39.

Figure 6-39   Criteria range for creating an advanced filter

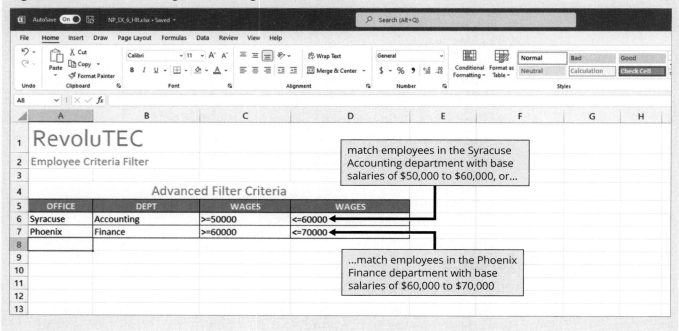

Amit stored wage data in a new table named Wages in the Wage Summary worksheet. You will use the criteria range to copy data from that table into the Criteria Filter worksheet.

To apply an advanced filter:

1. On the ribbon, click the **Data** tab, and then in the Sort & Filter group, click the **Advanced** button. The Advanced Filter dialog box opens.

2. Click the **Copy to another location** option button to copy matching records from the data range, and then press **TAB** to make the List range box active.

3. Go to the **Wage Summary** worksheet, click cell **A4**, and then press **CTRL+SHIFT+SPACEBAR** to select the entire data range. The external reference Wages[#All] appears in the List range box indicating that the entire Wages table is included in the list range.

    > **Tip** You can use the Advanced Filter tool to copy data from a table in one workbook to a data range in another workbook.

4. Press **TAB** to make the Criteria range box active.

5. Select the range **A5:D7** containing the advanced filter criteria. The reference 'Criteria Filter'!$A$5:$D$7 appears in the box.

6. Press **TAB** to make the Copy to box active, and then click cell **A9** to specify the location for inserting the copied records. Refer to Figure 6–40.

Figure 6–40   Advanced Filter dialog box

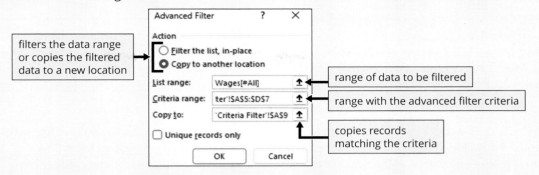

7. Click **OK** to copy the records that match the advanced filter criteria. Refer to Figure 6–41.

Figure 6–41   Advanced filter results

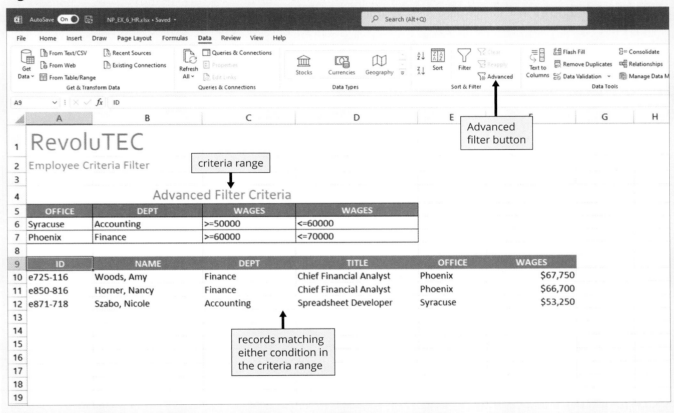

Three employees match either set of criteria: Nicole Szabo, a spreadsheet developer in the Syracuse Accounting department, and Amy Woods and Nancy Hormer who are chief financial analysts in the Phoenix Finance department.

There are limitations to advanced filtering. The data is copied in the order it appears in the list range. You cannot sort the data as it is copied and filtered. Another limitation is that because the data is copied, it will not automatically update as the data source changes. You must rerun the filter every time the data source is updated. Both limitations can be overcome using the FILTER function.

Filtering Data with the FILTER Function

The FILTER function is an example of a dynamic array function, which is a function that returns an array of values. You can use the FILTER function to create a table drawn from the contents of another table. The advantage of a dynamic array function is that it does not need to be recreated if the data source changes. A dynamic array function will always reflect the current content of the data source. The syntax of the FILTER function is

```
FILTER(array, include, [if_empty])
```

where `array` is a data range or table containing the data to be filtered, `include` specifies the criteria for including records from the data source, and `if_empty` is an optional argument that supplies either a value to be display or a function to run in the event that no matches are found. If you do not specify an `if_empty` value, the FILTER function returns the error value #CALC! when no matching records are found.

The following formula uses the FILTER function to return all records from the range A1:E100 for which values in the range A1:A100 are greater than 50. If no cells in the range A1:A100 match that criterion, the FILTER function displays the text string "No matching records found":

```
FILTER(A1:E100, A1:A100 > 50,"No matching records found")
```

The function does not need to return the entire table. If you only want to return the values from columns B and C for which the corresponding value in column A is greater than 50, limit the `array` argument to the B1:C100 range, as in the following formula:

```
FILTER(B1:C100, A1:A100 > 50,"No matching records found")
```

> **Tip** When filtering values in one array against values in a different array, the rows in the two arrays must match.

To use the FILTER function with an Excel table, enter references to table fields for the `array` argument and use table field names as part of the `include` argument. The following formula returns records for all employees in the Atlanta office using data from the Wages table; otherwise, it returns the text string "No employee records found" if there are no records for Atlanta employees:

```
FILTER(Wages, Wages[Office]="Atlanta", "No employee
records found")
```

You will use the FILTER function to generate a table showing the wages of all employees in the Phoenix office.

To use the FILTER function to generate a table of wages for the Phoenix office:

1. Go to the **Office and Dept** worksheet.

2. In cell **B4**, type **Phoenix** and press **ENTER**.

3. In cell **D5**, type the formula **= FILTER(Wages, Wages[Office] = B4, "No records found")** and press **ENTER**. Excel returns the wage records of all Phoenix employees. Refer to Figure 6–42.

Figure 6–42   FILTER function used to create a table of Phoenix employees data

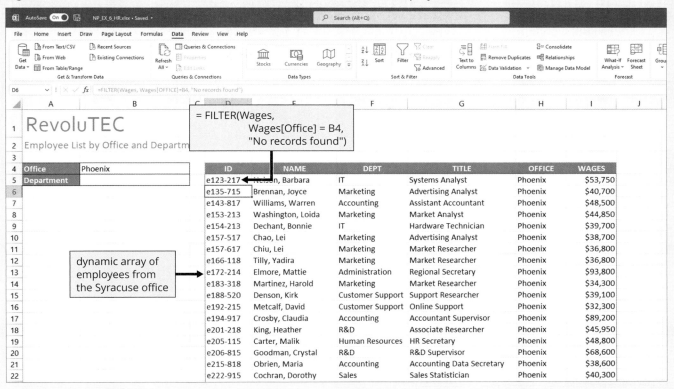

4. In cell **B4**, change the value to **Miami**. The formula in cell D5 returns the text string "No records found" because no Miami employees are listed in the Employees table.

5. In cell **B4**, change the value to **Houston** to display records of the Houston employees.

The FILTER function also works with data arranged in rows rather than columns. The formula

```
FILTER(A1:E100, A1:E1 > 25,"No matching records found")
```

would retrieve an array of columns from the range A1:E100 in which the values in the first row (A1:E1) are all greater than 25.

Filtering with Multiple Criteria

For filters that involve several criteria, join the criteria with a multiplication symbol (*) for an AND condition (so that records must match both criteria) or an addition symbol (+) for a OR condition (so that records can match either criteria.) The following expression would match all records in which the value in the range A1:A100 is greater than 50 AND the values in the range D1:D100 equal 5:

```
(A1:A100 > 50)*(D1:D100 = 5)
```

To change the criteria to an OR condition, change the symbol to +

```
(A1:A100 > 50)+(D1:D100 = 5)
```

to retrieve all records for which the value of a cell in the range A1:100 is greater than 50 OR a value in the range D1:D100 equals 5. You must enclose each criterion within a set of parentheses.

Amit wants the FILTER function to filter employee records by both Office and Department. You will modify the formula in cell D5 now using the * symbol to create an AND condition between the two criteria.

To use the FILTER function with multiple criteria:

1. Click cell **B5**, type **Marketing** as the department, and then press **ENTER**.

2. Click cell **D5**, and then press **DELETE** to remove the current formula.

3. In cell **D5**, type **= FILTER(Wages,** to begin the FILTER function.

4. Type **(Wages[OFFICE] = B4)** to specify the first condition that the office must match the value in cell B4.

5. Type ***(Wages[DEPT] = B5)** to specify the second condition that the department must match the value in cell B5.

6. Type **, "No records found")** to complete the formula = FILTER(Wages, (Wages[OFFICE] = B4)*(Wages[DEPT] = B5), "No records found")

7. Press **ENTER**. The 11 employees who work in the Houston Marketing department are displayed. Refer to Figure 6–43.

Figure 6–43　　FILTER function with multiple criteria

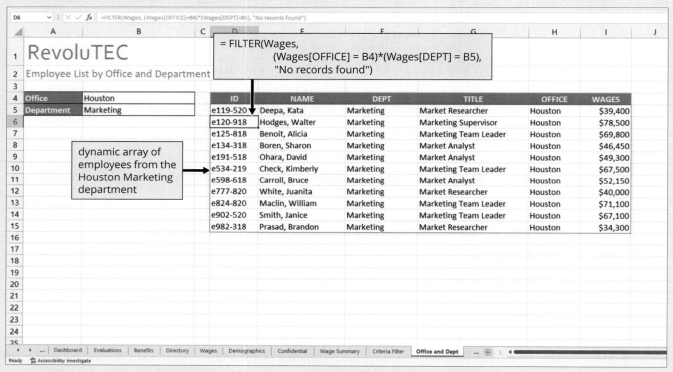

8. In cell **B4**, change the value to **Phoenix** and then in cell **B5**, change the value to **Sales** to list the 17 employees in the Phoenix Sales department.

By grouping the expressions using nested parentheses, you can define criteria involving several AND/OR conditions. The following expression matches any record in which the range A1:A100 is greater than 50 OR where the range D1:D100 equals 5 AND the range E1:E100 equals 0:

```
(A1:A100 > 50)*((D1:D100 = 5)+(E1:E100)=0)
```

In this way, a single FILTER formula can accomplish what would have required an Advanced Filter table with several rows of criteria to do. Because the FILTER function is dynamic, unlike Advanced Filter tables, it does not have to be rerun whenever the source data changes.

Proskills

Choosing Columns with the FILTER Function

In some applications, you might only want to retrieve a few select columns from a large and complicated table. This can be a challenge if those columns are not adjacent to each other. There are several workarounds you can apply to choose which columns to retrieve and which to omit.

To select which columns to retrieve, provide criteria with an array of numbers the same length as the number of columns. A value of 1 in the array will include the corresponding column in the filter; a value of 0 excludes it. For example, the following filter retrieves only column A, D, and E from the five columns in the range A1:E100:

```
= FILTER(A1:E100, {1,0,0,1,1})
```

By nesting one FILTER function within another you can choose both the columns and the rows from the data source. The following formula retrieves columns A, D, and E from the range A1:E100, but only for those rows in which the value in column A is greater than 50:

```
= FILTER(FILTER(A1:E100, A1:A100 > 50),{1,0,0,1,1})
```

If there are many columns in the data source, it would be cumbersome to insert a long array indicating whether each column should be included or excluded. A more compact approach is to use the CHOOSECOLS function, identifying the included columns by their index number. To choose the first, fourth, and fifth columns from the data source, use the following formula:

```
= CHOOSECOLS(FILTER(A1:E100, A1:A100 > 50), {1,4,5})
```

As with the previous example, this function will return columns A, D, and E from the range A1:E100, but only for rows in which the value is column A is greater than 50.

Sorting Data with the SORT Function

Another dynamic array function is the SORT function, which sorts values from a data range or table or the contents of another dynamic array. The syntax of the SORT function is

```
SORT(array, [sort_index], [sort_order], [by_col])
```

where *array* is a data range or table, *sort_index* provides indices of the columns or row to the sort the data by, *sort_order* specifies whether to sort the data in ascending (1) or descending (–1) order, and *by_col* indicates whether the data should be sorted by column (TRUE) or by row (FALSE). The default is to sort data using the first column (*sort_index* = 1), in ascending order (*sort_order* = 1), by row within each column (*by_col* = FALSE). The SORT function does not alter the original data; it only impacts the dynamic array it creates.

The following formula uses the SORT function to return a dynamic array of the values in the range A1:E100 sorted by the values of column C in ascending order:

```
SORT(A1:E100, 3)
```

To create a dynamic array of the same data sorted by column E in descending order, use the following formula:

```
SORT(A1:E100, 5, -1)
```

To sort by multiple columns (or rows) enclose the *sort_index* and *sort_order* values in a comma-separated array enclosed in curly braces. The following formula returns a dynamic array of the range A1:E100 values sorted first by column C (third column) in ascending order and within that sorted order, by column E (fifth column) in descending order:

```
SORT(A1:E100, {3,5}, {1, -1})
```

Amit wants to review the array of employee data sorted by Office and Department in ascending order by then by Wages in descending order. You will use the SORT function to generate that dynamic array.

To apply the SORT function:

1. Click cell **D5**, and then press **DELETE** to remove the FILTER formula.

2. In cell **D5**, type **= SORT(Wages,** to begin the function returning a dynamic array of the sorted data from the Wages table.

3. Type **{5, 3, 6},** to insert array of column indices for the Office (5), Dept (3), and Wages (6) fields.

4. Type **{1, 1, –1})** to sort the Office and Dept fields in ascending order and the Wages field in descending order. The complete text of the formula is: = SORT(Wages, {5,3,6}, {1,1,-1})

5. Press **ENTER**. A dynamic array of the employee data sorted by Office and Department in ascending alphabetical order and by Wages in descending numeric order is displayed. Refer to Figure 6–44.

Figure 6–44   SORT function applied to data from the Wages table

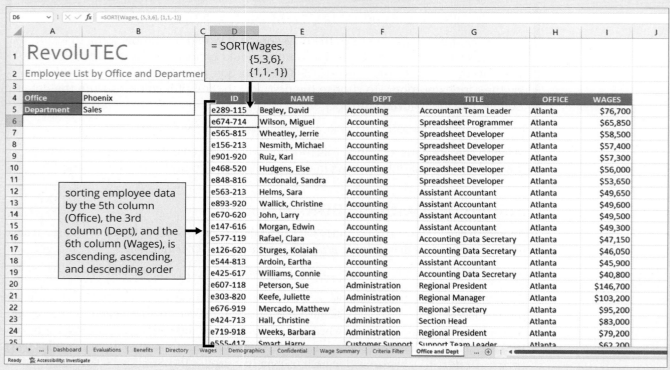

The SORT function can also work with records arranged by columns instead of by rows. To sort a data range in the horizontal direction, set the *by_col* value to TRUE.

Sorting Data with the SORTBY Function

The SORTBY function, which is similar to the SORT function, sorts data from a table or data range based on values from another array. The field to sort the data does not to be shown in the sorted array. This has advantages when that field contains confidential information, such as employee salary, that should not be visible to everyone. The syntax of the SORTBY function is

```
SORTBY(array, by_array1, [sort_order1],
    [by_array2, sort_order2], …)
```

where *array* is the data to be copied and sorted, *by_array1* references the range or array to sort by and *sort_order1* specifies whether to sort in ascending (1) or descending (–1) order. The optional arguments *by_array2*, *sort_order2*, and so on provide additional levels of sorting.

The following function uses the SORTBY function to create a dynamic array of the contents of the range A1:C100 sorted using corresponding data values in the ranges D1:D100 and E1:E100. The data will be copied and sorted in ascending order of the values in the D column and then descending of the column E values.

```
SORTBY(A1:C100, D1:D100, 1, E1:E100, -1)
```

The SORTBY function frees you from having to associate columns with index numbers because you reference the values to sort by using a range reference or a range name. The following function creates a dynamic array of the employee data, in descending order of Wages field:

```
SORTBY(Employees, Employees[Wages], -1)
```

Another advantage of the SORTBY function is that the Wages field can be moved to a new column within the Employees table without affecting the function results. This would not be true with the SORT function which references columns by a static index number. The SORTBY function does not require the array to be sorted and the array to be sorted by to be in the same table. You can create a dynamic array of sorted values from one table using fields arrays from an entirely different table.

Combining Sorting and Filtering

Because the FILTER, SORT, and SORTBY functions all return dynamics arrays as their output, they can be combined to both filter and sort the contents of a data range or Excel table. The FILTER function creates the dynamic array of filtered values which is then used as the input to the SORT or SORTBY function. The following formula uses this technique to first filter the range A1:E100, including only those rows where the values in column A are greater than 50, and then sorts those filtered values in ascending order of column C (the third column) and descending order of column E (the fifth column):

```
SORT(FILTER(A1:E100, A1:A100 > 50), {3, 5}, {1, -1})
```

Amit wants to create a dynamic array that first filters data from the Wages table by the Office and Dept fields, and then sorts that data in descending order of the Wages field. You will nest the FILTER function within a SORT function to generate that output for Amit.

To combine the FILTER and SORT functions to create a table:

1. Click cell **D5**, and then press **DELETE** to remove the SORT function within the cell.
2. In cell **D5**, enter the formula similar to the formula you created earlier **=FILTER(Wages, (Wages[OFFICE]=B4)*(Wages[DEPT]=B5))** and press **ENTER**.
3. Verify that Excel returns a table of employees in the Phoenix Sales department.

   > **Tip** The best practice when nesting dynamic array functions is to start with the innermost function, confirm that the correct dynamic array is generated, and then proceed to the outer functions.

4. Click cell **D5**, and then in the formula bar, click between = and FILTER. You will add the Sort function to the formula.
5. Type **SORT(** to begin the function.
6. Directly after the closing parenthesis of the FILTER function, type **, 6, -1)** to sort the dynamic array by the sixth column (Wages) in descending order. The complete formula is: = SORT(FILTER(Wages, (Wages[OFFICE]=B4)*(Wages[DEPT]=B5)), 6, -1)
7. Press **ENTER** to sort the dynamic array. Refer to Figure 6–45.

Figure 6–45   Filtered and sorted employee data

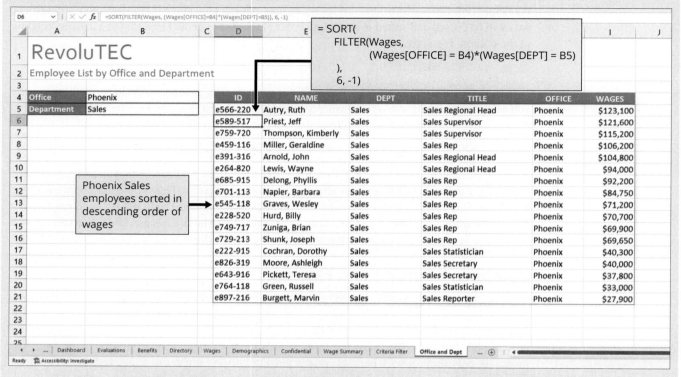

8. In cell **B4**, change the value to **Syracuse** and in cell **B5**, change the value to **Human Resources**. The dynamic array updates to show 14 employees from the Syracuse Human Resources department sorted in descending order of wages.

Note that index numbers for the sorted columns match the index numbers of the dynamic array returned by the FILTER function. For example, if the FILTER function removes column 2 through 4 of a 5-column data range leaving only columns 1, 5, and so forth, the second column referenced by the SORT function is column 5 of the original data range.

> **Tip** Dynamic arrays are arranged along the same columns and rows as the original data. To switch the columns and rows, nest the dynamic array within the TRANSPOSE function.

Exploring Other Dynamic Array Functions

Dynamic array functions are a useful tool for summarizing and analyzing data. Figure 6–46 lists some of the other dynamic array functions that can be applied to a data set.

Figure 6–46   Dynamic array functions

Function	Description
CHOOSECOLS(*array*, *col_num1*, [*col_num2*], ...)	Returns columns from an *array*, where *col_num1*, *col_num2*, etc. are the indices of the columns
CHOOSEROWS(*array*, *row_num1*, [*row_num2*], ...)	Returns rows from an *array*, where *row_num1*, *row_num2*, etc. are the indices of the rows
DROP(*array*, *rows*, [*columns*])	Removes rows or columns from an *array*, where *rows* is the number of rows to drop and *columns* is the number of columns. Positive row/column numbers drop from the start of the array, negative row/column numbers drop from the end of the array
TAKE(*array*, *rows*, [*columns*])	Extracts rows or columns from an *array*, where *rows* is the number of rows to extract and *columns* is the number of columns. Positive row/column numbers extract from the start of the array, negative row/column numbers extract from the end of the array
TOCOL(*array*, [*ignore*], [*scan_by_column*])	Converts an *array* into a single column, where *ignore* indicates whether to ignore blanks and error values, and *scan_by_column* indicates whether to scan the array in row order (FALSE), or column order (TRUE)
TOROW(*array*, [*ignore*], [*scan_by_column*])	Converts an *array* into a single row, where *ignore* indicates whether to ignore blanks and error values, and *scan_by_column* indicates whether to scan the array in row order (FALSE), or column order (TRUE)
RANDARRAY([*rows*], [*columns*], [*min*], [*max*], [*whole_number*])	Returns an *array* of random number, where *rows* and *columns* define the number of rows and columns in the array, *min* and *max* provide the minimum and maximum possible random number, and *whole_number* specifies whether to return a whole number (TRUE) or a decimal value (FALSE)
SEQUENCE(*rows*, [*columns*], [*start*], [*step*])	Returns an array of sequential numbers, where *rows* and *columns* define the number of rows and columns in the array, *start* is the starting number of the sequence, and *step* is the increment between consecutive numbers in the sequence
UNIQUE(*array*, [*by_col*], [*exactly_once*])	Extracts unique values form an *array*, where *by_col* specifies whether to compare values across columns (TRUE) or across rows (FALSE), and *exactly_once* specifies whether to return unique values that occur only once (TRUE) or any number of times (FALSE)

In large data sets, investigators are often interested in generating lists of unique values, such as a master list of store locations, product IDs, or departments. Such lists can be created from a data range or table using the UNIQUE function

```
UNIQUE(array, [by_col], [exactly_once])
```

where *array* is range or array from which to retrieve unique values, *by_col* specifies whether to compare values across columns (TRUE) or across rows (FALSE), and *exactly_once* specifies whether to return unique values that occur exactly once in the array (TRUE), or to return a list of all unique values (FALSE). The default values for *by_col* and *exactly_once* are both FALSE to compare values across rows and to return all unique values.

Because the UNIQUE function returns a dynamic array, it can also be nested within the SORT and FILTER functions to either sort the list of unique values or pare down the list to a select few values that match specified criteria.

RevoluTEC is expanding its operations to new offices and will reorganize its employee structure by adding new departments or renaming job titles. As the reorganization progresses, Amit wants to maintain a master list of offices, departments, and job titles. You will create that master list using the UNIQUE function taking data from the Employees table you created earlier.

To create a sorted list of offices, departments, and job titles:

1. Go to the **Field Lists** worksheet, and then click cell **A5.**

2. Type the formula **= SORT(UNIQUE(Employees[OFFICE]))** and then press **ENTER.** Excel returns a master list of the five departments, sorted in alphabetical order.

3. Click cell **C5**, type the formula **= SORT(UNIQUE(Employees[DEPT]))** and then press **ENTER.** Excel returns a list of nine departments in alphabetical order.

4. Click cell **E5**, type the formula **= SORT(UNIQUE(Employees[TITLE]))** and then press **ENTER.** Excel returns a long list of job titles in alphabetical order. Refer to Figure 6–47.

Figure 6–47   UNIQUE function applied to create lists of offices, departments, and titles

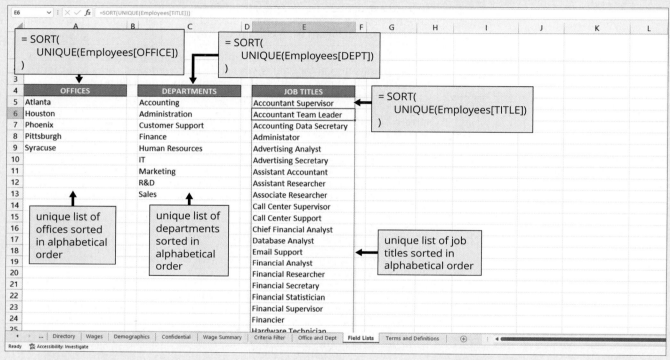

5. **sam** Save the workbook, and then close it.

Any changes you and Amit make to the Employees table in the Confidential worksheet will be reflected automatically in the master list of offices, departments, and job titles. These master lists can also act as lookup tables for other Excel functions and applications.

You have completed your work with the employee data. The tools and techniques you used in this workbook will prove useful in future reports for the HR department.

Part 6.3 Quick Check

1. What are two reasons for using slicers rather than filter buttons to filter data?

2. Write a formula to calculate the sum of the filtered values from the Price field in the Sales table.

3. Write a formula to calculate the average of the filtered values from the Price field in the Sales table.

4. Write a formula to retrieve the value of Customer field from the record in the Sales table whose PID field equals the value in cell B10.

5. Write a formula to create a dynamic array of the Sales table where the Product field equals "Washer" or "Dryer".

6. Write a formula to create a dynamic array of the Sales table sorted in descending order of the Date field and ascending order of the PID field. Assume that the PID field is the first column in the table and the Date field is the second column.

7. Write a formula to create a dynamic array of the Sales table sorted in descending order the Customer field in that table.

8. Write a formula to create a dynamic array of the Sales table where the Product field equals "Washer" and the records are sorted in descending order of the Date field. Assume that the Date field is the second column in the table.

9. Write a formula to list all the unique names of the Product field in the Sales table.

Practice: Review Assignments

Data File needed for the Review Assignments: NP_EX_6-2.xlsx

Amit in the Human Resources department of RevoluTEC needs to track the hiring process for new recruits, from the initial application stage, through the interview stages, and culminating in a final offer of employment. Amit compiled information on current candidates for positions in the soon-to-be-opened Nashville office and wants you to develop reports and summaries of the recruitment efforts. Complete the following:

1. Open the **NP_EX_6-2.xlsx** workbook located in the Excel6 > Review folder included with your Data Files. Save the workbook as **NP_EX_6_Hires** in the location specified by your instructor.

2. In the Documentation sheet, enter your name and the date in the range B3:B4.

3. Go to the Applications worksheet containing a list of applications made to the Nashville office for 12 positions. The worksheet lists the dates that each applicant completed each stage of the recruitment process from the date the application was received, through the phone screening, manager interview, onsite interview, offer date, and acceptance date. The value #N/A indicates that the applicant did not pass to that recruitment stage. Refer to the Table Data worksheet for a description of each field.

4. Use conditional formatting to locate records that have a duplicate Applicant ID in the range A5:A1043. Delete the second duplicate record. Do *not* remove the conditional formatting rule when you are finished.

5. One applicant record is duplicated for all fields except for the Applicant ID field. Use the Remove Duplicates command to remove the duplicate.

6. Convert the data range A4:N1041 into an Excel table named **Recruits**.

7. Make the following changes to the Recruits table:

   a. Insert a new field named **Full Name** between the Last Name and Position fields. In cell D5 enter the formula **= CONCAT([@[Last Name]],", ",[@[First Name]])** to display the full names of each applicant.

   b. Enter a new field named **Days to Hire** in cell P4. In cell P5, use your mouse to enter a formula calculating the value of the Acceptance Date field in cell M5 minus the Application Date field in cell G5.

   c. Apply the General number format to the results so that the values appear as days rather than dates and then resize the column to make the field name fully visible.

8. Show how applicants are tracked through the recruitment process by sorting the table by the Position field in A to Z order and then by Acceptance Date, Offer Date, Onsite Date, Manager Date, and finally Phone Date fields, with all dates sorted from newest to oldest. The sorted data should show applicants for each position that went farthest last.

9. Go to the Hires worksheet. In cell A5, use the FILTER function to create a dynamic array of the values of the Recruits table, selecting only those records where the Hired field equals Yes.

10. Modify the formula in cell A5 to use the SORT function to sort the dynamic array returned by the FILTER function in ascending order of the Position and Full Name columns (columns 5 and 4).

11. Freeze panes at cell A5 so that you can scroll vertically and horizontally through the hiring list keeping the data labels in view.

12. Copy the data for the Full Name through the Department columns and the Base Salary column and paste the values (not the formulas) into cell A5 of the Hiring Salaries worksheet.

13. In the Hiring Salaries worksheet, add subtotal rows at each change in the value of the Position field, showing the average of the Base Salary field within each Position.

14. Go to the IT and Marketing Hires worksheet and complete the following advanced filter:

   a. Complete the criteria range to create a list of new hires from the IT department with base salaries greater than $75,000 or from the Marketing department with base salaries greater than $65,000.

   b. Run the Advanced Filter using the copy data to another location option. Use the data in the range A4:P40 of the Hires worksheet as the list range, the range A4:B6 in the IT and Marketing worksheet as criteria range, and the range D4:S4 of the IT and Marketing Hires worksheet as the Copy to cell.

15. Go to the Applications worksheet and insert a slicer for the Position field. Move the slicer to the Metrics worksheet and resize it to fit in the range B4:B13. Display the slicer buttons in two columns.

16. In the range E5:E10 of the Metrics worksheet, do the following to count the number of applicants who reach each stage of the recruitment process:

   a. In cell E5, use the SUBTOTAL function with the COUNTA function to count the number of entries in the Applicant ID field of the Recruits table.

   b. In cell E6, use the SUBTOTAL function with the COUNT function to count the number of values in the Phone Date field.

   c. In cell E7, use the SUBTOTAL function with the COUNT function to count the number of values in the Manager Date field.

   d. In cell E8, use the SUBTOTAL function with the COUNT function to count the number of values in the Onsite Date field.

   e. In cell E9, use the SUBTOTAL function with the COUNT function to count the number of values in the Offer Date field.

   f. In cell E10, use the SUBTOTAL function with the COUNT function to count the number of values in the Acceptance Date field.

17. Calculate the following values to track certain Key Performance Indexes (KPIs) that indicate the efficiency of the recruitment process:

   a. In cell E11, calculate the number of applicants for each hire by dividing the value in cell E5 by the value in cell E10.

   b. In cell E12, calculate the number of interviews for each hire by dividing the sum of the values in cells E7 and E8 by the value in cell E10.

18. In the range F6:F10, calculate the percent of the original applicants that advance after each step in the process by dividing the number of applicants that made it to each step by the value in cell E5.

19. In the range E5:E10, use conditional formatting to add orange data bars with a gradient fill to the values to show how the number of applicants is trimmed during recruitment.

20. Go to the Applications worksheet and create a Histogram chart of the data in the range P4:P1041 to display the distribution for the number of days to hire new employees. Do the following to the chart:

   a. Move the chart to the Metrics worksheet, and then resize the chart to cover the range H3:M13.

   b. Change the chart title to **Days to Hire** and add data labels to the bars in the histogram.

   c. In the axis options, change the histogram's Bin width to 5 with an Overflow bin value of 50 and an Underflow bin value of 25.

21. Test the dashboard you created by showing the recruitment statistics for the Programmer position. Verify that the KPIs are updated to reflect this subset of the data and the histogram changes to show the distributions of the number of days required to fill that position.

22. Save the workbook, and then close it.

Apply: Case Problem 1

Data File needed for this Case Problem: NP_EX_6-3.xlsx

Harbor Outfitters Daria Magda is an inventory manager for Harbor Outfitters, a major manufacturer and distributor of boating parts and tools. Daria uses Excel to help manage the inventory at Harbor Outfitters warehouses, ensuring that products remain stocked and resupplied on a timely basis. At the Harbor Outfitters warehouses, the products are located by row number and bin number. Daria wants a report that indicates how many of the warehouse items need restocking and at what cost. The report also must track restocking needs by row number and bin number. You will create a dashboard that will display the answers that Daria needs. Complete the following:

1. Open the **NP_EX_6-3.xlsx** workbook located in the Excel6 > Case1 folder included with your Data Files, and then save the workbook as **NP_EX_6_Harbor.xlsx** in the location specified by your instructor.

2. In the Documentation sheet, in the range B3:B4, enter your name and the date.

3. Go to the Inventory worksheet. Use the Remove Duplicates tool to remove records for which every field value is duplicated. Verify that Excel reports that five duplicates are removed.

4. Convert the data range in the Inventory worksheet to an Excel table. Rename the table **Inventory_Tbl**.

5. Sort the table in ascending order of the Warehouse, Bin, and Part ID fields.

6. Insert a new field named **Inventory Value** between the Stock Qty and Reorder Qty fields. Calculate the inventory value by using your mouse to enter the formula that multiplies the Unit Cost field (cell E5) by the Stock Qty field (cell F5). If necessary, format the values using the Currency format and resize the column to fit the data.

7. In cell J4, add a new field named **Restock** that you will use to determine which items need to be restocked. Use your mouse to enter an IF function that displays a value of "Yes" if the Stock Qty field (cell F5) is less than or equal to the Reorder Qty field (cell H5) and "No" if it is not.

8. In cell K4, add the **Restock Indicator** field. Use your mouse to enter a formula that uses the IF function to display the value 1 if the Restock field (cell J5) equals "Yes" and the value 0 otherwise. Resize the column to fit the data.

9. In cell L4, add the **Restock Qty** field. In this field, determine the number of items to order for products that need to be restocked. Use your mouse to enter a formula equal to the Restock Indicator field (cell K5) times the difference between the Restock Level and Stock Qty fields (I5 – F5). Resize the column to fit the data.

10. In cell M4, add a new field named **Restock Cost** to calculate how much it will cost to restock the items that need restocking. Use your mouse to enter a formula that multiplies the Restock Qty field (cell L5) by the Unit Cost field (cell E5).

11. Go to the Restock List worksheet. In cell A5, use the FILTER function to show only those records where the Restock field in the Inventory_Tbl table equals "Yes".

12. Nest the formula in cell A5 within the SORT function to sort the dynamic array values by descending order of the restock cost (column 13).

13. Add a freeze pane to the Restock List worksheet at cell E5.

14. Go to the Inventory worksheet, and then create slicers for the Warehouse and Bin fields. Do the following:

    a. Move the slicers to the Report worksheet.

    b. Place the Warehouse slicer over the range A4:A7 with four columns in the button layout.

    c. Place the Bin slicer in the range A9:A16 with three columns in the button layout.

    d. Allow users to make multiple selections from both slicers.

15. Calculate the following summary statistics for the inventory data:

    a. In cell D5, enter the SUBTOTAL with the COUNTA function to count the number of records in the Part ID field of the Inventory_Tbl table.

    b. In cell D6, enter the SUBTOTAL function with the SUM function to the Stock Qty field to calculate the quantity of items in the warehouse.

    c. In cell D7, enter the SUBTOTAL function with the SUM function to the Inventory Value field to calculate the total value of items in the warehouse.

    d. In cell D8, enter the SUBTOTAL function with the SUM function to the Restock Indicator field to calculate the number of items requiring restocking.

    e. In cell D9, calculate the difference between cells D5 and D8, returning the total number of items that do not require restocking.

    f. In cell D10, enter the SUBTOTAL function with the SUM function to the Restock Costs field to calculate the total cost of restocking items that have low inventory.

16. Insert a pie chart of the data in the range C8:D9 and resize it to cover the range C11:D18. Remove the chart title and add data labels to the pie slices showing the percentage of items that need restocking.

17. Use the slicers to show a summary for items from warehouse rows 1 and 2 and from bins 1, 4, 7, and 10.

18. Save the workbook, and then close it.

Challenge: Case Problem 2

Data File needed for this Case Problem: NP_EX_6-4.xlsx

Mount Sinai Medical Center Miriam Cantor is the Quality-of-Care manager at Mount Sinai Medical Center located in White Plains, New York. Miriam wants to use Excel to monitor daily clinic appointments, looking at how many patients a doctor sees per day and how much time is spent with each patient. Miriam is also interested in whether patients are experiencing long wait times within particular departments or with specific doctors. She provided a worksheet containing the scheduled appointments from a typical day. Miriam wants you to create a dashboard that can be used to summarize the appointments from that day. Complete the following:

1. Open the **NP_EX_6-4.xlsx** workbook located in the Excel6 > Case2 folder included with your Data Files, and then save the workbook as **NP_EX_6_Sinai** in the location specified by your instructor.

2. In the Documentation sheet, enter your name and the date in cells B3 and B4.

3. In Patient Log worksheet, convert the data range listing the entire day's appointments from 8 AM to 5 PM at four departments into an Excel table using **Appointments** as the table name. Turn off the banded rows style.

4. In the Departments, Physicians, and Patients worksheets, convert each data range to a table, naming them **Department_List**, **Physician_List**, and **Patient_List**, respectively. You will use these tables to display names instead of IDs in the Appointments table.

5. In the Patient Log worksheet, create the following fields and use your mouse to enter formulas for the following calculated fields (resize the columns as needed):
   a. Between the Dept ID and Physician ID fields, insert the **Department** field and then enter an XLOOKUP function selecting cell B5 as the lookup value and using the Dept ID field from the Dept_List table as the lookup array and the Department field from the Dept_List table as the return array.
   b. Between the Physician ID and Patient ID fields, insert the **Physician** field. Use an XLOOKUP function to retrieve the value of the Physician Name field from the Physician_List table.
   c. Between the Patient ID and Patient Check In fields, insert the **Patient** field. Use an XLOOKUP function to retrieve the value of the Patient Name field from the Patient_List table.

6. In column K, create the **Patient Wait** field and then enter an IF function to calculate whether a patient had to wait past the scheduled appointment time. Test whether the value of the Exam Start field (cell I5) is greater than the Appt Time Field (cell A5); if it is, return the value 1; otherwise, return the value 0. Format the calculated values with the General number format.

7. Insert the **Wait Time** field in column L. Calculate how many minutes each patient had to wait by using your mouse to enter a formula that multiplies the value of the difference between the Exam Start (cell I5) and Appt Time (cell A5) fields by 24*60 (to express the difference in minutes). Format the calculated values with the General number format.

8. Insert the **Visit Length** field in column M. Calculate the visit length in minutes by using your mouse to enter a formula that multiplies the difference between the Exam End and Exam Start fields by 24*60. Format the calculated values with the General number format.

9. Resize the columns in the Appointments table so that no field values or columns labeled are truncated.

10. Insert slicers for the **Department** and **Physician** fields, and then do the following:
    a. Move both slicers to the Dashboard worksheet.
    b. Resize the Department slicer to cover the merged range A4:D7.
    c. Resize the Physician slicer to cover the merged range A8:D16.
    d. Set the layout of both slicers to five columns.

11. **Explore:** On the Slicer tab, in the Slicer group, in the Slicer Caption box, change the caption of the Department slicer to **Treating Department** and the caption of the Physician slicer to **Examining Physician**.

12. **Explore:** Select the Treating Department slicer, and then click the Slicer Settings button in the Slicer group to open the Slicer Settings dialog box. Click the Hide Items with no data check box to hide department names when they are not relevant to the dashboard report. Repeat for the Examining Physician slicer.

13. Calculate the following summary statistics in the Dashboard worksheet:

   a. In the merged cell A19, show the number of appointments behind schedule by applying the SUBTOTAL function with the SUM function to the Patient Wait field of the Appointments table.

   b. In the merged cell B19, show the number of appointments that were on time by entering the SUBTOTAL function with the COUNT function to the Appt Time field of the Appointments table and subtracting the value of cell A19.

   c. In the merged cell C19, enter the SUBTOTAL function to calculate the average value of the Wait Time field in the Appointments table.

   d. In the merged cell D19, enter the SUBTOTAL function to calculate the average value of the Visit Length field in the Appointments table.

14. Create a pie chart of the data in the range A18:B23, and then move the chart to cover the range A25:B34. Remove the chart legend. Add data labels positioned on the outside end of each slice, showing both the percentage and the category name. If two categories are not displayed in the pie chart, on the Chart Design tab, in the Data group click the Switch Row/Column button.

15. Create a histogram of the data in the Wait Time column in the Patient Log worksheet. Move the histogram to the Dashboard worksheet and then resize the chart to fit in the range C25:C34. Change the chart title to **Waiting Time**. Add data labels. Set the bin width to 5, the Overflow bin value to 10, and the Underflow bin value to 0.

16. Create a histogram of the data in the Visit Length column in the Patient Log worksheet. Move the histogram to the Dashboard worksheet and resize it to fit in the range D25:D34. Change the chart title to **Length of Visit** and add data labels. Set the bin width to 10, the Overflow bin value to 60, and the Underflow bin value to 20.

17. Test the slicer buttons by showing the results for Dr. Jacob Leiva of the Internal Medicine department.

18. Type **Dr. Leiva, Jacob** in cell G8.

19. In cell F11, use the FILTER function to create a dynamic array of appointments from the Appointments table where the Physician field equals the value in cell G8. Do not worry if the values are not formatted correctly. That will be fixed in the next step.

20. **Explore:** You do not need to display all the columns from the Appointments table. Nest the FILTER function in the previous step within another FILTER function. Set the value of the include parameter to the array {0,0,0,0,0,1,1,1,1,1,0,0,0} (five zeroes followed by five ones followed by three zeroes). Refer to the Pro Skills Box *Choosing Columns with the FILTER Function* for more information on filtering out columns.

21. Save the workbook, and then close it.

Summarizing Data with PivotTables

Creating a Customer Relationship Management Report

Case: Argyle Security

Jeannette Roselle is an accounts coordinator for Argyle Security, a business that develops and installs security systems for commercial and residential customers. Jeannette wants to examine the company's ability to attract and retain customers. You will use Excel to assist Jeannette in developing a report analyzing customer contacts during the current fiscal year, determining the company's success in growing its business.

Starting Data Files

Excel7	Case1
Module	NP_EX_7-3.xlsx
NP_EX_7-1.xlsx	**Case2**
Review	NP_EX_7-4.xlsx
NP_EX_7-2.xlsx	

Objectives

Part 7.1
- Perform an approximate match lookup
- Analyze scenarios with logical functions
- Calculate summary statistics with summary IF functions

Part 7.2
- Create a PivotTable
- Change a PivotTable layout
- Format a PivotTable
- Calculate summary statistics with a PivotTable

Part 7.3
- Create a PivotChart
- Apply a slicer to multiple PivotTables
- Create a Timeline slicer

Part 7.1 Visual Overview: XLOOKUP and Summary IF Functions

This IF function returns a value of the Proposed field if Status equals "Won" and 0 otherwise:

= IF([@Status]="Won", [@Proposed], 0)

This XLOOKUP function uses values in the Client field to return State values from the Contacts table:

= XLOOKUP([@Client], Contacts[Client], Contacts[State])

Values in the Client Type column use XLOOKUP to retrieve Client Type values from the Contract Type lookup table using an approximate match lookup.

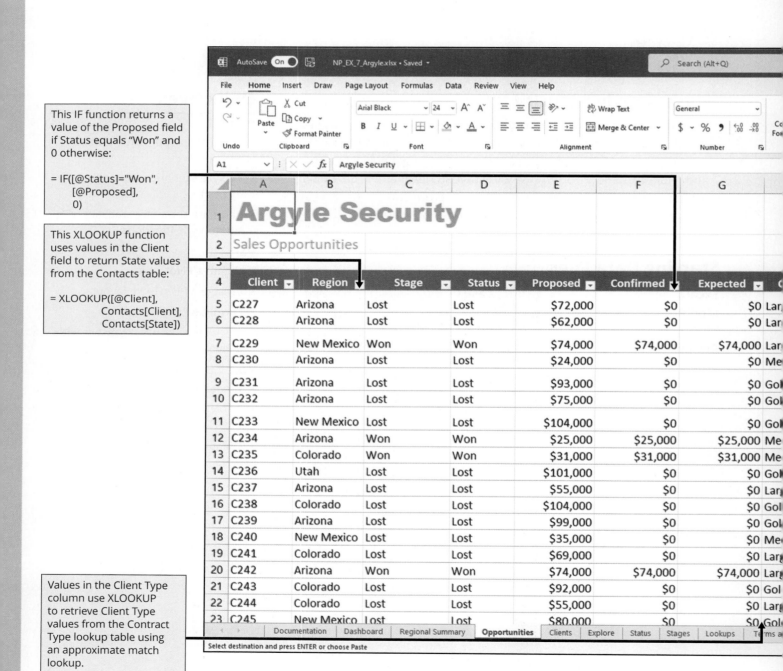

The **COUNTIF function** counts the number of cells that match a specified criteria. In this case, it counts the number of cells in the Arizona region.

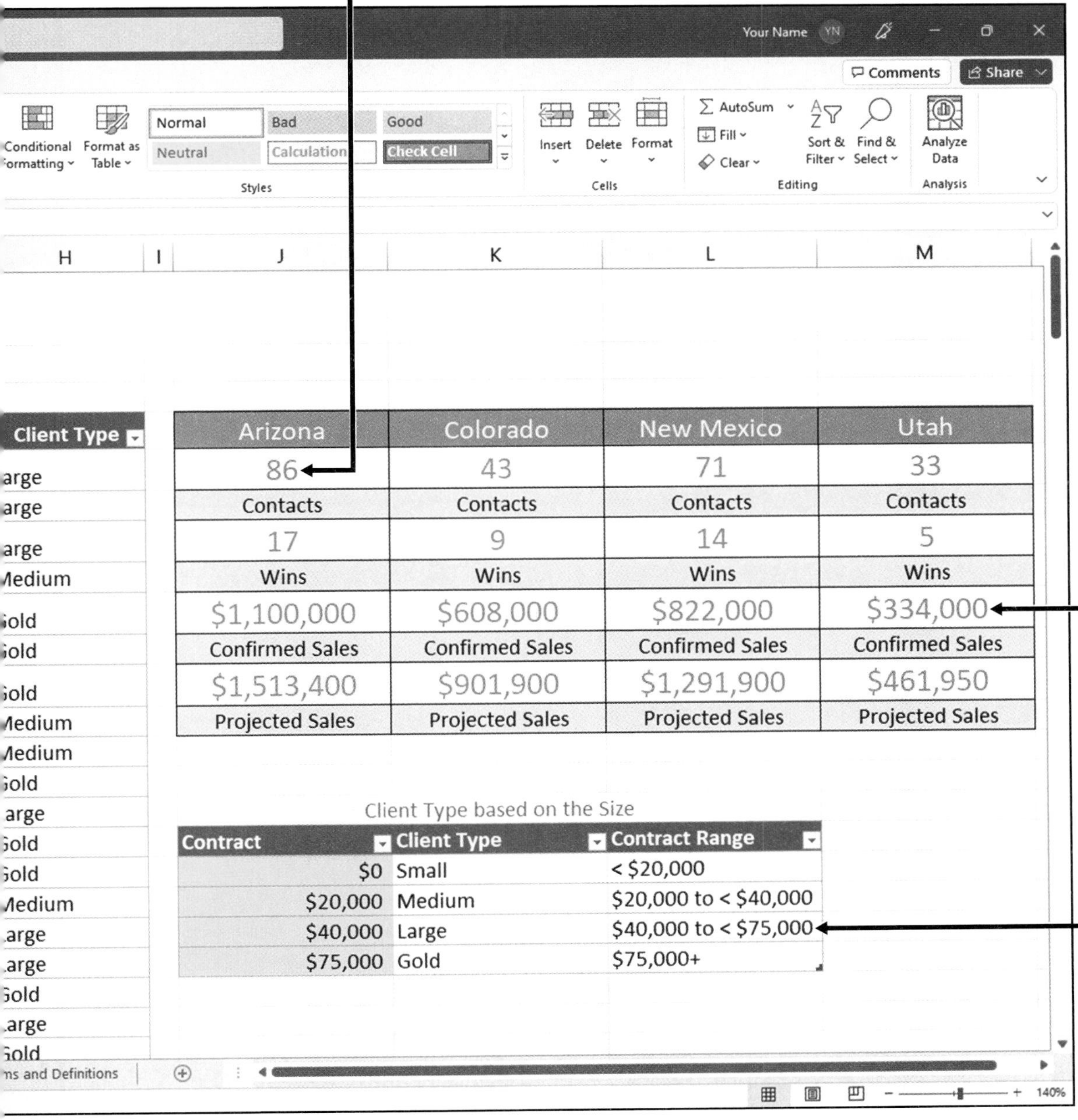

Your Name
Comments
Share
Conditional Formatting
Format as Table
Normal
Bad
Good
Neutral
Calculation
Check Cell
Styles
Insert
Delete
Format
Cells
AutoSum
Fill
Clear
Sort & Filter
Find & Select
Editing
Analyze Data
Analysis
H
I
J
K
L
M
Client Type
Arizona
Colorado
New Mexico
Utah
86
43
71
33
Contacts
17
9
14
5
Wins
$1,100,000
$608,000
$822,000
$334,000
Confirmed Sales
$1,513,400
$901,900
$1,291,900
$461,950
Projected Sales
Client Type based on the Size
Contract
Client Type
Contract Range
$0 Small < $20,000
$20,000 Medium $20,000 to < $40,000
$40,000 Large $40,000 to < $75,000
$75,000 Gold $75,000+
140%

The **SUMIF function** calculates the sum of values for cells that match a specified criteria. In this case, it calculates the sum of confirmed sales in the Utah region.

An **approximate match lookup** compares a lookup value to ranges of values, determining the range the lookup value falls within. In this case, the value $74,000 returns the value "Large" because it falls between $40,000 and $75,000.

Retrieving Data with Lookup Functions

Jeannette has compiled data on the interactions between Argyle Security's sales team and potential clients and wants to use that information for a customer relationship management report. **Customer Relationship Management** or **CRM** is technology for managing a company's interactions with customers and potential customers with the goal of enhancing profitability and quality of service. There are many aspects to CRM, including developing brand loyalty, locating trouble spots in recruiting clients, increasing overall profitability, and improving communication between the company and its customers. Jeannette wants to develop a CRM report focusing on the business opportunities of the past several months, determining where potential clients are located and how successful the company has been in moving prospective clients into paying customers.

But compiling data is the just the first step in developing a successful business analysis. The crucial next step is uncovering those important trends and factors needed to make thoughtful business decisions. You will start this process by opening Jeannette's workbook and exploring its contents.

To open Jeannette's workbook containing CRM data:

1. **sam** ↓ Open the **NP_EX_7-1.xlsx** workbook located in the **Excel7 > Module** folder included with your Data Files, and then save the workbook as **NP_EX_7_Argyle** in the location specified by your instructor.

2. In the Documentation sheet, enter your name in cell B3 and the date in cell B4.

3. Go to the **Opportunities** worksheet. This sheet contains an Excel table named Sales with a client ID number, the name of the sales rep managing the account, the date that the account was first initiated, the stage reached in negotiations between the company and the client, and the value of completed contract with the client. You will add formulas in the empty fields in this module. Refer to Figure 7–1.

Figure 7–1   Sales table in the Opportunities worksheet

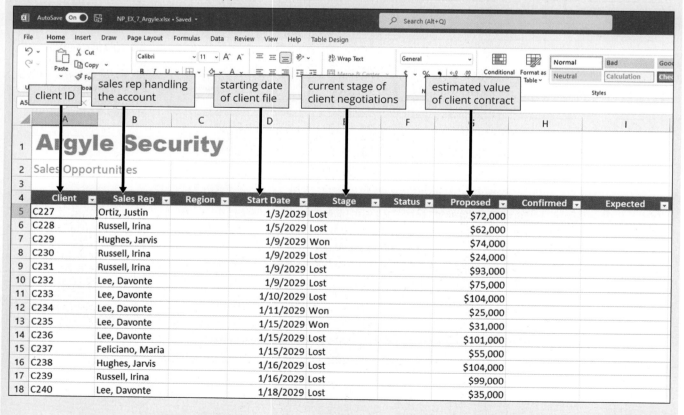

4. Go to the **Clients** worksheet. This sheet contains and Excel table named Contacts with contact information for each client including the client's primary contact.

5. Go to the **Lookups** worksheet. This sheet contains two Excel tables named StageProb and ContractSize. You will use these lookup tables as you complete this module.

6. Go to the **Terms and Definitions** worksheet and review the information about the tables and fields used in this project. The other worksheets are empty, and you will complete those in this module.

7. Go to the **Opportunities** worksheet.

Jeannette's report examines sales data from four sales regions: Arizona, Colorado, New Mexico, and Utah. The region associated with each client is stored in the Clients worksheet. You will use a lookup function to retrieve the client's region, adding that information to the Sales table in the Opportunities worksheet. Recall that data is retrieved from a table or data range, using the XLOOKUP function

```
XLOOKUP(lookup_value, lookup_array, return_array,
   [if_not_found], [match_mode], [search_mode])
```

where *lookup_value* is a value to match, *lookup_array* is the column or row containing the lookup values, *return_array* is the corresponding column or row containing return values where a match is found, *if_not_found* is an optional value returned if no match is found, *match_mode* is the type of match, and *search_mode* specifies how the lookup array will be searched for matches. By default, XLOOKUP does an exact match lookup, finding the one value in the lookup array that exactly matches a specified lookup value.

> **Tip** XLOOKUP supports dynamic arrays, so you can supply an array of lookup values to the function to generate an array of return values.

You will apply the XLOOKUP function in the Region field of the Sales table to retrieve each client's region from the Contacts table based on the value of the client's ID number. Because the data is stored in an Excel table, you will use field name references in your formula. To ensure accuracy, you will enter the formula using your mouse pointer.

To apply XLOOKUP to retrieve each client's sales region:

1. In the Opportunities worksheet, click cell **C5** to select the first cell in the Region column of the Sales table.

2. Type **= XLOOKUP(** to begin the XLOOKUP function.

3. Click cell **A5** to enter the field reference [@Client] for the value of the Client field in the current row.

4. Type **, Contacts[Client]** to reference the Client field from the Contacts table as the lookup array. As you type, the available Excel table and field names appear in a menu. You can insert a highlighted field name by pressing the TAB key.

5. Type **, Contacts[State])** to use the State field from the Contacts table as the return array.

6. Press **ENTER** to enter the complete formula = XLOOKUP([@Client], Contacts[Client],Contacts[State]). AutoFill enters that formula in the entire column, retrieving each client's sales region. Refer to Figure 7–2.

Figure 7–2   XLOOKUP performing an exact match

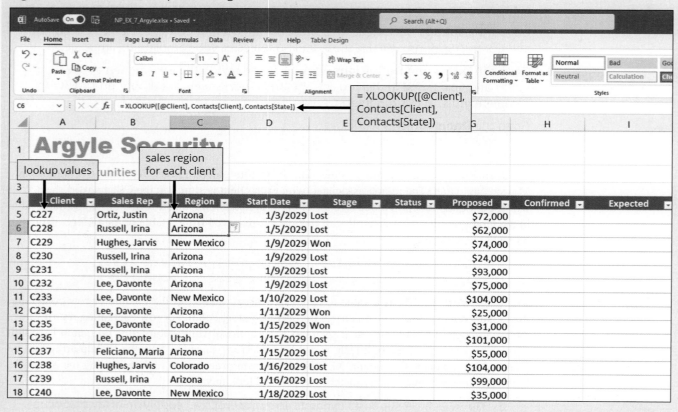

In an exact match lookup, Excel will return a value only if it finds an exact match between the lookup value and values in the lookup array. For other types of lookups, you can do an approximate match lookup.

Creating Approximate Match Lookups

An approximate match lookup is used when the lookup value falls within a range of possible values. For example, the test score of a B-level exam might fall in the range from 82% up to 87%. An approximate match lookup will return a value of B for any grade falling within that range. A lookup table for an approximate match lookup identifies either the lower end or the upper end of each range. Figure 7–3 shows a grading lookup table in which the lower end of each range is provided in the first column of the table.

Figure 7–3   Approximate match lookup table

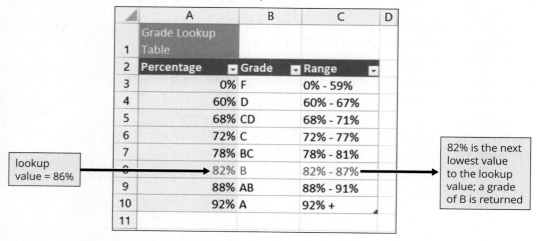

To retrieve the letter grade, Excel proceeds down the lookup array, locating either an exact match to the lookup value or the next lowest value if no exact match is found. A test score of 86% is matched to a value of 82% (the next lowest value in the lookup array), and a grade of "B" is returned from the second column of the table.

Tip Always include a column in an approximate match lookup table that describes the complete range of values for each category.

The XLOOKUP function uses the following values of *match_mode* argument to determine what constitutes a match:

- **match = 0**   (default) Exact match. If none is found, returns the error value #N/A or the value specified by the *if_not_found* argument.
- **match = –1**   Exact match or the next smaller value in the lookup array.
- **match = 1**   Exact match or the next larger value in the lookup array.
- **match = 2**   Wildcard match using the *, ? and ~ symbols to locate a match within the lookup array.

The XLOOKUP *search_mode* argument uses the following values to specify the search direction:

- **search = 1**   (default) Search from the first value in the lookup array.
- **search = –1**   Search from the last value in the lookup array.
- **search = 2**   Employ a binary search relying on lookup values sorted in ascending order.
- **search = –2**   Employ a binary search relying on lookup values being sorted in descending order.

If no values are provided for the *match_mode* and *search_mode* arguments, the XLOOKUP function performs an exact match lookup starting from the first value in the lookup array.

Tip Always sort the lookup table in ascending order of the lookup values if you intend to perform an approximate match lookup.

Jeannette wants to use approximate match lookup to categorize clients based on the size of the proposed contracts. The company rates client contracts as Small, Medium, Large, or Gold. As with the grading example, the lookup table specifies the lower end of each range. Small contracts start at $0 and go up to, but do not include, $20,000. Medium contracts start at $20,000, Large contracts start at $400,000, and Gold contracts start at $75,000. Figure 7–4 shows the contents of the lookup table stored as the ContractSize table in the Lookups worksheet.

Figure 7–4   ContractSize lookup table in the Lookups worksheet

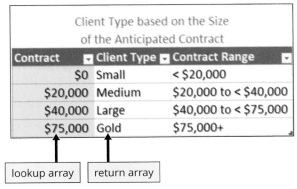

You will use the XLOOKUP function to retrieve each client's rating based on the size of their potential contracts.

To rate the clients using an approximate match lookup:

1. In the Opportunities worksheet, click cell **J5** to select the first cell in the Client Type column.

2. On the ribbon, click the **Formulas** tab. In the Function Library group, click the **Lookup & Reference** button, scroll down the list of functions, and then click **XLOOKUP**. The Function Arguments dialog box opens.

3. Make sure the insertion point is in the Lookup_value box, and then click cell **G5** in the Sales table. The table reference [@Proposed] references the value of the Proposed field in the current row.

4. Press **TAB** to move to the Lookup_array box, type **ContractSize[Contract]** to reference the Contract field in the ContractSize table.

5. Press **TAB** and then in the Return_array box, type **ContractSize[Client Type]** to reference the Client Type field in the ContractSize table.

6. Press **TAB** twice to move to the Match_mode box, and then type **–1** to specify that XLOOKUP will return the next smaller value from the lookup table if no match is found. You will not specify a value for the Search_mode box, accepting the default method of a search starting with the first entry in the column of lookup values. Refer to Figure 7–5.

Figure 7–5   Function arguments for an approximate match XLOOKUP function

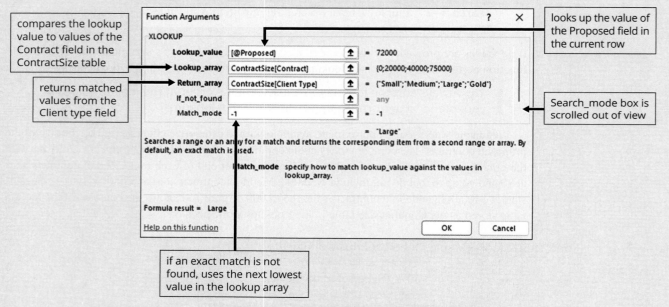

compares the lookup value to values of the Contract field in the ContractSize table

returns matched values from the Client type field

looks up the value of the Proposed field in the current row

Search_mode box is scrolled out of view

if an exact match is not found, uses the next lowest value in the lookup array

Key Step If you do not define a value for the *if_not_found* argument of the XLOOKUP function, you must still include the a comma placeholder (,,) if you define a value for the *match* or *search* arguments.

7. Click **OK** to insert the formula = XLOOKUP([@Proposed], ContractSize[Contract], ContractSize[Client Type],,-1) into the Client Type field. Refer to Figure 7–6.

Figure 7–6   XLOOKUP retrieves the client type

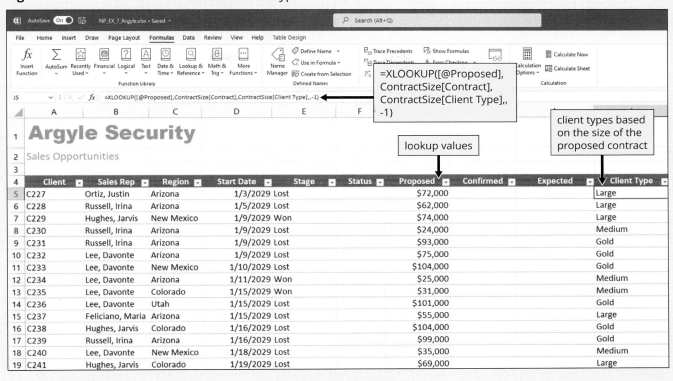

Excel displays the client type for each client listed in the Sales table. If the information on the potential size of the contract changes, the value returned by the XLOOKUP function will automatically update the client type.

Insight

Performing Partial Lookups with Wildcards

A **partial lookup** uses wildcards to match a character pattern rather than a specific value. For example, the following XLOOKUP function uses the * wildcard to match any string of characters that start with letters "WIL" using the lookup values in the LastNames array and returning values from the FirstNames array. If there is no match, the text string "No Name" is returned. The match argument value must equal two for XLOOKUP to interpret the wildcard symbols within the lookup value.

```
XLOOKUP("WIL*", LastNames, FirstNames, "No Name", 2)
```

Because XLOOKUP ignores case, values such as William, Willet, Will, or Willey are matched by this function. Excel will choose the first match it encounters in the table even if other entries would match the wildcard pattern. To combine a wildcard character with a cell value, use the & character. For example, the following function looks up values starting with the text stored in cell B10:

```
XLOOKUP(B10&"*", LastNames, FirstNames, "No Name", 2)
```

The * wildcard matches any number of characters. To match a specific number of characters, repeat the ? symbol for each character. The following function will match a text string starting with "WIL" followed by any three characters:

```
XLOOKUP("WIL???", LastNames, FirstNames, "No Name", 2)
```

Text strings such as Willet or Willey are matched, but not text strings like William or Will.

Approximate Match Lookups with VLOOKUP and HLOOKUP

In older workbooks, you might find lookups constructed using the VLOOKUP and HLOOKUP functions. The VLOOKUP function assumes that the lookup table is organized vertically with lookup values and return values arranged in columns. The HLOOKUP function assumes that the lookup table is organized horizontally with lookup and return values are arranged in rows. The syntax of each function is

```
VLOOKUP(lookup_value, table_array, col_index,
[range_lookup])

HLOOKUP(lookup_value, table_array, row_index,
[range_lookup])
```

where *lookup_value* is the lookup value to find in the first column of the lookup table (for VLOOKUP) or the first row (for HLOOKUP), *table_array* references the entire lookup table, *col_index* and *row_index* are the column and row indexes of the return values, and *range_lookup* is an optional argument specifying whether the lookup should be done as an exact match (*range_lookup* = FALSE) or an approximate match (*range_lookup* = TRUE).

> **Tip** The XLOOKUP function assumes exact matches by default, while VLOOKUP and HLOOKUP assume approximate matches.

XLOOKUP provides more control over how searches are accomplished and is much more flexible than VLOOKUP and HLOOKUP. You might encounter the VLOOKUP and HLOOKUP functions in older workbooks, so you should understand how they differ from XLOOKUP. For example, to retrieve a letter grade of B for an exam score of 86% using the lookup table shown in Figure 7–3, you can use either of the following XLOOKUP and VLOOKUP formulas:

```
XLOOKUP(86%, A3:A10, B3:B10,,-1)

VLOOKUP(86%, A3:C10, 2)
```

Note that VLOOKUP references the entire lookup table and uses the index number of the column to reference the return array while XLOOKUP directly references both the lookup array and the return array. With VLOOKUP the lookup array must always be in the first column of the lookup table while XLOOKUP allows the lookup array in any column. Finally, VLOOKUP assumes an exact match or the next smaller item in the lookup array, while that matching method must be explicitly defined in XLOOKUP by setting the match value to –1.

Using XLOOKUP with Multiple Lookup Values

The XLOOKUP function is not limited to a single lookup value. To use multiple lookup values, concatenate the lookup values and the lookup arrays using the & symbol. Figure 7–7 shows an example in which two lookup values are sent to a table of student grades, retrieving the letter grade matching both the student ID (in the range A3:A10) and the class name (in the range B3:B10).

Figure 7–7   XLOOKUP with two lookup values

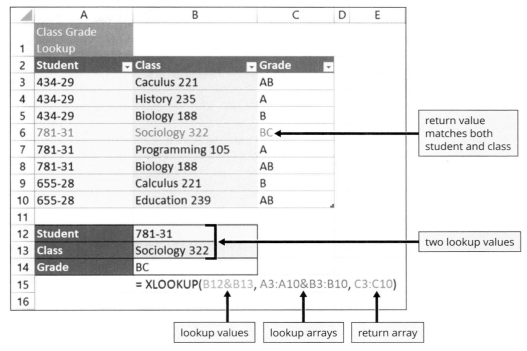

In this technique, the combination of the two lookup values must exactly match the combined values of the lookup arrays. Unless both lookup values are matched, no return value will be found.

You can develop more complex criteria for XLOOKUP under the general expression

```
XLOOKUP(1, criteria, return_array, [match_mode],
     [search_mode])
```

where `criteria` is an expression that is either true or false. The lookup table in Figure 7–8 contains the names of client projects and the percentage of the project completed by a specified date. A XLOOKUP function return the latest date by which a specified completion percentage is attained.

Figure 7–8   XLOOKUP with custom criteria

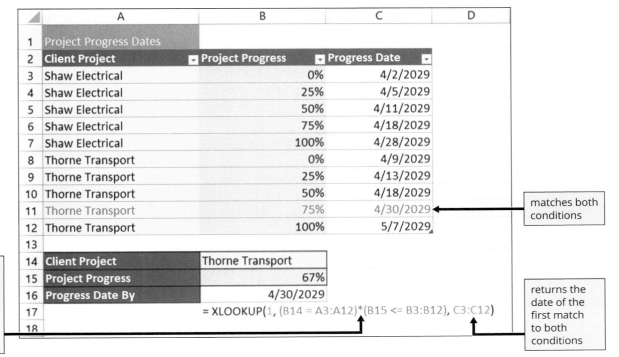

This XLOOKUP function takes advantage of how Excel handles conditional expressions. The expression `(B14=A3:A12)*(B15<=B3:B12)` returns a value of TRUE only when the value in cell B14 (Thorne Transport) exactly matches a value in the range A3:A12 and the value in cell B15 (67%) is less than or equal to a value in the range B3:B12. The * symbol joins the two conditions so that both conditions must be true for the entire expression to be true. The first record in the lookup table for which both criterion is true is in row 11 where the client project is Thorne Transport with 75% of the project completed by April 30, 2029. Argyle Security could inform the client that they expect that 67% of the project will be completed no later than April 30 (and in fact, they expect that 75% of the project will be completed by that date).

The syntax of the formula works because Excel stores a false value as 0 and a true value as 1. By multiplying the two expressions using the * character, a value of 1 can only be attained when both expressions are equal to 1 (or true). This technique can only be used when combining criteria with the * operator.

Two-Way Lookups with XLOOKUP

Another useful feature of XLOOKUP is the ability to match lookup values to the rows and columns of a lookup table, also known as a **two-way table**. The two-way table in Figure 7–9 lists client types in columns and regions in rows with the count of clients stored in the cell at the intersection of the client type and region. From the table, it is evident that there are 13 medium-sized clients in the New Mexico region.

Figure 7–9　　A two-way table of client region and client size

	A	B	C	D	E	F
1	Clients by Region and Size					
2	Region	Small	Medium	Large	Gold	
3	Arizona	12	17	24	33	
4	Colorado	6	6	18	13	
5	New Mexico	10	→13	19	29	
6	Utah	1	6	8	18	
7						

there are 13 medium-sized clients in the New Mexico region

To create a two-way lookup, you take advantage of the fact that, as with other Excel functions, XLOOKUP can return a dynamic array of values rather than a single value. Figure 7–10 shows how to use XLOOKUP to return a dynamic array of values showing the count of every client type in the New Mexico region.

Figure 7–10　　Dynamic array of values returned using XLOOKUP

	A	B	C	D	E	F
1	Clients by Region and Size					
2	Region	Small	Medium	Large	Gold	
3	Arizona	12	17	24	33	
4	Colorado	6	6	18	13	
5	New Mexico	10	13	19	29	
6	Utah	1	6	8	18	
7						
8	Region	New Mexico				
9	Return Array	10	13	19	29	
10		= XLOOKUP(B8, A3:A6, B3:E6)				
11						

dynamic array of return values

value to match to the first column of the table

lookup array from the first column of the table

range of return values covers all data in the two-way table

A dynamic array returned by XLOOKUP can be used as the return array for another XLOOKUP function by nesting one XLOOKUP function within another. The inner XLOOKUP function provides the dynamic array selected from one row in the two-way table, the outer XLOOKUP function selects a single column or cell from that array. The general syntax is

$$\text{XLOOKUP}(\textit{value1},\ \textit{column},\ \text{XLOOKUP}(\textit{value2},\ \textit{row},\ \textit{return}))$$

where *value1* is the value to be matched in a column of the two-way table, *value2* is the value to be matched in a row, *column* and *row* reference the column and row containing the lookup arrays, and *return* references the array of return values. Figure 7–11 shows how to apply nested XLOOKUP functions to retrieve client counts based on the client type and the region.

Figure 7–11   XLOOKUP retrieves a value from a two-way table

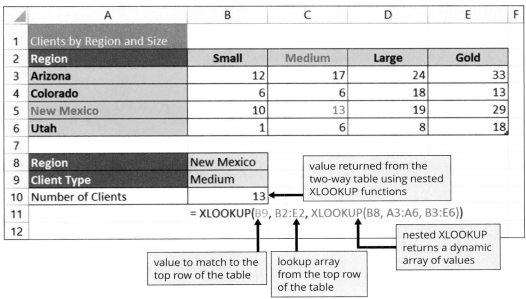

This process of nesting one XLOOKUP function within another can also be used with approximate match lookups in which the two-way table's row and column contain ranges of values rather than specific categories.

Retrieving Data with Index Match Lookups

Another way of retrieving data from a two-way table is with the INDEX and XMATCH functions. The INDEX function returns a value from a table by specifying the indexes, or positions, of the rows and columns. Its general syntax is

$$\text{INDEX}(\textit{array},\ \textit{row\_num},\ \textit{col\_num})$$

where *array* references the data range, *row_num* specifies the row number, and *col_num* specifies the column number. For example, the following INDEX function applied to the data shown in Figure 7–11 returns a value of 13, corresponding to the entry in the third row and second column of the data:

$$\text{INDEX}(\text{B3:E6},\ 3,\ 2)$$

The XMATCH function does the opposite. Given a value, XMATCH returns the index of the matching value within a row or column. The syntax of the XMATCH function is

```
XMATCH(lookup_value, array, [match_mode], [search_mode])
```

where `lookup_value` is the value to locate, `array` is a single row or column in which to search for that value, and `match` is an optional argument specifying how the search should be conducted. The `match` argument has three values, similar to the `match` argument in the XLOOKUP function:

- **match = 0**   (default) Exact match to the lookup value.
- **match = 1**   Exact match or the next larger value to the lookup value.
- **match = –1**   Exact match or the next smaller value.
- **match = 2**   Match using wildcard symbols.

The values of `search_mode` are the same as the values used with the XLOOKUP function. Applying the following XMATCH functions to table in Figure 7–11, the location of "New Mexico" in the first column of region labels is 3 and the location of the "Medium" within the first row of client types is 2:

```
XMATCH(B8, A3:A6, 0) // returns 3

XMATCH(B9, B2:E2, 0) // returns 2
```

By nesting two XMATCH functions within an INDEX function, you can retrieve data from a two-way table using the following general syntax

```
INDEX(array, columnMatch, rowMatch)
```

where `array` is the array of return values, `columnMatch` is the XMATCH function applied to the lookup labels in the table's first column, and `rowMatch` is the XMATCH function applied to lookup labels in the table's first row. The following expression combines the INDEX and XMATCH functions to retrieve the number of clients based on the region specified in cell B8 and the client type specified in cell B9:

```
INDEX(B3:E6,XMATCH(B8,A3:A6,0),XMATCH(B9,B2:E2,0))
```

XMATCH is the successor to the older MATCH function supported in Excel using the following syntax:

```
MATCH(lookup_value, array, [match_mode])
```

The MATCH function does not support a `search_mode` argument so that searches always start with the first item in the array. Also, the values of the `match_mode` argument are different than XMATCH:

- **match = 0**   Exact match to the lookup value.
- **match = 1**   (default) Exact match or the next smaller value.
- **match = –1**   Exact match or the next larger value.

If you update the MATCH function in older workbooks with XMATCH, note that the `match_mode` values are switched so that a value of 1 looks for an exact match or the next smaller value and a value of –1 looks for an exact match or the next larger value. Also, MATCH assumes a `match_mode` value of 1 by default while XMATCH assumes a default value of 0.

Reference

Retrieving Values from Lookup Tables

- To retrieve a value from a lookup table, apply the function

      XLOOKUP(*lookup_value*, *lookup_array*, *return_array*,
      [*if_not_found*], [*match_mode*], [*search_mode*])

  where *lookup_value* is a value to match, *lookup_array* is the column or row containing the lookup values, *return_array* is the corresponding column or row containing return values where a match is found, *if_not_found* is an optional value returned if no match is found, *match_mode* is the type of match, and *search_mode* specifies how the lookup array will be searched for matches. The default is an exact match lookup.

- In older versions of Excel, use the following functions to retrieve values from vertical or horizontal lookup tables

      VLOOKUP(*lookup_value*, *table_array*, *col_index*,
      [*range_lookup*])
      HLOOKUP(*lookup_value*, *table_array*, *row_index*,
      [*range_lookup*])

  where *lookup_value* is the lookup value to find, *table_array* references the entire lookup table, *col_index* and *row_index* are the column and row numbers containing the return values, and *range_lookup* is the type of match. The default is an approximate match lookup.

- To retrieve lookup values based on specified criteria, use

      XLOOKUP(1, *criteria*, *return_array*, [*if_not_found*],
      [*match_mode*], [*search_mode*])

  where *criteria* is a value that either true or false.

- To retrieve lookup values from a two-way table, use

      XLOOKUP(*value1*, *column*, XLOOKUP(*value2*, *row*, *return*))

  where *value1* is the value to be matched in the column of the two-way table, *value2* is the value to be matched in the row, *column* and *row* reference the column and row containing the lookup values and *return* references the array of return values from the two-way table.

  or

      INDEX(*array*, *columnMatch*, *rowMatch*)

  where *array* is the array of return values and *columnMatch* and *rowMatch* use the XMATCH function to match values in the two-way table's column and row labels.

Exploring Logical Functions

The XLOOKUP and XMATCH functions both involve logical expressions that return values only when specified criteria are met. Another function that uses logical expressions is the IF function

      IF(*criteria*, *value_if_true*, [*value_if_false*])

where *criteria* is an expression that is either true or false, *value_if_true* is the value returned if the expression is true, and *value_if_false* is the value returned if the expression is false. The IF function accepts logical operators such as * for the AND condition and + for the OR condition. For example, the following expression returns a value of "Arizona" if cell B1 equals either "Phoenix" or "Tucson." If neither of those conditions is true, the function returns the text string "Not Arizona":

```
IF((B1 = "Phoenix")+(B1 = "Tucson"), "Arizona",
"Not Arizona")
```

Jeannette wants to use the IF function to describe the status of negotiations between Argyle Security and potential clients. Negotiations go through several stages:

- **Lead**—The initial contact between Argyle Security and the client
- **Meeting**—A formal meeting between Argyle Security and the client where the client's needs are discussed
- **Planning**—The phase where a security plan for the client is discussed and formulated
- **Pitched**—The final pitch made to the client based on the security plan and its costs
- **Won**—The client has accepted a contract with Argyle Security
- **Lost**—The client has firmly rejected the Argyle Security proposal

Each client contract is either Won, Lost, or Open, where Open means that negotiations are ongoing and the final outcome is not settled. The negotiation stage has already been entered in the Sales table in the Stage column. You will apply an IF function to the Status column to indicate the contract's status.

To use the IF function to identify the status of each contract:

1. In the Opportunities worksheet, click cell **F5** to select the first cell of the Status column in the Sales table.

2. Type **= IF(** to begin the IF function.

3. Type **(** to start the first expression, click cell **E5** to insert [@Stage], and then type **="Lost")** to insert the expression ([@Stage]="Lost").

4. Type **+ (** to start the second expression, click cell **E5**, and then type **="Won")** to complete the criteria: ([@Stage]="Lost")+([@Stage] = "Won"). The IF criteria tests whether the current value of the Stage field is equal to "Lost" or "Won". If either of these two conditions is true, the Status is equal to the Stage (Won or Lost).

5. Type **,** and then click cell **E5** to insert the expression: , [@Stage]. If this condition is not true, then the status of negotiations is still open.

6. Type **, "Open")** to complete the IF function. The entire formula is:
= IF(([@Stage]="Lost")+([@Stage] = "Won"), [@Stage], "Open")

7. Press **ENTER** to insert the formula into the Status field. Refer to Figure 7–12.

Figure 7–12   IF function indicates the status of client negotiations

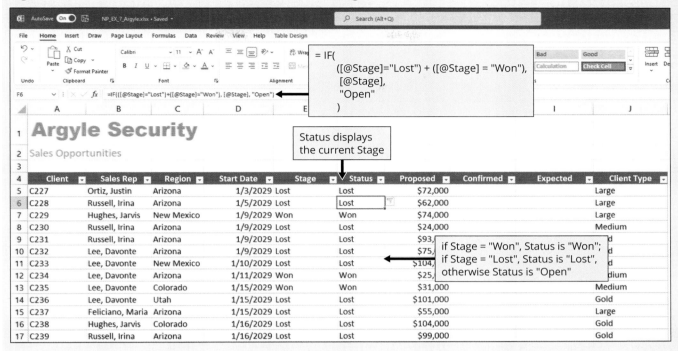

8. Scroll down the worksheet and notice that for more recent clients, the negotiations are still open without a final resolution.

When a contract is won, Jeannette will include the contract's value as a confirmed sale; otherwise, the current value of the contract is zero. You will use the IF function to enter the confirmed value of each contract.

To use the IF function to record the confirmed value of each contract:

1. Scroll up the workbook and click cell **H5** in the Confirmed column.

2. Type **= IF(** to begin the IF function.

3. Click cell **F5** and type **= "Won"** to enter the expression [@Status]="Won".

4. Type **,** and then click cell **G5** to enter the expression [@Proposed].

5. Type **, 0)** to complete the formula = IF([@Status]="Won", [@Proposed], 0).

6. Press **ENTER** to insert the formula into the Confirmed field. Refer to Figure 7–13.

Figure 7–13   Using the IF function to enter confirmed sales

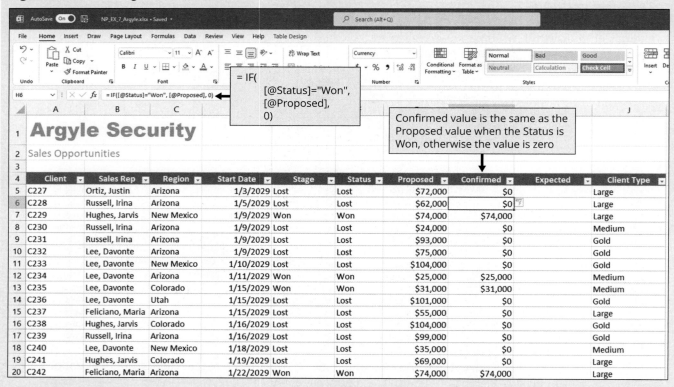

7. Scroll down the workbook and verify that only for Won contracts is the Confirmed value equal to the Proposed value. For all other records, the value is zero.

With so many contracts still open, Argyle Security has a lot of potential revenue. Of course, clients could reject Argyle Security at any stage in the negotiations, but the company is more likely to win a contract the longer the client stays interested and involved. Company history has shown that about 15% of contracts in Lead stage will be eventually won, but if negotiations reach the Pitched stage, 65% of those contracts will be won. Jeannette has created the lookup table shown in Figure 7–14 providing the probability of winning the contract after each stage of negotiations.

Figure 7–14   Lookup table for win probability by stage

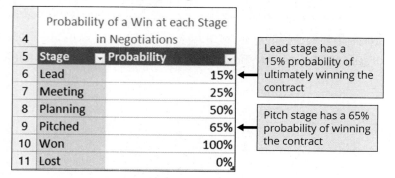

One way to place a value on an open contract is to multiply the contract's value by the probability that it will be eventually won. For example, a $100,000 contract at the Lead stage where the win probability is 15% has an expected value of 15% of $100,000 or $15,000. If that same contract reaches the Pitched stage, the estimated value increases to 65% of $100,000 or $65,000.

Jeannette wants to estimate the potential revenue from all open contracts. You will use the XLOOKUP function to write a formula that retrieves the win probability for each contract based on the value of the Stage field and then multiply that probability by the proposed value of the contract.

To project the value of each contract in the Sales table:

1. Scroll up the workbook and click cell **I5** in the Expected column.

2. Type **= [@Proposed]** to retrieve the proposed value of the contract.

3. Type ***XLOOKUP([@Stage], StageProb[Stage], StageProb[Probability])** to multiply the proposed contract value by the probability that it will be won.

4. Press **ENTER**. An estimated value of each contract is displayed in the Expected column.

5. Scroll down the worksheet to review the estimated value of the open contracts. Refer to Figure 7–15.

Figure 7–15   Expected value of each contract

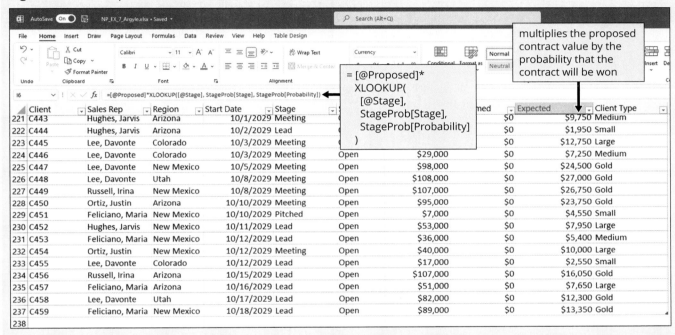

Because the most recent contracts are still open, a lot of potential revenue remains untapped. By estimating the value of those open contracts, Jeannette can get a more accurate projection of Argyle Security's sales income in the upcoming months.

Reference

Applying Logical Functions

- To test one condition for two possible outcomes, use

      IF(*criteria*, *value_if_true*, [*value_if_false*])

  where *criteria* is an expression that is either true or false, *value_if_true* is the value returned if the expression is true, and *value_if_false* is the value returned if the expression is false.

- To test multiple conditions for multiple possible either nest one IF statement inside of another or use

      IFS(*logical_test1*, *value_if_true1*, *logical_test2*, *value_if_true2*, …)

  where *logical_test1*, *logical_test2*, … are logical conditions, and *value_if_true1*, *value_if_true2* … are the values associated with each condition if the condition is true.

Generating Multiple Outcomes from a Logical Function

The IF function returns two possible values depending on whether the logical condition is true or false. To handle multiple values, nest one IF function within another. The following formula uses two IF functions to test the value of cell B10 resulting in three possible values:

```
= IF(B10 < 70%, "Fail", IF(B10 < 80%, "Poor", "Pass"))
```

If cell B10 is less than 70%, the formula returns the text string "Fail"; otherwise, if the cell value is less than 80%, it returns the text "Poor" and if neither of those conditions is true, it returns the text string "Pass." By adding more nested IF functions, you can test for as many possible conditions as you want. However, at some point the collection of nested IF functions will become so convoluted that you are better off using a lookup table to match each condition to a different value.

To avoid a series of nested IF function, use the **IFS function**, which has the syntax

```
IFS(logical_test1, value_if_true1, logical_test2,
    value_if_true2, …)
```

where *logical_test1*, *logical_test2*, … are logical conditions, and *value_if_true1*, *value_if_true2* … are the values associated with each condition if the condition is true. You could rewrite the nested IF function shown previously using the following IFS function specifying the same three possible values:

```
= IFS(B10 < 70%, "Fail", B10 < 80%, "Poor", B10 >= 80%,
  "Pass")
```

The IFS function tests the logical condition in the order in which they are listed. When a true condition is encountered, the function skips the remaining logical conditions. If none of the conditions are true, the function returns the error value #N/A. You can define a default value for the function by setting the final logical test to the value TRUE, as in the following expression:

```
= IFS(B10 < 70%, "Fail", B10 < 80%, "Poor", TRUE,
  "Pass")
```

If cell B10 is not less than 70% and not less than 80%, the function will use "Pass" as the default value of the function.

Using the AND, OR, and NOT Functions

Another way of combining multiple conditions is with the OR function and the AND function. The **AND function** returns a value of TRUE if all specified conditions are true, doing the same thing as the * logical operator for combining logical expressions. The following two expressions will return a value of TRUE if cell B10 equals 50% *and* cell C10 equals 20%, but they will return a value of FALSE otherwise:

```
(B10 = 50%)*(C10 = 20%)
AND(B10 = 50%, C10 = 20%)
```

The **OR function** tests whether at least one of the specified conditions is true, duplicating the action of the + operator. The following two expressions will return a value of TRUE if cell B10 equals 50% or if cell C10 equals 20%. If neither of those conditions is true, the expressions will return a value of FALSE:

```
(B10 = 50%) + (C10 = 20%)
OR(B10 = 50%, C10 = 20%)
```

Some logical statements test for inequalities in which two expressions are confirmed to be not equal to one another. For those types of statements you can use the **NOT function**, which reverses the value of a logical expression, changing a TRUE value to FALSE and a FALSE value to true. In place of the NOT function, you can also use the <> logical operator, which tests for inequalities. The following statements both return TRUE if cell B10 is not equal to 50%:

```
B10 <> 50%
NOT(B10 = 50%)
```

In many situations you will find that the *, +, and <> operators result in more compact and flexible formulas, but you might encounter the AND, OR, and NOT functions in older workbooks, so you should be familiar with both approaches.

Applying Summary IF functions

A summary IF function is a function that provides a summary statistic for an array of data values, subject to a logical condition. Excel supports summary IF functions for the following statistics: COUNT, SUM, AVERAGE, MAX, and MIN. Jeannette wants you to use summary IF functions to summarize the data from the different sales region in the CRM report. You will start by creating a conditional count.

Conditional Counting with COUNTIF and COUNTIFS

A **conditional count** tallies cells only if they match a specified value or condition. To create a conditional count, use the COUNTIF function

```
COUNTIF(range, criteria)
```

where *range* references a range of cells or table field to be counted and *criteria* defines which cells to include in that count. The following expression counts the number of cells in the Region field of the Sales table whose value equals "Utah":

```
COUNTIF(Sales[Region], "Utah")
```

Figure 7–16 provides other examples of the COUNTIF function for conditional counting. Note that the COUNTIF function works with both numeric values and text strings, unlike the COUNT function, which counts only numeric values.

Figure 7–16   Examples of the COUNTIF function

Function	Description
COUNTIF(A2:A100, "Utah")	Counts the cells in the range A2:A100 with the value "Utah"
COUNTIF(A2:A100, D1)	Counts the cells in the range A2:A100 with a value equal to the value of cell D1
COUNTIF(A2:A100, "> 50")	Counts the cells in the range A2:A100 with a value greater than 50
COUNTIF(A2:A100, ">" & D1)	Counts the cells in the range A2:A100 with a value greater than the value of cell D1

Jeannette wants a count of the clients broken down by region. You will use the COUNTIF function to count the number of contacts in each of four regions described in Jeannette's report.

To do conditional counting with the COUNTIF function:

1. Go to the **Regional Summary** worksheet and click cell **A6**.

2. Type **= COUNTIF(Sales[Region], A5)** to count the number of cells in the Region column of the Sales table with a value equal to cell A5 (Arizona).

3. Press **ENTER**. Excel returns a value of 86 indicating that there are 86 contacts made in the Arizona region.

4. Copy cell **A6** and paste the copied cell into the range **B6:D6** to count the number of contacts in the other three regions. Refer to Figure 7–17.

Figure 7–17   COUNTIF counts client contacts within a region

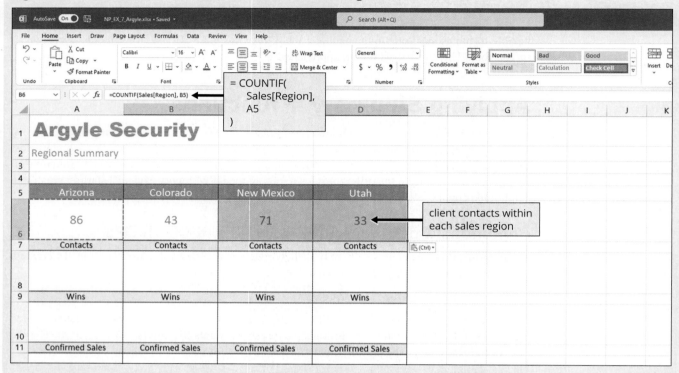

> **Trouble?** Do not use the fill handle to drag the formula in cell A6 through the B6:D6 range. Filling to the right will create formulas will shift the field reference in the COUNTIF function, counting other fields than the Region field.

The COUNTIF function is limited to a single logical condition. For multiple conditions, use the **COUNTIFS function**, which has the syntax

```
COUNTIFS(range1, criteria1, [range2, criteria2],
[range3, criteria3] …)
```

where $range1$, $range2$, $range3$, … are ranges to be counted and $criteria1$, $criteria2$, $criteria3$ … are the criteria applied to each range, respectively. You can include up to 127 $range/criteria$ pairs. Each additional range must have the same number of rows or columns as $range1$ and $criteria1$, though the ranges do not have to be adjacent. The following formula use two logical conditions to count the number of won contracts in the Utah sales region:

```
= COUNTIFS(Sales[Region], "Utah", Sales[Status], "Won")
```

You will use the COUNTIFS formula to count the winning contracts for each region in Jeannette's report.

To apply the COUNTIFS function:

1. Click cell **A8**.

2. Type the formula **= COUNTIFS(Sales[Region], A5, Sales[Status], "Won")** and then press **ENTER**. The formula returns a value of 17, indicating that there are 17 contracts won in the Arizona region.

3. Copy cell **A8** and paste it into the range **B8:D8** to display the number of won contracts for the other three regions. Refer to Figure 7–18.

Figure 7–18   COUNTIFS counts winning contracts within a region

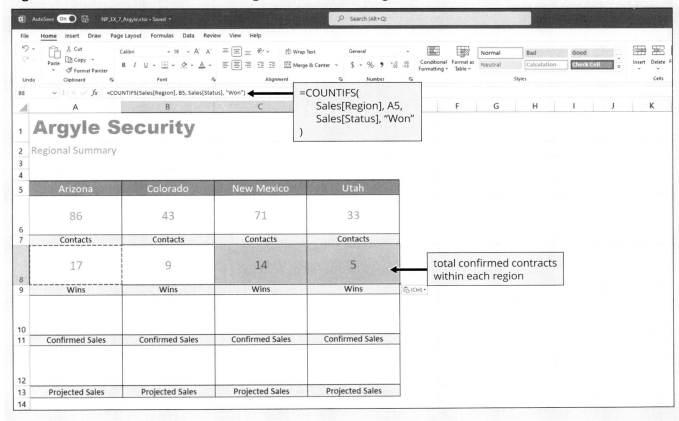

The COUNTIFS function combines criteria using the AND logical condition, so that all criteria must be true for the records to be counted. To combine the criteria using the OR logical condition, you can use arrays.

Proskills

Problem Solving: Conditional Counting with Arrays

The COUNTIF function allows arrays to be used in logical expressions so that multiple counts are returned by a single function. The following function returns an array of counts from the Sales[Region] column which equal "Arizona" or "Utah":

```
= COUNTIF(Sales[Region], {"Arizona", "Utah"})
```

This array formula returns the values of 86 and 33, representing the number of cells in the Region column which equal "Arizona" and the number which equal "Utah." To combine those two counts into a single count, nest the COUNTIF function within the SUM function as follows:

```
= SUM(COUNTIF(Sales[Region], {"Arizona", "Utah"}))
```

The formula returns a value of 119 representing the count of cells equalling "Arizona" or "Utah." This technique also works for the COUNTIFS function to combine several OR conditions into a single expression. The following formula counts the number of records in the Sales table in which the client comes from Arizona or Utah, and for which the contract size is either Gold or Medium:

```
= SUM(COUNTIFS(
        Sales[Region],{"Arizona","Utah"},
        Sales[Contract Size], {"Gold","Medium"})
    )
```

The great challenge with this approach is keeping track of the nested functions and arrays, so it often helpful to enter the formula on multiple lines within the formula bar. This technique will also work with the other conditional summary functions like SUMIF and SUMIFS.

Calculating Conditional Sums

To calculate a **conditional sum** of values matching specified criteria, apply the SUMIF function

```
SUMIF(range, criteria, [sum_range])
```

where `range` is the range of cells selected in the `criteria` argument, and `sum_range` is an optional argument specifying the values to sum. The following expression calculates the sum of values in the range A2:A100, including only those cells with a value greater than 50:

```
SUMIF(A2:A100, "> 50")
```

To calculate a conditional sum of values in another range, include the range as the last argument in the SUMIF function. The following formula calculates the sum of values in the Confirmed column of the Sales table, but only for those records where the Region field equals "Utah":

```
SUMIF(Sales[Region], "Utah", Sales[Confirmed])
```

You will use the SUMIF function to calculate the sum of confirmed sales in each of the four regions in Jeannette's report.

To calculate confirmed sales by region using SUMIF:

1. Click cell **A10**.
2. Type the formula **= SUMIF(Sales[Region], A5, Sales[Confirmed])** and then press **ENTER**. The formula returns a value of $1,100,000 confirmed sales in the Arizona region.

3. Copy cell **A10**, and then paste it into the range **B10:D10** to calculate the conditional sums for the other regions. Refer to Figure 7–19.

Figure 7–19　　SUMIF calculates total confirmed sales within a region

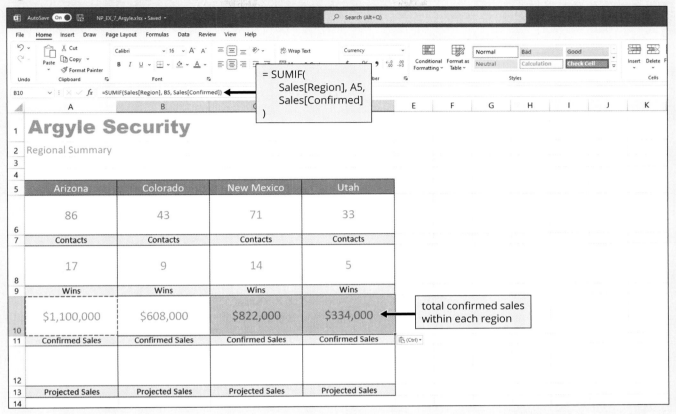

You can apply multiple criteria in a conditional sum using the **SUMIFS function**

```
SUMIFS(sum_range, range1, criteria1, [range2],
[criteria2] …)
```

where *sum_range* references the data range to sum and each subsequent *range*/*criteria* pair provides the criteria and the data ranges that determine which cells to include in the conditional sum. In the SUMIFS function, unlike in the SUMIF function, the data to be summed is the first argument in the function and not the last. Multiple criteria are combined using AND so that all criteria must be true for a data value to be included in the sum. The following formula uses SUMIFS to calculate the sum of the Confirmed sales, limited to Gold clients in the Utah region.

```
SUMIFS(Sales[Confirmed], Sales[Region], "Utah",
Sales[Client Type], "Gold")
```

Any record in the Sales table that does not match both criteria is not included in the conditional sum.

Reference

Using Conditional Summary Functions

- To count values subject to a logical condition, use

      COUNTIF(*range*, *criteria*)

  where *range* references the range of cells or table field to be counted and *criteria* is a value or a condition that defines which cells to include in the count.

- To count values subject to multiple criteria, use

      COUNTIFS(*range1*, *criteria1*, [*range2*, *criteria2*], [*range3*, *criteria3*] …)

  where *range1*, *range2*, *range3*, … are ranges to be counted and *criteria1*, *criteria2*, *criteria3* … are the criterion applied to each range.

- To calculate the sum of values subject to a logical condition, use

      SUMIF(*range*, *criteria*, [*sum_range*])

  where *range* is the range of cells selected in the *criteria* argument, and *sum_range* is an optional argument that specifies the values to sum.

- To calculate the sum of values subject to multiple criteria, use

      SUMIFS(*sum_range*, *range1*, *criteria1*, [*range2*], [*criteria2*] …)

  where *sum_range* references the data range to sum and each subsequent *range*/*criteria* pair provides the criteria and the data ranges that determine which cells to include in the conditional sum.

- To calculate conditional summaries of averages, minimums, and maximums, use AVERAGEIF, AVERAGEIFS, MINIF, MINIFS, MAXIF, and MAXIFS.

- For more general conditional summaries, use the FILTER function to filter the data array subject to logical criteria and the nest the FILTER function within the Excel summary function of your choice.

Calculating Other Conditional Statistics

The general form of the conditional sum functions can extended to **conditional averages** to calculate the average of data values subject to a specified criteria. The **AVERAGEIF function** and **AVERAGEIFS function** are used to calculate averages from a data range:

    AVERAGEIF(*range*, *criteria*, [*average_range*])

    AVERAGEIFS(*average_range*, *range1*, *criteria1*, [*range2*], [*criteria2*] …)

To calculate the average confirmed sales for all Utah clients and specifically for Gold clients in Utah, use the following AVERAGEIF and AVERAGEIFS functions:

    AVERAGEIF(Sales[Region], "Utah", Sales[Confirmed])

    AVERAGEIFS(Sales[Confirmed], Sales[Region], "Utah", Sales[Client Type], "Gold")

Note that the range to be averaged, Sales[Confirmed], is listed last in the AVERAGEIF function but first in AVERAGEIFS.

To calculate a conditional minimum or maximum value from a data array, use the following functions, which once again have a similar syntax to what is used with AVERAGEIF and AVERAGEIFS:

    MINIF(*range*, *criteria*, [*min_range*])

    MINIFS(*min_range*, *range1*, *criteria1*, [*range2*], [*criteria2*] …)

```
MAXIF(range, criteria, [max_range])

MAXIF(max_range, range1, criteria1, [range2], [criteria2] …)
```

For example, to display the largest confirmed sale in Utah and the largest sale for Gold clients in Utah, use the following MAXIF and MAXIFS functions:

```
MAXIF(Sales[Region], "Utah", Sales[Confirmed])

MAXIFS(Sales[Confirmed], Sales[Region], "Utah",
Sales[Client Type], "Gold")
```

To display the smallest sale, replace MAXIF and MAXIFS with MINIF and MINIFS in the formulas.

Summary Calculations Using the FILTER Function

The conditional summary functions have the following two limitations:

1. The criteria are combined using AND so that all criteria must be true. You cannot apply more complicated logical criteria selecting only those clients who are either from Utah or from New Mexico with a Gold contract.

2. The functions are limited to counts, sums, averages, minimums, and maximums. For example, there is no conditional summary function for medians or percentiles.

To overcome these limitations, use the FILTER function to filter the data and then apply the statistical function of your choice to the filtered data. For example, to filter the Sales data to include only the confirmed sales for Gold clients or for clients from Utah, you would first apply the following FILTER function to limit the records to be analyzed:

```
FILTER(Sales[Confirmed],
(Sales[Region]="Utah")+(Sales[Client Type]="Gold"))
```

Because the + operator is used in the logical expression, the dynamic array contains records of the Confirm column matching either condition. Next, apply an Excel statistical function to the filtered data. To calculate the median, or midpoint, of the filtered data, nest the FILTER function within the MEDIAN function:

```
= MEDIAN(
    FILTER(Sales[Confirmed],
(Sales[Region]="Utah")+(Sales[Client Type]="Gold"))
    )
```

You will use this technique to complete the contents of the Regional Summary worksheet by calculating the sum of the expected sales from the contracts in each of the four regions.

To calculate the sum of expected sales in each region:

1. Click cell **A12** and type **= SUM(** to begin the sum formula.

2. Type **FILTER(Sales[Expected], Sales[Region] = A5)** to filter the Expected column from the Sales table so that it includes only those values where the region is equal to the value of cell A5 (Arizona).

3. Type **)** and then press **ENTER** to insert the completed formula = SUM(FILTER(Sales[Expected], Sales[Region] = A5)) into cell A12. The formula returns $1,513,400, which is the expected sales from Arizona when all open negotiations have been concluded.

4. Copy cell **A12** and paste it into the range **B12:D12** to calculate the conditional sum of the other regions. Refer to Figure 7–20.

Figure 7–20   Nesting the FILTER function within the SUM function

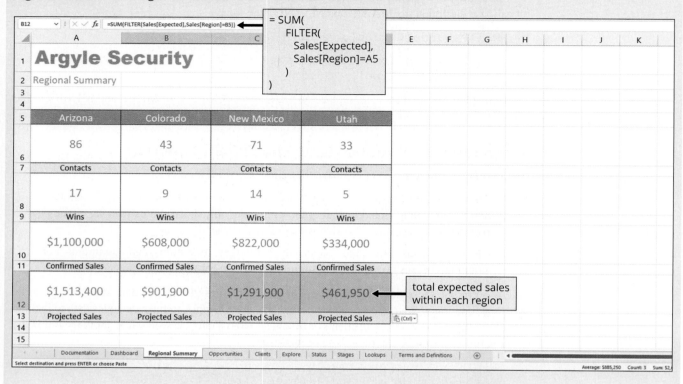

Based on your analysis, expected sales for the Arizona through Utah regions range from $1,513,400 down to $461,950. That information will prove useful as Jeannette projects future income for Argyle Security from contracts currently in negotiation.

The conditional summary functions and the FILTER function you worked with in this part are useful for analyses involving a few criteria. However, they quickly become unwieldy for more complex logical conditions or when they must be applied to several data ranges. A better approach to those challenges is a PivotTable.

Part 7.1 Quick Check

1. A lookup table has a lookup array in the range E2:E10 and a return array in the range G2:G10. Write a formula using the XLOOKUP function to do an exact match to the lookup value in cell A1.

2. Using the same lookup table and lookup value, write a formula using the XLOOKUP function to do either an exact match or a match to the next larger value from the lookup array.

3. How does XLOOKUP differ from VLOOKUP in the placement of the lookup array?

4. A two-way table has lookup arrays in the range B1:F1 and in the range A2:A10. The return array is in the range B2:F10. Using nested XLOOKUP functions, write the formula to retrieve a value from the two-way table using cell M1 as the lookup value for the values in the range B1:F1 array and cell M2 as the lookup value for values in the range A2:A10 array.

5. Write a formula using the IF function to return a value of "Pass" if cell A1 equals 2 or 3, and a value of "Fail" if otherwise.

6. Write a formula using the IFS function to return a value of "Fail" if cell A1 equals 1, "Pass if cell A2 equals 2, and "Excellent" if cell A1 equals 3.

7. Write a formula using the COUNTIF function to count the cells in the range E2:E100 with a value greater than or equal to the value of cell A1.

8. Write a formula using the SUMIF function to calculate the total of the values in the range F2:F100 for which the corresponding values in the range E2:E100 are greater than or equal to the value of cell A1.

9. Write a formula using the FILTER and SUM functions to calculate the sum of values in the range F2:F100 for which the corresponding values in the range E2:100 are greater than or equal to the value of cell A1.

Part 7.2 Visual Overview: PivotTables

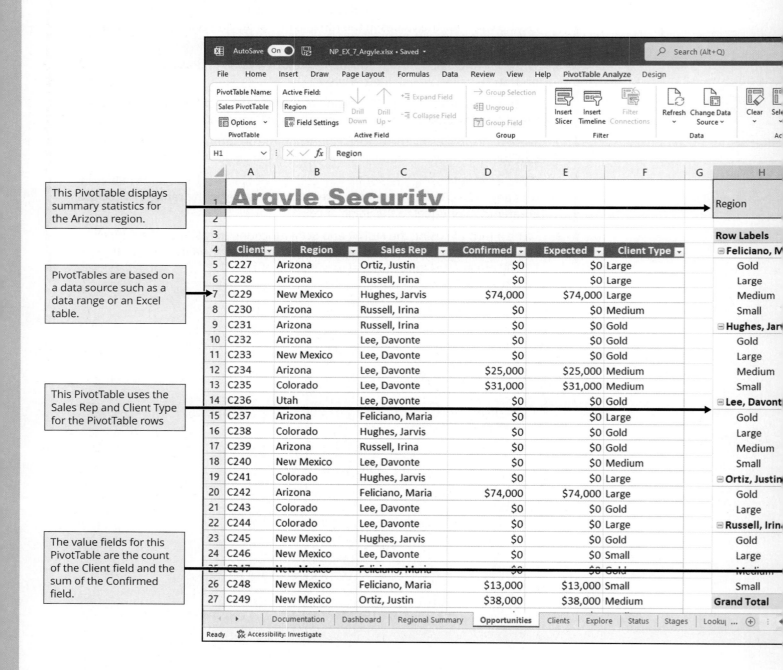

This PivotTable displays summary statistics for the Arizona region.

PivotTables are based on a data source such as a data range or an Excel table.

This PivotTable uses the Sales Rep and Client Type for the PivotTable rows

The value fields for this PivotTable are the count of the Client field and the sum of the Confirmed field.

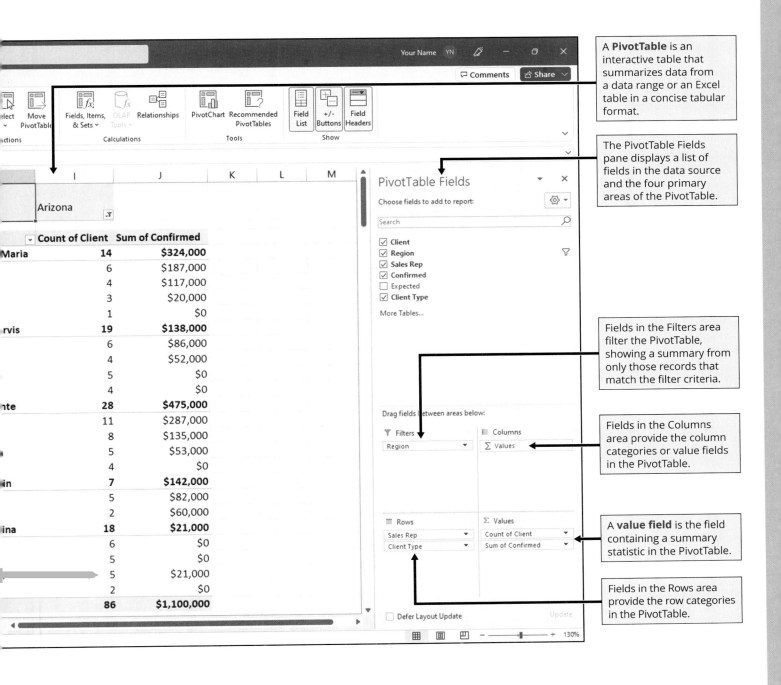

A **PivotTable** is an interactive table that summarizes data from a data range or an Excel table in a concise tabular format.

The PivotTable Fields pane displays a list of fields in the data source and the four primary areas of the PivotTable.

Fields in the Filters area filter the PivotTable, showing a summary from only those records that match the filter criteria.

Fields in the Columns area provide the column categories or value fields in the PivotTable.

A **value field** is the field containing a summary statistic in the PivotTable.

Fields in the Rows area provide the row categories in the PivotTable.

Creating a PivotTable

One of most useful Excel tools for data analysis and exploration is a PivotTable. A PivotTable is an interactive table that groups and summarizes data from a data range, Excel table, or external data source. A single PivotTable can do the work of multiple summary IF functions but with more ease and flexibility.

A PivotTable contains the following four primary areas:

- **Rows area**—displays category values from one or more fields arranged in separate rows
- **Columns area**—displays categories from one or more fields arranged in separate columns
- **Values area**—displays summary statistics for one or more fields at the intersection of each row and column category
- **Filters area**—contains a filter button limiting the PivotTable to only those values matching specified criteria

These four areas are identified in the PivotTable in Figure 7–21, which counts client contacts broken down by region and client type. The regions are placed the Columns area. Client Type categories appear in the Rows area. The COUNT function is applied to the Client field with counts of each region and client type displayed in the Values area. The Filters area displays a filter button, limiting the table to clients handled by Davonte Lee. The table also includes grand totals, summarizing the count of clients across all row and column categories.

Figure 7–21   Structure of a PivotTable

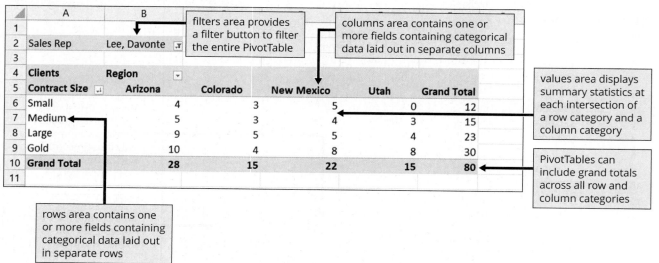

The PivotTable in Figure 7–21 reveals that Davonte Lee has 30 Gold clients: and 10 of them are in Arizona, four are in Colorado, eight are in New Mexico, and eight are in Utah. The table also provides a breakdown of other types of clients within each state. Overall, Davonte Lee is managing 80 client negotiations across all regions and client types.

Reference

Creating a PivotTable

- Click anywhere within a data range or Excel table
- On the Insert tab, in the Tables group, click the PivotTable button; or on the Table Design tab, in the Tools group, click the Summarize with PivotTable button.
- Specify whether to insert the PivotTable in a new worksheet or at a cell location within an existing worksheet.
- Click OK.
- Drag fields from the field list on the PivotTable Fields pane and drop them on the Filters, Columns, Rows, or Values area boxes.

Inserting a PivotTable

To create a PivotTable, click any cell within a data range or an Excel table, and then click the PivotTable button in the Tables group on the Insert tab. New PivotTables can be placed within a new or existing worksheet. Excel reserves a space 3 columns wide by 18 rows tall for the PivotTable. If the worksheet does not have enough empty space to accommodate the PivotTable, you will be prompted to overwrite the cell content.

Jeannette wants to analyze confirmed sales by the Region, Client Type, and Sales Rep fields. You will create a PivotTable from the data in the Sales table for this analysis.

To create a PivotTable from the Media table:

1. If you took a break at the end of the previous part, make sure the NP_EX_7_Argyle workbook is open.

2. Go to the **Opportunities** worksheet and click cell **A4** to select a cell in the Sales table.

3. On the ribbon, click the **Insert** tab, and then in the Tables group, click the **PivotTable** button. The PivotTable from table or range dialog box opens.

   Tip You can also click the Summarize with PivotTable button in the Tools group on the Table Design tab to open the PivotTable from table or range dialog box.

4. Verify that **Sales** appears in the Table/Range box. This specifies the Sales table as the source for the PivotTable.

5. Click the **Existing Worksheet** option button. You want to insert the PivotTable into the Explore worksheet starting at cell A6.

6. Click the **Explore** sheet tab, and then in the Explore worksheet, click cell **A6**. The 3-D reference Explore!$A$6 is entered in the Location box. Refer to Figure 7–22.

Figure 7–22   PivotTable from table or range dialog box

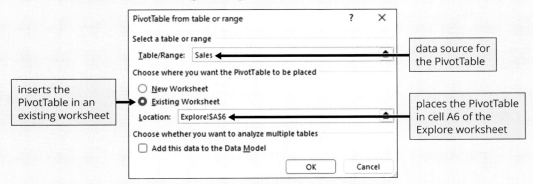

7. Click **OK**. The empty PivotTable report appears in the Explore worksheet. Refer to Figure 7–23.

Figure 7–23   PiviotTable features

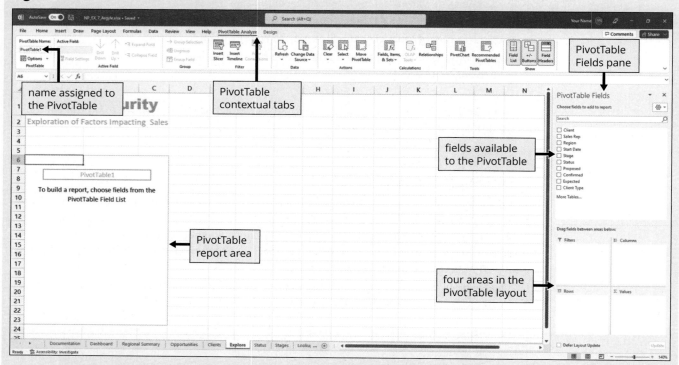

Trouble? If the PivotTable Fields pane is not open, you need to display it. On the ribbon, click the PivotTable Analyze tab, and then in the Show group, click the Field List button.

The empty PivotTable report section starts from cell A6 in the Explore worksheet. When any part of the PivotTable report section is selected, the PivotTable contextual tabs appear on the ribbon. You can select commands to populate and format the PivotTable from the PivotTable Analyze and Design tabs. The PivotTable Fields pane shows the fields from the Sales table. The boxes below the fields list represent the four areas of the PivotTable. You place the fields you want assigned to each area in these boxes.

Tip Click the Gear icon in the upper-right corner of the PivotTable Fields pane to choose a different layout for the area boxes.

Like Excel tables and charts, each PivotTable has a unique name. The first PivotTable created is named PivotTable1, the second is named PivotTable2, and so forth. You can give each PivotTable a more descriptive name by entering a new name in the PivotTable Name box in the PivotTable group on the PivotTable Analyze tab. PivotTable names have the same rules as Excel table names: The name can include spaces, but it cannot be any name reserved by Excel for other purposes.

Jeannette wants you to rename the PivotTable with a more descriptive name. You will change the name to Explore.

To change the PivotTable name:

1. On the PivotTable Analyze tab, in the PivotTable group, double-click the **PivotTable Name** box. The default name "PivotTable1" is selected.

2. Press **DELETE**, and then type **Explore** as the new name.

3. Press **ENTER**. The PivotTable is renamed.

Defining a PivotTable Layout

The layout of a PivotTable is defined by moving fields from the field list into one of the four area boxes. As fields are added to the area boxes, the content and calculations in the PivotTable are automatically updated. At any time, you can add, remove, or move the fields to arrange your data in a new way.

Jeannette wants this PivotTable to display the confirmed sales within each region, broken down by Client Type. You will place the Confirmed field in the Values area, the Region field in the Columns area, and the Client Type field in the Rows area.

To define the PivotTable layout:

1. In the PivotTable Fields pane, point to **Confirmed** in the field list to highlight it, and then drag the **Confirmed** field into the Values areas box. "Sum of Confirmed" appears in the Values box and the PivotTable shows a value of 2864000 as the total confirmed sales from all clients. Refer to Figure 7–24.

Figure 7–24   Field added to the Values area

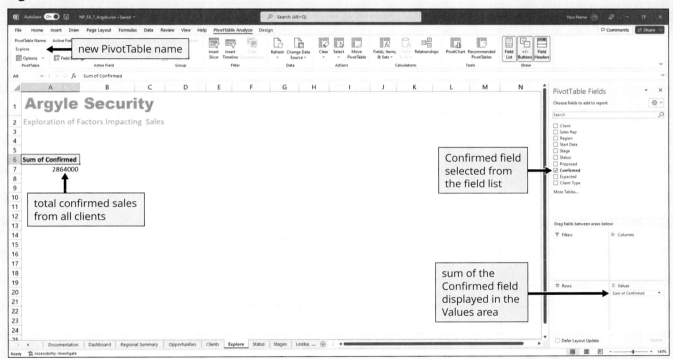

> **Tip** By default, Excel applies the SUM function to numeric fields placed in the Values area and the COUNT function to text fields. However, you can change the function used in the PivotTable.

2. Drag the **Region** field into the Columns area box. The total confirmed sales for each region is displayed in separate columns followed by the grand total of all confirmed sales across all regions. Note that these are the same values calculated using the SUMIF function (refer back to Figure 7–19).

3. Drag the **Client Type** field onto the Rows area box. The sum of the confirmed sales is broken down by both Region and Client Type. Refer to Figure 7–25.

Figure 7–25   Fields added to the Columns and Rows areas

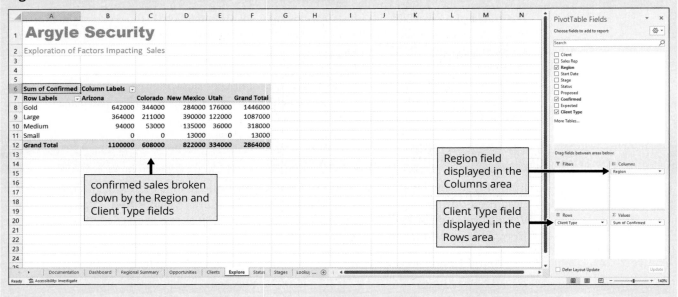

PivotTables are excellent for data exploration because you can quickly change the PivotTable layout to summarize data from different perspectives. To change the content of the PivotTable, drag fields out of any of the four area boxes to remove them from the table and drop new fields into the area boxes to add them. The PivotTable calculations are automatically updated to reflect the new layout.

Insight

Moving a PivotTable

You can move any PivotTable to a new location in the workbook. To move a PivotTable within its current worksheet, select the entire PivotTable range and then drag the table to a new location, being careful not to overwrite other content in the process. To move a PivotTable to a different worksheet, click anywhere within the PivotTable to select it, and then click the Move PivotTable button in the Actions group on the PivotTable Analyze tab. The Move PivotTable dialog box opens so you can choose the new location for the PivotTable. You can create a new worksheet for the PivotTable or choose an existing worksheet in the workbook. You can also select the entire PivotTable and then use the Cut and Paste buttons in the Clipboard group on the Home tab to move the PivotTable within the workbook.

Jeannette wants the expected sales from all clients broken down by status. You will modify the PivotTable now to show those calculations.

To modify the PivotTable to show expected sales by status:

1. Drag **Client Type** from the Rows area box and drop the icon on an empty section of the worksheet. The Client Type field is removed from the PivotTable.

2. Drag the **Status** field from the field list into the Rows area.

   Tip You can also remove a field from the PivotTable by deselecting its check box in the field list.

3. Click the **Confirmed** check box in the PivotTable Fields list to remove that field from the Values area of the PivotTable.

4. Click the **Expected** field in the field list to add it to the Values area. A numeric field, like the Expected field, is added to the Values area when you click its check box. Refer to Figure 7–26.

Figure 7–26   Expected sales by region and contract status

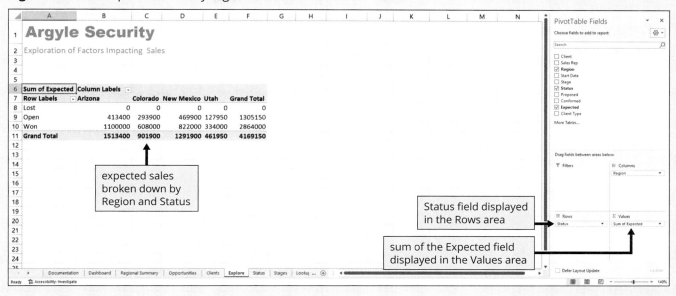

The total expected sales in row 11 of the PivotTable match the projected sales by region calculated earlier (refer back to Figure 7–20). The PivotTable also breaks down the expected sales by contract status, showing that the company expects another $1,305,150 in revenue from the open contracts (cell F9). All projected sales for lost contracts in row 8 are 0, which is to be expected.

Adding Multiple Fields to a Row or Column

PivotTables are not limited to a single field in the Rows or Columns area. You can place additional fields in each area, nesting one field within another. For example, placing the Status and Client Type fields in the same row or column will nest one field within another.

When two fields are placed within a row or column, the PivotTable will show subtotals for each category of the outer field. You can collapse and expand the outer field by clicking minus and plus boxes in the same way you can collapse and expand an outline in an Excel table.

You will add the Client Type field to the Rows area.

To nest the Client Type field in the Status field within a PivotTable:

1. Drag **Client Type** from the PivotTable Fields list and drop it directly below Status in the Rows area box. The PivotTable now shows the expected sales by region for each value of the Client Type field within the Status field. Subtotals are placed at the top of each Status category. Refer to Figure 7–27.

Figure 7–27   Nested PivotTable fields

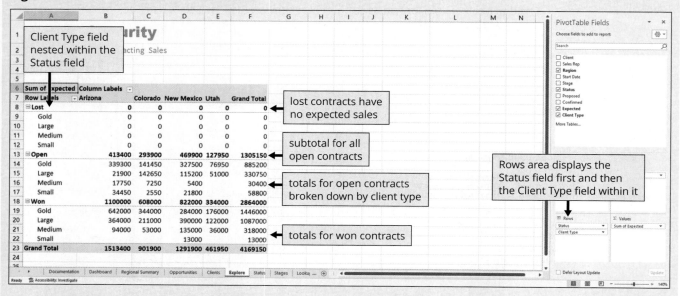

2. Click the **minus box** next to the Open category in cell A13. Excel collapses the PivotTable row to show only the subtotal of all open contracts.

3. Click the **plus box** next to the Open category in cell A13 to expand the PivotTable showing the expected sales for open contracts from all client types.

Based on the PivotTable, you can report to Jeannette $1,305,150 of sales are expected to come from open contracts (cell F13) with $885,200 of that total coming from Gold clients (cell F14). The largest expected sales come from Gold clients in Arizona with $339,300 (cell B14).

Notice that a few cells in the PivotTable are blank. This occurs when there is no data at the intersection of the row and column categories. Cell E16 is blank, indicating that there are no open contracts in Utah for medium-sized clients, and thus there is nothing to total.

> **Tip** To display a 0 in place of a blank, on the PivotTable Analyze tab of the ribbon, in the PivotTable group, click the Options button to open the PivotTable Options dialog box. On the Layout & Format tab, enter 0 in the For empty cells show box.

Filtering a PivotTable

The Filters area is a quick way to filter PivotTable data. When you add a field to the Filters area, a filter button appears two rows above the upper-left corner of the table. You can use the button to choose a value to filter the entire PivotTable by.

> **Tip** To select multiple items, click the Select Multiple Items check box and then click each item to include in the filter.

Jeannette wants to examine the expected sales managed by each of the company's sales representatives. You will add the Sales Rep field to the Filters area of the PivotTable.

To add the Sale Rep field as a filter to the PivotTable:

1. Drag the **Sales Rep** field from the PivotTable Fields list and drop it in the Filters area box. The filter label "Sales Rep" is displayed in cell A4, and the value (All) is displayed in cell B4, indicating that sales from all reps are shown in the PivotTable.

2. In cell B4, click the **Sales Rep filter** button to display a menu listing all the sales reps.

3. Click **Russell, Irina** in the list, and then click **OK**. The PivotTable updates to show only the expected sales from Irina Russell's clients. Refer to Figure 7–28.

Figure 7–28   Filtered PivotTable

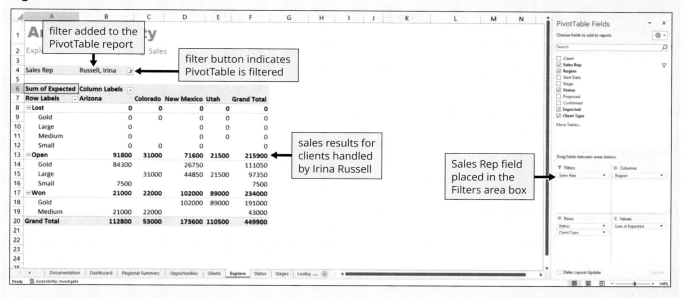

For more filter options, you can use the filter buttons next to the row and column labels in the PivotTable, choosing which row or column categories to include in the PivotTable. Jeannette suggests that including lost contracts in a PivotTable of expected sales can be confusing and asks that you remove that content from the PivotTable, showing only the won and open contracts.

To filter the PivotTable to show only won and open contracts:

1. In cell A7, click the **Row Labels filter** button. A menu opens displaying options for sorting and filtering the labels in the PivotTable row. Refer to Figure 7–29.

Figure 7–29   PivotTable field options

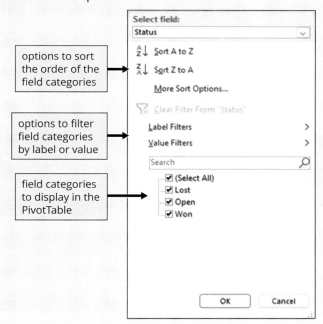

2. Click the **Lost** check box to remove the checkmark, and then click **OK** to apply the filter. Refer to Figure 7–30.

Figure 7–30   Filtered PivotTable row area

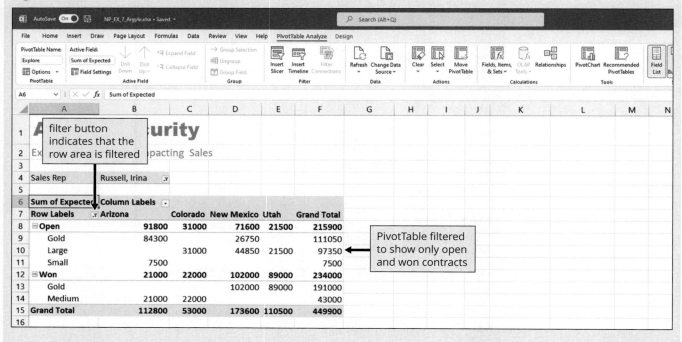

You can remove the filter by reopening the Select Field dialog box and reselecting the Lost check box. To remove all filters from a PivotTable, on the PivotTable Analyze tab of the ribbon, in the Actions group, click the Clear button arrow, and then the Clear Filters option.

Insight

Choosing a Recommended PivotTable

If you are not sure what to include in a PivotTable or how to structure it, you can use the Recommend PivotTables tool. To use the tool, select any cell within a data range or Excel table, and then click the Recommended PivotTables button in the Tables group on the Insert tab. A gallery of PivotTable layouts suitable for that data opens. Choose the one you find most useful and relevant. The PivotTable is inserted on a new sheet in the workbook using the layout you selected.

Formatting a PivotTable

Once you have decided on the contents and layout of your PivotTable, you can format the PivotTable so that its design is pleasing, and its contents are readable. Excel includes a gallery of PivotTable designs, and you can customize the appearance of your PivotTables to match the needs of your company or organization.

Jeannette wants to add PivotTables to a dashboard providing an overview of customer sales and projected income. The first PivotTable will display the number of won contracts, the total confirmed sales, and the average sale per client.

To create the PivotTable of won contracts:

1. Go to the **Opportunities** worksheet and click cell **A4** to select a cell in the Sales table.

2. On the Insert tab, in the Tables group, click the **PivotTable** button. The PivotTable from table or range dialog box opens.

3. Click the **Existing Worksheet** button.

4. With the Location box selected, click the **Dashboard** worksheet, and then click cell **A13**.

5. Click **OK** to insert PivotTable2 into the Dashboard worksheet.

6. On the PivotTable Analyze tab, in the PivotTable group, change the name of the PivotTable from PivotTable2 to **Won Contracts**.

Next, you will populate the PivotTable with fields from the Sales table.

To define a layout for the Won Contracts PivotTable:

1. Drag the **Status** field from the PivotTable Fields list to the Filters area.

2. In cell B11, click the **Status filter** button, click **Won** from the list, and then click **OK**. The PivotTable is filtered to show only won contracts.

3. Drag the **Client** field from the PivotTable Fields list box and drop it in the Values box. The count of won contracts (45) appears in cell A14.

4. Drag the **Confirmed** field from the PivotTable Fields list box and drop it in the Values area box. The sum of confirmed sales (2864000) appears in cell B14.

   Note that the two fields in the PivotTable are represented by ΣValues in the Columns area. Because ΣValues is placed in the Columns area, the two fields are displayed in separate columns.

5. Drag **ΣValues** from the Columns area box and drop it in the Rows area box. The two fields are now displayed in separate rows. Refer to Figure 7–31.

Figure 7–31   PivotTable with multiple value fields

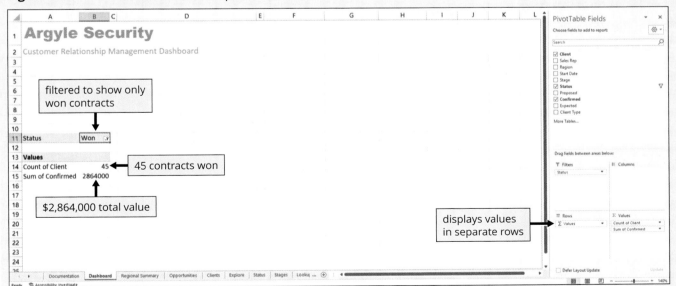

Changing PivotTable Labels

The default label for each PivotTable value contains the name of summary function applied to the field followed by the field name. The first label is "Count of Client" and the second label is "Sum of Confirmed." You can change these labels to any text except a reserved Excel name or the name of a PivotTable field. If you want to use a field name as a row or column label, type the field name and then add a blank space to the end of the field name text. The extra blank space will cause Excel to treat the label text as different from the field name text.

Jeannette wants the value labels changed to "Clients" and "Confirmed Sales." She also wants the label for the entire PivotTable changed from "Values" to "Summary."

To format the labels and values in the PivotTable:

1. Click cell **A13**, replace the Values label with **Summary** and then press **ENTER**. Notice that the label changed in the cell.

2. Click cell **A14**, replace the Count of Client label with **Clients** and then press **ENTER**. Note that the label changed in the cell and in the PivotTables Fields pane.

3. Change the label of cell **A15** from Sum of Confirmed to **Confirmed Sales**.

The PivotTable labels are easier to read. Jeannette also wants the Confirmed Sales values displayed in a currency format with no decimal places. You will format the values in the PivotTable to make them easier to interpret. Rather than changing the format applied to the cell, you will change the format applied to the PivotTable value itself.

To format Confirmed Sales as currency:

1. If necessary, click anywhere within the PivotTable to select it.

2. In the PivotTable Fields pane, click **Confirmed Sales** in the Values area box, and then click **Value Field Settings** on the menu.

> **Key Step** Always set the number format of a PivotTable value field using the Value Field Settings dialog box so that if the structure of the PivotTable changes, your number format is not lost.

3. In the Value Field Settings dialog box, click **Number Format**. The Format Cells dialog box opens.

4. In the Category box, click **Currency**.

5. In the Decimal places box, reduce the number of decimal places to **0**.

6. Click **OK** in each dialog box to return to the worksheet. Refer to Figure 7–32.

Figure 7-32   Formatted labels and values in the PivotTable

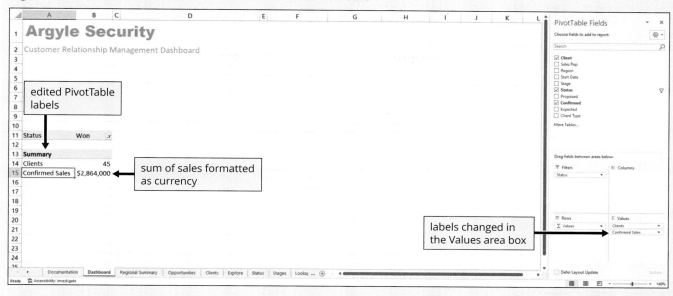

Changing a PivotTable Summary Function

By default, Excel uses the COUNT function to summarize non-numeric data and the SUM function for numeric data. However you can choose other summary functions such as AVERAGE, MIN, and MAX, from the Value Field Settings dialog box.

Jeannette wants the Won Contracts PivotTable to also show the average value of the contracts won by the company. You will add that statistic to the PivotTable now.

To display the average value of the Confirmed PivotTable field:

1. In the PivotTable Fields pane, drag **Confirmed** from the list of fields and add it to the Values area box.

2. In the Values area box, click **Sum of Confirmed**, and then click **Value Field Settings** on the menu. The Value Field Settings dialog box opens.

3. Click **Average** in the list of summary functions.

4. Double-click the **Custom Name** box to select the name "Average of Confirmed," and then type **Average Sale**. Refer to Figure 7-33.

Figure 7-33   Value Field Settings dialog box

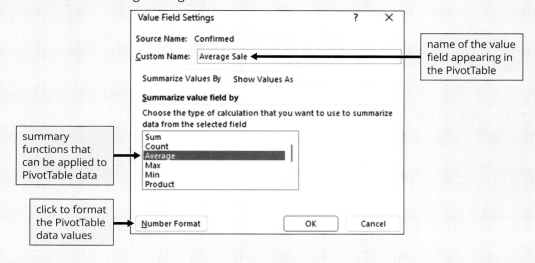

5. Click **Number Format** to open the Format Cells dialog box.

6. Click **Currency** from the list of format categories, and then reduce the number of decimal places to **0**.

7. Click **OK** in each dialog box to return to the workbook. Refer to Figure 7–34.

Figure 7–34   Average value of the Confirmed field

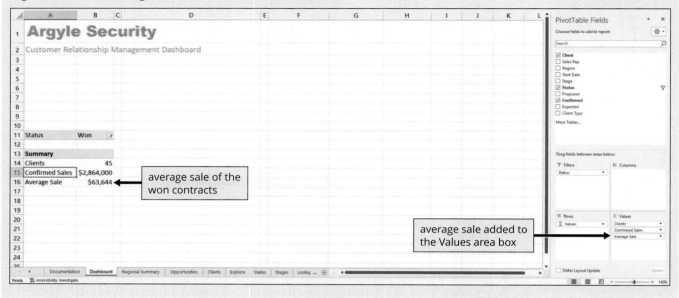

The PivotTable shows that the company won 45 contracts for total sales of $2,864,000 with an average sale of $63,644 per client.

Insight

Choosing a Report Layout

In addition to changing the structure of a PivotTable by moving fields into the different areas, you can change the overall table layout. PivotTables have possible three report layouts:

- **Compact Form** (default layout)—places all fields from the Rows area in a single worksheet columns and indents values to distinguish nested fields from other fields.
- **Outline Form**—places each field in the Rows area in its own column and includes subtotals above every field category group.
- **Tabular Form**—places each field in the Rows area in its own column and includes subtotals below every group.

To switch between PivotTable layouts, click the Report Layout button in the Layout group on the Design tab. Choose the PivotTable layout that presents the data in the most informative and effective format.

Choosing a PivotTable Style

Just as there are built-in styles for Excel charts and tables, there are built-in PivotTable styles. These styles are available in the PivotTable Styles gallery, which includes a variety of column and row colors. You can also set options such as adding or removing banded rows and banded columns to the PivotTable design and adding or removing column and row headings.

Jeannette wants you to use a built-in design to format the Won Contracts PivotTable.

To apply a PivotTable design to the Won Contracts PivotTable:

1. On the ribbon, click the **Design** tab to display tools for choosing a PivotTable style.

2. In the PivotTable Styles group, click the **Quick Styles** button, and then click **Light Orange, Pivot Style Medium 10**.

3. Select the range **A13:B16**.

4. On the ribbon, click the **Home** tab, and then in the Font group, increase the font size of the selected cells to **16** points.

5. Select the labels and values in the range **A14:B16**, and then change the font color to **Orange Accent 2**.

6. Increase the width of column A to **24 characters**.

7. Click cell **A13** to deselect the selected cells. Refer to Figure 7-35.

Figure 7-35   Formatted PivotTable

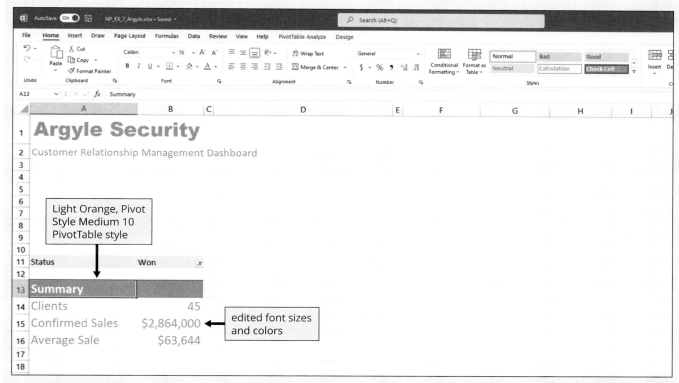

Formats applied directly to individual PivotTable cells override the formats used in the PivotTable styles gallery. If you change the PivotTable style for the Won Contracts PivotTable, the formatting applied directly to range A13:B16 will not change.

You can create a custom PivotTable style by opening the PivotTable Styles gallery on the Design tab and then clicking New PivotTable Style to open the New PivotTable Style dialog box. From that dialog box, you can format different parts of the table, such as formats for the rows, columns, first rows and columns, and header rows.

Setting PivotTable Options

Several default values and behaviors are associated with PivotTables. For example, Excel automatically sorts the row and column categories and displays missing combinations in the PivotTable as blank cells. If the layout of the PivotTable changes, the widths of the worksheet columns automatically increases or decreases to match the new PivotTable content. You can modify these defaults in the PivotTable Options dialog box.

Jeannette wants the columns of the Dashboard to remain fixed even if the layout and content of a PivotTable changes. Also, Jeannette wants empty cells to display a zero rather than a blank. You will use the PivotTable Options dialog box to make these changes to the Won Contracts PivotTable.

To define PivotTable Options for the Won Contracts PivotTable:

1. Make sure cell **A13** is still selected.

2. On the ribbon, click the **PivotTable Analyze** tab, and then in the PivotTable group, click the **Options** button. The PivotTable Options dialog box opens.

   Tip You can also open the PivotTable Options dialog box by right-clicking a PivotTable and clicking PivotTable Options on the shortcut menu.

3. Enter **0** in the For empty cells show list box.

4. Click the **Autofit column widths on update** check box to remove the checkmark. Refer to Figure 7–36.

Figure 7–36   PivotTable Options dialog box

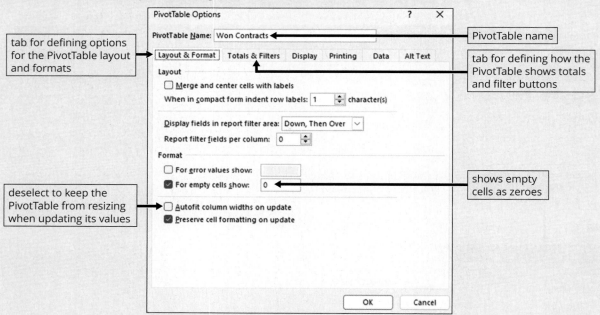

5. Click **OK** to close the dialog box and apply the changes.

Jeannette wants you to add another PivotTable to the dashboard showing the confirmed and projected sales broken down by client type.

To insert a PivotTable showing sales by client type into the dashboard:

1. Go to the **Opportunities** worksheet and verify that cell **A4** in the Sales table is selected.

2. On the ribbon, click the **Insert** tab, and then in the Tables group, click the **PivotTable** button. The PivotTable from table or range dialog box opens.

3. Click the **Existing Worksheet** option button to make the Location box active.

4. Click the **Dashboard** worksheet tab, and then click cell **F13** to enter the cell reference Dashboard!$F$13 in the Location box active, and then click **OK**. An empty PivotTable is added to the dashboard starting in cell F13.

5. Rename the PivotTable as **Confirmed and Projected Sales**.

6. Drag the **Confirmed** and **Expected** fields to the Values area box.

7. Drag the **Client Type** field to the Rows area box. The PivotTable shows the total confirmed and expected sales. Refer to Figure 7–37.

Figure 7–37   PivotTable of confirmed and expected sales

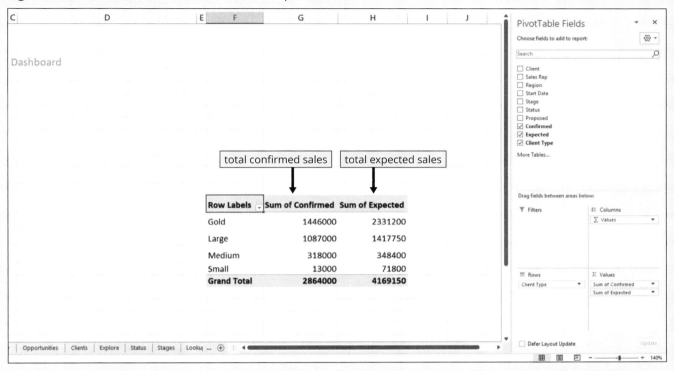

Jeannette wants you to format this PivotTable to match the style of the other PivotTable in the dashboard.

To format the PivotTable to match the dashboard style:

1. Click cell **G13** and change the label to **Confirmed Sales**.

2. Click cell **H13** and change the label to **Projected Sales**.

3. Right-click cell **G13**, click **Value Field Settings** on the shortcut menu to open the Value Field Settings dialog box.

4. Click the **Number Format** button, change the format to **Currency** with **0** decimal places, and then click **OK** in each dialog box.

5. Repeat Steps 3 and 4 for cell **H13** to display projected sales as currency with no decimal places.

6. On the ribbon, click the **Design** tab, and then in the PivotTable Styles gallery, click the **Quick Styles** button, and then click the **Light Orange, Pivot Style Medium 10**.

7. Right-click cell **F13**, click **PivotTable Options** on the shortcut menu to open the PivotTable Options dialog box.

> **Tip** You can hide a field header by deselecting the Field Headers button in the Show group on the PivotTable Analyze tab.

8. Enter **0** in the For empty cells show box, click the **Autofit column widths on update** check box to remove the checkmark, and then click **OK**.

9. With cell F13 still selected, change the text from "Row Labels" to **Client Type**. The PivotTable is fully formatted. Refer to Figure 7–38.

Figure 7–38   Formatted PivotTable

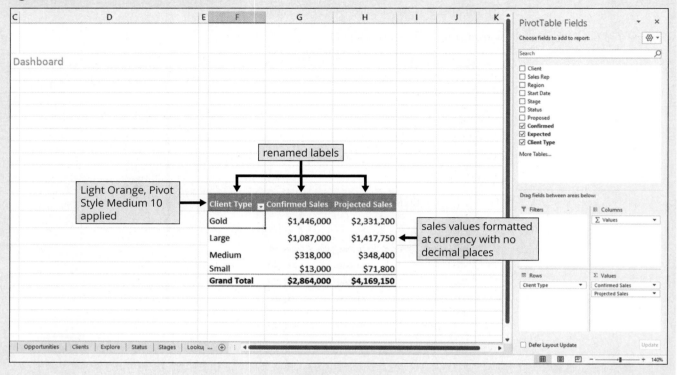

By default, PivotTables are displayed with filter buttons to allow users to quickly explore the impact of filtering the data. If you are preparing a final report in which you no longer need to filter your results, you might want to give your PivotTables a cleaner appearance by removing the filter buttons. You can hide the filter buttons by deselecting the +/- Buttons button located in the Show group on the PivotTable Analyze tab.

Proskills

Written Communication: Making PivotTables Accessible

Many companies and government agencies require documents to be accessible to users with visual impairments and special needs. Excel provides support for those users by making objects such as charts, graphics, and PivotTables accessible through alternate text.

To add alternate text to a PivotTable, open the PivotTable Options dialog box and go to the Alt Text tab. On the Alt Text tab, you can specify a title for the alternate text. The title provides a brief description of the alternate text so that the user can decide whether to continue to review the PivotTable content. Below the title box, you can insert a description of the PivotTable. The description can be a general overview of the table's contents or a detailed summary of the PivotTable numbers and summary statistics. There is no character limit on alternate text, though a general guideline is to limit the summary to about 160 characters.

If you want to include alternate text to many objects in your workbooks, you can add the Alt Text command to the Quick Access Toolbar. For information on modifying the Quick Access Toolbar, refer to Excel Help.

You have finished adding PivotTables to the dashboard. In the next session, you will complete the dashboard by adding PivotCharts and slicers to create a dashboard that users can interact with to explore customer relations at Argyle Security.

Part 7.2 Quick Check

1. What are the four primary areas of a PivotTable?

2. What default summary statistic is used for non-numeric data in the Values area of the PivotTable?

3. What default summary statistic is used for numeric data in the Values area of the PivotTable?

4. What does a blank in a PivotTable cell indicate?

5. Why should you set the number format of a PivotTable value using the Value Field Settings dialog box rather than defining the number format of the PivotTable cell?

6. Which has precedence: a format applied directly to a PivotTable cell or a format defined using a PivotTable style?

7. Field names are not allowed for row or column labels since they are reserved for other uses in the PivotTable, so how can you display the field name in a row or column label?

8. What are two ways of filtering a PivotTable?

9. How do you arrange multiple value fields in PivotTable rows rather than in columns?

Part 7.3 Visual Overview: PivotCharts and Slicers

The Report Connections button is used to connect a slicer or timeline to multiple PivotTables.

This slicer is used to filter PivotTables to show results from Arizona clients.

This timeline is used to filter PivotTables to show results only from June through August of 2029.

A **PivotChart** is a graphical representation of the data from a PivotTable.

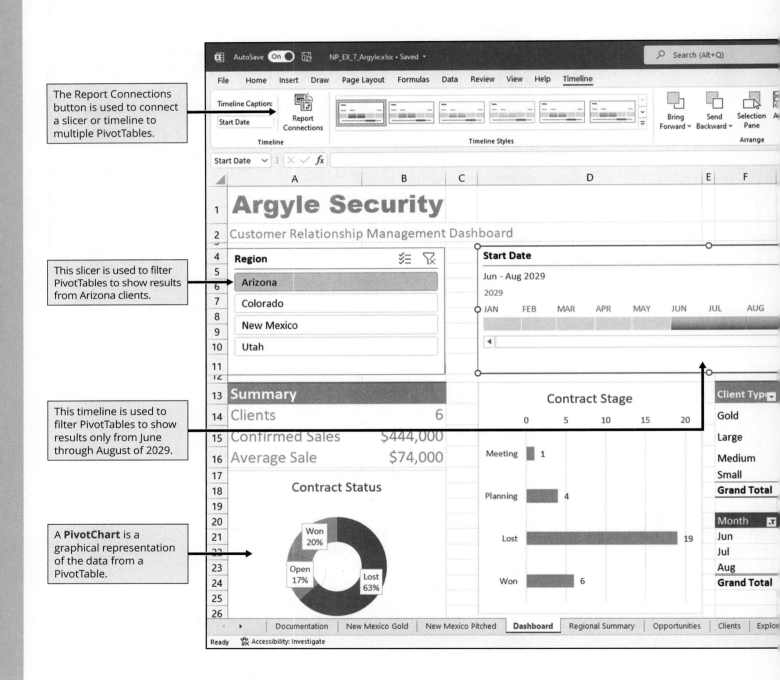

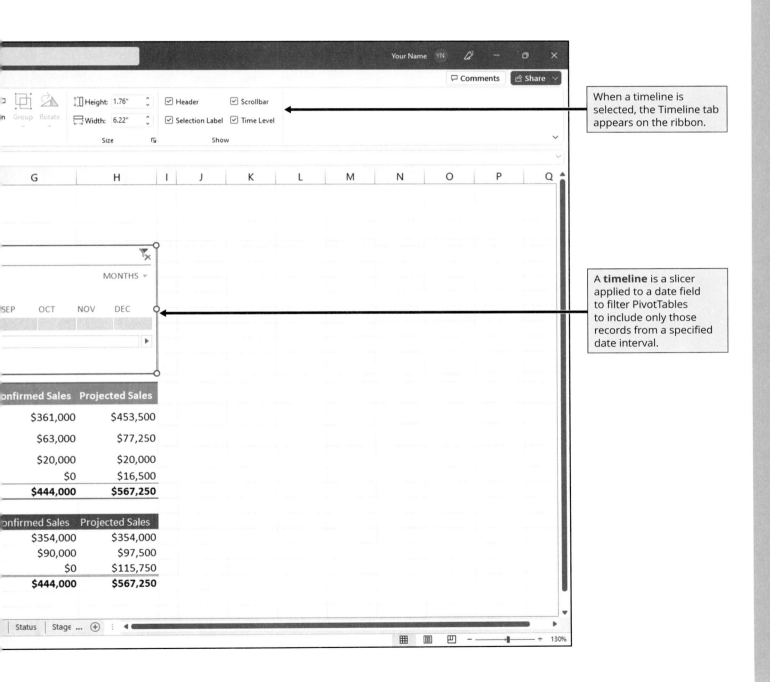

When a timeline is selected, the Timeline tab appears on the ribbon.

A **timeline** is a slicer applied to a date field to filter PivotTables to include only those records from a specified date interval.

Introducing PivotCharts

A PivotChart is a graphical representation of a PivotTable. Like PivotTables, you can explore PivotChart data by adding or removing fields from the different chart sections. You can also change the chart orientation, moving a field from a PivotChart axis into a PivotChart legend. A PivotChart has four primary areas:

- **Axis (Category) area**—displays categories that each data series is plotted against
- **Legend (Series) area**—breaks up the data values into separate data series
- **Values area**—contains the data values that are plotted on the PivotChart
- **Filters area**—contains a filter button that limits the PivotChart to only those values satisfying specified criteria

Figure 7–39 shows the structure of a PivotChart based on the PivotTable data shown earlier in Figure 7–21.

Figure 7–39   PivotChart Structure

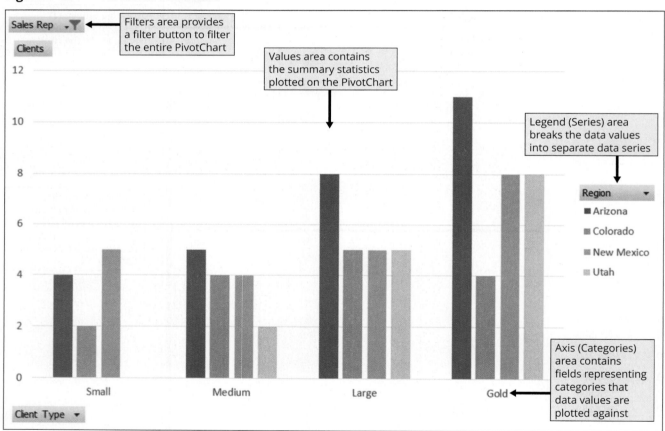

Reference

Creating a PivotChart

To insert a PivotChart:

- On the Insert tab, in the Charts group, click the PivotChart button.
- Specify whether to insert the PivotChart in a new worksheet or at a cell location in an existing worksheet.
- Drag fields from the field list on the PivotChart Fields pane and drop them on the Filters, Legend (Series), Axis (Categories), or Values area boxes.

To add a PivotChart to an existing PivotTable:

- Select a PivotTable in the workbook.
- On the PivotTable Analyze tab, in the Tools group, click the PivotChart button.
- Select the PivotChart chart type.
- If necessary, move the PivotChart to a different worksheet than the PivotTable.

Creating a PivotChart

A PivotChart is always based on data stored in a PivotTable. So, a PivotChart is either created from an existing PivotTable or created at the same time as its PivotTable. The layouts of a PivotTable and PivotChart always mirror one another. Any changes made to the structure and content of a PivotTable are reflected in the PivotChart, and vice versa.

Jeannette wants you to add a doughnut chart to the dashboard, showing the status of the contacts currently pursued by Argyle Security. You will add this chart as a PivotChart.

To begin building the PivotChart:

1. If you took a break at the end of the previous part, make sure the NP_EX_7_Argyle workbook is open.
2. Click the **Opportunities** sheet tab to make that worksheet active and verify that cell A4 is the active cell.
3. On the ribbon, click the **Insert** tab, and then in the Charts group, click the **PivotChart** button. The Create PivotChart dialog box opens.
4. Click the **Existing Worksheet** option button, click the **Status** sheet tab, and then click cell **A4** in the Status worksheet. The reference Status!$A$4 appears in the Location box.
5. Click **OK**. An empty PivotTable report and an empty PivotChart appear in the worksheet. Refer to Figure 7–40.

Figure 7–40   Empty PivotTable report and PivotChart

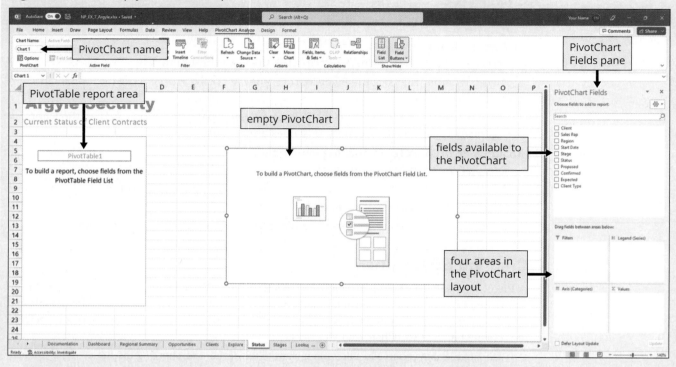

When a PivotChart is selected, the PivotChart Analyze, Design, and Format tabs appear on the ribbon. The Design and Format tabs include the same commands you have seen when working with other Excel charts. The PivotChart Analyze tab includes many of the same commands used for working with PivotTables. Once you know how to work with PivotTables, you have already learned many of the tools applicable to PivotCharts.

You will define the names of the PivotChart and PivotTable now.

To edit the PivotTable and PivotChart names:

1. With the PivotChart still selected, on the PivotChart Analyze tab, in the PivotChart group, change the name from Chart 1 to **Status Chart**.

2. Click cell **A4** to select the PivotTable.

3. Click the **PivotTable Analyze** tab, and then in the PivotTable group, change the name of the PivotTable to **Status Table**.

PivotCharts are built the same way as PivotTables: by choosing fields from the field list and dropping them into one of four PivotChart areas. Jeannette wants you to create a PivotChart doughnut pie chart with the Status field in the Axis (Category) area and the count of the Clients field in the Values area.

To lay out the PivotChart contents:

1. Click the **PivotChart** to select it.

2. Drag the **Status** field from the PivotChart Fields list into the Axis (Category) area box.

3. Drag the **Client** field from the field list into the Values area box.

   Tip The default PivotChart type is a clustered column chart.

4. On the ribbon, click the **Design** tab, and then in the Type group, click the **Change Chart Type** button. The Change Chart Type dialog box appears.

5. In the All Charts list, click **Pie**, and then click the **Doughnut** chart subtype (the rightmost subtype).

6. Click **OK** to insert the Doughnut chart into the worksheet. Refer to Figure 7–41.

Figure 7–41   Doughnut PivotChart

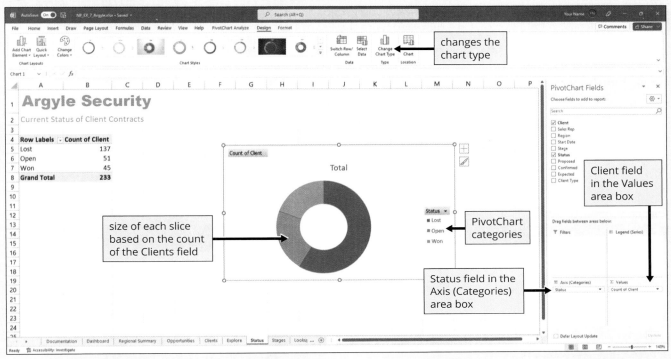

Not every Excel chart type can be created as a PivotChart. You can create PivotCharts only from the Column, Line, Pie, Bar, Area, Surface, and Radar chart types and from Combo charts created from those chart types. To use a chart type that is not a PivotChart, copy and paste the data from a PivotTable into a new data range and then create an Excel chart from the pasted values.

Moving a PivotChart to Another Worksheet

The PivotTable and PivotChart do not need to be on the same worksheet (though they must be in the same workbook). Jeannette wants the PivotChart moved to the Dashboard worksheet to be displayed alongside other summary tables and charts.

To move the PivotChart:

1. With the PivotChart still selected, click the **PivotChart Analyze** tab on the ribbon, and then in the Actions group, click the **Move Chart** button. The Move Chart dialog box opens.

2. Click the **Object in** option button If necessary to select it, click the **Object in** box, click **Dashboard** as the worksheet to place the PivotChart in, and then click **OK**. The PivotChart moves to the Dashboard worksheet.

3. In the Dashboard worksheet, move and resize the PivotChart to cover the range **A18:B29**.

Jeannette wants you to remove several chart elements, including field elements used with PivotTables. You will create a cleaner version of the PivotChart by removing these elements and adding data labels to chart showing the percentages of lost, open, and won contracts.

To format the PivotChart:

1. Make sure the PivotChart is still selected.

2. On the PivotChart Analyze tab, in the Show/Hide group, click the **Field Buttons** button to deselect it. All field buttons are removed from the PivotChart.

   > **Tip** You can remove select field buttons from a PivotTable or PivotChart by clicking the arrow on the Field Buttons button and deselecting only those field buttons you want hidden.

3. Change the PivotChart title from Total to **Contract Status**.

4. Click the **Chart Elements** button ⊞ and then click the **Legend** check box to remove the chart legend.

5. Click the **Data Label arrow**, and then click **Data Callout** to add callouts to the doughnut chart. Refer to Figure 7–42.

Figure 7–42   Revised PivotChart

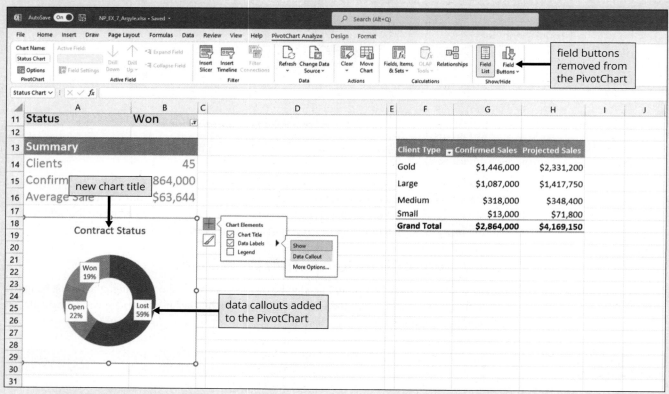

From the chart, Jeannette reports that 19% of the customer negotiations have resulted in a sale, 59% have been concluded without a sale, and 22% of negotiations are still open. Jeannette wants another PivotChart added to the dashboard—a bar chart showing the breakdown of the client contracts by the negotiation stage. You will create the PivotTable and PivotChart for this data.

To create a PivotChart of the Stage field:

1. Go to the **Opportunities** worksheet.

2. On the ribbon, click the **Insert** tab, and then in the Charts group, click the **PivotChart** button. The Create PivotChart dialog box opens.

3. Click the **Existing Worksheet** option button, press **TAB** to move to the Location box, click the **Stages** sheet tab, and then click cell **A4** in the. The cell reference Stages!$A$4 is entered in the Location box.

4. Click **OK** to insert the PivotTable and PivotChart in the Stages worksheet.

5. Rename the PivotChart as **Stages Chart** and rename the PivotTable as **Stages Table**.

6. With the PivotTable selected, drag the **Stage** field to the Rows area box and the **Client** field to the Values area box. The PivotTable and PivotChart are both updated to display the layout of the data.

7. Click the PivotChart, and then click the **Design** tab on the ribbon. In the Type group, click the **Change Chart Type** button.

8. In the All Charts box, click **Bar**, and then click **OK** to change the chart type to a bar chart. Refer to Figure 7–43.

Figure 7–43   PivotChart of the Stage field

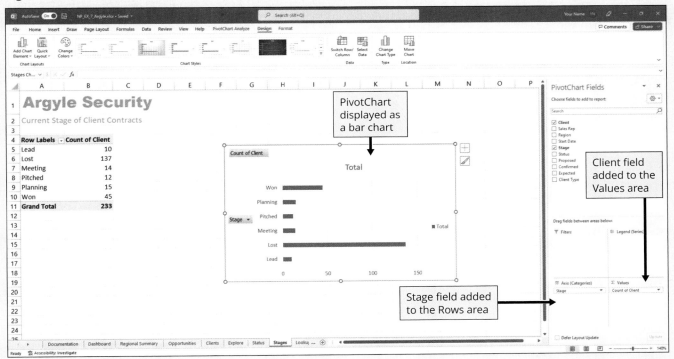

Jeannette wants you to move the PivotChart to the Dashboard worksheet and then format the chart so that it matches the design style of that sheet.

To move and format the bar chart:

1. Make sure the PivotChart is selected, and then on the Design tab, in the Location group, click the **Move Chart** button.

2. Click the Object in box, click **Dashboard**, and then click **OK**. The PivotChart moves to the Dashboard worksheet.

3. Move and resize the PivotChart so that it covers the range **D13:D29**.

4. On the PivotChart Analyze tab, in the Show/Hide ribbon, click the **Field Button** to remove all field buttons from the chart.

5. Change the chart title from Total to **Contract Stage**.

6. Click the **Chart Elements** button ⊞, and then click the **Legend** check box to remove the chart legend.

7. Click the **Data Labels** check box to show the client count for each negotiation stage, and then click the **Chart Elements** button ⊞ to close the menu.

8. Click the **Design** tab on the ribbon, and then in the Chart Styles group, click the **Change Colors** button.

9. Click **Monochromatic Palette 2** to change the fill color of the PivotChart bars to orange. Refer to Figure 7–44.

Figure 7–44   Formatted bar chart

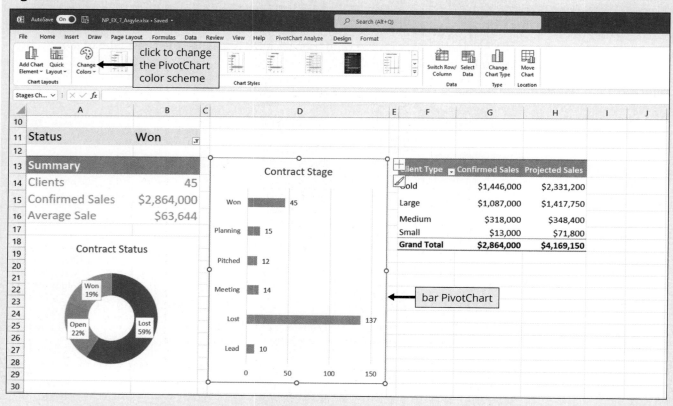

Jeannette likes the formatted chart but wants the chart categories reordered so that the list of negotiation stages is in chronological order. To make that change, you must reorder the categories in the PivotTable.

Sorting PivotTable Categories

The categories listed in a PivotTable row or column follow a predefined order. Text categories are listed alphabetically. Date categories are arranged from the earliest date to the latest. If a custom list has been defined for the field, the categories appear in the order of the custom list.

You can change the order of the categories by dragging and dropping the category labels in a new order or by typing the categories in the row or column in the order you prefer. You will reorder the categories in the PivotTable and by extension the categories in the PivotChart.

To reorder the PivotChart categories:

1. Go to the **Stages** worksheet.

2. Click cell **A6** in the PivotTable, and then type **Meeting** which is the second stage in negotiations between the company and a potential client. The Meeting category moves to the second item in the row, and the Lost category appears as the third row item in cell A7.

3. Click cell **A7**, and then type **Planning** which is the third stage in negotiations. The Lost category becomes the fourth row item in cell A8.

4. Click cell **A8**, and then type **Pitched** which is the fourth stage in negotiations when a formal offer is made to the client. The order of the row labels now matches the chronological order of the negotiations. Refer to Figure 7–45.

Figure 7–45   Rearranged PivotTable categories

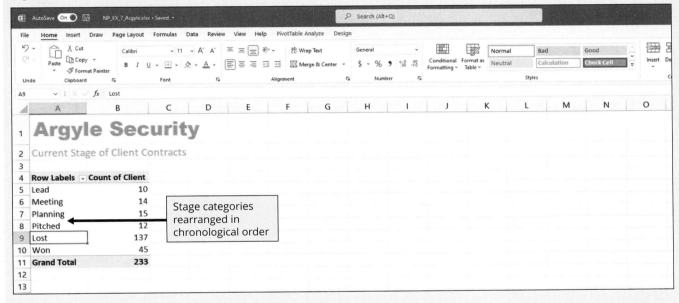

5. Go to the **Dashboard** worksheet and review the revised bar chart.

    The default order of bar charts is to place the first category at the bottom of the bar chart. You can reverse this default behavior by formatting the chart axis.

6. Right-click any label in the vertical chart axis, and then click **Format Axis** on the shortcut menu. The Format Axis pane appears.

7. Click the **Categories in reverse order** check box to display the categories from the top-down rather than from the bottom-up. Refer to Figure 7–46.

Figure 7–46   PivotTable categories in reverse order

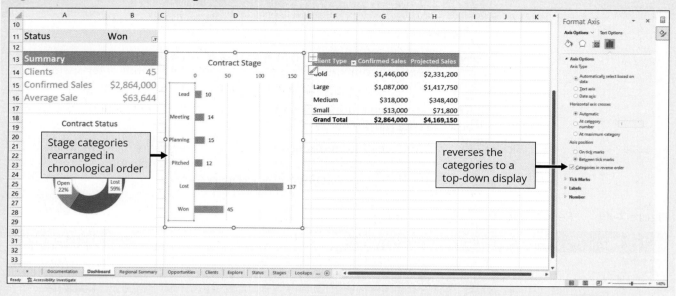

Once sorted, the order of categories in a row or column becomes part of the definition of the PivotTable. If that field is moved to another part of the PivotTable, the revised order is maintained. Even if you remove the field and add it back in later, Excel will retain the category order.

Adding Date Fields to PivotTables

PivotTables include special tools for date fields. When a field containing date values is added to a PivotTable row or column, Excel automatically provides subgroups for date values. If the values from a date field span several years, the dates are grouped by years, quarters, and then months within quarters. If the dates cover a single year, the dates are automatically grouped by months and then dates within months.

Jeannette wants a PivotTable to break down the customer information by the date that contact was first initiated. This information is stored in the Start Date field of the Sales table. You will create a PivotTable displaying the confirmed and projected sales totals by date.

To use a date field in the PivotTable:

1. Go to the **Opportunities** worksheet and make sure cell **A4** is selected.

2. On the ribbon, click the **Insert** tab, in the Tables group, click the **PivotTable** button. The PivotTable from table or range dialog box opens.

3. Click the **Existing Worksheet** button, go to the **Dashboard** worksheet and click cell **F20** to add the cell reference to the Location box, and then click **OK** to insert the PivotTable.

4. Rename the PivotTable as **Sales by Date**.

5. Drag the **Confirmed** and **Expected** fields to the Values area box.

6. For both fields, use the Value Field Settings dialog box to change the number format to **Currency** with **0** decimal places.

7. Change the value name Sum of Confirmed to **Confirmed Sales**, and then change the value name Sum of Expected to **Projected Sales**.

8. Drag the **Start Date** field to the Rows area box. The Sales by Date PivotTable is complete. Refer to Figure 7–47.

Figure 7–47   Date field in a PivotTable

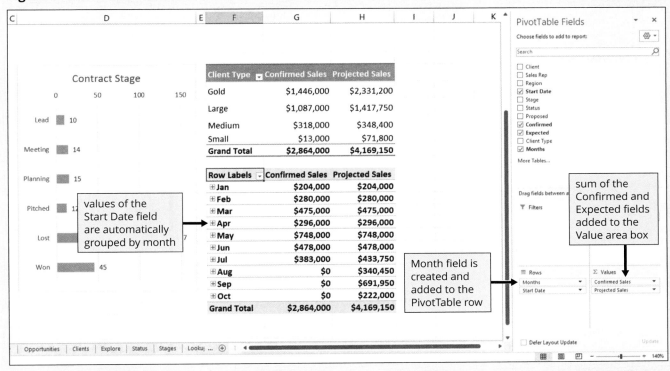

Trouble? Depending on your Excel installation, you might also see a Days (Start Date) field and a Months (Start Date) field in the Rows area.

When the Start Date field was added to the PivotTable row, a new grouping field named Months was automatically created and added to the field list. The Start Date values are nested within each month. You will expand the Jan group to review the sales made on specific dates.

To expand the Jan group of dates:

1. Click the **plus box** in front of Jan in cell F21 to expand the January values to individual starting dates within the month. The starting dates for each negotiation are shown in the PivotTable. Note that only four client contacts in January resulted in a sale. Refer to Figure 7–48.

Figure 7–48   Expanded date field

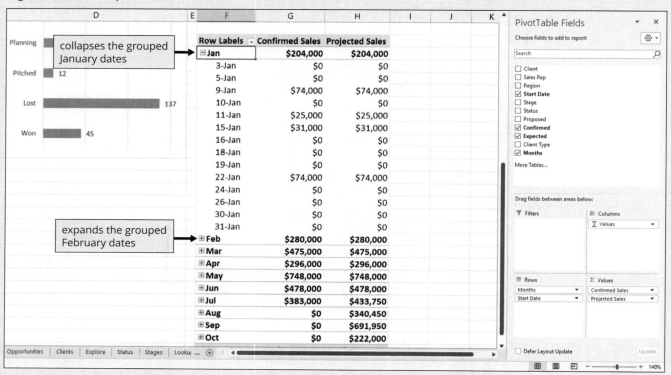

2. Click the **minus box** in front of Jan in cell F21 to collapse the January group.

> **Tip** To expand all grouped dates, go to the PivotTable Analyze tab and in the Active Field click the Expand Field button. To collapse all expanded groups, click the Collapse Field button.

Jeannette does not need the PivotTable shown at the level of individual dates. Now that Month field has been created, you can remove the Start Date field.

3. Drag all fields out of the Rows area, *except* the Months field, which you will leave as the only field remaining.

4. Click cell **F20**, type **Month** as the new column label, and then press **Enter** to make the change.

Date fields can be grouped at lower levels down to hours, minutes, and seconds. To enable other grouping levels, right-click any cell in the date field and click Group on the shortcut menu to open the Grouping dialog box. In the Grouping dialog box, choose the grouping levels to apply to the date field.

You will complete the Sales by Date PivotTable by applying a design style and setting the PivotTable options.

To format the PivotTable:

1. On the PivotTable Analyze tab, in the PivotTable group, click the **Options** button. The PivotTable Options dialog box opens.

2. Enter **0** in the For empty cells show box.

3. Click the **Autofit column widths on update** check box to deselect it.

4. Click **OK** to close the dialog box.

5. On the ribbon, click the **Design** tab, and then in the PivotTable Styles gallery, click the **Light Blue, Pivot Style Medium 6** to apply a light blue style of the PivotTable. The PivotTable is formatted. Refer to Figure 7–49.

Figure 7–49   Formatted PivotTable

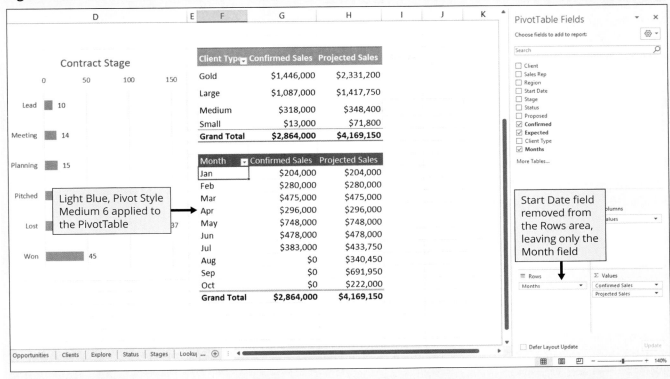

You have added all the tables and charts Jeannette requested be added to the Dashboard worksheet. Next you will use slicers to make the Dashboard truly interactive for the user.

Insight

Dynamic Referencing with the OFFSET Function

In working with data ranges and Excel tables, you referenced a range whose size and location were defined and static. In some Excel applications, you might need to reference a range whose size and location change based on the need of the application. For example, a formula might need to reference data in the range A1:A10 on one occasion and the range C11:E15 on another occasion.

You can create references whose location and size change by using the OFFSET function

```
OFFSET(reference, rows, cols, [height], [width])
```

where `reference` points to cells in the workbook, `rows` and `cols` are the number of rows and columns to shift that reference, and `height` and `width` set the size of the new reference in terms of rows and columns. For example, the following expression shifts the A1:A10 range reference 10 rows down and 2 columns across to point the range C11:C20:

```
OFFSET(A1:A10, 10, 2)
```

To resize the range to cover the range C11:E15, you specify the size of the new reference to be five rows high and three columns wide, as in the following expression:

```
OFFSET(A1:A10, 10, 2, 5, 3)
```

By modifying the parameters of the OFFSET argument, you can reference ranges of any location and size in a workbook, creating dynamic ranges that can change with your application.

Using Slicers with PivotTables

A third way of filtering PivotTables and PivotCharts is with a slicer. By clicking a slicer button, you can limit the PivotTable and PivotChart to a select group of records. Jeannette wants you to add a slicer to the dashboard containing values of the Region field and then to apply that slicer to the PivotTables.

To add a slicer for the Region field to a PivotTable:

1. On the Dashboard worksheet, click cell **A13** in the Won Contracts PivotTable.

2. On the ribbon, click the **Insert** tab, and then in the Filters group, click the **Slicer** button. The Insert Slicers dialog box opens, displaying the field list from the PivotTable.

3. Click the **Region** check box, and then click **OK**. The Region slicer appears on the Dashboard worksheet.

4. Move and resize the Region slicer to cover the range **A4:B11**, also covering the filter for the Won Contracts PivotTable.

5. In the Region slicer, click the **Arizona** button to filter the Won Contracts PivotTable to show only those won contracts from Arizona. The filtered PivotTable shows that there were 17 Arizona clients with confirmed sales of $1,100,000 with an average sale of $64,706. Refer to Figure 7–50.

Figure 7–50   Slicer added to a PivotTable

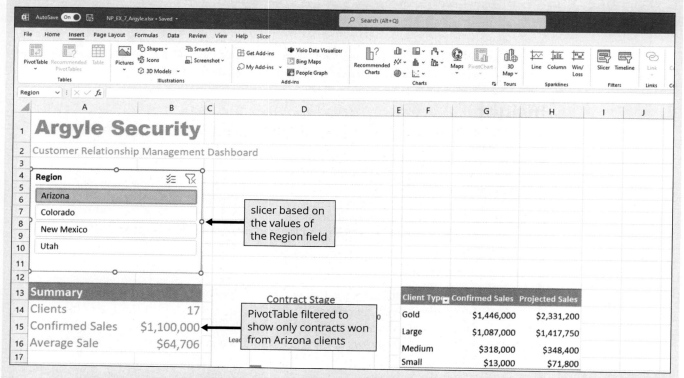

6. Click the other slicer buttons to confirm that with each region, different summary statistics are shown in the Won Contracts PivotTable.

7. Click the **Clear Filter** button 🔳 (or press **ALT+C**) to clear the filters and redisplay summary statistics for all topics.

The Region slicer applies to Won Contracts PivotTable only. Jeannette wants the slicer to apply to all the PivotTables and PivotCharts on the Dashboard worksheet.

Applying a Slicer to Multiple PivotTables

The same slicer can be applied to multiple PivotTables (and their associated PivotCharts), allowing you to filter several tables and charts based on the same criteria. The PivotTables do not need to be in the same worksheet, only the same workbook. Note that a slicer is not applied directly to a PivotChart, only to the PivotTable that PivotChart is based on.

Reference

Applying a Slicer to Multiple PivotTables

- Click the PivotTable slicer to select it.
- On the Slicer tab, in the Slicer group, click the Report Connections button.
- Click the check boxes for all the PivotTables to be associated with the slicer.
- Click OK.

Jeannette wants to know how a change in region would affect the other tables and charts on the dashboard. You will apply the Region slicer to other PivotTables in the workbook.

To apply the slicer to multiple PivotTables:

1. Click the **Region** slicer to select it.

2. On the ribbon, click the **Slicer** tab, and then in the Slicer group, click the **Report Connections** button. The Report Connections (Region) dialog box opens.

   Key Step To apply a slicer to a PivotChart, you must select the PivotTable on which the PivotChart is based.

3. Click the check boxes for the **Confirmed and Projected** and **Sales by Date** PivotTables in the Dashboard worksheet, the **Stages Table** PivotTable in the Stages worksheet, and the **Status Table** PivotTable in the Status worksheet. Every PivotTable is selected except the Explore PivotTable in the Explore worksheet. Refer to Figure 7–51.

Figure 7–51   Slicer linked to multiple PivotTables

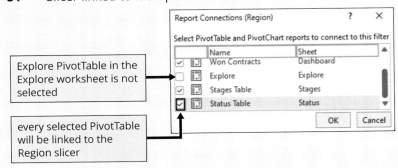

4. Click **OK** to apply the slicer to all the selected PivotTables.

5. In the Region slicer, click **Arizona** to filter the PivotTables and PivotCharts to Arizona clients. Refer to Figure 7–52.

Figure 7–52   Slicer applied to multiple PivotTables and PivotCharts

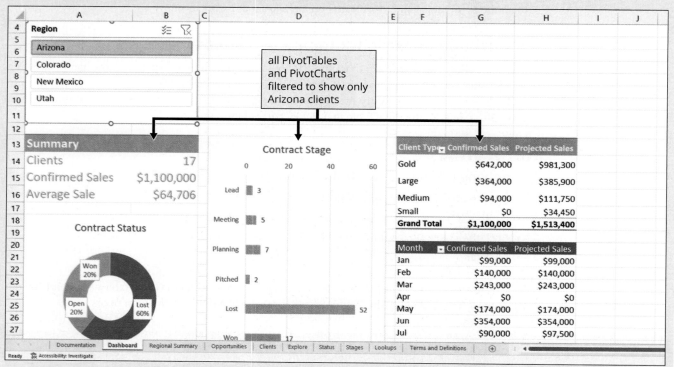

6. In the Region slicer, click **Colorado**, **New Mexico**, and then **Utah** to explore the client results for other regions.

7. Click the **Clear Filter** button 🔽 .

By applying the Region slicer to all the PivotTables and PivotCharts on the Dashboard worksheet, Jeannette can quickly examine how region affects client contracts and negotiations.

Proskills

Problem Solving: Consolidating Data from Multiple Worksheets

This module worked with PivotTables whose data is stored within a single data range or Excel table. However, some projects require PivotTables that analyze data spread across several worksheets.

One way of summarizing, or consolidating, data from multiple worksheets is with the Consolidate Data command. Click the Consolidate button in the Data Tools group on the Data tab to open the Consolidate dialog box. From the Consolidate dialog box, first choose the function for consolidating the data, such as average, count, minimum, and maximum, among others. Then, select a list of ranges from different worksheets containing the data to be consolidated, including any row or column labels to identify the data. Click the Add button to add multiple ranges to an All Ranges box. Once you have selected all the ranges, clicking OK will generate a table containing the statistical summary for the data from multiple data ranges.

Unlike PivotTables, the Consolidate command does not create an interactive table, so you must recreate the table each time you want to analyze your data from a different point of view. The consolidation table also does not interact with slicers or timelines, so you cannot filter the results. You can learn more about the Consolidate command in Excel Help.

Creating a Timeline Slicer

Another type of slicer is a timeline slicer, which filters a PivotTable to include only those records from a specified date interval. For example, you can limit the PivotTables only to those results between January and April or for an interval of specific years. Unlike slicers, which can be applied to both Excel tables and PivotTables, a timeline can be applied only to PivotTables.

Reference

Filtering a PivotTable with a Timeline Slicer

- Click anywhere in the PivotTable to select it.
- On the Insert tab, in the Filters group, click the Timeline button.
- Click the check boxes of the fields containing date values for which you want to create timelines.
- Click OK.
- Format the size, position, and appearance of the timeline.
- Select intervals within the timeline to filter the PivotTable.

Jeannette wants users to explore client interactions during specific time intervals. Are clients becoming more engaged at certain times of the year? Are efforts to improve sales working? To help analyze those kinds of questions, you will add a timeline slicer to the dashboard so that you can filter the PivotTables and PivotCharts by date as well as by region.

To create a timeline slicer:

1. In the Dashboard worksheet, click cell **A13** to select the first PivotTable.

2. On the ribbon, click the **Insert** tab, and then in the Filters group, click the **Timeline** button. The Insert Timelines dialog box opens. The Start Date field is the only field containing date information.

3. Click the **Start Date** check box, and then click **OK**. The Start Date timeline slicer is inserted into the dashboard.

4. Move and resize the timeline slicer to cover the range **D4:H11**.

   You want to link this timeline slicer to all the PivotTables and PivotCharts appearing on the dashboard.

5. On the Timeline tab, in the Timeline group, click the **Report Connections** button. The Report Connections (Start Date) dialog box opens.

6. Select all the entries in the list except the Explore PivotTable in the Explore worksheet, and then click **OK**. Refer to Figure 7–53.

Figure 7–53   Timeline slicer

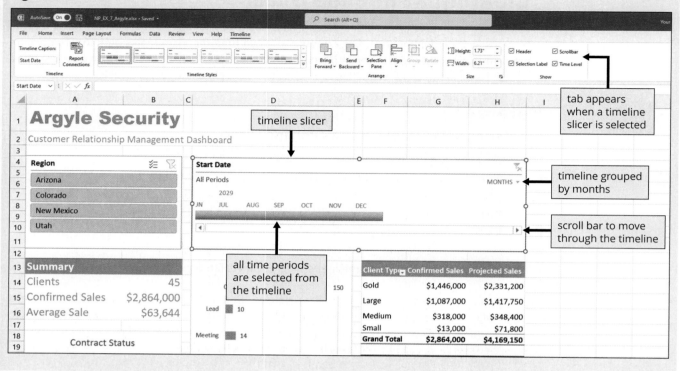

The timeline is laid out as a horizontal scroll bar grouped by months. You can filter the dashboard to show values only for specified time periods by selecting data ranges from the timeline. Jeannette wants to view the results for January 2029.

To filter the dashboard to January 2029:

1. Drag the timeline scroll bar to the left until JAN 2029 appears in the timeline slicer.

2. Click the **JAN** box located directly below JAN 2029, deselecting all other months in the timeline. The dashboard is filtered to show a client report only for those clients contacted in January 2029. Refer to Figure 7–54.

Figure 7–54   Dashboard filtered based on a timeline

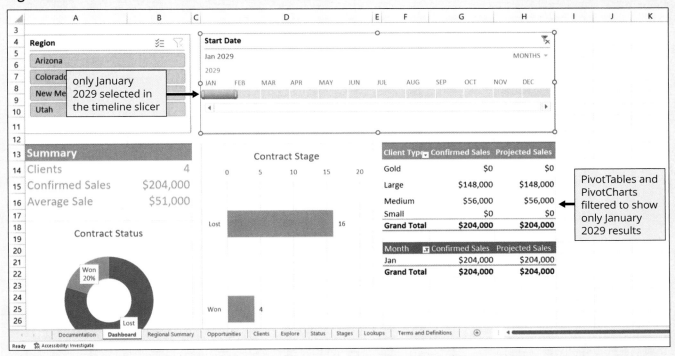

During January 2029, Argyle Security contacted 20 clients, of which four eventually signed a contract with the company and 16 did not. The revenue from those four clients was $204,000 with an average sale of $51,000.

You can drag across a timeline to select longer time intervals. Jeannette wants to collect information on Utah clients contacted between June and August. You will use the slicers to filter the dashboard by region and timeline.

To filter the dashboard based on timeline and region:

1. In the Start Date timeline slicer, click the **JUN** box, drag over the **JUL** and **AUG** boxes, and then release the mouse button. The dashboard is filtered to show the results from those three months.

   Tip To select a range of months, click the selection box in the timeline and drag the left or right selection handles over the range of months you want to cover.

2. In the Region slicer, click **Utah**. The dashboard is further filtered to include only the clients from the Utah region. Refer to Figure 7–55.

Figure 7–55   Dashboard filtered by region and timeline

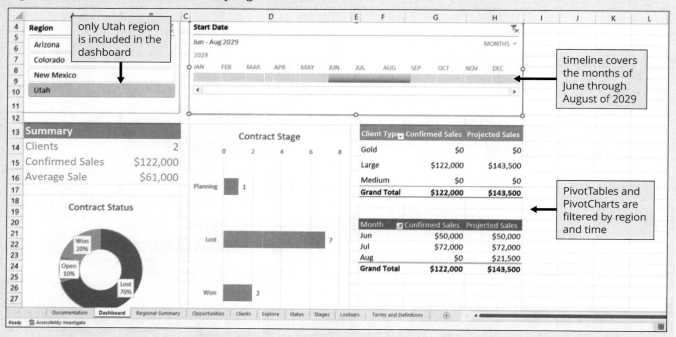

3. In the Region slicer, click **New Mexico**, and then in the Start Date slicer, select **SEP** through **DEC**. The dashboard displays only clients from New Mexico contacted from September through December in 2029.

Using the slicers, Jeannette learns that there 15 New Mexico client contacts from September through December. There are no sales yet, but of those 15 clients, two have been lost and the remaining 13 are in various stages of negotiations. The projected sales from those clients is $330,450.

You have completed your work on the dashboard. Using PivotTables, PivotCharts, and slicers, you have constructed a tool for Jeannette to interactively explore Argyle Security's ability to contact and retain interested and motivated clients.

Drilling Down a PivotTable

A PivotTable takes a data range or Excel table and creates a table summarizing that information. You can reverse that process by opening a cell from a PivotTable and displaying all records contributing to that cell's value. The process of recovering the data from a PivotTable is referred to as **drilling down** the table. You can double-click any cell from a PivotTable to drill down, showing detailed information about cells.

From the most recent exploration of the dashboard, Jeannette learned that there are no confirmed sales yet from New Mexico clients in the September through December time frame. But there are several open negotiations and some of those negotiations are with Gold-level clients. The projected value of those Gold contracts is $276,800. Who are those clients, and at what stage are the negotiations? Jeannette asks you to find out by drilling down the data from the PivotTables.

To drill down the PivotTable:

1. Make sure **New Mexico** is still selected in the Region slicer and **SEP** through **DEC** is still selected in the Start Date slicer.

2. Double-click cell **H14** ($276,800) in the Confirmed and Projected Sales PivotTable. A new worksheet named Sheet1 opens, containing an Excel table, listing eight Gold clients from New Mexico in the September through December time frame.

3. Rename the worksheet as **New Mexico Gold**.

4. Increase the zoom of the worksheet to **140%**.

5. In the range **G2:I9**, format the values as currency with no decimal places.

6. Resize the columns in the table so that all information is visible.

7. Click cell **A1** to select it. Refer to Figure 7–56.

Figure 7–56   Results of drilling down a PivotTable

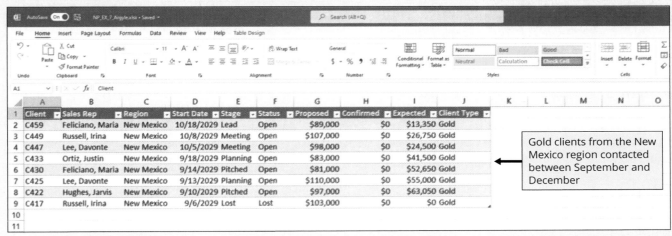

Gold clients from the New Mexico region contacted between September and December

Using the information in the New Mexico Gold worksheet, Jeannette has a list of the eight Gold clients, who they are, what stage has been reached in negotiations, and what are the proposed and expected values for each contract. Two clients have reached the Pitched stage (clients C430 and C422) with contract values of $81,000 and $97,000, respectively.

The Excel table generated with drilling down the PivotTable is not linked to the source data, so any changes made to the Sales table will not be carried over to the drilled down table. If you alter the source data, you must recreate the drilled down table.

Jeannette wants you to create a table of all New Mexico clients who are currently at the Pitched stage. This information is displayed in a PivotChart on the dashboard. You will drill down the PivotChart to retrieve data about the clients currently at the Pitched stage of negotiations.

To drill down the PivotChart:

1. Click the **Dashboard** worksheet to return to the dashboard.

2. In the Stage Chart PivotChart, click the bar for the four clients at the Pitched stage. All bars in the chart are selected.

3. Click the bar for the four Pitched clients again to select only that bar marker and no others.

4. Right-click the selected bar, and then click **Show Detail** on the shortcut menu. A new worksheet with detailed information on the four clients is created.

5. Rename the worksheet as **New Mexico Pitched** and increase the zoom to **140%**.

6. In the range **G2:I5**, format the values as currency with no decimal places.

7. Resize the columns in the table so that all information is visible.

8. Click cell **A1** to select it. Refer to Figure 7–57.

Figure 7–57   Results of drilling down a PivotChart

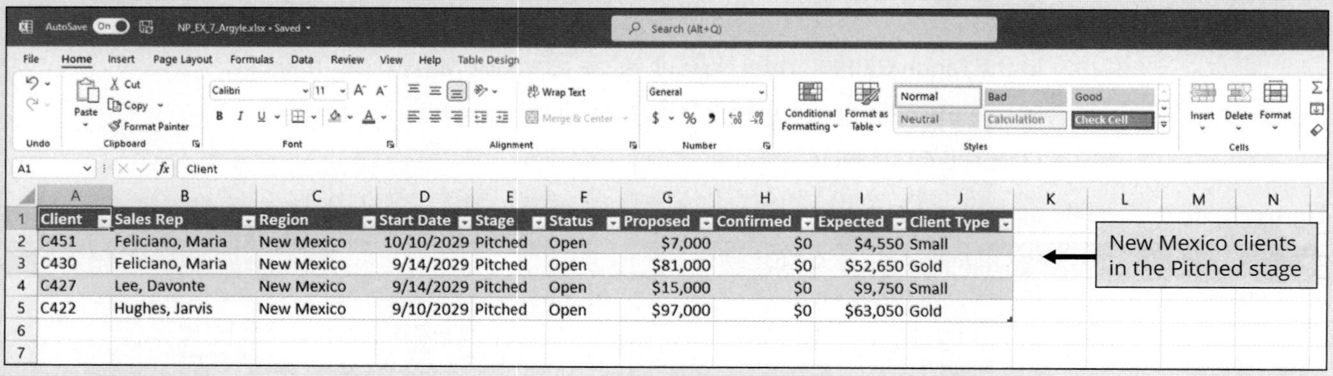

Client	Sales Rep	Region	Start Date	Stage	Status	Proposed	Confirmed	Expected	Client Type
C451	Feliciano, Maria	New Mexico	10/10/2029	Pitched	Open	$7,000	$0	$4,550	Small
C430	Feliciano, Maria	New Mexico	9/14/2029	Pitched	Open	$81,000	$0	$52,650	Gold
C427	Lee, Davonte	New Mexico	9/14/2029	Pitched	Open	$15,000	$0	$9,750	Small
C422	Hughes, Jarvis	New Mexico	9/10/2029	Pitched	Open	$97,000	$0	$63,050	Gold

New Mexico clients in the Pitched stage

9. **sam** Save the workbook, and then close it.

By drilling down, you can use PivotTables and PivotCharts to not only summarize data from your data sets but also to retrieve information about specific records that match defined categories.

Insight

Refreshing PivotTable Data

PivotTable data is stored in a memory location called the **PivotTable cache**. Each PivotTable is connected to a cache (and sometimes to the same cache) so that any changes made to the structure of the PivotTable relies on data from the cache and only indirectly from the data source (such as a data range or Excel table.)

PivotTables are quick and responsive because they get their data from the cache rather than from the original data source. The cost of this speed and flexibility is that changes made to the data source are not reflected in the contents of the PivotTable cache. If you add new data or revise data to the data range or Excel table, you must refresh the cache for those changes to appear in your PivotTables. To refresh the PivotTable cache (and by extension every PivotTable that uses that cache), click the Refresh button in the Data group on the PivotTable Analyze tab.

You can modify the PivotTable settings to have Excel automatically update a PivotTable every time the workbook is opened. Select the PivotTable, and then click the Options button in the PivotTable group on the PivotTable Analyze tab to open the PivotTable Options dialog box. On the Data tab, click the Refresh data when opening the file check box. Excel will then refresh the PivotTable each time the workbook is reopened.

If you do not refresh the cache each time your data changes—or each time your workbook is opened—your PivotTables might not accurately reflect the data. So always keep the cache up to date.

You have completed work on Jeannette's report on the success the company has achieved in recruiting and retaining clients. You will continue to use PivotTables and PivotCharts and other Excel tools to learn more about Argyle Security's efforts to import their customer relationship management system.

Drilling Down a PivotTable   EX 7-73

Part 7.3 Quick Check

1. What are the four areas of a PivotChart?

2. If you change the structure of a PivotTable, what happens to accompanying PivotChart?

3. Can any Excel chart type be turned into a PivotChart?

4. Describe two ways of reordering categories within a PivotTable field.

5. What does Excel do when a date field is added to a PivotTable row or column?

6. How do you apply the same slicer to multiple PivotTables?

7. Can a timeline slicer be used with Excel tables as well as PivotTables?

8. Describe how to drill down a PivotTable cell to view the source data used in that cell's calculations.

9. If you change the data in a PivotTable's data source, will the PivotTable automatically update to reflect the change?

Practice: Review Assignments

Data File needed for the Review Assignments: NP_EX_7-2.xlsx

Jeannette wants you to work on another customer relationship management report. This report will examine the factors that result in lost sales opportunities and compare the performance of five sales representatives in attracting and retaining customers. You will analyze 233 clients and potential clients in the Arizona, Colorado, New Mexico, and Utah regions. Complete the following:

1. Open the **NP_EX_7-2xlsx** workbook located in the Excel7 > Review folder included with your Data Files. Save the workbook as **NP_EX_7_CRM** in the location specified by your instructor.

2. In the Documentation sheet, enter your name and the date in the range B3:B4. Review the content of the rest of the worksheets in the workbook.

3. Go to the Sales worksheet containing the Sales table with information on contacts made with potential Argyle Security customers. The table will contain several calculated fields that you will have to write. Do the following:

    a. In cell G5 of the Sales table, determine the Negotiation Phase for the value of the Days field using the XLOOKUP function with [@Days] as the lookup value, Phase_Lookup[Days] as the lookup array, and Phase_Lookup[Negotiation Phase] as the return array. Do an approximate match lookup that returns either an exact match or the next smaller item.

    b. In cell J5, use an IF function that returns a value of 1 if the value of the Outcome field is "Lost" and 0 if otherwise. The purpose of this function is to mark those contracts that were lost to the company.

4. Go to the Lost Contracts worksheet where you will use summary IF functions to summarize the cost of losing contracts and track the reasons for losing those contracts (price, competition, features, or other). Use the Copy and Paste buttons, not AutoFill, to copy the formulas. (Using AutoFill will result in incorrect formulas in the pasted cells.) Do the following:

    a. In cell A5, use a COUNTIF function to count the number of clients lost because of price. Count the values of the Sales[Loss Reason] field whose value is equal to cell A4. Copy the formula in cell A5 into the range B5:D5.

    b. In cell A7, use a SUMIF function to calculate the total value of the lost contracts. Calculate the total using Sales[Loss Reason] as the range, cell A4 as the criteria, and Sales[Proposed] as the sum range. Copy the formula in cell A7 into the range B7:D7.

    c. In cell A9, use the AVERAGEIF function to calculate the average value of the lost contracts for each of the four reasons. Calculate the conditional average using Sales[Loss Reason] as the range, cell A4 as the criteria, and Sales[Proposed] as the average range. Copy the formula in cell A9 into the range B9:D9.

    d. In cell A11, calculate the median value of lost contracts by nesting a FILTER function within the MEDIAN function. In the FILTER function, use the Sales[Proposed] for the array argument and use Sales[Loss Reason] = A4 for the include argument so that the data is filtered to include only those records with the value of the Lost Reason field equal to the value of cell A4. Copy the formula in cell A11 into the range B11:D11.

5. How soon do negotiations reach the phase where a formula offer is pitched to a potential client? Jeannette wants a breakdown of how quickly negotiations are conducted by the sales rep. Do the following:

    a. Use the Sales table in the Sales worksheet to create a PivotTable in cell A6 of the Negotiation Progress worksheet.

    b. Rename the PivotTable as **Negotiation Table**.

    c. Put the Stage Reached field in the Rows area, the Negotiation Phase field in the Columns area, the Client field in the Values area, and the Sales Rep field in the Filter area.

    d. Reorder the column categories to 0 to 5 days, 5 to 15 days, 15 to 25 days, 25+ days.

    e. Reorder the row categories to: Lead, Meeting, Planning Pitched.

    f. There are five contracts that took more than 25 days to get to the Planning phase. Drill down that PivotTable cell to generate an Excel table of those five records in a new worksheet. Name the new worksheet as **Late Planning**.

    g. Return to the Negotiation Table PivotTable and filter it to show the negotiation history for Jarvis Hughes.

6. Summarize the confirmed and projected sales made in the current year by creating a PivotTable in cell A12 of the Dashboard worksheet using the Sales table as the data source. Do the following:

    a. Rename the PivotTable as **Summary**.

    b. In the PivotTable Options dialog box, deselect the Autofit column widths on update check box.

c. Place the Client, Confirmed, and Projected fields in the Values area. Move the ΣValues name filed to the Rows area so that each value appears in a separate row.

d. Change the label "Count of Client" to **Clients**, "Sum of Confirmed" to **Confirmed Sales**, and "Sum of Projected" **Projected Sales**. Display both sales totals in currency format with no decimal places.

e. Change the label in cell A12 to **Summary**.

f. Change the PivotTable design to the Light Blue, Pivot Style Medium 6.

7. Analyze the cost of lost contracts by creating a PivotTable in cell A17 of the Dashboard worksheet using the Sales table as the data source. Do the following:

a. Rename the PivotTable as **Loss Analysis**.

b. In the PivotTable Options dialog box, deselect the Autofit column widths on update check box.

c. Put the Loss Reason field in the Rows area. Put the Client and Proposed fields in the Values area.

d. Change the label "Count of Client" to **Clients** and "Sum of Proposed" to **Contract Value**. Display the contract values in currency format with no decimal places.

e. Change the label in cell A17 to **Loss Analysis**.

f. Change the PivotTable design to the Light Blue, Pivot Style Medium 6.

8. Use the Sales table in the Sales worksheet to create a PivotTable/PivotChart in cell A4 of the Contracts Status worksheet. Do the following:

a. Rename the PivotTable as **Contract Status**.

b. Place the Outcome field in the Rows area of the PivotTable and the Proposed Field in the Values area.

c. Display the Sum of Proposed values in currency format with no decimal places.

d. Move the PivotChart to the Dashboard worksheet and resize it to cover the range E12:H22.

e. Remove the chart legend, add data labels to the chart, change the chart title to **Contract Value**, and hide the Field Buttons.

9. Track the number of lost contracts throughout the year by creating a PivotTable in cell J4 of the Dashboard worksheet using the Sales table as the data source. Do the following:

a. Rename the PivotTable as **Lost Contracts**.

b. Move the Stage Date field to the Rows area and the Loss Indicator field to the Values area.

c. Change the label "Sum of Lost Indicator" to **Lost Contracts**.

d. Remove all fields from the Rows area *except* the Months field and then change the label in cell J4 to **Months**.

e. Change the PivotTable design to the Light Blue, Pivot Style Medium 6.

10. Insert a slicer for the Sales Rep field in the range A4:C10 of the Dashboard worksheet. Do the following:

a. Change the layout of the slicer buttons to two columns.

b. Connect the slicer to every PivotTable except the Negotiation Table from the Negotiation Progress worksheet.

11. Create a timeline slicer for the Stage Date (*not* the Start Date) field in the range E4:H10 of the Dashboard worksheet. Connect the timeline to every PivotTable except the Negotiation Table in the Negotiation Progress worksheet.

12. Test the slicer and timeline in the Dashboard by selecting sales reps for different time periods. Finalize your report by displaying the sales performance of Jarvis Hughes from June through August 2029.

13. Save the workbook, and then close it.

Apply: Case Problem 1

Data File needed for this Case Problem: NP_EX_7-3.xlsx

Jefferson Park Bistro Jiang Hui is the restaurant manager of Jefferson Park Bistro in Alexandria, Virginia. Jiang uses Excel as a tool for analyzing the restaurants annual budget in a competitive market. As the fiscal year ends, Jiang wants your help in writing a report comparing the restaurant's actual expenses to the budget. Jiang wants to identify expense items that exceed their budget but also wants to highlight areas where the restaurant saved money. Your work will help Jiang develop an action plan for the next fiscal year. Jiang's workbook includes a chart of accounts detailing each expense item and a ledger providing the expenditures made throughout the year in each account category. Complete the following:

1. Open the **NP_EX_7-3.xlsx** workbook located in the Excel7 > Case1 folder included with your Data Files, and then save the workbook as **NP_EX_7_Bistro.xlsx** in the location specified by your instructor.

2. In the Documentation sheet, enter your name and the date in the range B3:B4. Review the content of the other worksheets in the workbook.

3. Go to the Ledger worksheet and in the Ledger table, create the following calculated fields:

   a. In cell D5, use the XLOOKUP function to do an exact match lookup with the value of the Account field as the lookup value, the Account field from the Accounts table as the lookup array, and the Category field from the Accounts table as the return array.

   b. In cell E5, use the XLOOKUP function to do another exact match lookup but this time return the value of the Subcategory field from the Accounts table.

4. Summarize the expenditures made by the restaurant broken down by category by creating a PivotTable from the data in the Ledgers table, storing the PivotTable in cell A4 of the Annuals by Category worksheet. Do the following:

   a. Name the PivotTable as **Category Annuals**.

   b. Drag the Category field to the Rows area and the Amount field to the Values area.

   c. Change the label in cell A4 to **Category** and the label in B4 to **Expenditures**.

   d. Change the number format of the expenditures to the Accounting number format with no decimal places.

5. Compare the expenditures to their budgeted amounts. In cell D5, use the SUMIF function with a dynamic array to retrieve the budgets for each of the eight budget categories. Use the Category field of the Accounts table for the range, the array A5:A12 for the criteria, and the Budget field of the Accounts table for the sum range.

6. In cell D13, enter a formula to calculate the total budget across all categories in the range D5:D12.

7. In cell E5, enter the array formula **= (B5:B13 – D5:D13)/D5:D13** to calculate the percent difference between the actual expenditures and the budget.

8. Jiang wants to include a note identifying budget categories that were under budget or over budget. The status notes are found in the Expense_Lookup table. In cell F5, do an approximate match lookup with the XLOOKUP function using the range E5:E13 as the lookup values, the Percent field from the Expense_Lookup table as the lookup array, the Status field from the Expense_Lookup table as the return array, and the match_mode value of –1 to return either an exact match or the next smaller item.

9. Create a Pie chart that shows a graphical breakdown of expenditures by category. Do the following:

   a. Click cell A4 to select the PivotTable, add a Pie PivotChart to the worksheet.

   b. Move and resize the Pie chart to cover the range A15:F31.

   c. Remove the chart title, field buttons, and legend from the chart.

   d. Add data callouts to the Pie chart showing the percent of expenditures associated with each category.

10. Create another budget analysis examining expenditures by subcategory. In the Ledger worksheet, create another PivotTable from the data in the Ledgers table, storing the PivotTable in cell A4 of the Annuals by Subcategory worksheet. Do the following:

    a. Name the PivotTable as **Subcategory Annuals**.

    b. Drag the Subcategory field to the Rows area and the Amount field to the Values area.

    c. Change the label in cell A4 to **Subcategory** and the label in B4 to **Expenditures**.

    d. Change the number format of the expenditures to the Accounting format with no decimal places.

11. Compare the expenditures in each subcategory to the budget. Do the following:

    a. In cell D5, use the SUMIF function to retrieve the budgets for each subcategory. Use the Subcategory field of the Accounts table for the range, use the array reference A5:A41 for the criteria, and the Budget field of the Accounts table for the sum range.

    b. In cell D42, calculate the total budget from the values in the range D5:D41.

    c. In cell E5, enter the array formula **= (B5:B42 – D5:D42)/D5:D42** to calculate the percent difference within and across all subcategories.

    d. In cell F5, do an approximate match lookup with the XLOOKUP function, using the array E5:E42 as the lookup values, the Percent field from the Expense_Lookup table as the lookup array, the Status field from the Expense_Lookup table as the return array, and the match_mode value of –1 to return either an exact match or the next smaller item.

12. Jiang wants a budget summary for each month. In the Ledger worksheet, create a PivotTable from the Ledger table, saving the PivotTable to the cell A4 of the Monthly Expenses worksheet. Do the following:

    a. Rename the PivotTable as **Monthly Expenses**.

    b. Drag the Category and Subcategory fields to the Rows area. Drag the Date field to the Columns area. Drag the Amount field to the Values area.

   c. Change the label in cell A4 to **Expenditures**. Change the label in cell B4 to **Month**.

   d. Display the values of the expenditures in Accounting format with no decimals.

   e. Change the PivotTable options to show empty cells as zeroes.

   f. Remove all fields from the Columns area, *except* the Months field.

13. In December, an unusually large amount was spent on wine for the restaurant. Explore the source of the expenditures by doing the following:

   a. Drill down the PivotTable for cell M15, creating a worksheet listing the wine expenditures for December.

   b. Rename the worksheet as **Wine Expenditures** and increase the zoom to **140%**.

   c. Resize the columns so that no text in the cells is truncated.

   d. Format the values in the Amount column in Accounting format with no decimal places.

   e. Move the table from the range A1:E5 to the range A4:E8.

   f. Enter the text **Jefferson Park Bistro** in cell A1 and **A Large Wine Expenditure** in cell A2. Copy the formats from the range A1:A2 of the Accounts worksheet into the range A1:A2 of this worksheet.

14. Save the workbook, and then close it.

Challenge: Case Problem 2

Data File needed for this Case Problem: NP_EX_7-4.xlsx

Filmon Trucking and Delivery Robert Pederson manages drivers for Filmon Trucking and Delivery, a trucking company based in Florida and the Southeast United States. Robert has compiled a workbook containing the trucking deliveries from the past year for four different company trucks. Robert wants your assistance in compiling estimates on the total miles driven by the company trucks and their time on the road. Mileage and driving time estimates are stored in two-way tables on the Mileage Grid and Time Grid worksheets of Robert's workbook. Complete the following.

1. Open the **NP_EX_7-4.xlsx** workbook located in the Excel6 > Case2 folder included with your Data Files, and then save the workbook as **NP_EX_7_Filmon** in the location specified by your instructor.

2. In the Documentation sheet, enter your name and the date in cells B3 and B4. Review the contents of the workbook.

3. **Explore:** Go to the Driving Log worksheet. The worksheet contains the DrivingLog table detailing the starting and ending cities for each trip made by company trucks on each working day of the year. The table does not contain estimates of the miles driven nor the driving time. In cell E5, retrieve the distance between the cities by inserting a formula for looking up data from a two-way table using nested XLOOKUP functions. To create the nested XLOOKUP functions, do the following:

   a. In the outer XLOOKUP function, use the value of the Start field as the lookup value and the range name StartCity as the lookup array. Use a nested XLOOKUP function as the return array.

   b. In the nested XLOOKUP function, use the Destination field as the lookup value, the named array DestinationCity as the lookup array, and the named range MileageGrid as the return array.

   c. Repeat Step b for the driving time estimates in column F of the table, retrieving the data from the named range TimeGrid.

4. Robert wants a list of the cities that receive the most deliveries. To create the list, create a PivotTable from the DrivingLog table, storing the PivotTable in cell A4 of the Destinations worksheet. Do the following:

   a. Name the PivotTable as **Destination List**.

   b. Drag the Destination field to the Rows area of the PivotTable. Drag the Truck ID field to the Values area.

   c. Change the label in cell A4 to **City** and then change the label in cell B4 to **Visits**.

   d. Apply the PivotTable design Light Yellow, Pivot Style Medium 5 to the table.

5. **Explore:** Robert wants the PivotTable sorted in descending order of the Visits column. Do the following:

   a. Click the filter arrow in cell A4 and then click More Sort options on the menu.

   b. In the Sort (Destination) dialog box, click the Descending (Z to A) option button, and then select Visits from the box. Click OK to close the dialog box.

6. Robert wants to review the monthly driving totals for the four trucks both in a PivotTable and in a PivotChart. In the Driving Log worksheet, create a PivotChart from the table, storing the PivotTable in cell A4 of the Monthly Mileage worksheet. Do the following:

   a. Name the PivotTable as **Monthly Mileage**.

   b. Drag the Truck ID field to the Columns area, the Date field to the Rows area, and Mileage field to the Values area.

   c. Change the label in cell A4 to **Miles Traveled**, the label in cell B4 to **Truck**, and the label in cell A5 to **Month**.

   d. Format the Miles Traveled value field in the Number format with a thousands separator and no decimal places.

   e. Remove all fields from the Rows area, *except* the Months field.

7. Make the following changes to the PivotChart:

   a. Move and resize the chart to cover the range H4:N18.

   b. Remove the field buttons from the PivotChart.

   c. Change the chart type to a Line chart.

   d. Change the chart title to **Total Miles by Month**.

8. Robert also wants to analyze the monthly travel times. Repeat Steps 6 and 7 to store a PivotTable and PivotChart in the Monthly Travel Time worksheet. The report should appear similar to what you created for the monthly mileage data, except for the following:

   a. Move the Time field into the Values area of the PivotTable instead of the Mileage field.

   b. Name the PivotTable **Monthly Travel Time**.

   c. Change the cell A4 label to **Travel Time**, the cell B4 label to **Truck**, and the cell A5 label to **Month**.

   d. Change the chart title to **Total Travel Time by Month**.

9. **Explore:** Robert wants a worksheet in which he can enter the truck ID and the date and view the total mileage covered that day as well as the driving time. In the Driving Lookup worksheet, do the following to calculate total mileage and driving time:

   a. In cell B6, use the COUNTIFS function to calculate the total number of trips made by a truck on a specified date. Use the Truck ID field from the DrivingLog table as first criteria range and cell B4 as the first criteria value. Use the Date field from the DrivingLog as the second criteria range and cell B5 as the second criteria value.

   b. In cell B7, use the SUMIFS function to calculate the total mileage where the sum range is the Mileage field in the DrivingLog table, the first criteria range is the Truck ID field in the DrivingLog table, the first criteria is the value of cell B4, the second criteria range is the Date field in the DrivingLog worksheet, and the second criteria is the value of cell B5.

   c. Repeat Step b to use the SUMIFS function to calculate the total driving time using the Time field in the DrivingLog table as the sum range.

10. Robert wants the travel destinations to be displayed in the worksheet. In cell A12, enter a dynamic array FILTER function with the following properties:

   a. Filter the values of the Start through Time fields of the DrivingLog table.

   b. Retrieve values only if the value of the Truck ID field in the DrivingLog table equals cell B4 and the value of the Date field in the DrivingLog table equals cell B5.

   c. If the filter is empty, return the text string **"No trips that day"**.

11. Test the worksheet by retrieving the driving log for truck **TR032** on **4/19/2029**. Verify that the total number of trips, mileage, and driving time match the results show in the filtered table.

12. Save the workbook, and then close it.

Performing What-If Analyses

Maximizing Profits with the Best Product Mix

Case: Office Motion

Yuri David is a marketing and sales analyst for Office Motion, a manufacturer of office equipment with a special emphasis on ergonomics, comfort, and wellness. Standing desks are a new and important part of the Office Motion lineup of products. Yuri is analyzing the profitability of the new sales lines of standing desks to determine the number and type of each standing desk model the company must sell to maximize profits. Yuri wants to know whether the company can increase profits by reducing the selling price of the desks or by increasing the price of the desks even if that means a smaller sales volume. To explore these questions, you will use the what-if tools.

Starting Data Files

Excel8
Module
NP_EX_8-1.xlsx
Review
NP_EX_8-2.xlsx

Case1
NP_EX_8-3.xlsx
Case2
NP_EX_8-4.xlsx

Objectives

Part 8.1
- Create a one-variable data table
- Create a two-variable data table

Part 8.2
- Analyze scenarios with the Scenario Manager
- Generate a scenario summary report
- Generate a scenario PivotTable report

Part 8.3
- Find optimal solutions with Solver
- Create and apply constraints to a Solver model
- Create a Solver Answer Report
- Save and load a Solver model

Part 8.1 Visual Overview: Data Tables and What-If Analysis

A **one-variable data table** performs several what-if analyses by specifying one input cell and several result cells.

Input cells are the cells that contain values that are used in formulas of a what-if analysis.

Input values are values in a data table that are based on input cells. The values in the range D5:D12 are based on the input cell B4.

Result values are values in a data table that come from formulas applied to one or more input values. The values in the range D5:G12 are calculated from the result cells in the range B24:B26.

Result cells are the cells that contain the outcome of formulas involving input cells.

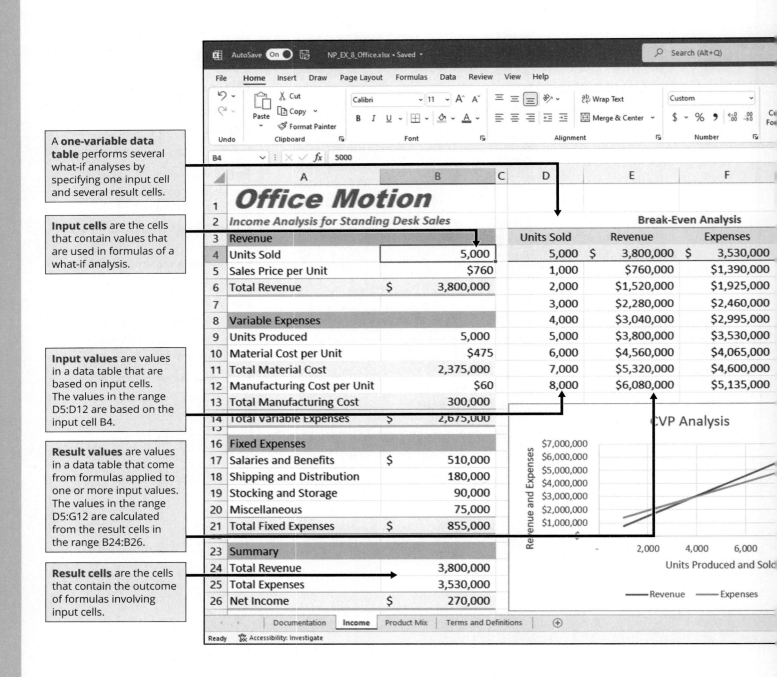

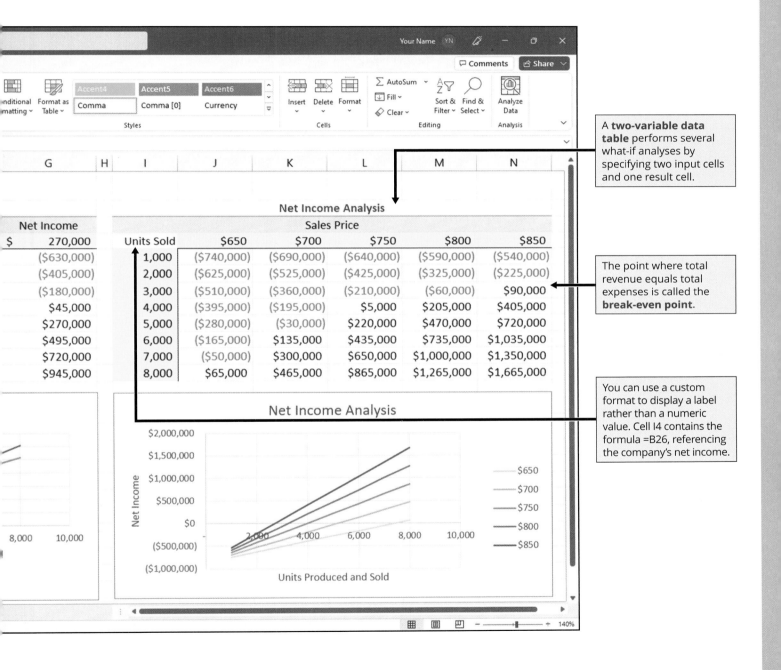

A **two-variable data table** performs several what-if analyses by specifying two input cells and one result cell.

The point where total revenue equals total expenses is called the **break-even point**.

You can use a custom format to display a label rather than a numeric value. Cell I4 contains the formula =B26, referencing the company's net income.

Net Income Analysis

Net Income		Units Sold	\$650	\$700	\$750	\$800	\$850
\$	270,000		Sales Price				
($630,000)		1,000	($740,000)	($690,000)	($640,000)	($590,000)	($540,000)
($405,000)		2,000	($625,000)	($525,000)	($425,000)	($325,000)	($225,000)
($180,000)		3,000	($510,000)	($360,000)	($210,000)	($60,000)	$90,000
$45,000		4,000	($395,000)	($195,000)	$5,000	$205,000	$405,000
$270,000		5,000	($280,000)	($30,000)	$220,000	$470,000	$720,000
$495,000		6,000	($165,000)	$135,000	$435,000	$735,000	$1,035,000
$720,000		7,000	($50,000)	$300,000	$650,000	$1,000,000	$1,350,000
$945,000		8,000	$65,000	$465,000	$865,000	$1,265,000	$1,665,000

Understanding Cost–Volume Relationships

One of the most powerful features of Excel is the ability to explore the impact of changing financial conditions on outcomes such as revenue, sales volume, expenses, and profitability. In this module, you will use Excel to investigate a variety of "what-if" scenarios. You will begin by exploring cost–volume–profit analysis.

Cost–volume–profit (CVP) analysis is a branch of financial analysis that studies the relationship between expenses, sales volume, and profitability. CVP analysis is an important business decision-making tool because it can help predict the effect of cutting overhead or raising prices on a company's net income. For example, Office Motion needs to determine a reasonable price to charge for the company's standing desks and how much added profit could be realized by increasing (or decreasing) the sales price.

Comparing Expenses and Revenue

The first component of CVP analysis is cost, or expense. Businesses usually deal with three types of expense: variable, fixed, and mixed. **Variable expenses** or **cost of goods sold** are expenses that change in proportion to production volume. For each additional desk the company produces, it spends more on parts, raw materials, and other expenses associated with manufacturing. On average, each desk produced by the company costs $475 in materials and $60 in manufacturing, for a total cost of $535 per unit. The company's total cost of goods sold with respect to its lineup of standing desks is equal to the cost of producing each standing desk multiplied by the total number of desks produced. The line graph in Figure 8–1 shows the total cost of goods sold as it relates to production volume. From the graph, you learn that Office Motion will incur about $2.7 million in variable expenses if it produces 5,000 desks.

Figure 8–1   Chart of cost of goods sold

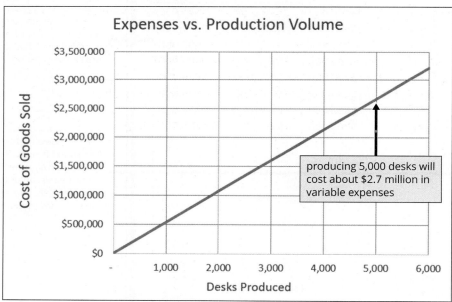

On average, the company sells a standing desk for $760, which is $225 more than it costs to manufacture each desk. At first glance, it might seem that the company earns a $225 profit on each sale, but that is incorrect. The sales price must also cover the company's fixed expenses. A **fixed expense** is an expense that must be paid regardless of sales volume. The company must pay salaries and benefits for the employees who build the desks as well as insurance, maintenance fees, and administrative overhead. Yuri tells you that manufacturing the standing desks costs the company more than $855,000 in fixed expenses and that cost must be paid even if the company does not sell a single desk.

Total expenses are calculated by adding variable and fixed expenses. The graph in Figure 8–2 shows the company's total expenses for a given number of standing desks produced each year.

From this chart, you learn that if the company produces 5,000 standing desks, its total expense would be about $3.6 million. Of this, about $2.7 million represents the cost of goods sold and about $0.9 million is from fixed expenses.

Figure 8–2   Chart of total expenses

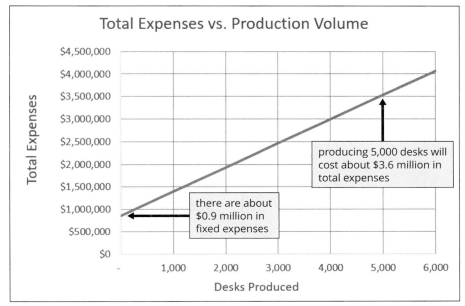

A third type of expense is a **mixed expense**, which is an expense that is part variable and part fixed. For example, if the salespeople at Office Motion receive commissions based on sales volume, their total compensation would be a mixed expense to the company because each salesperson has a fixed salary but also earns extra income as sales volume increases. You will not consider any mixed expenses in your analysis of standing desk sales by Office Motion.

Because Office Motion is a highly specialized company with a select but loyal clientele, the company sells almost all of what it produces. So, the company should bring in more revenue as it increases production. Figure 8–3 shows the increase in revenue in relation to increase in sales volume. For example, selling 5,000 standing desks at an average price of $760 per desk would generate about $3.8 million in revenue.

Figure 8–3   Chart of total revenue

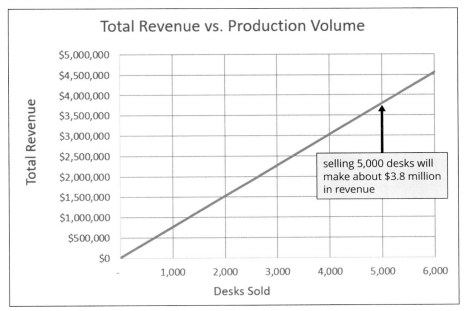

Exploring the Break-Even Point

The point where total revenue equals total expenses is called the break-even point. For this reason, CVP analysis is sometimes called **break-even analysis**. The more desks Office Motion sells above the break-even point, the greater its profit. Conversely, when sales volume falls below the break-even point, the company loses money.

You can illustrate the break-even point by graphing revenue and total expenses against sales volume on the same chart. The break-even point occurs where the two lines cross. This type of chart, shown in Figure 8–4, is called a **Cost–Volume–Profit (CVP) chart**.

Figure 8–4   Break-even point in a CVP Chart

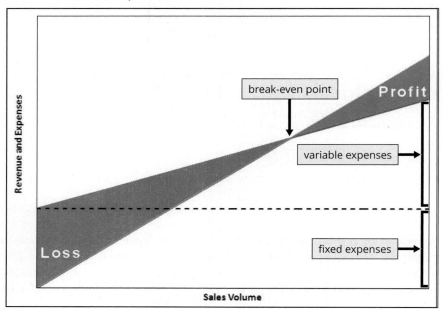

Yuri prepared an income statement for projecting the revenue, variable expenses, and fixed expenses for next year's sales of standing desks. You will review Yuri's data now. Later, you will use those projections to calculate the break-even point for sales of the company's line of standing desks.

To review the income statement for the line of standing desks:

1. **sam** ↓ Open the **NP_EX_8-1.xlsx** workbook located in the **Excel8 > Module** folder included with your Data Files, and then save the workbook as **NP_EX_8_Office** in the location specified by your instructor.

2. In the Documentation worksheet, enter your name and the date in the range B3:B4.

3. Go to the **Income** worksheet and review its contents and formulas. Refer to Figure 8–5.

Figure 8–5   Income statement for the line of standing desks

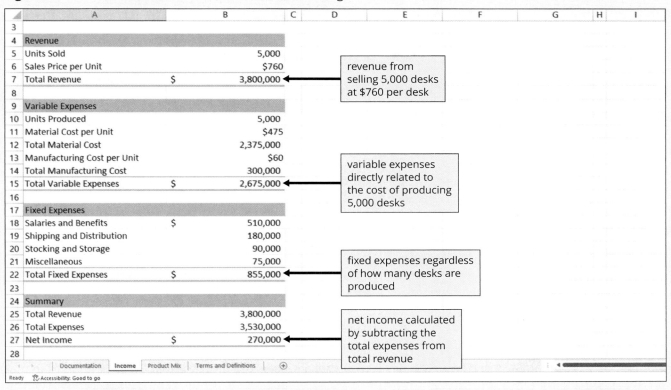

As itemized in the Income worksheet, the company projects that it will have a net income of $270,000 (cell B27) from producing and selling 5,000 standing desks. How will this bottom line be affected if the company produces and sells more desks or sells fewer desks? To answer that question, you will perform a what-if analysis on the data and formulas in the Income worksheet.

Finding the Break-Even Point with What-If Analysis

What-if analysis lets you explore the impact of changing different values in a worksheet. You can use such an analysis to explore the impact of changing financial conditions on a company's profitability. Yuri wants to know the impact on profits if the company's production and sales rises to 7,000 units or falls to 3,000 units.

To perform what-if analysis for different sales volumes:

1. In cell **B5**, enter **7000** to change the units produced and sold value. Increasing the sales volume to 7,000 units, the net income of the company shown in cell B27 increases to $720,000.

2. In cell **B5**, enter **3000**. If the units produced and sold drop to 3,000, the net income shown in cell B27 becomes –$180,000. The company will lose money with that low of a sales volume.

3. In cell **B5**, enter **5000** to return to the original units produced and sold projection.

How low can sales go and still have the company break even? Although you could hunt for that break-even point by entering other values for sales volume, using Goal Seek is quicker and more efficient. Recall that Goal Seek is a what-if analysis tool that finds the input value needed for an Excel formula to match a specified value. In this case, you will find out how many desks must be sold to set the net income value calculated in cell B27 to $0.

To use Goal Seek to find the break-even point:

1. On the ribbon, click the **Data** tab. In the Forecast group, click the **What-If Analysis** button, and then click **Goal Seek**. The Goal Seek dialog box opens with the cell reference in the Set cell box selected.

2. In the Income worksheet, click cell **B27** to replace the selected cell reference in the Set cell box with $B$27. The absolute reference specifies the Net Income cell as the cell whose value you want to set.

3. Press **TAB** to move the insertion point to the To value box, and then type **0** indicating that the goal is to set the net income value in cell B27 to 0.

4. Press **TAB** to move the insertion point to the By changing cell box, and then click cell **B5** in the Income worksheet to enter the cell reference $B$5. The absolute reference specifies that you want to reach the goal of setting the net income to 0 by changing the units produced and sold value in cell B5.

5. Click **OK**. The Goal Seek Status dialog box opens once Excel finds a solution.

6. Click **OK** to return to the worksheet. The value 3,800 appears in cell B5, indicating that the company must produce and sell 3,800 standing desks to break even. Refer to Figure 8–6.

Figure 8–6   Sales required to break even

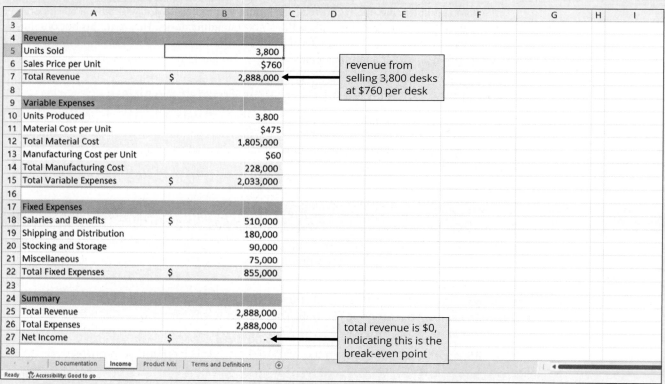

7. Click cell **B5** and enter **5000** to return to the original units produced and sold projection.

Yuri wants to continue to analyze the company's net income under different sales assumptions. For example, what would happen to the company's net income if sales increased to 6,000 desks? How much would the company lose if the number of sales fell to 2,500? How many desks must the company sell to reach a net income of exactly $500,000? You could continue to use Goal Seek to answer each of these questions in turn, but you could also answer all those questions at once using a data table.

Working with Data Tables

A **data table** is an Excel table that displays the results from several what-if analyses. The table consists of input cells and result cells. Input cells list the values to be changed in a what-if analysis. Result cells display the calculated values impacted by the changing input values. Excel supports one-variable data tables and two-variable data tables.

Creating a One-Variable Data Table

A one-variable data table contains one input cell and any number of result cells. The range of possible values for the input cell is entered in the first row or column of the data table, and the corresponding result values appear in matching rows or columns. One-variable data tables are particularly useful in business to explore how changing a single input value can impact several financial measures.

Reference

Creating a One-Variable Data Table

- In the upper-left cell of the table, enter a formula that references the input cell.
- In either the first row or the first column of the table, enter input values.
- For input values in the first row, enter formulas referencing result cells in the table's first column; for input values in the first column, enter formulas referencing result cells in the table's first row.
- Select the table (excluding any row or column headings).
- On the Data tab, in the Forecast group, click the What-If Analysis button, and then click Data Table.
- If the input values are in the first row, enter the cell reference to the input cell in the Row input cell box; if the input values are in the first column, enter the cell reference to the input cell in the Column input cell box.
- Click OK.

Yuri wants a one-variable data table of units sold matched to revenue, expenses, and net income. The first row of the data table references the input cell and the result cells to be used in the analysis. The next rows list units sold values ranging from 1,000 units to 8,000 units in 500-unit increments. You will create this data table structure now.

To set up a one-variable data table:

1. In cell **D3**, enter **Break-Even Analysis** as the table label, merge and center the range **D3:G3**, and then format the text with the **Heading 3** cell style.

2. In the range **D4:G4**, enter **Units Sold**, **Revenue**, **Expenses**, and **Net Income** as the labels, center the text in the selected cells, and then apply the **20% - Accent1** cell style to the cells.

3. In cell **D5**, enter the formula **= B5** to reference the input cell to be used in the data table.

4. In cell **E5**, enter the formula **= B25** to reference the result cell that displays the total revenue.

5. In cell **F5**, enter the formula **= B26** to reference the total expenses.

6. In cell **G5**, enter the formula **= B27** to reference the company's net income.

7. Format the range **E5:G5** using the **Accounting** format with no decimal places.

8. Format the range **D5:G5** with the **20% - Accent4** cell style and add a bottom border.

9. In the range **D6:D20**, enter Units Sold values from **1000** to **8000** in 500-unit increments, and then format the cells in that range with the **Comma** style and no decimal places.

10. Select cell **D5**. Refer to Figure 8–7.

Figure 8–7   Setup for the one-variable data table

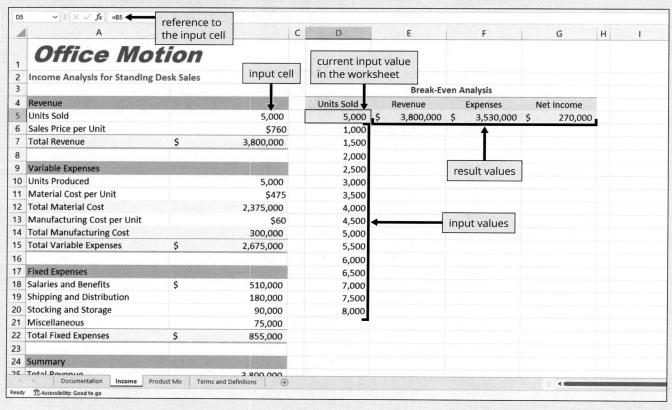

Data tables are arranged either vertically with input values listed in a single column or horizontally with input values listed in a single row. This data table lists the input values in the first column. To complete the table, you will use the Data Table tool to populate the matching columns with the calculated result values for revenue, expenses, and net income.

To complete the one-variable data table:

1. Select the range **D5:G20** containing the cells for the data table.

2. On the ribbon, click the **Data** tab. In the Forecast group, click the **What-If Analysis** button, and then click **Data Table**. The Data Table dialog box opens.

3. Press **TAB** to move the insertion point to the Column input cell box, and then click cell **B5** in the Income worksheet to indicate that all the result values in the data table first column should be matched with cell B5. The absolute reference $B$5 appears in the Column input box. Refer to Figure 8–8.

Figure 8–8   Data Table dialog box

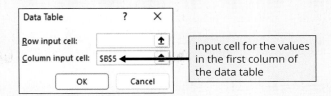

input cell for the values in the first column of the data table

4. Click **OK**. Excel completes the data table by displaying the revenue, expenses, and net income for each units sold value specified in the data table's first column.

5. Select the range **E6:G20** containing the Revenue, Expenses, and Net Income values for each Units Sold value.

6. Right-click the selected range, and then click **Format Cells** on the shortcut menu. The Format Cells dialog box opens.

7. Click **Currency** in the Category box, reduce the value in the Decimal place box to **0**, and then click the last entry in the Negative numbers list to display negative values in red parentheses.

8. Click **OK** to close the dialog box and return to the worksheet.

9. Click cell **G20**. Refer to Figure 8–9.

Figure 8–9   Completed one-variable data table

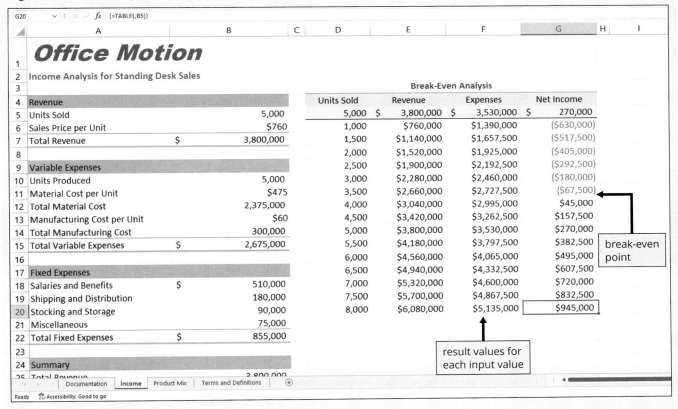

The data table shows the results of several what-if analyses. For example, producing and selling 4,500 standing desks results in $3,420,000 of revenue with $3,262,500 of expenses, yielding a net income of $157,500.

Charting a One-Variable Data Table

The one-variable data table gives important information about the cost–volume–profit relationship, but you will have a better picture of that relationship with a CVP chart. You will create a scatter chart displaying the revenue and total expenses against the total number of units sold.

To create the CVP chart of the data table:

1. Select the range **D4:F20** containing the data you want to chart.

2. On the ribbon, click the **Insert** tab.

3. In the Charts group, click the **Insert Scatter (X, Y) or Bubble Chart** button [icon], and then click **Scatter with Straight Lines** (the second option in the second row of the Scatter section). Each point in the data table is plotted on the chart and connected with a line. The break-even point occurs where the two lines cross.

4. Move and resize the chart so that it covers the range **D22:G36**.

5. Change the chart title to **CVP Analysis**.

6. Click the **Chart Elements** button [icon], and then click the **Axis Titles** check box to add axis titles to chart.

7. Change the vertical axis title to **Revenue and Expenses** and change the horizontal axis title to **Units Produced and Sold**. Refer to Figure 8–10.

Figure 8–10   CVP chart of one-variable data table

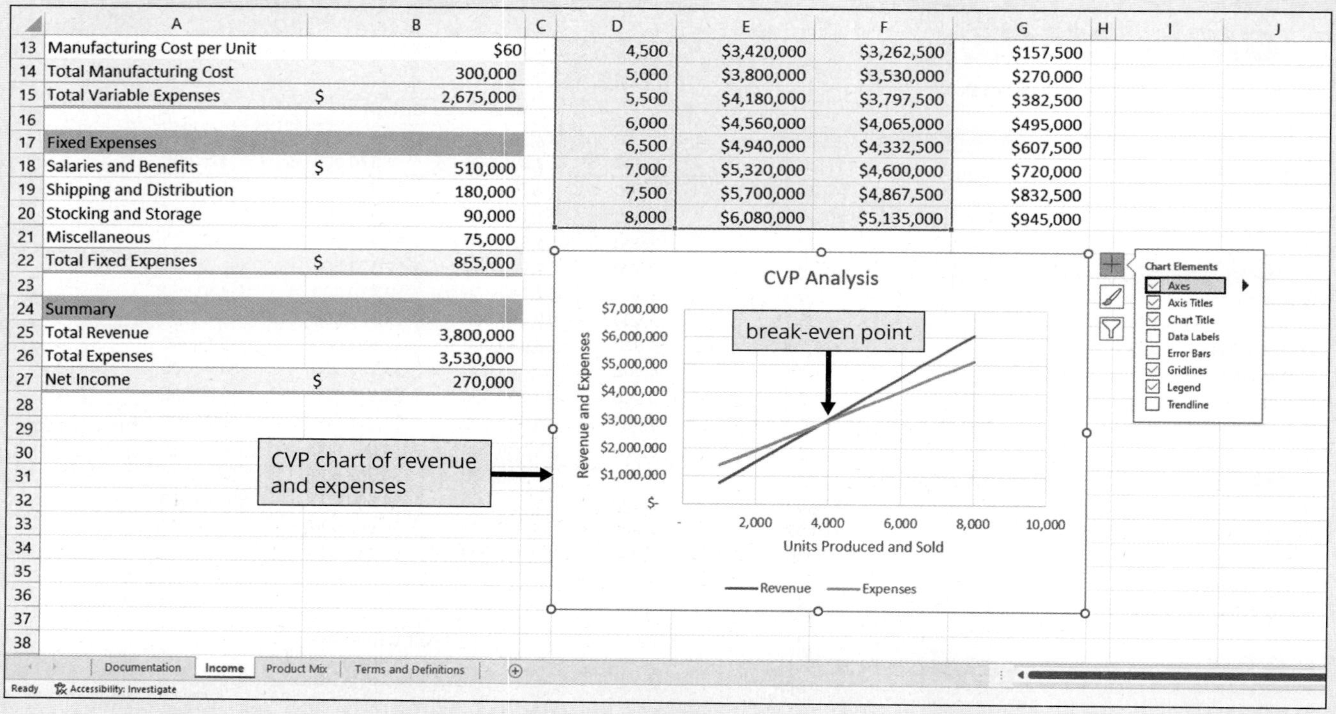

The line chart provides a visual representation of the break-even point that Yuri can use in reports presented to other members of the Office Motion sales team.

Modifying a Data Table

Data tables are dynamic so that changes in the input and result cells are automatically reflected in the table. Office Motion is considering lowering its prices to be more competitive with other manufacturers. Yuri wants you to perform another what-if analysis examining the effect of reducing the average sales price of their standing desks from $760 to $680. Changing the value in the Income worksheet will affect other results in the sheet, including the what-if analysis displayed in the one-variable data table and the break-even chart.

To view the impact of changing the sales price:

1. In cell **B6**, enter **$680** to reduce the average sales price of the company's line of standing desks. At this lower sales price, the break-even point moves to somewhere between 5,500 and 6,000 units—a fact reflected in both the data table and the CVP chart. Refer to Figure 8–11.

Figure 8–11   Impact of changing the sales price

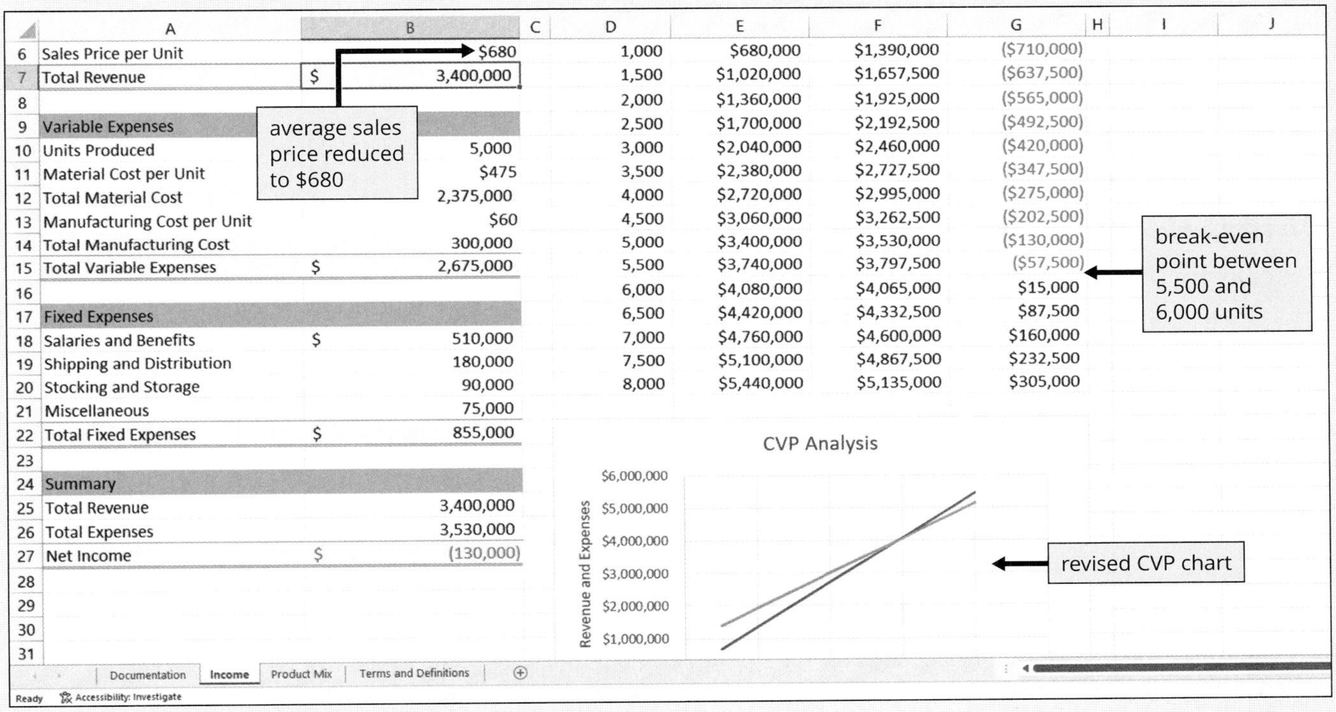

2. In cell **B6**, enter **$840** to view the impact of increasing the average sales price. At this higher price, the break-even point is somewhere between 2,500 and 3,000 units produced and sold.

3. Return the value in cell B6 to **$760**.

You could continue to perform what-if analyses with different sales prices to explore the relationship between sales volume and sales price on the break-even point, but another approach is to create a two-variable data table.

Insight

Directly Calculating the Break-Even Point

A CVP chart is a useful visual tool for displaying the break-even point. You can also calculate the break-even point directly by using the following formula:

$$\text{break-even point} = \frac{\text{fixed expenses}}{\text{sales price per unit} - \text{variable expenses per unit}}$$

For example, with a sales price of $800, fixed expenses of $900,000, and variable expenses of $620 per unit, the following equation calculates the break-even point:

$$\text{break-even point} = \frac{900,000}{800 - 620} = 5,000$$

Office Motion would have to sell 5,000 standing desks to break even. If the company sells more than that number, the company will show a profit.

Creating a Two-Variable Data Table

A two-variable data table shows the relationship between two input cells and one result cell. The input values are placed in the table's first row and first column. The result values are placed in cells at the intersection of each pair of input values. Unlike one-variable data tables in which you have several columns of result values, you can have only one result value with the two-variable data table.

Reference

Creating a Two-Variable Data Table

- In the upper-left cell of the table, enter a formula that references the result cell.
- In the first row and first column of the table, enter input values.
- Select the table (excluding any row or column headings).
- On the Data tab, in the Forecast group, click the What-If Analysis button, and then click Data Table.
- Enter the cell reference to the first-row input values in the Row input cell box, and then enter the cell reference to the first column input values in the Column input cell box.
- Click OK.

Yuri wants you to examine the impact of the sales price and the yearly sales volume on the net income from selling the Athena I. You will create a two-variable data table to explore this relationship.

To set up the two-variable data table:

1. In cell I3, enter **Net Income Analysis**, merge and center the range **I3:N3**, and then format the merged range with the **Heading 3** cell style.

2. In cell I4, enter **Sales Price**, and then merge and center the range **I4:N4**.

3. In the range **J5:N5**, enter the possible sales prices **$650** through **$850** in increments of $50.

4. Copy the values in the range **D6:D20**, and then paste them into the range **I6:I20**.

5. Select the two sets of input values in the nonadjacent range **J5:N5, I6:I20**, and then format the selected range with the **20% - Accent4** cell style.

6. Add a right border to the range **I6:I20** and a bottom border to the range **J5:N5**.

In two-variable data tables, the reference to the result cell is placed in the upper-left corner of the table at the intersection of the row and column input values. In this case, you will enter a formula in cell I5 that references the company's net income.

7. In cell **I5**, enter the formula **= B27**. The current net income value $270,000 is displayed in cell I5, Refer to Figure 8–12.

Figure 8–12   Setup for the two-variable data table

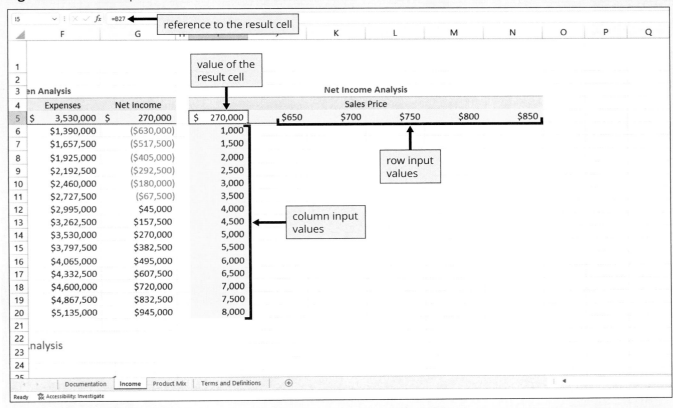

The two-variable data table is generated using the same Data Table command used with the one-variable data table, except that you specify both the row input cell (matched to the input values in the table's first row) and the column input cell (matched to the input values in the table's first column).

To generate table of result values:

1. Select the range **I5:N20** containing the row input values, the column input values, and the reference to the result cell.

2. On the ribbon, click the **Data** tab. In the Forecast group, click the **What-If Analysis** button, and then click **Data Table**. The Data Table dialog box opens.

3. In the Row input cell box, type **B6** to reference the sales price from the income statement.

4. In the Column input cell box, type **B5** to reference the number of units sold from the income statement.

5. Click **OK**. The data table values appear in the range J6:N20.

6. Use the Format Painter to copy the formatting from cell **G20** to the range **J6:N20**.

7. Click cell **J6** to deselect the highlighted range. Refer to Figure 8–13.

Figure 8–13   Completed two-variable data table

| | J6 | | × ✓ fx {=TABLE(B6,B5)} | | | | | | | | | | |

	F	G	H	I	J	K	L	M	N	O	P	Q	R
1													
2													
3	en Analysis					Net Income Analysis							
4	Expenses	Net Income				Sales Price							
5	$ 3,530,000	$ 270,000		$ 270,000	$650	$700	$750	$800	$850				
6	$1,390,000	($630,000)		1,000	($740,000)	($690,000)	($640,000)	($590,000)	($540,000)				
7	$1,657,500	($517,500)		1,500	($682,500)	($607,500)	($532,500)	($457,500)	($382,500)				
8	$1,925,000	($405,000)		2,000	($625,000)	($525,000)	($425,000)	($325,000)	($225,000)				
9	$2,192,500	($292,500)		2,500	($567,500)	($442,500)	($317,500)	($192,500)	($67,500)				
10	$2,460,000	($180,000)		3,000	($510,000)	($360,000)	($210,000)	($60,000)	$90,000				
11	$2,727,500	($67,500)		3,500	($452,500)	($277,500)	($102,500)	$72,500	$247,500				
12	$2,995,000	$45,000		4,000	($395,000)	($195,000)	$5,000	$205,000	$405,000				
13	$3,262,500	$157,500		4,500	($337,500)	($112,500)	$112,500	$337,500	$562,500				
14	$3,530,000	$270,000		5,000	($280,000)	($30,000)	$220,000	$470,000	$720,000				
15	$3,797,500	$382,500		5,500	($222,500)	$52,500	$327,500	$602,500	$877,500				
16	$4,065,000	$495,000		6,000	($165,000)	$135,000	$435,000	$735,000	$1,035,000				
17	$4,332,500	$607,500		6,500	($107,500)	$217,500	$542,500	$867,500	$1,192,500				
18	$4,600,000	$720,000		7,000	($50,000)	$300,000	$650,000	$1,000,000	$1,350,000				
19	$4,867,500	$832,500		7,500	$7,500	$382,500	$757,500	$1,132,500	$1,507,500				
20	$5,135,000	$945,000		8,000	$65,000	$465,000	$865,000	$1,265,000	$1,665,000				
21													
22													
23	nalysis												
24													

break-even point

result values show the net income for each combination of units sold and sales price

Documentation **Income** Product Mix   Terms and Definitions   ⊕

Ready   ※ Accessibility: Investigate

The break-even points for different combinations of price and units sold are easy to track because negative net income values are displayed in red and positive net income values are displayed in black. For example, if the sales price is set at $650, Office Motion must sell between 7,000 and 7,500 standing desks to break even. However, if the price is increased by $50 to $700, the company needs to only sell between 5,000 and 5,500 desks to break even.

Formatting the Result Cell

The reference to the result cell in the table's upper-left corner might confuse some users. To prevent that, you can hide the cell value using the custom cell format "*text*" where *text* is the label to display in place of the cell value. In this case, Yuri wants you to use a custom format to display "Units Sold" instead of the value in cell I5.

To apply a custom format to cell I5:

1. Right-click cell **I5**, and then click **Format Cells** on the shortcut menu (or press **CTRL+1**). The Format Cells dialog box opens.

2. If necessary, click the **Number** tab, and then in the Category box, click **Custom**.

   | **Key Step** Be sure to use opening and closing quotation marks around the custom text.

3. In the Type box, select the format code text, and replace it with the text string **"Units Sold"** (including the quotation marks) as the custom text to display in the cell. Refer to Figure 8–14.

Figure 8–14   Format Cells dialog box

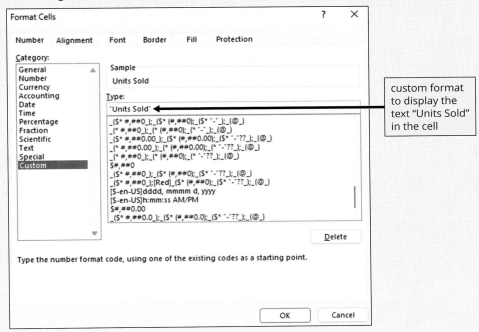

custom format to display the text "Units Sold" in the cell

> **Tip** You can also hide the reference to the result cell by applying the same font and fill color to the cell.

4. Click **OK**. The text "Units Sold" appears in cell I5 even though the cell's underlying formula is = B27.

> **Trouble?** If "Units Sold" does not appear in cell I5, you probably didn't include the quotation marks in the custom format. Repeat Steps 1 through 4, making sure that you include both opening and closing quotation marks.

Charting a Two-Variable Data Table

You can chart the values from a two-variable data table using lines to represent the different columns of the table. Yuri wants you to create a scatter chart based on the two-variable data table you just created.

To create a chart of the two-variable data table:

1. Select the range **I6:N20**. You will plot this range on a scatter chart. You did not select the unit prices in row 5 because Excel would interpret these values as data values to be charted, not as labels.

2. On the ribbon, click the **Insert** tab. In the Charts group, click the **Insert Scatter (X, Y) or Bubble Chart** button, and then click the **Scatter with Straight Lines** chart subtype (the second chart in the second row of the Scatter section).

3. Move and resize the chart so that it covers the range **I22:N36**.

4. Change the chart title to **Net Income Analysis**.

5. Position the chart legend to the right of the chart.

6. Add axis titles to the chart. Rename the vertical axis title **Net Income** and the horizontal axis title **Units Produced and Sold**. Refer to Figure 8–15.

Figure 8–15   Chart of net income values

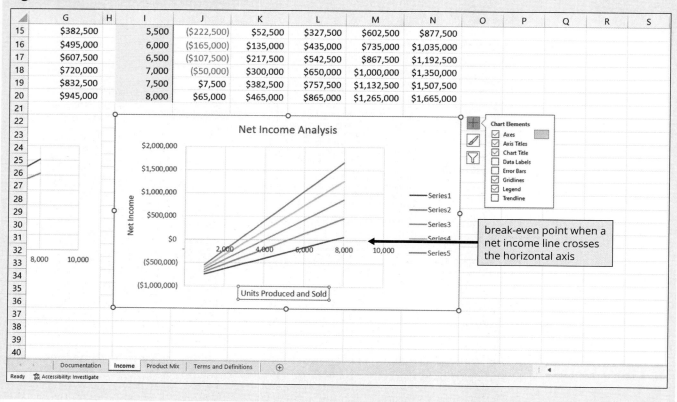

	G	H	I	J	K	L	M	N	O	P	Q	R	S
15	$382,500		5,500	($222,500)	$52,500	$327,500	$602,500	$877,500					
16	$495,000		6,000	($165,000)	$135,000	$435,000	$735,000	$1,035,000					
17	$607,500		6,500	($107,500)	$217,500	$542,500	$867,500	$1,192,500					
18	$720,000		7,000	($50,000)	$300,000	$650,000	$1,000,000	$1,350,000					
19	$832,500		7,500	$7,500	$382,500	$757,500	$1,132,500	$1,507,500					
20	$945,000		8,000	$65,000	$465,000	$865,000	$1,265,000	$1,665,000					

The chart shows a different trend line for each of the five possible values for unit price. However, the prices are not listed in the chart. Excel uses generic series names (Series1, Series2, Series3, Series4, and Series5) to identify each line. To display the unit prices rather than the generic names in the chart, you must add the unit price values as series names.

To edit the chart series names:

1. On the Chart Design tab, in the Data group, click the **Select Data** button. The Select Data Source dialog box opens.

2. In the Legend Entries (Series) box, click **Series1**, and then click **Edit**. The Edit Series dialog box opens.

3. With the insertion point in the Series name box, click cell **J5** to insert the reference =Income!$J$5, and then click **OK**. The Select Data Source dialog box reappears with the Series1 name changed to $650. Refer to Figure 8–16.

Figure 8–16   Select Data Source dialog box

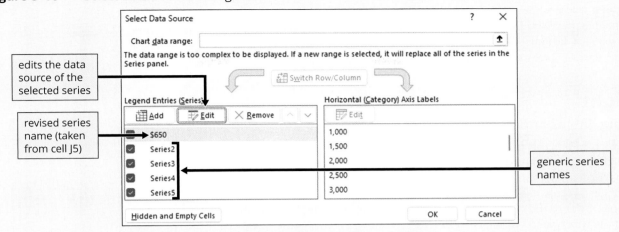

4. Repeat Steps 2 and 3 to edit Series2 to use cell **K5** as the series name, edit Series3 to use cell **L5** as the series name, edit Series4 to use cell **M5** as the series name, and edit Series5 to use cell **N5** as the series name. All the chart series are renamed to match the sales price values in row 5 of the two-variable data table.

5. Click **OK**. The Select Data Source dialog box closes, and the legend shows the renamed series.

6. On the Chart Design tab, in the Chart Styles group, click the **Change Colors** button, and then click **Monochromatic Palette 12** in the Monochromatic section. The line colors change to shades of blue, reflecting the increasing value of the unit price. Refer to Figure 8–17.

Figure 8–17   Final chart of net income values

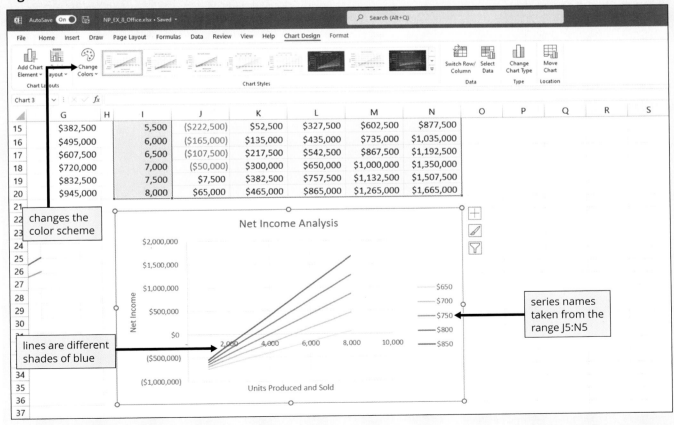

7. Save the workbook.

The chart shows the impact of price on the relationship between sales volume and net income. Each point where a line crosses the horizontal axis is a break-even point for a specific sales price. For example, the $800 line (the second highest of the five lines) crosses the horizontal axis near 3,000 units, indicating that with sales price of $800, the company will have to sell about 3,000 standing desks to break even.

Insight

Data Tables and Arrays

If you examine the cells in the two-variable data table you just created, you find that every cell displays a different value even though it has the same formula: {=TABLE(B6, B5)}. This expression is an example of an **array formula** that generates several values from a single formula. The syntax represents an older Excel standard for generating multiple values, prior to the introduction of dynamic arrays. Array formulas written in this syntax are always enclosed within curly braces.

The TABLE function is an array function that returns multiple values across multiple cells. Other array function include the TREND, MINVERSE, MMULT, and TRANSPOSE functions. To enter an array formula of this syntax, type the formula and then press CTRL+SHIFT+ENTER. Excel inserts the curly braces and applies the array formula to all the selected cells.

While many of their features have been supplanted by dynamic arrays, you might still encounter array formulas in legacy workbooks. Use Excel Help to learn more about array formulas and the functions that employ them.

So far, you have used what-if analysis with Goal Seek and data tables to analyze how units sold and sales price impact the company's net income. In the next session, you will use other what-if analysis tools to examine the impact of fixed expenses on the profitability of the standing desk line.

Part 8.1 Quick Check

1. Describe the difference between a variable expense and a fixed expense.

2. When does the break-even point occur?

3. What is a data table? What is an input cell? What is a result cell?

4. What is a one-variable data table? What is a two-variable data table?

5. How many result cells can you display with a one-variable data table? How many result cells can you display with a two-variable data table?

6. Cell E5 contains the formula = B10. You want to display the text "Profits" instead of the formula's value. What custom format would you use?

7. What is an array formula?

Part 8.2 Visual Overview: What-If Scenarios

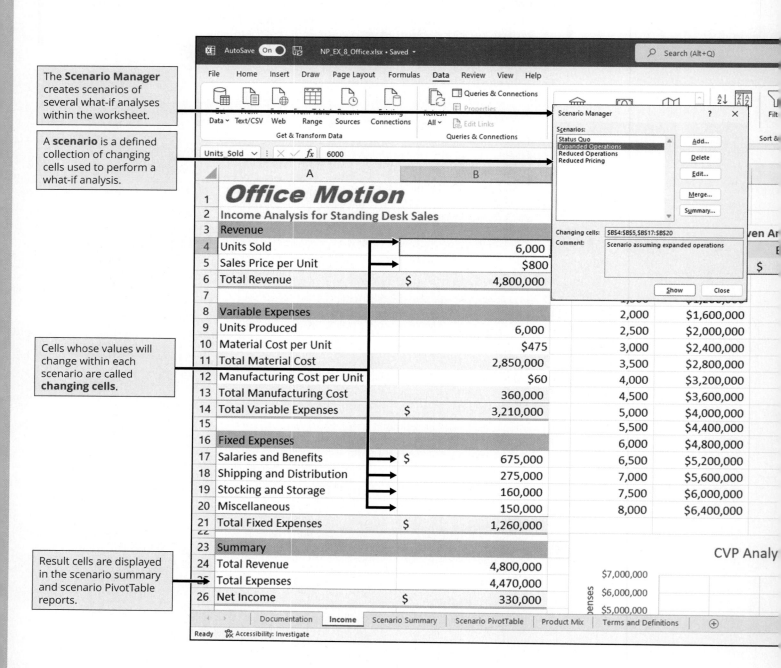

The **Scenario Manager** creates scenarios of several what-if analyses within the worksheet.

A **scenario** is a defined collection of changing cells used to perform a what-if analysis.

Cells whose values will change within each scenario are called **changing cells**.

Result cells are displayed in the scenario summary and scenario PivotTable reports.

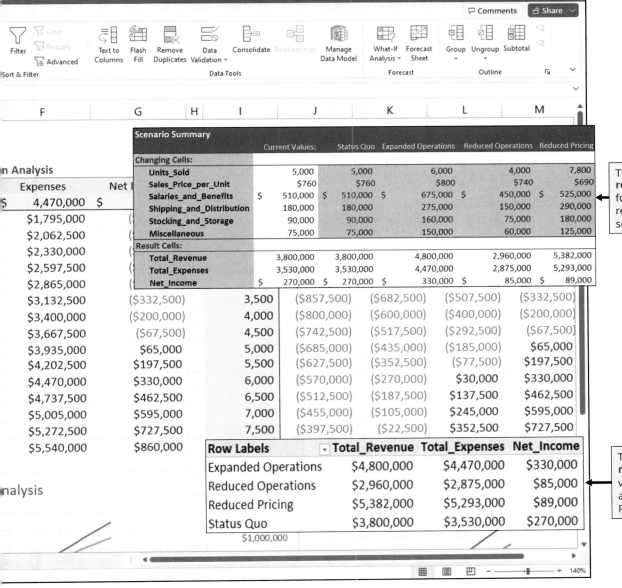

The **scenario summary report** lists the values for the changing and result cells within each scenario.

The **Scenario PivotTable report** displays the values for the changing and result cells within a PivotTable.

Scenario Summary

Changing Cells:	Current Values:	Status Quo	Expanded Operations	Reduced Operations	Reduced Pricing
Units_Sold	5,000	5,000	6,000	4,000	7,800
Sales_Price_per_Unit	$760	$760	$800	$740	$690
Salaries_and_Benefits	$ 510,000	$ 510,000	$ 675,000	$ 450,000	$ 525,000
Shipping_and_Distribution	180,000	180,000	275,000	150,000	290,000
Stocking_and_Storage	90,000	90,000	160,000	75,000	180,000
Miscellaneous	75,000	75,000	150,000	60,000	125,000
Result Cells:					
Total_Revenue	3,800,000	3,800,000	4,800,000	2,960,000	5,382,000
Total_Expenses	3,530,000	3,530,000	4,470,000	2,875,000	5,293,000
Net_Income	$ 270,000	$ 270,000	$ 330,000	$ 85,000	$ 89,000

(left partial table)

n Analysis		
Expenses	Net
$ 4,470,000	$
$1,795,000	(
$2,062,500	(
$2,330,000	(
$2,597,500	(
$2,865,000	(
$3,132,500	($332,500)
$3,400,000	($200,000)
$3,667,500	($67,500)
$3,935,000	$65,000
$4,202,500	$197,500
$4,470,000	$330,000
$4,737,500	$462,500
$5,005,000	$595,000
$5,272,500	$727,500
$5,540,000	$860,000

3,500	($857,500)	($682,500)	($507,500)	($332,500)
4,000	($800,000)	($600,000)	($400,000)	($200,000)
4,500	($742,500)	($517,500)	($292,500)	($67,500)
5,000	($685,000)	($435,000)	($185,000)	$65,000
5,500	($627,500)	($352,500)	($77,500)	$197,500
6,000	($570,000)	($270,000)	$30,000	$330,000
6,500	($512,500)	($187,500)	$137,500	$462,500
7,000	($455,000)	($105,000)	$245,000	$595,000
7,500	($397,500)	($22,500)	$352,500	$727,500

Row Labels	Total_Revenue	Total_Expenses	Net_Income
Expanded Operations	$4,800,000	$4,470,000	$330,000
Reduced Operations	$2,960,000	$2,875,000	$85,000
Reduced Pricing	$5,382,000	$5,293,000	$89,000
Status Quo	$3,800,000	$3,530,000	$270,000
	$1,000,000		

nalysis

Exploring Financial Scenarios with Scenario Manager

Usually multiple factors affect a financial result. Data tables are limited to at most two input cells. To go beyond two factors in your financial analysis, you can create scenarios, which can have more than two input cells.

After reviewing your data tables, Yuri wants to explore four other models or scenarios for the production and sale of Office Motion's line of standing desks. Figure 8–18 lists four scenarios, detailing input values for each scenario.

Figure 8–18   Standing desks what-if scenarios

Input Cells	Status Quo	Expanded Operations	Reduced Operations	Reduced Pricing
Units Sold (B5)	5,000	6,000	4,000	7,500
Sales Price (B6)	$760	$800	$740	$690
Salaries and Benefits (B18)	$510,000	$675,000	$450,000	$575,000
Shipping and Distribution (B19)	$180,000	$275,000	$150,000	$290,000
Stocking and Storage (B20)	$90,000	$160,000	$75,000	$180,000
Miscellaneous (B21)	$75,000	$150,000	$60,000	$155,000

Under the Status Quo scenario, Yuri assumes that the fixed expenses, units sold, and unit prices remain unchanged for the coming year. The Expanded Operations scenario assumes that the company will increase the total number of standing desks produced and sold while at the same time increasing its expenditures on salaries and benefits, shipping and distribution, stocking and storage, and miscellaneous expenses. The Reduced Operations scenario foresees a gradual phase-out of the current standing desk line with fewer units produced and sold accompanied by lower fixed costs for all categories. Finally, the Reduced Pricing scenario proposes cutting the sales price to $690, resulting in increased sales with slightly more fixed costs.

These scenarios require six input cells and are beyond the capability of a data table. However, you can explore these scenarios using the Scenario Manager. Rather than manually changing every input cell value, the Scenario Manager defines input values under each scenario, allowing you to switch the workbook between one scenario and another. The Scenario Manager can also be used to create reports summarizing the impact of each scenario on a set of result cells. The number of scenarios you can create is limited only by your computer's memory.

Before using the Scenario Manager, you should define range names for all input and result cells used in the scenarios. Although not a requirement, using range names makes it easier to work with the scenarios and for other people to understand the scenario reports.

To define names for the income statement values:

1. If you took a break after the previous part, make sure the NP_EX_8_Office workbook is open and the Income worksheet is the active sheet.

2. In the Income worksheet, select the range **A5:B6,A18:B21,A25:B27**. You will define names for each of these cells.

3. On the ribbon, click the **Formulas** tab, and then in the Defined Names group, click the **Create from Selection** button. The Create Names from Selection dialog box opens.

4. Click the **Left column** check box to insert a checkmark, if necessary, and then click any other check box that has a checkmark to deselect it.

5. Click **OK**. The cell values in column B are named using the labels in the corresponding cells in column A.

6. Click cell **A1** to deselect the range.

Defining a Scenario

Now that you have defined the names used in the worksheet, you will use the Scenario Manager to create scenarios based on the values listed in Figure 8–18. Each scenario includes a scenario name, a list of input or changing cells, and the values of each input cell under the scenario.

Reference

Defining a Scenario

- Enter the data values in the worksheet for the scenario.
- On the Data tab, in the Forecast group, click the What-If Analysis button, and then click Scenario Manager.
- Click Add in the Scenario Manager dialog box.
- In the Scenario name box, type a name for the scenario.
- In the Changing cells box, specify the changing cells.
- Click OK.
- In the Scenario Values dialog box, specify values for each input cell, and then click Add.
- Click OK.

You will start by creating the Status Quo scenario, whose values match those currently entered in the workbook.

To add the Status Quo scenario:

1. On the ribbon, click the **Data** tab. In the Forecast group, click the **What-If Analysis** button, and then click **Scenario Manager**. The Scenario Manager dialog box opens. No scenarios are defined yet.

2. Click **Add**. The Add Scenario dialog box opens.

3. In the Scenario name box, type **Status Quo**, and then press **TAB**. The cell reference in the Changing cells box is selected.

The Scenario Manager refers to input cells as "changing cells" because these worksheet cells contain values that are changed under the scenario. Changing cells can be located anywhere in the current worksheet. You can type the range names or locations of changing cells, but it is faster and more accurate to select them with the mouse.

Tip Scenarios are limited to a maximum of 32 changing cells.

The changing cells for each of the four scenarios are as follows:

- Cell B5: Units Sold
- Cell B6: Sales Price per Unit
- Cell B18: Salaries and Benefits
- Cell B19: Shipping and Distribution
- Cell B20: Stocking and Storage
- Cell B21: Miscellaneous

You will specify these cells as the changing cells for the Status Quo scenario.

To specify the changing cells for the Status Quo scenario:

1. With the Changing cells box still active, select the nonadjacent range **B5:B6,B18:B21**. Absolute references for the range appear in the Changing cells box. These are the changing or input cells.

2. Press **TAB** to select the default text in the Comment box, and then type **Scenario assuming no change in values** in the Comment box. Refer to Figure 8–19.

Figure 8–19   Edit Scenario dialog box

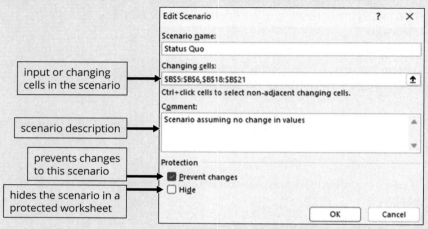

- input or changing cells in the scenario
- scenario description
- prevents changes to this scenario
- hides the scenario in a protected worksheet

3. Click **OK**. The Scenario Values dialog box opens so you can enter values for each changing cell you entered in the Changing cells box in the Edit Scenario dialog box. The Status Quo scenario values already appear in the dialog box because these are the current values in the workbook. Refer to Figure 8–20.

Figure 8–20   Scenario Values dialog box

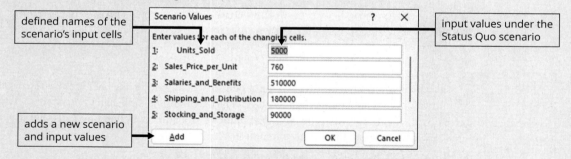

- defined names of the scenario's input cells
- input values under the Status Quo scenario
- adds a new scenario and input values

4. Click **OK**. The Scenario Manager dialog box reopens with the Status Quo scenario listed in the Scenarios box. Refer to Figure 8–21.

Figure 8-21   Scenario Manager dialog box

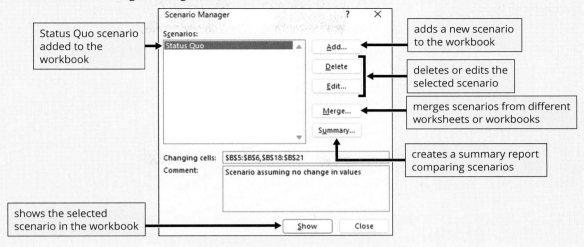

Status Quo scenario added to the workbook

adds a new scenario to the workbook

deletes or edits the selected scenario

merges scenarios from different worksheets or workbooks

creates a summary report comparing scenarios

shows the selected scenario in the workbook

You will use the same process to add the remaining three scenarios on Yuri's list—Expanded Operations, Reduced Operations, and Reduced Pricing.

To add the remaining scenarios:

1. In the Scenario Manager dialog box, click **Add**. The Add Scenario dialog box opens.

2. In the Scenario name box, type **Expanded Operations**, press **TAB** twice to go the Comment box, and then type **Scenario assuming expanded operations** in the Comment box.

   Note that the nonadjacent range you selected for the Status Quo scenario appears in the Changing cells box. Because you want to use the same set of changing cells, you did not edit the range.

3. Click **OK**. The Scenario Values dialog box for the Expanded Operations scenario opens.

   ▍**Key Step** Be sure you enter the values for the scenario. Do not simply accept the default values currently in the worksheet.

4. Enter the following values, pressing **TAB** to move from one input box to the next: **6000** for Units_Sold, **800** for Sales_Price_per_Unit, **675000** for Salaries_and_Benefits, **275000** for Shipping_and_Distribution, **160000** for Stocking_and_Storage, and **150000** for Miscellaneous.

5. Click **Add**. The Add Scenario dialog box reopens so you can enter the next scenario.

   ▍**Trouble?** If the Scenario Manager dialog box reopens, you clicked OK instead of Add. Click Add in the Scenario Manager dialog box to return to the Add Scenario dialog box, and then continue with Step 6.

6. Type **Reduced Operations** in the Scenario name box, press **TAB** twice, type **Scenario assuming reduced operations** in the Comment box, and then click **OK**.

7. Enter **4000** for Units_Sold, **740** for Sales_Price_per_Unit, **450000** for Salaries_and_Benefits, **150000** for Shipping_and_Distribution, **75000** for Stocking_and_Storage, and **60000** for Miscellaneous.

8. Click **Add** to enter the final scenario.

9. Type **Reduced Pricing** in the Scenario name box, press **TAB** twice, type **Scenario assuming a price reduction** in the Comment box, and then click **OK**.

10. Enter **7500** for Units_Sold, **690** for Sales_Price_per_Unit, **575000** for Salaries_and_Benefits, **290000** for Shipping_and_Distribution, **180000** for Stocking_and_Storage, and **155000** for Miscellaneous.
11. Click **OK**. The Scenario Manager dialog box reappears, listing all four scenarios.

Now that you have entered all four scenarios, you can view their impact on the income statement.

Viewing Scenarios

Scenarios are chosen by selecting them in the Scenario Manager dialog box. You switch from one scenario to another by clicking Show in the Scenario Manager dialog box. You do not have to close the dialog box to switch scenarios. You will start by viewing the results of the Expanded Operations scenario.

To view the impact of the Expanded Operations scenario:

1. In the Scenario Manager dialog box, in the Scenarios box, click **Expanded Operations**. The changing cells and the comment for the selected scenario appear at the bottom of the Scenario Manager dialog box.

   Tip You can double-click a scenario name in the Scenario Manager dialog box to view that scenario.

2. Click **Show**. The values in the Income worksheet change to reflect the scenario.
3. Click **Close**. The Scenario Manager dialog box closes. The income statement is updated to show expanded operations with increased fixed expenses. Refer to Figure 8–22.

Figure 8–22 Income statement under the Expanded Operations scenario

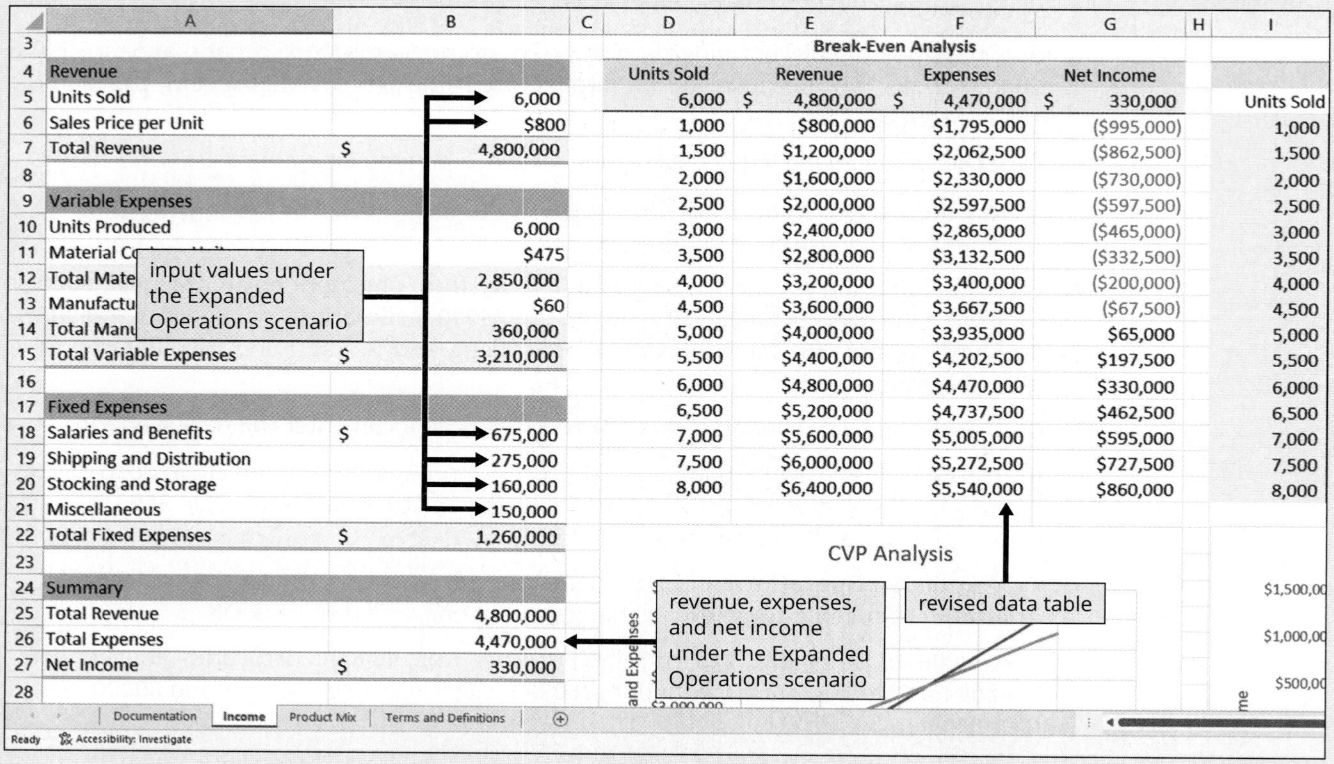

	A		B
3			
4	Revenue		
5	Units Sold		6,000
6	Sales Price per Unit		$800
7	Total Revenue	$	4,800,000
8			
9	Variable Expenses		
10	Units Produced		6,000
11	Material C…		$475
12	Total Mate…		2,850,000
13	Manufactu…		$60
14	Total Manu…		360,000
15	Total Variable Expenses	$	3,210,000
16			
17	Fixed Expenses		
18	Salaries and Benefits	$	675,000
19	Shipping and Distribution		275,000
20	Stocking and Storage		160,000
21	Miscellaneous		150,000
22	Total Fixed Expenses	$	1,260,000
23			
24	Summary		
25	Total Revenue		4,800,000
26	Total Expenses		4,470,000
27	Net Income	$	330,000
28			

Break-Even Analysis

Units Sold	Revenue	Expenses	Net Income
6,000	$ 4,800,000	$ 4,470,000	$ 330,000
1,000	$800,000	$1,795,000	($995,000)
1,500	$1,200,000	$2,062,500	($862,500)
2,000	$1,600,000	$2,330,000	($730,000)
2,500	$2,000,000	$2,597,500	($597,500)
3,000	$2,400,000	$2,865,000	($465,000)
3,500	$2,800,000	$3,132,500	($332,500)
4,000	$3,200,000	$3,400,000	($200,000)
4,500	$3,600,000	$3,667,500	($67,500)
5,000	$4,000,000	$3,935,000	$65,000
5,500	$4,400,000	$4,202,500	$197,500
6,000	$4,800,000	$4,470,000	$330,000
6,500	$5,200,000	$4,737,500	$462,500
7,000	$5,600,000	$5,005,000	$595,000
7,500	$6,000,000	$5,272,500	$727,500
8,000	$6,400,000	$5,540,000	$860,000

Trouble? If the values in your income statement do not match those in the figure, you probably entered the values for the scenario incorrectly. You will learn how to edit a scenario shortly and can then enter the correct values.

Excel automatically changes the values of the six input cells to match the scenario. Under the Expanded Operations scenario, the company's net income in cell B27 increases from the current value of $270,000 to $330,000. Note that the one-variable and two-variable data tables are also revised to reflect the changed values in the Expanded Operations scenario. You will review the other scenarios to examine their impact on the income statement and the data tables.

To view the impact of the remaining scenarios:

1. On the Data tab, in the Forecast group, click the **What-If Analysis** button, and then click **Scenario Manager**. The Scenario Manager dialog box opens.

2. In the Scenarios box, double-click **Reduced Operations** to update the worksheet, and then click **Close** to close the Scenario Manager dialog box. Under the Reduced Operations scenario, the company's net income will decline to $85,000 (cell B27). Refer to Figure 8–23.

Figure 8–23   Income statement under the Reduced Operations scenario

	A	B	C	D	E	F	G	H	I
3					Break-Even Analysis				
4	Revenue			Units Sold	Revenue	Expenses	Net Income		
5	Units Sold	4,000		4,000 $	2,960,000 $	2,875,000 $	85,000		Units Sold
6	Sales Price per Unit	$740		1,000	$740,000	$1,270,000	($530,000)		1,000
7	Total Revenue	$ 2,960,000		1,500	$1,110,000	$1,537,500	($427,500)		1,500
8				2,000	$1,480,000	$1,805,000	($325,000)		2,000
9	Variable Expenses			2,500	$1,850,000	$2,072,500	($222,500)		2,500
10	Units Produced	4,000		3,000	$2,220,000	$2,340,000	($120,000)		3,000
11	Material Cost per Unit	$475		3,500	$2,590,000	$2,607,500	($17,500)		3,500
12	Total Material Cost	1,900,000		4,000	$2,960,000	$2,875,000	$85,000		4,000
13	Manufacturing Cost per Unit	$60		4,500	$3,330,000	$3,142,500	$187,500		4,500
14	Total Manufacturing Cost	240,000		5,000	$3,700,000	$3,410,000	$290,000		5,000
15	Total Variable Expenses	$ 2,140,000		5,500	$4,070,000	$3,677,500	$392,500		5,500
16				6,000	$4,440,000	$3,945,000	$495,000		6,000
17	Fixed Expenses			6,500	$4,810,000	$4,212,500	$597,500		6,500
18	Salaries and Benefits	$ 450,000		7,000	$5,180,000	$4,480,000	$700,000		7,000
19	Shipping and Distribution	150,000		7,500	$5,550,000	$4,747,500	$802,500		7,500
20	Stocking and Storage	75,000		8,000	$5,920,000	$5,015,000	$905,000		8,000
21	Miscellaneous	60,000							
22	Total Fixed Expenses	$ 735,000			CVP Analysis				
23									
24	Summary			$7,000,000					$2,000,00
25	Total Revenue	2,960,000		$6,000,000					$1,500,00
26	Total Expenses	2,875,000			net income falls				
27	Net Income	$ 85,000	←		to $85,000				$1,000,00
28					$2,000,000				

Documentation | **Income** | Product Mix | Terms and Definitions   (+)

Ready   Accessibility: Investigate

3. Repeat Steps 1 and 2 to update the worksheet with the **Reduced Pricing** scenario. Under that scenario, the company would lose money with the net income (cell B27) falling to a negative $37,500. Refer to Figure 8–24.

Figure 8–24   Income statement under the Reduced Pricing scenario

	A	B	C	D	E	F	G	H	I
3					**Break-Even Analysis**				
4	Revenue			Units Sold	Revenue	Expenses	Net Income		
5	Units Sold	7,500		7,500 $	5,175,000 $	5,212,500 $	(37,500)		-Units Sold
6	Sales Price per Unit	$690		1,000	$690,000	$1,735,000	($1,045,000)		1,000
7	Total Revenue	$ 5,175,000		1,500	$1,035,000	$2,002,500	($967,500)		1,500
8				2,000	$1,380,000	$2,270,000	($890,000)		2,000
9	Variable Expenses			2,500	$1,725,000	$2,537,500	($812,500)		2,500
10	Units Produced	7,500		3,000	$2,070,000	$2,805,000	($735,000)		3,000
11	Material Cost per Unit	$475		3,500	$2,415,000	$3,072,500	($657,500)		3,500
12	Total Material Cost	3,562,500		4,000	$2,760,000	$3,340,000	($580,000)		4,000
13	Manufacturing Cost per Unit	$60		4,500	$3,105,000	$3,607,500	($502,500)		4,500
14	Total Manufacturing Cost	450,000		5,000	$3,450,000	$3,875,000	($425,000)		5,000
15	Total Variable Expenses	$ 4,012,500		5,500	$3,795,000	$4,142,500	($347,500)		5,500
16				6,000	$4,140,000	$4,410,000	($270,000)		6,000
17	Fixed Expenses			6,500	$4,485,000	$4,677,500	($192,500)		6,500
18	Salaries and Benefits	$ 575,000		7,000	$4,830,000	$4,945,000	($115,000)		7,000
19	Shipping and Distribution	290,000		7,500	$5,175,000	$5,212,500	($37,500)		7,500
20	Stocking and Storage	180,000		8,000	$5,520,000	$5,480,000	$40,000		8,000
21	Miscellaneous	155,000							
22	Total Fixed Expenses	$ 1,200,000							
23					CVP Analysis				
24	Summary								
25	Total Revenue	5,175,000							
26	Total Expenses	5,212,500		the company will lose $37,500 under this scenario					
27	Net Income	$ (37,500)							
28									

The different scenarios result in very different financial outcomes. The Expanded Operations scenario offers the greatest net income, but it also has total expenses of $4.47 million. If sales do not match projections, the company could lose a lot of money. The Reduced Operations scenario reduces the total expenses to $2.875 million but can only offer a net income of $85,000. Finally, the Reduced Pricing scenario will cost the company money in the long run unless some way is found to reduce total expenses.

Editing a Scenario

After you create a scenario, you can edit its assumptions to view other possible outcomes. When you edit a scenario, the worksheet calculations are automatically updated to reflect the revised input values.

The Reduced Pricing scenario is a net loser for the company. Yuri wants to examine the impact of decreasing some of the fixed expenses while increasing sales (assuming the company will sell more desks if it reduces the price). You will increase the units sold value and decrease fixed expenses in the Reduced Pricing scenario to examine those changes on profits.

To edit the Reduced Pricing scenario:

1. On the Data tab, in the Forecast group, click the **What-If Analysis** button, and then click **Scenario Manager**. The Scenario Manager dialog box opens.

2. In the Scenarios box, click **Reduced Pricing** if it is not already selected, and then click **Edit**. The Edit Scenario dialog box opens. You do not need to make any changes in this dialog box.

3. Click **OK**. The Scenario Values dialog box opens.

4. Change the Units_Sold value from $7500 to **7800**. Change the Salaries_and_Benefits value from $575,000 to **525000**. Change the Miscellaneous value from $155,000 to **125000**.

5. Click **OK** to return to the Scenario Manager dialog box.

6. Click **Show**, and then click **Close**. The Income worksheet updates to reflect the revised scenario, which results in net income increasing to a positive $89,000 (cell B27). Refer to Figure 8–25.

Figure 8–25   Income statement for a revised scenario

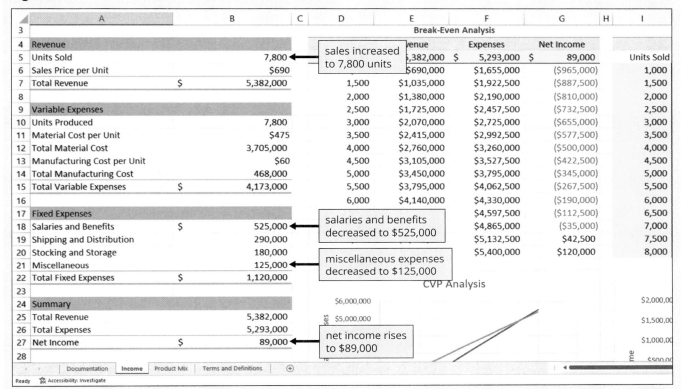

7. Open the Scenario Manager dialog box, and then double-click **Status Quo** in the Scenarios box to return the Income worksheet to the original values. Leave the Scenario Manager dialog box open.

The company is not losing money under the revised scenario, but its net income is not impressive, telling Yuri that the company is unlikely to be profitable if it reduces the average selling price of its standing desks.

Creating Scenario Summary Reports

Although scenarios can help you make important business decisions, repeatedly switching between scenarios is time-consuming. You can summarize all your scenarios in a single report, either as an Excel table or PivotTable. Yuri wants both types of reports for the scenarios you created, starting with a summary report in the form of an Excel table.

Reference

Creating a Scenario Summary Report or a Scenario PivotTable Report

- On the Data tab, in the Forecast group, click the What-If Analysis button, and then click Scenario Manager.
- Click Summary.
- Click the Scenario summary or Scenario PivotTable report option button.
- Select the result cells to display in the report.
- Click OK.

To create a scenario summary report, identify the result cells you want included in the report. Yuri is interested in the following results: total revenue (cell B25), total expenses (cell B26), and net income (cell B27). Your report will display these values along with the input values under each scenario.

To create the scenario summary report:

1. In the Scenario Manager dialog box, click **Summary**. The Scenario Summary dialog box opens, allowing you to create a scenario summary report or a scenario PivotTable report. You want to create a scenario summary report.

2. Verify that the **Scenario summary** option button is selected.

3. Make sure that the reference in the Result cells box is selected, and then in the Income worksheet, select the range **B25:B27** to enter the range reference for the result cells you want to display in the report.

4. Click **OK**. The scenario summary report is inserted in the workbook as a new worksheet.

5. Move the Scenario Summary worksheet directly after the Income worksheet.

6. Increase the Zoom factor of the worksheet to **140%** to better view its contents. Refer to Figure 8–26.

Figure 8–26   Scenario summary report

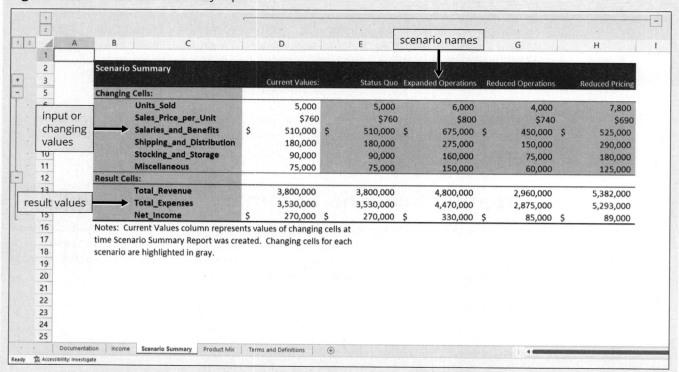

The scenario summary report displays the values of the changing cells and result cells under each scenario. The report uses the defined names you created earlier to identify the changing and result cells, making the report simpler to interpret. The report also includes outline buttons to expand and collapse different sections of the report, which is a useful feature for scenarios involving multiple input and result values.

Next, Yuri wants a PivotTable report of the scenario results. You will create that PivotTable report.

To create the Scenario PivotTable report:

1. Go to the **Income** worksheet and open the Scenario Manager dialog box.

2. Click **Summary** to open the Scenario Summary dialog box, and then click the **Scenario PivotTable report** option button. You will use the same result cells for this report.

3. Click **OK**. The Scenario PivotTable sheet is inserted in the workbook and contains the scenario values in a PivotTable.

4. Move the Scenario PivotTable worksheet after the Scenario Summary worksheet, and then change the zoom level of the worksheet to **140%**. Refer to Figure 8–27.

Figure 8–27   Scenario PivotTable report

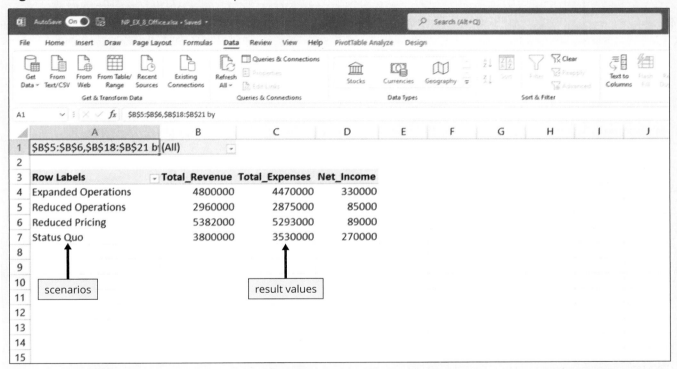

Yuri wants you to edit the scenario PivotTable to make it easier to read. You will do that now.

To edit and format the PivotTable report:

1. In the PivotTable Fields pane, in the FILTERS area box, click the **$B$5:$B$6,$B$18:$B...** button, and then click **Remove Field**. You will not filter the PivotTable.

   Tip The PivotTable filter button is useful only when you have merged scenarios from multiple users and want to filter scenarios by user.

2. In the Values area box, click the **Total_Revenue** button, and then click **Value Field Settings**. The Value Field Settings dialog box opens.

3. Click **Number Format** to open the Format Cells dialog box, click **Currency** in the Category box, change the number of decimal places to **0**, and then click the last entry **($1,234)** in the Negative numbers box to display negative currency values in a red font enclosed in parentheses.

4. Click **OK** in each dialog box to return to the worksheet. The currency format is applied to the Total_Revenue cells.

5. Repeat Steps 2 through 4 for the **Total_Expenses** and the **Net_Income** buttons to apply the same currency format.

6. In cell **A1**, enter **Scenario PivotTable**, and then format the text with the **Title** cell style. Refer to Figure 8–28.

Figure 8–28   Formatted scenario PivotTable report

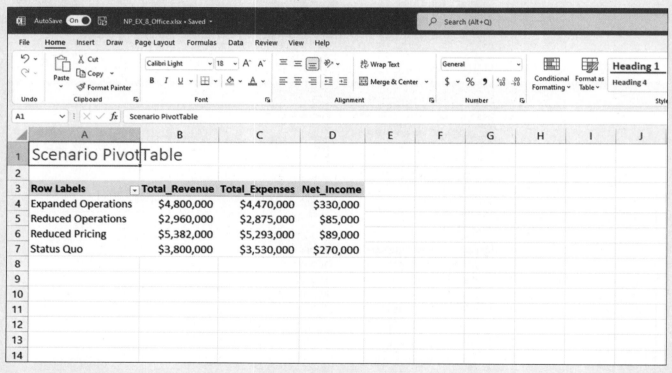

The Scenario Summary and Scenario PivotTable reports are both static reports. If you change the source data or the terms of the scenarios, those changes will not be reflected in either report. You must recreate the reports to reflect the impact of your edits.

Yuri wants you to augment the Scenario PivotTable report with a chart of the scenario results. You will add a PivotChart to the worksheet now.

To create a PivotChart with the scenario results:

1. Click cell **A3** to select the PivotTable.

2. On the ribbon, click the **PivotTable Analyze** tab, and then in the Tools group, click the **PivotChart** button. The Insert Chart dialog box opens.

3. On the All Charts tab, click the **Combo** chart type to create a combination chart.

4. Verify that the **Total_Revenue** and **Total_Expenses** series are displayed as clustered column charts and the **Net_Income** series is displayed as a line chart.

5. Click the **Secondary Axis** check box for the Net_Income series to chart those data values on a secondary axis.

6. Click **OK** to create the chart.

7. Move and resize the PivotChart to cover the range **A8:D22**.

8. On the ribbon, click the **PivotChart Analyze** tab, and then in the Show/Hide group, click the **Field Buttons** button. The field buttons in the chart are hidden.

9. Add the chart title **Scenario Comparisons**.

10. Position the chart legend at the bottom of the chart.

11. Add axis titles to the chart, and then name the primary vertical axis as **Revenue and Expenses**, name the secondary vertical axis as **Net Income**, and name the horizontal axis as **Scenarios**. Refer to Figure 8–29.

Figure 8–29   Scenario PivotChart

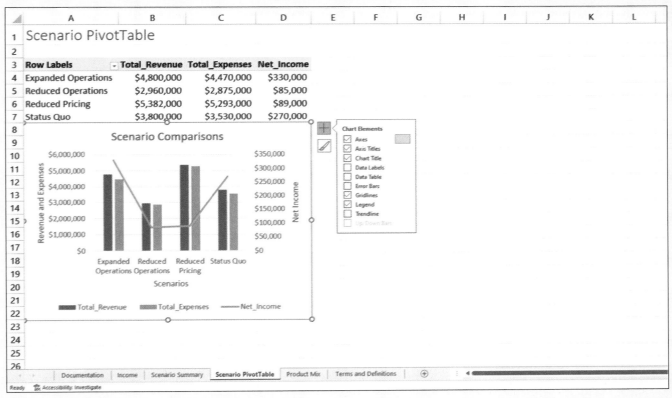

12. Save the workbook.

Yuri can now present an informative summary of the four scenarios to the financial team at Office Motion. Using that report the team can determine whether other scenarios need to be explored. At this time, the company might want to move to the Expanded Operations scenario if it can control its production costs.

Proskills

Teamwork: Merging Scenarios

In many businesses, several workbooks often track the same set of figures and evaluate the same set of scenarios. Colleagues can share scenarios by merging the scenarios from multiple workbooks into one workbook. The Scenario Manager dialog box includes a Merge button that you can use to merge scenarios from different workbooks. The scenarios will be merged into the active sheet, so they can be compared within a single document. It is easier to merge scenarios if all the what-if analyses on the different worksheets and workbooks are identical. All the changing cells from the merged scenario must correspond to changing cells in the active workbook and worksheet.

Once the scenarios are merged, they can be analyzed using a Scenario PivotTable report. One of the advantages of the Scenario PivotTable report over the Scenario Summary report is that you can use it with merged scenarios created by different users. For example, each member of the financial analysis team might propose different numbers for the various scenarios being considered. A Scenario PivotTable report can filter the four scenarios by user or show the average results across all users, giving the team a broader understanding of the various financial scenarios.

By sharing and merging scenarios, the team can more easily explore the impact of different financial situations, ensuring that everyone is always working from a common set of assumptions and goals.

In this part, you used scenarios to examine the impact of different financial scenarios on the profitability of Office Motion's line of standing desks. Office Motion offers several models of standing desks. Next, you will explore how promoting certain models over others can increase Office Motion's profitability.

Part 8.2 Quick Check

1. What is an advantage of scenarios over data tables?

2. What should you do before creating a scenario report to make the entries on the report easier to interpret?

3. What are changing cells in a scenario?

4. Where are the result cells in a scenario?

5. What are the two types of scenario reports?

6. If you change the values of the input cells, are those values automatically shown in scenario reports?

7. You are asked to explore the impact of changing the values of two input cells on a single result. Why would you use a data table instead of a scenario for your analysis?

8. You are asked to explore the impact of changing the values of four input cells on a single result cell. Why would you use a scenario instead of a data table for your analysis?

Part 8.3 Visual Overview: Optimal Solutions with Solver

Product mix is the combination of different products offered by a company for sale to the consumer.

Variable cells contain values that will be changed to reach an optimal solution. Here, the range B14:E14 contains variable cells.

The **objective cell** contains a value to maximize, minimize, or set to a specific value. Here, cell C27 is the objective cell.

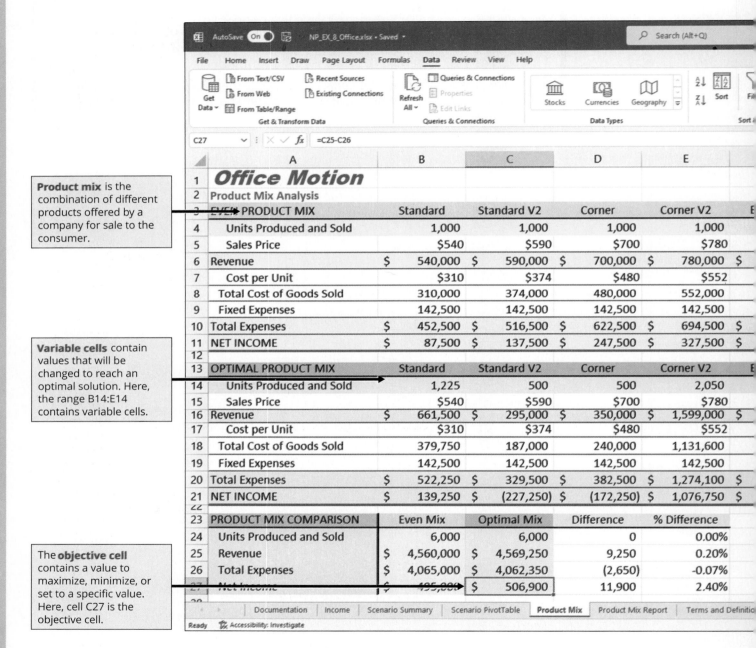

C27   =C25-C26

Office Motion
Product Mix Analysis

EVEN PRODUCT MIX	Standard	Standard V2	Corner	Corner V2
Units Produced and Sold	1,000	1,000	1,000	1,000
Sales Price	$540	$590	$700	$780
Revenue	$ 540,000	$ 590,000	$ 700,000	$ 780,000
Cost per Unit	$310	$374	$480	$552
Total Cost of Goods Sold	310,000	374,000	480,000	552,000
Fixed Expenses	142,500	142,500	142,500	142,500
Total Expenses	$ 452,500	$ 516,500	$ 622,500	$ 694,500
NET INCOME	$ 87,500	$ 137,500	$ 247,500	$ 327,500

OPTIMAL PRODUCT MIX	Standard	Standard V2	Corner	Corner V2
Units Produced and Sold	1,225	500	500	2,050
Sales Price	$540	$590	$700	$780
Revenue	$ 661,500	$ 295,000	$ 350,000	$ 1,599,000
Cost per Unit	$310	$374	$480	$552
Total Cost of Goods Sold	379,750	187,000	240,000	1,131,600
Fixed Expenses	142,500	142,500	142,500	142,500
Total Expenses	$ 522,250	$ 329,500	$ 382,500	$ 1,274,100
NET INCOME	$ 139,250	$ (227,250)	$ (172,250)	$ 1,076,750

PRODUCT MIX COMPARISON	Even Mix	Optimal Mix	Difference	% Difference
Units Produced and Sold	6,000	6,000	0	0.00%
Revenue	$ 4,560,000	$ 4,569,250	9,250	0.20%
Total Expenses	$ 4,065,000	$ 4,062,350	(2,650)	-0.07%
Net Income	$ 495,000	$ 506,900	11,900	2.40%

Documentation | Income | Scenario Summary | Scenario PivotTable | **Product Mix** | Product Mix Report | Terms and Definition

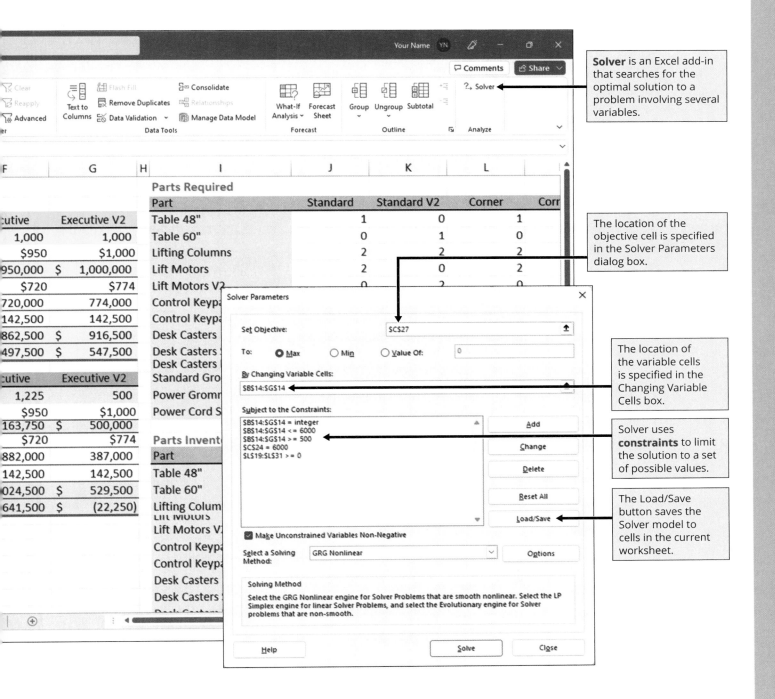

Solver is an Excel add-in that searches for the optimal solution to a problem involving several variables.

The location of the objective cell is specified in the Solver Parameters dialog box.

The location of the variable cells is specified in the Changing Variable Cells box.

Solver uses **constraints** to limit the solution to a set of possible values.

The Load/Save button saves the Solver model to cells in the current worksheet.

Optimizing a Product Mix

Not all products are alike. One product may differ from another in its sales price, its production costs, and its attractiveness to the consumer. Because of these differences, a company might find it more profitable to devote a large share of resources to promoting one product over another. For example, Office Motion might make a larger profit on each high-end standing desk it sells compared to its profit on less expensive models. The lineup of products and services offered by a company is known as the product mix.

Ideally, the product mix will maximize profits while still meeting the demands of the market. Even if Office Motion makes more money from some desks than from others, the demand for those desks might be smaller. Office Motion produces and sells six models of standing desks: the Standard and Standard V2 models selling for $540 and $590, respectively; the Corner and Corner V2 models selling for $700 and $780; and the Executive and Executive V2 models selling for $950 and $1,000.

Based on sales projections, Yuri estimates that Office Motion can sell 6,000 desks across the six models. If all the models were equally popular and equally profitable, the company would sell 1,000 of each type. However, that is not the case. Yuri wants you to find the optimal product mix, one that maximizes profits while still meeting consumer demand.

Yuri created the Product Mix worksheet listing the sales price, costs, and variable expenses of each desk model. He asks you to find the most profitable product mix if total sales across all models stays at 6,000 units. You will first explore how changing the number of desks produced and sold within each model affects the overall profitability of the line.

To explore a different product mix:

1. If you took a break after the previous part, make sure the NP_EX_8_Office workbook is open.

2. Go to the **Product Mix** worksheet. The worksheet contains a table showing financial numbers assuming an even product mix with each model producing and selling the same number of desks. A second table will be used to find an optimal product mix in which a different number of desks will be produced and sold across models.

3. In cell **B17**, enter **400** as the number of Standard desks produced and sold.

4. In cell **C17**, enter **1,600** for the number of Standard V2 desks produced and sold.

5. In cell **D17**, enter **500** for the number of Corner desks produced and sold.

6. In cell **E17**, enter **1,500** for the number of Corner V2 desks produced and sold.

7. In cell **F17**, enter **600** for the number of Executive desks produced and sold.

8. In cell **G17**, enter **1,400** for the number of Executive V2 desks produced and sold. Refer to Figure 8–30.

Figure 8–30 Different product mix evaluation

	A	B	C	D	E	F	G	H	I
11	Total Cost of Goods Sold	310,000	374,000	480,000	552,000	720,000	774,000		Desk Casters
12	Fixed Expenses	2,500	142,500	142,500	142,500	142,500	142,500		Desk Casters S
13	Total Expenses	2,500 $	516,500 $	622,500 $	694,500 $	862,500 $	916,500		Desk Casters H
14	NET INCOME	7,500 $	73,500 $	77,500 $	85,500 $	87,500 $	83,500		Standard Grom
15									Power Gromm
16	OPTIMAL PRODUCT MIX	Standard	Standard V2	Corner	Corner V2	Executive	Executive V2		Power Cord Se
17	Units Sold	400	1,600	500	1,500	600	1,400		
18	Sales Price	$540	$590	$700	$780	$950	$1,000		Parts Invento
19	Revenue	$ 216,000 $	944,000 $	350,000 $	1,170,000 $	570,000 $	1,400,000		Part
20	Units Produced	400	1,600	500	1,500	600	1,400		Table 48"
21	Material Cost per Unit	$270	$320	$420	$490	$650	$700		Table 60"
22	Manufacturing Cost per Unit	$40	$54	$60	$62	$70	$74		Lifting Column
23	Total Cost of Goods Sold	124,000	598,400	240,000	828,000	432,000	1,083,600		Lift Motors
24	Fixed Expenses	142,500	142,500	142,500	142,500	142,500	142,500		Lift Motors V2
25	Total Expenses	$ 266,500 $	740,900 $	382,500 $	970,500 $	574,500 $	1,226,100		Control Keypad
26	NET INCOME	$ (50,500) $	203,100 $	(32,500) $	199,500 $	(4,500) $	173,900		Control Keypad
27									Desk Casters
28	PRODUCT MIX COMPARISON	Even Mix	Optimal Mix	Difference	% Difference				Desk Casters S
29	Units Produced and Sold	6,000	6,000	0	0.00%				Desk Casters H
30	Revenue	$ 4,560,000 $	4,650,000	90,000	1.97%				Standard Grom
31	Total Expenses	$ 4,065,000 $	4,161,000	96,000	2.36%				Power Gromm
32	Net Income	$ 495,000 $	489,000	(6,000)	-1.21%				Power Cord Se

Callouts: "product mix with different units sold for different models"; "net income declines by $6,000 and 1.21% using the different product mix"; "net income with an even product mix"; "net income with a different product mix"

Under this product mix, total revenue increased by $90,000 to $4,650,000 (cell C30), but the total expenses also increased to $4,161,000 (cell C31). Therefore, the net income declined by 1.21% to $489,000 (cell C32). Perhaps, a product mix that emphasizes the more expensive models would result in higher net income.

To test a product mix for higher-end desks:

1. In cells **B17** and **C17**, change the units produced and sold values to **700** and **800**, respectively.

2. In cells **D17** and **E17**, change the units produced and sold values to **1,000** each.

3. In cells **F17** and **G17**, change the units produced and sold values to **1,200** and **1,300** respectively. Refer to Figure 8–31.

Figure 8–31   Product mix emphasizing more expensive desk models

	A	B	C	D	E	F	G	H	I
11	Total Cost of Goods Sold	310,000	374,000	480,000	552,000	720,000	774,000		Desk Casters
12	Fixed Expenses	142,500	142,500	142,500	142,500	142,500	142,500		Desk Casters S
13	Total Expenses	product mix 500 $	516,500 $	622,500 $	694,500 $	862,500 $	916,500		Desk Casters H
14	NET INCOME	emphasizing more 500 $	73,500 $	77,500 $	85,500 $	87,500 $	83,500		Standard Grom
15		expensive models							Power Gromm
16	OPTIMAL PRODUCT MIX	Standard	Standard V2	Corner	Corner V2	Executive	Executive V2		Power Cord Se
17	Units Sold	700	800	1,000	1,000	1,200	1,300		
18	Sales Price	$540	$590	$700	$780	$950	$1,000		Parts Invento
19	Revenue	$ 378,000 $	472,000 $	700,000 $	780,000 $	1,140,000 $	1,300,000		Part
20	Units Produced	700	800	1,000	1,000	1,200	1,300		Table 48"
21	Material Cost per Unit	$270	$320	$420	$490	$650	$700		Table 60"
22	Manufacturing Cost per Unit	$40	$54	$60	$62	$70	$74		Lifting Column
23	Total Cost of Goods Sold	217,000	299,200	480,000	552,000	864,000	1,006,200		Lift Motors
24	Fixed Expenses	142,500	142,500	142,500	142,500	142,500	142,500		Lift Motors V2
25	Total Expenses	$ 359,500 $	441,700 $	622,500 $	694,500 $	1,006,500 $	1,148,700		Control Keypad
26	NET INCOME	$ 18,500 $	30,300 $	77,500 $	85,500 $	133,500 $	151,300		Control Keypad
27									Desk Casters
28	PRODUCT MIX COMPARISON	Even Mix	Optimal Mix	Difference	% Difference				Desk Casters S
29	Units Produced and Sold	6,000	6,000	0	0.00%				Desk Casters H
30	Revenue	$ 4,560,000 $	4,770,000	210,000	4.61%				Standard Grom
31	Total Expenses	$ 4,065,000 $	4,273,400	208,400	5.13%	net income increases		Power Gromm
32	Net Income	$ 495,000 $	496,600	1,600	0.32%	by 0.32% to $496,600		Power Cord Se
33									
34									
35									
36		net income with an even product mix	net income for the more expensive models mix						

4. In the range **B17:G17**, enter **1,000** in each cell, restoring the model to an even product mix.

Under a product mix that emphasizes higher-end desks, the net income increased by 0.32% or 1,600 to $496,600 (cell C32), a marginal improvement. Perhaps another product mix would do even better. You could continue to use a trial-and-error approach by examining different product mixes, but there are so many combinations it would take time to answer the fundamental question: "Which product mix is the best?" Keep in mind that "best" does not simply mean the most profitable because the company still must meet consumer demand and have the resources to manufacture those desks. To find the best solution to this problem, you need to use Solver.

Finding the Optimal Solution with Solver

Solver is an **add-in**, which is a program that adds commands and features to Microsoft Office applications such as Excel. Solver works to find a numeric solution to a problem involving several input values, such as the problem of finding a product mix that maximizes profits. It can also be used for other problems such as scheduling employees subject to their availability or finding a travel route that minimizes time or distance traveled. Before you can use Solver, it must be activated.

Reference

Activating Solver

- On the Data tab, confirm whether Solver appears in the Analyze group. If it appears, Solver is already active. If it does not appear, continue with these steps.
- On the ribbon, click the File tab, and then click Options in the navigation bar.
- Click Add-ins in the left pane, click the Manage arrow, and then click Excel Add-ins.
- Click Go to open the Add-Ins dialog box.
- Click the Solver Add-in check box, and then click OK.
- Follow the remaining prompts to install Solver if it is not already installed.

Activating Solver

Solver is supplied with every desktop version of Microsoft Excel, but it might not be "turned on" or activated. You need to check whether Solver is already active on your version of Excel. If the Solver button does not appear in the Analyze group on the Data tab, the Solver add-in needs to be activated. If you are working on a network, you might need your instructor or network administrator to activate Solver for you. If you are working on a stand-alone PC, you can activate Solver yourself.

To activate the Solver add-in:

1. On the ribbon, click the **Data** tab, and then check for the Analyze group and the Solver button. If the Solver button is available (refer to Figure 8–32), Solver is active, and you should read but not perform the rest of this set of steps. If the Solver button is not on the ribbon, continue with Step 2.

Figure 8–32   Solver add-in button on the Data tab

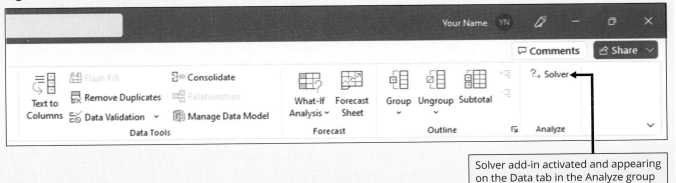

Solver add-in activated and appearing on the Data tab in the Analyze group

2. On the ribbon, click the **File** tab, and then click **Options** at the bottom of the navigation bar. The Excel Options dialog box opens.

   Tip You can also open the Excel Options dialog box by right clicking the ribbon, and then clicking Customize the Ribbon on the shortcut menu.

3. In the left pane, click **Add-ins**. Information about all the add-ins currently installed within Excel appears in the right pane.

4. If necessary, click the **Manage arrow** at the bottom of the dialog box, and then click **Excel Add-ins**.

5. Click **Go** next to the Manage arrow. The Add-ins dialog box opens and displays a list of all the available Excel add-ins. Although these add-ins are available, they might not have been activated.

6. Click the **Solver Add-in** check box to insert a checkmark.

   > **Trouble?** If Solver is not in the list of available add-ins, you may have to reinstall Excel on your computer. Ask your instructor or technical resource person for help.

7. Click **OK**. Solver is activated, and its button is added on the Data tab in the Analyze group. Refer back to Figure 8–32.

Now that Solver is activated, you can use it to find the optimal product mix.

Insight

Excel Add-Ins

Solver is only one of many available Excel add-ins. Other add-ins provide the ability to perform statistical analyses, generate business reports, and produce interactive maps. You can also create your own add-ins using the Visual Basic for Applications (VBA) macro language. The process for activating other add-ins is the same as the process you used to activate the Solver add-in. Most third-party add-ins provide detailed instructions for their installation and use.

Setting the Objective Cell and Variable Cells

Every Solver model needs an objective cell and one or more variable cells. An objective cell is a result cell that is maximized, minimized, or set to a specific value. A variable cell is an input cell that changes so that the objective cell can meet its defined goal.

In the Product Mix worksheet, cell C32, which displays the net income under the Optimal Mix model, is the objective cell whose value you want to maximize. The cells in the range B17:E17, which contain the number of standing desks of each model produced and sold by the company, are the variable cells whose values you want to change to maximize profits.

Reference

Setting Solver's Objective and Variable Cells

- On the Data tab, in the Analyze group, click the Solver button.
- In the Set Objective box, specify the cell whose value you want to set to match a specific objective.
- Click the Max, Min, or Value Of option button to maximize the objective cell, minimize the objective cell, or set the objective cell to a specified value, respectively.
- In the By Changing Variable Cells input box, specify the changing cells.

You will start Solver, and then define the objective cell and the variable cells.

To set up the Solver model:

1. On the Data tab, in the Analyze group, click the **Solver** button. The Solver Parameters dialog box opens with the insertion point in the Set Objective box.

2. Click cell **C32** in the Product Mix worksheet. The absolute reference to the cell appears in the Set Objective box.

3. Verify that the **Max** option button is selected. This option tells Solver to find the maximum value possible for cell C32.

4. Click the **By Changing Variable Cells** box, and then select the range **B17:G17** in the Product Mix worksheet. The absolute reference to this range tells Solver to modify the product mix values stored in these cells to maximize the value in cell C32. Refer to Figure 8–33.

Figure 8–33   Solver Parameters dialog box

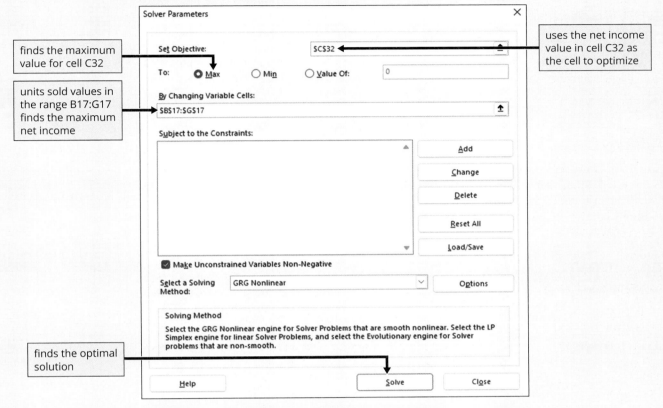

finds the maximum value for cell C32

units sold values in the range B17:G17 finds the maximum net income

uses the net income value in cell C32 as the cell to optimize

finds the optimal solution

▌ **Tip** Changing cells can contain only constant values, not formulas.

5. Click **Solve**. Solver attempts to find the maximum net income by evaluating different product mix combinations. The Solver Results dialog box opens, reporting that Solver was not able to arrive at a solution. Refer to Figure 8–34.

Figure 8–34   Solver Results dialog box

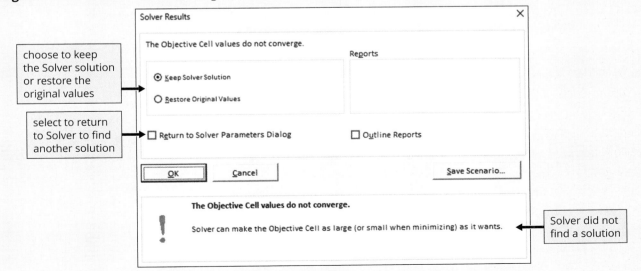

choose to keep the Solver solution or restore the original values

select to return to Solver to find another solution

Solver did not find a solution

6. Click the **Restore Original Values** option button to reset the original product mix numbers.

7. Click the **Return to Solver Parameters Dialog** check box if necessary to select it.

8. Click **OK**. The Product Mix worksheet returns to the original values for the optimal product mix cell, and the Solver Parameters dialog box reappears.

Solver could not find a solution because there were no limits on the number of desks produced and sold. With no limits, Solver kept increasing the values in the range B17:G17 to find the maximum net income since selling more units generally means more profit. To find a realistic solution, you must add constraints to the model.

Adding Constraints to Solver

Almost every model needs one or more constraints. A constraint is a condition limiting the solution to a set of possible values. For example, limiting the total number of desks produced to 6,000 units is a constraint on the possible solutions that Solver can find. Solver supports the six types of constraints described in Figure 8–35.

Figure 8–35   Solver constraint types

Constraint	Description	
<= , = , >=	Constrains the cell(s) to be less than or equal to a defined value, equal to a defined value, or greater than or equal to a defined value	
int	Constrains the cell(s) to be integers	
bin	Constrains the cell(s) to binary values (0 or 1)	
dif	Constrains the cells to be different integers within the range 1 to n, where n is the number of cells in the constraint	

You can use the <= constraint to limit the total number of desks produced and sold to a reasonable number, or you can use the = constraint to specify the exact number of desks produced and ultimately sold. Other constraints are used for special types of data.

The bin, or binary, constraint limits a cell value to 0 or 1 and is used to indicate the presence or absence of a property. For example, a binary constraint could be used in a work schedule to indicate whether an employee can work a particular shift or not. Finally, the dif, or All Different, constraint is used to limit cells to different integer values within the range of 1 to n and is often applied for factors that need to follow a defined order when 1 is assigned to the first factor and n is assigned to the last factor.

Reference

Setting Constraints on the Solver Solution

- In the Solver Parameters dialog box, click Add.
- Enter the cell reference of the cell or cells containing the constraint.
- Select the constraint type (<=, =, >=, int, bin, or dif).
- Enter the constraint value in the Constraint box.
- Click OK to add the constraint and return to the Solver Parameters dialog box.
- Repeat for each constraint you want to add to the model.

Yuri wants you to add two constraints to the model. The first is that the production run of each individual desk model cannot exceed 6,000 units. The second is that the total number of desks produced and sold across all models cannot exceed 6,000 units. You will add both constraints to the model and rerun Solver now.

To add constraints to a Solver model:

1. In the Solver Parameters dialog box, click **Add**. The Add Constraint dialog box opens.

2. With the insertion point in the Cell Reference box, select the range **B17:G17** in the Product Mix worksheet, containing the number of units sold for each of the six models. Excel inserts the absolute reference $B$17:$G$17 in the Cell Reference box.

3. Press **TAB** twice to move the insertion point into the Constraint box and type **6000**. Refer to Figure 8–36.

Figure 8–36   Limits the units sold of each desk model

> **Tip** Constraints can be applied only to adjacent ranges. For a nonadjacent range, apply separate constraints to each part of the range.

4. Click **Add** to add the constraint to the Solver model. The Add Constraint dialog box remains open. Next, you will set the total number of desks produced and sold to exactly 6,000 units.

5. Click cell **C29** in the Product Mix worksheet to enter the absolute cell reference to the Optimal Units Produced and Sold value in the Cell Reference box.

6. Click the **arrow** next to the constraint type box (the center box), and then click = in the list to specify an equal to constraint.

7. In the Constraint box, type **6000** to limit the value of cell C29 to exactly 6,000. Refer to Figure 8–37.

Figure 8–37   Constrains the total number of units sold

8. Click **OK** to add the constraint and return to the Solver Parameters dialog box. The Subject to the Constraints box shows two constraints added to the model: $B$17:$G$17 <= 6000 and $C$29 = 6000.

9. Click **Solve**. The Solver Results dialog box opens, indicating that the solution that Solver found satisfies the objective and constraints. Refer to Figure 8–38.

Figure 8–38　　Product mix limiting production to 6,000 units

	A	B	C	D	E	F	G	H	I
11	Total Cost of	0,000	374,000	480,000	552,000	720,000	774,000		Desk Casters
12	Fixed Expens	Standard desks are	142,500	142,500	142,500	142,500	142,500		Desk Casters Soft Roll
13	Total Expense	the only models	$ 516,500 $	622,500 $	694,500 $	862,500 $	916,500		Desk Casters Heavy Duty
14	NET INCOME	produced and sold	$ 73,500 $	77,500 $	85,500 $	87,500 $	83,500		Standard Grommet
15									Power Grommet
16	OPTIMAL PRODUCT MIX	Standard	Standard V2	Corner	Corner V2	Executive	Executive V2		Power Cord Set
17	Units Sold	6,000	-	-	-	-	-		
18	Sales Price	$540	$590	$700	$780	$950	$1,000		Parts Inventory
19	Revenue	$ 3,240,000 $	- $	- $	- $	- $	-		Part
20	Units Produced	6,000	-	-	-				
21	Material Cost per Unit	$270	$320	$420	$490				
22	Manufacturing Cost per Unit	$40	$54	$60	$62				
23	Total Cost of Goods Sold	1,860,000	-	-	-				
24	total number of desks	142,500	142,500	142,500	142,500				
25	produced and sold is	$ 2,002,500 $	142,500 $	142,500 $	142,500				
26	fixed at 6,000 units	$ 1,237,500 $	(142,500) $	(142,500) $	(142,500)				
27									
28	PRODUCT MIX COMPARISON	Even Mix	Optimal Mix	Difference	% Difference				
29	Units Produced and Sold	6,000	6,000	0	0.00%				
30	Revenue	$ 4,560,000 $	3,240,000	(1,320,000)	-28.95%				
31	Total Expenses	$ 4,065,000 $	2,715,000	(1,350,000)	-33.21%				
32	Net Income	$ 495,000 $	525,000	30,000	6.06%				
33									
34									
35									
36									

Solver Results dialog box:
Solver found a solution. All Constraints and optimality conditions are satisfied.
◉ Keep Solver Solution
○ Restore Original Values
☐ Return to Solver Parameters Dialog
Reports: Answer, Sensitivity, Limits
☐ Outline Reports
[OK] [Cancel] [Save Scenario...]

Solver found a solution. All Constraints and optimality conditions are satisfied.

When the GRG engine is used, Solver has found at least a local optimal solution. When Simplex LP is used, this means Solver has found a global optimal solution.

Tabs: Documentation | Income | Scenario Summary | Scenario PivotTable | Product Mix | Terms and Definitions

Ready　　Accessibility: Investigate

Solver has generated a solution in which only the Standard standing desk is produced and sold. Under this model, net income increases to $525,000 (cell C32), representing a 6.06% increase (cell E32) over the total income generated by an even product mix in which 1,000 of each model is produced and sold.

While this is an "optimal" solution and indicates that the Standard desk has the highest profit margin of all six models, it is not a reasonable solution. The company cannot limit its production to the Standard model because there is not enough demand for that product. Office Motion wants to diversify its product line to attract a wide range of customers and interests. In the long run, it would be counterproductive to focus on one product at the expense of all others.

You will fix this problem by adding the constraint that the company must produce at least 500 units of each model. Also, because the company cannot produce a fraction of a desk, you will add a constraint that the number of desks produced and sold must be an integer value.

To add more constraints to the model:

1. Click the **Restore Original Values** option button, verify that the **Return to Solver Parameters Dialog** check box is selected, and then click **OK** to return to the Solver Parameters dialog box.

2. Click **Add**. The Add Constraint dialog box opens with the insertion point in the Cell Reference box.

3. Select the range **B17:G17** in the Product Mix worksheet, select **>=** as the constraint type, and then enter **500** in the Constraint box. With this and the earlier constraint, you have set the number of each desk model to between 500 and 6,000 units.

4. Click **Add** to add the constraint to the Solver model. The Add Constraint dialog box remains open, so you can create another constraint.

5. Select the range **B17:G17** in the Product Mix worksheet, and then select **int** as the constraint type. The word "integer" is added to the Constraint box, specifying that each value in the range B17:G17 must be an integer.

6. Click **OK** to add the constraint to the model and return to the Solver Parameters dialog box. The Subject to the Constraints box now lists four constraints on the Solver solution.

7. Click **Solve**. Solver reports that it has found a solution that satisfies all the constraints.

8. Click the **Return to Solver Parameters Dialog** check box to remove the checkmark.

9. Click **OK**. The Solver Results dialog box closes, and the Solver solution remains in the worksheet. Refer to Figure 8–39.

Figure 8–39   Product mix with a production run of at least 500 units for each model

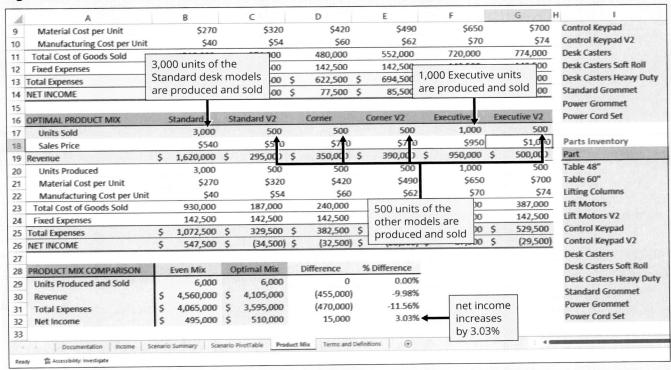

Under this product mix, Office Motion produces and sells 3,000 Standard desks, 1,000 Executive desks, and 500 each of the remaining four models. The company's net income grows to $510,000—an increase of 3.03% over the Even Product Mix model.

There is a problem with this model. Production runs are limited by the number of available parts. Yuri created a table listing the parts required by each of six standing desks and used this data to calculate the total number of parts in inventory, the total number required for the Optimal Product Mix, and the number of parts remaining after the production run. If there are not enough parts to satisfy demand, the undercount is displayed in the worksheet in red. The Optimal Product Mix that Solver found would leave the company short 1,400 48" tabletops, 1,800 lift motors, 900 control keypads, 7,100 desk casters, and 600 standard grommets. Refer to Figure 8–40.

Figure 8–40   Product mix exceeds the required parts in inventory

	E	F	G	H	I	J	K	L	M	N	O	P
12	142,500	table of parts	2,500		Desk Casters Soft Roll	0	4	4	4	0	0	
13	$ 694,500 $	required for	5,500		Desk Casters Heavy Duty	0	0	0	0	4	4	
14	$ 85,500 $	each standing	3,500		Standard Grommet	1	1	1	0	0	0	
15		desk model			Power Grommet	0	0	0	1	2	2	
16	Corner V2		e V2		Power Cord Set	1	1	1	1	1	1	
17	500	1,000	500									
18	$780	$950	$1,000		Parts Inventory							
19	$ 390,000 $	950,000 $	500,000		Part	In Stock	Used	Remaining				
20	500	1,000	500		Table 48"	3,100	4,500	(1,400)				
21	$490	$650	$700		Table 60"	3,400	1,500	1,900				
22	$62	$70	$74		Lifting Columns	14,200	12,000	2,200				
23	276,000	720,000	387,000		Lift Motors	7,200	9,000	(1,800)				
24	142,500	142,500	142,500		Lift Motors V2	7,800	3,000	4,800				
25	$ 418,500 $	862,500 $	529,500		Control Keypad	3,600	4,500	(900)				
26	$ (28,500) $	87,500 $	(29,500)		Control Keypad V2	3,400	1,500	1,900				
27					Desk Casters	4,900	12,000	(7,100)				
28	% Difference				Desk Casters Soft Roll	13,000	6,000	7,000				
29	0.00%				Desk Casters Heavy Duty	8,400	6,000	2,400				
30	-9.98%				Standard Grommet	3,400	4,000	(600)				
31	-11.56%				Power Grommet	5,500	3,500	2,000				
32	3.03%				Power Cord Set	7,800	6,000	1,800				

not enough parts in inventory to satisfy the demands of the optimal production mix

parts in stock   parts required   parts remaining

| Documentation | Income | Scenario Summary | Scenario PivotTable | **Product Mix** | Terms and ~~Definitions~~ |

Ready   Accessibility: Investigate

You need another constraint to ensure that the company has enough parts for the product mix. The constraint should test that the number of parts in inventory after the production run will be greater than or equal to zero for every desk part.

To add a constraint limiting the product mix to the available parts:

1. In the range **B17:G17**, change all the values back to **1,000**.

2. On the Data tab, in the Analyze group, click the **Solver** button. The Solver Parameters dialog box opens showing the current Solver model.

3. Click **Add** to open the Add Constraint dialog box.

4. Select the range **L20:L32**, containing the number of parts remaining after the production run, select **>=** as the constraint type, and then type **0** in the Constraint box to force all the values in the range L20:L32 to be greater than or equal to 0.

5. Click **OK**. The complete Solver model appears in the Solver Parameters dialog box. Refer to Figure 8–41.

Figure 8–41   Final Solver model

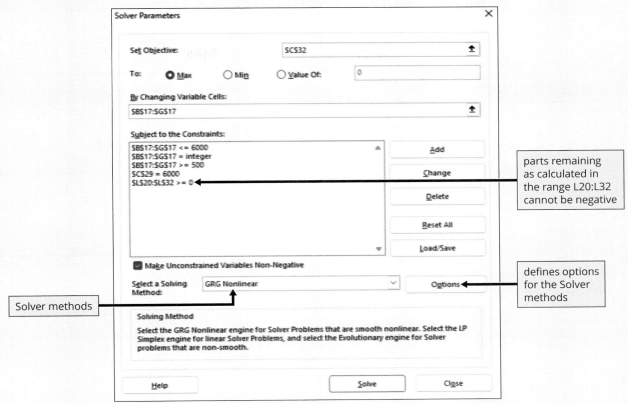

6. Click **Solve**, and then click **OK** in the Solver Results dialog box to accept the Solver solution and return to the worksheet.

7. Examine the worksheet to verify that this solution satisfies all the constraints, including that the production run does not exceed the number of available parts as indicated in the range L20:L32. Refer to Figure 8–42.

Figure 8-42   Final optimal product mix

	A	B	C	D	E	F	G	H
12	Fixed Expenses	142,500	142,500	142,500	142,500	142,500	142,500	
13	Total Expenses	$ 452,500	$ 516,500	$ 622,500	$ 694,500	$ 862,500	$ 916,500	
14	NET INCOME	units produced and sold of 00	$ 73,500	$ 77,500	$ 85,500	$ 87,500	$ 83,500	
15		each standing desk model						
16	OPTIMAL PRODUCT MIX	Standard	Standard V2	Corner	Corner V2	Executive	Executive V2	
17	Units Sold	1,225	500	500	2,050	1,225	500	
18	Sales Price	$540	$590	$700	$780	$950	$1,000	
19	Revenue	$ 661,500	$ 295,000	$ 350,000	$ 1,599,000	$ 1,163,750	500,000	
20	Units Produced	1,225	500	500	2,050	1,225	500	
21	Material Cost per Unit	$270	$320	$420	$490	$650	$700	
22	Manufacturing Cost per Unit	$40	$54	$60	$62	$70	$74	
23	Total Cost of Goods Sold	379,750	187,000	240,000	1,131,600	882,000	387,000	
24	Fixed Expenses	142,500	142,500	142,500	142,500	142,500	142,500	
25	Total Expenses	$ 522,250	$ 329,500	$ 382,500	$ 1,274,100	$ 1,024,500	$ 529,500	
26	NET INCOME	$ 139,250	$ (34,500)	$ (32,500)	$ 324,900	$ 139,250	$ (29,500)	
27								
28	PRODUCT MIX COMPARISON	Even Mix	Optimal Mix	Difference	% Difference			
29	Units Produced and Sold	6,000	6,000	0	0.00%			
30	Revenue	$ 4,560,000	$ 4,569,250	9,250	0.20%			
31	Total Expenses	$ 4,065,000	$ 4,062,350	(2,650)	-0.07%			
32	Net Income	$ 495,000	$ 506,900	11,900	2.40%			
33								
34								
35								
36								

net income of the optimal product mix has a 2.4% increase over the even product mix

Documentation | Income | Scenario Summary | Scenario PivotTable | **Product Mix** | Terms and Definitions | ⊕

Ready   ⚙ Accessibility: Investigate

In the optimal product mix, Office Motion will produce and sell 1,225 Standard desks, 500 Standard V2 desks, 500 Corner desks, 2,050 Corner V2 desks, 1,225 Executive desks, and 500 Executive V2 desks for a net income of $506,900 (cell C32) representing an increase of 2.4% over the even product mix model.

The income statement has a few interesting outcomes. The net income for the Standard V2, Corner, and Executive V2 desks is negative (cells C23, D26, and G26). The most profitable desk is the Corner V2 model with a net income of $324,900 (cell E26), accounting for 64% of the total net income of the entire production line. These results impact not only production but also marketing because the company needs to promote the Corner V2 model to increase demand for that model.

Exploring the Iterative Process

Solver arrives at optimal solutions through an **iterative process**, in which an initial solution is a basis to calculate a new solution. If that new solution improves the value of the objective cell, it will be used to generate the next solution; if it does not, Solver tries a different set of values as the starting point for the next step. With each step, or iteration, Solver attempts to improve the solution until a point is reached in which the new solutions are not significantly better than any previous solution. At that point, Solver will stop and indicate that it has found an "optimal" solution.

One way to think about this process is to imagine a hiker trekking a range of mountains to find the highest peak in the range. In an iterative process, the hiker could accomplish this by following the terrain upward until a high peak is climbed. One problem with this approach is that the hiker might simply find a peak that is high but not the highest point in the area. Solver refers to the overall high point as the **global optimum** and a nearby high point, which is not necessarily the highest overall point, as the **local optimum**.

To overcome this problem, Solver supports iterative processes that use multiple starting points. Using the hiker analogy, imagine several hikers starting from different locations and finding the nearest high point from their individual starting points. The more hikers involved, the more likely one of them will find the overall highest peak in the area. An issue with this approach is that the more starting solutions used by an iterative process, the longer the process takes to arrive at the optimal solution.

Depending on the problem, you might want to use iterative process over other processes. Solver provides the following iterative methods:

- The **Simplex LP method** is used for simple linear expressions involving only the operations of addition, subtraction, multiplication, and division. It will find the global optimum quickly if those conditions are met but might not converge to a solution for complicated models.

- The **GRG Nonlinear method** is used for complicated expressions involving nonlinear functions such as some exponential and trigonometric functions. It is very sensitive to your choice of initial values and might not always converge to the global optimum. You can set options for the method that employ multiple starting points.

- The **Evolutionary method** is used for complicated expressions that involve discontinuous functions that jump from one value to another. It converges to a solution from several starting points but is very time-consuming.

Tip To define options for the selected Solver method, click the Options button in the Solver Parameters dialog box.

If Solver fails to find a solution or you are not sure if its solution is the global optimum, you can try each method and compare the results to determine which solution is the best.

Creating a Solver Answer Report

Solver provides three reports to help you evaluate its solution—an answer report, a sensitivity report, and a limits report. The **answer report** is probably the most useful because it summarizes the results of a successful solution by displaying information about the objective cell, changing cells, and constraints as well as the initial and final values in the worksheet. The **sensitivity report** and **limits report** are often used in scientific research to document the mathematical aspects of the Solver result, allowing the investigator to quantify the reliability of the solution.

Tip You cannot display sensitivity and limits reports when the Solver model contains integer constraints.

As part of documenting the Solver solution, Yuri wants you to create an answer report providing information on the process used to determine the optimal product mix. To ensure that the answer report includes information on the entire process, you will change the current values in the range B17:G17 to start from an even product mix with 1,000 of each model produced and sold.

To create an answer report for the optimal product mix:

1. In the range **B17:G17**, enter **1,000** in each cell.

2. On the Data tab, in the Analyze group, click the **Solver** button to open the Solver Parameters dialog box, and then click **Solve** to run Solver using the conditions you specified earlier.

3. In the Solver Results dialog box, click **Answer** in the Reports box, and then verify that the **Keep Solver Solution** option button is selected.

4. Click the **Outline Reports** check box so that Solver returns its report using the outline tools. Refer to Figure 8–43.

Figure 8–43   Solver Results dialog box with the answer report selected

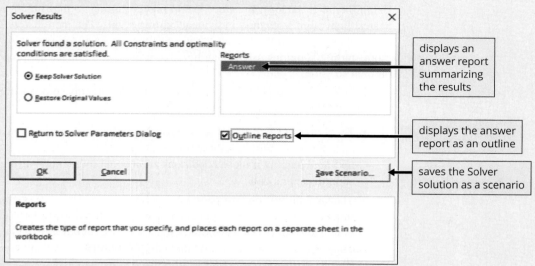

5. Click **OK** to accept the solution and generate the answer report in a new sheet named Answer Report 1.

    Tip Answer reports are named Answer Report 1, Answer Report 2, and so on; the newest report has the next highest number.

6. Move the **Answer Report 1** worksheet directly after the Product Mix worksheet, and then rename the worksheet as **Product Mix Report**. The answer report is long. With the outline tools turned on, some of the report is hidden.

7. Click the last three **expand outline** buttons ⊞ to view more detailed information about the variable cells and the constraints used in the solution.

8. Increase the Zoom factor to **140%** to better view the report contents. Refer to Figure 8–44.

Figure 8–44   Solver answer report

	Cell	Name	Cell Value	Formula	Status	Slack
31	Constraints					
33	$C$29	Units Produced and Sold Optimal Mix	6,000	$C$29=6000	Binding	0
34	$L$20:$L$32 >= 0					
35	$L$20	Table 48" Remaining	150	$L$20>=0	Not Binding	150
36	$L$21	Table 60" Remaining	350	$L$21>=0	Not Binding	350
37	$L$22	Lifting Columns Remaining	2,200	$L$22>=0	Not Binding	2,200
38	$L$23	Lift Motors Remaining	1,300	$L$23>=0	Not Binding	1,300
39	$L$24	Lift Motors V2 Remaining	1,700	$L$24>=0	Not Binding	1,700
40	$L$25	Control Keypad Remaining	650	$L$25>=0	Not Binding	650
41	$L$26	Control Keypad V2 Remaining	350	$L$26>=0	Not Binding	350
42	$L$27	Desk Casters Remaining	-	$L$27>=0	Binding	-
43	$L$28	Desk Casters Soft Roll Remaining	800	$L$28>=0	Not Binding	800
44	$L$29	Desk Casters Heavy Duty Remaining	1,500	$L$29>=0	Not Binding	1,500
45	$L$30	Standard Grommet Remaining	1,175	$L$30>=0	Not Binding	1,175
46	$L$31	Power Grommet Remaining	-	$L$31>=0	Binding	-
47	$L$32	Power Cord Set Remaining	1,800	$L$32>=0	Not Binding	1,800
49	$B$17:$G$17 <= 6000					
50	$B$17	Units Sold Standard	1,225	$B$17<=600C	Not Binding	4775
51	$C$17	Units Sold Standard V2	500	$C$17<=600C	Not Binding	5500
52	$D$17	Units Sold Corner	500	$D$17<=600C	Not Binding	5500
53	$E$17	Units Sold Corner V2	2,050	$E$17<=6000	Not Binding	3950
54	$F$17	Units Sold Executive	1,225	$F$17<=6000	Not Binding	4775

information about the impact of the constraints on the solution

binding constraint that limited the Solver solution

nonbinding constraints that did not affect the Solver solution

Documentation Income Scenario Summary Scenario PivotTable Product Mix **Product Mix Report** Terms and Definitions ⊕

Ready   Accessibility: Investigate

The answer report is divided into the following sections:

- The Title section identifies the worksheet containing the Solver model, the date on which the report was created, and whether Solver found a solution.
- The Solver Engine section provides technical information about how long Solver took to find a solution.
- The Solver Options section lists the technical options used by Solver in arriving at a solution.
- The Objective Cell section provides the original and final value of the objective cell.
- The Variable Cells section lists the original and final values of the variable cells used in the solution.
- The Constraints section lists the constraints imposed on the solution by Solver.

The status of each constraint is listed as either Binding or Not Binding. A **binding constraint** is a constraint that was a limiting factor in the solution. A **nonbinding constraint** is a constraint that was not a factor in the solution. Nonbinding constraints could be removed from the model without altering the solution. For example, the constraint that the number of units produced and sold be equal to 6,000 is a binding constraint that limits the solutions available to Solver. The constraint that the company produce and sell no more than 6,000 of each type of desk model turned out to be nonbinding. Once the company was limited to producing exactly 6,000 desks and was limited by the available parts on hand, the optimal product mix would have resulted in the company producing no more than 6,000 units of each desk anyway.

Identifying binding constraints helps production determine which elements have the greatest impact on manufacturing and profits. In the Office Motion parts lists, there are binding constraints for the number of desk casters (cell L27) and the number of power grommets (cell L31). If the company had more of those parts in inventory, it might be able to generate more revenue by manufacturing more desks with a higher profit margin.

The last column in the Constraints section shows the slack for each constraint. The **slack** is the difference between the value in the cell and the value at the limit of the constraint, showing how close the constraint came to be a binding constraint. A binding constraint will always have a slack of 0 because Solver pushed that constraint to limit finding a solution. For example, the slack for the number of 48" tables remaining (cell L20) is 150, indicating that when Solver found the optimal product mix, there were still 48" tables left, ready to be used if needed. The availability of 48" tables was not a limiting factor in the solution.

Proskills

Decision Making: Choosing a What-If Analysis Tool

Part of performing an effective what-if analysis is deciding which what-if analysis tool to use. Each tool has its own set of advantages and disadvantages. Data tables are best used when you want to perform several what-if analyses involving one or two input cells and you need to display the analysis in a tabular format. Data tables can also be easily displayed as charts, providing a visual picture of the relationship between the input values and the result values. For what-if analyses involving more than two input cells, you must create a scenario. Scenario summary tables and scenario PivotTables can be used to obtain a quick snapshot of several possible outcomes, and scenarios can be merged and shared among several workbooks. Data tables and scenarios can provide a lot of information, but they cannot easily deliver a single solution or "best outcome." If you need to maximize or minimize a value, you must use Solver. You can also use Solver to set a calculated cell to a specific value. However, if you do not need to specify any constraints on your solution, it is generally quicker and easier to use Goal Seek.

Saving and Loading Solver Models

You might want to apply different Solver models to the same data. For example, in addition to knowing what product mix maximizes the company's net income, Yuri wants to know what product mix minimizes the company's total material costs. To determine this, you could create another Solver model, but creating a new model in the worksheet overwrites the previous model. To avoid losing work, you can save the Solver parameters and retrieve them when needed.

Reference

Saving and Loading a Solver Model

- Open the Solver Parameters dialog box.
- Click Load/Save.
- Select an empty range containing the number of cells specified in the dialog box, and then click Save.
- Select the range containing the saved model, and then click Load.

Before running the second Solver problem for Yuri, you will store the parameters of the current model that maximizes the company's net income.

To save the current Solver model:

1. Go to the **Product Mix** worksheet.

2. On the Data tab, in the Analyze group, click the **Solver** button. The Solver Parameters dialog box opens.

3. Click **Load/Save**. The Load/Save Model dialog box opens, specifying that you need to select an empty range with eight cells to store the model.

4. Select the range **A36:A44** in the Product Mix worksheet. You will store the Solver parameters in this range.

    | **Key Step** Be sure the range of cells you select to save the Solver parameters is empty so you don't overwrite other information on the worksheet.

5. Click **Save**. The information about the Solver model is entered in the range A36:A44, and the Solver Parameters dialog box reappears.

6. Click **Close** to close the Solver Parameters dialog box.

7. In cell **A35**, enter **Maximum Net Income** and then format that cell with the **20% - Accent6** cell style. Refer to Figure 8–45.

Figure 8–45   Saved Solver model

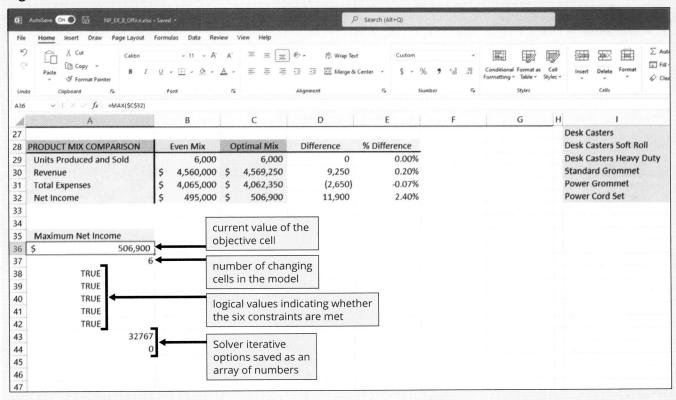

Cell A36 contains the formula = MAX($C$32), providing the information that the Solver model finds the maximum of cell C32, which in this case is the highest net income for product mix, $506,900. Cell A37 displays the value 6, which is the number of variable, or changing, cells in the model. The next four cells display TRUE, indicating that the four constraints in the model are all satisfied in the Solver solution. If you later change some of the worksheet data so that it violates a constraint, the Solver parameter cells will display FALSE. These cells provide a quick visual check that all the model's conditions are still being met as the worksheet is modified. The final two cells, cells A43 and A44, display technical information on the iterative process by which Solver arrives at a solution.

Now that you have saved this Solver model, you can create a second model to determine the product mix that minimizes the total expense of producing and selling these desks. Yuri wants to know what product mix has the lowest total expense under the constraints that 6,000 desks must be produced, at least 500 of each model must be produced, the number of desks produced must be integers, and the desks produced cannot exceed available parts. The objective cell for this model is cell C31 instead of cell C32.

To find the product mix that minimizes total expenses:

1. In the range **B17:G17**, change the value of each cell to **1,000**.

2. Open the Solver Parameters dialog box.

3. With the Set Objective box selected, click cell **C31** in the Product Mix worksheet. This cell contains the total material cost under the Optimal product mix.

4. Click the **Min** option button to find the minimum value for total expenses.

You can delete the constraint to keep the number of desks produced below 6,000 units.

5. From the Subject to the constraints list box, click the constraint **$B$17:$G$17 <= 6000** and then click **Delete** to remove it.

6. Click **Solve**. Solver finds the product mix that minimizes the total expenses.

7. Click **OK** to close the Solver Results dialog box and view the solution. Refer to Figure 8–46.

Figure 8–46   Solution to minimizing total expenses

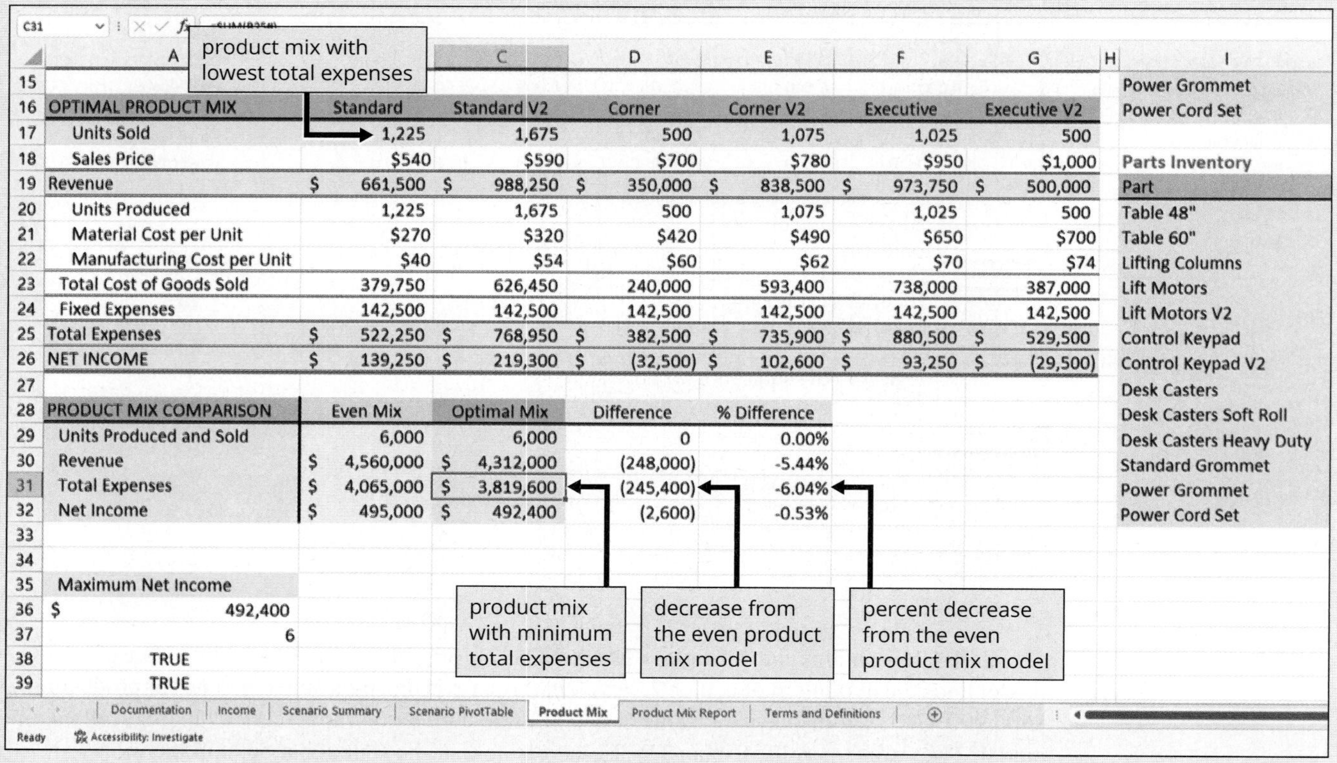

The company can reduce total expenses to $3,819,600 (cell C31), which is a 6.04% decrease from an even product mix (cell E31). However, this product mix will also result in a decrease of 0.53% (cell E32) in profit. You will save this model in the Product Mix worksheet.

To save the model that minimize total expenses:

1. In cell **A46**, enter **Minimum Total Expenses** and then format that cell with the **20% - Accent4** cell style.

2. Open the Solver Parameters dialog box, and then click **Load/Save**. The Load/Save Model dialog box opens.

3. Select the range **A47:A54** in the Product Mix worksheet to specify the eight cells in which to save the model.

4. Click **Save**. The current Solver model is saved in the Product Mix worksheet.

5. Click **Close** to close the Solver Parameters dialog box.

You have two Solver models saved in the Product Mix worksheet—the Maximum Net Income model and the Minimum Total Expenses model. You can quickly reload each of these Solver models in the worksheet from the Solver Parameters dialog box.

Yuri wants the final version of the worksheet to use the Solver model that maximizes net income for the company. You will load and rerun the Maximum Net Income model.

To load the Maximum Net Income model and run it:

1. In the range **B17:G17**, change the values in each cell to **1,000** as the initial product mix.

2. Open the Solver Parameters dialog box, and then click **Load/Save**. The Load/Save Model dialog box opens.

3. In the Product Mix worksheet, select the range **A36:A44** containing the parameters of the Maximum Net Income model.

4. Click **Load** to load the Solver parameters from the worksheet. The Load Model dialog box opens, asking whether you want to replace the current model or merge the new model with the current model.

   > **Tip** To combine the Solver model with the model currently used in the worksheet, click the Merge button.

5. Click **Replace**. The Solver Parameters dialog box appears. The parameters for the Maximum Net Income model have replaced the parameters for the Minimum Total Expenses model with the objective cell set once again to cell C32 and the Max option button selected in the dialog box.

6. Click **Solve**. Solver runs the Maximum Net Income model, and then the Solver Results dialog box opens.

7. Click **OK** to keep the Solver solution and return to the Product Mix worksheet.

8. **sam**⬆ Save the workbook, and then close it.

By saving the Solver model parameters to cells on the worksheet, you can create as many models as you need to effectively analyze the data. You can then load and apply these different models to your analysis as new data is entered.

You have finished analyzing how Office Motion can maximize its profits from its line of standing desks by modifying the product mix. Using data tables, Excel scenarios, and Solver models, you provided Yuri with several pricing and production options to increase the company's net income or minimize material costs for the upcoming year.

Part 8.3 Quick Check

1. What is an add-in?

2. What are three options for the objective cell using Solver?

3. What is an objective cell? What is a variable cell?

4. What are the six types of constraints you can put on a cell in a Solver model?

5. What is an iterative process?

6. What is the difference between a binding constraint and a nonbinding constraint?

7. In the Solver report, what is meant by the term "slack"?

8. What is the slack of a binding constraint?

Practice: Review Assignments

Data File needed for the Review Assignments: NP_EX_8-2.xlsx

Office Motion is planning to introduce a new standing desk model called the Royal. Yuri is preparing a financial analysis of the new product. The report should find the break-even point (in terms of units sold) for the model under different assumptions for sales price and variable expense.

As the sales price of an item rises, it generates more revenue with each unit sold. However, if the price rises too high, consumers are less likely to purchase the item, resulting in fewer sales and less profit. Office Motion wants to find the optimal price point for the Royal standing desk that maximizes profit. You will use Solver to find that price point subject to constraints on sales and expense. Complete the following:

1. Open the **NP_EX_8-2.xlsx** workbook located in the Excel8 > Review folder included with your Data Files. Save the workbook as **NP_EX_8_Royal** in the location specified by your instructor.

2. In the Documentation sheet, enter your name and the date in the range B3:B4, and then review the contents of the workbook.

3. Go to the Break-Even Point worksheet. Yuri wants you to create a two-variable table displaying the break-even point for different combinations of sales price and variable expense per unit produced. Do the following:
   a. In cell D5, enter the formula = **B26** to display the break-even point in the current income statement.
   b. Apply a custom format to cell D5 to display the text **"Variable Expense"** in place of the break-even value.
   c. Complete the two-variable table by selecting the range D5:J21, opening the Data Table dialog box, and using cell B6 as the Row input cell and cell B11 as the Column input cell.

4. Yuri wants a graph of the curves for the break-even points from the two-way table. To create the table, do the following:
   a. Select the range D6:J21 and create a scatter chart with smooth lines (the third subtype in the list of Scatter charts).
   b. Move and resize the scatter chart to cover the range D23:J36.
   c. Change the chart title to **Break-Even Point by Sales Price**.
   d. Add a vertical axis title with the label **Units Sold**. Add a horizontal axis title with the label **Variable Expense per Unit**.
   e. Change the scale of the horizontal axis to range from $**300** to $**700**.
   f. Move the chart legend to the right side of the chart.
   g. Using the Select Data command on Data group of the Chart Design tab, change the Series1 name to match the value of cell E5, the Series2 name to match cell F5, the Series3 name to match cell G5, the Series4 name to match cell H5, the Series5 name to match cell I5, and the Series6 name to match cell J5.

5. Yuri wants to examine the impact of different expense scenarios on the profitability of the Royal standing desk. Use Scenario Manager to create a scenario named **Standard** with the changing cells B6, B11, B15:B18 using the current values in the worksheet.

6. Add another scenario named **Trial Promotion** with the following values: Sales_Price_per_Unit = **750**, Variable_Expenses_per_Unit = **420**, Salaries_and_Benefits = **175000**, Shipping_and_Distribution = **50000**, Stocking_and_Storage = **25000**, Miscellaneous = **15000**.

7. Add a third scenario named **Favored Promotion** with the following values: Sales_Price_per_Unit = **875**, Variable_Expenses_per_Unit = **480**, Salaries_and_Benefits = **250000**, Shipping_and_Distribution = **70000**, Stocking_and_Storage = **45000**, Miscellaneous = **30000**.

8. Create a scenario summary report using B22:B24,B26 as the result cells. Move the Scenario Summary worksheet after the Break-Even Point worksheet and increase the zoom factor to **140%**.

9. Go to the Price Point worksheet containing the optimal price to charge for the Royal standing desk. In cell B5, enter the formula = **6000*EXP(−B6/500)** to estimate the number of units that would be sold at a price of $500 per desk.

10. Create a one-variable data table of Units Sold and Net Income for different price points by the doing the following:
    a. In cell D5 enter the formula = **B6**. In cell E5, enter the formula = **B5**. In cell F5, enter the formula = **B24**.
    b. Select the range D5:F26 and create a one-variable data table using cell B6 as the column input cell.

11. Yuri wants a chart showing the decline in sales with increasing price. Select the range D6:E26 and do the following:
    a. Insert a scatter chart using the Scatter with Smooth Lines chart subtype.
    b. Move and resize the chart to cover the range H4:M14.
    c. Change the chart title to **Units Sold vs. Selling Price**.
    d. Add a vertical axis title with the label **Units Sold**. Add a horizontal axis title with the label **Selling Price**.
    e. Change the horizontal scale to range from **$600** to **$1100**.

12. Yuri wants another chart of net income versus selling price. Select the nonadjacent range D6:D26,F6:F26 and do the following:
    a. Insert a scatter chart using the Scatter with Smooth Lines chart subtype.
    b. Move and resize the chart to cover the range **H16:M26**.
    c. Change the chart title to **Net Income vs. Selling Price**.
    d. Add a vertical axis title with the label **Net Income**. Add a horizontal axis title with the label **Selling Price**.
    e. Change the horizontal scale to range from **$600** to **$1100**.

13. The Net Income vs. Selling Price chart shows that profits rise and then fall as the sales price increases. Yuri wants to locate the price point that maximizes profits. Open Solver and do the following:
    a. Set cell B24 as the objective cell and choose the Max option button.
    b. Set cell B6 as the changing variable cell.
    c. Add a constraint that sets the total variable expenses (cell B12) to be at most $400,000.
    d. Add constraints to limit the units sold (cell B5) to between 500 and 1200 units.
    e. Run Solver to find the optimal price point that maximizes profits under the constraints. (Note: Depending on your initial values, the total revenue values in cell B7 might differ by one or two dollars.)
    f. If an employee has not made a schedule request, there are no constraints on the days that employee can work.

14. Create a Solver Answer report of your solution. Move the Answer Report 1 worksheet after the Price Point worksheet and increase the Zoom factor to **140%**.

15. Save the Solver model to the range O5:O11.

16. Save the workbook, and then close it.

Apply: Case Problem 1

Data File needed for this Case Problem: NP_EX_8-3.xlsx

Bright Star Foods Laura Holmes is a dispatch manager for Bright Star Foods. One of Laura's tasks is to schedule the shipping of products between warehouses and distribution centers. The company has warehouses located in Atlanta, Chicago, Pittsburgh, and Omaha. The distribution centers are in Cincinnati, Dallas, Denver, Nashville, and St. Louis. Products can be delivered from any warehouse to any distribution center, but it is less expensive when the overall distance between the warehouses and the distribution centers is minimized. Laura wants your help in finding a dispatch schedule that will save the most in delivery expenses. Complete the following:

1. Open the **NP_EX_8-3.xlsx** workbook located in the Excel8 > Case1 folder included with your Data Files, and then save the workbook as **NP_EX_8_Bright.xlsx** in the location specified by your instructor.

2. In the Documentation sheet, in the range B3:B4, enter your name and the date. Review the contents of the workbook.

3. In the Shipping worksheet, you will determine a dispatch schedule between the warehouses and the distribution centers. You will calculate the distance between each warehouse/distribution center pair. Do the following:
    a. In cell D6, enter the formula **= B7** to reference the distance between the two cities listed in the Distance Calculator between Cities section of the worksheet.
    b. Select the range D6:I10 and generate a two-variable data table using cell B5 as the row input cell and cell B6 as the column input cell.
    c. Use a custom format in cell D6 to display the text **"Warehouse"** in place of the value of cell B7.

4. The Dispatch Assignments table will be used to determine how products are dispatched from the warehouses to the distribution centers. Each warehouse has a specific number of items in stock. Each distribution center has requested a specific number of those items. Add the following values and calculations to the table:

   a. For each warehouse/distribution center pairing in the range E15:I18. enter **0** since no dispatch orders have been generated yet.

   b. In cell J15, calculate the sum of items shipped in the range E15:I15 from the Atlanta warehouse. Copy the cell J15 formula through the range J15:J18 to calculate the sum of items shipped from each of the four warehouses.

   c. In cell E19, calculate the sum of items received by the Cincinnati distribution center. Copy the cell E19 formula through the range E19:I19 to calculate the sum of items received by each of the five distribution centers.

5. The Cost of Delivery table will be used to calculate the cost of delivering items for each warehouse/distribution pairing. Do the following:

   a. In cell E25, calculate the cost of delivering items from Atlanta to Cincinnati by multiplying the values of cells E7 (the distance in miles), cell E15 (the number of items shipped), and cell B8 (the cost per miles). Use an absolute reference to cell B8 in your formula.

   b. Use the AutoFill handle to copy the formula in cell E25 through the range E25:I28. Do not copy the format of cell E26, only the formula.

   c. In cells J25 through J28, enter formulas to calculate the total cost of delivery from each of the four warehouses to the five distribution centers.

6. In cell B10, determine the total cost of all deliveries by calculating the sum of the values in the range J25:J28.

7. Use Solver to find a dispatch schedule that ensures that each distribution center gets all the items it orders and without exceeding any warehouse's inventory and does so in the cheapest way possible. Do the following:

   a. Have Solver find the minimum value for the total cost of deliveries (cell B10).

   b. Set the range E15:I18 as the cells to change in finding a solution.

   c. Add a constraint that every value in the range E15:I18 be an integer.

   d. Add a constraint that the values in the range J15:J18 be less than or equal to the values in the range K15:K18 so that no warehouse is asked to deliver more items than it has in stock.

   e. Add a constraint that the values in the range E19:I19 equal the values in the range E20:I20 so that every distribution center receives exactly what it needs.

   f. Run Solver to determine the dispatch schedule that results in the minimal total delivery cost between warehouses and distribution centers. Verify that all constraints have been met, ensuring that no warehouse is asked to deliver more than its inventory and every distribution will receive what it requested.

8. Laura wants to explore how changing the cost per mile value in cell B8 will impact the total delivery cost. Do the following:

   a. In cell A14, enter the formula **= B8** to reference the current Cost per Mile value.

   b. In cell B14, enter the formula **= B10** to reference the current delivery cost.

   c. Generate a one-variable data table in the range A15:B23 using cell B8 as the column input cell to show the impact of changing the cost per mile value on the total delivery cost.

9. Due to operational problems in the Nashville distribution center, the company might have to redirect deliveries for Nashville to either Lexington or Memphis. Laura wants to determine the impact of redirecting shipments to either of those two locations on the total delivery cost. Do the following:

   a. Assign cell B8 the range name **Cost_per_Mile**. Assign cell B10 the range name **Delivery_Cost**.

   b. Create a scenario named **Nashville** by changing the values in cells H6, H14, and H24. Add the comment **Delivery to Nashville Location** to the scenario. Accept the default values ("Nashville") for those cells.

   c. Add another scenario named **Lexington** with the scenario comment **Delivery to Lexington Location.** Change the values of cells H6, H14, and H24 to **Lexington**.

   d. Add a third scenario named **Memphis** with the scenario comment **Delivery to Memphis Location.** Change the values of cells H6, H14, and H24 to **Memphis**.

    e. Create a scenario summary report showing the values of the three delivery scenarios. Use cells B8 and B10 as the result cells.

    f. Rename the Scenario Summary worksheet **Cost of Replacing Nashville** and move the sheet directly after the Shipping worksheet. Increase the zoom factor of the worksheet to **140%**.

10. The company has decided to redirect shipments from Nashville to the Lexington location. Apply the Lexington scenario to show dispatch the final shipping schedule, under the assumption that all shipments previously directed to Nashville will be redirected to Lexington.

11. Save the workbook, and then close it.

Challenge: Case Problem 2

Data File needed for this Case Problem: NP_EX_8-4.xlsx

Meier Travel Celeste Florentin manages the work schedule for the call center of Meier Travel, a nationwide travel agency. There are 16 call center operators. Twelve of the operators are full-time employees seeking to work 40 hours per week. The other four operators are part-time and work 24 hours per week. One of Celeste's major challenges is to accommodate time-off requests for call center operators while still maintaining a sufficient workforce to handle customer support calls and requests. You will generate a work schedule that meets the needs of the call center while still satisfying the requests of the staff. Complete the following:

1. Open the **NP_EX_8-4.xlsx** workbook located in the Excel8 > Case2 folder included with your Data Files, and then save the workbook as **NP_EX_8_Meier** in the location specified by your instructor.

2. In the Documentation sheet, enter your name and the date in cells B3 and B4.

3. Review the Schedule worksheet, which contains the weekly schedule and information about employees who have requested time off. Cells in the range D5:J20 indicate filled shifts with 1 and unfilled shifts with a 0. Each shift is 8 hours. The work schedule is currently empty.

4. In cell K5, enter a formula to calculate the total hours worked by Claudia Arroyo by multiplying the sum of the values in the range D5:J5 by eight. Calculate the total hours worked by the other 15 employees by copying the formula in cell K5 through the range K5:K20 without copying the formatting.

5. Ten shifts need to be covered on Monday through Friday, and eight shifts need to be covered on Saturday and Sunday. In cell D23, calculate the sum of the shifts scheduled for Monday by adding the values in the range D5:D20. Calculate the total scheduled shifts for the rest of the days of the week by copying the formula in cell D23 through the range D23:J23.

6. Track the shortage of employees on each day in the range D24:J24 by calculating the number of operators required minus the number of operators scheduled for each cell.

7. In cell D26, calculate the total employee shortage for the entire week by summing the values in the range D24:J24.

8. **Explore:** Set up Solver to generate a work schedule for the upcoming week. Define the following objective and changing cells:

    a. Set cell D26 as the objective cell for the Solver model.

    b. Set cell D26 to a value of zero because Celeste wants to have no shortage of operators during the week.

    c. Define the range D5:J20 as the changing variable cells.

9. **Explore:** Values in the range D5:J20 will either be a 0 (no shift scheduled) or a 1 (shift scheduled). Add a constraint that limits the values in the D5:J20 range to binary numbers.

10. Full-time employees work no more than 40 hours. Add a constraint to limit values in the range K5:K16 to be less than or equal to 40. Part-time employees work at most 24 hours. Add a constraint to limit values in the range K17:K20 to less than or equal to 24.

11. Ensure that there are enough operators for each day by adding a constraint that the values in the range D22:J22 must equal the values in the range D23:J23.

12. The remaining constraints are used to accommodate employee requests. For these constraints, use the information in range C5:C20 and do the following:

    a. If an employee requests a day off, constrain the value of the cell for that day to 0.

    b. If an employee requests a range of days off, constrain the range of cells for those days to be equal to 0.

    c. If an employee requests a limited number of hours, constrain the total hours for that employee to be less than or equal to that number.

    d. If an employee is on leave, constrain the range of cells for that employee's entire week to 0.

13. Explore: Set the Solving Method to Evolutionary and run Solver. It might take Solver a minute to arrive at a solution. When Solver arrives at a solution, verify that the work schedule has met the staffing needs of the call center and satisfied all employee requests. It is possible there is more than one correct solution.

14. Celeste wants Excel to automatically generate a list of employees working on each day of the week. To create the list, do the following:

    a. Select the range A4:J20 and create range names using the labels in the top row of the selection so that the range name Operator references the employee names from the range A5:A20, Mon references the Monday schedule entered in the range D5:D20 and so forth.

    b. Go to the Assignment List worksheet. In cell A5, enter the dynamic array formula **= SORT(FILTER(Operator, Mon=1))** to create a sorted list of employees who are scheduled to work Monday.

    c. Create similar formulas for cells B5 through G5, replacing the range name "Mon" in the formula with range name for "Tue", "Wed", "Thu", "Fri", "Sat" and "Sun".

15. Save the workbook, and then close it.

Exploring Financial Tools and Functions

Analyzing a Business Plan

Case: Robuster

Kim Kapono is a financial analyst for Robuster, a startup tech company based in Birmingham, Alabama. The company is looking to produce a line of smart micro-robotic dusters, capable of cleaning surfaces and spaces inaccessible to bulkier cleaning equipment and fans. The company's products will be aimed at industrial markets that require clean, dust-free spaces to operate. If the technology proves successful and cost-effective, the company might branch into residential applications. Since this is innovative technology, it requires time and motivated investors to bring it to market. It might be several years before the company shows significant profits.

To obtain the capital that Robuster will need to start production, Kim must create a business plan detailing the financial challenges the company will face and the likely return investors can expect within the next five years of operation. Kim needs to project future revenue, expenses, and cash flow. To do those calculations, you will rely on the Excel library of financial tools and functions.

Objectives

Part 9.1
- Analyze loans and investments with Excel functions
- Create an amortization schedule
- Calculate interest and principal payments

Part 9.2
- Perform calculations for an income statement
- Interpolate and extrapolate a series of values
- Calculate a depreciation schedule

Part 9.3
- Determine a payback value
- Calculate a net present value
- Calculate an internal rate of return
- Trace a formula error to its source

Starting Data Files

Excel9
Module
NP_EX_9-1.xlsx
Review
NP_EX_9-2.xlsx

Case1
NP_EX_9-3.xlsx
Case2
NP_EX_9-4.xlsx

Part 9.1 Visual Overview:
Loan and Investment Functions

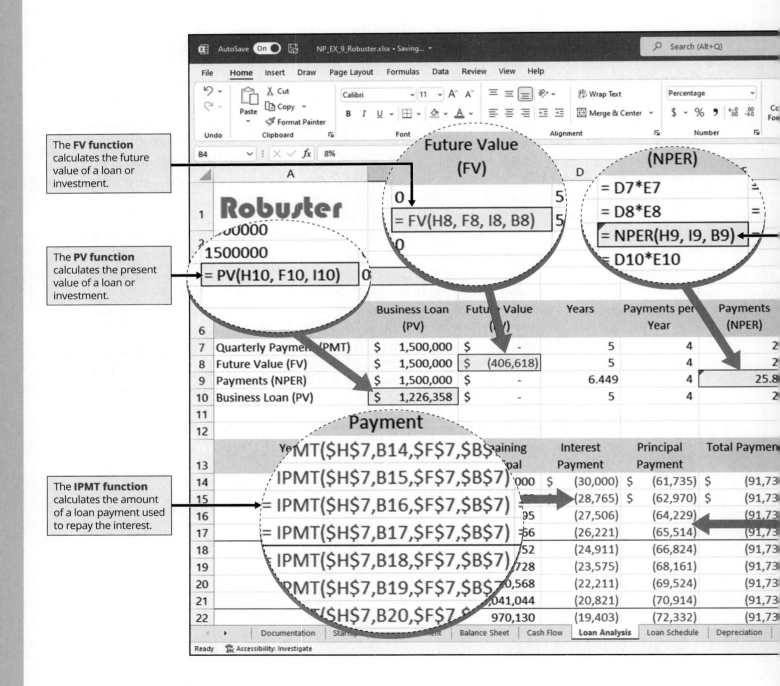

The **FV function** calculates the future value of a loan or investment.

The **PV function** calculates the present value of a loan or investment.

The **IPMT function** calculates the amount of a loan payment used to repay the interest.

Future Value (FV)

= FV(H8, F8, I8, B8)

(NPER)

= D7*E7
= D8*E8
= NPER(H9, I9, B9)
= D10*E10

= PV(H10, F10, I10)

Robuster

Payment

MT($H$7,B14,$F$7,B...
IPMT($H$7,B15,$F$7,$B$7)
= IPMT($H$7,B16,$F$7,$B$7)
= IPMT($H$7,B17,$F$7,$B$7)
IPMT($H$7,B18,$F$7,$B$7)
PMT($H$7,B19,$F$7,B...
($H$7,B20,$F$7,$...

	Business Loan (PV)	Future Value (FV)	Years	Payments per Year	Payments (NPER)
7 Quarterly Payment (PMT)	$ 1,500,000	$ -	5	4	2
8 Future Value (FV)	$ 1,500,000	$ (406,618)	5	4	2
9 Payments (NPER)	$ 1,500,000	$ -	6.449	4	25.8
10 Business Loan (PV)	$ 1,226,358	$ -	5	4	2

		Interest Payment	Principal Payment	Total Payment
13				
14	,000 $	(30,000) $	(61,735) $	(91,73...
15		(28,765) $	(62,970) $	(91,73...
16	...95	(27,506)	(64,229)	(91,73...
17	...56	(26,221)	(65,514)	(91,73...
18	...52	(24,911)	(66,824)	(91,73...
19	...728	(23,575)	(68,161)	(91,73...
20	...0,568	(22,211)	(69,524)	(91,73...
21	...,041,044	(20,821)	(70,914)	(91,73...
22	970,130	(19,403)	(72,332)	(91,73...

Documentation   Startu...   ...ment   Balance Sheet   Cash Flow   **Loan Analysis**   Loan Schedule   Depreciation

Ready   Accessibility: Investigate

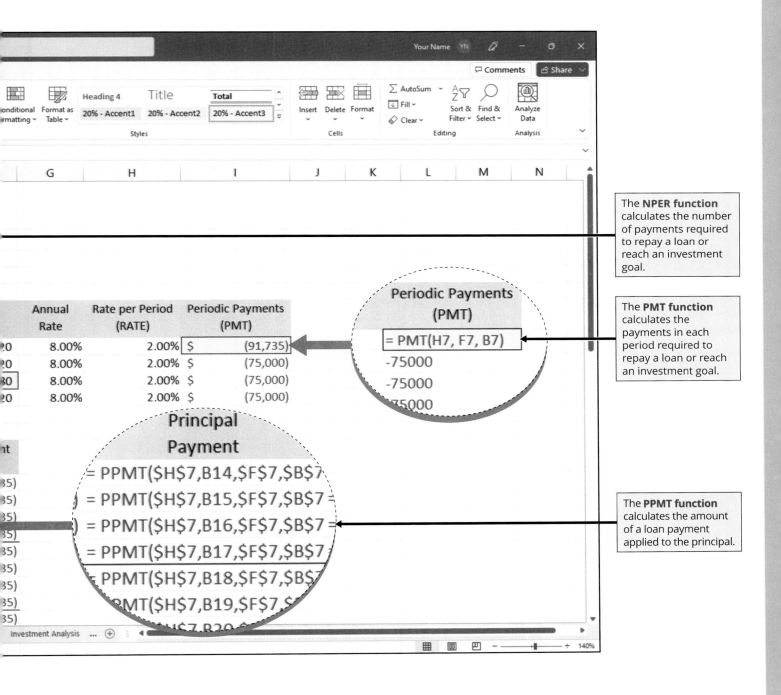

The **NPER function** calculates the number of payments required to repay a loan or reach an investment goal.

The **PMT function** calculates the payments in each period required to repay a loan or reach an investment goal.

The **PPMT function** calculates the amount of a loan payment applied to the principal.

	Annual Rate	Rate per Period (RATE)	Periodic Payments (PMT)
20	8.00%	2.00%	$ (91,735)
20	8.00%	2.00%	$ (75,000)
30	8.00%	2.00%	$ (75,000)
20	8.00%	2.00%	$ (75,000)

Periodic Payments (PMT)

= PMT(H7, F7, B7)

-75000

-75000

-75000

Principal Payment

= PPMT($H$7,B14,$F$7,$B$7)

= PPMT($H$7,B15,$F$7,$B$7

= PPMT($H$7,B16,$F$7,$B$7

= PPMT($H$7,B17,$F$7,$B$7

= PPMT($H$7,B18,B

PMT($H$7,B19,$F$7,$

Investment Analysis

Introducing Financial Functions

In this module, you will learn the Excel skills you need to apply financial calculations to business planning and analysis. In the process, you will explore how to evaluate financial aspects of a business plan. Note that this will be a simplified treatment of a very complicated financial challenge that usually involves hundreds of pages of financial reports and in-depth discussions with teams of accountants and lawyers.

You will start by opening the workbook Kim created for the Robuster business plan.

To open the Robuster workbook:

1. **sam**⬇ Open the **NP_EX_9-1.xlsx** workbook located in the **Excel9 > Module** folder included with your Data Files, and then save the workbook as **NP_EX_9_Robuster** in the location specified by your instructor.

2. In the Documentation worksheet, enter your name and the date in the range B3:B4.

3. Review the content of each worksheet in the workbook. Note that many worksheets are incomplete, and some contain error values. You will correct those issues in this module.

This module focuses on **financial functions**—the Excel functions used for analyzing loans, investments, and financial metrics. Many financial functions deal with **cash flow**, which is the direction of money to and from an individual or group. A **positive cash flow**, or **cash inflow**, represents money coming to an individual or group (cash received). A **negative cash flow**, or **cash outflow**, represents money that is leaving the individual or group (cash spent). Borrowing money is a positive cash flow to you but a negative cash flow to the lender. Repaying a loan is a negative cash flow to you but a positive cash flow to the lender. Money invested is a negative cash flow until the investment returns money as a positive cash flow to the investor. Many Excel functions automatically return positive or negative values depending on cash flow, so pay close attention to positive and negative currency values because they indicate the direction of the cash flow.

Another important concept in financial functions is the difference between present value and future value. **Present value** refers to the current value of a loan or investment, whereas **future value** is the value of the loan or investment at a future time. For example, if you take out a $100 loan at an annual interest rate of 5%, the present value is $100 (positive cash flow to you). In one year, the future value of that loan is –$105, a negative cash flow representing the money that must be repaid.

Kim wants to estimate the costs associated with business loans to the company. To do that, you will use the Excel financial functions associated with loans and investments.

Calculating the Cost of Borrowing

The cost of a loan to an individual or business is based on three factors: principal, interest, and time. **Principal** is the present value of the loan. **Interest** is an amount charged by the lender to borrower. You can think of interest as a "user fee" because the borrower is paying for the right to use the lender's money. Generally, interest is expressed as an annual percentage rate, or APR. For example, a 9% APR means that the annual interest rate on the loan is 9% of the principal owed to the lender.

An annual interest rate is usually divided by the number of payments per year (often monthly or quarterly). If a 9% annual interest rate is paid monthly, the resulting monthly interest rate is 1/12 of 9%, or 0.75% per month. If payments are made quarterly, then the interest rate per quarter would be 1/4 of 9%, or 2.25% per quarter.

The third factor in calculating the loan cost is the time required to repay the loan, which is specified as the number of payment periods. The number of payment periods is based on the length of the loan multiplied by the number of payments per year. A 10-year loan that is paid monthly has 120 payment periods. If that same 10-year loan is repaid quarterly, it has 40 payment periods.

Excel provides functions to calculate five values associated with loans and investments:

- The payment made during each period of the loan or investment (PMT)
- The future value of the loan or investment (FV)
- The total number of payments (NPER)
- The present value of the loan or investment (PV)
- The interest rate of the loan or investment per period (RATE)

Knowing any four of these values, you can use a financial function to calculate the fifth. You will start by exploring how to calculate the payment required for each period.

Calculating Payments with the PMT Function

To determine the size of payments made periodically to either repay a loan or reach an investment goal, use the PMT or payment function

PMT(Rate, Nper, Pv, [Fv = 0], [Type = 0])

where *Rate* is the interest rate per period, *Nper* is the total number of payment periods, *Pv* is the present value of the loan or investment, and *Fv* is the future value of the loan or investment after all the scheduled payments have been made. The *Fv* argument is optional and has a default value of 0. Finally, the optional *Type* value specifies whether payments are made at the end of each period (*Type* = 0) or at the beginning (*Type* = 1). The default is to assume that payments are made at the end of each period.

> **Tip** Excel financial functions automatically format calculated values as currency. Negative cash flows appear in a red font within parentheses.

If a company borrows $500,000 at 6% annual interest to be repaid quarterly over a five-year period, the *Rate* value would be 6%/4, or 1.5%, because the 6% annual interest rate is divided into four quarters. The *Nper* value is 4 $\times$ 5 (four payments per year for five years), resulting in 20 payments over the five-year period. The PMT function for this loan would be entered as

PMT(6%/4, 4*5, 500000)

returning the negative cash flow value –$29,122.87, indicating that the company must pay almost $30,000 each quarter to entirely repay the $500,000 loan plus interest in five years. Note that the $500,000 loan amount is a positive cash flow value because it represents money sent to the company, but quarterly payments are negative cash flows because they are monies spent repaying the loan. Also note that a default value of 0 is assumed for the *Fv* argument because the loan will be completely repaid and thus have a future value of 0.

If you were to use the PMT function to calculate the periodic returns from a one-time investment, you would use a negative *Pv* value because the present value is the money you invested. The PMT function would return a positive value for the money being received periodically from the investment.

Reference

Working with Loans and Investments

- To calculate the size of the monthly or quarterly payments required to repay a loan or meet an investment goal, use the PMT function

        PMT(Rate, Nper, Pv, [Fv = 0], [Type = 0])

    where *Rate* is the interest rate per period, *Nper* is the total number of payment periods, *Pv* is the present value, *Fv* is the future value, and *Type* specifies whether payments are made at the end of each period (*Type* = 0) or at the beginning (*Type* = 1).
- To calculate the future value of a loan or an investment, use the FV function

        FV(Rate, Nper, Pmt, [Pv = 0], [Type = 0])

- To calculate the number of payments required to repay a loan or meet an investment goal, use the NPER function

        NPER(Rate, Pmt, Pv, [Fv = 0], [Type = 0])

- To calculate the present value of a loan or an investment, use the PV function

        PV(Rate, Nper, Pmt, [Fv = 0], [Type = 0])

- To calculate the interest rate on a loan or an investment, use the RATE function

        RATE(Nper, Pmt, Pv, [Fv = 0], [Type = 0], [Guess = 0.1])

    where the optional *Guess* argument provides an initial guess of the interest rate value.

Robuster plans to take out a business loan of $1,500,000 to fund the startup expenses not already covered by existing assets and money from investors. Kim wants you to calculate the quarterly payment on a $1.5 million loan at 8% annual interest to be completely repaid in five years. A good practice is to enter the loan conditions into separate cells rather than including them in the PMT function. Making the loan conditions visible removes any ambiguity about the conditions of the loan and allows you to explore the impact of different loan conditions in a what-if analysis.

You will enter the loan conditions in the workbook Kim created, and then use the PMT function to calculate the quarterly payment.

To calculate a quarterly payment with the PMT function:

1. Go to the **Loan Analysis** worksheet. Kim already entered and formatted much of the content in this worksheet.

2. In cell **B4**, enter **8%** as the annual interest rate of the loan.

3. In cell **B7**, enter **$1,500,000** as the amount of the business loan.

4. In cell **C7**, enter **0** for the future value of the loan because the loan will be completely repaid by the company.

5. In cell **D7**, enter **5** as the length of the loan in years.

6. In cell **E7**, enter **4** as the number of payments per year, which is quarterly.

7. In cell **F7**, enter the formula **= D7*E7** to calculate the total number of loan payments. In this case, four loan payments per year for five years is 20.

8. In cell **G7**, enter the formula **= $B$4** to display the annual interest rate specified in cell B4.

9. In cell **H7**, enter the formula **= G7/E7** to calculate the interest rate for each payment. In this case, the annual interest rate divided by quarterly payments returns 2.00% as the interest rate per quarter.

    Key Step To apply the PMT function correctly, be sure to use the interest rate for that payment period rather than the annual interest rate.

10. In cell **I7**, enter the formula **= PMT(H7, F7, B7)** to calculate the payment due each quarter based on the rate value in cell H7, the number of payments specified in cell F7, and the amount of the loan in cell B7. The formula returns ($91,735), a negative value that indicates the company will need to make payments of $91,735 each quarter to pay off the loan in five years. Refer to Figure 9–1.

Figure 9–1   Quarterly payment required to repay a loan

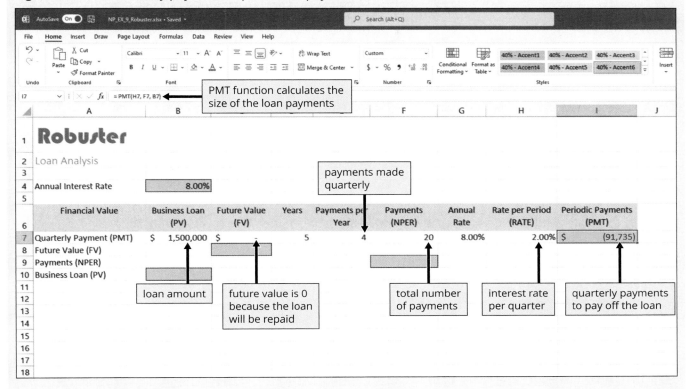

The $91,735 quarterly payments are higher than Kim anticipated. Kim was hoping for quarterly payments closer to $75,000 and asks you to determine how much of the loan would be unpaid with that payment schedule. You can calculate the amount left on the loan using the FV function.

Calculating a Future Value with the FV Function

In writing the PMT function, you used the default value of 0 for the future value because the intent was to completely repay the loan. However, if a loan will not be completely repaid, use the FV function to calculate the loan's future value after a specified number of periods. The future value is the principal remaining on the loan that is still owed to the lender. The syntax of the FV function is

```
FV(Rate, Nper, Pmt, [Pv = 0], [Type = 0])
```

where the `Rate`, `Nper`, `Pmt`, and `Type` values still represent the interest rate per period, the number of payments, the payment each period, and when the payment is due (beginning or end of the period). The `Pv` argument is optional and represents the present value of the loan or investment, which is assumed to be 0 by default.

The FV function is often used with investments to calculate the future value of a series of payments. For example, if you deposit $100 per month in a new savings account that has a starting balance of $0 and pays 1% interest annually compounded monthly, the FV function to calculate the future value of that investment after 10 years or 120 months is

```
FV(1%/12, 10*12, -100)
```

which returns $12,614.99. The extra $614.99 above the total amount of $12,000 you deposited is the interest earned from the money during that 10-year period. Note that the payment value is –100 because it represents the monthly deposit (negative cash flow), and the value returned by the FV function is positive because it represents money returned to the investor (positive cash flow). The *Pv* value in this example is assumed to be 0 because no money was in the savings account before the first deposit.

When used with a loan, the present value is positive because it is money received. If you borrow $10,000 at 4% annual interest and repay the loan at a rate of $250 per month, you would calculate the amount remaining on the loan after three years or 36 months as the future value

        FV(4%/12, 12*3, -250, 10000)

which returns ($1,727.33), a negative value, indicating that more than $1,700 is still owed to the lender after three years.

Kim wants to know how much the company would still owe after five years if the quarterly payments were $75,000. You will use the FV function to calculate this future value.

To calculate the future value of the loan:

1. In cell **B8**, enter **$1,500,000** as the size of the loan.

2. Copy the values and formulas from the range **D7:H7** and paste them in the range **D8:H8**.

3. In cell **I8**, enter **–$75,000** as the size of the quarterly payments. Again, the value is negative because it represents money that the company will spend (negative cash flow).

4. In cell **C8**, enter the formula **= FV(H8, F8, I8, B8)** to calculate the future value of the loan based on the rate value in cell H8, the number of payments specified in cell F8, the quarterly payments specified in cell I8, and the present value of the loan entered in cell B8. The formula returns ($406,618), a negative value that indicates the company will still owe the lender more than $400,000 at the end of the five-year period. Refer to Figure 9–2.

Figure 9–2   FV function to calculate the value of the loan after five years

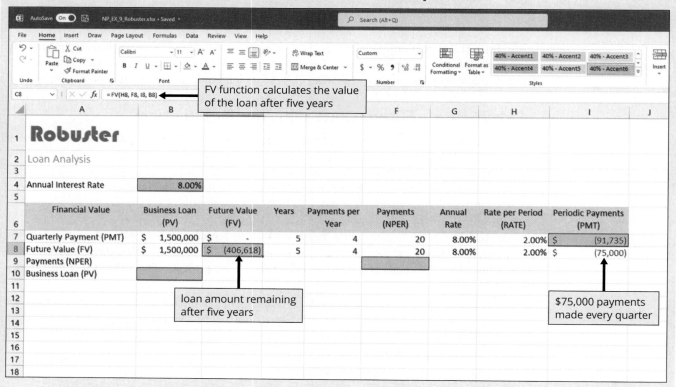

At 8% annual interest, about 27% of the original $1,500,000 loan will still need to be repaid at the end of five years if the quarterly payments are limited to $75,000.

Insight

Calculating Inflation with the FV Function

You can use the FV function to calculate future costs, adjusting for the effects of inflation. To project a future value of an item, use

```
FV(Rate, Years, 0, Present)
```

where `Rate` is the annual inflation rate, `Years` is the number of years in the future for which you want to project the cost of the item, and `Present` is the present-day cost. For example, if an item currently costs $15,000 and the inflation rate is 2.3%, the cost of the item in eight years is calculated using

```
FV(2.3%, 8, 0, 15000)
```

which returns –$17,992.70. The negative value is based on how Excel handles the FV function with positive and negative cash flows. For the purposes of predicting an inflated value, you can ignore the minus sign and use a value of $17,992.70 as the future cost of the item. Notice that you enter 0 for the value of the `Pmt` argument because you are not making payments toward inflation.

The FV function can also be used to express today's dollars in terms of yesterday's dollars by entering a negative value for the Years value. For example, the following function uses a value of –8 for years

```
FV(2.3%, -8, 0, 15000)
```

returning the value –$12,505.07, indicating that at an annual inflation rate of 2.3%, $15,000 today is equivalent to about $12,500 eight years ago.

Because a significant amount of the original loan would still be unpaid after five years, Kim wants to know how much more time would be required to repay the $1,500,000 loan assuming quarterly payments of $75,000. You can calculate the length of the payment period using the NPER function.

Calculating the Payment Period with the NPER Function

The NPER function calculates the number of payments required either to repay a loan or to reach an investment goal. The syntax of the NPER function is

```
NPER(Rate, Pmt, Pv, [Fv = 0], [Type = 0])
```

where the `Rate`, `Pmt`, `Pv`, `Fv`, and `Type` arguments are the same as described with the PMT and FV functions. For example, the following function calculates the number of $20 monthly payments needed to repay a $1,000 loan at 4% annual interest:

```
NPER(4%/12, -20, 1000)
```

The formula returns 54.7875773, indicating that the loan and the interest will be completely repaid in about 55 months.

> **Tip** The NPER function returns the number of payments, not necessarily the number of years.

To use the NPER function for investments, you define a future value of the investment along with the investment's present value and the periodic payments made to the investment. If you placed $200 per month in an account that pays 3% interest compounded monthly, the following function calculates the number of payments required to reach $5,000:

```
NPER(3%/12, -200, 0, 5000)
```

The formula returns 24.28, which is just over two years. Note that the `Pv` value is set to 0 based on the assumption that no money was in the account before the first deposit.

You will use the NPER function to calculate the time required to repay a $1,500,000 loan at 8% interest with quarterly payments of $75,000.

To calculate the number of payments for the loan:

1. Copy the present and future values of the loan in the range **B7:C7** and paste them into the range **B9:C9**.

2. In cell **E9**, enter **4** to specify that payments are made quarterly.

3. Copy the annual interest rate, rate per quarter, and the quarterly payments values and formulas in the range **G8:I8** and paste them in the range **G9:I9**.

4. In cell **F9**, enter the formula **= NPER(H9, I9, B9)** to calculate the required number of payments based on the interest rate per quarter in cell H9, the quarterly payments value in cell I9, and the present value of the loan in cell B9. The formula returns 25.80, indicating that about 26 payments are required to fully repay the loan.

   > **Tip** If the NPER function returns #NUM!, the loan cannot be repaid because the payments for each period are less than the interest due.

5. In cell **D9**, enter the formula **= F9/E9** to divide the total number of payments by the number of payments per year, which determines the number of years needed to repay the loan. The formula returns 6.44896, indicating that the loan will be repaid in about six and half years.

6. Select cell **F9**. Refer to Figure 9–3.

Figure 9–3   Payments required to repay the loan

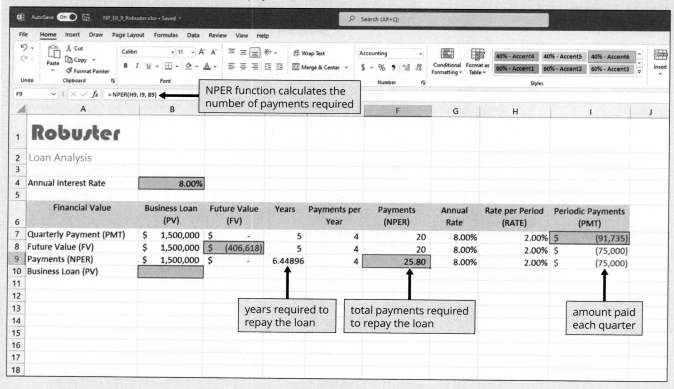

The company does not want to take more than six years to repay a business loan, so Kim wants you to calculate the size of the loan that could be repaid within five years at $75,000 per quarter.

Calculating the Present Value with the PV Function

The PV function calculates the present value of a loan or an investment. For a loan, the present value would be the current size of the loan. For an investment, the present value is the amount of money initially placed in the investment account. The syntax of the PV function is

```
PV(Rate, Nper, Pmt, [Fv = 0], [Type = 0])
```

where the `Rate`, `Nper`, `Pmt`, `Fv`, and `Type` arguments have the same meanings they had for the other financial functions. You can use the PV function to calculate the loan amount that you can afford given a set number of payments and an annual interest rate. For example, if you make $100 monthly payments at 4% annual interest for four years (or 48 months), the function to calculate the largest loan you can afford is

```
PV(4%/12, 48, -100)
```

which returns $4,428.88. Note that because you are paying $100 per month for 48 months, the total amount paid back to the lender is $4,800. The $371.12 difference between the total amount paid and the loan amount represents the cost of the loan in terms of the total interest paid.

You can also use the PV function with investments to calculate the initial payment required to reach a savings goal. For example, if you add $100 per month to a college savings account that grows at 4% annual interest and you want the account to reach a future value of $25,000 in 10 years (or 120 months), the following function returns the size of the initial payment:

```
PV(4%/12, 120, -100, 25000)
```

The function returns –$6,892.13, indicating you must start with almost $6,900 in the account to reach the $25,000 savings goal at the end of 10 years.

You will use the PV function to determine the largest loan that Robuster can afford if the company pays back the loan with quarterly payments of $32,000 made over a five-year period at 6% annual interest.

To apply the PV function to calculate the loan size:

1. Copy the loan condition values and formulas in the range **C7:H7** and paste them in the range **C10:H10**.

2. In cell **I10**, enter **–$75,000** as the quarterly payment amount.

3. In cell **B10**, enter **= PV(H10, F10, I10)** to calculate the size of the loan based on the interest rate per quarter value in cell H10, the number of payments specified in cell F10, and the size of the quarterly payments in cell I10. The formula results specify a loan amount of $1,226,358. Refer to Figure 9–4.

Figure 9–4   Present value of the loan

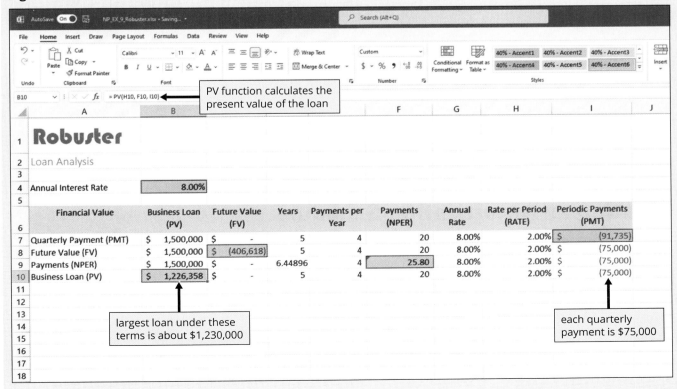

Kim will recommend a loan amount of $1,250,000 to be repaid at 8% interest in quarterly payments over the first five years of the company's operation. You will enter this loan amount in the Startup worksheet, which contains the company's startup costs and assets.

To enter the loan amount:

1. Go to the **Startup** worksheet.

2. In cell **B26**, enter **1,250,000** as the loan amount.

3. Review the Startup worksheet, noting the expenses and assets for starting up the company as well as other sources of funding. You will use some of these values later.

Kim wants you to provide more detailed information about the proposed business loan in the Loan Schedule worksheet. You will start by entering the terms of the loan and calculate the exact value of each loan payment.

To calculate the size of the loan payments:

1. Go to the **Loan Schedule** worksheet.

2. In cell **A5**, type **=** to begin the formula, go to the **Startup** worksheet, click cell **B26**, and then press **TAB**. The formula = Startup!B26 entered in cell A5 displays the loan amount of $1,250,000 from cell B26 in the Startup worksheet.

3. In cell **B5**, enter **8.00%** as the annual interest rate.

4. In cell **C5**, enter **4** as the number of payments per year because the company plans to make quarterly payments.

5. In cell **D5**, enter the formula **= B5/C5** to calculate the interest rate per quarter. The formula returns 2.00% as the interest rate.

6. In cell **E5**, enter **5** to indicate that the loan will be repaid in five years.

7. In cell **F5**, enter the formula **= C5*E5** to calculate the total number of payments, which is 20 payments in this case.

8. In cell **G5**, enter the formula **= PMT(D5, F5, A5)** to calculate the size of each payment. The formula returns –$76,466, which is the exact amount the company will have to spend per quarter to completely repay the $1,250,000 loan in five years.

Kim wants to examine how much of each $76,466 quarterly payment is spent on interest charged by the lender and how much is used in paying off the loan. To determine that value, you will create an amortization schedule.

Creating an Amortization Schedule

An **amortization schedule** specifies how much of each loan payment is devoted to paying interest and how much to paying off the principal. In most loans, the initial payments are usually directed toward interest charges. As more of the loan is repaid, the percentage of each payment devoted to interest decreases (because the interest is being applied to a smaller and smaller principal) until the last few payments are almost entirely devoted to repaying the principal. Figure 9–5 shows a typical relationship between the amount paid toward interest and the amount paid toward the principal over time.

Figure 9–5   Interest and principal payments

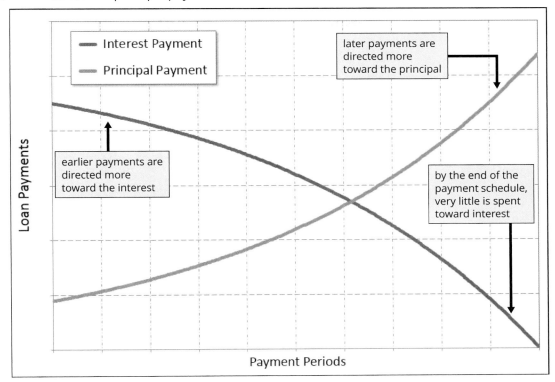

Calculating Interest and Principal Payments

To calculate the amount of a loan payment devoted to interest and to principal, use the IPMT and PPMT functions. The IPMT function returns the payment amount directed toward interest on the loan. It has the syntax

```
IPMT(Rate, Per, Nper, Pv, [Fv = 0], [Type = 0])
```

where the *Rate*, *Nper*, *Pv*, *Fv*, and *Type* arguments have the same meaning as they do for the PMT and other financial functions. The *Per* argument indicates the payment period for which the interest is due. For example, the following function calculates how much interest is due in the third payment of the company's $1,250,000 loan at 8% interest paid quarterly over five years:

```
IPMT(8%/4, 3, 20, 1250000)
```

The formula returns a value of –$22,921.59 or about $23,000 that is used solely for paying the interest on the loan and not on paying down the principal. You can calculate the principal payment using the PPMT function:

```
PPMT(Rate, Per, Nper, Pv, [Fv = 0], [Type = 0])
```

The principal payment for the third payment period is

```
PPMT(8%/4, 3, 20, 1250000)
```

returning a value of –$53,524.31. Because every dollar of the loan payment is directed toward either interest or repaying the principal, the sum of the IPMT and PPMT values ($76,445.90 or $76,446 rounded to the nearest dollar) is the total amount paid each quarter (cell G5 of the Loan Schedule worksheet). The total amount paid to the bank each quarter doesn't change. The only change is how that amount is allocated between interest and principal.

Kim wants you to complete an amortization schedule for the proposed loan. The Loan Schedule worksheet already contains the table in which you will enter the formulas to track the changing amounts spent on principal and interest over the next five years. You will use the IPMT and PPMT functions to create the amortization schedule.

To create the amortization schedule for the company's loan:

1. In cell **C9**, enter the formula **= A5** to display the initial value for the remaining principal on the loan (prior to any payments being made).

2. In cell **D9**, enter the formula **= IPMT($D$5, B9, $F$5, $A$5)** to calculate the interest due for the first payment, with $D$5, $F$5, and $A$5 referencing the loan conditions specified in row 5 of the worksheet, and cell B9 referencing the number of the period. The formula returns the value –$25,000, which is the amount of interest due in the first payment.

    | **Tip** Use absolute references to apply the same loan conditions to every payment period when you copy the formulas to the rest of the amortization schedule.

3. In cell **E9**, enter the formula **= PPMT($D$5, B9, $F$5, $A$5)** to calculate the portion of the payment applied to the principal in the first period. The formula returns the value –$51,446, which is the amount of the first payment directed toward reducing the principal.

4. In cell **F9**, enter the formula **= D9 + E9** to calculate the total payment for the first period of the loan. The formula returns –$76,466, matching the quarterly payment value in cell G5. Refer to Figure 9–6.

Figure 9–6   Initial payment in the amortization schedule

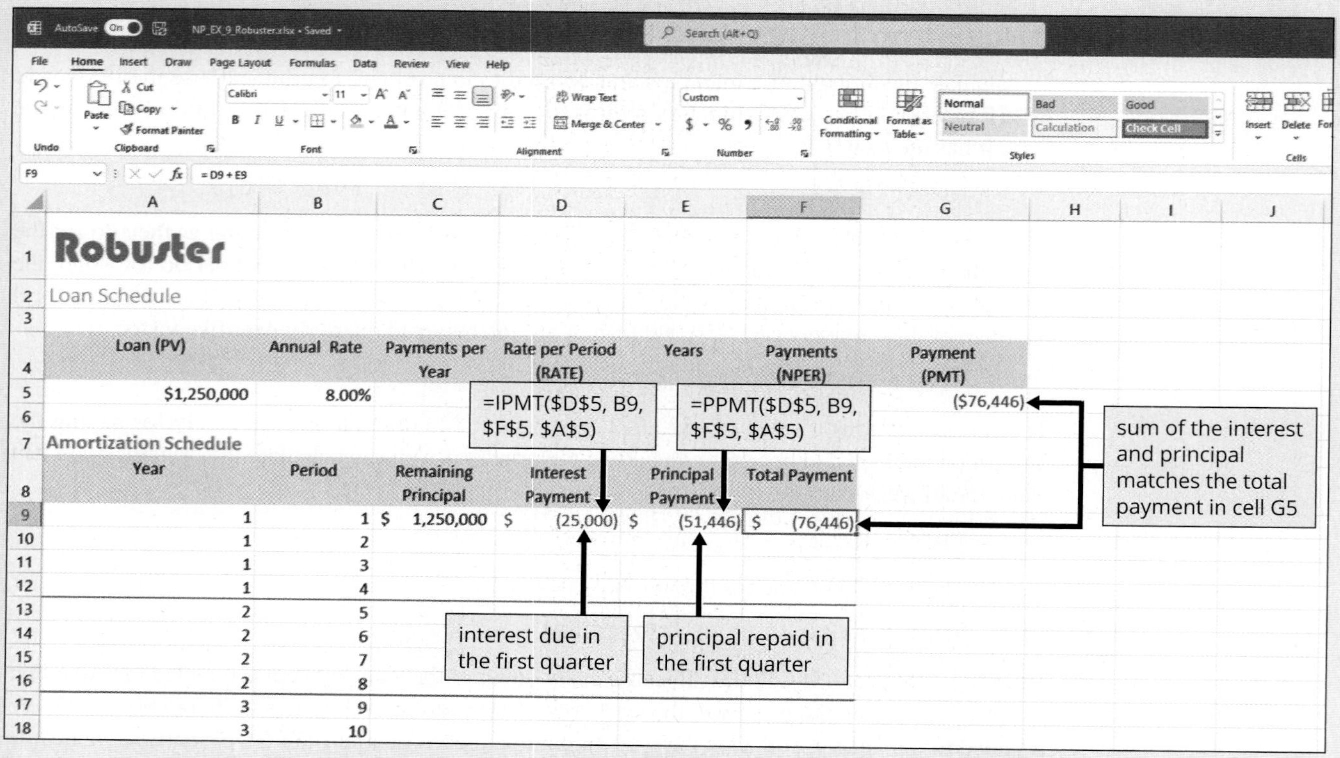

The formulas for the rest of the amortization schedule are like those used for the first quarter except that the remaining principal in column C must be reduced by the amount paid toward the principal from the previous quarter.

To complete the amortization schedule:

1. In cell **C10**, enter the formula **= C9 + E9** to add the principal remaining from the previous quarter to the principal payment. Excel returns the value 1,198,554.

2. Copy the formulas in the range **D9:F9** and paste them in the range **D10:F10** to calculate the interest, principal, and total payment for the quarter. The interest paid drops to –$23,971 because interest is charged on the smaller remaining principal, while the amount paid toward the principal increases to –$52,475. The total payment remains $76,446, a valuable confirmation that the formulas are correct.

3. Use the fill handle to extend the formulas in the range **C10:F10** through the range **C11:F28**. The formulas are copied into the rest of the rows of the amortization schedule to calculate the remaining principal, interest payment, principal payment, and total payment for each of the remaining 18 quarters of the loan.

4. Click the **Auto Fill Options** button 🔡, and then click the **Fill Without Formatting** option button. The formulas are entered without overwriting the existing worksheet formatting. Notice that in the last quarterly payment at the end of the fifth year, only $1,499 of the $76,446 payment is for interest on the loan. The remaining $74,947 pays off the principal.

5. In cell **C29**, enter the formula **= C28 + E28** to calculate the final balance of the loan after the final payment. The final balance is $0.00, verifying that the loan is completely repaid at the end of the five-year period. Refer to Figure 9–7.

Figure 9–7   Completed amortization schedule

	A	B	C	D	E	F	G	H	I	J
7	Amortization Schedule		remaining principal steadily declines							
8		Year	Period	Remaining Principal	Interest Payment	Principal Payment	Total Payment			
9		1	1	$ 1,250,000	$ (25,000)	$ (51,446)	$ (76,446)			
10		1	2	1,198,554	$ (23,971)	$ (52,475)	$ (76,446)			
11		1	3	1,146,079	(22,922)	(53,524)	(76,446)			
12		1	4	1,092,555	(21,851)	(54,595)	(76,446)			
13		2	5	1,037,960	(20,759)	(55,687)	(76,446)			
14		2	6	982,273	(19,645)	(56,800)	(76,446)			
15		2	7	925,473	(18,509)	(57,936)	(76,446)			
16		2	8	867,537	(17,351)	(59,095)	(76,446)			
17		3	9	808,441	(16,169)	(60,277)	(76,446)		constant payments of $76,446 per quarter		
18		3	10	748,164	(14,963)	(61,483)	(76,446)			
19		3	11	686,682	(13,734)	(62,712)	(76,446)			
20		3	12	623,970	(12,479)	(63,967)	(76,446)			
21		4	13	560,003	(11,200)	(65,246)	(76,446)			
22		4	14	494,757	(9,895)	(66,551)	(76,446)			
23		4	15	428,206	(8,564)	(67,882)	(76,446)			
24		4	16	360,325	(7,206)	(69,239)	(76,446)			
25		5	17	291,085	(5,822)	(70,624)	(76,446)			
26		5	18	220,461	(4,409)	(72,037)	(76,446)			
27		5	19	148,424	(2,968)	(73,477)	(76,446)			
28		5	20	74,947	(1,499)	(74,947)	(76,446)			
29			Final Balance	$0.00						
30										
31			final balance is 0 after the last payment							

Docu...   Balance Sheet   Investment Analysis ... ⊕ : ◀

interest payments decrease while principal payments increase

Ready   Accessibility: Investigate

Kim finds it helpful to know how much interest the company is paying each quarter. However, many financial statements also show the amount paid toward interest and principal over the whole year because this information is useful for creating annual budgets and calculating tax liability.

Calculating Cumulative Interest and Principal Payments

Cumulative totals of interest and principal payments can be calculated using the CUMIPMT and CUMPRINC functions. The **CUMIPMT function** calculates the sum of several interest payments and has the syntax

    CUMIPMT(Rate, Nper, Pv, Start, End, Type)

where *Start* is the starting payment period for the interval you want to sum and *End* is the ending payment period. This function does not specify a future value because the assumption is that loans are always completely repaid. Also, note that the *Type* argument is not optional. You must specify whether the payments are made at the end of the period (*Type* = 0) or at the start (*Type* = 1). For example, to calculate the total interest paid in the second year of the company's loan (at the end of quarters 5 through 8), you would enter the function

    CUMIPMT(8%/4, 20, 1250000, 5, 8, 0)

which returns –$76,265 as the total spent on interest in the second year of the loan.

To calculate the cumulative total of payments made toward the principal, you use the **CUMPRINC function**, which has a similar syntax:

    CUMPRINC(Rate, Nper, Pv, Start, End, Type)

The following function calculates the total amount spent on reducing the principal of the loan during the fifth to eighth quarters

    CUMPRINC(8%/4, 20, 1250000, 5, 8, 0)

returning a value of –$229,519, indicating that the amount remaining on the loan is reduced by almost $230,000 during the second year.

Kim wants you to add the total interest and principal payments for the loan for each of the five years in the amortization schedule. You will use the CUMIPMT and CUMPRINC functions to calculate these values. The table at the bottom of the Loan Schedule worksheet already has the starting and ending quarters for each year of the loan, which you will reference in the functions.

To calculate the cumulative interest and principal payments:

1. In cell **B36**, enter the formula **= CUMIPMT($D$5, $F$5, $A$5, B34, B35, 0)** to calculate the cumulative interest payments for the first year. The formula returns –$93,744, which is the amount of interest for the first year.

    Notice that the formula uses absolute references to cells D5, F5, and A5 for the *Rate*, *Nper*, and *Pv* arguments so that these arguments always reference the loan conditions at the top of the worksheet, which do not change throughout the loan schedule. The references to cells B34 and B35 for the start and end arguments are relative because they change based on the period over which the payments are made.

2. In cell **B37**, enter the formula **= CUMPRINC($D$5, $F$5, $A$5, B34, B35, 0)** to calculate the total principal payments in the first year. The formula returns –$212,040, which is the amount by which the principal will be reduced the first year.

3. Copy the formulas in the range **B36:B37** and paste them in the range **C36:F37** to calculate the cumulative interest and principal payments for each of the next four years.

4. Click cell **F37**. Refer to Figure 9–8.

Figure 9–8   Annual cumulative interest and principal payments

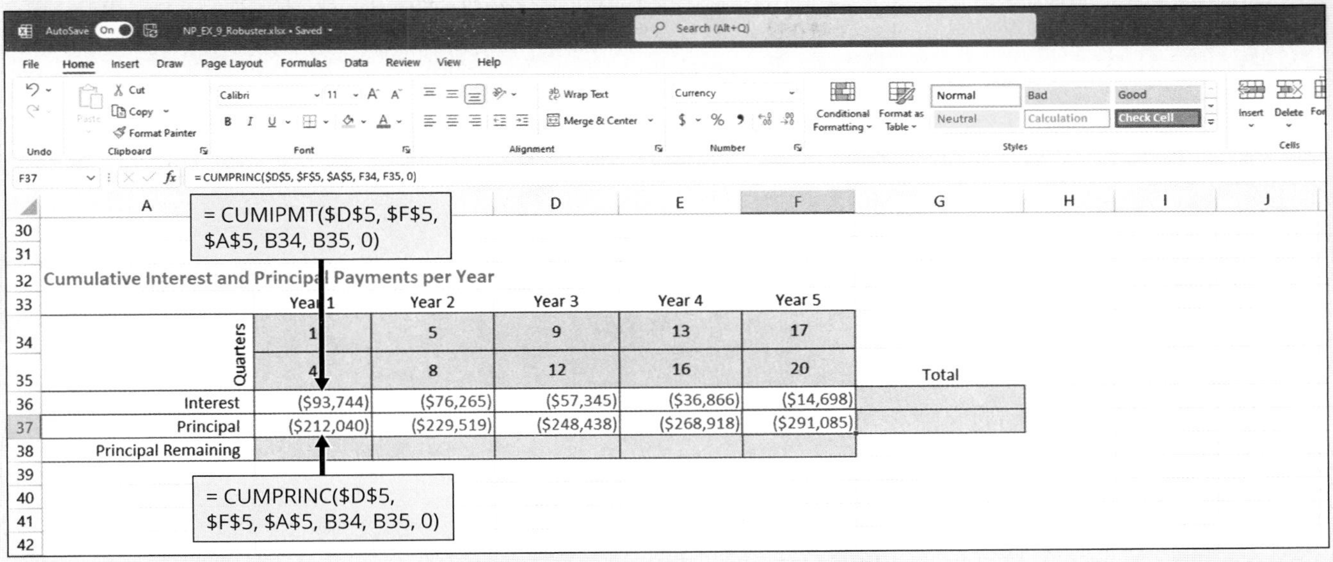

Each year, more money is spent reducing the principal. For example, in Year 5, the company will spend $14,698 on interest payments and will reduce the loan principal by $291,085. Next you will calculate the total interest and principal paid through the five years of the loan and the principal remaining at the end of each year.

To complete the cumulative payment table:

1. Select the range **G36:G37**.

2. On the Home tab, in the Editing group, click the **AutoSum** button to calculate the total interest and principal payments over the five years of the loan, which are $278,918 and $1,250,000, respectively.

   Finally, you will calculate the principal remaining at the end of each of the five years of the loan.

3. In cell **B38**, enter the formula **= $A$5 + B37** to add the cumulative principal payment to the initial amount of the loan in cell A5. The formula returns $1,037,960, which is the amount of the loan remaining to be paid after the first year.

4. In cell **C38**, enter the formula **= B38 + C37** to calculate the remaining principal at the end of Year 2 by adding the Year 1 principal to the Year 2 principal payments. The formula returns $808,441.

5. Copy the formula in cell **C38** and paste it in the range **D38:F38** to calculate the remaining principal at the end of each of the next three years. Note that at end of the fifth year, the principal remaining is zero because the entire loan is paid off.

6. Select cell **A31** to deselect the table. Refer to Figure 9–9 for the final table of cumulative interest and principal payments.

Figure 9–9   Total loan payments

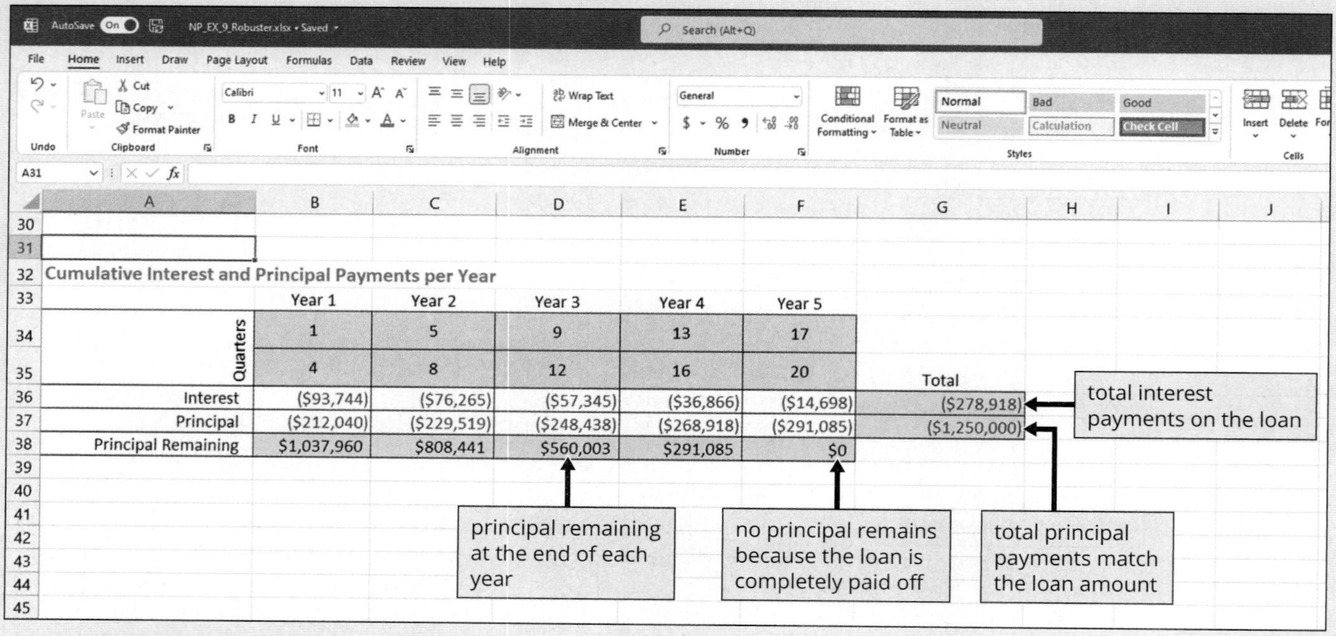

7. Save the workbook.

The Loan Schedule worksheet shows that the company will spend almost $280,000 in interest payments to finance this loan. Calculating the total principal payment verifies that the loan conditions are set up correctly. If the total payment toward the principal does not match the initial amount of the loan, there must be a mistake in the calculations used in the loan schedule.

Loan and Investment Schedules with Variable Interest Rates

The loan schedule you created assumes a constant interest rate during the duration of the loan or investment. However, many loans and investments employ variable interest rates that change throughout the duration of the financial transaction. To calculate the future value of loans and investments with variable interest rates, use the following **FVSchedule function**:

```
FVSCHEDULE(Principal, Schedule)
```

where `Principal` is the present value of a loan or investment and `Schedule` is an array of interest rates to apply to that principal. For example, if $1,000 is invested in an account for five years with annual interest rates of 4%, 4%, 6%, 3%, and 2%, the future value is calculated using the expression

```
FVSCHEDULE(1000, {0.04, 0.04, 0.06, 0.03, 0.02})
```

returning a future value at the end of those five years of $1,204.51.

> **Tip** If you enter the FVSCHEDULE interest rates directly within an array, enter the values as decimals rather than percentages to avoid Excel returning a #NUM error.

You can also place the `Schedule` values in a worksheet range. If the annual interest rates are placed in the range E1:E5, the expression

```
FVSCHEDULE(1000, E1:E5)
```

would also return a future value of $1,204.51. Note that unlike the FV function which would treat $1,000 as a positive cash flow and returning a negative cash flow (as payment on a loan), the FVSCHEDULE does not take cash flow into account and will return a positive value.

Proskills

Written Communication: Writing a Financial Workbook

A properly written financial workbook should concisely communicate key pieces of information to the reader. It should also be editable to allow exploration of what-if scenarios that analyze the impact of different assumptions on the financial bottom line. To help ensure that any financial workbook you create meets these goals, keep in mind the following principals:

- Place all important financial variables at or near the top of a worksheet so that they are visible to others. For example, place the interest rate you use in calculations in a clearly labeled worksheet cell.
- Use defined names with the financial variables to make it easier to apply them in formulas and functions.
- Clearly identify the direction of the cash flow in all your financial calculations by expressing the cash value as negative or positive. Using the wrong sign will turn the calculation of a loan payment into an investment deposit or vice versa.
- Place argument values in worksheet cells where they can be viewed and changed. Never place these values directly into a financial formula.
- When values are used in more than one calculation, enter them in a cell that you can reference in all formulas rather than repeating the same value throughout the workbook.
- Use the same unit of time for all the arguments in a financial function. When using the PMT function to calculate monthly loan payments, the interest rate and the number of payments should be based on the interest rate per month and the total months to repay the loan.

   A financial workbook that is easy to read and understand is more useful to yourself and others when making important business decisions.

You have finished analyzing the conditions for the company's business loan. Next, you will forecast the company's future earnings by developing a projection of the company's income statement over the next five years.

Part 9.1 Quick Check

1. Explain the difference between positive and negative cash flow. If you borrow $20,000 from a bank, is that a positive or negative cash flow? Explain your answer.
2. What is the formula to calculate how much a savings account would be worth if the initial balance is $5,000 with monthly deposits of $150 for 10 years at 3.8% annual interest compounded monthly? What is the formula result?
3. You want a savings account to grow from $5,000 to $15,000 within five years. Assume the bank provides a 3.5% annual interest rate compounded monthly. What is the formula to calculate how much you must deposit each month to meet your savings goal? What is the formula result?
4. A business takes out a loan for $750,000 at 7.8% interest compounded monthly. If the business can afford to make monthly payments of $10,000 on the loan, what is the formula to calculate the number of months required to repay the loan completely? What is the formula result?
5. If the business in Question 4 can afford only a $5,000 monthly payment, what is the revised formula and resulting value? How do you explain the result?
6. A business takes out a 10-year loan for $750,000 at 7.5% interest compounded monthly. What is the formula to calculate the monthly payment and what is the resulting value?
7. For the loan conditions specified in Question 6, provide formulas to calculate the amount of the first payment used for interest and the amount of the first payment used to repay the principal. What are the resulting values?
8. For the loan conditions specified in Question 6, what are the formulas to calculate how much interest the business will pay in the first year and how much the business will repay toward the principal? Assume that payments are made at the end of the month. What are the resulting values?
9. An investment of $25,000 is deposited in an account with annual interest rates during the first five years of 4.2%, 3.8%, 3.5%, 3%, and 4%. What is the formula to calculate the future value of the investment at the end of the five years? What is the result of that formula?

Part 9.2 Visual Overview:
Income Statements and Depreciations

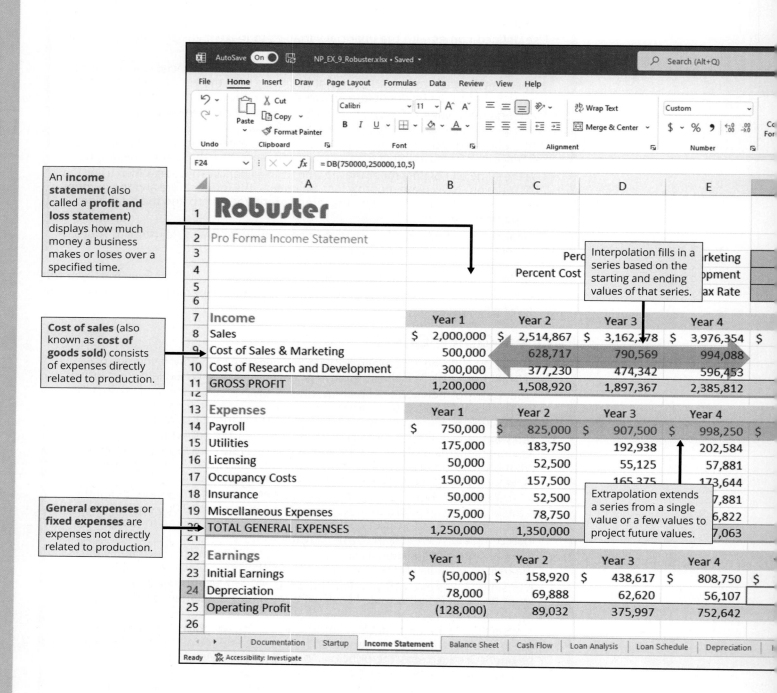

An **income statement** (also called a **profit and loss statement**) displays how much money a business makes or loses over a specified time.

Cost of sales (also known as **cost of goods sold**) consists of expenses directly related to production.

General expenses or **fixed expenses** are expenses not directly related to production.

Interpolation fills in a series based on the starting and ending values of that series.

Extrapolation extends a series from a single value or a few values to project future values.

F24   = DB(750000,250000,10,5)

Robuster

Pro Forma Income Statement

	Year 1	Year 2	Year 3	Year 4
Income				
Sales	$ 2,000,000	$ 2,514,867	$ 3,162,478	$ 3,976,354
Cost of Sales & Marketing	500,000	628,717	790,569	994,088
Cost of Research and Development	300,000	377,230	474,342	596,453
GROSS PROFIT	1,200,000	1,508,920	1,897,367	2,385,812
Expenses				
Payroll	$ 750,000	$ 825,000	$ 907,500	$ 998,250
Utilities	175,000	183,750	192,938	202,584
Licensing	50,000	52,500	55,125	57,881
Occupancy Costs	150,000	157,500	165,375	173,644
Insurance	50,000	52,500		7,881
Miscellaneous Expenses	75,000	78,750		6,822
TOTAL GENERAL EXPENSES	1,250,000	1,350,000		7,063
Earnings				
Initial Earnings	$ (50,000)	$ 158,920	$ 438,617	$ 808,750
Depreciation	78,000	69,888	62,620	56,107
Operating Profit	(128,000)	89,032	375,997	752,642

Documentation | Startup | Income Statement | Balance Sheet | Cash Flow | Loan Analysis | Loan Schedule | Depreciation

Ready   Accessibility: Investigate

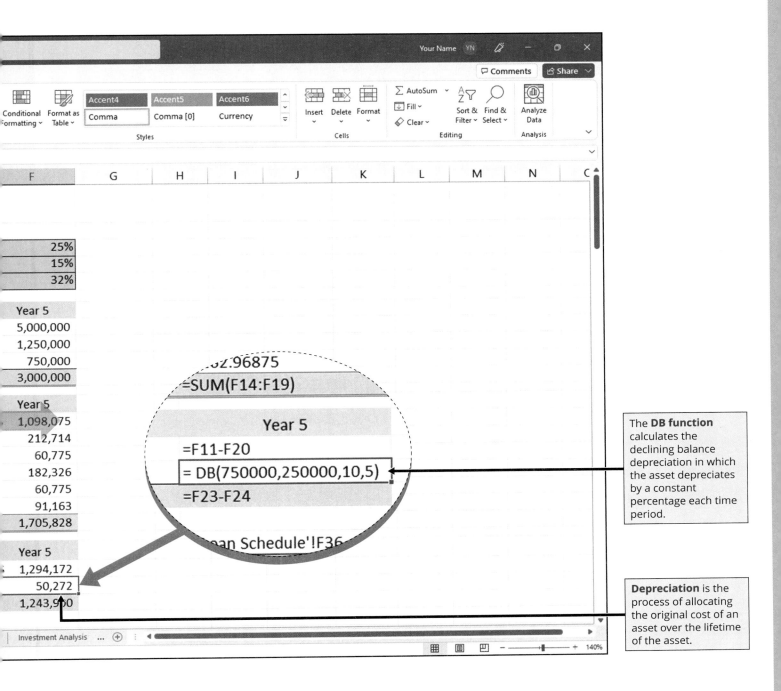

The **DB function** calculates the declining balance depreciation in which the asset depreciates by a constant percentage each time period.

Depreciation is the process of allocating the original cost of an asset over the lifetime of the asset.

Projecting Future Income and Expenses

A key part of any business plan is a projection of the company's future income and expenses in an income statement. Income statements, also known as profit and loss statements, are usually created monthly, semiannually, or annually.

Kim has an Income Statement worksheet projecting the company's income and expenses for its first five years of operation. The income statement is divided into three main sections. The Income section projects the company's income from sales of its line of robotic cleaners as well as the cost of sales, marketing, and development for those printers. The Expenses section projects the general expenses incurred by company operations regardless of the number of robotic cleaners it manufactures and sells. The Earnings section estimates the company's net profit and tax liability. You will review this worksheet.

To view the Income Statement worksheet:

1. If you took a break after the previous part, make sure the NP_EX_9_Robuster workbook is open.

2. Go to the **Income Statement** worksheet, and review the three main sections—Income, Expenses, and Earnings. Refer to Figure 9–10.

Figure 9–10   Income Statement worksheet

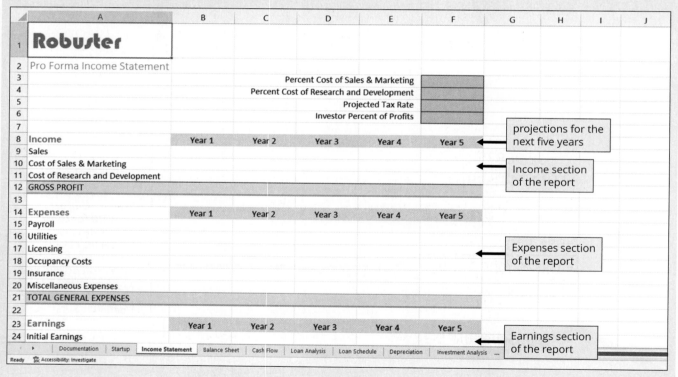

To project the financial future of the company, you will have to predict how the company's expansion will affect its future revenue, expenses, and net income. With Excel, you can project either a linear trend or a growth trend in those values.

Exploring Linear and Growth Trends

Assuming that Robuster will be a success and grow over the next five years, Kim foresees two possibilities: (1) Revenue will grow by a constant amount from one year to the next; or (2) Revenue will grow by a constant percentage each year. The first scenario, in which revenue changes by a constant amount, is an example of a **linear trend**. A linear trend appears as a straight line when plotted.

The second possibility, in which revenue changes by a constant percentage rather than a constant amount, is an example of a **growth trend**. A growth trend appears as a curve with the greatest numerical differences occurring near the end of the series. Figure 9–11 shows a linear trend and a growth trend for revenue that starts at $2,000,000 in Year 1 increasing to $4,000,000 by Year 5. Under the linear trend, the revenue increases by $500,000 per year, while under the growth trend the revenue increases by about 19% each year. The growth trend lags behind the linear trend in the early years but reaches the same revenue value by the end of the fifth year.

Figure 9–11   Linear and growth trends

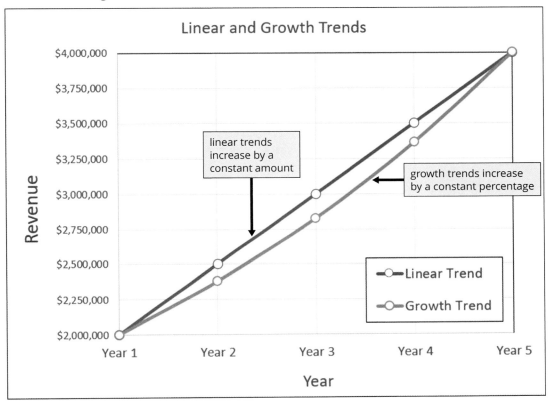

> **Tip** A growth trend is also called exponential growth in the fields of science, economics, and statistics.

To fill data within a linear or a growth trend, you use interpolation.

Interpolating from a Starting Value to an Ending Value

Interpolation is the process of estimating values between a defined starting and ending point. You can use AutoFill to interpolate values for both linear and growth trends. Kim wants you to estimate revenues for each of the company's first five years, assuming the company's revenue grows from $2,000,000 in Year 1 to $5,000,000 in Year 5. Kim first wants to determine how much revenue will be generated each year if the revenue grows by a constant amount annually. You will interpolate the company's revenue between Year 1 and Year 5 under a linear trend.

To project future revenue based on a linear trend:

1. In cell **B9**, enter **$2,000,000** as the Year 1 revenue.

2. In cell **F9**, enter **$5,000,000** as the Year 5 sales.

3. Select the range **B9:F9**, which includes the starting and ending sales values.

4. On the Home tab, in the Editing group, click the **Fill** button, and then click **Series**. The Series dialog box opens.

5. Verify that the **Rows** option button in the Series section and the **Linear** option button in the Type section are selected. Excel will fill the series within the same rows using a linear trend.

6. Click the **Trend** check box to insert a checkmark and apply a trend that interpolates between the starting and ending values in the selected range. Refer to Figure 9–12.

Figure 9–12   Series dialog box

7. Click **OK**. The values inserted in the range C9:E9 show the company's projected sales revenue based on a linear trend. Refer to Figure 9–13.

Figure 9–13   Linear trend values

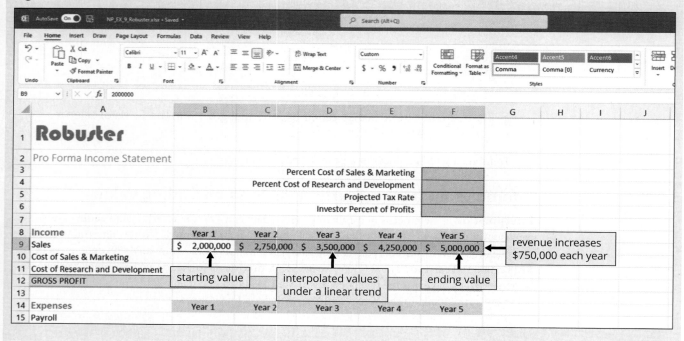

The linear trend projects an increase in the company's revenue of $750,000 per year. Next, you will interpolate the revenue in Year 2 through Year 4 assuming a growth trend.

To project future revenue assuming a growth trend:

1. Select the range **C9:E9** and press **DELETE** to clear the contents of those cells.

   > **Key Step** To interpolate between starting and ending values, the middle cells must be blank.

2. Select the range **B9:F9**.

3. On the Home tab, in the Editing group, click the **Fill** button, and then click **Series**. The Series dialog box opens.

4. In the Type section, click the **Growth** option button, and then click the **Trend** check box to select it, applying a growth trend to the interpolated values.

5. Click **OK**. The Year 1 through Year 5 revenue projections are now based on a growth trend. Refer to Figure 9–14.

Figure 9–14   Growth trend values

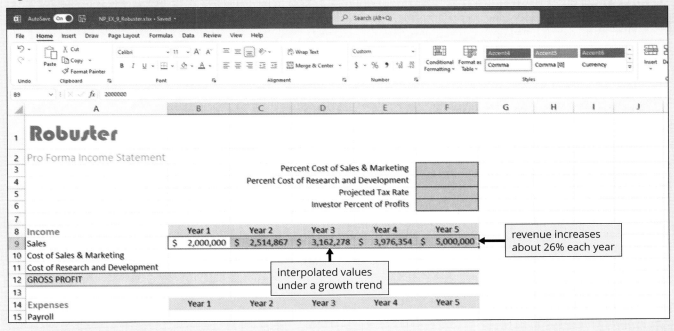

You can determine the percentage change in growth trend by dividing the current year's revenue by the previous year's revenue. Under the growth trend model, the company's revenue grows at a constant rate of about 26% per year. The largest revenue increase occurs at the end of the five-year period. For example, revenue grows by $514,867 from Year 1 to Year 2, but by $1,023,646 from Year 4 to Year 5.

Insight

Interpolating and Extrapolating in Charts

You can add interpolated values to any scatter chart by adding a trendline to the chart. To add a trendline, select the chart, click the Chart Elements button for the chart, and then click the Trendline check box. Excel supports trendlines for exponential (or growth) trends, linear (straight line) trends, logarithmic trends, polynomial trends, power trends, and moving averages. All these options can be found in the Format Trendline pane of the chart.

Trendlines can be extrapolated forward or backward from the points in the scatter chart by setting the forecast options in the Format Trendline pane. Again, these extrapolated values can be based on a wide variety of functions including linear and exponential functions. For more information, you can display the equation of the trendline on the chart itself.

Calculating the Cost of Goods Sold

The next part of the worksheet displays the cost of sales, also known as the cost of goods sold. Robuster needs to purchase the raw material to create the micro-robotic cleaners, and it also must invest time into the development and upgrade of the cleaners. Kim estimates that for every dollar of sales revenue, the company will need to spend 15 cents on sales and marketing and 10 cents on research and development. As the company's revenue increases, these costs will also increase. The difference between the company's sales revenue and the cost of goods sold is the company's **gross profit**.

Kim wants you to project the company's expenses and gross profit for each of the next five years using those cost of goods sold estimates.

To project the cost of goods sold and the gross profit:

1. In cell **F3**, enter **15%** as the percentage cost of sales and marketing.

2. In cell **F4**, enter **10%** as the percentage cost of research and development.

3. In cell **B10**, enter the formula **= B9*$F$3** to multiply the Year 1 revenue by the cost of goods percentage for sales and marketing. Excel returns a value of 300,000, which is the estimated cost of sales and marketing for Year 1.

4. In cell **B11**, enter the formula **= B9*$F$4**. Excel returns a value of 200,000, which is the estimated cost of research and development in Year 1.

5. In cell **B12**, enter the formula **= B9 – (B10 + B11)**. Excel returns a value of 1,500,000, which is the estimated gross profit in Year 1.

6. Copy the formulas in the range **B10:B12** and paste them in the range **C10:F12** to calculate the cost of goods sold and the gross profit for Year 2 through Year 5.

7. Deselect the selected range to better view the data. Refer to Figure 9–15.

Figure 9–15   Cost of goods sold and gross profit

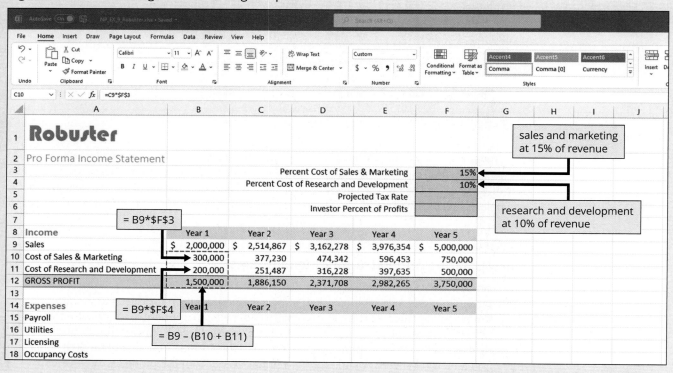

Based on these calculations, the company's gross profit is projected to increase from $1,500,000 in Year 1 to $3,750,000 in Year 5.

Reference

Interpolating and Extrapolating a Series

To interpolate a series of values between starting and ending values:

- Select the range with the first cell containing the starting value, blank cells for middle values, and the last cell containing the ending value.
- On the Home tab, in the Editing group, click the Fill button, and then click Series.
- Select whether the series is organized in rows or columns, select the type of series to interpolate, and then check the Trend check box.
- Click OK.

To extrapolate a series from a starting value:

- Select a range with the first cell containing the starting value followed by blank cells to store the extrapolated values.
- On the Home tab, in the Editing group, click the Fill button, and then click Series.
- Select whether the series is organized in rows or columns, select the type of series to extrapolate, and then enter the step value in the Step value box.
- Click OK.

The next section of the income statement contains the projected general expenses for the company. These expenses are not directly related to production. For example, the company must pay its employees, purchase insurance, provide for general maintenance, and pay for office space, regardless of the number of products it sells. You will add the Year 1 general expenses to the Income Statement worksheet.

To enter the Year 1 expenses:

1. In the range **B15:B20**, enter the following general expense values: **$750,000** in cell B15 for payroll, **150,000** in cell B16 for utilities, **50,000** in cell B17 for licensing, **100,000** in cell B18 for occupancy costs, **50,000** in cell B19 for insurance, and **40,000** in cell B20 for miscellaneous expenses.

2. In cell **B21**, enter the formula **= SUM(B15:B20)** to calculate the total expenses for Year 1. The formula returns the value 1,140,000.

From these Year 1 values, you will extrapolate the next four years of general expenses.

Extrapolating from a Series of Values

Extrapolation extends a data series from a single value or a few values to future values. Excel can extrapolate data based on either a linear trend or a growth trend. With a linear trend, the data are assumed to change by a constant amount. With a growth trend, they are assumed to change by a constant percentage.

To extrapolate a data series, you must provide a step value representing the amount by which each value is changed as the series is extended. For linear trends, the change measures the difference in values, while for growth trends the change measures the percent difference.

Kim estimates that the company's general expenses will grow by 4% each year. Since this growth is based on percentages, you will use Excel to extrapolate a growth trend.

To extrapolate the Year 1 expenses:

1. Select the range **B15:F20** containing the cells in which annual general expenses are entered.

2. On the Home tab, in the Editing group, click the **Fill** button, and then click **Series**. The Series dialog box opens.

3. Click the **Rows** option button to select it because the data will be extrapolate along the rows of the selected range and not along the column.

4. In the Type section, click the **Growth** option button to extrapolate the values assuming a growth trend.

5. In the Step value box, enter **1.04** so that the values are increased by 4% per year. Refer to Figure 9–16.

Figure 9–16   Series dialog box for extrapolation

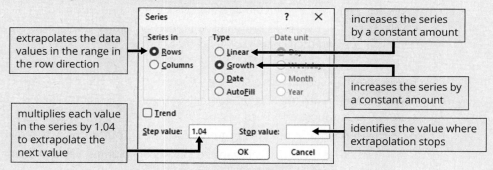

> **Tip** To extrapolate a decreasing trend, use a negative step value for a decreasing linear trend, and a step value between 0 and 1 for a decreasing growth trend.

6. Click **OK**. Excel extends the general expenses through the next four years, culminating in a Year 5 payroll expense of $877,394 and a utilities expense of $175,479.

7. Select the range **C21:F21** and on the Home tab in the Editing group, click the **AutoSum** button. This completes the expenses section by calculating the total general expenses from Year 2 through Year 5. Refer to Figure 9–17.

Figure 9–17   Projected general expenses

	A	B	C	D	E	F	G	H	I	J
1	**Robuster**									
2	Pro Forma Income Statement									
3				Percent Cost of Sales & Marketing		15%				
4				Percent Cost of Research and Development		10%				
5				Projected Tax Rate						
6				Investor Percent of Profits						
7										
8	Income	Year 1	Year 2	Year 3	Year 4	Year 5				
9	Sales	$ 2,000,000	$ 2,514,867	$ 3,162,278	$ 3,976,354	$ 5,000,000				
10	Cost of Sales & Marketing	300,000	377,230	474,342	596,453	750,000				
11	Cost of Research and Development	200,000	251,487	316,228	397,635	500,000				
12	GROSS PROFIT	1,500,000	1,886,150	2,371,708	2,982,265	3,750,000				
13										
14	Expenses	Year 1	Year 2	Year 3	Year 4	Year 5				
15	Payroll	$ 750,000	$ 780,000	$ 811,200	$ 843,648	$ 877,394				
16	Utilities	150,000	156,000	162,240	168,730	175,479				
17	Licensing	50,000	52,000	54,080	56,243	58,493				
18	Occupancy Costs	100,000	104,000	108,160	112,486	116,986				
19	Insurance	50,000	52,000	54,080	56,243	58,493				
20	Miscellaneous Expenses	40,000	41,600	43,264	44,995	46,794				
21	TOTAL GENERAL EXPENSES	1,140,000	1,185,600	1,233,024	1,282,345	1,333,639				
22										
23	Earnings	Year 1	Year 2	Year 3	Year 4	Year 5				
24	Initial Earnings									

extrapolated values assuming 4% annual growth

initial estimates of general expenses

Documentation | Startup | Income ... | ...sis | Loan Schedule | Depreciation | Investment Analysis | Terms and De ...

Ready   Accessibility: Investigate

Average: 1,258,652

The calculations show that the total general expenses will rise from $1,140,000 in Year 1 to $1,333,639 by the end of Year 5. Next, project the company's earnings during each of the next five years. Earnings are equal to the company's gross profit minus the total general expenses.

To calculate the company's earnings:

1. In cell **B24**, enter the formula **= B12 – B21** to subtract the total general expenses from the gross profit for Year 1. The estimate of earnings for the first year is $360,000.

2. Copy the formula in cell **B24** and paste it in the range **C24:F24** to project yearly earnings through Year 5. Refer to Figure 9–18.

Figure 9–18   Projected earnings

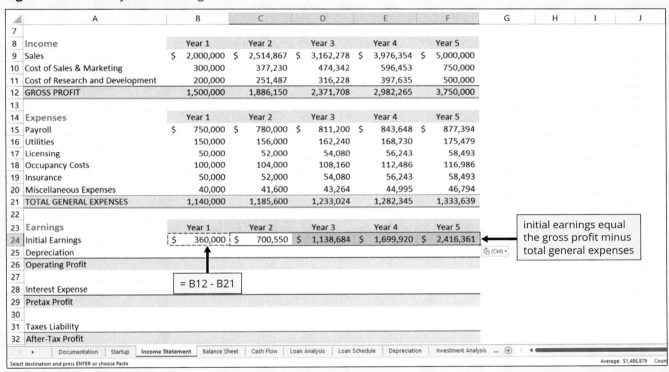

Projected earnings for the company will rise from $360,000 in Year 1 to more than $2,400,000 in Year 5. These projections assume that sales will increase by about 26% per year as the company establishes its brand and enlarges its clientele and that it can keep general expenses rising at only 4% per year. If those projections are too optimistic, the company might lose money during its five-year startup and go out of business. Many startups do.

Calculating Depreciation of Assets

The financial status of a company is not determined solely by its revenue, expenses, or annual earnings. Its wealth is also tied up in noncash assets such as equipment, land, buildings, and vehicles. These assets are known as **tangible assets** because they are long-lasting material assets not intended for sale but for use only by the company. Not all material assets are tangible assets. For example, assets such as the ingredients a restaurant uses when preparing its dishes are not considered tangible assets because although they are used in the cooking process, they are sold indirectly to the consumer in the form of a finished meal. However, items such as the cooking stove, refrigeration units, deep fryers, and so forth are tangible assets for that restaurant.

Tangible assets wear down over time and lose their value and thus reduce the company's overall worth. Tax laws allow companies to deduct this loss from reported earnings on the company's income statement, reducing the company's tax liability.

The loss of the asset's original value is usually spread out over several years in a process known as depreciation. An asset whose original value is $200,000 might be depreciated to $50,000 after 10 years of use. Different types of tangible assets have different rates of depreciation. Some items depreciate faster than others, which maintain their original value longer. In general, to calculate the depreciation of an asset, you need to know the following:

- The asset's original value
- The length of the asset's useful life
- The asset's salvage value, which is the asset's value at the end of its useful life
- The rate at which the asset depreciates over time

There are several ways to depreciate an asset. This example focuses on straight-line depreciation and declining balance depreciation.

Straight-Line Depreciation

Under **straight-line depreciation**, an asset loses value by equal amounts each year until it reaches the salvage value at the end of its useful life. You can calculate the straight-line depreciation value using the SLN function

```
SLN(cost, salvage, life)
```

where *cost* is the initial cost or value of the asset, *salvage* is the value of the asset at the end of its useful life, and *life* is the number of periods over which the asset will be depreciated. In most cases, life is expressed in terms of years. To calculate the yearly depreciation of an asset with an initial value of $200,000 and a salvage value of $50,000 after 10 years, use the function

```
SLN(200000, 50000, 10)
```

which returns a value of $15,000, indicating that the asset will decline $15,000 every year from its original value down to its salvage value.

Declining Balance Depreciation

Under **declining balance depreciation**, the asset depreciates by a constant percentage each year rather than a constant amount. The depreciation is highest early in the asset's lifetime and steadily decreases as the asset itself loses value. Figure 9–19 compares the yearly straight-line and declining balance depreciation over a 10-year lifetime as an asset declines from its initial value of $300,000 down to $75,000.

Figure 9–19   Straight-line and declining-balance depreciation

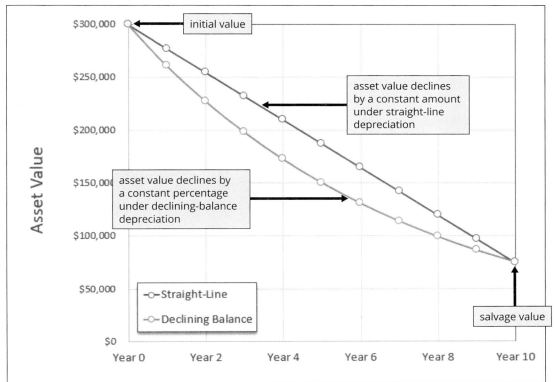

An asset shows a greater initial decline under declining balance depreciation than under straight-line depreciation. Declining balance depreciation is another example of a negative growth trend in which the asset decreases in value by a constant percentage rather than by a constant amount, as is the case with straight-line depreciation. A declining balance depreciation is calculated with the DB function

DB(*cost*, *salvage*, *life*, *period*, [*month* = 12])

where *cost*, *salvage*, and *life* are again the initial value, salvage value, and lifetime of the asset, respectively, and *period* is the period for which you want to calculate the depreciation. If you are calculating depreciation on a yearly basis, then *period* would contain the year value of the depreciation. For example, to calculate the fourth year of depreciation of a $200,000 asset that declines to a salvage value of $50,000 after 10 years, you would use the function

DB(200000, 50000, 10, 4)

which returns $17,048.03, indicating that the asset declines in value more than $17,000 during its fourth year of use. By contrast, the asset's depreciation in its fifth year is

DB(200000, 50000, 10, 5)

which returns $14,848.83. The depreciation is smaller in the fifth year because the asset has a lower value later into its useful life and thus will suffer less depreciation.

The DB function also supports an optional *month* argument, which is needed when the asset is used for only part of the first year. For example, if you are depreciating the $200,000 asset after using it for only two months in Year 1, you would calculate its depreciation in the fifth year as

```
DB(200000, 50000, 10, 5, 2)
```

which returns $16,681.50. The depreciated value is higher because the asset has not been subjected to wear and tear for a full five years, making it more valuable going into Year 5.

Kim estimates that Robuster will have $750,000 in tangible assets at its startup. The useful life of these assets is estimated at 10 years with a salvage value of $250,000. You will add this information to the company's startup figures and then apply it to the Depreciation worksheet.

To specify the values of the tangible assets:

1. Go to the **Startup** worksheet.

2. In cell **B13**, enter **750,000** as the initial value of the long-term assets.

3. Go to the **Depreciation** worksheet.

4. In cell **B4**, type **=** to begin the formula, go to the **Startup** worksheet, click cell **B13**, and then press **ENTER**. The formula = Startup!B13 is entered in cell B4, displaying the $750,000 long-term assets value from the Startup worksheet.

5. In cell **B5**, enter **$250,000** as the asset's estimated salvage value.

6. In cell **B6**, enter **10** as the useful life of the asset.

Next, you will calculate the depreciation of the company equipment using straight-line depreciation.

To calculate the straight-line depreciation:

1. In cell **B10**, enter the formula **= SLN($B$4, $B$5, $B$6)** to calculate the straight-line depreciation in Year 1 based on the cost value in cell B4, the salvage value in cell B5, and the life value in cell B6. The formula returns a depreciation value of $50,000, indicating the asset will decline in value by $50,000 in Year 1.

2. Copy the formula in cell **B10** and paste it in the range **C10:F10** to calculate the straight-line depreciation for the remaining years. Because the straight-line depreciation is a constant amount every year, the formula returns a depreciation value of $50,000 for Year 2 through Year 5.

    Next, you will calculate the cumulative depreciation of the asset from Year 1 through Year 5.

3. In cell **B11**, enter the formula **= B10** to display the depreciation for the first year.

4. In cell **C11**, enter the formula **= B11 + C10** to add the Year 2 depreciation to the depreciation from Year 1. The total depreciation through the first two years is $100,000.

5. Copy the formula in cell **C11** and paste it in the range **D11:F11** to calculate cumulative depreciation through the first five years. By Year 5, the asset's value will have declined by $250,000.

6. In cell **B12**, enter the formula **= $B$4 – B11** to calculate the depreciated asset's value after the first year. The asset's value is $700,000 after one year of use.

7. Copy the formula in cell **B12** and paste it in the range **C12:F12**. By Year 5, the asset's value has been reduced to $500,000.

8. Click cell **B10** to deselect the copied range. Refer to Figure 9–20.

Figure 9–20   Straight-line depreciation of the asset

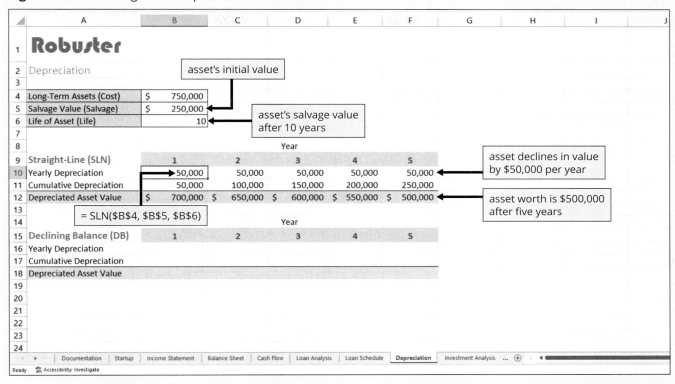

Kim also wants to explore the depreciation of the company's tangible assets under the declining balance depreciation method.

To calculate the declining balance depreciation:

1. In cell **B16**, enter the formula **= DB($B$4, $B$5, $B$6, B15)** to calculate the declining balance depreciation for Year 1 based on the initial cost of the asset in cell B4, the salvage value in cell B5, the life of the asset in cell B6, and the current period (or year) in cell B15. The formula returns $78,000, which is the amount that the assets will depreciate in Year 1.

2. Copy the formula in cell **B16** and paste it in the range **C16:F16** to calculate the depreciation in each of the remaining four years. The depreciation amount decreases each year under the declining balance schedule, dropping to $50,272 in Year 5.

3. Copy the formulas in the range **B11:F12** and paste it in the range **B17:F18** to calculate the cumulative depreciation and depreciated value of the asset.

4. Click cell **B16** to deselect the copied range. Refer to Figure 9–21.

Figure 9-21   Declining-balance depreciation of the asset

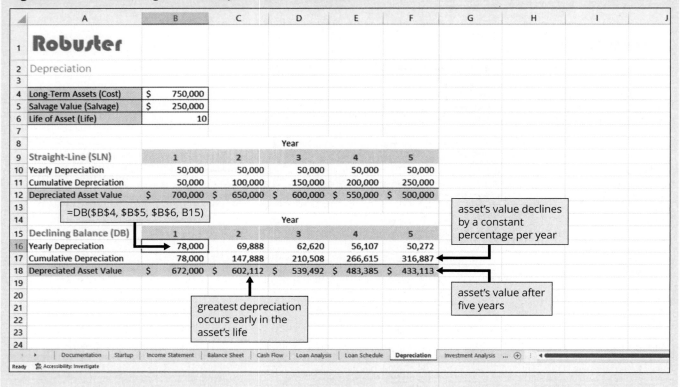

Based on the declining balance depreciation method, the value of the asset declines to $316,887 by the end of Year 5, which is lower than the Year 5 value under the straight-line depreciation model. Figure 9–22 describes several other depreciation functions that can be used to satisfy specialized accounting needs.

Figure 9-22   Excel depreciation functions

Function	Description
SLN(cost, salvage, life)	Returns the straight-line depreciation in which the asset declines by a constant amount each year, where cost is the initial cost of the asset, salvage is the salvage value, and life is the useful lifetime of the asset.
DB(cost, salvage, life, period, [month])	Returns the declining balance depreciation in which the asset declines by a constant percentage each year, where period is the year of the depreciation and month is an optional argument that defines the number of months that the asset was owned during Year 1.
SYD(cost, salvage, life, period)	Returns the sum-of-years' digit depreciation that results in a more accelerated depreciation than straight-line depreciation, but a less accelerated depreciation than declining balance depreciation.
DDB(cost, salvage, life, period, [factor = 2])	Returns the double-declining balance depreciation that doubles the depreciation under the straight-line method and applies that accelerated rate to the original asset value minus the cumulative depreciation. The factor argument specifies the factor by which the straight-line depreciation is multiplied. If no factor is specified, a factor of 2 (for doubling) is assumed.
VDB(cost, salvage, life, start, end, [factor = 2], [no_switch = FALSE])	Returns a variable declining depreciation for any specified period using any specified depreciation method, where start is the starting period of the depreciation, end is the ending period, factor is the rate at which the depreciation declines, and no_switch specifies whether to switch to the straight-line method when the depreciation falls below the estimate given by the declining balance method.

Adding Depreciation to an Income Statement

Depreciation is part of a company's income statement because even though the company is not losing actual revenue, it is losing value as its tangible assets depreciate, which reduces its tax liability. Kim wants to add the declining balance depreciation figures from the Depreciation worksheet to the projected income statement to project the company's operating profit, which represents the pretax company's profit.

To add depreciation to the income statement:

1. Return to the **Income Statement** worksheet.

2. In cell **B25**, type **=** to begin the formula, go to the **Depreciation** worksheet, click cell **B16**, and press **ENTER**. The formula = Depreciation!B16 is entered and displays the depreciation value $78,000 for Year 1.

3. Copy the formula in cell **B25** and paste it in the range **C25:F25** to show the annual depreciation for Year 2 through Year 5.

4. In cell **B26**, enter the formula **= B24 – B25** to subtract the depreciation from the company's earnings. The projected loss in operating profit for the company in the first year is $282,000.

5. Copy the formula in cell **B26** and paste it in the range **C26:F26** to calculate the operating profit for Year 2 through Year 5.

Even when depreciation of its assets is included, the company's operating profit increases throughout the five-year period, culminating in a Year 5 operating profit of $2,366,089.

Proskills

Decision Making: Choosing a Depreciation Schedule

How do you decide which method of depreciation is the most appropriate? The answer depends on the type of asset being depreciated. Tax laws allow different depreciation methods for different kinds of assets and different situations. In general, you want to choose the depreciation method that most accurately describes the true value of the asset and its impact on the company's financial status.

In tax statements, depreciation appears as an expense that is subtracted from the company's earnings. So, if you accelerate the depreciation of an asset in the early years of its use, you might be underestimating the company's profits, making it appear that the company is less profitable than it is. On the other hand, depreciating an asset slowly could make it appear that the company is more profitable than it really is. For this reason, the choice of a depreciation method is best made in consultation with an accountant who is fully informed of the financial issues and tax laws.

Adding Taxes and Interest Expenses to an Income Statement

Interest expenses are also part of a company's income statement. You have already projected the annual interest payments the company will have to make on its $1,250,000 loan (refer to row 36 in Figure 9–9). Rather than reenter these values, you can reference the calculated values from that worksheet in the income statement. Because those values were displayed as negative numbers, you will change the sign to match the format of the Income Statement worksheet in which those interest expenses are entered as positive values.

To include the interest expense in the income statement:

1. In cell **B28** of the Income Statement worksheet, type **= –** (an equal sign followed by a minus sign) to begin the formula.

2. Go to the **Loan Schedule** worksheet, click cell **B36**, which contains the total interest payments in Year 1, and then press **ENTER**. The formula = –'Loan Schedule'!B36 is entered in the cell, returning the value 93,744.

3. In cell **B29**, enter the formula **= B26 – B28** to subtract the interest expense from the operating profit for Year 1. The Year 1 pretax profit is $188,256.

4. Copy the formulas in the range **B28:B29** and paste them in the range **C28:F29** to calculate the interest payments and pretax profits for the remaining years. By Year 5, the company's pretax profits (including interest expense) is projected to be $2,351,391.

Finally, you need to account for the taxes that the company will pay on the money it makes. Kim estimates that the company will be subject, in general, to a 30% tax rate on its pretax income. You will add this tax rate to the Income Statement worksheet and then calculate the company's tax liability. The company will pay taxes only if it makes money, so you will use an IF function to test whether the pretax income is positive before calculating taxes. If the pretax profit is negative, the tax will be zero.

To calculate the company's tax liability:

1. In cell **F5** of the Income Statement worksheet, enter **30%** as the assumed tax rate.

2. In cell **B31**, enter the formula **= IF(B29 > 0, B29*$F$5, 0)** to test whether the pretax income in Year 1 is greater than 0. If it is, then the pretax income will be multiplied by the tax rate in cell F5; otherwise, the formula will return 0. Excel estimates Year 1 taxes at $56,477.

3. In cell **B32**, enter the formula **= B29 – B31** to subtract the taxes owed for Year 1 from the pretax income. Excel estimates the Year 1 after-tax profit at $131,779.

4. Copy the formulas in the range **B31:B32** and paste them in the range **C31:F32** to calculate the tax liability and after-tax profit for the remaining years. After accounting for taxes, Robuster will show an after-tax profit of $1,645,974 by the end of its fifth year.

5. Click cell **B30** to deselect the copied formulas. Refer to Figure 9–23.

Figure 9–23   Revised income statement

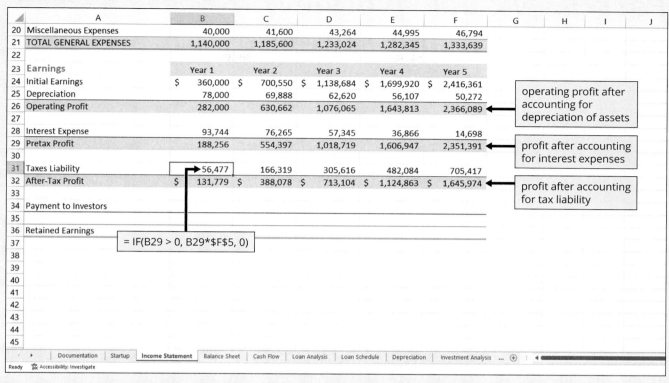

6.   Save the workbook.

With the initial financial planning laid out, the company needs to attract some investors. Next, you will evaluate the return on investment that the company will be able to offer investors and the impact it will have on the company's profitability.

Part 9.2 Quick Check

1.   The first value in a linear trend is 25, and the fifth value is 225. What are the values of the second, third, and fourth items?

2.   The first value in a growth trend is 3, and the fifth value is 48. What are the values of the second, third, and fourth items?

3.   By what percentage do the values you calculated in Question 2 grow?

4.   The first value in a series is 50. Extrapolate the next four values assuming a linear trend with a step size of 75.

5.   The first value in a series is 100. Extrapolate the next four values if each value grows by 24% over the previous value.

6.   A new business buys $180,000 worth of computer equipment. If the useful life of the equipment is 10 years with a salvage value of $30,000, what is the formula to determine the depreciation during the first year assuming straight-line depreciation? What is the formula result?

7.   What is the value of the asset in Year 1 through Year 5 using the depreciation schedule you created in Question 6?

8.   Assuming a declining balance depreciation for the computer equipment described in Question 6, what are the formula and result to determine the depreciation in the first year?

9.   What is the value of the asset in Year 1 through Year 5 using the declining balance depreciation schedule in Question 8?

Part 9.3 Visual Overview: NPV and IRR and Auditing

The **RATE function** calculates the per-period interest rate required to repay a loan or reach an investment goal.

The **payback period** is the time for an investment to recover its initial cost resulting a nonnegative net cash flow.

The **net present value** is the difference between the present value of an investment and the initial expenditure on that investment.

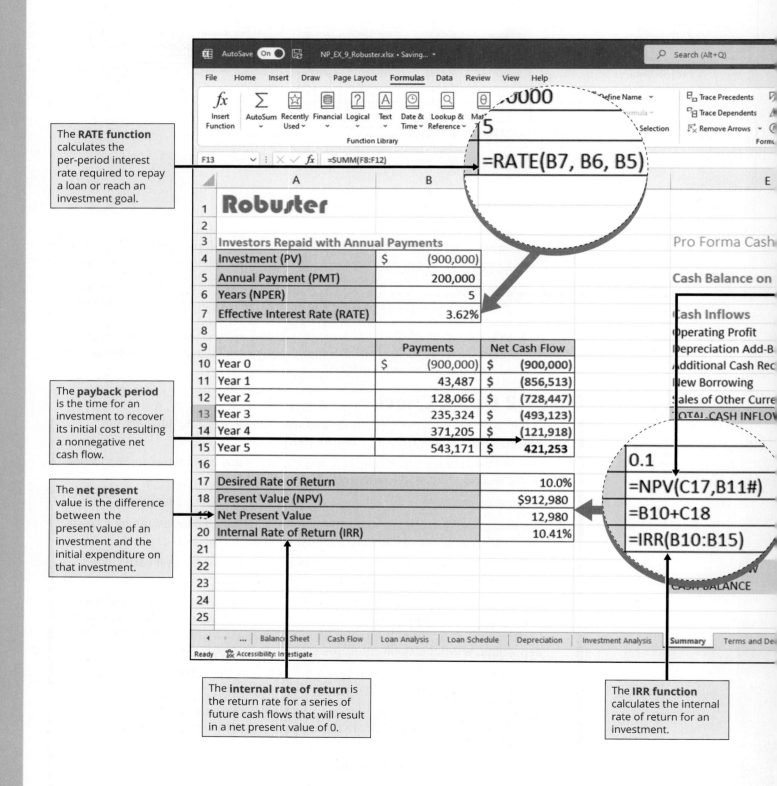

The **internal rate of return** is the return rate for a series of future cash flows that will result in a net present value of 0.

The **IRR function** calculates the internal rate of return for an investment.

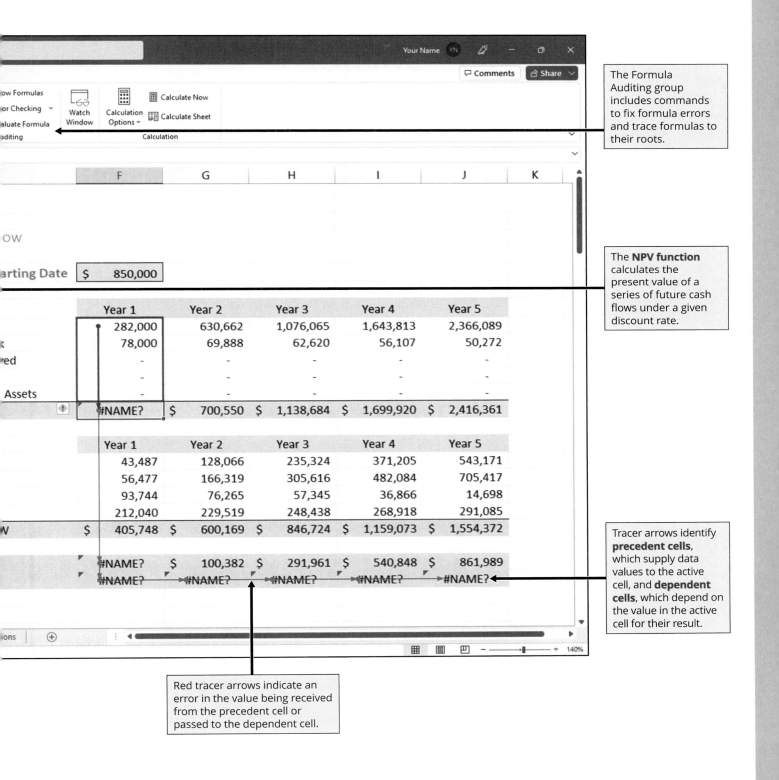

The Formula Auditing group includes commands to fix formula errors and trace formulas to their roots.

The **NPV function** calculates the present value of a series of future cash flows under a given discount rate.

Tracer arrows identify **precedent cells**, which supply data values to the active cell, and **dependent cells**, which depend on the value in the active cell for their result.

Red tracer arrows indicate an error in the value being received from the precedent cell or passed to the dependent cell.

Calculating Interest Rates with the RATE Function

When you evaluated potential loans in the Loan Analysis worksheet, you may have noticed that the *Pmt*, *Fv*, *Nper*, and *Pv* arguments match the PMT, FV, NPER, and PV functions. The *Rate* argument also has a matching RATE function that calculates the interest rate assuming equal periodic payments. The syntax of the RATE function is

        RATE(Nper, Pmt, Pv, [Fv = 0], [Type = 0], [Guess = 0.1])

where *Nper* is the number of equal payments, *Pmt* is the payment amount, *Pv* is the loan or investment's present value, *Fv* is the future value, and *Type* defines when the payments are made. The optional *Guess* argument is used when the RATE function cannot calculate the interest rate value and needs an initial guess to arrive at a solution.

The RATE function is used primarily to calculate the return from investments in which an initial investment is repaid with a series of smaller payments spaced out in time. The rate of a $14,000 initial investment returning $150 per month for 10 years (or 120 months) can be calculated using the function

        RATE(120, 150, -14000)

returning an interest rate of 0.43% per month or 5.2% annually. Note that the payment values of $150 are positive because the payments are made to the investor (positive cash flow), but the present value –14,000 is negative because it represents money initially spent in the investment (negative cash flow). The future value is 0 by default because once the initial investment has been completely paid back, no funds are left.

> **Tip** Always multiply the RATE function result by the number of payments per year. For monthly payments, multiply the rate value by 12.

When the RATE function is applied to loans, the positive and negative signs of the *Pmt* and *Pv* values are switched. The interest rate on a $14,000 loan repaid at $150 per month over 120 months is calculated as

        RATE(120, -150, 14000)

which again returns 0.43% per month or 5.2% annually. Notice that the payment value (–$150) is negative and the present value ($14,000) is positive because a loan is a positive cash flow to the borrower, but the payments represent a negative cash flow from the borrower back to the bank.

Not every combination of payments and present value will result in a viable interest rate. The interest rate for a $14,000 loan repaid with payments of $100 per month for 120 months is calculated with the function

        RATE(120, -100, 14000)

returning an interest rate of –0.25% per month or –3.0% annually. The interest rate is negative because a $14,000 loan cannot be repaid with $100 payments each month for 120 months. The total payments would amount to only $12,000.

Robuster needs $900,000 in startup capital from a group of investors. The company is considering repaying the group $200,000 per year for the first five years of the company's operation for a total return of $1,000,000. While this would represent a profit of $100,000 to the investors, Kim wants to calculate the annual interest rate associated with such a repayment schedule. You will use the RATE function to find out.

To calculate the interest rate of the investment:

1. If you took a break after the previous part, make sure the NP_EX_9_Robuster workbook is open.

2. Go to the **Startup** worksheet, and then in cell **B31**, enter **900,000** as the amount contributed by investors.

3. Go to the **Investment Analysis** worksheet. You will use this worksheet to analyze the returns from investing in the company.

4. In cell **B5**, type **= –** (an equal sign followed by a minus sign), go to the **Startup** worksheet, click cell **B31**, and then press **ENTER**. The formula = –Startup!B31 is entered in the cell.

   The formula displays the negative value $(900,000) in the cell. You want a negative cash flow because you are examining this investment from the point of view of the investment group, which is making an initial startup payment of $900,000 to the company in hopes of receiving a future return.

5. In cell **B6**, enter **200,000** as the payment back to the group. This positive cash flow is received by the investors each year.

6. In cell **B7**, enter **5** as the total number of payments made to the investors.

7. In cell **B8**, enter the formula **= RATE(B7, B6, B5)** to calculate the interest rate of this repayment schedule based on the number of payments in cell B7, the size of each payment in cell B6, and the present value of the investment in cell B5. Refer to Figure 9–24.

Figure 9–24   Interest rate of an investment

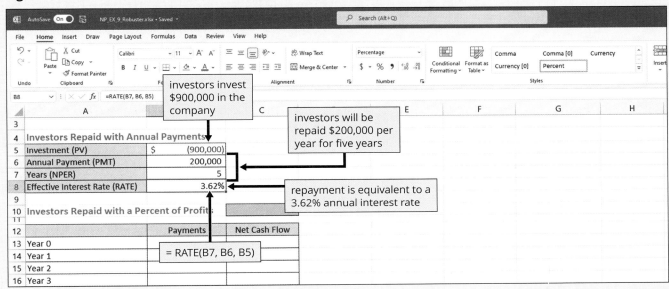

Based on these calculations, the annual interest rate to the investors for this repayment schedule is 3.62%. One way to interpret this rate is that it is equal to placing $900,000 in a savings account paying 3.62% annual interest.

The company does not believe it can attract investors with a 3.62% annual interest rate on a speculative and potentially risky venture. Nor does the company want to be responsible for a $200,000 annual payment to investors on top of what it is already paying for its business loan. Another way of paying back investors is to offer them a percentage of the profits. Kim wants you to calculate the Year 1 through Year 5 payments assuming that investors are paid 33% of the after-tax profits.

To calculate 33% of the profits for investors:

1. Go to the **Income Statement** worksheet.

2. Click cell **F6**, type **33%** and press **ENTER**.

   As with the tax estimate, investors receive payment only if there are profits. You will use an IF statement to test whether the after-tax profit is positive before calculating the investor payment.

3. Click cell **B34** and type **= IF(B32 > 0, B32*$F$6, 0)** and press **ENTER**. Excel returns a 43,487 as the Year 1 payment to the investor group.

4. In cell **B36**, and enter **= B32 – B34** to calculate the earnings retained by the company after paying its investors. The Year 1 retained earnings are $88,292.

5. Copy the range **B34:B36** and paste it into the range **C34:F36** to project both the investor payments and retained earnings through the company's first five years. Refer to Figure 9–25.

Figure 9–25   Payments to investors

	A	B	C	D	E	F	G	H	I	J
17	Licensing	50,000	52,000	54,080	56,243	58,493				
18	Occupancy Costs	100,000	104,000	108,160	112,486	116,986				
19	Insurance	50,000	52,000	54,080	56,243	58,493				
20	Miscellaneous Expenses	40,000	41,600	43,264	44,995	46,794				
21	TOTAL GENERAL EXPENSES	1,140,000	1,185,600	1,233,024	1,282,345	1,333,639				
22										
23	Earnings	Year 1	Year 2	Year 3	Year 4	Year 5				
24	Initial Earnings	$ 360,000	$ 700,550	$ 1,138,684	$ 1,699,920	$ 2,416,361				
25	Depreciation	78,000	69,888	62,620	56,107	50,272				
26	Operating Profit	282,000	630,662	1,076,065	1,643,813	2,366,089				
27										
28	Interest Expense	93,744	76,265	57,345	36,866	14,698				
29	Pretax Profit	188,256	554,397	1,018,719	1,606,947	2,351,391				
30										
31	Taxes Liability	56,477	166,319	305,616	482,084	705,417				
32	After-Tax Profit	$ 131,779	$ 388,078	$ 713,104	$ 1,124,863	$ 1,645,974				
33										
34	Payment to Investors	43,487	128,066	235,324	371,205	543,171				
35										
36	Retained Earnings	$ 88,292	$ 260,012	$ 477,779	$ 753,658	$ 1,102,802				
37										
38										
39										
40										
41										
42										

investors receive 33% of the after-tax profits

=IF(B32 > 0, B32*$F$6, 0)

retained earnings after paying investors 33% of the profits

Startup | Income Statement | Balance Sheet | Cash Flow | Loan Analysis | Loan Schedule | Depreciation | Investment Analysis | Terms and Defir ...

Ready   Accessibility: Investigate

Under this plan, investors will receive almost $44,000 on their $900,000 investment in Year 1, steadily increasing to more than $540,000 by Year 5. The company's earnings after paying its expenses, taxes, and investors will rise from more than $88,000 in Year 1 to more than $1.1 million in Year 5.

Is this series of payments a good deal for the investor group? Because the payments are unequal, you cannot evaluate the investment using the RATE function. One way to evaluate such an investment is with the payback period.

Viewing the Payback Period of an Investment

The payback period is the length of time required for an investment to recover its initial cost. For example, a $400,000 investment that returns $50,000 per year would have a payback period of exactly eight years to completely refund the initial investment.

In the first few years, the payments to Robuster investors will be very low, but they will steadily rise as the company's profits and client base increases. Kim wants you to examine the payback period so that investors will know how long they will have to wait until they recover their $900,000 investment.

To determine the payback period for the investment:

1. Go to the **Investment Analysis** worksheet.

2. In cell **C10**, enter the formula **= 'Income Statement'!F6** to document the 33% of profits investors will receive.

3. In cell **B13**, enter the formula **= –Startup!B31** to reference the initial investment from the Startup worksheet. Excel displays $(900,000), a negative number, because this is a negative cash flow to the investors.

4. Click cell **B14** and begin typing the dynamic array formula **= TRANSPOSE(** in the cell.

5. Click the **Income Statement** sheet tab, select the range **B34:F34**, and then type **)** to close the function.

6. Press **ENTER** to insert the dynamic array formula = TRANSPOSE('Income Statement'!B34:F34). The investor payments appear in the column range B14:B18.

   > **Tip** If the investor payments from the Income Worksheet change, they will be automatically updated in the transposed values in the range B19:B23.

7. Select the range **B13:B18**, click the **Quick Analysis** button 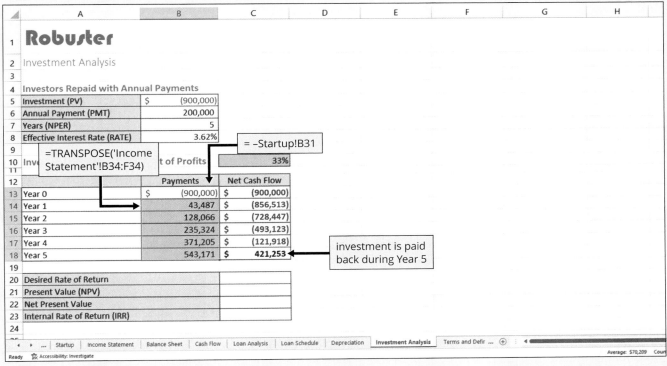, click **Totals**, scroll right to the end of the Totals tools, and then click **Running Total** to calculate a column of running totals for the net cash flow to investors. Refer to Figure 9–26.

Figure 9–26   Payback period of the investment

The payback period indicates that investors will have to wait for five years to recover their investment (when the value of the cumulative net cash flow changes from negative to positive). However, at the end of those five years, they will get a $421,253 return on their $900,000 investment. So, while the payoff seems substantial, the wait could be a problem. What would this investment be worth in current dollars?

Calculating Net Present Value

The major drawback of the payback period is that it does not consider the time value of money. To understand why, you must explore how time impacts financial decisions.

The Time Value of Money

The **time value of money** is based on the observation that money received today is often worth more than the same amount received later because you can always invest the money you receive today and earn interest on that investment. Inflation can also seriously erode the future value of money. The time value of money can be expressed by what represents a fair exchange between current money and future money.

To determine a future value of a loan or investment in terms of a present value, you need a rate of return. The **rate of return** or **discount rate** is a percentage that indicates how the value of money changes over time. The rate of return is what you expect, or hope for, in the value of future dollars and provides a standard for comparing investments.

For example, is it better to receive $100 today or $105 one year from now? The answer depends on what you could do with that $100 during that year. If you could invest it in an account paying a rate of return of 8% per year, the $100 would turn into $108, making it better to receive the $100 now rather than $105 a year from now. But, if you could expect a rate of return of only 3% on the $100, it would be better to wait a year and receive the $105 rather than $103 from the 3% interest.

You can use the PV function to calculate the time value of money under different rates of return. The following PV function calculates the present value of receiving $100 per year for the next five years at a 6% annual rate of return:

```
PV(6%, 5, 100)
```

The function returns a negative value of –$421.24, indicating that it would be a fair exchange to spend $421.24 today to receive $100 per year for each of the next five years. In other words, $421.24 today is worth the same as $500 spread over $100 annual payments if the rate of return is 6%. On the other hand, if the return rate were 8%, the present value would be $399.27 so that spending $399.27 today is equal to receiving $100 per year for the next five years. The higher the anticipated return rate, the lower the present value of the investment. Likewise, the lower the anticipated return rate, the higher the present value.

For investments that pay off at the end without any intermediate payments, enter 0 for the payment (*Pmt*) value and enter the amount returned by the investment as the future value. So, to calculate the present value of receiving $500 at the end of five years at a 6% rate of return, enter the PV function

```
PV(6%, 5, 0, 500)
```

which returns –$373.63, indicating that it would be a fair exchange to spend $373.63 today to receive $500 five years from now. If the return rate were 8%, this value would be –$340.29 so that spending $340.29 now is a fair exchange for receiving $500 after a five-year wait.

You also can use the FV function to estimate how much a dollar amount today is worth in terms of future dollars. To determine the future value of $100 in two years if the rate of return is 5%, enter

```
FV(5%, 2, 0, -100)
```

which returns a value of $110.25. The positive cash flow indicates that it is fair to spend $100 today in order to receive $110.25 in two years. Once again, the *Pmt* value is 0 because there are no payments prior to receiving $110.25 at the end of Year 2.

Using the NPV Function

The PV function assumes equal payments. If the payments are not equal, you must use the NPV function to determine the present value of an investment. The syntax of the NPV function is

```
NPV(Rate, value1, [value2, value3,…])
```

where *Rate* is the rate of return, and `value1`, `value2`, `value3`, and so on are the future payments. The NPV function assumes payments occur at the end of each payment period and the payment periods are evenly spaced.

For example, to calculate the present value of a three-year investment that pays $100 at the end of the first year, $200 at the end of the second year, and $500 at the end of the third year with a 6% annual rate of return, you would apply the NPV function

```
NPV(6%, 100, 200, 500)
```

which returns a value of $692.15, indicating that $800 spread out over this repayment schedule is equivalent to $692.15 today if the discount rate is 6%. If the discount rate were 8%, this value would decrease to $660.98 because the large payment of $500 is paid at a later date with dollars of lesser value.

Unlike the PV function, which returns a negative value for the investment's present value, the NPV function returns a positive value. This is because the PV function returns a cash flow value that indicates how much you need to invest now (a negative cash flow) to receive money later (a positive cash flow); whereas the NPV function calculates the value of those payments in today's dollars based on your chosen rate of return.

You can receive surprising results examining the time value of money. Consider an investment that has a 6% rate of return with these transactions: Year 1—investor receives $250; Year 2—investor receives $150; Year 3—investor receives $100; Year 4—investor pays $150; and Year 5—investor pays $400. At first glance, this seems to be a bad investment. The investor receives $500 in the first three years but spends $550 in the last two years, for a net loss of $50. However, that analysis does not consider the time value of money. When the present value of this transaction is calculated using the NPV function

```
NPV(6%, 250, 150, 100, -150, -400)
```

the present value of the investment is $35.59, a positive result. The investment is profitable because the investor receives the money early and repays later with dollars of lesser value.

Choosing a Rate of Return

Whether an investment is profitable or not often depends on the desired rate of return. The rate of return is related to the concept of risk—the possibility that the entire transaction will fail, resulting in a loss of the initial investment. Investments with higher risks generally should have higher rates of return. If an investor places $50,000 in a simple bank account (a low-risk venture), the investor would not expect a high rate of return. On the other hand, a speculative investment of $900,000 in a startup company merits a higher rate of return.

After discussing the issue with financial analysts, the company has settled on a 10% rate of return, promising investors a return at least as great as they would get by investing the $900,000 in an account paying 10% annual interest over five years. You will use that rate of return in the NPV function as you calculate the present value of the proposal that Kim will make to the investor group.

To calculate the present value of the investment:

1. In cell **C20**, enter **10.0%** as the desired rate of return.

2. In cell **C21**, enter **= NPV(C20, B14#)** to calculate the present value of the investment based on the desired rate value in cell C21 and the return paid to the investors for Year 1 through Year 5.

   The formula returns $912,980 which is the present value of the investment to the investor group. You will add this present value to the initial investment cost to calculate the net present value.

3. In cell **C22**, enter **= B13 + C21** to add the initial investment to the present value of the investment over the next five year. Refer to Figure 9–27.

Figure 9-27   Present value of an investment

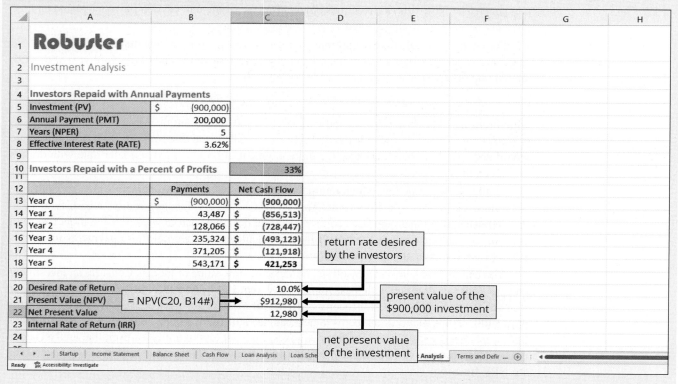

According to these results, the $900,000 investment in the company is worth $12,980 more than placing the same amount in a different investment paying 10% annual interest. Giving investors a share of the profits is a more attractive plan, assuming Robuster will reach the projected profits over the next five years. The company will need a thorough and detailed market analysis and business plan to make a successful sales pitch.

Insight

Understanding Net Present Value and the NPV Function

Net present value is the difference between the present value of a series of future cash flows and the current value of the initial investment. One source of confusion for Excel users is that despite its name, the NPV function does not actually return the net present value of an investment if the initial investment is made immediately. Instead, it returns the investment's present value based on the returns that the investment will provide in the future.

To calculate the net present value in Excel, the initial cost of the investment must be added to the present value of the returns from the investment using the formula

    = immediate investment + NPV value

where *immediate investment* is the cost of the investment made immediately and *NPV value* is the value of the NPV function applied to future returns. The initial investment is assumed to have a negative cash flow because that investment is being purchased, and it is assumed to be based on current, not future, dollars.

The exception to this formula occurs when the initial investment also takes place in the future. For example, if the initial investment takes place at the end of the current year and the returns occur annually after that, then the NPV function will return the net present value without having to be adjusted because the initial investment is also discounted.

In any financial analysis, it is a good idea to test other values for comparison. Kim wants you to rerun the analysis using return rates of 8% and 12%.

To view the impact of different rates of return:

1. In cell **C20**, change the value to **8%** to decrease the desired rate of return. The present value in cell C21 increases to $979,389, indicating that investment is almost $80,000 more profitable (in current dollars) than what could be achieved by an account bearing 8% annual interest.

2. In cell **C20**, change the value to **12%**, increasing the desired rate of return. The net present value of the investment declines to $852,538. Investing in the company would be less profitable than putting the money in an account bearing 12% interest by almost $50,000.

3. In cell **C20**, change the value back to **10%**.

Compared to investments with higher rates of return, the net present value of the company investment plan decreases. Remember that net present value only has meaning in relation to other investments. If the comparison made to investments with lower rates of return, the company's investment offer will appear to be more valuable.

Calculating the Internal Rate of Return

This analysis of net present value under different return rates illustrates an important principal: At some return rate, the net present value of an investment switches from positive (profitable) to negative (unprofitable). Figure 9–28 shows the change in net present value for the Robuster investment under different rates of return.

Figure 9–28   Locating the internal rate of return

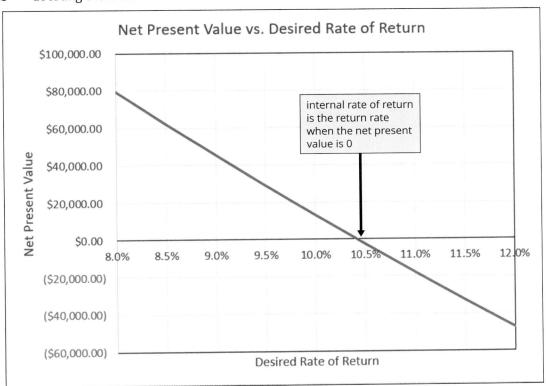

The point at which the net present value of an investment equals 0 is called the internal rate of return (IRR) of the investment. The IRR is another popular measure of the value of an investment because it provides a basis of comparison between investments. Those investments with higher IRRs are preferred to those with lower IRRs.

Using the IRR Function

The IRR function calculates the internal rate of return for an investment. Its syntax is

```
IRR(values, [guess = 0.1])
```

where values are the cash flow values from the investment, and guess is an optional argument in which you provide a guess for the IRR value. A guess is needed for financial transactions that have several possible internal rates of return. This can occur when the investment switches between negative and positive cash flows several times during its lifetime. For those types of transactions, an initial guess helps Excel locate the final value for the IRR. Without the guess, Excel might not be able to calculate the IRR. If you do not include a guess, Excel will use an initial guess of 10% for the IRR and proceed from there to converge to an answer.

For example, the internal rate of return for a $500 investment that pays $100 in the first year, $150 in the second and third years, and $200 in the fourth year is calculated using the IRR function

```
IRR({-500, 100, 150, 150, 200})
```

which returns a rate of 6.96% indicating that the return for this investment is equally profitable as depositing $500 in an account that pays 6.96% annual interest.

The order of payments affects the internal rate of return. In the above example, the total amount of money paid back on the investment is $600. However, if the payments were made in the opposite order—$200, $150, $150, and $100—the internal rate of return would be calculated as

```
IRR({-500, 200, 150, 150, 100})
```

which returns a rate of 8.64%. The increased rate of return is due to the larger payments made earlier with dollars of greater value.

The list of values in the IRR function must include at least one positive cash flow and one negative cash flow, and the order of the values must reflect the order in which the payments are made, and the payoffs are received. Like the NPV function, the IRR function assumes that payments and payoffs occur at evenly spaced intervals.

Reference

Calculating the Value of an Investment

- To calculate the net present value when the initial investment is made immediately, use the NPV function with the discount rate and the series of cash returns from the investment. Add the cost of the initial investment (negative cash flow) to the value returned by the NPV function.

- To calculate the net present value when the initial investment is made at the end of the first payment period, use the NPV function with the discount rate and the series of cash returns from the investment. Include the initial cost of the investment as the first value in the series.

- To calculate the internal rate of return, use the IRR function with the cost of the initial investment as the first cash flow value in the series. For investments that have several positive and negative cash flow values, include a guess to aid Excel in finding a reasonable internal rate of return value.

Kim wants you to determine the internal rate of return for the proposed series of payments made to investors for the $900,000 investment. You will use the IRR function to make this calculation.

To calculate the internal rate of return for the investment:

1. In cell **C23**, enter the formula **= IRR(B13:B18)** and press **ENTER** to calculate the internal rate of return, where the range B13:B18 contains the initial investment of $900,000 and the returns that investors can expect. The internal rate of return is 10.41%.

2. Select cell **C23**. Refer to Figure 9–29.

Figure 9–29   Internal rate of return

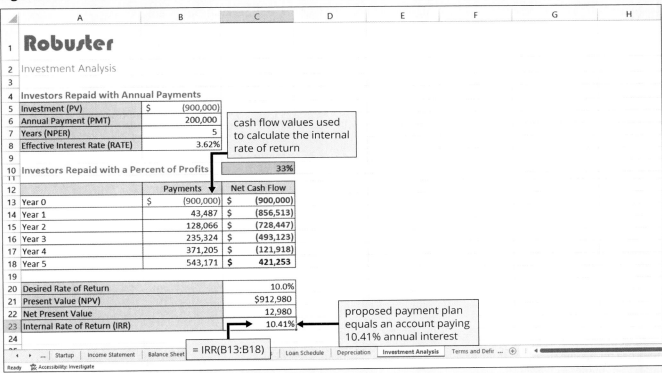

Based on the IRR calculation, the company can tell potential investors that they will receive a 10.41% return on their investments if the financial projections for the company are met.

Proskills

Decision Making: Using NPV and IRR to Compare Investments

Investors will often have several investment options. In comparing investments, investors usually want to select the one with the highest net present value or the highest internal rate of return. However, if investors rely solely on the net present value, they can receive different recommendations depending on the value of discount rate.

For example, consider the following two returns from an initial investment of $1,000. Investment A returns $1,900 on a $1,000 investment while Investment B returns $1,700.

Investment	Year 0	Year 1	Year 2	Year 3	Year 4	Year 5
A	–$1,000	$200	$200	$300	$400	$800
B	–$1,000	$500	$500	$400	$200	$100

Which is better? It depends on the chosen discount rate—in other words, the time value of money. Investment A has a higher net present value when discount rates are less than 8.5%, while Investment B has a higher net present value when the discount rate is greater than 8.5%. The reason is that if the discount rate is assumed to be low, more value is placed on later payments. Investment A is then the better choice because its payments are weighted toward the later years. If the discount rate is high, less value is placed on later payments. Investment B is then best because it returns most of its money early. You would choose Investment A when you want more dollars even if the payment is delayed, but Investment B when you want to be repaid sooner even if the total dollars are less.

Using the internal rate of return instead of the net present value can also lead to apparently contradictory results. This situation occurs when an investment switches several times between positive and negative cash flows during its history. For example, if the cash flow switches between negative and positive twice, there will be two possible internal rates of return.

A good guideline for comparing multiple investments is to graph the net present value for each investment against a range of discount rates. By comparing the graphs, you can reach an informed decision about which investment is the most profitable and under which conditions.

Exploring the XNPV and XIRR Functions

Both the NPV and IRR functions assume cash flows occur at evenly spaced intervals such as annual payments in which the cash receipts from an investment are returned at the end of the fiscal year. For cash flows that appear at unevenly spaced intervals, Excel provides the XNPV and XIRR functions.

The **XNPV function**, which calculates the net present value of a series of cash flows at specified dates, has the syntax

```
XNPV(Rate, Values, Dates)
```

where `Rate` is the desired rate of return, `Values` is the list of cash flows, and `Dates` are the dates associated with each cash flow. The series of values must contain at least one positive and one negative value. The cash flow values are discounted starting after the first date in the list, with the first value not discounted at all. Figure 9–30 shows an investment in which the initial deposit of $300,000 on September 8, 2028 is repaid with eight payments totaling $340,000 spaced at irregular intervals over the next two years. The net present value of this investment is $7,267.04 based on a 7.2% rate of return. Note that the net present value is not $40,000 (the difference between the initial deposit and the total payments) because the investment is repaid over time with dollars of lesser value.

Figure 9–30   The XNPV function

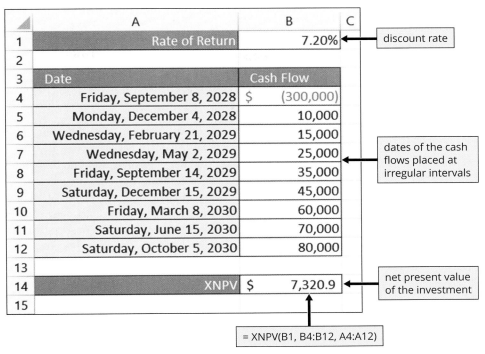

To calculate the internal rate of return for a series of cash flows made at specified dates, use the **XIRR function**

        XIRR(*Values*, *Dates*, [*Guess* = 0.1])

where *Values* is the list of cash flow values, *Dates* are the dates of each cash flow, and *Guess* is an optional argument that guesses at the internal rate of return when you have a complicated set of cash flows with multiple possible return rates. Figure 9–31 shows the internal rate of return for the transaction presented in Figure 9–30. This investment's internal rate of return is 9.01%.

Figure 9–31   The XIRR function

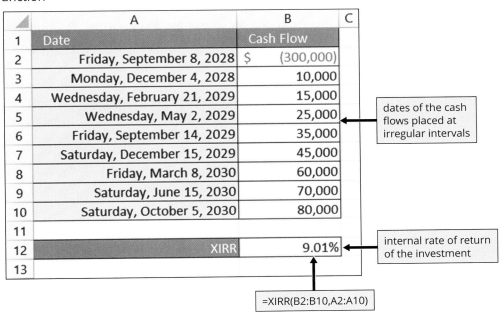

In the Robuster business plan, all payments to the investors are to be made at regular intervals, at the end of the upcoming fiscal years, so you do not need to use either the XNPV or the XIRR function.

Viewing the Modified Internal Rate of Return

The IRR function assumes that all cash flows are reinvested at the same rate as the IRR. Cash flows can also be reinvested or financed at different return rates. For those situations, you calculate the modified internal rate of return with the **MIRR function**

     MIRR(*values, finance_rate, reinvest_rate*)

where *values* is an array of cash flows (at least one of which is positive and one of which is negative), *finance_rate* is the interest rate paid on the cash flows, and *reinvest_rate* is the interest rate when the cash flows are reinvested. For example, an investor places $500 in an investment that pays off $100, $150, $150, and $200 over the next four years. The finance rate for the investment is 5%. Payments from the investment are reinvested in a more conservative fund paying 2%. To calculate the internal rate of return, use the function

     MIRR({-500, 100, 150, 150, 200}, 5%, 2%)

returning an internal rate of return of 5.32%. The MIRR function is useful in financial analysis where cash moves among several different investments.

At this point, Kim has settled on an investment proposal based on several projections regarding future sales, expenses, and taxes. As Kim works with teams of lawyers and financial analysts, those projections and assumptions will be argued and tested, but they represent a good first attempt at planning for the startup company's future.

Auditing a Workbook

In designing this workbook, Kim created several worksheets with interconnected values and formulas. The initial financial conditions entered in the Startup worksheet impact the company's loan repayment schedule. Values in the Depreciation worksheet are referenced in the Income Statement. The investor payments in the Income Statement worksheet are used in the Investment Analysis worksheet. This interconnectedness gives Kim the ability to view the impact of changing one or more assumption across several financial statements. Two of these statements are stored in the Balance Sheet and the Cash Flow worksheets.

The Balance Sheet worksheet projects what the company will own in both cash and tangible assets and what it will owe to banks and investors for each of the next five years. The Cash Flow worksheet projects the cash the company will have on hand through in its first five years of operation. You will review the contents of these worksheets now.

To review the Balance Sheet and Cash Flow worksheets:

1. Go to the **Balance Sheet** worksheet. Cells throughout the worksheet contain the #NAME? error value. Refer to Figure 9–32.

Figure 9–32   Error values in the Balance Sheet worksheet

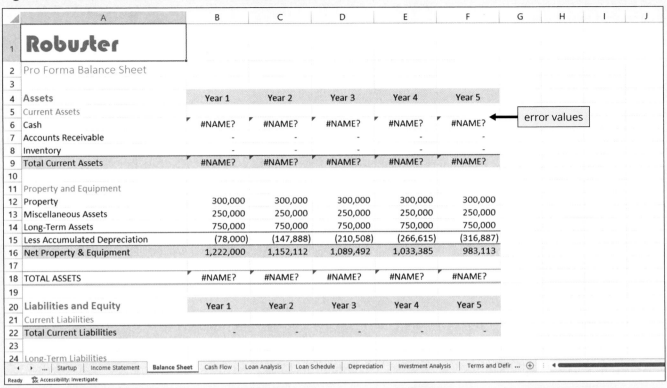

2. Go to the **Cash Flow** worksheet. At the bottom of the worksheet, notice that several cells also contain the #NAME? error value.

The downside of a workbook with many interconnected worksheets and formulas is that an error in one cell can create errors throughout the entire workbook. Does the error displayed in the Balance Sheet originate in that worksheet, or is it somewhere else? Kim wants you to locate the source of the #NAME error. To do that, you will use auditing tools.

Tracing an Error

One of most useful tools in fixing an error-filled workbook is the Trace Error tool. In tracing an error value to its source, you need to work with dependent and precedent cells. A dependent cell is one whose value depends on the values of other cells in the workbook. A precedent cell is one whose value is used by other cells. For example, if cell C15 contains the formula = C13 + C14, then cell C15 is a dependent cell because it relies on cells C13 and C14 for its value, making cells C13 and C14 precedent cells. Any error values in cell C13 or cell C14 would impact cell C15. A cell can be both dependent and precedent. In this example, if cell C15 is used by another cell in the workbook, then it becomes the precedent to that cell.

To locate the source of an error value, you select any cell containing the error value and trace that error back to its precedent cells. If any of those precedent cells displays an error value, you need to trace that cell's precedents and so on until you find the final error cell that has no precedents. That cell is the source of the error. After correcting the error, if other errors still exist, repeat this process until you have removed all the errors from the workbook.

Reference

Tracing Error Values

- Select the cell containing an error value.
- On the Formulas tab, in the Formula Auditing group, click the Error Checking arrow, and then click Trace Error.
- Follow the tracer arrows to a precedent cell containing an error value.
- If the tracer arrow is connected to a worksheet icon, double-click the tracer arrow, and open the cell references in the worksheet.
- Continue to trace the error value to its precedent cells until you locate a cell containing an error value that has no precedent cells with errors.

You will use the auditing tools to trace the #NAME? error values in the Balance Sheet worksheet back to their source or sources, and then correct the errors.

To trace the errors in the Balance Sheet worksheet:

1. Go to the **Balance Sheet** worksheet, and then click cell **F9**. You will start tracing the error from this cell.

2. On the ribbon, click the **Formulas** tab.

3. In the Formula Auditing group, click the **Error Checking arrow**, and then click **Trace Error**. A tracer arrow is attached to cell F9. Refer to Figure 9–33.

Figure 9–33   Error value being traced

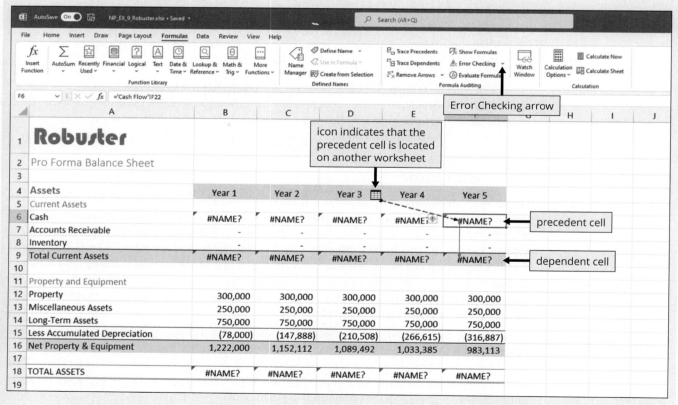

The tracer arrow provides a visual clue to the source of the error. A blue tracer arrow indicates that no error has been received or passed. A red tracer arrow indicates that an error has been received from the precedent cell or passed to the dependent cell. In this case, a red tracer arrow points from cell F6 to cell F9, indicating that cell F6 is the source of the error in cell F9. However, cell F6 also has a precedent cell. A black dashed tracer arrow points from a worksheet icon, indicating that the precedent cell for the value in cell F6 is in another worksheet in the workbook. You will follow the tracer arrow to that sheet.

To continue tracing the error to its source:

1. Double-click the **tracer arrow** that connects the worksheet icon to cell F6. The Go To dialog box opens, listing a reference to cell F22 in the Cash Flow worksheet.

2. In the Go to box, click the reference to cell **F22**, and then click **OK**. Cell F22 in the Cash Flow worksheet is now the active cell.

3. On the Formulas tab, in the Formula Auditing group, click the **Error Checking arrow**, and then click **Trace Error** to trace the source of the error in cell F22.

   The tracer arrows pass through several cells in row 22 before going to cell B22 and settling on cell B19. Cell B19 has a single precedent indicated by the blue arrow and the blue box, which surrounds the range that is the precedent to the formula in cell B19. Because blue is used to identify precedent cells that are error free, the source of the error must be in cell B19 of the Cash Flow worksheet, which is selected.

4. In the formula bar, review the formula for cell B19 in. Notice that the function name in the formula is entered incorrectly as SUMM, which is why the #NAME? error code appears in the cell. Refer to Figure 9–34.

Figure 9–34   Source of the error value

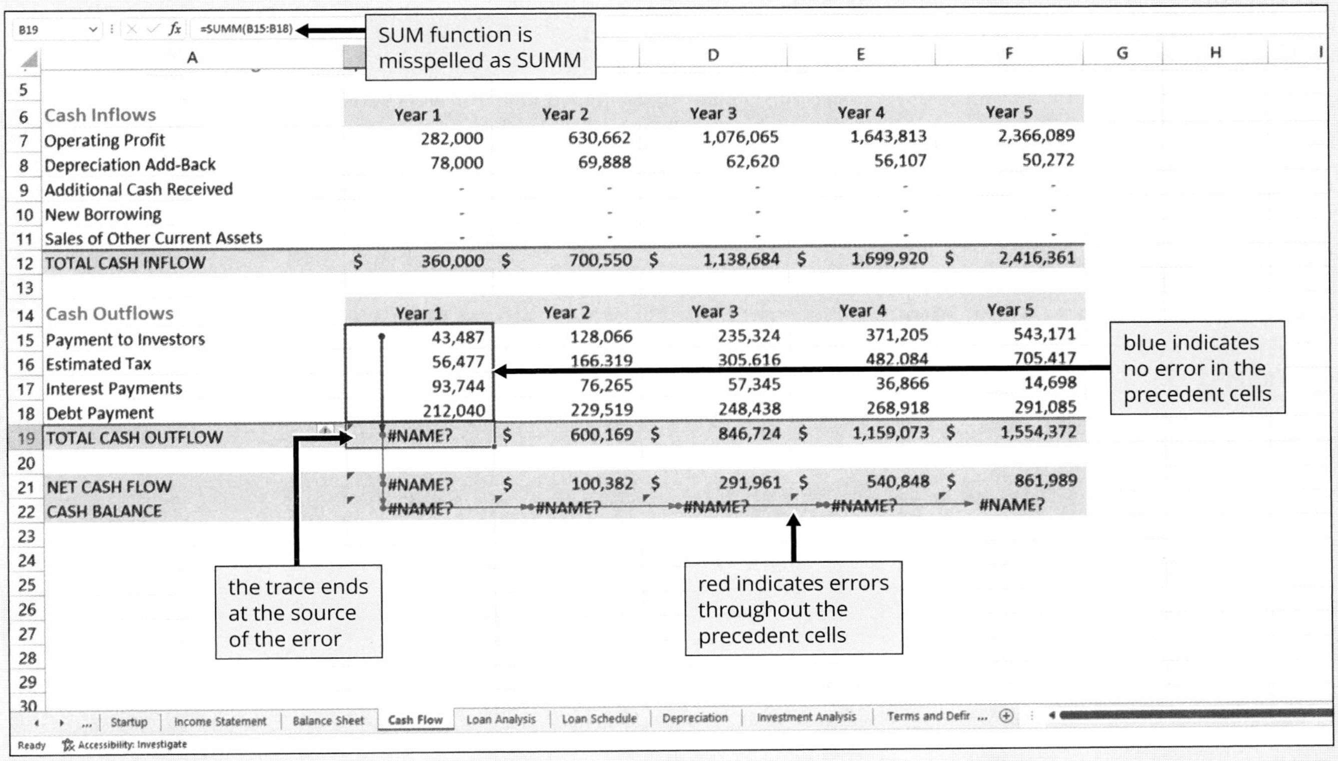

Trouble? If the tracer errors disappear, you can restore them by retracing the formulas in the workbook.

5. In cell **B19**, change the formula to **= SUM(B15:B18)** and then press **ENTER**. After you edit the formula, the #NAME? error values disappear from the worksheet.

6. On the Formulas tab, in the Formula Auditing group, click the **Remove Arrows** button if necessary to remove all the tracer arrows from the worksheet.

7. Return to the **Balance Sheet** worksheet and verify that no error values appear on that sheet.

8. Click the **Remove Arrows button**, if necessary, to remove the tracer arrows from the worksheet.

> **Trouble?** If the tracer arrows already disappeared from your workbook, it's not a problem. Excel removes tracer arrows automatically after a few seconds.

You can use the auditing tools to track any cell formula whether or not it contains an error. To trace the precedents of the active cell, click the Trace Precedents button in the Formula Auditing group on the Formulas tab (or press CTRL+[ ). To locate cells that are dependent upon the active cell, click the Trace Dependents button (or press CTRL+]).

Evaluating a Formula

Another way to explore the relationship between cells in a workbook is by evaluating formulas using the Evaluate Formula tool. From the Evaluate Formula dialog box, you can display the value of different parts of the formula or display other formulas in the cell references in the formula to discover the source of the formula's value. This is helpful for subtle worksheet errors that are not easily seen and fixed.

On a balance sheet, the value of the company's total assets should equal the value of the total liabilities and equity. Checking that these totals match is a basic step in auditing any financial report. In the Balance Sheet worksheet, the total assets in row 18 are equal to the total liabilities and equity in row 33 for Year 1 through Year 4. However, in Year 5 these values do not match. The company's Year 5 total assets shown in cell F18 are $3,582,544, but the Year 5 total liabilities and equity shown in cell F33 is $3,873,630. Because the values differ, there must be an error somewhere in the workbook. You will use the Evaluate Formula tool to evaluate the formula in cell F33 to locate the source of the error.

To evaluate the formula in cell F33 of the Balance Sheet worksheet:

1. Select cell **F33**, which contains the total liabilities and equity value for Year 5.

2. On the Formulas tab, in the Formula Auditing group, click the **Evaluate Formula** button. The Evaluate Formula dialog box opens with the formula in cell F33 displayed. Refer to Figure 9–35.

Figure 9–35   Evaluate Formula dialog box

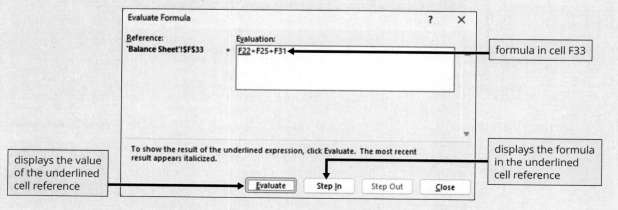

From the Evaluate Formula dialog box, you can evaluate each component of the formula in cell F33. To display the value of the underlined cell reference, click Evaluate. If the underlined part of the formula is a reference to another formula located elsewhere in the workbook, click Step In to display the other formula. Likewise, click Step Out to hide the nested formula.

You will use the Evaluate and Step In buttons to trace the formula in cell F33 to its sources.

To evaluate and step into a formula:

1. Click **Evaluate**. The selected cell reference F22 is replaced with the current liabilities for Year 5 (0). Cell F25 is now the underlined reference.

2. Click **Step In** to view the formula in cell F25. Below the original formula, the formula = 'Loan Schedule'!E38 appears, indicating that from that cell, F25 gets its value. Refer to Figure 9–36.

Figure 9–36   Stepping into a formula

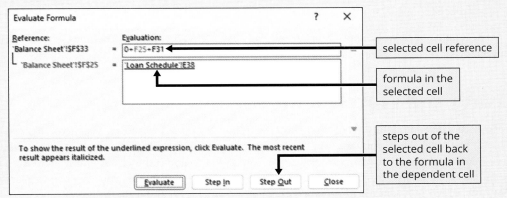

3. Click **Step In** to evaluate the formula in cell E38 of the Loan Schedule worksheet. Refer to Figure 9–37.

Figure 9–37   Source of the error found

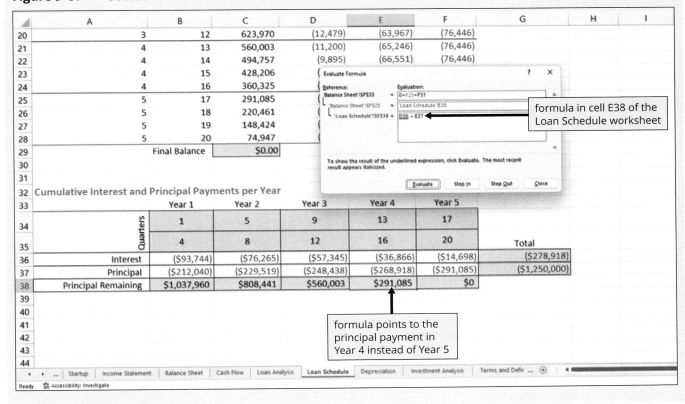

	A	B	C	D	E	F	G	H	I
20		3	12	623,970	(12,479)	(63,967)	(76,446)			
21		4	13	560,003	(11,200)	(65,246)	(76,446)			
22		4	14	494,757	(9,895)	(66,551)	(76,446)			
23		4	15	428,206						
24		4	16	360,325						
25		5	17	291,085						
26		5	18	220,461						
27		5	19	148,424						
28		5	20	74,947						
29			Final Balance	$0.00						
30										
31										
32	Cumulative Interest and Principal Payments per Year									
33			Year 1	Year 2	Year 3	Year 4	Year 5			
34		Quarters	1	5	9	13	17			
35			4	8	12	16	20	Total		
36		Interest	($93,744)	($76,265)	($57,345)	($36,866)	($14,698)	($278,918)		
37		Principal	($212,040)	($229,519)	($248,438)	($268,918)	($291,085)	($1,250,000)		
38		Principal Remaining	$1,037,960	$808,441	$560,003	$291,085	$0			
39										
40										
41										
42										
43										
44										

formula points to the principal payment in Year 4 instead of Year 5

Startup   Income Statement   Balance Sheet   Cash Flow   Loan Analysis   **Loan Schedule**   Depreciation   Investment Analysis   Terms and Defir ...

Ready   Accessibility: Investigate

You have located the source of the problem. As noted in Figure 9–37, cell E38 in the Loan Schedule worksheet is the Principal Remaining value for Year 4 of the loan payment schedule. However, it should be pointing to cell F38, which contains the Year 5 value, because you are examining liabilities and assets for Year 5. You will fix this error.

To fix the error in the calculation:

1. Click the **Step Out** button twice to hide the nested formula and redisplay the Balance Sheet worksheet.

2. Click **Close** to close the Evaluate Formula dialog box and return to the Balance Sheet worksheet with cell F25 selected.

3. In cell **F25**, change the formula to **= 'Loan Schedule'!F38** to change the cell reference from cell E38 to cell F38.

The total liabilities and equity value in cell F33 changes to $3,582,544, matching the total assets value in cell F18. The balance sheet is in balance again.

Using the Watch Window

Workbooks can contain dozens of worksheets with interconnected formulas. When you change a value in one worksheet, you may want to view the impact of that change on cell values in other worksheets. Moving among worksheets can be slow and awkward if the values you want to follow are spread across many sheets. Rather than jumping to different worksheets, you can create a **Watch Window**, which is a window displaying cell values located throughout the workbook. When you change a cell's value, a Watch Window allows you to view the impact of the change on widely scattered dependent cells. The window also displays the workbook, worksheet, defined name, cell value, and formula of each cell being watched.

Kim has projected a corporate tax rate of 30% for the next five years, but there are indications that the government might raises taxes. Kim wants to know how raising the tax rate from 30% to 34% will impact the company's Year 5 retained earnings, the Year 5 cash balance, and the internal rate of return offered to investors. You will use the Watch window to trace the impact of an increased tax rate on those outcomes.

To use the Watch Window to display values from multiple cells:

1. Go to the **Income Statement** worksheet and scroll to the top of the sheet.

2. On the Formulas tab, in the Formula Auditing group, click the **Watch Window** button. The Watch Window opens.

3. Click **Add Watch**. The Add Watch dialog box opens.

4. Click cell **F36** in the Income Statement worksheet, and then click **Add**. The Year 5 retained earnings value in cell F36 of the Income Statement worksheet is added to the Watch Window.

5. Click **Add Watch**, go to the **Balance Sheet** worksheet, click cell **F35**, and then click **Add**. The Year 5 net worth value from cell F35 of the Balance Sheet worksheet is added to the Watch Window.

6. Click **Add Watch**, go to the **Investment Analysis** worksheet, click cell **C23**, and then click **Add**. The internal rate of return for investors is added to the Watch Window.

Now you can tell the impact these three values have when the tax rate changes from 30% to 34%.

To modify the tax rate value:

1. In the Income Statement worksheet, click cell **F5** containing the projected corporate tax rate.

2. Change the tax rate value from 30% to **34%**. The Watch Window shows the impact of increasing the tax rate. Refer to Figure 9–38.

Figure 9–38   Watch Window

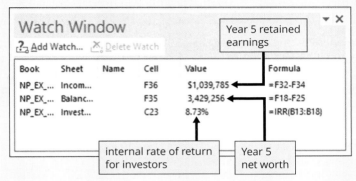

Tip You can assign range names to watched cells to make the Watch Window easier to interpret.

From the Watch Window, you can observe the effect of the revised tax rate by the end of the company's first five years. The Year 5 retained earnings amount in the Income Statement worksheet drops about $62,000 from $1,102,802 to $1,039,785; the Year 5 net worth value in the Balance Sheet worksheet falls about $150,000 from $3,582,544 to $3,429,256. Finally, the internal rate of return the company is promising to investors drops from 10.41% to 8.73%.

With operating margins so tight in a competitive market, those losses are a great concern. Kim will study this more closely and perhaps revise the business plan to deal with the possibility of increased corporate taxes. In the meantime, you will restore the tax rate to its original value.

To restore the 30% tax rate:

1. In cell **F5**, change the tax rate value back to **30%**.

2. Close the Watch Window.

3. **sam** Save the workbook, and then close it.

You have completed an initial financial analysis of Robuster's business plan. This is, of course, a preliminary rough estimate of the factors and issues involved with designing a five-year projection of the company's financial future. More in-depth analysis in consultation with financial analysts, lawyers, and others is Kim's next step.

Part 9.3 Quick Check

1. What is the formula to calculate the interest rate on a loan for $150,000 that must be repaid in 10 years with quarterly payments of $5,000? What is the quarterly interest rate? What is the annual interest rate?

2. If the annual rate of return is 5%, is $95 today worth more than, less than, or the same as $100 a year from now? What formula did you use to answer this question? What are the formula results?

3. From an investment, you receive $500 at the end of Year 1, $750 at the end of Year 2, and $1,000 at the end of Year 3. If the rate of return is 4.5%, what is the net present value of this investment? Show the formula you used to answer this question.

4. You spend $4,000 on an investment that pays $2,500 in Year 1, $1,000 in Year 2, $800 in Year 3, and $200 in Year 4. Assume a 4.5% rate of return. If you make the investment immediately, what is the net present value of the investment? Show the formula and formula results you used to answer this question.

5. Instead of spending $4,000 immediately on an investment in Question 4, you make the investment a year from now and then receive $2,500 in Year 2, $1,000 in Year 3, $800 in Year 4, and $200 in Year 5. What is the formula to calculate the present value of that investment and what is the result?

6. Calculate the internal rate of return for the investment in Question 4. If another investment is available that pays a 7.8% rate of return, should you take it? Show the formula and formula results you used to answer this question.

7. When would you use the MIRR function in place of the IRR function?

8. When tracing an error with the auditing tools, what do red tracer arrows indicate and what do blue tracer arrow indicate?

Practice: Review Assignments

Data File needed for the Review Assignments: NP_EX_9-2.xlsx

Kim has a new set of assumptions from the business planning team to analyze. Robuster can get slightly better loan conditions from another lender, so that the company will need less startup funds from an investor group. Also, the team believes that the five-year projections were a bit too optimistic and wants to examine more moderate projections for income, expenses, and depreciation. However, instead of a five-year window for those projections, Kim wants to provide an analysis for the next 10 years. You will determine the feasibility and profitability of the new business plan based on these financial considerations. The workbook also contains an error that Kim needs you to locate and fix. Complete the following:

1. Open the **NP_EX_9-2.xlsx** workbook located in the Excel9 > Review folder included with your Data Files. The workbook may open with a yellow security warning indicating the presence of disabled links. You will fix that problem in these assignments. Click the Close button at the right edge of the message bar to hide the warning message.

2. Save the workbook as **NP_EX_9_Plan2** in the location specified by your instructor.

3. In the Documentation sheet, enter your name and the date in the range B3:B4. Review the contents of the workbook.

4. Kim wants to investigate several possible loan scenarios assuming a 7.2% annual interest rate compounded quarterly from the lending institution. In the Loan Scenarios worksheet, do the following:

   a. The company wants to make quarterly payments of $45,000. In cell B7, apply the PV function to calculate the maximum loan that the company can assume given the number payments specified in cell F7 and the period payments specified in cell I7.

   b. The company wants to get a $1,500,000 loan. They plan to repay the loan at a rate of $45,000 per quarter. In cell C8, apply the FV function to calculate how much of the $1,500,000 will be left as principal after 10 years using the rate value in cell H8, the number of payments in cell F8, the payment amount in cell I8, and the present value in cell B8.

   c. The company wants to make $45,000 quarterly payments on the $1,500,000 loan. In cell F9, apply the NPER function to calculate the total number of payments required to completely pay back the loan using rate value in cell H9, the payment value in cell I9, and the present value in cell B9.

   d. The company wants to completely repay the $1,500,000 loan in 10 years. In cell I10, apply the PMT function to calculate the required quarterly payments, using the rate value in cell H10, the number of payments in cell F10, and the present value in cell B10.

5. The company has settled on a $1,400,000 loan to be repaid in 10 years at 7.2% annual interest compounded quarterly. In the Amortization Schedule worksheet, complete the table showing the amount spent on interest and on paying down the principal each quarter. As you fill in the amortization schedule, fill in the formulas without formatting. Do the following:

   a. In the range G4:G43, apply the IPMT function to calculate the interest payments each quarter, using the rate value in cell B8, the payment period from the adjacent cell in column E, the number payments in cell B10, and the present value in cell B5. Be careful to use absolute cell references for cells B8, B10, and B5.

   b. In the range H4:H43, apply the PPMT function to calculate payments on the principal each quarter using the same cell references you used for the IPMT function.

   c. In the range F5:F43, reduce the amount of principal remaining by the money spent the previous quarter on the principal.

   d. Verify that the loan is completely paid off by confirming that the value in cell F44 is zero once the schedule is completed.

6. In the Loan Payments worksheet, determine the amount spent on the $1,400,000 loan for interest and principal each year by doing the following:

   a. In the range B16:K16, apply the CUMIPMT function to calculate the cumulative interest payments for each of the 10 years, using the rate value in cell B8, the number payments in cell B10, the present value in cell B5, and the starting and ending periods from the adjacent cells in rows 14 and 15. Make sure you use absolute cell references for cells B8, B10, and B5. Assume that interest payments are made at the end of each quarter.

b. In the range B17:K17, apply the CUMPRINC function to calculate the cumulative payments made toward the principal for each of the 10 years using the same cell references you applied to the CUMIPMT function. Again, assume that principal payments are made at the end of the quarters.

c. In the range B18:K18, enter formulas that calculate the principal adding the loan amount by the principal payment for Year 1 and then for the remaining years by adding the principal remaining from the previous year to that year's principal payment. The principal remaining in cell K18 should be $0.

7. The company will start with $1.8 million in long-term material assets that will depreciate to $500,000 in 10 years. In the Depreciation worksheet, calculate the yearly depreciation using a declining balance depreciation model by doing the following:

a. In the range B10:K10, apply the DB function to calculate the depreciation amount for each year, using the cost value in cell B4, the salvage value in cell B5, the life value in cell B6, and the period value from the adjacent cell in row 9. Use absolute cell references to cells B4, B5, and B6 containing the depreciation conditions.

b. In the range B11:K11, calculate the cumulative depreciation for Year 1 through Year 10. Refer to Figure 9–21 as a guide for calculating the cumulative depreciation.

c. In the range B12:K12, calculate the depreciated value of the material assets at end of each year. Note that because of how the DB function rounds values in a declining deprecation calculation, the value in cell K12 will be close to, but not exactly equal to, $500,000.

8. The company needs to project income, expenses, and profits for the next 10 years. In the Income Statement worksheet, do the following:

a. In the range C9:J9, interpolate the projected sales in Year 2 through Year 9 assuming a geometric growth trend from Year 1 sales of $2 million to Year 10 sales of $7 million.

b. In the range C10:K10, enter formulas to calculate the annual cost of sales and marketing, assuming the cost of goods sold is 18% (cell B4) of the sales income.

c. In the range C11:K11, enter formulas to project the annual cost of research and development, assuming the cost of goods sold is 12% (cell B5) of the sales income.

d. In the range C12:K12, enter formulas to project the annual gross profit (equal to the total sales minus cost of good sold) for sales, marketing, research, and development.

e. In the range C15:K20, extrapolate general expenses through the next 10 years, assuming expenses grow by 5% each year. In the range C21:K21, enter formulas to sum the total general expenses for each year.

f. In the range B24:K24, calculate the initial earnings, which are equal to the gross profit minus total general expenses. In the range B25:K25, enter formulas to reference the annual depreciation of material assets calculated in cells B10 through K10 of the Depreciation worksheet. In the range B26:K26, calculate operating profit by subtracting deprecation from initial earnings.

g. In the range B28:K28, enter formulas to reference the annual interest payments on the loan, calculated in cells B16 through K16 of the Loan Payments worksheet as positive values rather than negative. In the range B29:K29, calculate the pretax profit by subtracting the interest expense from the operating profit.

h. In the range B31:K31, use an IF statement to test whether the pretax profit is greater than zero. If it is, calculate the tax liability by multiplying the pretax profit by the tax rate in cell E4. Otherwise, return a 0 value for the tax liability. In the range B32:K32, calculate the after-tax profit by subtracting the tax liability from the pretax profit.

i. The company proposes to pay investors 22% of the after-tax profit. In the range B34:K34, use an IF statement to test whether the after-tax profit is greater than 0. If it is, multiply the after-tax profit by the value of cell E5. Otherwise, return a value of zero.

j. In the range B36:K36, calculate retained earnings by subtracting the investor payments from the after-tax profits.

9. Kim wants to determine the return investors can receive from the company. In the Investment Analysis worksheet, do the following:

a. One proposal is to repay the $750,000 investment at a rate of $85,000 for 10 years. In cell B8, apply the RATE function to calculate the effective interest rate of that return, using cell B7 for the number of payments, cell B6 for the payment value, and cell B5 for the present value.

b. The other proposal is to repay investors using the 22% of profits calculated in the Income Statement worksheet. In cell B14, use the TRANPOSE dynamic array function to display the values from the range B34:K34 of the Income Statement worksheet.

   c. Investors need to know when the original $750,000 investment will be repaid. In the range C13:C23, calculate the cumulative net cash flow from the values in the range B13:B23.

   d. Investors want a rate of return of at least 10%. In cell C26, apply the NPV function to calculate the present value of the cash flow values, using cell C25 for the rate value and B14# to reference the dynamic array of payments.

   e. In cell C27, calculate the net present value of the investment by adding the present value in cell C26 to the original investment in cell B13.

   f. In cell C28, apply the IRR function to calculate the internal rate of return of the investment, using the cash flow values in the range B13:B23.

10. When you opened the workbook, a warning appeared that possible links existed the workbook. The Balance Sheet and Cash Flow worksheets contain multiple instances of the #REF! error value, which occurs when a formula references a cell or worksheet that does not exist in the current workbook. This error can often occur from mistyping a worksheet name. Starting from cell K19 in the Cash Flow worksheet, use the auditing tools to trace the error to its source. Correct the formula that is the source of the error.

11. Save the workbook, and then close it.

Apply: Case Problem 1

Data File needed for this Case Problem: NP_EX_9-3.xlsx

Cedar Creek Farm Elihu Waitkins is the owner of Cedar Creek Farm located in upstate New York. The farm needs to replace a high speed 12-row planter used to lay down seeds along predefined rows. New row planters of this type typically cost $170,000 and will last about 10 years before they should be salvaged. Elihu must choose between leasing the planter or buying it. If the farm leases the planter, it will have to pay monthly lease payments but will not own the equipment at the end of the 10 years. If the farm buys the planter, it will have to take out a business loan to cover most of the purchase cost and pay back the loan in 10 years. However, if the farm buys the planter, it will be able to sell it after 10 years to recoup part of the cost of owning. Elihu wants to analyze the cost of leasing versus buying in terms of the net present value of both options. Complete the following:

1. Open the **NP_EX_9-3.xlsx** workbook located in the Excel9 > Case1 folder included with your Data Files, and then save the workbook as **NP_EX_9_Cedar.xlsx** in the location specified by your instructor.

2. In the Documentation sheet, in the range B3:B4, enter your name and the date. Review the workbook. Elihu has already entered the conditions for different aspects of this financial analysis. You will use those assumptions to project the cost of leasing versus buying. In the following steps, pay careful attention to positive and negative cash flows that indicate whether an entry represents a cost to the farm or income to the farm.

3. In the Lease vs Buy worksheet, complete the entries in the Lease Options table to calculate the cost of leasing as follows:

   a. In cell E6, enter a reference to cell B17, displaying the value as a negative cash flow, for the nonrefundable deposit of $15,000 for the lease agreement. In the range E7:E16, enter **0** in each cell because the farm pays the $15,000 deposit only once.

   b. In the range F7:F16, enter a reference to cell B21 as a negative cash flow in each cell to display the cost to purchase a $3,000 annual service contract for maintenance and repair of the leased planter.

   c. In the range G7:G16, enter a reference to cell B18 as a negative cash flow to display the annual $11,000 payment the farm will pay to the leaser.

   d. In the range H6:H16, calculate the sum of the deposit, maintenance contract, and lease payment costs for Year 0 through Year 10 as a negative cash flow because these costs are all tax deductible.

   e. In the range I6:I16, calculate the tax deduction for Year 0 through Year 10 by multiplying the values in the range H6:H16, by the tax shield rate in cell B20. Enter the values as positive cash flows because they represent income to the farm.

   f. In the range J6:J16, add the deductible costs to the tax shield values to calculate the net income or loss to the farm of leasing the planter from Year 0 through Year 10.

4. In cell B5, calculate the net present cost of leasing the planter for 10 years by adding the value of cell J6 to the NPV of the values in the range J7:J16 using the discount rate in cell B4.

5. In the Loan Payments worksheet, calculate the present cost of buying the planter using a business loan and then selling the planter after 10 years. The farm proposes to make a $15,000 down payment on the planter while taking out a loan for the remaining $155,000 at a 6.2% annual interest rate compounded monthly for 10 years. Do the following:

   a. In cell B11, use the PMT function to calculate the monthly payment using the rate value in cell B9, the number of payments value in cell B10, and the present value in cell B7.

   b. In cell D14, use the CUMIPMT function to calculate the cumulative interest payments from Month 1 through Month 12 of Year 0, using the loan conditions specified in cells B9, B10, and B7, and the start and ending periods specified in cells B14 and C14. Assume that the payments are made at the end of each month. Make sure you use absolute cell references for the values in cell B9, B10, and B7. Copy the formula in cell D14 into the range D15:D23 to determine interest payments for Year 2 through Year 10.

   c. Repeat the previous step in the range E14:E23, using the CUMPRINC function to calculate the cumulative principal payments made in Year 1 through Year 10.

   d. In cells D24 and E24, calculate the total spent on interest and principal in Year 1 through Year 10. Verify that the total spent on principal in cell E24 matches the value of the loan in cell B7.

6. In the Lease vs. Buy worksheet, enter the financial data on buying the planter. Do the following:

   a. In cell E20, enter a reference to cell B17 containing the $15,000 down payment. Enter the value as a negative cash flow. In the range E21:E30, enter **0** in each cell because the farm makes the down payment is only once.

   b. In cell E31, multiply the salvage value in cell B13 by the percent at resale value in cell B25 to indicate that the farm will sell the planter at 90% of its salvage value at the end of the 10 years. Display the value as a positive cash flow because it represents income to the farm.

   c. In the range F21:F30, enter a reference to cell B26 as a negative cash flow to indicate the farm will do self-maintenance on the planter at an estimated cost of $2,100 per year.

   d. The farm will be able to deduct the depreciation of the planter. In cell G21, use the DB function to calculate the first year's declining balance depreciation, using cell B10 as the asset's cost, cell B13 as the salvage value, cell B14 as the planter's useful life, and cell D21 as the depreciation period. Use absolute cell references to cells B10, B13, and B14 and display the depreciation as a negative cash flow. Copy the formula in G21 through range G22:G30 to determine the depreciation cost for Year 2 through Year 10.

   e. Interest payments are also tax deductible. In the range H21:H30, enter a reference to the interest payments in the range D14:D23 of the Loan Payments worksheet.

   f. In the range I20:I31, calculate the sum of the deductible costs for down payments, maintenance, depreciation, and interest for Year 0 through Year 10 and after.

   g. In cell J20, calculate the Year 0 tax shield. Use an IF function to determine whether the value of cell I20 is greater than 0, if it is return a value of 0 (because you can only get a tax deduction for an expense), otherwise multiply the value of cell I20 by the tax shield value in cell B24. Use an absolute reference to cell B24. Display the tax shield value as a positive cash flow because it represents income to the farm. Copy the formula in cell J20 through the range J21:J31, calculating the tax shield for Year 2 through Year 10 and after.

   h. Principal payments are not tax deductible, but they are an expense to the farm. In the range K21:K30, enter a reference to the principal payments from the range E14:E23 of the Loan Payments worksheet.

   i. Calculate the annual total costs for purchasing and then selling the planter after 10 years. In cell L20, add the Buy/Sell, Maintenance, Interest Payment, Tax Shield, and Principal Payment values for Year 0. Copy the formula in cell L20 through the range L21:L31 to calculate the yearly cash flow through Year 10 and after.

7. In cell B6, calculate the net present cost of buying and then selling the planter by adding the value of cell L20 to the NPV of the values in the range L21:L31 using the discount rate in cell B4.

8. Choosing between leasing and buying often depends on the discount rate. If the discount rate is high, selling the planter 10 years in the future might not be an attractive option because money from the sale would be heavily discounted. If the discount rate is low, money from the sale would not be heavily discounted and be more valuable to the farm today. In the range N4:P22, complete a one-variable data table showing the net present cost of leasing versus buying for discount rates ranging from 4% up to 12%.

9. Create a scatter chart with smoothed lines of the data in the range N6:P22, and then do the following:
   a. Resize the chart to cover the range R4:X22.
   b. Change the chart title to **Net Present Cost of Leasing vs. Buying**
   c. Change the horizontal scale to go from 4% to 12%.
   d. Change the vertical scale to go from –110,000 to –70,000.
   e. Add a vertical axis label with the text **Net Present Cost**. Add a horizontal axis label with the text **Discount Rate**.
   f. Using the Select Data button from the Chart Design tab, edit Series1 to change its name to **Lease** and edit Series2 to change its name to **Buy**.
10. Save the workbook, and then close it.

Challenge: Case Problem 2

Data File needed for this Case Problem: NP_EX_9-4.xlsx

Eco Storage Trevor Schays is a financial planner for Eco Storage, a company that builds and manages landfills storing hazardous wastes in a way that is environmentally responsible and safe for surrounding communities. The company is bidding for a new environmental landfill to be placed in the Durham/Raleigh region of North Carolina. The landfill is required to handle waste for the next 20 years. After initial startup costs, the company will generate income via usage fees from local businesses and the government. At the end of the 20 years, the landfill will incur additional expenses when it is closed, and the land restored to a pristine condition. Trevor wants you to determine the financial costs of a proposed building project to determine under what conditions the project will be profitable to Eco Storage. Complete the following.

1. Open the **NP_EX_9-4.xlsx** workbook located in the Excel9 > Case2 folder included with your Data Files, and then save the workbook as **NP_EX_9_Eco.xlsx** in the location specified by your instructor.
2. In the Documentation sheet, in the range B3:B4, enter your name and the date. Review the rest of the workbook, examining the financial assumptions in the Landfill Project and Loan Schedule worksheets.
3. The company will get a $18 million business loan at 6.4% annual interest compounded quarterly for 20 years. In the Loan Schedule worksheet, complete the loan schedule by doing the following:
   a. In cell B11, calculate the quarterly payment for the loan. Multiply the quarterly payment value by $1,000,000 to express the payment in dollars instead of millions of dollars.
   b. In the range G6:G25, calculate the cumulative interest payments for each year. Assume that the payments are made at the end of each quarter. Multiply the value returned by the CUMIPMT function by $1,000,000 to express the cumulative payments in dollars instead of millions of dollars.
   c. Repeat step b in the range H6:H25 using the CUMPRINC function to calculate the cumulative principal payments for Year 1 through Year 20.
   d. In cells G26 and H26, calculate the total payments made to interest and principal. Verify that the total principal payment shown in cell H26 matches the loan amount.
4. In the Landfill Project worksheet, project the future income from the landfill by doing the following:
   a. In the range F6:F13, interpolate income from a Year 1 income of $3.2 million up to Year 10 income of $19.2 million using a geometric growth trend.
   b. In the range F15:F23, interpolate an income decline from $19.2 million in Year 10 to $6.6 million in Year 20 using a geometric growth trend.
   c. The cost of goods sold is 31% of the income generated. In the range G5:G24, multiply the Year 1 through Year 20 income values by the COGs percent in cell B11. Make sure it is a negative cash flow.
   d. Fixed costs will grow by 3% per year. Using the Year 1 fixed cost of $4.8 million, extrapolate the Year 2 through Year 20 costs in the range H6:H24 using a growth trend.
   e. In cell I5, reference the cumulative interest payments for Year 1, dividing the value by $1,000,000 so that it appears in millions of dollars rather than dollars. Copy the formula in cell I5 through the range I6:I24 to show the interest payments for Year 2 through Year 20.
   f. The landfill will have $12 million in material assets that depreciate over 20 years to a salvage value of $7.5 million. In cell J5, calculate the declining balance depreciation using the DB function with the depreciation parameters in cells B27, B29, and B28 and the period number in cell E5. Show the depreciation as a negative cash flow. Copy the formula and then paste it in the range J6:J24 to calculate depreciation for Year 2 through Year 20.

g. In cell K5, reference the cumulative principal payments for Year 1, dividing the value by $1,000,000 so that it appears in millions of dollars rather than dollars. Copy the formula in cell K5 and paste it in the range K6:K24 to show the principal payments for Year 2 through Year 20.

h. The company can deduct the expenses for cost of goods sold, fixed costs, interest, and depreciation. In the range L4:L25, calculate the sum of these expenses for each year including the startup and cleanup costs.

i. The company can deduct 31% of its business-related expenses. In cell M4, multiply the deductible expense in cell L4 by the tax shield rate in cell B16. Display the calculated value as a positive cash flow. Copy the formula in cell M4 and paste it in the range M5:M25 to show tax shield income Year 1 through Year 20, startup, and cleanup.

j. In cell N4, calculate the startup earnings by adding the values for income, cost of goods sold, fixed costs, interest, principal, and tax shield. Copy the formula in cell N4 and paste it in the range N5:N25.

k. In the range O4:O25, calculate the running total of the earnings value in column N. Where the cumulative earning is negative, the company lost money through that data (without considering the time value of money).

5. Create a scatter chart with smooth lines of the values in the range D4:D25, O4:O25. Complete scatter chart as follows:

a. Move and resize the chart to cover the range T3:Z13.

b. Change the chart title to **Cumulative Earnings ($mil)**.

c. **Explore:** The date values in the horizontal axis overlap. Double-click the horizontal axis containing the dates to open the Format Axis pane. On the Text Options tab, in the Number section, enter **yyyy** in the Format Code box and click **Add** to display only the year values in the chart.

6. **Explore:** The cumulative earnings chart appears to show that the company will eventually lose money in the Durham/Raleigh project. However, that analysis does not consider the time value of money. In cell B4, calculate net present value with the XNPV function using the discount rate in cell B15, the cash flow values in the range N4:N25, and the date values in the range D4:D25.

7. In the range Q3:R27, create a one-variable data table showing the net present value for different discount rates.

8. **Explore:** Graph the data in the range Q5:R27 as a scatter plot with smooth lines to display how the selection of discount rate affects the net present value. Note that the NPV curve crosses the horizontal axis twice, indicating that there are two possible internal rates of return depending on whether cash flows are lightly discounted or heavily discounted. Do the following to complete the chart:

a. Move and resize the chart to cover the range T14:Z27.

b. Change the chart title to **Net Present Value vs. Discount Rate**

c. Add a vertical axis label with the text **Net Present Value ($mil)**. Add a horizontal axis label with the text **Discount Rate**.

9. The Durham/Raleigh project will go forward only if the net present value of the project is greater than $2 million at discount rate of 4.5%. In cell B5, enter an IF function that displays "Approved" if the cell B4 is greater than 2 and "Disapproved" if otherwise.

10. Save the workbook, and then close it.

Analyzing Data with Business Intelligence Tools

Presenting Sales and Revenue Data

Case: Musiki

Adina Abrams is an accounts manager for Musiki, a retail chain selling musical instruments, books, and accessories at 10 brick-and-mortar stores located on the Pacific Coast, in Arizona, in Colorado, as well as from the company website. Adina is developing a report tracking the sales of specialty percussion instruments over the recent and long-term history of the company. Information from this report will be used to project future sales and revenue for the company. Adina has compiled several thousands of records of sales, detailing what instruments were purchased, where they were purchased, when they were purchased, and where the customers were located. This large volume of data will be retrieved from a variety of data sources, including text files and external databases. Adina wants to import this data into an Excel workbook and develop a report to present to other Musiki account managers at an upcoming sales meeting.

Starting Data Files

Excel10

Module

NP_EX_10-1.xlsx
Support_EX_10_Data.accdb
Support_EX_10_History.csv
Support_EX_10_TwoYear.csv

Review

NP_EX_10-2.xlsx
Support_EX_10_Keyboards.accdb
Support_EX_10_LongTerm.csv
Support_EX_10_Trends.csv

Case1

NP_EX_10-3.xlsx
Support_EX_10_Parks.csv
Support_EX_10_Survey.csv
Support_EX_10_Visits.csv

Case2

NP_EX_10-4.xlsx
Support_EX_10_Cases.csv
Support_EX_10_Counties.csv
Support_EX_10_Postal.csv

Objectives

Part 10.1

- Retrieve data with the Query Editor
- Create and edit a query
- Chart trends and forecast future values

Part 10.2

- Add data to the Data Model
- Manage table relations with Power Pivot
- Create a PivotTable with data from multiple tables

Part 10.3

- Drill through a field hierarchy
- Apply slicers to a Data Report
- Create map charts
- Create map presentations with 3D Maps

Part 10.1 Visual Overview: Queries and Trendlines

The **Power Query Editor** is an Office tool to write queries.

A **data query** is a request for information from a data source. This query retrieves information from the Year, Business Year, and Revenue ($mil) fields.

The Preview grid displays a preview of the query result.

The Query Settings pane displays the name of the query and a list of all the steps involved in defining the query.

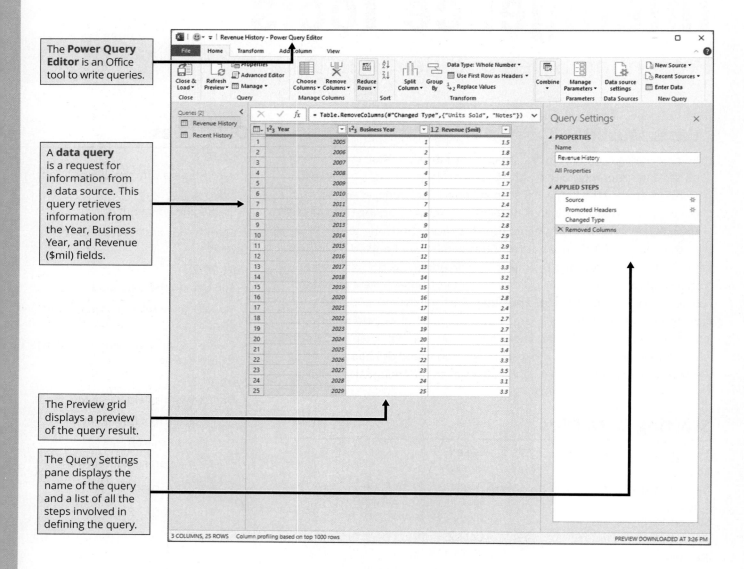

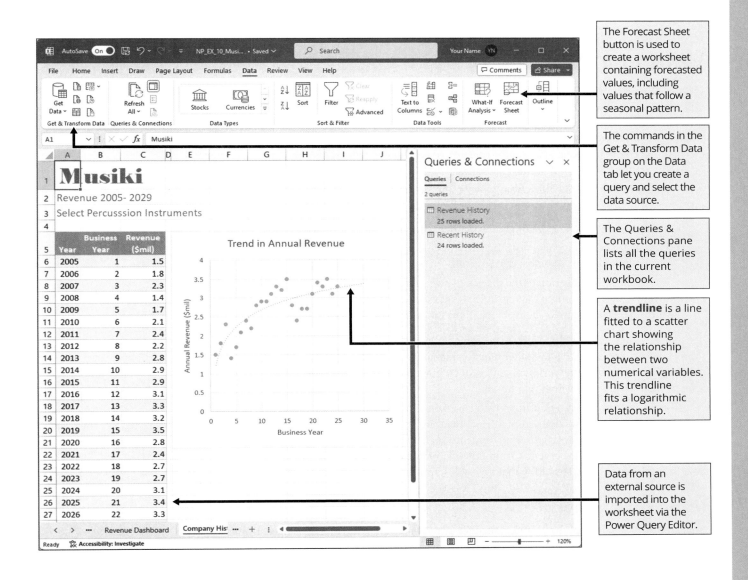

The Forecast Sheet button is used to create a worksheet containing forecasted values, including values that follow a seasonal pattern.

The commands in the Get & Transform Data group on the Data tab let you create a query and select the data source.

The Queries & Connections pane lists all the queries in the current workbook.

A **trendline** is a line fitted to a scatter chart showing the relationship between two numerical variables. This trendline fits a logarithmic relationship.

Data from an external source is imported into the worksheet via the Power Query Editor.

Introducing Business Intelligence

The business world is awash in data. The challenge for a data analyst is to organize and manage that data for informed decision making. The tools and techniques for extracting useful information from large data sets are referred to as **business intelligence** (or **BI**). Business intelligence seeks to answer questions of fact, such as *What happened?* and *When did it happen?* and *Where did it happen?* Business intelligence is often paired with **analytics**, which seeks answers to strategic planning questions, such as *Why did it happen?* and *How can we make it happen again?* When properly applied, business intelligence accelerates and improves decision making, resulting in a competitive advantage in the marketplace.

In this module, you'll learn the tools you need to turn Excel into an effective business intelligence platform. That process starts with data queries.

Writing a Data Query

Data is often stored in text files, online documents, and databases. To bring that data into Excel, you create a data query. Because data sources often contain thousands or even millions of records, a query will often reduce an external data set to a manageable size. A sales manager might construct a data query to retrieve sales of a few select products sold within a specified time window. Queries can also remove extraneous information, create new calculated data fields, sort and filter data, and generally get the data ready for analysis in Excel.

A query establishes a connection between the Excel workbook and the data source by doing one of the following tasks:

- Imports the data once, creating a "snapshot" of the data at a specific moment in time.
- Establishes a "live connection" that will be updated periodically, ensuring that the workbook contains the most current data.
- Establishes a connection to the data but leaves the data stored in the data source, creating a smaller, more manageable workbook, and avoids creating duplicate copies of the same data across multiple locations and documents.

For example, a climatologist interested only in temperature values from past epochs would need to import data only once. On the other hand, a financial analyst would probably want to establish a live connection between a workbook and a stock market data source so that the workbook always reflects the most current values and trends.

Musiki sells a wide range of musical instruments and accessories, including instruments that reflect the musical contributions from different culture and nationalities. One of these product lines is a selection of African percussion instruments such as udu drums, shakers, and djembes. Adina wants a report on the sales revenue from this line of specialty percussion instruments. Those data have been stored in an external file that you will import with Power Query.

Using Power Query

Power Query is a BI tool for writing data queries to almost any kind of data source, from text files to websites to large data structures. With Power Query, you can specify which parts of the data to import and how that data should be structured before it is brought into Excel.

Text files are the simplest and one of the most widely used data storage formats, containing only text and numbers without any internal coding, formulas, or graphics. The text file data are usually organized in columns separated by a character known as a **delimiter**. The most used delimiters are spaces, commas, and tabs. Text files with comma delimiters are known as **Comma Separated Values (CSV) files**.

Figure 10–1 shows the first lines of content from a financial document of data Adina wants imported into Excel. The data are arranged in five columns separated by commas. The column titles, shown in the first line, are Year, Business Year, Revenue ($mil), Units Sold, and Notes. The remaining lines of the file contain the annual sales figures and notes on the 25 years of sales data.

Figure 10-1   Data arranged in a CSV file

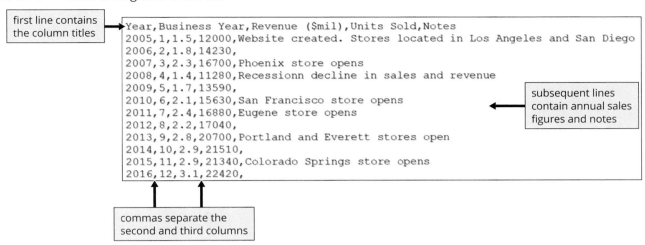

first line contains the column titles

```
Year,Business Year,Revenue ($mil),Units Sold,Notes
2005,1,1.5,12000,Website created. Stores located in Los Angeles and San Diego
2006,2,1.8,14230,
2007,3,2.3,16700,Phoenix store opens
2008,4,1.4,11280,Recessionn decline in sales and revenue
2009,5,1.7,13590,
2010,6,2.1,15630,San Francisco store opens
2011,7,2.4,16880,Eugene store opens
2012,8,2.2,17040,
2013,9,2.8,20700,Portland and Everett stores open
2014,10,2.9,21510,
2015,11,2.9,21340,Colorado Springs store opens
2016,12,3.1,22420,
```

subsequent lines contain annual sales figures and notes

commas separate the second and third columns

You want to be careful retrieving financial data from a CSV file because commas placed within currency values will be interpreted as column separators.

> **Tip** If your data values require commas, use a text file in which a tab character separates one column from another.

Another type of text file format is a **fixed width format** in which each column is placed in a fixed position with a specified number of characters. A delimiter is not required with fixed width data files.

Reference

Constructing a Query

- On the Data tab, in the Get & Transform Data group, click the Get Data button.
- On the Get Data menu, select a data source category, click the type of file or the data source, and then import the data source file.
- Click Transform Data, and then in the Power Query Editor, click toolbar commands to transform the data from the data source.
- In the Query Settings pane, edit the steps in the query.
- On the Home tab, in the Close group, click the Close & Load arrow, and then click Close & Load To.
- In the Load To dialog box, select how to load the data, and then click Load.

You will create a query to retrieve the data values from the CSV file presented in Figure 10–1.

To create a query to retrieve the revenue history data:

1. **sam** ⬇ Open the **NP_EX_10-1.xlsx** workbook located in the **Excel10 > Module** folder included with your Data Files, and then save the workbook as **NP_EX_10_Musiki** in the location specified by your instructor.

2. In the Documentation worksheet, in the range **B3:B4**, enter your name and the date.

3. Go to the **Company History** worksheet. You will place the revenue data that Adina has compiled in this worksheet.

4. On the ribbon, click the **Data** tab, and then in the Get & Transform Data group, click the **From Text/CSV** button. The Import Data dialog box opens.

> **Tip** You can also open CSV files directly in Excel using the Open command in Backstage view.

5. Navigate to the **Excel10 > Module** folder included with your Data Files, click the **Support_EX_10_History.csv** file, and then click **Import**. A dialog box opens with a preview of the data from the CSV file. Refer to Figure 10–2.

Figure 10–2   Preview of queried data

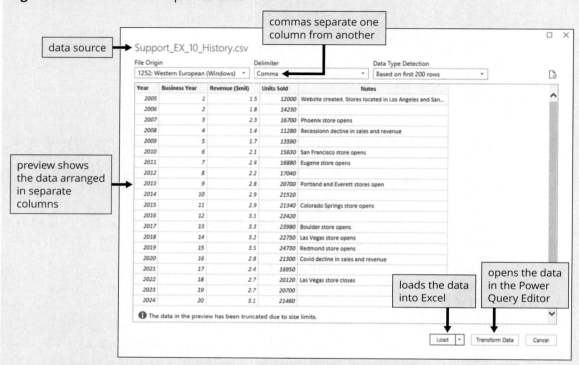

6. Click **Transform Data**. The Power Query Editor window for this data source opens. Refer to Figure 10–3.

Figure 10–3   Power Query Editor window

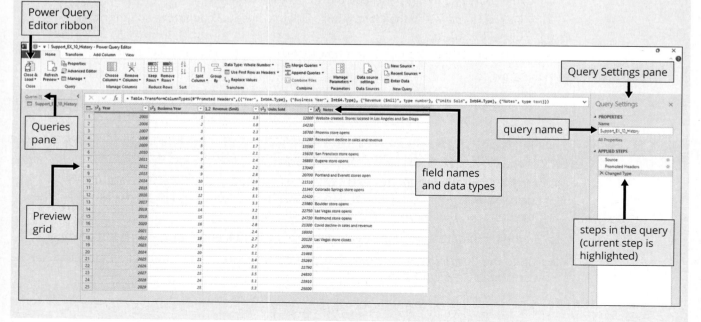

Power Query assigns each query a name. The default is the name of the data source, which in this case is the Support_EX_10_History file. You will change the name of the query to Revenue History.

To change the query name to Revenue History:

1. Near the top of the Query Settings pane, click the **Name** box.

2. Select the default name assigned to the query, and then press **DELETE**.

3. Type **Revenue History** as the query name, and then press **ENTER**. The query is renamed.

A query is defined by a list of commands appearing in the APPLIED STEPS box of the Query Settings pane. Power Query entered three commands to import the data from the CSV file. To better understand what Power Query is doing, you will view the impact of each step on the data query by viewing the status of the data in the Preview grid.

To view the first three steps of the query:

1. In the Query Settings pane, in the APPLIED STEPS box, click **Source**. The Source step establishes the connection to the Support_EX_10_History.csv file. The Preview grid displays the appearance of the data after this step but before the next step. At this point in the query process, the default column names are Column1 through Column5, and all fields are treated as containing only text values, as indicated by A^B_C .

2. In the APPLIED STEPS box, click **Promoted Headers**. In this step, Power Query uses the first line in the CSV file as a header row and assigns field names to the five columns of data.

3. In the APPLIED STEPS box, click **Changed Type**. The Changed Type step applies data types to the values in the five columns, with the Year, Business Year, and Unit Sold fields defined as containing whole numbers 1^2_3 , the Revenue ($mil) field as containing decimal numbers 1.2 , and the Notes field as containing text A^B_C .

You can modify a query step by selecting the step in the APPLIED STEPS box and clicking the Gear icon ⚙ to the right of the step title. You can also delete a step by clicking the Delete button ✕ that appears to the left of the selected step title. Be aware that editing or deleting a query step might cause subsequent steps to fail.

Insight

M: The Language of Power Query

All steps in Power Query are written in the language **M**, which is a mashup query language that extracts and transforms data from a data source. Each expression in M is applied as a function that creates or acts upon the connection to the data source. For example, the following Csv.Document() function from the M language retrieves the contents of the revenue.csv file located in the Excel folder of the user's MAIN computer, using a comma symbol as the delimiter to separate one column of data from the next:

```
=Csv.Document(File.Contents("\\MAIN\Excel\Revenue.csv"),
[Delimiter=",",Encoding=1252])
```

As your understanding of Power Query progresses, you may find it more efficient to write your own commands in M rather than having the Power Query Editor do it for you. You can view and edit all the M commands in a query by clicking the Advanced Editor button in the Query group on the Home tab of the Power Query Editor window.

Retrieving Data into an Excel Table

Once the data is in the form you want, you can load the data into your Excel workbook. Queried data can be imported into an Excel table, a PivotTable, or a PivotChart. You can also just create a connection to the data source. Adina wants you to load the financial history data into an Excel table on the Company History worksheet. You will import the data now.

To load the query data into an Excel table on the Company History worksheet:

1. On the Home tab, in the Close group, click the **Close & Load arrow**, and then click **Close & Load To**. The Import Data dialog box opens.

   > **Key Step** Be sure to click the Close & Load arrow so you can choose where to place the imported data.

   > **Trouble?** If Excel loaded the data into a new worksheet, you clicked the Close & Load button not the Close & Load To arrow. Cut and paste the Excel table into cell A3 in the Company History worksheet and then read but do not perform Steps 2 through 4.

2. Verify that the **Table** option button is selected, and then click the **Existing worksheet** option button.

3. If necessary, click cell **A5** to enter the expression ='Company History'!$A$5 in the cell reference box.

4. Click **OK**. After a few seconds, the data is loaded into a new table on the Company History worksheet. Refer to Figure 10–4.

Figure 10–4   Queried data loaded into an Excel table

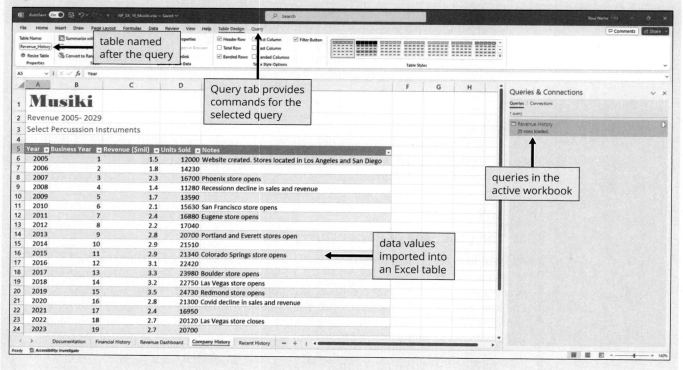

Excel assigns the new table the same name as the query that generated it. When the Revenue_History table is selected, the ribbon includes the Table Design tab and the Query tab, which contains commands for editing the selected query. The Queries & Connections pane also appears, listing all the queries in the active workbook.

Editing a Query

You can edit an existing query. When you point to that query in the Queries & Connections pane, a dialog box opens, displaying information about the selected query and options for modifying the query. Adina wants you to edit the Revenue History query, removing the Units Sold and Notes columns so the table focuses only the revenue data.

To edit the existing Revenue History query:

1. In the Queries & Connections pane, point to **Revenue History**. A dialog box appears with information about the query. Refer to Figure 10–5.

Figure 10–5   Revenue History dialog box

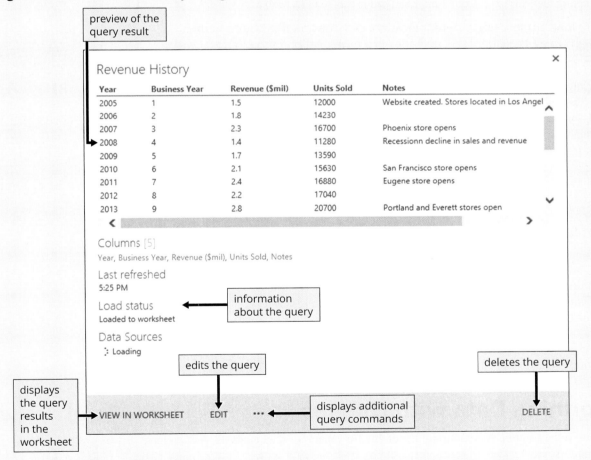

2. At the bottom of the dialog box, click **EDIT**. The Power Query Editor window for the Revenue History query opens.

> **Tip** You can also edit a query by going to the Query tab on the ribbon, and then clicking the Edit button in the Edit group.

3. Click the **Units Sold** column header, hold down **CTRL**, click the **Notes** column header to select both columns, and then release the **CTRL** key.

4. On the Home tab, in the Manage Columns group, click the **Remove Columns** button. The Units Sold and Notes columns are removed from the query, leaving only the Year, Business Year, and Revenue ($mil) columns.

5. On the Home tab, in the Close group, click the **Close & Load** button. The edited query is loaded, and the Revenue History table now shows only the first three columns from the data source.

Note that removing columns from a query does not affect the data in the data source. It affects only the data that was imported into Excel.

Refreshing Query Data

Loading data from a query into Excel creates a snapshot of that data. If the values in the data source change, the connection can be refreshed to show the most current information. You can refresh a query by clicking the Refresh button in the Load group on the Query tab.

> **Tip** To load a query to a different location, click the Load To button in the Load group on the Query tab, and specify a new location in the Import Data dialog box.

To automatically refresh a data query, click the Refresh All arrow in the Queries & Connections group on the Data tab, and then click Connection Properties. The Query Properties dialog box opens to the Usage tab. From that tab, you can view controls for the connection to the query's data source. You can have Excel automatically refresh external data on a periodic schedule or whenever the workbook is opened. In this way, you can ensure the workbook contains timely and accurate information.

Insight

Excel Tables as Data Sources

An Excel table or a data range can be a data source for other Excel workbooks. To create a query to an Excel table or data range, select the table or data range, and then click the From Table/Range button in the Get & Transform Data group on the Data tab.

One advantage of using Power Query for tables and data ranges is that you then have access to all the unique tools and commands in Power Query. You can filter, reorder, and transform the table or data range for use in the current workbook or in other workbooks. However, like all queries, any changes you make to the data in the query do not impact the content or structure of the table or data range itself.

Transforming Data with Queries

The structure of a data source is sometimes unsuitable for reports or data analysis. As you have learned, you can use Power Query to remove columns from the data source. Power Query also includes tools to create new columns, group data values, and calculate summary statistics. This capability is particularly useful for large datasets in which the analyst is interested in only overall measures and not individual values.

Adina has another CSV file with two years of daily revenue totals from Musiki's of line of specialty percussion instruments. Adina wants a query that totals this data by month. Rather than importing all the daily information, you will use Power Query to group and summarize the data from the CSV file before bringing it into Excel. First, you will access the data source.

To write a query to access the two-year revenue data source:

1. Go to the **Recent History** worksheet.

2. On the Data tab, in the Get & Transform Data group, click the **From Text/CSV** button. The Import Data dialog box opens.

3. If necessary, navigate to the **Excel10 > Module** folder included with your Data Files, click the **Support_EX_10_TwoYear.csv** file, and then click **Import**. The preview box for the CSV file opens.

4. Click **Transform Data** to open the Power Query Editor.

5. In the Query Settings pane, in the Name box, change the name of the query from Support_EX_10_TwoYear to **Recent History**. Refer to Figure 10–6.

Figure 10–6   Initial preview of the Recent History query

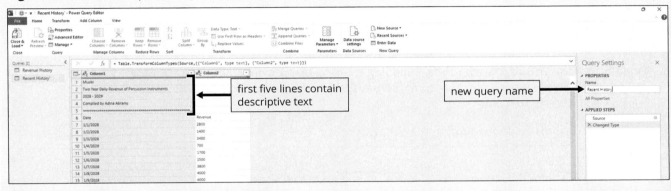

It is not uncommon for text files to include a few lines of introductory text before the data. However, the inclusion of an introduction means that Power Query cannot automatically locate the data columns. You must do that manually, indicating that data begins on the sixth row of the file. You then define the data types of column headers for the two data fields in the CSV file.

To set up the data query:

1. On the Home tab, in the Reduce Rows group, click the **Remove Rows** button, and then click **Remove Top Rows**. The Remove Top Rows dialog box opens.

2. In the Number of rows box, type **5**, and then click **OK**. The first five rows are removed from the data.

   Tip You can use the Remove Rows command to also remove bottom rows, duplicate rows, and blank rows from the data.

3. On the Home tab, in the Transform group, click the **Use First Row as Headers** button. The top row is used as the column headers for the two data columns.

Excel creates the Date and Daily Revenue fields, assigning the Date data type to the Date field and the Whole Number data type $\boxed{1^2_3}$ to the Daily Revenue field.

Adding a New Column

You can add new columns to the data query. Adina wants to know the monthly revenue totals, not the daily revenue totals shown in the data file. Because revenue figures are tallied at the end of each month, you will add a new column named Month displaying the date of the last day in each month—that is, 1/31/2029 for January, 2/28/2029 for February, and so forth.

To create a new column with the end-of-month dates:

1. If necessary, click the **Date** column heading to select that column.

   Tip To change a column's data type, select the column, then on the Home tab, in the Transform group, click the Data Type box and choose a different type.

2. On the ribbon, click the **Add Column** tab, and then in the From Date & Time group, click the **Date** button. A menu opens with date options.

3. On the menu, point to **Month**, and then click **End of Month**. The End of Month column is added to the data.

4. Double-click the **End of Month** column heading to select the current column name, type **Month** as the new column name, and then press **ENTER**. The column is renamed and resized. Refer to Figure 10–7.

Figure 10–7   Month column added to the data query

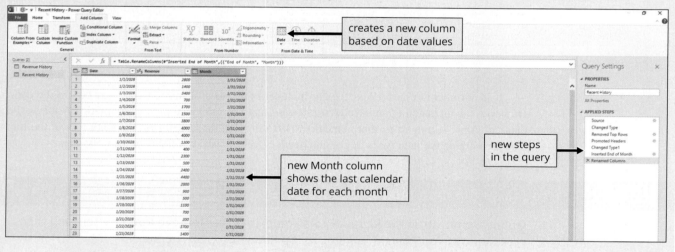

Grouping Values in a Query

You can group the data in a query by the values within one or more of its columns. When you create a grouping, Power Query adds a new column that summarizes the numeric values within each group by calculating statistics such as the sum, average, median, minimum, maximum, or count of those values.

Adina wants the query to return the total revenue within each month. You will group the query by the values in the Month column and create a new column containing the sum of the Revenue field.

To calculate the monthly revenues:

1. On the ribbon, click the **Transform** tab, and then in the Table group, click the **Group By** button. The Group By dialog box opens.

2. If necessary, click the top box, and then click **Month** to group the values by the dates in the Month column.

   > **Tip** To group by multiple columns, click the Advanced option button and choose additional columns and grouping options.

3. In the New column name box, double-click **Count**, type **Monthly Revenue** as the name of the new column to be added to the query, and then press **TAB**.

4. Click the **Operation** box, select **Sum** to apply the sum function to the column, and then press **TAB**.

5. Click the **Column** box, and then select **Revenue** as the column to sum within the Month group. Refer to Figure 10–8.

Figure 10–8   Group By dialog box

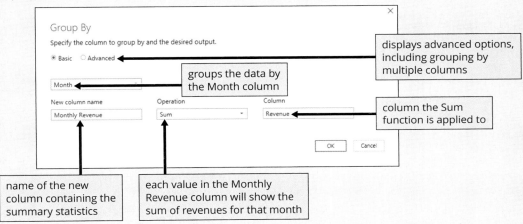

6. Click **OK**. The values in the data query are grouped in a new column named Monthly Revenue. The Daily Revenue column is removed from this new grouping.

You can now load queried data into an Excel table.

To close and load the Monthly Revenue query:

1. On the ribbon, click the **Home** tab. In the Close group, click the **Close & Load arrow**, and then click **Close & Load To**. The Import Data dialog box opens.

2. Verify that the **Table** option button is selected.

3. Click the **Existing worksheet** option button, and then click cell **A5** in the Recent History worksheet to load the Excel table containing the query data into that location.

4. Click **OK**. The 24 monthly revenue values appear in an Excel table in the Recent History worksheet.

5. Select the range **B6:B29**, and then format the selected cells with the Currency number format with no decimal places. Refer to Figure 10–9.

Figure 10–9   Imported monthly revenue values

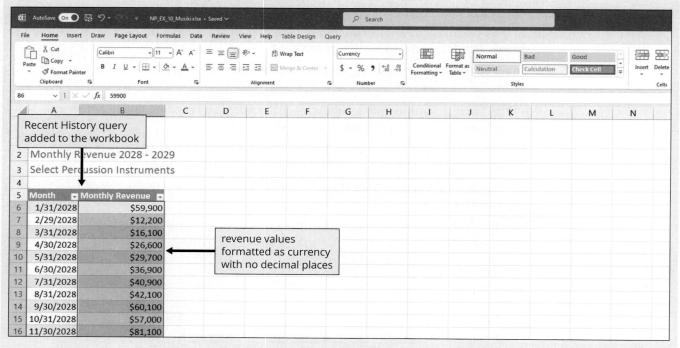

6. Close the Queries & Connections pane.

The recent history data provides Adina with valuable insight into how Musiki's sales vary throughout the year. For example, the lowest revenue total occurred in February 2029 in which Musiki had $10,500 (cell B6) in sales of specialty percussion instruments. The highest occurred in December 2028 in which the total revenue from percussion instruments was $164,000 (cell B17).

Insight

Moving a Query's Data Source

The connection between a workbook and a data source is lost when one or the other is moved to a new location. If the files are no longer stored in the original location, the data can no longer be refreshed. To update the path between the workbook and the data source, do the following:

1. Open the query in the Power Query.
2. Double-click the Source step from the list of query steps in the APPLIED STEPS box.
3. Specify the new location of the data source in the File path box.
4. Click OK to save the query with the new location of the data source.

After saving the query, you can refresh the query within Excel and verify that it can again connect to the data source without error.

Charting Trends

Recognizing trends and projecting future values is an important goal of business intelligence. One way of identifying a trend is with a trendline added to a chart.

Reference

Adding and Editing a Trendline

- Create a scatter chart of the data.
- Select the chart, click the Chart Elements button, click the Trendline arrow, and then select the type of trendline.
- Double-click the trendline in the scatter chart to open the Format Trendline pane.
- Select the option button for the type of trendline to fit to the data.
- Enter the number of future values in the Forward box to project future values along the same trend.
- Click the Display Equation on chart check box to display the equation of the trendline.
- Click the Display R-squared value on chart check box to display the R^2 value that indicates how well the trendline fits the data.

Adina wants you to create a scatter chart of the company's revenue from specialty percussion instruments over the past 25 years with a trendline indicating the general pattern of revenue growth. Adina is interested in learning whether revenues have grown by a constant amount each year or are levelling off.

To create a scatter chart of the company's annual revenue:

1. Go to the **Company History** worksheet, and then select the range **B5:C30**.

2. On the ribbon, click the **Insert** tab. In the Charts group, click the **Insert Scatter (X, Y) or Bubble Chart** button, and then click **Scatter** (the first chart in the gallery). A scatter chart plotting Revenue vs. Business Year appears in the worksheet.

3. Move the chart to the **Financial History** worksheet, and then move and resize it to cover the range A4:G20.

4. Add the title **Annual Revenue ($mil)** to the vertical axis and the title **Business Year** to the horizontal axis.

5. Change the chart title to **Trend in Annual Revenue**.

6. Click the **Chart Elements** button, and then click the **Trendline** check box.
   A straight line is added to the chart showing a general upward trend in the revenue figures over the past 25 years. Refer to Figure 10–10.

Figure 10–10   Linear trendline added to a scatter chart

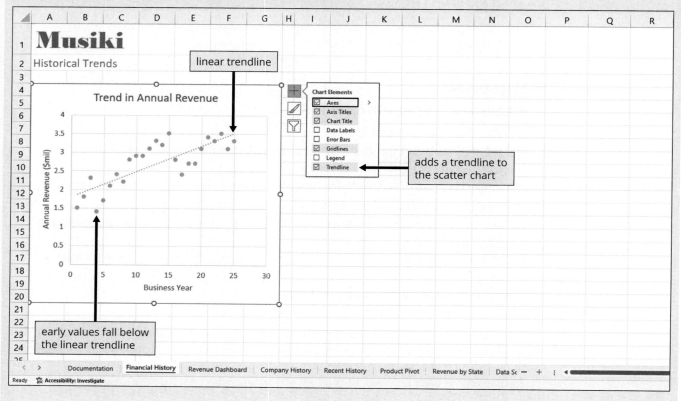

Excel scatter charts support the following trendline types:

- **Linear** for straight-line trends that increase or decrease by a constant amount (the default)
- **Exponential** for data values that rise or fall at increasingly higher rates
- **Logarithmic** for trends that increase or decrease quickly and then level out
- **Moving Average** to smooth out data by charting the average of consecutive data points
- **Polynomial** for trends that fluctuate between peaks and valleys defined by a polynomial equation
- **Power** for trends that increase or decrease by a constant multiple

The straight line in the chart you created for Adina is for a linear trend, based on the assumption that revenue increases by a constant amount each year. However, the linear trendline overestimates the revenue in the early years. Adina thinks that a logarithmic trendline would be more appropriate because revenues grew rapidly at the beginning and then levelled off in later years.

> **Tip** Power and Exponential trendlines cannot be used if the data contains zero or negative values.

You will add a logarithmic trendline to the chart and extend the trendline five years into the future so that Adina can project future revenue from this line of products.

To change the trendline to logarithmic and project future values:

1. With the chart still selected, click the **Chart Elements** button ⊞, and then click the **Trendline** check box. The linear trendline disappears from the chart.

2. Click the **Trendline arrow** to display a menu of trendline options, and then click **More Options**. The Format Trendline pane opens.

3. In the Trendline Options section, click the **Logarithmic** option button. The logarithmic trendline appears on the chart.

4. In the Forecast options, type **5** in the Forward box, and then press **ENTER**. The trendline extends to forecast the company's annual revenue for the next five periods, or years. Refer to Figure 10–11.

Figure 10–11   Revenue estimated using a logarithmic trend

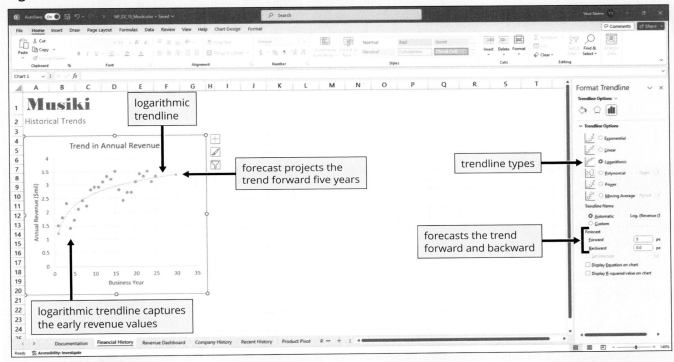

The logarithmic trendline appears to follow the general growth of revenue from the sale of percussion instruments better than the linear trend. Adina will use the logarithmic trendline going forward, which indicates that the company's annual revenue should reach $3.4 million in five years.

Insight

Judging a Trendline with R^2

How well a trendline fits the data can be evaluated using the R^2 **statistic**, which measures what percentage of the variability in the data can be explained by the trendline. The R^2 statistic is expressed as a decimal between 0 and 1 where an R^2 value such as 0.85 indicates that 85% of the variability of the data can be accounted for by the trendline. R^2 values close to 1 indicate much of the data can be fitted by the trendline. On the other hand, R^2 values close to 0 indicate there is little evidence of a trend in the data based on the fitted line. You can display the R^2 value for an Excel trendline by clicking the Display R-squared value on chart check box in the Format Trendline pane.

Creating a Forecast Sheet

Forecast sheets are another Excel tool used for displaying trends and projecting future values. One advantage of forecast sheets is that they can be used to analyze **seasonal data** in which the values follow a periodic pattern during the calendar year.

Reference

Creating a Forecast Sheet and Setting the Forecast Options

- Select the data range containing the date values and numeric values to be forecasted.
- On the Data tab, in the Forecast group, click the Forecast Sheet button.
- In the Create Forecast Worksheet dialog box, click Options.
- To add a seasonal trend to the forecasts, in the Seasonality group, click the Set Manually option, and then enter the number of periods in one season.
- To set the confidence interval for the forecasted values, enter a value in the Confidence Interval input box.
- To set the extent of the forecast, enter the ending date in the Forecast End box.
- Click Create.

Adina wants you to create a forecast sheet to track the seasonal changes in monthly revenue and project next year's monthly revenue.

To generate a forecast sheet of the monthly revenue:

1. Go the **Recent History** worksheet and select the range **A5:B29**.

2. On the ribbon, click the **Data** tab, and then in the Forecast group, click the **Forecast Sheet** button. The Create Forecast Worksheet dialog box opens, showing a preview of the forecasted values. Refer to Figure 10–12.

Figure 10–12   Create Forecast Worksheet dialog box

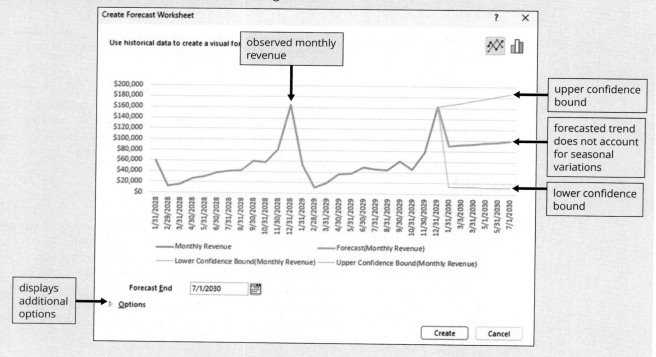

Excel uses two years of monthly revenue figures to project the revenue trend up to July 1, 2030. The trend is bracketed by upper and lower **confidence bounds**, which provide a measure of the uncertainty of the forecast by indicating within what range the forecasted values will lie. The default is to create 95% confidence interval in which one is 95% confident that the actual values will appear. For example, if the 95% confidence bound for a forecasted revenue ranges from $20,000 to $180,000, you would be 95% confident that the eventual revenue will be not less than $20,000 and not greater than $180,000. The fact that the upper and lower bounds are so far apart in Figure 10–12 indicates a large measure of uncertainty in the projected monthly revenue.

> **Tip** To change the confidence interval percentage, click Options in the Create Forecast Worksheet dialog box, and then enter a new value in the Confidence Interval box.

Adina notes that revenue follows a seasonal pattern with the highest sales totals occurring in November and December and lowest sales in February and March. The forecasted values have not picked up this trend. You will revise the forecast to account for seasonal variability.

To create a seasonal forecast of the monthly revenue:

1. In the lower-left corner of the Create Forecast Worksheet dialog box, click **Options**. The dialog box expands to display the forecast options.

2. In the Seasonality group, click the **Set Manually** option button, and then enter **12** in the Set Manually box. This specifies a seasonal pattern that will repeat itself every 12 months.

> **Tip** You need at least two complete years of data to project a seasonal trend for the next year.

3. In the Forecast End box, change the date to **12/31/2030** to forecast a year of monthly revenue. When the revenue follows a seasonal pattern, the confidence bounds are much smaller than when no seasonality was assumed. Refer to Figure 10–13.

Figure 10–13   Forecasts with a seasonal trend

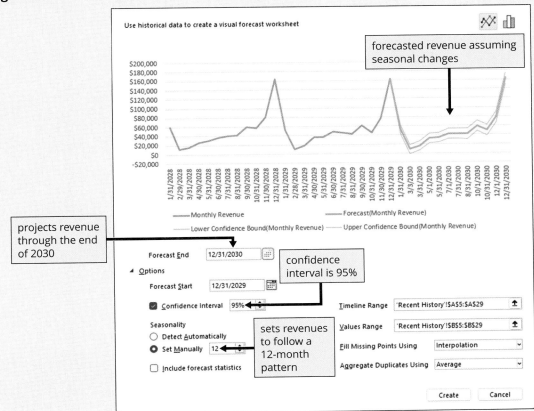

4. Click **Create**. A new worksheet containing the forecasted values is added to the workbook. The forecasted values have been placed within an Excel table.

5. If the Forecast Sheet dialog box opens, read the message, and then click **Got it!**

6. Rename the new worksheet as **Monthly Revenue Forecast** and then move the sheet directly before the **Data Sources** worksheet at the end of the worksheets.

7. Click the **Table Design** tab, and then in the Properties group, click the **Table Name** box, type **Forecast_Table**, and then press **ENTER** to change the table name.

8. Increase the zoom factor of the worksheet view to **140%**.

9. Increase the width of column A to **15** characters so that all dates are visible.

10. Scroll down to the bottom of the worksheet to view the projected revenue. Refer to Figure 10–14.

Figure 10–14   Forecast worksheet

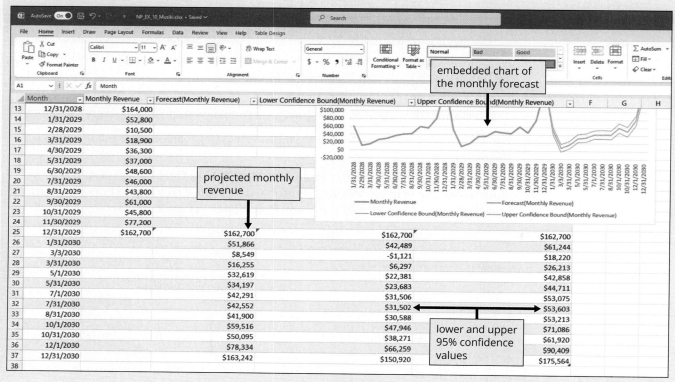

From the forecasted values, Adina projects December 2030 sales of specialty percussion instruments to be about $163,242 (cell C37) and is 95% confident that the revenue will be at least about $150,920 (cell D37) but not more than about $175,564 (cell E37).

You will complete this section of the report by moving the forecast chart into the Financial History worksheet and formatting it.

To move the monthly revenue chart:

1. Move the embedded chart on the Monthly Revenue Forecasts worksheet to the **Financial History** worksheet.

2. Move and resize the chart to cover the range I4:R20.

3. Remove the chart legend.

4. Add the chart title **Trend in Monthly Revenue**.

5. Add the axis titles **Monthly Revenue** and **Date** to the vertical and horizontal axes.

6. Close any open worksheet panes. Refer to Figure 10–15.

Figure 10–15　　Annual and Monthly Trends

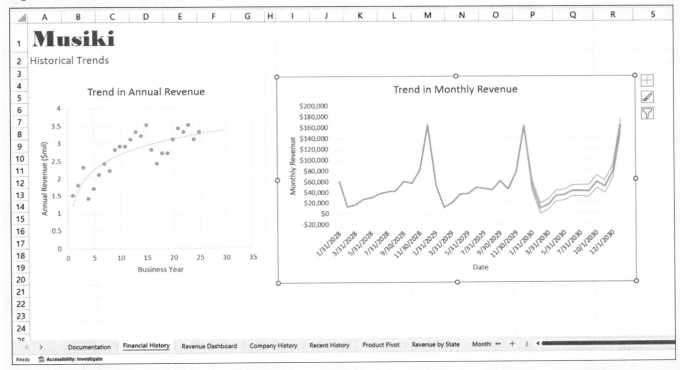

7. Save the workbook.

Adina will include both charts in a report projecting the company's revenue over the next few years.

Proskills

Teamwork: Maintaining Data Security

Data security is essential for any business to maintain the integrity of its data and retain the trust of its colleagues and customers. It is critical to secure data to prevent lapses in security. If your workbooks are connected to external data sources, keep in mind the following tips:

- **Apply data security controls.** Make sure your data files are set up with password controls to prohibit unauthorized access.

- **Keep software updated.** Be sure to diligently update the software that stores your data with the latest security patches.

- **Closely monitor data copying.** Have only one source of your data. When multiple copies of the data exist, data security, consistency, and integrity are compromised.

- **Encrypt your data.** Use data encryption to prevent hackers from gaining unauthorized access to sensitive information.

Maintaining data security requires that everyone with access to your data files knows how to retrieve and process that data appropriately. In the end, your data will be only as secure as the work habits of the people who access it.

You have completed the revenue estimates and projections using data retrieved with the Power Query Editor. Next, you'll perform analyses that involve combining data from several data sources within a single PivotTable and PivotChart.

Part 10.1 Quick Check

1. What is business intelligence?

2. What is a query?

3. What is a delimiter?

4. What is a CSV file?

5. How do you undo an action in the Power Query Editor?

6. What trendline should you add to a chart for data that increases or decreases quickly and then levels out?

7. What does a 95% confidence bound tell you about forecasted values?

Part 10.2 Visual Overview:
Power Pivot and the Data Model

The Power Pivot add-in provides access to the **Data Model**, which is a database attached to an Excel workbook.

The Diagram View button in Power Pivot displays the structure and relationships of the tables in the Data Model.

A **database** is a highly structured collection of data values organized into separate tables.

Tables in a database are associated with each other through **table relationships** in which common fields match a record from one table to a record from another table. Here the StoreID field is common to both the Orders and Stores tables.

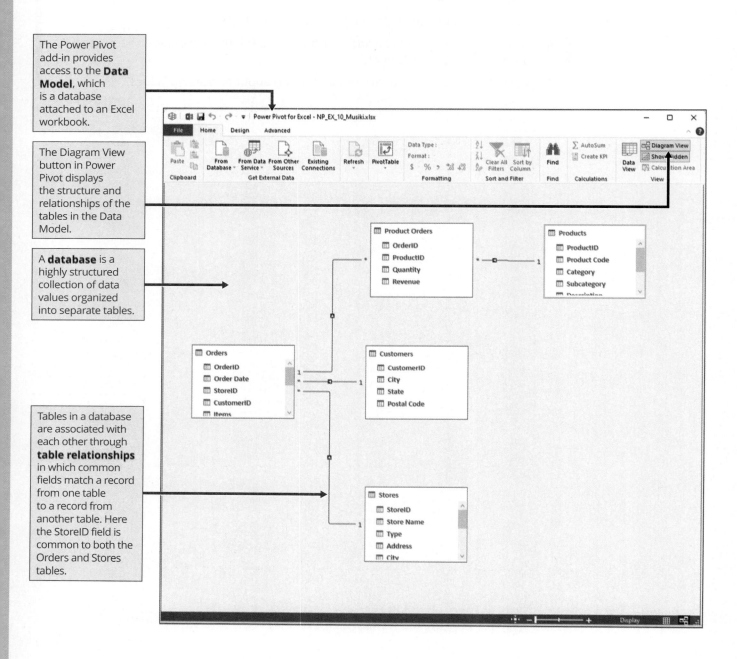

When the Power Pivot add-in is activated, the Power Pivot tab appears on the ribbon.

Click the Manage button to manage the contents of the Data Model.

PivotTables can retrieve data from multiple fields in different tables in the Data Model.

Slicers and timelines filter data from several tables connected in the Data Model. These filter data with fields from the Stores and Orders tables.

This PivotTable uses the Store Name field from the Stores table, the Category field from the Products table, and the Revenue field from the Product Orders table.

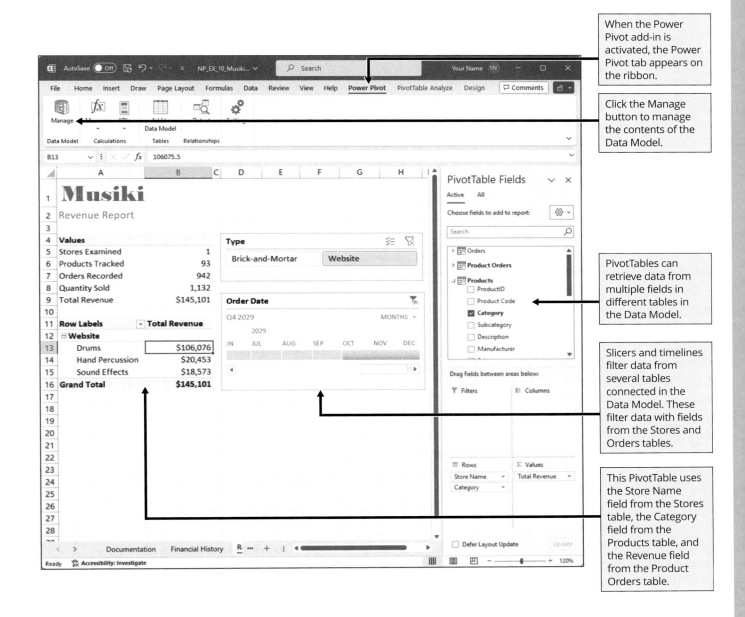

Introducing Databases

In this part, you will connect the Excel workbook to an external database. A database is a structured collection of data values, often organized into tables with each table focusing on a single subject. Database tables are very similar to Excel tables with each column a field describing a characteristic and each row a record of multiple fields. With their formal structure, databases help ensure data integrity and reliability. Microsoft Office includes the Microsoft Access database program for managing and storing large data collections.

Adina has an Access database file containing five tables describing different aspects of the sales transactions between Musiki and its customers. Figure 10–16 summarizes the contents of these tables.

Figure 10–16   Musiki database tables

Table	Contains
Customers	Data on customers that have bought items from Musiki, including the general location of the customer
Orders	Data on customer orders made at a Musiki store, including when the order was made, the ID of the store, the ID of the customer who made the order, the total quantity of items, and the costs associated with the order
Product Orders	Sales data on specific products purchased from Musiki, the quantity purchased, and the ID of the order in which the purchase occurred
Products	Product information on specific products offered by Musiki including the product category, subcategory, and a general description of the product
Stores	Data on Musiki stores located across the country and the company website

By extracting information from all five tables, Adina can learn what products customers have been purchasing, how many they purchased and for how much, as well as when they were purchased and from where. A complete inventory of Musiki sales would involve millions of records, so, for this analysis, you'll research only the percussion instruments sold over the past two years.

Relational Databases

In a database with multiple tables, the tables are connected through one or more fields that are common to each table. For example, the data in the Product Orders table connects with the data in the Products table through the common field ProductID. As shown in Figure 10–17, by matching the values of the ProductID, information from both tables can be combined into a single data structure providing information on the orders handled by the company and type of products contained in each order. This relationship is known as a **one-to-many relationship** because one record from the Products table is matched can be matched several records from the Product Orders table (because a single product might be purchased on several different customer orders).

Figure 10–17   Tables related by a common field

Product Orders table   Products table

combined data

Another type of relationship is the **one-to-one relationship**, in which one record from the first table can be matched to only one record from the second table. If the Musiki database had a table with information about the manufacturer of each product, it would have a one-to-one relationship with the Products table because each product would have only one manufacturer.

Databases with tables joined through common fields are known as **relational databases**. Because common fields are shared, you don't need to duplicate the same piece of information in multiple tables. Information about a product can be entered in one table and then made accessible to other tables by a table relationship. Removing duplication makes it easier to manage large datasets. It also improves data quality and integrity.

Querying an Access Database

Power Query supports almost all the popular database applications, including Microsoft Access, SQL Server, Oracle, IBM DB2, and MySQL. The Query Editor creates a query to extracts data from any one table or collection of tables within the database. You will use the Query Editor to extract data from several tables in the Musiki database.

To create a query to an Access database table:

1. If you took a break after the previous part, make sure the NP_EX_10_Musiki workbook is open.

   Trouble? If you reopen the workbook and a yellow bar appears below the ribbon with a Security Warning message about connecting to external data, click the Enable Content button to continue and then click Yes in the Security Warning dialog box to make this file a trusted document.

2. On the ribbon, click the **Data** tab, and then in the Get & Transform Data group, click the **Get Data** button. A menu of data options appears.

3. On the menu, point to **From Database** to display a list of database sources, and then click **From Microsoft Access Database**. The Import Data dialog box opens.

   Trouble? If a dialog box appears warning about accessing data from an external data source, click OK to continue.

4. Select the **Support_EX_10_Data.accdb** file located in the Excel10 > Module folder, and then click **Import**. The Navigator dialog box shows a list of the tables in the database.

5. Click **Customers** in the table list to preview the Customers table contents. Refer to Figure 10–18.

Figure 10–18   Navigator dialog box

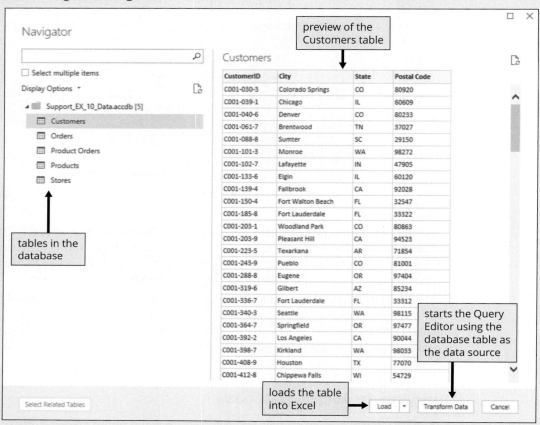

The Customers table has four fields. The CustID field uniquely identifies a Musiki customer, and the City, State, and Postal Code fields specify the customer's location. Though not shown in the dialog box, the Customers table has over 6,000 records. With so many records, Adina doesn't want to create a large Excel table to hold all the customer data. An alternative is to use the Excel Data Model.

Exploring the Data Model

The Data Model is database storage built into Excel workbook providing many of the tools found in database programs such as Microsoft Access. Because the Data Model is part of an Excel workbook, its contents are immediately available to PivotTables, PivotCharts, and other Excel tools. Data stored in the Data Model are compressed, resulting in a smaller file, queries that run faster, and PivotTables that load quicker. The drawback is that Data Model contents are not visible in the workbook. To view them, you must use Power Pivot—an Excel add-in for managing the Data Model contents.

Data can be stored in the Data Model using Power Query. Once placed in the Data Model, Excel establishes a connection between the Data Model contents and the workbook. Essentially, it's like having a connection to an external data source even though the Data Model is saved within the workbook file.

You will load the contents of the Customers table into the Data Model.

To load the Customers table into the Data Model:

1. With the Navigator dialog box still open and the Customers table still selected, click the **Load arrow**, and then click **Load To**. The Import Data dialog box opens.

2. Click the **Only Create Connection** option button to establish a connection between the external data and the workbook without loading the data into an Excel table, PivotTable, or PivotChart.

   | **Key Step** Be sure to only create a connection. Do not load the data into an Excel table, PivotTable, or PivotChart.

3. Click the **Add this data to the Data Model** check box to insert the contents of the Customers table into the data model of the NP_EX_10_Musiki workbook. Refer to Figure 10–19.

Figure 10–19   Data being added to the Data Model

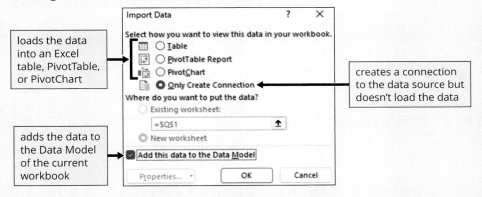

4. Click **OK** to establish the connection to the Data Model. When the data loading is complete, the Customers query appears in the Queries & Connection pane indicating that 6,045 rows have been loaded.

   | **Trouble?** If an Excel table containing the Items Purchased data appears, delete the table and the query, repeat the previous set of steps to recreate the query, and then repeat Steps 1 through 4, making sure to load the table only to the Data Model and not to an Excel table.

You will add the remaining tables from the database to the workbook's Data Model. Because the data have been structured within the Access database, you will not need to edit the data contents with Power Query. You'll load the remaining four tables in the Data Model.

To load the remaining database tables:

1. On the Data tab, in the Get & Transform Data group, click the **Get Data** button, point to **From Database**, and then click **From Microsoft Access Database** to select the database source. The Import Data dialog box opens.

2. Select the **Support_EX_10_Data.accdb** file, and then click **Import**. The Navigator dialog box opens.

3. Click the **Select multiple items** check box so you can select more than one table from the database. Check boxes appear before each table name.

4. Click the **Orders**, **Product Orders**, **Products**, and **Stores** check boxes to select those tables. As you select a check box, a preview of that table's contents appears in the Navigator dialog box.

5. Click the **Load arrow**, and then click **Load To**. The Import Data dialog box opens.

6. Verify that the **Only Create Connection** option button and the **Add this data to the Data Model** check box are selected to load the tables without placing them in Excel tables, PivotTables, or PivotCharts.

7. Click **OK** to load the four tables into the Data Model.

After several seconds, the four tables will be listed as queries in the Queries & Connections pane. There are 8,632 rows are loaded from the Orders table, 9,647 rows from the Product Orders table, 93 rows from the Products table, and 11 rows from the Stores table. Later, Adina might perform a more complete analysis involving the entire sales lineup, but even this sample of a few products results in a large dataset to manage.

Proskills

Written Communication: Designing a Database

Databases are great tools to organize information, track statistics, and generate reports. When used with Excel, a properly designed database can provide valuable information and help you make informed financial decisions. Whether you are creating a database in the Data Model or Microsoft Access, keep in mind the following guidelines:

- **Split data into multiple tables.** Keep each table focused on a specific topical area. Link the tables through one or more common fields.

- **Avoid redundant data.** Key pieces of information, such as a customer's address or phone number, should be entered in only one place in the database.

- **Use understandable field names.** Avoid using acronyms or abbreviations that may be unclear or confusing.

- **Maintain consistency in data entry.** Include validation rules to ensure that rules such as abbreviating titles (for example, Mr. instead of Mister) are always followed.

- **Test the database on a small subset of data before entering all the data.** The more errors you eliminate early, the sooner your database will be ready for use.

A badly designed or improperly used database will end up creating more problems rather than solving them.

Transforming Data with Power Pivot

Power Pivot is a BI tool built into Excel used for managing data from multiple sources in a single data structure. With Power Pivot you can define table relationships, reorganize and regroup data, and create new columns from calculations on existing fields. Many of the skills used with Excel tables and data ranges can also be applied to the tables in Power Pivot, but Power Pivot offers even more commands and options to manage your data.

> **Tip** Excel tables can be added to the Data Model by selecting the table, and then clicking the Add to Data Model button in the Tables group on the Power Pivot tab.

Because Power Pivot is an add-in, you must install it before using it to work with the contents of the Data Model. You can have Excel install the Power Pivot add-in by attempting to view the contents of the Data Model. If Power Pivot is not already installed, Excel will install it for you.

To install Power Pivot:

1. On the Data tab, in the Data Tools group, click the **Manage Data Model**. If Power Pivot is not installed, a dialog box opens, prompting you to enable the Data Analysis add-ins.

2. If prompted, click **Enable**. If it is not already present, the Power Pivot tab appears on the ribbon, and the Power Pivot window opens showing the contents of the Data Model.

3. If necessary, maximize the window to fill the entire screen. Refer to Figure 10–20.

Figure 10–20   Power Pivot window

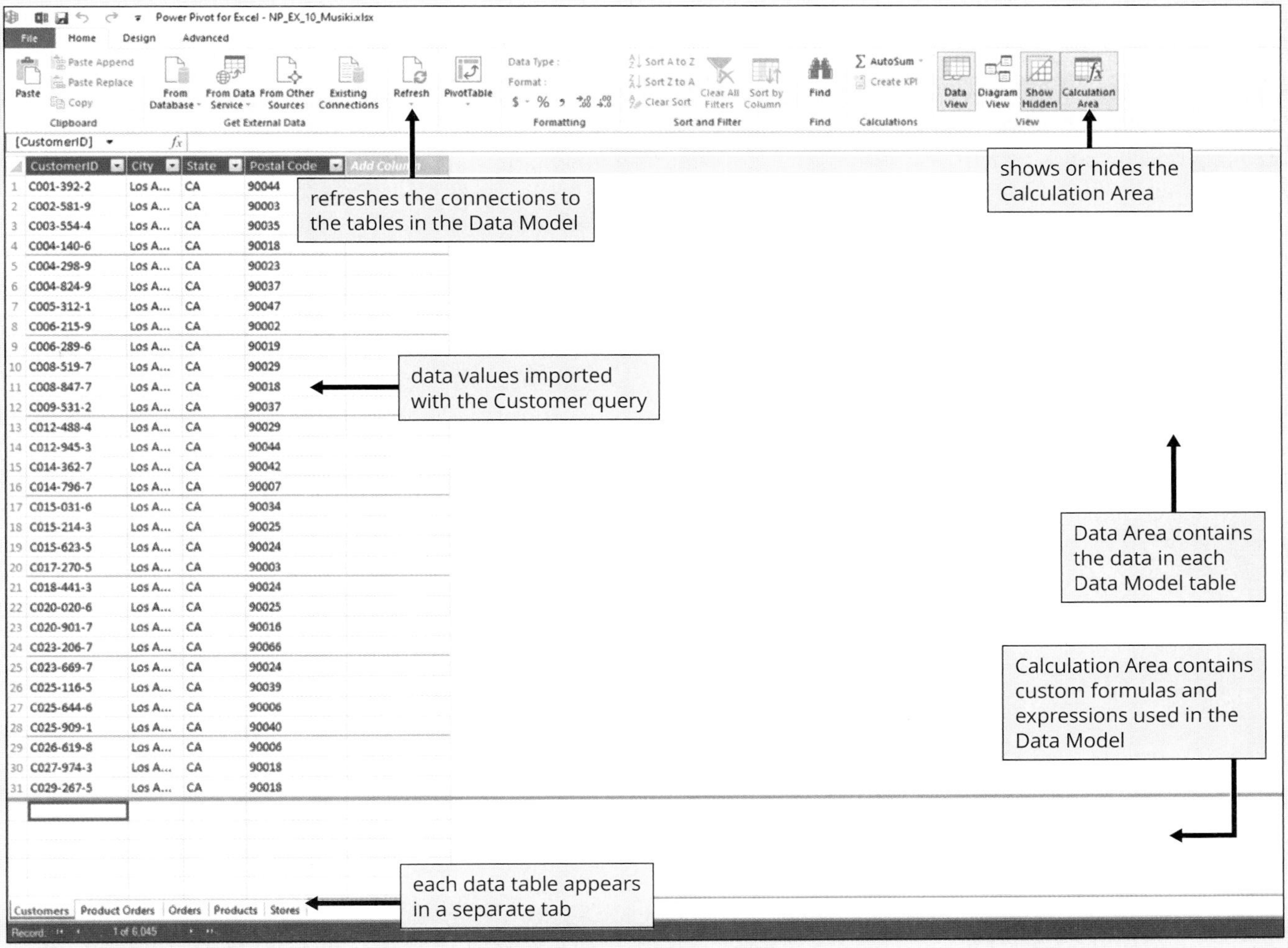

The Power Pivot window places each table in the Data Model on a separate tab. The Data Area displays the contents of each table. Below the table grid is the Calculation Area used for writing customized functions and expressions.

To view the contents of the Data Model:

1. Use the top vertical scroll bar to scroll up and down the rows of the Customers tab to view other customer records.

2. Click the **Orders** tab to view the contents of the Orders table.

3. Click the **Product Orders** tab to review records from the Product Orders table.

4. Click the **Products** tab to view information about select products sold by Musiki.

5. Click the **Stores** tab to view information and the 10 brick-and-mortar Musiki stores as well as the company's website.

6. Click to the **Customers** tab to return to the customer records.

Exploring the Data Model in Diagram View

So far, you have reviewed the Data Model in **Data view**, which displays the contents of each table in a separate tab. You can also examine the Data Model in **Diagram view**, which lists the fields within each table. Diagram view is useful when you want to work with the general structure of the Data Model. From Diagram view, you can quickly define the relationships that connect the tables. You will switch to Diagram view.

To switch to Diagram view and arrange the tables:

1. On the Home tab, in the View group, click the **Diagram View** button. Power Pivot displays each table in a separate box with the table name and a list of fields. Power Pivot initially lines up all the tables horizontally in the Diagram view window.

2. If necessary, use the scroll bars to scroll through Diagram view to review the table contents.

3. Drag the tables by their table names to arrange them to match the tables in Figure 10–21.

Figure 10–21   Power Pivot in Diagram view

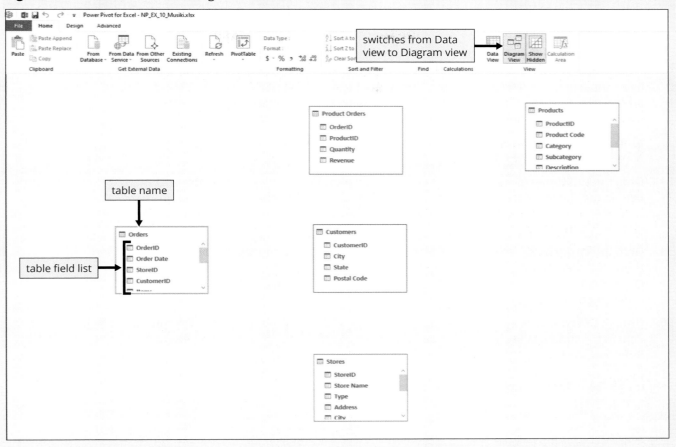

Managing Table Relationships

Table relationships are defined in Diagram View by dragging a common field between two tables. In a one-to-many relationship one of the tables acts as a lookup table for the other. For example, the Stores table acts as a lookup table for the Orders table, providing specific information about the store in which the purchase was made. Diagram View indicates the existence of a relationship by a line connecting the two tables.

Adina wants you to establish the following relations between the five tables, as follows:

- Orders table to the Customers table through the CustomerID field, matching every order with a customer
- Orders table to the Stores table through the StoreID field, matching every order with a store
- Orders table to the Product Orders table through the OrderID field, matching every order with products purchased on that order
- Product Orders table to the Products table through the ProductID field, matching every product order with information about that product

You will establish these relationships between the tables in the Data Model.

To define table relationships in Diagram View:

1. Click the **Orders** table to select it.

2. Drag the **StoreID** field from the Orders table and drop it onto the **StoreID** field in the Stores table. Power Pivot connects the two tables with a line. A "1" appears where the line connects to the Stores table and a "*" appears next to connection to the Orders table, indicating that this is a one-to-many relationship in which one store can be matched to many orders.

   > **Tip** You can also drag the field from the Stores table to the Orders table and Power Pivot will establish the same relationship.

3. Drag the **CustomerID** field from the Orders table and drop it onto the **CustomerID** field in the Customers table. Power Pivot establishes another one-to-many relationship between the Orders table (many) and the Customers table (one) because one customer can be matched to several orders.

4. Drag the **OrderID** field from the Orders table and drop it onto the **OrderID** field in the Product Orders table, establishing another one-to-many relationship. In this case, the Orders table is the "one" and the Product Orders table is the "many" because a single order might include several products.

5. Drag the **ProductID** field from the Product Orders table and drop it onto the **ProductID** field in the Products table, creating a one-to-many relationship between the two tables. Refer to Figure 10–22.

Figure 10–22   Table relationships defined in Power Pivot

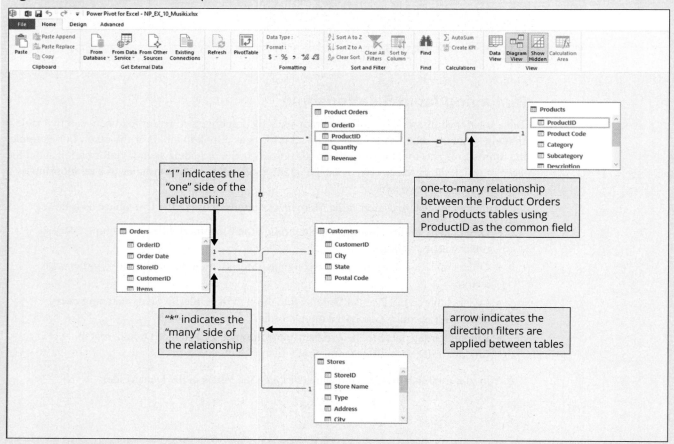

6. On the ribbon, click the **File** tab, and then click **Close** to close Power Pivot, returning to the Excel workbook window.

> **Trouble?** If a yellow Security Warning bar with the caption "External Data Connections have been disabled" appears in Excel, you can click the Enable Content button followed by the Yes button to enable the connection to the data model and to make this workbook a trusted document.

Arrows in the connecting lines indicate the direction in which filters propagate between tables. The arrow in the Stores and Orders table relation in Figure 10–22 points from Stores to Orders so that filtering the Stores table (perhaps to show records from a single store) also filters records in the Orders table. However, the reverse is not possible. Filtering the Orders table will not affect the Stores table. The arrow points in one direction only.

You can determine how a filter will affect other tables in the Data Model by following the arrows. The Orders table is connected to the Product Orders table, so that any filtering done to the Stores table will also pass through the Orders table to the Product Orders table. In this way, filters applied to one table will spread through the Data Model wherever there exists a connected path pointing from one table to the next.

> **Tip** You can also define table relationships in an Excel workbook by clicking the Relationships button in the Data Tools group on the Data tab.

With the table relationships defined, you can analyze the Musiki sales data, pulling information from any of the five tables in the Data Model.

Creating a PivotTable from the Data Model

Any of the tables in the Data Model can be displayed in a PivotTable or PivotChart. A single PivotTable or PivotChart might draw information from multiple tables if the tables are connected via table relationships.

Adina wants you to create a dashboard to view revenue totals for different combinations of stores, products, customer locations, and dates. The first PivotTable for this dashboard will provide a general summary of the items that Adina has compiled from the sample of Musiki products.

To create a PivotTable based on the Data Model:

1. Go to the **Revenue Dashboard** worksheet, and then click cell **A4** to select it.

2. On the ribbon, click the **Insert** tab. In the Tables group, click the **PivotTable arrow**, and then click **From Data Model** from the list of possible data sources for the PivotTable.

3. Click **OK**. A new PivotTable is added to the Revenue Dashboard worksheet. Five tables in the Data Model plus the tables you created earlier for the revenue forecast, the recent financial history, and the revenue history are displayed in PivotTable Fields pane.

4. On the ribbon, click the **PivotTable Analyze** tab. In the PivotTable group, click the **PivotTable Name** box, and then enter **Summary** as the PivotTable name.

5. In the PivotTable group, click the **Options** button. The PivotTable Options dialog box opens.

6. Click the **Autofit columns widths on update** check box to deselect it, preventing column widths in the PivotTable from resizing as the data changes.

7. Click **OK**. Refer to Figure 10–23.

Figure 10–23   Inserting a PivotTable from the Data Model

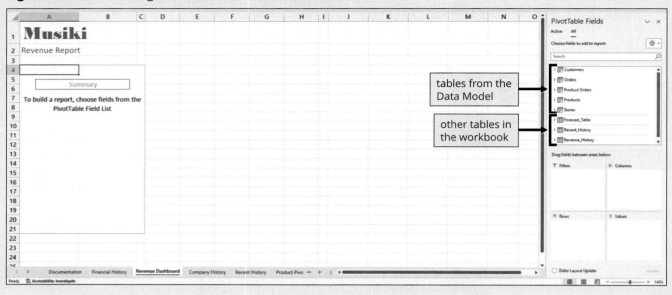

Adina wants you to add summary calculations to the PivotTable showing the number of stores examined, the number of products tracked, the number of customer orders placed, the total number of items ordered, and finally the total revenue generated. You will start with the count of the number of stores, the number of products, and the number of orders.

To display the summary calculations:

1. In the PivotTable Fields pane, scroll down the list of tables, and then click the **Stores** table. The list of fields in the table appears.

2. Drag the **StoreID** field into the Values area box, change the label "Count of StoreID" to **Stores Examined**, and then display the field using the Number format with no decimal places and a thousands separator.

3. Repeat Steps 1 and 2 for the **ProductID** field in the Products table, placing the ProductID field after the Stores Examined field, and changing its label name to **Products Tracked**.

4. Repeat Steps 1 and 2 for the **OrderID** field in the Orders table, placing the OrderID field after the Products Tracked field, and changing its label name to **Orders Recorded**.

5. Display the Orders Recorded value in the Number format with no decimal places and a thousands separator.

6. Drag the **∑Values** icon from the Columns area box to the Rows area box. The summary statistics are displayed in a single column on different rows. The report tracks 11 stores, 93 products, and 8,632 orders.

Next, you will display the quantity of items sold and the total revenue generated for the company.

To complete the PivotTable:

1. Click the **Product Orders** table in the table list to view its contents, and then drag the **Quantity** field into the Values area box, placing it below the **Orders Recorded** value field.

> **Trouble?** To drag the Quantity field to the bottom of the entries in the Values area box, you might need to scroll down the area box first.

2. Change the label name from "Sum of Quantity" to **Quantity Sold** and display the field value in the Number format with no decimal places and a thousands separator. The value 10,422 appears in cell B8.

3. Drag the **Revenue** field from Product Orders table into the Values area box after the Quantity Sold value field.

4. Change the name of the field from "Sum of Revenue" to **Total Revenue** and display the value in the Currency format with no decimal places. Refer to Figure 10–24.

Figure 10–24   PivotTable with data from the Data Model

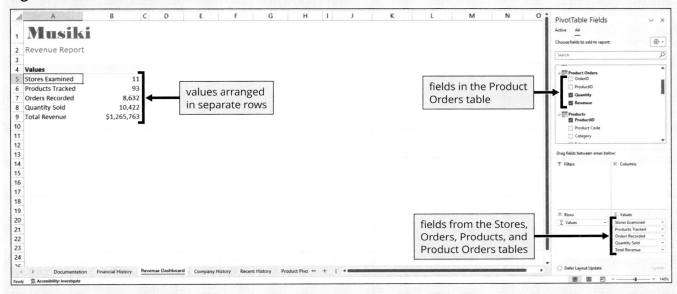

Tabulating Across Fields from Multiple Tables

PivotTables can tabulate values across Data Model tables so that a field in one table can be broken down by fields in the other tables (if a relationship between the tables has been established). Adina wants you to add another PivotTable to the worksheet showing the revenue totals broken down by store and product category.

To show revenue by store and product category:

1. Click cell **A11**, click the **Insert** tab on the ribbon, and then in the Tables group, click the **PivotTable arrow** to display menu of data sources for the new PivotTable.

2. Click **From Data Model**. The PivotTable from Data Model dialog box opens.

3. In Create PivotTable dialog box, verify that the range 'Revenue Dashboard'!$A$11 appears in the Location box, and then click **OK**.

4. On the PivotTable Analyze tab, in the PivotTable group, click the **PivotTable Name** box, and then change the PivotTable name to **Product by Store**.

5. In the PivotTable group, click the **Options** button. The PivotTable Options dialog box opens.

6. Click the **Autofit column widths on update** check box to deselect it, and then click **OK**.

7. In the PivotTable Fields pane, click the **Stores** table, and then drag the **Store Name** field into the Rows area box.

8. In the PivotTable Fields pane, click the **Products** table, and then drag the **Category** field into the Rows area box directly below the Store Name field.

9. In the PivotTable Fields pane, click the **Product Orders** table, and then drag the **Revenue** field into the Values area box.

10. Change the field name from "Sum of Revenue" to **Total Revenue** and display the values in Currency format with no decimal places. Refer to Figure 10–25.

Figure 10–25   Total revenue displayed by store and product category

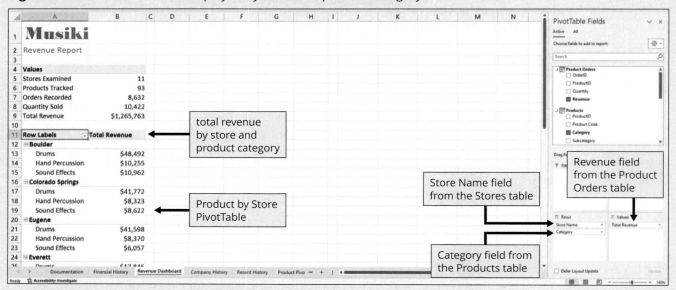

> **Trouble?** If your PivotTable shows blanks for the Store or Category fields, check your table relations in Power Pivot, verifying that you are connecting the tables through a common field.

From the PivotTable report, Adina learns that Musiki gets most of its revenue from sales of drums and drum-related products. Website sales account for a large portion of total sales. For example, the website brought in over $420,000 in drum sales (cell B53) compared to the brick-and-mortar stores, which brought in anywhere from $17,846 at the Everett location (cell B25) to $82,080 at the Los Angeles location (cell B29). The other product categories show a similar comparison between website sales and brick-and-mortar sales.

Applying Slicers and Timelines from the Data Model

Slicers and timelines can be applied across multiple tables if the tables are connected through a common field. Adina wants you to add a slicer to the dashboard that filters the PivotTables by company website and brick-and-mortar stores.

To add a slicer to the dashboard:

1. With the Product by Store PivotTable still selected, click the **Insert** tab on the ribbon, and then in the Filters group, click the **Slicer** button. The Insert Slicers dialog box opens.

2. On the Active tab, scroll down to the Stores table, and then click the **Type** check box. Refer to Figure 10–26.

Figure 10–26   Insert Slicers dialog box

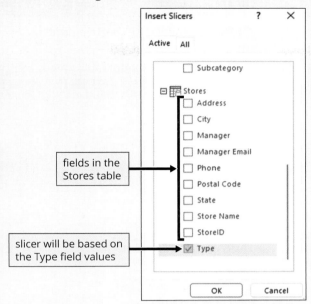

fields in the
Stores table

slicer will be based on
the Type field values

3. Click **OK** to insert the slicer.

4. Move and resize the slicer to cover the range D4:H7.

5. On the Slicer tab, in the Buttons group, change the Columns box to **2** columns. Refer to
    Figure 10–27.

Figure 10–27   Type slicer from the Stores table

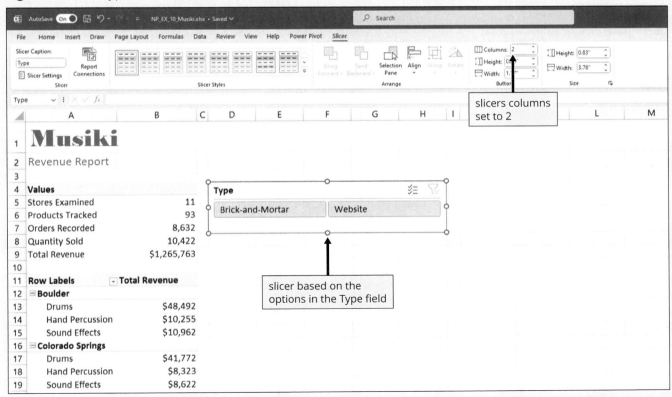

slicers columns
set to 2

slicer based on the
options in the Type field

Adina also wants to filter the sales values by date. You will add a timeline slicer to the dashboard,
basing it on the Order Date field from the Orders table.

To add the Order Date timeline to the dashboard:

1. On the ribbon, click the **Insert** tab, and then in the Filters group, click the **Timeline** button. The Existing Connections dialog box opens.
2. Click the **Data Model** tab, and then click **Open** to access the Data Model tables. The Insert Timelines dialog box opens.
3. Under the Orders table, click the **Order Date** check box.
4. Click **OK** to insert the timeline.
5. Move and resize the slicer to cover the range **D9:H16**. Refer to Figure 10–28.

Figure 10–28   Order Date timeline from the Orders table

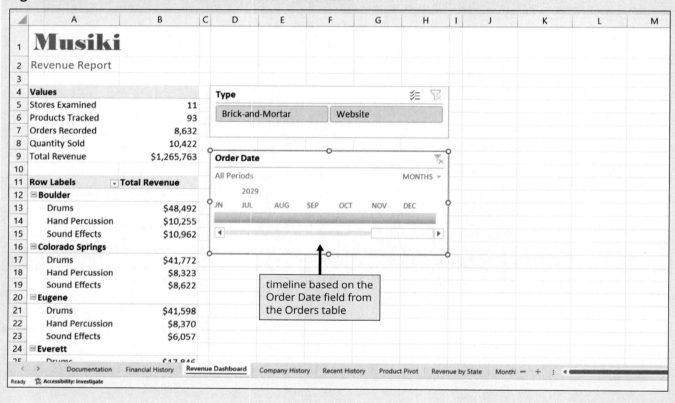

You'll connect the slicer and the timeline to the two PivotTables on the dashboard. Then, you'll use them to display revenue figures for the website in the fourth quarter of 2029.

To connect the slicer and timeline to the PivotTables:

1. With the timeline still selected, on the ribbon, click the **Timeline** tab.
2. In the Timeline group, click the **Report Connections** button. The Report Connections (Order Date) dialog box opens.
3. Click the **Product by Store** and **Summary** check boxes to apply the timeline to both PivotTables in the dashboard, and then click **OK**.
4. Click the **Type** slicer to select it, click the **Slicer** tab on the ribbon, and then in the Slicer group, click the **Report Connections** button. The Report Connections (Type) dialog box opens.
5. Click the **Summary** check box, verify that the check boxes for both PivotTables are selected, and then click **OK**.
6. In the Type slicer, click **Website** to filter the dashboard, showing results only from the Musiki website.

7. In the Order Date timeline, click **OCT** from 2029, and then drag over **NOV** and **DEC** to filter the dashboard for orders placed in Q4 2029, from October through December 2029. Refer to Figure 10–29.

Figure 10–29   Dashboard filtered by store type and order date

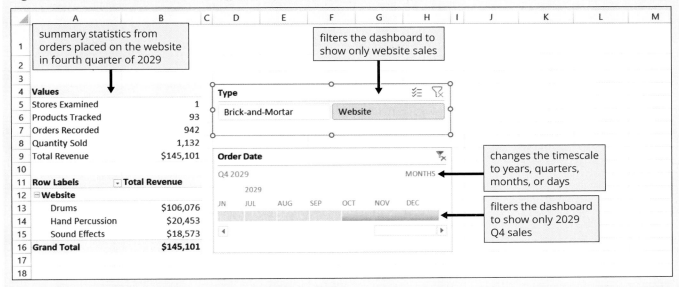

> **Tip** You can also select the fourth quarter of 2024 by changing the time scale of the timeline to QUARTERS and clicking Q4 from 2024.

8. Click the **Clear Filter** button 🗙 in both the slicer and timeline to show results from all the records in the Data Model.

9. Save the workbook.

Based on the filters applied through the Type slicer and the Order Date timeline, Adina learns that in the fourth quarter of 2029, the website generated more than $145,000 in revenue from the 93 select products with more than $106,000 coming sales of drums, $20,453 from hand percussion instruments, and $18,573 from sound effect instruments. The fact that filtering field values from one table affected the summary statistics of fields in the other tables is a consequence of the relationships you create in the Data Model.

In this part, you loaded data from an Access database into the Data Model and then analyzed data from fields spread across multiple tables in a PivotTable. In the next part, you'll continue to explore business intelligence tools by learning how to organize fields into a hierarchy and how to display data in geographic maps.

Part 10.2 Quick Check

1. What is a relational database?

2. What is a one-to-many relationship?

3. What is the advantage of placing large tables in the Data Model rather than in an Excel table that is visible in the workbook?

4. What is Power Pivot?

5. Describe how to create a table relationship in Power Pivot Diagram view.

6. In Diagram view, what does the arrow on the line connecting two tables indicate?

7. What is the advantage of using table relationships when creating a PivotTable report?

Part 10.3 Visual Overview: Hierarchies and Maps

Quick Explore is a feature of PivotTables and PivotCharts for drilling into a hierarchy or to explore the impact of other fields on your data outcomes.

A **hierarchy** is an organization of fields that start with the most general and go down to the most specific; the Product List hierarchy includes three fields.

A **map chart** displays data superimposed on a regional or world map.

A **value map** fills in map regions from a color gradient based on the numeric value associated with each region. These fill colors are based on total sales revenue per state.

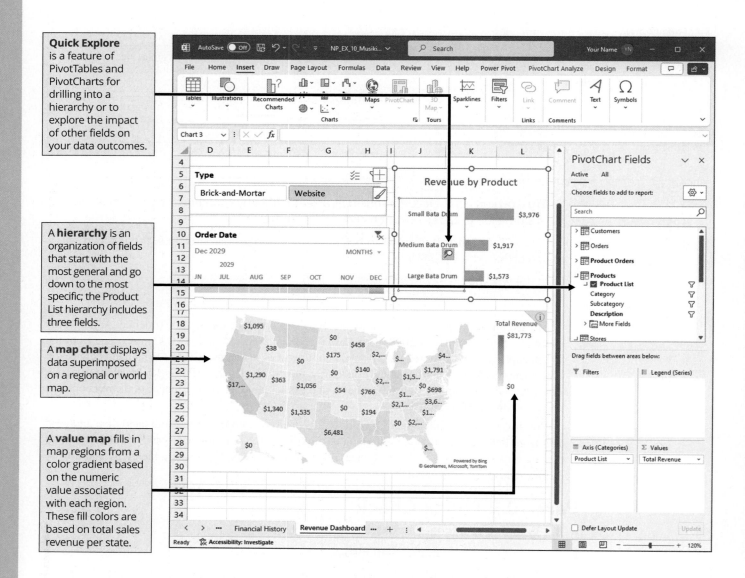

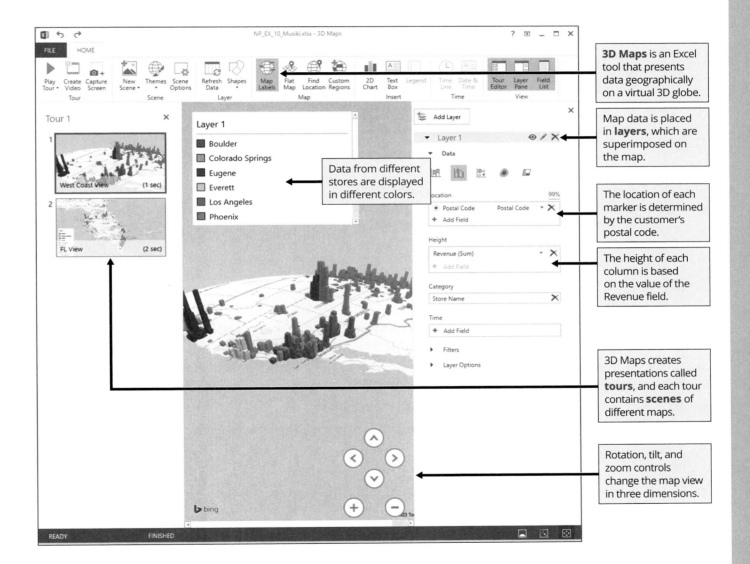

3D Maps is an Excel tool that presents data geographically on a virtual 3D globe.

Map data is placed in **layers**, which are superimposed on the map.

Data from different stores are displayed in different colors.

The location of each marker is determined by the customer's postal code.

The height of each column is based on the value of the Revenue field.

3D Maps creates presentations called **tours**, and each tour contains **scenes** of different maps.

Rotation, tilt, and zoom controls change the map view in three dimensions.

Working with Outlines and Hierarchies

Often in data analysis, you want to drill into the data, going from a general overview down to a more detailed view. Timelines provide this feature by allowing you to examine data across years, quarters, months, and down to individual days. You can do the same thing with PivotTable fields by nesting more specific fields inside of general ones.

Outlining a PivotTable by Nested Fields

When you nest fields within a PivotTable row or column, you can expand the view to display greater detail or collapse the view to display a more general level. Adina wants you to create a PivotTable that shows total revenue broken down by the following fields:

- **Category field**—specifying the general product category (Drums, Hand Percussion, and Sound Effects)
- **Subcategory field**—classifying products within each category so that a category like Drums is organized into Bongos, Congas, and so forth
- **Description field**—providing a general description of products within each Subcategory, such as "Natural Wood Quinto" and "Compact Conga" describing two different types of conga drums

You will add these three fields to the Rows area.

To insert the Product Revenue PivotTable:

1. If you took a break after the previous part, make sure the NP_EX_10_Musiki workbook is open.

2. Go to the **Product Pivot** worksheet.

3. On the ribbon, click the **Insert** tab. In the Tables group, click the **PivotTable arrow**, and then click **From Data Model**. The Create PivotTable from Data Model dialog box opens.

4. Click **Existing Worksheet**, click cell **A4** in the Product Pivot worksheet if necessary to select it, and then click **OK**. The PivotTable form is added to the worksheet.

5. On the PivotTable Analyze tab, in the PivotTable group, click the **PivotTable Name** box, and then enter **Product Revenue** as the PivotTable name.

6. In the PivotTable Fields pane, click the **Products** table to open it.

7. Drag the **Category**, **Subcategory**, and **Description** fields to the Rows area box.

8. In the PivotTable Fields pane, click the Product Orders table to open it, and then drag the **Revenue** field to the Values area box.

9. Change the value field name from "Sum of Revenue" to **Total Revenue**, and then change the number format to Currency with no decimal places. Refer to Figure 10–30.

Figure 10-30   Total Revenue by product category, subcategory, and description

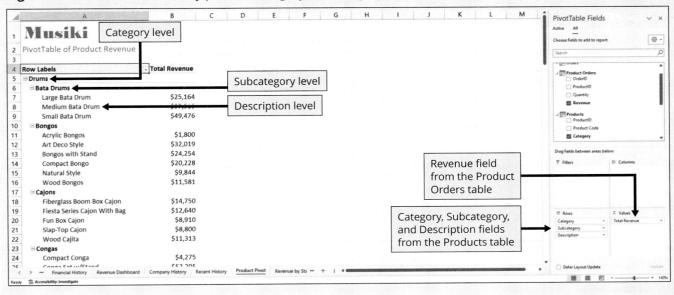

When a PivotTable contains multiple fields in the Rows or Columns area, Excel adds outline buttons to expand and collapse the list of visible fields. The default is to show all fields nested within each other. In Product Revenue table, the Description field is nested within the Subcategory field, which is nested within the Category field. You will use the outline buttons to collapse and then expand the list of visible fields.

To collapse and expand entries in the PivotTable:

1. To the left of Bata Drums, click the **Collapse Outline** button ⊟ . The Bata Drums category collapses and the PivotTable shows $132,150 as the total revenue for all Bata Drum sets.

2. To the left of Bongos, click the **Collapse Outline** button ⊟ . The Bongos category collapses and the PivotTable shows $99,725 as the total revenue for all bongos.

3. On the PivotTable Analyze tab, in the Active Field group, click the **Collapse Field** button. The entire PivotTable collapses to display revenue totals for all subcategories. Refer to Figure 10-31.

Figure 10–31   Collapsed PivotTable outline

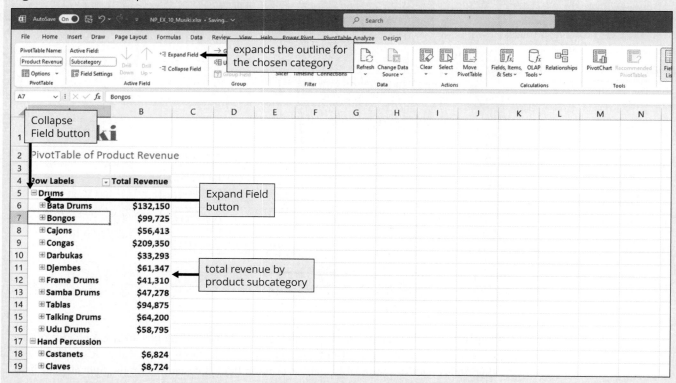

4. In the Active Field group, click the **Expand Field** button to expand all field levels so that the PivotTable again shows total revenue by product description.

Using the Expand and Collapse buttons, you can display revenue totals at any level of specificity. However, a PivotTable outline can be unwieldy if the table contains a lot of categories or nested levels. In that case, to display only the total revenue for single product, you would have to go down several field levels and at each level the table would show results for other categories you're not interested in. To limit the view to only those categories of interest, you can create a hierarchy.

Drilling Down a Field Hierarchy

A hierarchy is a named set of fields organized from the most general down to the most specific. Unlike outlines involving multiple fields nested within one another, a hierarchy displays only one field level at a time. To switch the PivotTable view from one field level to the next lower level, you **drill down** into the hierarchy. For example, you can drill down into a hierarchy of product fields, displaying revenue totals from all product categories and then revenue from all Drums products and, finally, revenue from all types of drums. To go from the most specific field to the most general, you **drill up** the hierarchy, going up from sales of specific drum types to all drum sales to sales of all products.

Reference

Creating a Hierarchy of Fields

- View the Data Model in Diagram view in the Power Pivot window.
- Click the Create Hierarchy button in the table box to create a hierarchy for the table.
- Specify a name for the hierarchy.
- Drag fields into the hierarchy, arranged in order from the most general down to the most specific.

Hierarchies are defined within Power Pivot, becoming part of the data structure of their tables. Once defined, a hierarchy is treated as any other PivotTable field and can be moved to different sections of the PivotTable. Adina wants you to create a hierarchy named "Product List" containing the Category, Subcategory, and Description fields from the Products table. You'll create this hierarchy in Power Pivot.

To create a hierarchy of the fields in the Products table:

1. On the ribbon, click the **Data** tab, and then in the Data Tools group, click the **Manage Data Model** button. The Power Pivot window opens.

2. On the Home tab, in the View group, click the **Diagram View** button, if necessary, to switch Power Pivot to Diagram view.

3. Point to the bottom border of the **Products** table box until the pointer changes to a double arrow pointer ↕, and then drag the bottom border until the table box is twice as high.

4. Point to the upper-right corner of the table box, and then click the **Create Hierarchy** button ⬚. A new entry named "Hierachy1" appears in the Products field list.

5. With the name selected, type **Product List** as the hierarchy name, and then press **ENTER**.

6. Click the **Category** field, hold down **SHIFT** and click the **Description** field to select the Category, Subcategory, and Description fields, and then release **SHIFT**.

7. Drag the select fields on top of the Product List hierarchy, placing the three fields into that hierarchy. Refer to Figure 10–32.

Figure 10–32   Fields in the Product List hierarchy

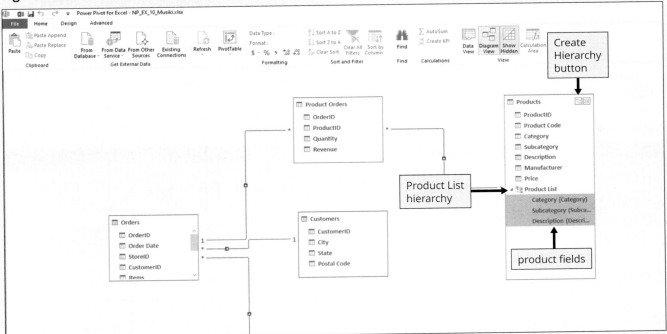

8. Close Power Pivot to return to the Excel workbook.

The Product List hierarchy is now part of the Products table and appears within the PivotTable Fields pane. You will replace the Category, Subcategory, and Description fields displayed in the PivotTable row with the Product List hierarchy, which contains all those fields.

To add the Product List hierarchy to the PivotTable:

1. Drag the **Category**, **Subcategory**, and **Description** fields out of the Rows area box, removing them from the PivotTable.

2. If necessary, click the **Products** table in the PivotTable Fields pane to display its contents.

3. Drag the **Product List** hierarchy from the field list and drop it into the Rows area box to add it to the PivotTable. The PivotTable displays the total revenue broken down by the Category field. The Expand Outline button 🅱 appears to the left of each product category (Drums, Hand Percussion, and Sound Effects).

Though it seems like nothing has changed in the PivotTable, you can now drill down into the Product List hierarchy, viewing the revenue totals within each category, subcategory, and description group. Adina wants you to use the Product List hierarchy to show the total revenue from sales of Musiki's line of tambourines.

To drill down and up the Product List hierarchy:

1. Click cell **A6**, containing the Hand Percussion label. You want to drill down this product category.

2. On the ribbon, click the **PivotTable Analyze** tab, and then in the Active Field group, click the **Drill Down** button. The column labels change, displaying the subcategories within the Hand Percussion category, starting with Castanets and ending with Wood Blocks.

   > **Tip** To view the PivotTable data in outline form, click the Expand buttons in front of the column or row labels.

3. In cell A9, click the **Tambourines** label, and then click the **Drill Down** button to view revenue from tambourine sales. Musiki sells four types of tambourines with revenues ranging from about $1,845 to $11,371. Refer to Figure 10–33.

Figure 10–33   PivotTable drilled down the Product List hierarchy

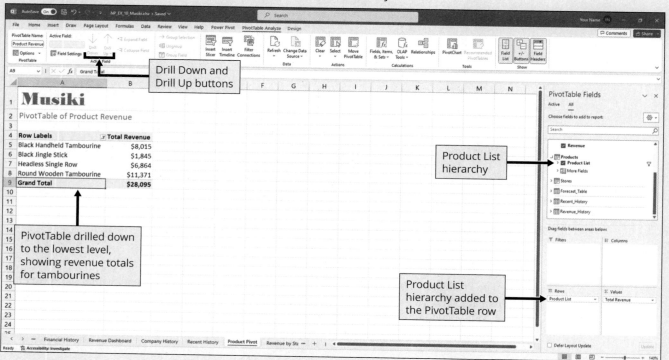

Next, you'll drill up the Product List hierarchy moving from the most specific categories to the most general.

4. Click cell **A5** to select the "Black Handheld Tambourine" label.

5. Click the **Drill Up** button twice to go up the hierarchy and back to the level containing the Category field. At each step in the process the labels in the PivotTable row are replaced with categories of the next highest level in the Product List hierarchy.

Using a hierarchy creates a simpler and cleaner PivotTable that focuses your attention on those details of most interest to you. If you don't want to create a hierarchy, you can always use the Expand Outline and Collapse Outline buttons to view the table outline across multiple fields.

Adina wants you to add product revenue information to the dashboard as a clustered bar chart. You'll create the PivotChart based on this table and add it to the Revenue Dashboard worksheet.

To create a PivotChart of product revenue:

1. With the PivotTable still selected, click the **PivotTable Analyze** tab on the ribbon if necessary, and then in the Tools group, click the **PivotChart** button. The Insert Chart dialog box opens.

2. On the All Charts tab, click **Bar** as the chart type, click **Clustered Bar** as the chart subtype, and then click **OK**. The bar chart is added to the worksheet.

3. Move the chart to the **Revenue Dashboard** worksheet, and then move and resize it to cover the range **J4:M16**.

4. Change the chart title to **Revenue by Product**.

5. Add data labels to the chart showing revenue totals for each category, and then remove the chart legend and chart gridlines.

6. Click the **Chart Elements** button ⊞, click the **Axes** arrow, and then click the **Primary Horizontal** check box to remove the horizontal axis from the chart.

7. On the PivotChart Analyze tab, in the Show/Hide group, click the **Field List** and **Field Buttons** buttons to deselect them, if necessary. The field list and buttons no longer appear on the chart and the worksheet. Refer to Figure 10–34.

Figure 10–34   Revenue by Product PivotChart

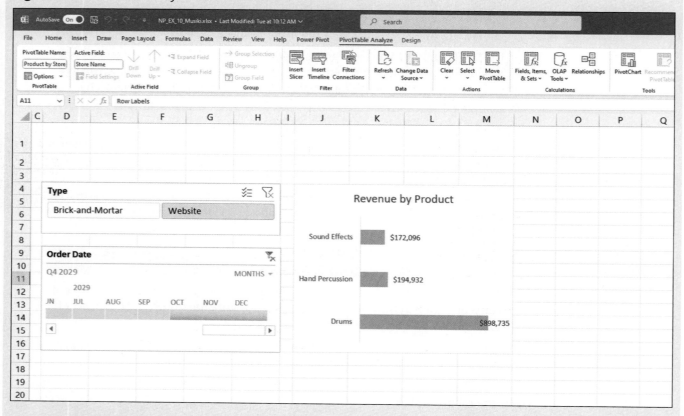

Finally, you will connect the Product Revenue PivotTable to both the slicer and the timeline on this worksheet.

8. Click the **Type** slicer to select it, click the **Slicer** tab on the ribbon, and then in the Slicer group, click the **Report Connections** button. The Report Connections (Type) dialog box opens.

9. Click the **Product Revenue** check box to add it to the list of connected PivotTables for the slicer, and then click **OK**.

10. Click the **Order Date** timeline, click the **Timeline** tab, and then in the Timeline group, click the **Report Connections** button. The Report Connections (Order Date) dialog box opens.

11. Click the **Product Revenue** check box to add it to the list of connected PivotTables for the timeline, and then click **OK**.

12. In the Type slicer, click **Website**, and then in the Order Date timeline, click **Dec 2029**. The PivotChart filters to show the Website revenue for December 2029, matching the results shown in the range A13:B15. Both the Sound Effects products and the Hand Percussion products showed more than $11,000 of sales in December 2029, while Drum products showed almost $60,000 of sales that month.

Viewing Data with the Quick Explore Tool

The Quick Explore Tool is a feature of PivotTables and PivotCharts used to drill into data at any level of specificity or to explore the impact of other fields on your analysis. As with PivotTables, drilling down or up a PivotChart replaces the categories from one field with those of another. You'll use the Quick Explore tool to drill down the Revenue by Product PivotChart to view sales data on Musiki.

To drill down the Revenue by Product PivotChart using the Quick Explore tool:

1. Click the **Drums** category in the Revenue by Product PivotChart twice so that it is the only bar selected in the PivotChart. The Quick Explore button 🔎 appears below the label.

    > **Trouble?** If the Quick Explore button does not appear, click the PivotChart Analyze tab and use the Drill Down and Drill Up buttons in the Active Field group to complete the following steps.

2. Click the **Quick Explore** button 🔎. The Explore box appears with options to drill down the Products table to the Subcategory field or to choose a different field to display in the PivotChart. Refer to Figure 10–35.

Figure 10–35   Quick Explore button

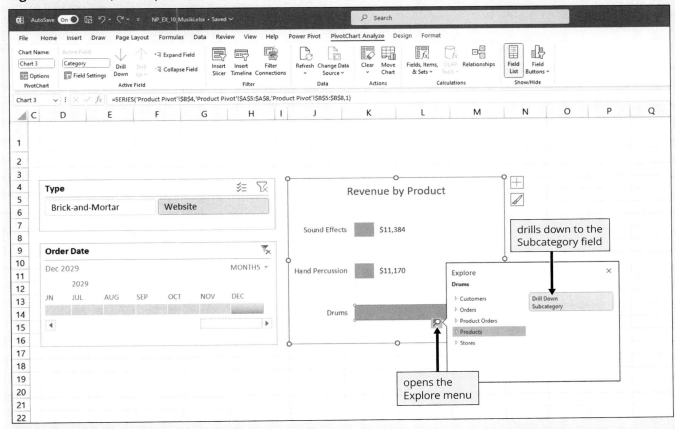

3. In the Explore box, click **Drill Down Subcategory**. The horizontal axis labels are replaced with Subcategory values ranging from Udu Drums to Bata Drums.

    > **Tip** You can drill up the PivotChart by clicking Drill Up Category in the Explore box.

4. In the PivotChart labels, click the **Congas** subcategory, click the **Quick Explore** button 🔎 that appears, and then click **Drill Down Description** in the Explore box. The PivotChart displays revenue totals for six brands of conga drums. Refer to Figure 10–36.

Figure 10–36   Conga drum sales

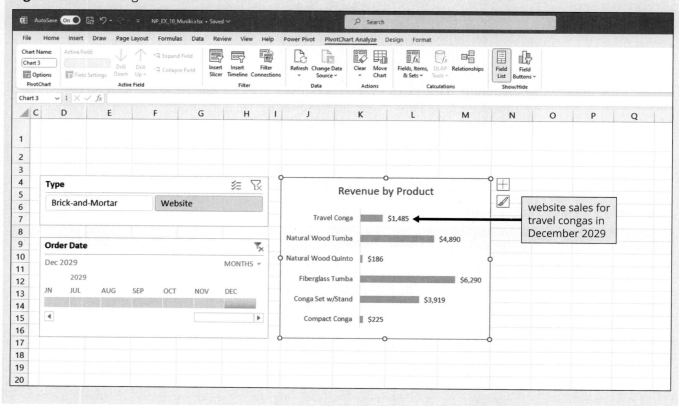

Drilling into the data, Adina learns that in December 2029, the website had more than $6,000 in sales of fiberglass tumbas. A customer support specialist wants to know the location of the customers making these purchases. You'll use Quick Explore to display revenue from that product by the State field in the Customers table.

To display the PivotChart by the CustID field:

1. Click the **Fiberglass Tumba** category label, and then click the **Quick Explore** button ⚲ .

   Trouble? If the Quick Explore button does not appear, right-click the category and then click Quick Explore on the shortcut menu.

2. In the list of tables, double-click **Customers** to view the field list. You can drill to any field within the field list.

3. In the field list, click **State**, and then click **Drill to State**. Drilling to a new field changes the structure of the PivotChart. A dialog box opens to confirm that you want to replace the data in the Product Pivot PivotTable.

4. Click **Yes**. Purchases of fiberglass tumbas were made by customers in WI (Wisconsin), NC (North Carolina), IL (Illinois), FL (Florida), and CA (California). Refer to Figure 10–37.

Figure 10–37   Fiberglass tumba revenue by state

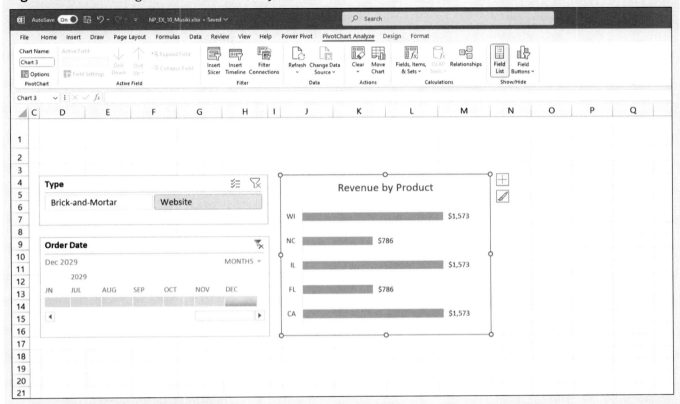

5. If necessary, on the ribbon, click the **PivotChart Analyze** tab, and then in the Show/Hide group, click the **Field List** button to display the PivotTable Fields pane.

6. Drag the **State** field out of the Axis (Categories) box to remove it, and then move the **Product List** hierarchy from the Filters box to the Axis (Categories) box. The PivotChart is restored to its original structure, showing total revenue charted against product category.

7. Close the PivotChart Fields pane.

8. Clear the filters from both the Type slicer and Order Date timeline to show revenue from all store types and all order dates.

The Quick Analysis Tool is useful for displaying important pieces of information such as who bought what products, when, and where. However, because it can change the PivotTable structure, you should be prepared to reorganize the PivotTable and PivotChart layouts when you are done using it.

Viewing Data with Map Charts

Location is another important aspect of data analysis. Financial analysts at Musiki want to know what products are generating revenue for the company. The Advertising department wants to know who is buying those products so that it can target advertising dollars to specific regions and the country. The Shipping department wants customer location data to better predict shipping expenses. If the company opens another brick-and-mortar store, it can use location data to place the new store in a region filled with customers already supportive of Musiki products.

Reference

Creating a Map Chart

- Create a data source with the first column or columns containing region names from countries down to states and counties.
- Enter data values in the last column of the data source.
- On the Insert tab, in the Charts group, click the Maps button.

You can create a map chart to plot data by location. Map chart data must be organized with the first column or columns indicating the map location and the last column containing the values to be charted. Excel supports two types of map charts. In a **value map**, regions are filled with a color gradient based on the numeric value associated with each region. In a **category map**, regions belonging to the same category share the same color. Colors are always applied at the region level, filling in entire counties, states, or countries. Refer to Figure 10–38.

Figure 10–38   Values and category maps

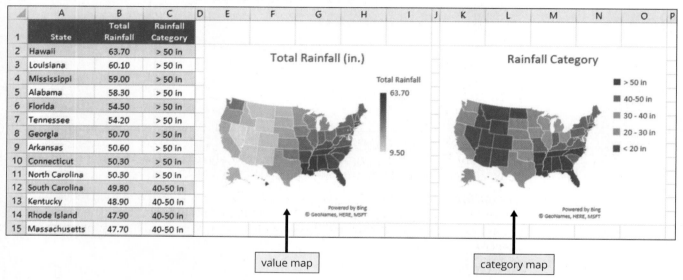

Creating a Value Map Chart

Adina wants you to add a value map to the dashboard showing revenue totals from each state. However, map charts are not supported by PivotTables like bar and pie charts are. To overcome this limitation, you will first create a PivotTable of revenue broken down by state, and then copy those PivotTable values into a data range, which *can* be displayed in a map chart.

To create a PivotTable of revenue by state:

1. Go to the **Revenue by State** worksheet.

2. On the Insert tab, in the Tables group, click the **PivotTable arrow**, and then click **From Data Model**. The PivotTable from Data Model dialog box opens.

3. Click the **Existing Worksheet** option button, click cell **A4** in the Revenue by State worksheet, and then click **OK**.

4. Rename the PivotTable as **State Revenue**.

5. Drag the **State** field from the Customers table into the Rows area box.

6. Drag the **Revenue** field from the Product Orders table into the Values area box.

Next, you will copy the contents of the PivotTable to a data range using Paste Link so that any changes to the PivotTable values will be reflected in the data range.

To create a PivotTable of revenue by state:

1. Select the range **A4:B55**, and then on the Home tab, in the Clipboard group, click the **Copy** button.

2. Click cell **E4**, and then in the Clipboard group, click the **Paste arrow** and click **Paste Special**. The Paste Special dialog box opens.

3. In the Paste Special dialog box, click the **Paste Link** button. The pasted PivotTable is linked to the original PivotTable.

   Key Step Be sure to use Paste Link so that the data range always updates as the PivotTable updates.

4. In cell **E4**, enter **State** as the column label, and then in cell **F4**, enter **Total Revenue** as the label.

5. Select the range **F5:F55** and format the selection as Currency with no decimal places. Refer to Figure 10–39.

Figure 10–39   PivotTable data pasted using Paste Link

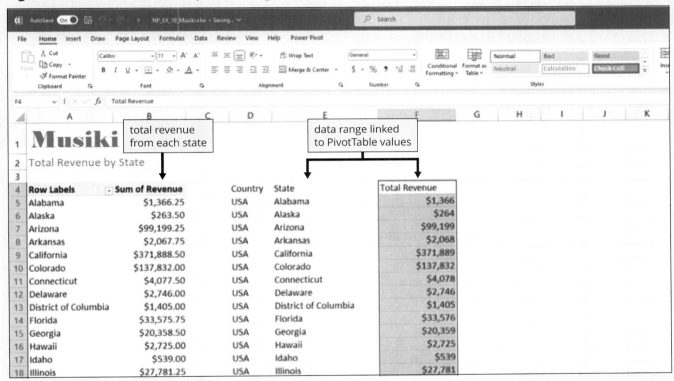

Notice that the workbook includes the name of the country (USA) alongside the state names. In general, you should always include all the regions in your map table so that there is no ambiguity about the region location. If you are mapping values by state, include the country of origin. If you are mapping values by county, include both the country name and the state name in the table.

You can use this Paste Link technique with other chart types that are not supported by PivotCharts. For example, you can link PivotTable results to a data range for use in creating a histogram or scatter chart.

Be careful about the effect of filters. Some states might not be represented under some filters and would not be listed in the PivotTable. For example, a filter that limits the PivotTable to sales from the Chicago store might not show any revenue from customers who live outside the state of Illinois. However, Adina wants all states represented in the data, even if their revenue is zero. You can set the PivotTable options so that the PivotTable always displays every state, even when there is no data for that state.

To display all state categories:

1. Right-click cell **A4**, and then click **PivotTable Options** on the shortcut menu. The PivotTable Options dialog box opens.

2. Click the **Display** tab.

3. Click the **Show items with no data on rows** and **Show items with no data on columns** check boxes so that the PivotTable always shows all rows and categories even when there is no data. Refer to Figure 10–40.

Figure 10–40   PivotTable Options dialog box

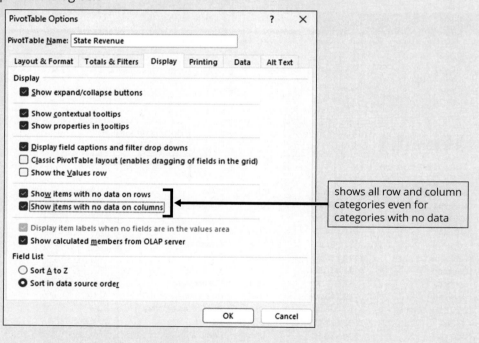

4. Click **OK**.

The PivotTable now will always show data for all 50 states, no matter how it is filtered, as will the data range linked to that PivotTable. You will create a map chart of the total revenue data using the values in the range D4:F55.

To map total revenue by state:

1. Select the range **D4:F55**.

2. On the ribbon, click the **Insert** tab, and then in the Charts group, click the **Recommended Charts** button. The Insert Chart dialog box opens.

3. Verify that the **Filled Map** chart type is selected, and then click **OK**. The map chart is inserted into the workbook.

   > **Trouble?** If you are prompted to send your data to Bing to create the map chart, click I Accept or OK to retrieve location data from Bing.

4. Move the chart to the **Revenue Dashboard** worksheet, and then move and resize the chart to cover the range **D18:M32**.

5. Remove the chart title, and then add data labels that will display total revenue superimposed over the state regions. Refer to Figure 10–41.

Figure 10–41   Revenue totals on the value map chart

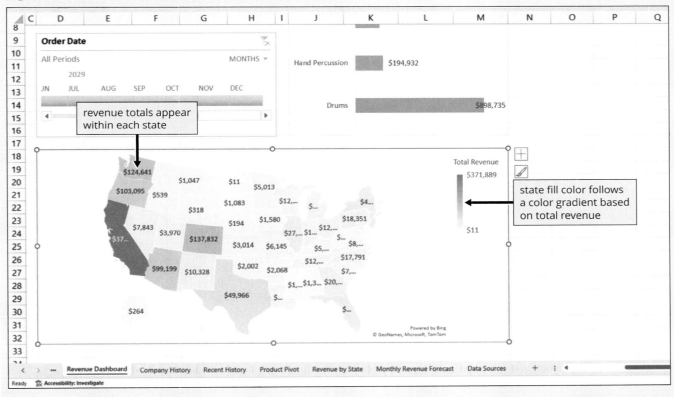

The darkest colors are found in or near the states that have Musiki stores (California, Washington, Arizona, and Colorado) as well as states with large populations. Adina wants to filter the map chart so that it shows only the state revenue totals for website sales from December 2029. You will connect the slicer and timeline to the State Revenue PivotTable and then use them to filter the map.

To connect the map chart to the slicer and timeline filters:

1. Scroll up the worksheet and click the **Type** slicer to select it.

2. On the ribbon, click the **Slicer** tab, in the Slicer group, click the **Report Connections** button, click the **State Revenue** check box to add that PivotTable to the list of connected tables, and then click **OK**.

3. Click the **Order Date** timeline to select it.

4. On the ribbon, click the **Timeline** tab, in the Timeline group, click the **Report Connections** button, click the **State Revenue** check box to connect the PivotTable to the timeline, and then click **OK**.

5. On the **Type** slicer, click the **Website** button, and then on the Order Date timeline, click **DEC 2029**.

6. Verify that the map chart shows revenue totals only for orders placed on the company website during December 2029. Refer to Figure 10–42.

Figure 10–42   Website revenue by state for December, 2029

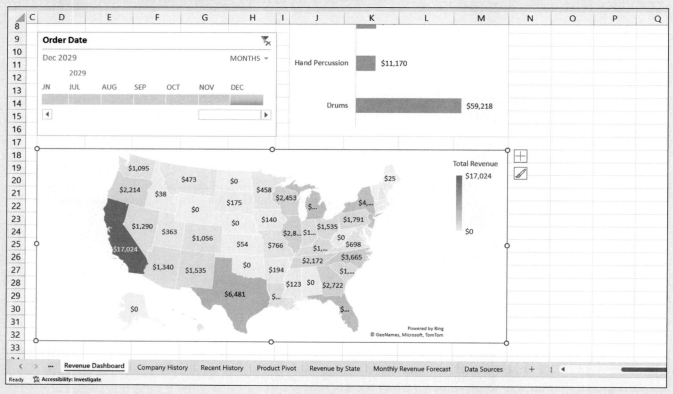

From the map chart, Adina learns that Texas has a good amount of revenue from the company website. As Musiki considers where to build a new store, a city in Texas might be logical place for that new location.

Proskills

Problem Solving: Specifying a Map Location

The map chart uses location names from the search site Bing to determine where to place data values. However, this can result in misplacing map locations when several regions share the same name. Does "Georgia" mean the state of Georgia in the United States or the country of Georgia located north of Turkey? Does "Norfolk" refer to the county in Massachusetts or the county in England? There are 31 different counties named "Washington" in the United States. Bing will use the context of other regions in your data list to decide on a location, but it can make mistakes.

To avoid confusion, include several columns in your data source: one to specify the country, another to specify the state, and a third to specify the county (if needed). You can also include a detailed region name such as "Georgia, United States" rather than "Georgia" to indicate that the location is a state within the United States and not an Eastern European country. Avoid abbreviations when possible. Spell out state names like Indiana rather than using the two-letter abbreviation IN. If you are mapping data from counties within states, include the word "County" after county name since many counties share common names with cities.

Your best option to ensure that Excel can locate your regions is to be as explicit as possible in identifying them. If your data is not mapped correctly (or at all), try different combinations of names and locations to correct the problem.

Formatting a Map Chart

Excel supports several formatting options specific to map charts. To access the map formatting options, right-click any of the map regions and click Format Data Series on the shortcut menu. In the Format Data Series pane, you can set the map projection; define the scope of the mapped area; add labels identifying counties, states, and countries; and define the fill colors used by the map.

The default map format uses a map projection that preserves the relative size of regions on the globe with the map area set just large enough to incorporate all regions listed in the data. Figure 10–43 shows a map chart using the Mercator map projection with the map area set to the entire world, adding labels as country names where they would fit.

Figure 10–43   Map chart formatting options

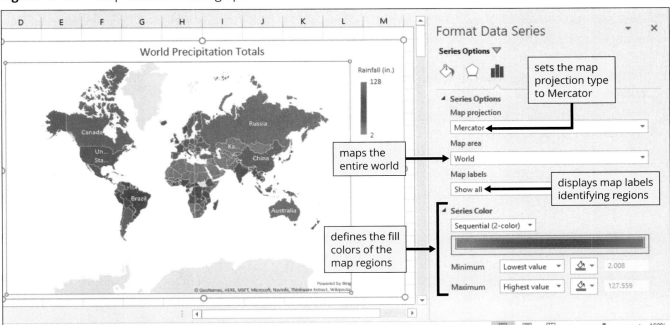

Map charts have several limitations: They cannot be used directly with PivotTables. They can plot only high-level regions like counties, states, and countries but not map points like cities, postal codes, or latitude and longitude. They cannot be zoomed in to smaller regional areas.

Insight

Using Linked Data Types

When analyzing geographic data, you will often want to include information about the regions being studied. For example, if you are reporting total sales revenue by state, it might be helpful to compare the revenue totals to state populations. **Linked data types** are data types linked to resources on the Internet. At the time of this writing, Excel supports two linked data types: Stocks for stock market information and Geography for geographic data. Microsoft plans to add more linked data types as it refines this Excel feature.

To retrieve data from a Linked Data Type, enter your stock symbols or map names into a worksheet, select the range containing those values, and then on the Data tab, in the Data Types group, click the Stocks or Geography linked data type. If Excel finds a match between your data and its online resources, it will convert your data to a Stocks or Geography data type. When you select your data, the Insert Data command appears, which you can use to choose the relevant stock market or geographic information you want to download from the Internet and add to your worksheet.

Visualizing Data with 3D Maps

Another type of Excel map is a 3D map, which instead opens in a separate window with a different set of ribbon tabs and commands. Presentations of 3D maps are called tours, and each tour contains one or more map scenes that can be played as a movie so one map scene transitions into another. For example, Adina could create a tour with a first scene displaying sales data from one region of the country and a second scene displaying sales data from a different region. A tour can be shown to colleagues and clients as part of a presentation or saved as a video file.

You will open 3D Maps and create a tour for Adina that shows the precise location of Musiki customers across the country.

To open 3D Maps:

1. In the Revenue Dashboard worksheet, click cell **A1** to deselect any charts or slicers currently selected.

2. On the ribbon, click the **Insert** tab, and then in the Tours group, click the **3D Map** button.

3. If necessary, click the **Tour 1** map in the Launch 3D Maps dialog box. The 3D Maps window opens. Refer to Figure 10–44.

Figure 10–44   3D Map window

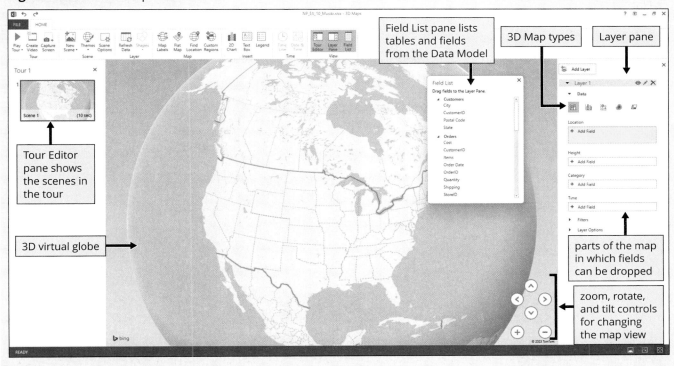

The 3D map window is organized into four sections: The Tour Editor pane lists the map scenes in the current tour. A map of the data is displayed in 3D view. The Field List pane shows tables and fields from the current workbook and Data Model. The Layer pane defines where and how data will be used in the map. A single map can contain multiple overlapping layers. You add data to a map scene by dragging fields into area boxes in the Layer pane.

The lower-right corner of the map has the following controls for changing the map view:

- The Zoom in ⊕ and Zoom out ⊖ controls increase and decrease the magnification of the map.
- The Tilt up ⌃ and Tilt down ⌄ controls tilt the map up and down.
- The Rotate Left ⌃ and Rotate Right ⌃ controls rotate the map from side to side.

You can also use the pointer to drag the virtual 3D globe into a new view of the data.

> **Tip** To rotate and tilt the map, press SHIFT+arrow in the direction you want the map to move. To zoom the map, press SHIFT+ + to zoom in and SHIFT+− to zoom out.

Adina wants a map showing the location of Musiki customers by their postal code. You will create this map scene using the Postal Code field from the Customers table.

To map the location of Musiki customers:

1. In the Field List box, drag the **Postal Code** field from the Customers table into the Location box in the Layer pane. Markers appear on the map at every location of a Musiki customer.

> **Trouble?** If all the markers plotted on the map don't appear right away, be patient. Depending on your connection speed, it might take several seconds for all the markers to be plotted on the map.

2. Click the **Zoom out** control ⊖ (or press **SHIFT+−**) until the entire continental United States is in view.

3. Drag the globe to the right, moving your view toward the states on the Pacific coast.

4. On the Home tab, in the Map group, click the **Map Labels** button. Descriptive labels appear on the map. Refer to Figure 10–45.

Figure 10–45 Customers mapped by postal code

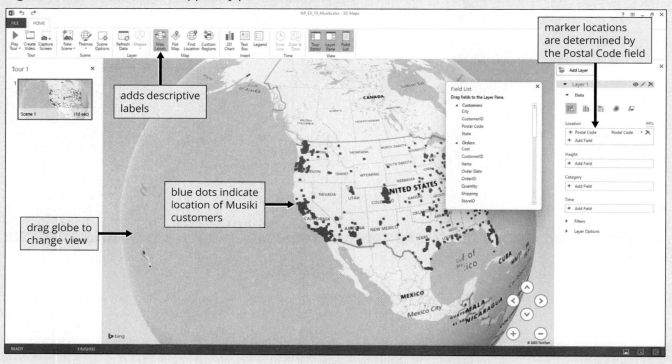

With very large data sets, the 3D map might plot only a representative sample of the data points.

Choosing a Map Style

Once you have the general map of customer locations, you can set how you want the data displayed. There are five ways of plotting data on a 3D map:

- The Stacked Column map ⬚ displays data values as column markers divided into categories.
- The Clustered Column map ⬚ displays data values as column markers with separate columns for each category value.
- The Bubble map ⬚ displays markers as bubbles with bubble sizes determined by the values of a numeric field.
- The Heat map ⬚ displays markers with colors of increasing intensity determined by the values of a numeric field.
- The Region map ⬚ fills in regions such as states and countries with colors determined by the values of a numeric or categorical field.

Adina wants you to create a Clustered Column map that indicates how sales revenue is distributed across the country for each store location. The height of the columns will be determined by the Revenue field and the categories determined by the Store Name field.

To create the Clustered Column map:

1. At the top of the Layer pane, click the **Clustered Column** icon [⊞].

2. Drag the **Revenue** field from the Product Orders table and drop it in the Height box in the Layer pane. The columns heights change to reflect how much money each customer spent.

3. Drag the **Store Name** field from the Stores table and drop it in the Category box in the Layer pane. The columns change color to indicate which store handled each customer's order.

4. In the Field List pane, click the **Close** button [✕] to view more of the 3D map.

5. Click the **Layer 1** legend box to select it, and then drag the sizing handles around the box so that all store names are displayed in a single column without excess space.

6. Use the map controls to change the view so that it points up from San Diego through the country to the Northeast region.

7. Move the Field List box off the map so you can view the entire map contents. Refer to Figure 10–46.

Figure 10–46   3D map with clustered columns

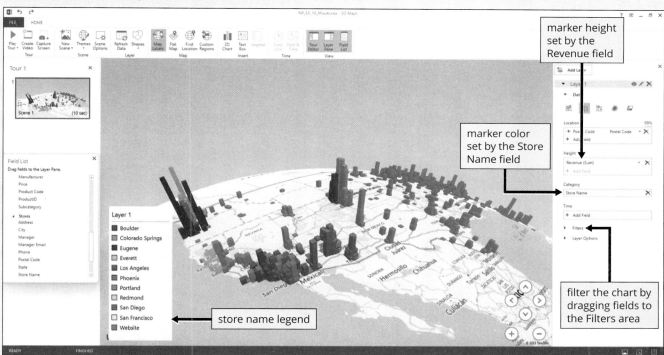

Musiki is considering opening a new store in Miami, Florida. As part of a presentation on this proposal, Adina wants another scene showing total revenue from potential store customers living in the Miami area.

Insight

Using Dates and Times in 3D Maps

If your data contains a date and time field like the date of a customer order, you can add that field to the Time box in the Layer pane. Adding a date/time field creates a play button on the map that you can use to view how the mapped data changes over time. For example, Adina could use the Order Date field to view changing revenue totals throughout the year in different regions of the country.

Creating New Scenes

New scenes can be created using an empty world map as the background—as you did when creating the first scene in this tour—or you can copy a current scene as the starting point for the next map. You can also create customized scenes with backgrounds of your choosing. For this new scene, you will copy the current scene and then change the view to show revenue in southern Florida.

To add a new scene showing Los Angeles revenue to the tour:

1. On the Home tab, in the Scene group, click the **New Scene** button. A second scene is added to the tour using the settings of the first scene.

2. On the Home tab, in the Map group, click the **Find Location** button. The Find Location dialog box opens.

3. Type **Miami, FL** in the location box, and then click **Find**. The map view shifts to a spot over Miami.

4. Close the Find Location dialog box.

5. Use the map controls to tilt and zoom out of the map to show the Florida and part of the southeast coast. Refer to Figure 10–47.

Figure 10–47   Revenue map as viewed from southern Florida

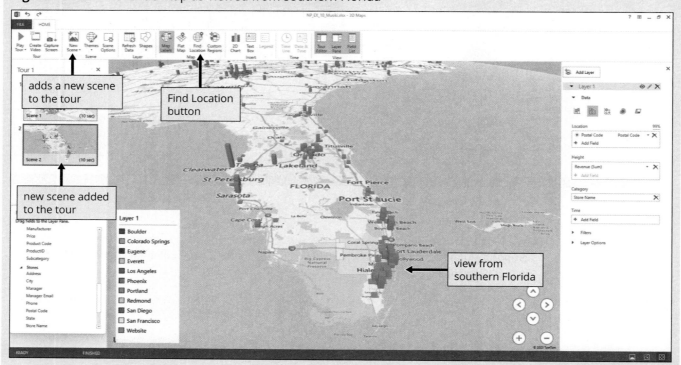

Setting Scene Options

Each scene in a tour has a duration of 10 seconds. You can change the duration by modifying the scene options. You can also change the length of time required to transition from one scene to the next. During the transition, the 3D maps tool gradually changes the values and styles associated with one scene to match the values associated with the next scene. For example, with the two scenes you created, the transition will gradually change from a view of the United States along the West Coast to a new view along the Southeast Coast. You can enhance the transition with the following effects:

- Circle and Figure 8 effects to add a repetitive circular motion to transition
- Dolly and Rotate Globe effects to move the map clockwise in a straight line
- Push In effect to zoom in on the scene
- Fly Over effect to move the map from top to bottom mimicking a camera flying over the object

You'll set the scene options of the two scenes in the tour.

To set the scene options:

1. With the second scene still selected in the Tour Editor, on the Home tab, in the Scene group, click the **Scene Options** button. The Scene Options dialog box opens. Because the second scene is selected, the changes you make in the Scene Options dialog box affect that scene.

2. In the Scene duration (sec) box, change the value to **2** so that the second scene lasts two seconds.

3. In the Scene Name box, type **FL View** to rename the scene.

4. In the Transition duration (sec) box, change the value to **4** so that the length of transition from Scene 1 to Scene 2 is 4 seconds.

   > **Tip** Transition durations are always measured from the previous scene; no transition is applied to the first scene in the tour.

5. Click the **Effect** button, and then click **Push In**. The Push In effect is added to the transition. Do not make any change to the effect speed. Refer to Figure 10–48.

Figure 10–48   Scene Options dialog box

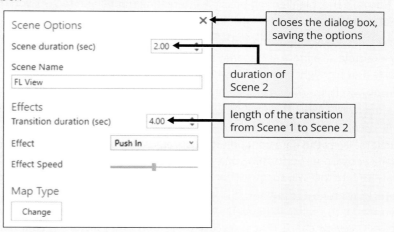

6. In the Tour Editor pane, click **Scene 1** to select it. Now you can set options in the Scene Options dialog box for the first scene.

7. Change the Scene duration to **1** second, and then change the Scene Name to **West Coast View**. You won't make any changes to the Effects options.

8. Click the **Close** button ☒ in the upper-right corner to close the Scene Options dialog box. The Scene 1 options are saved and applied.

Playing a Tour

Playing a tour presents all the scenes of the tour in order using the scene options you set. You will play the tour to view a presentation of revenue totals from across the United States on a 3D map.

To play the tour:

1. On the Home tab, in the Tour group, click the **Play Tour** button. The tour plays with the camera moving from the California to Florida over the United States. By default, tours are played in full screen view.

    Tip You can save the tour as video by clicking the Create View button in the Tour group on the Home tab.

2. Press **ESC** to return to the 3D Maps window.

3. In 3D Maps window, click the **Close** button ✕ . All changes are saved automatically, and you return to the workbook.

4. **sam** ⬆ Save the workbook, and then close it.

You can revise an existing tour and add new scenes. To do this, click the 3D Maps button in the Tours group on the Insert tab. The 3D Maps window opens with the existing tour.

Adina appreciates the tour you've created and will use it in a report on Musiki revenue and the prospects of opening a new store in the Los Angeles area.

Insight

Getting Ideas for Analysis

If you want ideas on how to present the information in a dataset, you can use the Excel Analyze Data tool, which examines data and uncovers trends and associations that you might want to highlight. To use the Analyze Data tool, place your data in an Excel table or data range, and then on the Home tab, in the Analysis group, click the Analyze Data button. The Analyze Data tool takes your data and previews several charts in an Analyze Data (Ideas) pane, highlighting possibly interesting trends and factors you might want to include in your analysis. Some of the things the Ideas tool searches for are:

*   **Ranks.** Do certain data categories result in outcomes significantly larger than others? For example, are there stores that are high sellers? The Analyze Data tool will preview charts that highlight those stores for further analysis.
*   **Trends.** Are there trends in the data? Are sales increasing, decreasing, or showing seasonal variability? The Analyze Data tool will preview scatter charts with trendlines that highlight important trends.
*   **Outliers.** Does the data contain unusual values or outliers? Is there a store that is significantly underperforming or a product that is exceeding expected sales? The Analyze Data tool will suggest charts that focus on those unusual outcomes.
*   **Majority Categories.** Is there a single factor that contributes to most of the outcomes? Are most of the sales associated with one store or one product line? The Analyze Data tool will preview charts that showcase those important factors in your data.

Once you've reviewed the suggested charts from the Analyze Data (Ideas) pane, you can select and insert those charts directly into your workbook to be used in any reports or dashboards you create. Remember, the Analyze Data tool should be the beginning of your analysis, providing you with insights and motivation to further pursue the stories hidden in your data.

You've completed the analysis of the large amount of data Adina had on the Musiki sales of percussion products. In the process, you've retrieved data from a variety of data sources, combined data from different sources in a single report, and presented that data using tables, charts, maps, and tours. This just touches on the power of Power Query, Power Pivot, and 3D maps. If you explore these BI tools in greater depth, you'll find they are powerful tools with many useful features.

Part 10.3 Quick Check

1. What is a hierarchy? How do you create a hierarchy?

2. What is the advantage of a hierarchy over an outline in a PivotTable design?

3. What are the two types of map charts?

4. Name three limitations of map charts.

5. What is a map tour?

6. Which 3D map type should you use to display locations with higher-sale totals in colors of greater intensity?

7. What is the Analyze Data tool?

Practice: Review Assignments

Data Files needed for the Review Assignments: NP_EX_10-2.xlsx, Support_EX_10_Keyboards.accdb, Support_EX_10_LongTerm.csv, Support_EX_10_Trends.csv

Adina wants a report on the sales of Musiki keyboards and keyboard-related products. The long-term and short-term history of sales has been stored in a pair of CSV files. Information on individual orders has been stored in an Access database. You will access data from those sources to create a report detailing what keyboard products have been sold, when they've been sold, and where the customer base is located. Complete the following:

1. Open the **NP_EX_10-2.xlsx** workbook located in the Excel10 > Review folder included with your Data Files. Save the workbook as **NP_EX_10_Keyboards** in the location specified by your instructor.
2. In the Documentation sheet, enter your name and the date in the range B3:B4. Review the contents of the workbook.
3. Use the Get Data button in the Get & Transform Data group on the Data tab to create a query to retrieve data from the **Support_EX_10_LongTerm.csv** file, loading the data as a table starting in cell A4 of the Long Term worksheet to display the sales of keyboard-related products over the past 15 years.
4. Create a scatter chart of the data in the range B4:C19. Do the following to the chart:
    a. Change the chart title to **Keyboard Revenue (2015 – 2029)**.
    b. Add the axis title **Revenue ($mil)** to the vertical axis and **Year** to the horizontal axis.
    c. Add a Power trendline to the chart and forecast the revenue values forward for the next four years. (**Hint:** To add a Power trendline, click the Trendline arrow in the Chart Elements box, and then click More Options. In the Format Trendline pane, click Power in the Trendline Options section.)
    d. Move the scatter chart to the Summary worksheet and resize it to cover the range A4:G16.
5. Create a query to retrieve data from the **Support_EX_10_Trends.csv** file of monthly sales of keyboard products from the last two years. Transform the data to make the following changes to the query within Power Query:
    a. Remove the top three rows from the data source.
    b. Use the new first row as headers for the query.
    c. Rename the query as **Monthly Keyboard Sales**.
    d. On the Add Column tab, in the From Date & Time group, click the Date button, point to Month, and then click End of Month to create the End of Month column storing the end-of-month dates for each record.
    e. On the Home tab, in the Transform group, click the Group By button, then and create a new column named **Monthly Revenue** containing the sum of the Revenue column grouped by the End of Month column.
    f. Close and load the transformed query data to the Short Term worksheet as a table in cell A4.
    g. Format the retrieved data in the range B5:B28 as currency with no decimal places.
6. In the Short Term worksheet, select the data in the range A4:B28, and then use the Forecast Sheet button in the Forecast group on the Data tab to create a Forecast sheet. Forecast keyboard revenue through 12/31/2030. Set seasonality manually for 12 periods (or months). Name the Forecast sheet as **Forecasts**.
7. Make the following changes to the forecast chart:
    a. Move the forecast chart to the Summary worksheet.
    b. Resize the chart to cover the range A18:G30.
    c. Remove the chart legend and add the chart title **Two-Year Forecast**.
    d. Add the axis titles, using **Monthly Revenue** for the vertical axis and **Month** for the horizontal axis.
    e. Change the scale of the vertical axis to 0 to 600,000.
8. Create a query to retrieve data from the Customers, Customer Orders, Items, Item Sales, and Stores tables in the **Support_EX_10_Keyboards.accdb** Access database. Create a connection to the database file and add the tables in the Excel Data Model. Do not load any tables in an Excel table, PivotTable, or PivotChart.

9. Click the Manage Data Model button in the Data Tools group on the Data tab to go to Power Pivot, and then in Diagram view, create the following table relations between the five database tables:
   a. Connect the Customer Orders and Customers tables through the CustID field.
   b. Connect the Customer Orders and Stores tables through StoreID field.
   c. Connect the Customer Orders and Item Sales tables through the OrderID field.
   d. Connect the Item Sales and Items tables through the ItemID field.

10. Add a hierarchy to the Items table named **Item List** and add the Class, Subclass, and Description fields to it in that order. Close Power Pivot and return to the workbook.

11. In the Items Pivot worksheet, in cell A4, insert a PivotTable from the Data Model, and then do the following:
   a. Rename the PivotTable as **Items Pivot**.
   b. Add the Item List hierarchy from the Items table to the Rows area box. Add the Type field from the Stores table to Columns area box. Add the Revenue field from the Item Sales table to the Values area box (displaying the Sum of Revenue).
   c. Change the number format of the revenue values to Currency format with no decimal places.

12. Create a clustered bar PivotChart from the Items Pivot PivotTable. Move the PivotChart to the Summary worksheet in the range I11:O30, and then do the following:
   a. Remove the field buttons, primary horizontal axis, and gridlines from the chart.
   b. Move the chart legend to the bottom of the chart area.
   c. Add data labels to the chart.
   d. Add the chart title **Digital Piano Sales** to the PivotChart.

13. Use the Quick Explore tool or the Drill Down buttons from the PivotChart Analyze tab to drill down the bar chart categories through the Pianos class and the Digital subclass down to the Description level showing the revenue from sales of six digital piano products.

14. In the State Revenue worksheet, do the following to view sales by state:
   a. Add a PivotTable from the Data Model to cell A4.
   b. Name the PivotTable as **State Revenue**.
   c. Place the State field from the Customers table to the Rows area box, and then add the Revenue field from the Item Sales table to the Values area.
   d. Open the PivotTable Options dialog box, and then on the Display tab, click the check boxes to show items with no data on the rows and columns.
   e. Copy the data in the range A5:B55, click cell E5, open the Paste Special dialog box, and then click Paste Link to paste references to the data values in the range E5:F55.
   f. Format the values in the range F5:F55 as currency with no decimal places.

15. Create a Map chart of the data in the range D4:F55, and then do the following:
   a. Move the map to the Summary worksheet in the range Q11:W30.
   b. Change the chart title to **Revenue by State**.
   c. Add data labels to the chart showing the revenue by state.
   d. Move the legend to the bottom of the chart area.

16. In the Summary worksheet, create a timeline using the Data Model's Order Date field from the Customer Orders table and do the following:
   a. Place the timeline across the range I4:W10.
   b. Create connections between the timeline and the Items Pivot and State Revenue PivotTables.
   c. Use the timeline to filter the PivotTables to show data only from July 2029 through December 2029.

17. Insert 3D Map presentation of this data, and then do the following to show the location of Musiki customers of keyboard products:
   a. In Scene 1, place the Postal Code field from the Customers table in the Location area, the Revenue field from the Items Sales table in the Height area, and the Store Name field from the Stores table in the Category area.
   b. Add map labels to the map.
   c. Change the view of the globe to a location above the East Coast, aiming toward the west.
   d. Resize the legend so that all items are visible and move the Layer 1 box to the top-left corner of the map.

18. Create a second scene of this data positioned above California, aiming northwest.

19. Change the durations of Scene 1 and Scene 2 to 1 second and play the tour, verifying that the viewpoint moves across the United States from the East Coast to California.

20. Close 3D Maps, save the workbook, and then close it.

Apply: Case Problem 1

Data Files needed for this Case Problem: NP_EX_10-3.xlsx, Support_EX_10_Parks.csv, Support_EX_10_Survey.csv, Support_EX_10_Visits.csv

Kentucky Parks Commission Sandra Wilkes is an administrator for the Kentucky Parks Commission. Part of Sandra's responsibilities is to monitor park usage and project future usage for budgeting. Sandra has compiled daily camping data from the previous five years at four prominent parks and wants to use that information to predict the visit pattern for the next year. The report should include information on the variation in usage during a typical week and from month-to-month. Sandra also has the results from a survey to show how park usage relates to the locations of campers in the state. Complete the following:

1. Open the **NP_EX_10-3.xlsx** workbook located in the Excel10 > Case1 folder included with your Data Files, and then save the workbook as **NP_EX_10_Park** in the location specified by your instructor.

2. In the Documentation sheet, in the range B3:B4, enter your name and the date.

3. Create a data query to retrieve data from the **Support_EX_10_Visits.csv** file located in the Excel10 > Case1 folder, and then transform the query as follows:
   a. Remove the top six rows and bottom five rows of text from the document.
   b. Use the new first row as the header for the column names.
   c. Remove the Wind, Humidity, and AQI columns from the query.
   d. Rename the query as **Usage**.
   e. Load the query, only creating a connection to the data and adding the data to the Data Model.

4. Create a data query to retrieve data from the **Support_EX_10_Parks.csv** file located in the Excel10 > Case1 folder, and then transform the query as follows:
   a. Remove the top four rows of text from the document.
   b. Use the new first row as the header for the column names.
   c. Rename the query as **Contacts**.
   d. Load the query, only creating a connection to the data and adding the data to the Data Model.

5. In PowerPivot, create a table relationship between the Usage and Contacts tables, using Park as the common field.

6. In the Years worksheet, in cell A4, insert a PivotTable using the Data Model, and then do following:
   a. Rename the PivotTable as **Year Pivot**.
   b. Place the Year field from the Usage table into the Rows area.
   c. Place the Campers field from the Usage table into the Values area.

7. Sandra wants a scatter chart of the total annual visits that will include a trendline. Because scatter charts are not a PivotChart type, first do the following:
   a. Copy the values in the range A5:B9 and paste a link to those values in the range D5:E9.
   b. Enter **Year** in cell D4, and then enter **Annual Visits** in cell E4.
   c. Format the values in the range E5:E9 in the Number format with a thousands separator but with no decimal places.

8. Create a scatter chart of the visit data in the range D4:E9, and then format the chart as follows:
   a. Add the axis title **Annual Total** to the vertical axis and **Year** to the horizontal axis.
   b. Add a linear trendline to the chart and extend the trendline forward two years.
   c. Move the scatter chart to the Overview worksheet and resize it to cover the range A12:F22.

9. In the Months worksheet, insert a PivotTable from data in the Data Model into cell A4, and then do the following:
   a. Rename the PivotTable as **Month Pivot**.
   b. Place the Date field from the Usage table into the Rows area to create a hierarchy of date fields. Remove all of them from the Rows area except the Date (Months) field.

c. Place the Campers field from the Usage table into the Values area.

d. Display the Sum of Campers in the Number format with a thousands separator and no decimal places.

10. Create a column chart PivotChart from the Month Pivot PivotTable, and then do the following:

   a. Move the PivotChart to cover the range A24:F34 in the Overview worksheet.

   b. Remove the chart legend and add data labels to chart.

   c. Remove the field buttons from the chart.

   d. Change the chart title to **Monthly Visits**, and then add the axis title **Monthly Total** to the vertical axis and **Month** to the horizontal axis.

11. In the Weekdays worksheet, insert a PivotTable from data in the Data Model into cell A4, and then do the following:

   a. Rename the PivotTable as **Weekday Pivot**.

   b. Place the Weekday field from the Usage table in the Rows area. Place the Campers field in the Values area.

   c. Change the Sum of Campers value field to display the average of the Campers field in the Number format with a thousands separator and no decimal places. Change the field label from Average of Campers to **Daily Average**.

12. Create a line chart PivotChart of the data in the Weekday Pivot PivotTable, and then do the following:

   a. Move the PivotChart to the Overview worksheet and resize it to cover the range H24:M34.

   b. Remove the Field Buttons and the legend from the chart.

   c. Change the chart title to **Daily Average**. Add the vertical axis title **Campers per Day** and the horizontal axis title **Day of the Week**.

   d. Add data labels to the chart.

13. In the Weather worksheet, insert a PivotTable using the Data Model into cell A4, and then do the following to compare park usage statistics to weather conditions:

   a. Rename the PivotTable as **Weather Pivot**.

   b. Move the Date (Month) field from the Usage table into the Rows area.

   c. Move the Temperature field and then the Campers field from the Usage table into the Values area (Temperature is the PivotTable's second column, and Campers is the third column).

   d. Change the field settings of the Sum of Campers and Sum of Temperature value fields to display their averages rather than the sums.

14. Create a scatter chart of Campers vs. Temperature by doing the following:

   a. Copy the Temperature and Campers values in the range B5:C16 and paste a link into the range E5:F16.

   b. Enter **Temperature** in cell E4, and then enter **Campers** in cell F4.

   c. Create a scatter chart of the data in the range E4:F16.

   d. Add a linear trendline to the scatter chart.

   e. Change the horizontal scale of the chart to go from 30 degrees up to 90 degrees. Change the vertical scale to go from 20 visits per day up 70 visits.

   f. Change the chart title to **Campers vs. Temperature**.

   g. Add the title **Campers per Day** to the vertical axis and the title **Temperature** to the horizontal axis.

   h. Move the scatter chart to the Overview worksheet and resize it to cover the range H12:M22.

15. Create a slicer from the Name field in the Contacts table in the Data Model. Resize the slicer to cover the range A4:C10 and increase the number of columns in the slicer to 2. Connect the slicer to all four PivotTables in the workbook.

16. Add a slicer for the Rain or Snow field in the Usage table in the Data Model. Resize the slicer to cover the range E4:F10. Connect the slicer to all four PivotTables in the workbook.

17. Add a timeline for the Date field in the Usage table in the Data Model. Resize the timeline to cover the range H4:M10. Connect the timeline to all four PivotTables in the workbook.

18. Create a data query to retrieve data from the **Support_EX_10_Survey.csv** file located in the Excel10 > Case1 folder. Transform the data to name the query as **Survey**. Load the query, only creating a connection to the data and adding the data to the Data Model. You'll use this to create a map showing the origins of park campers taken from a random survey of campers in the past year.

19. In PowerPivot, create a table relationship between the Survey and Contacts tables, using Park as the common field.

20. In the Survey worksheet, insert a PivotTable from the Data Model into cell A4, and then do the following:

   a. Rename the PivotTable as **Survey Pivot**.

   b. Place the County field from the Survey table into the Rows area of the PivotTable.

   c. Place the CamperID field from the Survey table into the Values area to show the count of campers from each county.

   d. On the Display tab of the PivotTable Options dialog box, click the Show items with no data on rows and Show items with no data on columns check boxes to select them.

21. Copy the range A5:B124 and paste a link of copied data into the range F5:G124.

22. Create a Filled Map from the data in the range D4:G124. Change the chart title to **Camper Origins**. Add data labels to the chart. Remove the chart legend. Move the chart to the Overview worksheet and resize it to cover the range O4:Y22.

23. Edit the Name slicer on the Overview worksheet and connect it to the Survey Pivot PivotTable.

24. Test the slicers so the Overview worksheet shows charts and maps for Blue Mountain Park when there is no rain nor snow from September through December of 2029.

25. Save the workbook, and then close it.

Challenge: Case Problem 2

Data Files needed for this Case Problem: NP_EX_10-4.xlsx, Support_EX_10_Cases.csv, Supprt_EX_10_Counties.csv, Support_EX_10_Postal.csv

Front Range Health Jamila Parker is a public health official for Front Range Health, a health research task force for the state of Colorado. Jamila is investigating the recent impact of a virus that spread through densely populated counties in central Colorado. Infection and demographic information have been stored in CSV files. Jamila wants you to load the data in Excel and create a summary report for use in a presentation that she will be giving next month on the virus and its spread. Complete the following.

1. Open the **NP_EX_10-4.xlsx** workbook located in the Excel10 > Case2 folder included with your Data Files, and then save the workbook as **NP_EX_10_Virus** in the location specified by your instructor.

2. In the Documentation sheet, in the range B3:B4, enter your name and the date.

3. Create a data query to retrieve demographic data from select counties in Colorado, accessing the **Support_EX_10_Counties.csv** file located in the Excel10 > Case2 folder. Remove the top 16 rows from the document. Use the new first row as the header for the column names. Rename the query as **Counties**. Load the query, only creating a connection to the data and adding the data to the Data Model.

4. Create a data query to retrieve information on postal codes in Colorado, accessing the **Support_EX_10_Postal.csv** file located in the Excel10 > Case2 folder. Remove the top 11 rows from the document and use the new first row as the header for the column names. Rename the query as **Postal**. Load the query, only creating a connection to the data and adding the data to the Data Model.

5. Create a data query to retrieve data on weekly virus cases by postal code. Use Power Query to access the **Support_EX_10_Cases.csv** file located in the Excel10 > Case2 folder. Remove the top 12 rows from the document and use the new first row as the header for the column names. Rename the query as **Cases**. Load the query, only creating a connection to the data and adding the data to the Data Model.

6. In Power Pivot, establish the following relationships between tables:

   a. Connect the Cases and Postal tables through the common Postal Code field.

   b. Connect the Postal and Counties table through the common County field. (Be sure to select the County field in the Postal table and not the Country field, which is very similar.)

7. In the Summary worksheet, where you will create a dashboard describing the infection of the virus over the past year, create a PivotTable in cell A4 using the tables from the Data Model, and then do the following:

   a. Rename the PivotTable as **Summary Pivot**.

   b. Open the PivotTable Options dialog box, and then on the Layout & Format tab, deselect the Autofit column widths on update check box.

   c. Place the County field from the Counties table and the Cases field from the Cases table in the Values area so that Count of County is in cell A4 and Sum of Cases is in cell B4.

   d. Move the ΣValues field from the Columns area to the Rows area.

   e. Change the label in cell A5 to **Counties** and the label in cell A6 to **Total Cases**.

   f. Display the Total Cases value in the Number format with a thousands separator and no decimal places.

8. Create another PivotTable in cell A8 using tables from the Data Model. Do the following:

   a. Rename the PivotTable as **Month Pivot**.

   b. In the PivotTable Options dialog box, on the Layout & Format tab, deselect the Autofit column widths on update check box.

   c. Move the Cases field from the Cases table into the Values area.

   d. Move the Date field from the Cases table in the Rows area. Excel will automatically generate a hierarchy of date fields. Remove the Date (Quarter) and Date fields from the Rows area.

   e. Expand the PivotTable rows to show both the Year and Month values in the table.

   f. Change the label in cell B8 to **Monthly Cases**. Display the Monthly Cases value in the Number format with a thousands separator and no decimal places.

9. In the Infection History worksheet, create a Pivot Table in cell A4 using the tables from the Data Model to summarize the rate of infection on a weekly basis for each of the seven counties. Do the following:

   a. Rename the PivotTable as **History Pivot**.

   b. Place the County field from the Postal table in the Columns area. Place only the Date field from the Cases table in the Rows area.

   c. Place the Cases field from the Cases table in the Values area to show the total number of cases per week and county over the past year.

10. Create a line chart of the data in the History Pivot PivotTable, and then do the following:

   a. Move the line chart to the Summary worksheet and resize it to cover the range D10:I23.

   b. Remove the field buttons from the chart.

   c. Add the chart title **Infection History**. Add a primary vertical axis title, **Virus Cases**.

11. Create a slicer from the County field in the Counties table to display detailed information on different counties, and then do the following:

   a. Move and resize the slicer so that it covers the range D4:I8.

   b. Increase the number of columns in the slicer to 4.

   c. Connect the slicer to the History Pivot, Month Pivot, and Summary Pivot PivotTables.

   d. Enable multi-select in the County slicer to display information from multiple counties.

   e. Use the slicer to display data only for the Arapahoe, Denver, and Boulder counties.

12. In the Elderly worksheet, in cell A4, create a PivotTable using the tables in the Data Model to explore whether there is a relationship between a county's infection rate and the percentage of its population which is over 65. Do the following:

   a. Name the PivotTable **Elderly Pivot**.

   b. Place the County field from the Counties table in the Rows area.

   c. Place the Over 65 field from the Counties table in the Values area to display the percent of the county population that is over 65. Place the Rate field from the Cases table in the Values area. (In the PivotTable, the values from the Over 65 field should be on the left and the values from the Rate field should be on the right.)

   d. Change the two fields in the Value area from sums to averages.

   e. Copy the data in the range B5:C11 and paste a link into the range E5:F11. Type **Over 65** in cell E4 and **Infection Rate** in cell F4.

   f. Format the values in the range E5:E11 as percentages with no decimal places.

13. Create a scatter chart of the data in the range E4:F11, and then do the following:

   a. Add the vertical axis title **Infection Rate per 100,000** and the horizontal axis title **Population 65 or Over**.

   b. Add a linear trend line to chart.

   c. Move the chart to the Summary worksheet, and then resize it to cover the range K10:O23.

14. **Explore:** Open a 3D Map tour and do the following to provide maps of where the infection rate was the highest:
    a. In the Layer pane, click the Heat Map icon (the fourth data visualization at the top of the pane).
    b. Place the Postal Code field from the Cases table into the Location box.
    c. Place the Cases field from the Case field into the Value box.
    d. Turn on the map labels for the map.
    e. Zoom into the map so that counties that Jamila is investigating fill the screen.
    f. Add map labels to the 3D map.

15. **Explore:** As the year progressed, the infection rate increased and declined. To visualize the changing inflection rate on the map, do the following:
    a. Place the Date field from the Cases table into the Time box.
    b. Directly above and to the right of the Time box, click the clock icon and click Data stays until it is replaced if it is not already selected.
    c. Click the Play button below the map to view the spread of the virus over the past year.

16. **Explore:** Save the animated map in a video file so it can be used in presentations by doing the following:
    a. On the Home tab in the Tour group, click the Create Video button.
    b. In the Create Video dialog box, select the Computer & Tablets option for the video quality.
    c. Click Create, and then save the MP4 video file as **NP_EX_10_Video.mp4** in the location specified by your instructor. It might take a few minutes to create the video file.
    d. When the file is finished saving, click Open to play the file and confirm that the video has been created by Excel. After it plays, close the video window, and then close the 3D Map window.

17. Save the workbook, and then close it.

Exploring PivotTable Design and Data

Tracking Daily Revenue Estimates

Case: Hogar Inn & Suites

Elian Morales is a regional manager for Hogar Inn & Suites, a worldwide chain of midsized hotels for budget-conscious travelers and conference organizers. Elian is preparing a sales report for an upcoming meeting on 24 Hogar franchises located in Florida. Elian's report will explore how revenue and occupancy rates have changed over the past two years and highlight those hotels and regions that are performing above or below expectations. To create this report, you'll develop PivotTables that will analyze the daily revenue and occupancy rates from the 24 hotels.

Starting Data Files

Excel11

Module

NP_EX_11-1.xlsx
NP_EX_11-2.xlsx

Review

NP_EX_11-3.xlsx
NP_EX_11-4.xlsx

Case1

NP_EX_11-5.xlsx

Case2

NP_EX_11-6.xlsx

Objectives

Part 11.1

- Change a PivotTable layout
- Display and hide PivotTable grand totals and subtotals
- Sort PivotTable contents
- Filter PivotTable contents
- Group items within a PivotTable

Part 11.2

- Apply PivotTables to calculations
- Create conditional formats for PivotTables
- Manage the PivotTable cache
- Create calculated items and fields in a PivotTable

Part 11.3

- Analyze PivotTable data from the Data Model
- Retrieve data from a PivotTable
- Analyze data with database functions
- Analyze data using linked data types
- Finding trends and insights with Analyze Data

Part 11.1 Visual Overview: Layouts, Sorting, Filtering, and Grouping

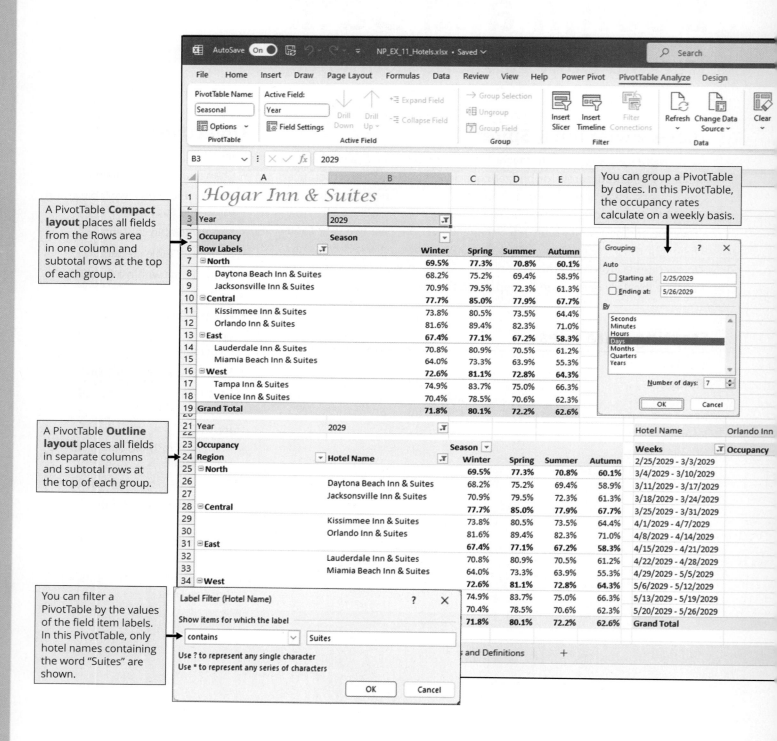

A PivotTable **Compact layout** places all fields from the Rows area in one column and subtotal rows at the top of each group.

A PivotTable **Outline layout** places all fields in separate columns and subtotal rows at the top of each group.

You can filter a PivotTable by the values of the field item labels. In this PivotTable, only hotel names containing the word "Suites" are shown.

You can group a PivotTable by dates. In this PivotTable, the occupancy rates calculate on a weekly basis.

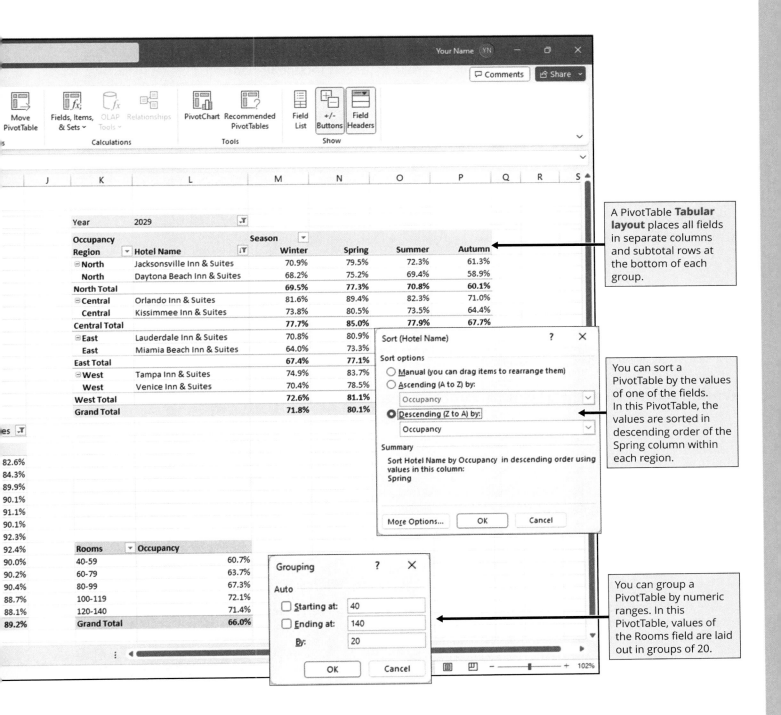

A PivotTable **Tabular layout** places all fields in separate columns and subtotal rows at the bottom of each group.

You can sort a PivotTable by the values of one of the fields. In this PivotTable, the values are sorted in descending order of the Spring column within each region.

You can group a PivotTable by numeric ranges. In this PivotTable, values of the Rooms field are laid out in groups of 20.

Laying Out a PivotTable

PivotTables are an indispensable tool for summarizing and analyzing data. In this module, you will explore PivotTable designs and features to present data in a wide variety of formats. You'll also learn how to edit PivotTables to include custom calculations. Elian has already created an Excel workbook detailing daily hotel occupancy and revenue over the past two years at 24 hotels located in Florida. You will start your work on Elian's report by opening this workbook.

To review Elian's workbook:

1. **sam** ↓ Open the **NP_EX_11-1.xlsx** workbook located in the **Excel11 > Module** folder included with your Data Files, and then save the workbook as **NP_EX_11_Hotels** in the location specified by your instructor.

2. In the Documentation worksheet, enter your name and the date in the range B3:B4.

3. Go to the **Hotels** worksheet. In this worksheet, Elian created an Excel table named Hotels containing 17,544 records of daily occupancy at the Florida hotels over the previous two years.

4. Review the fields in this table. Information on the fields is also included in the Terms and Definitions worksheet at the end of the workbook.

5. Review the other worksheets in the workbook. Some worksheets already include PivotTable report areas, which you will use in your report.

Elian wants to examine gross revenue and occupancy rates across different hotels, months, and seasons. He also wants to compare values from one year to the next. Elian will use this information to identify which hotels are succeeding in their location and which may be in trouble. You will start your analysis by exploring how hotel revenue varies between regions within Florida.

Working with Grand Totals and Subtotals

Elian wants a report showing the breakdown of revenue by year and sales region, showing the grand total across all regions and the subtotals within each region. You will create this report using an Excel PivotTable.

To create the PivotTable of hotel revenue:

1. Go to the **Revenue by Location** worksheet, and then make sure cell **A4** is selected to make the PivotTable report area active.

2. Drag the **Year** field to the Columns area, drag the **Region** and **Hotel Name** fields to the Rows area, and then drag the **Revenue** field to the Values area.

3. Use the Value Field Settings dialog box to change the value field for Revenue from "Sum of Revenue" to **Gross Revenue** and change the number format of the revenue values to Currency with zero digits after the decimal point. Refer to Figure 11-1.

Figure 11–1   PivotTable of Revenue by Location

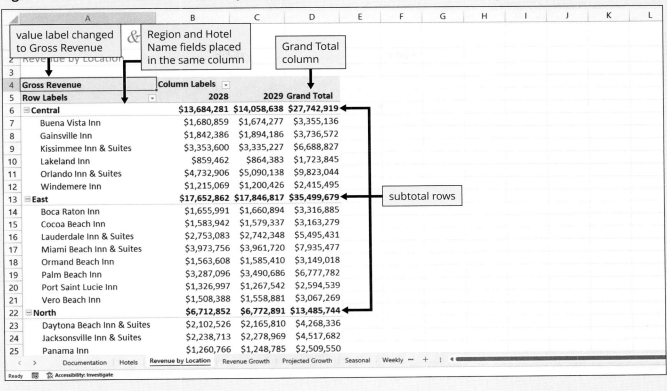

A PivotTable will, by default, show grand totals across all columns and rows. The grand totals in column D in this table provide the total revenues from 2028 and 2029 for each of the 24 hotels and the grand totals in row 34 display the totals across all hotels for each year. Based on this information, Elian can report that the chain had more than $96 million in gross revenue (cell D34) over the previous two years with revenue slightly higher in 2029 than in 2028. Not all hotels increased their revenue. The Buena Vista Inn (row 7) experienced a slight decline in gross revenue, decreasing from $1.68 million to $1.67 million. The Sarasota Inn (row 31) experienced a sharper drop of almost $200,000 in gross revenue between 2028 and 2029.

The PivotTable also includes subtotals for each of the four sales regions. Hotels in the Central region had $27.74 million in gross revenue over the past two years (cell D6). The East hotels brought in $35.50 million (cell D13), the North hotels brought in $13.49 million (cell D22), and the West hotels brought in $19.71 million (cell D27).

When grand totals and subtotals are not of interest, you can remove them from the PivotTable. You will remove both totals now.

To remove the grand totals and subtotals from the PivotTable:

1. On the ribbon, click the **Design** tab to display commands for changing the PivotTable's appearance, and then in the Layout group, click the **Grand Totals** button. A menu of options appears. You can turn off grand totals for the PivotTable rows and columns, keep the grand total values on for either rows or columns, or keep grand totals on for both (the default).

2. Click **Off for Rows and Columns**. The Grand Totals disappear from column D and row 34.

3. In the Layout group, click the **Subtotals** button. You can remove all subtotal calculations or move the subtotal rows to either the top of each group or the bottom.

4. Click **Do Not Show Subtotals** to remove the subtotals from the PivotTable. The subtotal calculations disappear from the PivotTable. Refer to Figure 11–2.

Figure 11–2   Grand total and subtotals removed from the PivotTable

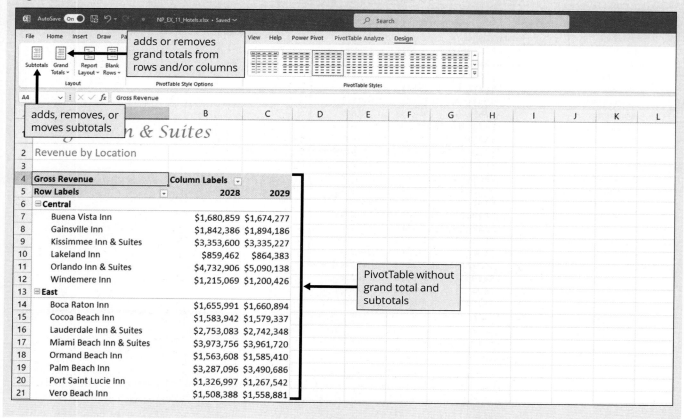

You will next explore how to change the layout of a PivotTable report.

Insight

Displaying Multiple Subtotals

PivotTables calculate subtotals using the same summary function applied to the individual table rows. A subtotal row will use the SUM function if the value field is summarized with sums and the AVERAGE function if the PivotTable shows averages of the value field.

If you want to show the results of more than one summary function, you can add multiple subtotal rows with different calculations to a PivotTable. First, open the Field Settings dialog box for the field over which the summary statistics are calculated. In the Field Settings dialog box, go to the Subtotal & Filters tab, and then click the Custom option button. Select one or more functions from the list of summary functions, which includes Sum, Count, Average, Max, Min, and Product. Click OK to close the Field Settings dialog box. The PivotTable will now show multiple summary statistics in each subtotal row.

If you want to display subtotals for some fields but not others, choose the None option button from the Subtotal & Filters tab. Note that you must have the PivotTable displayed in the Tabular layout.

Changing the PivotTable Layout

You can lay out PivotTables in one of three ways: Compact (the default; refer back to Figure 11–1), Outline, and Tabular, as described in Figure 11–3.

Figure 11-3   PivotTable layout options

Layout	Fields in the Rows Area	Subtotals
Compact	Placed together in the first column, separated by outlining buttons	Placed at the top of each row group
Outline	Placed in separate columns	Placed at the top of each row group
Tabular	Placed in separate columns	Placed at the bottom of each row group

The three layouts differ in how they arrange multiple fields placed in the Rows area and where they display subtotal rows.

> **Tip** Subtotals for a Tabular layout can only be placed at the bottom of a row group.

The Compact layout reduces the PivotTable width by placing all fields from the Rows area in one column. The Outline and Tabular layouts are best if you want to use values from the PivotTable in a subsequent analysis by placing each field value in its own PivotTable cell. You can also repeat field values in the Outline and Tabular layouts so that every row includes a field value.

Reference

Choosing a PivotTable Layout

- On the Design tab, in the Layout group, click the Report Layout button.
- Choose the Compact form to place all fields in the Rows area within a single column; choose the Outline or Tabular forms to place the fields in separate columns.
- To repeat item labels within a field, click the Report Layout button, and then click Repeat All Item Labels.

You will change the layout of the Revenue PivotTable to the Tabular form and repeat the field values within each row.

To display a PivotTable in Tabular layout:

1. On the Design tab, in the Layout group, click the **Report Layout** button, and then click **Show in Tabular Form**. The PivotTable changes to the Tabular layout.

2. In the Layout group, click the **Report Layout button** again, and then click **Repeat All Item Labels**. The name of the region is repeated for each row.

3. In the Layout group, click the **Blank Rows** button, and then click **Insert Blank Line After Each Item**. The PivotTable layout is more readable with each row group is separated by a blank row.

4. In the Layout group, click the **Subtotals** button, and then click **Show all Subtotals at the Bottom of Group** to restore subtotals to the PivotTable. Refer to Figure 11-4.

Figure 11–4   PivotTable in a Tabular layout

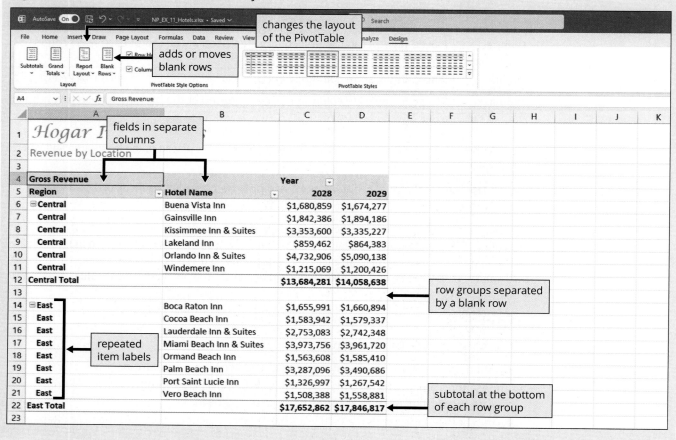

Elian finds the Tabular layout more readable for this data and more useful for the Revenue report.

Proskills

Written Communication: Setting Default PivotTable Options

Some professions enforce very specific design for reports. The default Compact layout might not match the standard for your profession. Rather than changing the PivotTable layout every time you create a report, you can set your own preferred layout options.

To define your PivotTable defaults, click Options in Backstage view. In the Options dialog box, click the Data tab, and then click the Edit Default Layout button in the Data options section to make changes to the default layout of PivotTables. In the Edit Default Layout dialog box, specify whether to show subtotals and, if so, where they should be placed, whether to show grand totals for PivotTable rows and/or columns, and finally whether new PivotTables should be created using the Compact, Outline, or Tabular layouts.

To save time, you can select a cell from an existing PivotTable and then click Import to use all the layout choices from that PivotTable as the defaults going forward. To set defaults for PivotTable options other than layouts, click the PivotTable Options button in the Edit Default Layout dialog box. In the PivotTable Options dialog box, you can set all the other PivotTable options for any new PivotTables you create.

By defining your own PivotTable options, you can reduce the time required to create a finished report and make your reports more consistent in design and appearance.

Sorting a PivotTable

PivotTables labels containing text are automatically sorted in alphabetical order, and PivotTable labels containing date/time values are sorted in chronological order. In the Revenue PivotTable, both the region names and the hotel names within region are sorted alphabetically (refer back to Figure 11–4). Elian wants the PivotTable to list the regions in the following order: North, Central, East, West. Within each region, Elian wants the busiest hotels listed first.

> **Tip** Month names are automatically sorted in calendar order, such as Jan, Feb, Mar, and so on. Weekday names are sorted in day order, such as Sun, Mon, Tue, and so on.

Manually Sorting a Field

To change the order of the field items, you can drag and drop the item labels into your preferred order. Another method is to select each item label and retype its name. The items will then be automatically resorted to match the names you enter. You will use the typing method to reorder the Region field, arranging the items in the order of North, Central, East, and then West.

To manually sort the Region field:

1. Click cell **A6** containing the text Central.

2. Type **North** to specify the first item you want to appear in the field, and then press **ENTER**.

   The four hotels in the North region are listed first in the table, starting with Daytona Beach Inn & Suites. The hotels for the Central region are next, followed by East and then West.

   > **Trouble?** If the category is renamed but not reordered, you probably mistyped the category name. Undo that action, and then repeat Steps 1 and 2, being sure to type the name of the category correctly.

Excel remembers your chosen order so that if you recreate this PivotTable or create another PivotTable with the Region field, you will not have to reorder the items again.

Reference

Sorting PivotTables

- To manually sort the items within a PivotTable field, drag the field items or type the item labels in the order you prefer.
- To sort the items in ascending or descending order, click the Filter button next to the field name, and then click Sort A to Z or Sort Z to A on the menu.
- To sort a field based on values from another field in the PivotTable, click the Filter button next to the field name, click More Sort Options, select the field the sorting is based on, specify the sorting options, and then click OK.

Sorting by Value

You can have Excel sort a field by clicking the Filter button next to the field name and selecting a sorting option from the menu. Elian wants you to sort the hotels within each region so that the hotels with the highest revenue appear at the top of each region. You will sort the values of the Hotel Name field in descending order of the 2029 revenue.

To sort the hotel names in descending order of revenue:

1. Click the **Filter** button in cell B5 of the PivotTable to open the filter menu.

2. Click **More Sort Options**. The Sort (Hotel Name) dialog box opens.

3. Click the **Descending (Z to A) by** option button, click the **Descending (Z to A) by** box, and then click **Gross Revenue**. Refer to Figure 11–5.

Figure 11–5   Sort (Hotel Name) dialog box

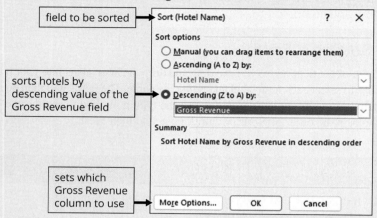

You can sort the hotels by the 2028 gross revenue, the 2029 gross revenue, or the grand total across both years (even if the grand total is hidden). Elian wants the hotels within each region sorted in descending order of the 2029 revenues.

4. Click **More Options**. The More Sort Options (Hotel Name) dialog box opens.

5. Click the **Values in selected column** option button, and then press **TAB** to select the cell reference.

> **Key Step** If you do not select the column to be sorted, Excel will sort the values by the grand total even if the grand total does not appear in the PivotTable.

6. Click cell **D6** to replace the cell reference. This will sort the hotel names by the 2029 revenue values in column D. Refer to Figure 11–6.

Figure 11–6   More Sort Options (Hotel Name) dialog box

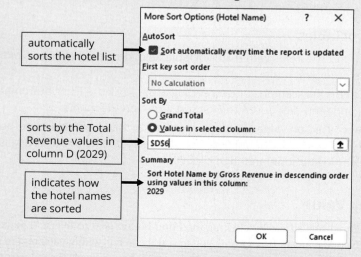

7. Click **OK** in each dialog box to return to the workbook. The hotel names within each region are sorted in descending order of the 2029 gross revenue. Refer to Figure 11–7.

Figure 11-7   Hotels sorted in descending order of gross revenue

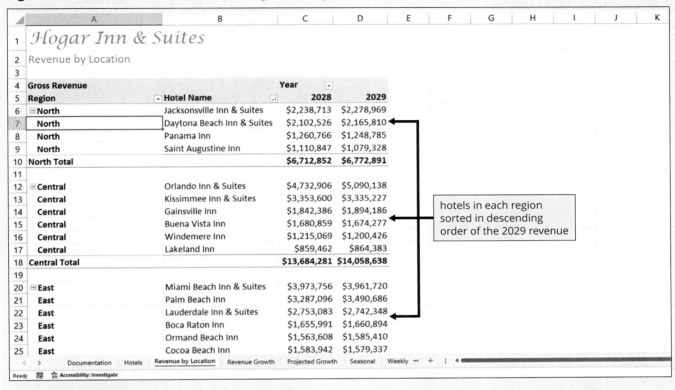

The PivotTable now effectively shows the information that Elian needs for the report. The top-selling hotel in the North region for 2029 is the Jacksonville Inn & Suites with $2.279 million in revenue, followed by the Daytona Beach Inn & Suites and then the Panama Inn with $2.166 million and $1.249 million, respectively. The hotel with the greatest gross revenue for the Central region is the Orlando Inn & Suites with over $5 million in 2029 revenue (cell D12), for the East region it is the Miami Beach Inn & Suites with about $3.962 million (cell D20), and for the West region it is the Tampa Inn & Suites with $2.619 million (cell D30).

Insight

Sorting a PivotTable by a Custom List

PivotTables can be automatically sorted alphabetically, by numeric value, or by date, in ascending or descending order. However, in some situations, you will want PivotTables automatically sorted based on a custom list. For example, Elian might always want PivotTables to sort the hotels by region in the order North, Central, East, and then West.

To create a custom sort order, click Options in Backstage view to open the Excel Options dialog box. Click the Advanced tab, scroll down to the General section, and then click the Edit Custom Lists button. The Custom Lists dialog box opens, from which you can create lists of items in any order to use with your PivotTables.

If later you want to prevent Excel from automatically sorting based on custom lists, go to the PivotTable Analyze tab, and then in the PivotTable group, click the Options button. In the PivotTable Options dialog box, on the Totals & Filters tab, deselect the Use Custom Lists when sorting check box, and then click OK.

The hotels in the Hogar chain are often marketed to different clientele. For example, the line of Inn & Suites hotels, such as the Orlando Inn & Suites, provides more spacious rooms and meeting facilities, perfect for the needs of business travelers and midsized conferences. The success of those hotels is of special interest to Elian, who wants an analysis of those types of hotels. You can narrow the scope of a PivotTable report using filters.

Filtering a PivotTable

Excel provides several ways of filtering PivotTables. Users can select values from the Filters area in a drop-down list. Slicers can be linked to a PivotTable to filter the table by one or more multiple categories or by timelines. Or, a filter can also be applied directly to the fields within the PivotTable using the following filter types:

- **Manual filters**, which select values from check boxes listing all of the unique field values
- **Date filters**, which select data based on specific dates or date ranges
- **Label filters**, which select data based on the labels of the items in the field
- **Value filters**, which filter data based on values of a numeric field elsewhere in the PivotTable

Elian wants the Revenue table to list only those hotels in the Inn & Suites line that had more than $2.5 million in gross revenue in 2029. To modify the report, you will first use a manual filter to narrow the focus of the PivotTable to 2029 revenue totals.

To apply a manual filter to the PivotTable:

1. Click the **Filter** button in cell C4 next to the Year label.

2. Click the **2028** check box to deselect it, leaving only the 2029 check box selected.

    Tip You can reduce the filter values by entering a search string in the Search box directly above the list of field item values.

3. Click **OK**. The 2028 revenue column is removed from the PivotTable, leaving only the 2029 gross revenues displayed in column C.

Manual filters are a quick way to filter data. However, if data contains a lot of field values, the list of filter values will be extremely long. Another approach is to use the Label filter in which you limit the field to only those labels whose value matches specified criteria. Narrow the PivotTable so that it only shows results from hotels with the word "Suites" in their name. You will filter the PivotTable now.

To apply a Label filter to the PivotTable:

1. Click the **Filter** button in cell B5 next to the Hotel Name label.

2. Click **Label Filters** on the menu. A list of criteria that can be applied to the labels of the selected field appears.

3. Click **Contains** from the list of filter options. The Label Filter (Hotel Name) dialog box opens with "contains" selected in the left box and the insertion point in the input box on the right.

4. In the input box, type **Suites** to limit the PivotTable to only those hotels containing the word "Suites" in their name. Refer to Figure 11–8.

Figure 11–8   Label Filter (Hotel Name) dialog box

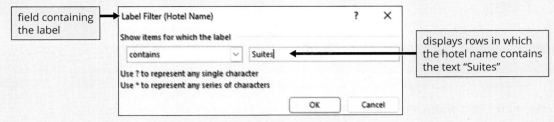

field containing
the label

displays rows in which
the hotel name contains
the text "Suites"

5.   Click **OK**.

The PivotTable is filtered to show 2029 revenue from eight Inn & Suites hotels located in Florida. Note that Label filters can also be applied to labels that have numeric values. For example, a field specifying the number of rooms in the hotel could be filtered to show only those hotels with more than 100 rooms or between 50 and 75 rooms. Label filters, whether used with text strings or numeric values, always apply the filter to the field associated with the filter button. To filter a field based on the values from another field in the PivotTable, use a Value filter.

> **Tip** You can view the sort and filter settings for your PivotTable by pointing to the Filter button in the PivotTable.

Elian wants to further filter this PivotTable to show only the hotels with $2.5 million or more revenue in 2029. However, there is a problem. By default, only one filter can be applied to a field at a time: You can apply a Label filter or a Value filter to the Hotel Name field, but not both. To apply multiple filters to a single field, you must first modify the PivotTable properties.

To allow multiple filters within the same field:

1.   Make sure the Revenue Location PivotTable is still selected.
2.   On the ribbon, click the **PivotTable Analyze** tab, and then, in the PivotTable group, click the **Options** button. The PivotTable Options dialog box opens.
3.   Click the **Totals & Filters** tab to view options for totals and filters.
4.   In the Filters section, click the **Allow multiple filters per field** check box. Refer to Figure 11–9.

Figure 11–9   PivotTable Options dialog box

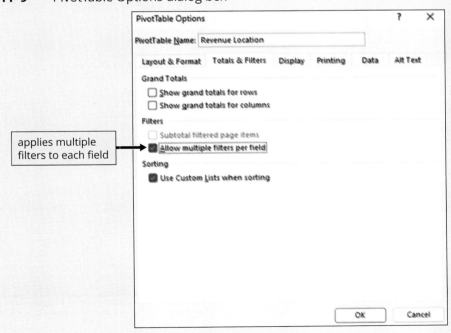

applies multiple
filters to each field

5.   Click **OK** to return to the workbook.

Next, you will add a second filter that limits the PivotTable to only those hotels with 2029 gross revenue of $2.5 million or more.

To apply a Value filter to the PivotTable:

1. Click the **Filter** button in cell B5 next to the Hotel Name label.

2. On the menu, click **Values Filters**. A submenu of filter options that can be applied to numeric values appears.

3. Click **Greater Than Or Equal To**. The Value Filter (Hotel Name) dialog box opens with Gross Revenue already chosen as the numeric field that "is greater than or equal to" a specified value.

   ▌ **Tip** Unlike sorting, filters cannot be based on specific columns within a field.

4. In the input box on the right, type **2,500,000** to limit the PivotTable to those Inn & Suites hotels with a gross 2029 revenue of $2.5 million or greater. Refer to Figure 11–10.

Figure 11–10   Value Filter (Hotel Name) dialog box

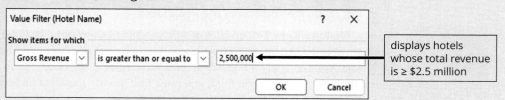

5. Click **OK**. The Value filter is applied to the table. Five hotels satisfy all the filter criteria. Refer to Figure 11–11.

Figure 11–11   Filtered revenue totals

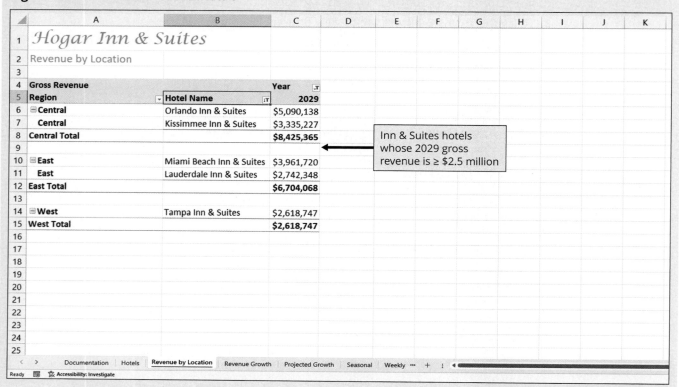

If you want to remove all the filters to include revenue totals for all hotels, you can click the Clear arrow in the Actions group on the PivotTable Analyze tab, and then click Clear Filters.

Insight

Generating Multiple PivotTables with Show Report Filter Pages

You can create multiple copies of a PivotTable with the **Show Report Filters Pages tool**. To apply the tool, first place a field in the Filters area of the PivotTable. Then, rather than using the Filter button to switch the PivotTable between values of the filter, do the following:

1. Click the PivotTable Analyze tab.
2. In the PivotTable group, click the Options arrow, and then click Show Report Filter Pages.
3. In the Show Report Filter Pages dialog box, select the field from which to generate the filter pages.
4. Click OK.

Excel will generate new worksheets with each sheet containing a copy of the original PivotTable, filtered to include a different field value and the sheets automatically named for their field value. The PivotTables are not linked to the original table so any changes you make to the original PivotTable will not be reflected in the copies. The Show Report Filter Pages tool is a great way of quickly generating reports for specific stores, regions, or time periods in data.

Grouping PivotTable Fields

Gross revenue is one metric to gauge the success or failure of a hotel. Another is the average occupancy rate, which measures the percentage of available rooms being occupied on an average night. A hotel in a small market might not return a lot in gross revenue, yet still be successful if it constantly rents out most of its rooms. On the other hand, a hotel in a large market might be underutilized even if it is bringing in a large amount of gross revenue.

Elian is interested in exploring how the occupancy rates of the Florida hotels vary throughout the year. You will create a new PivotTable report to calculate the average occupancy rate for each of the 24 hotels from January through December in 2029.

To report on average occupancy rates:

1. Go to the **Seasonal** worksheet.
2. Drag the **Year** field into the Filters area, drag the **Month** field into the Columns area, drag the **Hotel Name** field into the Rows area, and drag the **Occupancy Rate** field into the Values area. By default, Excel displays the sum of the occupancy rates, but Elian wants the average occupancy rate.
3. Modify the Value Field Settings for the Sum of Occupancy so that the PivotTable displays the average occupancy as percentages to one decimal place and change the name from "Average of Occupancy Rate" to **Average Occupancy**. The PivotTable displays the average occupancy rate per day broken down by hotel and month.
4. On the ribbon, click the **Design** tab. In the Layout group, click the **Report Layout** button, and then click **Show in Tabular Form** to apply the Tabular layout to the PivotTable.
5. On the Design tab, in the Layout group, click the **Grand Totals** button, and then click **On for Columns Only** to include the average occupancy rate by month but not across all months. Elian wants to focus on occupancy rates for 2029.

6. Click the **Filter** button in cell B4, click **2029** on the submenu, and then click **OK** to include the occupancy rates for only 2029. Refer to Figure 11–12.

Figure 11–12   Occupancy rates by month and hotel for 2029

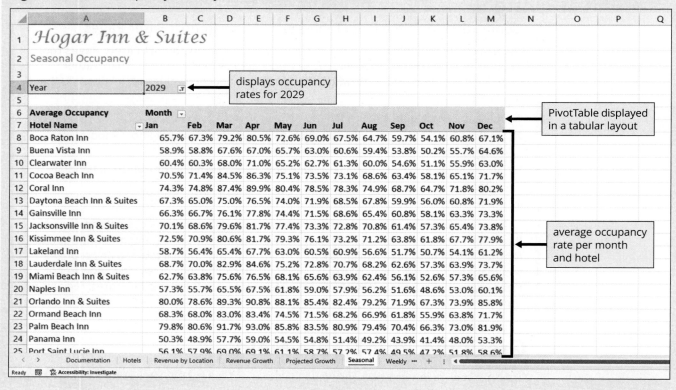

This PivotTable is 13 columns by 24 rows, not including the grand total row. As a PivotTable grows, the sheer number of cells of data can be overwhelming. You can reduce the PivotTable size by grouping common categories. For example, a PivotTable containing monthly sales data might be better understood if the months were grouped into quarters.

Elian is more interested in comparing seasonal rates. For Florida hotels, the peak season occurs during Spring as travelers from the north seek the beaches and warmer weather of Florida. Elian wants you to group the PivotTable to compare occupancy rates from different seasons.

Reference

Grouping PivotTable Fields

- To manually group items within a PivotTable field, select individual items, and then on the PivotTable Analyze tab, in the Group group, click the Group Selection button, and then enter a name for the group in the Active Field box.

- To group a date field, select the field, and then on the PivotTable Analyze tab, in the Group group, click the Group Selection button, and then in the Grouping dialog box, specify starting and ending dates for the field and select the levels from Seconds up to Years in which the dates should be grouped.

- To group a numeric field, select the field, and then on the PivotTable Analyze tab, in the Group group, click the Group Selection button, and then in the Grouping dialog box, specify the numeric intervals on which the groups are based.

Manual Grouping

One way of grouping a PivotTable is with a **manual group** in which items within a field are combined to create a new group that appears as a new field within the PivotTable. You will use manual grouping to combine values from different months into seasons.

To create a manual group:

1. Click cell **B7** containing the label "Jan" and hold down **CTRL**, click cells **C7** and **M7** to select the Feb and Dec labels, and then release **CTRL**.

2. On the ribbon, click the **PivotTable Analyze** tab, and then in the Group group, click the **Group Selection** button. A new grouped field named Month2 is added to the PivotTable.

3. On the PivotTable Analyze tab, in the Active Field group, click the **Active Field** box, and then change the name from Month2 to **Season**.

4. Click cell **B7**, type **Winter** to change the label from Group1, and then press **ENTER**.

5. Click cell **F8** containing the label "Mar" and hold down **CTRL**, click cells **H8** and **J8** to select the Mar, Apr, and May labels, and then release **CTRL**.

6. Click the **Group Selection** button to group these PivotTable columns.

7. Click cell **F7** and then enter **Spring** to change the label in the cell from Group2.

8. Click cell **J8**, hold down **CTRL**, click cells **L8** and **N8** to select the labels for Jun, Jul, and Aug, and then release **CTRL**.

9. Click the **Group Selection** button to group the columns, and then change the group label in cell J7 from Group3 to **Summer**.

10. Click cell **N8**, hold down **CTRL**, click cells **P8** and **R8** to select the labels for Sep, Oct, and Nov, and then release **CTRL**.

11. Click the **Group Selection** button to group the columns, and then change the group label in cell N7 from Group4 to **Autumn**.

12. Drag the **Month** field out of the Columns area of the PivotTable, leaving only Season as a Columns field. Refer to Figure 11–13.

Figure 11–13   Grouped PivotTable

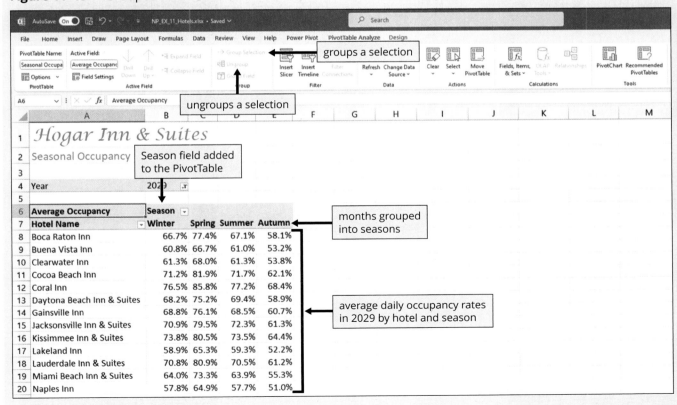

Elian is not surprised to learn that occupancy rates are the highest in the Spring. For example, the Boca Raton Inn will fill 77.4% of its rooms daily during the Spring (cell C8) but only 58.1% of those rooms will be filled in the Autumn (cell E8). The other hotels follow a similar seasonal pattern.

Tip Once a group has been manually created, it will act as a new PivotTable field and will be available to other PivotTables in the workbook.

Elian wants to sort the PivotTable so that the hotels with the highest Spring occupancy rates are listed first. You will sort the PivotTable by the Average Occupancy field in the Spring column.

To sort the PivotTable in descending order of Spring occupancy:

1. Click the **Filter** button in cell A7 next to the Hotel Name label.

2. Click **More Sort Options** on the menu. The Sort (Hotel Name) dialog box opens.

3. Click the **Descending (Z to A) by** option button, and then select **Average Occupancy** from the accompanying box.

4. Click the **More Options** button. The More Sort Options (Hotel Name) dialog box opens.

5. Click the **Values in selected column** option button, press **TAB**, and then click cell **C8** (containing the Spring occupancy rates for the Boca Raton Inn).

6. Click **OK** in each dialog box to return to the workbook. Refer to Figure 11-14.

Figure 11-14 Sorted PivotTable

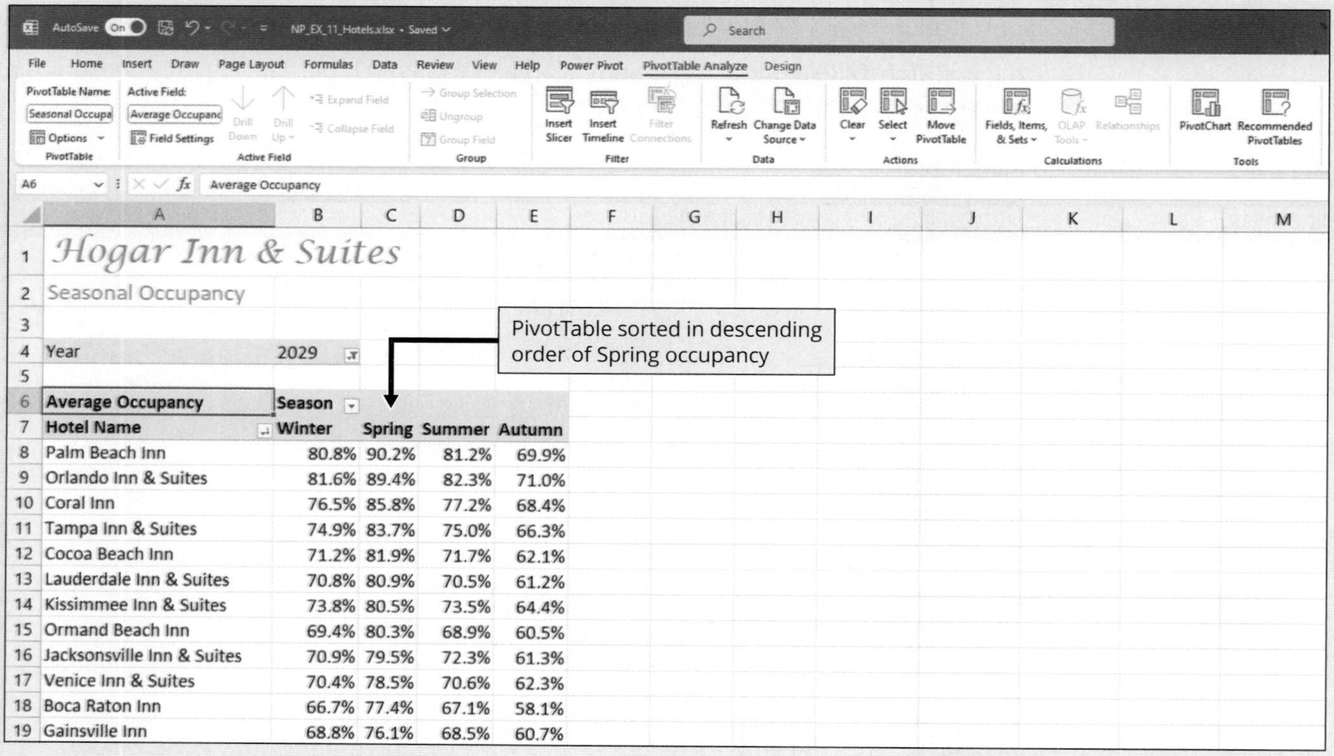

PivotTable sorted in descending order of Spring occupancy

Hotel Name	Winter	Spring	Summer	Autumn
Palm Beach Inn	80.8%	90.2%	81.2%	69.9%
Orlando Inn & Suites	81.6%	89.4%	82.3%	71.0%
Coral Inn	76.5%	85.8%	77.2%	68.4%
Tampa Inn & Suites	74.9%	83.7%	75.0%	66.3%
Cocoa Beach Inn	71.2%	81.9%	71.7%	62.1%
Lauderdale Inn & Suites	70.8%	80.9%	70.5%	61.2%
Kissimmee Inn & Suites	73.8%	80.5%	73.5%	64.4%
Ormand Beach Inn	69.4%	80.3%	68.9%	60.5%
Jacksonsville Inn & Suites	70.9%	79.5%	72.3%	61.3%
Venice Inn & Suites	70.4%	78.5%	70.6%	62.3%
Boca Raton Inn	66.7%	77.4%	67.1%	58.1%
Gainsville Inn	68.8%	76.1%	68.5%	60.7%

The busiest hotel in the Spring is the Palm Beach Inn with a daily average occupancy rate of 90.2%, followed by the Orlando Inn & Suites with 89.4%. The Panama Inn has the lowest Spring occupancy rate at 57.0% (cell C31).

Grouping by Dates

Within a season, some days are busier than others. Knowing the days and weeks of peak usage is extremely important for projecting costs and staffing needs. Elian wants you to examine daily usage rates by date. When Excel encounters a date field that spans more than one year, it automatically groups the date values into quarters, months, and years. With nested levels of date groups, you can analyze the data at any level of precision. You will begin creating the PivotTable to do that analysis now.

To create a PivotTable of occupancy rate versus date:

1. Go to the **Weekly** worksheet.

2. Drag the **Occupancy Rate** field to the Values area and drag the **Hotel Name** field to the Filters area.

3. Change the value field settings for the Occupancy Rate field to calculate the average rather than the sum of the occupancy rates.

4. Change the number format to display the averages as a percentage to one decimal place, and then change the Value field name to **Average Occupancy**. The average daily occupancy rate across all hotels and all days is 66.0%.

5. Drag the **Date** field to the Rows area. Excel creates an outline of nested fields, grouping the dates by year, quarter, month, and date. You want to view the nested fields in separate columns.

6. On the ribbon, click the **Design** tab. In the Layout group, click the **Report Layout** button, and then click **Show in Tabular Form**. Four columns labeled Years (Date), Quarters (Date), Months (Date), and Date appear in columns A through D.

7. Click the **expand outline** button in cell **A8** to expand the 2029 Year field into its subgroups consisting of quarters.

8. Click the **expand outline** button in cell **B8** to expand the Qtr1 field into its subgroups consisting of the months of Jan through Mar.

9. Click the **expand outline** button next to Jan in cell C8 to view the average occupancy rates across the 24 hotels for each day in January 2029. Refer to Figure 11–15.

Figure 11–15 Date groups in a PivotTable

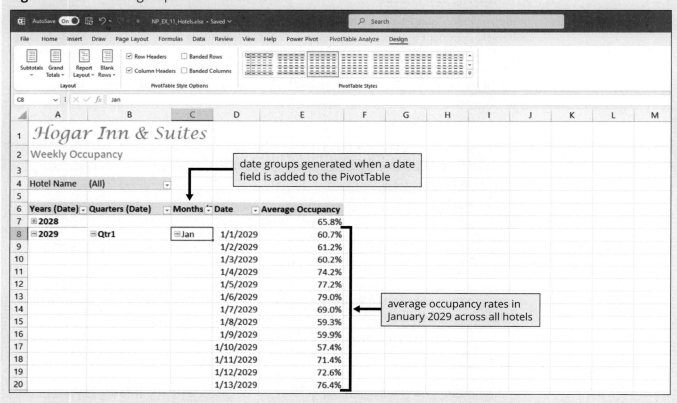

A PivotTable with occupancy rates per day is more detailed than Elian can use. Instead, he wants you to group the dates by weeks. Excel does not automatically add a Week (Date) to the PivotTable, so you must define that group yourself. Elian wants the PivotTable to focus only on those weeks during the Spring in which hotel usage is at its peak. He suggests you report the occupancy rates on weekly basis starting with February 25, 2029 (Sunday) and ending with May 26, 2029 (Saturday).

To group the occupancy data by weeks:

1. Click cell **D8** to select it.

2. On the ribbon, click the **PivotTable Analyze** tab, and then in the Group group, click the **Group Selection** button. The Grouping dialog box opens, covering dates starting with 1/1/2028 through 1/1/2030. The Months, Quarters, and Years options are selected to group the date values from months, quarters, and years.

3. In the Starting at box, change the starting date to **2/25/2029**.

4. Press **TAB** twice, and then change the ending date to **5/26/2029**.

5. In the By box, click **Days** to select it and add it as a date grouping level.

6. In the By box, click **Months**, **Quarters**, and **Years** to deselect and remove them as grouping levels.

> **Tip** To prevent Excel from generating date groups from a field, click any date in the date field, and then click the Ungroup button in the Group group on the PivotTable Analyze tab.

7. In the Number of days box, enter **7** so the PivotTable is grouped by 7-day weeks. Refer to Figure 11–16.

Figure 11–16   Grouping dialog box

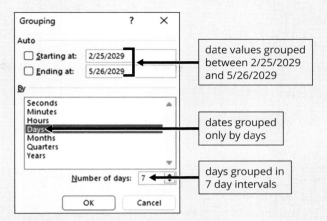

8. Click **OK** to create the grouping and return to the workbook.

The occupancy rates are grouped into weeks from 2/25/2029 through 5/26/2029. Dates before 2/25/2029 or after 5/26/2029 constitute their own groups. You will use a Date filter now to filter out those date ranges, focusing the PivotTable on the weeks during the Spring 2029. Then you will view the weekly occupancy rates for select hotels.

To apply a Date filter for dates:

1. Click the **Filter** button in cell A6.

2. On the Filter menu, click **Date Filters** to display a list of date filters that can be applied to the field.

3. Click **Between**. The Date Filter (Days[Date]) dialog box opens.

4. Enter **2/25/2029** in the first box, and then enter **5/26/2029** in the second box. Refer to Figure 11–17.

Figure 11–17   Date Filter (Days (Date)) dialog box

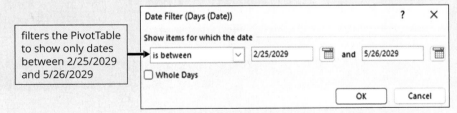

5. Click **OK** to return to the workbook and apply the filter.

6. Click the **Filter** button in cell B4, click **Orlando Inn & Suites**, and then click **OK** to review the average daily occupancy rates for the weeks between 2/25/2029 and 5/26/2029. Refer to Figure 11–18.

Figure 11–18   Average daily occupancy at the Orlando Inn & Suites in Spring 2029

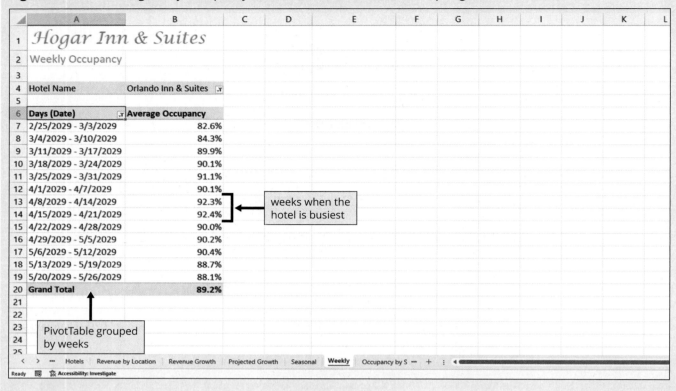

The Orlando Inn & Suites is the busiest in the second and third weeks of April when the occupancy rate tops 92%. After those weeks, the occupancy begins to drop slightly, but the hotel is still busy into the end of May. This kind of information will help Elian advise the hotel on its staffing needs for the upcoming year.

Grouping by Numeric Fields

Elian wants to explore whether occupancy rates are related to the size of the hotel. Are larger hotels less likely to have high occupancy rates or are they large because they attract more customers and rarely have vacancies? To answer that question, you will create another PivotTable comparing average occupancy to hotel size, where size is measured by the number hotel rooms.

To apply a Label filter for dates:

1. Go to the **Occupancy by Size** worksheet.

2. Drag the **Occupancy Rate** field to the Values area, and then drag the **Rooms** field to the Rows area.

3. Change the Sum of Occupancy Rate to display the average occupancy rate as percentages to one decimal place and change the Value field name to **Average Occupancy**.

4. On the ribbon, click the **Design** tab. In the Layout group, click the **Report Layout** button, and then click **Show in Tabular Form**. Refer to Figure 11–19.

Figure 11–19   Average occupancy rates vs. number of rooms

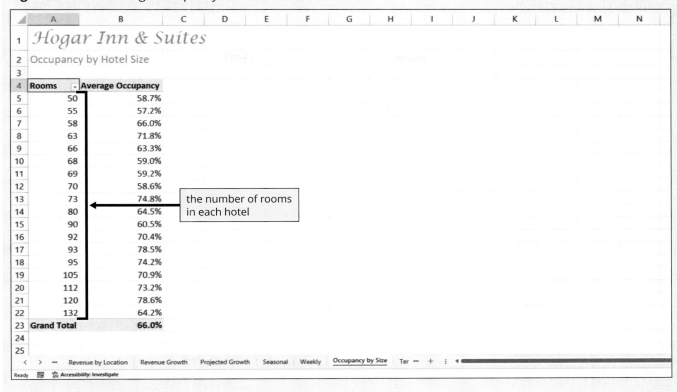

The PivotTable shows average occupancy rates for hotels with 50 rooms up to 132 rooms. With so many possible sizes, it's difficult to get a clear sense of the relationship (if any) between hotel size and occupancy. To create a simpler PivotTable, you can group the values of the Hotel Rooms field with each group category spanning an interval of hotel sizes.

Elian wants you to group the hotels in 20-room intervals, starting with hotels containing 40 to 59 rooms through hotels containing 140 rooms. You will generate the groups using the Grouping dialog box.

To group by number:

1. Click cell **A4** containing the Hotel Rooms label to select it.

2. Click the **PivotTable Analyze** tab, and then in the Group group, click the **Group Field** button. The Grouping dialog box opens.

3. In the Starting at box, enter the value **40** to indicate that the grouping starts with hotels containing at least 40 rooms.

4. In the Ending at input box, enter the value **140** to indicate that the grounding ends with hotels containing at most 140 rooms.

5. In the By input box, enter **20** as the group size. Refer to Figure 11–20.

Figure 11–20   Grouping dialog box

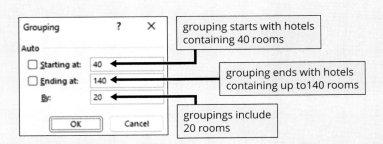

6. Click **OK** to return to the workbook. The occupancy rates are grouped by hotel size. Refer to Figure 11–21.

Figure 11–21   Hotels grouped by size

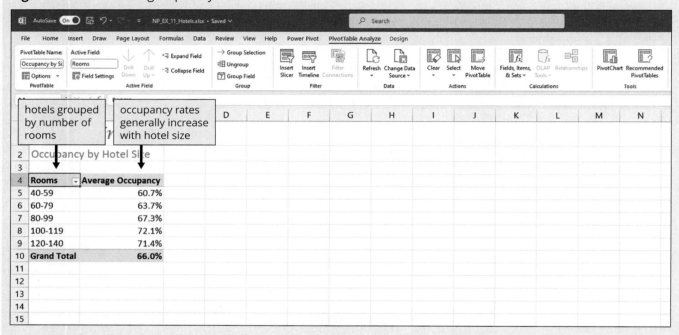

7. Save the workbook.

Presenting the hotel sizes in groups of 20 rooms gives a clear picture of the relationship between hotel size and occupancy. In general, as the size of the hotel increases, the occupancy rate also increases. This is not true for every hotel in the group (refer back to Figure 11–20). The larger hotels are often built in areas with more tourism and have access to more clientele.

The groups you create either manually or through the Grouping dialog box are retained with the PivotTable and available to all future PivotTables that share the same data source. Note that groups created through manual selection are stored as new fields, whereas groups created automatically or through the Grouping dialog box replace the PivotTable field that they group. Once you group the Date field by weeks, all future uses of the Date field will be grouped that way.

You've finished your initial analysis of the Florida hotel data, discovering when those hotels are busiest and which hotels have the greatest revenue. In the next part, you will use PivotTables to analyze this data in other ways.

Part 11.1 Quick Check

1. How does the Compact layout differ from the Tabular layout?

2. What are two ways of manually sorting a PivotTable field?

3. When sorting a PivotTable by values in a field, how are the field values sorted by default?

4. When would you use a Label filter in a PivotTable?

5. When would you use a Value filter in a PivotTable?

6. How do you allow a PivotTable field to include both a Date filter and a Value filter?

7. When a PivotTable field is manually grouped, how does Excel treat the grouped items?

8. What does Excel do to date fields that are added to a PivotTable?

Part 11.2 Visual Overview: Conditional Formats and Calculations

An **icon set** is a conditional format in which different icons are displayed in a cell based on the cell's value.

A **color scale** is a conditional format in which the fill color is based on a range of cell values where cells with larger values are filled with progressively darker (or lighter) shades.

PivotTables can include calculations from across fields and field items. Here, the Revenue field is expressed as the percentage difference between the 2028 and 2029 values.

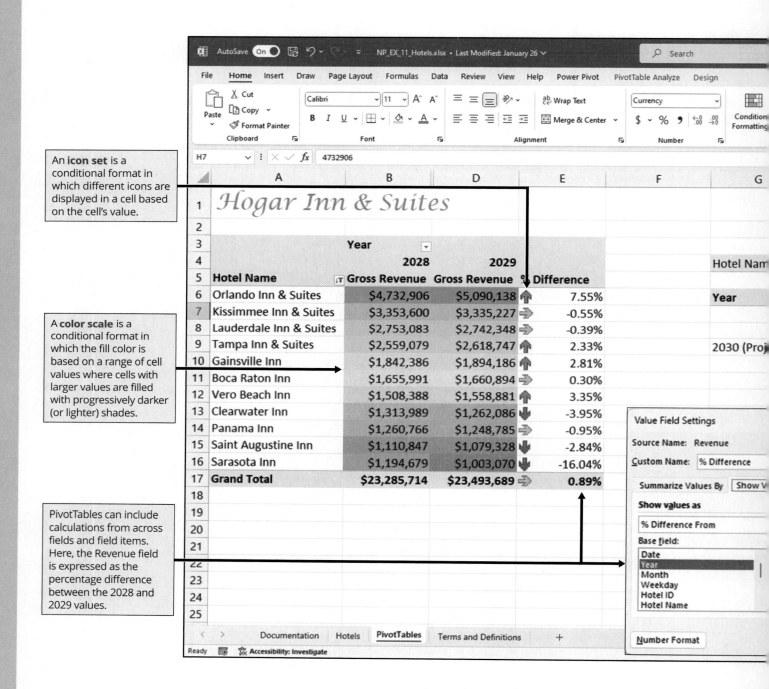

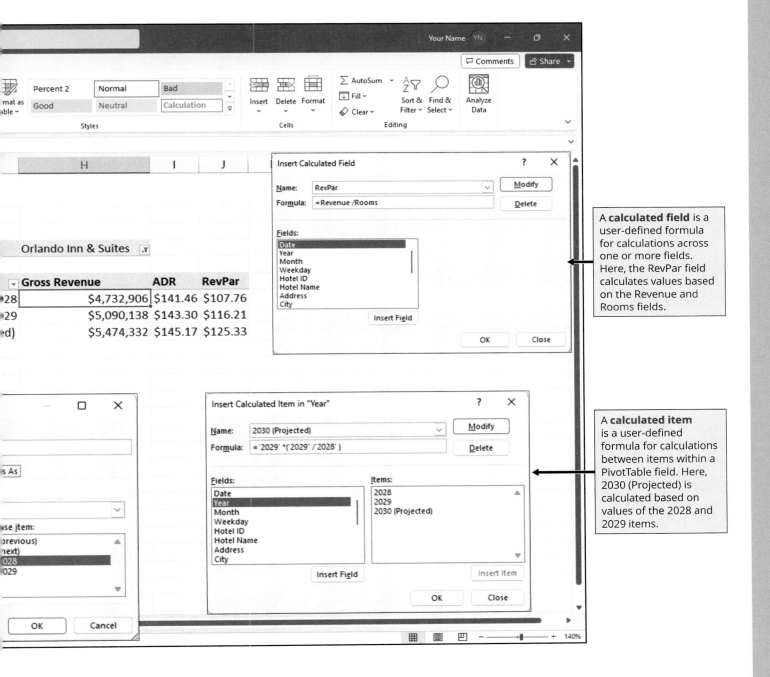

A **calculated field** is a user-defined formula for calculations across one or more fields. Here, the RevPar field calculates values based on the Revenue and Rooms fields.

A **calculated item** is a user-defined formula for calculations between items within a PivotTable field. Here, 2030 (Projected) is calculated based on values of the 2028 and 2029 items.

Calculations with PivotTables

PivotTables support the following statistical functions to summarize data within each PivotTable field: Sum, Count, Average, Max, Min, Product, CountNumbers, StdDev, StdDevP, Var, and Varp. Figure 11–22 describes other PivotTable operations that calculate values between fields or within items of the same field. With these operations, you can calculate the difference between one field and another or calculate a running total of the items within a field.

Figure 11–22   PivotTable calculations between and within fields

Calculation	Description
% of Grand Total	Calculates the value of each cell as a percentage of the grand total across all cells
% of Column Total	Calculates the value of each cell as a percentage of the total of its column
% of Row Total	Calculates the value of each cell as a percentage of the total of its row
% of Parent Row Total	With multiple fields in the Rows area, calculates the value of each cell as a percentage of the total of its parent field
% of Parent Column Total	With multiple fields in the Columns area, calculates the value of each cell as a percentage of the total of its parent field
% of Parent Total	With multiple fields in the Rows and/or Columns area, calculates the value of each cell as a percentage of its row and column parent
Running Total In	Calculates a running total within the cell's row or column
% Running Total In	Calculates a running total as a percentage within the cell's row or column
Rank Smallest to Largest	Calculates the rank of the cell within the cell's row or column with the smallest cell given a rank of "1"
Rank Largest to Smallest	Calculates the rank of the cell within the cell's row or column with the largest cell given a rank of "1"
% of	Calculates the percent of the cell value relative to another item in the PivotTable
Difference from	Calculates the difference of the cell value from another item in the PivotTable
% Difference From	Calculates the percent difference of the cell value from another item in the PivotTable
Index	Calculates the relative importance of the cell within the PivotTable

To apply these calculations, you will often have to identify a **base field** or **base item**, which is a field or item used as the basis for comparison. For example, if you calculate monthly revenue totals relative to the January total, January is the base item for that calculation.

The PivotTable in Figure 11–23 applies different calculations to the same Revenue field. The Rank Largest to Smallest column presents the total 2029 revenue for hotels in the West and East region ranked from the largest to smallest. The next column calculates the total gross revenue for each hotel. The final column calculates each hotel's revenue as a percentage of the total revenue from its region and the revenue of each region as a percentage of the grand total. The PivotTable provides a clear indication of how revenue totals are related across hotels and regions.

Figure 11–23   Calculated ranks and percentage of parent row totals

	A	B	C	D	E	
1	Year	2029				
2						
3	**Region**	**Hotel Name**	**Rank Largest to Smallest**	**Gross Revenue**	**% of Parent Row Total**	
4	⊟ East	Boca Raton Inn	4	$1,660,894	9.31%	
5		Cocoa Beach Inn	6	$1,579,337	8.85%	
6		Lauderdale Inn & Suites	3	$2,742,348	15.37%	
7		Ormand Beach Inn	5	$1,585,410	8.88%	
8		Palm Beach Inn	2	$3,490,686	19.56%	
9		Port Saint Lucie Inn	8	$1,267,542	7.10%	
10		Vero Beach Inn	7	$1,558,881	8.73%	
11		Miami Beach Inn & Suites	1	$3,961,720	22.20%	
12	**East Total**			**$17,846,817**	**64.42%**	subtotals show the percent of each region's total revenue compared to the grand total
13	⊟ West	Clearwater Inn	4	$1,262,086	12.80%	
14		Coral Inn	3	$1,799,414	18.25%	
15		Naples Inn	5	$1,220,952	12.38%	
16		Sarasota Inn	6	$1,003,070	10.17%	
17		Tampa Inn & Suites	1	$2,618,747	26.56%	
18		Venice Inn & Suites	2	$1,954,322	19.82%	
19	**West Total**			**$9,858,591**	**35.58%**	
20	**Grand Total**			**$27,705,409**	**100.00%**	
21						

revenue rank within each region | gross revenue | percent of total revenue within and across the regions

The PivotTable in Figure 11–24 contains the 2029 monthly revenue totals for the Orlando Inn & Suites. The columns present the total revenue per month, a running total of monthly revenue, the difference in revenue from one month and the next, and the monthly revenue as a percentage of March's total revenue.

Figure 11–24   Monthly revenue calculations

	A	B	C	D	E
1	Year	2029			
2	Hotel Name	Orlando Inn & Suites			
3					
4	**Month**	**Revenue**	**Running Total**	**Difference from Previous Month**	**% of March**
5	Jan	$421,849	$421,849		86.9%
6	Feb	$374,965	$796,814	($46,884)	77.3%
7	Mar	$485,238	$1,282,052	$110,272	100.0%
8	Apr	$480,428	$1,762,481	($4,809)	99.0%
9	May	$478,408	$2,240,889	($2,020)	98.6%
10	Jun	$446,658	$2,687,547	($31,750)	92.0%
11	Jul	$440,231	$3,127,778	($6,427)	90.7%
12	Aug	$418,999	$3,546,777	($21,231)	86.3%
13	Sep	$361,243	$3,908,020	($57,757)	74.4%
14	Oct	$345,847	$4,253,867	($15,396)	71.3%
15	Nov	$373,208	$4,627,075	$27,361	76.9%
16	Dec	$463,062	$5,090,138	$89,854	95.4%
17	**Grand Total**	**$5,090,138**			
18					

monthly gross revenue | running total of gross revenue | difference in revenue from the previous month | revenue as a percent of the March 2029 revenue

Each column provides a different insight into the hotel's monthly revenue. The running total indicates how quickly revenue is generated through the year and can aid in developing the hotel's budget. The difference from one month to the next calculation is useful for planning future expenditures. A hotel manager can quickly determine that September expenses must be cut to make up for nearly $58,000 drop in revenue that month.

Reference

Calculating Values for a PivotTable Field

- Open the Value Field Settings dialog box for the field and click the Show Values As tab.
- To show ranks of items within a field, choose Rank Smallest to Largest or Rank Largest to Smallest.
- To calculate a running total of items within a field, choose Running Total In or % Running Total In.
- To calculate the change from one field item to another, choose Difference From or % Difference From.
- To calculate percentages of PivotTable totals, choose % of Column Total, % of Row Total, or % of Grand Total.
- To calculate percentages of a parent item in the table, choose % Of, % of Parent Column Total, % of Parent Row Total, or % Parent Total.
- Click OK.

Calculating Ranks

In the previous part, you created a PivotTable showing weekly occupancy during the summer of 2029. You will supplement this table now by ranking those weeks in order from most busy to least busy.

To rank items within a field:

1. If you took a break after the previous part, make sure the NP_EX_11_Hotels workbook is open.

2. Go to the **Weekly** worksheet.

3. Drag the **Occupancy Rate** field into the Values area box directly below the Average Occupancy value.

4. Click cell **C6** to select it, click the **PivotTable Analyze** tab on the ribbon, and then in the Active Field group, click the **Field Settings** button. The Value Field Settings dialog box opens.

5. Click the **Show Values As** tab.

6. In the Show values as box, select **Rank Largest to Smallest** and then verify that **Days (Date)** is selected as the Base field because all ranks are determined relative to the occupancy rates within that field.

7. In the Custom name box, enter **Rank** as the name. Refer to Figure 11–25.

Figure 11–25   Ranks for the occupancy field calculation

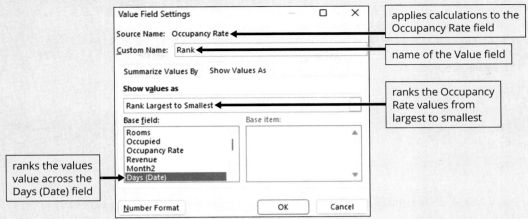

8. Click **OK**. A rank of each week is added to the PivotTable. Refer to Figure 11–26.

Figure 11–26   Weekly occupancy rates ranked

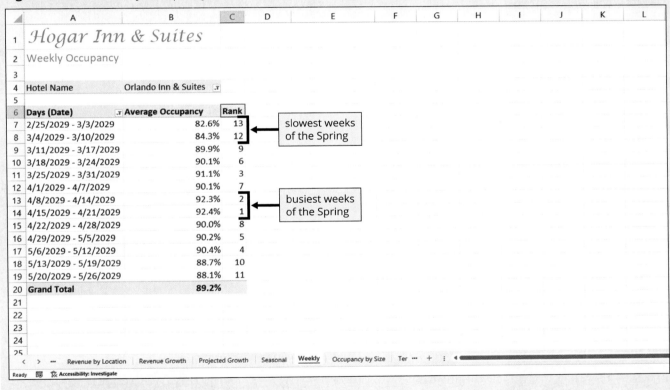

The PivotTable is enhanced by the inclusion of the rank columns, indicating which Spring months are the busiest and which months are the slowest. Elian can use that information when considering staffing and resource needs for each hotel.

Calculating Percent Differences

Elian has collected two years of data to identify which hotels are gaining and losing revenue. You will create a PivotTable comparing total gross revenue by year and hotel and display the percentage growth of each hotel's revenue from 2028 to 2029. First, you'll create the PivotTable of Total Revenue versus Hotel Name.

To create the Total Revenue versus Hotel Name PivotTable:

1. Go to the **Revenue Growth** worksheet.

2. Drag the **Year** field into the Columns area, drag the **Hotel Name** into the Rows area, and drag the **Revenue** field into the Values area.

3. Change Value field name "Sum of Revenue" to **Gross Revenue** and display the revenue totals as currency with no values after the decimal point.

4. Change the PivotTable report layout to a **Tabular layout** and turn on grand totals for the columns only.

Next, you will add a new column displaying the percentage growth in revenue for each hotel.

To calculate percentage growth in revenue for 2029:

1. Drag the **Revenue** field into the Values area directly below the Gross Revenue value field. The new value field as "Sum of Revenue" is added to the PivotTable.

2. Open the Value Field Settings dialog box for the "Sum of Revenue" value field.

3. Change name from Sum of Revenue to **% Change**.

4. Click the **Show Values As** tab.

5. In the Show Values as box, click **% Difference From**.

6. In the Base field box, click **Year** to calculate percentage differences across years.

7. In the Base item box, click **2028**, if necessary, to base all percentages relative to 2028 gross revenue. Refer to Figure 11–27.

Figure 11–27   Percentage changes in revenue calculation

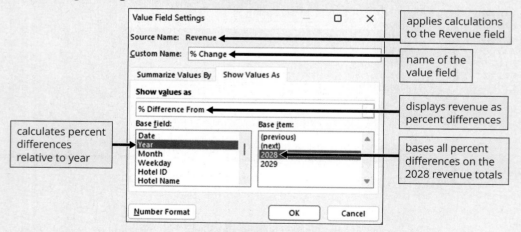

8. Click **OK** to calculate the percent change in revenue from 2028 to 2029.

Two new columns appear on the PivotTable. Column E shows the percent change in revenue from 2028 to 2029 for each hotel. Column C does the same calculation, but the column is blank because there is no percent change in 2028 revenue totals from themselves. To avoid confusing the reader, you will hide this column.

> **Tip** A hidden column is not removed from the worksheet. Instead, it is given a width of 0 pixels, effectively hiding it from view.

9. Right-click the **column C heading**, and then click **Hide** on the shortcut menu. Column C is hidden in the workbook. Refer to Figure 11–28.

Figure 11–28 Percent changes from 2028 to 2029

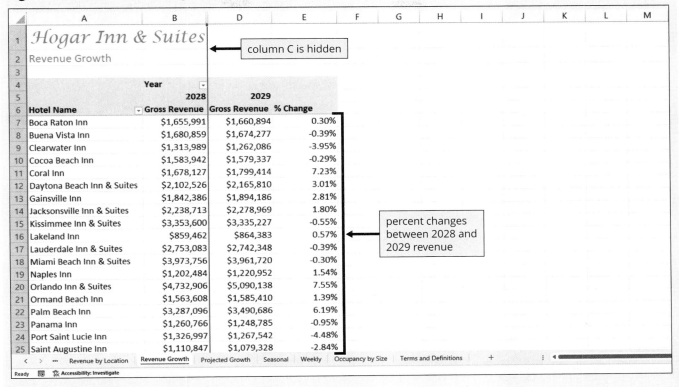

Overall, the Florida hotels saw a revenue increase of 1.34% (cell E31), but this result was not uniform across hotels. The revenue of the Sarasota Inn decreased by 16.04% (cell E26), while the revenue of Coral Inn increased by 7.23% (cell E11). With so many numbers and calculations, the PivotTable can be confusing. You can add a conditional format to make it easier to analyze.

Displaying PivotTables with Conditional Formats

PivotTables do a great job of summarizing large amounts of data, but sometimes it can be overwhelming to wade through all those numbers. One way of making PivotTables more accessible is with a conditional format that highlights key values, painting a visual picture of the data. You can apply a conditional format to the following parts of a PivotTable:

- **Selected Cells.** The conditional format is applied directly to cells selected from the PivotTable.
- **All Cells Showing a Field Value.** The conditional format is associated with a specific field, wherever that field is located within the PivotTable.
- **All Cells Showing Multiple Field Values.** The conditional format is applied to cells where multiple fields intersect, such as the cells representing revenue totals from hotels in each month.

A conditional format is applied within a PivotTable structure. As the PivotTable's layout changes, the conditional format adapts to that new layout, following the field values to their new locations. You will explore two conditional formats that are well suited to PivotTables: icon sets and color scales.

Reference

Creating Icon Sets and Color Scales

- To display a conditional format with icon sets or color scales, select the data range or PivotTable.
- On the Home tab, in the Styles group, click the Conditional Formatting button.
- Click New Rule on the Conditional Formatting menu.
- For PivotTables, select which part of the PivotTable the rule should be applied to.
- For icon sets, select Icon Sets in the Format Style box and specify the value or percent ranges for each icon.
- For color scales, select 2-Color Scale or 3-Color Scale in the Format Style box and specify the color scale for the values in the data range or PivotTable field.
- Click OK.

Creating an Icon Set

An icon set is a conditional format in which different icons are displayed in a cell based on the cell's value. Icon sets are useful for highlighting extreme values or trends in your data.

Elian thinks the PivotTable you just created would benefit from icon sets that include an up arrow if a hotel's revenue increased between 2028 and 2029, a down arrow if revenue declined, and a sideways arrow if the revenue stayed mostly the same. Elian wants to use the up arrow when the revenue increases by more than 1% and the down arrow when the revenue decreases by 1%. The other values should use the sideways arrow. For percentage values, you must enter decimals numbers in the conditional format dialog box. You will create this conditional format now.

To create the icon set conditional format:

1. Click cell **E7** to select a cell in the % Change column.

2. On the ribbon, click the **Home** tab. In the Styles group, click the **Conditional Formatting** button, and then click **New Rule**. The New Formatting Rule dialog box opens.

3. Click the **All cells showing "% Change" values** option button to apply the conditional format to every cell in the % Change column, including the cell displaying the grand total across all hotels.

4. In the Edit the Rule Description section, click the **Format Style arrow**, and then click **Icon Sets**.

5. Click the **Icon Style arrow**, and then click the **3 Arrows (Colored)** icon set with the red arrow pointing down, the yellow arrow pointing sideways, and a green arrow pointing up.

   > **Tip** To change or remove an icon in an icon set click the drop-down list arrow next to the icon image.

6. Click the upper **Type** box, select **Number** and then enter **0.01** in the Value box. The up arrow will appear for hotels that gained more than 1% in revenue.

7. Click the lower **Type** box, select **Number**, and then enter **–0.01**. The down arrow will appear for hotels that lost more than 1% in revenue. Refer to Figure 11–29.

Figure 11–29   Icon set defined for a conditional format

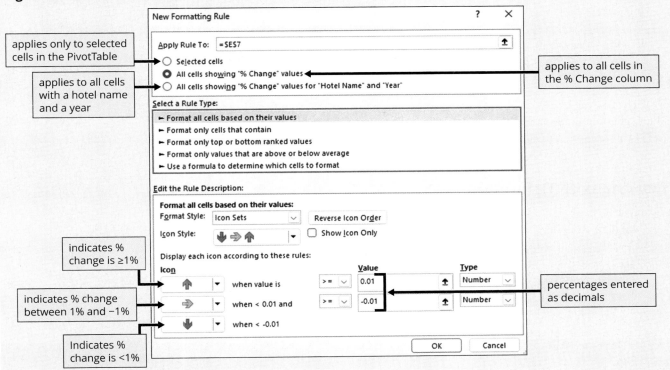

8. Click **OK** to apply the icons to all the values in the % Change column. Refer to Figure 11–30.

Figure 11–30   Icon sets applied to a PivotTable

	A	B	D	E	F	G	H	I	J	K	L	M
6	**Hotel Name**	**Gross Revenue**	**Gross Revenue**	**% Change**								
7	Boca Raton Inn	$1,655,991	$1,660,894 ⇨	0.30%								
8	Buena Vista Inn	$1,680,859	$1,674,277 ⇨	-0.39%								
9	Clearwater Inn	$1,313,989	$1,262,086 ⬇	-3.95%								
10	Cocoa Beach Inn	$1,583,942	$1,579,337 ⇨	-0.29%								
11	Coral Inn	$1,678,127	$1,799,414 ⬆	7.23%								
12	Daytona Beach Inn & Suites	$2,102,526	$2,165,810 ⬆	3.01%								
13	Gainsville Inn	$1,842,386	$1,894,186 ⬆	2.81%								
14	Jacksonsville Inn & Suites	$2,238,713	$2,278,969 ⬆	1.80%								
15	Kissimmee Inn & Suites	$3,353,600	$3,335,227 ⇨	-0.55%								
16	Lakeland Inn	$859,462	$864,383 ⇨	0.57%								
17	Lauderdale Inn & Suites	$2,753,083	$2,742,348 ⇨	-0.39%								
18	Miami Beach Inn & Suites	$3,973,756	$3,961,720 ⇨	-0.30%								
19	Naples Inn	$1,202,484	$1,220,952 ⬆	1.54%								
20	Orlando Inn & Suites	$4,732,906	$5,090,138 ⬆	7.55%								
21	Ormand Beach Inn	$1,563,608	$1,585,410 ⬆	1.39%								
22	Palm Beach Inn	$3,287,096	$3,490,686 ⬆	6.19%								
23	Panama Inn	$1,260,766	$1,248,785 ⇨	-0.95%								
24	Port Saint Lucie Inn	$1,326,997	$1,267,542 ⬇	-4.48%								
25	Saint Augustine Inn	$1,110,847	$1,079,328 ⬇	-2.84%								
26	Sarasota Inn	$1,194,679	$1,003,070 ⬇	-16.04%								
27	Tampa Inn & Suites	$2,559,079	$2,618,747 ⬆	2.33%								
28	Venice Inn & Suites	$1,898,220	$1,954,322 ⬆	2.96%								
29	Vero Beach Inn	$1,508,388	$1,558,881 ⬆	3.35%								
30	Windemere Inn	$1,215,069	$1,200,426 ⬇	-1.21%								
31	**Grand Total**	**$47,896,573**	**$48,536,938** ⬆	**1.34%**								

icons based on the percentage change in gross revenue

< > ⋯ Revenue by Location Revenue Growth Projected Growth Seasonal Weekly Occupancy by Size Ter ⋯ + ⋮ ◀

Ready   🔳   ♿ Accessibility: Investigate

Trouble? If your icons are different, you may have mistyped something in the Conditional Formatting Rules Manager. Click the Conditional Formatting button, click Modify Rules, select the conditional format for the Icon Set, click Edit Rule, check the settings in your dialog box against those shown in Figure 11–29, correct any mistakes, and then click OK.

The arrow icons clearly identify hotels whose revenue increased significantly and those with a significant drop in revenue. Green up arrows figure prominently throughout the worksheet, so it is quickly apparent that the Florida hotels are evenly split between those that had increased revenue, those that had decreased revenue, and those that stayed relatively unchanged.

Working with Color Scales

A color scale is a conditional format that uses progressively darker (or lighter) shades of fill color based on the values in a range of cell. The varying shades in the color scale quickly identify the extreme values of the PivotTable field and highlight important trends in the data. Remember to keep your audience in mind, as some people are unable to distinguish between colors.

Elian wants the PivotTable to highlight the seasonal occupancy rates with a color scale that goes from red (low occupancy) through yellow and up to green (high occupancy). As with icon sets, you can apply the color scale to entire fields within the PivotTable.

To apply a color scale to seasonal occupancy rates:

1. Go to the **Seasonal** worksheet and click cell **C8** to select it.

2. On the Home tab, in the Styles group, click the **Conditional Formatting** button, and then click **New Rule**. The New Formatting Rule dialog box opens.

3. Click the **All cells showing "Average Occupancy" values for "Hotel Name" and "Season"** to apply the conditional format to cells at the intersection of the Hotel Name and Season field values.

4. Click the **Format Style** arrow, and then click **3-Color Scale** to choose a color gradient going from red up to green. Refer to Figure 11–31.

Figure 11–31   Rule to define a color scale

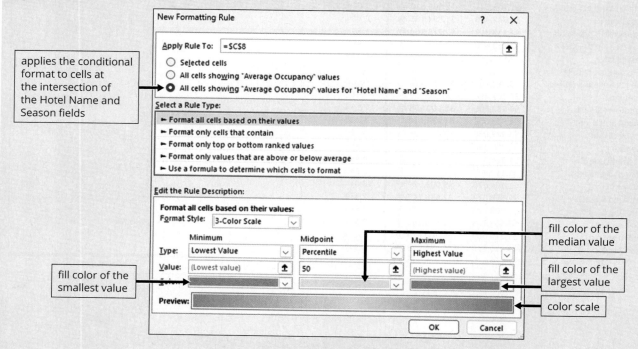

5. Click **OK**. A color scale is added to all the seasonal occupancy rates in the PivotTable. Refer to Figure 11–32.

Figure 11–32   Color scale applied to the seasonal occupancy rates

	A	B	C	D	E
6	**Average Occupancy**	**Season**			
7	**Hotel Name**	**Winter**	**Spring**	**Summer**	**Autumn**
8	Palm Beach Inn	80.8%	90.2%	81.2%	69.3%
9	Orlando Inn & Suites	81.6%	89.4%	82.3%	71.0%
10	Coral Inn	76.5%	85.8%	77.2%	68.4%
11	Tampa Inn & Suites	74.9%	83.7%	75.0%	66.3%
12	Cocoa Beach Inn	71.2%	81.9%	71.7%	62.1%
13	Lauderdale Inn & Suites	70.8%	80.9%	70.5%	61.2%
14	Kissimmee Inn & Suites	73.8%	80.5%	73.5%	64.4%
15	Ormand Beach Inn	69.4%	80.3%	68.9%	60.5%
16	Jacksonsville Inn & Suites	70.9%	79.5%	72.3%	61.3%
17	Venice Inn & Suites	70.4%	78.5%	70.6%	62.3%
18	Boca Raton Inn	66.7%	77.4%	67.1%	58.1%
19	Gainsville Inn	68.8%	76.1%	68.5%	60.7%
20	Daytona Beach Inn & Suites	68.2%	75.2%	69.4%	58.9%
21	Windemere Inn	65.8%	74.6%	65.0%	57.4%
22	Miami Beach Inn & Suites	64.0%	73.3%	63.9%	55.3%
23	Clearwater Inn	61.3%	68.0%	61.3%	53.8%
24	Vero Beach Inn	60.1%	68.0%	58.9%	51.5%
25	Buena Vista Inn	60.8%	66.7%	61.0%	53.2%
26	Port Saint Lucie Inn	57.5%	66.4%	57.8%	49.5%
27	Lakeland Inn	58.9%	65.3%	59.3%	52.2%
28	Naples Inn	57.8%	64.9%	57.7%	51.0%
29	Saint Augustine Inn	55.6%	62.2%	55.9%	48.5%
30	Sarasota Inn	51.7%	58.1%	53.4%	46.8%
31	Panama Inn	50.9%	57.0%	51.8%	44.4%

darker green indicates highest occupancy

darker red indicates lowest occupancy

The color scale provides additional visual information about the occupancy rates across seasons and hotels. For example, the Panama Inn (row 31) had low occupancy rates as indicated by the dark red fill across all four seasons, while the Palm Beach Inn had high or moderate occupancy rates in every season.

Exploring the PivotTable Cache

The information used to create a PivotTable is stored within a data structure called the **PivotTable cache**. The cache contains a copy of the PivotTable's data source optimized for calculation, which makes PivotTables very responsive to changes in content and layout. When you modify a PivotTable layout, Excel retrieves the data from the cache, not the original data source. If the data has been finalized and will not change, you could even delete the data source and work entirely from the information stored in the cache. (Be sure you no longer need the data source before doing that!) The existence of the cache is also why you must refresh PivotTables whenever the data changes. Refreshing a PivotTable repopulates the cache so that it reflects the most recent version of the data source.

Sharing a Cache Between PivotTables

The downside of having a PivotTable that will quickly recalculate as its layout changes is an increased file size because the same data is duplicated in both the workbook and the cache. Excel minimizes this problem by having all PivotTables operate from the same cache. The result is that all PivotTables also share the same fields and groups because that information is part of the cache. Refer to Figure 11–33.

Figure 11–33   PivotTable cache shared by multiple PivotTables

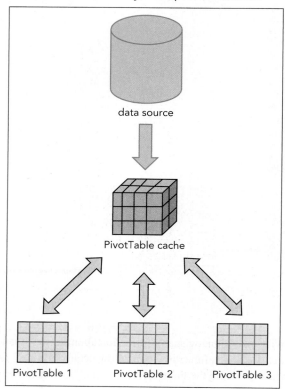

A consequence of sharing the same cache is that anything done in one PivotTable becomes part of the cache and is instantly applied to the other PivotTables. For example, if you manually group dates by months, that grouping will be reflected across all PivotTables sharing a common cache. If you change that grouping in any of those PivotTables, the same change will be automatically applied to all PivotTables.

One solution to this problem is to create separate caches for different PivotTables so that you can change the structure and contents of one PivotTable without affecting the others. Both caches connect to the same data source, so that the impact of refreshing the data source will still be reflected in both caches, but changing one cache has no impact on the other. A separate cache increases the size of the workbook file but will give you more flexibility in designing your PivotTables. Refer to Figure 11–34.

Figure 11-34   Multiple PivotTable caches

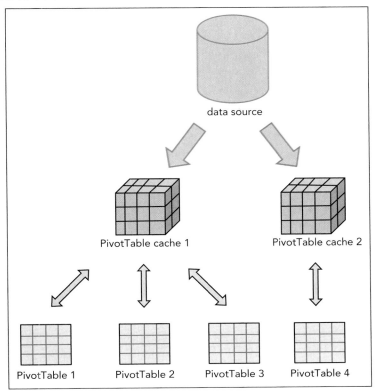

Creating a New Cache

To create a separate cache, you will use a tool that was available in older versions of Excel. Prior to Excel 2016, PivotTables were created using the **PivotTable Wizard** to step the user through the process of creating a PivotTable. One of the steps in the PivotTable Wizard is an option to create the PivotTable from an existing cache or from a new cache. The PivotTable Wizard is still available, though not directly accessible from the ribbon.

Reference

Creating a PivotTable from a New Cache

- Press ALT+D,P to open the PivotTable Wizard.
- Specify the type of data and the type of report to create in Step 1 of the wizard.
- Specify the data source in Step 2 of the wizard.
- Click No to create the report using a new PivotTable cache.
- Specify the location of the PivotTable report in Step 3 of the wizard.
- Click Finish to insert the PivotTable report.

Elian wants you to create a new PivotTable that will project future performance of the hotels in the QC Inn chain. Because the structure of this PivotTable will be different from the PivotTables you've already created, you will use a separate cache for it. You will create this PivotTable using the PivotTable Wizard.

To create a PivotTable from a new cache:

1. Go to the **Projected Growth** worksheet and click cell **A6** to select it, if necessary.

2. Press **ALT+D** and release both keys, and then immediately press **P** to launch the PivotTable Wizard. The PivotTable and PivotChart Wizard dialog box opens to the Step 1 of 3.

3. Verify that the **Microsoft Excel list or database** option button is selected as the data source and the **PivotTable** option button is selected as the type of report to create.

4. Click **Next**. The second step dialog box appears.

5. In the Range box, type **Hotels** (the name assigned to the Excel table containing the hotel data) as the data source of the PivotTable, and then click **Next**.

6. Click **No** when Excel prompts you to use an existing cache for the new PivotTable. This puts the new PivotTable you are creating in its own, separate cache. The Step 3 dialog box appears.

    > **Key Step** You must click No; otherwise, Excel will not base the new PivotTable on a new cache.

7. Verify that the **Existing worksheet** option button is selected and the expression **=$A$6** appears in the box.

8. Click **Finish** to create the new PivotTable report.

9. Change the name of the PivotTable to **Projected Growth**. Refer to Figure 11–35.

Figure 11–35   New PivotTable report based on its own cache

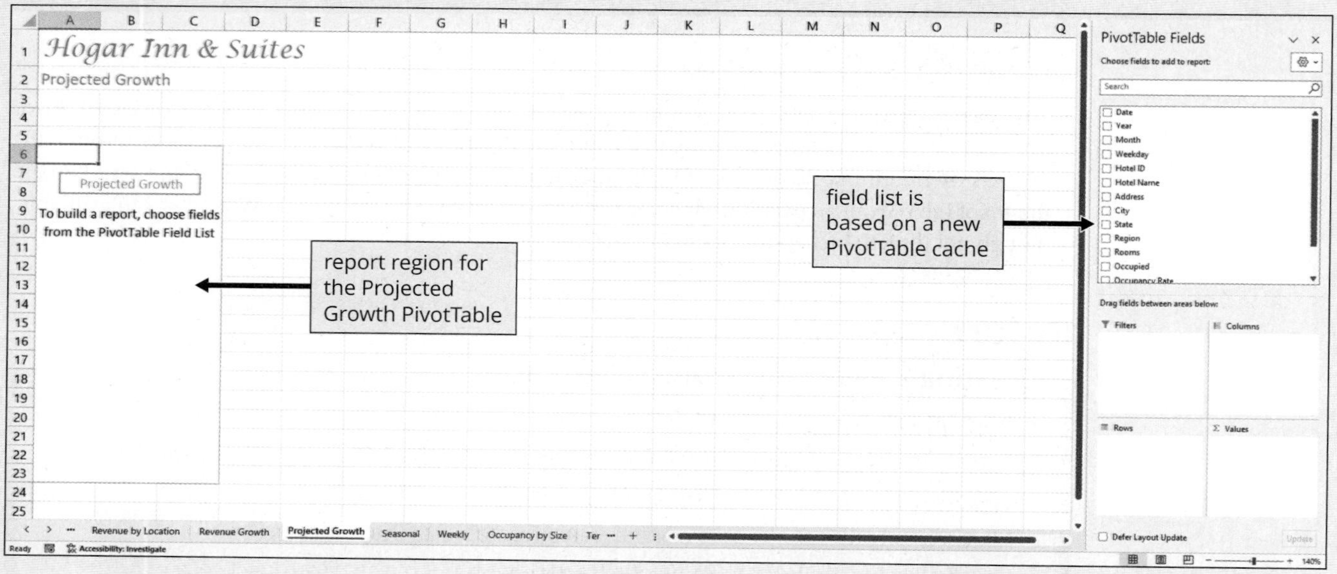

With the Projected Growth PivotTable generated from a new cache, you are ready to create a PivotTable projecting future revenue. That table will involve using calculated items and calculated fields.

Insight

Counting Your Caches

In a workbook with multiple PivotTables and multiple caches, you might want to know exactly how many caches are in use. Excel does not provide a direct way to get that information, but you can find out using the Excel programming language, Visual Basic for Applications (VBA). To find the total number of caches in a workbook, do the following:

1. Press ALT+F11 to open the Visual Basic Editor window.
2. Press CTRL+G to open a window in which you can enter VBA commands.
3. Type ?ActiveWorkbook.PivotCaches.Count and then press ENTER. Excel returns a count of caches in the workbook.
4. Press ALT+Q to close the Visual Basic editor and return to the workbook.

Each PivotTable cache is given an index number. The first PivotTable cache is given an index of 1, the second an index of 2, and so forth. To identify the index number of the cache used for a specific PivotTable, do the following:

1. Select any cell in the PivotTable and then press ALT+F11.
2. Press CTRL+G, and then enter the command ?ActiveCell.PivotTable.CacheIndex. Excel will return the index number of the cache.
3. Press ALT+Q to close the editor and return to the PivotTable.

You can automate this process so that you don't have to reopen the Visual Basic Editor window every time. You do this by creating custom functions using the language of VBA, which can then be called from any cell within the workbook. Writing custom VBA functions is beyond the scope of this module, but you can find examples of the code online.

Working with Calculated Items and Calculated Fields

PivotTables are not limited to the list of calculations supplied by Excel. You can enter your own formulas to create calculated items and calculated fields.

Creating a Calculated Item

A **calculated item** is a user-defined formula for calculations involving items within a PivotTable field. For example, within the Hotel Name field, you could create a calculated item that calculates the difference in revenue between one group of hotels and another. A calculated item appears as a new item within the field and can be moved, sorted, and filtered just like any field item. However, because it's a calculated item, any changes to the data are automatically reflected in its value.

Calculated items are part of the PivotTable cache. A calculated item in one PivotTable is shared by PivotTables using the same cache. Calculated items cannot be shared between PivotTables of different caches.

Reference

Creating a Calculated Item or Calculated Field

- Select any cell in a PivotTable field.
- On the PivotTable Analyze tab, in the Calculations group, click the Fields, Items, & Sets button.
- Click Calculated Item or click Calculated Field.
- Enter a name for the calculated item or field.
- In the Formula box, for a calculated item enter a formula that performs calculations on items within a field or for a calculated field, enter a formula that performs calculations between fields in the PivotTable's data source.
- Click OK.

Elian wants you to create a PivotTable that shows the revenue generated for each year and hotel. Then, he wants you to create a calculated item projecting next year's revenue for each hotel.

To create a PivotTable of 2028 and 2029 performance:

1. With the Projected Growth PivotTable still selected, drag the **Hotel Name** field to the Filters area box, drag the **Year** field to the Rows area box, and then drag the **Revenue** field to the Values area box.

2. Change Value field name from "Sum of Revenue" to **Gross Revenue** and display the revenue totals as currency with no digits after the decimal point.

3. Change the PivotTable report layout to **Tabular** form and turn off grand totals for both rows and columns. Refer to Figure 11–36.

Figure 11–36   Gross revenue from all hotels

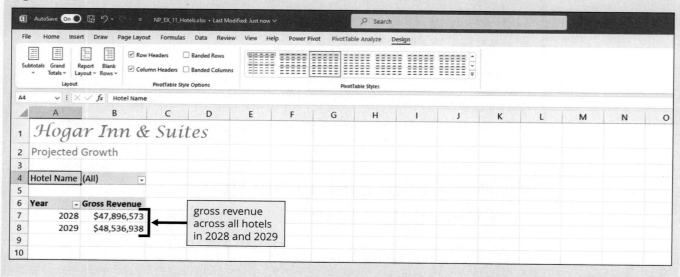

To project next year's revenue based on the 2028 and 2029 values, Elian assumes that revenues will increase at the same rate they increased between 2028 and 2029. The formula to calculate the 2030 revenue is:

$$2030\ revenue = (2029\ revenue) \times \frac{2029\ revenue}{2028\ revenue}$$

You will create a calculated item based on this formula and add it to the PivotTable.

To create a calculated item that calculates the 2030 revenue:

1. Click cell **A7** to select a cell in the Year column.

2. On the ribbon, click the **PivotTable Analyze** tab. In the Calculations group, click the **Fields, Items, & Sets** button, and then click **Calculated Item**. The Insert Calculated Item in "Year" dialog box opens.

3. In the Name box, replace the default name Formula1 with **2030 (Projected)** and then press **TAB** to go the Formula box.

4. Type **=** to begin the formula, click **2029** in the Items box, and then click **Insert Item**. Excel inserts = '2029' into the Formula box.

5. Type ***(** to continue the formula, click **2029** in the Items box, and then click **Insert Item**.

6. Type **/** for the division operator, click **2028** in the Items box, click **Insert Item**, and then type **)** to finish the formula. The complete formula ='2029'*('2029'/'2028') is entered the Formulas box. Refer to Figure 11–37.

Figure 11–37   Insert Calculated Item dialog box

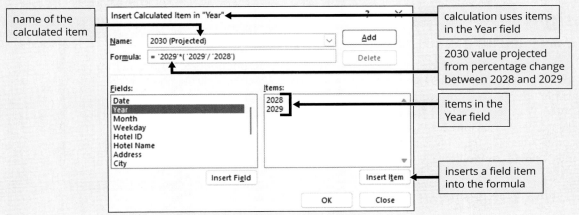

7. Click **OK**. The 2030 (Projected) formula is entered as a calculated item into the PivotTable and projected gross revenue across all hotels is displayed in cell B9. Refer to Figure 11–38.

Figure 11–38   Projected gross revenue from all hotels in 2030

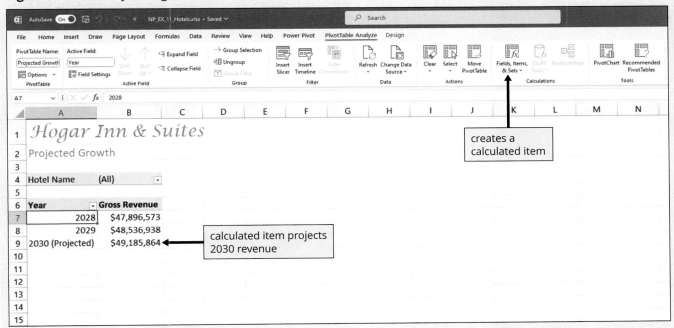

Next, you'll view projected revenues for individual hotels within Florida.

8. Click the **Filter** button in cell B4, select **Sarasota Inn** from the list of hotels, and then click **OK**. The 2030 revenue for this hotel is calculated in cell B9 as $842,192, which is a decline of more than $160,000.

9. Click the **Filter** button in cell B4, click **Coral Inn** in the hotel list, and then click **OK** to view the projected income for 2030. Under the current trend, annual gross revenue for this hotel is projected to increase to about $1.93 million, which is an increase of more than $130,000.

10. Click the **Filter** button in cell B4, select **(All)** to remove the filter, and then click **OK**. The PivotTable again shows projected revenue across all hotels.

Note that in the formula for the calculated item, you never specified that the revenue field should be used in the calculation. Calculated items can be applied to any numeric field from the PivotTable. The only exception is that you cannot use calculated items for fields summarized with the average, standard deviation, or variance functions.

Insight

Calculated Items and Grouping

A PivotTable can have calculated items and grouped fields, but not both. The structure of the PivotTable cache does not allow for it. This is true even if the calculated item is placed within one field and the grouping is done on an entirely separate field. If you need to use both calculated items and grouped fields in a report, the best option is to create separate PivotTable caches: one for PivotTables with calculated items and one for PivotTables containing grouped fields. If necessary, you can then copy and paste the PivotTable values into a single comprehensive report showing both features.

Creating a Calculated Field

A calculated item performs calculations on items within a field. A **calculated field** is a user-defined formula for calculations across one or more fields. For example, a calculated field could multiply the number of vacant rooms by the price of each room to calculate the total revenue lost from vacancies. Calculated fields are added to the list of PivotTable fields, appearing as just another set of fields. The effect would be the same as if you added them as calculated columns to the original data source.

A measure of a hotel's financial status is the hotel's Average Daily Rate (ADR), which measures the revenue generated per occupied room. The formula is:

$$ADR = \frac{revenue}{occupied\ rooms}$$

The ADR value tells a financial analyst how much the hotel is receiving from each occupied room and provides an indicator of the average room price. Another measure used in the hotel industry in the Revenue per Available Room (RevPar) which measures the revenue generated per room (whether occupied or not). The formula is:

$$RevPar = \frac{revenue}{rooms}$$

The RevPar value tells an analyst how the average price per room is affected by vacancies. A hotel might have a very high ADR value if its rooms are expensive, but a low RevPar value if it cannot fill those rooms. Such a situation might lead a hotel owner to reduce prices to attract more business, reduce vacancies, and increase total revenue even though less is charged per room.

The Hotels data source doesn't include an ADR or RevPar field. Elian wants you to add these to the PivotTable as calculated fields, showing values for 2028 and 2029 and projecting those values into 2030. You will start by creating a calculated field to calculate ADR.

To create a calculated field for ADR:

1. On the PivotTable Analyze tab, in the Calculations group, click **Fields, Items, & Sets**, and then click **Calculated Field**. The Insert Calculated Field dialog box opens.
2. In the Name box, replace the default Field1 name with **ADR**, and then press **TAB**.
3. In the Formula box, type **=** to begin the formula, click **Revenue** in the Fields list, and then click **Insert Field**.

   Tip Fields do not have to be displayed in the PivotTable to be accessible to a calculated field formula.

4. Type **/** for the division operator, click **Occupied** in the Fields list, and then click **Insert Field**. The formula = Revenue/Occupied appears in the Formula box. Refer to Figure 11–39.

Figure 11–39   ADR calculated field

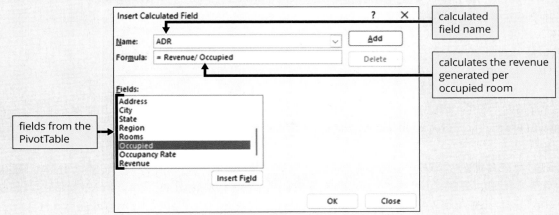

5. Click **OK**. The Sum of ADR is added to the PivotTable with ADR calculations based on all the hotels in the data source.

6. Click cell **C6** to select it, and then in the Active Field group, change the value of the Active Field box from Sum of ADR to **ADR** followed by a blank space to avoid conflict with the calculated field name.

7. On the PivotTable Analyze tab, in the Active Field group, click the **Field Settings** button, change the number format of the ADR field to currency with two decimal places, and then click **OK** in each dialog box to return to the worksheet. Refer to Figure 11-40.

Figure 11–40   Revenue per occupied room from all hotels

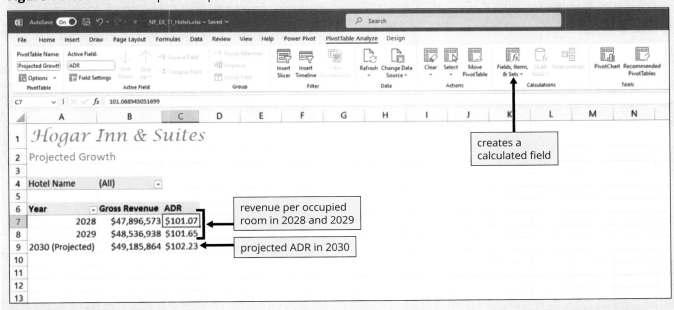

The average income from an occupied room across all hotels is $101.65 in 2029 and is projected to rise to $102.23 in 2030. Elian wants to know how individual hotels compare to this.

8. In the Hotel Name filter, select **Sarasota Inn**. The ADR value is $95.11 in 2029 and is projected to decrease to $94.40 in 2030. While that might not seem like much, remember that is revenue lost per occupied room for every day of the year. In a hotel with hundreds of occupied rooms, that can total up to thousands of dollars in a year.

9. In the Hotel Name filter, select **Coral Inn**. The ADR value in 2029 is $87.70 and is projected to rise to $88.79 in 2030, a projected increase of more than $1 per occupied room.

10. In the Hotel Name filter, select **(All)**, once again showing the ADR values from across all hotels in Florida.

You will use the same process to add RevPar as a calculated field to the PivotTable.

To create a calculated field for RevPar:

1. On the PivotTable Analyze tab, in the Calculations group, click the **Fields, Items, & Sets** button, and then click **Calculated Field**. The Insert Calculated Field dialog box opens.

2. In the Name box Enter **RevPar** as the field name, and then press **TAB**.

3. In the Formula box, enter **= Revenue/Rooms** as the formula, using the Fields box and the Insert Field button.

4. Click **OK** to create the calculated field and return to the workbook.

5. Click cell **D6** and change the value the Active Fields box from Sum of RevPar to **RevPar** followed by a blank space. Refer to Figure 11–41.

Figure 11–41   Revenue per room from all hotels

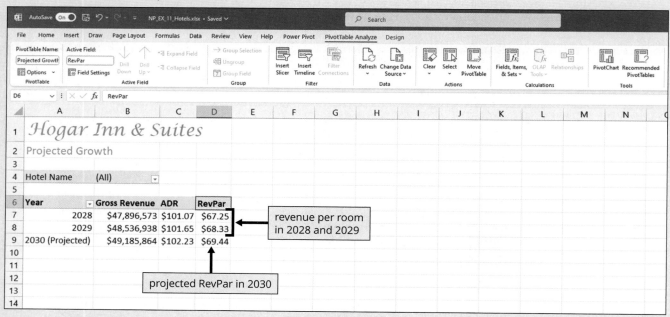

For all hotels, the revenue per room is projected to increase from $68.33 in 2029 to $69.44 in 2030. Elian wants you to compare this to individual hotels.

6. In the Hotel Name filter, select **Sarasota Inn**. The RevPar value for that hotel is $49.97 in 2029 and is projected to decrease by almost $8 per room to $42.07 in 2030.

7. In the Hotel Name filter, select **Coral Inn**. RevPar values for that hotel are projected to increase by more $5 per room between 2029 and 2030, rising from a 2029 value of $67.53 to $72.61 in 2030.

8. In the Hotel Name filter, select **(All)** to return to the RevPar values for all hotels in the chain.

9. **sam↑** Save the workbook, and then close it.

The projected RevPar numbers for the Sarasota Inn are particularly concerning to Elian as they indicate a hotel with too many vacancies for its size to bring in substantial revenue.

One possible solution is for the Sarasota Inn to lower its prices to attract more customers, reducing its vacancy rate. The other alternatives are to attract more customers with customer incentives and reward programs. The inn might also need to upgrade its facilities or use flexible pricing models that will take advantage of periods of high customer demand.

Behind the Math of Calculated Items and Fields

The formulas for calculated items and fields can accept any worksheet function that uses numbers as arguments and returns a numeric value, such as the AVERAGE, SUM, or COUNT functions. However, calculated items and calculated formulas cannot use text functions, nor can they reference data outside of the PivotTable. You could not, for example, include the VLOOKUP function in the formula for a calculated item or field because it will reference data outside of the PivotTable. Only data residing within another PivotTable field or entered explicitly as a constant is available.

The other important consideration is that calculated fields are always based on sums of fields. For example, the ADR calculations in Figure 11–40 are the equivalent of taking the sum of the revenue from all the hotels and dividing that sum by the total number of rented rooms. But because calculated fields are limited to sums, you could not, for example, create a calculated field from an average value, such as the average occupancy rate.

The fact that calculated fields are limited only to sums can lead to incorrect results. The PivotTable in Figure 11–42 displays the number of occupied rooms and the price per room for a select group of hotels on a single day. The Income field is calculated as the product of the Occupied by Price per Room fields.

Figure 11–42   Calculated formula applied to a grand total

	A	B	C	D	E	F	G	H	I	J
1	Date	4/15/2029 ⫟								
2										
3	**Row Labels** ⫟	**Occupied**	**Price per Room**	**Income**						
4	Daytona Beach Inn & Suites	67	$112.88	$7,562.63						
5	Jacksonville Inn & Suites	73	$95.13	$6,944.20						
6	Kissimmee Inn & Suites	97	$114.00	$11,058.00						
7	Lauderdale Inn & Suites	88	$103.50	$9,108.00						
8	Miami Beach Inn & Suites	106	$133.00	$14,098.00						
9	Orlando Inn & Suites	117	$150.33	$17,589.00						
10	Tampa Inn & Suites	87	$107.39	$9,343.34						
11	Venice Inn & Suites	63	$94.99	$5,984.21						
12	**Grand Total**	**698**	**$911.22**	**$636,029.19**						
13										
14			Sum of Income	$81,687.38						
15										
16										
17										
18										
19										

Income = Occupied*Price per Room

grand total incorrectly shows total income as the total occupied rooms multiplied by the sum of the price per room

correct total income

The income calculations are correct for each hotel, but the grand total makes no sense since you would not take the sum of the Price per Room field and multiply that value by the number of occupied rooms. Doing so gives a total income for that day of more than $636,000, while the correct value is closer to $81,000.

Always confirm that any field used in a calculated field formula makes sense when it is summed. The room price field does not make sense to sum in this text context, nor would a field such as the age of the hotel. In those cases, avoid displaying subtotals and grand totals for tables for the calculated field so you do not confuse anyone using your workbook. Another way to solve this problem is to create a calculated measure, which you'll do in the next part.

Proskills

Documenting Calculated Items and Fields

As PivotTables grow in size and complexity, it is helpful to document your work. You should always give PivotTable fields and calculations clear and descriptive names. Choose formats that are appropriate for the type of data you are displaying and apply conditional formats if appropriate to highlight key features in tables.

You should document any customized calculations used in a PivotTable somewhere in the workbook. You can create the documentation sheet, or you can have Excel create a list of calculated items and fields by doing the following:

1. Select the PivotTable whose calculated items and fields you want to document.
2. On the PivotTable Analyze tab, in the Calculations group, click the Fields, Items, & Sets button, and then click List Formulas.

Excel will create a new worksheet describing all the calculated items and fields, including the name of the items and the fields, the formulas involved, and the solution order. This is a static list, so if you add to or edit the calculated items and fields, you must regenerate the list of formulas.

You have finished designing PivotTables for the data in the Hotels table. In the next session, you will explore design issues involved with creating PivotTables from data stored in an Excel Data Model.

Part 11.2 Quick Check

1. How do you display the rank (smallest to largest) of a PivotTable field?

2. Conditional formats can be applied to which parts of a PivotTable?

3. What is the PivotTable cache?

4. If hotels are grouped by size in one PivotTable, how are they displayed in other PivotTables sharing the same cache?

5. How do you create a PivotTable with its own cache?

6. What is the difference between a calculated item and a calculated field?

7. How is the value of a calculated field summarized within a PivotTable?

8. What is a potential mistake you could make with calculated fields?

Part 11.3 Visual Overview: PivotTable Measures

Tables in the Data Model include **measures**, which are summary calculations made on fields in the table. Daily Revenue and Royalties are both measures in the Stays table.

The **Distinct Count function** counts the unique values within a field. Here, the Distinct Count function counts the number of days in each month.

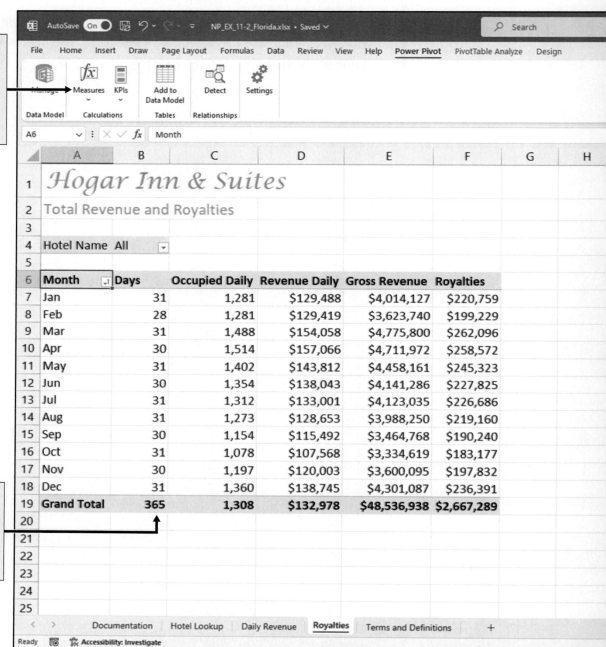

Month	Days	Occupied Daily	Revenue Daily	Gross Revenue	Royalties
Jan	31	1,281	$129,488	$4,014,127	$220,759
Feb	28	1,281	$129,419	$3,623,740	$199,229
Mar	31	1,488	$154,058	$4,775,800	$262,096
Apr	30	1,514	$157,066	$4,711,972	$258,572
May	31	1,402	$143,812	$4,458,161	$245,323
Jun	30	1,354	$138,043	$4,141,286	$227,825
Jul	31	1,312	$133,001	$4,123,035	$226,686
Aug	31	1,273	$128,653	$3,988,250	$219,160
Sep	30	1,154	$115,492	$3,464,768	$190,240
Oct	31	1,078	$107,568	$3,334,619	$183,177
Nov	30	1,197	$120,003	$3,600,095	$197,832
Dec	31	1,360	$138,745	$4,301,087	$236,391
Grand Total	**365**	**1,308**	**$132,978**	**$48,536,938**	**$2,667,289**

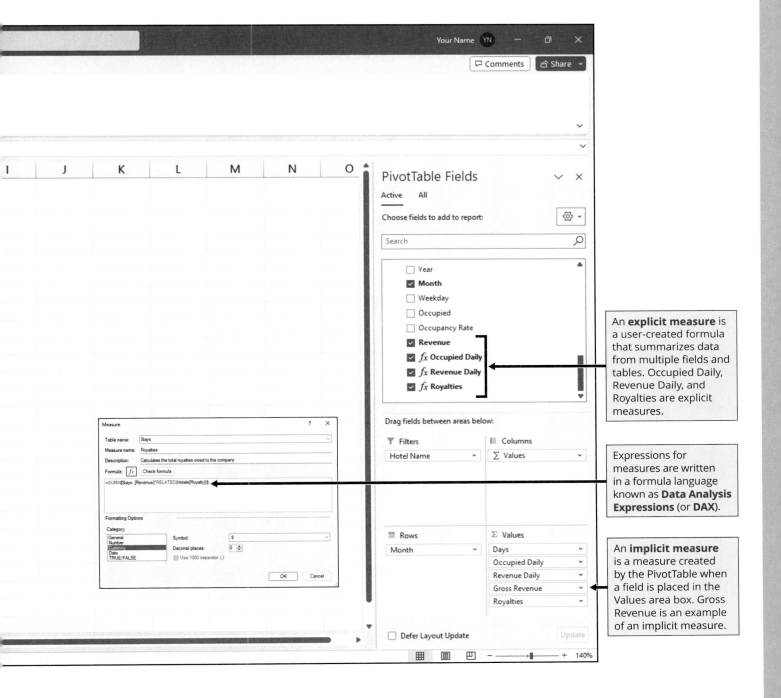

An **explicit measure** is a user-created formula that summarizes data from multiple fields and tables. Occupied Daily, Revenue Daily, and Royalties are explicit measures.

Expressions for measures are written in a formula language known as **Data Analysis Expressions** (or **DAX**).

An **implicit measure** is a measure created by the PivotTable when a field is placed in the Values area box. Gross Revenue is an example of an implicit measure.

Introducing PivotTable Design under the Data Model

So far, you have worked with PivotTables that summarized data from a single Excel table. This kind of PivotTable is referred to as a **standard PivotTable** because it relies on a data source within the workbook from an Excel table or a data range, and it includes many standard tools such as automatic sorting of dates, grouping, and calculated items and fields.

The downside to placing all the data into one table or range is that you duplicated a lot of information. For example, the Hotels table included the name of the hotel, its size, and its location in every table record. Re-entering the same data is inefficient and introduces opportunities for data-entry errors. From a data management perspective, it's much better to put hotel-specific information in one table, data on the daily operations in another table, and then connect the two tables via a common field using Power Pivot.

Standard PivotTables and PivotTables created from multiple tables in the Data Model do not support the same features. For example, you can create group field items in a standard PivotTable, but you can't with a PivotTable based on the Data Model. Figure 11–43 lists features that are supported by each type of PivotTable.

Figure 11–43   Features of standard PivotTables and PivotTables from the Data Model

Feature	Standard PivotTable	Data Model PivotTable
Product function	✔	
Count Numbers function	✔	
Distinct Count function		✔
Show Report Filter Pages tool	✔	
Drill into a PivotTable cell	✔	✔ (first 1000 rows)
Calculated items	✔	
Calculated fields	✔	
Grouping	✔	
Show Items with No Data option	✔	
Hierarchies		✔
Including filtered items in totals		✔
Connect multiple tables		✔
Calculated measures		✔
DAX functions		✔
Named sets		✔

The two PivotTable types are complementary. Sometimes you will use standard PivotTables, and other times you will use the Data Model. Standard PivotTables are quick to set up but do not support the more advanced features available through Power Pivot. So, you might use standard PivotTables for quick analyses and Power Pivot for large projects with custom applications.

Elian created another workbook providing detailed information on operations in 2029 using data stored in the Data Model. You will open that workbook to work with PivotTables in that in the Data Model.

To open the Data Model workbook:

1. **sam ⬇** Open the **NP_EX_11-2.xlsx** workbook located in the **Excel11 > Module** folder included with your Data Files, and then save the workbook as **NP_EX_11_Florida** in the location specified by your instructor.

2. In the Documentation worksheet, enter your name and the date in the range B3:B4.

3. On the ribbon, click the **Power Pivot** tab, and then in the Data Model group, click the **Manage** button. Power Pivot opens.

4. Review the contents of the Hotels and Stays tables.

5. On the Home tab, in the View group, click the **Diagram View** button to view the relationship between the Hotels and Stays tables.

6. Close Power Pivot and return to the workbook.

The Hotels table contains information about the 24 hotels in Florida. The Stays table describes daily stays at the hotels during 2029. The Hotels and Stays tables are connected via the common HotelID field in a one-to-many relationship.

Insight

Named Sets and the Data Model

In a standard PivotTable, the combination of fields is repeated for every PivotTable level. For example, you cannot choose to display one set of months for one year in your PivotTable and a different set of months for a different year. You must display the same set of months for both years.

PivotTables based on the Data Model allow for **named sets** to define which fields are displayed within each part of the PivotTable. The named set feature allows for asymmetric PivotTables in which the list of fields can differ within the same PivotTable. This means you could display one set of financial calculations for one year and a different set for another year.

To create a named set, on the PivotTable Analyze tab, in the Calculations group, click the Field, Items, & Sets button. You then define sets based on items in the PivotTable rows or PivotTable columns. Named sets are very useful in removing extraneous or irrelevant data from a final PivotTable report.

Calculating Distinct Counts

A **distinct count** is a count of the unique values from a field. This is different from the COUNT function, which counts both unique values and duplicates. The DISTINCTCOUNT function is available in PivotTables created from the Data Model.

Elian wants distinct counts used in a PivotTable analyzing daily sales across all the Florida hotels. You will begin creating a PivotTable displaying the number of days within each month the hotels were open.

To begin creating the PivotTable with the open days count:

1. Go to the **Daily Revenue** worksheet. A PivotTable report area named "Daily Revenue" is already set up in this worksheet.

2. Drag the **Month** field from the Stays table into the Rows area box, drag the **Date** field from the Stays table into the Values area box, and then drag the **Hotel Name** field from the Hotels table into the Filters area box.

3. Change the format of the Count of Date field to a number value with no decimal places.

   With Data Model PivotTables, month names are not automatically sorted in chronological order. You'll apply the custom sort list to sort by month.

4. Click the **Filter** button in cell A6, and then click **More Sort Options**. The Sort (Month) dialog box opens.

5. Click the **Ascending (A to Z)** by option button and verify that Month appears in the box.

6. Click **More Options**. The More Sort Options (Month) dialog box opens.

7. Click the **Sort automatically every time the report is updated** check box to deselect it.

8. Click the **First key sort order** box and click the **Jan, Feb, Mar...** custom list.

9. Click **OK** in each dialog box to return to the workbook. Refer to Figure 11–44.

Figure 11–44   PivotTable of Count of Date

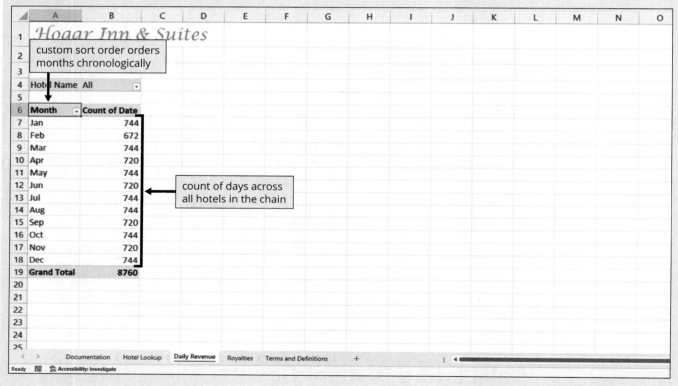

The PivotTable shows a count of days from every hotel within every month. The day count in January is 744 because there are 31 days in January multiplied by 24 hotels, which equals 744 total days. Because Elian wants to count the number of days across all hotels and doesn't want to count the same day more than once, you will replace the COUNT function in the PivotTable with the DISTINCTCOUNT function.

To calculate the distinct count of days:

1. Click cell **B6** containing the Count of Date label to select it.

2. On the ribbon, click the **PivotTable Analyze** tab, and then in the Active Field group, click the **Field Settings** button. The Value Field Settings dialog box opens.

3. Scroll down the list of summary functions and select **Distinct Count**.

4. In the Custom Name box, change the label from "Distinct Count of Date" to **Days**.

5. Click **OK** to return to the workbook. The number of days in each month is listed in column B.

You will use the distinct count of the days to determine the average number of customers per day at all Florida hotels. You can do this calculation by creating a measure.

Creating a Measure

Because PivotTables based on the Power Pivot Data Model do not support calculated fields, you must define a measure, which is a calculation summarizing data from a Data Model table. PivotTables use two types of measures: implicit and explicit.

An implicit measure is a measure created by the PivotTable when a field is placed in the Values area box. For example, placing the Revenue field in the Values area creates the implicit measure "Sum of Revenue" to calculate a total revenue for each cell in the PivotTable. Implicit measures are limited to the standard summary functions: SUM, COUNT, MIN, MAX, AVG, and DISTINCTCOUNT and can be used only within a PivotTable or PivotChart.

An explicit measure is a user-created formula that summarizes data from multiple fields and tables. Measures become part of a data table's structure and are available to PivotTables, PivotCharts, and any other application that can access the Data Model. An explicit measures acts like an implicit measure in that the calculation is applied across different cells within a PivotTable.

A crucial point to understand is that a measure provides the formula, but the data for that formula is determined by the PivotTable. A measure tells Excel how to calculate a value. The PivotTable determines where it is applied.

Introducing DAX

An explicit measure is written in the formula language Data Analysis Expressions, more commonly known as DAX. It's beyond the scope of this module to go deeply into the syntax of DAX. However, DAX uses many of the same functions used with Excel worksheets and Excel tables, so you can apply what you've learned about those topics to get started in writing measures in DAX.

Table and field references use the same syntax applied to Excel tables. So, a reference to the Occupied field within the Stays table would be written as Stays[Occupied]. To create a measure that calculates the sum of the Rooms field, you apply the formula = SUM(Stays[Occupied]). If you leave out the table name, Excel uses the table specified in the definition of the explicit measure.

Reference

Adding a Measure to a PivotTable

- On the Power Pivot tab, in the Calculations group, click the Measures button, and then click New Measure.
- In the Measures dialog box, specify the table that will contain the measure and the name of the measure.
- Enter the DAX formula for the measure.
- Specify the output format of the measure.
- Click OK to apply the measure to the table. Once a measure has been defined, it becomes part of the data table and can be used in any PivotTable.

DAX is a powerful language. As you develop your Excel skills, knowledge of DAX and its uses will be essential for creating powerful and sophisticated Excel reports and applications. In this section, you will learn the basics.

Adding a Measure to a Table

Measures are always associated with a table in the Data Model, and they become part of that table's definition. Elian wants you to create a measure for the Stays table that calculates the average number of hotel rooms occupied each day across all hotels. To calculate that value, you will divide the sum of the Occupied field by a distinct count of the number of days. The measure formula written in DAX is:

$$= \text{SUM([Occupied])/DISTINCTCOUNT([Date])}$$

You will create this measure using the Measure dialog box.

To create a measure calculating the daily average hotel rooms rented:

1. On the ribbon, click the **Power Pivot** tab. In the Calculations group, click the **Measures** button, and then click **New Measure**. The Measure dialog box opens.

2. Click the **Table Name** arrow, and then click **Stays** to add this measure to the Stays table.

   | **Key Step** You must select the Stays table even though it already appears in the Table name box so that the measure is associated with the correct table in the Data Model.

3. Press **TAB**, and then type **Occupied Daily** in the Measure name box.

4. Press **TAB**, and then type **Average daily occupation at Hogar Inn hotels** in the Description box.

5. Click after the **=** symbol in the Formula box, and then type **SUM(** to begin the formula. Note that as you type, Excel provides a list of functions, tables, and fields you can insert into the formula.

6. Double-click **[Occupied]** from the field list to insert this field into the formula, and then type **)** to complete the SUM function.

7. Type **/DISTINCTCOUNT(** as the next part of the formula, double-click **[Date]** in the fields list, and then type **)** to complete the formula. The formula = SUM([Occupied])/DISTINCTCOUNT([Date]) appears in the Formula box.

   ▌ **Tip** You can check for errors in a formula by clicking the Check formula button.

8. Click **Number** in the Category box, click **Whole Number** in the Format box, and then click the **Use 1000 separator (,)** check box to add a thousands separator. Refer to Figure 11–45.

Figure 11–45   Defining the Occupied Daily measure

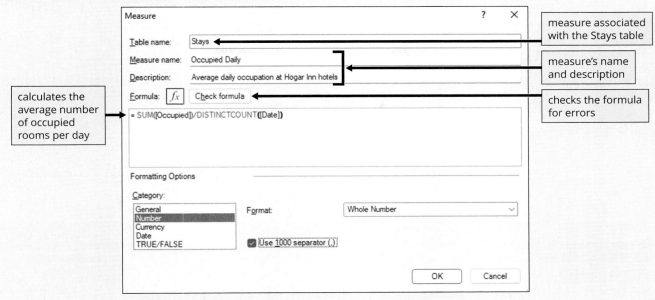

9. Click **OK** to create the Occupied Daily measure. The measure is added as a new column to the PivotTable. Refer to Figure 11–46.

Figure 11–46   Measure of occupied rooms per day

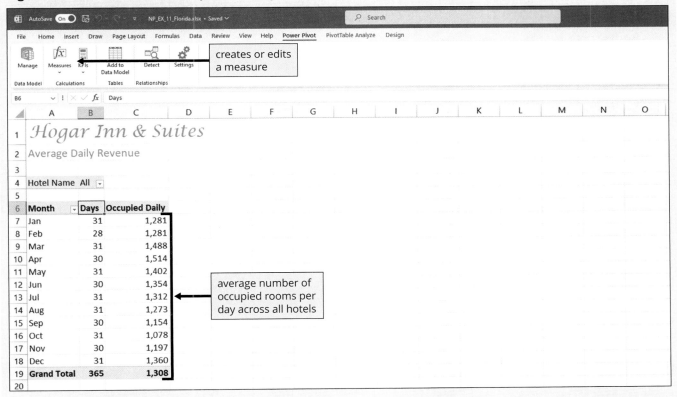

Based on the Occupied Daily measure, you learn that on average a total of 1,281 rooms across all 24 hotels are occupied daily during January and February 2029. That number rises to 1,488 rooms in March. The lowest daily occupancy occurs in October with 1,078 rooms typically occupied daily across the entire Florida chain. If Elian wanted to know the average daily occupancy for a specific hotel, he could select that hotel from the filter button in cell B4.

> **Tip** Measures become part of the table structure and are available to any PivotTable based on that table.

Notice that the Occupy Daily measure is added to the list of items in the Stays table. The f_x symbol indicates that Occupied Daily is a measure and not a table field. The measure is automatically added to the Values field, using the label name you specified in the Measure dialog box.

Next, you will create a measure named Revenue Daily that calculates the total revenue generated per day from the Florida hotels.

To create the Revenue Daily measure:

1. On the Power Pivot tab, in the Calculations group, click the **Measures** button, and then click **New Measure**. The Measure dialog box opens.

2. Select **Stays** in the Table name box, enter **Revenue Daily** in the Measure name box, and then enter **Average daily revenue at Hogar Inn hotels** in the Description box.

3. Click after the = symbol in the Formula box and type **SUM(** to begin the formula.

4. Double-click **[Revenue]** in the field list, and then type **)** to complete the SUM function.

5. Type **/DISTINCTCOUNT(** to continue the formula, double-click **[Date]** in the fields list, and then type **)** to complete the formula. The formula =SUM([Revenue])/DISTINCTCOUNT([Date]) appears in the Formula box.

6. Click **Currency** in the Category box to display the values as currency and reduce the number of digits after the decimal point to **0**. Refer to Figure 11–47.

Figure 11–47   Revenue Daily measure defined

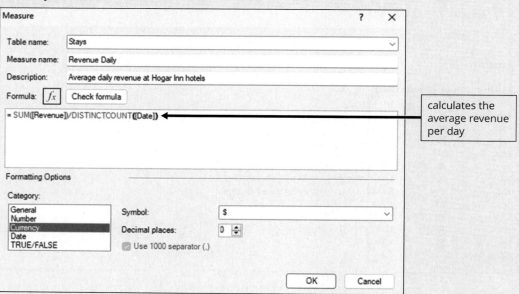

calculates the average revenue per day

7. Click **OK**. The measure of average revenue collected daily from across all hotels is shown in column D. Refer to Figure 11–48.

Figure 11-48   Measure of daily average revenue

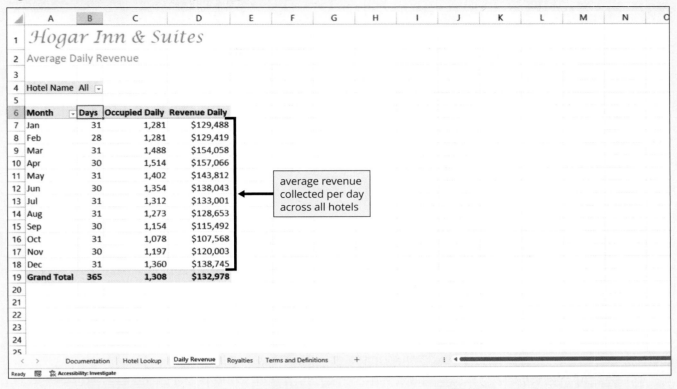

In January 2029, all the Florida hotels took in almost $130,000 on an average day. In April, at the height of the tourist season, the typical daily revenue collected was more than $157,000. To view average daily occupied rooms and revenues for other combinations of hotels and dates, Elian has only to change the structure of the PivotTable. The Occupied Daily and Revenue Daily measures will automatically recalculate for each cell in the new PivotTable.

Because the company franchises its hotels, the collected revenues do not all go to the corporate headquarters. Instead, the company receives a percentage, or royalty, of the revenue in exchange for administrative help, infrastructure, advertising, and the right to use the Hogar Inn name.

Elian wants to track the total royalties collected from the Florida hotels in the past year. To do that calculation, you will create a measure using data from multiple tables.

Calculating Measures Across Tables and Rows

The great power of DAX and Power Pivot becomes apparent when you need to perform calculations using fields from multiple tables. In this case, you want to combine data from two tables: the Revenue field from the Stays table that records the amount of daily revenue collected by each hotel and the Royalty field from the Hotels table that provides each hotel's royalty rate. Hotel franchises in the Hogar Inn chain will pay royalties from 4% of revenue up to 7% based on the contract between the franchise owner and the company.

Elian wants a PivotTable that shows the revenue and royalties for each hotel. You will start creating this PivotTable now by inserting a column of total revenue.

To create a PivotTable of total revenue:

1. Go to the **Royalties** worksheet.

2. In the PivotTable Fields pane, click **All** to display all the tables in the Data Model.

3. Drag the **Hotel Name** field from the Hotels table into the Rows area box.

4. Drag the **Revenue** field from the Stays table into the Values area, and then change the label from Sum of Revenue to **Gross Revenue**. Refer to Figure 11–49.

Figure 11–49   Gross revenue by hotel

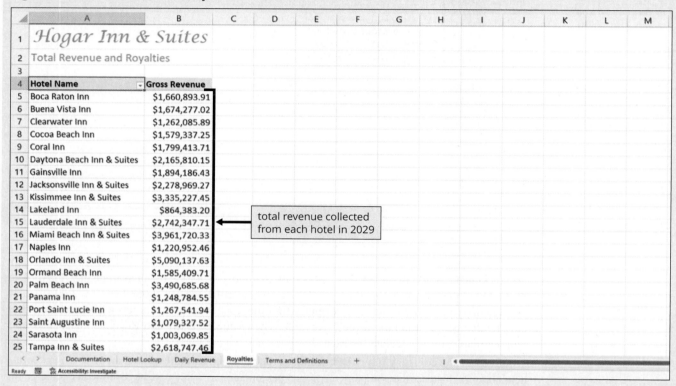

To calculate the total royalties owed to the company, you will multiply the revenue collected by the hotel's royalty rate. For example, if a hotel collects $10,000 in revenue at a 6% royalty rate, it will owe the company ($10,000) × (6%) = $600. Elian wants to use this calculation to sum the total royalties the company collects from its franchised hotels.

The RELATED Function

For every royalty calculation, you need to use the value of the Royalty field for the hotel. You can look up a value from a table in the Data Model using the RELATED function

        RELATED(*table*[*field*])

where *table* is the table and *field* is the field to retrieve the data from. So, to retrieve the value of the Royalty field in the Hotels table, the expression is:

        RELATED(Hotels[Royalty])

The RELATED function acts like a lookup table, but there is no lookup value. So how does the formula know where to find the correct royalty rate? The answer is that the relation between the Stays table and Hotels table has already been defined in the Data Model. If you know the hotel that generated the revenue, the table relation tells which record in the Hotels table to use for the royalty rate.

The SUMX Function

Royalties are calculated by multiplying revenue by the value of the royalty field. At first, you might try the following formula that multiplies the sum of the Revenue field in the Stays table by the value of the Royalty field in the Hotels table:

    = SUM(Stays[Revenue])*RELATED(Hotels[Royalty])

But this formula would not work. Nothing in the expression SUM(Stays[Revenue]) indicates which revenue figures are being summed. You could be adding revenues from one hotel or from several hotels, each with a different royalty rate. Remember that the measure provides the formula, but the PivotTable supplies the data. This formula provides no way to match the sum of the revenues to a single royalty rate.

Instead, you want to calculate the royalty owed each time revenue is collected by a hotel and then add those royalties to get the total royalties paid to the company. That kind of sum, which proceeds through a table row by row, is calculated using the SUMX function

    SUMX(*table*, *expression*)

where *table* is the table to go through row by row, and *expression* is an expression to calculate on each row of the table. SUMX then returns the sum of all those individual calculations. So, the expression

    [Revenue]*RELATED(Hotels[Royalty])

calculates the royalty on a single transaction. You nest that expression within the following SUMX function to sum all the calculations for every record in the Stays table:

    SUMX(Stays, [Revenue]*RELATED(Hotels[Royalty]))

This measure can then be added to a PivotTable to calculate total royalties for any combination of hotels or dates within the year. You will add this formula as a measure named Royalties to the PivotTable in the Royalties worksheet.

To create the Royalties measure:

1. On the ribbon, click the **Power Pivot** tab. In the Calculations group, click the **Measures** button, and then click **New Measure**. The Measure dialog box opens.

2. Select **Stays** in the Table name box.

3. Change the measure name to **Royalties** and enter the description **Calculates the total royalties owed to the company** in the Description box.

4. In the Formula box after the = symbol, type **SUMX(Stays, [Revenue]*RELATED(Hotels[Royalty]))** to enter the formula.

   > **Tip** You can avoid typing mistakes by selecting table names, field names, and function names from the box that appears within the Formula box.

5. Click **Check formula** to confirm the expression you entered contains no syntax errors.

   > **Trouble?** If Excel reports an error, you probably mistyped the formula. Common errors include missing parentheses or square brackets around the field names. Check your formula against the formula in Step 4, correct any mistakes, and then repeat Step 5. If you are still having problems entering the formula correctly, you can copy the expression from the Terms and Definitions worksheet.

6. In the Category box, click **Currency** to display the Royalties measure as currency, and then reduce the number of decimal places to **0**. Refer to Figure 11–50.

Figure 11–50   Royalties measure defined

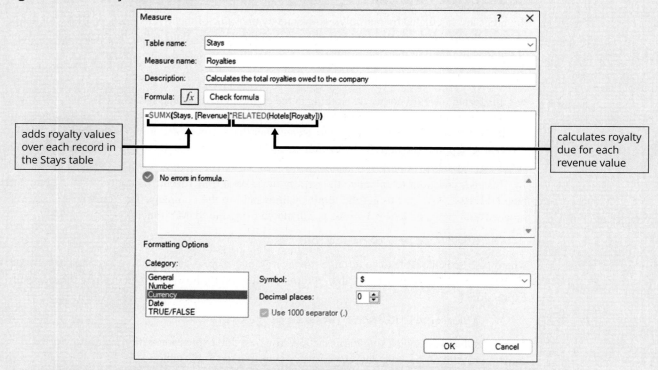

adds royalty values over each record in the Stays table

calculates royalty due for each revenue value

7. Click **OK**. The Royalties measure is added to the PivotTable.

8. Click the **Filter** button in cell A4, and then click **More Sort Options**. The Sort (Hotel Name) dialog box opens.

9. Click the **Descending (Z to A)** option button, and then select **Royalties** in the box.

10. Click **OK** to return to the PivotTable. The PivotTable is sorted in descending order of royalties. Refer to Figure 11–51.

Figure 11–51   Total collected royalties

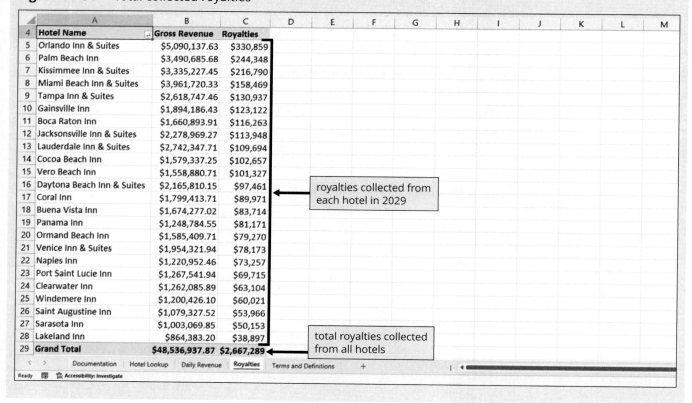

Hotel Name	Gross Revenue	Royalties
Orlando Inn & Suites	$5,090,137.63	$330,859
Palm Beach Inn	$3,490,685.68	$244,348
Kissimmee Inn & Suites	$3,335,227.45	$216,790
Miami Beach Inn & Suites	$3,961,720.33	$158,469
Tampa Inn & Suites	$2,618,747.46	$130,937
Gainsville Inn	$1,894,186.43	$123,122
Boca Raton Inn	$1,660,893.91	$116,263
Jacksonsville Inn & Suites	$2,278,969.27	$113,948
Lauderdale Inn & Suites	$2,742,347.71	$109,694
Cocoa Beach Inn	$1,579,337.25	$102,657
Vero Beach Inn	$1,558,880.71	$101,327
Daytona Beach Inn & Suites	$2,165,810.15	$97,461
Coral Inn	$1,799,413.71	$89,971
Buena Vista Inn	$1,674,277.02	$83,714
Panama Inn	$1,248,784.55	$81,171
Ormand Beach Inn	$1,585,409.71	$79,270
Venice Inn & Suites	$1,954,321.94	$78,173
Naples Inn	$1,220,952.46	$73,257
Port Saint Lucie Inn	$1,267,541.94	$69,715
Clearwater Inn	$1,262,085.89	$63,104
Windemere Inn	$1,200,426.10	$60,021
Saint Augustine Inn	$1,079,327.52	$53,966
Sarasota Inn	$1,003,069.85	$50,153
Lakeland Inn	$864,383.20	$38,897
Grand Total	**$48,536,937.87**	**$2,667,289**

royalties collected from each hotel in 2029

total royalties collected from all hotels

The most royalties were collected from Orlando Inn & Suites with more than $330,000 in royalties on a gross revenue of $5.09 million. The smallest royalty amount came from the Lakeland Inn with more than $38,000 in royalties from more than $864,000 in revenue (row 28). From all the Florida hotels about $2.67 million in royalties were collected from more than $48 million in gross revenue (row 29).

Insight

Exploring the X functions in DAX

SUMX is one of the summary X functions in DAX. The others are AVERAGEX, COUNTX, MINX, MAXX, and PRODUCTX. As with SUMX, each X function evaluates an expression row by row within a table, applying the summary function to the row-by-row values. For example, the following AVERAGEX function goes through every record in the Stays table, calculates the rooms rented divided by the total number of rooms in the hotel for each record, and then returns the average of those ratios:

```
= AVERAGEX(Stays, [Rooms Rented]/RELATED(Hotels[Total Rooms]))
```

Similarly, the following COUNTX function counts up the number of days in which every room was rented:

```
= COUNTX(Stays,IF([Rooms Rented]=RELATED(Hotels[Total Rooms]),1))
```

The measure goes through every record in the Stays table using the IF function to test whether the number of rooms rented equals the number of rooms in the hotel. If they are equal, the value 1 is returned; otherwise, no numeric value is given. The COUNTX function then counts the number of records containing a numeric value which is the same as counting the number of days the hotel was full.

DAX is a powerful language for constructing formulas using data from multiple tables, and the X functions are one of its more useful tools.

Retrieving PivotTable Data with GETPIVOTDATA

The reports you helped Elian create were limited to the 24 Florida hotels, but there are over 400 Hogar Inns spanning more than five countries and territories. A PivotTable providing summaries on each hotel would be large and unwieldy. One solution to that problem is to treat a PivotTable itself as a data source and extract information from it for use in a report using the **GETPIVOTDATA function**. The syntax of the function is:

```
GETPIVOTDATA(data_field, pivot_table, [field1, item1,
field2, item2,...])
```

where *data_field* is data to retrieve from the PivotTable, *pivot_table* is a reference to any cell within the PivotTable, and the *field1, item1, field2, item2*, and so on are optional *field/item* pairs that indicate the location of the cell within the PivotTable. The field names and item names are text strings and should be enclosed within double quotes.

Note that it doesn't matter how the PivotTable is structured. You can switch rows and columns, add subtotals, add grand totals, and so forth. The GETPIVOTDATA function will locate the calculated value in the PivotTable based on the data field and the list of field/item names.

The GETPIVOTDATA function works with both standard PivotTables and PivotTables created under the Data Model. Figure 11–52 provides an example of the GETPIVOTDATA function used with a standard PivotTable.

Figure 11–52 Data extracted from a PivotTable using the GETPIVOTDATA function

	A	B	C	D	E	F	G	H	I
1	Occupancy	Year ▾							Retrieve Data from the PivotTable
2	Hotel ▾	2028	2029	Grand Total					
3	Boca Raton Inn	67.0%	67.4%	67.2%		Grand Total			
4	Buena Vista Inn	60.5%	60.5%	60.5%		Occupancy	63.5%		= GETPIVOTDATA("Occupancy",$A$1)
5	Clearwater Inn	63.3%	61.1%	62.2%					
6	Cocoa Beach Inn	71.8%	71.8%	71.8%		Hotel	Coral Inn		
7	Coral Inn	72.5%	77.0%	74.8%		Year	2029		
8	Gainsville Inn	66.6%	68.5%	67.6%		Occupancy	77.0%		= GETPIVOTDATA("Occupancy",$A$1,"Year",2029,"Hotel","Coral Inn")
9	Lakeland Inn	58.5%	58.9%	58.7%					
10	Naples Inn	56.9%	57.9%	57.4%		Hotel	Naples Inn		
11	Panama Inn	51.4%	51.0%	51.2%		Year	2028		
12	Grand Total	63.2%	63.8%	63.5%		Occupancy	56.9%		= GETPIVOTDATA(F12&"",$A$1,F10,G10,F11,G11)
13									
14									
15									

The first function

```
= GETPIVOTDATA("Occupancy",$A$1)
```

retrieves the grand total of the Occupancy rate from across all hotels and years. The second function

```
= GETPIVOTDATA("Occupancy",$A$1,"Year",2029,"Hotel","Coral
Inn")
```

retrieves the 2029 occupancy rate for the Coral Inn. Finally, the third function

```
= GETPIVOTDATA(F12&"",$A$1,F10,G10,F11,G11)
```

uses cell references to specify the data field (cell F12), and the two field/item pairs (cells F10/G10 and F11/G11) to return the 2028 occupancy rate for the Naples Inn. Note that the data field must be appended with an empty text string, &"", to avoid a #REF! error from Excel. By using cell references, you can change the hotel name and the year value in G10 and G11 to retrieve PivotTable calculations from any hotel and year.

The GETPIVOTDATA function is more complicated when the PivotTable's data source is the data model. In that situation, the field names and items are entered as measures. For example, the GETPIVOTDATA function for the average of the Occupancy rate across all hotels and years is:

```
= GETPIVOTDATA("[Measures].[Average of Occupancy
Rate]",$A$1)
```

and the GETPIVOTDATA function for retrieving the average occupancy rate in 2029 for the Coral Inn is:

```
= GETPIVOTDATA("[Measures].[Average of Occupancy
Rate]",$A$1,"[Hotels].[Hotel Name]","[Hotels].[Hotel
Name].&[Coral Inn]","[Hotels].[Year]","[Hotels].
[Year].&[2029]")
```

Fortunately, you don't have to write these long and cumbersome formulas yourself. If you reference a PivotTable cell, Excel will automatically generate the GETPIVOTDATA function for you.

Elian included a worksheet in which you will use the GETPIVOTDATA function to retrieve data from the Royalties PivotTable. You will use the GETPIVOTDATA functions now to retrieve data from that table.

To insert the GETPIVOTDATA function:

1. Go to the **Hotel Lookup** worksheet.

2. Click cell **B5** and type **=** to begin the formula.

3. Click the **Royalties** sheet tab, click cell **B6** containing the gross revenue for the Palm Beach Inn, and then press **ENTER**. The GETPIVOTDATA function is entered into cell B5, returning the Sum of Revenue measure for the Palm Beach Inn.

   Next, you will retrieve the value of the Royalties measure for the Palm Beach Inn.

4. In cell **B6**, type **=** to begin the formula, click cell the **Royalties** sheet tab, click cell **C6**, and then press **ENTER**.

5. Select the range **B5:B6** containing the GETPIVOTDATA functions. Refer to Figure 11–53.

Figure 11–53   Data extracted from a PivotTable using the GETPIVOTDATA function

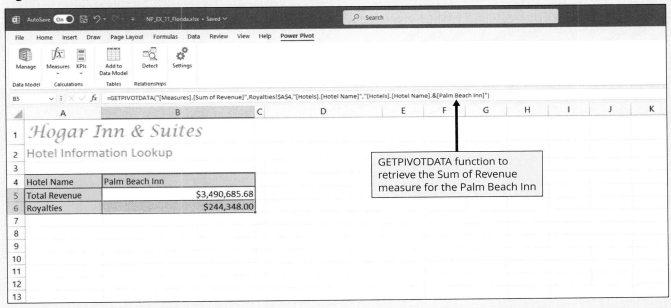

Elian wants the GETPIVOTDATA function to retrieve revenue and royalty values for any of the 24 hotels. You will modify the GETPIVOTDATA functions now, replacing the explicit reference to the Palm Beach Inn with a reference to whatever hotel is named in cell B4.

To view PivotTable data for any hotel:

1. With the range B5:B6 still selected, press **CTRL+H**. The Find and Replace dialog box opens.

2. Type **Palm Beach Inn** in the Find what box.

3. Press **TAB**, and then type **"&B4&"** in the Replace with box. Refer to Figure 11–54.

Figure 11–54   Find and Replace dialog box

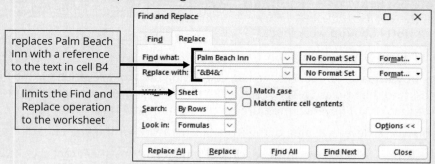

replaces Palm Beach Inn with a reference to the text in cell B4

limits the Find and Replace operation to the worksheet

4. Click **Replace All** to replace the text in the two selected cells. Excel reports that two replacements were made.

5. Click **OK**, and then click **Close** to return to the workbook.

6. In cell **B4**, enter **Gainsville Inn** as the hotel name. The worksheet updates to show the total revenue ($1,894,186.43) and royalties collected ($123,122.12) for the hotel. Refer to Figure 11–55.

Figure 11–55   PivotTable with the Gainsville Inn data

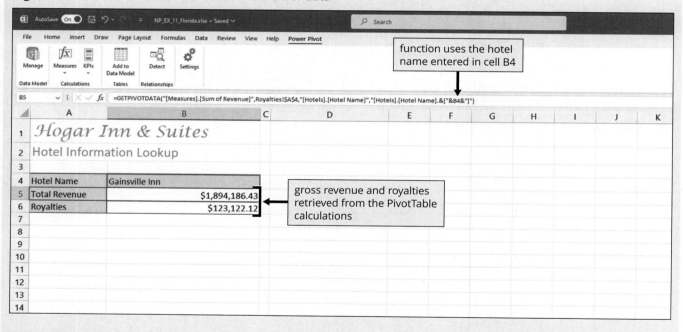

function uses the hotel name entered in cell B4

gross revenue and royalties retrieved from the PivotTable calculations

7. **sam** ⬆ Save the workbook, and then close it.

By default, Excel will generate a GETPIVOTDATA function whenever you reference a PivotTable cell. To replace that default action, select the PivotTable and within the PivotTable group on the PivotTable Analyze tab, click the Options arrow, and deselect the GetPivotData option. After that, if you link to a PivotTable cell, Excel will return the cell reference and not the GETPIVOTDATA function.

Elian can build upon this example to create a dashboard with PivotTable lookups. One of the great appeals of the GETPIVOTDATA function is that it gives you the flexibility to display PivotTable results in customized layouts and report styles.

Proskills

Retrieving Measures from OLAP Databases

When data is stored in the Data Model, you don't need a PivotTable to perform PivotTable calculations. The Data Model stores data in a multidimensional array of fields and measures called a **Data Cube**. Because this data structure is built into the Data Model, the type of calculations you would do through a PivotTable can be done without a PivotTable.

Data Cubes are a feature of an **Online Analytic Processing (OLAP) database**, which is a database designed for the efficient analysis of large datasets. Rather than calculating and recalculating a dataset with hundreds of thousands to millions of records, an OLAP database has all those measures pre-stored for quick retrieval.

To retrieve data from an OLAP database, use the CUBEVALUE function

= CUBEVALUE(*connection*, "*[expr1]*","*[exp2]*", *slicers*, …)

where *connection* is the connection to an OLAP database like the Data Model and *expr1*, *expr2*, and so on are OLAP expressions references the measures and filters applied to those measures. Finally, the optional *slicers* parameters connect the value returned by CUBEVALUE to slicers and timelines in the workbook. Button slicers should be prefaced with the text Slicer_ and timeline slicers should be prefaced with Timeline_.

For example, the following CUBEVALUE function calculates the Sum of Revenue measure for the Coral Inn during the month of April, extracting data from both the Hotels and Stays tables in the workbook's Data Model. The Year slicer is included so that whatever is selected in that slicer is applied to the CUBEVALUE function.

```
= CUBEVALUE("ThisWorkbookDataModel",
 "[Measures].[Sum of Revenue]",
 "[Hotels].[Hotel Name].[Coral Inn]",
 "[Stays].[Month].[Apr]",
 Slicer_Year)
```

Note that the connection and expressions should be enclosed within quotes, but slicers and timelines are not. If you use the CUBEVALUE function, you will usually create a PivotTable to assist in defining the measures used in the function. Once the measures have been created, you can delete the PivotTable.

Exploring Database Functions

Another way to summarize data from an Excel table or data range without using PivotTables is with a **Database function** (or **Dfunction**). Database functions calculate summary statistics including AVERAGE, COUNT, MAX, MIN, and SUM using criteria specified in a range. The general form of a Database function is

D*function*(*database*, *field*, *criteria*)

where *function* is the name of an Excel database function, *database* specifies the data range including both the data values and the field names, *field* is the name of a database field, and *criteria* references a range containing filter criteria to apply to the database function. Figure 11–56 lists some of the Database functions used to calculate summary statistics from a database.

Figure 11–56   Excel database functions

Function	Description
DAVERAGE(*database, field, criteria*)	Calculates the average of the values in the *field* column under criteria specified in the *criteria* range
DCOUNT(*database, field, criteria*)	Counts the numeric values in the *field* column for cells matching the *criteria*
DCOUNTA(*database, field, criteria*)	Counts the nonblank cells in the *field* column for cells matching the *criteria*
DMAX(*database, field, criteria*)	Returns the maximum value of the *field* column for cells matching the *criteria*
DMIN(*database, field, criteria*)	Returns the minimum value of the *field* column for cells matching the *criteria*
DSUM(*database, field, criteria*)	Calculates the sum of the *field* column for cells matching the *criteria*
DSTDEV(*database, field, criteria*)	Calculates the standard deviation of the *field* column for cells matching the *criteria*
DGET(*database, field, criteria*)	Returns the first cell from *field* column matching the *criteria*

Figure 11–57 provides examples of the DAVERAGE, DSUM, DMAX, and DMIN functions to calculate the average, sum, maximum, and minimum value of the Occupancy and Revenue fields during May 2028 from a sample database table.

Figure 11–57   Summary statistics calculated with database functions

The criteria range operates the same way for the Database functions as it did for the Advanced Filter tool in that:

1. Field names are listed in the first row of the table and must exactly match the field names used from the database. Field names can be repeated in the same row for multiple criteria.

2. Criteria for each field are listed in subsequent rows of criteria range.

3. Criteria within the same row are combined using the AND logical operator.

4. Criteria in different rows are combined using the OR logical operator.

The criteria range in Figure 11–58 has two rows so that the matching rows from the database match Occupancy and Revenue values for either the Coral Inn in 2028 or the Naples Inn in 2029.

Figure 11–58   Database functions with multiple criteria

	A	B	C	D	E	F	G	H	I	J
1			Database					Criteria		
2	Year	Month	Hotel	Occupancy	Revenue		Year	Hotel		
3	2028	Mar	Coral Inn	81.5%	$163,916		2028	Coral Inn		
4	2028	Mar	Gainsville Inn	73.5%	$174,014		2029	Naples Inn		
5	2028	Mar	Naples Inn	62.6%	$112,777					
6	2028	Apr	Coral Inn	82.7%	$160,871				Database Functions	
7	2028	Apr	Gainsville Inn	75.9%	$174,469		Average Occupancy	72.6%	= DAVERAGE(A2:E20, "Occupancy", G2:H4)	
8	2028	Apr	Naples Inn	66.1%	$115,355		Maximum Occupancy	82.7%	= DMAX(A2:E20, "Occupancy", G2:H4)	
9	2028	May	Coral Inn	76.4%	$150,339		Minimum Occupancy	61.8%	= DMIN(A2:E20, "Occupancy", G2:H4)	
10	2028	May	Gainsville Inn	72.5%	$171,345					
11	2028	May	Naples Inn	60.3%	$107,946		Average Revenue	$137,047	= DAVERAGE(A2:E20, "Revenue", G2:H4)	
12	2029	Mar	Coral Inn	87.4%	$177,622		Sum of Revenue	$822,282	= DSUM(A2:E20, "Revenue", G2:H4)	
13	2029	Mar	Gainsville Inn	76.1%	$181,402		Maximum Revenue	$163,916	= DMAX(A2:E20, "Revenue", G2:H4)	
14	2029	Mar	Naples Inn	65.5%	$118,019		Minimum Revenue	$110,982	= DMIN(A2:E20, "Revenue", G2:H4)	
15	2029	Apr	Coral Inn	89.9%	$178,432					
16	2029	Apr	Gainsville Inn	77.8%	$179,983					
17	2029	Apr	Naples Inn	67.5%	$118,155					
18	2029	May	Coral Inn	80.4%	$160,950					
19	2029	May	Gainsville Inn	74.4%	$176,282					
20	2029	May	Naples Inn	61.8%	$110,982					
21										

As with advanced filters, you can include operations in the criteria cells. An expression such as "> 150000" could be used to filter results to include only those rows in which revenues were greater than $150,000. If you want a quick way of calculating databases statistics, the Database functions might be a good choice.

Analyzing Data with Linked Data Types

In examining the hotel data, you used data stored in different formats or data types. Figure 11–59 describes the data types in both Excel and the Data Model.

Figure 11–59   Data types in Excel and the Data Model

Excel	Data Model	Description
Whole Number	64-bit Integer Value	Numbers with no decimal places, including integers and whole numbers
Decimal Number	64-bit Real Value	Numbers with a decimal value, including currencies and percentages
TRUE/FALSE	Boolean	Values which are either true or false
Text	String	Character text strings, used for names, addresses, and labels
Date	Date/Time	Date and time values stored internally as numeric values
	Blank	Blanks or null values
Error		Error values such as #REF!, #NAME?, #VALUE!, and #N/A

Beyond these data types, Excel also supports **linked data types**, which are data types linked to external data sources providing current information about the data value. For example, a linked data type can be created for stocks that displays current stock values and trading information. A linked data type for a geographic location will provide access to civic data about the selected city, state, country, or region.

Linked data types are found in the Data Types group on the Data tab. To create a linked data type, select the data value from a cell or field, and then click the corresponding data type in the Data Types group. The linked data types for the Florida hotels, such as the ones in in Figure 11–60, can display current information about the hotel's location.

Figure 11–60   Geography linked data type

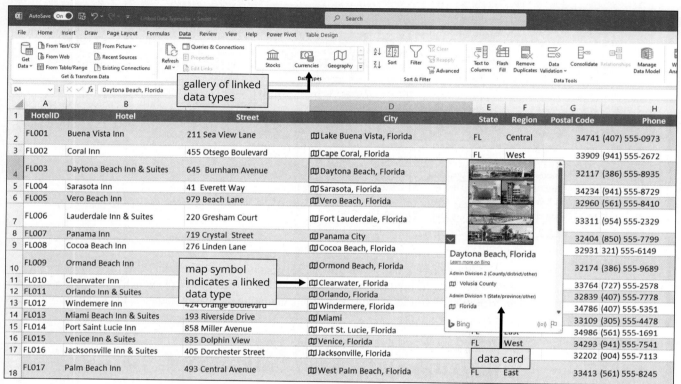

The linked information is stored in a **data card**, which is a scrollable popup window containing text, graphics, and links to information about the data value. The data card in Figure 11–60 provides additional information about Daytona Beach, Florida.

Excel provides three built-in linked data types for stocks, currencies, and geography. Third parties create other linked data types for such diverse subjects as climate research, medical reports, entertainment, and leisure activities.

You can also use Power Query to construct data types and data cards, collapsing several columns of data into a single data card. Figure 11–61 shows an hotel table in which all the hotel contact information been replaced with a single data card, reducing the complexity of the Excel table.

Figure 11–61   Data card with multiple data fields

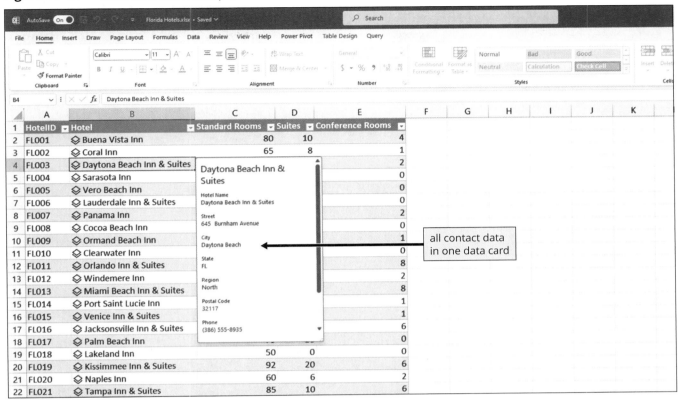

To construct a custom data type containing multiple fields, open the data source in Power Query, select all the fields to be combined into one data card, and then on the Power Query Transform tab, in the Structured Column group, click the Create Data Type button.

Getting Insights into Data

A database with thousands of records and dozens of fields can be overwhelming. Where do you start? What kind of tables, charts, and statistics should you examine? The Analyze Data tool provides suggestions to guide a data analysis project.

To start reviewing the suggestions, select any cell in the data table, and then on the Home tab, click the Analyze Data button. Excel generates a gallery of suggested PivotTables and PivotCharts. In Figure 11–62, Excel suggested a PivotTable to review Revenue and Occupancy rates by the Hotel ID field and a PivotChart that analyses Revenue by the day of the week.

Figure 11–62   Data analysis suggestions

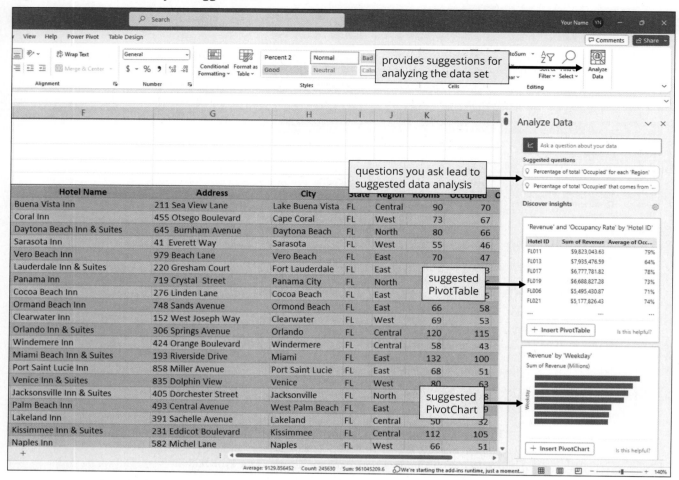

To direct Excel into specific areas of research, click the box at the top of the Analyze Data pane and enter a question about your data. Elian might ask such questions as, "On what weekdays is the hotel revenue the greatest?" or "What is the monthly trend in occupancy rate?" While Elian will still have to finetune the suggestions with his own insights, the Analyze Data button provides a good starting point.

At this point, you have completed the initial analysis of the hotel data for Elian. Elian will continue to use your work with PivotTables and data tools to investigate other aspects of the Florida hotel's performance over the past years in preparation for the upcoming sales meeting.

Part 11.3 Quick Check

1. What is a standard PivotTable?

2. What function should you use to count the number of unique values within a field?

3. What is the difference between an implicit measure and an explicit measure?

4. Write a DAX formula to calculate the average of the Revenue field values in the Stays table.

5. What DAX function do you use to retrieve a value from a Data Model table based on the table relation?

6. What is the difference between the SUM and SUMX functions?

7. What function do you use to retrieve values from a PivotTable?

8. What function do you use to retrieve calculated measures from the Data Model without the use of a PivotTable?

9. What are the three arguments of an Excel Database function?

Practice: Review Assignments

Data Files needed for the Review Assignments: NP_EX_11-3.xlsx, NP_EX_11-4.xlsx

Elian is continuing to explore the Florida hotel data and wants to analyze how occupancy rates change during a typical week, focusing on weekend occupancy (Friday through Sunday) versus weekday occupancy (Monday through Thursday). Elian also wants to know whether occupancy rates and revenue are higher for new hotels that might have more modern amenities. Finally, Elian wants a report on the number and percentage of days each hotel is completely booked during the year. Complete the following:

1. Open the **NP_EX_11-3.xlsx** workbook located in the Excel11 > Review folder included with your Data Files. Save the workbook as **NP_EX_11_Weekday** in the location specified by your instructor.

2. In the Documentation sheet, enter your name and the date in the range B3:B4.

3. In the Age worksheet, click cell A4, and then use the Group Field command in the Group group on the PivotTable Analyze tab to group the values in the Hotel Age column in 5-year groups starting at 0 and ending at 34 to determine whether there is a trend of older hotels having lower average revenue.

4. In the Weekend worksheet, manually group the Mon, Tue, Wed, and Thu items in the Weekday field of the PivotTable. Remove the Weekday field from the Columns area and rename Group1 as **Weekdays**. Manually group the Sun, Fri, and Sat items and rename Group2 to **Weekends**. Click cell B4, and then use the Active Field box in the Active Field group on the PivotTable Analyze tab to change the name of the grouped field from Weekday2 to **Days**.

5. Click cell C6, click the Conditional Formatting button in the Styles group on the Home tab, and then click New Rule. For all cells showing Occupancy values, format the values with a three-color scale going from red (low occupancy) through yellow and up to green (high occupancy).

6. In the Day of the Week worksheet, remove the Weekday2 group from the Rows area of the PivotTable. Click cell C5, and then click the Field Settings button in the Active Field group on the PivotTable Analyze tab. On the Show Values As tab, select the Difference From calculation with Weekday as the Base field and (previous) as the Base item. Change the Custom Name of the field from Occupancy2 to **Change in Rate**.

7. Create a new conditional formatting rule for All cells showing "Change in Rate" values for "Weekday" and use the red–yellow–green arrow icon set to indicate change in occupancy rate. If the cell value is greater than or equal to 0.03, display a green up arrow. If the cell value is between 0 and 0.03, display a yellow level arrow; otherwise, display a red downward arrow. Note that Sunday will not have an icon because it's the first day of the week.

8. Go to the RevPar worksheet, and then press ALT+D and then P to open the PivotTable and PivotChart Wizard. In Step 2, enter Hotels to use the data in the Hotels table, and then select No to create a PivotTable from a new cache. Place the PivotTable report in cell A6 of the RevPar worksheet. Rename the PivotTable as **RevPar Pivot**. Place the Hotel Name field in the Filters area and Weekday in the Rows area.

9. Change the PivotTable report layout to Tabular form, and then turn off the grand totals for the PivotTable rows and columns.

10. Click cell A6, click the Fields, Items, & Sets button in the Calculations group on the PivotTable Analyze tab, and then click Calculated Field. Create a calculated field named **RevPar** that is equal to the Revenue field divided by the Rooms field. Change the label of the value field from Sum of RevPar to **RevPar** followed by a blank space.

11. Click cell A6, click the Fields, Items, & Sets button in the Calculations group on the PivotTable Analyze tab, click Calculated Item, and then add the following calculated items:
    a. Name the calculated item as **Weekday Average** and then enter using the formula
       = AVERAGE(Mon, Tue, Wed, Thu) using the Insert Field button to enter the days.
    b. Name the calculated item as **Weekend Average** and then enter the formula
       = AVERAGE(Sun, Fri, Sat).

12. Save the workbook, and then close it.

13. Open the **NP_EX_11-4.xlsx** workbook located in the Excel11 > Review folder included with your Data Files. Save the workbook as **NP_EX_11_Booked** in the location specified by your instructor. You will use this workbook to examine how often and when the Florida hotels are completely booked.

14. In the Documentation sheet, enter your name and the date in the range B3:B4.

15. In the Vacancies worksheet, change the PivotTable report layout to a tabular form.

16. On the Power Pivot tab, in the Calculations group, click the Measures button, and then click New Measure. Add the new measure to the Stays table named **Days Filled** with the description **Count of days with no vacancies**, and then enter the following DAX formula:

```
= SUMX(Stays, IF([Occupied]=RELATED(Hotels[Rooms]),1,0))
```

(You can also copy this formula from the Terms and Definitions worksheet and paste it into the Measures dialog box. Be sure to type an equal sign (=) before the expression.)

17. In the Formatting Options section, select the Number category, and then display the measure as a decimal number with no decimal places.

18. Add a second measure to the Stays table named **Percent Filled** with the description **Percent of days with no vacancies** that calculates the percent of days in which the hotel was completely filled using the following DAX formula, and displays the value as a percentage number to one decimal place:

```
= [Days Filled]/[Count of Date]
```

19. Make sure that both the Days Filled and the Percent Filled measures are added to the PivotTable. Note that most hotels will not be completely booked except for the busiest hotels in the busiest months.

20. In the Day of Week worksheet, in cell A4, insert a PivotTable from the Data Model. Name the PivotTable **Booked Pivot**. Place the Month field from the Stays table in the Rows area and the Weekday field from the Stays table in the Columns area.

21. Change the PivotTable report layout to tabular form.

22. Sort both the Month and Weekday fields in ascending order (Jan to Dec and Sun to Sat).

23. Place the Percent Filled Measure from the Stays table in the Values area.

24. With the PivotTable still selected, insert a slicer to the worksheet. Add the Hotel Name field from the Hotels table to the slicer. Set the number of columns in the slicer to **2** and then resize the slicer to fit the range K4:N22. Use the slicer to display the booking percentages for the Orlando Inn & Suites hotel.

25. In the Vacancy Lookup worksheet, click cell B6, type **=** and then click cell D5 in the Vacancies worksheet to insert the GETPIVOTDATA function for that cell. Do the same with cell B7 to insert the GETPIVOTDATA function from cell E5 in the Vacancies worksheet.

26. Select the range B6:B7 and use the Find and Replace command to replace all occurrences within the selection of Boca Raton Inn with **"&B4&"** (include the quotation marks). With the range B6:B7 still selected, use the Find and Replace command to replace all occurrences of Jan with **"&B5&"** (include the quotation marks).

27. Test the vacancy lookup by entering **Coral Inn** in cell B4 and **Mar** in cell C5 to return the number and percent of days in March that the Coral Inn was completed booked.

28. Save the workbook, and then close it.

Apply: Case Problem 1

Data File needed for this Case Problem: NP_EX_11-5.xlsx

Riverside Day School Jan Dryer is an operations manager at Riverside Day School, a small 6–12 private school in Ohio. Jan is developing an Excel workbook to generate Profit and Loss statements for the school to help manage their revenue and expenditures as well as make projections for future years. Jan has entered the school's financial transactions in a ledger worksheet and wants your help in designing a PivotTable that will take the ledger data and construct a Profit and Loss statement tracking revenue, cost of goods sold, expenses, gross profit, and net profit. Complete the following:

1. Open the **NP_EX_11-5.xlsx** workbook located in the Excel11 > Case1 folder included with your Data Files, and then save the workbook as **NP_EX_11_Riverside** in the location specified by your instructor.

2. In the Documentation sheet, in the range B3:B4, enter your name and the date. Review the contents of the workbook, and then go to the Profit and Loss worksheet.

3. Insert a PivotTable in the Profit and Loss worksheet based on the entries in the Ledger table. Click the Add this data to the data model check box to deselect it, if necessary. Name the PivotTable **Profit and Loss**. Place the Account Type and then the Account ID Name fields in the Rows area of the PivotTable. Place the Actual and then the Budget in the Values area. Rename "Sum of Actual" as **2029 Actuals** and "Sum of Budget" as **2029 Budget**. Display both fields as currency.

4. Remove the grand totals from the PivotTable layout. Show all subtotals at the bottom of each group. Insert blank lines after each item using the Blank Rows button in the Layout group of the Design tab.

5. Rearrange the Account Type field so that Revenue is listed first, followed by Cost of Goods Sold and then by Expense.

6. Create a PivotTable calculated item named **Gross Profit** that is equal to Revenue minus 'Cost of Goods Sold'.

7. Collapse the Gross Profit field in the PivotTable, hiding the gross profit for individual account items, so that only the subtotal is visible in the PivotTable.

8. Move the Gross Profit item directly after the Cost of Goods Sold. (**Hint:** You can move the Gross Profit item by dragging and dropping it with your mouse.)

9. Create a PivotTable calculated item named **Net Profit** that is equal to Gross Profit minus Expense. Collapse the Net Profit field so only the Net Profit subtotal is visible.

10. Create a calculated field name **Difference** that is equal to (Actual – Budget)/Budget. Display the PivotTable values as percentages to two decimal places. Change the field label from Sum Difference to **% Difference**.

11. Click cell D6, and then create a conditional format for all cells showing '% Difference Values' for 'Account ID Name' showing green, yellow, and red direction arrows. Display the green (up) arrow when the Number is greater than 0.01. Display the yellow (level) arrow when the Number is between –0.01 and 0.01. Otherwise, display the red (down) arrow.

12. Open the PivotTable Options dialog box, and then on the Layout & Format tab, deselect the options to AutoFit column widths on update and Preserve cell formatting on update check boxes. On the Display tab, deselect the Show expand/collapse button check box and the Display field captions and filter drop downs check boxes.

13. Create a slicer using the Department field, and then resize the slicer to cover the range F4:H17. Test the slicer to verify that you can view a Profit and Loss statement for each department, and then clear the filter when you are finished, displaying the Profit and Loss statement for the entire school.

14. In the Account Info worksheet, in cell B5, use an XLOOKUP function to match the value in cell B4 to the value of the Account field in the Accounts table, and then return the Account ID Name value from the Accounts table. Do the same in cell B6 to retrieve the Account Type.

15. In cell B7, type = and then click cell B7 of the Profit and Loss PivotTable to insert the GETPIVOTDATA function, retrieving the 2029 Actuals for account 4006.

16. In cell B7, edit the GETPIVOTDATA function, replacing "2029 Actuals" with **A7&""**, replacing "4006 Scholarship Gifts" with **B$5** and replacing "Revenue" with **B$6**.

17. Copy and fill without formatting the revised formula in cell B7 through the range B7:B9. Confirm that the values in the B7:B9 range match their corresponding values in the Profit and Loss PivotTable.

18. Test the dashboard by display financial information for ledger account **4105**.

19. Save the workbook, and then close it.

Challenge: Case Problem 2

Data File needed for this Case Problem: NP_EX_11-6.xlsx

Celerity Mobile Chandra Mali is an inventory analyst with the mobile network company Celerity Mobile. Part of her job is verifying that the company warehouses are well stocked but not overstocked. If a warehouse has too few items, orders will have to be backordered, resulting in irritated customers and lost sales. If the warehouse has too many items, Celerity Mobile is wasting money as products sit idle, generating no revenue.

There are three measures of inventory efficiency Chandra wants you to explore:

1. **Stockout Rate**, which measures the percentage of customer orders which could not be immediately fulfilled but instead must be placed on back order. High percentages indicate that the inventory might be understocked.

2. **Turnover Ratio**, which measures the total number of orders divided by the average number of items in stock over a specified time period. A ratio of 5 would mean that the inventory would be restocked five times to meet demand during the specified time period. The higher the turnover ratio, the more often the inventory must be restocked to keep up with orders.

3. **Inventory Period**, which measures the expected number of days an item will remain in inventory before shipping out. The Inventory Period is equal to a length of days divided by the Turnover Ratio during those days. A low Inventory Period means that products are moving quickly out of inventory. A high Inventory Period indicates that the inventory might be overstocked.

Chandra has a sample database containing data on the daily inventory of 12 mobile products stored within the Data Model of an Excel workbook. The Inventory table contains information on the number of items at the warehouse each day of the year, the number that need to be shipped out, and the number which are on back order because the inventory ran short. The Products table contains data on the 12 products that Chandra wants tracked. Your job will be to finish the workbook by completing the PivotTables and adding measures to report inventory statistics. Complete the following:

1. Open the **NP_EX_11-6.xlsx** workbook located in the Excel11 > Case2 folder included with your Data Files, and then save the workbook as **NP_EX_11_Celerity** in the location specified by your instructor.

2. In the Documentation sheet, in the range B3:B4, enter your name and the date. Review the contents of the workbook, particularly the Terms and Definitions worksheet that describes the contents of the Inventory and Products table. Note that the workbook contains empty PivotTables based on the tables in the Data Model, which you will complete in these steps.

3. Open Power Pivot to become familiar with the contents of the two tables in the Data Model, but do not make any changes to their content or structure, and then return to the workbook.

4. In the Inventory worksheet, do the following to complete the Inventory PivotTable to track the number of items in stock as well as customer orders for each day of the current year:
    a. Move the Date field from the Inventory table in the Rows area, and then move the Items and Customer Orders fields from the Inventory table into the Values area.
    b. Remove the Date (Month) field from the Rows area so that the inventory and orders for all products on each date are shown in the table.
    c. Change the label in cell B4 to **Items in Stock** and the label in cell C4 to **Items Ordered**.

5. Create a line chart PivotChart from the Inventory PivotTable and do the following:
    a. Move the PivotChart to the Summary worksheet and resize it to cover the range A10:C24.
    b. Add the chart title **Inventory and Orders**.
    c. Hide the field buttons and move the legend to the bottom of the chart.

6. Chandra wants to report the percentage of orders each month that could not be immediately supplied from the inventory. In the Stockout worksheet, in the Stockout PivotTable, move the Date field from the Inventory table to the Rows area. Remove the Date field, leaving only the Date (Month) group in the Rows area.

7. Create a measure for the Inventory table named **Stockout Rate**. Include the description **The percent of orders which cannot be filled by the inventory**. Apply the following formula to the measure and display the calculated value as a percentage to one decimal place:
    = SUM([Shortage])/SUM([Customer Orders])

8. Create a clustered column PivotChart of the data in Stockout PivotTable, and then do the following:
   a. Move the chart to the Summary worksheet. Move and resize the chart to cover the range E14:G24.
   b. Change the chart title to **Stockout Rate** and remove the chart legend and hide the field buttons.

9. Chandra wants to report the monthly rate at which the inventory is completely turned over. In the Turnover worksheet, in the Turnover PivotTable, do the following to determine the inventory turnover ratio:
   a. Move the Date (Month) field from the Inventory table to the Rows area.
   b. Create a measure for the Inventory table named **Turnover Ratio** with the description **The rate at which the inventory turns over**, and then enter the following formula and display the calculated value as a number to two decimal places:

      = SUM([Customer Orders])/(SUM([Items])/DISTINCTCOUNT([Date]))

   c. Create a line PivotChart from the PivotTable and move the chart to the Summary worksheet, and then resize it to cover the range I14:K24.
   d. Remove the chart legend and field buttons from the PivotChart. Change the chart title to **Turnover Ratio**.

10. Chandra needs to track how long items wait in the inventory. In the Inventory Period worksheet in the Inventory Period PivotTable, do the following to determine how many days, on average, an item will wait in the inventory before being shipped out:
    a. Move the Date (Month) field in the Inventory table to the Rows area.
    b. Create a measure for the Inventory table named **Inventory Period** with the description **The expected days an item will wait in the inventory**, and then enter the following formula and display the calculated value as a number to 0 decimal places:

       = DISTINCTCOUNT([Date])/[Turnover Ratio]

    c. Create an area PivotChart from the PivotTable and move the chart to the Summary worksheet and resize it to cover the range M14:O24.
    d. Remove the chart legend and field buttons from the PivotChart, and then change the chart title to **Inventory Period (Days)**.

11. Chandra wants a statistical summary of the status of the inventory. Do the following to display summary statistics on the Summary dashboard for each of the three inventory measures:
    a. In the Summary worksheet, click cell **B5**, type **=** and then click cell B18 of the Stockout worksheet to enter the GETPIVOTDATA function to display the grand total of the Stockout measure.
    b. Repeat the previous step for cell B6 to display the grand total of the Turnover Ratio measure in cell B18 of the Turnover worksheet.
    c. Repeat the previous step for cell B7 to display the grand total of the Inventory Period measure in cell B18 of the Inventory Period worksheet.

12. **Explore:** Chandra needs to report how much money is tied up in the inventory. In the Scratch worksheet, do the following to define a measure that calculates the daily cash value of the inventory:
    a. With the PivotTable in the Scratch worksheet selected, define a new measure for the Inventory table named **Inventory Value** with the description **The average value of the inventory over the specified time period**.
    b. Enter the following formula that calculates the average of the number of items in the inventory multiplied by their cost from the Products table, and then display the calculated value as currency with 0 decimals places. (Note that you can copy this long and complex formula from the Terms and Definitions worksheet.)

       = SUMX(Inventory,[Items]*RELATED(Products[Cost]))/DISTINCTCOUNT([Date])

    c. Verify that the Scratch PivotTable displays the value $1,203,193, indicating that on a typical day, the value of all inventory items is about $1.2 million.

13. **Explore:** In the Summary worksheet, in cell B8, insert the following CUBEVALUE function from the Data Model, to display the Inventory Value measure without using a PivotTable, and then verify that the average daily value is once again about $1.2 million:

    = CUBEVALUE("ThisWorkbookDataModel", "[Measures].[Inventory Value]", Slicer_Product, Timeline_Date)

14. Chandra wants to track inventory data on individual products for specified dates. On the Summary worksheet, insert a slicer for the Product field from the Products table in the Data Model. Move and resize the slicer to cover the range E1:O5 and increase the number of columns to **4**. Connect the slicer to the following PivotTables in the Data Model: Inventory, Inventory Period, Stockout, and Turnover.

15. Insert a timeline for the Date field from the Inventory table in the Data Model. Move and resize the timeline to cover the range E6:O12. Connect the timeline to the following PivotTables in the Data Model: Inventory, Inventory Period, Stockout, and Turnover.

16. In the spring and summer, the company experienced severe supply chain problems with the Sportify X26 Smartwatch. Use the Product slicer and the Date timeline to display an inventory report on the Sportify X26 Smartwatch from April to September.

17. Save the workbook, and then close it.

Developing an Excel Application

Tracking Donations to a Nonprofit

Case: Chestnut Academy

Rebecca Barthold is a fundraising coordinator for Chestnut Academy, a nonprofit private school in Lancaster, Pennsylvania. Rebecca uses Excel to track fundraising efforts in a capital campaign for a multimillion-dollar building project. The workbook containing the fundraising results will be shared with Rebecca's development team. However, because many of her colleagues are not regular Excel users, Rebecca wants to develop a custom Excel application that will enable her team to analyze the fundraising data without introducing errors to the workbook or changing the Excel formulas already in use.

Starting Data Files

Excel12

Module

NP_EX_12-1.xlsx

Review

NP_EX_12-2.xlsx

Case1

NP_EX_12-3.xlsx

Case2

NP_EX_12-4.xlsx

Objectives

Part 12.1

- Hide error values with the IFERROR function
- Validate data entry
- Protect a worksheet
- Unlock worksheet cells

Part 12.2

- Define variables and functions with LET
- Define custom functions with LAMBDA
- Apply LAMBDA helper functions

Part 12.3

- Display the Developer tab
- Record and run a macro
- Create macros in the Visual Basic Editor
- Protect a workbook

Part 12.1 Visual Overview: Error Control and Data Validation

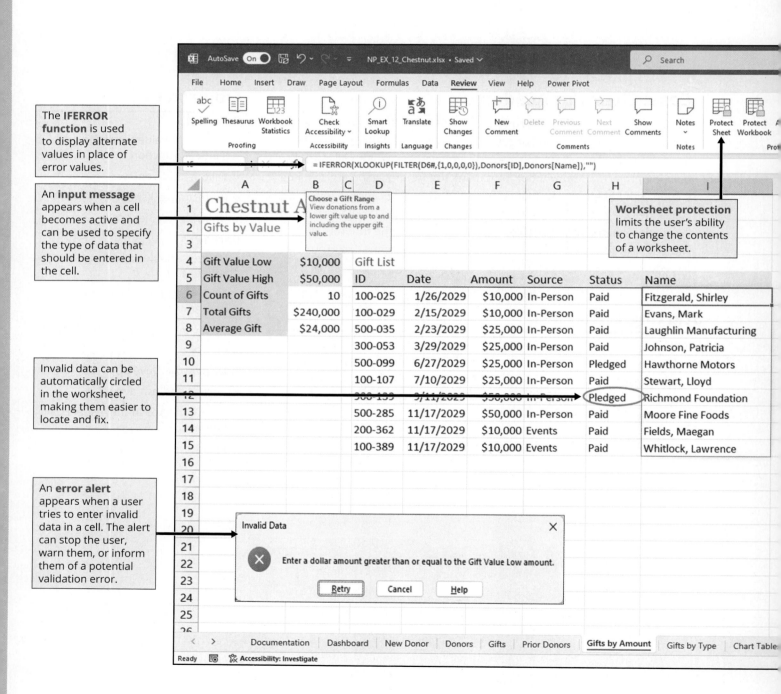

The IFERROR function is used to display alternate values in place of error values.

An **input message** appears when a cell becomes active and can be used to specify the type of data that should be entered in the cell.

Worksheet protection limits the user's ability to change the contents of a worksheet.

Invalid data can be automatically circled in the worksheet, making them easier to locate and fix.

An **error alert** appears when a user tries to enter invalid data in a cell. The alert can stop the user, warn them, or inform them of a potential validation error.

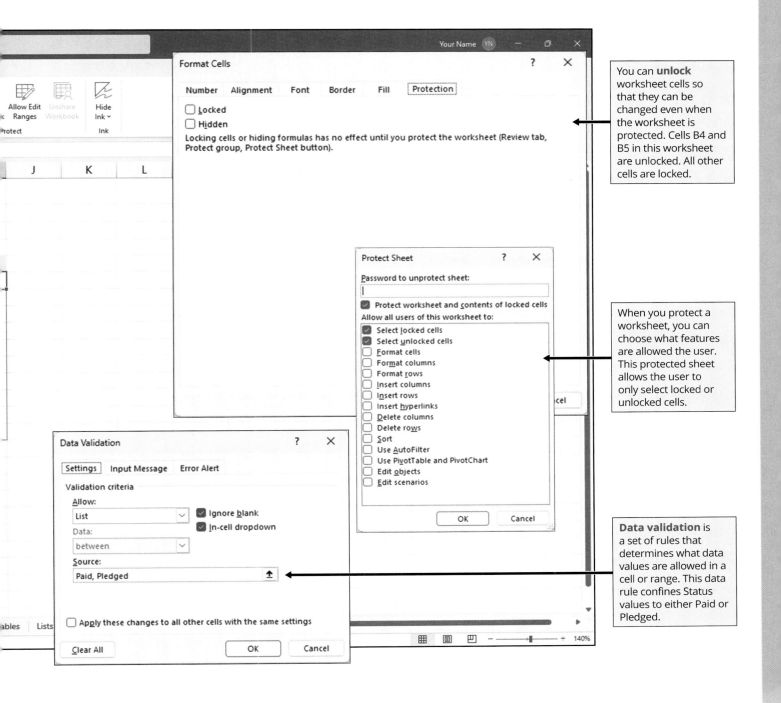

You can **unlock** worksheet cells so that they can be changed even when the worksheet is protected. Cells B4 and B5 in this worksheet are unlocked. All other cells are locked.

When you protect a worksheet, you can choose what features are allowed the user. This protected sheet allows the user to only select locked or unlocked cells.

Data validation is a set of rules that determines what data values are allowed in a cell or range. This data rule confines Status values to either Paid or Pledged.

Planning an Excel Application

An **Excel application** is an Excel workbook featuring error control, protected formulas, and automated data entry in a customized interface to make it easier for users to enter data and generate reports. One reason to create an Excel application is to unlock the power of Excel for users not experienced in Excel. Another goal is to protect the workbook so that formulas and data are not inadvertently changed by users.

You will help Rebecca create an Excel application to track donations to the Chestnut Academy capital campaign. Rebecca needs to evaluate the success of the campaign using industry-standard fundraising metrics. But she also wants members of the campaign team to be able to easily enter new donor contacts without altering formulas and tables already in the workbook. You'll start by reviewing Rebecca's workbook.

To review Rebecca's workbook:

1. **sam↓** Open the **NP_EX_12-1.xlsx** workbook located in the **Excel12 > Module** folder included with your Data Files, and then save the workbook as **NP_EX_12_Chestnut** in the location specified by your instructor.

2. In the **Documentation** worksheet, enter your name and the date in the range B3:B4.

3. Review the sheets in the workbook, but do not change any content.

4. After reviewing the workbook, go to the **Dashboard** worksheet.

Rebecca tracks the campaign's fundraising efforts in three tables stored in the workbook and in the Excel Data Model:

- The Donors table provides contact information for every donor to the current campaign.
- The Gifts table lists each donation made to the current campaign.
- The Prior table lists donors who contributed to a previous fundraiser and the amount they gave.

A donor might make several gifts to the current campaign, so the Donors and Gifts table are linked through a common ID field identifying the donor.

Donors fall into six categories: parents or guardians of a student at the academy, other involved family members, academy alumni, general benefactors, corporate benefactors, and grants from private or public institutions. Individual gifts are classified according to how the gift was solicited. The six possible gift sources are in-person contributions, gifts contributed through fundraising events, gifts solicited through a two-week phonathon, gifts given online via the academy website, gifts provided through payroll deductions, and gifts solicited through mail flyers.

The Dashboard worksheet (refer to Figure 12–1) provides an overview of the campaign's progress. The campaign is struggling. After a year of effort, the school has raised about $1.4 million of its $3.6 million target, putting it only 39% of the way toward its goal. Rebecca needs to determine the cause.

Figure 12–1   Fundraising dashboard

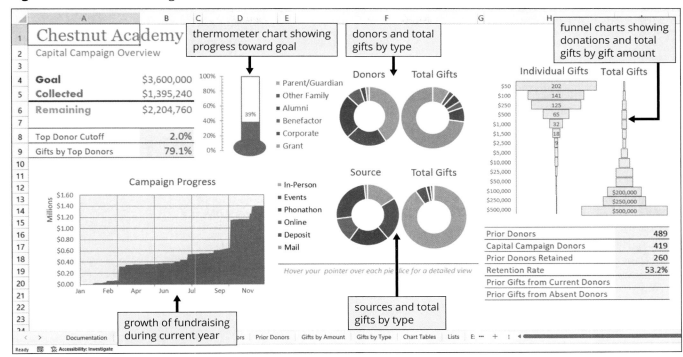

The dashboard provides important insights on the campaign. Most of the donors are students' parents or guardians, followed by extended family, alumni, and general benefactors. Although most donors fall into these categories, most of the money collected comes from private and public grants. Gifts to the campaign are roughly evenly split between in-person interviews, fundraising events, the school phonathon, online contributions, and direct deposits, but most of the money has come from in-person solicitations.

The dashboard also breaks down donors and donations by the gift amount. While most donors contribute gifts of $50 to $100, most of the money comes from a few individual gifts of $100,000 to $500,000. This information provides Rebecca and her team a better understanding of who is contributing to the campaign and how much they are contributing.

Insight

Creating Funnel Charts and Thermometer Charts

Rebecca used funnel charts and thermometer charts in her dashboard to provide crucial information on the capital campaign. A **funnel chart** is a chart comparing values within a hierarchy of category levels. Funnel charts get their name from the funnel shape that often appears when data are clustered at lower or upper categories. To create a funnel chart:

1. Select the data range containing the category levels and the numeric values within each category.
2. Open the Insert Chart dialog box, and then on the All Charts tab, select Funnel from the list of chart types.
3. Format the chart to provide the most useful information to the reader.

Funnel charts cannot be created as PivotCharts, but you can copy PivotTable data to another cell range and chart those linked values or use dynamic arrays to generate the table of funnel values.

A **thermometer chart** is a chart showing progress toward a goal in the form of a thermometer graphic, where a completion rate of 100% is indicated by a full thermometer. Excel does not include the Thermometer chart type, but you can create one as follows:

1. Enter the calculated progress towards the goal and the 100% goal value in a two-by-two table, such as:

   Progress   Goal
   38%   100%

2. Create a clustered column chart from the data range, and then on the Chart Design tab, in the Data group, click the Switch Row/Column button.
3. Double-click the Progress marker in the column chart to open the Format Data Series pane.
4. In the Series Option section, plot the Progress series on a secondary axis.
5. Set the range for both the primary and secondary axes to go from 0 to 1.

After these edits, the two columns of the column chart will be superimposed on each other. You can then change the fill colors and line colors to create the thermometer graphic. To improve the thermometer image, place an oval shape filled with the progress color at the base of the column.

The dashboard will be a valuable tool for the fundraising team, but only if the fundraising data is error-free.

Managing Error Values

Managing workbook errors is an important feature of any workbook, especially if that workbook is used by people with varying Excel abilities. Error control has three general components:

1. Managing error values in a way that is informative to the user.
2. Limiting cell values to predefined criteria to avoid data entry mistakes.
3. Limiting the cells users can edit to avoid adding unintentional errors to formulas and functions.

An error value can appear even when the formula seems simple and straightforward. For example, a workbook might contain the following formula to calculate the average of the data in the range D1:D100:

```
= AVERAGE(D1:D100)
```

But if the range D1:D100 does not contain numeric data, the #DIV/0! error value is returned. Error values can be disconcerting to users, and they also make a report look sloppy and unprofessional. Rebecca wants her workbook to handle errors of this type more gracefully.

Using the IFERROR Function

The IFERROR function catches error values and can display alternate text in place of the error values. The IFERROR function syntax is

```
= IFERROR(value, value_if_error)
```

where $value$ is the value returned by a formula when no errors are present, and $value\_if\_error$ is the value returned in place of the default error value. For example, the following formula returns the average of the values in the range D1:D100 but returns the text string "No data available" if that calculation results in an error:

```
= IFERROR(AVERAGE(D1:D100), "No data available")
```

In the Gifts by Amount worksheet, Rebecca wants her team to be able to identify gifts within a specified dollar range. In addition to identifying the individual donors, the worksheet also counts the total number of gifts, sums the total gift amount, and averages the gift amount. If no gifts were made in the specified range, the average gift calculation will return an error value because it cannot calculate an average with no gifts. Rebecca wants to avoid that distraction. You'll use the IFERROR function to display a blank text string in place of the error value.

To enter the IFERROR function to display a blank text string instead of an error value:

1. Go to the **Gifts by Amount** worksheet. Cell B8 displays the #DIV/0! error value because there are no gifts in the $3,000 and $4,000 range.

   The worksheet reports the number of donors (cell B6), the total gifts (cell B7), and the average gift amount (cell B8) for gifts between $3,000 and $4,000. Because there are no gifts in that range, the formula in cell B8, which calculates the value of cell B7 divided by B6 and returns the #DIV/0! error.

2. Click cell **B8** containing the formula = B7/B6, change the formula to **= IFERROR(B7/B6, "")** and then press **ENTER**. Cell B8 no longer displays any text.

3. Click cell **B8** to select it, verifying that the cell displays an empty text string rather than the #DIV/0! error value. Refer to Figure 12–2.

Figure 12–2   Error value prevented with IFERROR function

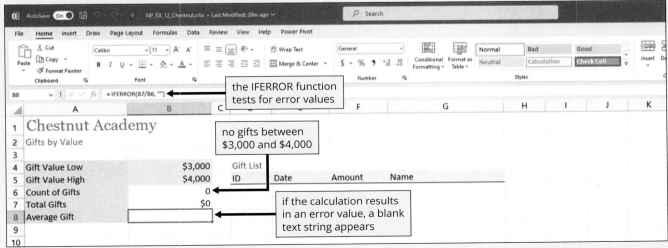

The IFERROR function can be applied to any function that returns an error, but some Excel functions provide their own parameters for handing errors.

Proskills

Written Communication: Identifying Data Types

Another useful error function is the following ISERROR function, which returns a value of TRUE if *value* is an error value and FALSE if it isn't:

```
ISERROR(value)
```

For example, the following expression tests whether cell B10 contains an error value:

```
ISERROR(B10)
```

The advantage of the ISERROR function is that you can enter the formula in one cell and then place an informative message about any errors in an adjacent cell. The following formula nests an ISERROR function within an IF function to display one message if cell B10 has error and a different message if not:

```
= IF(ISERROR(B10), "Input Error", "Input Valid")
```

The ISERROR function is part of a class of Excel functions that test cells for specified data types. Other functions include ISBLANK to test whether a cell is empty, ISNUMBER to test whether a cell contains a number, ISTEXT to test for the presence of text value, and ISFORMULA to test for presence of a formula. You can also test for a specific type of error value using ISNA to test for the #N/A error value.

A custom Excel application can make great use of these functions to confirm that users are not just entering data that is error free but also data that is the correct type.

Handling Errors in Dynamic Array Functions

Dynamic array functions, used to look up or filter values from an array, include an argument to handle error values without needing to nest the formula within the IFERROR function. For example, the XLOOKUP function includes the optional *if_not_found* argument:

```
XLOOKUP(lookup_value, lookup_array, return_array,
[if_not_found], [match_mode], [search_mode])
```

If Excel is unable to retrieve a matching value, the *if_not_found* argument provides a way to report that fact without an error value. For example, if Rebecca wanted to retrieve the name of the donor with the ID 100-999 from the Donors table, she could apply the following XLOOKUP function:

```
XLOOKUP("100-999", Donors[ID], Donors[Name],
"No donor found")
```

Excel will then return either the name of the donor or the text "No donor found". If there is no value included for the *if_not_found* argument, XLOOKUP will return the error value #N/A if no match is found.

> **Tip** The VLOOKUP and HLOOKUP functions do not support the *if_not_found* argument, so those functions must be nested within IFERROR to return alternate text instead of an error value.

The FILTER function includes the optional *if_empty* argument to handle the situation where filtering returns an empty array. The FILTER function has the syntax:

```
FILTER(array, include, [if_empty])
```

To filter the list of contributions in the Gifts table to show only those gifts from Donor 100-999, Rebecca could use the following expression to return either an array listing all gifts from Donor 100-999 or the text "No gifts from that donor":

```
FILTER(Gifts, Gifts[ID]="100-999", "No gifts from that
donor")
```

If Rebecca does not provide a value for the *if_empty* argument, Excel will return the #CALC! error value, indicating a failure to generate the array.

Rebecca wants to use the FILTER function in the Gifts by Amount worksheet to list the gifts matching the dollar range specified in cells B4 and B5. If no gifts are found, Rebecca wants Excel to display the text "No Gifts". The formula

```
= FILTER(Gifts[ID]:Gifts[Amount],
(Gifts[Amount]>=B4)*(Gifts[Amount]<=B5), "No Gifts")
```

will return only the ID through Amount columns from the Gifts table. Note that filter criterion specifies that the gift amount must be greater than or equal to the value of cell B4 and less than or equal to the value of cell B5. You will enter this formula into the worksheet.

To filter the donation list by dollar amount:

1. Click cell **D6**, and then type the formula:

   ```
   = FILTER(Gifts[ID]:Gifts[Amount],(Gifts[Amount]>=B4)*
   (Gifts[Amount]<=B5),"No Gifts")
   ```

   Tip Use the Autocomplete feature to insert the name of the Gifts table and fields within that table by pressing TAB after each AutoComplete suggestion.

2. Press **ENTER**. The formula returns the text "No Gifts" because there are no donations in the $3,000 to $4,000 range.

   Trouble? If Excel reports an error message, check your formula. Common mistakes include omitting a closing parenthesis or a quotation mark.

3. In cell **B4**, enter **5000** and then in cell **B5**, enter **10000** to list all donations from $5,000 up to $10,000. There are 16 gifts for a total of $105,000 and an average gift size of $6,563.

4. Click cell **D6** containing the FILTER formula. Refer to Figure 12–3.

Figure 12–3   Values filtered from the Gifts table

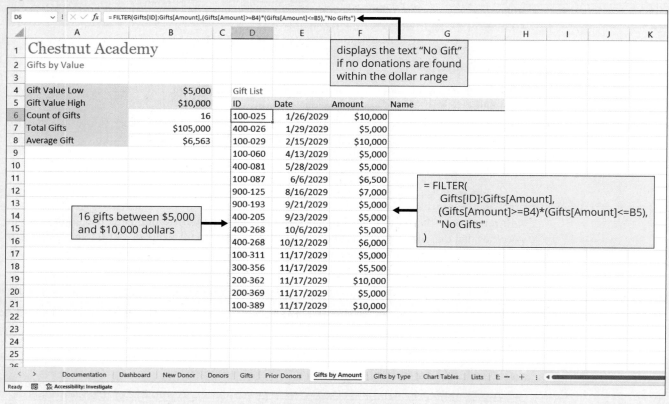

The gift list should also include the donor names. Because this information is stored in the Donors table, you will use the following formula to retrieve donor names based on donor IDs provided in the spill range starting at cell D6:

```
= XLOOKUP(FILTER(D6#,{1,0,0}),Donors[ID],Donors[Name])
```

The formula uses the FILTER function to generate a dynamic array based on the first column of the spill range using the array {1, 0, 0} to retrieve only the first column of donor IDs. That column of donor IDs is then used in the XLOOKUP function to retrieve the Name field from the Donors table.

There is one problem. If the spill range returns the text "No Gifts", the XLOOKUP function will return the #VALUE! error value. The simplest correction is to wrap the entire XLOOKUP function within IFERROR and return a blank text string in the place of the error value. The revised formula is:

```
= IFERROR(XLOOKUP(FILTER(D6#,{1,0,0}),Donors[ID],
Donors[Name]),"")
```

You will enter this formula into cell G6 of the Gifts by Amount worksheet to display the donor names associated with each donation.

To display the names of each donor in the list:

1. Click cell **G6** and then type the formula:

    ```
    = IFERROR(XLOOKUP(FILTER(D6#,{1,0,0}),Donors[ID],
    Donors[Name]),"")
    ```

2. Press **ENTER**. The names of each donor appear alongside their gift amount.

    Trouble? If Excel rejects the formula, check that you have closed all parentheses and used curly braces to enclose the {1, 0, 0} array.

3. Click cell **G6** containing the formula. Refer to Figure 12–4.

Figure 12–4   Names of the donors displayed

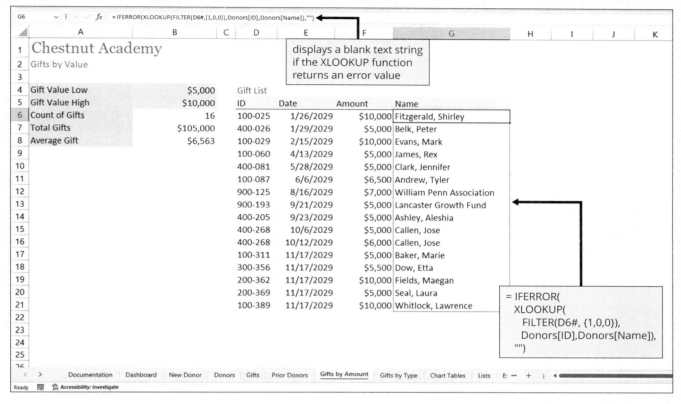

4. Delete the values in cell **B4** and **B5** to confirm that the gift list responds to the missing dollar range by displaying only the text "No Gifts".

Error functions hide distracting error values resulting from data entry errors. However, they do not remove data entry errors. Users can still enter invalid data but then not know that they have done it. Tracking down the source of a data entry error after the fact can be frustrating and time-consuming. You can use data validation to prevent invalid data from being entered.

Validating Data Entry

Error functions are an important tool for catching errors before they happen, but it is even better to catch those errors before they're made. You can guard against many data entry errors with a **validation rule**, defining what values are allowed in a cell range and what values are not. A validation rule might restrict a cell value to a range of numeric values or dates, to a list of categories, or to text strings of a certain length, or in general any value that matches specified criteria. Figure 12–5 describes the types of validation rules supported by Excel.

Figure 12–5   Validation criteria

Type	Description
Any value	Any number, text, or date; removes any existing data validation
Whole Number	Integers only; you can specify the range of acceptable integers
Decimal	Any type of number; you can specify the range of acceptable numbers
List	Any value in a range or entered in the Data Validation dialog box separated by commas
Date	Dates only; you can specify the range of acceptable dates
Time	Times only; you can specify the range of acceptable times
Text Length	Text limited to a specified number of characters
Custom	Values based on the results of a logical formula

Only one validation rule at a time can be applied to a cell range. However, you can customize a validation rule to handle a wide variety of user errors.

Reference

Validating Data

- Select a cell or range in which to apply data validation.
- On the Data tab, in the Data Tools group, click the Data Validation button.
- Click the Settings tab.
- Click the Allow arrow, click the type of data allowed in the cell, and then enter the validation criteria for that data.
- Click the Input Message tab, and then enter a title and text for the input message.
- Click the Error Alert tab, and then, if necessary, click the Show error alert after invalid data is entered check box to insert a checkmark.
- Select an alert style, and then enter the title and text for the error alert message.
- Click OK.

Validating Numbers

Rebecca wants to ensure that users enter only nonnegative numbers in cells B4 and B5. She also wants to verify that the value of cell B5 is greater than or equal to the value of cell B4. You will start by creating a validation rule for cell B4, limiting its value to numbers greater than or equal to zero.

To create a validation rule restricting cell B4 to nonnegative numeric values:

1. Click cell **B4** to select it.

2. On the ribbon, click the **Data** tab, and then in the Data Tools group, click the **Data Validation** button. The Data Validation dialog box opens.

3. If it is not already selected, click the **Settings** tab to display the criteria for the validation rule.

4. Click the **Allow** box, and then select **Decimal** to limit cell B4 to decimal values.

5. Click the **Data** box, and then select **greater than or equal to** to specify the lower range of acceptable cell B4 values.

6. Click the **Minimum** box and enter **0** to set $0 as the lower limit for cell B4. Refer to Figure 12–6.

Figure 12–6   Settings tab in Data Validation dialog box

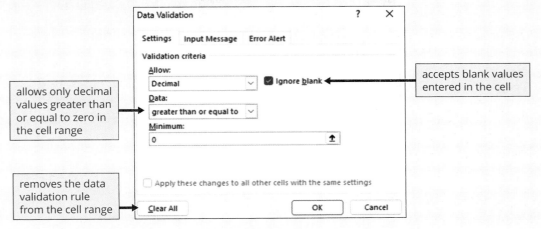

7. Click **OK** to close the Data Validation dialog box and apply the rule.

Validation rules are applied after the user has finished editing the cell and pressed ENTER to exit Edit mode. They are not applied while the user is typing, nor is the cell value tested when the user simply selects the cell and presses ENTER. You will test the validation rule by attempting to enter nonnumeric values and negative numbers in cell B4.

To test the validation rule in cell B4:

1. In cell **B4**, enter **school** as the value. A dialog box appears, indicating that this value fails the validation test. Refer to Figure 12–7.

Figure 12–7   Entered cell value fails the validation rule

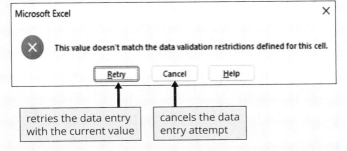

2. Click **Cancel** to return to cell B4.

3. In cell **B4**, enter **–10** as the value, and then verify that Excel also rejects this negative value.

4. Click **Cancel** to return to cell B4.

5. In cell **B4**, enter **5000** as the value. Excel does not display a warning because this value passes the validation test.

Next, you will create a validation rule for cell B5 to ensure that its value is greater than or equal to the value in cell B4.

To create a validation rule for cell B5:

1. Click cell **B5** to select it, and then on the Data tab, in the Data Tools group, click **Data Validation** button. The Data Validation dialog box opens.

2. Click the **Allow** box, and then select **Decimal** and click the **Data** box, and then select **greater than or equal to**.

    ▌ **Key Step** You must type the = symbol before to the cell reference so that validation rule refers to cell B4.

3. In the Minimum box, type **= B4** to restrict values of cell B5 to be greater than or equal to the value entered in cell B4. Refer to Figure 12–8.

Figure 12–8   Validation rule using a cell value

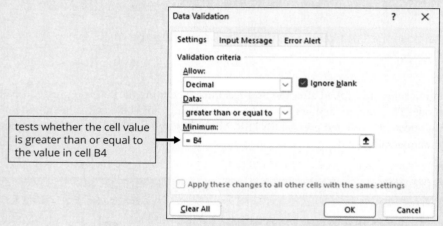

4. Click **OK** to apply the validation rule.

5. In cell **B5**, enter **50** to verify that Excel rejects that data as invalid because it is not greater than or equal to the value of cell B4.

6. Click **Cancel**, and then enter **10000** in cell B5 to confirm that Excel accepts the data value and reports all gifts from $5,000 up to $10,000.

A common data error is neglecting to enter data into cells that require a value. By default, validation rules will ignore blanks, but you can test for that condition by deselecting the Ignore Blanks check box in the Data Validation dialog box. However, that will only catch blanks if the user exits Edit mode with a blank cell value. It will not catch blanks if the user is never in Edit mode.

Insight

Validating Dates

Applications that track sales or shipping data need to limit dates to a specified range. The same validation rules applied to numeric values can be applied to dates. For example, you can require dates to fall within a specific date range. You can also create a validation rule based on the current date. To allow only dates on or before today's date, do the following:

1. Select the cells containing the date values.
2. Open the Data Validation dialog box.
3. Click the Allow box, and then click Choose Date.
4. Click the Data box, and then click "less than or equal to".
5. In the End date box, enter = TODAY().
6. Click OK.

Any date on or before the current date will be accepted. To allow only dates on or after today, change the value in the Data box to "greater than or equal to" and enter = TODAY() in the Start date box. The same technique can be used for time values by using the = NOW() function to reference the current date and time.

Creating a Validation Message

Some data entry errors are more serious than others. Excel provides three ways of responding to invalid data. In decreasing order of severity, they are:

1. **Stop**—The user is stopped, and no data entry is allowed in the cell unless it satisfies the validation rule (the default).

2. **Warning**—The user is warned. Data is allowed in the cell only after it is confirmed by the user as being acceptable.

3. **Information**—The user is informed of possibly invalid data and is given the opportunity to cancel the data entry but is not required to do so.

With each error response, you can create a custom message explaining in more detail why the data was invalid and what the user should do to correct the problem.

Rebecca thinks it would be less confusing to users if the Excel application displayed a warning message explaining the problem with values entered in cells B4 and B5. You will create a warning message for cell B4 that tells users to enter a value that is zero or higher.

To create a warning message for cell B4:

1. Click cell **B4** to select it, and then on the Data tab, in the Data Tools group, click the **Data Validation** button. The Data Validation dialog box opens.

2. Click the **Error Alert** tab.

3. Click the **Style** box, and then select **Warning**.

4. Click the **Title** box, type **Invalid Data** and then press **TAB**.

5. In the Error message box, type **Enter a dollar amount greater than or equal to zero.** (including the period). Refer to Figure 12-9.

Figure 12–9   Error Alert tab in the Data Validation dialog box

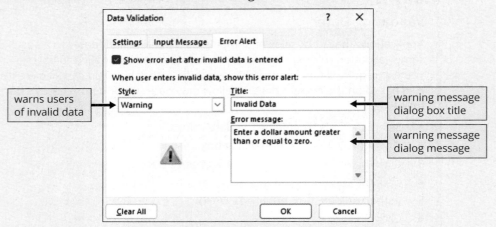

6. Click **OK** to close the dialog box, updating the validation rule.

7. In cell **B4**, type **school** and then press **ENTER**. The Invalid Data dialog box appears with the warning message you created. Refer to Figure 12–10.

Figure 12–10   Data validation warning message

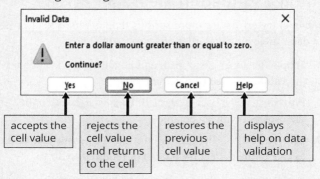

8. Click **Cancel** to return to cell B4, restoring the most recent value of $5,000.

Rachel wants to add a Stop message for cell B5, directing the user to enter a value greater than cell B4. You'll create that message now.

To create a Stop message for cell B5:

1. Click cell **B5** and then on the Data tab, in the Data Tools group, click the **Data Validation** button. The Data Validation dialog box opens.

2. On the Error Alert tab, click the **Style** box, and then select **Stop** if it is not already selected.

3. Click the **Title** box, type **Invalid Data** and then press **TAB**.

4. In the Error message box, type **Enter a dollar amount greater than or equal to the Gift Value Low amount.** (including the period).

5. Click **OK** to apply the validation rule and return to cell B5.

6. Type **0** in cell B5, and then press **ENTER**. The Invalid Data dialog box appears with the error message you created. Refer to Figure 12–11.

Figure 12–11   Data validation stop message

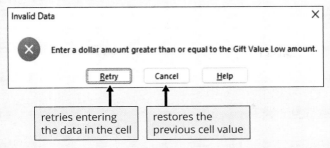

retries entering
the data in the cell

restores the
previous cell value

7. Click **Cancel** to restore cell B5 to its previous value of $10,000.

Any time you want to remove validation from a cell, select the cell, reopen the Data Validation dialog box, and then click the Clear All button.

Creating an Input Message

Rather than constantly notifying users of their errors, you can make an application more user-friendly by providing the validation rule prior to data entry. An input message is a pop-up message that appears next to a selected cell specifying the type of data expected in that cell.

Rebecca wants you to add an input message to cell B4 informing users to enter dollar amounts in cell B4 and B5.

To create an input message:

1. Click cell **B4** to select it, and then on the Data tab, in the Data Tools group, click the **Data Validation** button. The Data Validation dialog box opens.

2. Click the **Input Message** tab.

3. Click the **Title** box, type **Choose a Gift Range** and then press **TAB**.

4. In the Input message box, type **View donations from a lower gift value up to and including the upper gift value.** (including the period). Refer to Figure 12–12.

Figure 12–12   Input message being defined

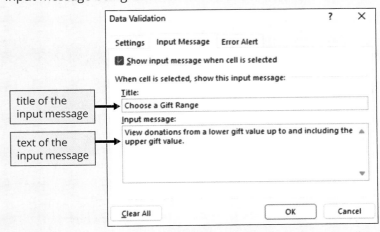

title of the
input message

text of the
input message

5. Click **OK** to close the Data Validation dialog box. Cell B4 remains selected in the worksheet and the input message appears in a box next to cell B4. Refer to Figure 12–13.

Figure 12–13   Input message for active cell

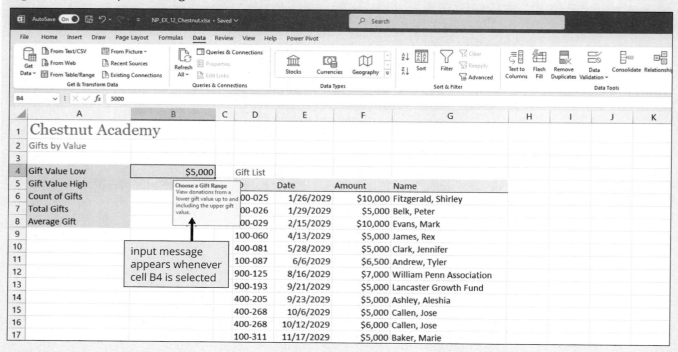

Rebecca is confident that the input message and validation rule will ensure users know what data to enter and will enter valid data into cell B4 and B5.

Validating Against a List

Another validation rule limits data values to a predefined list of accepted choices. A predefined list removes the possibility of mistyping an entry and speeds up data entry because users can select a data value from the drop-down list that appears within the cell. The list can be based on cells entries in the workbook or entered directly in the Data Validation dialog box as a comma-separated list.

Rebecca created a worksheet that lists donations by the type of donor (Parent/Guardian, Other Family, Alumni, Benefactor, Corporate, or Grant). She wants to ensure that users can enter only one of those six possible values. Rebecca has already placed error control functions into the worksheet. You'll add a validation rule based on the list of accepted donor types.

To validate the donor type based on a list:

1. Go to the **Gifts by Type** worksheet and select cell **B4** in which users specify the donor type.

2. On the Data tab, in the Data Tools group, click the **Data Validation** button. The Data Validation dialog box opens.

3. Click the **Settings** tab in the dialog box.

4. Click the **Allow** box, select **List**, and then press **TAB** to move the insertion point to the Source box.

5. Use your pointer to click the **Lists** sheet tab, and then select the range **F5:F10** containing the list of donor types. The reference = Lists!$F$5:$F$10 appears in the Source box.

> **Tip** You can simplify validation rules by assigning range names to all lists used in an Excel application.

6. Click the **Ignore Blank** check box so that users cannot enter a blank value into the cell. The validation rule is complete. Refer to Figure 12–14.

Figure 12–14   Validation rule based on a list

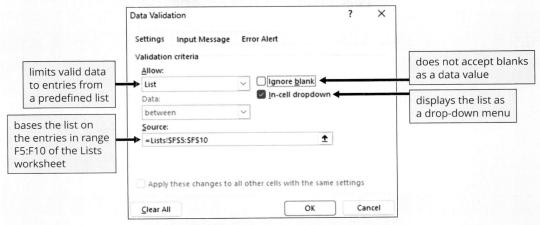

7. Click **OK** to apply the validation rule and return to cell B4.

8. Next to cell B4, click the **arrow** button, and then select **Corporate**. The worksheet displays all gifts from corporate donors. Refer to Figure 12–15.

Figure 12–15   List of donor types

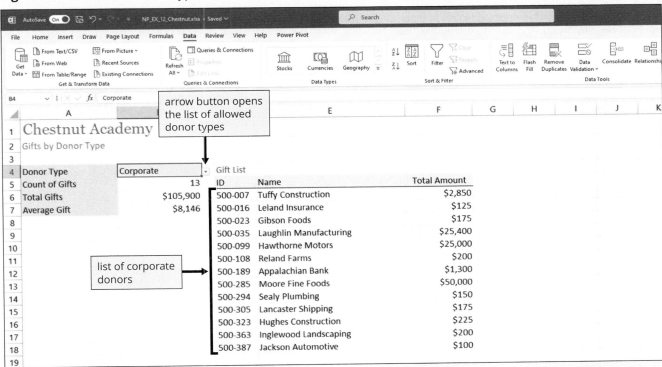

The campaign has 13 corporate donors, having contributed a total of $105,900 with an average gift of $8,146. The largest donation came from Moore Fine Foods, which donated $50,000 to the campaign.

Creating a Custom Validation Rule

In addition to the built-in data validation rules, you can create your own validation criteria using a formula that returns either TRUE (if the cell passes validation) or FALSE (if the cell fails the validation test). For example, to allow only even numbers to be entered into cell C10, you would use the following ISEVEN function as the custom validation rule:

    = ISEVEN(C10)

The ISEVEN function returns TRUE if the value in cell C10 is an even number and FALSE if not. If a user attempts to enter a text string or an odd number into the cell, the entry will be rejected as invalid.

Rebecca wants you to create a validation rule for the ID values in the Gifts table. The ID field references the donor who made the gift, so the ID must match an ID listed in the Donors table. Rebecca created the range name ID_List to reference a list of all donor IDs. To determine whether a cell value matches an item in that list, you can apply the custom validation rule

    = ISNUMBER(XMATCH(*ref*, ID_List))

where *ref* references a cell containing a donor ID. For example, the following formula tests whether the value in cell B5 contains a listed donor ID:

    = ISNUMBER(XMATCH(B5, ID_List))

The formula uses XMATCH to find a match for the value cell B5 in the ID_List range. If it finds a match, it returns the index number of the match, and the ISNUMBER function returns a value of TRUE. If there is no match, XMATCH returns an error value, and the ISNUMBER function returns a value of FALSE, marking the data as invalid.

> **Tip** Validation formulas can reference cells, range names, or spill ranges, but they cannot reference table fields.

You will enter this ISNUMBER formula as a validation rule for cell B5 of the Gifts table to test whether that cell contains a valid donor ID.

To create a custom validation rule for cell B5:

1. Go to the **Gifts** worksheet and click cell **B5** to select it.

2. On the Data tab, in the Data Tools group, click the **Data Validation** button. The Data Validation dialog box opens.

3. In the Settings tab, click the **Allow** box, select **Custom**, and then press **TAB**.

4. In the Formula box, enter **= ISNUMBER(XMATCH(B5, ID_List))** as the formula. Refer to Figure 12–16.

Figure 12–16 Custom validation rule

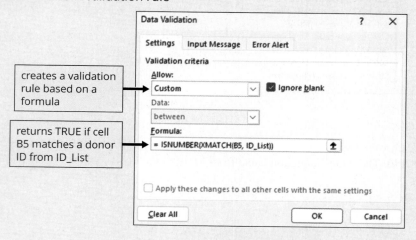

creates a validation rule based on a formula

returns TRUE if cell B5 matches a donor ID from ID_List

5. Click the **Error Alert** tab, and make sure **Stop** is selected in the Style box.

6. Click the **Title** box, type **Invalid ID** as the title, click the **Error message** box and then type **No Donor ID Found** as the error message.

7. Click **OK** to apply the validation rule.

8. In cell **B5**, type **100-999** as the ID, and then press **ENTER**. A dialog box indicates that this is not a valid donor ID.

9. Click **Cancel** to return to cell B5, restoring the previous valid donor ID 200-001.

A validation rule can be copied and pasted from one cell into an entire range. When the rule is copied, any cell reference from a custom validation formula will be automatically adjusted to match the new cell address. If you copy the validation rule in cell B5 to cell B6, the relative reference B5 will be changed to B6, and the validation rule will be applied to that cell.

> **Tip** If you want a reference in a validation formula to remain unchanged as it is copied to a new cell range, use either an absolute cell reference or a range name.

You will copy the validation rule in cell B5 to the remaining cells in column B of the Gifts table.

To copy and paste the validation rule in cell B5:

1. Click cell **B5** to select it, if necessary.

2. On the ribbon, click the **Home** tab, and then in the Clipboard group, click the **Copy** button. The cell contents are copied to the Clipboard.

3. Select the range **B6:B622**, and then in the Clipboard group, click the **Paste arrow** and then click **Paste Special**. The Paste Special dialog box opens.

4. Click the **Validation** option button, and then click **OK** to paste the validation rule into the selected cells.

5. Click cell **B15** and change the value from 300-012 to **100-999**. The donor ID is rejected.

6. Click **Cancel** to restore the cell value to 300-012.

You can apply the same validation rule to an entire range by selecting the range and writing the validation rule for the first cell in the range. Any cell references in the validation formula will be adjusted to match the address of each subsequent cell.

Validating Existing Data

All the techniques described so far have been used to catch errors when a user is entering values. Validation rules can also highlight errors already present in the workbook. Data entry errors are circled so you can easily identify and then fix.

The Gifts table includes a Status field indicating the status of the donation payments. Each gift should be marked as either Paid or Pledged. Rebecca is worried that some entries in the Gifts table do not follow this convention. You will create a validation rule for the entire column to highlight any invalid Status values.

To validate existing data in the Gifts table:

1. In the Gifts worksheet, select the range **F5:F622** containing the status of each gift.

2. On the ribbon, click the **Data** tab, and then in the Data Tools group, click the **Data Validation** button. The Data Validation dialog box opens.

3. Click the **Settings** tab, click the **Allow** box and select **List** from, and then press **TAB**.

4. In the Source box, enter the comma-separated list **Paid, Pledged** and then click **OK** to return to the worksheet.

5. In the Data Tools group, click the **Data Validation arrow**, and then click **Circle Invalid Data**.

6. Scroll down the worksheet and verify that only cells F85 and F94 are circled. Refer to Figure 12–17.

Figure 12–17   Invalid data

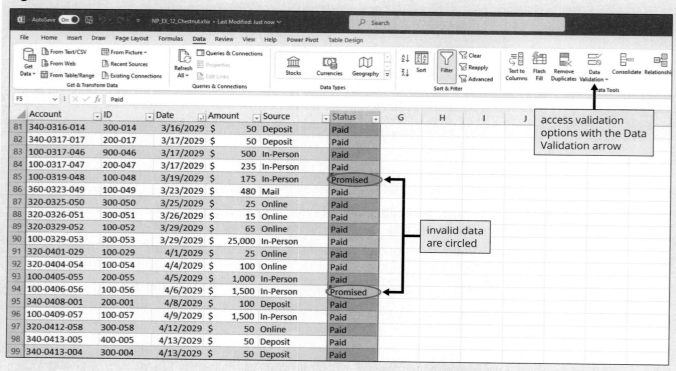

7. Change the value in cells F85 and F94 from Promised to **Pledged**, removing the circles and the data entry errors.

8. Verify that there are no other invalid Status values in the column.

Once you create a validation rule for a table field, that validation rule will be automatically applied to new table records.

Insight

Validating for Uniqueness

Some data fields, such as IDs, need to be unique. You can use a custom validation rule to test for uniqueness using the COUNTIF function

```
= COUNTIF(range, cell) = 0
```

where *range* references the cells containing the unique values and *cell* references the cell whose value should not already be in that list. For example, the following formula tests whether the value in cell B2 has already been entered in the range D1:D100:

```
= COUNTIF($D$1:$D$100, B2) = 0
```

If the cell you are validating is also part of the range containing the data values, the formula has a slightly different form that tests whether the cell value occurs exactly once in the selected range:

```
= COUNTIF(range, cell) = 1
```

The following formula validates the value in cell D1 against the entire range D1:D100.

```
= COUNTIF($D$1:$D$100, D1) = 1
```

By applying this custom validation rule to all cells in the range D1:D100, every cell in that range must be unique for the list to pass validation.

Protecting a Worksheet

Another way that errors can be introduced to a workbook is by users accidentally changing a formula or a data value. You can protect worksheets to prevent this type of error. Once a worksheet is protected, it can be modified only by users who know the password that opens the sheet for editing.

Enabling Protection

Setting worksheet protection allows you to manage what users can and cannot do. The default is to allow users only to select cells, but you can also give users the ability to perform other tasks such as formatting cells, inserting rows and columns, editing scenarios, sorting data, and deleting rows and columns. Such limits are enforced only when the worksheet is protected. Once the protection is removed, any user can edit the worksheet's contents and structure at any time.

Reference

Protecting a Worksheet

To protect a worksheet:
- On the Review tab, in the Protect group, click the Protect Sheet button.
- Enter a password (optional).
- Select all the actions you want to allow users to take when the worksheet is protected.
- Click OK.

To unprotect a worksheet:
- On the Review tab, in the Protect group, click the Unprotect Sheet button.
- Enter a password (optional).

To unlock cells that users can access in a protected worksheet:
- Select the range to unlock so that users can enter data in them.
- On the Home tab, in the Cells group, click the Format button, and then click Format Cells (or press CTRL+1).
- In the Format Cells dialog box, click the Protection tab.
- Click the Locked check box to remove the checkmark.
- Click OK.

Protecting a worksheet is usually only done once you are finished editing and are ready to make that worksheet available for general use. Rebecca has no more edits to make to several of the worksheets. She wants you to protect the content of those sheets, so users can only select cells but not edit them.

To protect the worksheets in Rachel's workbook:

1. Save the workbook.

   Key Step Whenever you are about to make a major change to a workbook, be sure to save the workbook. Then, if the workbook changes in unexpected ways, you can return to that earlier version.

2. Click the **Donors** sheet tab.

3. On the ribbon, click the **Review** tab, and then in the Protect group, click the **Protect Sheet** button. The Protect Sheet dialog box opens. You can specify a password that must be entered before the sheet can be unprotected. You can also go through a checklist of tasks that users are allowed to do within the protected sheet. The default is to allow users to only select cells.

4. Verify that only the **Select locked cells** and **Select unlocked cells** check boxes are selected. Refer to Figure 12–18.

Figure 12–18   Protect Sheet dialog box

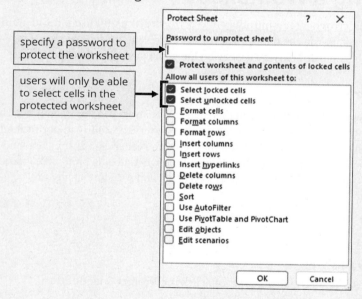

specify a password to protect the worksheet

users will only be able to select cells in the protected worksheet

5. Click **OK** to protect the sheet *without a password* and prevent users from doing anything other than selecting cells.

   Trouble? If you accidentally applied a password to the worksheet and are unable to unprotect the worksheet, close the workbook *without* saving, reopen the workbook, and repeat this set of steps starting with Step 2.

6. Repeat Steps 1 through 5 to protect the **Gifts**, **Prior Donors**, **Chart Tables**, and **Lists** worksheets.

7. Go to the **Donors** worksheet, and then click cell **A5**.

8. In cell A5, start typing. You cannot edit the contents of cell A5 because the worksheet is protected.

9. Click **OK** to close the dialog box.

If you don't include a password in the Protect Sheet dialog box, any user will be able to unprotect the sheet by clicking the Unprotect Sheet button in the Protect group on the Review tab.

> **Tip** If you do include a password, *do not lose it*. Without the password, you cannot unprotect the sheet. Passwords are case sensitive. The password "admin" is different from "ADMIN".

Locking and Unlocking Cells

You may want users to edit some cells, but not others, in a protected sheet. You can make cells in a protected sheet editable using the **locked property**, which defines whether or not a cell is editable when the worksheet is protected. Once a sheet is protected, only unlocked cells can be edited. Refer to Figure 12–19.

Figure 12–19   Locked and unlocked cells

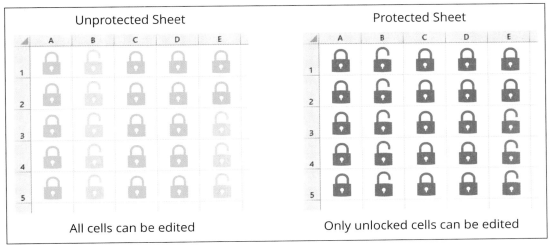

By default, every cell in a worksheet is locked, making them uneditable in a protected sheet. To allow users to edit certain cells, they must be unlocked. Rebecca wants you to unlock cells B4 and B5 in the Gifts by Amount worksheet so users can change those values but leave the rest of the sheet inaccessible.

To unlock a cells B4 and B5 in the Gift by Amount worksheet:

1. Go to the **Gifts by Amount** worksheet.
2. Select the range **B4:B5**. These are the cells you want to unlock.
3. On the ribbon, click the **Home** tab. In the Cells group, click the **Format** button, and then click **Format Cells** (or press **CTRL+1**). The Format Cells dialog box opens.
4. Click the **Protection** tab to display those options.
5. Click the **Locked** check box to deselect it and unlock the selected cells. Refer to Figure 12–20.

Figure 12–20   Protection tab in the Format Cells dialog box

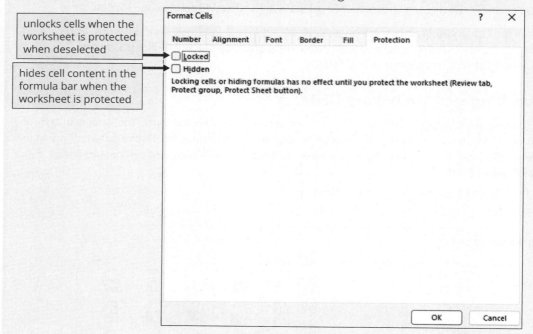

unlocks cells when the worksheet is protected when deselected

hides cell content in the formula bar when the worksheet is protected

6.   Click **OK**.

Next, you will protect the Gifts by Amount worksheet and then verify that you can edit cells B4 and B5 even when other cells are locked.

To edit unlocked cells:

1.   On the ribbon, click the **Review** tab. In the Protect group, click the **Protect Sheet** button. The Protect Sheet dialog box opens.

2.   Verify that only the **Select locked cells** and **Select unlocked cells** check boxes are selected, and then click **OK**. The worksheet is protected.

3.   In cell **B4**, enter **15,000** as the new value, and then in cell **B5**, enter **25,000** as the new value. Verify that the range shows four gifts of $25,000 each for a total of $100,000.

4.   Click cell **B6** and begin typing to verify that you cannot change the cell's content.

5.   Repeat Step 4 to attempt to edit other cells in the worksheet, confirming that the only cells you can edit while the sheet is protected are cells B4 and B5.

Cells containing drop-down lists can also be unlocked while the rest of the worksheet is protected. You'll unlock cell B4 so users can select an option from the drop-down list.

To unlock cell B4 to allow access to the drop-down list:

1. Go to the **Gifts by Type** worksheet.

2. Right-click cell **B4**, and then click **Format Cells** on the shortcut menu. The Format Cells dialog box opens.

3. On the **Protection** tab, click the **Locked** check box to deselect it and unlock cell B4, and then click **OK**. Cell B4 is unlocked.

4. In the Protect group, click the **Protect Sheet** button, make sure the **Select locked cells** and **Select unlocked cells** check boxes are selected, and then click **OK**.

5. Click cell **B4** and select **Grant** from the list to display the eight gifts from Grants.

6. Click cell **B5** and attempt to type, verifying that the cell is protected and cannot be edited.

7. Save the workbook.

If, at any point, you need to make more edits to these worksheets, you must first unprotect the sheets, then make the edits, and finally protect the worksheets again.

Highlighting Unlocked Cells

Locked and unlocked cells look alike. To make it clearer which cells are available for editing, you can highlight unlocked cells with conditional formatting. You use the CELL function

CELL(*info_type*, *reference*)

where *info_type* is a property of the cell and *reference* is the cell reference. For example, the following formula determines whether cell A1 is locked by returning a value of 1 if the cell is locked and 0 if it unlocked:

= CELL("protect", A1)

The steps for applying this formula in a conditional format are:

1. Unprotect the worksheet and select all cells in the sheet.

2. On the Home tab, in the Styles group, click the Conditional Formatting button, and then click New Rule.

3. In the New Formatting Rule dialog box, click Use a formula to determine which cells to format.

4. In the Format values where this formula is true box, enter the formula
= CELL("protect", A1) = 0.

5. Click Format to select a format for cells that are unlocked, and then click OK.

6. Click OK to apply the conditional format to all the cells.

Every unlocked cell in the worksheet will be formatted with the conditional format you chose, highlighting which cells are editable and which are not.

Proskills

Teamwork: Assigning Ranges to Users

The technique of unlocking cells does not distinguish between one user and another. The cells in a workbook are locked or unlocked for every user. When a workbook is shared, you might want to assign each user a different range to edit.

You can fine-tune access to the contents of a workbook using the Allow Edit Ranges button in the Protect group on the Review tab. This tool lets you define who can edit which ranges when the worksheet is protected. You can even create different passwords for each range. For example, you can let workers in one department edit one range of data and let workers in another department edit a different range.

Editable ranges are useful when you have several groups of employees accessing and editing the workbook. You can then control who has access to existing data and who has the clearance to enter new data.

In this part, you have better protected Rachel's workbook against data entry errors, which will make it more accessible to inexperienced Excel users and prevent unintended edits. In the next part, you will explore how to create custom Excel functions that will make it easier to write and maintain complicated formulas.

Part 12.1 Quick Check

1. Convert the formula =B1/B10 into a formula that calculates this value only if there is no error but otherwise displays the text "Error Found".

2. Write a formula that uses the FILTER function to filter the contents of the Gifts table to show only those records where the value of the Amount field is greater than 50000. If no record in the table matches this condition, display the text "No gifts greater than $50,000".

3. Write a formula to test whether cell B10 contains a numeric value.

4. What are the three types of validation messages?

5. Write a custom validation formula that validates the data only if the value of cell C10 is less than or equal to the value of cell D10.

6. When do you use the Circle Validation button?

7. What are the steps for protecting a sheet in the workbook?

8. When does locking a cell prevent the user from editing its contents?

9. Why would you unlock a cell?

Part 12.2 Visual Overview: LET and LAMBDA Functions

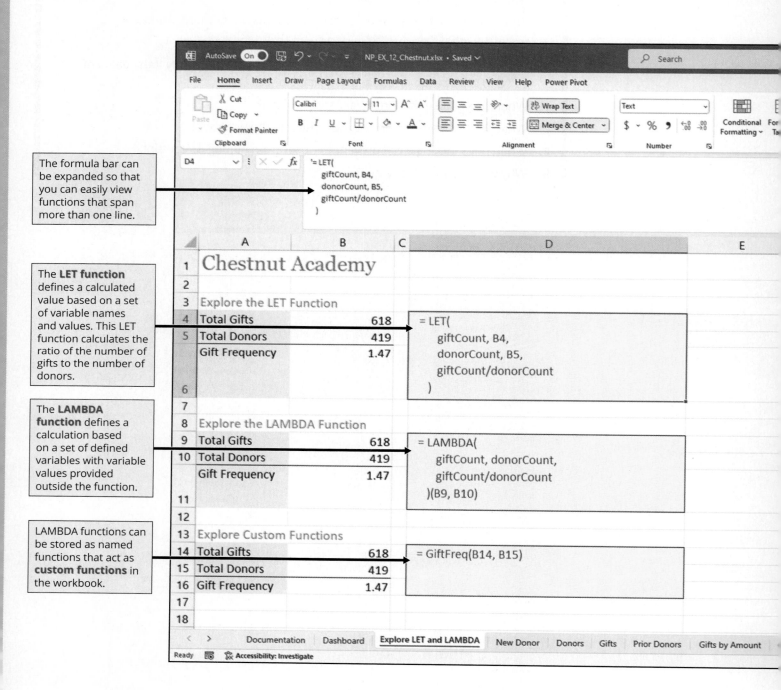

The formula bar can be expanded so that you can easily view functions that span more than one line.

The **LET function** defines a calculated value based on a set of variable names and values. This LET function calculates the ratio of the number of gifts to the number of donors.

The **LAMBDA function** defines a calculation based on a set of defined variables with variable values provided outside the function.

LAMBDA functions can be stored as named functions that act as **custom functions** in the workbook.

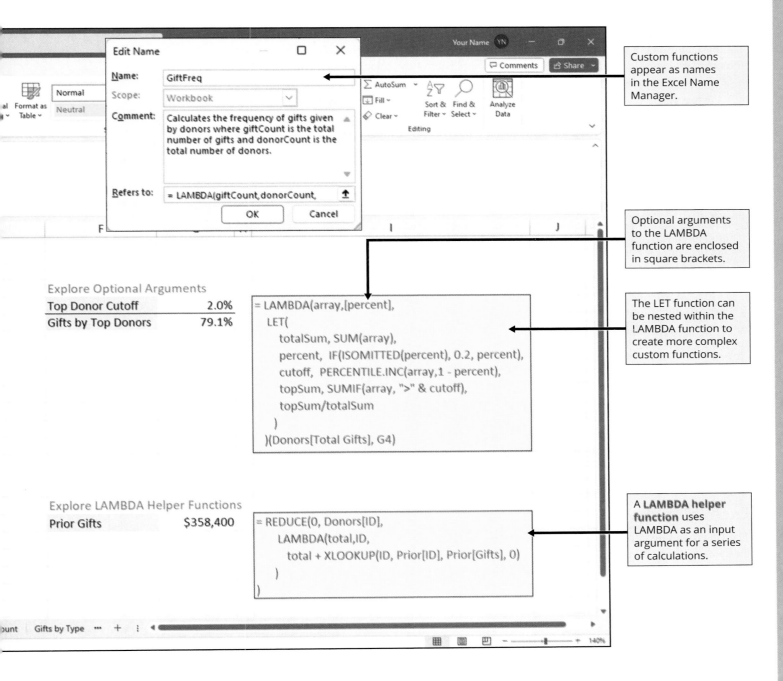

Edit Name

Name: GiftFreq

Scope: Workbook

Comment: Calculates the frequency of gifts given by donors where giftCount is the total number of gifts and donorCount is the total number of donors.

Refers to: = LAMBDA(giftCount,donorCount,

OK   Cancel

Custom functions appear as names in the Excel Name Manager.

Optional arguments to the LAMBDA function are enclosed in square brackets.

Explore Optional Arguments

Top Donor Cutoff	2.0%
Gifts by Top Donors	79.1%

```
= LAMBDA(array,[percent],
    LET(
        totalSum, SUM(array),
        percent,  IF(ISOMITTED(percent), 0.2, percent),
        cutoff,  PERCENTILE.INC(array,1 - percent),
        topSum, SUMIF(array, ">" & cutoff),
        topSum/totalSum
        )
)(Donors[Total Gifts], G4)
```

The LET function can be nested within the LAMBDA function to create more complex custom functions.

Explore LAMBDA Helper Functions

Prior Gifts	$358,400

```
= REDUCE(0, Donors[ID],
    LAMBDA(total,ID,
        total + XLOOKUP(ID, Prior[ID], Prior[Gifts], 0)
    )
)
```

A **LAMBDA helper function** uses LAMBDA as an input argument for a series of calculations.

Writing Formulas with the LET Function

Excel provides a large library of functions to handle most situations. You can nest functions to do even more complex tasks. But formulas involving several layers of nesting are often difficult to interpret or fix if something goes wrong.

For example, in Part 12.1, you used the following function to retrieve donor names from the Donors table using IDs found in the first column of a spill range starting at cell D6:

```
= IFERROR(XLOOKUP(FILTER(D6#,{1,0,0}),
Donors[ID],Donors[Name]),"")
```

Perhaps you had to retype this formula several times before catching all the errors. Long formulas like this can use up a lot of time as you locate and fix all errors. Instead of using a long formula, you can create a custom function that hides the complexity of the calculation from the user but is easier to interpret and edit.

Custom functions are created using the LET and LAMBDA functions. Both functions use a programming language approach where variables store values to be calculated and calculations are entered as expressions that work on those variables. Figure 12–21 describes the general difference between writing a formula using nested functions and writing a formula using LET and LAMBDA functions.

Figure 12–21   Nested functions compared to LET and LAMBDA functions

Nested Functions	LET and LAMBDA Functions
The formula is written on a single line with multiple layers of nested functions enclosed in parenthesis.	The formula is written as a series of expressions separated by commas, with expression storing a value or performing a calculation.
Calculations are performed from the innermost nested function outward.	Calculations are done sequentially in the order they are written.
Intermediate calculations are not stored and are only available to the next high-level function.	Intermediate calculations are stored in variables that can be referenced in any subsequent expression.
The formula must be rewritten in each cell it is used.	The formula can be saved as a custom function reused throughout the workbook.
Supported in all versions of Excel.	Not supported in older versions of Excel.

Before you can create a custom function, you will need to understand how LET and LAMBDA operate. You'll start by exploring the LET function.

Examining the Syntax of LET

The LET function defines a calculated value based on a set of variable names and values, using the syntax

```
LET(
    name1, value1,
    name2, value2,
    ...,
    calculation
)
```

where *name1*, *value1*, *name2*, *value2*, and so forth comprise the name/value pairs that are **LET variables** for storing variables and their values, and *calculation* is an expression that operates on those variables. You can provide up to 126 name/value pairs, but you must always provide both a variable name and its value, and the last argument in the LET function must be a single expression performing a calculation.

Although you can enter the entire LET function on a single line, it is often easier to enter the function on multiple lines with each name/value pair on its own line and the calculation on a final line within the function.

> **Tip** Common LET mistakes involve ending the function with several calculation arguments or not pairing each variable name with a variable value.

Variable names must begin with a letter and are not case-sensitive. A variable named "DonorID" is treated the same as "donorID" or "donorid". Variable names can contain numbers if the name cannot be interpreted as a cell reference. Thus "xValue1" is a legitimate name but "x1" is not. Although you cannot use spaces in a variable name, you can use the underscore character (_) to separate words. The name "Donor Name" is not a valid variable name, but "Donor_Name" is.

> **Tip** Because the last possible column label in an Excel workbook is XFD and the last possible row number is 1,048,576, practically any variable name that starts with three letters or less, followed by a number, will be invalid.

The following LET function defines two variables named GiftsAmt (the total amount of gifts) and GiftsCount (the total number of gifts) with initial values of $4,000 and 25, respectively. The final argument divides GiftsAmt by GiftsCount, returning an average gift size of $160.

```
= LET(
     GiftsAmt, 4000,
     GiftsCount, 25,
     GiftsAmt/GiftsCount
)
```

You could have performed this calculation without LET and with fewer characters, but LET provides several important advantages over the built-in Excel formulas:

1. Naming variables makes the code easier to read and interpret, particular for complex calculations.

2. With variables, you can define intermediate values before the final calculation, removing the need for nesting one function within another. (Nesting is a major source of error when writing formulas.)

3. Once you define a variable and its value, you do not have to recalculate it, removing redundancy from code and speeding up process time.

Removing redundancy is a major concern with larger data sets. The following IFS function shows the effect of redundancy by returning a different message based on the sum of gifts made to the campaign. If the sum is greater than $1,000,000, the function returns the text "Great". If the sum is greater than $500,000, the function returns the text "Good". If the sum is greater than or equal to zero, the function returns the text "Poor".

```
= IFS(SUM(Gifts[Amount]) > 1000000, "Great",
       SUM(Gifts[Amount]) > 500000, "Good",
       SUM(Gifts[Amount]) >= 0, "Poor")
```

The problem is that this formula calculates the same sum three separate times. If the Gifts table had thousands and thousands of records, that would require a lot of processing time. Rewriting the formula using LET requires only a single calculation stored in the GiftSum variable:

```
= LET(
     Outcome, Gifts[Amount],
     GiftSum, SUM(Outcome),
     IFS(GiftSum > 1000000, "Great",
         GiftSum > 500000, "Good",
         GiftSum >= 0, "Poor")
      )
```

Notice that the GiftSum variable references the value of the Outcome variable. Variable names have scope within the LET function and can be referenced, but the variable's scope does not extend beyond that. In other words, you cannot define a LET variable in one cell and reference it from a different cell.

Reference

Writing a LET Function

- To write a LET function, enter the function code:

```
= LET(
    name1, value1,
    name2, value2,
    ...,
    calculation
)
```

where each *name*, *value* pair defines the name of a LET variable and its value, and *calculation* is an expression returning a calculation based on those names and values.

- The variable names and values must be entered in a comma-separated list.
- The calculation must be the final expression in the function following all name and value pairs.
- You can enter a LET function on multiple lines in the formula bar by pressing ALT+ENTER after each line.

Writing a LET Function

Rebecca created several worksheets where you will use the LET and LAMBDA. A useful fundraising metric is Gift Frequency, which calculates the average number of gifts made by individual donors. The equation for Gift Frequency is:

```
Gift Frequency = (Count of Gifts)/(Count of Donors)
```

You will use LET to write this function.

To determine the gift frequency using a LET function:

1. If you took a break after the previous part, make sure the NP_EX_12_Chestnut.xlsx workbook is open.

2. Go to the **Explore LET** worksheet, and then click cell **B6** to select it.

3. In the right corner of the formula bar, click the **down arrow**. The formula bar height expands so you can review several lines of code.

   Tip You can quickly toggle between an expanded and collapsed formula bar by pressing CTRL+SHIFT+U.

4. Click the formula bar, type **= LET(** to begin the function, and then press **ALT+ENTER** to add a new line while remaining in Edit mode.

   Key Step If you press ENTER, you will exit Edit Mode and enter the incomplete function, resulting in an error message.

5. Press **SPACEBAR** six times, type **giftCount, B4,** to define the giftCount variable setting its value to the value of cell B4, and then press **ALT+ENTER**.

6. Press **SPACEBAR** six times to align the insertion point with the previous line, type **donorCount, B5,** to create the donorCount variable setting its value equal to the value of cell B5.

7. Press **ALT+ENTER** to add a new line, press **SPACEBAR** six times, and then type **giftCount/donorCount** to calculate the gift frequency.

8. Press **ALT+ENTER** to add a new line, and then type **)** to complete the LET function. Refer to Figure 12–22.

Figure 12–22   LET function in the formula bar

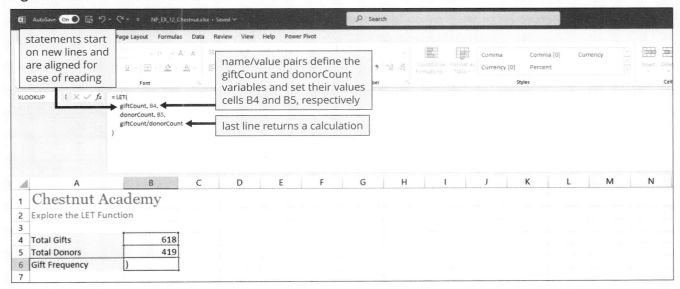

9. Press **ENTER** to enter the LET function. Excel returns a gift frequency of 1.47, indicating that on average, each donor has made about one-and-a-half separate gifts to the current campaign.

> **Trouble?** If Excel reports an error, check for the following possible causes: (1) a missing comma after each name value, (2) a mistyped variable name, (3) an incomplete LET function entered in the cell. Make the appropriate correction.

Using the SPACEBAR to align the statements within LET and LAMBDA is standard practice to make the code easier to read. In the steps that follow, we will continue that practice without mentioning it.

Writing Formulas with LAMBDA

The LAMBDA function defines a calculation based on a set of defined variables. Its syntax is

```
= LAMBDA(parameters,
      expression
   )
```

where *parameters* is a comma-separated list of **LAMBDA variables**, and *expression* is a calculated result based on those variables. As with the LET function, the entire LAMBDA function could be written on a single line, but you might find it easier to enter and to read by breaking it up into multiple lines, pressing ALT+ENTER after each line in the code.

To rewrite the previous formula using a LAMBDA function, you could enter:

```
= LAMBDA(GiftsAmt, GiftsCount,
    GiftsAmt/GiftsCount
      )
```

Notice that unlike LET, no values are defined for LAMBDA variables. Those values are passed to LAMBDA from outside the function by appending a list of values to the function enclosed within a set of parentheses

```
= LAMBDA(parameters,
    expression
) (parameter_values)
```

where *parameter_values* is a comma-separated list of values matched to each LAMBDA variable.

> **Tip** There should be no blank space between the closing parenthesis of the LAMBDA function and the opening parenthesis of the parameter values. If there is a space, Excel will return the #VALUE! error message.

To calculate the average gifts per donor from $4,000 of gifts spread among 25 donors, you could enter the following formula and LAMBDA would return an average gift size of $160:

```
= LAMBDA(GiftsAmt, GiftsCount,
    GiftsAmt/GiftsCount
) (4000, 25)
```

As with LET, there can be only one calculated expression in the LAMBDA function, and it must be the function's final argument coming from the variable name list.

Reference

Writing a LAMBDA Function

- Enter the function code:

```
= LAMBDA(parameters,
    expression
    )
```

  where each *parameters* is a comma-separated list of LAMBDA variable names, and *expression* is a calculated result based on the variables.
- The calculated expression must be the final expression in the function following the list of variable names.
- The calculated expression can itself be a LAMBDA or LET function.
- To supply values to a LAMBDA function, apply the code:

```
= LAMBDA(parameters,
    expression
    ) (values)
```

  where *values* is a comma-separated list of variable values matched to the list of parameters.

You will explore how to use LAMBDA to calculate the Gift Frequency value for the capital campaign.

To apply a LAMBDA function to calculate the Gift Frequency value:

1. Go to the **Explore LAMBDA** worksheet and double-click cell **B6** to select it in Edit mode.
2. Click in the expanded formula bar, type **= LAMBDA(giftCount, donorCount,** as the first line of the function, press **ALT+ENTER** to create a new line, and then press SPACEBAR six times to indent the next line.
3. Type **giftCount/donorCount** and then press **ALT+ENTER** to start a new line in the code.

4. Type **)** on the new line to complete the LAMBDA function, and then press **ENTER** to enter the function. Excel returns the #CALC! error value because no values have been provided for the giftCount and donorCount variables.

    > **Tip** The variable names you define in LAMBDA will appear as Autocomplete options when you type into the formula bar. Press TAB to insert the suggested names into the formula.

5. Double-click cell **B6** to edit the formula, and then type **(B4, B5)** after the final parenthesis in the LAMBDA function. Refer to Figure 12–23.

Figure 12–23   LAMBDA function entered in the formula bar

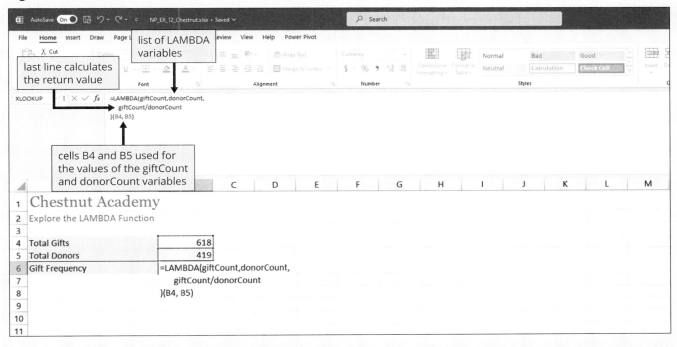

6. Press **ENTER**. The formula returns a Gift Frequency value of 1.47.

So far, the LET and LAMBDA functions you have created do not really benefit from those functions.

Combining LET and LAMBDA

The strength of LET and LAMBDA comes when they are combined in longer and more complex formulas. LAMBDA allows only the last argument to perform a calculation. But what if you need to perform several calculations on the variables? You can do that by using the LET function as the last argument and defining the additional variables and their calculated values you need to complete the calculation within LET.

For example, the following formula nests the SUM function and the FILTER functions to calculate the total contributions made by donors who contributed $5,000 to $20,000 each:

```
= SUM(
    FILTER(Donors[Total Gifts],
        (Donors[Total Gifts]>=5000)*(Donors[Total
        Gifts]<=20000)
    )
)
```

You can rewrite this function using LAMBDA and LET. First define the Amounts variable to store the amount to be summed and define the lowerVal, and upperVal variables to store the lower and upper values of the range of dollar amounts. The beginning of the formula is written as:

```
= LAMBDA(Amounts, lowerVal, upperVal,
    )
```

Next, insert a LET function, and within that function define the criteria variable to set the lower and upper limits of the dollar range. Also, create the resultArray variable to filter the gifts amount by the criteria variable. Finally, use the SUM function calculate the sum of the values in the resultArray variable:

```
= LAMBDA(Amounts, lowerVal, upperVal,
    LET(
        criteria,(Amounts >= lowerVal)*(Amounts <=
        upperVal),
        resultArray, FILTER(Amounts, criteria),
        SUM(resultArray)
    )
)
```

Although the LET/LAMBDA function has more lines, each line in the formula does a single thing, which makes it easier to edit and interpret. If you want to apply a different criterion to the FILTER function, you only need to edit the value of the criteria variable.

> **Tip** It will often make code easier to read if you list all LAMBDA variables on a single opening line and write the rest of the function code in subsequent lines.

Rachel wants you to combine the LAMBDA and LET functions to calculate the total gifts within a specified dollar range.

To combine LAMBDA and LET in a single formula:

1. Go to the **Explore LET and LAMBDA** worksheet and double-click cell **B7** to begin editing it.

2. In the expanded formula bar, type the following formula, pressing **ALT+ENTER** to add each new line and pressing **SPACEBAR** as needed to align the statements (refer to Figure 12–24):

```
= LAMBDA(Amounts, lowerVal, upperVal,
    LET(
        criteria,(Amounts >= lowerVal)*(Amounts <= upperVal),
        resultArray, FILTER(Amounts, criteria),
        SUM(resultArray)
    )
)
```

Figure 12–24   LAMBDA and LET function entered

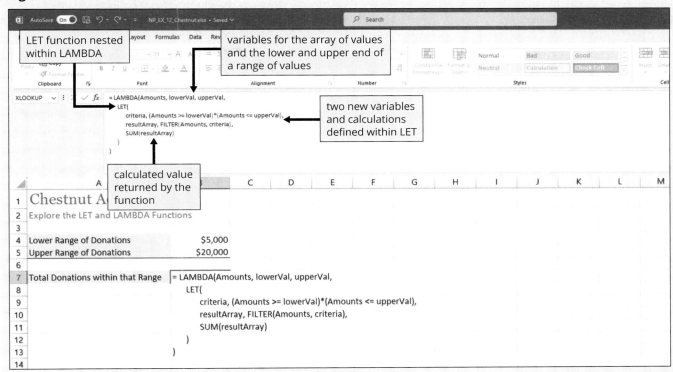

3. Press **ENTER**. The #CALC! error value appears because no values have yet been provided for the Amounts, lowerVal, and upperVal variables.

4. Double-click cell **B7** and after the closing parenthesis, enter the follow variable values using Donors[Total Gifts] as the value for the Amounts array, cell B4 for lowerVal variable, and cell B5 for the upperVal variable (refer to Figure 12–25):

    (Donors[Total Gifts], B4, B5)

Figure 12–25   Parameter values applied to the LAMBDA function

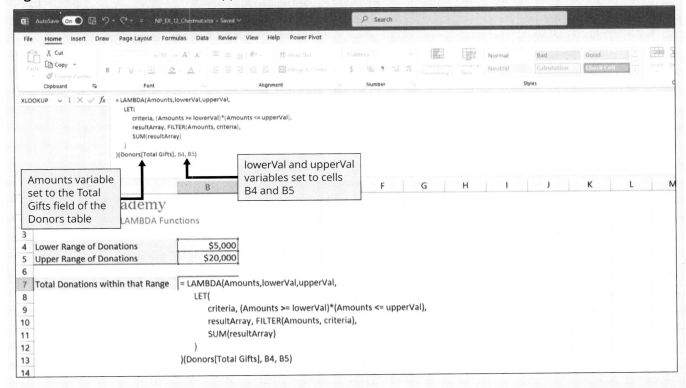

5. Press **ENTER**. Excel returns a value of $106,775, indicating the total amount from donors each contributing $5,000 to $20,000 is almost $107,000.

> **Trouble?** If Excel displays the #VALUE! error value, check your code against the code shown in the figure. Verify that you do not have a blank space between the ending parenthesis of the LAMBDA function and the opening parenthesis of the variable values. If you are still unable to find and fix the error, you can copy the text of the formula from the Terms and Definitions worksheet and paste it in cell B7.

If Rebecca wanted to use this formula elsewhere in the workbook, would she have to retype the entire long expression? No. The power of LAMBDA is that you can store this formula and reuse it as a custom function anywhere in the workbook.

Insight

Debugging Code

While LET and LAMBDA borrow many programming concepts, they are not programming languages. They do not have the debugging tools common to the development tools programmers use to catch errors in their code.

If you are confronted by a mysterious #VALUE! or #NAME? error value in LET or LAMBDA code that you are *sure* is correct, look for these common errors:

- **Invalid variable names**. A variable name cannot be a cell reference. Although the variable name "Top10" doesn't look like a cell reference, it is. If you want to append a number to a variable name, use at least four characters in the name.
- **Missing commas**. Every expression within LET and LAMBDA is an argument to the function and must be separated from other arguments with a comma.
- **Missing parentheses**. While LET and LAMBDA reduce the amount of nesting functions, you will still have some nesting. Make sure that every function ends with a parenthesis and that all values required by the function are present.
- **Unrecognized names**. If Excel returns the #NAME? error value, you might have mistyped a variable name. Check your code to make sure you have referenced all variables correctly.
- **Unexpected values**. If Excel returns the #VALUE! error value, you might have specified the wrong data type for a function, such as using a text string when the function was expecting a numerical value.

If you still cannot locate the source of the error, try reducing the code. Take out everything except the opening and closing lines to ensure that they work. Then, slowly add each line to isolate the line containing the error. Excel will help. When Excel encounters an error, it will place the insertion point within the code before the location where the error occurred.

Finally, use the Autocomplete feature whenever you can so that you don't make a mistake typing the name of a function, table, field, or variable. LET and LAMBDA are great tools for expanding the power of Excel, but you will have to carefully enter the function carefully. As you gain experience, errors will happen less frequently.

Creating Custom Functions with LAMBDA

Using Excel names, any LAMBDA function can be stored as a **custom function** that acts like a built-in Excel function. Just as with range names, named LAMBDA functions have workbook scope so that your custom functions can be used anywhere in your workbook. Once the function is named, you do not have to retype the code for the LAMBDA function, and you apply values to the custom function just as you would with a built-in Excel function.

Reference

Creating a Custom Function with LAMBDA

- Write the LAMBDA function in a worksheet, verifying that the formula returns the correct value for a set of input values without error.
- Copy the code of the formula from the equals sign to the closing parenthesis, but not including the list of variable values.
- On the Formula tab, in the Defined Names group, click the Define Name button.
- In the New Name dialog box, enter the name you want assigned to the custom function, enter a comment describing the function, and paste the copied code in the Refers to box.
- Click OK.
- In any cell of the worksheet, type the function name followed by a comma-separated list of values for each variable in the function.

After you have verified that the LAMBDA function returns the correct value without error, you will store the code as a named function using the Excel Name Manager. You will start by copying the code of the formula.

To copy the LAMBDA function code:

1. Double-click cell **B7** to select it and open it in Edit mode.
2. Select the code of the LAMBDA function from the equal sign through the closing parenthesis of the function, but do *not* select the parameter values.
3. Press **CTRL+C** to copy the code. Refer to Figure 12–26.

Figure 12–26   LAMBDA code selected for copying

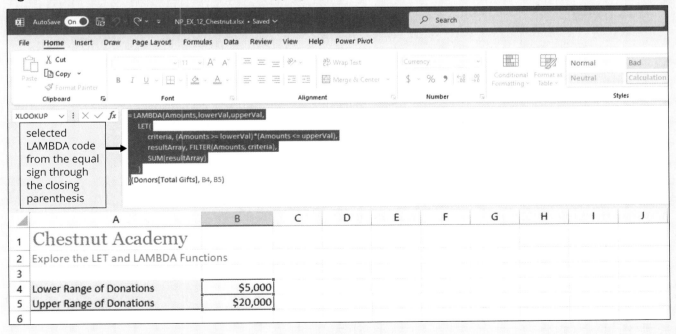

4. Press **ESC** to exit Edit mode, returning to the workbook.

Next you will paste the copied formula into a new Excel name in the Name Manager, creating a custom function. You will name this new function MY_SUMBETWEEN.

To create the custom MY_SUMBETWEEN function:

1. Click the **Formulas** tab on the ribbon, and in the Defined Names group, click the **Define Name** button. The New Name dialog box opens.

2. In the Name box, type **MY_SUMBETWEEN** as the custom function name, and then press **TAB** twice to go to the Comment box.

   > **Tip** Give custom function names a common preface such as "MY_" to easily distinguish your functions from built-in Excel functions.

3. In the Comment box, type **Calculate the sum of an array of values between lower and upper endpoints.** (including the period).

4. Press **TAB** to move to the Refers to box.

5. Press **CTRL+V** to paste the copied LAMBDA code. Refer to Figure 12–27.

Figure 12–27 New Name dialog box

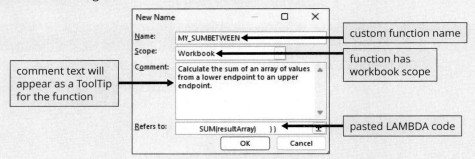

6. Click **OK** to close the dialog box and create the custom function.

Now that you have created the MY_SUMBETWEEN function, you can apply it to calculate the sum of any numeric array of values from a lower end of values to an upper end. The function has workbook scope, so it can be used in any worksheet. You will enter the function in the Explore Custom Functions worksheet to calculate the sum of donations made by donors who contributed from $1,000 up to $2,000.

To enter the MY_SUMBETWEEN function:

1. Go to the **Explore Custom Functions** worksheet.

2. Click cell **B7** to select it and type **=MY_SUMBETWEEN(** to begin the function. As you type, the custom function appears in the list of function and range names along with the comment describing the function. After you type the open parenthesis, Excel display the list of the parameters you defined for the function.

3. Type **Donors[Total Gifts], B4, B5)** to complete the formula. Refer to Figure 12–28.

Figure 12-28   MY_SUMBETWEEN custom function entered in cell B7

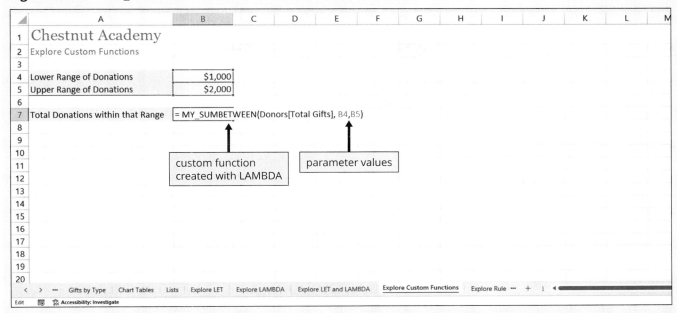

4. Press **ENTER**. The formula returns a value of $44,775, indicating that donors who contributed between $1,000 and $2,000 to the campaign accounted for almost $45,000 in total donations.

The MY_SUMBETWEEN function can be used with any array of numerical values by referencing the range or table field containing the values and the lower and upper limits to be summed.

Creating a Custom Function for the 80|20 Rule

Rebecca wants you to test the campaign donations against the 80|20 Rule. The **80 | 20 Rule** is an observation that 80% of a result often comes from 20% of the population. For example:

- 80% of the work is done by 20% of the employees.
- 80% of worktime is spent on 20% of the projects.
- 80% of business expenses come from 20% of the expense categories.
- 80% of social media traffic comes from 20% of the subscribers.

In fundraising, 80% of donations will often come from 20% of the donors. This holds true for Chestnut Academy, for which most of the donations came from a few large gifts (refer back to the funnel charts in Figure 12–1). Knowing how the 80|20 Rule applies to Chestnut Academy's capital campaign will help Rebecca decide where to best focus future fundraising. Because the 80|20 Rule appears so often in different applications, Rebecca wants you to create the following custom function to return the percentage of gifts from the top 20% of donors:

```
= MY_RULE8020(array)
```

where *array* is a range of numeric values. The code for the LAMBDA function on which MY_RULE8020 will be based is:

```
= LAMBDA(array,
     LET(
       totalSum, SUM(array),
       percent, 0.2,
       cutoff, PERCENTILE.INC(array,1 - percent),
       topSum, SUMIF(array, ">" & cutoff),
       topSum/totalSum
     )
  )
```

Figure 12–29 describes each expression in this formula.

Figure 12–29   Expressions for the Rule 80|20 formula

Expression	Description
`LAMBDA(array,`	Start the LAMBDA function, storing an array of numeric values in the array variable.
`LET(` `  totalSum, SUM(array),`	Calculate the sum of the array values, storing that sum in the totalSum variable.
`percent, 0.2,`	Store 20% in the percent variable as the cutoff representing the upper range value of values.
`cutoff,` `PERCENTILE.INC(array,1-percent),`	Use the PERCENTILE.INC function to determine the array value at the 80th percentile (1 − percent).
`topSum, SUMIF(array, ">" &` `cutoff),`	Use the SUMIF function to calculate the sum of all values in the array greater than the 80th percentile, storing that sum in the topSum variable.
`topSum/total` `)`	Divide topSum by totalSum to calculate the percent of the total sum contributed by the top 20%.
`)`	End the LAMBDA function.

Before turning a formula into a custom function, you should always first enter it as LAMBDA function, confirming that the formula works correctly. You will test the LAMBDA function code in the Explore Rule8020 worksheet.

To insert the LAMBDA function for the 80|20 Rule:

1. Go to the **Explore Rule8020** worksheet.

2. Double-click cell **B5** and then enter the following formula in the expanded formula bar, pressing **ALT+ENTER** to enter each expression on a new line and pressing **SPACEBAR** to align the expressions as shown:

```
= LAMBDA(array,
     LET(
       totalSum, SUM(array),
       percent, 0.2,
       cutoff, PERCENTILE.INC(array,1 - percent),
       topSum, SUMIF(array, ">" & cutoff),
       topSum/totalSum
     )
  )(Donors[Total Gifts])
```

3. Press **ENTER** to complete the expression. The formula returns a value of 95.5%.

> **Trouble?** If the formula returns an error value, check your code against the code shown above for typing errors, missing parentheses, or missing commas. If you still cannot find and fix the error, you can copy the code from the Terms and Definitions worksheet and paste it into cell B5.

4. Double-click cell **B5** to open the cell in Edit mode. Refer to Figure 12–30.

Figure 12–30   LAMBDA function for calculating the 80|20 Rule

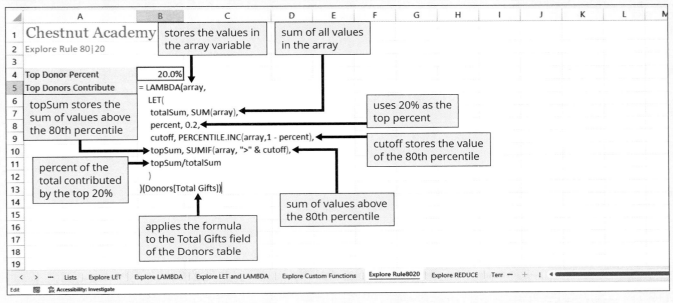

From the formula results, Rebecca learned that the top 20% of donors contribute 95.5% of the donations. Now that your formula works, you will store it as a custom function named MY_RULE8020.

To create the MY_RULE8020 function:

1. Copy the LAMBDA formula in cell **B5** from the = sign through the closing parenthesis, but not including (Donors[Total Gifts]).

2. Press **ENTER** to exit Edit mode.

3. On the Formulas tab, in the Defined Names group, click the **Define Name** button. The New Name dialog box opens.

4. In the Name box, type **MY_RULE8020** to enter the custom function name, and then press **TAB** twice, accepting workbook scope for the custom function.

5. In the Comment box, type **Apply the 80|20 Rule to the data array.** (including the period), and then press **TAB**.

6. In the Refers to box, press **CTRL+V** to paste the copied formula, and then click **OK**. The custom function is created without workbook scope.

Rebecca wants the result of applying the MY_RULE8020 to donor contributions to be displayed on the Dashboard worksheet. You will enter the formula to do that.

To apply the MY_RULE8020 function:

1. Go to the **Dashboard** worksheet.

2. In cell **B8**, enter **20.0%**.

3. Click cell **B9**, type **= MY_RULE8020(Donors[Total Gifts])** and then press **ENTER**. The same value as before, 95.5%, is returned in the cell.

4. Click cell **B9** to select it and display the formula.

5. Press **CTRL+SHIFT+U** to collapse the formula bar. Refer to Figure 12-31.

Figure 12-31   MY_RULE8020 function applied in cell B9

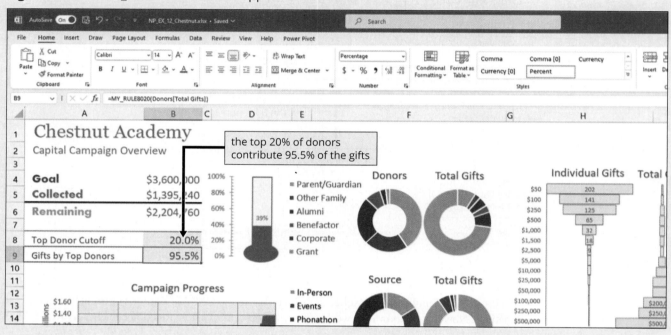

The 80|20 Rule is a general guideline describing the distribution of values within a population. You can also create a function that works with cutoffs other than 20%. For the Chestnut Academy data, Rebecca wants to know the percentage of all gifts contributed by the top 10% of the donors or the top 3%. You can modify the MY_RULE8020 to include the top percentage of donors as an optional argument.

Creating an Optional Argument

Just as with built-in Excel functions, custom functions support optional arguments. To create an optional argument for LAMBDA, enclose the variable name within a set of square brackets as follows

```
LAMBDA(arg1, arg2, [arg3], [arg4],
    expression
)
```

where *arg1* and *arg2* are required parameters and *arg3*, *arg4*, and so forth are optional and can be included in the function or omitted. Optional arguments must always be listed after the required parameters. You can determine whether the user supplied a value for an optional argument using the **ISOMITTED function**

```
ISOMITTED(arg)
```

where arg is the name of an optional argument listed in the LAMBDA function. The ISOMITTED function returns the value TRUE if the user did *not* supply a value for the function and FALSE if the user did. If the user did not supply a value, the formula should supply a default value by applying the IF function

```
IF(ISOMITTED(arg), default, notOmitted)
```

where *default* is the default value of the optional argument and *notOmitted* is the value supplied by the user. For example, the following LAMBDA function increases the value of the xValue variable by an amount supplied by the user, but increases that value by 1 if the user does not provide a stepUp value:

```
= LAMBDA(xValue, [stepUp],
     IF(ISOMITTED(stepUp), xValue + 1, xValue + stepUp)
   )
```

If the user supplies an xValue of 5, then the function returns the value 6:

```
= LAMBDA(xValue, [stepUp],
     IF(ISOMITTED(stepUp), xValue + 1, xValue + stepUp)
   )(5)
```

But, if the user supplies an xValue of 5 and a stepUp value of 3, the function returns the value 8:

```
= LAMBDA(xValue, [stepUp],
     IF(ISOMITTED(stepUp), xValue + 1, xValue + stepUp)
   )(5, 3)
```

Rebecca wants you add an optional argument to MY_RULE8020 function that by default calculates the contribution of the 20% of donors unless the user supplies a different top percent to use in the calculation. The code to set the percent value applies the IF function

```
percent, IF(ISOMITTED(percent), 0.2, percent),
```

so that if the user omits a percent value, the function uses the default 20% value, but otherwise it uses the value supplied by the user. You will modify the LAMBDA function to use this optional percent argument.

To create an optional argument for the MY_RULE8020 function:

1. Return to the **ExploreRule8020** worksheet.

2. Press **CTRL+SHIFT+U** to expand the formula bar, and then double-click cell **B5** containing the LAMBDA function.

3. Directly after the array argument in the first line, type **[percent],** as an optional argument.

   | **Key Step** You must include a comma directly before and directly after the [percent] argument to avoid a syntax error.

4. Replace the line percent, 0.2, with `percent, IF(ISOMITTED(percent), 0.2, percent),` so that the percent variable is equal to 0.2 if no percent value is supplied by the user but equal to the value of the percent argument if otherwise. Refer to Figure 12–32.

Figure 12–32   Revised MY_RULE8020 function

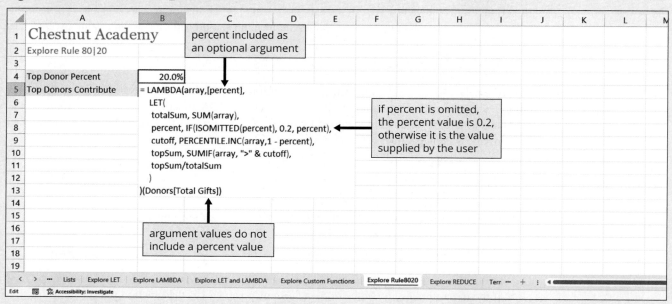

5. Press **ENTER** to apply the function. The function returns the same 95.5% because no value was supplied for the percent argument and the function applies the 80|20 Rule.

6. In cell **B4**, enter **10.0%** as the value.

7. In cell **B5**, edit the LAMBDA formula to change the parameter values from (Donors[Total Gifts]) to **(Donors[Total Gifts], B4)**. The function returns a value of 92.8%, indicating that the top 10% of the donors contributed 92.8% of all the money collected by the campaign.

As you update a function, you can copy and paste the revised code into the custom function's definition within the Name Manager. You will update the MY_RULE8020 in the Name Manager with the new code.

To update the custom function code in the Name Manager:

1. Double-click cell **B5** to put the cell in Edit mode.

2. In the expanded formula bar, select the function code from the initial equal sign through the closing parenthesis, but not including (Donors[Total Gifts], B4).

3. Press **CTRL+C** to copy the selected code, and then press **ESC** to exit the cell.

4. On the Formulas tab, in the Defined Names group, click the **Name Manager** button. The Name Manager dialog box opens.

5. Double-click **MY_RULE8020** in the name list. The Edit Name dialog box opens.

6. Using the mouse, select all the text in the Refers to box.

7. Press **CTRL+V** to paste the copied code, overwriting the previous text.

8. Click **OK** to close the dialog box, and then click **CLOSE** to close the Name Manager.

As with new formulas, you should also test revised formulas. You will test the updated custom function in the Dashboard worksheet.

To test the revised MY_RULE8020 function:

1. Go to the **Dashboard** worksheet.

2. In cell **B8**, change the value to **2.0%**.

3. Click cell **B9**, change the formula to = `MY_RULE8020(Donors[Total Gifts], B8)` and then press **ENTER**. The function returns a value of 79.1%, indicating that the top 2% of the donors contribute 79.1% of the donations.

4. Press **CTRL+SHIFT+U** to collapse the formula bar to a single line.

5. Click cell **B9** to select it. Refer to Figure 12–33.

Figure 12–33   MY_RULE8020 applied with an optional cutoff

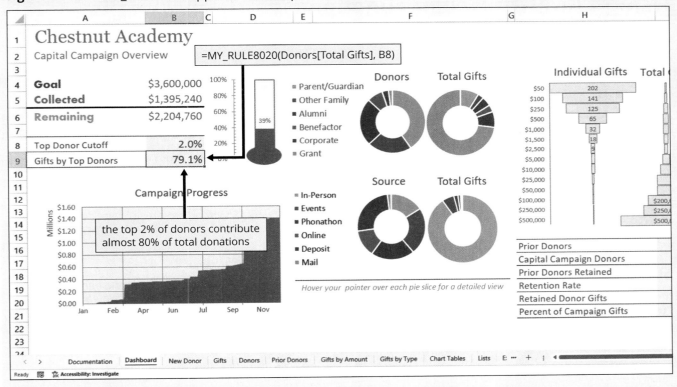

From the results of the custom function, Rebecca has learned that almost 80% of money collected by the campaign come from the top 2% of the donors. This is cause for concern because the campaign is relying on so few donors. Rebecca wants to expand the base of donors at the smaller gift amounts but needs to find those donors. You will explore that issue next.

Proskills

Teamwork: Sharing a Library of Custom Functions

Custom functions have scope throughout a workbook, but that scope does not extend to other workbooks. To create a custom function library that can be used in other workbooks, do the following:

1. Copy a worksheet from the workbook containing your custom functions.
2. Paste that sheet into a new workbook.

Along with the worksheet, every defined name from the first workbook will be copied into the second workbook, including all named LAMBDA functions and their formulas. To avoid confusion, you should only have named functions in the original workbook because range names will also be copied into the new workbook. Best practice is to document the custom functions you created in the copied worksheet. If you modify one of your custom functions or create new functions, you will have to copy and paste the worksheet again.

Using LAMBDA Helper Functions

The ISOMITTED function is an example of a **LAMBDA helper function**, which is a function that works with LAMBDA to calculate a value or return a result. Figure 12–34 describes the seven LAMBDA helper functions supported by Excel.

Figure 12–34   LAMBDA helper functions

Function	Description	Syntax
ISOMITTED	Returns TRUE if a LAMBDA argument value is omitted.	`ISOMITTED (argument)` where `argument` is a parameter value from LAMBDA

BYROW	Applies LAMBDA to each array row, returning a row of results.	`BYROW array,`
		`   LAMBDA(row, expression)`
		`)`
		where `array` an array, `row` is a variable representing each row in the array, and `expression` is a calculation applied to each row.

BYCOL	Applies LAMBDA to each column, returning a column of results.	`BYCOL(array,`
		`   LAMBDA(col, expression)`
		`)`
		where `array` an array, `col` is a variable representing each column in the array, and `expression` is a calculation applied to each column.

MAP	Applies LAMBDA to each array value, returning an array of results.	`MAP(array,`
		`   LAMBDA(item, expression)`
		`)`
		where `array` an array, `item` is a variable representing each item in the array, and `expression` is a calculation applied to each item.

REDUCE	Applies LAMBDA to each array value, accumulating a single summary value.	`REDUCE([initial], array,`
		`   LAMBDA(accumulator, item, expression)`
		`)`
		where `initial` is the starting value for a variable that will store the accumulated values, `array` is an array, `accumulator` is the variable storing the accumulated valued, `item` represent each item in the array, and `expression` is a calculation applied to each item.

SCAN	Applies LAMBDA to each array value, accumulating an array of partial values.	`SCAN([initial], array,`
		`   LAMBDA(accumulator, item, expression)`
		`)`
		where `initial` is the starting value for a variable that will store the accumulated values, `array` is an array, `accumulator` is the variable storing the accumulated valued, `item` represent each item in the array, and `expression` is a calculation applied to each item.

MAKEARRAY	Returns a calculated array of a specified row and column size, by applying a LAMBDA function to item in the array.	`MAKEARRAY(rows, cols,`
		`   LAMBDA(row, col, expression)`
		`)`
		where `rows` and `cols` are the total rows and columns in the array, `row` and `col` are variables representing the row and column index of each array item, and `expression` is a calculated applied to each array item.

Figure 12–35 provides an example of the BYCOL helper function in which LAMBDA is applied to every column of an array to return the name of the top fundraising within each month. In each column, LAMBDA uses the XLOOKUP function to match the name of the fundraiser in the range A4:A8 with top fundraising amount for that month.

Figure 12–35   BYCOL function applied

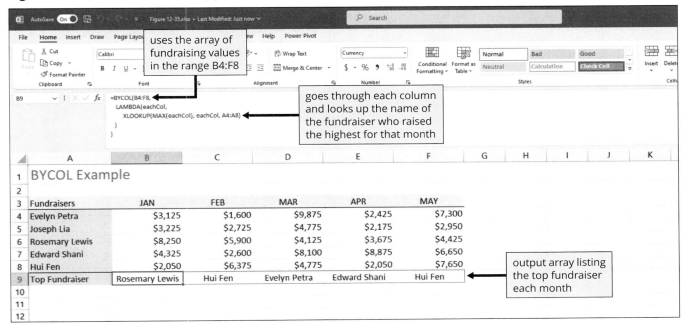

Another useful LAMBDA helper function is the REDUCE function, which reduces an array of values to a single summary statistic by applying a LAMBDA calculation to each item in the array and keeping an accumulated total of those calculations. The general syntax of the REDUCE function is

```
REDUCE([initial], array,
    LAMBDA(accumulator, item,
        expression)
    )
)
```

where *initial* is an optional argument providing the initial value of the accumulation, *array* is the array to which the function is applied, *accumulator* is a variable that stores an accumulated total, *item* is a variable that references the current cell in the array, and *expression* is a calculation applied to current cell in the array.

Rebecca has created a worksheet that explores the operation of the REDUCE function. The worksheet contains a column of numbers. An operation is applied to each number in the column to double the number if it is odd and leave it unchanged if it is even. The total of the revised numbers is then calculated. However, calculating the final total involves generating a column of calculated values—a wasted step if the only calculation of interest is the final sum of the revised values. With the REDUCE function, you can replace that column of revised values with a single cell and formula.

To explore the REDUCE function:

1. Go to the **Explore REDUCE** worksheet. Cell B15 calculates the total of the revised numbers in the range B5:B14. By doubling the odd numbers and leaving the even numbers unchanged, the sum of the revised numbers is 218. You can do the same calculation in a single cell using the REDUCE function.

2. Press **CTRL+SHIFT+U** to expand the formula bar, and then double-click cell **E4**.

3. In the expanded formula bar, type the following formula, pressing **ALT+ENTER** after each line and pressing **SPACEBAR** to align the entries:

```
= REDUCE(0, A5:A14,
    LAMBDA(total, number,
        IF(ISODD(number), total + 2*number, total + number)
    )
)
```

4. Press **ENTER** to insert the function. The function returns a value of 218, matching the value of cell B15.

> **Tip** The SCAN function is similar to the REDUCE function except that it returns an array of intermediate accumulation calculation rather than the final accumulation.

5. Click cell **E4** to select it. Refer to Figure 12–36.

Figure 12–36   REDUCE function applied

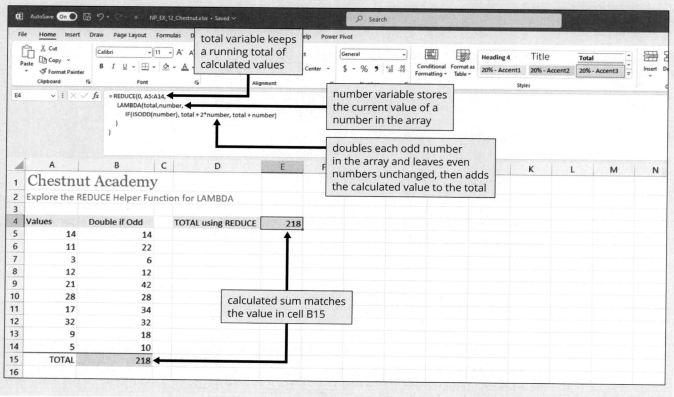

Next, you will use the REDUCE function to estimate how much might still be collected from previous donors who have not contributed to the current campaign.

The previous fundraiser had 489 donors. Of those, 260 have already contributed to the current campaign, for a retention rate of 53.2%. Rebecca wants to determine how much these retained donors contributed to the last fundraiser. To answer that question, you will use the REDUCE function to examine every donor in the current campaign and look up what they contributed to the previous fundraiser.

Figure 12–37 describes the expressions in the REDUCE function that you will use to calculate the total gifts active donors made to the previous fundraiser.

Figure 12-37   Expressions to determine what active donors contributed to the prior fundraiser

Expression	Description
`= REDUCE(0, Donors[ID],`	Use the REDUCE function to go through every donor ID in the Donors table. Set the initial value of the accumulation to 0.
`    LAMBDA(total, ID,`	The total variable will store the running total of gifts and the ID variable will store the current ID of each donor.

`        total + XLOOKUP(ID, Prior_Donors[ID],`
`        Prior_Donors[Total Gifts], 0)`
`    )`
	For each donor, look up their ID in the Prior_Donors table. If a match is found, add that donor's previous gift to the total; otherwise, add 0 to the total.

`)`	Complete the REDUCE function, reporting total gifts from the prior campaign from all active donors.

You will add this REDUCE function to the Dashboard worksheet.

To apply the REDUCE function:

1. Go to the **Dashboard** worksheet, and then double-click cell **I20**.

2. In the expanded formula bar, type the following code, pressing **ALT+ENTER** to start a new line and pressing **SPACEBAR** to align the contents:

```
= REDUCE(0, Donors[ID],
    LAMBDA(total, ID,
        total + XLOOKUP(ID, Prior[ID], Prior[Gifts], 0)
    )
)
```

3. Press **ENTER** to insert the function. The function returns a value of $358,400.

Current donors gave almost $360,000 to the previous fundraiser. Whatever is left from that last fundraiser is money contributed by donors who have not yet contributed to the current campaign but might do so if presented with the right sales pitch. You will calculate the amount those "lost donors" contributed in the past.

To calculate the amount that inactive donors previously contributed:

1. In cell **I21**, enter the formula **= SUM(Prior[Gifts]) - I20** to calculate past contributions. The formula returns a value of $919,550.

2. Click cell **I20** to select it. Refer to Figure 12-38.

Figure 12–38   REDUCE function applied

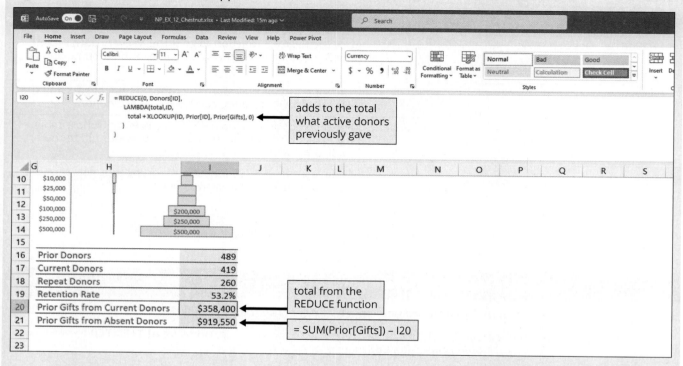

3. Press **CTRL+SHIFT+U** to collapse the formula bar.

4. Save the workbook.

Based on your analysis, Rebecca now knows that there is pool of potential donors who have previously contributed almost $920,000 to the school. If the team can make inroads with this group, they could get much further along in reaching the campaign's $3.2 million target and expand the campaign's base of support.

Insight

Generating Data with MAKEARRAY

Some workbooks require a large table of generated values. Rather than typing each number, you can generate the table using MAKEARRAY. For example, to create a 20x20 multiplication table, you can apply the following MAKEARRAY formula:

```
= MAKEARRAY(20, 20, LAMBDA(x, y, x * y))
```

To create a 4x10 table of random integers from 1 to 100, you can enter the formula:

```
= MAKEARRAY(4,10, LAMBDA(x, y, RANDBETWEEN(1,100)))
```

And to create 50-row column of zeroes, you can use:

```
= MAKEARRAY(50,1, LAMBDA(x, y, 0))
```

The following formula generates a 100-row column of text string with "Donor1" and ending with "Donor100":

```
= MAKEARRAY(100, 1, LAMBDA(x, y, "Donor" & x))
```

As you become more comfortable with LAMBDA, you can populate tables with more complicated calculations. The following formula creates a 5x6 table consisting of randomly chosen state abbreviations:

```
= MAKEARRAY(5, 6,
    LAMBDA(x, y,
        CHOOSE(RANDBETWEEN(1, 3), "PA", "OH", "MI")
    )
)
```

If you find yourself typing a lot of sample data, MAKEARRAY might be able to save you time.

In the next part, Rebecca wants to enroll new donors in the campaign. You will use Excel macros to do this.

Part 12.2 Quick Check

1. Write a LET function that has returns the sum of two variables named xVal and yVal with values of 10 and 20.

2. Explain how LET can reduce redundancy in calculations.

3. What keyboard combination should you press to start a new line in an expanded formula bar?

4. Write a LAMBDA function that returns the sum of two variables named xVal and yVal with the variable values supplied stored in cells E1 and E2.

5. The LAMBDA function allows only one argument for performing a calculation. How can you insert additional calculated values into a LAMBDA function?

6. Where are LAMBDA functions stored so that they can be repeatedly accessed as custom functions?

7. How do you indicate an optional argument within the LAMBDA function?

8. How do you test whether an optional argument was supplied a value in a LAMBDA function?

9. What LAMBDA helper function is used to apply a calculation to every cell within a row?

Part 12.3 Visual Overview: Macros and Visual Basic for Applications

The Developer tab provides tools for developers of Excel applications.

The Record Macro button opens the Record Macro dialog box lets you store a series of actions in a macro.

To view macro code, you open the **Visual Basic for Applications Editor**, which is a separate application to edit and manage VBA code.

The Macros button opens the Macro dialog box, which you use to run or edit macros.

The **macro security settings** control the security level workbooks containing macros.

A macro button runs the assigned macro when clicked.

In the Record Macro dialog box, you specify a name, shortcut key, location, and description of a macro.

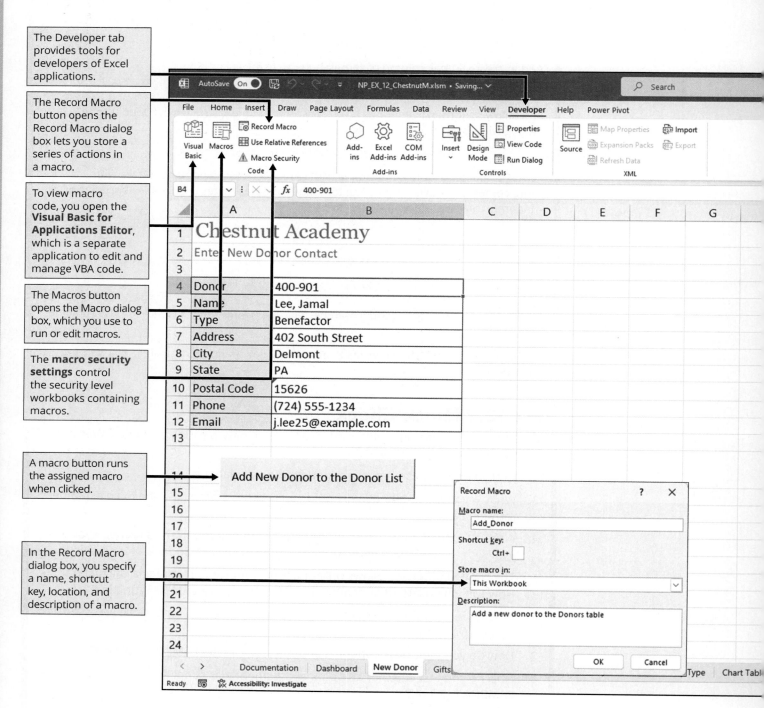

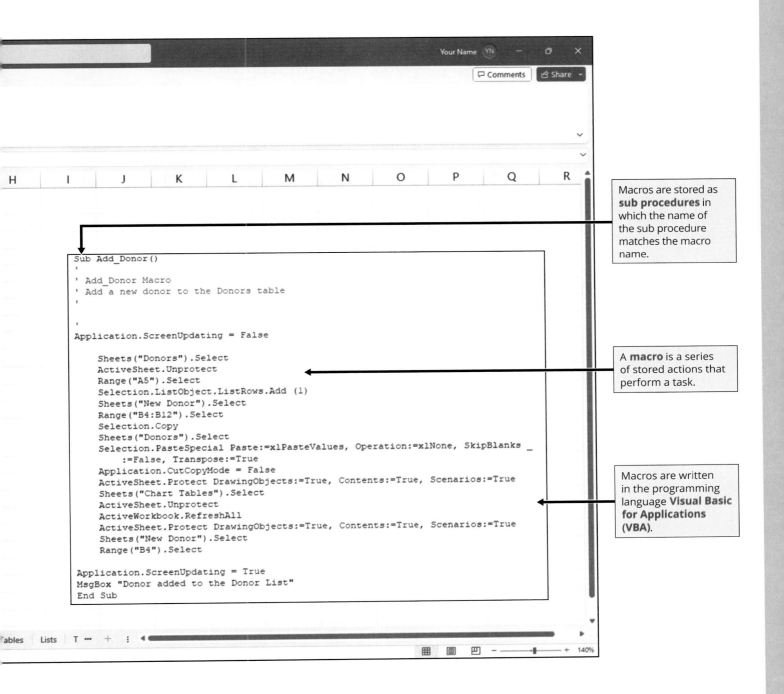

Your Name YN — ⌗ ✕

💬 Comments   🔗 Share ⌄

H	I	J	K	L	M	N	O	P	Q	R

Macros are stored as **sub procedures** in which the name of the sub procedure matches the macro name.

```
Sub Add_Donor()
'
' Add_Donor Macro
' Add a new donor to the Donors table
'

'
Application.ScreenUpdating = False

    Sheets("Donors").Select
    ActiveSheet.Unprotect
    Range("A5").Select
    Selection.ListObject.ListRows.Add (1)
    Sheets("New Donor").Select
    Range("B4:B12").Select
    Selection.Copy
    Sheets("Donors").Select
    Selection.PasteSpecial Paste:=xlPasteValues, Operation:=xlNone, SkipBlanks _
        :=False, Transpose:=True
    Application.CutCopyMode = False
    ActiveSheet.Protect DrawingObjects:=True, Contents:=True, Scenarios:=True
    Sheets("Chart Tables").Select
    ActiveSheet.Unprotect
    ActiveWorkbook.RefreshAll
    ActiveSheet.Protect DrawingObjects:=True, Contents:=True, Scenarios:=True
    Sheets("New Donor").Select
    Range("B4").Select

Application.ScreenUpdating = True
MsgBox "Donor added to the Donor List"
End Sub
```

A **macro** is a series of stored actions that perform a task.

Macros are written in the programming language **Visual Basic for Applications (VBA)**.

Tables   Lists   T ⋯   +   ⋮   ◀

⊞ ▣ ⊡   − ——⬤— +   140%

Getting Started with Macros

Analyzing data sometimes involves repetitive tasks such as copying and pasting values, updating PivotTables, or entering new rows of data values. These tasks can be streamlined through the use of macros.

A **macro** is a series of stored actions that can be run using a single action such as a mouse click. These actions could be short and straightforward, such as switching between one worksheet and another. Or, they can be long and involved, such as inserting a new record to an Excel table, generating reports and charts, or retrieving data from an external data source.

To create a macro, you must first enable the Developer tools.

Loading the Excel Developer Tab

All the tools for creating macros are on the **Developer tab** of the ribbon. Because most Excel users do not write macros, this tab is usually not displayed on the ribbon. You will check whether this tab appears on the ribbon and add it if necessary.

To add the Developer tab to the ribbon:

1. If you took a break after the previous part, make sure the NP_EX_12_Chestnut workbook is open.

2. Look for the **Developer** tab on the ribbon. If the Developer tab is not on the ribbon, continue with Step 3. If the Developer tab is already on the ribbon, read but do not perform the rest of these steps.

3. Right-click a blank spot on the ribbon, and then click **Customize the Ribbon** on the shortcut menu. The Excel Options dialog box opens.

   Tip You can also click Options in Backstage view to open the Excel Options dialog box.

4. In the right pane, click the **Developer** check box to select it. Refer to Figure 12–39.

Figure 12–39   Customize Ribbon category in the Excel Options dialog box

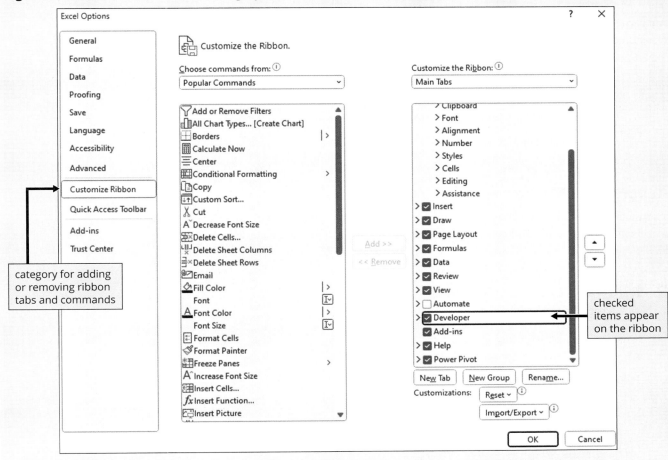

5. Click **OK**. The dialog box closes, and the Developer tab is added to the ribbon.

Saving a Macro-Enabled Workbook

Workbooks containing macros pose a security risk for Excel because macros could contain viruses or malicious software. The default Excel file format does not support macros. To use macros in an Excel workbook, it must be saved in the macro-enabled workbook format. If you create macros in an Excel workbook that is not macro-enabled, Excel will prompt you to save it in the macro-enabled format when you try to save that workbook. Because you know you will be adding macros to the workbook, you will save it as a macro-enabled workbook before you create the macros.

To save the workbook as a macro-enabled workbook:

1. On the ribbon, click the **File** tab, and then in the navigation bar, click **Save As**.

2. Type **NP_EX_12_ChestnutM** in the File name box.

3. Click **Save as type** box below the File name box, and then click **Excel Macro-Enabled Workbook (*.xlsm)**.

4. Click **Save**.

The file extension is .xlsx for Excel workbooks and .xlsm for macro-enabled workbooks. Workbook files can share a common name as long as they have different file extensions.

Creating an Excel Macro

A macro is stored as lines of code attached to the workbook. When you run a macro, Excel accesses that stored code, executing every command in the macro. There are two ways of creating an Excel macro:

1. Use the macro recorder to record actions and keystrokes, storing them within a macro that can be rerun at a later time.

2. Use the macro editor to directly enter the macro commands.

A good way to start learning about macros is with the macro recorder. Once you have recorded a macro, you can study its code in the macro editor and make additional changes to macro.

Recording a Macro

The macro recorder works like any other kind of recorder: You start the recorder, perform whatever tasks you wish, and then stop the recorder. All your actions are recorded as macro code for later playback.

Reference

Recording a Macro

- Save the workbook before you start recording.
- On the Developer tab, in the Code group, click the Record Macro button.
- Enter a name for the macro.
- Specify a shortcut key (optional).
- Specify the location to store the macro.
- Enter a description of the macro (optional).
- Click OK to start the macro recorder.
- Perform the tasks you want to automate.
- Click the Stop Recording button.

Rebecca's workbook has 17 worksheets. Such a large workbook can be overwhelming for users to navigate. Rebecca wants to give users the ability to jump to the last worksheet—the Terms and Definitions sheet—in a single step without having to scroll through all the tabs in the workbook. You will record a macro for that purpose now.

To start the macro recorder:

1. Save the workbook.

   > **Key Step** Always save your workbook before recording a macro. If you make a mistake in the recording, you can close the file without saving your changes and try again.

2. Go to the **Documentation** worksheet. This is the starting point of the macro recording.

3. On the ribbon, click the **Developer** tab.

4. In the Code group, click the **Record Macro** button. The Record Macro dialog box opens.

5. Type **Show_Terms** in the Macro name box, and then press **TAB** twice to go to the Store macro in box.

6. If it is not already selected, select **This Workbook** from the Store macro in box to store the macro in the current workbook, and then press **TAB** to go to the Description box.

7. Type **Go to the Terms and Definitions worksheet** in the Description box. Refer to Figure 12–40.

Figure 12–40   Record Macro dialog box

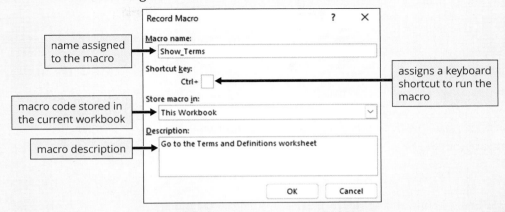

You are ready to begin recording. Once you start the recorder, every action you perform will be recorded as part of the Show_Terms macro. In any macro recording, you want to be very careful and precise in following the steps because every action will be recorded in the order you perform them in. You will start recording the macro.

To record the Show_Terms macro:

1. Click **OK** to begin the recorder.

2. Scroll through the list of sheet tabs and click the **Terms and Definitions** worksheet to make it the active sheet in the workbook.

3. Click cell **A1** to make it the active cell in the worksheet. Note that even if cell A1 is already the active cell, you still click it to ensure that is always the active cell when a user switches to the worksheet.

4. On the Developer tab, in the Code group, click the **Stop Recording** button. The macro recording is turned off and no additional tasks will be added to the macro code.

> **Key Step**   Be sure to turn off the macro recorder when you are done. Otherwise, the recorder will add every additional task you perform to the macro code.

The Show_Terms macro that you recorded is stored in the current document.

Insight

Creating a Macro Library with the Personal Macro Workbook

Excel has three options for storing macro code: in the current workbook where the macro was recorded, in a new workbook, or in the Personal Macro workbook. The Personal Macro workbook is a hidden workbook named Personal.xlsb that opens whenever you start Excel. Every macro in the Personal Macro workbook is accessible to any open workbook, making the Personal Macro workbook an ideal location for a macro library.

The Personal.xlsb file is stored in the Excel XLSTART folder. If you want to share your macro library, you can send colleagues a copy of the workbook or you can make that workbook available on a shared server. An IT department might have such a macro library stored on a shared server with macros tailored to specific needs of its organization or company.

Running a Macro

After recording a macro, you should run it to verify that it works as intended. In running the macro, Excel runs the same commands in the same order that they were recorded, including any mistakes you may have made during the recording.

Reference

Running a Macro

- Press the shortcut key assigned to the macro.

or

- On the Developer tab, in the Code group, click the Macros button.
- Select the macro from the list of macros.
- Click Run.

You will run the Show_Terms macro to verify that it is working correctly.

To run the Show_Terms macro:

1. Go to the **Dashboard** worksheet as your starting point. The macro should work from any sheet in the workbook.

2. On the Developer tab, in the Code group, click the **Macros** button (or press **ALT+F8**). The Macro dialog box opens. Refer to Figure 12–41.

Figure 12–41   Macro dialog box

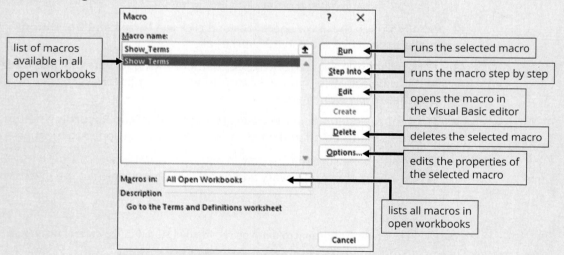

3. Select the **Show_Terms** macro if necessary, and then click **Run**. The Terms and Definitions worksheet becomes the active sheet in the workbook and cell A1 is selected.

> **Trouble?** If the macro does not go to the Terms and Definitions worksheet, you probably made a mistake in recording the actions. Close the workbook without saving, and then reopen the workbook and repeat both set of steps in the previous section to record the macro again.

Having verified that the Show_Terms macro works as intended, you will enable the macro to be run using a single mouse click.

Assigning a Macro to a Graphic Object

Macros can be assigned to graphic objects and command buttons so that you and others can quickly run macros by clicking those objects.

Rebecca suggests you insert an arrow shape into the Documentation sheet that users can click to jump to the Terms and Definitions worksheet.

To insert an arrow shape into the workbook:

1. Go to the **Documentation** sheet.

2. On the ribbon, click the Insert tab, and then in the Illustrations group, click the **Shapes** button to open a gallery of shapes.

3. Click the **Arrow: Right** graphic shape (the first arrow listed in the Block Arrows section).

4. Drag the pointer over the range **A7:B11**. As you drag the pointer, the block arrow increases in size to cover the select range.

5. With the block arrow still selected, type **View Terms and Definitions** to insert that text into the arrow. Refer to Figure 12–42.

Figure 12–42   Graphic shape inserted in worksheet

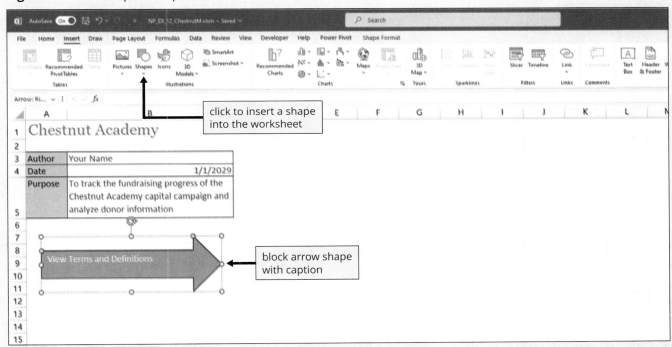

Next, you will assign the Show_Terms macro to the arrow and verify that you can jump to the Terms and Definitions worksheet by clicking it.

To assign the Show_Terms macro to the arrow graphic object:

1. Right-click the selected block arrow, and then click **Assign Macro** on the shortcut menu. The Assign Macro dialog box opens.

2. Click **Show_Terms** in the list of macros, and then click **OK**. The dialog box closes.

3. Click any cell outside of the block arrow to deselect it.

4. Click the **View Terms and Definitions** block arrow to run the macro. The Terms and Definitions worksheet becomes the active sheet.

You can both record a macro and assign it to a graphic shape at the same time. You will do this to create another graphic arrow to return the user to the Documentation sheet.

To create a macro to return to the Documentation sheet:

1. Save the workbook.

2. On the Insert tab, in the Illustrations group, click the **Shapes** button to display the shapes gallery.

3. Click the **Arrow: Left** shape (the second arrow listed in the Block Arrows group).

4. Drag the pointer to create a block arrow over the range **C1:C4**.

5. With the arrow still selected, type **Return to the Documentation Sheet**. Refer to Figure 12–43.

Figure 12–43   Block arrow to return to the Documentation sheet

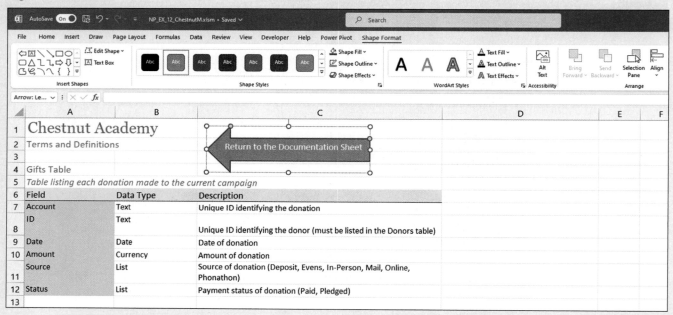

6. Right-click the selected block arrow, and then click **Assign Macro** on the shortcut menu. The Assign Macro dialog box opens.

7. Click **Record**. The Record Macro dialog box opens.

8. Type **Show_Documentation** in the Macro name box, type **Go to the Documentation worksheet** in the Description box, and then click **OK** to begin recording.

9. Scroll through the sheet tabs and click the **Documentation** sheet tab, and then click cell **A1**.

10. On the ribbon, click the **Developer** tab, and then in the Code group, click the **Stop 10 Recording** button.

11. Test the Show_Documentation and Show_Terms macros by clicking the block arrows in the Documentation and Terms and Definitions worksheet to verify that you can jump between the two sheets.

12. Go to the **Dashboard** worksheet.

The macros you created can be added to any sheet in the workbook so users can quickly move to the first and last sheets in the workbook.

Insight

Assigning Keyboard Shortcuts to Macros

Another way to quickly run a macro is with a keyboard shortcut. You can assign a shortcut key to run the macro within the Record Macro dialog box by selecting CTRL plus a letter or by selecting CTRL+SHIFT plus a letter. If you use a shortcut key combination that is already assigned to a default Excel shortcut, the new shortcut you create overrides the default Excel shortcut for the workbook. For example, using CTRL+p to run a macro overrides the default keyboard shortcut for opening the Print screen (CTRL+P).

Some users find macro shortcut keys a quick way to run a macro. Others dislike them because they can sometimes override the original function of a shortcut key, confusing users who use the built-in Excel keyboard shortcuts. The keyboard shortcut you create for a macro exists as long as the macro-enabled workbook is opened. Once you close the workbook, the keyboard shortcut for the macro disappears and any Excel commands assigned to the keyboard combination return.

Creating a Data Entry Worksheet

Now that you are familiar with the macro recorder, you will use it to store a more complicated action. Rebecca has created a worksheet for entering new donors. Using data validation and error control, she has built several safeguards into the worksheet:

1. The sheet is protected so that users cannot modify the layout and contents of the sheet.

2. The only cells which are unlocked and can be edited that those cells used for data entry.

3. Cells employ data validation tests to ensure that proper data is entered. For example, a new donor cannot use an ID already assigned to another donor. The donor type is limited to Alumni, Benefactor, Corporate, Grant, Other Family, and Parent/Guardian.

Rebecca wants other users to be able to enter contact information on new donors. Usually, this would be done by inserting a new row into the Donors table. But with all the safeguards and protections that have been created for the worksheet, Rebecca wants users to be able to enter new donors only through a macro.

Rebecca has contact information for Lisa Gonzalez, an alumnus of the school who wishes to contribute the current campaign. The contact information passes all the validation tests built into the worksheet, but Lisa has not been added yet as a new donor.

Recording a Macro to Enter Donor Information

You will create a macro named Add_Donor that will copy Lisa's contact information and insert it as a new row in the Donors table.

Note that this macro contains several steps, so take it slow and perform every action precisely as described. It's often a good idea to practice any set of steps before doing them with the macro recorder. If you do practice the steps, be sure to reset the workbook back to its original conditions before you start the actual recording.

The macro will record the following actions:

1. Unprotect the Donors worksheet and insert a blank row at the top of the Donors table.

2. Copy the donor information from the New Donor worksheet and paste the transposed values into the blank first row of the Donors table.

3. Protect the Donors worksheet.

4. Unprotect the Chart Tables worksheet containing the PivotTables used in the Dashboard.

5. Refresh the data in the PivotTables.

6. Protect the Chart Tables worksheet, return to the New Donor worksheet, and select cell B4.

When those actions are completed, the Lisa's information will be added to the Donors table and the information on the Dashboard will be updated with the revised donor list.

You will start recording that macro now.

To start the Add_Donor macro:

1. Save the workbook. If you make a mistake, you can retrieve the previous version of the workbook.

2. On the Developer tab, in the Code group, click the **Record Macro** button. The Record Macro dialog box opens.

3. Verify that **This Workbook** appears in the Store macro in box.

4. Type **Add_Donor** in the Macro name box, and then type **Add a new donor to the Donors table** in the Description box.

5. Click **OK** to start the macro recorder.

You will record the actions of the Add_Donor macro. *Caution!* If at any time you make a mistake as you perform these steps, you can stop the recording, close the workbook without saving changes. Then, you can reopen the workbook and try again starting from the previous set of steps. Another option is to stop the macro, click the Macros button in the Code group on the Developer tab, select Add_Donor from the list of macros, click Delete to remove the macro, and then repeat the previous set of steps to begin creating the macro again. If you choose this method, make sure that you have reset the workbook to its original condition prior to recording the macro.

To record the Add_Donor macro:

1. Go to the **Donors** worksheet.

2. Click the **Review** tab on the ribbon, and then in the Protect group, click the **Unprotect Sheet** button to unprotect the sheet so you can edit the Donors table.

3. Click cell **A5** to select it.

4. Click the **Home** tab. In the Cells group, click the **Insert arrow**, and then click **Insert Table Rows Above** to insert a new tab row at the top of the table.

5. Click the **New Donor** sheet tab to go to the New Donor worksheet.

6. Select the range **B4:B12**, and then on the Home tab, in the Clipboard group, click the **Copy** button.

7. Click the **Donors** sheet tab, and verify that cell is A5 still selected. If it is *not* selected, click cell A5 to select it.

8. In the Clipboard group, click the **Paste arrow**, and then click **Paste Special** to open the Paste Special dialog box.

9. Click the **Values** options button, click the **Transpose** check box to select it, and then click **OK** to insert the data on Lisa Gonzalez into the table.

10. Click the **Review** tab on the ribbon. In the Protect group, click the **Protect Sheet** button to protect the contents of the worksheet, and then click **OK**.

The PivotTables used in the Dashboard should be updated to reflect the new entry in the Donors table. To refresh the PivotTable cache for those PivotTables you must unprotect the worksheet.

11. Click the **Chart Tables** sheet tab.

12. On the Review tab, in the Protect group, click the **Unprotect Sheet** button.

13. On the ribbon, click the **Data** tab, and then in the Queries & Connections group, click the **Refresh All** button.

14. Click the **Review** tab on the ribbon, and then in the Protect group, click the **Protect Sheet** button to protect the contents of the Chart Tables worksheet, and then click **OK**.

15. Click the **New Donor** sheet tab, and then click cell **B4**.

16. Click the **Developer** tab on the ribbon, and then in the Code group, click the **Stop Recording** button.

You have completed recording the macro. Before continuing, you will verify that the steps you recorded create the correct results.

To verify the steps you recorded in the macro:

1. Click the **Donors** sheet tab, and then verify that Lisa Gonzalez appears in row 5 of the Donors table followed by **Carrie Walker**. Note that Lisa's total gifts (cell J5) are $0 because no donations have been entered for her.

2. Go to the **Dashboard** worksheet. Verify that there are 420 current donors (cell I17) and 261 repeat donors retained (cell I18).

   Trouble? If you do not have the same results, you might have made a mistake while recording the macro. Close the workbook without saving, and then reopen the workbook to the saved version prior to recording the macro. Repeat the three sets of steps in this section to record and test the macro again. If you still cannot get the macro to work correctly, you can use the code from Terms and Definitions worksheet.

3. Return to the **New Donor** worksheet.

Assigning a Macro to a Form Button

The Developer tab includes options for creating **form controls**, which are form elements used for entering data and running commands. You can create form controls for buttons, input boxes, check boxes, spinners, and list boxes among other choices. The controls can also be linked to worksheet cells so that a user can set or change a cell value by clicking a form control.

   Tip You can create a customized menu interface for an Excel application by inserting form controls from the Developer tab.

You will add a button to the New Donor worksheet that can be clicked to run the Add_Donor macro for the next donor.

To create a macro button for the Add_Donor macro:

1. On the ribbon, click **Review** tab, and then in the Protect group, click the **Unprotect Sheet** button so that you can add a form control to the New Donor worksheet.

2. On the ribbon, click the **Developer** tab, and then in the Controls group, click the **Insert** button. A gallery of Form Controls appears with a variety of form controls that can be placed in the worksheet. Refer to Figure 12–44.

Figure 12–44   Gallery of Form Controls and ActiveX Controls

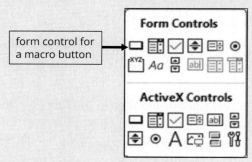

form control for a macro button

3. Click the **Button (Form Control)** icon in the first row and first column of the Form Controls section.

4. Click and drag the pointer over the range **A14:B15**. When you release the mouse button, the Assign Macro dialog box opens.

5. Click the **Add_Donor** macro in the list of macros, and then click **OK**. The macro button appears with the label Button 1.

6. With the macro button still selected, type **Add New Donor to the Donor List** as the new button label. Refer to Figure 12–45.

Figure 12–45   Macro button inserted

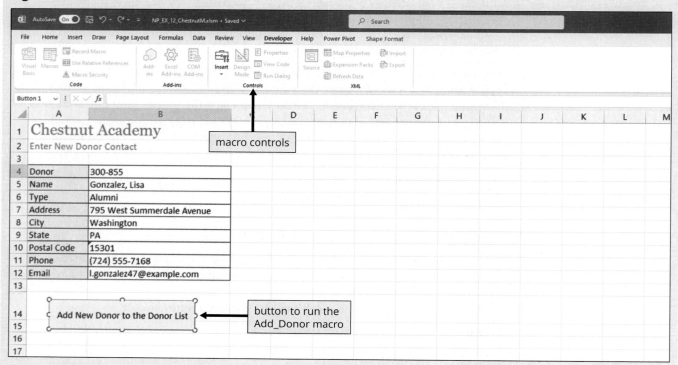

macro controls

button to run the Add_Donor macro

7. On the ribbon, click the **Review** tab, and then in the Protect group, click **Protect Sheet**. The Protect Sheet dialog box opens.

8. Click **OK** to protect the worksheet.

You will test the macro button and the Add_Donor macro now by adding a new donor to the Donations table.

To test the Add_Donor macro:

1. On the New Donor worksheet, in the range **B4:B12**, enter the donor information for Nick Eng listed in Figure 12–46.

Figure 12–46   Donor information for Nick Eng

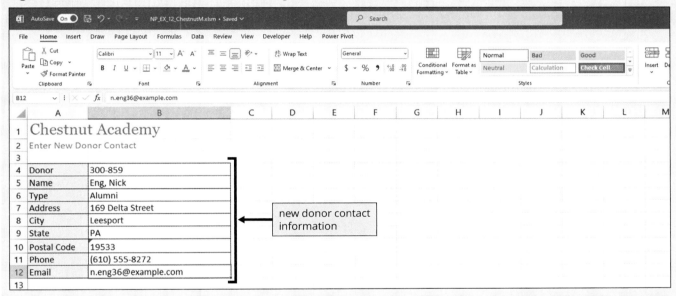

2. Save the workbook.

3. Click the **Add New Donor to the Donor List** button to add Nick Eng to the list of donors.

4. Click the **Donors** sheet tab and verify that Nick Eng has been inserted as a new donor in the Donors table. Refer to Figure 12–47.

Figure 12–47   Donor table includes Nick Eng entry

Nick Eng added to the list of donors

ID	Name	Type	Address	City	State	Postal Code	Phone	Email	Total Gifts
300-859	Eng, Nick	Alumni	169 Delta Street	Leesport	PA	19533	(610) 555-8272	n.eng36@example.com	$0
300-855	Gonzalez, Lisa	Alumni	795 West Summerdale Avenue	Washington	PA	15301	(724) 555-7168	l.gonzalez47@example.com	$0
200-001	Walker, Carrie	Other Family	120 South Keway Street	Lancaster	PA	17602	(717) 555-9564	c.walker99@example.com	$1,200
100-002	Wherry, Karen	Parent/Guardian	213 Lessing Street	Lancaster	PA	17603	(717) 555-4707	k.wherry14@example.com	$1,500
100-003	Fleming, Andre	Parent/Guardian	982 Frontier Way	Lancaster	PA	17602	(717) 555-7998	a.fleming43@example.com	$2,000
300-004	Gomes, Harry	Alumni	11 Crilly Street	Lancaster	PA	17603	(717) 555-1511	h.gomes76@example.com	$600
400-005	Sanders, James	Benefactor	191 Leonard Lane	Lancaster	PA	17602	(717) 555-3455	j.sanders14@example.com	$600
100-006	Carrigan, Richard	Parent/Guardian	976 West New Street	Lancaster	PA	17602	(717) 555-7406	r.carrigan22@example.com	$1,025
500-007	Tuffy Construction	Corporate	324 North Lake Shore Street	Lititz	PA	17543	(717) 555-3789	p.tuffy13@example.com	$2,850
400-008	Johnson, Pat	Benefactor	322 Stave Street	Lancaster	PA	17603	(717) 555-9241	p.johnson61@example.com	$600
300-009	Thacker, Evelyn	Alumni	138 Cullom Street	Paradise	PA	17562	(717) 555-4024	e.thacker6@example.com	$600
300-010	Mares, Joseph	Alumni	142 Nashville Avenue	Elizabethtown	PA	17022	(717) 555-9525	j.mares83@example.com	$600
200-011	Fuller, Patrick	Other Family	133 Mohawk Avenue	Bethlehem	PA	18015	(610) 555-1089	p.fuller10@example.com	$600
300-012	Hinton, Linnie	Alumni	169 Armitage Way	Ephrata	PA	17522	(717) 555-7894	l.hinton14@example.com	$600
100-013	Adams, Raymond	Parent/Guardian	975 North Natchez Street	Lancaster	PA	17602	(717) 555-1106	r.adams93@example.com	$600
300-014	Nelson, Patricia	Alumni	174 East Leamington Street	Chula Vista	CA	91911	(619) 555-3459	p.nelson63@example.com	$600
100-015	Hillman, Natalie	Parent/Guardian	97 Inda Avenue	Lancaster	PA	17601	(717) 555-4383	n.hillman14@example.com	$600
500-016	Leland Insurance	Corporate	685 Public Avenue	New Holland	PA	17557	(717) 555-3164	s.leland11@example.com	$125
200-017	Johnston, Sheila	Other Family	136 Hoey Avenue	Sylmar	CA	91342	(818) 555-8938	s.johnston7@example.com	$1,600
200-018	Martin, Sandra	Other Family	139 La Salle Way	Denver	PA	17517	(717) 555-8915	s.martin13@example.com	$600
300-019	Wells, Gary	Alumni	178 Gole Court	Manheim	PA	17545	(717) 555-1174	g.wells44@example.com	$75

5. Go to the **Dashboard** worksheet and verify that the number of current donors has increased to 421 (cell I17) and the number of repeat donors has increased to 262 (cell I18).

The Add_Donor macro will make it easier for Rebecca's colleagues to enter new donors without having to work with Excel tables, protected worksheets, or PivotTable caches. To put the finishing touches on this macro, you will review and edit the content of the macro code you generated with the macro recorder.

Insight

Data Entry with a Data Form

Another way of automating the data entry process is with an Excel data form, which is a dialog box containing the field names from the table or data range along with input boxes for entering new data. To create a data form from an Excel table or data range, do the following:

1. Make sure each column in the structured range of data or the Excel table has column headers. These headers become the labels for each field on the form.
2. Make sure the Form button is on the Quick Access Toolbar. If not, click the Customize Quick Access Toolbar button, and then click More Commands. In the Quick Access Toolbar options, click the Choose commands from box, click Commands Not in the Ribbon, click the Form button in the box, click the Add button, and then click OK.
3. Select the range or table for which you want to create the data form.
4. On the Quick Access Toolbar, click the Form button. The data form opens with the selected fields ready for data entry.
5. Enter data in each box, and then click New to add the complete record to the end of the range or table and create a new record.
6. Click Close to close the data form.

Data forms can be helpful when people need to enter data, especially when a worksheet is very wide and requires repeated horizontal scrolling.

Working with the VBA Editor

Macro code is written in a programming language called Visual Basic for Applications (VBA), which is the programming language used by all Microsoft Office apps. Once you know the basics of VBA in one Office program, you can apply much of what you learn to create applications for the other programs in the Office suite.

Opening the VBA Editor

The content of a macro code can be accessed in the Visual Basic for Applications editor. The editor is a separate application that works with Excel and other Office programs to fix, edit, and manage VBA code. You'll open the VBA Editor to review the code of the Add_Donor macro.

To review the code of the Add_Donor macro:

1. On the Developer tab, in the Code group, click the **Macros** button.

2. Click **Add_Donor** in the list of macros to select it if necessary, and then click the **Edit** button. The Visual Basic for Applications editor opens showing the code of the Add_Donor macro. Refer to Figure 12–48.

Figure 12–48   The Visual Basic Editor

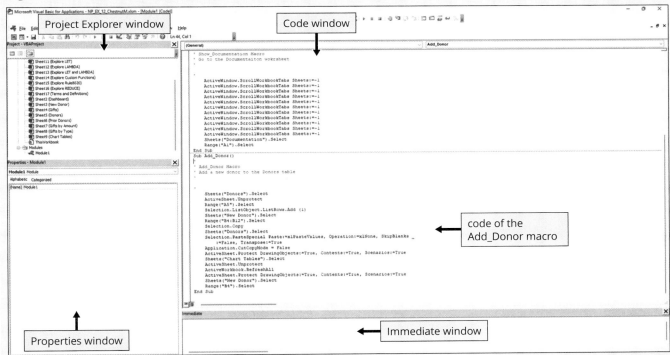

Trouble? Depending on how your computer is configured, the layout and contents of your window might differ from the one in Figure 12–48. If all the windows of the VBA editor are not shown, you can display them by selecting the name of the window on the View menu.

The VBA Editor opens with the four windows: The Project Explorer window displays a treelike diagram consisting of every open workbook. The Properties window shows the properties associated with the selected object in the Project Explorer window. The Code window contains the VBA code, including the code of every recorded macro. The Immediate window lets you enter and run VBA commands. For this project, you will only work with the contents of the Code window.

▌ **Tip** You can also open the VBA Editor by pressing ALT+F11.

Understanding Sub Procedures

In VBA, macros are stored in blocks of code called sub procedures, which have the general syntax

```
Sub procedure(arguments)
'comments
commands
```

where *procedure* is the name of the macro, *arguments* are any arguments used in the macro, *comments* are descriptive comments about the macro, and *commands* are the actions run by the macro.

▌ **Tip** Every VBA comment line begins with the ' character.

Even without knowing VBA syntax, you can often interpret the actions of the macro by examining the macro code. For example, the following commands select the Donors worksheet to make it the active sheet, unprotects it, and then selects cell A5.

```
Sheets("Donors").Select
ActiveSheet.Unprotect
Range("A5").Select
```

Sub procedures are organized in a folder called a **module**. A VBA project could have multiple modules, and multiple sub procedures within each module. The first module is named Module1, the second is called Module2, and so forth. Modules are primarily a way of grouping related macros.

Editing a Macro with the VBA Editor

Learning the syntax of VBA is beyond the scope of this module, but you can add some simple tasks to the code generated by the macro recorder. To enter a VBA command, write the text of the command in the Code window. As you type, the editor will provide pop-up windows to help you write error-free code.

Reference

Editing a Macro

- On the Developer tab, in the Code group, click the Macros button, select the macro in the Macro name list, and then click Edit; or on the Developer tab, in the Code group, click the Visual Basic button.
- Use the Visual Basic Editor to edit the macro code.
- On the menu bar, click File, and then click Close and Return to Microsoft Excel.

When the Add_Donor macro is running, the screen shows each action you recorded. Rebecca thinks this is distracting and slows down the macro. She would prefer that the macro hide its operations until it is finished. You can turn off the screen updating as the macro runs by adding the following command to the macro:

```
Application.ScreenUpdating = False
```

To turn screen updating back on, you add the command:

```
Application.ScreenUpdating = True
```

You will add these commands to the start and the end of Add_Donor macro.

To turn screen updating off and on:

1. Directly before the Sheets("Donors").Select command, insert the following command:

   ```
   Application.ScreenUpdating = False
   ```

   Tip As you type the command, the editor will offer Autocomplete suggestions to help you write error-free code.

2. Directly before the End Sub line, insert the following command (refer to Figure 12–49):

   ```
   Application.ScreenUpdating = True
   ```

Figure 12–49   Code added to turn screen updating on and off

```
Application.ScreenUpdating = False ◄──  turns off screen
                                        updating
    Sheets("Donors").Select
    ActiveSheet.Unprotect
    Range("A5").Select
    Selection.ListObject.ListRows.Add (1)
    Sheets("New Donor").Select
    Range("B4:B12").Select
    Selection.Copy
    Sheets("Donors").Select
    Selection.PasteSpecial Paste:=xlPasteValues, Operation:=xlNone, SkipBlanks _
        :=False, Transpose:=True
    Application.CutCopyMode = False
    ActiveSheet.Protect DrawingObjects:=True, Contents:=True, Scenarios:=True
    Sheets("Chart Tables").Select
    ActiveSheet.Unprotect
    ActiveWorkbook.RefreshAll
    ActiveSheet.Protect DrawingObjects:=True, Contents:=True, Scenarios:=True
    Sheets("New Donor").Select
    Range("B4").Select

Application.ScreenUpdating = True ◄──  turns on screen
End Sub                                updating
```

Macro commands can also create variables and store variable values. A useful command in a macro is to the store the value of a selected cell in a variable. To store the value of a selection, use the command

```
variable = Selection.Value
```

where *variable* is the name assigned to a variable. Once you have stored a value in a variable, that variable can be referenced elsewhere in the macro code.

Displaying a Message Box

Rebecca is concerned that there is no indication that the macro has completed its tasks. She wants the macro to display a message box indicating that the donor has been added. You can display a message box using the following VBA command:

```
MsgBox message
```

where *message* is the text of the message to display in a dialog box. For example, the following VBA command creates a dialog box displaying the message "Donor added":

```
MsgBox "Donor added"
```

You will add this command to the end of the Add_Donor macro.

To display a message box using VBA:

1. Directly before the End Sub line, insert the command `MsgBox "Donor added to the Donor List"` (refer to Figure 12–50).

Figure 12–50   Code to display a message box

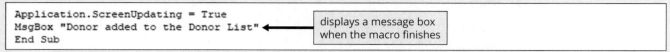

```
Application.ScreenUpdating = True
MsgBox "Donor added to the Donor List"    ◄———  displays a message box
End Sub                                          when the macro finishes
```

2. On the menu bar, click **File**, and then click **Close and Return to Microsoft Excel** (or press **CTRL+Q**).

The message box command is added to the Add_Donor macro. You will test the revised macro with new donor info.

To add a new donor to the list using the Add_Donor macro:

1. Go to the **New Donor** worksheet, and then enter the donor information for Jamal Lee listed in Figure 12–51.

Figure 12–51   Donor information for Jamal Lee

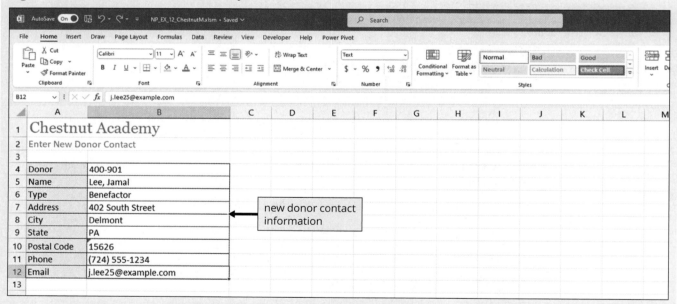

2. Save the workbook. You want to save before running the macro in case you have introduced an error to the macro code.

3. Click the **Add New Donor to the Donor List** button to add Jamal Lee to the donor list.

4. As the macro runs, it hides its actions from the user. When the macro is concluded, it displays the message box confirming that the donor was added to the donor list. Refer to Figure 12–52.

Figure 12–52   Macro message box

5. Click **OK**.

6. Go to the **Donors** worksheet and confirm that Jamal Lee has been inserted as a new donor.

7. Go to the **Dashboard** worksheet and confirm that the number of current donors has increased to 422 (cell I17). Because Jamal Lee is not a repeat donor, the number of repeat donors stays at 262 (cell I18).

You have finished creating and editing macros. Because you no longer need the Developer tab, you will remove this tab from the ribbon.

To remove the Developer tab from the ribbon:

1. Right-click an empty area of the ribbon, and then click **Customize the Ribbon** on the shortcut menu.

2. In the Main Tabs box on the right, click the **Developer** check box to deselect the Developer tab.

3. Click **OK** to apply the changes to the ribbon. The Developer tab no longer appears on the ribbon.

Rebecca will continue to work with macros, adding new features and making the macro easier to use and free from errors. But this initial Add_Donor macro is a good first step.

Proskills

Decision Making: Planning and Recording a Macro

Planning and practice help to ensure you create an error-free macro. First, decide what you want to accomplish. Then, consider the best way to achieve those results. Next, practice the keystrokes and mouse actions before you begin recording. This may seem like extra work, but it reduces the chance of error when you actually record the macro. As you set up a macro, consider the following:

- Choose a descriptive name that identifies the macro's purpose.
- Weigh the benefits of selecting a shortcut key against its drawbacks. Although a shortcut key is another way to run a macro, you are limited to one-letter shortcuts, which don't identify the shortcut's purpose. Your macro shortcut key might override another shortcut key provided by Microsoft Office.
- Store the macro with the current workbook unless the macro can be used with other workbooks.
- Include a description that provides an overview of the macro and perhaps your name and contact information.

Good decision making includes thinking about what to do and what not to do as you progress to your goals. This is true when developing a macro as well.

Finishing an Excel Application

You have completed much of the development of the fundraising app for Chestnut Academy. There are a few more tasks to accomplish before releasing the workbook. One of these is to hide any content that should not be visible to other members of Rebecca's team.

Hiding Workbook Content

A good app should allow access only to those things that the user has a right to or needs to access. This often means hiding confidential financial information and worksheets containing data, formulas, and lists used to create PivotTables or charts, but which are not of direct interest to the user. Hiding content in one part of a workbook does not affect content in other parts of the workbook. A PivotTable, formula, or chart will operate the same whether its data source is visible or hidden.

Reference

Hiding Workbook Content

To hide a worksheet row or column:
- Select a range of row or column headers.
- Right-click the selection, and then click Hide on the shortcut menu.

To unhide a worksheet row or column:
- Select the row or column headers surrounding the hidden content.
- Right-click the selection, and then click Unhide on the shortcut menu.

To hide a worksheet:
- Select the sheet tabs of the worksheets you want hidden.
- Right-click the selection, and then click Hide from the shortcut menu.

To unhide a worksheet:
- Right-click any sheet tab in the workbook, and then click Unhide on the shortcut menu.
- Click the sheets you want unhidden from the list in the Unhide dialog box.
- Click OK.

You can hide worksheet rows, columns, and entire worksheets without affecting the rest of the workbook. For example, the Prior Donors worksheet contains contact information on past donors. Rebecca wants her colleagues to review the gift totals but also wants to protect the privacy of those donors. You will help her maintain donor confidentiality by hiding the columns containing their names and contact information.

To hide worksheet columns:

1. Go to the **Prior Donors** worksheet.
2. Click the **Review** tab on the ribbon, and then in the Protect group, click the **Unprotect Sheet** button.
3. Select columns **B** through **I** containing the names and contact information for each donor.
4. Right-click the selected columns, and then click **Hide** on the shortcut menu. Excel hides columns B through I, leaving only the donor ID and the total amount of gifts. Refer to Figure 12–53.

Figure 12-53   Hiding worksheet columns

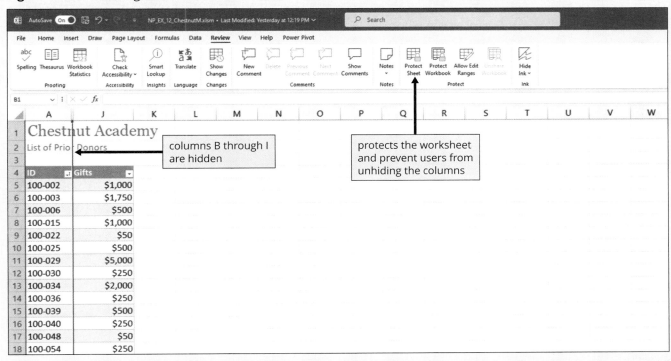

5. In the Protect group, click the **Protect Sheet** button, and then click **OK** so that the sheet is again protected.

Hiding a column or row does not remove it from the workbook; it merely sets the width or height to 0 pixels. To unhide a group of hidden columns or rows, select the visible column or rows headers around the hidden content, right-click the selection, and then click Unhide on the shortcut menu.

> **Tip** If the worksheet is protected, hidden columns and rows cannot be unhidden unless the protection is removed.

In developing this workbook, you explored different aspects of the LET and LAMBDA functions in a collection of worksheets. Although Rebecca wants to keep these worksheets as a reference for future projects, she doesn't want them visible to her colleagues. You will hide these worksheets.

To hide a group of worksheets:

1. Click the **Explore LET** sheet tab.

2. Use the sheet scrolling tabs to scroll through the worksheet tabs to the end of the workbook.

3. Hold down **SHIFT** as you click the **Explore REDUCE** sheet tab, grouping all the Explore worksheets.

4. Right-click the worksheet group, and then click **Hide** on the shortcut menu. The Explore worksheets are hidden, and no worksheets appear between the Lists worksheet and the Terms and Definitions worksheet.

To unhide the hidden worksheets, you right-click any sheet tab in the workbook, and then click Unhide on the shortcut menu. The Unhide dialog box opens, listing the names of all hidden sheets. You then click the names of the sheets you want to make visible and click OK.

Setting Macro Security

If you plan on distributing a macro-enabled workbook to a larger audience, you need to consider how Excel manages macro security to ward off viruses. A **virus** is a computer program designed to copy itself into other programs with the intention of causing mischief or harm. When unsuspecting users open these infected workbooks, Excel automatically runs the attached virus-infected macro. **Macro viruses** are a type of virus that uses a program's own macro programming language to distribute the virus. Macro viruses can be destructive and can modify or delete files that may not be recoverable.

> **Tip** To manage how Excel opens macro-enabled documents, click the Macro Security button in the Code group on the Developer tab and choose an option for whether Excel enabled or disables macro-enabled documents by default.

One of the ways Excel protects you from macro viruses is to disable macros until you explicitly agree that they should be enabled. You will explore this now by closing and reopening your workbook.

To close and reopen a macro-enabled workbook:

1. Save the **NP_EX_12_ChestnutM** workbook.

2. Close the workbook.

3. Open the **NP_EX_12_ChestnutM** workbook. A security warning opens, indicating that macros have been disabled. Refer to Figure 12–54.

Figure 12–54   Security warning for a workbook containing a macro

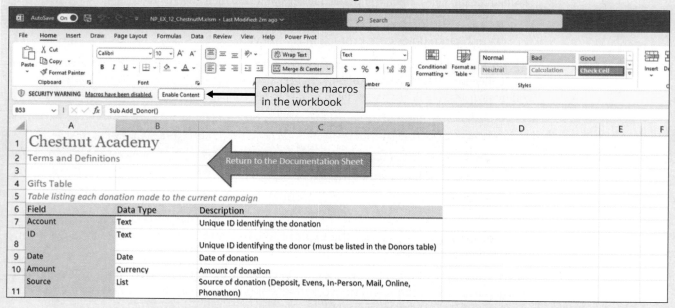

Trouble? If the security warning does not open, it could be that your version of Excel treats this workbook as a trusted document or that it comes from a trusted location. If that is the case, you do not have to do anything to enable the workbook content. Read but do not perform Steps 4 and 5.

4. Click the **Enable Content** button to enable the macros stored in the workbook. A dialog box opens, prompting you to make this document a trusted document.

5. Click **Yes**.

A **trusted document** is a document that Excel trusts as being free of macro viruses and will not prevent you from opening and will not prompt you to confirm that it can be opened. Once you identify a document or location as being trustworthy, Excel will not prompt you with a security warning as you open the workbook.

You can define how Excel manages the security of your documents in the **Trust Center**, which is a collection of settings that define how macros are managed by Excel. You can review the Trust Center by clicking the File tab on the ribbon, and then clicking Options in the navigation bar to open the Excel Options dialog box. Click Trust Center from the list of Excel options, and then click the Trust Center Settings button to review your Microsoft Office security options.

Insight

Creating a Digital Signature

Another way to mark a trusted workbook is to assign it a **digital signature**, which marks the workbook as coming from a trusted author. Digital signatures are added one of the last steps before distributing a workbook to a wide audience of users. Before you can add a digital signature to a workbook, you need to obtain a digital ID (also called a digital certificate) that proves your identity. Digital certificates are typically issued by a certificate authority. After you have a digital certificate, do the following to digitally sign your workbook:

1. On the ribbon, click the File tab, and then, in the navigation bar, click Info.
2. On the Info screen, click the Protect Workbook button, and then click Add a Digital Signature.
3. If the Get a Digital ID dialog box opens, asking if you would like to get a digital ID from a Microsoft Partner, click Yes. Your browser opens to a website with information about digital signature providers and available digital IDs.
4. Select a provider and follow the steps to obtain a digital ID from that provider.

Digitally signing workbooks assures others that the workbook has not been altered since its creation by the document's author. A digital signature is removed any time the workbook is saved, ensuring that no one (including the original workbook author) can modify the document without removing the digital signature. In this way, a chain of custody is established from document creation to document distribution, ensuring that no third party has altered the Excel application.

Protecting a Workbook

Protecting the workbook prevents other users from renaming, deleting, hiding, or inserting worksheets into the document. As with worksheet protection, you can password-protect the workbook to provide an additional level of security. The last step before making the fundraising workbook available to other members of Rebecca's team is to protect the workbook itself. You will protect Rebecca's workbook *without* providing a password.

To protect the workbook:

1. Click the **Review** tab on the ribbon.

2. In the Protect group, click the **Protect Workbook** button. The Protect Structure and Windows dialog box opens.

3. Click **OK** without entering enter a password in the Password (optional) box.

4. Click the **Terms and Definitions** sheet tab and attempt to drag it to a new location in the workbook. You cannot move the worksheet.

5. Right-click the **Terms and Definitions** sheet tab in the workbook and verify that options for inserting, deleting, removing, hiding, and unhiding the sheet are grayed out and unavailable to the user.

6. **sam**⬆ Save the workbook, and then close it.

To remove workbook protection, go to the Review tab and in the Protect group, click the Unprotect Workbook button, providing a password if necessary.

You have completed your work on the first draft of Rebecca's fundraising workbook. She will share this workbook with other team members and continue to revise and refine its features based on their feedback, creating an Excel application that is user-friendly, efficient, and protected from data entry errors.

Part 12.3 Quick Check

1. What is the Developer tab?

2. How do the file extensions differ between workbooks and macro-enabled workbooks?

3. What is one thing you should always do before starting the macro recorder?

4. How do you insert a form button into a worksheet?

5. What is VBA?

6. What action is accomplished by the following VBA command?

    ```
    ActiveSheet.Unprotect
    ```

7. Provide the VBA command to display a message box with the text "New donation added to the donation list."

8. What is a trusted document?

9. How do you prevent users from deleting or renaming worksheets in your workbook?

Practice: Review Assignments

Data File needed for the Review Assignments: NP_EX_12-2.xlsx

In the months since you worked with Rebecca on the fundraising workbook, the campaign has contacted many of its missing donors and is halfway to the $3.6 million goal. Rebecca wants you to create another workbook in which she can enter individual gifts to the campaign using a macro. Rebecca also wants a custom function that will estimate the date at which the fundraising goal will be reached given the current rate of contributions. The workbook you develop should contain features for error control, data validation, and protection of both the worksheets and the workbook itself. Complete the following.

1. Open the **NP_EX_12-2.xlsx** workbook located in the Excel12 > Review folder included with your Data Files. Save the workbook as **NP_EX_12_Progress** in the location specified by your instructor.
2. In the Documentation sheet, enter your name and the date in the range B3:B4 and then review the contents of the worksheets and the information in the Terms and Definitions worksheet.
3. In the Gifts by Date worksheet, do the following to display information on gifts made within a specified date interval:
   a. In cell B4, change the date to **3/10/2030** and in cell B5, change the date to **3/31/2030**. The worksheet will show error values in cells B8, D6, and J6 because no donations were made on those dates.
   b. In cell B8, apply the IFERROR function to show a zero in place of the #DIV/0! error value.
   c. In cell D6, revise the FILTER function to display the text "**No gifts during these dates**" if the filter returns an empty array.
   d. In cell J6, apply the IFERROR function to show a blank in place of the #VALUE! error value.
4. In cell B4, add the following validation test to ensure users enter a valid date:
   a. Create a validation test that verifies that the date entered in cell B4 is greater than or equal to 2/2/2029, which is the campaign start date.
   b. Add an input message with the title **Start Date** and the text **Enter the initial date of your date range.** (including the period).
   c. Add an error alert to show a Warning alert if a user enters an invalid date with the title **Possible Invalid Date** and the error message **The campaign began on 2/2/2029.** (including the period).
5. In cell B5, add the following validation test to ensure users enter a valid date:
   a. Create a validation test that verifies the date in cell B5 is greater than or equal to the value of cell B4.
   b. Add an error alert to show a Stop alert if the user enters an invalid date with the title **Invalid Date** and the message **The ending date must be greater than or equal to the starting date.** (including the period).
6. In the Explore LET and LAMBDA worksheet, in cell B9, create a LAMBDA function with the variables **StartDate**, **CurrentAmt**, **Goal**, and an optional parameter **CurrentDate**.
7. Expand the formula bar, and then within the LAMBDA function, insert a LET function with the following variables and calculations:
   a. If the user does not provide a value for the CurrentDate parameter, apply the following expression to set CurrentDate to the value returned by the TODAY() function: **CurrentDate, IF(ISOMITTED(CurrentDate), TODAY(), CurrentDate),**
   b. Define the **Days** variable equal to CurrentDate minus StartDate.
   c. Define the **DollarsPerDay** variable equal to the CurrentAmt variable divided by the Days variable.
   d. Define the **AmtRemaining** variable equal to the Goal variable minus the CurrentAmt variable.
   e. Define the **DaysToGoal** variable equal to the AmtRemaining variable divided by the DollarsPerDay variable.
   f. In the final line of the LET function, insert the following calculation that determines that date on which the fundraising goal will be met rounded up to the nearest day: **ROUNDUP(CurrentDate + DaysToGoal, 0)**
8. In cell B9, include cells B4, B5, B6, and B7 for the values StartDate, CurrentAmt, Goal, and CurrentDate variables. You should get a date of 5/9/2031.
9. In cell B4, enter the formula **= TODAY() – 10** to return a date that is 10 days before the current date and leave cell B7 blank. Change the list of parameter values used in the LAMBDA formula in cell B9 from (B4, B5, B6, B7) to **(B4, B5, B6)**. Verify that the value returned by the function is 10 days after your current date or 20 days after the date in cell B4.

10. Once you have verified that your LAMBDA/LET formula works, copy the text of the formula (but not the values) and create a function named **MY_GOALDATE** with workbook scope and the comment: **Estimate the date that the fundraising goal will be met given the current rate of fundraising.** (including the period).

11. Apply the MY_GOALDATE function to cell B10 in the Dashboard worksheet, using cells B8, B5, B4, and B9 for the values of the StartDate, CurrentAmt, Goal, and CurrentDate variables. You should get an estimated date of 5/9/2031.

12. In the Dashboard worksheet, do the following to calculate what repeat donors have given to the current campaign:
    a. In cell I20, insert the REDUCE function with an initial value of zero and Prior[ID] as the array.
    b. Within the REDUCE function, run the following LAMBDA function to lookup the total gifts by repeat donors, calculating the sum of the total gifts:

```
LAMBDA(total, ID,
    total + XLOOKUP(ID, Donors[ID], Donors[Total Gifts], 0)
)
```

    c. Close the REDUCE function with an ending parenthesis.

13. In cell I21, calculate the value of cell I20 minus cell I19 and divide that difference by the value of cell I19 to get the percent increase in donations by repeat donors between the previous current campaigns.

14. Before you create a macro, save the workbook in case you need return to the previous version, and then save the workbook as a macro-enabled workbook named **NP_EX_12_ProgressM** in the location specified by your instructor. Display the Developer tab on the ribbon.

15. In the **New Donation** worksheet, do the following to create a macro that copies the gift shown in the worksheet to a new entry in the Gifts table:
    a. Record a macro named **Add_Gift** stores in this workbook with the description **Add a new gift to the Gifts table**.
    b. Click the Gifts worksheet tab and then click cell A5 in the worksheet.
    c. Click the Home tab on the ribbon. In the Cells group, click the Insert arrow, and then click Insert Table Rows Above to insert a new table row at the top of the table.
    d. Click the New Donation worksheet tab, select the values in the range B4:B9. On the Home tab, in the Clipboard group, click the Copy button.
    e. Click the Gifts tab and make sure cell A5 is still selected. On the Home tab, in the Clipboard group, click the Paste arrow and then click Paste Special.
    f. Click the Values options button, click the Transpose check box, and then click OK.
    g. Click the Data tab, and then in the Queries & Connections group, click the Refresh All button.
    h. Click the New Donation worksheet tab.
    i. Click the Developer tab on the ribbon, and then in the Code group, click the Stop Recording button.

16. In the New Donation worksheet, insert a form control button over the range A10:B13 of. Assign the Add_Gift macro to the button and add the label **Add a New Gift to the Campaign** to the button.

17. In the range B4:B9, enter the following information for a new gift: cell B4: **500-0310-555**, cell B5: **500-626**, cell B6: **3/10/2030**, cell B7: **$5,000**, cell B8: **In-Person**, and cell B9: **Paid**.

18. Save the workbook, and then click the Add a New Gift to the Campaign button. In the Gifts worksheet, verify that the gift was added at the top of the table. In the Dashboard worksheet, verify that the total collected shown in cell B5 increased to $1,806,165.

19. Open the Visual Basic Editor and go to the Add_Gift macro located in the Module1 folder. Directly above the End Sub line, insert the command **MsgBox "Gift Added"** to display a message box when the macro is done running.

20. Close the Visual Basic Editor and return to the New Donation worksheet and unlock the cells in the range B4:B9. Protect the worksheet but do NOT provide a password.

21. Hide the Explore LET and LAMBDA worksheet.

22. Protect the workbook, but do NOT provide a password.

23. Save the workbook, and then close it.

Apply: Case Problem 1

Data File needed for this Case Problem: NP_EX_12-3.xlsx

Agir Electronics Lydia Gil is an HR manager for Agir Electronics, a manufacturer of electronic equipment and software. The company is expanding rapidly and is interviewing and hiring candidates for a variety of positions. Applicants go through several stages, starting with a phone screening to eliminate applicants who don't match the company's needs, followed by two interviews at different levels of management. After the second interview, an applicant might receive a job offer, which might or might not be accepted, resulting in a new hire.

Lydia uses Excel to track the application process. Her workbook includes more than 1,500 applications from the current year for 12 position categories across the company. Each application includes an application ID, the general position applied for, the current stage of the application, a code indicating the current stage, the dates at which stage was achieved by the applicant, and the number of days between each stage and the initial application date.

Lydia wants you to develop an Excel app that will calculate the number of candidates who reach each stage in the application process broken down by position. Lydia is concerned that the hiring process is too slow and wants your app to determine the average number of days applicants need to reach each stage. Your app will be used by several employees in the HR department, so it needs error control and document protection. Complete the following:

1. Open the **NP_EX_12-3.xlsx** workbook located in the Excel12 > Case2 folder included with your Data Files, and then save the workbook as **NP_EX_12_Agir** in the location specified by your instructor.

2. In the Documentation sheet, in the range B3:B4, enter your name and the date. Review the contents of the workbook including the Terms and Definitions worksheet.

3. In the Summary worksheet, add data validation to cell B4 to display the list of positions from the Positions range name. Verify that the list includes 12 positions.

4. Add data validation to cell B5 to display the list of stages from the Stages range name. Verify that the list includes six stages.

5. In cell F8, the FILTER function creates an array of candidates who reach the stage shown in cell B5 for the position shown in cell B4. If no candidates match those criteria, the array shows the value #CALC! Modify the FILTER function to display the text **No Applicants** when the FILTER function returns an empty array.

6. In the Explore LAMBDA1 worksheet, in cell B7, use LAMBDA and LET to calculate the number of employees who reach each application stage for a position. Do the following:
   a. Create a LAMBDA function in cell B7.
   b. Within the LAMBDA function, insert two variables named **Position** and **Stage**.

7. Insert a LET function within the LAMBDA function that does the following:
   a. Define a variable named **Applicants** that references those fields in the Log table containing applicants. Set the value of the Applicants variable to:

      `INDIRECT("Log[" & Stage & "]")`

   b. Define a variable named **AppPos** that filters the Applicants variable to include only those applicants for a specified position. Set the value of the AppPos variable to:

      `FILTER(Applicants, (Log[Position]=Position))`

   c. Complete the LET function by adding the following line to calculate the number applicants listed in the AppPos variable:

      `COUNT(AppPos)`

8. Test the function by applying the parameter values **(B4, B5)** to the LAMBDA function, to count the number of applicants to the Systems Analyst position that reached at least the second interview. Verify that the function returns a value of 35.

9. Create another custom function that calculates the average number of days to reach a specified stage for a given position. Days are calculated in fields of the Log table named DaysToScreen through DaysToHire. Do the following:

   a. Copy the formula in cell B7, and then paste it into cell B7 of the Explore LAMBDA2 worksheet.

   b. Change the name of the Applicants variable to **Days** and change the value of the Days variable to **INDIRECT("Log[DaysTo" & Stage & "]")**

   c. Change the name of the AppPos variable to **DaysPos** and set its value to **FILTER(Days, (Log[Position]=Position))**

   d. In the last line of the LET function, change COUNT(AppStage) to **AVERAGE(DaysPos)** and then verify that the function returns a value of 38.8 as the average number of days for candidates to the Systems Analyst position to reach the second interview stage.

10. Copy the function you created in cell B7 of the Explore LAMBDA1 worksheet, paste it as a new function named **MY_APPS** and with the comment **Calculate the number of applicants**. Do NOT copy the cell references to B4 and B5.

11. Copy the function in cell B7 of the Explore LAMBDA2 worksheet (but do not copy the parameter values (B4, B5)), pasting the copied code as a new function named **MY_APPDAYS** with the comment **Calculate the average number of days**.

12. In the Summary worksheet, in cell B8, enter the formula **=MY_APPS($B$4, $A8)** to calculate the total number of applicants for the Content Editor position. Copy and fill, without formatting, the formula in cell B8 through the range B8:B13 to calculate the number of Content Editor candidates that reach each stage. Verify the formula returns the values 106, 77, 49, 18, 0, and 0.

13. In cell C8, enter the formula **= B8/$B$8** to calculate the percentage of applicants who reached the Apply stage. Copy and fill the formula, without formatting, through the range C8:C13. Verify the formula returns the percentages 100%, 72.6%, 46.2%, 17.0%, 0.0%, and 0.0%.

14. Enclose the formulas in the range C8:C13 within an IFERROR function that will display blank text in place of an error value.

15. In cell D9, enter the formula **=MY_APPDAYS($B$4, $A9)** to calculate the average number of days for Content Editor candidates to reach the screening stage. Copy and fill, without formatting, the formula cell D9 through the range D9:D13. Verify the formula returns the values 14.8, 27.7, 39.1, #DIV/0!, and #DIV/0!

16. Apply the IFERROR function to the formulas in the range D9:D13 to display blank text if an error value is encountered.

17. In cell B4, change the value to **Sales Agent** and in cell B5, change the value to **Hire** and confirm the table lists the four candidates who have been hired as sales agents.

18. Use conditional formatting to add solid green data bars to the values in the range B8:B13.

19. Save the workbook, and then save it as a macro-enabled workbook named **NP_EX_12_AgirM** in the location specified by your instructor.

20. Create a macro to jump to a candidate's contact information when their ID is selected in column F of the Summary worksheet.

   a. Click cell F11 containing the ID A810-47418-410.

   b. Save the workbook with cell F11 of the Summary worksheet selected.

   c. Start the macro recorder, naming the macro as **Show_Contact** with the description **Display contact information for a selected ID.** (including the period).

21. Record the following steps in the macro:

   a. On the Home tab, in the Clipboard group, click the Copy button.

   b. Click the Contacts worksheet tab

   c. On the Home tab, in the Editing group, click the Find & Select button, and then click Find.

   d. In the Find and Replace dialog box, paste the copied ID into the Find what box, click Find Next, and then click Close.

   e. Press CTRL+SHIFT+RIGHT ARROW to select the entire row of information on Dorothy Doss.

   f. Stop the macro recorder.

22. Edit the macro as follows so that it will work with any ID that is selected by the user:

   a. On the Developer tab, in the Code group, click the Macros button, select Show_Contact from the list of macros, and click then Edit to open the Visual Basic for Applications editor.

   b. Directly below the line Selection.Copy, insert the following line to store the value of the selected cell in the ID variable: **ID = Selection.Value**

c. In the line containing the Cells.Find() method, replace What:="A810-47418-410" with **What:=ID**

d. Directly above the End Sub line, insert the following command to display a message box with the ID of the selected applicant: **MsgBox "Contact information for " & ID**

e. Exit the Visual Basic for Applications editor and return to the Summary worksheet.

23. In the range F5:G6, insert a form control button for the Show_Contact macro with the label **Show Selected ID Contact** in the button.

24. Click cell F8 containing the ID A810-47249-408, and then click the Show Selected ID Contact macro button. Verify that a message box with the caption "Contact information for A810-47249-408" appears and the table for Mildred Walker is selected. Click OK.

25. In the Summary worksheet, unlock cells B4 and B5.

26. Protect the Summary worksheet WITHOUT a password to protect its contents except for unlocked cells B4 and B5.

27. Hide the Explore LAMBDA1 and Explore LAMBDA2 workbooks.

28. Protect the workbook WITHOUT a password.

29. Use the Summary worksheet to list all candidates for a Programmer position that reached the Offer stage.

30. Click cell F20 and then click the Show Selected ID Contact button to show contact information for applicant A630-47446-503.

31. Return to the Summary worksheet. Save the workbook, and then close it.

Challenge: Case Problem 2

Data File needed for this Case Problem: NP_EX_12-4.xlsx

Wingait Farms Jackson Ross is a production analyst for Wingait Farms, a large farming operation based in central Iowa. Jackson is analyzing the growth of various corn hybrids, predicting their date of harvest and their yield. One way of tracking produce growth is with Growing Degree Days, or GDD, which measures growth as a function of days in which the daily temperature falls within a range of values that optimizes growth. The GDD statistic is calculated as

$$GDD = \frac{Tmin + Tmax}{2} - base$$

where $Tmin$ and $Tmax$ are the minimum and maximum temperatures in which crop growth occurs and $base$ is a baseline temperature. Different crops have different $Tmin$, $Tmax$, and $Base$ values. For corn, those values are 50°, 86°, and 50°, respectively, indicating that corn grows best when the daily temperature is between 50° and 86°. Produce will be ready for harvest when the crop has accumulated a specific number of growing degree days. A fast growth corn hybrid might be ready for harvesting when it has accumulated 2500 growing degree days, while a slow growth hybrid might require 3000 growing degree days to reach maturity.

Because GDD is such an important statistic, Jackson wants you to create a GDD function for Excel. He wants to incorporate that function in a workbook that charts the total GDD for the farm's collection of corn hybrids, estimating the date on which each hybrid reaches maturity and is ready for harvesting. Complete the following:

1. Open the **NP_EX_12-4.xlsx** workbook located in the Excel12 > Case2 folder included with your Data Files, and then save the workbook as **NP_EX_12_Wingait** in the location specified by your instructor.

2. In the Documentation sheet, in the range B3:B4, enter your name and the date. Review the contents of the workbook including the Terms and Definitions worksheet.

3. In the Hybrids worksheet, do the following:
   a. Add a validation test for the Yield values in the range B5:B12, restricting those values to Good, Very Good, or Excellent.
   b. Add a validation test for the Height values in the range C5:C12, restricting those values to Medium, Medium Tall, or Tall.
   c. Unlock the cells in the range A5:I12, and then protect the worksheet without a password.

4. **Explore:** In the Explore GDD worksheet, in cell B9, create a LAMBDA function with variables **lowTemp**, **highTemp**, and optional variables **Tmin**, **Tmax**, and **Base**.

5. Within that LAMBDA function, insert a LET function with the following lines:
   a. If Tmin is omitted, set its values to 50; otherwise use the Tmin value specified by the user.
   b. If Tmax is omitted, set its value to 86; otherwise use the Tmax value specified by the user.
   c. If Base is omitted, set its value to 50; otherwise use the Base value specified by the user.
   d. As the final line in the LET function, insert the following calculation that will return the GDD value given the temperature values:

   ```
   (MAX(lowTemp, Tmin) + MIN(highTemp, Tmax))/2-Base
   ```

6. Test the formula in cell B9, as follows:
   a. Use cell B4 for the lowTemp variable and cell B5 for the highTemp variable. Do not specify values for the Tmin, Tmax, and Base variables. Verify that the formula returns a GDD of 31.
   b. Use cells B4, B5, B6, B7, and B8, for the lowTemp, highTemp, Tmin, Tmax, and Base variables. Verify that the function returns a GDD value of 20.

7. Save the LAMBDA LET formula in cell B9 as the custom function named **MY_GDD** with the comment **Calculate the Growing Degree Day value for the range of temperatures.** (including the period).

8. In the Growth worksheet, in column D, apply the MY_GDD function to calculate the GDD for each day given the lowTemp value in column B and the highTemp value in column C. Verify that the first four GDD values are 1, 7, 10, and 13, and the first four cumulative GDD values in column E are 1, 8, 18, and 31.

9. **Explore:** In the Explore Harvest worksheet, in cell B5, enter a LAMBDA formula and then do the following to return the date at which a crop reaches a specified total GDD:
   a. Add the following variables to the LAMBDA function: **GDD, Dates, TotalGDD** where GDD will be the GDD value, Dates is an array of dates, and TotalGDD is an array of cumulative GDD values.
   b. Apply the following calculation to the LAMBDA function to return the date on which the GDD is level is reached:

   ```
   XLOOKUP(GDD, TotalGDD, Dates, "Not Reached", 1)
   ```

10. Test the formula in cell B5 using cell B4 for the GDD value, Growth[Date] for the Dates array, and Growth[Total GDD] for the TotalGDD array. Verify that the formula returns the date 8/27/2029 (the estimated date on which the crop will reach maturity).

11. Save the LAMBDA formula in cell B5 as the custom function named **MY_HARVEST** with the comment **Return the date on which the crop reaches maturity for a specified GDD level.** (including the period).

12. In the Dashboard worksheet, in cell B15, apply the MY_HARVEST function using cell B9 for the GDD value, Growth[Date] for the Dates array, and Growth[Total GDD] for the TotalGDD array. Verify that the formula returns the date 8/5/2029.

13. Add data validation to cell B5 to restrict the values to the list of corn hybrids specified in the Hybrid_List range name. Use the list in cell B5 to change the hybrid to CS6489, verifying that the harvest date changes to 9/6/2029.

14. In the Growth worksheet, add a table column named **Maturity** in column F, setting all values in the column to the value of cell $B$9 in the Dashboard worksheet to specify the GDD level at which the crop is ready for harvest.

15. Create a scatter chart of the values in the range A4:A163,E4:F163 using the Scatter with Smooth Lines chart subtype, and then modify the chart as follows:
   a. Move the chart to the Dashboard worksheet and then resize it to cover the range E4:L18.
   b. Change the chart title to **Growing Degree Days**.
   c. Add the vertical axis title **Total GDD** and the horizontal axis title **Date** to the chart.
   d. Remove the chart legend.

16. Click cell B5 to deselect the chart, and then save the workbook.

17. The date labels in the horizontal axis overlap, making them difficult to read. You will create a macro that Jackson can use to quickly change the scale of the horizontal axis. Save the workbook as a macro-enabled workbook named **NP_EX_12_WingaitM** in the location specified by your instructor.

18. **Explore:** Start the macro recorder, create a macro named **Adjust_Chart** with the description **Adjust the date range shown in the chart**, and then record the following steps in the macro:
    a. Click cell O5 of the Dashboard worksheet and copy its value.
    b. Click the chart to select it and then double-click the dates in the horizontal axis.
    c. From the Format Axis pane, go to the Axis Options section, and paste the copied date into the Minimum box. Press TAB to change the lower range of the charted dates.
    d. Click cell O6 and copy its value.
    e. Click the chart and double-click the dates in the horizontal axis.
    f. From the Format Axis pane in the Axis Options section, paste the copied date into the Maximum box and press TAB.
    g. Click cell O7 and copy its value.
    h. Click the chart and double-click the dates in the horizontal axis.
    i. From the Format Axis pane, in the Units section, paste the copied value into the Major box and press TAB.
    j. Click cell N4 and then stop the recording.

19. **Explore:** On the Developer tab, in the Code group, click the Macros button. Select the Adjust_Chart macro, click Edit, and then edit the macro as follows so it uses the copied values in adjusting the chart:
    a. Directly below the first Selection.Copy line (after the Range("O5").Select command), enter the command: **MinDate = Selection.Value**
    b. Go to the line with property MinimumScale = 47253 and change the text to: **MinimumScale = MinDate**
    c. Directly below the second Selection.Copy line (after the Range("O6").Select command), enter the command: **MaxDate = Selection.Value**
    d. Go to the line with property MaximumScale = 47376 and change the text to: **MinimumScale = MaxDate**
    e. Directly below the third Selection.Copy line (after the Range("O7").Select command), enter the command: **Days = Selection.Value**
    f. Go to the line with property MajorUnit = 30 and change the text to: **MajorUnit = Days**
    g. Directly after the initial line Sub Adjust_Chart(), enter the following command to turn off screen updating as the macro is running: **Application.ScreenUpdating = False**
    h. Directly before the end line End Sub, enter the following command to turn on screen updating as the macro finishes: **Application.ScreenUpdating = True**

20. Close the Visual Basic Editor and return to the Dashboard worksheet. Insert a macro button form control in the range N8:O10 for the Adjust_Chart macro with the label **Modify the Date Range**.

21. Change the date in cell O5 to **7/1/2029**, change the date in cell O6 to **8/1/2029** and change the value in cell O7 to **7**. Click the Modify the Date Range macro button and verify that the chart's date range changes to roughly match the values in the range O5:O7.

22. Change the hybrid in cell B5 to **CS6389** to show the growth tracker for that corn hybrid from July 1 to about August 1.

23. Hide the Explore GDD and Explore Harvest worksheets.

24. Protect the workbook without a password. Save the workbook, and then close it.

Index

Note: Page numbers in **bold** indicate keyterms.

A

absolute cell references, **EX 3-3**, EX 3-11–3-12
  formulas, EX 3-11–3-12
Access database
  query, EX 10-27–10-28
Accounting format, **EX 2-12**
  apply, EX 2-12–2-14
activate Solver, EX 8-43–8-44
active cell, **EX 1-3**
active sheet, **EX 1-2,** EX 1-7
add
  footers, EX 2-59
  headers, EX 2-59
add-in, EX 8-42
advanced filter, EX 6-58–6-61
  criteria range, EX 6-60
  defined, **EX 6-59**
Advanced Filter dialog box, EX 6-61
align cell content, EX 2-23–2-27
amortization schedule, create,
  EX 9-12–9-19
analysis
  ideas, EX 10-66
analytics, **EX 10-4**
Analyze Data (Ideas) pane, EX 10-66
Analyze Data tool, EX 10-66
AND function, EX 7-20
  defined, **EX 7-20**
answer report, EX 8-53
  create, EX 8-53–8-55
approximate match lookups, **EX 3-3**
  create, EX 7-6–7-9
arguments, **EX 1-36**
arithmetic operators, **EX 1-32**
Arrange All button, EX 5-2
array, **EX 3-14**
array formula, EX 8-20
ascending order sort, **EX 6-13**
asset(s)
  calculate depreciation,
    EX 9-30–9-35
  declining-balance depreciation,
    EX 9-34
  material, EX 9-30
  noncash, EX 9-30
  straight-line depreciation, EX 9-33
  tangible, EX 9-30
audit workbook, EX 9-52–9-58
AutoComplete, **EX 1-20**–1-21
AutoFill, **EX 3-2**
  explore options, EX 3-7–3-8
  extend series, EX 3-9

  fill series, EX 3-8–3-11
  formula, EX 3-6–3-7
  formulas and data patterns,
    EX 3-6–3-11
  options menu, EX 3-8
AutoFit, **EX 1-27**
automatic page break, **EX 2-33**
AutoSum, **EX 1-31**
  insert functions, EX 1-37–1-39
AVERAG
  EX function, EX 11-63
average, **EX 3-26**
Average Daily Rate (ADR)
  calculated field, EX 11-45
AVERAGE function, EX 2-6, **EX 3-22**,
  EX 11-47
  3-D reference, EX 5-15
AVERAGEIF function
  calculate conditional averages,
    EX 7-26
  defined, **EX 7-26**
AVERAGEIFS function
  calculate conditional averages,
    EX 7-26
  defined, **EX 7-26**
averages, calculate, EX 2-43–2-44
AVG function, EX 11-55. *See also*
  AVERAGE function
axis titles
  add, EX 4-29–4-30
  added to chart, EX 4-30
  defined, **EX 4-29**

B

background
  image, add, EX 2-10–2-11
  work, EX 2-9–2-12
Backstage view, EX 1-4
banded rows, **EX 6-25**
bar charts, **EX 4-18**
base field, **EX 11-28**
base item, **EX 11-28**
bind constraint, EX 8-55
bins, **EX 4-44**
blank cell(s)
  calculations, EX 3-34–3-35
  role, EX 3-34–3-35
border(s), EX 1-30
Border styles, work with,
  EX 2-20–2-23
borrowing cost, calculate,
  EX 9-4–9-12
boxplot, EX 6-57

break-even analysis, EX 8-6
break-even point, EX 8-3
  CVP chart, EX 8-6
  directly calculate, EX 8-14
  explore, EX 8-6–8-7
  find with what-if analysis,
    EX 8-7–8-9
bubble chart, **EX 4-37**
Bubble map, EX 10-62
business intelligence (BI),
  EX 10-4
  charting trends, EX 10-15–10-17
  introduce, EX 10-4
BYCOL function, EX 12-51

C

calculate
  averages, EX 2-43–2-44
  borrowing cost, EX 9-4–9-12
  cost of goods sold, EX 9-26–9-27
  cumulative interest and principal
    payments, EX 9-16–9-19
  depreciation of assets,
    EX 9-30–9-35
  distinct counts, EX 11-53–1-55
  formulas, EX 1-32–1-35
  functions, EX 1-36–1-39
  future value with FV function,
    EX 9-7–9-9
  inflation with FV function,
    EX 9-9
  interest and principal payments,
    EX 9-13–9-15
  interest rates with RATE function,
    EX 9-40–9-42
  internal rate of return,
    EX 9-47–9-52
  measures across tables and
    rows, EX 11-59–11-63
  monthly revenues in query,
    EX 10-13
  net present value, EX 9-44–9-47
  payment period with NPER
    function, EX 9-9–9-10
  payments with PMT function,
    EX 9-5–9-7
  percent differences,
    EX 11-31–11-33
  present value with PV function,
    EX 9-10–9-12
  ranks, EX 11-30–11-31
  values for PivotTable field,
    EX 11-30

calculated fields, **EX 11-44**. *See also*
  field(s)
  behind the math, EX 11-47–11-48
  create, EX 11-44–11-47
  defined, **EX 6-38**
  Excel table, EX 6-38–6-42
  work, EX 11-41–11-49
calculated items, **EX 11-41**
  behind the math, EX 11-47–11-48
  create, EX 11-41–11-44
  group, EX 11-44
  work, EX 11-41–11-49
calculation(s)
  blank cells and zeroes, EX 3-34–3-35
  dates and times, EX 3-6
  design workbook, EX 3-4–3-5
  document, EX 3-5
  dynamic arrays, EX 3-14–3-18
  measures of central tendency,
    EX 3-27
  minimums and maximums,
    EX 3-24–3-26
  PivotTables, EX 11-28–11-33
  Quick Analysis Tool, EX 3-18–3-20
cascade layout
  workbook window, EX 5-7
cash flow, EX 9-4
  negative, EX 9-4
  positive, EX 9-4
cash inflow, EX 9-4. *See also*
  positive cash flow
cash outflow, EX 9-4. *See also*
  negative cash flow
category axis, **EX 4-18**
Category field, EX 10-44
category map, **EX 10-54**
category values, **EX 4-3**
cell(s), **EX 1-3**
  change, EX 8-22
  edit, EX 1-18–1-20
  find and select, EX 6-26–6-27
  find by type, EX 6-27
  format text selections, EX 2-8–2-9
  highlighting unlocked, EX 12-27
  highlight with top/bottom rule,
    EX 2-47–2-48
  input, EX 8-2
  locate, within worksheet,
    EX 6-26–6-27
  locking, EX 12-25–12-27
  merge, EX 2-25–2-26
  move worksheet, EX 1-40–1-41
  objective, EX 8-44–8-46
  selected, EX 11-33

cell(s), (Continued)
  show field value, EX 11-33
  show multiple field values,
    EX 11-33
  unlocking, EX 12-25–12-27
  variable, EX 8-44–8-46
  wrap text, EX 1-27–1-28
cell borders, add, EX 1-49
cell content
  align, EX 2-23–2-27
CELL function, EX 12-27
cell range, **EX 1-2**
  selecting, EX 1-9–1-13
cell references, **EX 1-9**
  absolute, **EX 3-3**, EX 3-11–3-12
  conditional format with, EX 2-50
  explore, EX 3-11–3-14
  mixed, **EX 3-12**, EX 3-12–3-14
  relative, EX 3-11
cell styles, **EX 2-33**
  apply, EX 2-34–2-38
  create custom, EX 2-36–2-37
  defined, EX 2-34
cell text
  indent, EX 2-24–2-26
central tendency, **EX 3-26**
change
  cells, EX 8-22
  PivotTable layout, EX 11-6–11-8
characters, wildcard, EX 6-33
chart(s), EX 4-4. See also specific
    types
  add data callout, EX 4-40–4-41
  add data tables, EX 4-22–4-23
  add gridlines, EX 4-22–4-23
  add trendlines, EX 4-40
  axis titles added, EX 4-30
  change color scheme,
    EX 4-15–4-16
  choose style, EX 4-14–4-15
  communicate effectively, EX 4-27
  dynamic, EX 6-54–6-56
  extrapolate, EX 9-25
  funnel, **EX 12-6**
  hierarchy, EX 4-43
  histogram, **EX 4-44**
  insert graphic shape, EX 4-41–4-42
  interpolate, EX 9-25
  move, EX 4-8–4-10
  net income values, EX 8-18
  Pareto, EX 4-43–4-44
  perform what-if analyses,
    EX 4-17–4-18
  resize, EX 4-8–4-10
  revenue, EX 8-5
  sunburst, EX 4-43
  templates, create, EX 5-49
  thermometer, **EX 12-6**
  total expenses, EX 8-5
  treemap, **EX 4-43**
  variable expenses, EX 8-4
  waterfall, **EX 4-45**

chart area, **EX 4-3**
chart data source
  dialog box, EX 4-39
  edit, EX 4-38–4-40
  modify, EX 4-38
chart design theory, EX 4-49
chart elements
  common, EX 4-10–4-11
  defined, **EX 4-10**
  format, EX 4-11–4-14
  overlay, EX 4-17
  work, EX 4-10–4-17
chart formats
  copy, EX 4-38
  paste, EX 4-38
charting trends, EX 10-15–10-17.
    See also trendlines
"chart junk," EX 4-49
chart legend, **EX 4-2**
  chart area, EX 4-13
  fill color, EX 4-14
chart sheet, **EX 1-7**
chart style
  choose, EX 4-14–4-15
  preview, EX 4-15
chart title, **EX 4-2**
  edit, EX 4-21
choose
  PivotTable layout, EX 11-7
  rate of return, EX 9-45–9-47
clear, **EX 1-44**
Clear Filter button, EX 6-44
Clipboard, **EX 1-35**
clustered column chart, **EX 4-19**
  create, EX 4-19–4-21
Clustered Column map
  create, EX 10-63
Collapsed PivotTable outline, EX 10-46
color scales, **EX 11-26**
  create, EX 11-34
  defined, EX 11-36
  work, EX 11-36–11-37
column(s)
  add multiple fields, EX 7-37–7-38
  add new, EX 10-12
  choose with FILTER function,
    EX 6-65
  delete, EX 1-43–1-44
  freeze, in worksheet, EX 6-9
  hide, EX 1-47
  insert, EX 1-43–1-44
  insert and delete, EX 1-43–1-44
  resize, EX 1-25–1-29
  unhide, EX 1-47
column chart, **EX 4-18**
  clustered, EX 4-19–4-21
  compare subtypes, EX 4-18–4-19
  create, EX 4-18–4-23
  and pie charts with the same
    data, EX 4-18
  set gap width, EX 4-21–4-22
  subtypes, EX 4-18–4-19

column headings, **EX 1-3**
combination chart, **EX 4-3**
  add axis title, EX 4-29–4-30
  create, EX 4-27–4-31
  edit value axis scale,
    EX 4-30–4-31
Comma Separated Values (CSV) file,
    EX 10-4
  data arranged, EX 10-5
Comma style, **EX 2-3**
Compact layout, **EX 11-2**
compare expenses and revenue,
    EX 8-4–8-5
comparison operator, **EX 3-37**
conditional averages
  calculate with AVERAGEIF
    function, EX 7-26
  calculate with AVERAGEIFS
    function, EX 7-26
  defined, **EX 7-26**
conditional count, **EX 7-21**
  COUNTIF function, EX 7-21–7-22
  COUNTIFS function,
    EX 7-22–7-23
conditional formats, **EX 2-33**
  with cell references, EX 2-50
  display PivotTables,
    EX 11-33–11-37
  document, EX 2-50–2-51
  duplicate values, EX 6-10–6-11
  edit, EX 2-48–2-50
  highlight data, EX 2-44–2-52
  use effectively, EX 2-52
conditional formatting rule
  clear, EX 2-51
conditional statistics, calculate,
    EX 7-26–7-27
conditional summary functions
  use, EX 7-26
conditional sums
  calculate with SUMIF function,
    EX 7-24–7-25
  defined, **EX 7-24**
  with SUMIFS function, EX 7-25
confidence bounds, **EX 10-19**
Conga drum sales, EX 10-52
constant(s)
  decide where to place, EX 3-5
  defined, **EX 3-5**
  units, EX 3-5
constraints, EX 8-39
  binding, EX 8-55
  nonbinding, EX 8-55
copy formats, EX 2-16–2-20
cost of goods sold, EX 9-20.
    See also cost of sales
  calculate, EX 9-26–9-27
cost of sales, EX 9-20. See also cost
    of goods sold
Cost-Volume-Profit (CVP)
  analysis, EX 8-4
  chart, EX 8-6

cost-volume relationships, EX 8-4–8-9
count caches, EX 11-41
COUNT function, EX 11-53–11-55
  counting numeric values with,
    EX 1-41–1-43
  3-D reference, EX 5-15
COUNTIF function, **EX 7-3**
  conditional count, EX 7-21–7-22
  examples, EX 7-21
COUNTIFS function
  apply, EX 7-23
  conditional count, EX 7-22–7-23
  defined, **EX 7-22**
COUNTX function, EX 11-63
Create Forecast Worksheet dialog
  box, EX 10-19
Create PivotTable dialog box,
  EX 10-37
criteria filters, EX 6-30–6-32
  defined, **EX 6-30**
  text, number, and date, EX 6-31
criteria range, **EX 6-59**
CUBEVALUE function, EX 11-67
CUMIPMT function, EX 9-16
CUMPRINC function, EX 9-16
cumulative interest
  calculate, EX 9-16–9-19
Currency format, **EX 2-12**
  apply, EX 2-12–2-14
custom
  validation rule, create,
    EX 12-20–12-21
Custom AutoFilter dialog box,
  EX 6-32
custom cell styles
  create, EX 2-36–2-37
  merge, EX 2-7–2-38
custom colors, create, EX 2-7
customer relationship management
  (CRM) technology, **EX 7-4**
custom function, EX 12-40–12-50
  code selection, EX 12-41
  80|20 Rule, EX 12-43–12-46
  MY_SUMBETWEEN function,
    EX 12-42–12-43
  optional arguments,
    EX 12-46–12-49
Customize Ribbon category in the
  Excel Options dialog box,
  EX 12-59
custom list, **EX 6-17**
Custom Lists dialog box, EX 6-17
  delete, EX 6-18
  sort PivotTables, EX 11-11

D

dashboard, **EX 6-44**
  add histogram, EX 6-55
  add Order Date timeline, EX 10-40
  add slicers, EX 10-38–10-39
  create, EX 6-48–6-51

create dynamic charts,
EX 6-54–6-56
design, EX 6-51
filtered by store type and order
date, EX 10-41
slicer, EX 6-45
SUBTOTAL function, EX 6-51–6-54
data
date, **EX 1-18**
filter, EX 6-27–6-33
filter, with slicer(s), EX 6-46–6-48
filter with advanced filter,
EX 6-58–6-61
filter with FILTER function,
EX 6-62–6-63
filter with multiple criteria,
EX 6-63–6-65
highlight with conditional
formats, EX 2-44–2-52
look up, EX 3-42–3-47
look up, with tables,
EX 6-57–6-58
manage in Excel, EX 6-4–6-5
numeric, **EX 1-18**
pie and column charts, EX 4-18
retrieve with Index Match
lookups, EX 7-13–7-14
retrieve with lookup function,
EX 7-4–7-15
sort with SORTBY function,
EX 6-66–6-67
sort with SORT function,
EX 6-65–6-66
text, **EX 1-18**
time, **EX 1-18**
transpose, EX 2-20
use pane, for navigation,
EX 6-6–6-10
validate, EX 12-15
data analysis, EX 11-69–11-72
Data Analysis Expressions (DAX),
EX 11-51
introduce, EX 11-55–11-56
X functions, EX 11-63
data bar rule, modify, EX 4-46–4-47
data bars, **EX 4-32**
create, EX 4-45–4-47
database, **EX 10-24**
calculations with multiple
criterion, EX 11-69
design, EX 10-30
introduce, EX 10-26–10-28
tables, EX 10-24
Database functions, **EX 11-67**
explore, EX 11-67–11-69
summary statistics calculated,
EX 11-68
data callouts, **EX 4-33**
add to chart, EX 4-40–4-41
defined, **EX 4-40**
data card, **EX 11-70**
Data Cube, **EX 11-67**

data definition table, **EX 6-5**
employee data, EX 6-5
data entry, EX 6-6
create custom validation rule,
EX 12-20–12-21
create input message,
EX 12-17–12-18
create validation message,
EX 12-15–12-17
create worksheet, EX 12-65–12-70
data form, EX 12-70
validate, EX 12-11–12-23
validate against list, EX 12-18–12-19
validate date, EX 12-15
validation numbers, EX 12-12–12-15
data form
data entry, EX 12-70
data label, **EX 4-3**
data markers, **EX 4-2**
format, EX 4-25–4-27
Data Model, **EX 10-24**
advantages of storing data,
EX 10-28–10-29
apply slicers and timelines in
Power Pivot, EX 10-38–10-41
calculate distinct counts,
EX 11-53–11-55
create PivotTable, EX 10-35–10-41
data types, EX 11-69
drawback of storing data, EX 10-29
explore, EX 10-28–10-30
explore in Diagram view,
EX 10-32–10-33
import Data dialog box to load
data, EX 10-29
introduce PivotTable design
under, EX 11-52–11-53
load Customers table, EX 10-29
named sets, EX 11-53
Power Pivot with data, EX 10-37
view contents, EX 10-32
data patterns, and AutoFill,
EX 3-6–3-11
data query
edit, EX 10-9–10-10
month column, add, EX 10-12
refresh, EX 10-10
retrieve data into Excel table,
EX 10-8–10-9
set up, EX 10-11
use Power Query, EX 10-4–10-7
write, EX 10-4–10-10
data range
add subtotal, EX 6-18
convert, into table, EX 6-33–6-35
defined, **EX 6-2**
highlight duplicate values,
EX 6-10–6-11
make more accessible, EX 6-43
remove duplicate records,
EX 6-12–6-13
sort records, EX 6-13–6-18

data security, maintain, EX 10-22
data series, **EX 4-6**
data source(s), **EX 4-2**
Excel table, EX 10-10
move query, EX 10-14
select, EX 4-6
data tables
arrays, EX 8-20
defined, EX 8-9
modify, EX 8-13
one-variable, EX 8-9–8-12
two-variable, EX 8-14–8-20
work, EX 8-9–8-14
data types, linked, EX 10-69–11-71
data validation, **EX 12-3**
Data Validation dialog box, EX 12-14
data validation warning message,
EX 12-16
data values, round, EX 3-29–3-32
Data view, **EX 10-32**
date(s)
calculate, EX 3-6
calculations with working days,
EX 3-36
create validation rule, EX 12-15
enter, EX 1-22–1-25
format, EX 2-15–2-16
group, EX 11-19–11-22
date and time functions,
EX 3-35–3-37
date data, **EX 1-18**
date fields
add to PivotTables, EX 7-60–7-63
Date Filter dialog box, EX 11-21
date filters, EX 11-12
DB function, EX 9-21
declining balance depreciation,
EX 9-30–9-34
asset, EX 9-34
calculate, EX 9-33
definition, EX 9-30
straight-line, EX 9-30
default PivotTable options, EX 11-8
defined name, **EX 5-34**
existing formulas, EX 5-44–5-46
save time, EX 5-41
written communication, EX 5-41
delete, **EX 1-44**
range, EX 1-45–1-47
records, in Excel table,
EX 6-37–6-38
rows and columns, EX 1-43–1-44
worksheets, EX 1-17
delimiter, **EX 10-4**
dependent cells, EX 9-39
depreciation of assets
add to income statement,
EX 9-35
calculate, EX 9-30–9-35
declining balance depreciation,
EX 9-30–9-34
defined, EX 9-21

schedule, EX 9-35
straight-line, EX 9-30
descending order sort, **EX 6-13,**
EX 6-14
Description field, EX 10-44
design
workbook for calculations,
EX 3-4–3-5
design database, EX 10-30
destination workbook, **EX 5-22**
Developer tab, EX 12-56, **EX 12-58**
load, EX 12-58–12-59
Dfunction, **EX 11-67**. *See also*
Database functions
Diagram view, **EX 10-32**
explore Data Model,
EX 10-32–10-33
Power Pivot, EX 10-33
switch, EX 10-32–10-33
table relationships,
EX 10-34–10-10–35
Diagram View button, Power Pivot,
EX 10-24
dialog box
chart data source, EX 4-39
edit series, EX 4-39
digital certificates, EX 12-79
digital signature, **EX 12-79**
DISCOUNT COUNT function,
EX 11-53–11-54
discount counts
calculate, EX 11-53–11-55
discount rate, EX 9-44
display
all state categories in PivotTable,
EX 10-56
multiple subtotal functions,
EX 11-6
PivotChart by Cust ID field,
EX 10-52–10-53
PivotTables with conditional
formats, EX 11-33–11-37
summary calculations, Power
Pivot, EX 10-36
total revenue by store and
product category, EX 10-37–10-38
Distinct Count function, **EX 11-50**
DISTINCTCOUNT function, EX 11-55
document calculations, EX 3-5
document conditional formats,
EX 2-50–2-51
document PivotTables, EX 11-48
drag and drop, **EX 1-40**
drill down, **EX 7-70**
field hierarchy, EX 10-46–10-50
hierarchy, **EX 10-46**
PivotTable, EX 7-70–7-72
revenue by Product PivotChart
using Quick Explore Tool,
EX 10-51–10-52
drill up
hierarchy, **EX 10-46**

duplicate records
  highlight duplicate values,
    EX 6-10–6-11
  locate, EX 6-10–6-13
  remove, EX 6-12–6-13
duplicate values
  conditional formatting highlights
    cells, EX 6-11
  highlight, EX 6-10–6-11
dynamic
  charts, EX 6-54–6-56
  reference with OFFSET function,
    EX 7-63
dynamic array functions,
    EX 6-68–6-70, EX 12-8–12-11
dynamic arrays, EX 3-14
  calculations, EX 3-14–3-18
  multiplication table,
    EX 3-14–3-15
  referencing spill range,
    EX 3-16–3-18
  spill ranges, EX 3-15–3-16

E

edit
  category axis, EX 4-24–4-25
  cells, EX 1-18–1-20
  chart data source, EX 4-38–4-40
  chart title, EX 4-21
  conditional format, EX 2-48–2-50
  data query, EX 10-9–10-10
  Links dialog box, EX 5-27
  macro with VBA editor,
    EX 12-72–12-73
  Revenue History query,
    EX 10-9–10-10
  scenario, EX 8-30–8-31
  trendline, EX 10-15
  value axis scale, EX 4-30–4-31
Edit Custom Lists button,
    EX 11-11
Edit Default Layout dialog box,
    EX 11-8
Edit mode, EX 1-19
80|20 Rule, EX 12-43,
    EX 12-43–12-46
email address
  link, EX 5-31–5-32
error
  handling, EX 12-8–12-11
  trace, EX 9-53–9-56
error alert, EX 12-2
error values, EX 3-20
  common, EX 3-20
  components, EX 12-6
  dynamic array functions,
    EX 12-8–12-11
  interpret, EX 3-20–3-21
  source, EX 9-55
  trace, EX 9-54
  traced, EX 9-54

use IFERROR function to catch,
    EX 3-41
  using IFERROR function,
    EX 12-7–12-8
evaluate, formula, EX 9-56–9-58
Evolutionary method, EX 8-53
exact match lookup, EX 3-42
  find with HLOOKUP function,
    EX 3-45–3-47
  find with VLOOKUP function,
    EX 3-45–3-47
  find with XLOOKUP function,
    EX 3-42–3-45
Excel, EX 1-4
  AutoComplete, EX 1-20–1-21
  calculate with formulas,
    EX 1-32–1-35
  calculate with functions,
    EX 1-36–1-39
  close workbook, EX 1-13
  data analysis functions,
    EX 3-24–3-37
  depreciation functions, EX 9-34
  enter dates, EX 1-22–1-25
  enter dates and numeric values,
    EX 1-22–1-25
  enter text, EX 1-18
  generating text with Flash Fill,
    EX 1-47–1-48
  keyboard shortcuts, EX 1-6
  linked data types, EX 11-69–11-71
  manage data, EX 6-4–6-5
  move worksheet cells,
    EX 1-40–1-41
  navigation keyboard shortcuts,
    EX 1-10
  programming language, EX 11-41
  resize worksheet columns and
    rows, EX 1-25–1-29
  start new workbook, EX 1-13–1-15
  in Touch Mode, EX 1-6–1-7
  using Excel Interface,
    EX 1-4–1-7
  using Help, EX 1-6
Excel add-ins, EX 8-44
Excel application, EX 12-4
  plan, EX 12-4–12-5
Excel charts
  get started, EX 4-4–4-5
  types and subtypes, EX 4-4
Excel data form, EX 12-70
Excel Developer tab, load,
    EX 12-58–12-59
Excel Filter tools
  advanced filter, EX 6-58–6-61
  create Excel table, EX 6-58–6-70
  FILTER function, EX 6-62–6-63
  filter with multiple criteria,
    EX 6-63–6-65
Excel functions
  calculate minimums and
    maximums, EX 3-24–3-26

data analysis, EX 3-24–3-37
  date and time functions,
    EX 3-35–3-37
  measures of central tendency,
    EX 3-26–3-29
  nested, EX 3-33–3-34
  role of blanks and zeroes,
    EX 3-34–3-35
  round data values, EX 3-29–3-32
Excel Ideas tool, EX 10-66
Excel Options dialog box, EX 11-11
  Customize Ribbon category,
    EX 12-59
Excel table, EX 6-24
  add and delete records,
    EX 6-37–6-38
  add Total row, EX 6-36–6-37
  calculated field creation,
    EX 6-38–6-42
  convert range to table,
    EX 6-33–6-35
  create, EX 6-33–6-43
  create with Excel Filter tools,
    EX 6-58–6-70
  data source(s), EX 10-10
  filters, EX 6-25
  load query data, EX 10-8
  make more accessible, EX 6-43
  retrieve data, EX 10-8
  structural elements, EX 6-35
  structural references,
    EX 6-41–6-42
  styles, use, EX 6-35–6-36
Excel templates, EX 5-47
Excel workbook
  return, EX 10-35
expenses
  fixed, EX 9-20
  general, EX 9-20
  interest, EX 9-35–9-37
  projected general, EX 9-28
  project future, EX 9-22–9-29
  revenue, EX 8-4–8-5
explicit measure, EX 11-51
exploded pie chart, EX 4-10
explore
  Data Model, EX 10-28–10-30
  Data Model in Data view,
    EX 10-32–10-33
  growth trend, EX 9-22–9-23
  linear trend, EX 9-22–9-23
  PivotTable cache,
    EX 11-37–11-41
  XIRR function, EX 9-50–9-52
  XNPV function, EX 9-50–9-52
exponential trendline, EX 10-16
external reference, EX 5-20
  create, EX 5-22–5-25
  enter, EX 5-23
  formula, EX 5-24
  profit and loss values, EX 5-25
  security concerns, EX 5-25–5-26

external workbooks
  link, EX 5-22–5-28
extrapolate
  charts, EX 9-25
  series, EX 9-27
  series of values, EX 9-27–9-29
extrapolation, defined, EX 9-20

F

field(s)
  create a hierarchy of, EX 10-46
  defined, EX 6-3
  manually sort, EX 11-9
  outline by nested,
    EX 10-44–10-46
  primary sort, EX 6-14
  secondary sort, EX 6-14
  sort by multiple, EX 6-14–6-16
  sort by single, EX 6-13–6-14
  tabulate from multiple tables,
    Power Pivot, EX 10-37–10-38
Field List pane, 3D Map window,
    EX 10-61
Field Settings dialog box, EX 11-6
field value
  cells show, EX 11-33
fill colors, EX 2-3
  change, EX 2-9–2-10
  change sheet tab color,
    EX 2-11–2-12
  work, EX 2-9–2-12
fill handle, EX 3-6
filter
  based on multiple field,
    EX 6-29–6-30
  based on one field, EX 6-27–6-29
  buttons, EX 6-48
  data, EX 6-27–6-33
  data with slicers, EX 6-46–6-48
  PivotTable, EX 7-38–7-40,
    EX 11-12–11-15
filter data
  with advanced filter, EX 6-58–6-61
  with FILTER function, EX 6-63–6-65
  with multiple criteria, EX 6-63–6-65
filtered pie chart, EX 4-17
FILTER function, EX 6-45, EX 7-27–7-28
  choose columns, EX 6-65
  filter data, EX 6-62–6-63
  summary calculations,
    EX 7-27–7-28
  use with multiple criteria, EX 6-64
filters
  apply advanced, EX 6-58–6-61
  clear, EX 6-32
  criteria, EX 6-30–6-32
  Excel table, EX 6-25
  text, EX 6-33
financial functions
  defined, EX 9-4
  introduce, EX 9-4

financial workbook, EX 1-5, EX 9-19
Find and Replace commands, EX 2-40–2-42
Find and Replace dialog box, EX 6-26–6-27, EX 11-66
fixed expenses, EX 8-4, EX 9-20
fixed width format, **EX 10-5**
Flash Fill, **EX 1-47**
  generating text with, EX 1-47–1-48
font(s), **EX 2-2**
  color, apply, EX 2-7–2-8
  sans serif, **EX 2-5**
  standard, **EX 2-5**
  theme, **EX 2-5**, EX 2-39
font color
  apply, EX 2-7–2-8
font size, EX 1-30
  change, EX 1-49–1-50
font styles, **EX 2-2**
footer(s)
  add, EX 2-59
  defined, **EX 2-59**
Forecast Sheet button, EX 10-3
Forecast sheets, **EX 10-18**
  create, EX 10-18–10-23
  generate, EX 10-18
Forecasts with seasonal trend, EX 10-19
Forecast worksheet, EX 10-20
format, **EX 1-48**
  change labels formats, EX 7-42–7-43
  chart elements, EX 4-11–4-14
  conditional and duplicate values, EX 6-10–6-11
  data markers, EX 4-25–4-27
  dates and times, EX 2-15–2-16
  map chart, EX 10-59–10-60
  monetary values, EX 2-13
  numbers, EX 2-12–2-216
  PivotTable, EX 7-40–7-49
  result cell, EX 8-16–8-17
  slicer(s), EX 6-49–6-50
  sparkline, EX 4-50–4-51
  text, EX 2-4–2-9
  text selections within cell, EX 2-8–2-9
  workbook for print, EX 2-52–2-63
  workbooks for readability and appeal, EX 2-30–2-31
  worksheet, EX 1-48–1-50
Format Cells dialog box
  alignment, EX 2-28
  border, EX 2-28
  explore, EX 2-28–2-31
  fill, EX 2-28
  font, EX 2-28
  number, EX 2-28
  protection, EX 2-28
Format pane, **EX 4-3**

Formats
  copy, EX 2-16–2-20
  copy with Format Painter, EX 2-16–2-18
  copy with Paste Options button, EX 2-18
  find and replace, EX 2-40–2-42
  highlight data with conditional, EX 2-44–2-52
  paste, EX 2-16–2-20
form controls, **EX 12-67**
formula(s)
  3-D reference apply, EX 5-14–5-18
  absolute references, EX 3-11–3-12
  AutoFill, EX 3-6–3-11
  calculate, EX 1-32–1-35
  copy, EX 1-35–1-36
  defined, **EX 1-31**
  defined names, EX 5-44–5-46
  evaluate, EX 9-56–9-58
  external references, EX 5-24
  paste, EX 1-35–1-36
  perform what-if analyses, EX 3-47–3-50
  simplify with named ranges, EX 5-36–5-46
  step, EX 9-57
  use absolute references, EX 3-11–3-12
  use mixed references, EX 3-12
  use relative references, EX 3-11
  using range names, EX 5-38–5-41
  write effective, EX 1-39
formula bar, EX 1-2
formula view, **EX 1-55**
freeze pane(s), EX 6-8–6-10
  defined, **EX 6-8**
  freeze rows and columns, EX 6-9
function(s)
  3-D reference apply, EX 5-14–5-18
  calculate, EX 1-36–1-39
  calculate future value with FV, EX 9-7–9-9
  calculate inflation with FV, EX 9-9
  calculate interest rates with RATE, EX 9-40–9-42
  calculate payment period with NPER, EX 9-9–9-10
  calculate payments with PMT, EX 9-5–9-7
  calculate present value with PV, EX 9-10–9-12
  defined, **EX 1-31**
  display multiple subtotal, EX 11-6
  Excel depreciation, EX 9-34
  explore XIRR, EX 9-50–9-52
  explore XNPV, EX 9-50–9-52
  insert with AutoSum, EX 1-37–1-39
  perform what-if analyses, EX 3-47–3-50
  syntax, EX 1-36
  XLOOKUP function, EX 6-57–6-58

funnel chart, **EX 12-6**
future value, EX 9-4
  calculate with FV function, EX 9-7–9-9
FV function, EX 9-2
  calculate future value, EX 9-7–9-9
  calculate inflation, EX 9-9
FVSchedule function, EX 9-18

G

gap width, set, EX 4-21–4-22
general expenses, EX 9-20. *See also* fixed expenses
General format, **EX 2-12**
generate multiple PivotTables with Show Report Filter Pages, EX 11-15
GETPIVOTDATA function, **EX 11-63**
  data extraction, EX 11-64
  insert, EX 11-65
  retrieve PivotTable data, EX 11-63–11-67
Get & Transform Data group, EX 10-3, EX 10-10
global optimum, EX 8-52
global scope, **EX 5-35**
Goal Seek, **EX 3-48**–3-50
  perform, EX 3-48
grand totals
  calculated formulas applied, EX 11-47
  removed from PivotTable, EX 11-6
  work, EX 11-4–11-6
graphic objects
  add to workbook, EX 4-40–4-42
  assign macros, EX 12-63–12-65
graphic shape, insert, EX 4-41–4-42
GRG Nonlinear method, EX 8-53
gridlines, EX 1-30, **EX 4-2**
  add to chart, EX 4-22–4-23
gross profit, EX 9-26
group
  calculated items, EX 11-44
  dates, EX 11-19–11-22
  manual, EX 11-16–11-18
  numeric fields, EX 11-21–11-24
  PivotTable fields, EX 11-15–11-25
Group By dialog box, EX 10-13
Group dialog box, EX 11-23
grouped worksheets, EX 5-11
groups, **EX 1-2**
growth trend, EX 9-23
  explore, EX 9-22–9-23

H

header(s)
  add, EX 2-59
  defined, **EX 2-59**

header row, **EX 6-5**
Heat map, EX 10-62
Help, EX 1-6
hide, **EX 1-47**
  columns, EX 1-47
  rows, EX 1-47
  workbook content, EX 12-76–12-78
  worksheets, EX 1-47
hierarchy, **EX 10-42**
  create, EX 10-46
  define, EX 10-47
  drill up, **EX 10-46**
  work with, EX 10-44–10-53
hierarchy charts, **EX 4-43**
hierarchy of fields
  create, EX 10-46
highlight unlocked cells, EX 12-27
histogram, **EX 4-44**
histogram charts, EX 4-44
HLOOKUP function, **EX 3-45**, EX 12-8
  approximate match lookups, EX 7-10
  find exact match, EX 3-45–3-47
  syntax, EX 7-10
horizontal layout
  workbook window, EX 5-7
horizontal lookup tables, **EX 3-42,** EX 7-15
100% stacked column chart, **EX 4-19**
hyperlink(s), **EX 5-21**
  create, EX 5-28–5-32
  link to email address, EX 5-31–5-32
  link to location within workbook, EX 5-29–5-31
  work, EX 5-29
Hyperlink dialog box
  inserting, EX 5-30

I

icon sets, **EX 11-26**
  create, EX 11-34–11-36
IFERROR function, **EX 3-2**, **EX 12-3,** EX 12-7–12-8
IF function, EX 7-2, EX 7-15–7-19
IF logical function, **EX 3-23**
  work, EX 3-37–3-41
IFS function
  apply summary, EX 7-21–7-29
  defined, **EX 7-20**
  use, EX 7-20
implicit measure, **EX 11-51**
improper scale, EX 4-52
income
  project future, EX 9-22–9-29
income statement, **EX 5-4**, EX 9-20. *See also* profit and loss (P&L) statement
  add depreciation, EX 9-34
  add taxes and interest expenses, EX 9-35–9-37
  revised, EX 9-37

indent cell text, EX 2-24–2-26
INDEX function, EX 7-13–7-14
Index Match lookups
    retrieve data, EX 7-13–7-14
index match lookups, retrieve data,
    EX 7-13–7-14
indirect reference, **EX 5-46**
inflation, calculation with FV
    function, EX 9-9
input cells, EX 8-2
input message, **EX 12-2**
    create, EX 12-17–12-18
input value(s), EX 8-2
insert
    GETPIVOTDATA function,
        EX 11-65
    graphic shape, EX 4-41–4-42
    Hyperlink dialog box, EX 5-30
    PivotTable, EX 7-33–7-34
    range, EX 1-45–1-47
    rows and columns, EX 1-43–1-44
    worksheets, EX 1-16
Insert Slicers dialog box,
    EX 10-39
interest, EX 9-4
    calculate, EX 9-13–9-15
interest payments, calculate,
    EX 9-13–9-15
interest rates
    calculate with RATE function,
        EX 9-40–9-42
    investment, EX 9-41
internal rate of return, EX 9-38
    calculate, EX 9-47–9-52
    locating, EX 9-46
    modified, viewing, EX 9-52
    use IRR function, EX 9-48–9-50
international date formats,
    EX 1-23
interpolate
    charts, EX 9-25
    series, EX 9-27
    start value to end value,
        EX 9-23–9-25
interpolation, defined, EX 9-20
interpret error values,
    EX 3-20–3-21
INT function, **EX 3-32**
investment(s)
    calculate value, EX 9-48
    use NPV and IRR to compare,
        EX 9-50
    view payback period, EX 9-42–9-43
IPMT function, EX 9-2
IRR function, EX 9-38
    use, EX 9-48–9-50
    use to compare investments,
        EX 9-50
ISOMITTED function, **EX 12-46**
iterative process
    defined, EX 8-52
    explore, EX 8-52–8-53

K

keyboard shortcuts, **EX 1-6**
key performance indicator (KPI),
    EX 3-39
Key Tips, **EX 1-6**

L

Label Filter (Hotel Name) dialog box,
    EX 11-13
label filters, EX 11-12
labels, change, EX 7-42–7-43
LAMBDA function
    custom function, EX 12-40–12-50
    helper functions,
        EX 12-50–12-55
    vs. LET, EX 12-37–12-40
    nested functions, EX 12-25
    writing formulas,
        EX 12-35–12-37
LAMBDA helper functions, **EX 12-50,**
    EX 12-50–12-55
LAMBDA variables, **EX 12-35**
landscape orientation, **EX 1-52**
language
    mashup query, **EX 10-7**
    Power Query, EX 10-7
Layer pane, 3D Map window,
    EX 10-61
layers, **EX 10-43**
lay out PivotTable, EX 11-4–11-8
LET function
    vs. LAMBDA function,
        EX 12-37–12-40
    nested functions, EX 12-32
    syntax of, EX 12-32–12-34
    writing, EX 12-34–12-35
LET variables, **EX 12-32**
limits report, EX 8-53. See also
    sensitivity report
linear trend, EX 9-22
    explore, EX 9-22–9-23
linear trendline
    add to scatter chart, EX 10-16
    definition, EX 10-16
line chart, **EX 4-2**
    create, EX 4-23–4-27
    edit category axis, EX 4-24–4-25
    format data markers,
        EX 4-25–4-27
link(s), **EX 5-22**
    email address, EX 5-31–5-32
    external workbooks,
        EX 5-22–5-28
    hyperlinks to location within
        workbook, EX 5-29–5-31
    manage workbooks, EX 5-25–5-28
    review within workbooks,
        EX 5-27
linked data types, **EX 10-70,**
    EX 11-69–11-71

Links dialog box
    editing, EX 5-27
list, validate against, EX 12-18–12-19
Live Preview, **EX 2-5**
load
    Customers table into Data Model,
        EX 10-29
    Excel Developer tab,
        EX 12-58–12-59
    Monthly Revenue query,
        EX 10-13–10-14
    query data into Excel table,
        EX 10-8
    remaining database tables,
        EX 10-30
    Solver models, EX 8-56–8-59
loan(s)
    calculate future value, EX 9-8
    calculate number of payments,
        EX 9-10
    future value, EX 9-8
    payments required to repay,
        EX 9-10
    present value, EX 9-11
    quarterly payment required to
        repay, EX 9-7
    work, EX 9-6
local optimum, EX 8-52
    material assets, EX 9-30
local scope, **EX 5-35**
locked property, **EX 12-25**
locking cells, EX 12-25–12-28
logarithmic trendline
    definition, EX 10-16
    revenue estimated use,
        EX 10-17
logical comparison operators,
    EX 3-37
logical functions
    apply, EX 7-19
    defined, **EX 3-37**
    explore, EX 7-15–7-21
    generate multiple outcomes,
        EX 7-20
    use AND, OR and NOT functions,
        EX 7-20–7-21
    use IFS function, EX 7-20
Long Date format, **EX 2-15**
lookup array, **EX 3-42**
lookup functions, **EX 3-42**
    retrieve data, EX 7-4–7-15
lookup tables, **EX 3-42**
    exact match returned, EX 3-42
    retrieve values, EX 7-15

M

macro(s), **EX 12-58**
    assign keyboard shortcuts,
        EX 12-65
    assign to graphic object,
        EX 12-63–12-65

    create data entry worksheet,
        EX 12-65–12-70
    creating an Excel, EX 12-60–12-65
    edit with VBA editor, EX 12-72–12-73
    plan, EX 12-75
    record, EX 12-75
    run, EX 12-62
Macro dialog box, EX 12-62
macro-enabled workbook
    save, EX 12-59
macro security set, EX 12-78–12-79
macro security settings, **EX 12-56**
Macro Settings in Trust Center,
    EX 12-79
macro viruses, **EX 12-78**
    create digital signature for
        workbook, EX 12-79
    macro security set, EX 12-78–12-79
    protect against, EX 12-79–12-80
major tick marks, **EX 4-30**
manual filters, EX 11-12
manual group, **EX 11-16**–11-18
manually sort field, EX 11-9
manual outlines, create, EX 6-22
manual page break, **EX 2-33**
map(s)
    customers mapped by postal
        code, EX 10-62
    location of customers by postal
        code, EX 10-61–10-62
    specify location, EX 10-59
    total revenue by state, EX 10-57
    value, **EX 10-54**
    as viewed from southern Florida,
        EX 10-64
map chart, **EX 10-42**
    connect to slicer and timeline
        filters, EX 10-58
    create, EX 10-54
    format, EX 10-59–10-60
    format options, EX 10-59
    limitations, EX 10-60
    view data, EX 10-53–10-67
map style
    selection, EX 10-62–10-63
margin
    defined, **EX 2-60**
    set top, EX 2-61
mashup query language, **EX 10-7**
MAX function, **EX 3-22,** EX 11-55
    3-D reference, EX 5-15
MAXIFS function, EX 7-27
Maximize button, **EX 1-3**
MAXX function, EX 11-63
mean, **EX 3-26**
measure(s), **EX 11-50**
    add to table, EX 11-56–11-59
    calculate across tables and rows,
        EX 11-59–11-63
    create, EX 11-55–11-59
    explicit, EX 11-51
    implicit, EX 11-51

measure, create
  add measure to table,
    EX 11-56–11-59
  introduce DAX, EX 11-55–11-56
measures of central tendency,
  EX 3-26–3-29
  average, **EX 3-26**
  calculate, EX 3-27
  mean, **EX 3-26**
  median, **EX 3-26**
  mode, **EX 3-26**
median, **EX 3-26**
MEDIAN function, **EX 3-22**
  3-D reference, EX 5-15
merge, **EX 2-2**
  cells, EX 2-25–2-26
  custom cell styles, EX 2-7–2-38
  scenarios, EX 8-36
Microsoft Access database
  program, EX 10-28
Microsoft Excel, **EX 1-4**
MIN function, **EX 3-**22, EX 11-55
  3-D reference, EX 5-15
MINIFS function, EX 7-27
Minimize button, **EX 1-3**
minimums and maximums calculate,
  EX 3-24–3-26
Mini toolbar, **EX 2-8**
minor tick marks, **EX 4-30**
MINX function, EX 11-63
MIRR function, EX 9-52
mixed cell references,
  EX 3-12–3-14
  formulas use, EX 3-12
mixed expense, EX 8-5
M language, **EX 10-7**
mode, **EX 3-26**
MODE.MULT function, **EX 3-26**
MODE.SNGL function, **EX 3-22**
modify
  chart data source, EX 4-38
  data bar rule, EX 4-46–4-47
  data table, EX 8-13
  PivotTable(s), EX 7-36–7-37
module, **EX 12-72**
money
  time value, EX 9-44
Monthly Revenue query
  close and load, EX 10-13–10-14
  import values, EX 10-14
monthly revenue values
  calculate, EX 10-14
  import, EX 10-14
More Sort Options (Hotel Name)
  dialog box, EX 11-10
Mouse Mode, **EX 1-6**–1-7
move
  monthly revenue chart, EX 10-21
  query data source, EX 10-14
  worksheet cells, EX 1-40–1-41
  worksheets, EX 5-4
Move or Copy dialog box, EX 5-6

moving average trendline,
  EX 10-16
MROUND function, **EX 3-32**
multiple fields sort, EX 6-14–6-16
multiple field values, cells show,
  EX 11-33
multiple PivotTable caches,
  EX 11-39
multiple sheets, unhide, EX 12-76
Multi-Select button, EX 6-44
MY_SUMBETWEEN function,
  EX 12-42–12-43

N

Name box, **EX 1-2**
named range, **EX 5-34**
  define, EX 5-36–5-38
  defined in Name box, EX 5-37
  defined using labels in adjacent
    cells, EX 5-38
  determine scope, EX 5-41–5-43
  formulas, EX 5-38–5-41
  scope, **EX 5-35**
  simplify formulas, EX 5-36–5-46
named sets, **EX 11-53**
  Data Model, EX 11-53
Navigator dialog box, EX 10-28
negative cash flow, EX 9-4.
  See also cash outflow
nested fields
  outline by PivotTable,
    EX 10-44–10-46
nesting functions, **EX 3-33**–3-34
net present value, EX 9-38
  calculate, EX 9-44–9-47
  choose rate of return,
    EX 9-45–9-47
  time value of money, EX 9-44
  understand, EX 9-46
  use NPV function, EX 9-44–9-45
NETWORKDAYS function, **EX 3-36**
New Formatting Rule dialog box,
  EX 11-34
New Window button, EX 5-2
nonadjacent range, **EX 1-2**
nonbinding constraint, EX 8-55
noncash assets, EX 9-30
Normal view, **EX 1-31**
NOT function, EX 7-20–7-21
  defined, **EX 7-20**
NPER function, EX 9-3
  calculate payment period with
    function, EX 9-9–9-10
NPV function, EX 9-39
  understand, EX 9-46
  use, EX 9-44–9-45
  use to compare investments,
    EX 9-50
number(s)
  format, EX 2-12–2-216
  format percentages, EX 2-14–2-15

numeric data, **EX 1-18**
numeric fields, group, EX 11-21–11-24
numeric value(s)
  enter, EX 1-22–1-25

O

objective cell
  defined, EX 8-38
  set, EX 8-44–8-46
OFFSET function
  dynamic reference, EX 7-63
OLAP Cube
  retrieve measures, EX 11-67
one-to-many relationship,
  EX 10-27
one-variable data table, EX 8-2
  chart, EX 8-12
  completed, EX 8-10–8-11
  create, EX 8-9–8-12
  setup, EX 8-9–8-10
Online Analytic Processing (OLAP)
  database, **EX 11-67**
open
  3D maps, EX 10-60–10-61
  VBA editor, EX 12-71–12-72
operators, **EX 1-32**
optimize product mix, EX 8-40–8-42
Options dialog box, EX 11-8
OR function
  defined, **EX 7-20**
outline(s)
  Collapsed PivotTable, EX 10-46
  PivotTable by nested fields,
    EX 10-44–10-46
  work with, EX 10-44–10-53
Outline layout, **EX 11-2**
outline view
  create, EX 6-22
  subtotals, EX 6-21–6-22

P

Page Break Preview, **EX 1-31**
  use, EX 2-52–2-53
page breaks, move, add and
  remove, EX 2-56–2-58
Page Layout, EX 1-30
Page Layout tab, **EX 2-32**
Page Layout view, **EX 1-31**
page margins, setting,
  EX 2-60–2-63
page orientation, **EX 1-52**
  change, EX 1-52–1-53
pane(s)
  defined, **EX 6-2**
  divide workbook window,
    EX 6-6–6-8
  freeze, EX 6-8–6-10
  unfreeze, in workbook window,
    EX 6-9
  use, for navigating data, EX 6-6–6-10

Pareto charts, **EX 4-43**–4-44
partial lookups
  defined, **EX 7-9**
  perform with wildcards, EX 7-9
paste, **EX 1-35**
  chart formats, EX 4-38
  formats, EX 2-16–2-20
  formulas, EX 1-35–1-36
Paste Link
  PivotTable data pasted,
    EX 10-55
  use of, EX 10-56
Paste Options button
  copy formats, EX 2-18
Paste Special command
  copy formats, EX 2-18–2-19
  perform special tasks, EX 2-19
path, **EX 5-22**
payback period, EX 9-38
  view for investment,
    EX 9-42–9-43
payment period
  calculation with NPER function,
    EX 9-9–9-10
payments
  calculate interest and principal,
    EX 9-13–9-15
  calculation with PMT function,
    EX 9-5–9-7
  quarterly, required to repay loan,
    EX 9-7
  required to repay loan, EX 9-10
  total loan, EX 9-18
percentages, format, EX 2-14–2-15
Percent style formats, **EX 2-3**
Personal Macro workbook,
  EX 12-61
  create macro library, EX 12-61
Personal.xslb file, EX 12-61
pie chart(s), **EX 4-3**
  chart with Quick Analysis tool,
    EX 4-7–4-8
  color schemes, EX 4-16
  and column charts with the same
    data, EX 4-18
  create, EX 4-6–4-10
  exploded, **EX 4-10**
  filtered, EX 4-17
  move and resize chart, EX 4-9
  select data source, EX 4-6
PivotCharts
  create, EX 7-53–7-55
  create, product revenue,
    EX 10-49–10-50
  defined, **EX 7-50**
  display by Cust ID field,
    EX 10-52–10-53
  introduce, EX 7-52–7-58
  move to another worksheet,
    EX 7-55–7-58
  revenue by product, EX 10-50
  structure, EX 7-52

PivotTable(s), EX 7-30
  add date fields, EX 7-60–7-63
  add multiple fields to row or
    column, EX 7-37–7-38
  add Product List hierarchy,
    EX 10-48
  all cells showing field value,
    EX 11-33
  all cells showing multiple field
    values, EX 11-33
  apply slicer to multiple,
    EX 7-65–7-66
  calculate percent differences,
    EX 11-31–11-33
  calculate ranks, EX 11-30–11-31
  calculations, EX 11-28–11-33
  change labels and number
    formats, EX 7-42–7-43
  change PivotTable layout,
    EX 11-6–11-8
  change summary function,
    EX 7-43–7-44
  choose recommended, EX 7-40
  choose report layout, EX 7-44
  choose style, EX 7-44–7-45
  collapse and expand categories,
    EX 10-45–10-46
  columns area, EX 7-32
  Count of Date, EX 11-54
  create, EX 7-32–7-40
  create icon set, EX 11-34–11-36
  data analysis, EX 11-69–11-72
  data pasted using Paste Link,
    EX 10-55
  defined, **EX 7-31**
  define layout, EX 7-35–7-36
  display all state categories,
    EX 10-56
  display with conditional formats,
    EX 11-33–11-37
  document, EX 11-48
  drill down, EX 7-70–7-72
  filter, EX 7-38–7-40,
    EX 11-12–11-15
  filters area, EX 7-32
  filter with timeline slicer,
    EX 7-67
  format, EX 7-40–7-49
  grand total removed, EX 11-6
  group fields, EX 11-15–11-25
  insert, EX 7-33–7-34
  inserted, from the Data Model,
    EX 10-36
  insert Product Revenue,
    EX 10-44–10-45
  lay out, EX 11-4–11-8
  linked data types,
    EX 11-69–11-71
  make accessible, EX 7-48
  manually sort field, EX 11-9
  modify, EX 7-36–7-37
  move, EX 7-36

  outline by nested fields,
    EX 10-44–10-46
  PivotTable cache shared by
    multiple, EX 11-38
  reorder categories,
    EX 7-58–7-59
  retrieve data with GETPIVOTDATA
    function, EX 11-63–11-67
  revenue by location,
    EX 11-5
  rows area, EX 7-32
  selected cells, EX 11-33
  set options, EX 7-45–7-48
  share cache, EX 11-38–11-39
  sort by custom list, EX 11-11
  sort by value, EX 11-9–11-11
  sort categories, EX 7-58–7-60
  standard, EX 11-52
  structure, EX 7-32
  subtotals removed, EX 11-6
  Tabular layout, EX 11-8
  use slicers, EX 7-64–7-70
  values area, EX 7-32
  work with color scales,
    EX 11-36–11-37
  work with grand totals and
    subtotals, EX 11-4–11-6
PivotTable caches, **EX 7-72**
  count, EX 11-41
  create new, EX 11-39–11-40
  create PivotTable from new,
    EX 11-40
  explore, EX 11-37–11-41
  multiple, EX 11-39
  new PivotTable report based on
    its own cache, EX 11-40
  share cache between
    PivotTables, EX 11-38–11-39
  shared by multiple PivotTables,
    EX 11-38
PivotTable design
  introduce under Data Model,
    EX 11-52–11-53
PivotTable fields
  calculate values, EX 11-30
  group, EX 11-15–11-25
  group by dates, EX 11-19–11-22
  group by numeric fields,
    EX 11-21–11-24
  manual group, EX 11-16–11-18
PivotTable Fields pane, EX 7-31
PivotTable layout
  change, EX 11-6–11-8
  choose, EX 11-7
  define, EX 7-35–7-36
  options, EX 11-7
PivotTable Options dialog box,
  EX 10-8, EX 11-13
PivotTables from the Data Model
  features, EX 11-52
PivotTables options, set,
  EX 7-45–7-48

PivotTable Tools Analyze tab,
  EX 11-53
PivotTable Wizard, **EX 11-39**
pixel, EX 1-26
PMT function, EX 9-3
  calculate payments,
    EX 9-5–9-7
point, EX 1-28
polynomial trendline, EX 10-16
portrait orientation, **EX 1-52**
positive cash flow, EX 9-4. *See also*
  cash inflow
Power Pivot
  apply slicers and timelines from
    Data Model, EX 10-38–10-41
  BI tool, EX 10-31
  connect slicer and timeline,
    EX 10-40–10-41
  create from Data Model,
    EX 10-35–10-41
  data from Data Model,
    EX 10-37
  Data Model, EX 10-25
  Diagram view, EX 10-33
  Diagram View button,
    EX 10-24
  display summary calculations,
    EX 10-36
  install, EX 10-31
  table relationships, EX 10-34
  tabulate across fields from
    multiple tables, EX 10-37–10-38
  transform data, EX 10-31–10-32
Power Pivot window, EX 10-31
Power Query, **EX 10-4,**
  EX 10-12
  data query, EX 10-4–10-7
  language, EX 10-7
Power Query Editor, **EX 10-2,**
  EX 10-3
Power Query Editor window,
  EX 10-6, EX 10-9
power trendline, EX 10-16
PPMT function, EX 9-3
precedent cells, EX 9-39
present value, EX 9-4
  calculation with PV function,
    EX 9-10–9-12
preview
  queried data, EX 10-6
  Recent History query,
    EX 10-11
Preview grid, EX 10-2
primary axis, **EX 4-27**
primary sort field, **EX 6-14**
principal, defined, EX 9-4
principal payments, calculate,
  EX 9-13–9-15, EX 9-16–9-19
print
  format workbook, EX 2-52–2-63
  workbook, EX 1-50–1-55
  worksheet groups, EX 5-14

print area
  defined, **EX 2-32**, EX 2-53–2-54
print options, set, EX 1-54–1-55
print titles, **EX 2-32**
  set, EX 2-55–2-56
problem solving
  3-D reference, EX 5-15
Product List hierarchy
  add to PivotTable, EX 10-48
  drill down, EX 10-48–10-49
  drill up, EX 10-48–10-49
  fields, EX 10-47
  PivotTable drilled down, EX 10-48
product mix
  assume increasing sales for
    higher-end models, EX 8-41–8-42
  defined, EX 8-38
  optimize, EX 8-40–8-42
  test for higher-end desks, EX 8-41
Product PivotChart
  drill down revenue by using Quick
    Explore Tool, EX 10-51–10-52
Product Revenue PivotTable
  insert, EX 10-44–10-45
Products table
  create hierarchy of fields,
    EX 10-47
PRODUCTX function, EX 11-63
profit and loss (P&L) statement,
  EX 5-4, EX 9-20. *See also* income
  statement
  open workbook, EX 5-4
  templates, EX 5-48
project
  future income and expenses,
    EX 9-22
protect
  against macro viruses,
    EX 12-79–12-80
  Protect Sheet dialog box,
    EX 12-24
  worksheet, EX 12-21–12-28
PV function, EX 9-2
  calculate present value,
    EX 9-10–9-12

Queries & Connections pane,
  EX 10-3
query, **EX 10-2**
  Access database,
    EX 10-27–10-28
  add new column, EX 10-12
  calculate monthly revenues,
    EX 10-14
  construct, EX 10-5
  create Access database table,
    EX 10-27–10-28
  create to revenue history data,
    EX 10-5–10-6
  group values, EX 10-12–10-14

import monthly revenue values, EX 10-14

move data source, EX 10-14

preview of data, EX 10-6

set name, EX 10-7

transform data, EX 10-10–10-14

trendline, **EX 10-3**

view steps, EX 10-7

Query Settings pane, EX 10-2

Query tab, EX 10-8, EX 10-9, EX 10-10

Quick Analysis tool, EX 10-53

chart, EX 4-7–4-8

performing calculations, EX 3-18–3-20

Quick Explore, **EX 10-42**

Quick Explore button, EX 10-51

Quick Explore Tool

drill down revenue by Product PivotChart, EX 10-51–10-52

view data, EX 10-50–10-53

R

R2 statistic, **EX 10-17**

random data, generate, EX 3-46–3-47

range, **EX 1-2**

insert and delete, EX 1-45–1-47

move, EX 1-41

nonadjacent, **EX 1-2**

range names

determine scope, EX 5-41–5-43

in formulas, EX 5-38–5-41

range reference, **EX 1-11**

rank(s)

calculate, EX 11-30–11-31

occupancy field calculation, EX 11-31

weekly occupancy rates, EX 11-31

RATE function, EX 9-38

calculate interest rates, EX 9-40–9-42

rate of return, EX 9-44

choose, EX 9-45–9-47

Recent History query

initial preview, EX 10-11

record(s)

add and delete, in Excel table, EX 6-37–6-38

defined, **EX 6-3**

sort, in data range, EX 6-13–6-18

record macro, EX 12-60–12-61

Record Macro button, EX 12-56

Record Macro dialog box, EX 12-65

REDUCE function, EX 12-51–12-54

refresh

data query, EX 10-10

PivotTable data, EX 7-72

Region map, EX 10-62

RELATED function, EX 11-60

relational databases, EX 10-26–10-27, **EX 10-27**

relationship(s)

one-to-many, **EX 10-27**

table, **EX 10-24**

relative cell references, **EX 3-3,** EX 3-11

formulas use, EX 3-11

Remove Duplicates tool, EX 6-12–6-13

rename worksheets, EX 1-16

Report Connections button, EX 7-50

report layout in PivotTables, choose, EX 7-44

resize

charts, EX 4-8–4-10

worksheet columns and rows, EX 1-25–1-29

Restore Down button, **EX 1-3**

result cells, EX 8-2

format, EX 8-16–8-17

result values, EX 8-2

retrieve

data into Excel table, EX 10-8

retrieve data with lookup functions, EX 7-4–7-15

return array, **EX 3-42**

revenue

chart, EX 8-5

compare expenses, EX 8-4–8-5

Revenue History dialog box, EX 10-9

Revenue History query, EX 10-9–10-10

revenue trends, annual and monthly, EX 10-21

RGB Color model, **EX 2-7**

ribbon, **EX 1-2**

Robuster, EX 9-1

rotate text, EX 2-26–2-27

round data values, EX 3-29–3-32

ROUNDDOWN function, **EX 3-29**

ROUND function, **EX 3-22,** EX 3-29

ROUNDUP function, **EX 3-29**

row(s)

add multiple fields, EX 7-37–7-38

banded, EX 6-25

calculate measures across, EX 11-59–11-63

change heights, EX 1-28

delete, EX 1-43–1-44

freeze, in worksheet, EX 6-9

hide, EX 1-47

insert, EX 1-43–1-44

insert and delete, EX 1-43–1-44

resize worksheet, EX 1-28–1-29

Total, EX 6-25

unhide, EX 1-47

row headings, **EX 1-2**

row heights, change, EX 1-28

run macro, EX 12-62

run total(s)

calculate with Quick Analysis Tool, EX 3-18–3-20

S

sans serif fonts, **EX 2-5**

save

macro-enabled workbook, EX 12-59

Solver models, EX 8-56–8-59

theme, EX 2-39

workbook, EX 1-17–1-18

scale, **EX 1-53**

data values differently, EX 4-52

improper, EX 4-52

printed page, EX 1-53

secondary axis, EX 4-30–4-31

scatter chart, **EX 4-32**

create, EX 4-34–4-38, EX 10-15

insert graphic shape, EX 4-41–4-42

linear trendline, add, EX 10-16

preview, EX 4-35

removing elements, EX 4-36–4-37

return rate *vs.* volatility, EX 4-34

Scenario Manager, EX 8-22

explore financial scenarios, EX 8-24–8-31

scenario PivotTable report, EX 8-23

scenarios

define, EX 8-25–8-28

edit, EX 8-30–8-31

merge, EX 8-36

view, EX 8-28–8-30

scenario summary reports, EX 8-23

create, EX 8-31–8-36

scene(s), **EX 10-43**

create, EX 10-64

play tour, EX 10-66–10-67

set options, EX 10-65

show Los Angeles revenue, EX 10-64

Scene Options dialog box, EX 10-65

scope, **EX 5-35**

determine, range names, EX 5-41–5-43

ScreenTip, **EX 1-6**

Search box, **EX 1-2**

seasonal data, **EX 10-18**

seasonal forecast, create, EX 10-19–10-20

secondary axis, **EX 4-27**

secondary sort field, **EX 6-14**

sensitivity report, EX 8-53. *See also* limits report

series

AutoFill used to extend, EX 3-9

extrapolate, EX 9-27

fill, EX 3-8–3-11

interpolate, EX 9-27

patterns extended with AutoFill, EX 3-9

values, extrapolate, EX 9-27–9-29

serif fonts, **EX 2-5**

set

forecast options, EX 10-18

query name, EX 10-7

scene options, EX 10-65

set up data query, EX 10-11

share cache between PivotTables, EX 11-38–11-39

sheet(s), **EX 1-2**

navigating between, EX 1-7–1-9

sheet tab, **EX 1-2**

sheet tab color, change, EX 2-11–2-12

shortcut menu, **EX 1-17**

Short Date format, **EX 2-15**

Show Report Filters Pages tool, **EX 11-15**

generate multiple PivotTables, EX 11-15

significant digits

defined, **EX 3-32**

display, EX 3-32

Simplex LP method, EX 8-53

single field sort, EX 6-13–6-14

slack, EX 8-55

slicer(s), **EX 6-44,** EX 7-64–7-70, EX 10-25

add to dashboard, Power Pivot, EX 10-38–10-39

apply from Data Model, Power Pivot, EX 10-38–10-41

apply to multiple PivotTables, EX 7-65–7-66

choose between filter buttons and, EX 6-48

connect map chart, EX 10-58

create, EX 6-46

dashboard, EX 6-45

vs. filter buttons, EX 6-48

filter data, EX 6-46–6-48

format, EX 6-49–6-50

Slicer tab, EX 6-44

Solver

activate, EX 8-43–8-44

add constraints, EX 8-46–8-52

add-in, EX 8-42

constraint types, EX 8-46

defined, EX 8-39

find optimal solution, EX 8-42–8-52

Solver answer report, create, EX 8-53–8-55

Solver models

activate Solver, EX 8-43–8-44

add constraints to Solver, EX 8-46–8-52

load, EX 8-56–8-59

save, EX 8-56–8-59

set objective cell and variable cells, EX 8-44–8-46

sort

ascending order, EX 6-13

custom list, EX 6-16–6-18

descending order, EX 6-13

multiple fields, EX 6-14–6-16

sort (*Continued*)
  options, choose, EX 6-16
  PivotTable, EX 11-9–11-11
  PivotTable categories,
    EX 7-58–7-60
  PivotTables by custom list,
    EX 11-11
  records in data range,
    EX 6-13–6-18
  single field, EX 6-13–6-14
  value, EX 11-9–11-11
sort and filter, combine,
  EX 6-67–6-68
SORTBY function
  sort data, EX 6-66–6-67
Sort (Hotel Name) dialog box,
  EX 11-10
SORT function, **EX 6-45**
  sort data, EX 6-65–6-66
source workbook, **EX 5-22**
sparkline(s)
  create, EX 4-48–4-53
  defined, **EX 4-33**
  format, EX 4-50–4-51
  types, EX 4-48
sparkline axes, EX 4-51–4-53
sparkline groups, EX 4-51–4-53
spill ranges, **EX 3-3**
  dynamic arrays, EX 3-15–3-16
  multiplication table, EX 3-16
  reference, EX 3-16–3-18
split bar, **EX 6-2**
Split button, EX 6-8
spreadsheet(s), **EX 1-4**
stacked column chart, **EX 4-19**
Stacked Column map, EX 10-62
standard colors, **EX 2-7**
standard fonts, **EX 2-5**
standard PivotTable, **EX 11-52**
  features, EX 11-52
status bar, **EX 1-2**
Stores table, Type slicer, EX 10-39
straight-line depreciation, EX 9-30
  asset, EX 9-33
  declining-balance depreciation,
    EX 9-30
  defined, EX 9-30
structural references
  defined, **EX 6-41**
  Excel table, EX 6-41–6-42
Subcategory field, EX 10-44
sub procedures, **EX 12-57**
  edited, EX 12-72–12-73
  understand, EX 12-72
Subtotal button, EX 6-3
Subtotal dialog box, EX 6-19
Subtotal & Filters tab, EX 11-6
SUBTOTAL function, **EX 6-44**
  apply, EX 6-52–6-53
  dashboard, EX 6-51–6-54
  display multiple, EX 11-6
  function numbers, EX 6-52

subtotals
  calculate, EX 6-18–6-22
  defined, **EX 6-18**
  outline view, EX 6-21–6-22
  removed from PivotTable, EX 11-6
  work, EX 11-4–11-6
Subtotal tool, EX 6-2
SUM function, **EX 1-31**, EX 11-6,
  EX 11-55
  3-D reference, EX 5-16
SUMIF function
  calculate conditional sums,
    EX 7-24–7-25
  defined, **EX 7-3**
SUMIFS function
  calculate conditional sums,
    EX 7-25
  defined, **EX 7-25**
summary calculations with FILTER
  function, EX 7-27–7-28
summary IFS functions
  apply, EX 7-21–7-29
SUMX function, EX 11-61–11-63
sunburst charts, **EX 4-43**
switch, to Diagram view,
  EX 10-32–10-33
Synchronous Scrolling button,
  EX 5-3
  between windows, EX 5-9–5-10
syntax, **EX 1-36**

T

tab, **EX 1-2**
table(s)
  add measure, EX 11-56–11-59
  calculate measures,
    EX 11-59–11-63
Table Design tab, EX 10-9
table relationships, **EX 10-24**
  defined in Power Pivot, EX 10-34
  Diagram view, EX 10-34–10-35
  manage, EX 10-33–10-35
Tabular layout, **EX 11-3**
  PivotTable, EX 11-8
tangible assets, EX 9-30
template(s), **EX 1-4**–1-5, EX 5-34
  chart, EX 5-49
  copy styles, EX 5-50
  create workbook, EX 5-49–5-52
  profit and loss statements,
    EX 5-48
  workbooks created, EX 5-49–5-52
text
  enter, EX 1-18
  find, EX 2-40–2-42
  format, EX 2-4–2-9
  replace, EX 2-40–2-42
  rotating, EX 2-26–2-27
  wrap within cell, EX 1-27–1-28
text data, **EX 1-18**
text filters, EX 6-33

text string, **EX 1-18**
theme(s), **EX 2-4**
  apply, EX 2-38–2-39
  save, EX 2-39
  set theme colors and fonts, EX 2-39
  work, EX 2-38–2-39
theme colors, **EX 2-7**
  set, EX 2-39
theme fonts, **EX 2-5**
  set, EX 2-39
thermometer charts, **EX 12-6**
3-D distortions, EX 4-52
3D maps, **EX 10-43**
  with clustered columns, EX 10-63
  open, EX 10-60–10-61
  use Dates and Times, EX 10-64
  visualize data, EX 10-60–10-67
3D Map window, EX 10-61
3-D reference, **EX 5-3**
  apply to formulas and functions,
    EX 5-14–5-18
  enter, EX 5-15
  problem solving, EX 5-15
  SUM function, EX 5-16
  wildcards, EX 5-18
  write, EX 5-14–5-18
tiled layout
  workbook window, EX 5-7
time(s)
  calculate, EX 3-6
  format, EX 2-15–2-16
time data, **EX 1-18**
timeline(s), **EX 7-51**, EX 10-25
  add Order Date to dashboard,
    Power Pivot, EX 10-40
  apply from Data Model, Power
    Pivot, EX 10-38–10-41
  connect map chart, EX 10-58
  connect slicer and, Power Pivot,
    EX 10-40–10-41
timeline slicer, EX 7-67–7-70
  create, EX 7-67–7-70
time value of money, EX 9-44
TODAY function, **EX 3-36**
top/bottom rule, EX 2-47–2-48
total expenses, chart of, EX 8-5
Total row, **EX 6-25**
  add, in Excel table, EX 6-36–6-37
Totals & Filters tab, EX 11-11
Touch Mode, **EX 1-6**
  use Excel, EX 1-6–1-7
Tour Editor pane, 3D Map window,
  EX 10-61
tours, **EX 10-43**
trace error, EX 9-53–9-56
transpose data, EX 2-20
transposed pasted range, EX 2-20
treemap chart, **EX 4-43**
trendlines, EX 9-3, **EX 10-3**
  add, EX 10-15
  add to charts, EX 4-40
  defined, **EX 4-40**

edit, EX 10-15
exponential, EX 10-16
judge with R2 statistic, **EX 10-17**
linear, EX 10-16
logarithmic, EX 10-16
to logarithmic and project future
  values, EX 10-17
moving average, EX 10-16
polynomial, EX 10-16
power, EX 10-16
queries, EX 10-3
types, EX 10-16
trial and error, **EX 3-47**
  use, EX 3-47–3-48
  what-if analysis, EX 3-47–3-48
Trust Center, **EX 12-79**
  Macro Settings, EX 12-79
trusted document, **EX 12-79**
Tufte, Edward, EX 4-49
two-variable data table, **EX 8-3**
  chart, EX 8-17–8-20
  completed, EX 8-16
  create, EX 8-14–8-20
  example, EX 8-16
  format result cell, EX 8-16–8-17
  setup, EX 8-15–8-16
two-way lookup table, **EX 7-12**
  value retrieved, EX 7-13

U

ungroup
  worksheet groups, EX 5-13
  worksheets, EX 5-10
unhide, **EX 1-47**
  columns, EX 1-47
  multiple sheets, EX 12-76
  rows, EX 1-47
  worksheets, EX 1-47
uniqueness, validate, EX 12-23
units, and constants, EX 3-5
unlocking cells, EX 12-25–12-28
unlock worksheet cells, **EX 12-3**

V

validate
  data entry, EX 12-11–12-23
  existing data, EX 12-21–12-22
  against list, EX 12-18–12-19
  uniqueness, EX 12-23
validation criteria, EX 12-12
validation error message
  create, EX 12-15–12-17
validation numbers, EX 12-12–12-15
validation rule, **EX 12-11**
value(s)
  interpolate from start to end,
    EX 9-23–9-25
  series of, extrapolate,
    EX 9-27–9-29
  tracing error, EX 9-53

value axis, **EX 4-18**
value axis scale, edit,
    EX 4-30–4-31
value field, EX 7-30, **EX 7-31**
Value Filter (Hotel Name) dialog
    box, EX 11-14
value filters, EX 11-12
value map, **EX 10-54**
value map chart
    create, EX 10-54–10-58
    revenue totals, EX 10-57
variable cells
    defined, EX 8-38
    set, EX 8-44–8-46
variable expenses, EX 8-4
    chart, EX 8-4
VBA editor
    displaying a message box,
        EX 12-73–12-75
    edit macro with VBA editor,
        EX 12-72–12-73
    open, EX 12-71–12-72
    understand sub procedures,
        EX 12-72
    work, EX 12-71–12-75
verify
    pretax profits and percentages in
        other sheets, EX 5-13
vertical layout
    workbook window, EX 5-7,
        EX–5–9
vertical lookup table, **EX 3-42**
view
    contents of Data Model,
        EX 10-32
    data with map chart,
        EX 10-53–10-67
    data with Quick Explore Tool,
        EX 10-50–10-53
    payback period for investment,
        EX 9-42–9-43
    scenarios, EX 8-28–8-30
    steps of query, EX 10-7
    workbook, multiple windows,
        EX 5-6–5-10
virus, **EX 12-78**
Visual Basic for Applications (VBA),
    EX 11-41, **EX 12-57**
    editor, **EX 12-56**, EX 12-71
    macro language, EX 8-44
visualize
    data with 3D maps,
        EX 10-60–10-67
VLOOKUP function, **EX 3-45,**
    EX 11-8
    approximate match lookups,
        EX 7-10
    find exact match, EX 3-45–3-47
    syntax, EX 7-10
volatile functions, **EX 3-47**

W

Watch Window
    definition, EX 9-58
    use, EX 9-58–9-60
waterfall charts, **EX 4-45**
what-if analysis, **EX 3-47**
    cost-volume relationships,
        EX 8-4–8-9
    create scenario summary
        reports, EX 8-31–8-36
    create Solver answer report,
        EX 8-53–8-55
    create two-variable data table,
        EX 8-14–8-20
    data tables, work, EX 8-9–8-14
    explore financial scenarios
        with Scenario Manager,
        EX 8-24–8-31
    explore iterative process,
        EX 8-52–8-53
    find break-even point,
        EX 8-7–8-9
    find optimal solution with Solver,
        EX 8-42–8-52
    optimize product mix, EX 8-40–8-42
    perform with charts, EX 4-17–4-18
    perform with formulas and
        functions, EX 3-47–3-50
    save and load Solver models,
        EX 8-56–8-59
    tool, EX 8-55
    use Goal Seek tool, EX 3-48–3-50
    use trial and error, EX 3-47–3-48
what-if scenarios, EX 8-24
wildcard characters, EX 6-33
wildcards, **EX 5-18**
    3-D reference, EX 5-18
    perform partial lookups, EX 7-9
workbook(s), **EX 1-2**
    add graphic objects,
        EX 4-40–4-42
    arrange multiple windows, EX 5-9
    arrange Windows dialog box,
        EX 5-8
    audit, EX 9-52–9-58
    change page orientation,
        EX 1-52–1-53
    change worksheet views,
        EX 1-50–1-52
    close, EX 1-13
    created from templates,
        EX 5-49–5-52
    create effective, EX 1-14
    create new viewing window,
        EX 5-7
    decision making while link, EX 5-28
    delete worksheets, EX 1-17
    design for calculations,
        EX 3-4–3-5

edit cells, EX 1-18–1-20
evaluate formula, EX 9-56–9-58
financial, EX 9-19
format for print, EX 2-52–2-63
hide content, EX 12-76–12-78
insert and delete rows and
    columns, EX 1-43–1-44
link external, EX 5-22–5-28
link hyperlinks to location within,
    EX 5-29–5-31
macro-enabled, EX 12-59
manage links, EX 5-27–5-28
move worksheets, EX 1-16–1-17
print, EX 1-50–1-55
protect, EX 12-21–12-28,
    EX 12-79–12-80
rename and insert worksheets,
    EX 1-16
review links, EX 5-26–5-27
save, EX 1-17–1-18
scale printed page, EX 1-53
set print options, EX 1-54–1-55
start new, EX 1-13–1-15
template, EX 5-34
trace error, EX 9-53–9-56
use color to enhance, EX 2-9–2-10
use COUNT function, EX 1-41–1-43
view, multiple windows,
    EX 5-6–5-10
Watch Window, use, EX 9-58–9-60
window layout, EX 5-7
windows in vertical layout,
    EX 5-8–5-9
workbook contents
    hide, EX 12-76–12-78
workbook templates
    explore, EX 5-46–5-52
    set up, EX 5-47–5-48
workbook window, **EX 1-3**
    divide, into panes, EX 6-6–6-8
    panes, EX 6-3
    split, EX 6-7–6-8
    unfreeze pane(s), EX 6-9
WORKDAY function, **EX 3-36**
worksheet(s), **EX 1-3**, EX 1-7
    add cell borders, EX 1-49
    change font size, EX 1-49–1-50
    change views, EX 1-50–1-52
    consolidate data from multiple,
        EX 7-66
    copy, EX 5-4–5-6
    data definition, EX 6-5
    data entry, EX 12-65–12-70
    delete, EX 1-17
    enter dates and numeric values,
        EX 1-22–1-25
    enter text, EX 1-18
    format, EX 1-48–1-50
    freeze column(s), EX 6-9
    freeze row(s), EX 6-9

group and ungroup, EX 5-11
hide, EX 1-47
insert, EX 1-16
locate cells within, EX 6-26–6-27
move, EX 1-16–1-17
Move or Copy dialog box, EX 5-6
move PivotChart to another,
    EX 7-55–7-58
protect, EX 12-21–12-28
reference cells in other,
    EX 5-14
rename, EX 1-16
selecting cells, EX 1-9–1-13
unhide, EX 1-47
view formulas, EX 1-55–1-56
worksheet formulas, EX 1-55–1-56
worksheet group, **EX 5-2**, write
    3-D references, EX 5-14–5-18
    editing, EX 5-12–5-13
    print, EX 5-14
    ungroup, EX 5-13
worksheet protection, **EX 12-2**
work with VBA editor,
    EX 12-71–12-5
write
    data query, EX 10-4–10-10
    financial workbook, EX 9-19

X

XIRR function
    defined, EX 9-51
    explore, EX 9-50–9-52
XLOOKUP function, EX 6-57–6-58,
    EX 7-2, EX 12-8
    array of values returned, EX 7-13
    call center metrics, EX 3-45
    with custom criteria, EX 7-11
    defined, **EX 3-42**
    Function Arguments dialog box,
        EX 3-44
    function arguments for
        approximate match, EX 7-8
    perform two-way lookups,
        EX 7-12–7-13
    retrieve value from two-way
        table, EX 7-13
    use with multiple lookup values,
        EX 7-10–7-12
XMATCH function, EX 7-13–7-14
XNPV function
    defined, EX 9-50
    explore, EX 9-50–9-52

Z

zeroes
    calculations, EX 3-34–3-35
    role, EX 3-34–3-35
Zoom controls, **EX 1-3**